A Review of the Events of 1978

The 1979 World Book Year Book

The Annual Supplement to The World Book Encyclopedia

World Book–Childcraft International, Inc.

A subsidiary of The Scott & Fetzer Company

Chicago London Paris Sydney Tokyo Toronto

Staff

Editorial Director
William H. Nault

Editorial Staff
Executive Editor
Wayne Wille

Managing Editor
Paul C. Tullier

Chief Copy Editor
Joseph P. Spohn

Senior Editors
Marsha F. Goldsmith
Beverly Merz
Jay Myers
Edward G. Nash
Foster P. Stockwell

Copy Editor
Irene B. Keller

Senior Index Editor
Marilyn Boerding

Index Editor
Bruce A. Davis

Editorial Assistant
Madelyn Krzak

**Executive Editor,
The World Book Encyclopedia**
A. Richard Harmet

Art Staff
Executive Art Director
William Dobias

Art Director
Roberta Dimmer

Senior Artists
Joe W. Gound
Marge Kathan
Richard B. Zinn

Artists
Free Chin
Stanley A. Schrero

Photography Director
Fred C. Eckhardt, Jr.

Photographer
Stephen Hale

Photo Editing Director
Ann Eriksen

Senior Photographs Editors
Blanche Cohen
John A. Marshall
Carol A. Parden
Paul Quirico
Jo Anne M. Ticzkus

Research and Services
Head, Editorial Research
Jo Ann McDonald

Senior Researcher
Robert Hamm

Head, Research Library
Indrani Embar

Head, Cartographic Services
H. George Stoll

Pre-Press Services
Director
J. J. Stack

Manager, Manufacturing Liaison
John Babrick

Supervisor, Keyboarding Section
Lynn Iverson

Manager, Film Separations
Alfred J. Mozdzen

Assistant Manager, Film Separations
Barbara J. McDonald

Supervisor, Art Traffic
Sandra Grebenar

Supervisor, Scheduling
Barbara Podczerwinski

Manufacturing Staff
Executive Director
Philip B. Hall

Production Manager
Joseph C. LaCount

Manager, Research and Development
Henry Koval

Year Book Board of Editors
Harrison Brown, Alistair Cooke, Lawrence A. Cremin, John Holmes, Sylvia Porter, James Reston, Walter (Red) Smith

World Book Advisory Board
Phillip Bacon. Professor of Geography, University of Houston; Rebecca T. Bingham, Director of Media Services, Jefferson County (Ky.) Public Schools; George B. Brain, Dean, College of Education, Washington State University; Anne Campbell, Commissioner of Education, State of Nebraska; Frank D. Drake, Goldwin Smith Professor of Astronomy and Director, National Astronomy and Ionosphere Center, Cornell University; Raymond Grew, Professor of History and Director, Center for Western European Studies, The University of Michigan; William E. McManus, Chairman, Committee on Education, United States Catholic Conference; A. Harry Passow, Jacob H. Schiff Professor of Education and Director, Division of Educational Institutions and Programs, Teachers College, Columbia University; William M. Smith, Professor of Psychology and Director, Office of Instructional Services and Educational Research, Dartmouth College.

Printed in the United States of America
ISBN 0-7166-0479-5
Library of Congress Catalog Card Number: 62-4818

Preface

We talked a lot about change and transition at the 1978 annual meeting of the YEAR BOOK Board of Editors. Change, of course, is what THE YEAR BOOK is all about. Each yearly edition helps update and supplement THE WORLD BOOK ENCYCLOPEDIA by presenting a review of the events and developments—the changes—of the preceding year. The year we discussed at our meeting, 1978, was as always one of changes completed and changes in progress. Proposition 13 had passed in California, and what changes would the taxpayers' revolt bring? The leaders of Egypt and Israel had met at Camp David, Maryland; what would that mean to the Middle East and the entire world? What changes would come from scientists' new knowledge about gene transplants? China was undergoing dramatic changes. We discussed these and many other developments of 1978.

So, in many ways it was business as usual at the Board meeting as we discussed the content of the Focus articles that would try to capture the meaning of the events of 1978. And then, near the end of the meeting, because there is "nothing permanent except change," as the Greek philosopher Heraclitus said, we turned our attention to the Focus section itself and what it should be in years to come.

It was a good discussion. Almost all of the Board members have been with us since the 1962 YEAR BOOK, when the Focus format was introduced. Their devotion to the book and to its role in education was never so apparent as in the lively flow of suggestions they made when we talked about a new approach to interpreting the year's events. The result of our discussion of the past year appears in the Focus reports in this book; the result of our talk about the future will show up in the 1980 edition of THE YEAR BOOK.   WAYNE WILLE

The YEAR BOOK Board of Editors and members of the book's editorial staff discuss the Focus reports on 1978 and the Focus section in years ahead.

Contents

A chronology of some of the most important events of 1978 appears on
pages 8 through 16.

A tear-off page of cross-reference tabs for insertion in THE WORLD
BOOK ENCYCLOPEDIA appears after page 16.

Contributors

Contributors not listed on these pages are members of THE WORLD BOOK YEAR BOOK editorial staff.

Adachi, Ken, M.A.; Literary Editor, *The Toronto Star.* [LITERATURE, CANADIAN]

Adams, James F., B.A., Ed.M., Ph.D.; Professor of Psychology, Temple University. [WORLD BOOK SUPPLEMENT: ADOLESCENT]

Alexiou, Arthur G., M.S., E.E.; Research Associate, Scripps Institution of Oceanography. [OCEAN]

Anderson, Virginia E., B.A., M.S.W.; Free-Lance Writer. [COMMUNITY ORGANIZATIONS; HANDICAPPED; PARENTS AND TEACHERS, NATIONAL CONGRESS OF; SOCIAL SECURITY; SOCIAL WELFARE; YOUTH ORGANIZATIONS]

Anderson, Leo S., B.A.; Editor, *Telephony Magazine.* [COMMUNICATIONS]

Araujo, Paul E., Ph.D.; Assistant Professor, Human Nutrition, University of Florida. [NUTRITION]

Banovetz, James M., Ph.D.; Chairman, Department of Political Science, Northern Illinois University. [CITY; City Articles; HOUSING]

Barber, Margaret, B.A., M.L.S.; Director, Public Information Office, American Library Association. [AMERICAN LIBRARY ASSOCIATION]

Beaumont, Lynn, Travel and Public Relations Consultant. [FAIRS AND EXPOSITIONS; TRAVEL]

Beckwith, David C., J.D.; Managing Editor, *Legal Times of Washington.* [COURTS AND LAWS; CRIME; PRISON; SUPREME COURT; SUPREME COURT (Close-Up)]

Benson, Barbara N., A.B., M.S., Ph.D.; Assistant Professor, Biology, Cedar Crest College. [BOTANY; ZOOLOGY]

Berkwitt, George J., B.S.J.; Chief Editor, *Industrial Distribution Magazine.* [MANUFACTURING]

Bornstein, Leon, B.A., M.A.; Labor Economist, U.S. Dept. of Labor. [LABOR]

Boyum, Joy Gould, Ph.D.; Professor of English, New York University. [MOTION PICTURES]

Bradsher, Henry S., A.B., B.J.; Foreign Affairs Writer, *Washington Star.* [Asian Country Articles]

Brown, Kenneth, Editor, *United Kingdom Press Gazette.* [EUROPE and European Country Articles; EUROPE (Close-Up)]

Cain, Charles C., III, B.A.; Automotive Editor, Associated Press. [AUTOMOBILE]

Carlson, Eric D., Ph.D.; Senior Astronomer, Adler Planetarium. [ASTRONOMY]

Clark, Phil, B.A.; Free-Lance Garden and Botanical Writer. [GARDENING]

Coble, Harold D., B.S., M.S., Ph.D.; Associate Professor of Crop Science, North Carolina State University. [WORLD BOOK SUPPLEMENT: PESTICIDE]

Cook, Robert C., former President, Population Reference Bureau. [POPULATION]

Cromie, William J., B.S.; Executive Director, Council for the Advancement of Science Writing. [SPACE EXPLORATION]

Csida, June Bundy, former Radio-TV Editor, *Billboard* Magazine. [MUSIC, POPULAR (Close-Up); RADIO; TELEVISION]

Cuscaden, Rob, Editor, *Home Improvement Contractor Magazine;* Architecture critic, *Chicago Sun-Times.* [ARCHITECTURE]

Cviic, Chris, B.A., B.Sc.; Editorial Staff, *The Economist.* [Eastern European Country Articles]

Dale, Edwin L., Jr., B.A.; Writer, Business Analyst. [INTERNATIONAL TRADE AND FINANCE]

Dawson, Terence J., B.Rur.Sc., Ph.D., Professor of Zoology, University of New South Wales, Australia. [Special Report: AUSTRALIA'S LIVING POGO STICKS]

Deffeyes, Kenneth S., M.S.E., Ph.D.; Professor of Geology, Princeton University. [GEOLOGY]

DeFrank, Thomas M., B.A., M.A.; Correspondent, *Newsweek.* [ARMED FORCES]

Delaune, Lynn de Grummond, M.A.; Assistant Professor, College of William and Mary; Author. [LITERATURE FOR CHILDREN]

Derickson, Ralph Wayne, Public Information Associate, Council of State Governments. [STATE GOVERNMENT]

Dewald, William G., Ph.D.; Professor of Economics, Ohio State University. [Finance Articles]

Dixon, Gloria Ricks, B.A.; Director of Public Affairs/Education, Magazine Publishers Association. [MAGAZINE]

Eaton, William, J., B.S.J., M.S.J.; Washington Correspondent, *Los Angeles Times.* [U.S. Political Articles]

Ebert, Roger J., B.S., M.A.; Film Critic, *Chicago Sun-Times.* [Special Report: WHERE THERE'S HOPE, THERE'S LIFE]

Esseks, John D., Ph.D.; Associate Professor of Political Science, Northern Illinois University. [AFRICA and African Country Articles]

Evans, Earl A., Jr., Ph.D.; Professor of Biochemistry, University of Chicago. [BIOCHEMISTRY]

Farr, David M. L., D. Phil.; Professor of History, Carleton University, Ottawa. [CANADA and Canadian Province Articles; LÉGER, JULES; TRUDEAU, PIERRE ELLIOTT]

Feather, Leonard, Author, Broadcaster, Composer. [MUSIC, POPULAR; RECORDINGS]

French, Charles E., Ph.D.; Study Director, President's Reorganization Project. [AGRICULTURE]

Gayn, Mark, B.S.; Member, Editorial Board, *The Toronto Star;* Author. [ASIA and Asian Country Articles]

Goldner, Nancy, B.A.; Critic, *Dance News, The Nation,* and *Christian Science Monitor.* [DANCING]

Goldstein, Jane, B.A.; Publicity Director, Santa Anita Park. [HORSE RACING]

Goy, Robert W., Ph.D.; Director, Wisconsin Regional Primate Research Center; Professor of Psychology, University of Wisconsin. [PSYCHOLOGY]

Graubart, Judah L., B.A.; former Columnist, *Jewish Post and Opinion* (Chicago). [JEWS AND JUDAISM]

Griffin, Alice, Ph.D.; Professor of English, Lehman College, City University of New York. [THEATER]

Gwynne, Peter, M.A.; Science Editor, *Newsweek.*[Special Report: COLDER WEATHER AHEAD—UNLESS IT'S WARMER]

Hales, Dianne Rafalik, B.A., M.S.; Editor/Writer. [HEALTH AND DISEASE; HOSPITAL; MEDICINE; MENTAL HEALTH; PUBLIC HEALTH]

Hechinger, Fred M., B.A.; Vice-President, *The New York Times* Company Foundation, Inc. [EDUCATION]

Hesburgh, Theodore M., C.S.C.; Ph.D.; President, University of Notre Dame. [DEATHS OF NOTABLE PERSONS (Close-Up)]

Huenergard, Celeste H., M.A.; Midwest Editor, *Editor and Publisher.* [NEWSPAPER; PUBLISHING]

Jacobi, Peter P., B.S.J., M.S.J.; Professor, Medill School of Journalism, Northwestern University. [MUSIC, CLASSICAL]

Jessup, Mary E., B.A., former News Editor, *Civil Engineering* Magazine. [BUILDING AND CONSTRUCTION; DRUGS; STEEL]

Joseph, Lou, B.A.; Manager, Media Relations, American Dental Association. [DENTISTRY]

Karr, Albert R., M.S.; Reporter, *The Wall Street Journal.* [TRANSPORTATION and Transportation Articles]

Kind, Joshua B., Ph.D.; Associate Professor of Art History, Northern Illinois University; Author, *Rouault;* Contributing Editor, *New Art Examiner.* [VISUAL ARTS]

Kisor, Henry, B.A., M.S.J.; Book Editor, *Chicago Sun-Times.* [LITERATURE]

Kitchen, Paul, B.A., B.L.S.; Executive Director, Canadian Library Association. [CANADIAN LIBRARY ASSOCIATION]

Koenig, Louis W., Ph.D., L.H.D.; Professor of Government, New York University; Author, *Bryan: A Political Biography of William Jennings Bryan.* [CIVIL RIGHTS]

Langdon, Robert, Research Fellow, Research School of Pacific Studies, Australian National University. [PACIFIC ISLANDS]

Leonard, Joseph W., B.S., M.S., P.C.; Professor of Mining Engineering and Director, Coal Research Bureau, West Virginia University. [WORLD BOOK SUPPLEMENT: COAL]

Levy, Emanuel, B.A.; Editor, *Insurance Advocate.* [INSURANCE]

Lewis, Ralph H., M.A.; Volunteer, Division of Museum Services, National Park Service. [MUSEUMS]

Litsky, Frank, B.S.; Assistant Sports Editor, *The New York Times.* [Sports Articles]

Livingston, Kathryn, B.A.; Senior Editor, *Town and Country.* [FASHION]

Maki, John M., Ph.D.; Professor of Political Science, University of Massachusetts. [JAPAN]

Martin, Everett G., A.B.; Latin American Correspondent, *The Wall Street Journal.* [LATIN AMERICA and Latin American Country Articles]

Marty, Martin E., Ph.D.; Fairfax M. Cone Distinguished Service Professor, University of Chicago. [PROTESTANTISM; RELIGION]

Mather, Ian, M.A.; Special Writer, *The Observer* (London). [GREAT BRITAIN; IRELAND; NORTHERN IRELAND]

McElroy, D. L., B.S., M.S., Ph.D.; Senior Research Staff Member, Union Carbide Corporation, Nuclear Division. [WORLD BOOK SUPPLEMENT: INSULATION]

Miller, J. D. B., M.Ec.; Professor of International Relations, Australian National University. [AUSTRALIA; NEW ZEALAND]

Mullen, Frances A., Ph.D.; Secretary-General, International Council of Psychologists, Inc. [CHILD WELFARE]

Murray, G. E., M.A.; Poetry Columnist; Free-Lance Writer. [POETRY]

Nelson, Larry L., Ph.D.; President, Snyder Associates, Inc. [AGRICULTURE]

Newman, Andrew L., M.A.; Information Officer, U.S. Department of the Interior. [CONSERVATION; ENVIRONMENT; FISHING; FISHING INDUSTRY; FOREST AND FOREST PRODUCTS; HUNTING; INDIAN, AMERICAN; WATER]

Oatis, William N.,; United Nations Correspondent, The Associated Press. [UNITED NATIONS; UNITED NATIONS (Close-Up)]

O'Connor, James J., P.E.; Editor in Chief, *Power* Magazine. [ENERGY]

Offenheiser, Marilyn J., B.S.; Free-Lance Writer. [ELECTRONICS]

O'Leary, Theodore M., B.A.; Special Correspondent, *Sports Illustrated* Magazine. [BRIDGE, CONTRACT; CAT; CHESS; COIN COLLECTING; DOG; GAMES, MODELS, AND TOYS; HOBBIES; STAMP COLLECTING]

Pankhurst, Richard, B.Sc., Ph.D.; Scholar, Institute of Ethiopian Studies, National University. [WORLD BOOK SUPPLEMENT: DJIBOUTI]

Pearl, Edward W., Meteorologist, Geophysical Research and Development Corporation. [WEATHER]

Plog, Fred, Ph.D.; Professor of Anthropology, Arizona State University. [ANTHROPOLOGY; ARCHAEOLOGY]

Plotkin, Manuel D., B.S., M.B.A.; Director, U.S. Bureau of the Census. [CENSUS]

Poli, Kenneth, Editor, *Popular Photography.* [PHOTOGRAPHY]

Price, Frederick C., B.S., Ch. E.; Free-Lance Writer. [CHEMICAL INDUSTRY]

Rabb, George B., Ph.D.; Director, Chicago Zoological Park. [ZOOS AND AQUARIUMS; ZOOS AND AQUARIUMS (Close-Up)]

Rowen, Joseph R., A.B.; Vice-President, National Retail Merchants Association. [RETAILING]

Rowse, Arthur E., I.A., M.B.A.; President, Consumer News, Inc. [CONSUMER AFFAIRS]

Schmemann, Alexander, S.T.D., D.D., LL.D., Th.D.; Dean, St. Vladimir's Orthodox Theological Seminary, New York. [EASTERN ORTHODOX CHURCHES]

Schubert, Helen C., B.S.; Home Furnishings Writer. [INTERIOR DESIGN]

Sederberg, Kathryn, B.A., M.A.; Features Editor, *Advertising Age.* [ADVERTISING]

Shaw, Robert James, B.S., B.A.; former Editor, *Library Technology Reports,* American Library Association. [LIBRARY]

Shearer, Warren W., Ph.D., J.D.; former Chairman, Department of Economics, Wabash College. [ECONOMICS]

Sheehan, Edward R. F., A.B.; Research Fellow, Center for International Affairs, Harvard University. [Special Report: ALLAH'S WILL AND OIL WELLS]

Sheerin, John B., C.S.P., A.B., M.A., LL.D., J.D.; General Consultor, American Bishops' Secretariat for Catholic-Jewish Relations. [ROMAN CATHOLIC CHURCH]

Sidar, Alexander G., Jr., B.S., Ed.M.; Executive Director, New Jersey Association of Colleges and Universities. [Special Report: HOW TO COPE WITH RISING COLLEGE COSTS]

Skalka, Patricia, B.A.; Free-Lance Writer. [Special Report: AID FOR YOUR ACHING BACK]

Smith, Gregory R., B.S.; Editor, *Skating* magazine. [WORLD BOOK SUPPLEMENT: ICE SKATING]

Spencer, William, Ph.D.; Professor of Middle East History, Florida State University; Author, *Land and People of Algeria.* [MIDDLE EAST and Middle Eastern Country Articles; North Africa Country Articles]

Summers, Larry V., Ph.D.; Agricultural Economist, U.S. Department of Agriculture. [FOOD]

Thompson, Carol L., M.A.; Editor, *Current History* Magazine. [U.S. Government Articles]

Thompson, Ida, Ph.D.; Assistant Professor, Department of Geological and Geophysical Sciences, Princeton University. [PALEONTOLOGY]

Tiegel, Eliot, B.A.; Managing Editor, *Billboard Magazine.* [MUSIC, POPULAR; RECORDINGS]

Tinkle, Donald W., B.S., M.S., Ph.D.; Professor of Zoology; Director, Museum of Zoology and Division of Biological Science, University of Michigan. [WORLD BOOK SUPPLEMENT: SNAKE]

Tofany, Vincent L., B.L.; President, National Safety Council. [SAFETY]

Verbit, Lawrence, Ph.D.; Professor of Chemistry, State University of New York. [CHEMISTRY]

Wade, Nicholas, M.A.; Staff Writer, *Science* Magazine. [SCIENCE AND RESEARCH]

White, Thomas O., Ph.D.; Lecturer in Physics, Cambridge University, Cambridge, England. [PHYSICS]

Wills, Garry, Ph.D.; Adjunct Professor, Johns Hopkins University. [Special Report: HOW REAL IS AMERICA'S RELIGIOUS REVIVAL?]

Chronology 1978

January

S	M	T	W	T	F	S
1	2	3	4	5	6	7
8	9	10	11	12	13	14
15	16	17	18	19	20	21
22	23	24	25	26	27	28
29	30	31				

1   **Canadian Prime Minister** Pierre Elliott Trudeau warns Quebec province that a unilateral declaration of independence would be met by federal force.
Air India Boeing 747 explodes shortly after take-off in Bombay, killing 213 persons.

3   **India's Congress Party ousts** former Prime Minister Indira Gandhi and her followers after they formed a rival group, named Congress Party-I.

4   **Chile's first election in five years** gives President Augusto Pinochet Ugarte a vote of confidence.

Jan. 4

Jan. 6

6   **The United States returns** St. Stephen's crown, Hungary's national symbol, which had been in U.S. custody since the end of World War II.

10   **Vietnam and China sign** a trade agreement.

11   **Nuclear export safeguards,** rules for exporting nuclear technology so that there will be no spread of atomic weapons, are agreed to by 15 nations, including the United States and Russia.

13   **Senator Hubert H. Humphrey dies of cancer.**

15   **The Dallas Cowboys** defeat the Denver Broncos, 27-10, in Super Bowl XII.

15-16   **Finnish voters elect** President Urho Kekkonen to a fifth term.

16   **Italian government resigns,** refusing to add Communists to the Cabinet.

17   **Belgium's coalition government** agrees to transform the nation into a federated state in the mid-1980s.

18   **Egypt suspends political talks with Israel,** recalls its delegates from Jerusalem.

19   **State of the Union message** by President Jimmy Carter stresses economy, calls United States "sound."

20   **Evidence exists of wrongdoing** by congressmen, reports Leon Jaworski, special counsel to the House committee investigating South Korean lobbying.

24   **Russian satellite falls to earth,** and radioactive debris is found in Canada.

25-26   **A raging blizzard,** 1,000 miles (1,600 kilometers) wide, dumps up to 31 inches (79 centimeters) of snow on six Midwestern states.

26   **New Portuguese Cabinet** is formed by Prime Minister Mario Soares' Socialist minority government after he lost a parliamentary vote of confidence.
Spyros Kyprianou wins a five-year term as president of Cyprus after the opposition fails to name a candidate.
Rules allowing federally funded abortions in limited cases are issued by the U.S. Department of Health, Education, and Welfare.

30   **A record $26.72-billion trade deficit** for 1977 is reported by U.S. Department of Commerce.

February

S	M	T	W	T	F	S
			1	2	3	4
5	6	7	8	9	10	11
12	13	14	15	16	17	18
19	20	21	22	23	24	25
26	27	28				

2   **Secretary of Defense Harold Brown warns** the House Armed Services Committee that Russian military build-up calls for increased U.S. defense spending.

5   **Rodrigo Carazo Odio** is elected president of Costa Rica.

5-7   **Blizzard paralyzes New England,** with record snowfalls in Boston and Providence, R.I.

7   **General strike in Nicaragua,** aimed at ousting

President Anastasio Somoza Debayle, ends in failure.

8 **House of Representatives rejects** a bill to create a consumer agency.

9 **Canada expels 11 Russian diplomats** on charges of operating a spy ring.

14 **U.S. says it will sell** jet warplanes to Egypt, Saudi Arabia, and Israel.

15 **Leon Spinks defeats Muhammad Ali** to become heavyweight boxing champion of the world.

16 **Japan and China sign** an eight-year, $20-billion trade pact.

21 **China spares the "Gang of Four,"** including Mao Tse-tung's widow, from execution.

23 **Environmental Protection Agency** reports that 103 of the 105 U.S. urban areas with more than 200,000 population fail to meet at least one of the five federal standards for air quality.

March

S	M	T	W	T	F	S
			1	2	3	4
5	6	7	8	9	10	11
12	13	14	15	16	17	18
19	20	21	22	23	24	25
26	27	28	29	30	31	

2 **President Carter** announces a plan to reform the civil service system.

3 **Rhodesian agreement** to transfer power to the black majority by December 31 is signed by Prime Minister Ian D. Smith and three black leaders.

4 **The *Chicago Daily News* ceases** publication. The newspaper was founded in 1875.

5 **Chinese National Congress adjourns** after reappointing Premier Hua Kuo-feng, adopting a new Constitution, and drafting a 10-year economic plan.

6 **President Carter invokes Taft-Hartley Act** in an effort to end the 91-day strike by the United Mine Workers Union.

7 **Carter signs** a bill canceling an appropriation to build two B-1 bombers.

9 **Helsinki accords review session** ends with 35 nations agreeing to establish a group to arrange a method to settle disputes peacefully.
Somalia withdraws troops from the Ogaden area of Ethiopia.

11 **New Italian Cabinet is formed** by Prime Minister Giulio Andreotti with Communist support.

13 **Guatemala's Congress elects** General Fernando Romeo-Lucas Garcia president because no candidate won a majority in the March 5 election.

14 **Dutch marines free 70 hostages** from South Moluccan terrorists in Assen, the Netherlands.
Israel attacks Palestine Liberation Organization bases in Lebanon, in retaliation for a guerrilla assault in which 37 Israeli civilians were killed.
Rhodesian settlement is rejected by the United Nations (UN) Security Council as "illegal and unacceptable."

Feb. 5-7

Feb. 9

March 3

March 7

9

March 17

March 22

| 16 | **U.S. Senate ratifies** Panama Canal Neutrality Treaty with a reservation that allows U.S. troops to enter Panama if the canal is closed after the year 2000. |

Italian terrorists kidnap former Prime Minister Aldo Moro in Rome after killing his five bodyguards.

17   **Tanker *Amoco Cadiz* hits a reef** off France, begins spilling a record 1.6 million barrels of crude oil.

Bolivia ends diplomatic ties with Chile, citing lack of progress in negotiations for an outlet to the Pacific Ocean.

President Carter warns Russia about its military build-up and intervention in Africa.

19   **French leftists lose** in the parliamentary election, ending the left's most serious threat in 20 years.

21   **Taiwan's National Assembly elects** Premier Chiang Ching-kuo president.

22   **UN peacekeeping troops enter** southern Lebanon after Israel declares a truce.

25   **U.S. coal strike ends** in its 110th day with a new three-year contract.

26-27   **Demonstrations delay** the opening of Tokyo airport.

30   **Ghana votes** for a union government of civilians, police, and military officers to replace the military government.

31   **Record trade deficit** of $4.52 billion in February is reported by the U.S. Department of Commerce.

April

S	M	T	W	T	F	S
						1
2	3	4	5	6	7	8
9	10	11	12	13	14	15
16	17	18	19	20	21	22
23	24	25	26	27	28	29
30						

April 27

3   **China signs five-year trade pact** with the European Community (Common Market).

***Annie Hall* wins** Oscar as the best picture and awards for the best actor and best actress go to Richard Dreyfuss and Diane Keaton.

Tong Sun Park tells the U.S. House ethics committee that he gave U.S. politicians $850,000 in gifts and campaign contributions, but denies acting for the South Korean government.

6   **The mandatory U.S. retirement age** is raised from 65 to 70.

7   **President Carter defers** production of the neutron bomb.

Philippines President Ferdinand E. Marcos wins control of the interim National Assembly in the first national elections since 1972.

9   **A Somali Army rebellion is crushed** in a two-hour battle.

10   **Arkady Shevchenko,** the highest-ranking Russian in the UN, defects to the United States, citing "differences" with his government.

12   **Solar energy can meet** one-fourth of U.S. energy needs by the year 2000, the President's Council on Environmental Quality reports.

13-14	**Turkish Cypriot negotiators** present UN Secretary-General Kurt Waldheim with a plan for Greek and Turkish states on Cyprus.
17	**Bill Rodgers wins the Boston Marathon** in 2 hours 10 minutes 13 seconds. Gayle Barron is first among the women, in 2:44:52.
18	**U.S. Senate ratifies** the Panama Canal Treaty, dealing with the operation and defense of the canal through 1999.
21	**President Carter criticizes Cambodia** as "the worst violator of human rights in the world today."
Chile government shuffle gives the nation its first civilian-majority Cabinet since 1973.
Japan tells plans to reduce its trade surpluses. It posted a record $20.57-billion surplus in fiscal 1977.
24	**U.S. Supreme Court declines** to review Patricia Hearst's robbery conviction.
25	**South Africa accepts** the Western plan for the independence of Namibia.
27	**President Mohammad Daoud is killed** in Afghanistan. Coup leaders abolish the Constitution.
30	**About 70,000 Muslims flee** from Burma to Bangladesh in three weeks, Bangalee authorities report.
Former President Richard M. Nixon's memoirs admit that he took part in the Watergate cover-up and misled the public.

18	**Italian Parliament passes** liberalized abortion law.
Russian court sentences physicist Yuri Orlov to seven years in prison for "anti-Soviet agitation." Orlov founded a group that monitored Russian compliance with the 1975 Helsinki accords.
19	**First-class postage goes up** from 13 cents to 15 cents per ounce (28 grams) in the United States.
19-20	**French and Belgian paratroopers** enter Kolwezi, Zaire, to rescue 2,500 Europeans trapped in conflict between Zairian troops and secessionist rebels.
20	**U.S. launches a spacecraft to orbit Venus.**
23	**UN General Assembly special session** on disarmament begins.
24	**China accuses Vietnam** of the "persecution and expulsion" of ethnic Chinese.
26	**The first legal gambling casino** in Atlantic City, N.J., opens.
Dominican Republic's election board declares Silvestre Antonio Guzman Fernandez the winner over President Joaquin Balaguer in the May 16 election.
27	**U.S. railroads report a record deficit** of $274 million in the first quarter of 1978.
28	**China announces** an eight-year program to improve its scientific and technological development.

May

S	M	T	W	T	F	S
	1	2	3	4	5	6
7	8	9	10	11	12	13
14	15	16	17	18	19	20
21	22	23	24	25	26	27
28	29	30	31			

1	**Japanese explorer Naomi Uemura** reaches the North Pole in the first solo overland journey.
Yasir Arafat, Palestine Liberation Organization leader, says that U.S. and Russian guarantees for Israel and a Palestinian state are "the only possible solution" in the Middle East.
2	**Rhodesian interim government** lifts the 1962 ban on two political parties, promises amnesty to guerrillas and release of political prisoners.
3	**Sun Day activities** throughout the United States promote solar energy.
4	**South African troops attack** guerrilla bases in Angola.
5-10	**Chinese Premier Hua Kuo-feng** visits North Korea in the first foreign trip by a Chinese Communist Party chairman since 1957.
8-11	**Riots sweep 34 Iranian cities** as Muslims protest Shah Mohammad Reza Pahlavi's modernization policies.
9	**Body of Aldo Moro** is found. Terrorists kidnapped and murdered the former prime minister of Italy.
15	**U.S. Senate approves the sale of warplanes** to Egypt, Saudi Arabia, and Israel.
15-23	**Riots and general strike in Peru** follow drastic price increases.
16	**Ethiopian troops begin an offensive** against rebels in Eritrea province.

May 3

May 8-11

June

S	M	T	W	T	F	S
				1	2	3
4	5	6	7	8	9	10
11	12	13	14	15	16	17
18	19	20	21	22	23	24
25	26	27	28	29	30	

1 **France starts to phase out price controls.**

3 **Bangladesh voters elect** Major General Ziaur Rahman as president.

5 **China releases 110,000 persons** detained since an "antirightist" campaign in 1957, Hong Kong reports say.

6 **California voters approve Proposition 13,** an initiative to cut property taxes 57 per cent. Coauthor Howard Jarvis and Governor Edmund G. Brown, Jr., meet later to discuss changes.

East African nations ask for help against plague of locusts.

8 **Writer Alexander I. Solzhenitsyn** tells a Harvard University commencement audience that "the Western world has lost its civil courage."

12 **Canadian Prime Minister Trudeau** outlines a plan for a constitution to replace the 1867 British North America Act.

13 **"Son of Sam" killer** David R. Berkowitz receives maximum prison term for six murders.

15 **U.S. Supreme Court upholds** a construction halt on a $116-million dam because it would endanger a rare fish. The dam was 80 per cent finished.

Colombia's election board declares that Julio Cesar Turbay Ayala, a Liberal, won the June 4 presidential election.

Italy's President Giovanni Leone resigns because of allegations of illegal private financial activities.

18 **Peruvians vote** for the first time in 10 years, elect a Constituent Assembly.

21 **U.S. balance-of-payments deficit** hit a record $6.95 billion for the first quarter of 1978, says Commerce Department.

22 **Pluto's moon is discovered** by U.S. Naval Observatory astronomer James W. Christy.

25 **Argentina wins soccer's World Cup,** defeating the Netherlands, 3-1.

28 **Supreme Court says Allan P. Bakke** must be admitted to the University of California Medical School. He had sued, claiming "reverse discrimination."

29 **Vietnam joins** the Council for Mutual Economic Assistance, Russia's Communist economic bloc.

June 6

June 25

July 8

July

S	M	T	W	T	F	S
						1
2	3	4	5	6	7	8
9	10	11	12	13	14	15
16	17	18	19	20	21	22
23	24	25	26	27	28	29
30	31					

1-4 **Memphis, Tenn., fire fighters strike,** and National Guard is called in to operate firehouses. At least 350 fires are reported during the strike.

1-6 **Syrian troops, Lebanese Christian militiamen** fight in and around Beirut.

3 **China ends economic aid to Vietnam.**

5 **Frederick William Kwasi Akuffo** replaces Ignatius Kutu Acheampong as Ghana's head of state.

Egypt offers peace plan calling for Israeli withdrawal from the West Bank, East Jerusalem, and the Gaza Strip.

6-7 **European Community monetary zone** is proposed by France and West Germany to stabilize currencies.

7 **Upper Volta Parliament** elects Joseph Conombo as prime minister.

8 **Martina Navratilova and Bjorn Borg win** Wimbledon tennis titles.

Alessandro Pertini is elected president of Italy.

8-13 **Basque riots,** demonstrations, and strikes sweep through northern Spain.

9 **Israel rejects Egyptian peace plan,** but agrees to discuss differences in London meeting.

10 **Military junta** deposes Mauritania's President Moktar Ould Daddah.

11 **India charges** former Prime Minister Indira Gandhi with the illegal arrest of opposition leaders in 1975.

12 **South-West Africa People's Organization** accepts the Western plan to end South African control over Namibia (South West Africa).

13 **China ends all aid to Albania.**

14 **Russia convicts Anatoly Shcharansky,** Jewish dissident, of treason, espionage, and "anti-Soviet agitation."

Canadian land rights settlement gives Inuit (Eskimos) $45 million and 37,000 square miles (96,200 square kilometers) of land in the Northwest Territories.

15 **President Carter rebukes Andrew Young,** UN ambassador, for saying there are "hundreds, perhaps even thousands, of political prisoners in the U.S."

Thailand and Cambodia settle their border dispute.

16-17 **Economic conference in Bonn** draws leaders of Canada, France, Great Britain, Italy, Japan, U.S., and West Germany.

18-19 **Israeli and Egyptian foreign ministers** discuss peace terms at London meeting.

18-22 **Organization of African Unity** discusses the presence of foreign troops in Africa at its annual meeting in Sudan.

20 **Peter G. Bourne resigns** as President Carter's special assistant for health affairs after admitting he wrote a prescription for a controlled drug for a fictitious person.

21 **Bolivian military junta seizes power,** appoints General Juan Pereda Asbun president.

24 **U.S. dollar declines** to 199.05 yen in Tokyo trading.

25 **U.S. repositions *Skylab*** satellite to keep it in orbit longer.

First baby conceived outside a woman's body is born—a girl, to John and Lesley Brown in Oldham, England.

U.S. Senate votes to lift the arms embargo against Turkey. House also agrees on August 1.

25-30 **Foreign ministers** of 87 nonaligned nations meet in Belgrade, Yugoslavia, to discuss threats to the neutrality of the nonaligned movement.

27 **Portuguese government falls** when Social Democratic Center Party withdraws from coalition with Socialists.

August

S	M	T	W	T	F	S
		1	2	3	4	5
6	7	8	9	10	11	12
13	14	15	16	17	18	19
20	21	22	23	24	25	26
27	28	29	30	31		

1 **Grand jury indicts** seven in connection with the 1976 assassination of Orlando Letelier, former Chilean ambassador to the United States.

2 ***Star Wars* surpasses *Jaws*** as the all-time leader in worldwide film rentals.

4 **Jeremy Thorpe,** former British Liberal Party leader, is arrested on a murder conspiracy charge.

6 **Pope Paul VI dies** in the 15th year of his reign, and is buried on August 12.

July 25

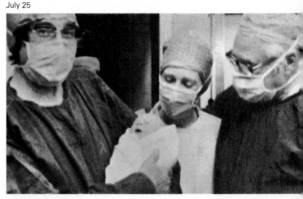

Aug. 6 and 12

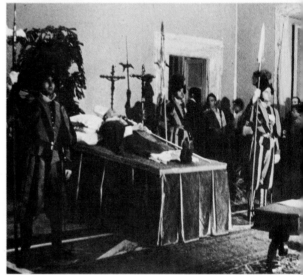

Aug. 17 and 25

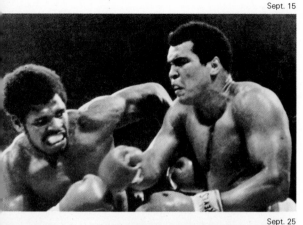

Sept. 15

Sept. 25

Sept. 20 and 28

7   **Honduran military junta deposes** Chief of State Juan Alberto Melgar Castro.

8   **U.S. launches *Venus 2,*** the second spacecraft headed for Venus.
    President Carter signs a bill giving New York City $1.65 billion in federal long-term loan guarantees.

9   **Pressmen's strike** shuts down *The New York Times,* the *Daily News,* and the *New York Post.*

12 **China and Japan sign a peace treaty** in Peking, China.

13 **Cleveland Mayor** Dennis J. Kucinich wins a recall election.
    Henry Ford II fires Lee A. Iacocca as president of Ford Motor Company.

15 **House of Representatives extends deadline** for Equal Rights Amendment ratification 39 months and rejects a proposal to let states rescind approval.

17 **Three Americans** complete the first transatlantic balloon crossing. They return from France in a supersonic jetliner on August 25.

22 **U.S. Senate approves** a proposed constitutional amendment to give the District of Columbia full voting representation in Congress.
    President Jomo Kenyatta dies. He was a leader of Kenya's fight for independence.

25 **Lower airfares** are permitted by the Civil Aeronautics Board.

26 **College of Cardinals elects** Albino Cardinal Luciani, patriarch of Venice, pope of the Roman Catholic Church. He takes the name John Paul I.

27 **Shah Mohammad Reza Pahlavi** of Iran appoints Jafar Sharif-Emami prime minister. Emami says his government "will respect religious society and the Islamic rules."

31 **Olafur Johannesson** becomes Iceland's prime minister as head of a left-of-center coalition.

September

S	M	T	W	T	F	S
					1	2
3	4	5	6	7	8	9
10	11	12	13	14	15	16
17	18	19	20	21	22	23
24	25	26	27	28	29	30

1   **First trip to Europe** by Chinese Communist head of state is completed by Premier Hua Kuo-feng.

3   **Japan announces economic measures** to meet its goal of 7 per cent growth in 1978.

4   **Vietnam accuses China** of invading its land, airspace, and territorial waters.

6   **Camp David summit talks start** among President Carter, Egyptian President Anwar al-Sadat, and Israeli Prime Minister Menachem Begin.
    Kennedy assassination probe opens in House of Representatives.

7   **Government wiretapping is prohibited** in most cases by bill that passes U.S. House.
    House upholds Carter's veto of $37-billion weapons bill.

8   **Iran declares martial law** in 12 cities after 100,000 demonstrate in Teheran.

12　**Major Australian ports close** for four days as dockworkers strike.

13　**Huge uranium deposit** is discovered under lake in Saskatchewan, Canada.

14　**Portuguese government falls** as National Assembly rejects Prime Minister Alfredo Nobre da Costa's program.

15　**Ali wins title third time.** Regains World Boxing Association heavyweight championship from Leon Spinks.

16　**Earthquake kills 25,000 persons in Iran.**

17　**Middle East peace framework is signed** by Israel's Prime Minister Begin, Egypt's President Sadat, and President Carter.

18　**UN extends peacekeeping force's term** in Lebanon by four months.

20　**Space-flight endurance record** is broken by Russian cosmonauts Vladimir Kovalyonok and Aleksander S. Ivanchenko in their 96th day.
Italian Red Brigades leader Corrado Alunni receives a 12-year jail sentence.
Prime Minister Vorster resigns in South Africa, is succeeded on September 28 by Pieter Willem Botha.

25　**144 die in air collision** of jetliner and single-engine plane over San Diego.

28　**Pope John Paul I dies** in the 34th day of his reign.

15　**João Baptista de Figueiredo is elected** president of Brazil, the fifth consecutive army general to be president since 1964.
95th Congress adjourns after passing an $18.7-billion tax cut and an energy bill.

16　**College of Cardinals elects** Karol Cardinal Wojtyla, archbishop of Kraków, Poland, as the first non-Italian pope since 1523. He takes the name John Paul II.

17　**Yankees win the World Series,** beating the Los Angeles Dodgers, four games to two.
Anatoly Karpov remains world chess champion by defeating Viktor Korchnoi in the 32nd game.

18　**Cambodia fights Vietnamese** invaders in the Parrot's Beak area.

20　**Recall of 10 million tires** is announced by Firestone Tire & Rubber Company. Recall is later raised to 13 million.
Paul vanden Boeynants succeeds Leo Tindemans as prime minister of Belgium.

24　**Carter unveils anti-inflation plan.**

25　**Carlos Mota Pinto** is named prime minister of Portugal.

27　**Nobel Peace Prize** is awarded to Egypt's President Anwar al-Sadat and Israel's Prime Minister Menachem Begin.

29　**Rhodesian election delay** for "mechanical reasons" is announced by Prime Minister Ian D. Smith.

31　**Iranian oil strike affects 40,000 workers.**

October

S	M	T	W	T	F	S
1	2	3	4	5	6	7
8	9	10	11	12	13	14
15	16	17	18	19	20	21
22	23	24	25	26	27	28
29	30	31				

3　**Second "test tube" baby** is born — a girl, to Bela Agarwal and her husband, Pravat, in Calcutta, India.

4　**Turkey allows U.S. to reopen bases** on its soil in return for the lifting of the arms embargo.

5　**Swedish government resigns** over nuclear power issue.

6　**Bill phasing out airline regulation** by the federal government clears congressional conference committee.
U.S. Senate extends deadline for Equal Rights Amendment ratification to 1982 and rejects amendments to allow states to rescind earlier approval.

7-20　**U.S. tour by Ian D. Smith,** prime minister of Rhodesia, fails to win support for his interim government.

10　**Belgian government resigns** over details of changeover to a federal state.
Rhodesia ends official racial discrimination.

11　**Aristides Royo is elected** president of Panama.

12　**Largest parks bill in history** clears Congress.

13　**Carter signs civil service reform act.**
Ola Ullsten becomes prime minister of Sweden.
U.S. House reprimands three congressmen for official misconduct, ending the 18-month inquiry into South Korean lobbying.

Oct. 16

Oct. 17

November

S	M	T	W	T	F	S
			1	2	3	4
5	6	7	8	9	10	11
12	13	14	15	16	17	18
19	20	21	22	23	24	25
26	27	28	29	30		

1 **Carter announces dollar defense** by currency-market intervention, gold sales, and discount-rate increases.
Uganda seizes 700 square miles (1,800 square kilometers) of Tanzanian territory after October 30 invasion.

2 **Space-flight endurance record** of 139 days and 15 hours is set by Russian cosmonauts Vladimir Kovalyonok and Aleksander S. Ivanchenko, who land safely in Russia.

5 **Austria rejects opening nuclear plant** in referendum.
Indira Gandhi wins a seat in India's Parliament, a comeback for the former prime minister.

6 **Martial rule is imposed in Iran** by Shah Mohammad Reza Pahlavi in an attempt to end violent demonstrations.

New York City newspaper strike ends after 88 days as *The New York Times* and the *Daily News* resume publishing.

7 **Republicans gain** 3 U.S. Senate seats, 12 House seats, and 6 governorships in midterm vote.

8 **Carter signs transportation bill** providing $54 billion for highways and mass transit through fiscal year 1982.

18 **U.S. Representative Leo J. Ryan** (D., Calif.) is killed in Guyana by members of the People's Temple, a California-based cult. Some 911 members of the cult then die in a mass suicide-murder. Ryan's body is returned to the U.S. on November 21.

19 **Peking poster accuses Mao Tse-tung** of supporting China's "Gang of Four," the first such accusation against the former Communist Party chairman.

24 **Bolivian coup d'état** ends the four-month presidency of Juan Pereda Asbun.

27 **Japan's Prime Minister Takeo Fukuda loses** party election; Masayoshi Ohira succeeds him as prime minister.
San Francisco's Mayor George Moscone and Supervisor Harvey Milk are assassinated.

30 **London newspaper *The Times* suspends** publication because of labor problems.

Nov. 5

Nov. 18 and 21

Dec. 8 and 12

December

S	M	T	W	T	F	S
					1	2
3	4	5	6	7	8	9
10	11	12	13	14	15	16
17	18	19	20	21	22	23
24	25	26	27	28	29	30
31						

1 **Carter places 56 million acres** (23 million hectares) of Alaska wilderness in the National Park System.

3 **Venezuela elects** Luis Herrera Campins, an opposition Social Christian, as president.

4-8 **Namibians vote** in elections run by South Africa without UN approval.

5 **European Monetary System is agreed** on by Belgium, Denmark, France, Luxembourg, the Netherlands, and West Germany. Ireland and Italy later decide to join.

8 **Golda Meir dies at age 80.** She was Israel's prime minister from 1969 to 1974. Her funeral is on December 12.

11 **Thieves take $5 million** from Kennedy International Airport in New York City, in the largest cash theft in U.S. history.

15 **President Carter** announces the U.S. will recognize China on Jan. 1, 1979.
Cleveland defaults on $15.5 million in loans.

17 **Organization of Petroleum Exporting Countries** announces price of oil will increase by a total of 14.5 per cent in 1979.

19 **India's Parliament expels Indira Gandhi,** sends her to jail until session ends.
Power failure strikes most of France.

27 **Algeria's President Houari Boumediene dies.**

Here are your

1979 YEAR BOOK
Cross-Reference Tabs

For insertion in your WORLD BOOK

Each year, THE WORLD BOOK YEAR BOOK adds a valuable dimension to your WORLD BOOK set. The Cross-Reference Tab System is designed especially to help youngsters and parents alike *link* THE YEAR BOOK's new and revised WORLD BOOK articles, its Special Reports, and its Close-Ups to the related WORLD BOOK articles they update.

How to Use These Tabs

First, remove this page from THE YEAR BOOK. Begin with the first Tab, "Adolescent."

Then, turn to the *A Volume* of your WORLD BOOK set and find the page of the "Adolescence" article. Moisten the gummed Tab and affix it to that page.

For the Close-Up on "Bakke Case," mount the Tab in the *B Volume* where the article should appear in alphabetical sequence.

Section One

The Year
In Focus

In this section, members of THE YEAR BOOK Board of Editors analyze some of the significant developments of 1978. The Related Articles list at the end of each Focus report directs the reader to THE YEAR BOOK's additional coverage of the subject.

John Holmes

Focus on The World

**Relations among states — large and small — were
changing, and the power game was being played
at different tables, in ways not always foreseen**

As the decade of the 1970s neared its close, we were clearly
moving into a new season in the relations among states, large and
small. The power game was being played at separate tables and in
ways not always foreseen. "In the midst of such complexity," said one
observer, commenting on the demonstrations against the shah in Iran,
"it is tempting to look at every eruption through the lens of the Cold
War. But that is an escape from today's complexity to the certainties
of a bygone era." In Southeast Asia, Communist Vietnam was fighting
with Communist China and Communist Cambodia. Whatever the
game, it was not dominoes.

Asia was on the move. The most portentous events of the year may
have been the Treaty of Peace and Friendship China signed with
Japan in August and its agreement in December to establish normal
diplomatic relations with the United States. These moves greatly
strengthened the sense of security of China, Japan, and the United
States. Japan and China had opened the prospect of an unrivaled
center of economic power, based on Chinese oil and Japanese industry. Vice-Premier Teng Hsiao-p'ing, now emerging as the strongman
of China, and his associates had committed their vast country to the
"four modernizations": the mechanization of agriculture, the building
of a strong national defense, the advancement of industry, and the fur-
thering of science and technology. They pursued also a huge mining
deal with West Germany, nuclear assistance from France, and aircraft
from Great Britain. China would not be transformed overnight, but
ideological obstacles, even adulation of the great Mao Tse-tung himself, were being removed at a dizzying pace.

The Chinese were not the only Asians reaching for industrial power.
South Korea was becoming a second Japan. Taiwan, Hong Kong,
Malaysia, Singapore, Iran, and even India were largely responsible for
a phenomenon noted as follows in the World Bank's *Annual Report
1978*: "With their expanding industrial capability, increasing numbers of developing countries are now involved in the massive re-

John Holmes

arrangement of international comparative advantage that started among the industrialized countries." There were in Asia, nevertheless, powerful forces opposing modernization, particularly within the Muslim states, where a resurgence of religious zeal has become an important factor of both internal and international politics.

For the time being, however, the world was still largely "managed" by the superpowers–Russia and the United States–occasionally in tandem. In arms, the superpowers remained in a class by themselves. They still had responsibilities for international security they could not escape, even though, for Americans at least, the burdens of superiority were perhaps looming larger than the advantages. This so-called condominium–or twin-power control–based on an arms balance, was maintained in a year of great tension. It was hardly a joint enterprise, of course. The superpowers were antagonists with a mutual recognition that at some unspecified point competition must be restrained. The condominium comes into action only in times of crisis. In February, when events in Ethiopia were particularly disturbing, U.S. Secretary of State Cyrus R. Vance said Russia had assured him Ethiopian troops would not cross the border of Somalia. They did in fact stop at the border, not simply because of an implied threat of Western intervention, but also because they would otherwise have offended almost all African opinion. Management by the superpowers cannot be entirely arbitrary. It must take into consideration prevailing circumstances and the attitudes of regional states.

Neither superpower was playing chess. Neither could control the pawns. An opposition leader in Nicaragua, for example, complained that "the United States can hardly call itself a superpower if it fails against a tiny Central American dictator." When bloody rebellion broke out against the Nicaraguan government, the United States found itself obliged to do something to promote more acceptable government. Since intervention had been renounced, the United States shared the mediation exercise with other American states. The United States continued to seek formulas for a peaceful transition to majority rule in Rhodesia, but it preferred to act with Great Britain. It collaborated also with the other Western powers in the United Nations (UN) Security Council, who, in a team of five, tried to reconcile South African policies with UN intentions in Namibia. The United States and its friends could persuade or cajole the parties, but they could no more command black or white Africans to peaceful settlement than they could force the prime minister of Israel or the president of Egypt to a treaty.

How the Russians managed their "clients" was harder to appraise. In the West, however, there was little tendency to see what was happening in Indochina or Africa simply as proxy wars instigated at long distance. Vietnam was dependent on Soviet help but was no one's satellite. Even Cuba, though an invaluable collaborator in Soviet policy in Africa, was fulfilling its chosen role as leader of the Third World radicals. The leaders of Mozambique and Angola still pro-

Asian leaders

fessed rousing Marxist rhetoric and gratitude to the Soviet Union, but for their own African reasons they worked with their neighbors of the "front line states" to seek negotiated settlements in Rhodesia and Namibia. Russia might like tension in Africa, but postrevolutionary states desperately needed economic help and, for the time being at least, some measure of tranquillity. Economic assistance was more likely to come from the West; the Russians specialized in providing arms. The African states expressed their concern lest the Cubans, as the Nigerians put it, "overstay their welcome in Africa," which was not about to "exchange one colonialist yoke for another." They would not, however, condemn these interventions in the cause of "liberation" so long as the Western powers, as they saw it, failed to oust the "racists" in the "unliberated" states. They professed confidence in their own ability to handle the Russians, and they saw the Soviet "alternative" as their best means of inducing the West to get tough with the white Africans.

It was not a very good year for Russia in politics or in economics

Russia, while cautious, had not ceased to compete. Its increasing store of arms and its advancing military technology continued to cause alarm. Although the North Atlantic Treaty Organization Council rededicated itself to the pursuit of détente and peaceful settlement, it reaffirmed the need to maintain security, develop technology, and spend more on arms.

But while Russia strengthened itself militarily in 1978, it was not a very good year politically and economically. China's rapprochement with Japan and the United States obviously affected the balance of forces. The Soviet Union made some strategic gains of doubtful value. Afghanistan became even more dependent on Moscow. The Arab states that rejected the Camp David accords on the Middle East inevitably turned back to Russia for military assistance and counterforce – but not for ideological sustenance. In spite of a good harvest, the Soviet Union's trade deficit with the West jumped sharply in 1978, and its growth rate lagged. While other countries resisted the temptation to join China in anti-Soviet alliance, China's Premier Hua Kuo-feng was received as an honored guest in Europe, even in such Communist countries as Yugoslavia and Romania. An important Soviet spokesman warned that if a country improved its relations with China on a clearly anti-Soviet basis it "could lay the cornerstone of an absolutely new set of international relationships that would make nobody very happy."

Moscow continued to lose what ideological authority it once had over the world Communist movement. In Poland, the Roman Catholic Church achieved the status of a loyal opposition without whose at least passive acceptance the government could not govern. Romanian foreign and defense policy became even more boldly independent. The Eurocommunists in Italy, France, and Spain lost ground in elections but did not revert to pro-Soviet positions. Typical of trends in leftist thinking were the so-called New Philosophers in France. Provoked by the bloody aftermath in Vietnam and Cambodia, they

Rhodesian leaders

turned their critical attention to tyranny and oppression committed in the name of socialism–without, however, rejecting socialism. Was the choice, a writer in *Nouvel Observateur* asked, between "a capitalist Africa, corrupt, police-ridden and often bloody, and a so-called Socialist Africa, anarchic, tyrannical, and no less bloody?" It was a time when it was less easy to identify the good guys and the bad guys –and that may well be a measure of progress.

What were the Russians after? Soviet Foreign Minister Andrei A. Gromyko gave one answer when he claimed that as of now "no question of any significance…can be decided without the Soviet Union or in opposition to it." The validity of that claim was being tested in the Middle East. The United States could not yet avoid being regarded when necessary as a kind of substitute UN. "Lebanon is being destroyed," cried a political leader in Beirut, "and the United States is doing nothing about it." The extraordinary Egyptian-Israeli sessions at Camp David illustrated dramatically the role a superpower could play with the encouragement of a large part of the world. This assumption of an American responsibility for peace in the world was revealed poignantly by the apparent expectation of Israelis and Arabs that the United States would not only arrange a settlement, but would also cover a good deal of the cost.

Although it was former Secretary of State Henry A. Kissinger who had set the United States on the path of mediation in the Middle East and Africa, America's restored authority in the world owed much to the image of President Jimmy Carter. His concern for human rights had caught him up in the ambiguities that beset that question, but the campaign he stimulated was irrepressible. He told the Organization of American States in June that his government "would not be deterred from our open and enthusiastic policy of promoting human rights," but he also pledged that the United States would not intervene during what he recognized as the difficult transition from authoritarian to democratic rule.

The Carter Administration continued its efforts to forestall conflict and avoid polarizations. Whether the Congress of the United States would support that posture was a question, however, that worried some foreigners. Russia's skeptical attitude toward the Panama Canal Treaties prompted concern over the possible fate of any new Strategic Arms Limitation Treaty (SALT). On the other hand, there were those abroad, as well as in the United States, who worried more about the will and capacity of Washington to retain its power and intervene here, there, and everywhere. A superpower may be respected, but it is not universally envied.

The Russians were clearly anxious to keep détente on the rails. Supreme Soviet Presidium Chairman Leonid I. Brezhnev went to Bonn, West Germany, to pursue practical arrangements with the rich and powerful West Germans. A group of U.S. senators engaged in some tough and candid dialogue in Moscow and other East European capitals. President Carter held off on the neutron bomb, though he

Carter's image had much to do with restoring U.S. authority in the world

Middle East leaders

was clearly using the threat of production to induce the Russians to cooperate in a second SALT agreement. The United States and its allies specifically decoupled the human rights campaign from the effort to get SALT II. The meetings in Belgrade, Yugoslavia, to review progress on the Helsinki agreements that had linked human rights to security finally concluded early in 1978. A brief communiqué noted simply that the European and North American signatories had met and differed, and would meet again in two years in Madrid, Spain. Although the session was widely regarded as a failure, it could hardly have been expected that the Russians would confess sin in a communiqué. Sin had been publicized, the non-Communists had refused to pretend that all was well, but the dialogue on European security was not broken off.

The time left to achieve any "world order" may be running out

The continuing search for SALT II held the superpowers in their curious duet. Opposition to any such agreement was gaining in the United States, and probably also in the Soviet Union. Some advocates feared that the advance of technology made the proposed terms almost meaningless. Nevertheless, most governments recognized that SALT had become a symbol. The commitment to restraint was what mattered, and the consequences of breaking off the quest were indeed fearsome. But SALT also isolated the superpowers. When the UN held a special session on disarmament in the spring, there was an almost universal demand across ideological divisions that the superpowers delay no longer dismantling their capacity for overkill. The fact that many of the critics were themselves buying or selling arms at an extravagant pace did not diminish their zeal to end "the arms race." Everyone seemed desperate to get off the treadmill. This pressure, coinciding as it did with shriller demands in First, Second, and Third World countries to divert resources to welfare and development, has become a political force of real consequence.

Time to achieve any "world order" may be running out. We could look back on the 1970s as the last chance to discipline ourselves—before arms proliferate beyond control and before blood and passion are unleashed in such quantities in Africa, the Middle East, or Asia that the world staggers beyond management. In 1978, the fate of Lebanon, destroyed by mindless wars, the eruption of bloodletting in Zaire in an invasion none of the powers seemed to want, and the suicidal genocide in Cambodia provided grim portents of a world no one could control.

Related Articles

For further information on international relations in 1978, see Section Two, SAUDI ARABIA: ALLAH'S WILL AND OIL WELLS. See also articles on the various countries and the following in Section Four: AFRICA; ASIA, EUROPE; INTERNATIONAL TRADE AND FINANCE; LATIN AMERICA; MIDDLE EAST; PACIFIC ISLANDS; UNITED NATIONS.

SALT negotiators

James Reston

Focus on
The Nation

**Going into the last year of the 1970s, America
was more thoughtful, pausing to sort things out
before confronting the problems of the 1980s**

Nations, like nature, have their seasons, and for the United
States, 1978 was a year of discontent. Going into the last year of the
1970s, the nation was not at war anywhere in the world, but it was not
at peace with itself, either. It was in a cautious and uncertain mood—
not thinking everything was going to get bigger and better, but in an
attitude of retrenchment and even self-doubt.

In some ways, this was a surprising reaction to the history of the
1970s. The nation had come through the long and divisive Vietnam
War and the constitutional crisis of the Watergate scandals in fairly
good order. One President (Lyndon B. Johnson, a Democrat) had
virtually abdicated, and another (Richard M. Nixon, a Republican)
had resigned under threats of impeachment and conviction.

But none of the pessimistic predictions attending these two crises
in the middle 1970s had actually come to pass by the last year of the
decade. The United States did not lose its influence in Asia. It established diplomatic relations with the Communist regime in China at
the beginning of 1979 after 30 years of unremitting opposition to
Peking in the Korean and Vietnamese wars.

Despite all its differences with the Soviet Union over human rights
and the conflicts of Africa, the United States seemed on the verge of
signing a second Strategic Arms Limitation Treaty with Russia, and,
as 1978 ended, was preparing to welcome the leaders of both of the
major Communist nations to Washington, D.C., in 1979.

Mainly as a result of Washington's diplomacy under the administrations of Nixon, Gerald R. Ford, and Jimmy Carter, the prospect of
peace in the Middle East was infinitely brighter in the last year of the
1970s than it had been in the first year. And yet, the American people
seemed divided, puzzled, and hesitant as they faced the 1980s.

James Reston

25

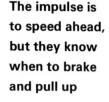

**The impulse is
to speed ahead,
but they know
when to brake
and pull up**

The 1960s were a time of civil rights within the nation, easing, if not removing, the tensions between the races. The 1970s saw the dramatic entrance of women into the work force of the nation, and a wider reform movement for women's rights. But by the end of the decade there seemed to be a vague feeling among the people that it was time to pause and think about where they had been and where they were going.

These cycles of reform and retreat, or at least reappraisal, are typical of the American people. Their impulse is to speed ahead, but they have usually known when to brake down and pull up. The late Richard Hofstadter, professor of history at Columbia University, dramatized this tendency in his study of *The Age of Reform.*

"Just as the cycle of American history running from the Civil War to the 1890s can be thought of chiefly as a period of industrial and continental expansion and political conservatism," Hofstadter wrote, "so the age...running from about 1890 to the second World War can be considered an age of reform.

"The surge of reform, though largely turned back in the 1890s and temporarily reversed in the 1920s, has set the tone of American politics for the greater part of the 20th century."

But Hofstadter also noted a reaction to this progressivism that occurs from time to time. He defined it as "a rather widespread and remarkable good-natured effort of the greater part of society to achieve some not very clearly specified self-reformation.

"Its general theme was the effort to restore a type of economic individualism and political democracy that was widely believed to have existed earlier in America and to have been destroyed by the great corporation and the corrupt political machine; and with that restoration to bring back a kind of morality and civic purity that was also believed to have been lost."

President Carter

Something of this same conservative impulse that challenged the reformers at the end of the last century and the "new freedom" and world visions of Woodrow Wilson in the 1920s reappeared in the closing years of the 1970s.

There were federal budget deficits running over $50 billion a year; vast expenditures for social welfare programs that didn't seem to be redeeming their promise; rising prices leading to more demands for higher wages; higher taxes; and higher rates of inflation until the confidence in the money of the United States and the political leadership of the United States began to be discounted in the other financial and political capitals of the world.

Accordingly, in the last couple of years of the 1970s, there was a popular revolt, primarily within the dominant middle class, of the people against the high cost and low efficiency of all government—federal, state, and local. It was encouraged by a new generation of investigative newspaper and electronic-media reporters who were exposing the failures and corruption of American political and commercial leaders.

For example, beginning in California, powerful forces were mobilized to cut property taxes and limit the rise in government spending. President Carter, who came into office in 1977 as a populist former governor of Georgia, fought the 1978 congressional elections on a platform of fiscal caution, austerity, and even frugality.

These were traditional Republican Party themes, but by anticipating the popular anxiety over higher prices, interest rates, and inflation rates, the Democrats managed to keep their congressional losses well below the normal midterm election average, and maintained large majorities in the Congress, which they have controlled for 41 out of the last 45 years.

Carter made control of inflation his top priority for 1979

Taking these election results as an accurate measure of American public opinion, the Carter Administration made the control of inflation its major objective in 1979, cut the normal rise in social expenditures, and insisted that it would come to the end of the 1970s with no more than a 2 or 3 per cent rise in the growth of the economy in 1979. This led to protests from blacks, labor union leaders, and intellectual liberals—all traditional supporters of the Democratic Party.

As another indication of this more conservative trend, the political power of the labor union leaders, so impressive since the New Deal days of the 1930s, actually declined in the last half of the 1970s. In 1978, union membership dropped to only 20.1 per cent of the labor force, the lowest percentage since World War II. And in the years since 1974, the total of union members fell by half a million, while the economy in this same period actually added 6 million new jobs.

This was not generally regarded as anything more than a temporary period of reflection and stocktaking, a lull before a revival of the progressive and reformist tradition in the 1980s. But in the last years of the decade, the people seemed to sense that the government had been too spendthrift and that even they themselves had been wasteful and self-indulgent and were beginning to lose their normal technological and productive advantages in the export markets of the world.

This was dramatized, for example, by staggering deficits in the nation's balance of trade. In the years from 1975 to 1979, the United States bought $50 billion worth of goods abroad more than it sold abroad—much of it by the purchase of foreign oil. Despite all the talk of "austerity," the consumption of oil actually increased by 17 per cent, and there was no evidence that this problem was going to get better. In the last years of the decade, President Carter pleaded with the people to reduce their consumption of foreign oil in order to reduce the inflation and improve the value of the nation's currency, but they consumed more and more each year.

Americans

In December 1978 the major oil-producing countries raised their prices for 1979 by 14.5 per cent, and this alone threatened to push the rate of inflation in the United States up to 8 per cent at the beginning of 1979 and to depress further the value of the dollar.

One of the most striking and disturbing developments of the late 1970s was the growth of special-interest groups, combined with a decline in the political activity of those who normally vote, not for a single issue, but for the general public interest.

For example, only 37 per cent of the eligible voters went to the polls in the November 1978 congressional elections–the lowest turn-out in 35 years.

New York City almost went bankrupt in 1977, and the city of Cleveland actually defaulted on payment of $15.5 million of debts in December 1978 to become the first major city to do so since the Great Depression of the 1930s. Thousands of Cleveland city workers faced lay-offs as the city's mayor tried to deal with the crisis of confidence.

This was not an entirely new experience in the political conflicts within the cities and states of the nation. The Constitution of the United States assumed a continuing struggle between different factions and regions of the nation, assuming that this competition would eventually serve the national interest. But there was some anxiety at the end of the 1970s that this factionalism was creating a host of embittered minorities and eroding confidence in the government and the common purposes of the people.

Presidential authority was not destroyed in this struggle with single-issue factions, but it was increasingly under challenge. In the foreign field, President Carter was able to establish normal diplomatic relations with China after 30 years of estrangement. He was also able, by the narrowest of margins, to get the consent of the Senate to transfer the Panama Canal to Panama at the end of the century. But while he defeated his opponents on these issues, he did not convince them, and left behind pockets of regret and even resentment.

This was the troubling problem within the nation as it came to the end of the 1970s: a general anxiety about the priorities and common purposes of the people; a widespread distrust in the institutions of government; a decline of confidence in the political parties, the press, and other instruments of communication; and therefore a tendency for all factions to concentrate on their own special interests rather than the general welfare.

The political controversies of 1978 and early 1979 illustrate this drift toward a transformation of the people into new, isolated but powerful factions and the fragmenting of the nation's politics.

In his efforts to bring the inflation under control and to restore the value of the dollar and the United States competitive position in the markets of the world, President Carter introduced an austerity budget for 1978-1979 that infuriated the liberals, the major labor union leaders, and the blacks.

In his efforts to bring about some kind of reconciliation between the state of Israel and the Arab states in the Middle East, and prevent the infiltration of the Soviet Union into the oil-producing states of that region, he alarmed most of the pro-Israeli leaders of the United States–normally supporters of his Democratic Party.

In short, though the executive power of the federal government usually managed to prevail, especially on foreign policy issues, the

Factionalism was creating some anxiety at the end of the 1970s

Arms talks

President left behind a number of aggrieved minorities and had to face the beginning of the 1980s with an increasingly puzzled and divided nation.

There were, however, some consolations. The conflict between the generations in the United States, so evident at the start of the 1970s, was less embittered at the end. University students, alarmed by the need to find jobs and by the disturbing results of drug experimentation, were working harder and even showing more interest in marriage and religion.

In sum, the United States was a more thoughtful, if less cocky nation as 1979 began. It had been humiliated by Vietnam and startled by Watergate and the decline of its economy at home and abroad. It was reflecting about the past, about its institutions, and even about itself, and was pausing to sort things out before facing the problems of the 1980s.

The conflict between the generations was not as embittered

Related Articles

For further information on United States affairs in 1978, see also Section One, Focus on The Economy; Focus on Education; and Focus on Science; Section Two, How Real is America's Religious Revival?; and the following articles in Section Four:

Sylvia Porter

Focus on The Economy

Mere decades ago, the U.S. dollar was the most respected currency in the world, but relentless inflation has caused its chaotic deterioration

The chaotic deterioration in the value of the United States dollar through most of 1978 created an almost insoluble dilemma for this nation and threatened disaster for the entire Western world. The Carter White House's inexperience and ineptitude were prime factors that brought the country to this near-crisis. And no matter how much could be attributed to President Jimmy Carter's prolonged learning on the job, his Administration could not escape the blame.

The fundamental force behind the demoralization in the U.S. dollar –the most revered, desired currency in the world mere decades ago– was the relentless and, in 1978, accelerating rate of inflation. This is the evil above all other economic evils. No paper currency can long survive the vicious impact of a steep inflation upon the moral standards, confidence, and leadership of its issuing nation. None ever has. The United States dollar cannot either.

Inflation has placed us in the horrible dilemma of damned if we do, damned if we don't. And although we could have escaped the dilemma–with appropriate policies and timing–we didn't.

On the one side, if U.S. economic policy is designed to substantially curb inflation and the equally dangerous psychology of inflation, then the danger of a business downturn in 1979-1980 becomes very real–with all that implies about rising joblessness, business bankruptcies, and so forth. And the business recession danger did indeed intensify as the Federal Reserve System, determined to do all it could on its own to control the price-wage spiral, aggressively tightened the screws on credit from mid-1978 on. The discount rate–the interest the Federal Reserve charges its own member banks that borrow funds from the system, and the pivot rate of the nation–was jerked up to a record 9½ per cent in early November with an abruptness obviously

Sylvia Porter

designed to shock the world. The prime rate–the rate banks charge their most credit-worthy customers–was boosted to 11¾ per cent. The federal funds rate–the rate at which banks borrow overnight funds from each other–went to a startling 10 per cent. All other rates spiraled up from here.

On the other side, if U.S. economic policy is geared to maintaining production, profits, sales, and employment at what are deemed tolerable "political" levels, then the almost certain result is persistent inflation, culminating in what could be the worst depression since the catastrophic 1930s.

Despite the contempt for U.S. economic policy fumbling that other national leaders (West German, Swiss, and Japanese, in particular) displayed at various international conferences during 1978, there was as yet no other money powerful enough to replace the U.S. dollar and support the expansion of global trade so imperative if world prosperity is to be sustained.

Of course, the economic shilly-shallying within the United States could not go on. Thus, the President's Phase II anti-inflation policy was initiated in late October. For in a mere 10 years, your dollar's buying power would be slashed more than in half if it were to continue losing value at "only" an 8 per cent pace–and the loss was running at a much worse annual rate than 8 per cent as 1978 closed.

This is not tolerable. You couldn't make long-term plans for anything worthwhile on the basis of an inflation rate of this magnitude. Meanwhile, perhaps the most insidious aspect of the pernicious inflation was the spreading expectation that inflation is becoming permanent–a "psychology of inflation" that is dangerously self-fulfilling. For as millions of Americans become resigned to the prospect that the price spiral is a fact of life to be accepted for the indefinite future, these unhealthy developments follow:

■ More and more workers demand wage hikes to keep up with past price increases and to get a jump ahead of future price increases–thereby adding to the current inflation rate.

■ More and more union leaders insist on cost-of-living adjustment clauses in their union contracts to give them automatic pay raises as the Consumer Price Index climbs. (In 1978, an estimated half of the total U.S. population–Social Security and welfare recipients as well as workers–were covered by such automatic raises.)

■ More and more businesses boost prices in anticipation of the wage demands and of the imposition of mandatory wage-price controls.

■ The whole sick pyramid collapses into a business slump, which leads to "reflation" policies and a new round of inflation.

Only an all-out courageous attack can brake inflation at its source as well as break the inflation psychology. President Carter's Phase II anti-inflation plan–centering on voluntary wage-price guidelines and introducing the new concept of a Tax-based Incomes Policy (TIP) via a request to Congress to vote a tax rebate to workers who obey the wage ceilings–went about as far as the White House could go under

No other money is strong enough to replace the U.S. dollar in global trade

What 8 Per Cent Inflation Will Do To the Dollar

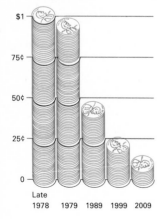

$1
75¢
50¢
25¢
0

Late
1978   1979   1989   1999   2009

its 1978 powers. Yet, voluntary though it is, the program can work if it gets the three "C's":

Compliance. The great power centers in organized labor and in business will have to agree voluntarily to accept the "flexible" overall standards of annual hikes in wages and fringe benefits not to exceed 7 per cent and price increases in 1979 limited to 0.5 per cent below their average annual rate during 1976-1977.

Clout. To back up the voluntary standards, the President will have to use his enormous authority to award juicy government contracts only to businesses that comply with the standards. And he will have to demonstrate his own fiscal austerity, too, by slamming the lid on federal spending, reducing the federal payroll, and so on. These are all potentially effective moves.

Congressional approval. The so-called wage insurance Carter promised to workers who hold down wage demands must set the stage for a full-scale debate on TIP in Congress.

But while Carter rejected outright the alternative of a "deliberate recession," the "extreme alternative" of a recession well may turn out to be the crucial factor in curbing the price spiral. For it was against the background of the following two sobering facts that Carter introduced Phase II.

Sobering Fact Number One. As 1978 ended, this economic expansion went into its 46th month. By any yardstick, this made it "aged." With the single exception of the artificially prolonged 50-month boom of the 1960s, no post-World War II upturn has lasted this long. And this expansion was clearly flashing signals of impending weakness. Its age alone suggested a marked slowdown, if not a stall, and then a downturn.

Sobering Fact Number Two. The inflation rate in 1978 speeded up even as the expansion aged and the Federal Reserve System clamped down on credit. The combination of an aged expansion, a fearful rate of inflation, and defiantly high interest rates made the threat of recession very real.

A business recession would indeed cool the inflation (temporarily, anyway). For, barbaric and cruel though it is to make the unemployed and bankrupt a first line of defense against inflation, a business slump has been the one sure answer to inflation throughout history.

What are some bold approaches through which we might conquer the inflation that is tearing apart the fabric of our society (without relying on the "certain" solution of a slump)? First, the "real wage insurance" program that Carter asked Congress to approve in its 1979 session is among the few truly innovative anti-inflation concepts to emerge in years. Under Carter's version, a worker who accepted the wage-benefit guideline of an annual increase of 7 per cent or less and then was hit by an annual rise in the cost of living of more than this limit would receive a tax rebate to make up the difference.

To illustrate, say you earn $20,000 a year and you get a pay-benefit increase in 1979 of $1,400 or 7 per cent. Then the Consumer Price

A number of factors made the threat of recession a very real one

President Carter

Index jumps 10 per cent. You would receive a check for $600 from the federal government (3 per cent of your base pay and equal to the difference between your pay increase and your cost of living increase). Your total pay boost would come to $2,000, or 10 per cent—and you would have been "insured" against 1979's inflation.

But as Congress debates Carter's wage insurance proposal, it undoubtedly will probe into the whole theory. And what may emerge at the end could be an entirely different program of curbing inflation.

TIP would make use of the U.S. tax system to fight inflation

Just what is TIP? It would use tax rebates as a "carrot" to encourage unions and business to moderate wage-price increases—or it would slap on tax increases as a "stick" to punish them if their actions add to inflation. The rationale is that if the tax system can be used to spur business spending on new plants and equipment, or to encourage insulation of homes, why can't it be used to combat inflation?

A second approach to fighting inflation lies in the fact that the weakness in the U.S. dollar was a prime factor in fueling inflation in 1978 by pulling up prices of once-cheap imports. Every 1 per cent decline in the dollar's buying power in terms of Japanese yen, West German Deutsche marks, or other major currencies added an estimated 0.1 of 1 per cent to consumer prices across-the-board.

But the already powerful drive toward protectionism is intensifying. Instead of being geared to fighting inflation, U.S. trade policies are swinging toward stimulating inflation. Quotas, tariffs, "voluntary" restraints, and other similar barriers are not really necessary to safeguard American jobs. Within any given industry, more jobs are estimated as lost through technological change (automation) than through imports. Trade protection tends to encourage the industries that are involved to delay the technological changes and cost-cutting steps they inevitably must take to prosper.

Average Yearly Growth In Productivity, 1962-77

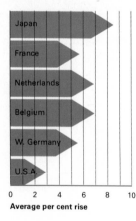

0   2   4   6   8   10
Average per cent rise

Direct, temporary payments—wage subsidies—would be a less costly, less inflationary, more efficient way to help workers in dying industries to move into new jobs. The U.S. government could pay more than $3,750 to each of the roughly 360,000 hourly workers in the steel industry, for example, and the total cost to U.S. taxpayers would be no greater than what current protectionist policies now cost in the form of higher prices. And substituting direct payments for the import protection now given the meat, steel, and sugar industries would lead to a drop in prices that could total as much as $2.7 billion a year.

A third bold approach to fighting inflation would be a postponement of the stiff increases in Social Security taxes scheduled to start in January 1979, increase again in 1980, and jump again in 1981. If the Social Security tax hikes remain written into the law as it now stands, there is no doubt that much of the added Social Security tax burden on employers simply will be passed along to consumers in the form of higher prices. But only Congress, which voted the Social Security tax increases, can change the law.

A fourth step would call for a review of future minimum-wage increases, now in the law—with particular emphasis on a two-tier minimum wage (under which young workers would get a lower minimum than adults). Carter can't do this on his own, either. It's Congress that writes the law.

And fifth, if you—a typical U.S. worker—could turn out 10 widgets per hour instead of eight, because you have new machinery, a modern plant, and a generally more congenial atmosphere, could you get a hefty pay increase of as much as 25 per cent without cutting one penny of your corporation's net profits? You bet you could. Your higher productivity (efficiency per worker, per work-hour) would be the key answer to an ever-rising standard of living for you and your fellow workers, an ever-improving profit position for your employer— and stable prices for our nation and all of us, as consumers.

Once the United States led the world in its rate of growth in productivity. But as the decade of the 1970s wore on, our growth rate plunged to an almost unbelievable 1.6 per cent a year—far behind the rising rates of our major trading partners. Clearly, something has gone terribly wrong. To correct it, we must expand business investment in new plants and equipment (as the 1978 tax law begins to do) by means of capital gains tax cuts and investment incentives; support all efforts that encourage technological innovations (as we formerly did so successfully); and foster cooperation toward these desirable ends between management and labor and between business and government. In addition, industry and labor must be consulted in the development of new government rules and in the elimination of outmoded regulations that are unnecessary barriers to productivity. Public managers and elected officials must also be held accountable for improvement in productivity of government services. And there must be improvement in the measurement of nationwide productivity. Also crying out for serious consideration are steps to:

■ Reform current agricultural programs, under which farmers are paid not to plant and minimum prices are set for certain crops to boost farmers' income by raising our grocery bills.

■ Write hospital cost containment into law.

■ Speed up deregulation of such industries as trucking and coastal maritime trade (in addition to airlines). If more firms enter these fields, fares would be more competitive—and lower.

This is merely a sampling of the ideas. They tumble out, one on top of the other. And they add up to one giant achievement: a return to a tolerable rate of inflation. But who in the White House or Congress is really listening, truly dedicated? Or must our nation wait for America's next generation of leaders to tackle—and finally win—the economic battle of the closing half of the 20th century?

Must we wait for the next generation to win the battle?

Inflation forum

Related Articles

For further information on economics in 1978, see Section Four, AGRICULTURE; BANKS AND BANKING; ECONOMICS; INTERNATIONAL TRADE AND FINANCE; LABOR; MANUFACTURING; STOCKS AND BONDS.

Harrison Brown
Focus on Science

We now know in molecular detail how living things work, but the question is whether we will be able to cope with this new knowledge

One of the great triumphs of biology in recent years has been the finding out in molecular detail how living things work. We now know that the reason a cell can pass on its characteristics to its descendants is that each cell contains a complete recipe that tells it how to manufacture the ingredients needed for it to reproduce itself. The recipe exists as a very complex molecule known as deoxyribonucleic acid (DNA). Each such molecule directs the manufacture of enzyme molecules that transform the available food molecules into materials that enable the DNA molecule to *replicate* (exactly reproduce) itself.

In the entire human body there are only 5 grams (0.18 ounce) of DNA, and this contains all of the information necessary for humans to multiply. Not only does each of the 10 trillion cells in the human body contain the same amount of DNA, it also contains all the genetic information needed to make the entire creature. This has been vividly demonstrated by scooping out the nucleus of a cell from the intestine lining of a South African clawed toad and injecting it into the *cytoplasm* of an egg from the same toad. (Cytoplasm is all the cell except the nucleus.) The nucleus from the body cell immediately starts to make more DNA and to divide. From this egg, there develops a tadpole and eventually an adult clawed toad that is genetically identical to the original toad used in the experiment.

This process is known as *cloning*. In 1978 the possibility of applying the technique to human beings received considerable attention. A motion picture, *The Boys from Brazil*, had as its theme the cloning of Adolph Hitler, which led to the creation of several dozen genetic duplicates of Hitler who were set loose in the world. A book, *In His Image, The Cloning of a Man*, dealt with a wealthy (and obviously vain) man who paid large sums of money to have a duplicate of himself created. The book seemed to be presented as truth, but the scientific community denounced it as pure fiction.

Geneticists agree that we are far removed from the time when a human being can be cloned. Cloning a human being is a far cry from

Harrison Brown

cloning a South African clawed toad, and it may well be several decades before the cloning of humans is a reality. But we can rightfully ask—so what? We can hardly imagine our society being greatly improved by such a practice, even if our future Shakespeares, Mozarts, and Einsteins were to be made near immortal in this way.

Far more important than cloning for the potential improvement of society are some recent developments in transplantation of *genes*, the units of heredity that determine particular characteristics. In 1978, Stanford University's Paul Berg, a leading research worker in DNA, announced the first transplant of a functional gene from one mammal to another. Berg and his colleagues, Richard Mulligan and Bruce Howard, spliced a segment of DNA containing codes for a specific chain of rabbit *hemoglobin* (a substance in blood) into a DNA virus known as SV 40. Cells from an African green monkey were then infected with this hybrid virus DNA to permit the newly incorporated gene segments to multiply. The scientists found that the rabbit hemoglobin was manufactured in these infected cells from the green monkey.

Thus, the new *recombinant DNA* (gene splicing) techniques were used for the first time to cause a gene of one species of mammal to function in another species. In announcing this important development, Berg said, "It is quite clear that the isolation of genes and the ability to manipulate them puts us at the threshold of a new form of medicine, the treatment of crippling genetic diseases through replacement of defective genes by their normal counterpart."

Over the ages, genetic diseases have caused inestimable human agony, ranging from that of parents whose children suffer from incapacitating genetic defects, to that of those who suffer themselves from hemoglobin disorders, diabetes, or other diseases. Although genetic counseling for prospective parents has become generally available, it was not until 1969 that significant help was forthcoming. In that year, a group at the University of Wisconsin successfully analyzed the amniotic fluid of a 22-week fetus and diagnosed it as a mutant male. Such techniques were rapidly improved and have been applied to the detection of a wide range of genetic abnormalities at early stages of fetal development. But the testing primarily provides peace of mind to worried parents-to-be. When serious genetic defects are found, and in the absence of corrective treatment of the developing fetus, the parents have to choose between the sad alternatives of abortion or giving birth to a mutant child.

Now, the observations of Berg and his co-workers suggest that if the code sequence of a given defective gene can be deciphered, it might be possible to synthesize a segment of DNA with the corrected sequence and replace it in the genetic apparatus. But much more work must be done before this possibility is transformed into reality.

Intimately related to the subject of human genetics and the treatment of genetic defects was the birth in 1978 of the first child to be conceived outside of the human body. The child, an apparently normal girl, was born in Oldham, England, on July 25. Her parents are

We are at the threshold of a new form of medicine, replacement of defective genes

Researcher Paul Berg

John and Lesley Brown. Two doctors, Patrick C. Steptoe and Robert G. Edwards, had brought the father's sperm and the mother's eggs together in the laboratory under carefully controlled conditions conducive to fertilization. A fertilized egg that had developed into a tiny embryo was then implanted in the mother's womb, where it developed normally until birth.

In the immediate future, these new techniques will be primarily useful in cases where the female is unable to conceive in the usual way because of some biological defect. But looking to the longer-range future, a number of possibilities present themselves. In theory, a selected embryo could be implanted in another woman's womb, raising the possibility of surrogate mothers for those unable or unwilling to carry a child the normal period of pregnancy. But far more important is the possibility of using the technique in conjunction with possible treatments for genetic defects.

While such possibilities may become realities in the distant future, other advanced applications of genetic engineering are already with us. An outstanding example is the application of recombinant DNA technology to the production of insulin for possible use by diabetics.

Diabetes mellitus is a disease that is usually inherited—in other words, it results from a genetic defect. It afflicts some 3 per cent of the population, but the number of diabetics in the United States is estimated to be increasing at the alarming rate of 6 per cent each year.

Diabetes results from insufficient manufacture of the hormone insulin by the pancreas. This lack of insulin prevents the body from utilizing sugar as an energy source and from storing it as starch. Until such time as the genetic defect that gives rise to diabetes can be repaired, the most effective therapy is to replace the missing hormone with insulin obtained from nonhuman sources.

Insulin is too complex a molecule to be synthesized economically in a chemical factory. Our present supplies are obtained from the pancreases of slaughtered cattle and hogs. There is serious danger, however, that demand for insulin may soon outstrip supply.

In 1978, a group at Harvard University headed by Walter Gilbert reported that—using recombinant DNA technology—they created a form of the bacterium *Escherichia coli* (*E. coli*) that could manufacture and secrete rat *proinsulin* (an immediate precursor of insulin in the pancreas). This is an important step toward developing industrial systems that can produce complex chemicals by making use of bacteria rather than large animals as the basic production units.

Rat insulin cannot be utilized by humans, but Gilbert and his colleagues believe that *E. coli* can be developed that will produce human insulin directly. Indeed, there is every reason to suppose that complex hormones such as insulin will be produced from bacteria on an industrial scale someday, and that they will prove to be less expensive than the products we now obtain from the slaughterhouse.

Thus, in an astonishingly short period of time, recombinant DNA technology has been applied in ways that give promise of improving

Recombinant DNA techniques can be used to produce insulin for diabetics

Doctors Edwards and Steptoe

39

the human condition. Only four years prior to these developments, however, a group of 11 molecular biologists who had been brought together by the National Academy of Sciences called for a temporary ban on certain types of recombinant DNA research. The group's main concern was that new types of bacteria and viruses, to which human beings have not been exposed, can now be created. The scientists foresaw the danger that these new viruses and bacteria might infect the human population. They urged the director of the National Institutes of Health (NIH) to consider establishing an advisory committee to evaluate the potential hazards of recombinant DNA molecules and develop procedures and guidelines to minimize the dangers.

Reports were issued dealing with problems of recombinant DNA research

Shortly after this guarded warning, the NIH formed a high-level advisory group that developed guidelines for recombinant DNA research in the United States. In 1976, the International Council of Scientific Unions created the Committee on Genetic Experimentation (COGENE) to serve as a source of advice across national boundaries concerning recombinant DNA activities. Initially, the new international body drew heavily upon the findings of the NIH, but it soon developed its own approaches to the problems. In 1978, COGENE issued reports dealing with the problems of risk assessment, guidelines for research using recombinant DNA technology, and the potential benefits of recombinant DNA technology.

Analysis of numerous experiments led the group to conclude that *E. coli K-12* (by far the most widely used bacterium in recombinant DNA experiments) has a limited prospect of survival and therefore probably cannot be converted by laboratory DNA manipulations into an agent capable of causing a dangerous epidemic or harming the environment. This reassuring conclusion that the original estimates of danger had been exaggerated came four years after the original warning had been made public by the scientists. Environmental activists had entered the discussion during the intervening period, and the entire issue of recombinant DNA research quickly became a matter of serious public concern. Regulations began to appear, and, among other developments, the city of Cambridge, Mass., refused to let Harvard build a special laboratory for recombinant DNA research.

Strands of DNA

The COGENE report on guidelines for research estimated that at least 367 recombinant DNA projects were underway in 155 laboratories in 15 countries by early 1978. Seven of these projects were being conducted at a high level of containment, and 76 were at a moderate level, but the remainder were being conducted at a low level of containment—which means that if anything goes wrong, there is little that can be done to keep the effects localized. Nevertheless, virtually all of the nations involved with recombinant DNA research in 1978 had drawn up guidelines for experimentation. Only 16 of the recombinant DNA projects were in nations where no guidelines exist.

For the most part, the various national guidelines for research are intended to deal with the risk of a major epidemic. The COGENE report emphasized that the chance of initiating an epidemic by recombinant DNA experimentation using *E. coli K-12* appears negligible. It emphasized further that the level of containment required for work with recombinant DNA from known *pathogens* (disease-producing organisms) is often greater than is specified for work with the original intact pathogenic organism. Indeed, some nations now effectively prohibit recombinant DNA work with genes from medically important disease-producing organisms.

The COGENE report on the applications of recombinant DNA technology stressed the enormous potential benefits for the development on an industrial scale of new or improved sources of medicines, foods, and industrial chemicals. It concluded that the genetically engineered microorganisms that will have to be constructed to realize these benefits will not pose any special hazards that cannot be contained by measures already used in the industrial fermentation industry.

Thus, the prospects for utilizing genetic engineering to improve human well-being had become obvious by the end of 1978, and the same scientists who had warned in 1974 that there were potential dangers were now saying that the dangers were not so serious. But in the meantime, the danger signals had become embedded in the public mind. Many questions were being asked. To what extent were scientists asking for relaxation of the rules in their own self-interest? Were the potential hazards now being deliberately underemphasized? Were the potential benefits being exaggerated?

Clearly, humankind stands at the threshold of a new age in human biology. Our present knowledge and that which we can obtain in the near future through our research efforts give promise of greatly improving the human condition. But there are also dangers associated with this new knowledge. Scientists might say that certain dangers are negligible, but if an improbable accident ends up killing a large part of the population, it is no longer negligible.

All of us would agree that the elimination of genetic diseases such as diabetes or Down's syndrome would be a good thing. But certainly the drive to "improve" the human species will not stop there. Many modifications of our genetic patterns will be proposed. But who will judge what is good or what is bad for us? Who will make the decisions?

Humankind has traveled a long pathway since the power of conceptual thought first appeared some 2 million years ago. Today we are still children, excited by each new toy we discover, no matter whether that toy be beneficial or dangerous. Our new biological knowledge is quickly bringing our childhood to an end. Will we be able to cope with our new knowledge as adults? That is the overwhelming question that confronts us.

Related Articles

For further information on science and technology in 1978, see the articles on the various sciences in Section Four.

Who is to make the decisions about what is good or what is bad for us?

DNA research lab

Lawrence A. Cremin

Focus on Education

**Two sets of decisions about American education
were made in very different places in 1978, raising
fundamental questions about policy and purposes**

We often talk about the way in which Americans "make up their
minds" about matters of educational policy, as if there were some
sort of immense town meeting at which 220 million people gather to
discuss issues and then take votes. Actually, Americans make up their
minds about education in a thousand places and in a thousand ways—
in rulings of the Supreme Court of the United States, in laws passed
by state legislatures, in policies made by local school boards, in agreements reached by college faculties, in selections made by textbook
publishers, and in decisions reached by thousands of individuals and
their families across the country about how, when, and where they
will pursue their education.

The year 1978 witnessed two sets of decisions about American
education made in very different places by very different sorts of
people according to very different procedures. Yet both raised fundamental questions of policy and purposes that would ultimately affect
the character of the American community and the values Americans
held in common.

The first set of decisions could be associated with a specific date;
namely, June 28, 1978, when the United States Supreme Court handed
down its opinion in the case of *Regents of the University of California
v. Allan Bakke*. Bakke, a resident of Los Altos, Calif., was a 38-year-old
aerospace engineer who decided somewhat later in life than most
people that he wanted to be a physician. In 1972 and again in 1973,
he applied to the School of Medicine at the University of California,
Davis. He was rejected both times. That, of course, was not unusual.
In 1972-1973, the Davis medical school received 2,464 applications
for 100 places, and in 1973-1974, 3,737 applications for 100 places.
What troubled Bakke, as a white male, was that as part of its affirmative action program to bring more members of minority groups into
the practice of American medicine, the medical school had created a
special committee to evaluate the applications of blacks, Chicanos,
Asians, and American Indians, and that committee had reserved for it

Lawrence A. Cremin

43

16 places in the entering class of 100 for such minority applicants. Moreover, the standards by which the committee judged these candidates were somewhat different from the standards applied generally. In fact, Bakke discovered that he received higher composite ratings on his grades, test scores, and interview performances than some of the minority-group candidates who had been admitted. As a consequence, Bakke sued the university in the California Superior Court, charging that the medical school had excluded him on the basis of race, in violation of the equal protection clause of the 14th Amendment to the United States Constitution (that clause provides that no state shall "deny to any person within its jurisdiction the equal protection of the laws"). In his suit, Bakke demanded that he be admitted to the medical school.

The Superior Court held that the special program operated as a racial quota and therefore violated the federal Constitution; but it refused to order Bakke's admission, maintaining that he had not proved conclusively that he would have been admitted if the special program had not been in existence. Both the university and Bakke appealed the decision, the university insisting that the special program was not illegal and Bakke insisting that he should have been admitted. The California Supreme Court, which next reviewed the case, concurred in the Superior Court's ruling that the special program was illegal, and also ordered Bakke's admission to the medical school. The university then appealed the case to the United States Supreme Court.

The United States Supreme Court heard the case on Oct. 12, 1977, in a context of widespread public concern. Many *amicus curiae* (friend of the court) briefs were filed on both sides, by organizations and institutions that were not directly involved but believed that important principles were at stake. Those who backed the university maintained that affirmative action programs are a vital instrument for providing true equality of opportunity to members of minority groups and thereby ensuring their entry into the mainstream of American life. Those who supported Bakke maintained that an individual's right to be judged on his or her own merits, wholly apart from considerations of race, color, creed, or national origin, is the very essence of the American conception of equal opportunity.

The Supreme Court's decision, which was heralded in advance as the most important since the *Brown* decision of 1954 ordering racial desegregation in the nation's schools, came by the narrowest possible majority. Five of the nine justices (Warren E. Burger; Lewis F. Powell, Jr.; William H. Rehnquist; John Paul Stevens; and Potter Stewart) concurred in the California Supreme Court's opinion that the special admissions program of the Davis medical school, with its quota of reserved places, was unconstitutional and that Bakke, given the conditions of his rejection, should be admitted. But five justices (Harry A. Blackmun; William J. Brennan, Jr.; Thurgood Marshall; Powell; and Byron R. White) also took partial issue with the California court, holding that matters of race and ethnicity may be considered as one

The court heard the Bakke case in a context of widespread public concern

Bakke at medical school

element of an admissions program, provided that strict quotas are not enforced.

In effect, both sides won. Bakke's right to be judged on his merits was upheld, as was the university's right to maintain an affirmative action program. Professor A. E. Howard of the University of Virginia Law School called the decision a "Solomonic compromise"; while Professor Alan Dershowitz of the Harvard University Law School called it an "act of judicial statesmanship."

The other set of decisions that came in 1978 could not be associated with any single date, because the decisions were made individually by dozens of college and university faculties across the country. They concerned what ought to be the common requirements for under-graduate degrees, and what was at stake was whether a college degree should mean anything more than that an individual had studied at some recognized institution for two or four years following high school graduation.

The drift during the decade from 1968 to 1978 had been unmis-takable. In the first place, the number of students (full time and part time) attending American junior and senior colleges had increased steadily, from 7.5 million in 1968 to 11.8 million in 1978. Second, as more and more students had come into the colleges, more and more programmatic options had been developed to meet their varying needs and interests—departments of ethnic studies, for example, and special vocational training programs, and work-study arrangements away from the campus, and student-taught courses, and the like. Third, as knowledge had proliferated, college departments had be-come more specialized and had been broken into subdepartments, with the result that students who wished to develop command of a subject area had been required to spend increasing amounts of time in ever narrower fields of study. And fourth, as students had de-manded more and more freedom from what they perceived to be unreasonable academic and parietal controls, the requirement of par-ticular courses or course distributions for graduation had also come to seem increasingly unjustifiable to them. The result had been a growing formlessness about American higher education, and a consequent in-ability to assume any particular competence on the part of college graduates—in the English language, or in mathematics, or in litera-ture, or in the sciences.

As often happens in such cases, concern about the problem arose simultaneously in many places during the mid-1970s. By way of ex-ample, institutions as different and as widely separated as Stanford University, Harvard University, New York University, and Miami-Dade Community College began to turn their attention to what undergraduates ought to know in common upon completion of their studies. The discussion proceeded differently in different institutions, and with varying results; but the predominant question across the country was essentially the same: What should be the character of educated men and women?

Concern about the growing formlessness of education began to grow

College science laboratory

**What were the
characteristics
that educated
men and women
should share?**

Given the pre-eminence of Harvard as the country's oldest and most prestigious institution, the discussions there were of unusual interest. They began in 1974, with an open letter from Dean Henry Rosovsky to the 800 members of the faculty of arts and sciences that pointed to the problem of fragmentation and asked for suggestions. That Dean Rosovsky chose to initiate the process in that particular way was absolutely appropriate, since it is the faculties of American colleges and not their deans or presidents who decide what programs, standards, and requirements will prevail. Rosovsky also appointed a number of faculty committees to look into various aspects of undergraduate life at Harvard—admissions, advisement, quality of teaching, and degree requirements—and asked them to report back to the faculty. The committee on degree requirements issued a statement in 1976-1977, recommending a required core curriculum for all students. The report was submitted to the faculty, informally debated at several meetings during the spring of 1977, and then approved in principle, with a request that the dean prepare specific recommendations. To comply with the request, Dean Rosovsky appointed several new faculty committees and asked them to work out the details. Their recommendations were embodied in a single report to the faculty in February 1978; after debate, the recommendations were approved in May. The process had taken four academic years.

The report the Harvard faculty accepted in 1978 contained few surprises. It affirmed that an educated person should have (1) an ability to think and write clearly and effectively; (2) a critical appreciation of the ways in which knowledge of the universe, of society, and of ourselves is developed and applied; (3) a knowledge and appreciation of other cultures; (4) an understanding of moral and ethical problems; and (5) a knowledge in depth of some field of learning. On the basis of these affirmations, the report set forth an undergraduate core requirement that embraced five fields—literature and the arts, history, social and philosophical analysis, science and mathematics, and foreign languages and cultures—and, associated with all of them, expository writing.

Harvard's proposal focused on five areas of study and the skill of expository writing. Stanford's focused on the common requirement of a university-wide course in Western culture. New York University's focused on a 10-element requirement that ran the gamut from mathematical competence to appreciation of the visual and performing arts. And Miami-Dade's focused on the individual's relationships with other people and groups, with society as a whole, with natural phenomena, with language, and with personal aspirations. A hundred other institutions doubtless developed a hundred other formulations. But, once again, the essential goal had been the same, to determine the common characteristics of educated men and women. And indeed, even though many of the efforts would ultimately founder on the shoals of academic politics, the substantive discussion they engendered would be valuable in their own right.

Supreme Court Building

Now, at first glance the issue of whether Allan Bakke should be admitted to the Davis medical school seemed to have little in common with the requirements for undergraduate degrees at Harvard, Stanford, New York University, and Miami-Dade Community College. At bottom, however, they involved similar questions: What should be the nature of American society, and how might education contribute to that society? More than a century ago, the French commentator Alexis de Tocqueville in his classic work *Democracy in America* wrote of the tremendous power of individualism in American life, deriving from the fact that Americans had never lived under feudalism and were attempting to build a new society based on equality for all. And he predicted that subsequent generations would have to give special attention to developing a community capable of containing the potentially destructive force of that individualism. Ultimately, both the *Bakke* decision of the United States Supreme Court and the curriculum decisions of college faculties across the country were addressing themselves to Tocqueville's problem.

The decisions symbolized a concept of community that was important

The *Bakke* opinion was not a stellar example of closely reasoned legal argument but rather a sensitive exercise in judicial pragmatism. To a country equally committed, on the one hand, to justice for minority groups too long excluded from full participation in the national life and, on the other hand, to justice for individuals irrespective of racial, religious, or national origins, the Supreme Court ruled that education would be permitted to serve both, in delicate balance and tension, neither to the exclusion of the other. Similarly, the various curriculum reports were not stellar examples of closely reasoned pedagogic argument but sensitive exercises in educational pragmatism. In a country that had fashioned a system of popular higher education designed to serve the commonwealth at the same time that it fostered individual development and technical expertise, faculties were ruling that a balance should be maintained, with neither commitment excluding the other. Both sets of decisions attracted strident critics; but the middle ground they sought to occupy symbolized a concept of community that Americans were finding it increasingly important to nurture during the final quarter of the 20th century.

Related Articles

For further information on education in 1978, see Section Two, How to Cope with Rising College Costs. In Section Four, see Education; Supreme Court of the United States (Close-Up).

Making school decisions

Alistair Cooke

Focus on The Arts

**It seems to be a good, if rash, idea to look back
to our preoccupations of the 1960s and see
how far we've come and where we went wrong**

In an early Focus piece, I quoted the Greek critic Longinus, who
died just over 1,700 years ago. He was known in his time as "the first
of critics" and "a living library and a walking museum." In old age,
he looked over all the poetry, the songs, the plays, and philosophical
treatises of his time and tried to answer the question that is implied
in every act of criticism or commentary: What makes for the best, and
what makes it most likely to become immortal? He ended with a confessional sigh: "The judgment of contemporary work is the last and
ripest fruit of much experience . . . and even then can be no more than
tentative."

That ought to give pause to all cocksure commentators who simply
lay down that so-and-so is the greatest of modern Presidents, or the
best painter or novelist, or that Muhammad Ali would surely have
"whupped" Joe Louis. Journalists, being fly-by-night critics, are
luckier than most in that their stuff, however crisp and bold it may
appear at a first reading, is seldom read again. It vanishes into the
pulp from which it grew. So journalists are able to go on believing
themselves to be fairly infallible, and so preserve their self-esteem, or
what might better be called *chutzpah*.

However, the opportunity is at hand for me to risk a resurrection
job on myself. These reports on the arts, like most other Focus articles,
started nearly 20 years ago. Since this is to be the last of them from me,
it seems to be a good, if rash, idea to look back to our preoccupations
of the early 1960s and see how far we've come, where we went wrong,
what recent novelties had never crossed our mind.

Although some of my pieces down the years have dealt with such
interesting oddities as op art, the financing woes of the Metropolitan
Opera, the arrival of the Beatles and rock music, "in-flight entertainment" on airplanes, the Highway Beautification Act (of fond, sad
memory), and the mania for dancing the twist, I find that there are
four recurring themes that seem to reflect most steadily the trends of
the times. They are: (1) the question of who is to be the patron or

Alistair Cooke

49

sponsor of the arts in the United States; (2) the revolution in American painting; (3) the bankruptcy of Hollywood; and (4) the problem of pornography and the First Amendment to the Constitution of the United States.

Other arts might look to public TV's method of financing

It is easy for an American tourist in Europe to forget that most of the European heritage in the arts–in architecture, painting, and music–was established first by the Roman Catholic Church and then by royal patrons. The great buildings we flock to see, from Dresden's Zwinger to Versailles to Hampton Court, were commissioned by kings and princes. Bath, the British resort, was commissioned by George IV of England; St. Petersburg (now named Leningrad) was founded and designed by Peter the Great. The Soviet Union quickly expunged the accursed memory of these royal benefactors by turning their houses into museums and schools, so that the czars' Winter Palace is an extension of the Hermitage, and the Cathedral of Our Lady of Kazan is now the Museum of Religion and Atheism. In music, certainly throughout the 18th century and on into the 19th, most of the great works, and all the dance music, of Handel, Mozart, and Beethoven were commissioned and paid for by some princeling. The rise of the opera house and the concert hall freed such later giants as Verdi and Wagner from the pleasant bondage to a sponsor at court.

Once the kings lost their taste, or their thrones, it became the European custom to hand the patron's obligation over to the state, so that whatever taxes the German or the Briton boggles at, he does not begrudge those that pay for the state opera houses or the British Arts Council.

But in America, as few people need to be told, there is a popular prejudice, uniting the early distrust of monarchy with the late fear of socialism, against having the state–the government–sponsor the arts. Into the breach of kingship stepped the "robber barons," their heirs, and later fortunes more respectably acquired. We have only to look through the catalogs of our city museums and galleries to realize what a pitiable state we would be in if we had not received the beneficences of the Rockefellers, the Carnegies, the Vanderbilts, the Morgans, Fricks, Mellons, Gardiners, DeYoungs, Corcorans, Gettys, and their like. However, since taxation has doomed the probability of a hereditary line of rich patrons, the remaining rich were urged in the early 1960s to pool their charities and set up cultural centers, from New York City to Atlanta to Los Angeles. In the intervening years, they have all been in financial trouble. The Lincoln Center for the Performing Arts had to close its New York State Theatre. All of them had to beg, in an annually mounting panic, for more private funds to pay the interest on the mortgages, with little hope of ever increasing their investment. Public television devised an alternative that might well come to be embraced by other arts: one-third of their funding guaranteed by the federal government, another third by business corporations, and the rest by voluntary contributions from the viewers.

From the artists' point of view, however, the great danger is that

Lincoln Center

their struggle to keep up the payments may obliterate their primary function, which is not only to perform, but also to create works of art. And that is something all the money in Arabia cannot buy. In the past decade, San Francisco has sharpened the point. It did not build a cultural center. It set up, modestly at first, an acting company and a ballet company. It trained a generation in the repertory classics; it slaved away at the disciplines of ballet. Without the investment of glittering new buildings, carrying huge overheads to maintain, it has produced in the American Conservatory Theater the best repertory company in the country, and a ballet company that has been favorably compared, if not with the glories of New York, at least with the best being done in London. The moral is simple and brutal: Creativeness is achieved by talent and hard work and cannot be bought with million-dollar buildings.

Art schools turned from big hamburgers to landscapes and portraits

In the early 1960s, we were all agog over the soaring reputation of American abstract art and the new international pre-eminence of the New York School: Jackson Pollock, Mark Rothko, Willem De Kooning, Franz Kline. No sooner had they acquired the respectability–and the fortunes–of masters than along came Robert Rauschenberg and Andy Warhol, the heralds of pop art, which somebody strange to our language could be forgiven for thinking meant the slavishly photographic painting of a Coca-Cola bottle.

Already the counterrevolution has set in with a vengeance. Art schools that in 1963 abandoned classes in drawing and commissioned such courtyard masterpieces as an enormous hamburger in concrete have returned to figure drawing, portraits of Highland cattle, and worthy imitations of the Hudson River School of landscape. This gear shift, though very agreeable to puffing oldsters, may itself be a bad sign or a proof of Kenneth Clark's contention that modern painting after postimpressionism had nowhere to go. At any rate, the change in painting fashions went along with a retreat, on the part of the museums, into nostalgia. Nobody could have suggested to me in 1964, at the risk of a coarse put-down, that not only would Andrew Wyeth soon have a retrospective show at New York City's Metropolitan Museum of Art but that, in 1978, the trendy young everywhere in Europe and America would be drooling over the lachrymose maidens, the macho Romans, and the meticulous draperies of Lord Leighton, Alma Tadema, G. F. Watts, and all the Pre-Raphaelites who in my youth were considered by experts to be the epitome of nonart.

Acting company acting

One of the worst, but historically one of the most significant, movies of the early 1960s was the Richard Burton-Elizabeth Taylor *Cleopatra*. It was originally budgeted, I believe, at the preposterous figure of $5 million. It did not recover its costs (though it may in a year or two through its sale on video cassettes). Its failure was widely attributed to the pre-emptive power of television. It took us several years to appreciate that what we were seeing was not so much the bankruptcy of Hollywood as the end of the studios' stable of stars signed to long-term contracts. Way back there, it appeared to be a basic law of economics that new movies were made from the profits of the old. But once the stars began to scorn a fat fee and demand the fatter booty of a percentage of the gross receipts, Hollywood ceased to be the financing capital of the movies and was threatened as the center of production. The arrival of the jet airplane and the cheaper labor to be found in Europe transferred much production to genuine locations abroad. (It was cheaper to build *Julia*'s Cape Cod cottage on the Norfolk coast of England and work with an English crew than film an existing cottage on Cape Cod with an American crew.)

Since labor costs followed, or perhaps charted, the dizzy rise of inflation, and since the newest movie stars, after one thumping success, began to demand the earth, investment in movie production had to spread among outside "angels." (As an example, a nubile redhead who never attained the earlier popularity of, say, Clara Bow or Ann Sheridan, could ask, and get—for what turned out to be a negligible movie—$350,000 in living expenses, a $1-million fee, and 5 per cent of the gross. This amounts to remuneration beyond the dreams of Gary Cooper or Greta Garbo or, for that matter, Walt Disney's seemingly indestructible Mickey Mouse, who celebrated his 50th anniversary as a star this year.) The new financier of the movies is known as an "independent," who is not to be thought of as a regular investing firm but is most often a wildcat investor in a one-shot deal. The latest projected epic is a sort of underwater *Star Wars*, provisionally called *Aquarius Mission*. It was at first to be produced by Columbia pictures in association with the Soviet Union. For complicated reasons, having to do with the extremely complex technology required, the Soviets backed out, and so did Columbia. At this writing, it is to be produced by the Guinness (stout) brewery and the Japanese, and to be filmed in Florida. The budget is figured at a conservative $16 million. The already released *Superman,* intended to elevate Christopher Reeve to godhead, was calmly budgeted at *$40 million!* It remains to be seen whether the Arab oil producers' continuing price hikes will make $80-million productions the regular thing or abolish once and for all the multimillion-dollar movie.

There is very little to add to the limitations I have been reciting in recent years about the spread of pornography in the theater, in books, and most of all in the movies, and the seeming inability of our system of justice to define obscenity and mark the spot where it becomes socially intolerable.

If the return to fashion of Pre-Raphaelite painters was inconceivable 20 years ago, the suggestion that copulation would soon become a standard feature of our movies would have seemed like the prediction of a lunatic. Yet in less than 20 years, the courts of the Western world have moved from the rigidity of the Victorians to the boundless tolerance of the Babylonians. In the 1930s, the criterion of obscenity as anything "likely to corrupt a minor" had been abandoned in the landmark decision of Judge John M. Woolsey, who decided that

Cleopatra

in sexual matters the test of excitation should be the instincts of "the average sensual man." Twenty-five years after the admission of James Joyce's *Ulysses* to the bookstores, D. H. Lawrence's *Lady Chatterley's Lover* was freed for publication in both Britain and the United States on the ground that its explicit sexual content was transcended, if not sanctified, by a high social purpose. Since then, the Supreme Court of the United States has abandoned also the requirement of a worthy social purpose and, leaving the definition of obscenity to the states, has retreated into a position of helpless neutrality in which anything that actually happens in the pathology of human relations may be considered an assertion of liberty and a vindication of the Founding Fathers' broad-mindedness.

Law must have its roots in some generally approved system of morality

What the courts first ignored and then abdicated was their duty to mark the line where liberty moves over into license. The very idea of license, is, of course, a moral concept. But unless law has its roots in some generally approved system of morality, in a code of things people agree not to do for the general good, it is no more than a roster of arbitrary rules.

I do not believe things will stay as they are. And it will not be enough to forego the marketing of obscenity simply because people may grow bored with it. The galloping tolerance of visible sex and violence has extended to television, and a federal judge has ruled that the networks' voluntary tradition of restraint, which bans such horrors from "family viewing time," is a violation of the right to a free press.

If we are not to follow the experience of the Germans half a century ago, when a berserk sexual permissiveness was brought to heel by the jackboot and the lash, the courts will sooner or later have to decide the limits of "freedom" that a healthy society can tolerate. They must face the problem they have ducked, of saying whether Sodom and Gomorrah were societies that should have been protected in all their vileness by the First Amendment to the Constitution.

Mickey

Related Articles

For further information on the arts in 1978, see Section Two, WHERE THERE'S HOPE, THERE'S LIFE; and the following articles in Section Four:

Architecture	Literature for Children	Poetry
Canadian Literature	Motion Pictures	Television
Dancing	Music, Classical	Theater
Literature	Music, Popular	Visual Arts

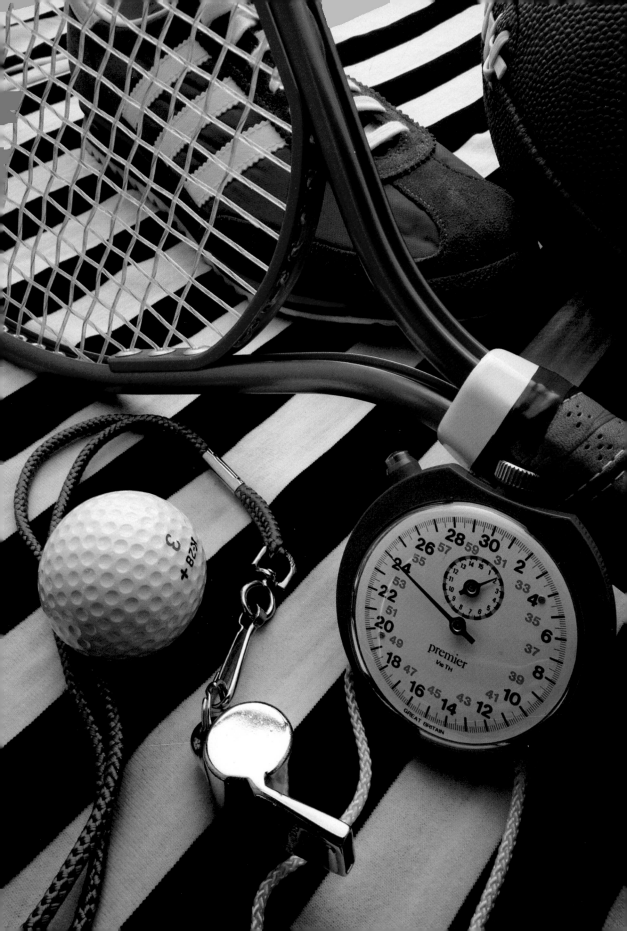

Red Smith

Focus on Sports

It was an absorbing baseball season, and its most engrossing aspect was the saga of Billy Martin — a talented leader and a genius at getting fired

"It was a great year to be a Yankee fan," a follower of the New York Yankees said of the 1978 baseball season. It was, Roger Angell wrote in *The New Yorker*, "one of the most absorbing, surprising, and painful—painful above all—baseball campaigns ever." Roger Angell is a fan of the Boston Red Sox. The season was indeed absorbing, even to a neutral who was neither elated by the Yankees' success nor dejected by the failure of the Red Sox, and its most engrossing aspect was the saga of Billy Martin.

Although he hasn't been around long enough to become a figure of legend like Casey Stengel, John McGraw, or Connie Mack, Martin is one of the most successful managers who ever lived. His talent for leadership is exceeded only by his genius for getting himself fired.

He was an able and combative infielder who became an able and combative manager of the Minnesota Twins, the Detroit Tigers, and the Texas Rangers before he moved to New York as an employee of an able and combative capitalist named George M. Steinbrenner III. Under Martin's direction the Twins and Tigers won divisional championships and the Rangers moved from last place to second. At every stop he clashed with his employers and lost his job.

In 1976, his first full season as manager in New York, the Yankees won the championship of the American League but lost the World Series. It was the club's first pennant in 12 years, and Steinbrenner, exultant, spent $12,000 buying $300 gift certificates on a men's clothing store for everybody on the squad. Martin was chosen the league's Manager of the Year in a poll taken by the Associated Press.

The next summer was made clamorous by discord in the Yankee clubhouse, but the feuding players won another pennant and defeated the cuddly Los Angeles Dodgers in the World Series, proving once again that brotherly love is not an indispensable ingredient of a winning team. That was 1977. The Yankees opened the 1978 season as defending champions of North America but came upon hard times early, and in spite of Martin's record his job was soon in jeopardy.

Red Smith

Teams like Detroit and Milwaukee made trouble for a while but as the race in the American League East took shape, the Red Sox moved into first place and set a punishing pace. Hobbled by injuries, the Yankees had trouble holding second place.

Starting in 1975 when they invested something like $3.75 million in Jim (Catfish) Hunter, the Yankees had spent so heavily for free agents that they came to be known, a trifle derisively, as "the best team money can buy." They had no glaring weakness at any position and seemed especially rich in pitching. However, sore arms subtracted Andy Messersmith and Don Gullett from the pitching staff; management disposed of Rawly Eastwick and Ken Holtzman; Catfish Hunter and Ken Clay were laid up; Ed Figueroa had his ups and downs; and Sparky Lyle's relief work was nowhere near as effective as in 1977, when he won the Cy Young Award as the league's Most Valuable Pitcher.

Some said the Yankees were "the best team money can buy"

In addition to the pitchers, other key players were disabled for various periods, including Thurman Munson, the splendid catcher; Mickey Rivers, the center fielder; and the second base-shortstop combination, Willie Randolph and Bucky Dent.

If Martin enjoyed any peace of mind it must have been when Ron Guidry was on the mound. That remarkable left-hander won his first 13 decisions and would complete the season with 25 victories and only three defeats. He would win another game in the pennant play-off and another in the World Series. His winning percentage of .893 was the highest for any 20-game winner ever. After the season he was a unanimous choice for the Cy Young Award.

However, except when Guidry was working, it was obvious to most observers that what the Yankees needed was not new leadership but a mess of medical miracles. This did not seem obvious to Steinbrenner or his executive vice-president, Al Rosen.

In the circumstances and in view of past performances, another owner might have announced that he was extending the manager's contract or at least might have touted him for Manager of the Year. Steinbrenner said Rosen would make the decision on Martin's future, adding that his own patience was wearing thin.

"Billy is a professional manager," Rosen said, "and he knows managers are hired to be fired. He's got to turn things around."

"It hurts me," Martin said. "I get tired of it. After winning two straight pennants and a World Series, why should I have to be on the block all the time?"

Things didn't turn around. At the midsummer intermission for the All-Star Game, the Yankees were in third place, 11½ games behind Boston. The decline continued until they were 14 games back, then came a five-game winning streak, then an explosion.

Reggie Jackson, demigod and demioutfielder, refers to himself as "the stick that stirs the drink," the catalyst that makes things happen. He made things happen in July by openly flouting the manager's authority, bunting when Martin had signaled for him to swing for a

Slugger Jackson

base hit. He was suspended for five days. When he returned, it was in the role of unrepentant martyr.

Martin boiled over. "If he doesn't shut his mouth he won't play!" he said, "I don't care what George says!" Jackson was a special favorite of Steinbrenner's. "The two of them deserve each other," Martin said. "One's a born liar and the other's convicted."

Billy was technically in error. Steinbrenner never was convicted of lying. Charged with illegal campaign contributions to political parties, he pleaded guilty of lying and trying to get employees to lie for him. Billy was in error tactically, too. You don't call a prominent sportsman a liar if you work for him. Rosen flew to join the club in Kansas City. Martin called a press conference, tried to read a statement of resignation, and broke down in tears.

Martin "quit," returned as "adviser," and Lemon arrived

Bob Lemon, dismissed earlier in the season as manager of the Chicago White Sox, was Martin's successor. The Yankees couldn't have found a leader more unlike his predecessor. Martin is tough, resourceful, and emotional. Lemon is quietly humorous and outwardly tranquil. Nobody will ever know whether the change in managers had anything to do with the change in the team's fortunes. A greater influence was the injured players' return to health. With Rivers, Munson, Randolph, and Dent all in the line-up and with Hunter winning six games in a row, the Yankees took out after the Red Sox.

First, though, Steinbrenner dropped the other shoe. A few days after Martin's "resignation," the owner announced that Billy would return as manager in 1980. At that time Lemon would move into the office as general manager. Meanwhile, Martin would serve in some vaguely described advisory capacity at $80,000 a year.

Not even scholars steeped in Steinbrenner lore could figure that one out. The most popular theory held that Steinbrenner, upset by the adverse reaction of fans to the departure of Martin, made the announcement to appease the customers, reassuring himself that anything could happen before 1980.

Boston was in trouble. Butch Hobson, the third baseman, bothered all summer by bone chips floating in the elbow of his throwing arm, had to leave the line-up. Carleton Fisk, the catcher, Jerry Remy, the second baseman, and all three outfielders—Fred Lynn, Dwight Evans, and Carl Yastrzemski—were hurting. Their lead dwindled to five games, showed brief improvement, then shriveled.

The Yankees were only four games back when they visited Boston's Fenway Park in September. In four games they scored 42 runs against nine. They left town tied for first place. Thereafter, games were won and games were lost and when the long season ended the teams were tied again.

When National League teams finish a season in a tie for first place, they play off the deadlock, two games out of three. With sounder logic and less concern for gate receipts, the American League holds that if you can't establish a champion in 162 games there is no point in prolonging the agony. The Americans play it off in a single game.

Manager Lemon

57

This one, played in Boston, was a beauty. The Yankees won, 5-4. Then they beat the Kansas City Royals, champions of the American League West, three times in four games. Then, for the second consecutive year, they met the Dodgers in the World Series.

Hardly anybody had expected them to be playing ball in October, and in the first two games they seemed to feel they didn't belong there. In the opening game they fell behind with alacrity, 6-0, and lost, 11-5. The Dodgers won the second game, too, but this was enriched by a curtain scene of high drama.

No other team had won in four straight after losing the first two

With Los Angeles in front, 4-3, Yankees on first and second base and two out in the ninth inning, Reggie Jackson went to bat against a big rookie named Bob Welch. A year earlier, when Welch was a 20-year-old graduate of Eastern Michigan University sitting at home in Ferndale, Mich., Jackson had won the deciding World Series game in outrageously flamboyant style, hitting three home runs with three consecutive swings. Now in this game he had driven in all the Yankee runs. An outfield single would tie the score; a double might put New York ahead.

The count went to three balls, two strikes. Welch pitched, the runners took off, Reggie swung, and the ball wasn't there. The Yankees were down, two victories to none.

The series moved to New York, where Guidry started the third game. Naturally, the Yankees won. They had to go 10 innings to win the fourth and square the series. The Dodgers may have begun to doubt themselves, for in the fifth game they committed three errors, there were two passed balls, their pitchers gave up 18 hits and a wild pitch, and the Yankees won, 12-2.

Back in Los Angeles, the Yankees wrapped it up, 7-2, with only token resistance. No team had ever won a World Series in four straight after losing the first two games. This was 1978, though, the year of the Yankees.

Even when the last game was over, echoes of this troubled and fascinating season could be heard. When a team qualifies for the World Series, the players always vote on how to cut up the loot. Often an individual's popularity will influence the vote. In the Martin-Lemon popularity contest, the Yankees waffled.

First they voted a half-share to Martin and a half-share to Lemon. When this got into the newspapers, they had second thoughts. The list they sent to the baseball commissioner's office had Martin still down for a half-share amounting to $15,618, but there was a blank space after Lemon's name. Bowie Kuhn, the commissioner, filled in the figure for a full share – $31,236.

Martin and Steinbrenner

Related Articles

For further information on sports in 1978, see also Section Five, ICE SKATING; and the following articles in Section Four: BORG, BJORN; LOPEZ, NANCY; NABER, JOHN; OLYMPIC GAMES; SPINKS, LEON; SPORTS; STENMARK, INGEMAR; UNSER, AL; and the articles on individual sports.

Section Two

Special Reports

Seven articles give special treatment to subjects
of current importance and lasting interest.

Aid for Your Aching Back

By Patricia Skalka

Medical science is finding better ways to treat the pain that various stresses cause in that miracle of engineering — the back

No matter who you are—man or woman, adult or child, laborer or office worker—the chances are excellent that you will suffer back pain at some time in your life. It may be only a temporary discomfort, or it may be an excruciating, incapacitating pain that virtually takes over your life.

According to medical estimates, some 80 per cent of all people in the United States, Canada, Australia, and Europe will share this woe. And the cost is high. Back problems account for more than 17 million physician visits each year in the United States, for example. They are the second most frequent health problem and second only to the headache as the leading cause of work time lost. Nearly 25 per cent of all disability payments go to workers with back injuries, while an additional $12 billion is eaten up annually in lost productivity and health-care costs. The picture is just as staggering and costly in other industrialized countries.

Most back pain is minor and temporary, involving a few days—or even hours—of discomfort. There are many possible causes, including too much exercise (or too little), poor posture, improper lifting, bending, reaching, and even mental stress. Much back pain is caused by simple muscle strain. But if the pain is severe, or persists, the first step is to see your doctor.

Severe and persistent back pain is not a new problem, but doctors have found it to be more complex than they once thought it to be. They now realize that this problem often involves much more than the physical components of the back and that treatment may reach far beyond the confines of the doctor's office. Medical science has made progress in recent years in untangling the complicated puzzle of back pain. At the same time, government, industry, and unions are paying more attention to working conditions in an effort to eliminate potentially damaging situations.

This new interest has come about because of growing concern over the high national cost of back pain, and demands for occupational safety. And you are the beneficiary. Whether or not you have ever felt annoying twinges or harsh stabbing pains in your back, you stand to gain from the growing sophistication and knowledge about the back. The more you know, the better you will understand the nature of the problem and the complexities of the solutions. You will learn what only a handful of health professionals suspected a few years ago—that much of this pain can easily be prevented and a good part of it can be cured, given prompt, correct diagnosis and treatment.

Scientists and medical experts offer two basic reasons for the high incidence of human back pain. The basic cause, some experts say, is directly linked to the evolutionary change in the human line from quadrupeds, or four-footed creatures, to bipeds, who walk on only two feet. "The spine was not made to be erect," suggests Alon P. Winnie, professor and head of the Department of Anesthesiology at the University of Illinois Medical Center in Chicago. "In becoming erect, we put stress on the back not experienced by quadrupeds."

Weight distribution and muscular demands, for example, both change when the body shifts from the horizontal to the vertical position. In the horizontal position, the weight is spread equally along the length of the spinal column and then divided between two sets of limbs before being transferred ultimately to the ground. But in the vertical position, the weight is concentrated in the lower back and is then transferred to one set of limbs—the legs.

Our two-footed stance is not the only reason for the high incidence of back pain, however. Our life style is a more immediate factor. Those of us who live in the highly industrialized Western world pay the price of prosperity with our backs. We slump in soft chairs instead of sitting erect on our haunches; we toss clothes into the dryer rather than hanging them on lines to dry; we ride elevators instead of climbing stairs; and we sleep on soft mattresses, not on firm floors or mats.

The author:
Patricia Skalka is a Chicago free-lance science writer who specializes in medical research and practice.

In short, we pamper our bodies and do not exercise enough, allowing such muscles as the large networks that layer our backs to become weak. "Then we expect too much of these muscles on sudden notice," says Kenneth Washburn, director of the Spinal Rehabilitation Clinic at the University of Texas in Austin.

The back, an anatomical marvel of structural engineering, is composed of hard and soft tissue. Hard tissue is bone – the 24 vertebrae of the spinal column plus the 5 fused vertebrae of the *sacrum*, a large triangular bone at the base of the spine, and the 4 fused bones of the *coccyx* (tailbone). The first 7 vertebrae of the spinal column are in the *cervical* (neck) region; the next 12 are in the *thoracic* (chest) region; and the last 5, the largest of all the vertebrae, are in the *lumbar* (lower back) region. The sacrum connects through joints to the wings or sides of the pelvis and leads through another joint to the coccyx.

The spinal column is an important part of the body's framework. It supports the head at the top, anchors the ribcage in the center, and joins the pelvis at the bottom. It also houses and protects the spinal cord, the massive array of nerves through which the brain communicates with the various parts of the body. Seen from the front or back, the normal spine looks straight; viewed from the side, it has four

Avicenna, an Arab doctor of the 11th century, described several ways to treat an ailing back in his book, *Canon of Medicine*.

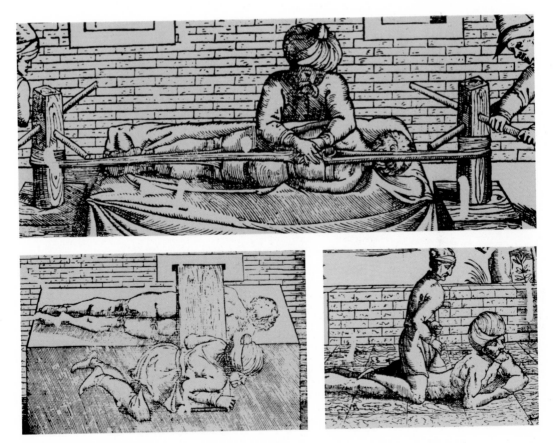

curves. These curves enable the column to carry more weight and handle more stresses than it could if it were perfectly straight.

What you feel when you press your hand against your back are bony rearward projections of the vertebrae—only a small part of the spinal structure. Other projections, called *processes* by anatomists, extend up and down, and left and right. The projections provide joint surfaces between the vertebrae and attachment areas for the numerous muscles and *ligaments* (strong connective tissue) required to make the vertebrae into a supportive, yet flexible, spinal column. The main, rounded part of the vertebral bone is deeper in the body. It bears the weight. Extending out from the main bone, the projections form a ringlike protective structure through which the spinal cord passes.

The back's soft tissues maintain and adjust its curvature to handle stresses. The ligaments stretch from the bony projections of the verte-

Back Basics
From the atlas vertebra that supports the head to the coccyx, or tailbone, the back, *below,* gives support and flexibility to the attached layers of muscle that move the body, *below right.*

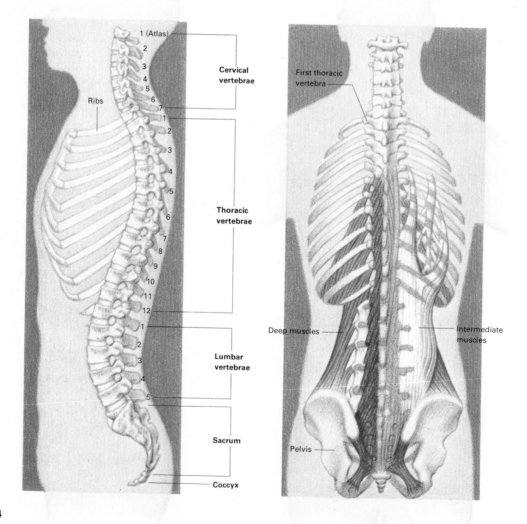

Ribs

1 (Atlas)
2
3
4
5
6
7

Cervical vertebrae

1
2
3
4
5
6
7
8
9
10
11
12

Thoracic vertebrae

1
2
3
4
5

Lumbar vertebrae

Sacrum

Coccyx

First thoracic vertebra

Deep muscles

Intermediate muscles

Pelvis

brae like guy wires. They attach bone to bone–backbone to rib, and vertebra to vertebra, running vertically and horizontally around the spinal column. Also reaching out from the backbone are tendons that attach to muscles.

The nerves extend from the brain down the spinal cord to the rest of the body, carrying commands from the brain and sending messages of irritation or pain to the brain. Thus, there are hundreds of potential causes of back problems. Any injury or disease of the backbone, the vertebral joints, the ligaments, muscles, tendons, or nerves can result in pain and disability.

Only about 10 percent of all serious back problems are caused by structural defects or disease. Structural defects may be *congenital* (present at birth) or acquired. In congenital conditions, vertebrae may be missing, incompletely developed, or fused. The two most common acquired conditions are lumbar lordosis (swayback) and scoliosis. Swayback affects all age groups and generally results from excessive chest-out, stomach-in posture. Scoliosis is a side-to-side curving of the spine that usually strikes teen-agers. It is six times more common in young girls than in young boys, and it seems to occur with the same frequency throughout the world–about 25 of every 1,000 young people can be expected to develop some degree of scoliosis. Scoliosis almost always begins during the adolescent growth period–but doctors do not know what causes it.

Diseases of the spine include tumors; spondylitis, or inflammation of the backbone; meningitis, or infection of the spinal cord; and arthritis, especially osteoarthritis caused by natural wear and tear, poor posture, and prolonged stress. Back pain can also result from disease or injury in other parts of the body. This is called *referred pain* and happens when the brain confuses signals coming from the vast network of nerves and misinterprets their origin.

Only about 10 per cent of back pain–much less than is commonly thought–is caused by disk problems. Disks separate each rounded main vertebral bone of the spinal column from its neighbors. These tough, flexible structures are heavy gelatinous masses surrounded by fibrous cartilage. The disks aid motion and act as cushions or shock absorbers. Without disks, you would be considerably shorter and you would feel the grind of bone on bone each time you bent over, sat up, twisted, or turned. Trouble occurs when the gelatinous nucleus of the disk herniates, or breaks through its cartilage covering. The cartilage then gradually wears away. But the pain of a slipped disk is generally produced by the pressure of the ruptured material on adjacent nerves, particularly as they emerge from the spinal cord.

About 80 per cent of back pain–some experts put the figure even higher–is associated with muscles and is usually linked to poor body conditioning and general muscular weakness. There are many contributing factors–tension keeps muscles taut and reduces their natural flexibility; poor posture can shift the body's natural weight loads or

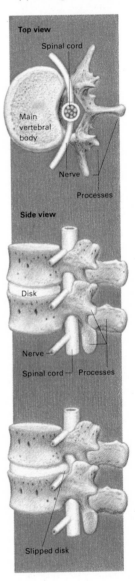

Disk Data
Disks cushion the bones that protect the spinal cord and are attached to muscles, ligaments, and tendons. Slipped disks become painful when they press against nerves.

Top view
Spinal cord
Main vertebral body
Nerve
Processes

Side view
Disk
Nerve
Spinal cord
Processes

Slipped disk

contribute to improper weight-lifting positions; bad working conditions may force workers to perform repetitive tasks in awkward positions or to carry loads that are too heavy for human handling; and obesity increases the burden that back muscles must bear.

"Most of the people doctors see wouldn't have as much of a problem if they had better conditioning in their backs," explains Stephen H. Butler, assistant professor of anesthesiology at the University of Washington in Seattle. "Unfortunately, we are taught that instant cure is the thing to expect. That's the way people feel about back pain. They strain their backs and they want a quick, easy solution."

According to Butler, patients must learn to accept some of the responsibility for treating back pain. They can do so by exercising—using exercises prescribed by a doctor.

"An exercise routine involving 15 minutes, twice a day, is sufficient for most people and should be done either to prevent or treat back pain," Butler says. "But it is easier from the physician's point of view to write out another prescription—and some maybe don't know what else to do—and it is easier from the patient's point of view to pop a pill than to exercise."

In 1961, John J. Bonica, an Italian-born physician, established the first multidisciplinary pain clinic at the University of Washington and the door began to open on an entirely new way to deal with long-term, seemingly incurable pain of all kinds, including back pain. Patients with back pain were treated there by a team of experts representing many different disciplines—anesthesiology, neuroscience, orthopedics, physical therapy, psychology, and others—rather than by one physician at a time, each representing only one specialty. The team then decided on the treatment deemed best for each patient. The results were encouraging and physicians soon began to get the message: The team concept works and offers new and concrete hope to pain patients. Today, more than 46 multidisciplinary pain clinics including six or more different specialties exist in the United States and 12 other countries, and there are 200 with three to five specialties.

"Before we knew some of the new techniques and the things we're doing now, doctors had two choices," says Lucien L. Trigiano, director of the Department of Rehabilitation Medicine at St. Francis Memorial Hospital in San Francisco, where the team approach has been used for five years. "One was rest and medication—considered conservative treatment—and the other was surgery. Now we're offering an alternative. And we're winning about 85 to 90 per cent of those backaches. We're getting them better, getting the patients back to work, back to society as productive people."

The battery of treatments offered by multidisciplinary clinics runs the gamut from the traditional and conservative to the experimental and controversial. Among the more established nonsurgical techniques are hydrotherapy, heat packs, and *diathermy* (applying heat by sending high-frequency electronic currents through the body). Some

Patients at the Chicago
Rehabilitation Institute's
Low Back and Pain Clinic
perform special exercises,
top, then study their
performance on videotape,
center left. Therapy
also includes a session
in the pool, *left.* Staff
members demonstrate the
correct posture for such
simple tasks as opening
an oven door, *above.*

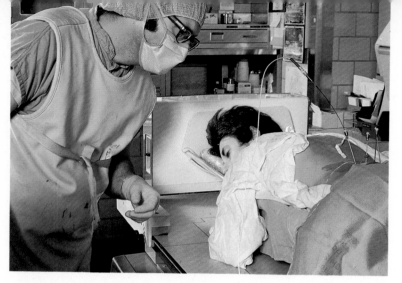

A dorsal-column receiver, *above,* implanted in a patient's back, *right,* allows the patient to block back pain at will by sending an electrical impulse to spinal nerves.

patients are taught to reduce tension with such newer methods as biofeedback, meditation, and even hypnosis. In some cases, tension or injury has caused *trigger points* (nodes of weakened pain-producing muscle fiber) to develop long after the original injury, and sometimes in a different area of the back. Injections are used to destroy these nodes so that the patient can exercise and condition weak muscles without pain.

Other experimental techniques include the nerve block—injecting an anesthetic into a weakened or painful muscle to stop the pain impulse temporarily and relax the muscle. With exercise, the muscle can function normally again. Electronic pain suppressors are also used. Doctors implant a device called the dorsal-column stimulator under the skin, and the transcutaneous nerve stimulator is placed on the skin surface over the painful muscle area.

These devices, which the patient controls, produce results that support the "gate-control" theory of pain, some experts believe. This theory holds that messages traveling via the nerve system to the brain pass through a series of gatelike points where the nerves enter the spinal column. These gates can let in either pain messages, which come on small nerve fibers, or touchlike messages, which come on large fibers. When messages on the large fibers outnumber those on the small fibers, they block the transmission of the pain messages. The electronic pain suppressors stimulate these large fibers, thus blocking pain messages on the small fibers. They may be used for temporary relief or regularly over a long period of time, almost like pain pills.

Traditional drug treatments are still used, but doctors are not as quick now to prescribe painkillers and tranquilizers, for example. Instead, they may prescribe anti-inflammatory agents or even antidepressive drugs, the latter because of their known pain-blocking abilities and also because depression may masquerade as pain in many patients who have been immobilized and cut off from their normal routine. Some physicians have reduced pain by limiting drug therapy to simple aspirin and aspirinlike medication.

Surgery, once the most common treatment for many back problems, is used less. At San Francisco's St. Francis Hospital, for example, fewer than 2 per cent of the first 1,200 back patients ended up in the operating room. Surgery is still recommended when there is serious nerve damage or when bone fusion or the insertion of a steel rod along the side of the spine is considered necessary to stabilize the spinal column, as in spinal fracture or advanced scoliosis, but it is no longer routinely accepted as the only way to treat a degenerating or herniated disk. Statistics show that surgery relieves pain in only 60 to 70 per cent of back patients with slipped disks in the lumbar region of the spine and in only 40 to 60 per cent of those who have slipped disks in the cervical region.

Patients with slipped disks should not be surprised if the recommended treatment is one or more of the following: extensive bed rest, traction, steroid injections, and—in some experimental situations—the use of chymopapain, an enzyme believed effective in dissolving ruptured disk material. Chymopapain is used extensively in Canada, Europe, Russia, and South America, but it has not been approved for general use in the United States.

Although scientists still do not fully understand how pain registers in the brain or why similar injuries produce varying amounts of pain in different people, they now recognize two separate kinds of pain—acute and chronic. Each must be approached differently.

"*Acute* simply means it happened recently—yesterday, this morning, a few days ago," explains psychologist William E. Fordyce of the University of Washington pain clinic. "*Chronic* means the problem has persisted for four to six months or longer." Treatment that would be appropriate for acute pain, such as rest and medication, is not appropriate for chronic pain. "In fact," says Fordyce, "it tends to make the problem worse."

Acupuncture, *below left,* and biofeedback therapy, *below,* are now being used experimentally to alleviate back pain.

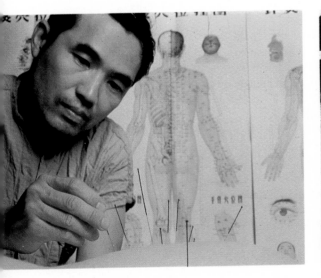

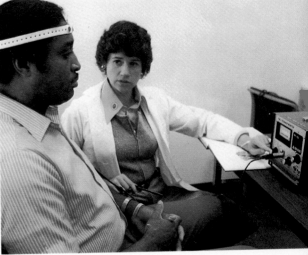

69

For one thing, chronic pain can be reinforced—that is, the patient must suffer to justify taking a pill or resting. Over an extended period, the result is an addicted patient with poor muscle tone and coordination, a person who feels pain simply because physical activity is taxing. The chronic patient may also acquire new pain behavior—a limp, a grimace, a sigh that says "I hurt"—and learns that there can be tangible rewards for hurting. Such a patient does not have to go to work, cut the grass, or paint the porch; the family is more sympathetic than usual; and the employer or the government may provide disability payments. Pain eventually becomes a way of life.

Breaking the cycle means changing the patient's behavior, an approach some doctors termed "irrelevant to the treatment of back pain" as late as 1971. However, multidisciplinary pain clinics throughout the world are now using this approach to varying extents. They first break the pain-pill association by prescribing medication on a schedule. The patient takes the medicine at the appointed times whether there is pain or not. Dosage is steadily decreased during this time, and physicians have found that in up to one-third of all habituated or addicted chronic-pain patients the pain disappears when drug dependency is eliminated.

Then doctors try to get the patient to become more active. Individualized, progressive physical therapy is important. The patient and the family can see that activity does not cause physical damage. It also gives the patient something positive to look forward to. Activity is essential, says Fordyce, because "people with lots to do tend to hurt less than people who have nothing to do."

Getting and staying in good physical condition, improving posture, and following a simple daily exercise program will help many people relieve back pain and strain. Others are not so fortunate. Their work and other activities may contribute directly to back injury. Housework, for example, is notorious for tasks that are potentially damaging to the human back.

Many office workers suffer back pain because of the unusual postures they assume on the job. Lifting the shoulder and twisting the body and the neck to hold a telephone may not seem harmful but constantly repeating these movements can injure the back. Also, according to industrial designer William Stumpf of Minneapolis, Minn., most office workers sit on chairs that are designed more for appearance than for comfort. Stumpf says the ideal chair is a tilt-swivel chair on wheels that allows lateral and angular movement. It should also have arms large enough to support some body weight, a back support reaching at least to the shoulder blades, a seat 22 to 24 inches (56 to 61 centimeters) wide, and a height-adjustment range of about 5 inches (13 centimeters). In West Germany, employers are required by law to provide chairs of different sizes so that employees can choose the right one for their own needs, an approach Stumpf is trying to persuade U.S. firms to take.

To prevent back strain while driving, sit back, adjust the seat so that the pedals are close, and keep the knees slightly higher than the hips.

Of greater concern to industry, however, is the fate of the employee who lifts, shoves, carries, and moves loads routinely as part of the job. "About one-third of all workers in the United States perform occasional, if not frequent, exertion that is hazardous—most because they are poorly matched to their jobs," explains Don B. Chaffin, director of the University of Michigan's occupational health and safety-engineering program. As a result, 400,000 workers suffer back injuries on the job each year. Nearly 1 million Americans have been permanently disabled by back injuries suffered while working.

"We feel that back injury is the single most important industrial medical problem," says safety expert Donald Badger. "And there is universal agreement among engineers that loading of the spinal column—picking up a load and transferring that weight to the [spinal] column—is somehow related to incidence of the injuries." Badger is chief of the work and environmental physiology section in the physiology and ergonomics branch of the National Institute of Occupational Safety and Health (NIOSH).

Until recently, however, neither industry nor science could effectively measure strength capabilities. Many industries gave job applicants back X rays, general medical examinations, and grip-strength tests, or assigned employees to jobs on the basis of their stature and weight. None of these methods are really effective, says Chaffin. Effective strength-measuring procedures have been developed and tested only in the last three years. These form the basis for the NIOSH Work Practices Guidelines.

The guidelines set maximum limits for workers handling materials. Badger says firms will have to find other ways to handle loads that

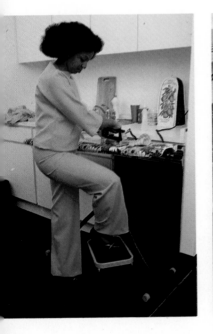

Vary the height of the legs to ease back strain while ironing, *far left.* When lifting objects, hold them close to the body and bend the knees, *left.* Experts recommend sleeping on the side with knees bent, *above.*

exceed the limits—buying a hoist or splitting a load into two or more portions, for example. Industry will be asked to evaluate specific lifting requirements, such as posture, size of load, and frequency of lifting and use these to develop strength-testing procedures. Employees can then be tested and placed on jobs they can safely handle.

If you are interested in learning more about proper back care and prevention of back injury and pain, ask your employer or a community organization about setting up a "back school," a training program based on an approach pioneered by physician Alf Nachemson, Sweden's leading back expert. Or check to see if your local Young Men's Christian Association is one of more than a thousand centers

Screening For Scoliosis

Although X ray is the only sure test for teen-age scoliosis, visual screening can detect early stages of abnormal spinal curvature—if you know what to look for. Hazel Bramson, Spinal Screening Coordinator at Northwestern University's McGaw Medical Center in Chicago, offers the following suggestions.

Step 1. Have the child stand with at least the upper portion of the body unclothed and with the back toward you. Note any of the following: uneven shoulders, uneven shoulder blades, uneven hips, uneven waist, one side of the ribcage fuller than the other, or one side of the lumbar region protruding more than the other.

Alone, none of these irregularities is indicative of scoliosis, says Bramson. However, a combination could mean trouble. If you find two or more of these signs, consult a physician.

Step 2. Have the child bend forward from the waist, hands together, and observe the posture from both the front and the back. You are looking for only one sign—a rib hump on either side of the body. "This is the acid test," says Bramson. "If you notice the hump, the child should be referred to a doctor, even if none of the other signs are present."

The Scoliosis Research Society, an affiliate of the American Academy of Orthopedic Surgeons, is sponsoring a nationwide screening program, encouraging school nurses and physical-education teachers to make this two-step examination annually on all children between 10 and 15 years of age.

According to Bramson, who is also a representative of the Scoliosis Research Society, the defect can be effectively treated, if caught in time, by using a Milwaukee brace—a neck-to-hip girdlelike device that halts the progression of the curve. Surgery is recommended only when the condition is advanced or when the patient's spine is very weak. If not treated, scoliosis can lead to disfigurement and may contribute to the development of osteoarthritis. Severe cases can produce abnormal and harmful pressure on soft internal organs, such as the lungs.

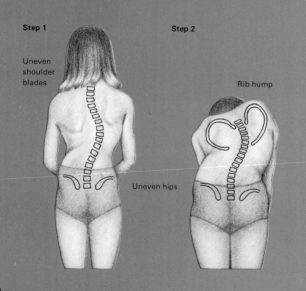

Step 1

Uneven shoulder blades

Step 2

Rib hump

Uneven hips

offering a special 10-week course entitled "Y's Way to a Healthy Back." Most such programs focus on back anatomy and on the three basics of good back care: exercise, proper lifting, and good posture.

Meanwhile, much work remains to be done on many fronts. Medical experts continue to try to crack the code of pain: The more they understand about how pain functions, the better equipped they will be to counter it. Researchers are testing and developing more sophisticated diagnostic and treatment methods—even the possibility of replacing a degenerating disk with an artificial one is not discounted. Others continue to study the human back, using the best in modern technology from miniature pill-shaped radio transmitters to computers, trying to determine just how the back does its job and how various stresses affect it.

In one laboratory at Surrey University in England, volunteer subjects swallow mercury-powered radio transmitters, then lift and shove loads while researchers measure the stresses created in their bodies. A team of biomechanical engineers headed by Albert Schultz, professor of mechanical engineering at the University of Illinois Circle Campus in Chicago, used a computer to create a model of a human spine, and then programmed in different forces or stresses. "It's as if a computer put together a spine that we can push on and pull on," he explains. "We can measure what happens inside the spine, what happens to a specific vertebra, something we can't do with human subjects."

The growing interest of the medical and scientific community in back-pain research is encouraging but still not equal to the need. In the United States, for example, there is no single organization devoted to back problems, no central clearing house of information or group to lobby for research funds. But there are indications that this may soon change, with the establishment of a group similar to or even linked with Great Britain's Society for Back Pain Research. And John Bonica founded the International Society for the Study of Pain, which held its first congress in 1973, to focus more attention on the problem of pain and the most effective means of combating it.

Attitudes are crucial. As doctors learn there are ways to heal their most frustrating group of patients, their interest will grow. As industry learns it does not have to live with thousands of back injuries, perhaps it will devote more time and money to research and training programs. As people realize that back pain can be prevented and treated, they, too, will demand action. In this way, the human race may eliminate one of its most common woes—the painful back.

For further reading:

Kraus, Hans. *Backache, Stress and Tension: Cause, Prevention, and Treatment.* Simon and Schuster, 1965.

Mines, S. *The Conquest of Pain.* Grosset and Dunlap, 1975.

Root, Leon and Kiernan, Thomas. *Oh, My Aching Back: A Doctor's Guide to Your Back Pain.* New American Library, 1973.

How to Cope
With Rising
College Costs

By Alexander G. Sidar, Jr.

It's never too early to start planning how to pay for a college education, and a wide range of aid programs can ease the financial burden

"How much does it cost, and how can we afford it?" These are questions on the minds of parents with children nearing college age.

The cost of a college education in the United States has almost tripled since the mid-1960s. One year's tuition and fees at a public four-year institution rose from an average of $225 for the 1964-1965 school year to an estimated $651 for 1978-1979, an increase of 189 per cent. The situation is as startling at private four-year institutions, where tuition costs averaged $1,000 in 1964-1965, but for 1978-1979 were an estimated $2,647, up 165 per cent. Add to this the expense of room and board, books and supplies, transportation, and pocket money and the cost of maintaining a student at a public college or university for one year rises to an estimated average of $3,054; at a private one, $5,110. It is safe to assume that these total costs will increase by another 5 to 7 per cent for the 1979-1980 school year. The climb in college costs is shown in the chart on page 77.

How does a family with college-age children meet current costs? How will a family with younger children be able to face the even higher costs projected for years ahead? Answers to these questions were the subject of controversy and congressional debate during 1978 as pressure increased to ease the financial burden by allowing parents to deduct part of college costs from their taxes or increasing the amount of educational grants so that families at higher income levels would be eligible. See Section Four, EDUCATION.

The traditional methods of building up funds to pay for a future college education have been insurance policies and savings accounts. But an insurance policy purchased 10 or 15 years ago, which was then sufficient to pay for four years of college, may not cover even one year at today's prices. Savings accounts are not the answer either for middle-income families already struggling to keep pace with inflation. The days of saving up to pay the entire cost of college are over. Most families will need outside help to finance a four-year education that, for just one child, could total $30,000 at a private institution. The cost of an education at some selected private, state, and community colleges is shown in the charts on pages 78, 79, and 80.

This does not mean that families will not have to save or make some financial sacrifices. It simply means that these measures alone will not do the job. Most families will have to seek aid to finance their children's higher education.

Nevertheless, there are bright spots in the college picture. Even though costs per student continue to increase, fewer and fewer students are and will be competing for the financial aid available, because college enrollments are declining. The situation has reversed since the mid-1960s, when the competition for admission to U.S. colleges was probably heavier than it has ever been. More than a million new college places were created to accommodate the children of the post-World War II baby boom. But the number of youngsters graduating from high school reached a peak of 3,140,000 in 1974 and has begun to decline. This alone means fewer college applicants. The number of freshmen entering college peaked at 1,955,000 in 1978 and is expected to drop to 1,709,000 by the mid-1980s. In addition, a tight job market for college graduates during the 1970s has discouraged many high school graduates from attending college. Consequently, colleges must now compete vigorously for students.

It will become progressively easier for students to get into colleges. Many of the 3,200 two-year and four-year college-level institutions in the United States provide superb educational opportunities, and most will admit students who have modest grades and average Scholastic Aptitude Test or American College Testing Program scores.

However, there are still about 60 highly prestigious colleges and universities, such as Yale, Princeton, Harvard, and Stanford, where aspiring students will run into stiff competition for admission. These institutions are very costly, but when a student who qualifies for admission needs financial aid, these schools can usually help with sufficient loans, grants, and part-time jobs to meet the high costs.

Loans are one of the most basic ways to pay for college. The Guaranteed Student Loan Program, backed by federal, state, or private

The author:
Alexander G. Sidar, Jr., former executive director of College Scholarship Service, is executive director of the New Jersey Association of Colleges and Universities.

Soaring Public and Private College Costs

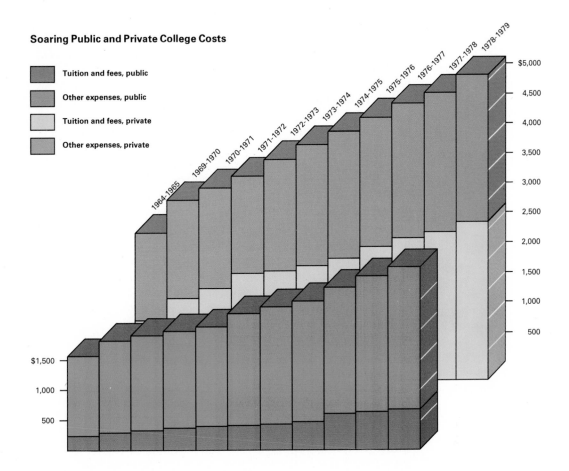

Legend:
- Tuition and fees, public
- Other expenses, public
- Tuition and fees, private
- Other expenses, private

agencies, is the largest U.S. educational-loan source. There are 20,000 authorized lenders in this program, most of them local banks. Students can borrow up to $7,500 for their undergraduate education at 7 per cent interest if their parents' taxable income is $25,000 or less. Students from families with taxable incomes above $25,000 may borrow under this program only if the school submits a recommendation certifying that the student is in financial need. The federal government's National Direct Student Loans program can provide up to $5,000 for four years of college at a 3 per cent interest rate. Under both of these programs the student is responsible for repayment, which begins after he or she graduates or leaves school.

There are other sources for loans, some of them relatively new. For example, United Student Aid Funds, Incorporated, of New York City provides loans directly to parents at prevailing interest rates. Payments start one month after the student begins college. Harvard University also has a loans-to-parents plan, and other institutions will undoubtedly begin this kind of loan program in the near future.

Other traditional sources of funds are federal or state grants and scholarships from corporations, religious organizations, the National Merit Scholarship Corporation, and colleges and universities. In addition, there are federal subsidy programs for which sons and daughters of federal workers, members of the armed services, and railroad employees may be eligible. A number of such aid sources are listed in the chart on pages 82 and 83.

College applicants can obtain specific information about financial-aid programs from the colleges they are interested in attending. Almost every college in the United States now has a financial-aid administrator to counsel students.

Most colleges require the family to submit a need-analysis form from one of the two national agencies that evaluate the ability of families to pay college costs–the College Scholarship Service of the College Entrance Examination Board or the Financial Aid Services of the American College Testing Program. These forms can be obtained from the high school or college.

In preparing the student's college budget on which the amount of aid will be based, families should take into consideration the full costs. They should include room and board, books and supplies, travel, and out-of-pocket expenses. Even students who plan to live at home while attending a local college should consider such expenses as the cost of commuting daily. A sample budget is on page 84.

A Sampling of College Costs
According to figures compiled by the College Scholarship Service, 1978-1979 costs vary widely among state, private, and community institutions, *overleaf.* For cost information on schools not listed, write directly to the school.

State University	Tuition & fees	Room & board	Other expenses*	Total
Alabama, University of	$ 670	$1,290	$ 640	$2,600
Arkansas, University of	500	1,195	770	2,465
College of William and Mary	1,031	1,614	670	3,315
Colorado, University of	800	1,575	775	3,150
Florida, University of	710	1,765	885	3,360
Illinois, University of	814	1,628	918	3,360
Indiana University, Bloomington	870	1,464	811	3,145
Iowa, University of	750	1,390	790	2,930
Kentucky, University of	550	1,545	605	2,700
Massachusetts, University of	845	1,750	600	3,195
Michigan, University of	1,020	1,780	1,030	3,830
Rutgers University	950	1,650	1,000	3,600
North Carolina, University of	529	1,621	800	2,950
Ohio State University	915	1,578	735	3,228
Oregon, University of	750	1,320	1,010	3,080
Pennsylvania State University	1,263	1,509	1,011	3,783
South Dakota, University of	688	1,150	800	2,638
New Mexico, University of	576	1,650	1,050	3,276
Texas, University of	410	2,040	900	3,350
Vermont, University of	1,355	1,670	675	3,700
Virginia, University of	805	1,600	750	3,155
Washington, University of	687	1,650	1,086	3,423
West Virginia University	450	1,700	950	3,100
Wisconsin, University of	705	1,650	725	3,080
Wyoming, University of	434	1,520	586	2,540

*The average expenditure for travel, books, supplies, and miscellaneous expenses.

Private Schools	Tuition & fees	Room & board	Other expenses*	Total
Amherst College	$4,620	$1,854	$ 726	$7,200
Barnard College	4,330	1,950	900	7,180
Bowdoin College	4,680	1,880	690	7,250
Brandeis University	4,740	2,025	685	7,450
Brown University	5,125	2,100	855	8,080
Bryn Mawr College	4,925	2,110	650	7,685
California Institute of Technology	4,338	2,160	1,111	7,609
Centenary College of Louisiana	1,920	1,380	826	4,126
Colby College	4,525	1,670	650	6,845
Columbia University	4,700	2,450	800	7,950
Concordia College, Moorhead, Minn.	2,995	1,145	600	4,740
Cornell University	4,850	2,085	775	7,710
Dartmouth College	4,920	2,260	770	7,950
Denison University	4,185	1,500	550	6,235
Drew University	3,685	1,585	910	6,180
Fairfield University	3,305	1,800	700	5,805
Goucher College	3,700	2,000	900	6,600
Grinnell College	4,415	1,255	500	6,170
Hampshire College	5,450	1,700	750	7,900
Harvard University	4,850	2,650	800	8,300
Haverford College	4,450	1,950	600	7,000
Hope College	3,080	1,450	750	5,280
Idaho, College of	2,820	1,300	930	5,050
Knox College	4,070	1,510	900	6,480
Massachusetts Institute of Technology	4,880	2,750	870	8,500
Middlebury College	4,988	1,350	650	6,988
Morehouse College	2,150	1,586	875	4,611
Mount Holyoke College	4,250	2,050	800	7,100
Muhlenberg College	3,700	1,350	775	5,825
Occidental College	4,250	1,900	600	6,750
Ottawa University	2,695	1,365	990	5,050
Pennsylvania, University of	4,825	2,475	750	8,050
Princeton University	5,100	2,117	850	8,067
Puget Sound, University of	3,500	1,650	1,000	6,150
Rollins College	3,390	1,600	1,000	5,990
Samford University	1,792	1,120	563	3,475
Scripps College	4,340	2,060	700	7,100
Smith College	4,745	1,900	705	7,350
Spalding College	1,968	1,260	670	3,898
Stanford University	5,130	2,169	700	7,999
Trinity College, Hartford, Conn.	4,556	1,770	674	7,000
Trinity College, Washington, D.C.	3,225	1,800	850	5,875
Union College, Schenectady, N.Y.	4,675	1,800	675	7,150
Valparaiso University	2,796	1,440	550	4,786
Vassar College	4,233	2,125	900	7,258
Wellesley College	4,367	2,300	700	7,367
Wesleyan University	4,995	1,895	600	7,490
Wheaton College, Norton, Mass.	4,550	1,800	550	6,900
Williams College	4,560	2,025	825	7,410
Yale University	5,150	2,350	800	8,300

*The average expenditure for travel, books, supplies, and miscellaneous expenses.

Costs in 1978-1979 in Some Community Colleges

■ Tuition and fees   □ Other

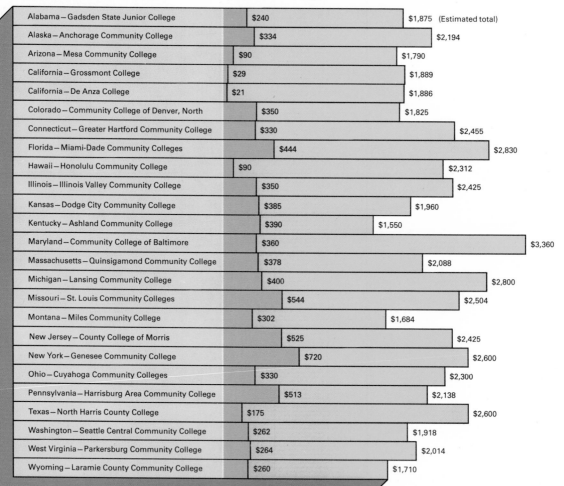

College	Tuition and fees	Other
Alabama — Gadsden State Junior College	$240	$1,875 (Estimated total)
Alaska — Anchorage Community College	$334	$2,194
Arizona — Mesa Community College	$90	$1,790
California — Grossmont College	$29	$1,889
California — De Anza College	$21	$1,886
Colorado — Community College of Denver, North	$350	$1,825
Connecticut — Greater Hartford Community College	$330	$2,455
Florida — Miami-Dade Community Colleges	$444	$2,830
Hawaii — Honolulu Community College	$90	$2,312
Illinois — Illinois Valley Community College	$350	$2,425
Kansas — Dodge City Community College	$385	$1,960
Kentucky — Ashland Community College	$390	$1,550
Maryland — Community College of Baltimore	$360	$3,360
Massachusetts — Quinsigamond Community College	$378	$2,088
Michigan — Lansing Community College	$400	$2,800
Missouri — St. Louis Community Colleges	$544	$2,504
Montana — Miles Community College	$302	$1,684
New Jersey — County College of Morris	$525	$2,425
New York — Genesee Community College	$720	$2,600
Ohio — Cuyahoga Community Colleges	$330	$2,300
Pennsylvania — Harrisburg Area Community College	$513	$2,138
Texas — North Harris County College	$175	$2,600
Washington — Seattle Central Community College	$262	$1,918
West Virginia — Parkersburg Community College	$264	$2,014
Wyoming — Laramie County Community College	$260	$1,710

Colleges pull together the various aid funds available to a student from different sources in a system called *packaging*. In its simplest form, packaging combines grants or scholarships with loans and summer or part-time jobs to meet a student's financial needs.

One of the criteria colleges use to determine the amount of grant aid included in the package is a student's academic index—a combination of admissions test scores, high school class rank, and grades. The better the index, the more grant aid is included in the package.

Many families are concerned about how much—if any—aid they might receive and how their financial need is determined. Sometimes families do not even apply for aid because of certain misconceptions. One is that a middle-income family cannot get aid based on need. Another is that a family that owns a home cannot qualify for college-education aid. Neither is true. Family need is determined by a nationally accepted formula that takes into consideration the total cost at the college, family size, number of children to be in college, whether both parents work, the family's taxes, and medical or other extraordinary expenses. No family with college-age children—whether in the low-, middle-, or upper-middle-income bracket—should simply assume that they cannot get college-education aid.

Grants, loans, and scholarships are the most common sources of aid for students who go directly to college from high school. But there are other ways to reduce the costs of a higher education. Some students begin at a local two-year community college, then transfer to a four-year institution for their final two years. Others take advantage of the Advanced Placement Program of the College Entrance Examination Board. In this program, students take college-level courses in high school and receive college credit for the courses after passing Advanced Placement tests, thus reducing the number of college credits for which they must pay. High school counselors are the best sources of information about this program.

The College Level Examination Program of the College Board is another way to reduce college costs. Students receive credits acceptable at almost 1,800 institutions after passing examinations that show they have attained college-level knowledge in a subject through work or other experience. Forty-seven subject examinations and five general examinations covering basic knowledge of the liberal arts are available. For information about this program, write to College Level Examination Program, Box 2815, Princeton, N.J. 08540.

Still another way to cut college costs and even earn money while learning is provided by a cooperative education program in which students study part time and work part time in areas related to their major fields of study. Students can find out more details about such work-study opportunities by consulting college admissions offices or by examining college bulletins and catalogs.

There is one more factor to consider in planning for college. Determining a college's admissions procedures will help students to avoid

Major Financial Aid Sources

Program	Source and Criteria
Basic Educational Opportunity Grants (BEOG)	A federal program based strictly on financial need. Awards limited to half of total educational costs
Supplementary Educational Opportunity Grants	A federal program administered by colleges, which must match the BEOG grant with other aid
National Direct Student Loans	A federal loans-to-students program based on financial need, with a 10-year repayment period
College Work-Study Program	A federal program providing jobs in the student's major area of study through the college
Guaranteed Student Loan Program	Loans backed by federal or state agencies or private financial institutions at 7 per cent interest
State Grant and Loan Programs	Programs funded by the states, the District of Columbia, and Puerto Rico, with awards based on need, merit and need, or merit alone
Institutional Aid Programs	Loans, grants, or jobs sponsored by the individual college or university and based on need or merit
National Merit Scholarships	Administered by National Merit Scholarship Corporation for top academic students, minority-group members, and students whose parents work for certain corporations or industries
Aid Association for Lutherans	Religious organization makes awards based on test scores, school grades, and financial need
Knights of Columbus	Five awards made by Roman Catholic organization, based on academic excellence alone
National Presbyterian Scholarships	Awards made by religious organization based on test scores, school grades, and financial need
United Methodist Scholarships	One-year tuition and fees awards only, made by religious organization
National 4-H Council	Awards sponsored by 60 businesses, corporations, and foundations, administered by the 4-H for state winners in 4-H projects
National Association of Secondary School Principals	Awards sponsored by principals' association and the National Honor Society for society members
Elks Foundation Scholarship Awards	Awards made by the Elks Foundation to U.S. citizens on the basis of ability, financial need, and leadership
Evans Scholars Foundation Caddy Scholarships	Awards made by Western Golf Association on the basis of rank in high school class and financial need
American Legion and Legion Auxiliary Scholarships	Awards made by American Legion and auxiliaries according to criteria that vary with state posts
Armed Forces Service Associations, Scholarships, and Loans	About 25 service associations of the armed forces award grants or loans, mainly to children of deceased servicemen
Reserve Officer Training Corps Program	A service training program of the Army, Navy, or Air Force for college students
Local, regional, or corporate scholarships	Usually awarded to local students by women's organizations, Kiwanis, Lions, and Rotary clubs, Jaycees, local churches, and high schools or to children of employees by unions, businesses, and corporations

Amount	Who Can Apply	Where To Apply
Grants from $200 to $1,800 per year	Students from low- to middle-income families enrolled at least half time	Obtain appropriate forms from high school or college
Grants from $200 to $1,500 per year	Students from low- to middle-income families enrolled at least half time	Contact college of your choice to file required form
Loans up to $5,000 for a bachelor's degree	Students from lower-income families enrolled at least half time	Contact college of your choice to file required form
Jobs usually pay $600 to $1,000 per year	Students in financial need	Contact college of your choice to file required form
Loans up to $2,500 per year to maximum of $7,500	Students from middle- and upper-middle-income families	Local bank, savings & loan association, or college-approved lenders
Grants from $100 to $2,700 per year; loans up to $2,500	Criteria vary by state from need only to merit only	See high school or college aid counselor for state agency address
Awards vary, ranging up to $4,000 per year	Top academic students or those in financial need	College of your choice
Grants from $250 to $1,500 for four years	High school juniors	See high school counselor for test information
Grants total from $500 to $1,750	Students who have made a contribution to society	Aid Association for Lutherans, Appleton, Wis. 54919
Grants total $1,000	Students who wish to attend Catholic University of America	Columbus Plaza, P.O. Drawer 1670, New Haven, Conn.
Grants total $100 to $1,400	Students with financial need; honors only to winners without need	National Presbyterian Scholarship, 475 Riverside Drive, New York, N.Y. 10027
Grants up to $500	Outstanding students	United Methodist Scholarships, P.O. Box 871, Nashville, Tenn. 37202
Grants total from $500 to $1,000	Current 4-H members	National 4-H Council, 150 North Wacker Drive, Chicago, Ill. 60606
Grants of $1,000	High school seniors who are National Honor Society members	Local National Honor Society
Grants total from $600 to $3,000	High school seniors in the jurisdiction of the Benevolent & Protective Order of Elks	Local Elks Lodge
Cost of tuition and room	Students in upper 25% of class who have caddied for at least two years	Evans Scholars Foundation Golf, Ill. 60029
Awards vary with state post	Varies with state post	Obtain pamphlet "Need a Lift?" from American Legion Education and Scholarship Program, American Legion Headquarters, Box 1055, Indianapolis, Ind. 46206
Awards vary	Children or other eligible relatives of members of armed services	Obtain pamphlet "Need a Lift?" from American Legion Education and Scholarship Program
$100 per month while in training	Students in or entering college	Army ROTC, Ft. Monroe, Va. 23651; Navy Opportunity Information Center, Pelham Manor, N.Y. 10803; Air Force ROTC, Maxwell Air Force Base, Ala. 36112
Awards vary	Varies	See your high school counselor

Many expenses besides tuition and fees must be figured into the total cost of a higher education, including transportation and various personal items.

Counting All the Costs of Going to College	Example for a community college	Example for a state university	Example for a private college	Estimate your costs	Estimate your costs
Tuition and fees	$ 375	$ 625	$2,500		
Books and supplies	175	200	200		
Room	Live at home	700	700		
Meals	850	700	700		
Personal expenses (laundry, clothing, recreation)	450	500	450		
Transportation	400	200	250		
Special expenses (such as for child care, physical handicap)	0	0	0		
Total	$2,250	$2,925	$4,800		

difficulties and even loss of money. Colleges in the United States use three basic types of procedures. The first is known as *rolling admissions*. In this procedure, a college accepts applications early in the high school student's senior year. Qualified students are notified between November and February that they will be admitted for the next school year. Students then have until May to decide whether they want to attend that school. The school also tells needy students how much financial aid they have been awarded so they can decide if they can afford to attend that institution.

Under another procedure, called *rolling forced admissions*, students are notified of acceptance between November and March, but then have only about two weeks after notification to inform the college whether they will attend. Those who decide to attend usually have to pay nonrefundable deposits of from $75 to $300.

About 35 or 40 highly prestigious colleges or universities use the *delayed admissions* procedure. These institutions wait until April 15 to notify applicants as to whether they have been accepted and how much financial aid the school is offering. Students who have been accepted have until about May 1 to respond.

Delayed admissions in itself does not place any particular pressure on an applicant. But the student may be in a difficult situation if he or she has applied to several colleges, and one of these has a delayed admissions procedure while the others use rolling forced admissions. Let us assume that a more prestigious institution practicing delayed admissions is the student's first choice and one that practices rolling forced admissions is the second choice. The second-choice college accepts the student in December, and the student must decide then whether to pay that school's deposit while awaiting a decision from the first choice. Students almost have to pay the deposit, because if they do not and the first-choice school rejects them, they will have no other place to go. But if they pay it, they forfeit the money if they are later admitted to their first-choice college.

Students and parents should ask college admissions officers what kind of admissions procedures they use and carefully calculate what to do if a situation such as the one described arises. For example, the high school counselor may call or write the college on behalf of the student and ask for an extension of the reply and deposit date.

Considering the expense and effort required for a student to spend four years acquiring a degree, many people ask, "Is it worth it?" The social and cultural benefits of a college education are real but are difficult to measure. Financial rewards *can* be measured, however. And the difference in total earning power between college and high school graduates from age 25 to retirement is still substantial. In 1976, the median annual income for heads of families 25 years of age and over with a high school diploma was $15,866. But for college graduates it was $22,019—a difference of $6,153. College graduates will earn over $200,000 more in their working lifetime.

Obviously, a four-year college education is still worthwhile. It continues to be one of the best financial investments that a family can make for the future of a son or daughter.

For further reading:

Chronicle Student Aid Annual, 1977-1978 Edition. Chronicle Guidance Publications, Inc.

S. Norman Feingold and Marie Feingold. *Scholarships, Fellowships, and Loans, Volume VI.* Bellman Publishing, 1977.

Gene R. Hawes and David M. Brownstone. *How to Get the Money to Pay for College.* David McKay, 1978.

Meeting College Costs, 1978 Edition. College Scholarship Service of the College Entrance Examination Board.

Elizabeth W. Suchar. *Financial Aid Guide for College.* Simon & Schuster, 1978.

Saudi Arabia: Allah's Will And Oil Wells

By Edward R. F. Sheehan

A country trying to reconcile a rigorous religion with its quest for modernization, Saudi Arabia has become a key part of the Western system

In the days when Great Britain ruled a global empire upon which "the sun never set," few corners of the world were as crucial to British interests as the Middle East. The United States never had an empire, but the Middle East is as vital to American interests now as it was to Britain in its time of glory. The Kingdom of Saudi Arabia in particular, repository of more than one-fourth of the non-Communist world's known oil reserves, has achieved an interdependence with the United States that puts the old connection between Britain and the Arabs in the shade.

During the 1800s and well into the 1900s, Britain dominated the Arab world so completely that it turned many countries into British protectorates. The purpose was clear and compelling—for its own prosperity, Britain had to protect the trade route to India that ran through the Suez Canal, and it dominated Egypt, the Sudan, Palestine, Jordan, Iraq, and the Persian Gulf sheikdoms to do this. As oil flowed in ever greater quantities from the Persian Gulf, the lifeline through Suez and the pipelines across the land at the eastern end of the Mediterranean Sea became ever more important to Britain.

The British Empire's sun went down in the Middle East in 1956, when Egypt nationalized the Suez Canal, and Russian and U.S. influence became dominant in the area. Russia is still important there, but U.S. influence has predominated in recent years.

A historic turning point occurred in July 1972 when President Anwar al-Sadat expelled Soviet military personnel from Egypt. Since then, Sadat has looked to the United States for help in ending the conflict between the Arabs and Israel. Sadat remains important on the stage of Middle East politics, but his country has been overshadowed by the rising wealth, influence, and power of Saudi Arabia.

Unlike Egypt, Saudi Arabia was never a protectorate of Britain or of any other European power. Yet its oil, extraordinary holdings in dollars, investments in America, ardent anti-Communism, and moderate stand in Arab politics make Saudi Arabia's association with the United States one of the paramount factors in international relations.

To appreciate the importance of this connection, we must first glimpse the essence of Saudi Arabia and of Saudi society. We must put aside the romantic legend of sheiks in tents, of Bedouins on camels, of a nomadic race who now happen to be blessed by the accident of riches from oil. We must take the Saudis seriously.

It is impossible to understand the Saudis today without knowing about their past, because Saudi Arabia is a place where the past is turning into the future with the speed of shifting desert sands. To be sure, the story *started* with Bedouins on camels who wandered "the trackless sands" and lived in tents. In 1902, a desert warrior, Abdul Aziz ibn Saud, and 40 companions on camels galloped out of Kuwait on the Persian Gulf and conquered Riyadh, the capital of the Najd, the sandy wasteland in the heart of the Arabian Peninsula. Abdul Aziz was more than a destitute nomad. The Saud family had ruled in the Najd from the mid-1700s until 1890, when a rival tribe drove them from Riyadh, so the young warrior's return was triumphant. Like all of the Saud dynasty, Abdul Aziz was also a religious reformer—an apostle of Wahhabism, a puritanical movement that preached submission to the will of Allah, a revival of Muslim simplicity, and a fundamentalist fidelity to the teachings of the Koran, the sacred book of Islam. The creed was uncompromising; it forbade most earthly pleasures and strictly regulated the rest.

Conquering rivals and making Wahhabi followers of them was not only allowed but encouraged, so, within 25 years, Abdul Aziz ruled most of the Arabian Peninsula, an area three times as large as Texas. He ensured the loyalty of the warring tribes by marrying their maid-

The author:
Edward R. F. Sheehan is a Research Fellow at the Center for International Affairs at Harvard University, where he conducts seminars on the Middle East.

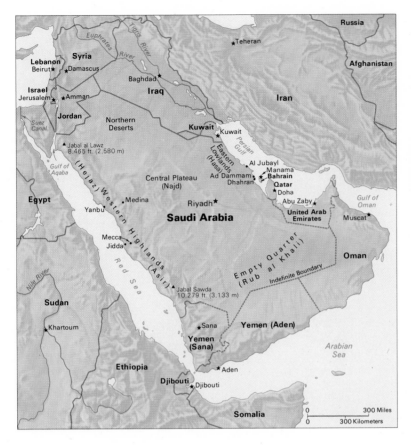

The Arabian Peninsula is about three times as big as Texas and annually produces about three times as much petroleum. Sand and gravel cover the Eastern Lowlands, the core of the oil industry.

ens—about 300 of them—and sired more than 40 sons who survived childhood. There may now be 4,000 Saudi princes and at least that many princesses. Six of his sons dominate the present Saudi government. The very vastness of the royal family serves as the cement of Saudi society and holds the country together.

In 1925, Abdul Aziz conquered the Hejaz, the western portion of the peninsula that borders the Red Sea and contains the two holiest cities of Islam: Mecca, where the founder of Islam, the Prophet Muhammad, was born, and Medina, where he took refuge. In Islam, the possession of Mecca and Medina is of great importance, because their ruler becomes the protector of the most sacred shrines and ranks first among Muslim monarchs. It is toward Mecca that all Muslims turn to pray. But Abdul Aziz and his kingdom were poor until American prospectors discovered oil at Dhahran in his eastern province in 1938.

The impact of that discovery can hardly be exaggerated. It has transformed Saudi Arabia from medieval backwardness into a still-developing nation of astonishing wealth and has produced extraordinary paradoxes and contradictions that have yet to be resolved.

The fact that Americans and not Britons unearthed Saudi oil coincided with Britain's decline and America's rise as the world's strong-

About 1.5 million Muslims make the *hajj* (pilgrimage) to Mecca each year. The Saudis wish to preserve traditional religious values while still gaining the abundance of modern technology.

est power. The Arabian American Oil Company (Aramco), an association of U.S. oil firms, introduced the Saudis not only to petroleum technology, but also to American medicine, efficiency, and education. Saudi fixation on things American increased as royal princes were sent to the United States to study and as the royal family looked to the United States for political and military protection.

King Abdul Aziz died in 1953. He was succeeded by his oldest son, Saud, who wasted much of the country's new wealth in extravagance. In 1964, Saud was succeeded by his half-brother, Faisal.

King Faisal was the opposite of Saud–frugal, taciturn, and remarkably patient. Faisal was no isolated sheep-herding sheik. He was a sophisticated, serious man who had traveled widely and knew how the Christian democracies functioned. He detested ostentation and lived in a villa, not a palace. Saud had married a hundred times, but Faisal remained with Queen Effat for more than 40 years. As king, he embarked upon reform and saved the country from financial disaster.

King Khalid, at left, *opposite page,* and Crown Prince Fahd, in center, preside over the Saudi policy of seeking stability and moderation in the Middle East.

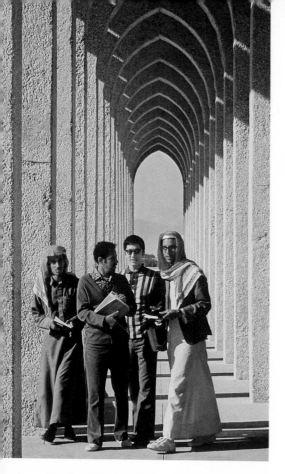

Faisal was as fervently religious as his father, and he aspired to avoid a clash between Wahhabi morality and Western materialism. He hoped to bestow upon Saudi Arabia all the blessings of technology while maintaining social guidelines set by the *ulema,* the established religious leaders. He wanted to create a welfare state for his people while he protected them from the coercion of socialism, the godlessness of Communism, and the decadence of the liberal democracies.

For example, Faisal wanted Saudi women to be educated, but to insulate them from the temptations he had observed in Western society, he insisted that they be taught separately from men. Even today, women students in Saudi universities may have no contact with their male professors, who lecture to them over closed-circuit television. In the 1960s, Faisal approved the introduction of public television to Saudi Arabia, but he was determined that his people would not be exposed to the violence and sex that make up so much of Western entertainment. Programs concentrated on readings from the Koran and lectures on Islam, and women were never shown. "There were some cartoons," a Saudi told me, "but even Minnie Mouse was for-

The Saudi budget for education is second only to its military spending. Dhahran's University of Petroleum and Minerals, *above,* opened in 1964 under the guidance of eight U.S. universities. The girls studying in a Jidda chemistry lab, *right,* typify the new opportunities being given to Saudi women.

bidden because she was a girl." That has changed; Saudi television now boasts a few modestly dressed women announcers.

Faisal also resolved to immunize his kingdom against every microbe of Marxist politics, and to prevent the radicalization of the Arab world at large. For that he needed an alliance with a great power. He chose the United States because of U.S. leadership in the conflict with Communism and the American corporate monopoly of Saudi oil. Although he made it clear that he disliked America's support of Israel, Faisal forged a friendship with Washington that resembled an alliance. He accepted U.S. arms despite radical Arab accusations that he was a reactionary and a "stooge."

Faisal proved he was not an American stooge during the Arab-Israeli war of October 1973. Angered by Washington's failure to heed his warnings of a crisis and then by added U.S. military support for Israel, Faisal slashed oil production and forbade any export to the United States. He lifted the oil embargo a few months later, as the United States tried to mediate the Arab-Israeli conflict, but the war and the embargo made the United States more dependent than ever on Saudi Arabia. Washington needed the Saudis to exercise moderation in Arab councils and to finance Egypt and other American friends in the Middle East, and it needed Saudi dollar earnings from oil to be recycled in the U.S. economy. Above all, America needed Saudi oil.

At the height of the embargo, on Dec. 22, 1973, the Organization of Petroleum Exporting Countries (OPEC), of which Saudi Arabia is the most important member, raised the price of oil to $11.65 per barrel —five times the 1970 cost. The Saudis argued for a more modest increase, but they acceded to pressure from the shah of Iran. The increase thrust Saudi Arabia, already rich, into the realm of opulence.

Overnight, the Saudis were compelled to contemplate the prospect of accumulating one-third of the holdings on European currency markets and much of the world's central bank reserves. A few basic statistics are illuminating: The Saudis now pump between 7 million and 9-million barrels of oil a day for export, which earns them about $700-million per week and $40 billion per year. In 1978, their total foreign assets approached $70 billion and were increasing at the rate of $1-billion per month. Their development plan calls for spending $142-billion by 1980—though that may prove impossible to do. In the United States alone, the Saudis hold more than $11 billion in U.S. Treasury certificates, and their total investments, bank deposits, and expenditures for goods and services may exceed $50 billion.

In March 1975, after a deranged nephew assassinated King Faisal in Riyadh, senior members of the royal family within hours selected the crown prince, Khalid ibn Abdul Aziz al-Saud, to be the new king and prime minister. Khalid is a tall, benevolent, genial man of simple tastes. He seems much loved by his people, but heart trouble limits his activity. His approval is required for all major decisions, but he reigns in consensus with the senior princes.

Crown Prince Fahd, Khalid's half-brother, wields executive power as first deputy prime minister. A large man in his 60s with the keen eyes of a falcon, Prince Fahd is an urbane, sophisticated activist. He came to power with a reputation as a "liberal," but has not carried out his expressed intention of establishing a parliamentary body.

Government as we practice it is unknown to the Saudis. They have no political parties, no uncensored press, and no trade unions. The Koran and the *sharia* (Muslim law) take the place of a constitution. Civil codes govern trade and finance. Ordinary citizens, however, enjoy what Saudis call "direct democracy": any Saudi can approach the king or crown prince in his *majlis* (council) on designated days to beg favors, plead grievances, or demand justice.

Fahd has the strongest voice in determining policy on oil, foreign affairs, and relations with the United States. Saudi foreign policy has not changed basically since the reign of Faisal. Its objectives are to oppose Communism throughout the Middle East, prevent radicaliza-

Only about 1 per cent of Saudi Arabian land is used to grow crops. Before irrigation let farmers diversify, dates were the chief crop. This date-palm oasis is at Qatif.

tion, promote stability and moderation, and remain neutral in inter-Arab conflicts and mediate them if possible.

"Dollar diplomacy" is an outstanding feature of Saudi foreign policy. We do not know exactly how much money Saudi Arabia loans or gives to nations in the Middle East, Asia, and Africa, but it appears to have distributed several billion dollars per year since 1973. Saudi Arabia is also a major lender to the World Bank, the United Nations International Bank for Reconstruction and Development.

Above all, the Saudis serve as a moderating force in the Arab-Israeli conflict. They were astonished by President Sadat's visit to Israel in November 1977 and watched the September 1978 meeting in Camp David, Maryland, with great wariness, but they support the basic bargain that Sadat has proposed to Israel–peace in exchange for Israeli withdrawal from Arab territory. The Saudis yearn to be free of the costly conflict with Israel so that they can concentrate on developing their country. Accordingly, they have encouraged other Arab states to cooperate with the United States in mediating the conflict, just as they have encouraged Sadat and other Arab leaders to settle their quarrels in the name of Arab unity.

It would be difficult to name a nation that has been more accommodating to global U.S. interests than Saudi Arabia. Time and again since 1973, the Saudis have resisted OPEC attempts to boost oil prices substantially or to drop the declining American dollar as the international base for oil prices. In return, the Saudis have sought greater U.S. protection. They are spending billions on defense of their vulnerable oil fields, and want the United States to provide the military equipment. When President Jimmy Carter fought and won a major battle in the U.S. Senate on May 15, 1978, to provide Saudi Arabia with 60 F-15 aircraft in the 1980s, his decision caused consternation in Israel, which will also receive F-15s. But given the scope of U.S. interdependence with the oil kingdom, the sale appeared imperative.

The present scale of civil and military development in Saudi Arabia is staggering. Much of the country resembles a vast construction site. Schools and hospitals are being established everywhere. Illiteracy among the young is being abolished and health care is much better than it was 20 years ago. Riyadh and Jidda were little more than mud-brick villages before World War II. Today they are large cities, filled with villas and apartment buildings, skyscrapers and supermarkets. When the cranes and rubbish are cleared away, these cities may be handsome. Still, less than half of all Saudi Arabians live in cities. The rest reside in farm villages or oases, tilling the soil or tending flocks of sheep or goats. But oil affects their lives, too.

"You simply cannot imagine," an Aramco executive told me recently, "how much this country has changed. When our first oil prospectors came here only 40 years ago, there was nothing." I first visited Saudi Arabia in 1973, after the October war and at the height of the oil embargo. Riyadh, the capital, was then being rapidly modern-

Lawrence of Arabia knew the *Rub al Khali* (the Empty Quarter), a tract of deep, drifting sands about as big as Texas. Only about 250 Bedouins, mostly camel breeders, eke out a living in this hostile land in southern Saudi Arabia.

Supertankers wait to take on Saudi Arabian oil at the Persian Gulf port of Ras Tanura. The Saudis pump 7 million to 9 million barrels of oil per day for export.

ized. On my last visit, five years later, the transformation was vast and the pace had become frantic. A constant cloud of dust hung over the sprouting underpasses, overpasses, boulevards of Parisian scope, apartment houses, and futuristic government buildings. Yemenis and Pakistanis, the country's hewers of wood and drawers of water, labored in the searing sun with pickaxes, shovels, and bulldozers while affluent Saudis in immaculate *kaffiyehs* (headcloths) and *thawbs* (flowing robes), chattering of business transactions, glided past in air-conditioned Cadillac, Mercedes-Benz, and Rolls-Royce limousines.

The Saudi government has built asphalt roads across much of the desert to connect major towns, and is speedily erecting new refineries, airports, and seaports. At Yanbu on the Red Sea and at Al Jubayl on the Persian Gulf, for example, tens of billions of dollars are being spent to build cities, harbors, and mammoth petroleum complexes.

Here again, American and Saudi interests interlock. More than 200 U.S. firms are benefiting from such expenditure. The Bechtel Corporation is responsible for the huge Al Jubayl and Yanbu projects. Ray-

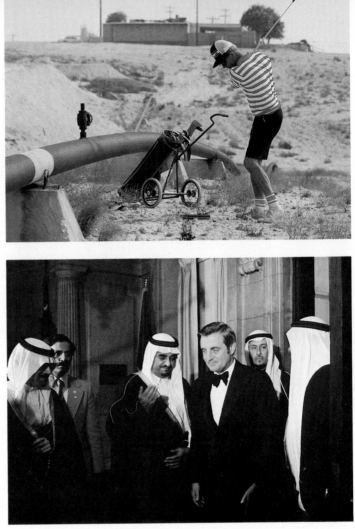

America's involvement with Saudi Arabia takes many forms. The oil company worker playing golf on the desert at Dhahran is one of the thousands of U.S. citizens who hold jobs there. On a more formal level, Crown Prince Fahd, visiting America, welcomes Vice-President Mondale to a luncheon.

theon, Lockheed, and Northrop corporations have $1-billion military and civil contracts. The U.S. Army Corps of Engineers is supervising construction of military complexes that will cost more than $17 billion, much of that going to American contractors. Telecommunications, water desalination, petrochemical, industrialization, and gasliquefaction projects that will cost more than $50 billion are being supervised by corporations such as Arthur D. Little, Bendix, Sanderson and Porter, Ralph Parsons, and Fluor of California. More than 30,000 Americans were living in Saudi Arabia in 1978, and more are arriving every month. In the United States, several hundred thousand jobs depend on Saudi contracts.

Conversely, many younger Saudi princes, several commoners in the king's Cabinet, and thousands of middle-management government and business officials have been educated in U.S. universities. Such training increases the Saudi appetite for American technology. But while Western firms may find it lucrative to work in Saudi Arabia, they do not always find it easy. The profits—and the problems—are not

The feverish building pace has transformed
Saudi Arabia. Riyadh, the capital, *above,*
is now a bustling metropolis. In Hofuf,
below, past and present stand side by side.

only American. Saudi development is so vast that
there is plenty of work for firms from France, West
Germany, Japan, the Netherlands, South Korea,
and other nations.

Although Saudi efficiency is increasing, there is
still the confusion that one might expect in a developing nation struggling to accomplish so much so
soon. In the past, such building projects as roads,
ports, electrification, and water and sewerage systems lacked coordination, and the effect seemed
chaotic. But conditions have improved steadily.

As recently as late 1976, for example, Saudi seaports were so crowded that ships had to wait for
months on the fringes of the harbors before they
could unload. I remember standing on Jidda's
docks, on the Red Sea, squinting in the blazing sun
at scores of ships unable to discharge nearly a million tons of food and merchandise.

Today, much of that chaos has been corrected.
After an edict by Crown Prince Fahd, a vigorous
director of ports imposed stern measures. Fayez
Badr, the president of the Ports Authority who attended the University of Southern California,
cleared all of the harbor traffic jam by March 1977.

Saudi Arabia now blends old and new. A sheik displays his falcon and sleek limousine, *top left*. A Saudi technician monitors patients at Riyadh's King Faisal Medical City, *above*. Oil men shop in an oil company supermarket, *left*, while others, *below*, enjoy legendary Arab hospitality.

A new sense of restraint governs planning and development. For example, the government cut back on some vast, uncoordinated projects, such as the proposed manufacture of automobiles, in favor of large investments of capital and moderate amounts of manpower in a few key industries, such as petrochemicals. Still, Saudi ambitions remain immense, and to skeptics who worry about "too much too fast," Minister of Industry Ghazi al-Qusaibi says, "Many economists tell us that we cannot compress the century-long process of development—creation of an infrastructure [foundation], manpower training, industrialization—into a few decades. But since no nation with our resources has ever tried to do so, no one really knows if it can be done. We shall try."

At the heart of many of Saudi Arabia's troubles in its struggle to modernize is a vexing cultural problem. The royal family and many Saudi citizens want to acquire all the abundance of technology while preserving their traditional values based on the Koran. This is extremely difficult to do. But the Saudis are trying. Prayer the required five times a day, pilgrimages to Mecca, and fasting during Ramadan, the holy month of the Muslim calendar, continue to coexist with the quest for modernization.

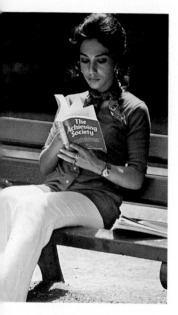

Life is slowly changing for Saudi women. This young Saudi abandoned the traditional veil and *abha* (floor-length robe) when she traveled to the U.S. to earn a master's degree in sociology.

There are simply not enough native Saudis to erect their modern state, so they have been obliged to recruit almost a million foreign workers; more will come before the task is finished. The impact of this influence has yet to be measured, but surely it has increased the tension between traditional values and those of the outside world. Since the royal family is so large, it may well absorb whatever future shock Saudi society may produce and go on governing indefinitely. But it is hardly likely that the younger generation of Saudis, exposed as they are to Western education and the temptations of wealth and liberal politics they have seen in their travels, will always be content with the cultural and social restrictions they now accept.

The status of women in Saudi Arabia, for example, is bound to change. Indeed, it is already changing, however slowly by Western standards. Saudi women are still veiled in public, because of the Muslim custom that adult females must not expose their faces to the gaze of strange men. Women have been secluded in their homes from male visitors for the same reason. According to tradition, they exist to serve their husbands, to bear children, and to manage the household—*not* to excite temptation in men to whom they are not married or betrothed. Saudi women still may not drive automobiles, travel without the protection of a male relative, or work in most public positions. But now they are being educated, and a few have begun to challenge these barriers. Unveiled wives, some of whom speak English, now mingle with men in the homes of the rich and of younger technocrats.

In public, though, the sexes are still kept rigidly apart. There are no motion-picture theaters, dance halls, or even soft-drink bars where boys and girls can meet. In the homes of the well-to-do, however, teenagers gather for parties, drink soda pop, and watch cassette television.

But such liberties are confined to the upper levels of society; most Saudi youths cannot mix with girls until (and unless) they go abroad.

Among the middle class, the poor, and the more traditional, the old restrictions remain in force, and even among the rich, many marriages are still arranged by elders. I have heard wealthy Saudi women rail against the old restrictions. They vow that they will assert themselves, work, take part in public affairs, and someday even drive automobiles down the main avenues. I believe they will succeed, because all these customs are certain to change. But there is that great cultural dilemma —at what cost? How will the Saudis avoid a damaging collision between the new awareness of the world beyond and the old values? Essentially, that is a problem they must resolve for themselves.

Could any two societies be bound more by common interest than the Saudi Arabian and the American and still be so different? The question, intriguing though it is, pales into insignificance for Americans when we remind ourselves of the political and economic facts.

Financially, Saudi Arabia has become an integral component of the Western, and particularly the American, system. In 1978, the United States was consuming about 18 million barrels of oil a day and importing 8 million barrels of this. About 2 million barrels of the imported oil came from Saudi Arabia, which must remain the chief source of new oil for the United States. By the early 1980s, the United States may be importing 5 million barrels a day from Saudi Arabia. Already the U.S. trade deficit, due mainly to oil expenditures, approaches $45-billion yearly. By the early 1980s, it could reach $60 billion.

Politically, the United States is fortunate that Saudi Arabia has become the chief Arab power, and that we have the Saudi leadership to deal with. In the past, Americans have tended to consider Arabs as emotional, impetuous hotheads. But the Saudis are the "cool" Arabs. If they have any particularly vexing fault, it is that they are so reflective, so cautious, that they shy away from decisions or take months, or years, to make up their minds. And yet they may be the shrewdest of all Arabs in international politics with their pragmatism, their responsible behavior, and their keen sense of how the world is run.

In the past, many Arabs under British and other colonial rule felt inferior, suitors to the men and governments who controlled their destinies. The Saudis, who were never colonized, may have felt uncomfortable with Westerners, but never inferior. In many respects, Americans have now become the suitors in that desert kingdom—with good reason. An American lifeline runs through Saudi Arabia, as surely as Great Britain's did through Suez only short decades ago.

For further reading:

Azzi, Robert. *Saudi Arabia*. Addison House, 1979.
Bulliet, Richard W. *The Camel and the Wheel*. Harvard University Press, 1975.
Howarth, David. *A Desert King: Ibn Saud and His Arabia*. McGraw Hill, 1964.
Iseman, Peter A. "The Arabian Ethos," *Harper's*, February 1978.
Thesiger, Wilfred. *Arabian Sands*. E.P. Dutton, 1959.

Australia's Living Pogo Sticks

By Terence J. Dawson

Kangaroos have evolved an admirable set of traits for survival in hot, dry grasslands

We were crouching in the predawn Australian darkness when a huge male red kangaroo suddenly appeared, hopping toward our trap. His arrival set off so much excitement in us that the buck did not stand a chance. The big kangaroo became entangled in the rope netting that lined our catching yard, and six people pounced on top of him. Our aim was to get him before he got us with his powerful hind legs or the claws on his forepaws.

The only safe way to catch a large kangaroo is to get behind it and grab its thick tail and a back leg, then roll it over; on their backs, kangaroos are relatively harmless. Once upended, all our red buck did was look up at us in a rather bemused way. He gave us very little trouble as we slipped an identifying collar around his furry neck. He was the first of many kangaroos we were to catch and collar at our research station in New South Wales, Australia. Our work there is still going on, producing many new details about the life of the kangaroo.

Growing up in inland Australia almost automatically produces a fascination concerning the ways of kangaroos. A mob—a group of kangaroos—loping across the plains or a lone kangaroo grazing in a mountain forest are sights not easily forgotten. However, my real enthusiasm and appreciation for kangaroos did not develop until I became involved in catching and collaring them.

With some colleagues and a small group of research students, I began studying the kangaroos that live in the Australian desert in the mid-1960s. To gain more detailed information, we decided in 1969 that we would have to study individually marked animals. So we built a trap on a water hole at our University of New South Wales research station at Fowlers Gap in the far west of New South Wales. The two species of kangaroo we were studying—the red kangaroo and the euro—came there to drink at the same large water hole.

About Christmas during the hot summer of 1969—seasons south of the equator are the reverse of seasons north of the equator—we built a high fence around the water hole as part of our plan for capturing kangaroos. The trap we made had one-way entrances and a chute leading into a small catching yard.

We captured the first red buck early in January 1970, but not all our experiences were that easy. The confidence of our team was shattered soon after, when a mob of six or eight red and euro females charged down on us. Although they were much smaller than the buck, they bounded all over the place, bit us, knocked us over in the dust, and generally made life very unpleasant until we subdued them and stuffed them into bags, along with their *joeys* (babies).

Since then, we have periodically captured kangaroos at Fowlers Gap. We measured and weighed our catches and outfitted them with white plastic collars having different patterns of colored reflective tape so that we could identify individuals even at night. Some were injected with radioactive water so that we could measure their water loss and estimate their water requirements if we caught them again. After the radioactive water mixed with the blood, we took a blood sample and kept a record of the radioactive concentration. If we caught the animal again, we took another sample and compared it with the first. This enabled us to determine how much water the animal had lost.

After all this, most kangaroos bounded off into the distance when we released them, but not the euro bucks. They merely lay down in the shade of our truck and watched the proceedings. One, whom we called Fred, stood for about 20 minutes peering over the shoulder of a student who was recording data. She did her best to ignore him, but her nerve finally cracked, and we had to drag Fred unceremoniously

The author:
Terence J. Dawson is professor of zoology at the University of New South Wales in Australia.

Australian scientists take blood samples from a euro kangaroo to determine how much water it consumes.

off by the tail, point him toward the hills, and give him a shove to persuade him to go home. We caught Fred regularly during the study, and the data we collected on him suggest that he really did not need to come in to drink; he probably came just for the excitement.

For weeks, we observed the kangaroos each morning, and we came to know many by their individual peculiarities. With such close personal contact in the field, we soon developed a greater appreciation for these animals and how they manage to thrive in the rather harsh environment of Australia's grasslands.

Many people explain the odd characteristics of kangaroos by simply declaring that kangaroos are primitive animals, a throwback to prehistoric times. But, actually, kangaroos have evolved steadily, finding other solutions to the problems of living on dry grasslands than those found by cattle or sheep.

Kangaroos are herbivores that feed on grasses and other plants. In the arid range country of Australia, the *graziers* (ranchers) generally have a tolerant attitude toward the kangaroos, which live on the same range with sheep and cattle. But when the inevitable summer drought comes to the rangelands, the graziers begin to fear that the kangaroos are getting the last of the water and sparse grass. Under drought conditions, the kangaroos can be doing very well while the sheep and cattle are losing weight rapidly.

Our continuing work at Fowlers Gap has two primary aims. We hope to learn more about how the kangaroo lives and relates to its environment so that conservation measures can be designed that will allow graziers and kangaroos to continue coexisting. And we want to understand the evolutionary and adaptive forces that have shaped these most unusual and successful animals.

Some Notable Members of the Kangaroo Family

 Where they live

Western gray kangaroo

Wallaroo

Western gray kangaroo

Wallaroo (euro)

Eastern, or great gray, kangaroo

Eastern, or great gray, kangaroo

106

Antelope kangaroo

Antelope kangaroo

Red kangaroo

Red kangaroo

Tree kangaroo

Tree kangaroo

Kangaroos are marsupial mammals—the females carry and nurse their young in a pouch on the abdomen. Kangaroos move about by hopping on their two large hind feet. There are five species of large kangaroos that belong to the hopping marsupial family *Macropodidae*, which literally means *big feet*. Red kangaroos live in semiarid grasslands; great gray and western gray kangaroos, in woodlands; wallaroos, in rocky hills; and antelope kangaroos, on the savannas of northern Australia. Euros are a subspecies of wallaroo found in dry areas across central and western Australia. Gray and red kangaroos are the largest species. Males average 6 feet (180 centimeters) in height and weigh about 150 pounds (68 kilograms). Females are considerably smaller, rarely weighing more than 60 pounds (27 kilograms).

Other members of the kangaroo family include the tiny rat kangaroo, *top,* and the rock wallaby, *above,* which has feet that are adapted for running on rough ground.

The kangaroo family includes about 40 other species, ranging from the wallabies, which are somewhat smaller than the large kangaroos, to the tiny musk rat-kangaroo, which I once mistook for a rat as it scurried around the jungle floor in tropical Queensland. Another unusual member of the family is the tree kangaroo, which lives almost entirely in trees and has forelimbs and hindlimbs more equal in length than do other kangaroos.

We know very little about the behavior of kangaroos, partly because most of them are largely *nocturnal* (active at night). Only the musk rat-kangaroo is known to be fully *diurnal* (active in daytime). Most kangaroos and wallabies are active from late afternoon until early morning. At Fowlers Gap, the various species of kangaroo spend summer days lying or standing in the shade of a rock or tree. During the winter, they like to lie in the sun in some sheltered spot.

Gregariousness seems to be a characteristic of kangaroos. During the day, we usually found them resting in groups. But the strength of group organization apparently varies among species. The great gray kangaroos on our research station seem to form more closely knit groups than the others, especially the euros. Research elsewhere in Australia supports this observation. But the factors that determine social organization are not yet clear. The most common and tightest group among red kangaroos and euros seems to be that of a female with one or two of her large offspring from the previous couple of years; bucks apparently are not involved in this family grouping and take no part in rearing the young. Large mobs of more than 100 red kangaroos form from time to time. It is possible that these mobs gather on better feeding areas.

The groupings that we understand best are those surrounding *does* (females) during the mating season. Often a doe with a large buck dominant in this social grouping will be surrounded by up to 12 other bucks. Most of the action occurs among these subordinate male kangaroos. They fight one another by clawing and grappling with their forepaws and, supporting themselves on their thick tails, they kick their opponent in the abdomen with their powerful hindlimbs. Injuries are rare, however, and the outcome is determined when one

A kangaroo cools off by licking an area on its forepaw, *left.* The dense network of blood vessels in that area is shown by a latex cast, *below.*

animal breaks off the encounter by turning away. These fights may determine position on the kangaroos' social ladder.

The subordinate bucks also make conspicuous threats toward one another. The most notable threat is grass pulling. They tear grass or bushes from the ground and vigorously beat them against their chests. Oddly, while all this activity is going on, the dominant buck and his doe quietly feed together in apparent indifference. This grouping may last for a day or two until the couple mate.

We still do not understand how dominant male kangaroos maintain their social rank, but size may be important. The dominant buck is usually the biggest. Age may also be involved, because kangaroos continue to grow after they reach sexual maturity at 3 to 4 years of age. Growth continues for about 10 years of their 18- to 23-year life span, so a very big buck may also be quite old.

The history of the kangaroo begins with the origins and separation of the marsupial and placental mammals. Placental females give birth to well-developed young that have grown in the uterus, nourished through an organ called the placenta. Most mammals, including human beings, are placentals.

The first advanced mammals appeared in the early Cretaceous Period (130 million to 65 million years ago). They were tiny insect-eating animals. The separation that gave rise to the marsupials and the placentals took place sometime later in the Cretaceous Period, and the two groups then developed independently.

Scientists believe the first marsupials developed in North America and then appeared in South America about 70 million years ago. The Australian marsupials apparently descended from ancient South

A mother kangaroo can have three offspring in her care at any given time—one inside her pouch, one outside, and an embryo arrested in its early development.

American marsupials that migrated to Australia via Antarctica, which linked the two land masses until about 50 million years ago.

How the early marsupials came to be on the island continent of Australia without contemporary placentals is still a mystery. There were many placental mammals in South America then. But fossils of them have not been found in Australia. Rodents, the first placentals known to inhabit Australia apart from bats, did not migrate from Asia until much later, and such other placentals as rabbits and *dingoes* (wild dogs) were brought in by humans. It is possible that early placentals did exist in Australia along with the marsupials, but that marsupials squeezed them out in the competition for living space and food.

Unfortunately, scientists have not yet found fossils in Australia that go back far enough to answer this question. But the fossil record does tell us that by 25 million years ago several major groups of Australian marsupials had become established. One of these groups was the macropodids, represented at that time by small rat-kangaroos. The major expansion of the macropodids came about 10 million to 15 million years ago, after the spread of the grasslands.

The spread of grasslands to the drier interiors of most continents began some 25 million years ago and provided a vast potential food resource. Cellulose is the principal carbohydrate in grass, however, and no mammal can produce the enzymes that are needed to break down cellulose. To overcome this problem, a symbiotic association evolved between mammals and microorganisms that have the necessary enzymes.

The microorganisms live in expanded sections of the mammalian gut and use cellulose and other plant products in a fermentation process that produces a by-product used by the mammal for energy. In *ruminants* (cud-chewing animals with special digestive chambers in their stomachs), these microorganisms live in sections of the animal's foregut and stomach. There are marked advantages in allowing the plant material to ferment in such chambers before it reaches the stomach; both the products of fermentation and the continually growing supply of microorganisms themselves can be digested and absorbed along the entire length of the small intestine.

Kangaroos have also evolved foregut fermentation so that they share the benefits of this type of digestion with such modern ruminants as cows, sheep, goats, deer, and camels. These benefits also include a lower requirement for protein. Urea, an organic compound formed by the breakdown of protein in the body, is excreted in the urine of most mammals. But it is returned in the saliva of kangaroos and ruminants to the foregut, where the microorganisms turn it back into nutritive protein. This recycling enables kangaroos and ruminants not only to gain full nourishment from dry, low-protein grasses, but also to conserve body water that would otherwise be needed to excrete the urea.

Marsupials, including kangaroos, have a low metabolic rate—that is, their bodies break food down into energy slowly, so they need less food. This low rate of metabolism combined with their efficient mode of digestion gives the kangaroos a formidable array of characteristics for surviving successfully in the dry grasslands.

A newborn joey attaches to a nipple in the pouch, *top,* while an older one nurses at another, *center.* A joey still in the pouch learns to graze, *right.*

How Kangaroos Shift Gears

Slow speed

Moderate speed

High speed

Kangaroos move at slow speeds by using the tail as a fifth leg. At higher speeds, they hop on the powerful hind legs, bouncing like a pogo stick in a gait that uses less energy than is used by running animals.

Because they live in an arid climate where water is scarce and rainfall unpredictable, kangaroos have had to become experts at conserving body water. Water plays a key role in regulating the body temperature of mammals. Sweating, for example, cools the body as the sweat evaporates from the surface.

Kangaroos are among the most talented mammals when it comes to regulating temperature, particularly in guarding against overheating. To cool off, kangaroos pant, sweat, and lick certain areas on their forelegs. A resting kangaroo gives off excess heat primarily by panting; in terms of saving water, this is the most economical way of keeping cool in a hot, dry environment.

When the kangaroo generates extra heat through some exercise or activity, such as hopping, it sweats. When the activity stops, the sweating also stops. To continue sweating would waste water in an environment where water is scarce.

Kangaroos sometimes lick the back of their forelegs to cool off, because this area contains a great concentration of blood vessels. My colleagues and I discovered this by injecting liquid latex into the foreleg of a dead kangaroo. The resulting latex cast revealed an intricate network of blood vessels. We also discovered that when the animal is hot, blood flow to this area increases. Passing blood through a single area is a highly efficient way to cool the whole body when water, in the form of saliva, is evaporating from that area and providing a cooling effect on the high concentration of blood.

As expected, we found that kangaroos living in desert areas can concentrate their urine to high levels. Our studies of the animals we collared at Fowlers Gap showed that red kangaroos and euros require only 25 per cent as much water as sheep require during the hot, dry summer. Most of the kangaroos we studied came to the water hole and drank only once every four to seven days, whereas the sheep drank at least once a day.

So far, most of the characteristics I have discussed evolved both in kangaroos and in placental mammals that live in arid climates. From our research, we concluded that many of the basic requirements for life in this dry environment are common to all large mammals, and kangaroos do have fundamental similarities to the placentals in their physiology; after all, they are both advanced mammals. But the puzzling question that still remains is: Why do you end up with such a unique animal as the kangaroo as a model for life in Australia's open country? Placentals elsewhere in the world have come up with entirely different models, from deer and antelope to sheep and cattle. To answer this question, it is probably best to look at the major differences between kangaroos and placentals.

Rearing their young in a pouch is one obvious difference between kangaroos and their placental counterparts. Being a marsupial, the kangaroo female bears her young after a shorter pregnancy than placental females of similar size. As a result, kangaroo young are born at a virtual embryonic stage.

In the red kangaroo, pregnancy lasts only 33 days. The newborn joey weighs less than 0.03 ounce (1 gram) and is only about 1 inch (2.5 centimeters) long. It has a lot of growing to do after it climbs from the birth canal to its mother's pouch. This trip is one of the marvels of marsupial reproduction, because the joey has to make it completely unaided. The mother rests on her back with her tail between her legs while her newborn crawls up to the pouch by grasping her fur with its clawed forelegs. The baby kangaroo's hind legs are mere stumps at this stage of development. Nevertheless, it makes this journey of about 7.9 inches (20 centimeters) in a remarkably short time—usually one to

A kangaroo hops on a treadmill and breathes through an oxygen mask so that scientists can measure the energy it expends in hopping.

four minutes. Within about 10 minutes, the joey is firmly attached to a nipple in its mother's pouch. It does not leave the pouch permanently until about 235 days later.

The joey possibly has some advantages over young placentals because it has the opportunity for "trial births." The red kangaroo joey leaves the pouch for a short, tentative look around at about 190 days. By the time it vacates the pouch permanently, it has become much more adventurous, spending about half its time outside. When it tires of the outside world or becomes frightened, it can retreat to the pouch. This period of slow adjustment has decided advantages over being dropped unprepared into a hard world, like a lamb or a fawn.

Even after a red kangaroo joey has been evicted from the mother's pouch to make way for a new occupant, it continues suckling. It puts its head back into the pouch to suckle from its original nipple while the new joey in the pouch is attached to another nipple. At this time, the mother's milk changes, and two kinds of milk are secreted by the two nipples to suit each joey's different nutritional requirements. How this is achieved baffles scientists.

Some scientists suggest that all early mammals used this pattern of giving birth to underdeveloped young. Why marsupials retained it and why it developed so highly in kangaroos is a puzzle. Some researchers theorize that marsupials have failed to develop a way to keep the pregnant animal's immune system from attacking the foreign tissue of the embryo. The developing embryo is foreign because it consists of tissues derived from the father as well as the mother. Placentals have developed a way to thwart this immune reaction, but marsupials

One of the greatest pleasures of kangaroo life is having a good scratch, and they often take the time to do it.

have not. In marsupials, an eggshell surrounds the embryo until late in pregnancy and apparently blocks attacks from the mother's immune system. Once the embryo grows large enough to break the shell, it must quickly leave the birth canal before a full-fledged immune attack is launched against it.

In some species, including red kangaroos and euros, the female can have three young at various stages at one time. Within a day or two after the large young has been evicted and a new joey has taken up residence in the pouch, the mother mates. The newly fertilized egg develops in her uterus to a size of between 70 and 100 cells, then stops growing for about 200 days while the nursing joey is in her pouch. Within 30 days after growth resumes, the embryo is born and crawls into her pouch. Then the mother mates again, and the cycle continues. There are some variations among kangaroo species on this theme of having young at various stages of development, and continued debate among scientists about its purpose. But, at least in the desert species, it appears to provide a way for kangaroo populations to recover rapidly after their ranks are depleted by serious drought. If the joey outside dies, the one in the pouch may survive on milk alone. If it does not, there is always an embryo in the mother's uterus waiting to resume its development.

Another obviously unusual characteristic of kangaroos is that they move primarily by hopping. Many small desert mammals, especially rodents, hop. But kangaroos are the only animals in evolutionary history weighing more than 6.5 to 11 pounds (3 to 5 kilograms) that hop. Why do kangaroos hop, and what are the problems and advantages in using this form of movement?

A scientific appreciation of the characteristics of hopping was not possible until recently, because there was no way to compare the efficiency of body energy in hopping with other forms of locomotion. Now this comparative framework is being developed by researchers such as zoologist C. Richard Taylor of Harvard University in Cambridge, Mass., and physiologist Knut Schmidt-Nielsen of Duke University in Durham, N.C.

Taylor and I shared common interests in several aspects of kangaroo energy use and temperature regulation, and we decided to collaborate. So I took four of my quietest kangaroos to Harvard, and we trained the two smaller ones to hop on a large treadmill there. In time, we also trained them to wear a gas mask so that we could measure their oxygen consumption to determine how much food they were burning for energy.

But the larger kangaroos apparently had a conceptual problem with the treadmill. Even though they would have stayed at the same spot because the tread was moving backward, they were unwilling to hop. They evidently feared that their hop would be longer than the treadmill and that this would place them in some unknown danger. One very large chap was so upset by this illusion that he preferred to hop off the treadmill, usually landing on top of the operator – me.

Our treadmill studies with the kangaroos that did cooperate showed that hopping was markedly different from normal running in terms of energy required. When the kangaroos were traveling at moderate to high speeds, they used less energy than two-footed or four-footed animals of similar size used in running. This obviously would be an advantage for the kangaroo on the plains when it had to flee from such four-footed predators as the dingo. We believe hopping is so efficient

Kangaroos are most active at night. As the Australian sun goes down, a mob of wallabies prepares for another "day."

at higher speeds because the kangaroo stores an increasing amount of energy in its tendons and other elastic fibrous tissues, much as energy is stored in the spring of a pogo stick.

If hopping is so efficient, why is it so rare in large animals? The answer probably lies in the kangaroo's type of locomotion at low speeds. At speeds below 3.7 miles per hour (mph) or 6 kilometers per hour (kph), kangaroos usually do not hop. Instead, they move in an odd way using their heavy tail as a support. This gait we called *penta-pedal* (five-footed) because the tail acts as a fifth leg, helping the fore-limbs support the kangaroo while the large hindlimbs move forward together. The slow pentapedal gait requires the kangaroos to expend a great deal of energy, however, and it is also relatively clumsy. Kanga-roos apparently use this gait simply because it would take even more energy to hop at slow speeds.

All things considered, it is clear that hopping has advantages for the kangaroo in spite of shortcomings at low speed. Kangaroos can sustain speeds up to about 22 mph (35 kph), and observers have estimated dashes at more than 40 mph (65 kph).

There is still the question of why hopping came to be so developed in the kangaroos. What was wrong with four-legged running? The answer may lie in the fact that marsupials in general have a low metabolic rate, about 70 per cent that of advanced placentals. How can a low metabolic rate be reconciled with the energy required for hopping? Here we must consider two aspects of locomotion. One is maximum sustained speed for escaping danger. The other is economy in long-distance travel. Because of its low metabolism, the kangaroo's ability to sustain maximum oxygen consumption or energy output may be somewhat limited. If so, hopping could be a way to overcome this limitation, and the kangaroo might actually use hopping to its energy advantage. For maximum speed, for example, the kangaroo does not move its hindlimbs faster and thus burn up more energy; it merely takes longer bounds, staying off the ground longer. And for economy in long-distance travel, kangaroos make use of stored energy as they bounce like pogo sticks. When all these factors are considered, it seems that kangaroos certainly make efficient use of their energy as they range over the semiarid interior of Australia.

The picture of kangaroos that we have seen developing is one of recently evolved mammals responding to a changing environment. Kangaroos still possess some characteristics that may be considered primitive, but they have adopted ways of getting around these limita-tions. And the fact that their solutions to the problems of grassland living are so different from those of sheep and cattle is one more example of nature's infinite variety.

For further reading:

Dawson, T. J. "Kangaroos," *Scientific American*, August 1977.
Frith, H. J. and Calaby, J. H. *Kangaroos*. Humanities Press, 1969.
Tyndale-Biscoe, Hugh. *Life of Marsupials*. American Elsevier Publishing, 1973.

Where There's Hope, There's Life

An interview with
Bob Hope,
conducted by Roger Ebert

**Bob Hope interrupts an amazingly busy schedule to
talk about his many years in show business — the
work and travel, the people and places, and the laughs**

Bob Hope at 75 is a legend — one of the best-known and most successful performers in the history of modern entertainment. He is also
an institution, representing many things to many people, which he
admits with one of the wisecracks that have become his trademark:
"We hate to use the word 'institution'. . ." we began to say, during our
conversation with Hope. He interrupted with a grin, "Don't be afraid.
They use it a lot."

They do. During the more than half a century since his vaudeville
debut as a song-and-dance man, Hope has become much more than a
very popular performer — as the unique May 1978 congressional tribute to him on his 75th birthday testified. A House of Representatives
resolution praised Hope for "enhancing national unity with unfailing
commitment and humor." Born in Eltham, England, in 1903, a naturalized United States citizen since the age of 4, he has come to repre-

The author and interviewer:
Roger Ebert, *at right above* with Bob Hope, has won a Pulitzer Prize as film critic of the *Chicago Sun-Times*.

sent in many ways a kind of cocky, confident, engaging streak in our national character.

And he has represented it with more success in more media than his contemporaries. No one else has had Bob Hope's ability to be at home in the movies, on radio, on TV, on the stage, on recordings, between the covers of his half-dozen best sellers, and in front of millions of people in thousands of personal appearances throughout the world.

To the hundreds of thousands of servicemen and servicewomen he entertained on his overseas tours during and since World War II – during periods of war and peace – he was a brash and irreverent visitor who somehow managed to thumb his nose at authority and deliver a patriotic message, both at once.

To radio audiences, he was the comedian with all the one-liners and the breakneck delivery. On television, his several specials consistently get top ratings every year. As a master of ceremonies on more Academy Awards presentations – 15 – than anyone else, he is known to a global television audience. And to motion-picture audiences, he's remembered most frequently as the traveling companion of Bing Crosby and Dorothy Lamour, as they traveled the roads to Singapore, Zanzibar, Morocco, Utopia, Rio, Bali, and Hong Kong.

Hope and his friends never seemed to arrive at their destinations at the end of the "Road" pictures – that was one of the running gags in the series – and Hope himself has never stopped traveling. He guesses he has flown more than 8 million miles (13.5 million kilometers) in his years in show business, and during one recent year he made more than 250 personal appearances.

The WORLD BOOK YEAR BOOK talked with Leslie Townes Hope after one of those appearances late in 1978. On a day when he was also scheduled to videotape scenes for a TV special, he flew in a private jet from Burbank, Calif., to San Francisco to do a surprise morning walk-on before a roomful of businessmen. That was typical scheduling for Hope, who says he works harder at 75 than he did 10 years ago. After his appearance, he returned to the airport, took off his coat and settled back as the small jet took off, ready to discuss his ideas on humor and look back over an extraordinary show-business career.

Roger Ebert: This is still the beginning of your day; now you're flying back to Los Angeles to go to work. You must like audiences.

Bob Hope: Yeah. The last couple of years, I've gone crazy. I've just been playing all over the place.

Ebert: Why do you work so hard?

Hope: Because I enjoy it. I mix it all in together, working, playing golf, travel. This summer, for example, I did a five-week tour in the East. And when you go to Philadelphia in June and you play at Valley Forge, you do your show at around 9:30 at night. So the whole day is yours to have fun or do whatever you want to do. You go sailing or play golf. You have your dinner. And you saunter over to the theater about 9:30. You walk on to a great audience. There's nothing like laughs; it's therapy for everybody. I asked Jack Benny once what he was doing for the summer, and he said he was going over to London and rent a theater. That laughter was his therapy. Mine too.

Ebert: Was there ever a time when you were starting out and it didn't all seem quite so easy?

Hope: Yes, but I always enjoyed it. I'm a natural ham, I'd say. I don't remember one time when I've really suffered by being in front of an audience, except when we broke the record at the Paramount Theater in New York City in 1950 with [actress] Jane Russell and [bandleader] Les Brown, and we had to do six shows a day and seven on the weekends. We did that many because we *wanted* to break the record. It made a funny story – they would have a movie along with the stage show in those days, and I remember Paramount had a sea epic that ran 98 minutes. We cut out about 12 minutes of waves, so that every day we could squeeze in another show.

What I love to do is have fresh material for every appearance. Flying up this morning, I worked on some new stuff about President Carter and Camp David, stuff like that, out of today's papers. Fresh. That's why I hate to do a second show. I can handle the first show; it's all fresh and everything. But I hate that second show, starting cold again. That's why I've never played Las Vegas. They've made me

Rehearsing a TV special, old pro Bob Hope checks camera angles and the lighting, *below left,* then works out a comedy sketch about baseball with Danny Kaye, *below.*

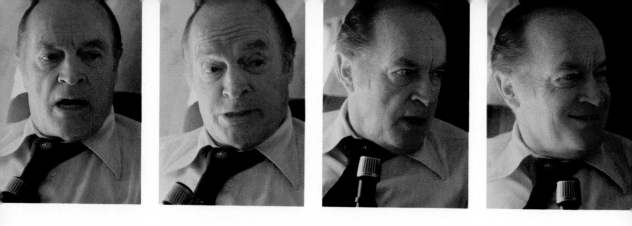

tremendous offers but I've never played it. But audiences–any kind of audience–I love them.

Ebert: What makes audiences laugh? What kinds of things–of material –do you depend on?

Hope: Well, as far as a philosophy of comedy, there's a whole range, from somebody gentle like James Thurber to a satirist like Mort Sahl or a slapstick guy like Mel Brooks. What do they have in common? It'd be hard to say, except that the point is to make people laugh.

What I've done over the years has been pretty simple. I do words. I keep them topical, and I try not to offend. If I have a gift, it lies in the timing. I don't use many gimmicks. I use my face a little to help out a joke here and there, but my strong point is probably the speed of delivery, and the timeliness of the joke. The joke has to be topical to make it for me. When I'm doing a TV show, for example, I always save the taping of the monologue until the very last minute, to keep the material fresh.

Ebert: You've played in front of audiences all over the world, people speaking a lot of different languages. Are there any universals in humor? Anything that everybody seems to laugh at?

Hope: Well, you have to get past the language barrier. You can stand up there with an interpreter, waiting for a laugh, and your clothes go out of style. That's happened to me. Sometimes, even if you speak the same language, it's tough. Once, in Australia, after we'd had a forced landing there during one of our tours, we did a special show–partly because we were so happy to be alive. And the Australians, they'd seen me in pictures for about seven years, and they just stood there and smiled politely.

I was doing a routine that was sure-fire with our guys, but I guess the Australians didn't understand a word I said. So I finally said I was in Brisbane, it was raining, and there was a lady there with her dress up over her hat. I said, "Lady, you're getting your legs wet." She said, "I don't care. My legs are 50 years old, but my hat is brand new." Well, they laughed like hell. And why? Maybe because I said the lady was from Brisbane; that made it local. Australian audiences are marvelous. I went down there again in March. And the Canadians. I've played Calgary twice in the past year and they keep inviting me back. They understand what's going on in the U.S. because they get our television but, of course, I do local things, too.

The movies were silent,
the laughter was not,
when the world watched
such great comedians
as Buster Keaton, *left;*
the Keystone Cops, *below
left;* Laurel and Hardy,
bottom left; and
Charlie Chaplin, *right.*

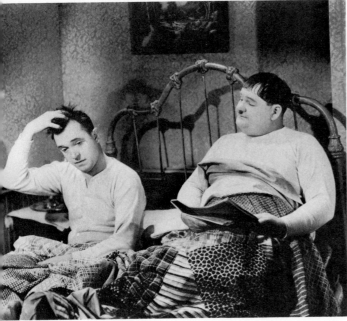

Sometimes, though, a foreign audience will do something amazing, really make you feel at home. We played in Osaka, Japan, in 1950, for example. And *Paleface* had just been released over there, and was a big success, with that hit song in it that I sing, "Buttons and Bows." They had the record for sale in Japanese. And at Osaka, I started the number, and all the Japanese came in on "buttons and bows" every time. We fell down, it was so unexpected. They didn't know the rest of the English lyrics, but they could do "buttons and bows."

Ebert: Is there a difference between what people laughed at when you started out in show business, and what they laugh at now? Are there old things that don't work, and new things that do?

Hope: I think, with a few exceptions, people will still laugh at what they laughed at then. I've actually tried it out, you know, using old jokes just to see if people think they're still funny. I used to open my vaudeville act with this story:

I was eating in the restaurant next door and when I got up to the cashier I found out that I didn't have any money. So I told the girl, "I left my money in my clothes in the dressing room and I'll pay you the next time I come in." She says, "That's all right, we'll just write your name on the wall until the next time you come in." I say, "Wait a minute, I don't want my name on the wall where everyone can see it." She says, "Don't worry about that. Your coat will be hanging over it."

Now that joke still plays, because once in a while I'll try it out with an audience and explain how I used to tell it. A lot of jokes still play, if you just bring them up to date. I used to say that so-and-so had his eye on the presidential seat, but look what Roosevelt has on it. Now you just say Teddy Kennedy has his eye on the seat, but look at Carter, and they still laugh.

Ebert: In terms of your specifically topical humor, are there things that you've noticed changing over the years?

Hope: Well, in terms of the material you're allowed to use, almost anything is acceptable. On television now, a guy might say his girl is pregnant. Shocking, because in radio we couldn't even say "damn." Now it's wide open. Audiences are much more sophisticated because of their exposure to television.

But I don't take advantage of a lot of that. On a TV show I might do things that are a little teeny bit suggestive. I change subjects and fool around. But you look out and you see a mother with two or three kids in the audience, and you don't want to embarrass her, you know. So I don't do stuff that's too far over the line.

Ebert: You sort of play the material in response to the audience?

Hope: Yes, whenever possible. When you're taping for TV, for example, if you do it in front of a live audience, they time the material for you. And that's a natural reaction that you're going to benefit from. Some guy trying to tune those laughs in, the mechanical laugh, and make it sound right—it takes a hell of a lot of work.

Ebert: One of your admirers is Woody Allen, who started out, of course, writing for the Sid Caesar show on television, when it was done before a live audience. And he has a theory that a whole young gener-

Many comics, such as Weber and Fields, *above left,* learned their trade in vaudeville, while singer-comedian Gracie Fields, *above,* started in English music halls. Later, such musical comedy revues as *The Ziegfeld Follies* were vehicles for great comedians, including Fanny Brice and a young, brash Bob Hope, *left.*

ation of comedy writers may have been short-changed because they've never really had to work for their laughs. That the writers who came up in radio and in early TV, before live audiences, tried material out and people either laughed or they didn't laugh. But now the recorded laugh track produces laughs whether it's funny or not.

Hope: That sounds right. You can almost detect from the chemistry on a show whether they have a live audience or not. For my TV shows, I work with a live audience all the time. I demand it, you know. I helped to design the NBC studio at Burbank. I wanted them to put the cameras in places where the audience wasn't really aware of them. Just the audience and the performers. They didn't do that, but they do have the audience right there in the studio, so it's like playing to a theater.

Ebert: Is that why you and Bing Crosby were known for being happy to have visitors on the set when you were making the "Road" movies—as opposed to performers who like closed sets and nobody watching?

Hope: We just weren't the type who worried about having people on the set. We were both personal-appearance people, and it's only peo-

Talkies brought the zany antics of the Marx brothers, *below,* and a wacky, courtly romance between Mae West and W. C. Fields, *below right.*

ple who are a little uptight about appearing in front of people who'd be self-conscious in front of an audience. Clark Gable, for example–I had him on a radio show once. He was on the other side of the mike, and his hand was shaking so much I had to reach across and grab his hand so he could read. That's how nervous he was, working up this thing about a personal appearance. But of course he was great in a movie. Crosby and myself, we didn't care. We never closed a set. We had so many of our friends who'd drop in.

Ebert: When you see the "Road" pictures today, you feel as if they must have been fun to make.

Hope: They were the most fun of all. And they're practically a documentary that goes on and on; I see myself all over the country on TV, because they send the film back for new sprocket holes and run them over and over.

Ebert: Many of the "Road" scenes seem almost improvised. Were they?

Hope: Yeah. Bing and I used to play tricks on each other where we'd steal each other's lines. And we'd ad lib. So there was that spontaneity and freshness about the thing, you know. The audiences grabbed it, too. The electricity carried over. In *The Road to Morocco*, when the camel spit in my eye, I asked the director if he wanted to shoot that scene over. "No," he says, "that's it." And so you see the picture today and the camel's still spitting in my eye. And the director went around telling people it took months to train that camel.

Ebert: When you were at Paramount, there were a lot of great people on the lot–W. C. Fields, for example.

Hope: And he was marvelous. Fields was very popular and all he ever really wanted to do in the movies was take bits that had worked for him in vaudeville and work them into the movies just the same way. I was one of the fellows he sometimes invited into his dressing room for a

Ad lib clowning by Bob Hope, Dorothy Lamour, and Bing Crosby gave a freshness to *The Road to Bali* and the six other "Road" movies.

drink. He didn't like too many people. He didn't want people around. But he liked me, and I got to know him.

They'd send him a script, and he'd read it and say, "I can fix this screenplay for $50,000." And they'd say, "How?" And he'd say he wanted to put this bit in, and of course it was something right out of his vaudeville act. In one of the *Big Broadcast* movies he put in his golf-game bit from vaudeville. It had nothing to do with the movie, but who cared? They knew he was going to do this, and they already had the $50,000 in the budget. Which was all right with them, because he was probably worth about five times what he was getting.

Ebert: Do you subscribe to the fairly popular theory that a lot of comedians are secretly sad? That inside every comic is someone who's depressed much of the time?

Hope: No, I don't. Not that they're depressed, that is. What does seem to be happening is that some of the new comedians are doing pretty serious material. I guess you can't go around laughing all the time. A guy like Steve Martin, who is the new young fellow, he's a very serious guy. He's thinking all the time when he's not on.

Jack Benny, *below,* made silent pauses an eloquent part of his comic style, even on radio. Jerry Colonna used a different method in skits, *below right* with Frances Langford, on Hope's show.

Then he changes characters immediately when he's on–he's a different guy. He does a little nutty thing and he's got the audience. Everybody is that way, you know. Groucho Marx had a lot of serious moments–everybody does, thinking about what they're going to do.

Ebert: Are you personally more or less the way you appear to people? In a good frame of mind most of the time?

Hope: I try to be. I keep in shape, I take a walk every night of my life, play golf, try not to worry about anything. But that's partly to do with the fact that I had four operations on my eye. Very serious. And they said the eye was reacting to tension. I was doing too many things.

Ebert: And you call 250 appearances a year slowing down?

Hope: No, but I've slowed down in my thinking about how I'm going to live. When I got my eye thing I was doing pictures, a radio show five times a week, a weekly radio show, television, personal appearances. I'd lie in bed and read these scripts I had to record. I used to do three at one time, two at another. And, boy, I tell you, it took its toll.

Bob Hope was 75 on May 29, 1978, and the occasion was marked by one of the most unusual weeks in the history of Washington, D.C. There was a White House reception hosted by President Jimmy Carter, a special tribute in the House of Representatives, and a salute by the United Service Organizations (USO) at the Kennedy Center for the Performing Arts to honor Hope's many years of entertaining United States and Allied military personnel.

The congressional tribute was particularly moving–and unprecedented. As congressmen trooped to the podium to praise Hope, they broke at least three House rules: Members of Congress are not to recognize people in the gallery; they are not to tell jokes on the floor; and they are not to sing. "If you can call that singing," Hope quips.

Early television clowns used the techniques of movies and vaudeville. Lucille Ball, *below left* with Edward Everett Horton and Desi Arnaz, was a daffy "Lucy," and the broad burlesque humor of Milton Berle, with Duke Ellington *below*, made him the first of the big television stars.

Hope served his country by entertaining U.S. troops all over the world in peacetime and in three wars. His bright topical humor delighted both weary veteran and raw recruit.

Robert Michel (R., Ill.) at least tried, in a paraphrase of Hope's long-time theme song:

> Thanks for the memory
> Of places you have gone,
> To cheer our soldiers on,
> The President sent Kissinger
> But you sent Jill St. John,
> We thank you so much.

Ebert: Do you ever get tired of that song, just like Harry Truman with "The Missouri Waltz"?

Hope: No way, no way. It represents a great moment in my life.

Ebert: People remember the song and they think of you?

Hope: I mean for me, for me. It's the first tune, the first foot of film I did in the movies, and I've been using it ever since, on radio, television.

Ebert: Nothing like the congressional tribute has ever been done for an entertainer before. It must have been a great day.

Hope: I was delighted. They gave me a plaque. You know, it's not very often that Congress gives something back to the taxpayers. No, it was a great moment in my career. I've had some great moments, but that was something.

Ebert: You've been friendly with so many Presidents. Which one were you closest to?

Hope: Probably Eisenhower. I met him in Africa when he was the head man, and then I met him when he was the chief of staff. We played golf. Then I met him when he was President. We played golf. Then he moved to Palm Springs. And we played a *lot* of golf. I got to know him very well. But all the Presidents I've known have been interesting. You don't get into a high position like that without really having something.

Ebert: Is there any inhibition about joking with a President?

Hope: They love it. One time, for example, in the early 1960s, my son graduated from Georgetown and I got an honorary degree. I went to give an address. Actually, I wasn't doing the commencement address, but I had fixed up a lot of things to say about the honorary degree. And when the priest met me, he said all I had to do was say thanks. And I said, "Well, 'thank you' is not my business; I've been working on a speech for two weeks." So they let me talk.

And I talked about Kennedy walking around without a coat and hat at the Army-Navy game, and I said I didn't care, they could put it on my tax bill and buy him a coat—we didn't want a blue President. Well, Kennedy heard about that and loved it. Invited me to the White House for just a quiet little dinner. It was very pleasant, he was wonderful company. He loved the relaxation of that sort of thing.

And then, I'll never forget his sense of humor. There was a Football Hall of Fame dinner at the Waldorf. Fifteen thousand men. And I had to go to the washroom. I got up, and they had the men's room blocked

Nightclubs sharpened the skills of many of today's comics, including the zany Steve Martin, *below left;* streetwise Bill Cosby, *bottom left;* and Carol Burnett, *below* with Vicki Lawrence and Harvey Korman. Others, like Mel Brooks, *bottom right* with Bernadette Peters, started as writers for other comics.

Hope cannot resist a few wisecracks during a 1978 White House ceremony honoring him for his contributions to the national morale in three wars. President Jimmy Carter; Rosalynn Carter; Dolores Hope, his wife for more than 40 years; and General Michael S. Davison, head of the USO, respond as millions have for over 50 years.

off by the Secret Service, for the President, and so I had to use the ladies' room. And when I got back to the table–I was sitting right next to him–I said, "They got the men's room blocked off for you; I had to use the ladies'." And he said, "How did it feel?"

Lyndon Johnson was funny, too–loved to joke. One of the funniest things–this was after his presidency–I ran into him down in Acapulco, and we had dinner with Lyndon and Lady Bird. In the middle of the dinner somebody tapped me on the shoulder and said President Nixon wanted to talk to me from Shanghai. So I said to Lyndon, "I've got to take this call. After all, *he's* working."

So the next day–I think he was planning to get even with me–we played some golf, and then he was picked up at the 18th hole by a limousine, and in the car he had his autobiography. "I autographed it to your wife," he says, "but I think you'll enjoy the pictures."

Ebert: When it comes right down to it, you've traveled across the United States...you've probably been in more cities than most Presidents. Do you have any impressions about our national state of mind?

Hope: Well, I find them so optimistic, the people of America. God, they're in great shape. That's the great thing about this country, year in and year out, we're doing pretty good.

You're right, the places I've been. I remember once in 1942 I was on an Indian reservation and an Indian chief put a headdress on me and named me Chief Running Nose or something. And then he turns to the guy next to me and asks, "Is he a Republican or a Democrat?" He thought I was running for office, because it was always the candidates who turned up for the headdresses–starting with Coolidge.

132

Ebert: You've never wanted to run for office?

Hope: No way, no way. It's a lot of work. They wanted me to run about 12 years ago. No way. I send money to whomever I think is worthy. That's it. Our biggest problem is that our country keeps getting bigger and bigger. But I've been through depressions, recessions, wars; we always solve them one way or another.

Ebert: Maybe we could go back a little to the congressional tribute. As you were there, in the gallery of the House of Representatives, what did you think about? Was it the proudest day of your life?

Hope: What did I think about? I found myself thinking back a few more years, to 1963, to the year I got the congressional Gold Medal from President Kennedy. And as I was standing in the Cabinet Room waiting to go out into the Rose Garden to receive this medal–maybe it was the fact that suddenly I was all alone, nobody else in the room. But I thought about a day in 1928 when I stood in front of the Woods Theater on Randolph Street in Chicago, and I looked across the street at a restaurant–Henrici's. I thought, they're eating, and I'm not. That was the day I decided to change my name from Leslie to Bob.

Ebert: Why?

Hope: I thought that would maybe get me work. It sounded chummier. But, anyway, standing all alone in the Cabinet Room, that's when I thought of that moment. There I was, alone on the street, not eating, and here I was in the White House, going out to get this high medal, you know? And then when Congress had their session, that reminded me again of that day.

Ebert: And now you're an–I hate to use the word–"institution."

Hope: Don't be afraid. They use it a lot. But what it is, you know–in the 54 years I've been in show business I've met a lot of people and done a lot of things. It just sort of piles up. But the only way I've found to react to it is to worry about my next show, whatever it is I have to do next. I want to do a better job all the time. That's the fun of it all, you know, to try and get better all the time.

The plane touched down at Burbank Airport about an hour after it left San Francisco. There were a few parting words and a handshake for the interviewer and a few more shots by the YEAR BOOK photographer. Then, with that familiar jaunty yet relaxed step, somewhere between a stride and an amble, Hope walked across the runway to his car. After lunch and a makeup session at home, he was back at work, taping a TV special at NBC's Burbank Studios. At 10:30 P.M., he was still at work, rewriting his material before a live audience, dealing with lighting and camera angles and guest stars. He was polishing and refining, getting better all the time, because "that's the fun of it all, you know."

For further reading:

Hope, Bob, and Martin, Pete. *The Last Christmas Show*. Doubleday, 1974.

Hope, Bob, and Thomas, Bob. *The Road To Hollywood: My Love Affair With the Movies*. W. H. Allen, 1977.

Morella, J., and others. *The Amazing Careers of Bob Hope*. W. H. Allen, 1974.

Colder Weather Ahead– Unless It's Warmer

By Peter Gwynne

Extremely cold winters and hot summers may point to a major climate change, but scientists lack data to solve this puzzler

What in the world is happening to the weather?

Buffalo, N.Y., was completely isolated by a raging snowstorm that buried automobiles and people in dunelike snowdrifts in January 1977. The mighty Mississippi River was choked with ice, closed to all shipping for the first time in 30 years. Lake Erie was frozen from bank to bank. No one could recall such a hard winter, and some said it was the start of a new ice age.

Because of the bitter cold, President Jimmy Carter asked for emergency legislation to relieve gas shortages in parts of the United States. Fuel shortages closed schools and factories and idled workers in New York, Pennsylvania, Ohio, Georgia, Tennessee, and Mississippi. Even the South was hit. Alabama, North Carolina, and South Carolina shivered through their hardest winter in 100 years. Frost destroyed crops in Florida, and Miami recorded lower temperatures on January 20 than did Anchorage, Alaska.

That unusually cold season might have been dismissed as just a freak weather event if the winter of 1977-1978 had not turned out to be much the same. Again, cities were snowed in, traffic snarled, and commerce halted by extreme cold. In Connecticut, Governor Ella T. Grasso suspended all but emergency driving after a major storm. And these happenings were only part of the story of changing weather conditions all over the world.

The summer of 1977 was the hottest on record throughout most of Europe. Lawns and agricultural crops dried to a brittle brown, and water shortages plagued some countries. From 1966 to 1974, Africa's Sahel region, just south of the Sahara, suffered a prolonged famine, brought about by drought from which it has still not recovered. And Antarctica went through a marked warm spell in the early 1970s. A Russian research station on the Antarctic coast recorded unprecedented temperatures—over 50° F. (10° C) at one point.

What indeed is happening to the world's weather? Meteorologists are almost as confused as the general public. They agree that some type of major climatic change is taking place, but they disagree sharply on the direction of that change.

Some weathermen argue that these climatic changes signal the onset of a long cold spell like the one that kept Europe and North America in its grip for most winters between 1500 and 1850. They picture a return to the painful cold that almost froze George Washington's tiny Continental Army to death in 1778 and 1779.

Other meteorologists disagree. They point out that excessive heat has been just as common as extreme cold in recent years, and they suggest that the world is really becoming warmer. Furthermore, they contend that we are causing the warming trend. By burning vast amounts of fossil fuels—coal and oil—we are pouring increasing quantities of carbon dioxide into the atmosphere. This gas absorbs more of the sun's incoming energy than do other constituents of the atmosphere, causing the atmosphere to grow warmer.

As yet, neither side can prove it is right. The long-term meteorological data needed for proof are not available and, so far, the temperature changes are too small to establish whether the earth is cooling or warming. Either change would cause serious problems, however, inevitably shifting the planet's food-growing zones and forcing farmers to grow crops in less productive soil. If the world becomes colder, for example, presently arid lands in Egypt and Mexico could become major food producers, while Canada, Russia, and parts of the United States would produce far less. The net result would be major changes in the world's balance of trade, perhaps a drop in food production, and possibly political unrest.

Change is an intimate component of the weather, of course. Variations in temperature, atmospheric pressure, rainfall, and wind strengths occur daily. And the overall pattern of heat, cold, and precipitation alters from season to season. Climatic change is quite different—and much rarer. Climate is a summary of general weather conditions over a long period of time, perhaps thousands of years. The onset and retreat of an ice age is a typical—if spectacular—example of climatic change. The last Ice Age began about 1.75 million years ago and lasted until about 10,000 years ago. Climate is, in effect, a measure of the average weather, so the factors that influence it are not quite the same as those affecting the daily weather.

The author:
Peter Gwynne is science editor of *Newsweek* magazine.

Weather is produced fundamentally by the sun, which pumps heat energy into the atmosphere. The heat strikes different parts of the earth at different angles because our planet is inclined at an angle to its orbital path around the sun. As a result, the sun's rays do not heat

Vast quantities of carbon dioxide, which absorbs some of the sun's energy, pour into the atmosphere from factory smokestacks and volcanic eruptions. Some climatologists say that this causes the atmosphere to warm up.

all the upper atmosphere evenly. They are most effective at the equator, where they strike straight on, and least effective at the two poles, where they hit at the most oblique angle.

This variation in heating effect causes the predominant wind patterns on earth. Hot air rises from the earth near the equator, and cooler air sweeps in from the two polar regions to replace it. Meanwhile, the hot air flows toward the North and South poles, thus creating circulatory wind patterns.

Local weather is also controlled by a number of basic factors that combine with the sun. The spin of the earth on its axis, for example, churns up the steady movement of air between the equator and the poles, producing air masses of various sizes and pressures. Topography is another vital factor. Mountain ranges, wide oceans, ice-covered lands and seas, and other types of terrain all have some influence on the weather in different ways.

The earth's climate, over decades and centuries, is controlled by a multitude of factors, too, but we understand the factors that influence the weather better. Once again, the sun is the dominant force. The angle at which the sun hits the upper atmosphere influences seasonal climates just as it does the daily weather. Tropical regions, where the sun's rays strike at much the same angle throughout the year, experience little change in climate from season to season. Subtropical regions, such as Mexico, and parts of the world at greater latitudes, such as Canada, have seasonal climate changes because the sun's rays strike at a much lower angle in winter than in summer.

Scientists are still trying to identify other factors that cause climate change. It is possible that slight wobbles in the earth's axis affect

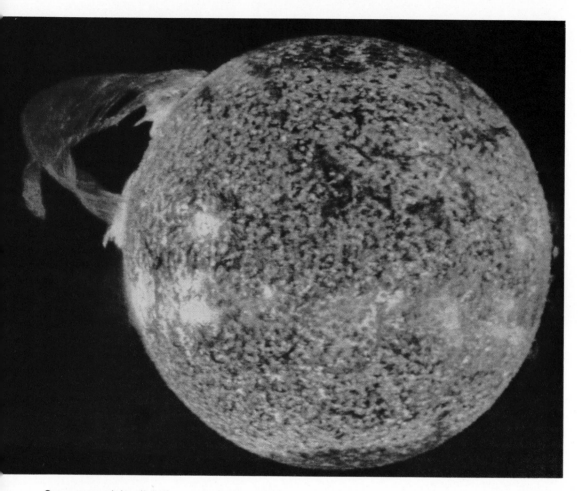

Some research has linked droughts with sunspots, the violent eruptions on the sun that occur in 11-year cycles and affect the earth's magnetic field. Records show that drought hits the Western United States about two years after the minimum period in every other cycle—that is, about every 22 years.

Sunspot and Drought Relationship

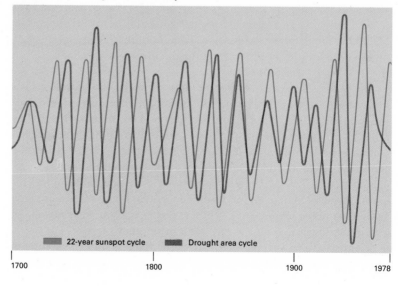

22-year sunspot cycle   Drought area cycle

1700   1800   1900   1978

climate. Wobbles slightly alter the angle of the earth's orbit around the sun and may therefore have some effect. And physicist John Eddy of the Smithsonian Astrophysical Observatory in the Harvard University Center for Astrophysics has suggested that sunspot activity may be involved.

Combing historical records and observations of weather made over the past 500 years, Eddy has detected an apparent link between the disappearance of sunspots and periods of extreme cold. Sunspots are the dark areas on the sun's surface. Because they are associated with violent eruptions on the sun, their occurrence can affect the earth's magnetic field. But we do not understand why their absence might affect the earth's climate. Eddy found that one prolonged sunspot-free period coincided with the start of a "mini ice age" that lasted from the 1500s to the 1800s.

Studies of sunspot cycles have led other scientists to a promising means of forecasting some droughts. The total number of spots generally reaches a maximum and then declines to a minimum over a fairly regular cycle of 11 years. Meteorologists J. Murray Mitchell of the National Oceanic and Atmospheric Administration in Washington, D.C., and Charles Stockton of the University of Arizona at Tucson found what seems to be an important connection between the 11-year sunspot cycle and droughts west of the Mississippi River. They report that droughts occur in that area about two years after the minimum periods of sunspot activity in every other cycle—that is, about every 22 years. The 1977 California drought, for example, followed the 1974-1976 solar-sunspot minimum. According to their calculations, another drought should hit the Western United States about 1999. But Mitchell and Stockton do not know why such a connection exists.

Studying another facet of climatic change, geologist James D. Hays of Columbia University's Lamont-Doherty Geological Observatory in Palisades, N.Y., has formed a theory of how the ice ages originated. He believes that ice from the North Pole began to move south when the earth's orbit around the sun changed slightly, taking the planet farther from the sun. Because of the greater distance, the earth received less heat energy from the sun, and the amount of ice and snow increased. This, in

University of Arizona climatologist Charles Stockton measures the rings in a cross section from a pine tree to identify the drought years during times before written records were kept.

By gathering data from tree rings, ice-core samples, and ancient writings, Hubert H. Lamb, climatologist at East Anglia University in England, traces climate patterns that are centuries old.

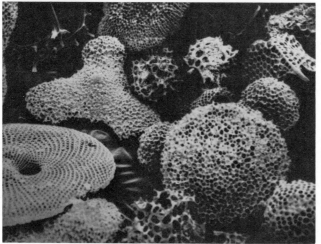

The earth's orbit has fluctuated over the centuries, occasionally taking our planet farther from the sun and causing it to cool, so that glaciers crept down from the Arctic toward warmer areas. Scientists find a record of such times by measuring the concentrations of oxygen-18 atoms in fossil plants and animals that form sea-floor sediments.

Variations in Earth's Climate and Orbit

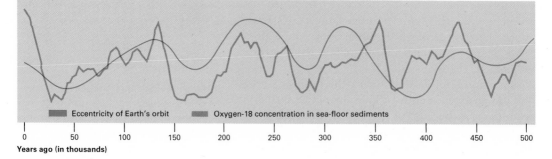

Eccentricity of Earth's orbit   Oxygen-18 concentration in sea-floor sediments

0   50   100   150   200   250   300   350   400   450   500

Years ago (in thousands)

turn, accelerated the cooling trend. White snow reflects more heat away from the earth's surface than do other types of land cover, while sea ice prevents the oceans' reservoir of heat from surging up to the atmosphere.

Speculations such as these deal with periods of thousands of years, and can never be truly confirmed. The speculations of most meteorologists—weather forecasts—are more open to proof and second-guessing by critics. Day-to-day weather forecasting is fast evolving from an art helped along by scientific data into a full-scale science in its own right. The reason for this change, which has provided short-term forecasts that are clearly more accurate, is the use of space satellites to gather data and computers to compile the information.

The first task of meteorological forecasters is to determine the weather conditions and wind-circulation patterns in all parts of the world. In the past, forecasters had measuring instruments only at ground stations and on a few ships, so they could not gather the extensive information they needed. Meteorologists' charts had huge blanks over ocean regions where there were no weather ships. Such omissions were critical because oceans cover more than 70 per cent of planet earth. Today, however, weather satellites provide meteorologists with a much more detailed global picture. With computers to collate the millions of pieces of data gathered by satellites, it is relatively simple to make short-term forecasts of the weather for any specific region. In fact, the National Weather Service now boasts an accuracy of 85 per cent for its two-day forecasts. "If you know what the winds are today, there are certain rules to tell you what they'll be like tomorrow," explains Mitchell.

Forecasting climatic changes from one season to the next is obviously more difficult, and no professional meteorologist would venture predictions for individual days several months ahead. Mitchell compares the problem to that of predicting the destination of a car passing by on a highway. "You may have a pretty good idea of where it will be five minutes from now," he says, "but if you try to say where it will be in half an hour, you'll probably flub it."

Nevertheless, meteorologists can and do predict climatic *trends* for forthcoming seasons, mainly by studying the patterns of seasonal change in past years when the weather resembled that of the season in which the forecast is made. Using this technique, the National Weather Service's long-range-forecast team has attained an accuracy of about 65 per cent for its three-month forecasts.

Predicting the climate for the next 100 years or even 10 years is an even more complicated and inexact matter. For one thing, seasonal fluctuations effectively mask the onset of any long-term climatic change. This is why experts are now hotly disputing whether the earth has entered a heating or a cooling phase.

Average global temperatures, a measurement climatologists often use to describe climate, vary within a certain range even when the

Today's weather data is more exact and complete because giant computers compile it as fast as weather satellites in space collect it from every part of the earth.

climate is not changing. For example, the average yearly temperature in both San Francisco and St. Louis is about 55°F. (13°C). Yet these cities have quite different climates. San Francisco has relatively mild, rainy winters and cool, almost rainless summers, while St. Louis has cold winters and hot summers with some rainfall throughout the year.

Average global temperatures have not exceeded or fallen below a relatively small range for the past 50 years. For this reason, climatologists who believe that the climate is changing—that our planet is either cooling or heating—must rely on indirect evidence.

Those who believe the earth is cooling point to a series of satellite surveys of the snow and ice cover of the Northern Hemisphere taken during recent winters. Starting in the early 1970s, says climatologist George Kukla of Columbia University in New York City, the cold white blanket has increased measurably. Climatologist Reid A. Bryson of the University of Wisconsin in Madison, one of the leading proponents of climatic cooling, believes this evidence indicates that the earth has entered another little ice age of the type that held Europe and North America in its chilly grip between the 1500s and 1800s. British paintings of that time show people skating and roasting meat over fires on the frozen River Thames—something unheard of in this century. Bryson points out that a drop of only 6° F. (3°C) in the average global temperature would trigger a full-scale ice age. Bryson calculates that the earth has gone one-sixth of the way toward that since 1900.

Those who believe that the earth is warming up point to the chemicals that modern technology is putting into the atmosphere. They argue that a number of substances that are now reaching the atmosphere in increasing amounts cause the *greenhouse effect*. That is, they allow sunlight and the heat energy it contains to pass through the atmosphere without interference. But the light reflects from the earth's surface as infrared light, the type of energy that the greenhouse compounds absorb. So, much of the reflected energy does not escape into space. Instead, it is absorbed by the greenhouse compounds, causing the atmosphere to become slightly warmer.

Recent scientific studies have revealed a number of man-made greenhouse compounds, including chlorofluorocarbons, the chemicals that powered most aerosol sprays until they were banned in 1978, and nitrous oxide, or laughing gas, a by-product of chemical-fertilizer production. But the most effective greenhouse compound by far is carbon dioxide (CO_2), the gas that humans and animals exhale.

Normally, trees and green plants remove carbon dioxide from the atmosphere. They use it as the raw material for *photosynthesis*, the process by which plants produce oxygen. Yet, the atmosphere may soon be overloaded with carbon dioxide, because the burning of coal and oil also releases CO_2—and these sources are freeing steadily increasing amounts of the gas into the atmosphere.

Scientists have made reliable measurements of the atmosphere's carbon dioxide levels for only about 20 years. But, during that time,

The Many Places for Weather Work

Meteorologists' work may take them many places. A meteorologist may gather data from a ship at sea, work at a desk preparing TV weather forecasts, use computers to process data, or work at a weather station.

Need Grows For Weather Experts

Meteorology and climatology offer interesting careers to anyone fascinated by cloud formations, weather changes, and instruments that measure wind speed and barometric pressure. There are about 9,000 meteorologists in the United States, and more are needed. Government agencies, including the National Weather Service, and the armed forces account for most of the jobs in the field at the present time. Private forecasting companies also employ meteorologists, however, and increasing numbers of weather analysts will probably find their way into private employment now that budget cuts are forcing the National Weather Service to reduce its staff.

Some private companies, such as airlines, utilities, and brokerage houses, employ their own meteorologists. Others pay private firms to provide forecasts that are tailored to their individual needs. They require more specialized information than is usually provided in the generalized weather analyses produced for the public at large. For example, the Geophysical Research and Development Corporation, better known as the GRD Weather Center, issues specific weather forecasts for the Denver Broncos professional football team. The predictions help the Broncos to prepare for games, wherever they may be played, and to decide on what special equipment will best suit field conditions.

GRD informed the Broncos more than a day before the team's Sept. 17, 1978, game against the San Diego Chargers that localized showers would soak the Denver playing field during the game. As a result, the forewarned Broncos wore shoes with longer cleats and Rick Upchurch returned a punt 75 yards for a touchdown while San Diego players slipped on the wet turf. That run was a turning point in the game, won by Denver, 27-14.

Research can be quite stimulating and challenging. Private companies often conduct meteorological research in cooperation with government agencies. The research entails analysis of data that have been collected on private or government field projects, using highly sophisticated computers and meteorological instruments, including those on satellites and other remote sensors.

The related field of climatology should not be overlooked, though breakthroughs in climatology are much less common because long-range forecasts, projected many years ahead, are open to many kinds of interpretation. Only a few private companies are likely to venture into this field, but climatological research in universities and under government sponsorship will undoubtedly expand. Forecasting long-term climate changes can be an important tool in improving world food production and predicting needs for fossil fuels.

Weather observers may work in exotic places, such as Antarctica, or they may work in your hometown. Physics, mathematics, and chemistry are important subjects for those planning to become meteorologists. They provide the background needed in cloud dynamics, cloud physics, climatology instrumentation, thermodynamics, and related studies. While schooling is important, experience is also valuable. On-the-job training while in school or on summer jobs at weather offices is a good way to acquire such experience.

A master's degree and a doctorate in the field are job getters in weather research but are not necessary for the trained weather forecaster. Like any specialized profession, meteorology has its old and well-established learning centers, such as the four originals in the field—Massachusetts Institute of Technology in Cambridge, Pennsylvania State University in State College, the University of Chicago, and the University of California, Los Angeles. The University of Wisconsin in Madison has one of the largest departments and a growing number of other colleges and universities now offer majors in the science of meteorology.

Only about 3 per cent of the meteorologists now active are women, but more women are studying in the field. Some people believe meteorology is a particularly promising field for women simply because there are so few active in the field.   Edward W. Pearl

145

the level has increased from 312 to 330 parts per million (ppm)—an increase of almost 6 per cent. Experts estimate that the atmosphere held 285 ppm of carbon dioxide in 1860, when the Industrial Revolution started to accelerate. Some scientists fear that if present trends continue, the proportion may reach 580 ppm by the year 2050.

Botanist George M. Woodwell of the Marine Biological Laboratory at Woods Hole, Mass., warns that the rate at which carbon dioxide increases in the atmosphere may be even higher than experts calculate because of another facet of industrialization. He believes that logging operations throughout the world are removing so many trees that the planet's greenery cannot take up carbon dioxide from the atmosphere as fast as it once did.

While there is small doubt that the amount of carbon dioxide in the atmosphere is increasing, scientists differ on how this increase will affect global temperatures. Bryson believes that carbon dioxide's greenhouse effect is balanced by a cooling process induced by dust particles in the atmosphere. He says the dust reflects incoming solar energy away from the earth—solar energy that would otherwise penetrate the atmosphere and heat the globe. And because dust is just as much a by-product of industry as is carbon dioxide, the greenhouse and cooling effects cancel each other. Therefore, Bryson concludes, the net effect of industrial pollution on the earth's climate is zero—and the atmosphere will continue on a natural cooling trend.

Bryson's argument has been disputed by a number of climatologists, notably Stephen H. Schneider of the National Center for Atmospheric Research in Boulder, Colo. Schneider agrees that natural dust, such as that emanating from volcanoes, reflects enough sunlight away from the earth to cool the atmosphere slightly. But he contends that industrial dust is different because much of it is darker than the land areas on earth. Industrial dust reflects less heat away from the atmosphere than does the land, according to Schneider. In effect, more heat can get into an atmosphere choked with industrial dust than gets into an atmosphere that contains no such dust. And the increasing amounts of carbon dioxide cause yet more heating. Climatologist David Gates of the University of Missouri in Columbia estimates that the earth could be 5.5°F. (3°C) warmer in the year 2050 than it is today.

The immediate effect of any change in climate would be to disturb agricultural patterns. Unfortunately, meteorologists will not be sure if the climate is changing—and, if so, how—until about the year 2000. And many scientists believe that by then it will be too late to take the necessary steps to stabilize the world's crop production.

How could a climate change disrupt agriculture? Scientists gain some insight from geologic studies of past eras when the earth was cooler or warmer than it is today. Extreme cold such as occurred during the ice ages, when glaciers traveled southward from the north polar regions to cover most of Europe and large areas of North America, would destroy the granaries of Russia and Canada, forcing the world to rely more heavily on growing regions in the United States and the southern continents.

As far as we know, an excess of carbon dioxide has never before warmed up the earth. However, scientists do have records from a time when the earth was much warmer than it is today—a period known as the altithermal era, between 4,000 and 8,000 years ago. Climatologist Will Kellogg of the National Center for Atmospheric Research reports that many of today's subtropical deserts, such as the Sahara, received relatively heavy rainfall during that period. On the other hand, some of today's most productive farming regions, such as the Corn Belt of the United States and Canada, were nothing more than arid prairies. Scientists have pieced together the picture by studying records of tree-ring size, microscopic fossils, and layers of snowfall in ice cores.

A warmer climate over the next 50 to 100 years would not greatly affect the world's food supply, but it probably would change world trade patterns because transportation and other industries related to agricultural production are now located and geared to serve today's granaries. A shift in growing areas from North America to the Sahara nations in Africa plainly would change the world's agricultural economy. Furthermore, as Gates points out, "The new growing regions won't necessarily have better, or even adequate, soils."

The result of a prolonged warm-up would be even more drastic. Russian calculations suggest that a worldwide increase of 7°F. (4°C) might melt the Arctic icecap, opening up the Arctic Ocean as a sea lane for the first time in more than a million years. That probably would not increase sea levels because the ice already floats atop the Arctic Ocean. But the melting of the ice could disrupt the climate.

Can climatic change be slowed or stopped? Political leaders and some meteorologists are reluctant to act because no one can be certain which direction the change is taking. Kellogg and his colleagues say that little could be done to overcome a natural cooling effect. But man-made heating, produced by carbon dioxide, might be slowed if less carbon dioxide is spewed into the atmosphere. That, says Kellogg, could be done by developing nonfossil sources of energy.

Meanwhile, the weather patterns remain erratic, scientists disagree over what this means, and government officials hesitate to alter energy policies on the basis of a climatic threat that may never materialize. So there is little that you and I can do to prepare for the future. Nobody can tell us whether we should stock up on suntan lotion or snowshoes.

For further reading:

Bryson, Reid A. and Murray, Thomas J. *Climates of Hunger: Mankind & the World's Changing Weather*. University of Wisconsin Press, 1977.
Calder, Nigel. *The Weather Machine*. Viking Press, Inc., 1975.
Claiborne, Robert. *Climate, Man & History: An Irreverent View of the Human Environment*. W. W. Norton & Co., Inc., 1970.
Green, H. Fitzhugh. *A Change in the Weather*. W. W. Norton & Co., Inc., 1977.
Gribbin, John. *Forecasts, Famines & Freezes*. Walker & Co., 1976.
Schneider, Stephen H. and Mestrow, Lynne E. *The Genesis Strategy: Climate & Global Survival*. Plenum Publishing Corp., 1976.

How Real Is America's Religious Revival?

By Garry Wills

The "born again" phenomenon, affecting both Protestants and Catholics, has deep roots in America's revivalist heritage

I t sounds like the plot of a bad novel. The United States has a "born-again Christian" as its President, and he occasionally takes time to teach a Bible class in a Baptist church. The President's sister, a faith healer, attracts attention with her preaching, particularly after she converts a pornographic-magazine publisher. Then, when the publisher is shot, she flies to his bedside to comfort him. It sounds like the "old-time religion" days of Sinclair Lewis' book *Elmer Gantry,* or some other sensational novel dealing with religion, power, violence, and sex.

Yet this was just part of the growing story of evangelical "rebirth." America looked, by some accounts, like a born-again nation in 1978. A former White House assistant to President Richard M. Nixon, Charles W. Colson, having served a jail sentence for his role in the Watergate scandal, was conducting revival crusades to bring prison inmates to Jesus. Former black activist Eldridge Cleaver was preaching his new-found faith to large audiences and attending prayer breakfasts with Christian businessmen. Olympic athletes, beauty queens, television and movie stars, generals, politicians, and what must have been more than half of the National Football League were all proclaiming themselves converts to *evangelism*, a movement that emphasizes the need for personal religious experience.

At a time when young people were still responding to such exotic religions as Sun Myung Moon's Unification Church, other Christians suddenly were no longer embarrassed to profess their faith publicly. Overt piety and fundamentalist dogma, as put forward by conservative evangelicals, became an exciting new religious fad.

But is it only a fad? Religion in the United States seems to reflect, superficially at least, the larger swings in national mood. In the conformist 1950s, for example, the more established, "respectable" Christian churches—Lutheran, Episcopalian, Methodist, Presbyterian, and Roman Catholic, to name a few—flourished. Membership rose and collection plates bulged. Families seeking "togetherness" attended church together. Evangelical and Roman Catholic forms of piety were tailored to these mainline tastes and beamed into homes from television screens in weekly half-hour segments by evangelist Billy Graham and then-Monsignor Fulton J. Sheen.

In the 1960s, respectability yielded to turbulence. Protests in the streets and on college campuses were accompanied by a search for new life styles. A reflection of this national mood was the growing interest that American young people showed in Eastern religions and mysticism. Some theologians speculated about the "death of God," and the militant Black Muslim sect posed an exotic challenge in black communities to the traditional Baptist-preacher style of civil rights leader Martin Luther King, Jr.

In the 1970s, a conservative mood of relief from the turmoil of the previous decade became visible in politics, in the schools, and in renewed stress on family discipline. A return to basic Biblical injunctions and to simple outward expressions of belief, long advocated by evangelicals, is now seen by many as a part of this shift in mood.

The author:
Garry Wills is a news columnist, professor of humanities at Johns Hopkins University in Baltimore, and author of many books, including *Inventing America: Jefferson's Declaration of Independence.*

The trouble with such an interpretation is that the spotlight of attention may be highlighting a momentarily congenial, but essentially minor, part of the total religious scene. Because of media attention, evangelical religion is suddenly "in" and everywhere visible. Theologians showed little interest in the phenomenon until the mid-1970s, but now they seem to see little else.

I do not mean that the evangelical phenomenon is minor—only that the idea that it is now making a great and sudden advance may be a trick of the eye. There has always been a strong evangelical strain in religion in the United States. It reached a fever pitch in the Great Awakening of colonial times, which began in the Middle Colonies of New York, New Jersey, Pennsylvania, and Delaware in the 1720s and spread for more than a decade throughout New England and some

parts of the South. After the American Revolution, the second Great Awakening lasted from about 1790 to 1810. And, even today, the strength of the revivalist influence can be seen in the fact that Billy Graham stands high in every popularity poll.

A nation that glorifies individual initiative and the common man has a built-in sympathy for the democratic aspects of the evangelical "conversion" experience–something equally open to all people. Catholicism was once considered "un-American" because it had a learned and elite priesthood to explain theological principles for the laity and an elaborate liturgy to mediate God's sacramental action to man. Evangelicals, on the other hand, believe that all men and women can grasp the simple Biblical injunctions and moral fundamentals on their own, and that the Holy Spirit acts directly on those who are open to God's action, without the need for priestly intermediaries or prescribed rituals.

The United States was formed without an established church. During the American Revolution, the people overthrew a king, and out of this experience there naturally developed a suspicion of religious "monarchs"–priests and bishops. Furthermore, anyone who took the title of preacher was allowed to fill that role by common consent, since in the beginning there was no hierarchy to "certify" clergy. It was a trade of opportunity.

So spontaneity became the mark of the evangelical response. According to this way of thinking, anyone can be instantly filled with the warming action of God's Holy Spirit–sinners, laypersons, the uneducated, even those who have just been introduced to the Bible. The evangelical believes in immediacy of experience, equality of opportunity for that experience, and a fraternal sharing rather than a priestly ministration. Evangelicals see themselves, in older expressions of the American spirit, as enthusiasts, "go-getters" who exude religious exhilaration, "live wires" transmitting the Holy Spirit.

So congenial is this approach to religion that Baptists, who have expressed this attitude better than most other sects, have long been the most populous among American Protestants. Baptists make up about one-fifth of the churchgoing public. America, of course, has also spawned a number of unique religions of its own, each based on private revelation and initiative–religions such as Mormonism and Christian Science. And aspects of the evangelical approach have long been evident in religious groups that might seem to stand furthest from it, groups such as the Quakers and the Roman Catholics.

Modern Quakers, for instance, do not have the undemonstrative quietism of their forebears. And, according to historian Jay P. Dolan of the University of South Carolina, author of *Catholic Revivalism: The American Experience, 1830-1900,* parish records and preachers' diaries reveal that many evangelical traits can be found in the American Catholic practices of parish mission weekends and retreats. Emotional peaks were sought at such retreats, much as they are in an evangelical prayer service, with visions of hellfire leading to a choice for Christ in the confessional.

So it is not surprising that, after the change from a Latin Mass to an English one, Catholics have adopted even more of the evangelical style. There is now a large group of Catholic "charismatics" who pray to the Holy Spirit aloud and demonstratively, just as many evangeli-

Catholic charismatics have adopted the style of demonstrative worship formerly used only by Protestant evangelicals.

Members of Hare Krishna, a form of Hinduism, hold a street parade in New York City. Such exotic sects, though far from the mainstream of American traditions, have attracted many young people to them.

cals do. In other words, Catholics have been gradually Americanized in their religious practices. And that process has quickened since the changes resulting from Vatican II, the Vatican Council held between 1962 and 1965 that tried to reform and renew the Roman Catholic Church on the basis of modern thought.

Until recently, the *normative*, or standard-setting, nature of evangelical beliefs and practices was obscured, however, because those practices were most prevalent in rural and poor areas, particularly in the South and Midwest. These areas were far away from the media centers of the nation, and so their activities went unreported. Although evangelicalism was always "out there," secular scholars and sophisticated theologians did not take it seriously. The question now is whether we are noticing for the first time something that has always been there, or whether something new is actually occurring.

Public opinion pollster George H. Gallup, Jr., believes something new is occurring. When I visited Gallup recently in Princeton, N.J., he offered as evidence of the new phenomenon the fact that an astounding number of Americans now call themselves born-again Christians—one-third of the churchgoing population in 1978 compared with one-fifth of churchgoers in 1963.

The figures are impressive. But we should remember that Baptists make up one-fifth of the churchgoing population in the United States

Evangelists now use trucks and vans to get to revival meetings, but they express the same immediacy of religious experience preached by the old-time evangelists traveling on horseback.

and that the term "born again" was almost exclusively used by that sect back in 1963. Since that time, it has had much wider currency. The language of black Baptist congregations, which included this term, spread throughout the nation during the civil rights campaign of the late 1960s. The term was also used extensively during President Jimmy Carter's 1976 presidential election campaign, and it was widely disseminated by the popularity of Colson's 1976 best-selling confessional book, *Born Again*.

The results of another opinion poll, taken in 1973 by the National Opinion Research Center of Chicago, suggest that the current use of this term may signify a new willingness among Americans to apply it to experiences they have long shared. In the study, roughly half of the Protestants and one-fourth of the Catholics questioned said that they had undergone some sort of mystical religious experience. Perhaps the most interesting finding of this poll is that those Americans most ready to admit to such mystical experiences were in the 50-year-old bracket —they were not, as might be expected, the young people, who are usually most responsive to fads.

Today's evangelicals spread the word in a variety of ways. The television preacher is Robert Schuller of Garden Grove, Calif. The basketball players attend Oral Roberts University, founded by revivalist Oral Roberts.

Did these 50-year-olds report such experiences simply because they had lived longer and had experienced a greater variety of life's events? If so, such experiences must have occurred with some regularity among the population over a long period of time, not just in recent years. Did the poll reflect a new openness about personal experience among people who had previously been more guarded in their religious language? Or is the outcome a combination of long-term experience, frankness, and other factors not yet recognized? In any case, we must read the polls with an intelligent allowance for such reservations.

It is interesting that much of the claim for a religious revival rests on the findings of opinion polls. Yet the polls show that Americans have always been a highly religious people, and that the rate of religious commitment has been relatively steady throughout history, both in periods of apparent secularity and in periods of renewed piety.

Noted faith healer Jean Carter Stapleton uses psychological therapy as well as inspirational evangelism in her work.

Polls taken during the 1960s showed that many Americans thought religion was in a period of decline. This was at the time when scholarly advocates of "secularity," such as theologian Harvey G. Cox of Harvard University, were saying that the old styles of religious mystery had died. Cox's widely read book *The Secular City* (1965) made this point strongly. This was also the time when some theologians talked about the "death of God" and argued that the felt influence of God's demise was the principal mark of modern religion.

But the same polls that recorded this perception of religious decline showed an increase in religious belief among those interviewed, not a decrease. The increase reached an all-time peak in 1968, when 98 per cent of those questioned professed religious faith. Apparently, those who were telling the pollsters that they saw a decrease in religious influence among their neighbors were getting these impressions from the media, the colleges, and other places that were humming with the new concepts of "secularity," not from the neighbors. Those interviewed were experiencing for themselves the opposite of what they thought was happening to others. If such was true of the pollsters' finding of a "fading" religious influence in the 1960s, might it not be equally true of the pollsters' records of increased religiosity in the 1970s? Media reporting, in other words, must be considered as a factor that may influence the answers on all religious polls.

During this century, however, polls have revealed an amazingly steady belief in God and the afterlife. In a 1975 study, 94 per cent of those asked said they believed in God, and 69 per cent believed in an afterlife. In 1948, 94 per cent professed belief in God and 68 per cent in an afterlife. Church attendance has held steady, too. The only exception is attendance among Catholics, whose decline from 74 per cent in 1955 – abnormally high by American standards – brought them nearer in 1976 to Protestant attendance – 56 per cent for Catholics compared with 41 per cent for Protestants.

Nor is this high rate of church attendance a purely 20th-century finding. It was thought that belief and church attendance in the 1800s

Mormonism is one of
the religions founded
in the United States
and based on private
revelation and initiative.
Mormon missionaries
have made converts in
many other countries.

were considerably below the modern level. But social historian Seymour Martin Lipset of Harvard University found that earlier studies
confused church membership with church attendance. Those early
studies drew on parish registers instead of the attendance figures reported in newspapers, travelers' journals, and books on religion. Lipset's more careful reading of the records, published in his 1963 book
The First New Nation, shows that the "data testify to an almost universal religious adherence by Americans in the 1830s, comparable to the
results obtained by public-opinion surveys in the past few decades."
Lipset also found that "the United States has experienced a continuous boom in religious adherence and belief." And that has been true
from the very beginning of this country. America was always a God-
obsessed nation, and continues to be one.

I am not denying that some kind of revival exists—a revival that is in
fact a new stage in the "continuing revival." But it is one thing to say
that long-term trends differ from perceived shifts; it is another thing
altogether to say that such perceptions do not affect reality. Heightened attention to one area of religion or another often gives that area
power to influence lives, usually in unforeseen ways. Catholic perceptions of a new spirit of tolerance among Protestants during the presidency of John F. Kennedy, for example, probably led many Catholics

to accept the 1960s fashion of "cool" secularity. Paradoxically, this flexibility also enabled them quickly to accept the "hot" fashion of charismatic revivalism in the 1970s.

If we now ask what produced the sudden awareness of evangelical religion in the 1970s, then we must look at how such styles of religious experience spread out from the more traditional centers of "conservative" evangelicalism in the South and Midwest. The evangelical phenomenon is tied to the social movements of the 1960s. It did not even become a subject of interest among academic scholars and newspaper columnists until it made an impact on the social movements of the day.

The principal factor was Martin Luther King, Jr., and the other civil rights leaders. They used an evangelical preaching style to motivate their followers, a style that university sophisticates at first considered "outmoded." White civil rights workers, traveling south from Northern universities, found something fresh and authentic in communities that prayed as well as marched together for freedom. The spontaneity and enthusiasm of the black evangelical congregations inspired and vitalized the white onlookers.

Whether in a Southern Baptist church like the one in Culpeper, Va., *above,* or at a Jesus Rally of Boston youths, *below,* the worship service is both spontaneous and enthusiastic.

A faith-healing service in a private residence, complete with the laying on of hands, is part of the evangelistic movement that never was confined within church walls.

This impetus of evangelical-inspired activism has continued into the 1970s. There are now evangelical communes, evangelical journals of protest, and evangelical marches against nuclear warfare. *Katallagete* (Greek for *Be Reconciled*), an evangelical magazine started in the 1960s by white activists, now unites many types of churchmen behind liberal causes in the South. Evangelical congregations that were once considered socially repressive and theologically backward supply most of the volunteers for a commune noted for its involvement in social and political issues and its journal called *Sojourners*, both based in Washington, D.C. A surprising number of evangelical believers, coming as they do from a branch of American religion traditionally opposed to the theologically liberal "social gospel," signed "A Call to Faithfulness," a 1978 document addressed to President Carter protesting the continuation of the nuclear arms race.

A similar ferment of demonstrative piety has occurred among Catholics since the 1960s. Union organizer Cesar Chavez, the migrant workers' champion in California's fruit farms, holds services that have a distinct evangelical flavor for workers in the grape fields. And Catholic liberals of the sixties adopted from Spanish-speaking immigrants the *Cursillo* (Little Course), a new kind of retreat that resembles the emotional revivals and missions of the past. A charismatic assembly for

Catholics at the University of Notre Dame near South Bend, Ind., in August 1978 drew more than 20,000 participants.

But this radical component in the evangelical movement, which puts a concern for social justice and political action at the center of their beliefs, coexists with the more traditional evangelical thrust that is totally focused on individual salvation. It also joins another development that was to be expected – the popularizing of pietism in a somewhat diluted form.

Theological concepts have often been made acceptable to great numbers of people by changing their meaning slightly. Billy Graham, for example, has been able to influence many people whom the old-style preachers of "hellfire" could not reach because he talks of a "spiritual cure" in modern, almost psychoanalytic terms. This shift from a fundamentalist to a Freudian approach offended many of the old-style preachers but "brought many souls to Christ." Norman Vincent Peale's "positive thinking" was more a form of psychology than of religious faith healing. And the President's sister, Ruth Carter Stapleton, has even adopted Freudian therapy techniques that are not theological for her faith-healing sessions. She has also freed her ministry from connection with any organized church.

The same subtle changes are evident in the adoption of Madison Avenue promotional methods to spread the evangelical gospel in such movements as the Campus Crusade, headed by California evangelist Bill Bright, and Youth for Christ. Bright's attempt to reach every American with television, telephones, billboards, bumper stickers ("I Found It!"), and the press is impressive. But the wide application of such promotional techniques inevitably leads to subtle changes in the original evangelical message.

What we are witnessing, then, in the "born-again revolution" is a new tapping of an old and relatively stable reservoir of religious belief –a fresh channeling of ancient energies. The roots of American religious faith are deep and tangled, and this is not the place to straighten them out. But even a cursory examination reveals a continuing American inclination toward religious piety. Religion in America is not "risen from the dead." It never died. Religion in America is no Lazarus returned to life. It is Methuselah, a miracle of longevity.

For further reading:

Ahlstrom, Sydney E. *A Religious History of the American People.* Yale University Press, 1972.

Dayton, Donald W. *Discovering an Evangelical Heritage.* Harper & Row Publishers, Inc., 1976.

Dolan, Jay P. *Catholic Revivalism: The American Experience, 1830-1900.* University of Notre Dame Press, 1977.

Quebedeaux, Richard. *The New Charismatics: The Origins, Development & Significance of Neo-Pentecostalism.* Doubleday & Co., 1977.

Wills, Garry. *Bare Ruined Choirs.* Dell Publishing Co., 1974.

A Year
In Perspective

THE YEAR BOOK casts a backward glance at
the furors, fancies, and follies of yesteryear. The
coincidences of history that are revealed offer
substantial proof that the physical world may
continually change, but human nature—with all
its inventiveness, amiability, and even perversity—
remains fairly constant, for better or worse,
throughout the years.

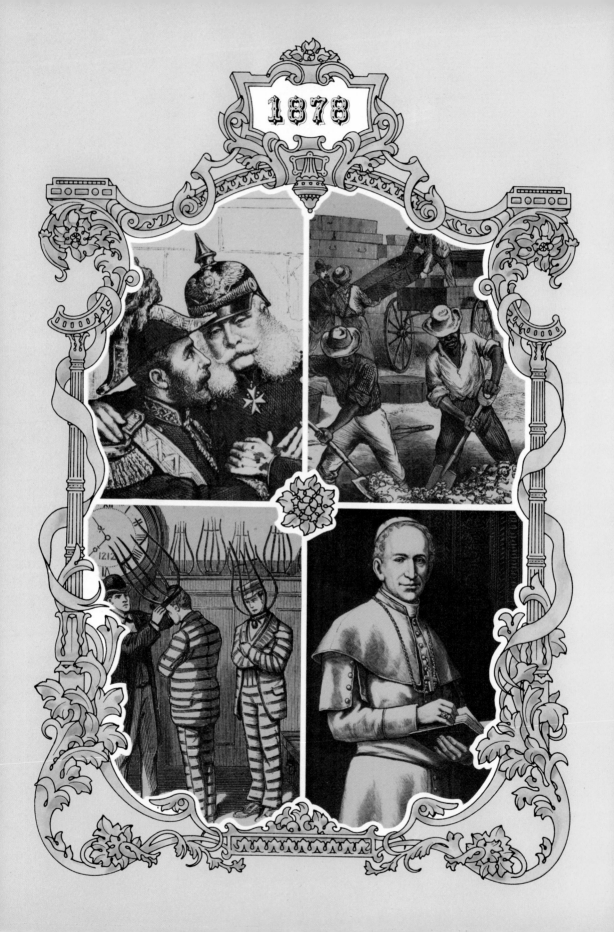

The Never-Ending Chain of History

By Paul C. Tullier

As the year 1878 demonstrates, no moment in history stands alone; each sliver of present time echoes the past and foreshadows the future

Years are like the links of a chain. Just as each link joins with the next to form a continuous, interdependent sequence, so years interlock in the chain of history. No one year stands alone; the strengths and flaws of one are the strengths and flaws of all. Today's fancies are tomorrow's foibles; yesteryear's trials are today's tribulations.

A hundred years ago, in 1878, world affairs seemed in a hopeless muddle, even as today. Members of the Will-of-the-People terrorist movement were stalking key government leaders in Moscow, Berlin, and Rome. Political division had all but paralyzed the government in France. For most of the year, a ministerial crisis in Italy had created near-anarchy in the Chamber of Deputies. Antipapal ill will in France, Italy, and Germany was temporarily eased by the death of Pope Pius IX and the election of Leo XIII as his successor. In Asia, China was massing troops along the Sino-Russian border to forestall

News highlights of 1878 included, *clockwise from upper left,* an attempt to murder the emperor of Germany; a yellow fever epidemic in the United States; a changeover in the Roman Catholic papacy; and prison brutality.

Russian territorial aggression. War held Afghanistan in its grip. Malaya's troops were ousting thousands of Chinese merchants who had illegally infiltrated the borders. India seethed with indignation over a newly passed Press Act that prohibited any criticism of the government. In the Western Hemisphere, relations between the United States and Canada were strained over rights to certain fishing grounds. Canada was bedeviled, too, by internal stress: Nova Scotia and New Brunswick were conferring informally on a possible union of the two provinces into a larger one named Acadia.

Nature was its usual unpredictable self in 1878. Spring floods in California devastated thousands of acres of valuable farmland. Hundreds of lives—as well as the year's coffee crop—were wiped out by floods in Ceylon. Famine plagued China and Morocco. A major earthquake in Venezuela snuffed out 16,000 lives.

Epidemics were as uncontrollable as they were unpredictable. Typhus was sweeping through Turkey, Romania, and Russia. Smallpox was a virulent killer in the African Congo, according to explorer Henry M. Stanley, who was recuperating after an arduous journey to the source of the Congo River. Typhoid fever raged in Bristol, England. But the most vicious killer of all in 1878 was yellow fever. It struck first in South America, and by June the burial grounds of Brazil, Venezuela, and the Central American countries overflowed with thousands of unburied corpses. By July, the disease had moved north to the United States, where it first struck New Orleans. Within weeks, the killer had spread to most of the other Southern states. In one week alone in August, the population of Grenada, Miss., was reduced from 2,200 to 300. In New Orleans, an estimated 11,000 persons perished before the epidemic finally abated.

Death and disease, like international dissension, were the larger issues that linked 1878 with 1978. But Americans, however great their concern over global affairs, found plenty of domestic issues to occupy them. Two of these centered on education. One, a major issue in 1878, was whether the nation's schools should introduce bilingual classroom instruction. It was a particularly hot issue in such cities as Cleveland and St. Louis, where a large number of German immigrants had settled. Advocates of foreign-language classes argued that they would ease the transition from alien to citizen. This policy was favored mostly by naturalized citizens such as 31-year-old Joseph Pulitzer, a Hungarian-born journalist who, near the end of 1878, purchased for $2,500 the *St. Louis Dispatch* (which he then merged with the *St. Louis Evening Post*). But a New York City weekly newspaper, writing with its city's large Italian population in mind, editorialized that "if [the immigrants] are to become full-fledged American citizens, they must learn to read, write, and think in English. Teaching them...in their former native tongue will only perpetuate their old ways and prevent accommodation to the new." The advocates of bilingual teaching in the nation's classrooms lost the battle.

The author:
Paul C. Tullier is Managing Editor of THE WORLD BOOK YEAR BOOK.

New York City's new 6th Avenue Elevated Railroad was one of many rapid-transit systems being built to meet urban needs.

The second controversy centered around free college education, a policy favored by educators in many states. Opponents focused their wrath on archetypal New York College—formerly known as the Free Academy. Its cost, critics said, was astronomical; for each student completing a free, four-year course, the city was spending $4,000, which came out of the taxpayers' pockets. The argument was particularly persuasive with New York City taxpayers—who were already up in arms about the city's finances. The New York Board of Apportionment estimated that $30 million would be required to run the city's government during the next fiscal year. Only three-fifths could be counted on from existing tax sources; the remaining two-fifths would have to come from new sources, tax increases, or cost cutting.

Many taxpayers favored cutbacks, especially after a study of the city's payroll was made public. "Officials and employees of New York City now number over 7,500," said the study, "and their total yearly pay is more than $11,000,000. There are 52 [employees] who draw each $5,000 or over; two get $15,000 apiece. Most certainly this band of bureaucratic banditti in City Hall could be greatly reduced without hindering services."

Some New Yorkers argued that economies could be effected in other ways. The city, like too many others in the United States, was

165

Environmental pollution was a growing problem. Garbage scows dumped New York City's refuse in Long Island Sound, forcing nearby bathing resorts to shut down.

investing its tax dollars in frivolous ways, they complained. Expensive experiments were being conducted with newfangled street hydrants allegedly capable of throwing jets of water upon burning buildings without the use of fire-engine pumps; transportation was being expanded beyond all reasonable future need—New York City's new 6th Avenue Elevated Railroad was one outstanding example.

Rising costs were not the only frustrations encountered by city dwellers. Strikes by labor unions for more pay often disrupted city services. The feminist movement, too, was a disruptive force as more and more women demonstrated not only for the right to vote, but also for equal work rights with men. Some employers sympathized with their plight. So did some labor groups, such as the Noble Order of the Knights of Labor, which in 1878 adopted a new constitution "to secure for both sexes equal pay for equal work, an eight-hour workday, and weekly pay." But the Knights were the exception rather than the rule. And even appeals to Congress for backup legislation on women's rights met with vacillation.

"The ability of Congress to veer from pro to con," wrote Mark Twain in the *Atlantic Monthly*, "is matched only by a side-winder caught between rocks and the river." Yet when Congress *did* act decisively, it aroused even more venomous criticism. Its vote to restore its

Soaring costs of coal and other energy sources caused French scientists to explore such cheaper alternatives as heating with the sun's rays.

franking privileges–despite its promises to the contrary–was deplored as self-interest; funds it appropriated to expand facilities at the Library of Congress, where 50,000 volumes were allegedly piled on the floor for lack of shelving, were called recklessly extravagant. Worse yet, it had authorized funds to establish schools and medical facilities for American Indians–an affront, critics said, to "those whose dear ones had been slaughtered by the savages at Little Bighorn" just two years earlier. Congress was even tinkering with the postal rates, to the despair of publishers who argued that there should be one uniform rate of 2 cents per pound (0.45 kilogram) on all publications, rather than a rate scale that fluctuated according to whether a publication appeared daily, weekly, monthly, or quarterly. Worst of all, to many critics, was congressional approval of the Bland-Allison Act, which required the Treasury to buy and mint a minimum of $2 million and a maximum of $4 million worth of silver per month. Holders of U.S. paper money, or greenbacks as they were called, could then redeem it in silver as well as gold. Farm and labor groups believed that increasing the amount of money in circulation would boost income. But by thus doubling the money supply, said August Belmont, a New York financier, Congress "has only added to the upward spiral of an already runaway inflation," which was then running at about 7 per cent.

The act had been passed over the veto of President Rutherford B. Hayes, who, even more than Congress, faced growing criticism of his policies. Under his Administration, the United States had developed a balance-of-trade problem; imports in fiscal 1878 had exceeded exports by $167 million. His recommendation that a new department of agriculture be created and placed under a Cabinet officer was belittled as just another executive boondoggle. So was his authorization of an ecological study of the Great Lakes. There was a greater need, his critics argued, for a solution to water-pollution problems, which, in 1878, forced a temporary shut-down of seaside resorts in Brighton, N.Y., and Atlantic City, N.J., and the bathing beaches of San Francisco Bay. Conservationists were aroused over Hayes's signing of the Timber Cutting Act, under which miners and settlers in the West could cut timber on public land free of charge – for their own use. Even Hayes's own Republican Party was blocking his efforts to reform the Civil Service. As one staunchly conservative journal editorialized, "We have squandered our forest resources and are even now seeking timber supplies from our northern neighbors; we have wasted our natural gas supplies in a most foolish and prodigal manner...we have foolishly trifled with our finances and with our civil and consular

War in Afghanistan typified the turbulent ethnic and political problems besetting much of Asia in 1878.

Hens were cooped up in stacked cages in 1878's "egg farms." Forced feeding of the chickens was thought by many to be a good technique for obtaining larger eggs.

services in a way to bring contempt and loss of confidence...and overburdened the people with taxation that brings profit only to the coffers of our millionaires."

Nor was the President's personal life beyond public comment. His wife Lucy's strict enforcement of a "no liquor" policy in the White House had been accepted grudgingly, but she was praised for starting in 1878 what would eventually be an annual egg-rolling contest on the White House lawn at Easter. But the shenanigans of the Hayeses' 9-year-old daughter, Fannie, were a different matter. She was being "pampered," "mollycoddled," and "overdressed," said the critics. Worse, because she was "permitted to dine with her elders and their visitors," she was "growing too old too fast for her years." Even the President's personal conversations found their way into public print, and his allegedly expressed approval of an 1878 ruling by the Supreme Court of the United States that a state law outlawing segregation of the races in railroad travel was unconstitutional raised a storm of criticism. It was considered a low blow to the cause of "full emancipation" by a man in the nation's highest office.

"We are living in a corrupt social state," wrote William Cullen Bryant, the influential editor of New York City's *Evening Post*, "which we have all helped to create by looseness in our commercial dealings, by connivance at small frauds, the persistent pursuit of low aims, and neglect of our fellow human beings."

Bryant's sentiments were shared by many, for the nation's sense of morality appeared to be deteriorating alarmingly. Divorce was increasing. Saloons were proliferating. Alcoholic consumption was on the rise. News reports of wife beating, usually winked at as a private matter between mates, were beginning to appear sporadically in some journals. Cases of child abuse were also being aired in print; there were reports of children being brutally beaten with broomsticks, burned with cigar butts, or kept chained to bedposts. Waifs roamed the streets of the nation's cities; in New York City alone, an estimated 22,000 runaways under the age of 10 called the city's paving stones their home. Alarmed, the American Humane Association—which had been formed in 1877—adopted a new constitution at a meeting held in Baltimore on Nov. 11, 1878. It dedicated itself to the prevention of cruelty to children as well as animals. Earlier in the year, Grace Church of New York City had set a precedent by establishing a nursery for the care of children of working mothers. The newly renamed Salvation Army—founded in London in 1865 as the Christian Mission—widened its scope to include underage youths. Traveling "tent" evangelists toured the hinterlands preaching against child abuse; one itinerant preacher, Judy (Big Sis) Oberger of Philadelphia, preached that a "rebirth" of harmony in the home would cure all of society's ills, including crime.

There was no doubt that a cure for crime was urgently needed. So were adequate prison facilities to house the convicted criminals. "Overcrowded prisons," read the first official statement of the newly formed National Prison Association, "are poorly managed, moral pesthouses. They are schools for crime. Three men are locked in one cell 7 feet long and 3½ feet wide. Open buckets are used for waste. Torture is not uncommon. Many are illiterate miscreants," the report went on, "who have no lawyers because either they do not know such professionals exist, do not trust the scalawags with which the legal profession abounds, or cannot afford their exorbitant fees." Whether by chance or design, Judge Simeon Eben Baldwin announced the formation of the American Bar Association following an informal meeting held in Saratoga, N.Y., on Aug. 21, 1878. One of the avowed goals of the original 291 members was to improve and enforce the standards of the profession.

Professionalism was becoming more and more a requirement, not only in the social sciences, but in other fields as well. Building and construction were booming. The first all-steel bridge—a 2,700-foot (820-meter) structure built by the Chicago & Alton Railroad Company—was opened for use across the Missouri River at Glasgow, Mo. Late in the year, the Tidewater Oil Company created a sensation when it began pumping oil over the Allegheny Mountains in pipes instead of shipping it in barrels. The government of Colombia granted a 99-year franchise to a French adventurer named Lucien Napoleon Bonaparte Wyse; he was planning to build a canal across the Isthmus of Panama. In Paris, the Great World's Fair opened on May 1. A mixture of Romanesque, Greek, Oriental, and Early American architecture, it attracted thousands of visitors. Its amusement park featured balloon rides at $4 each, of which $2 was to ascend and $2 to descend. The balloon was nicknamed *L'Aiglon* – The Eagle – after Napoleon Bonaparte's legitimate son, the Duke of Reichstadt.

In the sciences, American physicist Albert A. Michelson, using measuring apparatus of his own design, was breaking new ground in measuring the speed of light. In Switzerland, French chemist Raoul Pictet's experiments with the liquefaction and solidification of sulfur dioxide would contribute greatly to the refrigerators and air conditioners of the future. Germany's Adolph von Baeyer's successful synthesizing of indigo in 1878 would open up a whole new world of synthetic dyestuffs.

In England, Sidney Gilchrist Thomas and his cousin Percy Gilchrist developed the basic process for removing phosphorus from iron ore, thus making such ore usable for steel manufacture. Another Englishman, William Crookes, invented the cathode-ray tube; it would eventually be used in television cameras and sets. In the United States, a young Ohio engineer named Charles R. Brush made artificial outdoor illumination possible with his development of a practical arc light. Thomas A. Edison was hot on the trail of an incandescent lamp, which he envisioned as a replacement for the oil or gas lamps used in most homes; to help finance the project, the Edison Electric Light Company was incorporated on Oct. 15, 1878.

One new product that would become both a business and a household necessity was Alexander Graham Bell's telephone. On Jan. 28, 1878, the first commercial telephone exchange was installed in New Haven, Conn. It served 21 subscribers. By February 21, when the first telephone directory was issued, the list of subscribers had grown to 28. By year's end, Boston, New York City, and Philadelphia were installing telephone facilities. "Ahoy-ahoy" was the user's first experimental shout rather than the eventually triumphant "Hello."

Other ways to better the lot of the average citizen were being explored. In 1878, the Procter & Gamble Company introduced a new kind of soap that floated. It was called "White Soap" but was later renamed Ivory Soap and promoted with the sales slogan "99^{44}/$_{100}$% Pure." An enterprising dairyman named Alexander Campbell became the first to deliver milk in glass bottles to his customers in Brooklyn, N.Y. A New Orleans coffee-bean importer introduced "compressed coffee"; freshly roasted, fine-ground beans were put in molds and, under pressure, formed into cakes resembling chocolate bars. A housewife, harried for time, need only break off a teaspoon-sized piece and add water to produce a cup of "instant" coffee. Another household device was known as a "solar cooker." It was made of copper – tinned inside, painted black outside, and covered with glass. Solar rays passing through the glass cover heated the copper and tin to

1878

Thomas A. Edison's new "talking" machine, *top*, drew widespread public praise; public anger was beginning to surface over false advertising claims that touted fake medical cures.

create a blanket of hot air that was supposed to cook the food placed inside. (In France, experiments were being conducted with solar reflectors that would convert solar heat into energy for industrial use.)

Despite heavy advertising, neither the instant coffee nor the solar cooker caught on with the public. Consumers were becoming skeptical over the exaggerated, often false claims being advertised in various publications. So were the publishers. At least two publications, *Leslie's Illustrated Weekly Newspaper* and *Harper's Bazar*, ran frequent editorials deploring the spread of dishonest or misleading advertising. As well they might have. There was a product called "Hair Revivum. The Great Hair Restorer," which promised a luxuriant growth not only on bald heads, but also on youthful chests and chins. Another, "Rodway's Ready Relief," promised "A Cure For Every Pain," as did "Collins Voltaic Electric Plasters," which, as the "Curative Marvel of the Ages," could "be used efficaciously for lumbago, pleurisy, croup, and vapors," as well as for "rheumatism, chilblains, and vertigo." "Allen's Brain Food" proclaimed itself a "Botanical Extract that strengthens the brain, cures all nervous effections and restores lost power and manhood." The Chelsea China Company offered restaurateurs a service that printed advertisements on china so that, after finishing a meal, guests might read in the bottom of the plate "a message from the host or a theatrical troupe."

Advertisers by and large ignored the carpers. Some, however, began using big-name product-endorsement to improve sales. Lillie Langtry, a British actress, was a big favorite. Artificial hairpieces called Lillie Langtry bangs sold for $3.50 in department stores such as Marshall Field's in Chicago and John Wanamaker's Grand Depot Emporium in Philadelphia. The "Jersey Lily," as Langtry was also known, endorsed fans, shawls, and even a toothpaste.

In fashionable clothing accessories, an innovative fashion accessory called "Madame Foy's Corset Skirt Supporter" guaranteed a smooth figure for generously proportioned women. For the lesser endowed, there was the "American Elastic Bosom," which was also known as the "Gay Deceiver." For men, the newest "in" things were stiff paper collars. The most popular one was named for George Washington. It came boxed with a tiny hatchet, which, instructions said, was "to be worn in the lapel by the truthful as a charm." The runner-up in the neckwear sweepstakes was the William Riley collar. Its name derived from a popular song of the day, "Oh Rise Up, William Riley, and Come Along with me." Fast becoming popular but unrelated to sartorial splendor were the just-published songs "Baby Mine," "Carry Me Back to Old Virginny," "A Flower for Mother's Grave," and "Where Was Moses When the Lights Went Out."

People were reading more than ever. There were books suited to all tastes, ranging from Thomas Hardy's *The Return of the Native* and Henry James's *Daisy Miller: A Study* to Nate Robinson's *Born on the Deep or, which is The Heiress. The Leavenworth Case*, by Anna Katherine

1878

Greene, introduced the modern detective novel to American literature. When reading palled, there were outdoor activities to fall back on for diversion, including bicycling, soccer, and croquet. But baseball remained unchallenged as America's most popular sport. To the joy of many fans, Boston won the National League pennant under manager Harry Wright with 41 wins and 19 losses. Paul Hines of Providence, R.I., was the batting champion with a .356 average. He was also the home-run king—with four—and led in runs batted in with 50.

The arts remained an ongoing institution. The U.S. première of Georges Bizet's *Carmen* was given at the Academy of Music in New York City in 1878, with Minnie Hauk in the title role. The opera was sung in Italian rather than in the original French. Ole Bull, the distinguished Swedish violinist, was enthralling audiences in New York City, Chicago, New Orleans, and San Francisco. In France, Charles Gounod was at work on a five-act opera based on the immortal love story of Abelard and Héloïse; unfortunately, his latest opera, *Polyeucte*, which opened at the Grand Opera House in Paris in October, drew lukewarm reviews. Russia's Nicholas Rimsky-Korsakov was struggling with the score of *A Night in May*, an opera based on a story by Nikolai V. Gogol. Famous prima donnas like Maria Rôze were condescendingly recording operatic arias on Edison's new phonograph cylinders; recording would eventually be simplified through use of the first true microphone, which David Edward Hughes invented in 1878.

Theatergoers in New York City flocked to see *H.M.S. Pinafore,* the new Gilbert and Sullivan operetta, when an unauthorized version opened in late 1878.

Theatrical entertainment was flourishing on Broadway with such international stars as Genevieve Ward portraying Queen Catherine in *Henry VIII* at New York City's Booth Theatre and Ada Cavendish playing the lead in *Mercy Merrick* at the Broadway Theatre. At a less lofty level were female minstrel shows, which, needless to say, attracted mostly male audiences. The big attractions were "Blanche Selwyn's Red Riding Hood Minstrels" and "May Fiske's English Blondes, Living Art Pictures and Grand Specialty Combination." A leading producer of these exhibitions was E. E. Rice. It was in a Rice production in 1878 that actress Lillian Russell began her career—as a chorus girl.

There was one theatrical production during the season that put all others in the shade: a new operetta by William S. Gilbert and Arthur S. Sullivan called *H.M.S. Pinafore*. It opened at London's Opera Comique on May 25, 1878, to a wildly enthusiastic reception by British theatergoers. Its first U.S. performance—in an unauthorized version—was on Nov. 15, 1878, at the Boston Museum Theater. Other pirated versions quickly appeared. Before the year was out, 150 companies, including one all-black cast, were performing the operetta in more than 60 U.S. cities. San Francisco's newly completed Tivoli Opera House chose *Pinafore* as its initial presentation.

The theater world did not have a monopoly on imagination in 1878, however. From Brazil came news of an incredible monster reportedly living in the Amazon forest. The fact that monstrous beings had once walked the earth had been authenticated by the excavation of a reptilian skeleton 117 feet (36 meters) long in Colorado. This lent credibility to the tales seeping out of Brazil, where an enormous worm called a Minhocão was reportedly sighted on several occasions. Unidentified Christian missionaries claimed it was 150 feet (46 meters) long and covered with bones "as with a great coat of armor." It was said to be "powerful enough to uproot mighty pine trees as if they were blades of grass." When crossing a stream, its bulk often "diverted the course, turning surrounding dry land into a morass."

News of the Minhocão reached the New York City press in June; by August, rumors of other reprehensible creatures were spreading throughout the nation: A gigantic molelike creature with a human face was seen in the rain-drenched forests of the African Congo River Basin; a huge hairy behemoth had forced "the Esquimaux to flee their native habitat in the Arctic Circle."

Little attention was paid, however, to a marine creature that was reportedly roiling the waters of Loch Ness, a lake in Scotland. The Loch Ness monster was, relatively speaking, old hat by 1878. It had first been noted 13 centuries earlier. Some persons believed it a fact; some believed it a fantasy. Few saw in its resurfacing at intervals over the centuries one of those recurring interlocks that—like war, famine, plague, political unrest, and social upheaval—form the never-ending chain of history.

The Year On File, 1978

Contributors to THE WORLD BOOK YEAR BOOK report on the major developments of 1978. The contributors' names appear at the end of the articles they have written, and a complete roster of contributors, listing their professional affiliations and the articles they have written, is on pages 6 and 7.

Articles in this section are arranged alphabetically by subject matter. In most cases, the article titles are the same as those of the articles in THE WORLD BOOK ENCYCLOPEDIA that they update. The numerous cross references (in **bold type**) guide the reader to a subject or information that may be in some other article or that may appear under an alternative title. "See" and "See also" cross references appear within and at the end of articles to direct the reader to related information elsewhere in THE YEAR BOOK. "In WORLD BOOK, see" references point the reader to articles in the encyclopedia that provide background information to the year's events reported in THE YEAR BOOK.

ADVERTISING

ADVERTISING in the United States surged in 1978 for the third consecutive year, chalking up an estimated 13 per cent increase, two percentage points higher than overall economic growth. Total U.S. volume was put at $43 million by Robert J. Coen, vice-president of McCann-Erickson in New York City, in that agency's annual study on ad volume.

Ad growth also continued strong throughout the world, with international ad agencies reporting an increase of 26 per cent in income as they headed into 1978, according to *Advertising Age's* annual survey of agency income. The largest international agency was Japan's Dentsu, with gross income of $212-million on billings of $1.4 billion. The J. Walter Thompson Company in New York City was second, with gross income of $189 million on billings of $1.3 billion.

Airlines spent heavily in 1978 to promote ever-multiplying discount fares. American Airlines offered 30 per cent off on weekends and 40 per cent off midweek fares to 52 cities, while United Airlines included 108 cities in its Super Saver fares. United Airlines backed its new fares with more than $1-million in ad spending on network television. By year-end, several airlines, including American and TWA, had started to provide – and advertise – extra conveniences to mollify full-fare business travelers.

Commercial Clutter. Television station executives expressed concern in March over the Procter & Gamble Company's use of odd-length TV spots – teaming two 45-second spots or a 45-second and a 15-second spot. The station officials feared this might pave the way for 15-second commercials, adding to television clutter.

Agency media buyers, on the other hand, saw shorter commercials as the wave of the future – not just the 10-second company identifications shown now, but actual selling messages. They also charged that the networks were a prime source of clutter with their various promotional plugs.

Federal Decisions. The Supreme Court of the United States gave a boost to corporate advertising in April when it allowed issue-oriented advertising to come under the protection of the First Amendment. The ruling extended First Amendment protection to include corporate advertising on political issues.

At issue was the right of corporations to spend corporate funds to speak out on public referendum issues, such as energy or ecology, that do not relate directly to their businesses. Justice Lewis F. Powell, Jr., said in the majority opinion: "The First Amendment goes beyond protection of the press and self-expression of individuals to prohibit the government from limiting the stock of information on which members of the public may draw. A commercial advertisement is protected not so much because it pertains to the seller's business as because it furthers

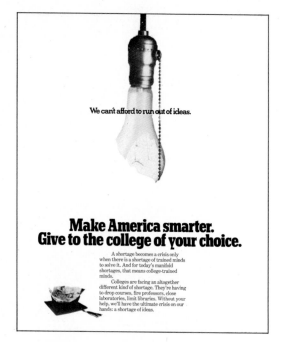

We can't afford to run out of ideas.

Make America smarter. Give to the college of your choice.

A shortage becomes a crisis only when there is a shortage of trained minds to solve it. And for today's manifold shortages, that means college-trained minds.

Colleges are facing an altogether different kind of shortage. They're having to drop courses, fire professors, close laboratories, limit libraries. Without your help, we'll have the ultimate crisis on our hands: a shortage of ideas.

A cartoon cliché brightens a public-service advertisement aimed at persuading people to support higher education in the United States.

the societal interest in the free flow of information."

The ruling does not apply to corporate ads for political candidates, which are still forbidden. Another restraining influence on corporate issue advertising was a ruling by the Internal Revenue Service that public-issue ads are not deductible expenses.

A federal grand jury in March handed down a 747-count indictment against the Joseph Schlitz Brewing Company of Milwaukee and its advertising agencies. The indictment charged Schlitz with conspiring with its wholesalers and retailers to violate the Alcohol Administration Act by giving inducements such as free fixtures and supplies to retailers and distributors to feature Schlitz beer.

In November, Schlitz agreed to pay $750,000 in civil penalties on four charges and pleaded no contest to two criminal misdemeanor charges. As part of the agreement, three felony charges and 743 other misdemeanor charges were dropped. Nine other beer and liquor companies were assessed similar penalties in out-of-court settlements, but Schlitz was the only one to have faced criminal charges.

In May, singer Pat Boone agreed to a landmark settlement with the Federal Trade Commission (FTC) holding him personally accountable for an acne product he endorsed. The FTC charged that ads for the product falsely implied that it was better than other acne products and could cure acne. The FTC sued Boone and the manufacturer of the product. Boone was the first product endorser to accept responsibility for a product claim and could be held personally liable for as much as 2.5 per cent of any refund ordered.

Major Account Shifts. Doyle Dane Bernbach lost the $15-million Bayer aspirin account in early February, just after the U.S. Food and Drug Administration (FDA) rebuked the Sterling Drug Company for running ads said to misrepresent an FDA report on the safety of aspirin versus nonaspirin products. The account was subsequently assigned to the SSC&B Inc. agency.

In other major account shifts, Grey Advertising got the $20-million American Motors passenger car account from Cunningham and Walsh; J. Walter Thompson Company lost 7-Up's $15-million billing to NW Ayer ABH; and Schlitz beer, billing $20-million, moved from Leo Burnett Company to Thompson.

Deaths. John H. Crichton, president of the American Association of Advertising Agencies since 1962, died on Dec. 27, 1977, at age 58. Leonard Matthews, president of Young and Rubicam's national division, was named to succeed him in August 1978.

Morris, the long-time feline spokesman for 9-Lives cat food, died on July 7 of cardiac complications related to old age. Kathryn Sederberg

In WORLD BOOK, see ADVERTISING.

AFGHANISTAN. President Mohammad Daoud was killed during a military coup d'état on April 27, 1978, five years after he had overthrown the monarchy and ousted his cousin, King Mohammad Zahir Shah. The 1973 coup was bloodless, but the 1978 uprising produced two days of violent street battles.

The coup climaxed widespread dissatisfaction over Daoud's failure to make political reforms or improve the economy. Earlier in April, the assassination of a prominent trade union leader set off a government crackdown on alleged Communist conspirators. Ordered to put down protest demonstrations, army units reacted by joining them.

The coup leaders, headed by former air force commander Colonel Abdul Qadir, organized a Revolutionary Council to rule but chose a civilian, Noor Mohammad Taraki, as prime minister and president of the council. Taraki's Cabinet, also civilian, were members of the leftist Khalq Party. Most of the coup leaders were rightist, but also pro-Russian. See TARAKI, NOOR MOHAMMAD.

The rivalry came to a head on September 29 with the arrest of Colonel Qadir and six Afghan ambassadors. They were charged with conspiring to overthrow Taraki. On December 5, Taraki signed a treaty of friendship with Russia. William Spencer

See also ASIA (Facts in Brief Table). In WORLD BOOK, see AFGHANISTAN.

An army tank guards a checkpoint in Kabul, the capital of Afghanistan, after President Mohammad Daoud was killed in a coup d'état on April 27.

AFRICA

Africa continued to be a setting for strife during 1978. African nations waged wars of annexation, civil wars raged between ethnic groups, and nationalist guerrillas continued their efforts to topple the remaining white-dominated governments. Meanwhile, the United States criticized Russia and Cuba for their continuing military presence in Africa.

Somalia and Ethiopia fought over control of the Ogaden region in southeastern Ethiopia; Libya and Chad over the Azou area in northern Chad; and Uganda and Tanzania over the Kagera River region in northwestern Tanzania. Civil war persisted in Angola and Ethiopia and flared again briefly in Zaire. Negotiations for peaceful transition to black rule in Rhodesia and Namibia foundered, increasing the chances of further escalation of guerrilla wars.

Rhodesia and Namibia. Ian D. Smith, Rhodesia's white prime minister, joined forces on March 3 with black political leaders Bishop Abel Muzorewa, Ndabaningi Sithole, and Jeremiah Chirau in an interim biracial government. This transitional regime pledged to hold parliamentary elections and to hand power over to a black-majority government by December 31.

The United States and Great Britain opposed this approach to black rule because black guerrilla leaders Joshua Nkomo and Robert Mugabe had no role in forming the interim government. A peaceful transition seemed unlikely without their support and that of some 40,000 guerrilla troops they commanded. In fact, the guerrilla war intensified after the interim government was established.

As a result of American and British prodding, Smith and the three black leaders agreed in mid-October to attend an all-party conference. However, Nkomo formally rejected such negotiations in December, arguing that the future of Zimbabwe (the African name for Rhodesia) could be settled only on the battlefield. See RHODESIA.

Western diplomatic efforts were also fruitless in Namibia (South West Africa). Although South Africa had agreed to grant it independence following elections, the South West Africa People's Organization (SWAPO), Namibia's major black nationalist party, refused to participate in elections conducted by the South African government. More than 90 per cent of Namibia's population is black.

A United Nations (UN) contact group composed of delegates from France, Great Britain, Canada,

Zaire's President Mobutu Sese Seko briefs his troops at Kolwezi, the battle-scarred capital of Shaba province, during May guerrilla invasion.

the United States, and West Germany proposed that elections be supervised by the UN and that most of the 18,000 South African troops stationed in Namibia be replaced by a UN peacekeeping force. South Africa agreed to the basic principles that were contained in the Western proposal in April, but it rejected specific plans for implementing the plan in September. South Africa argued that they favored SWAPO. South Africa conducted its own elections for a constituent assembly for Namibia from December 4 to 8. SWAPO boycotted the elections, and the South African-backed Democratic Turnhalle Alliance received 82 per cent of the vote. SWAPO continued to wage a guerrilla war against South African rule. See NAMIBIA; SOUTH AFRICA; UNITED NATIONS (UN).

The wars against white domination in Namibia and Rhodesia spilled over into neighboring African countries where black governments permitted nationalist guerrillas to maintain bases. South African forces attacked SWAPO camps in both Zambia and Angola. Rhodesian planes bombed guerrilla bases in Mozambique and Zambia.

Civil Wars. Angola's President Agostinho Neto and President Mobutu Sese Seko of neighboring Zaire met in June and August and pledged to stop aiding each other's internal opposition. Zaire had been providing military aid to three guerrilla groups opposed to Neto. See ANGOLA.

A stately military escort accompanies the cannon-mounted coffin of Jomo Kenyatta, the "father of Kenya," to its tomb in Nairobi.

Facts in Brief on African Political Units

Country	Population	Government†	Monetary Unit*	Foreign Trade (million U.S. $) Exports	Imports
Algeria	19,029,000	Acting President Rabah Bitat	dinar (3.9 = $1)	5,812	7,085
Angola	7,819,000	President Agostinho Neto	kwanza (47.6 = $1)	1,057	666
Benin	3,462,000	President & Chief of Government Mathieu Kerekou	CFA franc (216.6 = $1)	46	150
Bophuthats-wana	1,719,000	President Lucas Mangope	rand (1 = $1.15)	no statistics available	
Botswana	796,000	President Sir Seretse M. Khama	pula (1 = $1.20)	127	184
Burundi	4,150,000	President Jean-Baptiste Bagaza	franc (90 = $1)	95	74
Cameroon	6,898,000	President Ahmadou Ahidjo; Prime Minister Paul Biya	CFA franc (216.6 = $1)	658	994
Cape Verde	317,000	President Aristides Pereira; Prime Minister Pedro Pires	escudo (47.6 = $1)	2	28
Central African Empire	2,939,000	Emperor Bokassa I; Prime Minister Henri Maidou	CFA franc (216.6 = $1)	58	54
Chad	4,379,000	President F. Malloum Ngakoutou Bey-Ndi; Prime Minister Hissen Habre	CFA franc (216.6 = $1)	70	133
Comoros	338,000	President Abdellah Mohamed	franc (216.6 = $1)	8	22
Congo	1,485,000	President Joachim Yhombi-Opango; Prime Minister Louis Sylvain Goma	CFA franc (216.6 = $1)	182	177
Djibouti	116,000	President Hassan Gouled Aptidon; Prime Minister Barkat Gourad Hamadou	franc (187 = $1)	18	67
Egypt	40,619,000	President Anwar al-Sadat; Prime Minister Mustafa Khalil	pound (1 = $2.56)	1,726	4,823
Equatorial Guinea	326,000	President Macias Nguema Biyogo Negue Ndong	ekpwele (73.7 = $1)	25	21
Ethiopia	30,968,000	Provisional Military Government Chairman Mengistu Haile Mariam	birr (2.1 = $1)	330	349
Gabon	1,039,000	President Omar Bongo; Prime Minister Leon Mebiame	CFA franc (216.6 = $1)	1.136	498
Gambia	578,000	President Sir Dawda Kairaba Jawara	dalasi (2.1 = $1)	48	72
Ghana	10,975,000	Supreme Military Council Chairman Frederick William Kwasi Akuffo	new cedi (2.8 = $1)	760	805
Guinea	4,855,000	President Ahmed Sekou Toure; Prime Minister Lansana Beavogui	syli (20.3 = $1)	288	199
Guinea-Bissau	557,000	President Luis de Almeida Cabral; Prime Minister Joao Bernardino Vieira	peso (47.6 = $1)	6	36
Ivory Coast	7,897,000	President Felix Houphouet-Boigny	CFA franc (216.6 = $1)	2,170	1,761
Kenya	15,366,000	President Daniel T. arap Moi	shilling (7.5 = $1)	656	941
Lesotho	1,133,000	King Motlotlehi Moshoeshoe II; Prime Minister Leabua Jonathan	rand (1 = $1.15)	14	124
Liberia	1,871,000	President William R. Tolbert, Jr.	dollar (1 = $1)	447	464
Libya	2,881,000	General People's Congress Secretary General Muammar Muhammad al-Qadhaafi; General People's Congress Chairman Abd al-Ati Al-Ubaydi	dinar (1 = $3.38)	9,561	3,212
Madagascar	8,138,000	Supreme Revolutionary Council President Didier Ratsiraka; Prime Minister Desire Rakotoarijaona	franc (216.6 = $1)	292	363

The agreement between Neto and Mobutu followed the May invasion of Zaire's southeastern Shaba province by anti-Mobutu exiles based in Angola. About 2,000 to 2,500 guerrillas took part in the attack, captured Kolwezi, Zaire's chief mining town, and held it for a week before they were driven out by French and Belgian paratroopers. See ZAIRE.

United States President Jimmy Carter charged on May 25 that Cubans stationed in Angola aided the Shaba invaders. Cuba denied this charge and allegations that its troops helped Ethiopia's Marxist military government to fight secessionist rebels in Eritrea, Ethiopia's northernmost province.

At the start of 1978, Eritrean nationalists controlled an estimated 95 per cent of the province.

However, the Ethiopian government launched a counteroffensive in March and wiped out the last major line of resistance by November 29. At the time, there were from 15,000 to 16,000 Cuban soldiers and more than 1,000 Russian military advisers in Ethiopia. See ETHIOPIA.

Wars of Annexation. Despite its defeat by Ethiopia in March, Somalia did not renounce its claim to the Ogaden, a region bordering on Somalia and inhabited mainly by ethnic Somalis. Moreover, the Somali government provided covert assistance to guerrillas operating in the Ogaden against Ethiopian and Cuban troops. See SOMALIA.

Chad broke off diplomatic relations with neighboring Libya on February 6 after Libya occupied

Country	Population	Government†	Monetary Unit*	Foreign Trade (million U.S. $) Exports	Imports
Malawi	5,589,000	President H. Kamuzu Banda	kwacha (1.2 = $1)	195	235
Mali	6,288,000	President & Prime Minister Moussa Traore	franc (433.2 = $1)	70	148
Mauritania	1,461,000	Military Committee for National Recovery President & Chief of Government Moustapha Ould Mohamed Saleck	ouguiya (46.2 = $1)	151	207
Mauritius	954,000	Acting Governor General Dayendranath Burrenchobay; Prime Minister Sir Seewoosagur Ramgoolam	rupee (6 = $1)	312	442
Morocco	19,483,000	King Hassan II; Prime Minister Ahmed Osman	dirham (4 = $1)	1,300	3,197
Mozambique	10,119,000	President Samora Moises Machel	escudo (47.6 = $1)	202	417
Namibia (South West Africa)	1,027,000	Administrator-General M. T. Steyn	rand (1 = $1.15)	no statistics available	
Niger	5,117,000	Supreme Military Council President Seyni Kountche	CFA franc (216.6 = $1)	91	100
Nigeria	69,667,000	Head of State Olusegun Obasanjo	naira (1 = $1.56)	11,772	11,306
Rhodesia	7,482,000	Acting President Henry Everard; Executive Council members Ian D. Smith, Abel Muzorewa, Ndabaningi Sithole, and Jeremiah Chirau	dollar (1 = $1.38)	345	370
Rwanda	4,670,000	President Juvenal Habyarimana	franc (92.8 = $1)	92	114
São Tomé and Príncipe	86,000	President Manuel Pinto da Costa; Prime Minister Miguel Trovoada	dobra (35.9 = $1)	7	11
Senegal	4,078,000	President Leopold Sedar Senghor; Prime Minister Abdou Diouf	CFA franc (216.6 = $1)	461	576
Seychelles	63,000	President France Albert Rene	rupee (6.9 = $1)	5	27
Sierra Leone	3,440,000	President Siaka Stevens	leone (1.1 = $1)	112	153
Somalia	3,513,000	President Mohamed Siad Barre	shilling (6.3 = $1)	89	162
South Africa	28,115,000	President Balthazar Johannes Vorster; Prime Minister Pieter Willem Botha	rand (1 = $1.15)	6,158	5,893
Sudan	19,600,000	President & Prime Minister Gaafar Muhammed Nimeiri	pound (1 = $2.50)	661	1,060
Swaziland	560,000	King Sobhuza II; Prime Minister Maphevu Dlamini	lilangeni (1 = $1.15)	152	151
Tanzania	16,850,000	President Julius K. Nyerere; Prime Minister Edward Moringe Sokoine	shilling (7.5 = $1)	459	566
Togo	2,453,000	President Gnassingbe Eyadema	CFA franc (216.6 = $1)	105	201
Transkei	5,916,000	President Botha Sigcau; Prime Minister Kaiser Matanzima	rand (1 = $1.15)	no statistics available	
Tunisia	6,346,000	President Habib Bourguiba; Prime Minister Hedi Nouira	dinar (1 = $2.42)	910	1,767
Uganda	13,151,000	President Idi Amin Dada	shilling (7.7 = $1)	359	80
Upper Volta	6,729,000	President Aboubakar Sangoule Lamizana; Prime Minister Joseph Conombo	CFA franc (216.6 = $1)	58	219
Zaire	27,810,000	President Mobutu Sese Seko; Prime Minister Mpinga Kasenda	zaire (1 = $1.28)	982	606
Zambia	5,553,000	President Kenneth D. Kaunda; Prime Minister Daniel Lisulo	kwacha (1 = $1.23)	897	670

*Exchange rates as of Dec. 1, 1978. † As of Dec. 31, 1978.

about 27,000 square miles (70,000 square kilometers) of Chad's territory. It also charged that Libya gave military aid to Chadian rebels. The land in question, called the Azou Strip, borders on Libya and reportedly has rich uranium deposits. The rebels were Muslim and received Russian arms via Libya. Chad's government under President F. Malloum Ngakoutou Bey-Ndi received most of its political support from Christians and other groups in the south and received military aid from France. Malloum agreed to restore diplomatic ties with Libya, but the guerrilla war and Libya's occupation of the Azou Strip continued.

Uganda invaded northwest Tanzania on October 31 and announced the next day that it was annexing a 710-square-mile (1,840-square-kilometer) region north of the Kagera River. Uganda's President Idi Amin Dada charged that Tanzania used the territory to infiltrate revolutionary guerrillas into Uganda. Amin withdrew his troops on November 17 under pressure from other African governments and Russia, Uganda's principal supplier of arms. See TANZANIA.

U.S.-Communist Conflict. The involvement of Russia and its close ally, Cuba, in African trouble spots alarmed the U.S. government. Particularly disturbing to the Carter Administration was the strong Communist military presence in two strategic African areas – Ethiopia and Angola. Ethiopia borders on the Red Sea, and Russian bases there could

Jimmy Carter, the first U.S. President to visit a black African nation, reviews Nigerian troops during the ceremonies honoring his arrival on March 31.

threaten Western use of that key waterway. In Angola, Cubans apparently aided in the May invasion of Zaire as well as in helping guerrillas from Rhodesia and Namibia.

Somalia appealed to the United States in mid-January and early February for help in its war with Communist-backed Ethiopia. In June, Carter Administration advisers advocated arms aid to Angolan anti-Communist guerrillas led by Jonas Savimbi. Carter rejected both proposals.

United States diplomacy contributed to a relaxation of tensions between Zaire and Angola. Ethiopia agreed to resume diplomatic relations with the United States. However, Russia and Ethiopia signed a peace and friendship treaty on November 20.

The first trip to sub-Saharan Africa by a U.S. President took place between March 31 and April 3, when President Carter visited Nigeria and Liberia.

Economic Sanctions. At year's end, the Carter Administration faced a difficult decision over proposals to impose economic sanctions on South Africa. India and the three African countries represented on the UN Security Council called for the Council to impose a mandatory trade embargo and other economic penalties if South Africa did not agree to UN-supervised elections in Namibia. The United States had supported UN sanctions against Rhodesia since 1966 and enacted legislation of its own against Uganda on October 10. However, the Unit-

ed States and its allies, especially Great Britain, have major business investments in South Africa.

The Uganda trade embargo by the United States was aimed particularly at coffee imports. Coffee accounted for over 90 per cent of Uganda's foreign exchange earnings, and the United States had been buying about one-third of Uganda's total coffee exports. Opponents of Uganda's Idi Amin claimed that his government was brutally repressive and that the funds received from exports to America helped him to survive politically. Earlier in the year, America's two largest coffee companies voluntarily stopped buying coffee from Uganda in protest against Amin's alleged human-rights violations.

Organization of African Unity. The 15th annual summit conference of the Organization of African Unity (OAU) met in Khartoum, Sudan, in July. Thirty-four of the 49 OAU member countries were represented by their heads of state, the largest number to attend since the organization's founding in 1963. The conference rejected, by a 21 to 20 vote, a resolution calling on foreign powers to remove their military forces from Africa. Adopted instead was a resolution recognizing the right of African states to take any measures necessary to protect their territories. By implication, foreign military intervention could be invited.

The East African Community (EAC), an organization for regional economic cooperation, collapsed in 1978. The ties among EAC members – Kenya, Tanzania, and Uganda – had been gradually weakened by quarrels over EAC policy and other issues. Kenya formally withdrew from the community on June 30.

Drought and Famine. Parts of Ethiopia and the Sahel region of West Africa reported famine conditions in 1978. The low harvests brought on by poor rains in 1977 yielded too little grain to feed the people until the next harvests.

The hardest-hit West African countries were Cape Verde, Gambia, Mauritania, and Senegal. Mauritania's 1977 rainfall was less than half the normal level, and Senegal's rainfall was only one-third to one-half the usual amount. Thousands of people had died in the Sahel region in 1973-1974 as the result of drought-caused famine, so the Sahel countries recognized the importance of assessing food needs early to ensure that foreign aid could arrive in time to prevent starvation. The Sahel governments and the UN's Food and Agriculture Organization surveyed local harvests in late 1977, estimated their needs, and appealed for help. By August 1978, commitments by all donors grew to 450,000 short tons (408,000 metric tons).

Coups and Attempted Coups. The Comoros government was overthrown on May 13. Marxist President Ali Soilih was deposed and taken into custody in a coup d'état spearheaded by officers and politicians from a previous government. The new president was Abdellah Mohamed. Soilih was killed in an escape attempt on May 23.

A bloodless coup on July 10 toppled the government of Moktar Ould Daddah, Mauritania's president since 1961. The leader of the coup, Moustapha Ould Mohamed Saleck, inherited Mauritania's serious economic difficulties and a war.

The war was being waged against the Polisario guerrillas, who were fighting Morocco as well as Mauritania for control of the Spanish Sahara. Morocco and Mauritania divided the territory in 1975 when Spain relinquished its colonial control. Polisario attacks on the iron-mining region in the Sahara held by Mauritania had driven out most of the European technicians working there, disrupting the industry. In addition, ore prices were generally depressed on the world market. Saleck pledged to negotiate an end to Mauritania's part in the war.

Units of Somalia's army, angry over Somalia's defeat by Ethiopia, staged an unsuccessful coup on April 9. About 20 persons were killed in the skirmish.

Ghana's supreme military council chairman, Ignatius Kutu Acheampong, was forced to resign on July 5. His fall from power followed several months of shortages of essential goods, high inflation, and antigovernment agitation. He was replaced by Frederick William Kwasi Akuffo. See AKUFFO, FREDERICK WILLIAM KWASI.   John D. Esseks

In WORLD BOOK, see AFRICA.

AGRICULTURE in the United States was buoyant and prosperous in 1978, with farm incomes up substantially. Farm prices overall reached a record level, and livestock prices zoomed up almost 25 per cent over 1977. Farm exports also hit record levels, furnishing more than $13 billion toward reducing the overall U.S. trade deficit.

World agriculture improved in 1978, and grain supplies were at record levels. Harvest seasons worldwide were favorable. Southern Hemisphere wheat crops rebounded, and the planting of coarse grains went well. Asia had a good rice crop, despite flood damage in Southeast Asia, and a world-record rice crop was in the making. World grain stocks had built back to levels not seen since the early 1970s.

But agriculture still had problems. The United States Department of Agriculture (USDA) spent $169 million to help livestock producers buy feed in fiscal 1978 under the emergency feed program designed to give financial aid to farmers. The program applied where livestock were threatened by natural disasters. Secretary of Agriculture Bob Bergland called the shortage of railcars available to transport the large harvest the "worst in history." American Agriculture Movement farmers, who staged a farm strike in December 1977, met with Bergland on several occasions, and served notice that they would be back in Washington, D.C., at policy-making time early in 1979. Widespread interest was expressed in the need to develop a national food and nutrition policy that gave more emphasis to nutritional needs in food production. This change in policy was accelerated by internal USDA reorganization. Bergland and Carol Tucker Foreman, of USDA's Food and Consumer Services, both supported the policy revision, and a study submitted to President Jimmy Carter at year's end also addressed the issue.

Inflation problems plagued world agriculture. Trade negotiations that had started the year with great promise were stalled at the end of the year, in many cases by monetary considerations. Global grain stocks were larger than in previous years, but most of the grain was in U.S. hands. Even with the many improvements in the world's agricultural outlook, many economic and technical difficulties remained to be solved.

U.S. Farm Output continued near the all-time high achieved in 1977 as farmers harvested a bumper crop again in 1978. Output of all crops was less than 1 per cent below 1977's level and almost 6 per cent above 1976. New production records were established for several major crops. Corn was up 8 per cent; soybeans, up 3 per cent; rice, up 39 per cent; peanuts, up 7 per cent; and potatoes, up 1 per cent. The slight drop in total production was caused primarily by a 12 per cent decline in the wheat harvest, an 11 per cent drop in sorghum, and a 24 per cent cutback in cotton.

U.S. farmers, protesting imports of Mexican produce, halt a truck carrying onions on the international bridge at Hidalgo, Tex.

Livestock production was up slightly, led by an 11 per cent jump in broiler production, a 5 per cent increase in turkey, and a 1 per cent increase in pork output. Beef production was down 4 per cent, and total red-meat output was down 3 per cent.

The overall efficiency of U.S. agriculture was highlighted by a USDA study showing that farm-labor productivity jumped 7 per cent from 1976 to 1977. Farm output per unit of input increased nearly 3 per cent, reflecting the continuing adoption of improved production techniques by U.S. farmers.

Farm Prices were a pleasant surprise to many as they rebounded sharply from the depressed levels of 1977 in spite of continued high production. For all of 1978, crop prices went up an average of 5 per cent and livestock prices an average of 23 per cent. All prices received by farmers were up 14 per cent. The strong livestock prices are illustrated by a comparison of November 1978 and November 1977 prices in some categories. Beef cattle were $51.50 per hundredweight (cwt.; 45.4 kilograms), up from $34.30 in 1977; hogs were $46.70 per cwt., up from $37.80; broilers were 24.7 cents per pound (0.45 kilogram), up from 21.3 cents; turkeys were 46.6 cents per pound, up from 39 cents; eggs were 56.8 cents per dozen, up from 51.2 cents; and milk was $11.50 per cwt., up from $10.20.

The surprise to many farm experts came in crop prices, however. Even with record production levels,

all major crops except rice and potatoes showed substantial price increases. Soybeans sold in November for $6.31 per bushel, compared with $5.61 in November 1977; wheat was up to $3.05 per bushel from $2.46 a year earlier; and corn was $2.03 per bushel, up from $1.88.

Farmers' Financial Status received a big boost from the combination of high production levels and improved prices for their products. With overall production near 1977 levels, the higher prices boosted total cash receipts 13 per cent to $109 billion. A 9 per cent rise in production expenses cut into this gain, but it still left net income of all farmers at $25-billion, up 21 per cent.

The average American farm had assets of $264,-502 on Jan. 1, 1978, a 9 per cent increase from a year earlier. However, farm debt was up a whopping 18 per cent to $44,661 per farm, reflecting the profit pinch experienced by many farmers in 1977. The debt-to-asset ratio – total debts divided by total assets – was almost 17 per cent, the highest in more than 30 years but still low compared to most other industries.

Agricultural Trade. The United States continued its role as the world's largest exporter of farm products. Total agricultural exports of $27.3 billion set another record in 1978, up 14 per cent from 1977. With agricultural imports totaling $13.9 billion, a 4 per cent gain, the agricultural sector contributed a trade surplus of $13.4 billion, also a record.

The gain in exports was generally across-the-board, with most major commodities except dairy products showing increases. Major contributors were wheat, which was up 36 per cent; rice, up 21 per cent; cotton, up 11 per cent; soybeans, up 10 per cent; and feed grains, up 7 per cent.

Farm exports are vital to both United States farmers and to the rest of the world. Exports accounted for 31 per cent of all U.S. harvested crops. On the other hand, U.S. farmers supplied over 90 per cent of the world's soybean trade, 57 per cent of its coarse grain trade, 25 per cent of its cotton trade, 24 per cent of its rice trade, and 20 per cent of the tobacco trade.

World Agricultural Production headed up again after the moderate decline of 1977. The world's total grain harvest in 1978 was estimated at a record 1.55-billion short tons (1.4 billion metric tons), up more than 6 per cent and 4 per cent above the 1976 record of 1.49 billion short tons (1.35 billion metric tons). In addition to a bumper crop in the United States, Russia set grain-production records with 255 million short tons (230 million metric tons), as did the European Community (EC or Common Market) with 126 million short tons (114 million metric tons).

In spite of the increased production, world grain prices were generally well above 1977 levels, paralleling the U.S. situation. This 1978 price strength was attributable to several factors, including higher import demand from China; farmers withholding their grain from market, hoping for still better prices; putting grain into the U.S. reserve programs; and the decline of the U.S. dollar, which resulted in increased grain use in some countries.

Output of other agricultural products also increased. The world broiler output was up more than 6 per cent, and turkeys were up 5 per cent. Tea set a new record of 1.57 million short tons (1.42 million metric tons), up slightly from its 1977 record, and coffee rose almost 9 per cent to 74.5 million bags.

An August cold snap in Brazil damaged some of that country's coffee crop. However, the freeze will affect only the 1978 crop – unlike the 1975 freeze, which permanently ruined many coffee trees.

U.S. Farm Policy in 1978 was oriented toward strengthening farm incomes, especially by supporting grain prices. Storage payments to farmers who participated in the producer-held reserve were raised. Set-aside programs to take some acreage out of production also helped to restrain production and bolster prices. President Jimmy Carter formalized a 10 per cent feed-grain set-aside on February 8 complementing a wheat set-aside announced earlier. Cotton price protection was available for farmers who voluntarily reduced planting at least 20 per cent below 1977 levels.

The Carter Administration proposed on March 29 to remove the ceiling on farmer-held wheat and grain. Producers participating in the feed-grain set-aside would receive payments for diverting additional acreage. The loan rate on 1978 crop soybeans was set at $4.50 per bushel, up from $3.50 in 1977.

On May 15, President Carter signed the Emergency Agricultural Act of 1978. The act established a new minimum cotton price level for Commodity Credit Corporation loans and gave the secretary of agriculture discretionary authority to raise target prices – market prices below which farmers may receive government payments or loans – for wheat, feed grains, and cotton. Almost 1.2 million, or 51 per cent, of eligible farmers signed up for these programs. Government payments neared a record $3-billion.

Price supports for eligible tobacco were increased 6.3 per cent on June 30. In late July, a federal flaxseed purchase agreement plan, at $4.50 per bushel, was offered for the first time since 1974.

The USDA announced in August that these support programs would continue in 1979. Provisions were similar to those in 1978. The 1977 Food and Agriculture Act and the Emergency Agriculture Act of 1978 provided continuation of most farm programs for four years.

The Agricultural Credit Act of 1978 became law on August 4 and provided $4 billion in additional credit for farmers. The act provided larger loans to individual farmers and stimulated commercial loans by guaranteeing them at current interest rates.

Agricultural Statistics, 1978

World Crop Production
(million units)

Crop	Units	1977	1978	% U.S.
Corn	Metric tons	344.2	358.7	48.2
Wheat	Metric tons	381.1	422.5	11.5
Rice	Metric tons	366.2	376.5	1.7
Barley	Metric tons	164.3	178.6	5.3
Oats	Metric tons	51.3	48.8	17.8
Rye	Metric tons	23.6	26.3	2.0
Soybeans	Metric tons	72.3	77.0	62.3
Cotton	Bales**	63.5	59.4	24.2
Coffee	Bags***	63.5	74.5	0.3
Sugar (centrifugal)	Metric tons	92.1	90.2	6.5

**480 lbs. (217.7 kilograms) net
***132.276 lbs. (60 kilograms)

Output of Major U.S. Crops
(millions of bushels)

Crop	1962–66*	1977	1978**
Corn	3,876	6,370	6,890
Sorghums	595	790	704
Oats	912	748	595
Wheat	1,229	2,025	1,778
Soybeans	769	1,761	1,810
Rice (a)	742	992	1,337
Potatoes (b)	275	354	357
Cotton (c)	140	143	109
Tobacco (d)	2,126	1,912	2,007

*Average; **Preliminary
(a) 100,000 cwt. (4.54 million kilograms)
(b) 1 million cwt. (45.4 million kilograms)
(c) 100,000 bales (50 million lbs.) (22.7 million kilograms)
(d) 1 million lbs. (454,000 kilograms)

U.S. Production of Animal Products
(millions of pounds)

	1957–59*	1977	1978**
Beef	13,704	24,986	23,936
Veal	1,240	794	611
Lamb & Mutton	711	341	299
Pork	10,957	13,051	13,164
Eggs (a)	5,475	5,403	5,525
Turkey	1,382	1,892	1,983
Total Milk (b)	123	123	122
Chicken	4,880	10,130	10,785

*Average; **Preliminary
(a) 1 million dozens
(b) Billions of lbs. (454 million kilograms)

The Agricultural Trade Act of 1978, signed by Carter on October 21, was designed to improve sales of U.S. farm commodities abroad by new loan provisions through the Commodity Credit Corporation. The act provided three-year sales credits to the People's Republic of China, increased the status of agricultural attachés, and provided for the establishment of agricultural trade offices abroad. The first of these offices was established in London on May 26.

Foreign policy affecting agriculture saw food aid directed not only to feed the starving, but also to encourage creation of new jobs and to discourage violations of human rights. Domestic agriculture programs were designed to cushion hunger problems in other countries from disastrous swings in the

PBB Case:
A Tragedy
Of Errors

Farmers and state officials agonized in 1978 over how to get rid of PBB, a dangerous chemical that was accidentally added to the feed of dairy cattle, chickens, pigs, and sheep in Michigan in 1973. It took almost a year to discover that the PBB—polybrominated biphenyl—poisoned the animals, and longer yet before anything was done to protect the humans who ate the tainted meat, eggs, and dairy products.

The problem began when workers at the Michigan Chemical Corporation (now Velsicol) of St. Louis, Mich., accidentally shipped 500 to 1,000 pounds (225 to 450 kilograms) of Firemaster, a fire-retardant chemical, to Michigan's Farm Bureau Services, Incorporated, near Battle Creek. Farm Bureau workers, assuming from their appearance that the sacks contained a livestock-feed supplement, mixed the poisonous additive with feed that was sold to farmers.

Farm animals that ate the contaminated feed became ill. Milk production dropped, cows aborted, and some animals died. Farmers complained to the Farm Bureau, and the feed was tested. But veterinarians, unfamiliar with the lethal chemical, failed to detect it even after some of the feed killed laboratory rats at Michigan State University.

The poison was not identified until a farmer who had lost faith in the state's probe hired his own toxicologist in April 1974. By a stroke of luck, this toxicologist had previously worked with PBB and recognized it in the feed supply. He notified the chemical company and the feed distributor.

However, the state did not begin testing animals for PBB contamination until early in 1975, seven months after the poison had been identified. Since then, officials have destroyed and buried more than 35,000 cows, 150,000 chickens, hundreds of pigs and sheep, and millions of eggs. By the end of 1978, the Farm Bureau and Velsicol had paid millions of dollars in damages to farmers, and more than 300 claims were still pending. One of the largest public health surveys in United States history was conducted to determine the effects of PBB on Michigan's 9.1 million residents. It

PBB-contaminated cow

was announced in October that 8-million people in the state of Michigan are now carrying the chemical in their bodies.

Many Michigan farm families blame their sudden illness—fatigue, weight loss, and susceptibility to infection—on PBB. One of the victims is Carlton Warren of Oscoda County, who unwittingly fed the poisoned feed to his chickens and ate the contaminated meat and eggs. He says he has lost weight and suffers from constant fatigue, aching joints, headaches, sleeplessness, and dizziness.

The state legislature, sensitive to charges that it ignored earlier warnings about the dangers of PBB, passed a bill in 1977 lowering the permissible levels of the chemical in cattle from the federal standard of 300 parts per billion (ppb) to only 20 ppb. Cattle that might be considered fit for sale in the other 49 states are being identified and destroyed in Michigan. The state's other main actions so far have been to tighten reporting procedures in case of chemical contamination and to impose more stringent poison labeling laws on manufacturers.

Some Michigan farmers have criticized the state's methods of disposing of the poisoned animals—killing them and burying them in specially selected areas.

"You put that many dead animals in one area, over the water table, and you will have pollution," says Harry Seffer of Mio, Mich., a member of the PBB Action Committee, a group of farmers opposed to the burial. The committee wants the animals burned, but state officials argue that burning the cows might not destroy the poison. In July, the Michigan Supreme Court rejected the committee's suit to block the burial of contaminated animals, and the first of 1,300 PBB-tainted cows were put into a deep pit in a state forest in Oscoda County in August.

In October, a judge in Wexford County, Michigan, threw out a damage suit brought by one farmer against the chemical company on the grounds that there was no evidence presented that the defendant acted willfully and wantonly, and that the plaintiff failed to prove that PBB decimated his herd.　　**Foster Stockwell**

prices of agricultural products, particularly from the United States. Development assistance abroad was increased. Bilateral aid other than food rose 23 per cent over 1977. Late in the year, President Carter announced the formation of a Public Commission on Hunger to seek new ways to eliminate hunger and malnutrition in the United States and throughout the world. The United States proposed to establish an international system of nationally held grain reserves related to the new international wheat agreements. A U.S. wheat reserve was proposed to meet emergency food needs and to guarantee U.S. food aid commitments abroad.

Technology. Semidwarf soybeans were grown for the first time in 1978 in Illinois and Ohio. The plants yielded well and resisted falling over. Farmers, well aware that semidwarf wheat varieties revolutionized the world's wheat industry in recent years, were excited by the development.

Food technologists at the USDA Western Regional Research Center have designed new equipment and techniques to remove whole kernels from sweet corn for canning and give 20 per cent more corn per ear than the present wasteful cutting method. They also developed a new process for commercial tomato peeling that uses only heat and water.

Energy Research in agriculture took many forms. Congress approved spending of up to $24 million for research on farm-produced energy. USDA scientists were working on solar-powered grain dryers; solar-heated poultry, hog, and dairy houses; solar-heated greenhouses; solar processes to cure burley tobacco; and even a photovoltaic cell-powered insect trap.

A University of Missouri agricultural engineer has found that the excess heat given off by 10 cows or 2,000 chickens can heat a well-insulated, average-sized house. Heat pumps could carry the heat to the house, duplicating in principle the combined structures used in Europe for centuries. Extensive research is underway to assess the feasibility of making fuel from plant residues, chicken and animal manure, and even surplus grain.

Secretary Bergland on January 31 declared the United States free of hog cholera. This report came 99 years after the USDA began cholera research and 17 years after the agency started an extensive eradication campaign. Agricultural scientists considered the elimination of hog cholera to be one of their finest success stories. Scientific patience also paid off in another experiment. USDA entomologists reported that insecticides that were applied 13 years ago were effective in halting the emergence of cicadas that lived on a 13-year cycle and that were expected to emerge in 1978.   Charles E. French and Larry L. Nelson

See also FOOD. In WORLD BOOK, see AGRICULTURE; FARM AND FARMING.

AIR FORCE. See ARMED FORCES.
AIR POLLUTION. See ENVIRONMENT.
AIRPORT. See AVIATION.

AKUFFO, FREDERICK WILLIAM KWASI (1937–), was sworn in as Ghana's head of state on July 6, 1978. He replaced Supreme Military Council Chairman Ignatius Kutu Acheampong, who was forced to resign on July 5. Akuffo was deputy of the Supreme Military Council (SMC), Ghana's ruling body. See GHANA.

Akuffo immediately released political prisoners who had been arrested for accusing Acheampong of cheating on a March referendum on his plan for a union government. Akuffo promised that the SMC would hand over power to civilians on July 1, 1979. He also emphasized the need for national unity and stability and granted amnesty for all Ghanaian political exiles. He said his government would step up production and arrange foreign loans to restructure the economy.

Born in March 1937 in Akropong, Ghana, Akuffo attended the Royal Military Academy in Sandhurst, England, from 1958 to 1960, studied at the Army Staff College in England in 1967, and attended the India Defense College in India in 1973. Since 1962, he has held various military positions in Ghana.

Akuffo is a member of the Akan tribal group. The group dominated Ghana's Progressive Party, which headed the government from 1969 to 1972. Akuffo is married and has four children.   Madelyn Krzak

ALABAMA. See STATE GOVERNMENT.
ALASKA. See STATE GOVERNMENT.

ALBANIA completed its break with China in 1978. China suspended all further aid to Albania on July 7 and said that it had given Albania $5 billion in aid since 1954 by helping with 142 projects, sending 6,000 specialists to work in Albania, and training 2,000 Albanians in China. Albania charged on July 30 that China tried to make Albania appease Russia in 1964 and that China tried to force Albania into an anti-Russian alliance with Romania and Yugoslavia in 1968 and 1975. It denounced China's closer relations with the United States and stopped its broadcasts of Chinese propaganda in August.

Communist Party First Secretary Enver Hoxha repeated his criticisms of China on November 8, denounced Yugoslavia, and accused Albanian leaders purged in 1974 and 1975 of having tried to import "Titoist revisionist self-management." Politburo member Hysni Kapo denounced China for trying to overthrow the Albanian government.

Albania announced good results in prospecting for chromium, copper, ferronickel, coal, and other raw materials on August 31. The search for coking coal, iron without nickel, phosphates, and asbestos was intensified. The 1976-1980 plan was expected to raise chromium ore production 47 per cent; copper ore, 55 per cent; ferronickel, 230 per cent; and coal, 100 per cent.   Chris Cviic

See also EUROPE (Facts in Brief Table). In WORLD BOOK, see ALBANIA.

ALBERTA hosted the XI Commonwealth Games from Aug. 3 to 12, 1978. Queen Elizabeth II and members of the royal family officially opened the games after touring northern Alberta. Forty-eight Commonwealth members sent 2,000 athletes. The only Commonwealth nations that were not represented at the competition were Uganda, which was not welcome, and Nigeria, which withdrew to protest apartheid practices in sports. Six of Canada's 45 gold medals were won by Edmonton swimmer Graham Smith.

The 1978-1979 budget, presented on March 17, abolished taxes of 10 and 12 cents per gallon (4.5 liters) on gasoline and diesel oil, respectively, confirming Alberta's position as the most lightly taxed province in Canada. The only province without a sales tax on consumer purchases, Alberta owes its buoyant financial condition to its petroleum wealth. A major addition to the extraction of this wealth went into operation on September 15 when the giant $2.1-billion Syncrude Canada Limited plant opened. The biggest construction project ever undertaken in Alberta, Syncrude recovers oil from the tar sands near Fort McMurray on the Athabasca River in northern Alberta. Current production is 50,000 barrels per day (bpd), and production by 1982 is projected at 120,000 bpd, filling 5 per cent of Canada's oil requirements.   David M. L. Farr

See also CANADA. In WORLD BOOK, see ALBERTA.

ALGERIA. President Houari Boumediene, 53, entered an Algiers hospital on Nov. 18, 1978, with a rare form of blood cancer. He lapsed into a coma and died on December 27. He had ruled Algeria since 1965. Rabah Bitat, chairman of the National People's Assembly, was appointed temporary president.

Several national organizations such as the trade unions and farmers held congresses in 1978 that furthered Boumediene's plan to establish a system of popular government that would be neither one-party rule nor multiparty factionalism and confusion. Each group passed resolutions and elected delegates to a congress of the National Liberation Front, the only legal political organization in Algeria. The National People's Assembly, elected in 1977 in the final stage of a series of local, regional, and provincial elections, assumed legislative and budget responsibilities in April.

In Foreign Affairs, Algeria's dispute with Morocco over the former Spanish Sahara worsened. Algeria's support for Polisario, the Saharan guerrilla movement that seeks to establish an independent state and has been recognized by 12 countries as the Saharan Arab Democratic Republic, led to armed clashes between Moroccan and Algerian forces in August and September. Algeria received unexpected support for its position from Libyan General People's Congress Secretary General Muammar Muhammad al-Qadhaafi.

Economic Gains. Neither the dispute with Morocco nor aid to Polisario had much effect on Algeria's growing economic development, which is based on oil and natural gas production. The first liquefied natural gas plant and the world's largest methane plant went into production at Arzew in February. A shipment of 138,000 short tons (125,000 metric tons) of liquefied natural gas from Arzew was delivered to the El Paso Gas Company on March 13. In May, the state oil company, Sonatrach, started a 30-year, $30-billion investment program to develop new oil fields and gas reserves.

Agriculture remained the weak link in Algeria's economy. Drought and the uneven distribution of water resources hampered production. A separate ministry of water was set up in May to tackle the problem. Boumediene opened the Es-Saada Dam near Mostaganem in February, which will irrigate 3,200 acres (1,300 hectares) of farmland.

Boumediene opened the second 400-mile (640-kilometer) leg of the Trans-Saharan Highway on June 19, the anniversary of the 1965 revolution that brought him to power. The road, from Salah to Tamanrasset, opened up the Saharan region, the poorest part of Algeria, for development. The 1978 budget earmarked $1.7 billion for new programs in the region.   William Spencer

See also AFRICA (Facts in Brief Table). In WORLD BOOK, see ALGERIA; BOUMEDIENE, HOUARI.

ALLEN, WOODY (1935-   ), dominated the Academy of Motion Picture Arts and Sciences annual awards on April 3, 1978. His film *Annie Hall* won Oscars for best picture, best actress, best director, and best screenplay. Allen directed, co-authored, and starred in the movie, a "nervous romance" based on his real-life relationship with his co-star Diane Keaton (see KEATON, DIANE). Allen did not attend the awards ceremony, remaining in New York City to play clarinet with his Monday-night jazz group.

Allen Stewart Konigsberg was born on Dec. 1, 1935, in Brooklyn, N.Y. He began to submit jokes to newspaper columnists during high school, and at 17 he was hired by the National Broadcasting Company as a staff writer for such comedians as Sid Caesar and Jack Paar.

While working for "The Garry Moore Show," Allen performed in nightclubs, building his act around his supposed inability to cope with the world at large. His success as a stand-up comic provided the opportunity to make his first movie, *What's New, Pussycat?* (1965), which was followed by a series of other comedies, including *Bananas* (1971) and *Sleeper* (1973). Allen's latest film, *Interiors*, a bleak, intense character study, was released in August.

In 1978, Allen also received an O. Henry Award for short-story writing.   Beverly Merz

AMERICAN LEGION. See COMMUNITY ORGANIZATIONS.

AMERICAN LIBRARY ASSOCIATION (ALA).
More than 11,700 librarians, publishers, trustees, and friends of libraries met in Chicago for the ALA's annual conference in June 1978. Columnist Daniel L. Schorr; United States Commissioner of Education Ernest L. Boyer; Donald J. Urquhart, creator of the National Lending Library for Science and Technology in Great Britain; and journalist Ben H. Bagdikian addressed the conference on the theme "Toward a National Information Policy."

Russell Shank, university librarian at the University of California, Los Angeles, took office as ALA president. His inaugural address focused on Proposition 13, the California taxpayers' revolt, and on new information technology. He urged librarians to protest the practice of charging service fees.

ALA members passed resolutions to inform California Governor Edmund G. Brown, Jr., state legislators, and national media of the need for continued free and equal library access, and called for a campaign to alert the public to the effects on libraries of Proposition 13. They also established a committee to explore public financing alternatives for libraries in crisis situations.

Other Activities. A panel of experts informed librarians and educators in the South and Southwest of their rights under the new U.S. copyright law on February 7 when 15 public broadcasting stations aired an ALA-produced teleconference.

Groundbreaking ceremonies for new ALA headquarters on November 1 were another highlight of the year. The association will occupy six of the 56 floors in the $24-million structure in Chicago.

The Association of College and Research Libraries, oldest and largest of ALA's 11 divisions, held its first independent annual conference in Boston in November. Two other divisions, the Association of State Library Agencies and the Health and Rehabilitative Library Services Division, merged to form the Association of Specialized and Cooperative Library Agencies.

National Awards. The Association for Library Service to Children received the 1978 J. Morris Jones-Bailey K. Howard-World Book Encyclopedia-ALA Goals Award. The grant will finance 10 regional conferences to help librarians learn how to make the best use of their limited budgets.

Katherine Paterson, the author of *Bridge to Terabithia*, received the 1978 Newbery Medal for the most distinguished contribution to American literature for children. Peter Spier, who was the illustrator of *Noah's Ark*, won the 1978 Caldecott Medal for the most distinguished American picture book for children.   Margaret Barber

See also CANADIAN LIBRARY ASSOCIATION (CLA); LIBRARY; LITERATURE FOR CHILDREN. In WORLD BOOK, see AMERICAN LIBRARY ASSOCIATION.

ANDORRA. See EUROPE.

ANGOLA. Guerrilla opposition to President Agostinho Neto's government persisted throughout 1978. Neto's forces were aided by more than 20,000 Cuban soldiers stationed in Angola. United States President Jimmy Carter sent senior diplomat Donald F. McHenry to negotiate with Angolan leaders in June. Angola agreed to ease tensions with Zaire and to cooperate in achieving independence peacefully for Namibia (South West Africa). See NAMIBIA; ZAIRE.

Neto met with Zaire's President Mobutu Sese Seko in July and August and agreed to disarm refugees who had invaded Zaire's borderland Shaba province from bases in Angola. Mobutu pledged to stop supporting anti-Neto Angolan groups operating in Zaire. Angola had agreed on July 17 to reopen its Benguela Railway, the most economic route for shipping copper to the ocean, which had been closed to Zaire since 1975.

Neto and Portuguese President Antonio Dos Santos Ramalho Eanes agreed in June to a pact on general cooperation. As a result, hundreds of refugees who had fled to Portugal in 1975 during the civil war began to return to Angola.   John D. Esseks

See also AFRICA (Facts in Brief Table). In WORLD BOOK, see ANGOLA.

ANIMAL. See AGRICULTURE; CAT; CONSERVATION; DOG; ZOOLOGY; ZOOS AND AQUARIUMS; Section Five, SNAKE.

ANTARCTICA. An airborne radar survey conducted in 1978 by the Scott Polar Research Institute of Cambridge, England, revealed that the terrain under Antarctica's relatively smooth covering of ice is extremely rugged. The survey showed entombed mountains, lakes, and deep troughs that resulted from ancient upheavals in the earth. The lakes under the ice produced echoes that were easily recognized on the radar screen. The water in them is apparently warmed by heat flowing up from the earth's interior.

Geologists from the United States National Science Foundation and the National Aeronautics and Space Administration announced in February that they had found an abundance of microscopic life in rocks taken from an ice-free region of Antarctica. The microbes, algae, and fungi within these rocks from one of the earth's harshest environments significantly extend the known limits of life on this planet.

A tentative agreement to protect the vast Antarctic marine resources was drafted when representatives of the 13 Antarctic Treaty nations met in Canberra, Australia, from February 27 to March 16. The pact provided for a commission, representing all treaty signers, to set annual fishing catch quotas.

A boy, Emilio, was born to Captain Jorge Palma and his wife, Maria Silvia, on January 7 at an Argentine army base in Antarctica. He was the first child born on the icy continent.   Foster Stockwell

In WORLD BOOK, see ANTARCTICA.

ANTHROPOLOGY

ANTHROPOLOGY. Mary Leakey and her son Philip found the earliest known footprints of a humanlike creature at the Laetolil site in Tanzania, near Olduvai Gorge, in 1978. The Leakeys reported in February that the footprints, about 3½ million years old, are 6 inches (15 centimeters) long and 4½ inches (11.5 centimeters) wide. They are wider than human footprints or those of the Neanderthals, the producers of the earliest known humanlike footprints prior to this discovery.

The Leakeys believe that a plodding creature about 4 feet (122 centimeters) tall left the prints. They also suggest that the creature probably was not a hunter but ate plants and dead animals.

Dental Anthropology. David Ganff of Washington University in St. Louis, David Pilbeam of Yale University in New Haven, Conn., and Gregory Steward of Southern Illinois University in Carbondale reported in March that they have developed a technique for using teeth in investigating human ancestry. The scientists studied small particles of tooth enamel from modern and prehistoric humans and apes through a scanning electron microscope. Their detailed examinations revealed a "prismatic" pattern in the tooth enamel that varied from species to species.

The scientists found keyhole-shaped prisms in modern human enamel, while gorilla and chimpanzee teeth bore circular or hexagonal prisms. Enamel from teeth of the primate *Ramapithecus*, which lived about 8 million years ago, proved to be keyhole shaped, suggesting that *Ramapithecus* was an early member of the line leading to humans and that gorillas and chimpanzees either had a contemporary ancestor or represent a late change from the human line.

Jerome Rose of the University of Arkansas at Fayetteville, George Armelagos of the University of Massachusetts at Amherst, and John Lallo of Cleveland State University also studied the prismatic structure of tooth enamel, but they used the new technique to understand variations in the incidence of disease and malnutrition among prehistoric peoples who lived in the eastern United States. When teeth are growing in childhood, diseases and nutritional difficulties affect the enamel's prismatic structure and cause bands, called *Wilson bands*, to form. These indicators remain throughout life, so scientists can determine the stresses that individuals survived by studying their teeth.

By examining the teeth of prehistoric Woodlands and Mississippi peoples, the investigators showed that greater dietary and disease problems were associated with greater dependence on maize agriculture, a rise in population density, and growing social complexity.

Tribes and Territories. Anthropologists Rada Dyson-Hudson and Eric Smith of Cornell University in Ithaca, N.Y., disagree with the theory that humans are innately aggressive and try to maintain territory that is uniquely their own. They have completed a study of the territorial behavior of tribal groups in different parts of the world and have found great variation in the degree to which human groups defend territory. They say that humans usually aggressively defend territory that has abundant resources available in predictable quantities season after season and year after year.

The Philippine government acknowledged on May 23 that the discovery of a remote tribe of cave dwellers reported a week earlier actually was made at least 15 years earlier. The group, identified by the government press agency as Tao't Bato, or Stone Men, is the Ken-ey tribe reported found in 1963. They are cliff dwellers who live on the island of Palawan, 430 miles (690 kilometers) southwest of Manila in an area isolated by high mountains, deep ravines, and dense jungle. The people live in caves a few months and spend the rest of the year in forests near the caves.

Once discovered, primitive tribes become vulnerable to extinction. Their culture may be absorbed into the surrounding society, they may die of "civilized" diseases against which they have no immunity, or their natural habitat may be destroyed. Fred Plog

In WORLD BOOK, see ANTHROPOLOGY; PREHISTORIC MAN.

Peter Jones of the Leakey team lifts latex cast of footprints found in Tanzania. The prints may be those of a human ancestor of 3.5 million years ago.

ARCHAEOLOGY. Two excavations, one in Israel and the other in the United States, revealed in 1978 that early tribal hunting societies had unexpected social class patterns and were not always the classless societies that archaeologists assumed they were. Scientists had based their assumption on the fact that most present-day hunting and gathering groups are classless bands.

Archaeologist Gary Wright of the State University of New York at Albany excavated burial sites in Israel where the Natufian people lived about 12,000 years ago. Archaeologist Thomas King of the Micronesian Archaeological Survey excavated ancient grave sites in the Buchanan Reservoir in the San Joaquin Valley of California, an area occupied about 1,400 years ago.

Burial practices are especially helpful in distinguishing between classless and ranked societies. When a prehistoric society had distinct classes, those of high rank were usually buried apart from the rest of the people and with more belongings surrounding them in the grave. Infants and children of high-ranking individuals were buried in the same manner as their parents. The diggers found substantial evidence of ranking in both the Israel and California burials, even though the prehistoric people had been hunting and gathering tribes. The evidence strongly suggests that social classes developed because of economic or demographic pressures, but not as the result of a change from a hunting and gathering society to an agricultural one.

Early Calendar. Evidence of the early use of astronomical observations for a calendar of the seasons came from yet another part of the world in June. Archaeologists B. Mark Lynch and Lawrence H. Robbins of Michigan State University in East Lansing described their research in an area north of Lake Turkana (Rudolph) in Kenya, where they discovered a circular arrangement of 19 stone columns that they tentatively dated at around 300 B.C.

The people who now live in the region use a calendar that depends on the rising of seven stars and constellations, so Lynch and Robbins hypothesized that the stones might be aligned on the same heavenly bodies. When they computed the apparent locations of the bodies in 300 B.C., they found that their sightings across the columns aligned with these astronomical positions.

Prehistoric Agriculture. G. Lennis Berlin, Richard Ambler, and Richard Hevly of Northern Arizona University at Flagstaff and Gerald Schaber of the United States Geological Survey used remote sensing photography and soil and pollen analysis to study the prehistoric farming practices of the Sinagua Indians of central Arizona.

The archaeologists photographed the land from an airplane using *thermographic* techniques (heat-sensitive film) to identify the areas these people had cultivated. Then they compared soil samples from these areas with samples from land that they knew had never been cultivated. The samples from fields farmed in prehistoric times were found to have fewer small soil particles than samples from uncultivated land, a condition that can result when vegetation is stripped from an area. They also contained less potassium and nitrogen salts, indicating soil depletion. Finally, studies of pollen samples from the fields showed that corn and squash were once grown there.

Stephen Chomko of the University of Missouri in Columbia and Gary Crawford of the University of North Carolina in Chapel Hill examined evidence for the cultivation of squash at several archaeological sites in Missouri and Kentucky that were occupied as early as 2300 B.C. Scientists had always assumed that archaeological evidence of any corn, beans, and squash used and eaten by the people at this early date in the eastern and midwestern parts of North America came through trade from Mexico and other Central American areas. It was also assumed that the only crops cultivated locally were plants such as marsh elders and sunflowers. However, Chomko and Crawford proved that people cultivated squash at the midwestern sites at that time. The discovery raised the possibility that agriculture based on corn, beans, and squash began earlier in eastern and midwestern parts of North America than in the west. Fred Plog

In WORLD BOOK, see ARCHAEOLOGY.

ARCHITECTURE. The American Institute of Architects (AIA) voted on May 24, 1978, to allow its members to advertise. Acting at the annual convention in Dallas, 82 per cent of the delegates favored changing the AIA code of ethics so that, as of July 1, architects could advertise in a "dignified" fashion in magazines and newspapers. They were prohibited from advertising on television and radio, and from using photographs in advertisements.

The AIA action eliminated the threat of antitrust suits by the Department of Justice, which had warned earlier that it considered the ban on advertising an illegal restraint of trade. Both the American Bar Association and the American Medical Association had previously voted to allow their members to advertise.

Contractor Role. In another landmark decision, AIA delegates voted 3 to 1 to permit members to engage in a "design-build" practice. This action enables architects to participate in building contracting. Opponents questioned whether an architect could professionally serve a client as designer when he stood to profit from potential savings in labor and construction materials. Supporters argued that the architect is the person best qualified to direct the building process from design to completion.

AIA members will be allowed to operate a "design-build" practice over a three-year experimental period under monitoring by the institute.

The new East Wing of the National Gallery of Art in Washington, D.C., provides a spacious and dramatic setting for the works it houses.

Awards. The AIA's annual award for a significant building designed at least 25 years ago went to the Charles and Ray Eames Home in Pacific Palisades, Calif. Designed by Charles Eames and built in 1949, it was one of the first residences with a structural frame of prefabricated steel (including interior exposed trusses) and a facade of squared-off planes. (Charles Eames died August 21 at age 71.)

The AIA Architectural Firm Award went to Harry Weese & Associates of Chicago. Philadelphia architect Robert Venturi received an AIA medal for his book *Complexity and Contradiction in Architecture*, published in 1966 and revised in 1977.

The AIA's prestigious Gold Medal honoring a lifetime of design accomplishment, which is rarely awarded to a living architect, went to Philip C. Johnson of New York City. It came at a time of great controversy in the career of the 72-year-old architect, who has severed his affiliation with the steel-and-glass school of building design.

The Johnson Controversies. Johnson stunned the profession — and other interested observers — when his firm, Johnson & Burgee, unveiled the design of the American Telephone & Telegraph Company's headquarters building on March 30. The $110-million, 37-story granite tower will occupy a prominent midtown site in New York City.

Its main entrance is an 80-foot (24-meter) arch surmounted by thin, unbroken vertical piers capped by Doric-looking columns. However, it is the top of the structure, a *pediment* (gable) 30 feet (9 meters) high and shaped like a piece of Chippendale furniture, that has provoked responses ranging from amusement to outrage.

Early in June, Johnson stirred another furor, this time in Miami, Fla., with his proposal for a $22-million Dade County Cultural Center. The Johnson & Burgee design, which Johnson termed "Mediterranean," is nearly windowless. It is a complex of three buildings — library, art gallery, and museum — grouped around a central plaza. It has arched openings revealing shaded porticos, and will be faced with coral stone and roofed in red clay tile.

Critics complained that the complex would be incompatible with other new buildings in the vicinity. Johnson countered that his design suited Miami's climate better than a glass and steel building.

The National Gallery. President Jimmy Carter dedicated the new East Wing of the National Gallery of Art in Washington, D.C., on June 1. Designed by I.M. Pei & Partners, the building was universally proclaimed one of the finest works of architecture of the decade. The $94-million building is a strikingly bold composition in severe planes of marble and concrete. Its structure is crisply and cleanly apparent — a geometry of interlocking triangles within a trapezoid and roofed by a cluster of pyramid-shaped skylights. Inside, the galleries are connected by a series of courtyards featuring a constantly changing panorama of waterfalls and natural light. See PEI, I. M.

Barrier-Free Design. A particularly successful example of a public facility designed to accommodate the handicapped is the Illinois Regional Library for the Blind and Physically Handicapped and the Community Library in Chicago. The $1.9-million building, designed by Stanley Tigerman, opened in February.

The library's linear interiors make its plan easier for the blind to memorize. The furniture is built-in so that the chairs and tables are easier to locate, and all corners are round. Its single, undulating window is low in areas used by people in wheelchairs, and higher in areas used by library personnel.

Preservation. Two architecturally important downtown U.S. movie palaces, which had been struggling with rising costs and failing patronage, were given reprieves in 1978.

The Fox Theater in Atlanta, Ga., a 4,000-seat structure built in 1929 and noted for its neo-Arabian interior, was purchased by a nonprofit citizens' group. Radio City Music Hall, a 6,200-seat theater built in New York City in 1932, was saved by the New York Urban Development Corporation, which took over the art deco masterpiece and will operate it for at least one year. Rob Cuscaden

In WORLD BOOK, see ARCHITECTURE.

ARGENTINA was the center of world attention when it hosted the World Cup soccer finals from June 1 to June 25, 1978. The Argentine team's capture of the cup prompted a wave of pride and euphoria that temporarily helped the nation forget its severe economic crisis, left wing terrorism, and the oppressive rule of the military dictatorship. See SOCCER.

There had been serious doubts at home and abroad that Argentina would be able to host such a major international event. It was feared that the Montoneros, a terrorist group, would try to embarrass the junta by disrupting the games.

Human rights groups, too, objected to the games being played in Argentina, and in May the United States chapter of Amnesty International announced it would hold vigils in several U.S. cities to prevent the games from overshadowing the junta's treatment of political prisoners.

On entirely different grounds, the junta's own finance minister, Juan Alemán, objected to the games. He argued that the $700 million it would cost to stage them would further fuel inflation, which was running at an annual rate of about 120 per cent. Although it was down from the 1977 rate of 160 per cent, it was still one of the world's highest rates and double the junta's 1978 target of 60 per cent. Although Economy Minister José Martínez de Hoz had severely cut government expenditures, he com-

plained that his efforts had been sabotaged by the huge sums spent on the World Cup and by businessmen raising prices, expecting more inflation.

Other critics charged that the military must share some of the blame for inflation because it had spent nearly 15 per cent of the $11.3-billion national budget on armaments in anticipation of a possible military confrontation with Chile over disputed territorial rights in the Beagle Channel and the South Atlantic Ocean. See LATIN AMERICA.

The inflationary spiral had also affected the labor force. Its purchasing power in the first three months of 1978 was 33.3 per cent below that of 1977.

International Relations. The junta's relations with President Jimmy Carter's Administration in Washington, D.C., continued to be marred by U.S. charges that the junta was violating human rights in Argentina. On March 6, the American delegate to the United Nations Commission on Human Rights in Geneva, Switzerland, singled out Argentina as a country where human rights were consistently being violated. On March 21, a commission of Argentine Roman Catholic archbishops reportedly met with President Jorge Rafael Videla to ask him to free all prisoners not yet brought to trial. The government had begun releasing the names of some 2,000 political prisoners on February 3. President Videla told the archbishops on April 10 that 3,600 Argentines

Thousands of Argentines throng the Plaza de la República in Buenos Aires to celebrate their team's victory in the World Cup soccer finals.

were still being held without trial, but that they were "subversives or economic delinquents," not political prisoners.

Terrorist Attacks. The government claimed to have "decimated" the terrorists, but a labor specialist in the economy ministry was gunned down near his home in Buenos Aires on April 11, and two policemen were killed on April 6 in a bombing attack on their headquarters in the city. The 15-year-old daughter of Vice-Admiral Armando Lambruschini, naval chief of staff, was killed by a bomb meant for her father on August 1.

Videla retired from the army on July 31 and General Roberto Viola was appointed to his place in the junta. Videla, however, was to continue as president until March 1981, when—the junta claims—it will establish a more broadly based representative government.

On March 29, Videla said he wanted to have a "working dialogue" with civilian political leaders, but when 40 members of the Radical Civic Union published a document on April 23 praising his statement and criticizing the junta's economic policies, two members of the group were immediately seized for questioning.   Everett G. Martin

See also LATIN AMERICA (Facts in Brief Table). In WORLD BOOK, see ARGENTINA.

ARIZONA. See STATE GOVERNMENT.

ARKANSAS. See STATE GOVERNMENT.

ARMED FORCES. President Jimmy Carter triggered another national defense furor on April 7, 1978. Less than a year after he canceled the B-1 strategic bomber program, he deferred production of the controversial neutron bomb. The neutron bomb is a nuclear warhead that kills by radiation instead of by blast and fire, thus destroying human beings while leaving buildings intact. Carter ordered the United States Department of Defense to continue modernizing the Lance missiles that would ultimately carry the neutron warhead, but he said a production decision on the warhead itself would be influenced by Russia's restraint in its own nuclear arms programs.

Carter's decision was denounced by defense hard-liners and greeted with dismay in Western Europe, where the warhead would eventually be deployed. Carter reportedly was influenced by a desire to use the weapon as a bargaining chip in arms talks with Russia and by what he considered lukewarm support in Western Europe for its deployment. However, in October the President ordered production resumed on key neutron bomb components to reduce delays in case he later decided on full production of the weapon.

Strategic Systems. The United States and Russia worked to extend their 1974 SALT accord on strategic arms limitations, and a new SALT treaty was reportedly in sight by late December. Never-

theless, both sides continued research and development on a variety of weapons. The United States began plans to speed development of a new intercontinental ballistic missile (ICBM) that could be launched either from submarines or from land bases. It also considered accelerating air-launched cruise-missile development and modernizing the strategic bomber force. Russia began testing a new generation of ICBM's, neared completion of the prototype for a new long-range bomber, and began deploying more sophisticated submarine-launched missiles.

Arms Developments. Two studies released in 1978 concluded that the United States retains military superiority over the Soviet Union. A study by the Department of Defense, issued on March 6, rated America superior in ballistic missiles, heavy bombers, carrier-based aircraft, combat aircraft, air-to-surface missiles, and antisubmarine technology. Russia was rated superior in surface ships, antiship missiles, tanks, and surface-to-air missiles. A U.S. Arms Control and Disarmament Agency study released in August said U.S. nuclear strength was superior to Russia's, but that the two nations could be "essentially equal" by the mid-1980s.

United States arms sales to other nations continued to climb, despite an $8.6-billion annual ceiling on sales to nonallied nations imposed by the Carter Administration on February 1. White House officials acknowledged at the time that total 1978 sales to all nations would probably be more than $13-billion, a $2-billion increase. Two weeks later, the Administration announced plans to sell warplanes worth $4.8 billion to Egypt, Israel, and Saudi Arabia. The most controversial aspect of the package was the proposal to sell 60 of the sophisticated F-15 jet fighters to Saudi Arabia. The U.S. Senate approved the deal on May 15 after prolonged debate.

Military Strength. The United States trimmed its military forces slightly again in 1978. On September 30, troop strength stood at 2,062,402, the lowest level since World War II. More than 468,000 troops were stationed overseas, including 236,000 in West Germany and Berlin, 46,000 in Japan and Okinawa, 43,000 in South Korea, 15,000 in the Philippines, and 56,000 at sea.

The Carter Administration pledged to maintain U.S. military readiness while eliminating waste and reducing the size of the defense establishment. Nevertheless, Secretary of Defense Harold Brown reported to Congress in February that U.S. military spending would have to increase by more than $56-billion over the next five years simply to keep pace with the steady Russian military build-up.

Defense Budget. President Carter submitted a defense-budget request for fiscal 1979 (Oct. 1, 1978, to Sept. 30, 1979) on January 23. It asked for $115.2-billion, $9.9 billion over the previous budget request.

F-15 jet fighter planes are assembled in St. Louis for shipment to Egypt, Israel, and Saudi Arabia in a controversial arms sale.

In a clear departure from President Gerald R. Ford's emphasis on accelerating the development of strategic weapons, Carter's proposed budget placed priority on improving conventional forces.

The budget would support 16 Army and 3 Marine divisions, 26 Air Force tactical wings, 28 Navy and Marine air wings, and a Navy fleet of 458 vessels. Strategic forces would remain constant at 450 Minuteman II and 550 Minuteman III missiles, 54 Titan II missiles, and 656 Polaris-Poseidon submarine-launched missiles. An estimated $9.8 billion was allocated for strategic forces, $46.9 billion for general purpose forces, $11 billion for research and development, and $8.3 billion for military intelligence and communications. The Navy was scheduled to receive the largest share of the budget, $36.6 billion; the Air Force, $32.4 billion; and the Army, $28.2 billion.

The Navy asked for $2.8 billion for the *Trident* nuclear submarine and ballistic missile, $1.5 billion for guided missile frigates, $864.8 million for the F-18 Hornet carrier-based jet fighter, $674.4 million for the F-14 Tomcat jet fighter, and $152.1 million for the Tomahawk submarine-launched missile.

The Air Force requested $1.6 billion for the F-16 jet fighter, $1.4 billion for the F-15 Eagle jet fighter, $924.9 million for the A-10 close-support jet fighter, $490.2 million for the cruise missile, and $158.2-million for the M-X strategic missile.

The Army asked for $497 million for the XM-1 main battle tank and $411.7 million for M-60 tanks, $379.9 million for the Blackhawk utility helicopter, $307.1 million for the SAM-D (Patriot) air-defense missile, and $114 million for ballistic-missile defense.

Congress passed a $37-billion weapons authorization bill on August 4, but Carter vetoed the measure on August 17. Carter became the first President to veto a major defense measure in more than 100 years. He objected to the bill's inclusion of $2 billion for a fifth nuclear-powered aircraft carrier, arguing that the funds should have been allocated to improve the readiness of conventional forces, particularly those in Western Europe. Congress sustained Carter's veto by a wide margin on September 7 and subsequently deleted funds for the carrier.

Shipbuilding Flap. Citing severe budget constraints, the Carter Administration drastically curtailed its Navy shipbuilding program on March 24. The revised schedule more than halved the Ford Administration's plans to build 156 warships in five years. The Carter plan envisioned building 70 new ships and modernizing 13 others by 1983. The plan was bitterly opposed by congressional sea-power advocates and the Navy's admirals.

Personnel Developments. Faced with severe shortages in its reserve forces, the Army began offering cash bonuses for enlistment and re-enlistment in the Army Reserve and National Guard on January 1. The $5-million test program was aimed at reversing a steady decline in reserve levels since the end of the draft—a decline that experts believe has jeopardized the ability of the United States to mobilize rapidly in the event of war. The Defense Department asked Congress in March to repeal legislation prohibiting the use of women in combat. It said that growing personnel shortages and equal-opportunity considerations dictated that women serve aboard combat craft.

Command Changes. General George S. Brown retired as chairman of the Joint Chiefs of Staff in June and was succeeded by General David C. Jones, who was replaced as Air Force chief of staff by General Lew Allen. Brown died in December. Admiral Thomas B. Hayward succeeded Admiral James L. Holloway III as chief of naval operations. Colonel Margaret A. Brewer became the first woman general in the U.S. Marine Corps on May 11. Major General John K. Singlaub, relieved as chief of staff of U.S. forces in South Korea in 1977 after criticizing Carter's Korean troop withdrawal, retired from the Army under pressure after criticizing Carter's cancellation of the B-1 bomber and deferral of the neutron bomb.   Thomas M. DeFrank

In WORLD BOOK, see DISARMAMENT and articles on the service branches.

ARMY. See ARMED FORCES.

ART. See ARCHITECTURE; DANCING; LITERATURE; MUSIC, CLASSICAL; POETRY; VISUAL ARTS.

ASIA

Asia was a world of startling surprises in 1978. The sound of gunfire still echoed across wide areas in Vietnam and Cambodia, but this time United States troops were not involved. Communists were making war on other Communists. At the same time, the non-Communist governments of Southeast Asia, which U.S. analysts in the early 1970s were sure would topple like dominoes before the Marxist victors, continued to stand solid. Washington observers had also expected the two allies, China and

Vietnam, to dominate the region once U.S. troops left. But they erred. In the realignments of the post-Vietnam War era, the two friends were transformed into bitter enemies.

Enter the Giants. Three elements went into forming these realignments. One was the U.S. troop withdrawal from Southeast Asia. The second was China's emergence from the self-isolation of the Cultural Revolution. The third was the fact that Marxist dogma had yielded to nationalism, to ancient fears and hatreds, and to newly perceived national interests in all the Communist countries of Southeast Asia.

Rivalries largely ignored during the Vietnam War came out into the open. In 1978, Cambodians

Cambodians herded out of the cities in 1975 at gunpoint by the Communist government work in labor gangs planting rice and building dikes.

were bloodily fighting their old Vietnamese enemies, and the Vietnamese stood mobilized for war with their historic foe, China. In Vietnam's capital, Hanoi, a museum glorified victories scored against the Chinese invaders centuries ago. No longer allies, the Chinese ended their aid to Vietnam in July.

China and Russia moved into the power vacuum left by the withdrawal of U.S. troops, making Southeast Asia yet another battlefield in their global struggle. Indeed, some argued that in their savage war, Cambodia and Vietnam were really proxies for China and Russsia. But the rivalry between these giants was not confined to just one corner of Asia. They verbally fought each other across much of the continent, from North Korea to Iran.

The "China Card." The realignments also embraced Japan and the United States. After concluding its treaty of peace and friendship with China in August, Japan established trade agreements that in effect wedded its technological genius to China's vast and urgent needs. In addition, the industrial leaders of Japan made it clear that they stood ready to help China become a major military power.

When the last U.S. troops flew out of South Vietnam on April 30, 1975, a stunned U.S. Congress seemed determined never again to become involved in a land war in Asia. The modest goal of U.S. policy thereafter was to use diplomatic tools to prevent the dominance of Asia by any nation. But by 1978, the objective was changed. After a visit to China in May by President Jimmy Carter's National Security Adviser Zbigniew Brzezinski, the United States began to speak of playing the "China card," which could be used as a bargaining counter against Russia.

On December 15, Carter announced an agreement to establish normal diplomatic relations between China and the United States on Jan. 1, 1979. Following three lean years, U.S. trade with China soared in 1978, and there was wide technical cooperation. For the first time in decades, the United States enjoyed friendly ties with both Japan and China, instead of siding with one against the other. See CHINA.

Competitive Wooing. The day Hanoi's armies completed their take-over of South Vietnam, neighboring non-Communist countries wondered how long it would be before they themselves would be threatened. The Vietnamese did go to Indonesia, Malaysia, the Philippines, Singapore, and Thailand—members of the Association of Southeast Asian Nations (ASEAN)—but not as conquerors. They went to talk of friendship and trade. Vietnam's Prime Minister Pham Van Dong, who toured these countries in the fall, did his best to warn them of China's alleged iniquity. But right behind him came China's Deputy Premier Teng Hsiao-p'ing with the cautionary word that Vietnam meant to destroy them and that Vietnam was Russia's bridgehead in Southeast Asia. The competitive wooing left the non-Communists skeptical but delighted.

The Poverty Problem. The ASEAN countries formed one of Asia's rare pockets of prosperity. Much of the rest of the continent lived its life of accustomed agony. A United Nations expert estimated in October that more than 532 million Asians were living in "absolute poverty"—most of them in India, Pakistan, Bangladesh, and Indonesia. In India alone, 290 million persons were said to be living below the poverty line.

After signing a peace treaty, China's Deputy Premier Teng Hsiao-p'ing, left, visited Tokyo to talk of trade with Japan's Prime Minister Takeo Fukuda.

India and Indonesia made notable progress in industrialization. But experts agreed that the answer to their economic problems lay not in more steel mills but in greater farm yield – and in economic reforms.

The bleakness of the poverty scene was reflected in a report issued in late summer by a study group commissioned by the Asian Development Bank, headquartered in Manila, the Philippines. Rural poverty, the report said, "has considerably worsened in the past decade," and it was aggravated by the widening inequality of incomes. The new technology, it said, does "nothing to curtail the growing number of landless laborers."

The miracle of the Green Revolution, the report indicated, was limited. Rather, the food-grain deficits would be six times larger in 10 years than they were in the 1970s; most Asian nations would find it even more difficult to pay for the imported food they needed; and unemployment would soar.

One-third of all the farmers in Pakistan, Sri Lanka, and the Philippines were sharecroppers in 1978. In India, where tenant farmers number in the tens of millions, there were also millions of "bonded" farm laborers, whose plight was only a little better than that of slaves.

What was needed, therefore, the Development Bank study suggested, was not more tractors, water, and fertilizer, but a change in the will of the rulers – and birth control.

Colonels as Reformers. By and large, 1978 was not a vintage year for democracy in Asia. Democratic governments remained at the helm in India and Sri Lanka. However, they shied away from any economic changes that might break the power of the landed gentry, one of the pillars of their political support. But in most of non-Communist Asia, power lay in the hands of dictatorial military men, who either rejected reform outright or managed to temper their reformist zeal. Such measures as breaking the power of the rural elite and redistributing land were never close to their hearts.

The Communist nations also found it difficult to feed their people, if for different reasons. Not the least of these – as Chinese revelations showed in 1978 – was brutal exploitation of rural workers.

Family planning was as essential to economic stability as rural reforms. But its successes were few in 1978. Even in China, where the government can enforce birth control, the population kept growing – to an estimated 1 billion persons on Jan. 1, 1979, according to a U.S. congressional committee, though about 870 million was a more commonly accepted figure.

The situation was worse elsewhere in Asia. India's birth-control program, once one of the most promising on the continent, had broken down, in part because the government of Prime Minister Morarji Desai seemed half-hearted about it. Family-

Facts in Brief on the Asian Countries

Country	Population	Government†	Monetary Unit*	Foreign Trade (million U.S. $) Exports	Imports
Afghanistan	21,199,000	Revolutionary Council President & Prime Minister Noor Mohammad Taraki	afghani (45 = $1)	327	308
Australia	14,336,000	Governor General Sir Zelman Cowen; Prime Minister John Malcolm Fraser	dollar (1 = $1.13)	13,002	12,175
Bangladesh	84,459,000	President Ziaur Rahman	taka (14.7 = $1)	414	764
Bhutan	1,275,000	King Jigme Singye Wangchuck	Indian rupee	no statistics available	
Burma	34,483,000	President U Ne Win; Prime Minister U Maung Maung Kha	kyat (6.7 = $1)	223	185
Cambodia (Kampuchea)	9,057,000	Communist Party Secretary & Prime Minister Pol Pot; President Khieu Samphan	riel (1,610 = $1)	7	43
China	869,424,000	Communist Party Chairman & Premier Hua Kuo-feng	yuan (1.7 = $1)	7,200	6,000
India	649,940,000	President Neelam Sanjeeva Reddy; Prime Minister Morarji Desai	rupee (8.1 = $1)	5,412	5,798
Indonesia	152,582,000	President Suharto	rupiah (625 = $1)	10,853	6,230
Iran	37,019,000	Shah Mohammad Reza Pahlavi; Prime Minister Shahpour Bakhtiar	rial (69.4 = $1)	24,250	13,750
Japan	116,375,000	Emperor Hirohito; Prime Minister Masayoshi Ohira	yen (201.5 = $1)	80,470	70,660
Korea, North	17,635,000	President Kim Il-song; Premier Yi Chong-ok	won (2 = $1)	133	365
Korea, South	37,547,000	President Chung Hee Park; Prime Minister Choe Kyu-ha	won (476 = $1)	10,062	10,798
Laos	3,603,000	President Souphanouvong; Prime Minister Kayson Phomvihan	kip (200 = $1)	11	65
Malaysia	13,664,000	Paramount Ruler Yahya Petra ibni Sultan Ibrahim; Prime Minister Datuk Hussein Onn	ringgit (2.3 = $1)	6,507	4,966
Maldives	145,000	President Maumoon Abdul Gayoom	rupee (9 = $1)	1	3
Mongolia	1,625,000	People's Revolutionary Party First Secretary & Presidium Chairman Yumjaagiin Tsedenbal; Council of Ministers Chairman Jambyn Batmonh	tughrik (5.1 = $1)	105	146
Nepal	13,769,000	King Birendra Bir Bikram Shah Dev; Prime Minister Kirti Nidhi Bista	rupee (12 = $1)	99	162
New Zealand	3,328,000	Governor General Sir Keith J. Holyoake; Prime Minister Robert D. Muldoon	dollar (1 = $1.04)	3,142	3,363
Pakistan	79,078,000	President & Chief Martial Law Administrator Zia-ul-Haq	rupee (9.9 = $1)	1,149	2,447
Papua New Guinea	2,983,000	Governor General Sir Tore Lokoloko; Prime Minister Michael Somare	kina (1 = $1.45)	635	497
Philippines	47,663,000	President & Prime Minister Ferdinand E. Marcos	peso (7.3 = $1)	3,151	4,219
Russia	266,403,000	Communist Party General Secretary & Supreme Soviet Presidium Chairman Leonid Ilich Brezhnev; Council of Ministers Chairman Aleksey Nikolayevich Kosygin	ruble (1 = $1.46)	45,161	40,817
Singapore	2,397,000	President Benjamin Henry Sheares; Prime Minister Lee Kuan Yew	dollar (2.2 = $1)	8,241	10,472
Sri Lanka	15,258,000	President Junius Richard Jayewardene; Prime Minister R. Premadasa	rupee (15.6 = $1)	714	695
Taiwan	17,350,000	President Chiang Ching-kuo; Premier Sun Yun-hsuan	new Taiwan dollar (36 = $1)	9,326	8,510
Thailand	47,768,000	King Bhumibol Adulyadej; Prime Minister Kriangsak Chamanan	baht (20 = $1)	3,491	4,612
Vietnam	50,690,000	President Ton Duc Thang; Prime Minister Pham Van Dong	dong (2.4 = $1)	227	831

*Exchange rates as of Dec. 1, 1978. †As of Jan. 6, 1979.

Ethnic Chinese who say they are leaving their homes in Vietnam because of harassment wait at the border for official admittance into China.

planning campaigns had also slackened in such Muslim countries as Pakistan and Bangladesh.

The "Boat People." The ordeal of 2,500 Vietnamese who arrived off Malaysia's port city of Klang in October on the decrepit steamship *Hai Hong* – and were denied permission to land – helped to focus attention on the problem of people driven from their homelands by war, Communism, and inflamed nationalism. Six weeks passed before 600 of these refugees, short of water, food, and medical supplies, were accepted by Canada. Other governments were even slower to act – and Malaysia, with 42,000 refugees already in its camps, was adamant in keeping its doors barred.

The price was cruel. When a fishing tug, crammed with refugees, arrived in Kuala Terengganu in late November, the townspeople turned the boat back, only to see it capsize and 200 persons drown before their eyes. Later that month, Malaysian warships went out to turn back 30 small ships carrying 22,500 refugees from Vietnam, most of them Chinese.

The first refugees were active anti-Communists. But these were soon followed by politically neutral farmers and fishermen escaping collectivization and lean rations. Urban Chinese who had been "resettled" in the Vietnamese jungle joined the exodus early in 1978. Some 140,000 of them fled overland to China, but others bribed Communist officials to let them escape by boat to other havens.

They were welcomed nowhere. Thailand was perhaps the most generous, with 136,000 refugees from Vietnam, Cambodia, and Laos in its crude camps. In the face of these figures, the United States agreed to accept 25,000 refugees a year; France, 12,000; and Australia, 10,000. But, if perhaps 330,000 persons fled from Vietnam, some 150,000 Cambodians, escaping war and the brutality of their government, fled to Vietnam.

Natural Disasters complemented the human calamities. Six provinces in China, with a total population of 100 million persons, experienced the worst drought in 100 years, with even drinking water in short supply. To the south, there were floods. The rampaging Mekong River killed hundreds of persons in Laos and inundated some of the richest rice provinces. In Vietnam, the worst floods in a third of a century submerged 2.3 million acres (930,000 hectares) of land and brought official talk of famine and unprecedented appeals for foreign help. Similar tales of devastation came from Thailand, Cambodia, the Philippines, Pakistan, and Bangladesh. But nowhere was the destruction as widespread as in India. Floods, fed by monsoon rains that started in June, killed some 2,000 persons in Bihar and West Bengal states, left millions homeless, and caused damage estimated at $2 billion.   Mark Gayn

See also the various Asian country articles. In WORLD BOOK, see ASIA.

ASTRONOMY. *Pioneer Venus 1*, the first United States National Aviation and Space Administration (NASA) probe of Earth's "sister planet," went into orbit around Venus on Dec. 4, 1978. *Pioneer Venus 2* put five instrumented probes into the planet's atmosphere on December 9. Both Pioneers supported the theory that a "greenhouse effect" of trapped solar energy accounts for Venus' scorching surface. A surprise finding was the very high level of the gases neon and argon on Venus, much higher than on Earth.

Later in December, two Russian spacecraft – *Venera 11* and *Venera 12* – landed on Venus. Their mission was to record data as well as to start investigating the possibility of an Earth-to-Venus route for future spaceships.

Pluto's Moon. Astronomer James W. Christy of the United States Naval Observatory in Washington, D.C., on June 22 discovered a moon orbiting Pluto, the planet most distant from the Sun. It is the first moon of Pluto to be found since that planet was discovered in 1930.

Christy noticed that photographs made on two nights during April and May 1978 showed a somewhat elongated image of Pluto. Checking earlier photographs, he found a similar elongation on seven nights in 1965 and 1970. A moon orbiting at a distance of about 12,000 miles (19,000 kilometers) from Pluto could account for the elongated images.

Christy theorized that he had discovered a moon and sent predictions of the object's next appearance to other observers. Their reports soon confirmed the moon's existence. The body is so small, so faint, and so close to Pluto that it can be photographed only at certain times, even with the largest telescopes and under the best conditions. It cannot be seen through a visual telescope.

The new moon has been tentatively named Charon. In Greek mythology, Charon was the ferryman who rowed the souls of the dead across the River Styx to reach Hades.

Charon orbits Pluto in the same length of time that Pluto takes to spin once on its axis – 6 days 9 hours 17 minutes. Its diameter is estimated to be about 40 per cent that of Pluto, and its mass is estimated at about 5 per cent to 10 per cent of Pluto's mass. Pluto's own diameter is not known for certain, but it is estimated at 1,500 to 2,000 miles (2,400 to 3,200 kilometers). This would give Charon a diameter of 600 to 800 miles (1,000 to 1,300 kilometers).

Pluto's mass formerly was estimated to be comparable to that of Mars, or about twice that of Mercury and 10 per cent that of Earth. But astronomers used Charon's orbital period around Pluto to calculate the planet's mass, and the results were astonishing. Pluto's mass is 30 times less than that of Mercury and 600 times less than that of Earth. This means that Pluto "weighs" less than 14 per cent as much as our own Moon. The densities of both Pluto and Charon (about 0.7) are less than the density of water, which makes them as light as comets.

More Uranus Rings. After the 1977 announcement of the discovery of five rings around Uranus, further findings have brought the total to nine rings. Hale Observatories astronomers observed four more rings on April 10, 1978, confirming observations James Elliot made in 1977. All the rings lie between 25,000 and 32,000 miles (40,000 and 52,000 kilometers) from the center of Uranus. The space between Uranus and the innermost ring is about 8,000 miles (13,000 kilometers), about one-fourth the planet's diameter. The rings are extremely narrow and dark, and probably consist of countless bits of rubble orbiting Uranus in narrow zones. Most of the rings are no more than 3 miles (4.8 kilometers), and possibly less than 1 mile (1.6 kilometers), wide. But the outermost ring, Epsilon, is about 37 miles (60 kilometers) wide. Its shape is slightly elliptical, and after measuring its precessional rate, astronomers have estimated the spin rate of Uranus at 15 hours.

Super Black Hole? Two groups of astronomers reported on May 1 that they have found evidence that an invisible mass equal to 5 billion times the Sun's mass lies at the core of the galaxy M87. They believe the central mass could be a supermassive black hole, an object with gravity so strong that not even light can escape it.

Using the Hale Observatories' 200-inch (508-

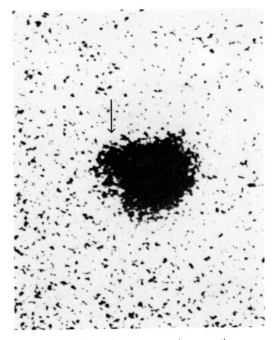

Pluto's moon, Charon, here seen as a bump on the left side of the planet, is so faint and so close to Pluto that it was not discovered until June.

centimeter) reflector on Mount Palomar and the 157-inch (398-centimeter) telescope at the Kitt Peak National Observatory in Arizona, the astronomers measured the speed of stars close to the galaxy's center and obtained an estimate of the central mass. They estimate the mass lies within a region that is at most 700 light-years across, but it may be much smaller.

A giant elliptical galaxy, M87 lies at the center of the famous Virgo cluster, the nearest cluster to the Earth, lying about 60 million light-years away. The brightest galaxy in the cluster and much bigger than Earth's Milky Way Galaxy, M87 is known to be a strong source of radio and X-ray energy, and a visible jet extends from its nucleus a distance of 5,000 light-years. The nucleus of M87 is presumed to be the source of the jet and the radio and X-ray energy.

Closed Universe? Melville P. Ulmer of Northwestern University in Evanston, Ill., and seven U.S. Naval Research Laboratory astronomers announced in September that they have discovered an immense gas cloud between the clusters of galaxies. They estimated the cloud's mass at 1 trillion times that of the Sun or at least five times the mass of our Milky Way. If every cluster of galaxies in the universe is surrounded by such gas clouds, the pull of gravity resulting from the density of the matter would be great enough to stop the expansion of the universe and pull the galaxies back together.

The first High Energy Astronomy Observatory (HEAO-1), a satellite orbiting above the Earth's atmosphere, detected X rays coming from the gas between and around two clusters of galaxies, Abell 399 and Abell 401. The scientists announced their discovery at the meeting of the High Energy Astrophysics Division of the American Astronomical Society in San Diego.

Multiple-Mirror Telescope. A long-standing dream of astronomers became a reality in 1978 when an optical instrument that combines six telescopes into one was completed on Mount Hopkins, near Tucson, Ariz. The telescope is a joint project of the Smithsonian Astrophysical Observatory in Cambridge, Mass., and the University of Arizona in Tucson.

The device consists of six mirrors, each 72 inches (183 centimeters) in diameter, arranged in a circle. Because of Earth's rotation, the instrument's rotation and tilt must constantly be changed, so the structure housing the mirrors performs like a gun mount. Lasers keep the mirrors aligned, and computers process their observations. The combination of the six images gives the instrument the light-gathering power of a telescope with a 175-inch (445-centimeter) mirror, making it the third most powerful telescope in the world.   Eric D. Carlson

See also SPACE EXPLORATION. In WORLD BOOK, see planet articles; ASTRONOMY; TELESCOPE.

A January fire destroys Loew's Grand Theater, the 85-year-old Atlanta landmark where the film *Gone With the Wind* premièred in 1939.

ATLANTA continued to feel the effects of its four-year real estate recession in 1978 as the city's major new business complex and its largest bank suffered financial reverses. The owners of Omni International, Atlanta's "city within a city," announced on February 10 that their financial backers were planning a foreclosure sale of the complex to recover unpaid debts. The complex includes a 500-room hotel, 15 restaurants, two office towers, specialty shops, and an indoor ice rink.

Omni International had failed to repay $77 million in loans and $14 million in interest to a group of banks led by Morgan Guaranty Trust Company of New York City. Foreclosure proceedings were called off in April, however, when Morgan Guaranty agreed to allow Omni International more time to find new long-term credit.

Citizens & Southern National Bank, the largest bank in Georgia, announced in February that it held $11 million in bad loans that would be charged against its 1977 earnings, resulting in a loss of $7.8-million for that year. Citizens & Southern had been more heavily involved in real estate lending than any other bank in the city.

Strong Economy. Otherwise, Atlanta's economy was surprisingly healthy. Nonresidential construction in the Atlanta area rose 78 per cent during the first five months of 1978. Residential construction was up 9.5 per cent during the period.

Living costs rose 6.3 per cent during the 12 months ending in April, but food costs rose 9.7 per cent for the year ending in May. A U.S. Department of Labor report issued on April 26 noted that an average family of four needed $15,483, or 9.5 per cent less than the national average, to live in moderate comfort in the Atlanta area. A Congressional Budget Office study released on September 10 listed Atlanta as a "moderate-need city" in terms of its "composite measure of social need."

Law Enforcement. A scandal over alleged cheating on promotions in the Atlanta Police Department led to the dismissal of Public Safety Commissioner A. Reginald Eaves on March 10. Eaves, a black who had been instrumental in carrying out affirmative action programs, reducing police brutality, and lowering the city's crime rate, was accused of allowing a group of black officers to study a promotion examination before taking it. Mayor Maynard H. Jackson appointed Lee P. Brown, former Director of the Department of Justice Services for Multnomah County, Oregon, to replace Eaves.

The *Atlanta Journal* reported in its May 31 edition that Federal Bureau of Investigation (FBI) documents revealed that the FBI had maintained a series of wiretaps on the Southern Christian Leadership Conference's Atlanta headquarters from 1963 to 1966.   James M. Banovetz

See also CITY. In WORLD BOOK, see ATLANTA.

AUSTRALIA. The Liberal-National Country Party coalition of Prime Minister John Malcolm Fraser stayed firmly in power in 1978, despite embarrassing internal difficulties. One problem began on April 24, when the government began a judicial inquiry into charges that federal Finance Minister Eric Robinson had improperly influenced the redrawing of electoral boundaries in Queensland.

The inquiry exonerated Robinson in August, but it implicated Minister of Administrative Services Reginald G. Withers, a close political ally of Fraser. Fraser denied that he had any part in the affair and fired Withers on August 7.

A second embarrassing incident involved Fraser's appointment on February 9 of former Governor General Sir John Kerr as ambassador to the United Nations Educational, Scientific, and Cultural Organization. Kerr resigned within a month because of attacks in the press and in Parliament. Kerr had aroused Australians in 1975 when, as governor general, he dismissed the Labor government of Gough Whitlam and appointed Fraser to succeed Whitlam.

The Ranger Project. The government's main political problem, however, arose from its dealings with Aborigines in the Northern Territory over the mining of the Ranger uranium project deposits. The Northern Territory contains the world's largest un-

Explosives experts examine the debris after a bomb blast killed three men outside a Sydney hotel where Commonwealth leaders were meeting.

developed uranium deposits. After agreeing on August 25 that mining could proceed, the Aborigines changed their minds. They finally agreed to a 4.25 per cent royalty for the use of their land. The project was delayed further in September, however, when the government and the mining companies could not agree on who should pay the royalty. An agreement signed on November 3 opened the way for mining, which was expected to begin in April 1979.

State Affairs. On June 17, about 84 per cent of the voters in New South Wales approved a proposal that the people elect the Legislative Council, the upper house of the state parliament. The oldest parliamentary assembly in Australia, its membership had always been elected by members of parliament. The state's Labor Party government was re-elected on October 7 with a larger majority in the Legislative Assembly, the lower house.

The Northern Territory took a step toward self-government on July 1 when the federal government handed over some functions to the local parliament. Others were promised for the future.

Citizens in Canberra, the federal capital, voted on the question of self-government in a referendum held on November 25. Sixty-three per cent voted for no change in the existing system of control by ministers and officials.

Sir Robert G. Menzies, prime minister from 1939 to 1941 and again from 1949 to 1966, died on May 15. Queen Elizabeth II was represented at his funeral in Melbourne by Prince Charles, and President Jimmy Carter by W. Averell Harriman.

Foreign Affairs Minister Andrew Peacock announced Australia's acceptance of East Timor as part of Indonesia on January 20. Peacock also reached an agreement in May with Papua New Guinea on maritime boundaries and other matters concerning the Torres Strait, including the seabed, fisheries, and sovereignty over local islands. Australia also agreed to accept more refugees from Indochina, and expected to admit about 10,000 persons in 1978 and 1979.

Prime Minister Fraser and Peacock advocated the claims of developing nations for aid and for a common commodity fund. A regional meeting of leaders of the Asian and Pacific Commonwealth nations in Sydney was interrupted on February 13 when a bomb exploded outside the hotel where the meeting was being held. The explosion killed three and injured nine.

Problems with the United States and the European Economic Community (EC or Common Market) illustrated Australia's economic relations with the industrial countries of the Northern Hemisphere. Among the issues were possible U.S. restrictions against the import of Australian beef and the U.S. proposal that Continental Airlines should share the Pacific air route with Pan American World Airways and Qantas Airways Limited, the Australian airline.

The Australian government continued to be highly critical of EC protectionist policies. The government and the EC agreed on May 11 on the pricing and level of Australian steel exports to the EC, but the EC refused to settle other trade issues, saying that they must be dealt with during multilateral trade negotiations in Geneva, Switzerland.

The Economy showed signs of expanding toward the end of 1978. Domestic demand was rising, and retail sales and private capital expenditure increased. The federal budget presented on August 15 by Treasurer John Howard was intended to continue to reduce inflation and to restrict government spending. Income taxes and excise taxes on beer, spirits, and tobacco were increased. On the other hand, the sales tax on cars was reduced and the duty on imported cars raised 12.5 per cent to assist the automobile industry.

There were some encouraging signs of economic progress. On May 7, Kevin Newman, minister for national development, reported that Australia might have more oil in the 1980s than previously thought, because of the discovery of new wells and a reduction in the rate of consumption. Oil was discovered in September in Bass Strait and in South Australia's Cooper Basin. An agreement in October between Australia and West Germany called for a study to determine if Australian coal can be converted economically into liquid fuel.

Major iron ore and coal sales to Japan failed to materialize because of the slow growth rate of Japan's steel industry. Lack of increased investment in manufacturing emphasized the problems of this area of the Australian economy as pressure from imports increased. The Association of Southeast Asian Nations criticized Australia for protecting its clothing and textile industries.

Plentiful rainfall followed the widespread droughts of early 1978 and brought farmers the prospect of better returns in crops, livestock, and wool. Farm income was estimated to be 22 per cent higher than 1977.

The balance-of-payments deficit continued to cause anxiety. The government announced on February 5 that it would support the Australian dollar with substantial overseas borrowing, if necessary, and it borrowed heavily during the rest of the year.

On June 8, the government issued new guidelines for mining investments, in the hope of attracting more overseas investors. A company may now start a major project with only 25 per cent Australian participation, if it guarantees that this will eventually rise to 51 per cent.

Other Developments. Australian science received worldwide attention in April when the International Civil Aviation Organization adopted Interscan, a microwave aircraft-landing system, for use at all international airports. Interscan was developed by the Commonwealth Scientific and Industrial Research Organization, the Australian Department of Transport, and Amalgamated Wireless Australasia, Limited, with some U.S. assistance.

Immigration remained low because of unemployment. Michael J. R. Mackellar, minister for immigration and ethnic affairs, announced on June 6 that a new system for assessing potential immigrants would begin in 1979. Based in part on the Canadian points system, it would take into account the immigrants' family ties with Australia, skills, literacy in their own language, knowledge of English, and prospects of successful settlement.

On May 30, the prime minister announced a $50-million increase in spending on services to immigrants in 1979, 1980, and 1981. Improvements were planned in immigrant education and housing.

The federal government continued to provide further land rights and improved services to Aborigines and reached a compromise in April with Queensland on the control of Aboriginal reserves in that state. After bauxite was discovered there, the Queensland government tried to take over management of two communities, Aurukun and Mornington Island, which had been operated by the Uniting Church. The federal government wanted the Aborigines to manage the land themselves under a government advisory board.   J. D. B. Miller

See also ASIA (Facts in Brief Table). In WORLD BOOK, see AUSTRALIA.

AUSTRIA narrowly rejected a plan to open its first nuclear power plant in a Nov. 5, 1978, referendum. The $560-million plant had been nearly finished for more than a year. Opponents claimed it was unsafe because it is near an earthquake fault, and raised questions about radioactive-waste disposal. Although the vote was not constitutionally binding, the government agreed not to open the plant.

Truckdrivers protested a transit tax introduced on July 1 by blockading Austria from July 2 to 7. Vacationers and immigrant workers heading home could not cross the borders when 9,000 trucks blocked all roads connecting Austria with neighboring Yugoslavia, Italy, Switzerland, West Germany, Czechoslovakia, and Hungary. The tax, of about 1.2 cents per mile (2 cents per kilometer) per metric ton, was imposed on vehicles over 5.5 short tons (5 metric tons). It could total $200 for a truck with a big trailer. The tax was imposed after Chancellor Bruno Kreisky's government decided that other Europeans who use Austria's roads should help pay for them.

Kreisky and his ministers talked to the truckers' representatives on July 6, and the blockade was lifted the next day when the drivers saw there was no chance of the tax being canceled.

Imported Energy. Austria continued to import large quantities of energy from its eastern neighbors: oil and natural gas from Russia, electricity from the Council for Mutual Economic Assistance (COME-

CON) network, and coal from Poland. Plans call for creating a European energy pool by adding to the pipelines that connect COMECON countries via Austria with countries of the European Community (EC or Common Market). Although Austria has not exploited its energy potential fully, it imports energy to balance trade with the COMECON countries. These countries account for about one-fifth of Austria's foreign trade.

Strong Schilling. The Austrian monetary unit, the schilling, retained its strength, following closely the neighboring West German Deutsche mark. Since 1973, the schilling has appreciated about 25 per cent against the U.S. dollar. Although he could have helped exports by devaluing the schilling, Finance Minister Hannes Androsch refused to do so. With the support of bankers, he introduced an austerity package in January 1978 that increased the value-added tax from 18 to 30 per cent on luxury imported items including automobiles, cut social-welfare subsidies, and tightened credit restrictions. Having to face a general election in 1979 also made devaluation seem unwise.

Austria and Hungary agreed on May 5 to abolish visas for travelers between the two countries, effective Jan. 1, 1979, opening up what was Europe's most heavily guarded frontier.　　　Kenneth Brown

See also EUROPE (Facts in Brief Table). In WORLD BOOK, see AUSTRIA.

AUTOMOBILE. The United States automobile industry had one of its better years in 1978 despite a host of problems including inflation, recalls, emission standards, and other government controls. New car production was expected to reach about 9.2-million vehicles, almost identical with 1977's output. United States sales were estimated at 9.3 million 1978-model domestic cars and 2 million imports for a combined total of 11.3 million units.

Truck sales also continued at a high plateau – 4-million 1978-model vehicles, up 15 per cent over the 3.5 million sold in 1977.

Price tags on 1979 U.S. models went up an average of 4.7 per cent, compared with 5.7 per cent in the 1978 model year. As usual, it was difficult to figure the increases exactly because the auto companies shuffled standard and optional equipment on their cars. General Motors Corporation (GM) President Elliott M. Estes noted that the industry had made a commitment to President Jimmy Carter to forego any additional price increases in the 1979 model year.

GM said its price hike on 1979 models was 5.7 per cent, or $302 on the average; the Ford Motor Company and Chrysler Corporation set their average increases at 4.2 per cent. In dollars, the average Ford boost was $297, while Chrysler went up $293.

Model Mix. In 1978, the year of the home-grown small car, compact and subcompact cars captured almost 45 per cent of the market, up 5 per cent over 1977. The declining dollar helped offset the traditional price advantage enjoyed by foreign cars.

Most import car lines shuffled their prices at least twice during the model year to keep up with fluctuations in the dollar against the Japanese yen and the West German Deutsche mark. Full-sized cars virtually held their own in the U.S. market, but mid-sized cars fell below the 1977 pace.

Illustrating the variations in pricing, GM boosted the price on its Chevette four times during the model year for a total increase of $380, while the sticker price on the average Toyota jumped $512 over the same period. Volkswagen of America (VW) posted introductory price increases 4.1 per cent over final 1978 prices, compared with the 6.9 per cent increase on the 1979 Japanese Toyota. A VW spokesman said the weakness of the dollar, inflated costs, and improvements in the product caused the increase in his firm's line.

On the international front, Chrysler sold its European holdings in August to Peugeot-Citroën of France for $230 million and a 15 per cent share in the French automaker's operations. The deal meant that Peugeot-Citroën became the largest automotive operation in Europe, moving ahead of Volkswagen. Prior to the sale, Chrysler was the world's fifth-largest auto producer; Peugeot ranked seventh.

Copyright Draper Hill, from King Features Syndicate, Inc., 1978

The last Volkswagen "beetle" built in West Germany rolls off the assembly line in Enden on January 19. The car will still be built in other countries.

Market Mix. United States automakers offered 247 models as the 1979 model year began. It was the smallest offering since 1960, when 244 choices were available. New to the automotive scene in 1978-1979 were the American Motors Corporation (AMC) Spirit, which succeeded Gremlin; the Mercury Capri; the Dodge St. Regis in the standard-sized field; and the American-built Volkswagen. VW began operations at its New Stanton, Pa., assembly plant, producing its first car in April.

Problems and Changes. The auto industry continued to complain that government-imposed fuel-economy standards strain its physical and financial abilities. The industry predicted it would have major problems in trying to raise fuel-economy standards from 19 miles per gallon (mpg), or 8 kilometers per liter (kpl), in 1979 to the 1985 figure of 27.5 mpg (11.7 kpl).

Top-level changes came thick and fast in the auto industry. Ford, Chrysler, and American Motors all got new presidents. The most spectacular change was the ouster of Lee A. Iacocca as president of Ford and his move across town to take over as president of Chrysler. The 54-year-old Iacocca left Ford in July after a rift with board chairman Henry Ford II. Iacocca, often described as the "father of the Ford Mustang," took over at Chrysler in November.

Ford promoted Vice-President Philip Caldwell to the presidency of the number-two U.S. auto company. W. Paul Tippett, Jr., who formerly worked for Ford, was named AMC president in October.

Profit Picture. Chrysler Corporation lost $247.8-million, equal to $4.15 per share, in the first nine months of 1978. This compared with earnings of $219.9 million, or $3.53 a share, in the same period in 1977.

General Motors earned $2.5 billion, or $8.73 a share, in the opening nine months of 1978, compared with $2.4 billion, or $8.36 a share, in the first nine months of 1977. Estes said the GM profit margin for the first nine months was 5.5 per cent, below the 6 per cent earnings in the previous year.

Ford, though troubled by a strike at its plants in Great Britain, reported earnings of $1.31 billion, or $11 a share in the first nine months of 1978, compared with $1.28 billion, or $10.84 a share, in the same 1977 period.

American Motors, smallest of the U.S. auto firms, reported its fiscal year was in the black for the second year in a row. Earnings came to $36.7 million, up 342 per cent from fiscal 1977's $8.3 million.

Diesels. General Motors announced plans to triple its use of diesel engines in 1979, upping output to 190,000 units on some Oldsmobile and Cadillac cars. Ford continued to show little interest in the diesel. Volkswagen has a diesel option on its Rabbit line and claims 45 mpg (20.8 kpl) compared with 29 mpg (12.3 kpl) for the regular Rabbit. But diesels are more expensive. For example, the 1978 Olds Diesel 88 costs $850 more than its conventional counterpart.

Research on electric cars continued. General Electric Company (GE) rolled out an experimental car that it said could sell for about $6,000. GE said it had no plans to market the car but would be willing to tell other manufacturers how the automobile was made. The GE car has a range of 45 miles (72 kilometers), with power coming from 18 batteries.

An Elkhart, Ind., grand jury indicted the Ford Motor Company in September for reckless homicide and criminal recklessness. The charges stemmed from the deaths of three teen-age girls in the fiery crash of a Ford Pinto. Ford asked in December that the indictment be dismissed. Charges that the Pinto – and the similar Mercury Bobcat – had poorly designed and positioned gas tanks had been made earlier. Ford recalled almost 2 million of the subcompacts in June to correct flaws in the fuel system.

The average hourly auto worker's pay rose to $8.40 thanks to an increase of $1.03 in the cost-of-living allowance negotiated in 1976 between the automakers and the United Automobile Workers. For assembly-line workers, the largest category in the industry, the hourly rate averaged $8.10, including fringe benefits.   Charles C. Cain III

See also CONSUMER AFFAIRS. In WORLD BOOK, see AUTOMOBILE.

AUTOMOBILE RACING. The Lotus factory team of England signed Mario Andretti of Nazareth, Pa., and Ronnie Peterson of Sweden to drive in the 1978 Formula One races for the world drivers' championship. Andretti won the title. Peterson died after an accident.

The sophisticated, single-seated roadsters competed from January to October in 16 Grand Prix races. Andretti had six victories, one second place, one fourth, and one sixth, and became the first American to win the world championship since Phil Hill in 1961.

The 38-year-old Andretti started racing stock cars in his teens and had been successful in all types of road and oval racing. Peterson, 34, had started in 123 Formula One races, more than any other active driver. In the right car, he was perhaps the fastest driver, but he was not happy.

"It used to be more fun," he said. "The Formula One business has turned tougher and tougher in recent years."

The 14th of the 16 races was the Italian Grand Prix on September 10 at Monza. The drivers disliked the track, calling it old and dangerous. Seconds after the race started, Peterson's car was hit by another, struck the guardrail, and caught fire. In seconds, 10 cars were involved in the accident. Peterson died the next day after surgery. He was the only driver who could have overtaken Andretti for the title.

Lotus signed Carlos Reutteman of Argentina to replace Peterson in 1979. Driving a Ferrari in 1978, Reutteman won four races, including the two in the United States – on April 4 at Long Beach, Calif., and on October 1 at Watkins Glen, N.Y. Gilles Villeneuve of Berthierville, Canada, won the Canadian Grand Prix in a Ferrari on October 8.

The Indianapolis 500. As usual, the world's richest race was the Indianapolis 500 on May 28. Except for their turbocharged engines, the cars were strikingly similar to the Formula One racers.

Al Unser of Albuquerque, N. Mex., the Indianapolis winner in 1970 and 1971, was not a favorite this time. His Penske-Cosworth was erratic, and twice during the year it came apart and caused accidents.

Despite the problems, Unser won the race, beating Tom Sneva by 8.19 seconds, and earned $250,-364 from the record purse of $1,145,225. Unser also won the $370,450 Schaefer 500 on June 25 at Mt. Pocono, Pa., by 24.42 seconds. Then he won the $300,000 California 500 on September 3 at Ontario, Calif., by 14 miles. It was the first time a driver had swept the three United States Auto Club (USAC) 500-mile races in one year. Unser set a USAC record by earning $591,599 in one year. See UNSER, AL.

NASCAR Series. The Grand National series of the National Association for Stock Car Auto Racing (NASCAR) involved late-model stock cars that

Al Unser happily raises the traditional bottle of milk in celebration of his third victory in the Indianapolis 500-mile race on May 28.

looked like showroom models. Cale Yarborough of Timmonsville, S.C., the series champion in 1976 and 1977 in a Chevrolet, won again in an Oldsmobile. He finished first in 10 of the 30 races and earned $436,980 before year-end bonuses.

Bobby Allison of Hueytown, Ala., who had not won a race in three years, took the richest race of the series, the $457,500 Daytona 500 on February 19.

Other Races. There were 11 endurance races in Europe and North America for the world manufacturers' championship. Porsche won the title for the third straight year. Porsches took the first seven places in the 24 Hours of Daytona on February 4-5 at Daytona Beach and five of the first eight places in the Six Hours of Endurance on July 8 at Watkins Glen. A French Renault Alpine driven by two Frenchmen won the world's best-known endurance race, the 24 Hours of Le Mans on June 10-11 in France.

In the United States and Canada, the Can-Am series produced few surprises. The 3-liter Lola in which Patrick Tambay of France won the 1977 title won again, driven by Alan Jones of Australia.

In drag racing, Don (Big Daddy) Garlits of Seffner, Fla., won a record fifth title in the top-fuel class of the United States Nationals August 31 to September 3 in Indianapolis. Kelly Brown of Hollywood, Calif., won the world championship in this, the fastest class in a high-speed sport.   Frank Litsky

In WORLD BOOK, see AUTOMOBILE RACING.

AVIATION companies prospered in 1978 as fare-trimming spread, boosting air travel and filling planes. The International Air Transport Association (IATA) estimated that scheduled airlines carried 22.6 per cent more paying passengers on North Atlantic routes in the first nine months of 1978, and cargo increased 16.6 per cent, compared with the first nine months of 1977. The international traffic carried by United States airlines increased 24.2 per cent through October. Marring this picture was the worst airline disaster in U.S. history; a jetliner and a small private plane collided over San Diego on September 25, killing 144 persons.

George W. James, the industry's chief economist, estimated in December that the carriers would show profits of nearly $1.3 billion for 1978. Domestic-airline passenger traffic through October was 16.6 per cent ahead of 1977, air freight increased 9.6 per cent, domestic air freight went up 13.3 per cent, and international air freight was up 3.7 per cent.

Airlines went on a buying spree for new aircraft that was prompted by rising profits, higher passenger loads, and U.S. government requirements for quieter planes. United Airlines ordered 30 of the Boeing Company's new 767 wide-body jets on July 14, and 30 of its 727s, for $1.6 billion, the largest purchase of commercial planes in history.

Worldwide Competition. President Jimmy Carter's Administration announced a new aviation policy on August 21, emphasizing lower fares and fewer restrictions on routes and capacities. United States agreements with Belgium, Great Britain, Israel, Poland, and West Germany lifted restrictions on fare cuts, charter service, and flight capacity, and gave other countries' airlines more U.S. landing rights.

The Civil Aeronautics Board (CAB) opened more overseas routes. Los Angeles joined New York City as the second U.S. city to be served by two U.S. airlines on London routes when the CAB switched Pan American World Airways' London service from Boston to Los Angeles on June 9. Four airlines, including two previously all-charter carriers, won rights to fly between the United States and the Netherlands or Belgium. United Airlines won routes linking Seattle and Portland, Ore., with Tokyo, pending Japanese approval.

Britain's Laker Airways, which initiated fare slashing on North Atlantic routes in 1977 with its New York City-to-London Skytrains, began similar Los Angeles-London service on September 26.

IATA loosened its grip on international airline fares. No IATA-set fare had been in effect on the North Atlantic since the 1977 fare cutting began. The CAB proposed on June 12 to end IATA fare setting by withholding approval of the joint-fare agreements of IATA members. Chief executives of major airlines voted in Montreal, Canada, in July to let IATA members cut fares individually. IATA made participation in fare coordination optional at its November meeting in Geneva, Switzerland.

Deregulation Begins. President Carter signed the Airline Deregulation Act on October 24. The measure stressed competition, cheaper air travel, and freer route policies. It gave airlines more freedom to add routes and to change fares without CAB approval, while ensuring continued service for small cities. The bill ends CAB's control over routes and fares by 1983, and it provides for the abolition of the CAB.

The CAB began to abandon its practice of choosing among applicants for new routes, instead allowing all airlines to offer the routes they wished. In a key case, the CAB opened Chicago's Midway Airport to connections with six Midwest points in July. It proposed 18 new routes to and from Midway and unlimited service on 15 new routes to and from Oakland, Calif.

The CAB moved to give PanAm and two charter airlines—World Airways and Trans International Airlines—low-fare coast-to-coast routes.

Under the new law, the CAB in November and December granted airlines about 350 unused routes of other airlines. The routes were available on a first-come, first-served basis. The CAB eliminated most restrictions on charter flights on August 17, to promote competition with scheduled airlines.

The agency let airlines discount or cut fares up to 70 per cent, or raise them up to 10 per cent on

A landing jetliner glides past protest banners at Tokyo's new $2.4-billion Narita airport in May. Demonstrations delayed the opening for months.

September 1, without CAB approval. American Airlines extended its "Super Saver" fare, up to 45 per cent below coach, at all U.S. mainland cities it serves, and other airlines offered similar plans. Western Airlines and National Airlines cut their basic fares 35 per cent between Miami and Los Angeles on April 13. Delta Air Lines cut first-class fares 13 to 20 per cent on May 18. American Airlines and Trans World Airlines (TWA) introduced a three-tier fare system on October 15. TWA dropped it in December, and American planned to drop it on Jan. 8, 1979. Other lines offered it on international routes.

The CAB approved a 3 per cent increase in the basic coach fare for all airlines effective on May 1, and let airlines boost coach fares by 3.2 per cent in November. Most airlines sought a 2.5 per cent increase, effective on November 10, and the other 0.7 per cent later.

One response to the new competition was a move toward mergers. PanAm, Eastern, and Texas International Airlines bid to merge with National, which agreed to join with PanAm, subject to CAB approval. North Central Airlines and Southern Airways agreed in July to merge, and Western Airlines and Continental Air Lines agreed in August.

CAB Chairman Alfred E. Kahn left the agency on October 25 to become President Carter's anti-inflation chief. His successor was Marvin S. Cohen, a Tucson, Ariz., lawyer.

Aircraft Noise. Airlines failed to gain federal support for using part of the passenger ticket tax to pay for noise reduction. The U.S. House of Representatives approved on September 14 a plan to permit use of 25 per cent of the funds from the 8 per cent tax for muffling or replacing noisy planes. But the Senate Finance Committee rejected a similar plan on October 3.

Air Safety. Airline fatalities declined throughout the world in 1978, but increased in the United States. Preliminary figures from the Flight Safety Foundation, a private U.S. group, indicated that there were 978 world deaths, excluding Russia and China, in 1978, compared with 1,507 deaths in 1977. There were 159 deaths in the United States in 1978, compared with 81 in 1977.

Tokyo International Airport opened in May after years of violent opposition by environmentalist protesters. Saudi Arabia began to build what is reported to be the world's largest airport at Jidda on the Red Sea. It will cover 41 square miles (106 square kilometers), compared with the 27.5 square miles (71.2 square kilometers) of Dallas-Fort Worth Airport in Texas, the largest in the United States. Leaders of seven Western countries agreed in July to cut off all flights to and from countries failing to act against hijackers (see EUROPE [Close-Up]).   Albert R. Karr

See also TRANSPORTATION. In WORLD BOOK, see AVIATION.

AWARDS AND PRIZES presented in 1978 included the following:

Arts Awards

Academy of Motion Picture Arts and Sciences. *"Oscar" Awards: Best Picture, Annie Hall,* United Artists, Charles H. Joffe, producer. *Best Actor,* Richard Dreyfuss, *The Goodbye Girl. Best Actress,* Diane Keaton, *Annie Hall. Best Supporting Actor,* Jason Robards, *Julia. Best Supporting Actress,* Vanessa Redgrave, *Julia. Best Director,* Woody Allen, *Annie Hall. Best Original Screenplay,* Woody Allen and Marshall Brickman, *Annie Hall. Best Cinematography,* Vilmos Zsigmond, *Close Encounters of the Third Kind. Best Film Editing,* Paul Hirsch, Marcia Lucas, and Richard Chew, *Star Wars. Best Original Music Score,* John Williams, *Star Wars. Best Feature Documentary, Who Are the DeBolts? And Where Did They Get Nineteen Kids?,* John Korty, Dan McCann, and Warren Lockhart, producers. *Best Visual Effects,* John Stears, John Dykstra, Richard Edlund, Grant McCune, and Robert Blalock, *Star Wars. Irving Thalberg Award,* Walter Mirisch. *Jean Hersholt Humanitarian Award,* Charlton Heston. *Honorary Award,* Maggie Booth, editor. See ALLEN, WOODY; DREYFUSS, RICHARD; KEATON, DIANE.

American Institute of Architecture. *Gold Medal,* for life's work, Philip C. Johnson, of Johnson and Burgee, New York City. *Architectural Firm Award,* Harry Weese & Associates, Chicago. *Medal,* Robert Venturi, Philadelphia, for his book *Complexity and Contradiction in Architecture. Design Award,* for a significant building at least 25 years old, Charles Eames, for the Charles and Ray Eames home in Pacific Palisades, Calif., built in 1949.

Antoinette Perry (Tony) Awards. *Drama: Best Play, Da,* by Hugh Leonard. *Best Actor,* Barnard Hughes in *Da. Best Actress,* Jessica Tandy in *The Gin Game. Best Director,* Melvin Bernhardt for *Da. Musical: Best Musical, Ain't Misbehavin'. Best Actor,* John Cullum in *On The Twentieth Century. Best Actress,* Liza Minnelli in *The Act. Best Choreography,* Bob Fosse for *Dancin'. Best Book,* Betty Comden and Adolph Green for *On The Twentieth Century. Best Score,* Cy Coleman for *On The Twentieth Century. Best Director,* Richard Maltby, Jr., for *Ain't Misbehavin'. Most Innovative Revival, Dracula* by John Lloyd Balderston and Hamilton Deane.

Cannes International Film Festival. *Golden Palm Grand Prize, The Tree of Clogs,* Italy. *Best Actor,* Jon Voight in *Coming Home. Best Actress* (tie), Jill Clayburgh in *An Unmarried Woman* and Isabelle Huppert in *Violette. Best Director,* Nagiosa Oshima for *Empire of Passion. Special Jury Prize* (tie), *The Shout,* Great Britain, and *Ciao Mascio,* Italy.

Capezio Foundation. *Capezio Dance Award,* Hanya Holm, choreographer, for "her contribution to modern dance and the American musical theater."

John F. Kennedy Center for the Performing Arts. *Honors,* "to build more enthusiasm for the performing arts and to bring the public's attention to the artist's true place in society," Marian Anderson, singer; Fred Astaire, dancer; George Balanchine, choreographer; Richard Rodgers, composer; and Arthur Rubinstein, pianist.

National Academy of Recording Arts and Sciences. *Grammy Awards: Record of the Year,* "Hotel California," The Eagles. *Album of the Year,* "Rumours," Fleetwood Mac. *Song of the Year* (tie), "Evergreen," Barbra Streisand and Paul Williams; "You Light Up My Life," Joe Brooks. *Best New Artist of the Year,* Debby Boone. *Best Jazz Vocal Performance,* "Look to the Rainbow," Al Jarreau. *Best Jazz Performance, Solo,* "The Giants," Oscar Peterson. *Group,* "The Phil Woods Six – Live from the Showboat," Phil Woods. *Big Band,* "Prime Time," Count Basie and his Orchestra. *Best Pop Vocal Performance, Female,* "Evergreen," Barbra Streisand. *Male,*

"Handy Man," James Taylor. *Duo, Group, or Chorus,* "How Deep Is Your Love," The Bee Gees. *Best Pop Instrumental Recording,* "Star Wars," London Symphony Orchestra, John Williams. *Best Rhythm and Blues Vocal Performance, Female,* "Don't Leave Me This Way," Thelma Houston. *Male,* "Unmistakably Lou," Lou Rawls. *Instrumental,* "Q," Brothers Johnson. *Best Rhythm and Blues Song,* "You Make Me Feel Like Dancing," Leo Sayer, Vini Poncia. *Best Country Vocal Performance, Female,* "Don't It Make My Brown Eyes Blue," Crystal Gayle. *Male,* "Lucille," Kenny Rogers. *Duo or Group,* "Heaven's Just A Sin Away," The Kendalls. *Instrumental, Country Instrumentalist of the Year,* Hargus (Pig) Robbins. *Best Country Song,* "Don't It Make My Brown Eyes Blue," Richard Leigh. *Album of the Year, Classical,* "Concert of the Century," with various artists. *Best Classical Orchestral Performance,* Mahler: *Symphony No. 9,* the Chicago Symphony Orchestra, Carlo Maria Giulini conducting. *Best Opera Recording,* Gershwin: *Porgy and Bess,* the Houston Grand Opera. *Best Choral Performance, Classical,* Verdi: *Requiem,* Chicago Symphony Orchestra and Chorus, Sir Georg Solti conducting; Margaret Hillis, choral director. *Best Chamber Music Performance,* Schoenberg: *Quartets for Strings,* Juilliard Quartet. *Best Instrumental Solo, with Orchestra,* Vivaldi: *The Four Seasons,* the London Philharmonic Orchestra, Itzhak Perlman, conductor and violinist. *Best Classical Performance, Solo,* Beethoven: *Sonata for Piano No. 18;* Schumann: *Fantasiestücke,* Arthur Rubinstein, pianist. *Best Classical Vocal Soloist Performance,* Bach: *Arias,* Janet Baker.

National Academy of Television Arts and Sciences. *Emmy Awards: Best Comedy Series,* "All in the Family." *Lead Actress, Comedy Series,* Jean Stapleton, "All in the Family." *Lead Actor, Comedy Series,* Carroll O'Connor, "All in the Family." *Best Drama Series,* "The Rockford Files." *Lead Actress, Drama Series,* Sada Thompson, "Family." *Lead Actor, Drama Series,* Edward Asner, "Lou Grant." *Best Limited Series,* "Holocaust." *Lead Actress, Limited Series,* Meryl Streep, "Holocaust." *Lead Actor, Limited Series,* Michael Moriarty, "Holocaust." *Continuing or Single Performance by a Supporting Actor in Variety or Music,* Tim Conway, "The Carol Burnett Show." *Continuing or Single Performance by a Supporting Actress in Variety or Music,* Gilda Radner, "NBC's Saturday Night Live." *Best Comedy-Variety or Music Show,* "The Muppet Show." *Best Special, Comedy or Drama, The Gathering.*

New York Drama Critics Circle Awards. *Best Play, Da* by Hugh Leonard. *Best Musical, Ain't Misbehavin',* music and lyrics by Thomas (Fats) Waller, directed by Richard Maltby, Jr.

Journalism Awards

American Society of Magazine Editors. *National Magazine Awards: Specialized Journalism, Scientific American,* for an article on microelectronic memory chips. *Essays and Criticism, Esquire* magazine, for Michael Herr's "High on War." *Fiction, The New Yorker,* for Mavis Gallant's "Potter" and Peter Taylor's "In the Miro District." *Public Service, Mother Jones,* for Mark Dowie's "Pinto Madness." *Reporting, The New Yorker,* for John McPhee's six-part series on Alaska. *Service to the Individual, Newsweek,* for "The Graying of America." *Visual Excellence, Architectural Digest.*

Loeb Foundation. *Gerald Loeb Awards,* for distinguished business and financial writing, Hobart Rowen, *The Washington Post;* Harold Chucker, *The Minneapolis Star;* Paul Steiger, Robert Rosenblatt, Ronald Soble, Murray Seeger, and Sam Jameson, *The Los Angeles Times.*

Long Island University. *George Polk Memorial Awards,* Carey McWilliams, retired editor of *The Nation,* for professional integrity; Red Smith, *The New York Times* sports columnist, for analyzing a "major American industry with candor and grace." **News Photography,** Eddie Adams, Associated Press, for pictures of Vietnam refugees. **Foreign Reporting,** Robert C. Toth, *The Los Angeles Times,* for coverage of the treatment of dissidents in Russia. **National Reporting,** Walter Pincus, *The Washington Post,* for stories on U.S. Department of Defense plans to develop the neutron bomb. **Local Reporting,** Len Ackland, *The Des Moines Register,* for articles on redlining – the refusal by certain banks to give mortgages in rundown urban areas. **Magazine Reporting,** Daniel Laing, *The New Yorker,* for an analysis of current German attitudes toward the Nazi Third Reich. **Radio and Television Reporting,** Barry Lando, producer of CBS's "60 Minutes" for investigative reporting. **Local Radio and Television,** John Stossel, WCBS-TV, for news on consumer abuse. **Science,** *The New England Journal of Medicine,* for medical coverage. **Criticism,** Peter S. Prescott, *Newsweek,* for book reviews. **Editorial Cartoons,** Jeffrey K. MacNelly, *The Richmond News Leader,* for astuteness and craftsmanship.

The Newspaper Guild. Heywood Broun Award, Fredric N. Tulsky and David Phelps, the *Jackson* (Miss.) *Clarion-Ledger,* for exposing police brutality and the maladministration of justice by the police-court system.

The Society of Professional Journalists, Sigma Delta Chi. Newspaper Awards: General Reporting, Fredric N. Tulsky and David Phelps, *The Jackson* (Miss.) *Clarion-Ledger,* for a series of articles on police harassment of the poor, particularly blacks, in the community. **Editorial Writing,** Desmond Stone, *The Rochester* (N.Y.) *Democrat & Chronicle,* for a series of 23 editorials called "The Violence Around Us" that covered aspects of social violence in such areas as police procedures, prisons, and private life. **Washington Correspondence,** Gaylord Shaw, *The Los Angeles Times,* for reporting on the hazards of dams throughout the United States. **Foreign Correspondence,** Robert Toth, *The Los Angeles Times,* for his reporting on the dissident movement in Russia and accounts of his own arrest by the Russian intelligence agency, KGB, for receiving "state secrets." **News Photography,** Eddie Adams, the Associated Press, for a series of pictures of a fishing boat filled with Vietnamese refugees. **Editorial Cartooning,** Don Wright, *The Miami News,* for a series of cartoons on a variety of subjects. **Public Service in Newspaper Journalism,** *The Philadelphia Inquirer,* for its reporting of systematic police violence in Philadelphia. **Magazine Reporting,** John Conroy, free-lancer, for a series entitled "Mill Town" in *Chicago* magazine. **Public Service in Magazine Journalism,** *Mother Jones,* for documentation of the safety hazards involved in the mounting of the Ford Motor Company's Pinto gasoline tank. **Radio Reporting,** Paul McGonigle, KOY Radio, Phoenix, Ariz., for his coverage of a bank robbery and the seizing of hostages in Yarnell, Ariz. **Public Service in Radio Journalism,** WSGN-AM News, Birmingham, Ala., for its investigation of insurance fraud in Alabama. **Editorializing on Radio,** Jay Lewis, Alabama Information Network, for a series of reports on the misuse of state vehicles by state authorities. **Television Reporting,** KPIX-TV Eyewitness News Team, San Francisco, for coverage of the eviction of 45 elderly residents of the International Hotel in the city's Chinatown area. **Public Service in Television Journalism,** KOOL-TV, Phoenix, Ariz., for its broadcast of the documentary *Water: Arizona's Most Precious Resource.* **Editorializing on Television,** Rich Adams, WTOP-TV, Washington, D.C., for an editorial entitled "Changes Needed in Housing Care Statutes" dealing with unsatisfactory medical care, particularly for the poor and elderly. **Research in Journalism,** Peter Braestrup, Sabillasville, Md., for his two-volume book, *Big Story: How the American Press and Television Reported and Interpreted the Crises of Tet 1968 in Vietnam and Washington.* **Public Service: Special Award,** Investigative Reporters and Editors, Incorporated, for a six-month investigation of corruption in

Arizona, prompted by the 1976 murder of Don Bolles, a reporter for *The Arizona Republic.* The result was a 23-part series called "The Legacy of Murder: The Arizona Story." **Edward Weintal Awards,** for distinguished reporting on American foreign policy and diplomacy, Flora Lewis and C. L. Sulzberger, *The New York Times;* Keyes Beech, the *Chicago Daily News;* and Eric Sevareid, CBS News.

Literature Awards

Academy of American Poets. Lamont Poetry Selection Award, Ai, for her collection of poems, *Killing Floor.* **Walt Whitman Award,** Karen Snow, for her first book of poems, *Wonders.* **Harold Morton Landon Award for Translation,** Galway Kinnell for *The Poems of François Villon* and Howard Norman for *The Wishing Bone Cycle: Narrative Poems of the Swampy Cree Indians.*

American Library Association. Beta Phi Mu Award, for distinguished services to education for librarianship, Frances E. Henne, librarian and educator. **Caldecott Medal,** Peter Spier, for *Noah's Ark.* **Francis Joseph Campbell Citation,** for outstanding contribution to the advancement of library service to the blind, Richard Kinney and the Hadley School for the Blind. **Melvil Dewey Medal,** for creative professional achievement of a high order, Frederick G. Kilgour, executive director, Ohio College Library Center, Columbus. **Joseph W. Lippincott Award,** for distinguished service in the profession of librarianship, Henry R. Drennan, senior program officer for research, Office of Libraries and Learning Resources, U.S. Office of Education, Washington, D.C. **Newbery Medal,** for the most distinguished contribution to children's literature, Katherine Paterson, for *Bridge to Terabithia.*

Association of American Publishers. National Book Awards; Biography, W. Jackson Bate, for *Samuel Johnson.* **Contemporary Thought,** Gloria Emerson, for *Winners and Losers: Battles, Retreats, Gains, Losses, and Ruins from a Long War.* **Fiction,** Mary Lee Settle, for *Blood Tie.* **History,** David McCullough, for *The Path Between the Seas: The Creation of the Panama Canal, 1870-1914.* **Poetry,** Howard Nemerov, for *The Collected Poems.* **Children's Literature,** Judith and Herbert Kohl, for *The View from the Oak: The Private Worlds of Other Creatures.* **Translation,** Richard and Clara Winston, for their translation of Uwe George's *In the Deserts of This Earth.*

Canadian Library Association. English Medal Award, for the best English-language Canadian children's book, *Garbage Delight,* to Dennis Lee. **Amelia Frances Howard-Gibbon Medal,** for the best illustrated children's book, *The Loon's Necklace,* Elizabeth Cleaver.

Columbia University. Bancroft Prizes, for books of exceptional merit and distinction in American history and diplomacy, Alfred D. Chandler, Jr., Harvard University, for *The Invisible Hand: The Managerial Revolution in American Business,* and Morton J. Horwitz, Harvard University, for *The Transformation of American Law: 1780-1860.*

Ernest Hemingway Award, for the best first novel by an American writer, Darcy O'Brien, for *A Way of Life, Like Any Other.*

National Arts Club. Medal of Honor for Literature, Saul Bellow, for his life's work.

Seal Books. First Novel Award, Aritha van Herk of Alberta, Canada, for *Judith.*

University of Chicago. Harriet Monroe Poetry Award, to an American poet of distinction or of distinguished promise, Richard Wilbur.

Nobel Prizes. See NOBEL PRIZES.

Public Service Awards

Aspen Institute for Humanistic Studies. Statesman-Humanist Award, Alberto Lleras Camargo, twice president of Colombia, for his "lifelong commitment to the principles of freedom."

Association for the Promotion of Humor in International Affairs. *Noble Prize,* John Kenneth Galbraith, for his "North Dakota Plan." See PERSONALITIES.

Boys' Clubs of America. *Herbert Hoover Award,* for outstanding service to youth, to DeWitt Wallace, founder of *Reader's Digest,* and J. Paul Lyet, chairman and chief executive officer of Sperry Rand Corporation.

Louis Dembitz Brandeis Medal, Edward M. Levi, president emeritus of the University of Chicago and former United States attorney general, for distinguished legal services.

Department of Energy. *Award for Exceptional Public Service,* Dennis Hayes, chairman of Solar Action.

Order of Victory, Leonid I. Brezhnev, chairman, Presidium of the Supreme Soviet, for his contributions in World War II.

Pahlavi Environment Prize, Thor Heyerdahl, Norwegian explorer and ethnologist, and Mohamed El-Kassas, Egyptian plant ecologist.

Pulitzer Prizes

Journalism. *Public Service,* The Philadelphia Inquirer, and two of its reporters, William K. Marimow and Jonathan Neumann, for reports exposing the abuse of police powers by the Philadelphia police. *General Local Reporting,* Richard Whitt, *The Louisville (Ky.) Courier-Journal,* for coverage of the Beverly Hills Supper Club fire in Southgate, Ky., on May 28, 1977, which killed 164 persons. *Special Local Reporting,* Anthony R. Dolan, *The Stamford* (Conn.) *Advocate,* for reports on municipal corruption in Stamford. *National Reporting,* Gaylord Shaw, *The Los Angeles Times,* for reports on unsafe dams that led the government to release funds for dam inspection. *International Reporting,* Henry Kamm, *The New York Times,* for articles on the "boat people," refugees from Vietnam, influencing the U.S. government to admit more refugees. *Editorial Writing,* Meg Greenfield, *The Washington Post,* for a wide range of editorials. *Spot News Photography,* John Blair, free-lance, Evansville, Ind., for a photo of an Indianapolis broker being held hostage by an armed man. *Feature Photography,* J. Ross Baughman, Associated Press, for pictures of guerrilla prisoners held by Rhodesian soldiers. *Editorial Cartooning,* Jeffrey K. MacNelly, *The Richmond News Leader,* for a number of cartoons. *Distinguished Commentary,* William Safire, *The New York Times,* for his columns on former Budget Director Bert Lance. *Distinguished Criticism,* Walter Kerr, *The New York Times,* for the "whole body of his critical work" on the theater. *Special Citation,* Richard L. Strout, for his 56-year career at *The Christian Science Monitor,* and his years as a columnist with *The New Republic.*

Letters. *Biography,* Walter Jackson Bate, Harvard University, for *Samuel Johnson. Drama,* Donald L. Coburn, for *The Gin Game. Fiction,* James Alan McPherson, University of Virginia, for his book of short stories, *Elbow Room. General Nonfiction,* Carl Sagan, Cornell University, for *The Dragons of Eden. History,* Alfred D. Chandler, Jr., for *The Invisible Hand: The Managerial Revolution in American Business. Music,* Michael Colgrass, for *Déjà Vu for Percussion Quartet and Orchestra. Poetry,* Howard Nemerov, for his *Collected Poems. Special Citation,* E. B. White, writer, for his life's work.

Science and Technology Awards

American Association for the Advancement of Science (AAAS). *AAAS-Rosensteil Award in Oceanographic Science,* Henry M. Stommel, professor of oceanography, Massachusetts Institute of Technology.

American Chemical Society, *Arthur C. Cope Award,* Orville E. Chapman, professor of chemistry, University of California, Los Angeles.

American Chemical Society, Chicago Section. *Willard Gibbs Medal,* William O. Baker, president, Bell Telephone Laboratories.

American Institute of Physics. *Dannie Heineman Prize for Mathematical Physics,* Elliot H. Lieb, Princeton University. *Davisson-Germer Prize,* Vernon Hughes, Yale University.

Columbia University. *Vetlesen Prize,* J. Tuzo Wilson, director general, Ontario Science Center, Toronto. *Louisa Gross Horwitz Prize,* David H. Hubel and Torsten N. Wiesel, Harvard University; Vernon B. Mountcastle, Johns Hopkins University.

Franklin Institute. *Franklin Medal,* Cyril M. Harris, acoustical engineer. *Albert A. Michelson Medal,* Albert V. Crewe, professor of physics, University of Chicago.

Gairdner Foundation. *Gairdner Awards,* K. Frank Austen, Harvard Medical School; Sir Cyril A. Clarke, Nuffield Unit of Medical Genetics, Liverpool, England; Jean Dausset, Institute for Research on Blood Diseases, Paris, France; Henry G. Friesen, The University of Manitoba, Winnipeg; Victor A. McKusick, The Johns Hopkins School of Medicine, Baltimore.

Geological Society of America. *Penrose Medal,* Robert M. Garrels, Northwestern University, Evanston, Ill. *Arthur L. Day Medal,* Samuel Epstein, California Institute of Technology, Pasadena.

Albert and Mary Lasker Foundation. *Albert Lasker Medical Research Award,* Hans W. Kosterlitz, University of Aberdeen, Scotland, and John Hughes, the Imperial College of Science and Technology, London. *Albert Lasker Clinical Medical Research Award,* Michael Heidelberger, New York University School of Medicine; Robert Austrian, University of Pennsylvania School of Medicine; Emil C. Gotslich, Rockefeller University, New York City. *Special Public Service Award,* Elliot L. Richardson, former secretary of Health, Education, and Welfare; Theodore Cooper, former director of the National Heart, Lung, and Blood Institute.

National Medal of Science, Morris Cohen, Massachusetts Institute of Technology, for research in metallurgy; Kurt O. Friedrichs, New York University, for mathematical research on the theory of flight; Peter C. Goldmark, Goldmark Communications Corporation, for contributions to communications sciences (posthumous); Samuel A. Goudsmit, University of Nevada, for the discovery of electron spin as the source of a new quantum number; Roger C. L. Guillemin, Salk Institute for Biological Studies, for showing the presence of a new class of brain hormones; Herbert S. Gutowsky, University of Illinois, for important studies in nuclear magnetic resonance spectroscopy; Erwin W. Mueller, Pennsylvania State University, for the invention of the field-emission, field-ion, and atom-probe microscopes (posthumous); Keith R. Porter, University of Colorado, for his work in electron microscopy; Efraim Racker, Cornell University, for work on oxidative and photosynthetic energy in living cells; Frederick D. Rossini, Rice University, for studies in chemical thermodynamics; Verner F. Suomi, University of Wisconsin, for research in meteorology; Henry Taube, Stanford University, for studies on the reaction mechanisms in inorganic chemistry and nitrogen fixation; George E. Uhlenbeck, Rockefeller University, for the discovery of electron spin as the source of a new quantum number; Hassler Whitney, Institute for Advanced Studies in Princeton, N.J., for founding the study of differential topology; Edward O. Wilson, Harvard University, for studies of insect societies.

Pepperdine University. *Tyler Ecology Award,* Russell E. Train, president, World Wildlife Fund. Edward G. Nash

BAHAMAS. See WEST INDIES.

BAHRAIN. See MIDDLE EAST.

BAKKE CASE. See SUPREME COURT OF THE UNITED STATES.

BALLET. See DANCING.

BALTIMORE appeared on two federal government lists of cities with severe social and economic problems in 1978. A study of 39 cities, released by the Congressional Budget Office on September 10, listed Baltimore as a "high-need city" in terms of a "composite measure of social need," based on such factors as unemployment and per capita income.

Baltimore also made the list of cities that qualified as "distressed areas" under President Jimmy Carter's proposed urban program. The list was released on May 26 by the U.S. Department of the Treasury. Baltimore's inclusion meant that, over the last five years, its rate of increase in employment and population was below the national average, its unemployment rate was above the national average, and the increase in its per capita income was below average.

Living Costs in the Baltimore area rose 6.6 per cent and the cost of food alone rose 7.4 per cent during the year ending in May. Bureau of the Census statistics revealed that wage earners and clerical workers had to contend with an overall 7.4 per cent cost-of-living increase during that period.

A Census Bureau report released in the spring placed Baltimore 22nd among U.S. cities in terms of crowded living conditions, with a density of 951 persons per square mile (367 per square kilometer). A report issued in November indicated that area population fell 6.8 per cent from 1970 to 1976.

Baltimore's Coldspring, a development subsidized by the city, features handsome, low-priced town houses to attract middle-income families.

A Civil Aeronautics Board (CAB) judge ruled on August 23 that World Airways, a West Coast charter airline, should be allowed to start scheduled transcontinental flights between Baltimore and Oakland and Ontario-Long Beach in California for a fare of only $99. The case was awaiting final action by the full CAB at year's end.

Crime Rate. A Federal Bureau of Investigation report released on October 18 ranked Baltimore fourth among the nation's metropolitan areas in the number of violent crimes reported to police in 1977. The report defined violent crime as murder, rape, robbery, and aggravated assault.

A Roman Catholic priest, Guido John Carcich, a former chief fund-raiser for the Pallottine Fathers, pleaded guilty on May 9 to "fraudulent intent" to misappropriate funds. Irregularities had been uncovered in an audit ordered by the Baltimore Roman Catholic archdiocese. Carcich was accused of sending less than 3 per cent of more than $20 million raised for overseas missions to other countries, and of using some of the funds to help pay the divorce costs of former Maryland Governor Marvin Mandel.

James H. Watkins, Baltimore's former deputy police chief, was convicted of official misconduct in November. Watkins allegedly failed to arrest a drug dealer and also filed false reports to mislead investigators. James M. Banovetz

See also CITY. In WORLD BOOK, see BALTIMORE.

BANGLADESH seemed to bear out in 1978 a gloomy forecast made four years earlier. Back in 1974, a secret World Bank report predicted that the most Bangladesh could hope for in the future was "to substitute stagnation for decline."

The 1978 food grain harvest reached 13.4 million short tons (12 million metric tons), 1.5 million short tons (1.4 million metric tons) better than in 1977. Sales of jute, the major export item, set a record of more than 500,000 short tons (454,000 metric tons). In addition, President Ziaur Rahman had restored law and order. But all these achievements merely substituted stagnation for decline.

Bangladesh still needed more than 1.5 million short tons of imported grain to ensure that each of its 84.4 million citizens would receive 15.5 ounces (434 grams) of cereals per day. Other countries provided just over $1 billion in annual aid, some 70 per cent of the nation's budget. So Bangladesh survived, but its basic condition did not improve.

Western studies showed that 60 per cent of the nation's families did not have enough to eat. About 60 million persons lived on a per-capita income of less than 25 cents per day, and the population was increasing rapidly. The gap between the rich and the poor kept widening, and the old-time landed barons in the countryside were joined by a new elite of army and police officers and senior bureaucrats who had invested in land.

A woman wearing the traditional Muslim
veil casts her ballot in June in the first
presidential election held in Bangladesh.

Strongman. Presiding over this scene was Rahman, popularly known as General Zia, who came to power in an army-led coup d'état in November 1975. He acquired electoral legitimacy on June 3, 1978, by winning the presidency in a national election with the backing of a coalition dominated by Muslim conservatives.

Under martial law, Zia had reduced corruption, nepotism, lawlessness, shortages, and prices. But the press was muzzled, opposition political activity was rigidly restricted, and the jails were packed with 30,000 political prisoners.

Hopes and Problems. Zia's economic plans emphasized developing the country's only major resource, natural gas, with aid from abroad. He also sought grants to expand wheat acreage, power-transmission lines, and a steel plant in Chittagong. The biggest benefactor, the United States, pressed Zia to cut the birth rate, but the Muslim priests blocked a family-planning program.

An unexpected blow came in April when some 200,000 Muslims fled from Burma into Bangladesh. Zia's government supplied them with a lean ration on the condition that the grain would be replaced by the United Nations – which provided emergency grants – and that the refugees would eventually go back to Burma. See BURMA.   Mark Gayn

See also ASIA (Facts in Brief Table.) In WORLD BOOK, see BANGLADESH.

BANKS AND BANKING. United States monetary authorities moved on Nov. 1, 1978, to halt the dollar's plunge and slow the inflationary spiral. The Federal Reserve System's Board of Governors authorized Federal Reserve Banks to raise the discount rate charged on loans to member banks from 8.5 to 9.5 per cent, an all-time high. And the U.S. Department of the Treasury arranged a $30-billion standby credit with other governments to permit it to bolster the sagging dollar. When the United States acted, interest rates were high and still rising as credit demands soared in a boom environment. There was a high level of economic activity, inflation was accelerating, and the dollar was depreciating rapidly in value against other currencies, particularly the West German Deutsche mark, the Japanese yen, and the Swiss franc, all from countries with low inflation rates compared with the United States and Canada.

Savings and Checking Accounts. The Federal Reserve Board authorized member banks to make automatic transfers from savings to checking accounts that would otherwise be overdrawn. This regulation was simultaneously extended to all insured banks by the Federal Deposit Insurance Corporation (FDIC), which insures the deposits of 97 per cent of the banks in the United States. The regulation effectively permitted payment of interest on deposits that can be withdrawn by check, which had been prohibited since the 1930s. The Federal Home Loan Bank Board, which regulates insured savings and loan institutions (S&L's), proposed "payment order accounts." Holders could write payment orders merchants would cash at S&L's.

Many banks offered automatic transfer accounts at the authorized 5 per cent maximum-interest rate. Most imposed minimum-balance requirements or charges on each transfer from a savings account, or both. Interest-rate ceilings for banks and thrift institutions ranged from zero on checking accounts to 8 per cent on long-term certificates of deposit. Certificates in denominations of $100,000 or more were not subject to a ceiling. And, if issued by commercial banks, variable-rate savings deposits in denominations of $10,000 to $100,000 and at least six months maturity had ceilings at the six-month U.S. Treasury bill rate and 0.25 per cent more if issued by S&L's or mutual savings banks.

Interest on Checking Accounts. Even without the new regulation, the prohibitions against paying interest on demand deposits had been breaking down. For example, many banks and thrift institutions permitted telephone transfers from savings to checking accounts. In New England, financial institutions had been authorized experimentally to issue special interest-bearing accounts from which Negotiable Orders of Withdrawal could be made. New York banks were granted this authority in 1978.

In spite of these measures, demand deposits paid poor returns on the average, compared with other

This scene in a broker's office in Frankfurt, West Germany, typifies the feverish activity triggered by the declining U.S. dollar.

federal-tax cut, but it was expected to be more than offset by increases in the Social Security tax, and by inflation putting taxpayers in higher tax brackets.

Monetary Growth. Federal Reserve chairmen had testified before congressional committees that the Fed was aiming at M1 monetary growth in the range of 4 to 6.5 per cent annually in 1977 and 1978, but actual growth averaged more than 8 per cent. Such a comparatively high monetary growth rate had a twofold effect on interest rates.

First, investors interpreted above-target monetary growth as an indication that the Federal Reserve would have to allow interest rates to rise by purchasing fewer securities. Attempts by investors to sell securities in anticipation of rising rates forced the rates up immediately.

Second, rapid monetary and bank-credit growth fueled increases in spending and inflation. And inflation, the major factor linked to the year's high interest rates, accelerated from 6 per cent in 1977 to between 7 and 8 per cent. A high inflation rate made interest rates high in dollar terms but low in real terms. Inflation depreciates the purchasing power of money over the period of a loan, so there is less real value in terms of purchasing power repaid by borrowers. Since the dollar was depreciating in value at more than 7 per cent in 1978, interest rates at 10 per cent translated into only 3 per cent in real terms. It

assets. This was a factor in demand deposits losing ground to other financial assets over the 1960s and 1970s. They fell from about 30 per cent of liquid assets in 1958 to less than 15 per cent in 1978. In the interim, interest rates on short-term liquid assets more than doubled while the ceiling rate on demand deposits remained at zero. Liquid assets include *M1* money balances (currency and demand deposits) as well as interest-bearing time and savings deposits held by banks and thrift institutions, U.S. savings bonds, and other short-term securities. Thrift institutions, such as S&L's, deal principally with time or savings deposits.

Inflation. Although interest rates rose during most of 1978, paradoxically, monetary policy was highly expansionary. The Federal Reserve purchased large amounts of U.S. government securities, adding almost $20 billion to its $100-billion portfolio of 1977. Such open-market purchases have the effect of financing part of the federal government's deficit by money issue. The deficit was nearly $50 billion in the fiscal year ending Sept. 30, 1978. The balance of the deficit had to be financed by issuing government securities to other buyers. This had the effect of driving up interest rates. As part of the anti-inflation program President Jimmy Carter announced in October, the Administration planned to cut the deficit by $10 billion in fiscal 1979 and $10 billion more in fiscal 1980. Congress passed an $18-billion

Arthur F. Burns, left, retiring chairman of the Federal Reserve Board, greets his successor, G. William Miller, and Mrs. Miller.

was no surprise in such a situation that lenders demanded to be compensated for high expected inflation, and the demand for credit was sustained by borrowers who were willing to pay high nominal interest rates for funds. The prime rate on loans to preferred borrowers from banks was advanced 14 times to a level of 11.75 per cent and the Federal funds rate was 10.3 per cent at year-end. The Federal funds rate is the interest rate on overnight loans of bank reserves—the rate Federal Reserve open-market operations in the government securities market seek to control.

Only 40 per cent of the more than 14,000 commercial banks in the United States are members of the Federal Reserve System, though member banks tend to be large and account for over 70 per cent of total commercial bank deposits. Nevertheless, their market share has been eroded. In 1950, there were about as many nonmember as member banks, and the members had 85 per cent of deposits.

Member banks are entitled to a variety of services from the Federal Reserve, such as loans at the discount rate, free check collections, and telegraphic transfers of securities and funds. But membership also entails costs, and the cash-reserve requirements are tougher than those imposed by state regulators on nonmember banks. In addition, small banks prefer to do their wholesale banking with correspondent banks with Federal Reserve services.

The Federal Reserve proposed in July that all banks insured by the FDIC—and almost all are—become member banks. The proposal, which won approval of the U.S. House of Representatives Banking Committee, would eliminate requirements against demand deposits at small banks but charge for services that are now free. Also, for the first time, member banks would be allowed to count balances with correspondents as legal reserves. The correspondents would simply pass the funds on to the Federal Reserve. Since required reserve ratios would be lowered for all banks on the average under the proposal, the Federal Reserve would have to sell securities in the open market to offset the effect on money and credit markets. The result, in effect, would transfer earning assets to banks in place of non-earning cash previously required. The Federal Reserve could also consider paying interest on cash reserves as a membership inducement.

President Jimmy Carter's appointment of G. William Miller to replace Arthur F. Burns as chairman of the Federal Reserve Board was confirmed by the U.S. Senate on March 3, 1978 (see MILLER, G. WILLIAM). Nancy H. Teeters, an economist, was also appointed to the seven-person board and became its first woman member. William G. Dewald

See also ECONOMICS; Section One, FOCUS ON THE ECONOMY. In WORLD BOOK, see BANKS AND BANKING.

BARBADOS. See WEST INDIES.

BASEBALL. The New York Yankees repeated in 1978. They repeated everything. As in 1976 and 1977, they won the American League pennant. As in 1977, they won the World Series from the Los Angeles Dodgers. And as in 1977, they won despite almost endless turmoil involving their manager, Billy Martin; their principal owner, George Steinbrenner; and their slugger, Reggie Jackson.

There was one different twist in 1978. Martin quit as manager on July 24 with 10 weeks left in the season and the Yankees 10½ games out of first place. Bob Lemon, fired about four weeks earlier by the Chicago White Sox, replaced Martin, calmed everyone, and made the Yankees winners.

In years past, the volatile Martin was fired as manager by the Minnesota Twins, Detroit Tigers, and Texas Rangers. He made each team a winner, but he always antagonized the front office. He had the same problem with the Yankees in 1977, when he bickered constantly with Steinbrenner and Jackson and almost had a fistfight with Jackson.

Then on July 17, 1978, with a man on base against the Kansas City Royals, Martin ordered Jackson on three successive pitches to hit away rather than bunt. Jackson bunted three times unsuccessfully. After the game, the Yankees suspended Jackson for five days.

When Jackson returned to the Yankees on July 23, Martin was still simmering. He talked to sports

Former batting star Tommy Holmes congratulates Pete Rose after Rose hit safely in his 38th straight game. Rose's streak ended at 44 games.

writers about Jackson, who earned almost $600,000 a year, and Steinbrenner, who once pleaded no contest to federal charges of making illegal political contributions.

"The two of them deserve each other," Martin said. "One's a born liar, the other's convicted."

The next day, on a Kansas City hotel mezzanine, a tearful Martin read a resignation statement at an impromptu news conference. He said in part, "I owe it to my health and my mental well-being to resign."

There was an O. Henry twist to come. On July 29, during Old-Timers' Day ceremonies at Yankee Stadium, the Yankees announced that Martin would return as manager in 1980. Lemon would become general manager when Martin returned. See Section One, FOCUS ON SPORTS.

The American League, meanwhile, had a pennant race. On July 19, the Boston Red Sox led the Yankees by 14 games. But the Red Sox lost 14 of 17 games in early September. The Yankees caught up, led by 3 1/2 games, then slipped a bit as the Red Sox won their last eight games.

The two teams ended the regular season tied for first place in the American League East with won-lost records of 99-63, the best in the major leagues. The Yankees won the one-game play-off on October 2 in Boston, 5-4. The winning pitcher was left-hander Ron Guidry, and the victory made his season record 25-3, the best in history for a 20-game winner.

Kansas City won its third straight American League West championship. Its pitching was strong as Dennis Leonard won 21 games; Paul Splittorff, 19; Larry Gura, 16; and rookie Rich Gale, 14. But the Yankees won the play-offs, 3 games to 1.

The National League West was expected to produce a battle between the Dodgers and the Cincinnati Reds, who had won five division titles, four pennants, and two World Series in the 1970s. The Reds took the division lead on August 6, then lost 15 of the next 21 games. The surprising San Francisco Giants made a strong run, but the Dodgers won 22 of the last 37 games and gained the division title by 2 1/2 games over the Reds. The Dodgers also set an all-time major-league home-attendance record of 3,347,845.

The Philadelphia Phillies and Pittsburgh Pirates staged their usual struggle in the National League East. Although their hitting was spotty, the Phillies led from June 23 on, and they clinched their third straight division title on the next-to-last day of the season. The Dodgers beat them, 3 games to 1, in the pennant play-offs.

The World Series. The Dodgers were favored in the 75th World Series. They dedicated it to Jim Gilliam, their long-time coach and former second

Final Standings in Major League Baseball

American League
Eastern Division

	W.	L.	Pct.	GB.
New York	100	63	.613	
Boston	99	64	.607	1
Milwaukee	93	69	.574	6 1/2
Baltimore	90	71	.559	9
Detroit	86	76	.531	13 1/2
Cleveland	69	90	.434	29
Toronto	59	102	.366	40

Western Division

	W.	L.	Pct.	GB.
Kansas City	92	70	.568	
California	87	75	.537	5
Texas	87	75	.537	5
Minnesota	73	89	.451	19
Chicago	71	90	.441	20 1/2
Oakland	69	93	.426	23
Seattle	56	104	.350	35

Offensive Leaders

Batting Average—Rod Carew, Minnesota	.333
Runs—Ron LeFlore, Detroit	126
Home Runs—Jim Rice, Boston	46
Runs Batted In—Jim Rice, Boston	139
Hits—Jim Rice, Boston	213
Stolen Bases—Ron LeFlore, Detroit	69

Leading Pitchers

Games Won—Ron Guidry, New York	25
Win Average—Ron Guidry, New York (25-3) (162 or more innings)	.893
Earned-Run Average—Ron Guidry, New York	1.74
Strikeouts—Nolan Ryan, California	260
Saves—Rich Gossage, New York	27

Awards
* Most Valuable Player—Jim Rice, Boston
* Cy Young—Ron Guidry, New York
* Rookie of the Year—Lou Whitaker, Detroit
† Manager of the Year—George Bamberger, Milwaukee

National League
Eastern Division

	W.	L.	Pct.	GB.
Philadelphia	90	72	.556	
Pittsburgh	88	73	.547	1 1/2
Chicago	78	83	.488	11
Montreal	76	86	.469	14
St. Louis	69	93	.426	21
New York	66	96	.407	24

Western Division

	W.	L.	Pct.	GB.
Los Angeles	95	67	.586	
Cincinnati	92	69	.571	2 1/2
San Francisco	89	73	.549	6
San Diego	84	78	.519	11
Houston	74	88	.457	21
Atlanta	69	93	.426	26

Offensive Leaders

Batting Average—Dave Parker, Pittsburgh	.334
Runs—Ivan DeJesus, Chicago	104
Home Runs—George Foster, Cincinnati	40
Runs Batted In—George Foster, Cincinnati	120
Hits—Steve Garvey, Los Angeles	202
Stolen Bases—Omar Moreno, Pittsburgh	71

Leading Pitchers

Games Won—Gaylord Perry, San Diego	21
Win Average—Gaylord Perry, San Diego (21-6) (162 or more innings)	.778
Earned-Run Average—Craig Swan, New York	2.43
Strikeouts—J. Rodney Richard, Houston	303
Saves—Rollie Fingers, San Diego	37

Awards
* Most Valuable Player—Dave Parker, Pittsburgh
* Cy Young—Gaylord Perry, San Diego
* Rookie of the Year—Bob Horner, Atlanta

* Selected by Baseball Writers Association of America.
† Selected by *The Sporting News.*

baseman, who died of a cerebral hemorrhage at age 49 on the eve of the series.

The Dodgers won the first two games, on their home field, 11-5 and 4-3. Then the series moved to New York City, where the Yankees won the three games, 5-1, 4-3 in 10 innings, and 12-2. They went back to Los Angeles, and the Yankees won there, 7-2, on October 17 to win the World Series, 4 games to 2. It was the first time a team had won four straight after having lost the first two games.

There were many Yankee heroes. Shortstop Bucky Dent, who batted .417, was voted Most Valuable Player. Brian Doyle, replacing the injured Willie Randolph at second base, batted .438. Rich Gossage, pitching in three games in relief, allowed only one hit in six innings. Graig Nettles made one sensational stop after another at third base.

Ron Cey, the Dodger third baseman, said, "They had better pitching, defense, and hitting. What else is there?" Bill Russell, the shortstop, batted .423 but fielded erratically. He said, "We couldn't get hits when we had runners on base. The Yankees could."

The Stars. Guidry led major-league pitchers in victories (25), winning percentage (.893), earned-run average (1.74), and shutouts (9), and he struck out 18 in one game. Jim Rice, the Red Sox outfielder-designated hitter, led in home runs (46), runs batted in (139), hits (213), triples (15), total bases (406), and slugging percentage (.600).

On May 5, Pete Rose, Cincinnati's 37-year-old third baseman, became the 13th player in major-league history to make 3,000 hits in a career. On July 31, Rose hit safely in his 44th straight game, tying the all-time National League record set by Wee Willie Keeler in 1897. After the season, Rose became a free agent. He signed a four-year, $3.2-million contract with the Phils in December. In November, the Reds fired manager George (Sparky) Anderson.

Rod Carew, the Minnesota Twins first baseman, batted .333 and won his second straight American League batting title, his sixth in seven years, and his seventh overall. Only Ty Cobb (12) and Honus Wagner (8) have won more. Carew, who earned $170,000 a year, said he would play out his option in 1979 because of racial slurs by Calvin Griffith, the Twins' owner. Right-hander Bob Forsch pitched a no-hit game on April 16 in beating the Phillies 5-0. Tom Seaver pitched his first no-hitter on June 16 when the Reds beat St. Louis 4-0. California Angels outfielder Lyman Bostock was shot to death on September 23 in Gary, Ind.

The Baseball Hall of Fame received three new members. Baseball writers elected Eddie Mathews, who played third base for the Braves and hit 512 home runs. The veterans committee chose Larry MacPhail, who headed the Reds, Brooklyn Dodgers, and Yankees, and Addie Joss, a Cleveland Indians' pitcher from 1902 to 1910.　　Frank Litsky

In WORLD BOOK, see BASEBALL.

BASKETBALL. The Washington Bullets, who did not win one of the four division titles during the regular season, became the National Basketball Association (NBA) champions in 1978. The University of Kentucky, heavily favored at the start of the season, became the college champion.

NBA Season. In the regular season, each of the 22 teams played 82 games from October 1977 to April 1978. The defending champion Portland Trail Blazers, Philadelphia 76ers, San Antonio Spurs, and Denver Nuggets won the division titles. They advanced to the play-offs with eight other teams, including the Bullets, second in their division, and the Seattle SuperSonics, third in their division.

Surprisingly, Washington and Seattle advanced to the finals. It was a major turnabout for Seattle, which won only five of its first 22 games. At that point, Lenny Wilkens replaced Bob Hopkins as coach, and he formed a starting team of relatively inexperienced players. Washington, coached by Dick Motta, finally started playing as a team, especially on defense.

The finals went the full seven games. Washington won the deciding game, 105-99, on June 7, snapping Seattle's 22-game winning streak on its home floor. Washington center Wes Unseld, who almost retired before the season because of chronic knee trouble, was voted the Most Valuable Player in the play-offs.

Washington Bullets' Bob Dandridge, right, eludes Seattle SuperSonics' Gus Williams, left, and John Johnson as Bullets win NBA title.

The Most Valuable Player during the regular season was Portland center Bill Walton. Walton helped the Trail Blazers win 50 of their first 60 games before he was sidelined by foot injuries. He returned for two play-off games before breaking an ankle. Later, he asked Portland to trade him, saying the Blazers had insisted he take painkillers and play despite injuries. When the 1978-1979 season began, he was still unable to play.

George Gervin of San Antonio won the scoring title with an average of 27.22 points per game to 27.15 for David Thompson of Denver. On the final afternoon of the regular season, Thompson apparently won the championship by scoring 73 points against Detroit. That night, Gervin passed him by scoring 63 points against New Orleans.

The all-star team consisted of Walton, Gervin, Thompson, Leonard (Truck) Robinson of New Orleans, and Julius Erving of Philadelphia. Kareem Abdul-Jabbar of the Los Angeles Lakers, the Most Valuable Player for five of his eight NBA seasons, was named to the second team.

Court Violence. Abdul-Jabbar was the key figure in the first of two violent incidents. In the season opener in Milwaukee on October 18, he punched Kent Benson, the Milwaukee Bucks center. The punch broke Abdul-Jabbar's right hand, and he was sidelined for seven weeks. Commissioner Lawrence O'Brien fined him $5,000.

The second incident happened on December 12 in Los Angeles. Kermit Washington of the Lakers, apparently thinking Rudy Tomjanovich of the Houston Rockets was about to punch him, threw a punch himself. Tomjanovich suffered a concussion, broken nose, double fracture of the jaw, and massive facial damage. He was hospitalized for 15 days and did not play the rest of the season.

O'Brien suspended Washington for 60 days and fined him $10,000, the largest such fine in sports history. Two weeks later, Los Angeles traded Washington to Boston. After the season, Boston sent him to the San Diego Clippers in a seven-man trade.

Team, Player Moves. The Clippers were an old team (the Buffalo Braves) with a new name and new home for the 1978-1979 season. The team was moved after the owners of the Braves and Boston Celtics had traded franchises, but not rosters.

There were other notable player shifts for the new season. The movers included Rick Barry from the Golden State Warriors to Houston and Marvin Webster from Seattle to the New York Knickerbockers. Both were free agents.

The College Season. The final wire-service polls were taken after the regular season. The Associated Press poll of writers and broadcasters placed Kentucky first; the University of California, Los Angeles (UCLA) second; DePaul, third; Michigan State, fourth; and Arkansas, fifth. The United Press International ratings by coaches showed Kentucky first;

National Basketball Association
Final Standings

Eastern Conference

Atlantic Division	W.	L.	Pct.
Philadelphia	55	27	.671
New York	43	39	.524
Boston	32	50	.390
Buffalo	27	55	.329
New Jersey	24	58	.293

Central Division			
San Antonio	52	30	.634
Washington	44	38	.537
Cleveland	43	39	.524
Atlanta	41	41	.500
New Orleans	39	43	.476
Houston	28	54	.341

Western Conference

Midwest Division	W.	L.	Pct.
Denver	48	34	.585
Milwaukee	44	38	.537
Chicago	40	42	.488
Detroit	38	44	.463
Kansas City	31	51	.373
Indiana	31	51	.373

Pacific Division			
Portland	58	24	.707
Phoenix	49	33	.598
Seattle	47	35	.573
Los Angeles	45	37	.549
Golden State	43	39	.524

Leading Scorers	G.	FG.	FT.	Pts.	Avg.
Gervin, San Antonio	82	864	504	2,232	27.22
Thompson, Denver	80	826	520	2,172	27.15
McAdoo, New York	79	814	469	2,097	26.5
Abdul-Jabbar, Los Angeles	62	663	274	1,600	25.8
Murphy, Houston	76	852	245	1,949	25.6
Westphal, Phoenix	80	809	396	2,014	25.2
Smith, Buffalo	82	789	443	2,021	24.6
Lanier, Detroit	63	622	298	1,542	24.5
Davis, Phoenix	81	786	387	1,959	24.2
King, New Jersey	79	798	313	1,909	24.2

College Champions

Conference	School
Atlantic Coast	North Carolina (regular season)
	Duke (ACC tournament)
Big Eight	Kansas (regular season)
	Missouri (Big 8 tournament)
Big Sky	Montana (regular season)
	Weber State (BSC tournament)
Big Ten	Michigan State
Eastern 8	Rutgers-Villanova (tie) (regular season)
	Villanova (E-8 tournament)
Ivy League	Pennsylvania
Metro	Florida State (regular season)
	Louisville (Metro tournament)
Mid-American	Miami (Ohio)
Missouri Valley	Creighton
Ohio Valley	East Tenn. State-Middle Tenn. (tie) (regular season)
	W. Kentucky (OVC tournament)
Pacific Coast Athletic	Fresno State-San Diego State (tie) (regular season)
	Fullerton State (PCAA tournament)
Pacific-8	UCLA
Southern	Appalachian State (regular season)
	Furman (SC tournament)
Southeastern	Kentucky
Southwest	Arkansas-Texas (tie) (regular season)
	Houston (SWC tournament)
West Coast Athletic	San Francisco
Western Athletic	New Mexico

College Tournament Champions

NCAA Division I	Kentucky
NCAA Division II	Cheyney State (Pa.)
NCAA Division III	North Park (Chicago)
NAIA	Grand Canyon (Ariz.)
NIT	Texas
NJCAA	Independence (Kans.)
AIAW (Women)	UCLA

UCLA, second; Marquette, third; New Mexico, fourth; and Michigan State, fifth.

The official champion was decided in the 32-team National Collegiate Athletic Association (NCAA) tournament. In the national semifinals on March 25 in St. Louis, Kentucky beat Arkansas, 64-59, and Duke held off Notre Dame, 90-86.

Kentucky was favored in the March 27 final because it was bigger, stronger, and more physical. Duke had the youngest team ever in an NCAA final, starting two freshmen, two sophomores, and one junior. Kentucky won, 94-88.

The national scoring champion for the second straight year was Freeman Williams of Portland (Ore.) State, who averaged 35.9 points per game. He finished his college career with 3,249 points.

The wire services chose Marquette guard Butch Lee as Player of the Year and Eddie Sutton of Arkansas as Coach of the Year. The consensus all-America team placed Lee and Phil Ford of North Carolina at guard, Mychal Thompson of Minnesota at center, and Larry Bird of Indiana State and David Greenwood of UCLA, both juniors, at forward.

In the Association of Intercollegiate Athletics for Women (AIAW) final, UCLA defeated Maryland, 90-74. Montclair (N.J.) State placed third, and its star, Carol Blazejowski, finished her college career with 3,199 points, an AIAW record.   Frank Litsky

In WORLD BOOK, see BASKETBALL.

BELGIUM. The government resigned three times in 1978. The coalition government of Prime Minister Leo Tindemans resigned first on June 15, when the coalition failed to agree on his economic austerity program for dealing with a threatened budget deficit of $3.34 billion. King Baudouin I rejected the resignation and asked Tindemans to resolve the issue. The coalition then backed Tindemans' request for power to cut public spending without Parliament's approval. In return, Tindemans offered to set a timetable for resolving the federalism issue – granting limited autonomy to the cultural regions of Brussels, Flanders, and Wallonia. The compromise ended the crisis on June 19.

However, when the Supreme Court found fault with some of the government's federalism proposals, Tindemans put the issue before Parliament. The coalition split again, and Tindemans resigned on October 11.

A coalition led by Paul vanden Boeynants took over on October 20. He resigned on December 18 after elections failed to resolve the federalism issue. The king asked him to stay until a new Cabinet could be formed. SEE VANDEN BOEYNANTS, PAUL.

Rescue in Zaire. Intervention in Zaire, a former Belgian colony in Africa, caused a government crisis in May. Belgian and French paratroops were dropped into Kolwezi, Zaire, on May 19 and 20 to evacuate 2,500 Europeans caught between rebels and government forces fighting in Zaire's Shaba province. But when the first European refugees reached Brussels on May 21, they said that quicker military intervention with greater secrecy would have saved many people from being massacred. President Mobutu Sese Seko of Zaire broke off diplomatic relations with Brussels on May 22, as Belgium started pulling out its paratroops. He said that Belgium had delayed answering Zaire's call for aid. See ZAIRE.

Nationalized Steel. The government on November 24 announced a plan to nationalize and trim Belgium's debt-ridden steel industry. By converting its loans to equity holdings, the government will have a 60 per cent ownership of the two largest steel groups, which are in Wallonia, and a 25 per cent holding in a Flanders plant. Then, if the trade unions approve, it will cut the payroll from 42,000 to 30,000 by closing plants. It will set aside $2 billion to pay industry debts, buy modern equipment, and promote new industry where it closes plants. Because most closings will be in Wallonia, the government promised similar help for Flanders' shipbuilding and textile industries.   Kenneth Brown

See also EUROPE (Facts in Brief Table). In WORLD BOOK, see BELGIUM.

BELIZE. See LATIN AMERICA.

BENIN. See AFRICA.

BHUTAN. See ASIA.

BIOCHEMISTRY. Ten scientists from the City of Hope National Medical Center in Duarte, Calif., and Genentech, Incorporated, in South San Francisco, Calif., made the first artificial human insulin on Aug. 9, 1978. Robert Crea and Keiichi Itakura of the City of Hope, David Goeddel and Dennis Kleid of Genentech, and six others used *recombinant DNA* techniques. In recombinant DNA, scientists break apart a chain of deoxyribonucleic acid (DNA), the material that contains the genetic code for transmitting inherited traits, insert genetic material from another type of cell, recombine the chain (put it back together again), and then put it into a cell like the one from which it came. The recombined genetic material becomes part of the cell and is duplicated when the cell duplicates itself.

The California scientists inserted synthetic genetic material that produces two types of protein chains that combine to form insulin into a laboratory strain of *Escherichia coli (E. coli),* a common bacterium found in the human intestine. The bacterium and its duplicates produced the two types of protein chains, which the scientists then separated from the bacteria and combined to form insulin. The major problem remaining for the scientists is to improve the chain-combining technique.

P-4 Lab. The National Institutes of Health (NIH) opened a laboratory in Frederick, Md., on March 17 to evaluate the dangers of recombinant DNA tech-

Scientist uses glove boxes at Frederick, Md.,
P-4 genetic-research laboratory, the first lab
used for the riskiest recombinant DNA research.

nology. The lab is the first to be approved for the P-4 category of containment, the strictest of four categories described in guidelines set by NIH, the federal government's main agency for conducting and supporting biomedical research. The scientists will first evaluate the danger that genetic material from an animal-cancer virus might cause cancer when incorporated into bacteria.

Rat Insulin. Howard Goodman and William Rutter of the University of California Medical School, San Francisco, had reported in June 1977 on their attempts to make rat proinsulin in bacteria. Proinsulin is produced by the pancreas, and enzymes then make it into insulin. The scientists synthesized the gene that produces proinsulin, then inserted it into a *plasmid* – a small, doughnut-shaped piece of genetic material – from an *E. coli* bacterium, and transferred the plasmid into an intact *E. coli*. The bacterium did not produce proinsulin, because the inserted gene had not been put where it could be "turned on"; that is, where the genetic factors inhibiting proinsulin synthesis could be removed.

Walter Gilbert and his colleagues at Harvard University in Cambridge, Mass., used a slightly different technique. They reported in August 1978 that they put the proinsulin-producing gene into a plasmid-carried gene that produces a protein that normally migrates into the *periplasmic space,* the space between the bacterium's outer wall and the plasma membrane. The Gilbert group hoped that the recombined plasmid would produce a stable, hybrid protein that they could extract from the periplasmic space.

The Harvard scientists obtained 48 *E. coli* bacteria whose plasmids carried the proinsulin gene. Only one secreted a hybrid protein that incorporated nearly all of the maximum obtainable proinsulin and two-thirds of the maximum obtainable protein. They extracted it, then used a protein-splitting enzyme to obtain the proinsulin. The amount of proinsulin is small – about 100 molecules per cell.

Ovalbumin Gene Cloned. Bert W. O'Malley, Savio Woo, and Achilles Dugaiczyk of Baylor College of Medicine in Houston *cloned* (produced genetically identical groups of) a hormone-regulated gene in *E. coli* in March. The cloned gene produced ovalbumin, which is found in egg whites, when under the control of steroid hormones from hens' oviducts. The Baylor group's cloning technique can multiply by 1 quadrillion (1 million billion) the amount of this gene available for study. Such a limited amount was previously available that scientists could not examine enough of it to see how it works. One question they now hope to answer is how hormones cause genes to produce substances in cells.

"Test-Tube" Babies. Two babies conceived outside the body of a woman were born in 1978. Louise Brown was born on July 25 to Lesley Brown and her husband, John, in Oldham, England. A girl was born on October 3 to Bela and Pravat Agarwal of Calcutta, India. See BIOLOGY (Close-Up).

David M. Rorvik, an American author, published *In His Image: The Cloning of a Man* in March, a book claiming to describe the duplication of an elderly millionaire by cloning. In this type of cloning, a surgical team would replace the nucleus of a human egg cell with the nucleus of a cell from the donor – in this case, the millionaire – then implant the egg cell in a human uterus. The cell would then develop into a baby who would be a duplicate of the donor as a baby. Rorvik claimed that he had seen the duplicate human, then a healthy 14-month-old, but he offered no proof. Scientists expressed strong doubts that human cloning was possible using current techniques.

Poison Probed. Anthony T. Tu and Jon B. Bjarnason of Colorado State University in Fort Collins reported in August that they had isolated and identified five poisonous compounds in rattlesnake venom. All five contain zinc, are relatively large compounds, and break down essential protein molecules in the membranes of blood vessels. Zinc is common in protein-destroying enzymes. When the scientists removed the zinc, the venom's protein destruction capacity declined greatly. Restoring the zinc restored the effect partially.   Earl A. Evans, Jr.

See also Section One, FOCUS ON SCIENCE. In WORLD BOOK, see BIOCHEMISTRY.

BIOLOGY. The scientists who discovered a "third life form" in 1977 identified two more members of it in 1978. The third form, in addition to animals and plants (in which many biologists include bacteria) is *archaebacteria,* far simpler than bacteria and probably an older form. Geneticist Carl R. Woese of the University of Illinois in Urbana-Champaign reported in 1977 on *methanogens,* which live on carbon dioxide and hydrogen. The new members are the *halophile,* which lives on sodium salts of calcium and magnesium; and the *thermoacidophile,* one type of which lives in an environment of 200° F. (93°C), far too hot for most organisms. The three members have common ribosomal and transfer ribonucleic acids, a peculiar cell-wall structure, common types of fats, and live in environments far different from those of the other two forms of life.

Thomas Langworthy of the University of South Dakota in Vermillion has isolated thermoacidophiles from a pool of hot water in Yellowstone National Park and from smoldering coal refuse in Kentucky. He intended to look for other archaebacteria in highly alkaline surroundings, because finding them would increase the likelihood that life exists in harsh environments elsewhere in the universe.

Instant Twins. The Institute of Animal Physiology in Cambridge, England, developed an egg-transfer technique that may boost meat production dramatically. Researchers at the institute took pieces of ovaries containing egg cells from recently slaughtered ewes and treated them with hormones to mature them. Within 24 hours, the cells were ready to fertilize. The scientists transferred them with a pipette into the oviducts of recently mated ewes, where they were fertilized along with these ewes' own eggs, increasing the number of offspring.

The cells can be used any time during their maturing stages. Previous experimenters had been able to transfer the cells at only a certain level of maturity. The technique had not succeeded in large animals. Used with cows, it would double calf production by providing twin births. It could be used to fertilize egg cells of pedigreed cows too old for breeding. The technique differs from that used for the "test-tube" babies born in 1978 in that the human mothers received their own eggs after the eggs were fertilized externally. See Close-Up.

Brain Transplant. West German scientists transferred memory from one animal to another by implanting a piece of brain. Ulla Martin, Herman Martin, and Martin Lindauer at the Institute of Zoology, University of Frankfurt, trained a group of bees to a feeding schedule by letting them fly out to a bowl of sugar water at a set time for a week. They then anesthetized each bee, decapitated it, removed the mushroom body portion of its brain, and implanted it into the *haemolymph* space near the brain of another bee. Haemolymph is the bee's equivalent of blood. A control group received the mushroom bodies of untrained bees, and another control group underwent surgery but received no implant.

After two or three days, the first group started to approach the food at the donor's feeding time. More than 60 per cent of their visits fell within that short period. Neither control group changed its feeding time. After the tests, the scientists found no nerve connection from a bee's brain to its implanted mushroom body. The haemolymph must have transmitted the signals that changed its feeding pattern.

Sleeping Evolution? A study by two University of Houston biologists shed light on the evolution of sleeping patterns. Studies of electroencephalograph (EEG) brain-wave patterns show two principal sleep patterns for mammals and birds. Passive sleep is characterized by slow waves; active sleep by fast waves, rapid eye movements, and other movements. B. F. Warner and J. E. Huggins wanted to learn whether mammals' and birds' sleep patterns originated in their common ancestors, the reptiles. They attached EEG equipment to crocodiles and let them sleep. The crocodiles showed no characteristic of active sleep. Because they have changed little in 180 million years, it is likely that active sleep evolved in another group of reptiles.   Jay Myers

In WORLD BOOK, see BIOLOGY.
BIRTHS. See CENSUS; POPULATION.
BLINDNESS. See HANDICAPPED.

Life has been found in cold Antarctic sandstone. The arrow points to algae, fungi, and microbes (dark line) living just under the rock's surface.

"Test-Tube" Babies

Louise Joy Brown, a blond, blue-eyed baby girl, was born on July 25, 1978, in the sleepy British mill town of Oldham. She was a healthy 5-pound 12-ounce (2.6-kilogram) infant, normal in all respects except one — Louise was the world's first "test-tube" baby. Her arrival gave birth to an international debate that was to occupy scientists, government commissions, religious leaders, and the public for months.

Louise's distinction as a "test-tube" baby refers to her conception in a laboratory vessel known as a Petri dish. An egg cell extracted from Louise's mother was fertilized by a sperm cell donated by her father. The egg cell was held in the Petri dish until it had divided into an eight-celled embryo, and then the embryo was reimplanted in her mother's uterus, where it developed.

This "test-tube" conception was the culmination of a series of events that had begun months earlier. Louise's parents, Lesley and John Brown, had tried for years to have a child, but Lesley Brown's Fallopian tubes, the tiny ducts leading from the ovaries to the uterus, were blocked. Although the ovaries continued to produce eggs, the eggs could not reach the uterus to become fertilized and develop further.

After an operation to open her Fallopian tubes failed, Lesley Brown was referred to gynecologist Patrick C. Steptoe, who, with his colleague, physiologist Robert G. Edwards, had made 100 or more attempts to implant an embryo developed outside the womb.

Steptoe used much the same procedure on Lesley Brown as he had on other patients. He first removed the obstructed Fallopian tubes, thus destroying any possibility of a natural conception. Then, he injected hormones to promote egg production. When a ripe egg developed, he removed it from the ovary with a suction instrument called a laparoscope and extracted it through a small incision in her abdomen.

The egg was placed in a Petri dish with samples of John Brown's sperm, and the egg and the sperm combined. Fertilization was accomplished with-

Louise Joy Brown

in 12 hours. The doctors then transferred the embryo to a special laboratory solution to help it grow. After 2½ days, the embryo was transplanted into Lesley Brown's uterus.

Edwards attributes the success of the Brown case after so many failures to the short period of time that elapsed before the embryo was implanted in the uterus. By allowing it to reach only the eight-cell stage, the doctors reduced risks to the embryo involved with further development outside the mother's body.

To the Browns, Louise was a nine-year dream come true. To others, she was an emissary from a "brave new world" in which human life could be engineered almost as readily as computer programs. Many childless couples viewed the process as one last chance to produce their own offspring, while a member of the British Parliament declared that it opened "Hitlerian" possibilities. "Test-tube" conception was approved by the Anglican and Jewish communities in Great Britain, but several Roman Catholic churchmen opposed it as "unnatural." The procedure also poses the same question as the abortion issue: at what stage of development should an embryo be considered a human being?

The scientific community was hesitant to endorse the procedure because Steptoe and Edwards had not yet published their methods in a scientific journal. Some scientists also suggested that the possible risks of damage to the infant are still unknown.

The Browns' greatest fear for Louise — that her uniqueness would subject her to undue publicity as she grew up — was alleviated on October 3 when a second "test-tube" baby was born, in Calcutta, India.

The conception of the second child, born to Bela and Pravat Agarwal, was reportedly similar to the first. However, in the Agarwal case, the eggs removed were frozen and stored until conditions favorable to implantation existed in the uterus 53 days later.

With two "test-tube" babies born and several pregnancies announced by Steptoe in December, "test-tube" conception may soon be just another fact of life.　　Beverly Merz

BOATING. Two Californians, Betty Cook, 55, from Newport Beach, and Bill Muncey, 49, from La Mesa, won powerboating's major United States championships in 1978.

Cook, the 1977 world champion, captured the seven-race series from March to September for the national offshore title. From June to September, Muncey won six of the seven races and took his sixth national unlimited hydroplane championship.

The Offshore Series involved boats 35 to 38 feet (10.7 to 11.6 meters) long, carrying two stern-drive engines (MerCruiser or Kiekhaefer Aeromarine) up to 428 cubic inches (7,014 cubic centimeters) each. Joey Ippolito of Hallandale, Fla., won three races; Billy Martin of Clark, N.J., two; and Cook, two. Cook was the most consistent all season. Martin won six races from January to April en route to the South American title.

Muncey, a corporate vice-president of Atlas Van Lines, drove a boat named *Atlas Van Lines.* Although he scored six victories in nine races in 1977, he lost the title on points to *Miss Budweiser.* In 1978, Muncey led from the first race and lost only once, when he blew an engine. His victories included the $110,000 Gold Cup – the richest hydroplane race ever – on July 2 at Owensboro, Ky. His boat was 28.6 feet (8.7 meters) long, weighed 5,100 pounds (2,313 kilograms), and was powered by a 12-cylinder supercharged Rolls-Royce airplane engine.

Yachting. The Newport-to-Bermuda biennial race of 635 miles (1,022 kilometers) was actually two races. Ninety of the newest and fastest yachts sailed under the International Offshore Rule. The handicap winner was *Acadia,* a 51-foot (15.5-meter) sloop owned by Burt Keenan of New Orleans.

The other 72 yachts sailed in the same fleet under the new Measurement Handicap System, which is designed to put the sport in the hands of skippers rather than designers. The handicap winner under this rule was *Babe,* a 39-foot (11.9-meter) Concordia Class wooden yawl owned by Arnie Gay of Annapolis, Md.

The big winter competition was the six-race series in Florida and the Bahamas of the Southern Ocean Racing Conference. The 88 ocean yachts that competed cost from $100,000 to $400,000 each. There was no official winner. The unofficial title went to *Williwaw,* a new 46-foot (14.1-meter) sloop designed by Doug Peterson of San Diego, owned by Seymore Sinett of Perth Amboy, N.J., and sailed by Dennis Conner of San Diego.

The National Association of Engine and Boat Manufacturers said there were 52.6 million boaters in the United States in 1977, the last year for which full statistics were available. Boaters spent $5.9-billion on boats, accessories, and boating services, an increase of almost $600 million. There were 10.5-million recreational boats, up 400,000.   Frank Litsky

In WORLD BOOK, see BOATING; SAILING.

BOLIVIA added two more chapters to its chaotic political history in 1978. On July 21, former Air Force General Juan Pereda Asbun seized the presidency in a bloodless military coup d'état. Pereda had apparently won the presidential election only 12 days earlier, but because of widespread charges of fraud the election had been annulled and a new one scheduled. Pereda's own rule was brief. On November 25, the armed forces announced that he had in turn been ousted and replaced by General David Padilla Arancibia. It also announced that general elections would be held at some time during the first six months of 1979.

President Hugo Banzer Suarez, the man Pereda overthrew, had himself taken over in a coup seven years earlier, but had promised that Bolivia would have an elected government in 1980. President Jimmy Carter's Administration had pressured Banzer into moving the election up to 1978, however. Critics in Bolivia, who feared a return to the old political system that has seen 150 presidents in 153 years of independence, bitterly called it "Mr. Carter's election."

The military chose Pereda, a moderate on human rights who had also been interior minister, as their candidate. He was opposed by six candidates on the left, three of them former presidents. Of these, the front-runners were Hernan Siles Zuazo, heading a leftist coalition that included the Communist and the Social parties, and Victor Paz Estenssoro, who was nominated for president by the Revolutionary Nationalist Movement and the Authentic Revolutionary Party.

The Election. Only Pereda's advertisements were run on the state-controlled television station, and his adherents continually harassed opposition politicians. On one occasion, Paz Estenssoro was prevented from attending a rally in Cobija because the air force put heavy equipment on the runway to keep his plane from landing.

Two separate teams of international observers invited to witness the July 9 elections denounced the vote as a fraud. They said soldiers intimidated voters and that ballots for the opposition candidates were not available in many rural polling places. Siles supporters charged that ballot boxes from La Paz were thrown into Lake Titicaca. An incomplete count gave Pereda a little over 50 per cent of the vote, but fraud charges finally compelled the National Electoral Court to annul the elections.

Pereda Acts. It was reported that Pereda agreed to a new election in six months, provided Banzer would hand over power to a military junta in the interim. Banzer agreed at first, then changed his mind. Pereda then launched his coup from Santa Cruz, a conservative stronghold in the country's eastern lowlands that has shown little patience with the left wing politicians who dominate the major cities in the populous mountain region.

Bolivian soldiers patrol a street near the presidential palace in La Paz during an uprising that ousted President Hugo Banzer Suarez in July.

Banzer stepped down on July 21 to avoid bloodshed between rebels and troops who were loyal to him. He gave an emotional farewell address on television and the next day strolled down the main street of La Paz chatting amiably with well-wishers.

Pereda, who said he acted to stop a Communist take-over, named three military officers and 12 civilians to his Cabinet on July 24. In August he scheduled elections for 1980.

Pereda characterized his government as "transitional," while the U.S. Department of State expressed its regrets over the events and declared that it hoped the "interruption was temporary." Some 100 politicians, labor leaders, and students were arrested after the coup, but Pereda ordered them released on July 26.

On March 17, the Banzer government broke diplomatic relations with Chile and sent troops to various points along the Chilean border. Banzer was protesting the stalemate in the talks with Chile over granting landlocked Bolivia an outlet corridor to the sea. Chile downplayed the break and said it was still willing to continue the talks.   Everett G. Martin

See also LATIN AMERICA (Facts in Brief Table). In WORLD BOOK, see BOLIVIA.

BOOKS. See CANADIAN LITERATURE; LITERATURE; LITERATURE FOR CHILDREN; POETRY; PUBLISHING.

BOPHUTHATSWANA. See AFRICA.

BORG, BJORN (1956-   ), Sweden's biggest athletic hero, won his third consecutive Wimbledon men's singles title in July 1978, becoming the second player in history to do so. England's Fred Perry won at Wimbledon in 1934, 1935, and 1936. In addition to his Wimbledon triumph, Borg won the French and Italian opens. However, he lost his bid for a Grand Slam when Jimmy Connors beat him in the U.S. Open finals in September. See TENNIS.

In his last two Wimbledon victories, Borg beat Connors in the finals. He won a memorable 1977 final that lasted three grueling hours. He needed only 1 hour 49 minutes to crush Connors 6-2, 6-2, 6-3 in 1978.

Born on June 6, 1956, in Södertälje, Sweden, Borg played both hockey and tennis as a boy. He abandoned hockey and began to concentrate on tennis when he was 13. As a 14-year-old, he won all Sweden's junior tennis titles. He won the Swedish men's title and also played for Sweden against New Zealand when he was 15.

Borg stands 5 feet 10 inches (178 centimeters) tall and weighs about 150 pounds (68 kilograms). On the court, he wears a headband to hold his long blond hair in place. He seldom shows any emotion, even in tense situations.

Borg lives in Monaco, where his parents operate a boutique. He is engaged to Mariana Simionescu, a Romanian tennis player.   Joseph P. Spohn

BOSTON

BOSTON. Massive winter blizzards dropped record-breaking snowfalls on the Boston area twice during the early weeks of 1978. The first storm hit on January 20, dumping about 20 inches (50 centimeters) of snow on the city and forcing Logan International Airport to shut down operations.

A second storm, the worst in Boston's history, struck on February 5, depositing another 27 inches (69 centimeters) of snow over a two-day period.

The accumulation stopped all traffic, and debris blown by the winds shorted out main electrical lines. The blackout left some 100,000 persons without power, some for up to 23 hours. Massachusetts Governor Michael S. Dukakis closed roads and streets to private traffic and called out the National Guard to cope with the emergency.

Boston's Schools opened without racial turmoil in September for the first time in five years. Federal controls, in effect since December 1975, had been lifted a week earlier from South Boston High School, once the center of opposition to court-ordered busing to integrate the city's schools.

A one-day walkout on July 7 by 4,200 subway, bus, and trolley operators left 500,000 commuters stranded. The strikers were protesting a bill pending before the state legislature that would have made salaries of public transit workers comparable to those paid in the private sector. The union complied with a back-to-work order by Superior Court Judge John Greaney, and workers returned to their jobs.

Traffic was banned from a 10-block area in Boston's central business district on September 5 when work began on a federally financed $3.3-million project designed to attract shoppers and eliminate traffic congestion. The zone gave pedestrians exclusive use of parts of Washington Street, where major stores are located. Truck deliveries were restricted to the hours before 11 A.M., and taxis to evening hours in some areas.

Quality of Life. Boston retained the doubtful distinction of being the most expensive large city for middle-income families in the continental United States. According to figures released by the U.S. Department of Labor on April 26, an average family of four would need an annual income of $20,609 to live comfortably in the city. The cost-of-living index, however, rose only 4.7 per cent in Boston during the 12-month period ending in May 1978.

Residential construction was down 16 per cent and nonresidential construction off by 26 per cent in the city during the first five months of the year.

U.S. Department of Commerce statistics showed Boston to be the nation's 16th most crowded urban region with a density of 1,257 persons per square mile (485 per square kilometer).   James M. Banovetz

See also CITY. In WORLD BOOK, see BOSTON.

Boston residents dig their cars out of deep drifts after a January blizzard buried the area under 20 inches (50 centimeters) of snow.

BOTANY. Researchers reported new discoveries in 1978 on how substances commonly found in the air and in certain soils affect plants. In some cases, substances now known to be harmful may interact to cause even greater damage.

Thomas W. Ashenden and Terence A. Mansfield of the University of Lancaster in England reported in May on research showing that the interaction of nitrogen dioxide (NO_2) and sulfur dioxide (SO_2) damages meadow grass. Both NO_2 and SO_2 are often found in the air and can be harmful to plants in extremely high concentrations, but not in the small amounts usually found in nature. Until these studies, however, no one realized that a combination of the two substances, even in relatively small amounts, could damage meadow grass.

In experiments conducted under carefully controlled greenhouse conditions, the researchers cultivated four pasture grasses — cocksfoot, Italian ryegrass, timothy, and smooth-stalked meadow grass — for 20 weeks. The grasses subjected to filtered air and air mixed only with SO_2 or NO_2 in concentrations of 0.068 parts per million grew normally. Those subjected to a combination of air, NO_2, and SO_2 in the same low concentrations had much smaller leaves and the dry weight was lower.

Nitrogen Fixation. Botanists Jochen Kummerow, James V. Alexander, James W. Neel, and Kathleen Fishbeck of San Diego State University in California studied several shrubs of the genus *Caenothus* to assess the ecological significance of the nitrogen-fixing fungus that lives in the plants. They studied plants that grow in the Echo Valley, an area of shrubby thickets called *chaparral* east of San Diego.

The shrubs have nodules on their roots in which a fungus, *Frankia*, lives. The fungus fixes nitrogen from the air into a form that the plants can use. In return, the fungus derives nutrients from the plants.

To measure the level of nitrogen-fixing activity in the shrub-fungus association, the scientists carefully dug trenches to excavate the roots so they could weigh the root nodules. Then they used a laboratory technique called acetylene reduction by nitrogen gas to determine the rate of nitrogen fixation and measured it by gas chromatography. Their measurements showed that the shrub-fungus association could fix 3.5 ounces per 2.5 acres (100 grams per hectare) of nitrogen per year. The botanists estimated that this is probably enough to replace all the nitrogen the chaparral ecological system loses by drainage and runoff.

Ancient Leaves. Botanists at the New York Botanical Garden in New York City and the University of North Carolina in Chapel Hill examined perfectly preserved fossil leaves found in volcanic ash deposits in Oregon that are 16 million to 36 million years old. The leaves were still green and intact down to the cell nuclei and chloroplasts.   Barbara N. Benson

In WORLD BOOK, see BOTANY; NITROGEN CYCLE.

Douglas fir plantlets, cloned from leaf tissue, prove to be identical and genetically superior in a forestry breeding-by-test-tube program.

BOTHA, PIETER WILLEM (1916-   ), became South Africa's eighth prime minister on Sept. 28, 1978. He succeeded Balthazar Johannes Vorster, who retired because of illness. See SOUTH AFRICA.

Botha was born on Jan. 12, 1916, at Telegraaf Farm in the Paul Roux district of the Orange Free State, a province of South Africa. After elementary school in Paul Roux and Voortrecker Secondary School in Bethlehem, he studied law at the University of the Orange Free State in Bloemfontein.

Entering politics at 20, Botha became organizer of the National Party in Cape of Good Hope Province and rose to national campaign manager. When the Nationalists came to power in 1948, he served as the party's chief secretary in Cape Province until 1958, when he was named deputy minister of the interior. In 1961, he became minister of community development, public works, and colored affairs.

Botha gained the nickname "Piet Wapen" (Pete the Weapon) for his characteristic outbursts of temper. It also fits his position from 1965 to 1978 — minister of defense. A military hard-liner, he made South Africa self-sufficient in arms.

Botha has never criticized South Africa's policy of white domination, but once startled his followers by declaring that "all men are equal before God."

Botha married Elize Rossouw in 1943, and they have five children.   Marsha F. Goldsmith

BOTSWANA. See AFRICA.

BOWLING. Mark Roth, a 26-year-old right-hander from North Arlington, N.J., and Earl Anthony, a 40-year-old left-hander from Tacoma, Wash., were major winners on the 1978 Professional Bowlers Association (PBA) tour. The tour was the richest in its 19-year history, with 35 tournaments carrying total prize money of $2.9 million.

Roth won three of the first five tournaments, six by the end of June, seven by the end of the summer tour, eight by the end of October. Only Billy Hardwick in 1969 and Anthony in 1976 had won seven tournaments in one year. Roth also led in earnings for the second straight year. He collected $134,500, breaking Anthony's 1976 record of $110,833.

Roth's Victories came at Torrance, Calif., and Grand Prairie, Tex., in January; Overland Park, Kans., in February; Windsor Locks, Conn., in April; Portland, Ore., and San Jose, Calif., in June; Cranston, R.I., in August; and Rochester, N.Y., in October. He finished third in the PBA national championship (Warren Nelson of Downey, Calif., won), fourth in the Firestone Tournament of Champions (Anthony won), and seventh in the United States Open (Nelson Burton, Jr., of St. Louis won).

Anthony, the outstanding bowler of the 1970s, had an eventful year. He won tournaments in January and April for a record total of 30 career victories. In February, he broke Dick Weber's career record of $555,753 in tournament earnings. Then in June he suffered a heart attack and was hospitalized for 10 days. Nine weeks later he bowled in the Waukegan (Ill.) Open and finished third.

The all-America team chosen by the *National Bowlers Journal* consisted of Roth, Anthony, Burton, Marshall Holman of Medford, Ore., and Mike Berlin of Muscatine, Iowa. The women's team comprised five Californians — Donna Adamek of Monrovia, Pat Costello of Union City, Vesma Grinfelds of San Francisco, Betty Morris of Stockton, and Virginia Norton of South Gate.

The Women's Tour was conducted for years by the Professional Women Bowlers Association. In 1977, the newly formed Ladies Professional Bowlers Association ran a rival tour. In 1978, the organizations merged into the Women's Professional Bowlers Association and ran one tour. The 17 tournaments carried $600,000 in prize money. Adamek was top money winner with $31,000.

Adamek won the United States Open, Loa Boxberger of Russell, Kans., the Queens title. Pat Costello finished 13th in the Metroplex Open in Dallas and earned only $600, but her first three games in the qualifying round made bowling history. Those games of 298, 266, and 299 totaled 863, breaking the women's three-game record of 817, which was set by Bev Ortner of Galva, Iowa, in 1968. Allie Brandt of Lockport, N.Y., set the men's record of 886 in 1939. *Frank Litsky*

In WORLD BOOK, see BOWLING.

BOXING. At the start of 1978, Muhammad Ali of Chicago reigned as the undisputed heavyweight champion of the world. In midyear, he was champion nowhere. At year's end, he was champion in part of the world.

These strange turns took place because the 36-year-old Ali lost the title, then regained part of it. He became the first man in history to win the heavyweight championship three times. And Leon Spinks of St. Louis, who took the title from him and then lost it to him, enjoyed the shortest reign of any heavyweight champion — seven months.

Ali Upset. Spinks hardly seemed ready to become heavyweight champion. A 24-year-old former marine who won the light-heavyweight title in the 1976 Olympic Games, he had fought only seven professional fights. See SPINKS, LEON.

Ali trained lightly, boxing only 50 rounds in training camp. Yet, the bookmakers thought so little of Spinks that they refused to take bets. But when Ali and Spinks fought on February 15 in Las Vegas, Nev., Spinks won easily in 15 rounds.

Spinks had agreed that if he won, he would make his first defense against Ken Norton of San Diego. When he declined, waiting for a more lucrative return bout with Ali, the World Boxing Council (WBC) took the title away on March 18 and gave it to Norton. The World Boxing Association (WBA)

World Champion Boxers

Division	Champion	Country	Year Won
Heavyweight	†Larry Holmes	U.S.A.	1978
	*Muhammad Ali	U.S.A.	1978
Light-heavyweight	†Marvin Johnson	U.S.A.	1978
	*Mike Rossman	U.S.A.	1978
Middleweight	Hugo Corro	Argentina	1978
Junior-middleweight	†Rocky Mattioli	Australia	1977
	*Masashi Kudo	Japan	1978
Welterweight	†Carlos Palomino	U.S.A.	1976
	*José Cuevas	Mexico	1976
Junior-welterweight	†Kim Sang-Hyun	South Korea	1978
	*Antonio Cervantes	Colombia	1977
Lightweight	Roberto Duran	Panama	1972
Junior-lightweight	*Samuel Serrano	Puerto Rico	1976
	†Alexis Arguello	Nicaragua	1978
Featherweight	†Danny Lopez	U.S.A.	1976
	*Eusebio Pedrozo	Panama	1978
Junior-featherweight	†Wilfredo Gomez	Puerto Rico	1977
	*Ricardo Cardona	Colombia	1978
Bantamweight	†Carlos Zarate	Mexico	1976
	*Jorge Lujan	Panama	1977
Flyweight	†Miguel Canto	Mexico	1975
	*Betulio Gonzalez	Venezuela	1978
Junior-flyweight	*Yoko Gushiken	Japan	1976
	†Kim Sung Jun	South Korea	1978

*Recognized by World Boxing Association
† Recognized by World Boxing Council

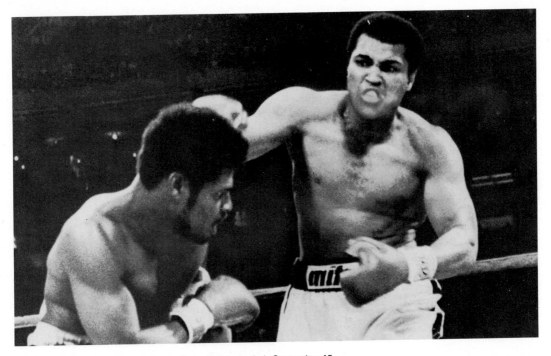

Muhammad Ali thoroughly dominates Leon Spinks in their September 15 rematch and regains the heavyweight title he lost to Spinks in February.

continued to recognize Spinks. Norton's reign was short. Larry Holmes of Easton, Pa., outpointed him June 9 in Las Vegas in a fight so close that all three judges had Holmes winning by 143 points to 142. In his first defense, Holmes knocked out Alfredo Evangelista of Spain in Las Vegas on November 10.

The Ali-Spinks return bout for the WBA share of the title was staged on September 15 in the New Orleans Superdome, with Spinks getting $3.75 million and Ali $3.25 million (for their first fight, Ali was paid $3.5 million; Spinks $320,000). There were 15,000 ringside seats at $200 each.

While Ali trained seriously this time, Spinks allegedly spent some of his evenings the week before the fight in night spots. So it was no surprise when Ali, despite a lack of sharpness, won decisively.

Other Champions. The most successful champion of the year was Wilfredo Gomez of Puerto Rico. He defended the WBC junior featherweight title five times and knocked out all five challengers.

There were four American co-champions in other weight classes—light-heavyweights Mike Rossman of Turnersville, N.J., and Marvin Johnson of Indianapolis, Ind.; welterweight Carlos Palomino of Huntington Beach, Calif.; and featherweight Danny Lopez, Alhambra, Calif.   Frank Litsky

In WORLD BOOK, see ALI, MUHAMMAD; BOXING.

BOY SCOUTS. See YOUTH ORGANIZATIONS.
BOYS' CLUBS. See YOUTH ORGANIZATIONS.

BRAZIL. President Ernesto Geisel confirmed on Jan. 5, 1978, that General João Baptista de Figueiredo, head of the nation's intelligence service, was his choice as presidential successor in 1979. Brazil's unique system of rotating military dictatorships allowed Geisel to serve for only five years, but under new rules Figueiredo will serve six years.

One of Geisel's advisers, General Hugo de Andrade Abreu, resigned after the January announcement and reportedly circulated a document arguing that Figueiredo was unfit for the post. But Figueiredo's election was never in serious doubt, if only because the government's tightly controlled political party, the Alliance for National Renewal (ARENA), held a 130-seat majority in the electoral college that selected the president on October 15. On August 23, General Euler Bentes Monteiro became the presidential candidate of the rival Brazilian Democratic Movement (MBD), but offered only token opposition to Figueiredo in the electoral college. Bentes promised to speed up the process of returning Brazil to democratic rule by governing for only three years and immediately convening an assembly to rewrite the Constitution.

Goals Announced. Figueiredo declared on June 28 that he would "make this country a democracy over all opposition, wherever it comes from." He warned, however, against the opposition's "radical" positions and "exaggerated" demands to move so

229

Presidential candidate João Baptista de Figueiredo delays casting his ballot
to discuss issues with two Xavante Indians at polling place in Brasília.

quickly that it might provoke the armed forces to slow down the process. The 61-year-old Figueiredo is the son of General Euclydes Figueiredo, a Brazilian hero who in 1932 tried unsuccessfully to overthrow a military dictator and restore constitutional rule. President Geisel had selected Figueiredo because he was one of Geisel's small inner circle of advisers as well as a man he could trust to "carry on the process of institutionalization of the nation . . . eliminate arbitrary laws and . . . make sure that our democracy is perfected more and more, not just on paper but in real life." See FIGUEIREDO, JOÃO BAPTISTA DE.

Geisel called the process he had introduced "the political opening," by which Brazil was to be led back to civilian rule at some undetermined future point. On June 9, he lifted the last vestiges of prior political censorship on all publications except a few small opinion magazines. On June 23, he submitted constitutional reforms to the Congress to end some of the harshest measures of the arbitrary military government and re-establish the right of *habeas corpus* for political prisoners.

Many observers believed that Geisel's policy of doling out more political freedom was designed to relieve discontent over the high inflation rate and the restrictive economic measures that the government took to contain it. For the second year in a row, inflation – which was caused largely by the rapid rise in world petroleum prices – hit 40 per cent, ending a rapid-growth period in the Brazilian economy that had kept most levels of society content under military rule.

Labor Unrest. Throughout April and May, workers unhappy with their declining purchasing power staged a series of strikes. It was the first labor unrest in the large industrial plants in the state of São Paulo since 1968. Some 50,000 employees of all the major automobile manufacturers, as well as many supplier plants, left their jobs in a series of short wildcat strikes, demanding wage increases above the government's 41 per cent increase in the minimum wage granted on April 28. In the past, the country's security forces had violently put down such uprisings, but Geisel instead allowed the companies to negotiate wages with the workers, calling the incidents "a sign of the times."

Lifting press censorship unleashed many reports of police brutality that previously would have been suppressed. Most major newspapers had been free of censorship since April 1977, and the president of the Brazilian Bar Association stated in an interview on February 22 that mistreatment of prisoners had declined since then. But, he added, charges of torture and abuse still surface.   Everett G. Martin

See also LATIN AMERICA (Facts in Brief Table). In WORLD BOOK, see BRAZIL.

BRIDGE. See BUILDING AND CONSTRUCTION.

BRIDGE, CONTRACT. The United States women's team defeated Italy by 89 international match points to win the Venice Cup at the World Bridge Federation tournament held in New Orleans in June 1978. It was the first world team championship for a United States women's team. Members of the team were Jacqui Mitchell, Gail Moss, and Dorothy H. Truscott of New York City; Emma Jean Hawes of Fort Worth, Tex.; Marilyn Johnson of Houston; and Mary Jane Farell of Los Angeles. Poland won the open team championship, defeating Brazil.

Gabino Cintra and Marcelo Branco of Rio de Janeiro won the world open pair championship; the world women's pair championship went to Judi Radin and Kathy Wei of New York City; and Barry Crane of Studio City, Calif., and Kerri Shuman of Los Angeles were victors in the world mixed pair championship. The Charles Solomon trophy for the best record in pair events went to the United States.

At the American Contract Bridge League (ACBL) spring championships in March in Houston, the Harold A. Vanderbilt knockout team championship was won by Malcolm Brachman, Mike Passell, and Bob Goldman of Dallas and Bill Eisenberg, Eddie Kantar, and Paul Soloway of Los Angeles. The same team, but without Eisenberg, took the Spingold knockout team title in Toronto, Canada, on August 2.   Theodore M. O'Leary

In WORLD BOOK, see BRIDGE, CONTRACT.

BRITISH COLUMBIA. Jack Davis, minister of energy, transport, and communications in the Social Credit government of Premier William R. Bennett, was fined $1,000 in September 1978 for defrauding the government by misrepresenting his travel expenses. Davis was charged with converting first-class airfares into economy class and pocketing the difference. He had been asked to resign from Bennett's cabinet on April 3, and he gave up his seat in the legislature on September 17. Davis had previously served for six years as a Liberal minister of the environment and fisheries. Chief Justice John Farris resigned effective December 31 after evidence suggested "contact with an alleged prostitute."

In a budget presented on April 10, Finance Minister Evan Wolfe reduced the consumer sales tax from 7 to 5 per cent in a move to stimulate the economy and combat unemployment. The balanced budget of $4.3 billion included measures to encourage the private sector to create new jobs.

The federal government vetoed a $750-million oil port and pipeline at Kitimat to handle Alaskan oil shipments. From Kitimat, a pipeline would have been constructed to Edmonton, Alta., to move the oil to the United States. Ottawa decided that the project was premature and risked polluting the waters off the British Columbia coast. David M. L. Farr

See also CANADA. In WORLD BOOK, see BRITISH COLUMBIA.

BUILDING AND CONSTRUCTION. After devastating quakes struck Greece, Iran, and Japan in 1978, earthquake-proof construction took on increased importance. Japanese officials announced plans to build an underwater double-track railroad tunnel that will be 2,483 feet (757 meters) long. The tunnel, part of the Daiban Railway Tunnel, will run under a strait between two islands. It will have flexible joints that are expected to enable it to adapt to movement in the earth. Post-tensioned cables will be used to seal the rubber joints – instead of welded steel or reinforced concrete – to give the tunnel flexibility.

One of the most quake-proof structures was being built relatively close to California's San Andreas Fault. The Olive View Medical Center in southern California's San Fernando Valley will have steel and concrete walls that should withstand an earthquake of much greater intensity than any recorded in California.

Earthquake Research by the U.S. Geological Survey more than doubled during 1978. About $80-million was appropriated for research on the reduction of earthquake hazards, $18 million more than in 1977. The 1978 research focused on improving earthquake-predicting capabilities, determining the earthquake-triggering potential of large reservoirs, and evaluating hazards and risks in earthquake-

The 106-room Ekofisk Hotel rises on stilts in the North Sea near Norway. For oil workers, it is linked with drilling platforms by a catwalk.

"You the new man?"

Steiner in *Saturday Review*

prone regions from Alaska and Hawaii to the New England States and South Carolina.

Spending for Construction in the United States rose 13 per cent in 1978 to an estimated $195.8-billion. Spending for housing units, exclusive of mobile homes, reached an estimated $92 billion, up 40 per cent from the $65.5 billion spent in 1977. *Engineering News-Record*'s annual construction cost index for 20 major cities in the United States was 7 per cent higher than in 1977.

The unemployment rate dropped to 9.1 per cent in August, the lowest since March 1974, and average wage pacts, such as those reached in New Jersey, Florida, and northern California, increased hourly pay substantially. Building trades workers across the country received wage gains of 6.7 per cent for the year ending July 8, 1978. The average pay per hour for all trades was $13.01.

Codes and Specifications. The National Institute of Building Sciences in May announced three major studies of building technology and regulations. The studies are expected to lay the groundwork for a more rational system of building regulations that could save billions of dollars. They will cover the collection, storage, and dissemination of technical data for use by builders and regulatory agencies; the evaluation of existing methods of developing and publishing performance standards as a basis for housing and building codes; and the

evaluation and prequalification of technology for producers, builders, and users.

New Building Techniques. The wholesale merchandising complex at the Dallas Market Center will expand to a total of 165 acres (67 hectares) of interior space, making it the largest such facility in the world. Eight stories will be added to a seven-story building and two to the four-story Apparel Mart. Additional floors will be cantilevered beyond the existing rectangular structure. Lighter material than the present precast concrete panels will be used for the facade to reduce weight on the cantilever.

In April, the American Telephone and Telegraph Company announced plans for a new 37-story, $110-million headquarters building in New York City. The building will feature a huge broken pediment, a common gablelike feature of Roman and baroque architecture. See ARCHITECTURE.

Bridges. The Texas Turnpike Authority announced plans to build a concrete box-girder bridge 10,450 feet (3,200 meters) long across the Houston Ship Channel. The $102-million, four-lane structure is slated for completion in 1982. The design was chosen because it will not disrupt channel traffic.

In January, the British firm of Freeman Fox & Partners won a contract to design and supervise construction of a second bridge over the Bosporus Strait in Turkey. The first bridge was opened in 1973, but is already approaching capacity because of increased truck traffic to and from oil-producing countries.

The world's longest floating bridge, providing a vital road link across the Demerara River in Guyana, opened in April. The two-lane, 6,074-foot (1,850-meter) crossing cost $15 million, about half the cost of a fixed structure.

In March, the New York City Planning Commission called for a $350-million rehabilitation program for 135 of the city's crossings and highways. The most critical projects, cited for early attention with a $100-million appropriation of city, state, and federal funds, include the heavily traveled Queensboro and Manhattan bridges and East River Drive.

Dams. An unusual combination of a curved-earth embankment, a concrete gravity-thrust block, and a concrete thin-arch prestressed with embedded vertical flat jacks went into the construction of Nambe Falls Dam on the Rio Nambe near Santa Fe, N. Mex. The first mechanically prestressed arch dam in the United States, it is a principal feature of the Bureau of Reclamation's San Juan-Chama Project. The project diverts water from the San Juan River in Colorado through the Continental Divide to the Rio Grande Basin in New Mexico, providing supplemental irrigation water and recreational opportunities. The dam began impounding water in 1976, and by October 1978 had peaked at an elevation of 6,809 feet (2,075 meters).

In July, Congress killed a Corps of Engineers plan to build the controversial Tocks Island Dam in the middle Delaware River. Conservationists had long sought to block the dam.

Tunnels. The American Society of Civil Engineers nominated the new Hampton Roads bridge-tunnel for its 1978 Outstanding Civil Engineering Achievement Award. The bridge-tunnel crosses 3.5 miles (5.6 kilometers) of water between Hampton and Norfolk, Va., paralleling a similar crossing built in 1957.

Officials in Philadelphia broke ground in June for a $308-million, 1.8-mile (2.9-kilometer) rail tunnel to connect the city's two commuter rail terminals. The U.S. Urban Mass Transportation Administration approved a $240-million grant to build the tunnel, which will link former Penn Central and Reading Railroad commuter lines.

Hong Kong transportation officials called for bids for a 7-mile (11-kilometer), $897.5-million extension of its $1-billion subway system. The 9.7-mile (15.6-kilometer) subway that runs from Hong Kong's central business district to the Kowloon Peninsula is now under construction. The extension will branch out from Prince Edward Station in Kowloon to the heavily industrialized Tsuen Wan area. The project is scheduled for completion in 1982. Mary E. Jessup

In WORLD BOOK, see BRIDGE; BUILDING CONSTRUCTION; DAM; TUNNEL.

BULGARIA held major trade discussions with Greece, Iran, and Turkey in 1978, but relations with Yugoslavia deteriorated. Turkey's Prime Minister Bulent Ecevit visited Bulgaria in May to discuss joint construction of a port in Turkey and a dam in Bulgaria; cooperation in energy, agriculture, trade, and industry; and joint ventures in other markets. After Shah Mohammad Reza Pahlavi of Iran visited Bulgaria in March, Iran loaned Bulgaria $150-million to finance Bulgarian agricultural exports to Iran, and signed a five-year trade agreement. Greek Prime Minister Constantine Karamanlis visited Bulgaria in July. Trade with Greece is to increase from $40 million in 1978 to $300 million in 1979.

Political Battles. Bulgaria took a vigorous part in the Russian bloc's propaganda campaign against the August visit of China's Premier Hua Kuo-feng to Romania and Yugoslavia. However, Bulgaria did not denounce Romania, and Prime Minister Stanko Todorov visited that country in October to discuss joint economic projects. Bulgaria sided with Albania in its disputes with China and offered to resume diplomatic relations with Albania, but Albania did not respond.

Relations with Yugoslavia worsened suddenly after State Council Chairman Todor Zhivkov spoke in Blagoevgrad, a Bulgarian Macedonian city, on June 15. Zhivkov said Bulgaria wanted no Yugoslav territory and offered to sign an agreement requiring each country to respect the other's national boundaries. Yugoslavia rejected the offer, saying there could be no agreement if Bulgaria did not acknowledge its Macedonian minority.

Bulgaria arrested four suspected West German terrorists on June 21 and returned them to West Germany within hours. This was the first such action by a Russian-bloc country. See EUROPE (Close-Up).

Business Freedom. Bulgaria gave state-owned business enterprises more independence after the national party conference in April, but said it would increase controls if the enterprises did not function well. The government also announced the average wage would be gradually increased from 80 leva ($73) per month in 1978 to 90 leva ($82) in 1980.

Industrial output increased 5.9 per cent in the first half of 1978 over the same period in 1977. The planned increase was 7.9 per cent. Foreign trade increased 7.9 per cent, almost 5 per cent less than planned. Deputy Foreign Trade Minister Boris Tsvetkov led a delegation to the United States in November to discuss expanding trade and technological cooperation.

The Austrian newspaper *Die Presse* published a Bulgarian dissident group's declaration on April 3 demanding the restoration of such human and civil rights as freedom of the press and religion, freer travel abroad, and greater social benefits. Chris Cviic

See also EUROPE (Facts in Brief Table). In WORLD BOOK, see BULGARIA.

BURMA. For the third consecutive year, Burma's rice fields yielded a rich harvest in 1978. The inflation rate fell to below 10 per cent from its 40 per cent record rate in 1975, and the volume of exports inched up.

But the improvements were short-range. In an attempt to end corruption, abuse of power, and economic problems, President U Ne Win in late 1977 had fired the prime minister. The ministers of finance and transportation were given life prison terms for misusing $140 in political party funds and for "corruption," respectively. Ne Win also eased controls in hopes of luring investments from other countries.

However, Ne Win dropped the experiment with relaxed controls early in 1978. As a result, the economy continued to be stagnant, shortages remained acute, and three-fourths of the trade in the country was done in the black market.

New Purges. Burma continued to feel the effects of purges. Ne Win was re-elected president on January 5. In February, he ousted the newly appointed liberal prime minister and his deputy – to the dismay of the World Bank, which saw a promise of progress in their liberal economic views. With the liberals done in, Ne Win next struck at the Socialist hard-liners. Western observers suggested that Ne Win was eliminating potential rivals.

Burmese farmers, who must sell almost half their rice to the government, pile harvested grain they have sold by a road to Mandalay.

Elections to the rubber-stamp assembly were held in January. The ruling Burmese Socialist Program Party was the only legal party, and the press and radio were rigidly censored. More important, the ruling circle appointed a new 29-member Council of State, 10 of whom were army officers previously linked with the feared army intelligence.

Rebels and Refugees. Ne Win's greatest danger came from internal insurrection. The best-organized enemy was the Communist guerrilla force, possibly 12,000 strong, armed by the Chinese and given sanctuary in China's Yunnan province. When China's Deputy Prime Minister Teng Hsiao-p'ing visited Rangoon in January, Ne Win pleaded with him in vain to halt aid to Burma's Communists.

Another crisis came in February, when the government began to register residents of border provinces. The move was aimed in part at Muslims who had fled to Burma during the turmoil in Bangladesh. Possibly with encouragement, Burmese Buddhists burned Muslim villages, and some 200,000 refugees fled to Bangladesh. In July, the two governments agreed on the return of the refugees.   Mark Gayn

See also ASIA (Facts in Brief Table). In WORLD BOOK, see BURMA.

BURUNDI. See AFRICA.

BUS. See TRANSIT; TRANSPORTATION.

BUSINESS. See ECONOMICS; LABOR; MANUFACTURING; Section One, FOCUS ON THE ECONOMY.

CABINET, UNITED STATES. The U.S. Senate on Sept. 28, 1978, approved President Jimmy Carter's proposal to create a new Cabinet-level Department of Education. If approved by the House of Representatives, the new department would start with an annual budget of $17.5 billion.

The Department of Education would oversee 164 programs currently under the jurisdiction of other government departments and agencies and would receive the funds allotted to these programs. Most of the programs would be transferred from the Department of Health, Education, and Welfare (HEW). The new department would take over most of HEW's education programs, budgeted at $12.9-billion, as well as the $680-million Project Head Start for preschool children.

The remainder of the budget would be made up of funds taken from other departments, including almost $3 billion from the Department of Agriculture for child nutrition; $271 million from the Department of the Interior for American Indian education; $350 million from the Department of Defense for schools for the dependents of military personnel stationed in other countries; and $111 million from the Department of Housing and Urban Development for college housing. The new department would incorporate the science-education program of the National Science Foundation, an independent agency with a $56-million budget.

Big Bird celebrates the Department of Health, Education, and Welfare's 25th birthday with HEW Secretary Joseph Califano and his daughter Claudia.

Pro's and Con's. President Carter's proposal won the support of Senator Abraham A. Ribicoff (D., Conn.), a former HEW secretary, and the 1.8-million-member National Education Association. It was opposed by HEW Secretary Joseph A. Califano, Jr., and the 447,000-member American Federation of Teachers. Proponents said a smaller department would be more manageable and would provide greater visibility for education issues. Opponents argued that education is naturally allied with health and welfare as an issue and would lose attention if isolated in a separate department.

Other Changes. In November, President Carter's reorganization staff suggested replacing two other Cabinet departments – the Department of Housing and Urban Development and the Department of the Interior – with a Department of Economic Development and a Department of Natural Resources, respectively. The new departments would have a broader range than their predecessors. The Department of Commerce was also being considered for revision. The proposal was to be reviewed by Director of the Budget James T. McIntyre, Jr., before going to the President. Beverly Merz

See also EDUCATION. In WORLD BOOK, see CABINET; HEALTH, EDUCATION, AND WELFARE, DEPARTMENT OF (HEW).

CALIFORNIA. See LOS ANGELES-LONG BEACH; SAN FRANCISCO-OAKLAND; STATE GOVERNMENT.

CAMBODIA and Vietnam fought a limited border war through most of 1978. In their border skirmishes, Vietnam used captured United States weapons and newly supplied Russian arms, while Cambodia resisted with guerrillas and some regular forces equipped with Chinese weapons. Then Vietnam suddenly escalated the fighting on December 25, advancing quickly into Cambodia. By Jan. 8, 1979, Vietnamese troops captured Phnom Penh, the capital, in the name of Cambodian rebels and claimed that the government had been overthrown.

Throughout 1978, Cambodia accused Vietnam of trying to force it into an Indochinese federation controlled by Hanoi. Vietnam accused Cambodia of committing atrocities against it. Behind these charges lay centuries of ethnic conflict and a history of Vietnamese encroachment upon ancient Cambodian territory in the Mekong River Delta.

Vietnam appeared at first to be trying to destroy the Cambodian forces, rather than penetrate deep into the country–possibly in the hope of inciting an uprising against Prime Minister Pol Pot. Hanoi reported insurrections in Cambodia, but it was hard to judge the spontaneity of the uprisings because Hanoi was known to be supporting Cambodian opponents of Pol Pot.

Each side made cease-fire proposals that the other found unacceptable. Cambodia said its survival was at stake, while Vietnam said it was using restraint in the face of alleged provocations. In June, Cambodia charged that Vietnam collaborated with the U.S. Central Intelligence Agency (CIA) in an attempt to overthrow Pol Pot. Hanoi denied the charge.

More Purges. The third major wave of purges since the Communist victory in 1975 swept Cambodia in 1978. The first purge had killed members of the losing Lon Nol regime, the second killed some middle- and upper-ranked Communist leaders, and the third hit lower-ranked Communist officials and workers. The continued bloodshed brought new condemnations of the Pol Pot regime.

International Relations. Only China and North Korea openly supported Cambodia. After a visit, Teng Ying-chao, a member of China's Communist Party Central Committee and the widow of Chinese Premier Chou En-lai, said on January 22 that China considered Cambodia a victim of "Vietnamese aggression." But a visit to Peking in early August by Cambodian Deputy Premier Son Sen apparently failed to win full Chinese military backing. China was believed to have urged Pol Pot to moderate internal policies and improve Cambodia's image. For the first time in two years, and possibly as a result of China's urging, Prince Norodom Sihanouk was publicly mentioned in 1978. Henry S. Bradsher

See also ASIA (Facts in Brief Table). In WORLD BOOK, see CAMBODIA.

CAMEROON. See AFRICA.

CAMP FIRE GIRLS. See YOUTH ORGANIZATIONS.

CANADA

National unity, the issue that had dominated public life in Canada since the separatist Parti Québécois (PQ) victory in the Quebec elections of November 1976, receded somewhat in 1978. Premier René Lévesque's PQ government in Quebec moderated its stance, announcing in October that it planned to use its promised referendum to win a mandate to negotiate "sovereignty-association" with the rest of Canada, rather than to seek support for secession. Under this strategy, the task of working out a new relation-

ship with Quebec promised to be a lengthy one. The other provinces showed more interest in formulating a new division of powers with the federal government in Ottawa than in negotiating a new link with Quebec.

Constitutional revision was overshadowed, however, by concern over the feeble state of the economy. Real material growth was marginal as high unemployment, inflation, steep interest rates, and policies of fiscal restraint characterized the economic scene. Inevitably, the discontent created by the nation's economic difficulties led to criticism of Prime Minister Pierre Elliott Trudeau's federal Liberal government. Trudeau marked his 10th anniversary in office in April, and his administration

Canada's Prime Minister Pierre Elliott Trudeau,
left, greets Quebec Premier René Lévesque
at meeting of provincial government leaders.

appeared increasingly tired and uncertain. Over the years, many of its strongest members had left politics, leaving Trudeau as the continuing symbol of 10 years of federal leadership. Public-opinion polls revealed that support for the prime minister and the Liberal Party had slumped badly. Trudeau on September 15 postponed a general election probably until the spring of 1979, though his chief opponents, the Progressive Conservatives led by 39-year-old Joseph Clark, demanded a test at the polls. The

government's five-year term ends in July 1979. Canada's uncertain mood as 1978 ended suggested the possibility of impending political change.

One upcoming change that surprised almost everyone was Trudeau's announcement on December 7 that Canada would have a new governor general in January. He is Edward R. Schreyer, premier of Manitoba from 1969 to 1977.

Anti-Trudeau Feeling? Conventional political wisdom holds that governments are not elected, they are defeated. Many observers wondered if this adage would be borne out in the political history of Canada. The Liberal Party, which held federal power for 37 of the last 43 years, suffered a number of sharp election setbacks in 1978. The most painful occurred on October 16, when the Liberals lost five seats in 15 by-elections to fill House of Commons vacancies. The Liberals won only 2 contested seats, both in Quebec. The Conservatives, with 6 of their seats at stake, lost 2 and kept 4, but won 6 more from the Liberals to emerge with 10 seats. The New Democratic Party (NDP) took a seat in Newfoundland for the first time and held on to another in Toronto, Ont. The Social Credit Party retained the constituency of André Fortin, who was killed in an automobile accident in 1977. Following the by-elections, standings in the 264-seat House of Commons were: Liberals, 136; Progressive Conservatives, 97; NDP, 17; Social Credit, 9; and Independent, 5.

While some commentators saw in the election results an English-Canadian backlash against a French-Canadian prime minister committed to policies of biculturalism, other conclusions seemed more plausible. Voters judged the Trudeau government's performance after 10 years in office, and its management of the economy was awarded low marks. The prime minister's arbitrary approach to constitutional reform had alienated people in western Canada. In addition, there was a general sense of a loss of direction and efficiency in the federal administration. All these factors hurt the government.

Cabinet Reorganization late in 1978 appeared to some observers to be Trudeau's response to the general dissatisfaction. In a surprise move on November 24, the prime minister shuffled his Cabinet and created a new federal ministry to be known as the Board of Economic Development Ministers. Robert K. Andras, who previously oversaw government spending as president of the Treasury Board, was named to head the powerful new department. All economic development proposals going to the Cabinet and the Treasury Board will have to be approved by the ministry, which will coordinate Canada's industrial strategy in an effort to improve trade and restrain inflation.

The appointment of a number of new ministers as the year neared an end served to restructure a Cabinet that had been in a state of flux throughout 1978. Embarrassing circumstances abounded. Francis Fox quit as solicitor-general in January after it was revealed that he forged another man's name on a hospital document to help a friend get an abortion. John Munro, minister of labor, had to resign on September 8 because he called a provincial court judge on behalf of a constituent who was about to be sentenced.

Fox, whose post encompassed supervision of the Royal Canadian Mounted Police, then under investigation for illegal practices, was replaced by Postmaster General Jean-Jacques Blais, a bilingual lawyer from northern Ontario. Gilles Lamontagne, former mayor of Quebec City and a newcomer to the Cabinet, succeeded Blais. Later, Ronald Basford, a member of the Cabinet since 1968, resigned as minister of justice for personal reasons. Trudeau gave the position on an interim basis to his veteran colleague Otto E. Lang, who was already serving as minister of transport and as the member of the government responsible for the Canadian Wheat Board. André Ouellet, minister of state for urban affairs, became acting labor minister.

Finally, the November appointments resulted in the following men holding office at the end of 1978: J. Judd Buchanan, president of the Treasury Board; Marc Lalonde, minister of justice and attorney general; André Ouellet, minister of public works; Martin O'Connell, labor minister; Pierre De Bané,

supply and services minister; and John Reid, minister of state for federal-provincial relations.

Canada's Economy continued to suffer in 1978. Wage and price controls applied by the Trudeau government in October 1975 expired in 1978 after achieving mixed results. The weakness of the economy led to a balance-of-payments deficit, a decline in foreign capital inflow, and a downward trend in the value of the Canadian dollar.

The government tried to reduce the rate of increase in federal spending. On August 1, Trudeau announced that he would change current and planned government spending patterns to cut expenditures by $2 billion. Proposed steps included returning some government operations to the private sector, prohibiting growth in the federal public service, and making the dispute-ridden post office into an autonomous public corporation. Family-allowance payments would be made more equitable, and the number of unemployment-insurance claimants would be reduced by 10 per cent.

The federal deficit caused concern in 1978. In the first of two budgets, Finance Minister Jean Chrétien on April 10 estimated revenues of $36 billion and expenditures of $46.9 billion for the 1978-1979 fiscal year. Taking into account nonbudgetary items, a deficit of $11.5 billion was estimated. This was later revised to $11.8 billion, the largest in Canadian

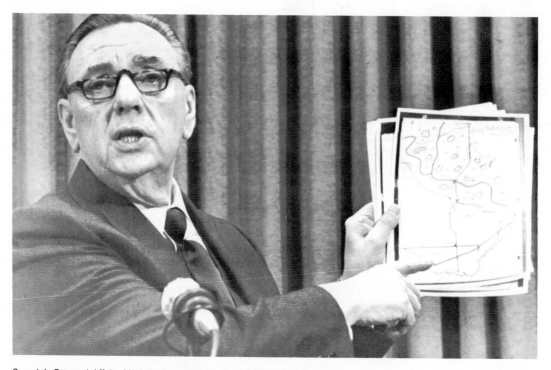

Canada's External Affairs Minister Donald C. Jamieson uses map to explain how government gathered evidence on a Russian spy ring.

history. A decline to $9.7 billion, later revised to $10.75 billion, was projected for 1979-1980.

The increase in real economic growth during 1978 was expected to be a disappointing 3 per cent. The few hopeful signs included a slowdown in the consumer price index's rate of increase and a somewhat brighter employment picture.

The Canadian dollar, after an orderly adjustment downward in 1977, fell more drastically in 1978. In early October, it fell from 90 cents (U.S.) to a little below 84 cents (U.S.) and then recovered slightly. This drop reflected uncertainty about the level of interest rates in Canada and poor merchandise trade returns during the summer.

The government borrowed abroad to support the reserves and raised the prime lending rate, which in practice has to be about one percentage point above the U.S. level in order to attract foreign capital. The Bank of Canada raised its bank rate – the rate of interest the central bank charges on loans to the chartered banks – to a record 10.75 per cent on November 5. This was the sixth increase during a year that began with a rate of 7.5 per cent. The move reflected the need to keep Canadian interest rates in line with U.S. rates, which were also rising.

Federal Budgets. Taxation changes were limited and, in some cases, temporary. Finance Minister Chrétien's April 10 budget offered to compensate the provinces if they would immediately reduce their consumer sales taxes. Two options were offered: a reduction of 2 per cent for a nine-month period, chosen by British Columbia and Saskatchewan, or a 3 per cent reduction for six months, chosen by Manitoba, New Brunswick, Newfoundland, Nova Scotia, Ontario, and Prince Edward Island. The federal government offered to make up all or part of the surrendered revenue, depending upon the province's financial state. Alberta, having no sales tax, could not respond to the offer, while Quebec demanded compensation on a different basis.

Chrétien's second budget, on November 16, tried to stimulate the economy while maintaining the cost competitiveness gained earlier. The federal manufacturing sales tax was reduced from 12 to 9 per cent, while personal tax exemptions and the employment expense deduction increased. Revenue was expected to fall short by $1.38 billion, providing a deficit for fiscal 1979-1980 of $10.75 billion.

Federal Legislation. Parliament's achievements were limited during the third session, which ended on October 10. A new session, the fourth, began the next day. The government's program for the new session concentrated on economic remedies and constitutional reforms. Several items not passed earlier were reintroduced. These included legislation to equalize public- and private-sector pay levels and put a ceiling on public-service pensions, create a federal ombudsman, and change the family-allowance and unemployment-insurance programs.

Parliament ended a bitter 10-day postal strike on October 18 by sending inside workers back to their jobs, and later ordered 375 engineers serving on lake carriers back to work to complete the last seven weeks of the Great Lakes shipping season.

Constitutional Progress. Trudeau made his third attempt to win a national consensus on changes in the British North America Act of 1867, the statute defining federal and provincial powers in the Canadian federation. He introduced legislation on June 20 aimed at modifying federal institutions and enacting a charter of rights and freedoms. Earlier attempts drew an unsympathetic response from the provinces, and Trudeau's latest initiative, including provisions for minority language rights, seemed

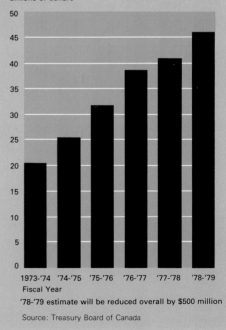

Federal Spending in Canada

Estimated Budget for Fiscal 1979*

	Billions of Dollars
Health and welfare	16.805
Public debt	6.500
Economic development and support	5.134
Defense	5.072
Transportation and communications	3.163
Fiscal transfer payments to provinces	2.801
General government services	2.236
Education assistance	1.729
Internal overhead expenses	1.700
Foreign affairs	1.033
Culture and recreation	1.023
Total	46.476

*April 1, 1978, to March 31, 1979

Spending Since 1973

Billions of dollars

'78-'79 estimate will be reduced overall by $500 million

Source: Treasury Board of Canada

The Ministry of Canada
In order of precedence

Pierre Elliott Trudeau, prime minister

Allan Joseph MacEachen, president of the queen's privy council and deputy prime minister

Jean Chrétien, minister of finance

Donald Campbell Jamieson, secretary of state for external affairs

Robert Knight Andras, president of the board of economic development ministers

Otto Emil Lang, minister of transport

Alastair William Gillespie, minister of energy, mines, and resources and minister of state for science and technology

Martin Patrick O'Connell, minister of labor

Eugene Francis Whelan, minister of agriculture

W. Warren Allmand, minister of consumer and corporate affairs

James Hugh Faulkner, minister of Indian affairs and northern development

André Ouellet, minister of public works

Daniel Joseph MacDonald, minister of veterans affairs

Marc Lalonde, minister of justice and attorney general of Canada

Jeanne Sauvé, minister of communications

Raymond Joseph Perrault, leader of the government in the Senate

Barnett Jerome Danson, minister of national defense

J. Judd Buchanan, president of the treasury board

Roméo LeBlanc, minister of fisheries

Marcel Lessard, minister of regional economic expansion

Jack Sydney George Cullen, minister of employment and immigration

Leonard Stephen Marchand, minister of state for the environment

John Roberts, secretary of state of Canada

Monique Bégin, minister of national health and welfare

Jean-Jacques Blais, solicitor general of Canada

Anthony Chisholm Abbott, minister of state for small business and minister of national revenue

Iona Campagnolo, minister of state for fitness and amateur sport

John Henry Horner, minister of industry, trade, and commerce

Norman A. Cafik, minister of state for multiculturalism

Gilles Lamontagne, postmaster general

John M. Reid, minister of state for federal-provincial relations

Pierre De Bané, minister of supply and services

Premiers of Canadian Provinces

Province	Premier
Alberta	Peter Lougheed
British Columbia	William R. Bennett
Manitoba	Sterling R. Lyon
New Brunswick	Richard B. Hatfield
Newfoundland	Frank Moores
Nova Scotia	John Buchanan
Ontario	William G. Davis
Prince Edward Island	Bennett Campbell
Quebec	René Lévesque
Saskatchewan	Allan Blakeney

Commissioners of Territories

Northwest Territories	Stuart M. Hodgson
Yukon Territory	Frank Fingland

destined for the same fate. The premiers examined the Trudeau plan at their annual conference in Regina, Sask., on August 9 and 10, but could not agree with it. A first ministers' conference held in Ottawa from October 30 to November 1 also failed to make progress. They decided to hold another conference on the subject in February 1979. A committee of selected ministers was named to study the proposed changes.

U.S. Relations. Fisheries and maritime boundaries became a controversial issue in 1978. The declaration of 200-nautical-mile offshore economic zones in 1977 by both countries made it necessary to define fishing limits and to draw boundaries across the continental shelf in contiguous areas.

United States fishing vessels were ordered out of Canadian coastal waters on June 4, a move that signaled the collapse of the 1977-1978 interim reciprocal agreement. The United States immediately closed its waters to Canadian fishermen. Differences concerned the conservation of fish stocks and access to rich inshore fisheries on both coasts of the continent. Drawing a maritime boundary across the Gulf of Maine, the site of valuable cod and haddock fisheries as well as promising oil and gas fields, constituted the most serious issue. Special negotiators appointed in mid-1977 to hammer out a comprehensive settlement, continued to meet with little success. Strong pressures on each side from state and provincial authorities raised the possibility that the boundary disputes could be settled only by third-party arbitration.

Canada and the United States also competed for a $535-million engine plant to be built by the Ford Motor Company in either Ohio or Ontario. It was announced on August 3 that Ontario had won the prize, aided by $68 million in grants to Ford from the federal government and Ontario. The new plant, to be built outside Windsor, was expected to employ about 2,600 workers, starting in April 1981.

The Canadian Senate's Foreign Affairs Committee issued a comprehensive study on August 10 recommending that Canada adopt free trade with the United States. By abandoning tariff protection, Canada could overcome structural weaknesses in its economy arising from a small domestic market, limited production runs, and a fragmented manufacturing industry. The government made no immediate response to the far-reaching proposal.

Foreign Affairs. Fragments from a nuclear-powered Russian satellite came down in the Northwest Territories on January 24. Canadian and U.S. aircraft joined in an expensive search for the radioactive debris and found about 220 pounds (100 kilograms) of fragments, most of them around the northeast corner of Great Slave Lake. The reactor core of the satellite was not found. Canada claimed some of the expenses of the search from Russia.

On February 9, Canada expelled 11 Russian

officials and barred two others from returning to Canada for plotting to infiltrate the security division of the Royal Canadian Mounted Police. Donald C. Jamieson, minister for external affairs, canceled a proposed visit to Russia after issuing the largest expulsion order in Canadian history for diplomatic espionage offenses.

Jamieson and other officials also worked on a team with representatives from Great Britain, France, West Germany, and the United States that tried to work out arrangements for the independence of Namibia (South West Africa). The group visited South Africa in October for talks on the plan, which was based on elections to be supervised by the United Nations (UN). Canada also supplied 80 communications specialists to the UN peacekeeping mission in southern Lebanon from April to October.

Facts in Brief: Population: 23,901,000. Government: Governor General Jules Léger; Prime Minister Pierre Elliott Trudeau. Monetary unit: Canadian dollar. Foreign trade: exports, $41,452,000,000; imports, $39,561,000,000. David M. L. Farr

See also Canadian provinces articles; CANADIAN LIBRARY ASSOCIATION (CLA); CANADIAN LITERATURE; LÉGER, JULES; MCDERMOTT, DENNIS; MCINTOSH, CAMERON IRWIN; ROGERS, HARRY; TRUDEAU, PIERRE ELLIOTT. In WORLD BOOK, see CANADA; CANADA, GOVERNMENT OF; CANADA, HISTORY OF.

CANADIAN LIBRARY ASSOCIATION (CLA)

took strong positions on postal rates, public access to information, and constitutional proposals in 1978. CLA protested the April 1 increase in the library-book postage rate, the first such rise in 27 years. Book-mailing costs, though still subsidized by the postal system, increased as much as 150 per cent.

In a June 13 brief to the parliamentary Joint Committee on Regulations and Other Statutory Instruments, CLA advocated more openness of government records and files, and recommended that the federal government's network of departmental libraries be responsible for easing public access to information. CLA also recommended appointing an information commissioner to resolve disputes when a government agency denies a citizen's request for information.

CLA sent a brief on September 29 to the Special Joint Committee on the Constitution of Canada, established to examine constitutional proposals of the government of Canada. The brief said the constitution should provide a federal role in coordinating and developing labraries as cultural institutions.

Project: Progress. With $130,000 raised, CLA ended its fund-raising campaign for "Project: Progress," a study to be made in 1979 on the future of Canadian public libraries. The study will provide a development plan for the next 20 years. The federal secretary of state will provide such information as

sociological and demographic profiles on 1,000 communities and data on national reading habits, community awareness, and use of libraries in 18 cities.

Awards. The CLA presented two book awards in June 1978: the English Medal Award for the best English-language Canadian children's book of 1977 to Dennis Lee for *Garbage Delight* (Macmillan) and the Amelia Frances Howard-Gibbon Medal for the best illustrated children's book to Elizabeth Cleaver for *The Loon's Necklace* (Oxford).

The CLA awarded the Howard V. Phalin-World Book Graduate Scholarship in Library Science to Sieglinde Stieda-Levasseur of Corner Brook, Nfld.; the H. W. Wilson Education Foundation Scholarship to April Covey of Prescott, Ont.; and the Elizabeth Dafoe Scholarship to Ellen Clarke of Toronto, Ont. The Canadian School Library Association presented the Margaret B. Scott Award of Merit to Lyle Evans King of Regina, Sask., and the Distinguished Service Award for School Administrators to Michael Kindrachuk of Saskatoon, Sask. A third Saskatchewan resident, Phoebe Bunnell of Swift Current, received the Canadian Library Trustees' Association Merit Award.

The CLA attracted 1,375 delegates to its annual conference, in Edmonton, Alta., from June 15 to 20. CLA memberships on June 30 totaled 3,700 individuals and 1,000 institutions. Paul Kitchen

In WORLD BOOK, see CANADIAN LIBRARY ASSN.

CANADIAN LITERATURE

faced economic and censorship problems in 1978, but offered plenty of variety and depth in all fields. A sluggish economy, reflected in inflation, the falling value of the dollar, and high unemployment, prompted the federal government to reduce its support of translation, children's books, public readings, and publication grants.

The Canada Council, which provides grants for the arts, was attacked for supporting the writing and publication of allegedly pornographic material. Some recognized literary works, such as Margaret Laurence's *The Diviners* and Alice Munro's *Lives of Girls and Women,* were removed from school libraries and literature courses in some communities.

Biography. The most visible title was *Trudeau* by George Radwanski, a psychological profile of Prime Minister Pierre Elliott Trudeau. For balance, there was David Humphries' *Joe Clark,* a biography of the Conservative Party leader. Peter Stursberg contributed another oral history, *Lester Pearson and the Dream of National Unity,* re-creating highlights in the career of the former prime minister.

Treating the careers of business tycoons were best-selling novelist Richard Rohmer's plodding but valuable *E. P. Taylor;* Michael Bliss's *A Canadian Millionaire,* which traced the rise and fall of Joseph Flavelle, the industrial magnate whose career was flecked by scandal; and Peter Newman's *Bronfman*

Aritha van Herk, 23, mounts a Montreal scaffold to get the $50,000 prize for her novel, *Judith,* winner of the Seal Books first-novel competition.

Dynasty, a lively, anecdotal account of the wealthy family's founder.

Other biographies and memoirs of well-known Canadians included *Bethune: The Montreal Years* by Wendell MacLeod, about a pivotal segment in the life of the noted surgeon; *The Making of a Secret Agent* by Frank Pickersgill, based on the letters of the remarkable war hero who was tortured and hanged by the Nazis in 1944; and *Fun Tomorrow* by John Morgan Gray, the publisher who nurtured the careers of such outstanding writers as Hugh Mac-Lennan, Morley Callaghan, and Donald Creighton. The life and work of painters Jean Paul Lemieux and J. E. H. MacDonald were examined by writers Guy Robert and Paul Duval, respectively, in a pair of lavishly illustrated books, *Lemieux* and *The Tangled Net.*

History. Many works dealt with Canada's destiny, especially the possibility of Quebec province separating from the rest of Canada. *Quebec: The People Speak,* edited by Rick Butler, contained interviews with 100 residents of the province; Heather Menzies' *The Railroad's Not Enough* plumbed the fears and aspirations of grass-roots Canadians; and Douglas Fullerton's *The Dangerous Delusion* denounced the aims and activities of the political architects of Quebec's aspirations to independence. Other books included the more optimistic *Has Canada a Future?,* by Marie-Josée Drouin and Barry

Bruce-Briggs, and *Together We Stand* by Donald Swinburne.

Pierre Berton published his 25th book in 24 years, *The Wild Frontier,* which again popularized and dramatized Canada's past. Historian Arthur Lower took up the theme of Western civilization in *A Pattern for History,* and Joseph Schull's focus was *Ontario Since 1867.* Graham Metson's *The Halifax Explosion* detailed the 1917 tragedy in which 1,659 persons died, James McWilliams and James Steel's *The Suicide Battalion* was an absorbing account of a Canadian infantry group cut to pieces in the European battlefields of World War I, and Joyce Hibbert's *The War Brides* gave first-person accounts of some of the 41,351 women who married Canadian soldiers based overseas in World War II.

Fiction. Short stories flourished in 1978 more than in any other recent year. Alice Munro again demonstrated her polished prose style in her fourth collection, *Who Do You Think You Are?;* and Margaret Gibson, a brilliant young talent, dealt again with darkly symbolic themes of madness and alienation. Other collections included works by Matt Cohen, Dave Godfrey, George Bowering, W. D. Valgardson, and Gunther Plaut. Anthologies included *78: Best Canadian Stories,* edited by John Metcalf and Clark Blaise; *The Best Modern Canadian Short Stories,* edited by Ivon Owen and Morris Wolfe; and *Canadian Short Stories,* edited by Robert Weaver.

In a year when major novels were sparse, there was a rich crop of books by well-known writers and some newcomers. Marian Engel followed her 1976 Governor General's Award-winning novel *Bear* with her sixth novel, *The Glassy Sea,* typically rich in style. Morley Callaghan contributed a publishing oddity in *No Man's Meat* and *The Enchanted Pimp,* two novellas written 47 years apart. Other noteworthy novels included *A Casual Affair* by Sylvia Fraser and *No More into the Garden* by David Watmough. The most publicized novel was Aritha van Herk's *Judith,* winner of the $50,000 Seal Books first-novel competition. Set on an Alberta pig farm, the novel spun several variations on the theme of woman's plight in modern society.

Poetry. The best of the collections was Al Purdy's *Being Alive,* idiosyncratic poems on a variety of subjects including nature, travel, beer halls, hockey, and love, gathered from 20 years of accomplished writing. *Fall by Fury* by Earle Birney, *Two-Headed Poems* by Margaret Atwood, *The Works* by Phyllis Gotlieb, and *The Ghosts Call You Poor* by Andrew Suknaski were other distinguished works.

Miscellaneous. Poet-novelist Leonard Cohen's first book in six years, *Death of a Lady's Man,* aroused much interest with its "mono-dialogue" about despair and the urgings of the flesh. *The Other Side of Hugh MacLennan,* edited by Elspeth Cameron, offered thoughtful essays on a wide range of subjects by the major Canadian novelist. Bernard Ostry contributed *The Cultural Connection,* a timely analysis of government cultural policy. Among many books on travel was poet Gwendolyn MacEwen's *Mermaids and Ikons,* a memoir of Greece.

Governor General's Literary Awards for books published in 1977 went to Timothy Findley for *The Wars* (English fiction); D. G. Jones for *Under the Thunder the Flowers Light up the Earth* (English poetry); Frank Scott for *Essays on the Constitution* (English nonfiction); Gabrielle Roy for *Ces enfants de ma vie* (French fiction); Michael Garneau for *Les Célébrations* and *Adidou Adidouce* (French drama); and Denis Monière for *Le dévelopement des idéologies au Quebec des origines à nos jours* (French nonfiction).

The Sir John A. Macdonald Prize for the historical work that made the most significant contribution to understanding the Canadian past went to Robin Fisher for *Contact and Conflict: Indian-European Relations in British Columbia 1774-1890.* Frank Scott won a Canada Council Translation Prize for his English translation of *Poems of French Canada* and Jean Paré won for his French translation of *The Weekend Man,* a novel by Richard Wright. The Stephen Leacock Memorial Award for humor was presented to Ernest Buckler for *Whirligig,* a collection of essays and light verse.   Ken Adachi

In WORLD BOOK, see CANADIAN LITERATURE.

CAPE VERDE. See AFRICA.

CARAZO ODIO, RODRIGO (1926-   ), candidate of the conservative opposition Union Party, was elected president of Costa Rica on Feb. 5, 1978. Carazo defeated Luis Alberto Monge of the National Liberation Party (PLN), which had been in power for eight years. Carazo was sworn in as president on May 8.

President Carazo, an economics expert and businessman, was born in Cartago on Dec. 27, 1926. After attending various schools, he graduated from the University of Costa Rica in 1954 with a degree in economics.

During his college years, Carazo became interested in politics and joined the PLN. In 1948, he was elected as a deputy to the Legislative Assembly, where he later served as president. He switched parties in 1969, joining the Democratic Renovation Party. He ran unsuccessfully as the party's candidate in the 1974 presidential election.

The president, who is firmly anti-Communist, announced after his election that he would recall Costa Rica's ambassador to Russia. He also indicated he would expel fugitive American financier Robert Vesco, who had been living in Costa Rica. Vesco was wanted by U.S. authorities on charges of fraudulent financial transactions. When Vesco went to the Bahamas on business, Carazo barred his return in May. Then in July, Vesco's application for Costa Rican citizenship was rejected.   Paul C. Tullier

CARTER, JAMES EARL, JR. (1924-   ), was more at ease in his second year in the White House in 1978. Early in the year his popularity sank in public-opinion polls, and many Americans thought he was not doing his job well. But following his successful intervention in the Middle East peace talks in September, Carter's popularity rating rose 11 per cent.

"My first year in office, maybe year and a half, I think I was overly cautious, timid about exerting the innate authority and influence of the President," he said after the Camp David conference. "I think that in the last few months I have been more at ease with it and have used it more forcefully, and it has proven to be more effective."

The Carter Staff. One reason for the President's new image was the addition to his staff on July 1 of advertising man Gerald R. Rafshoon. Rafshoon advised the President to appear more forceful in public and worked to coordinate the public statements of top-level White House staff members and Cabinet officials, to avoid the appearance of indecision and dissension in the Administration.

President Carter was angry when he discovered that his special assistant for health affairs, Peter G. Bourne, had made out a prescription to a fictitious person when prescribing a sleeping pill for a White House staff member. Bourne resigned from his White House post in July.

President Carter and his party float down the Salmon River in a rubber raft during a 10-day vacation trip to Idaho and Wyoming in August.

Camp David. At the presidential retreat in the mountains at Camp David on September 6, the President took personal charge of a secluded 13-day meeting with Israeli Prime Minister Menachem Begin and Egypt's President Anwar al-Sadat. Dressed in casual jeans and shuttling from cabin to cabin in the woods, he drew on the enormous prestige of the presidency and on his personality to persuade Begin and Sadat to reach an agreement. In a moving television appearance on September 17, Carter, Sadat, and Begin signed agreements preliminary to – but not guaranteeing – a peaceful settlement of the long Egyptian-Israeli Middle East conflict.

Relations with Congress. The President also took a more forceful position in his relationship with Congress, warning that he would not approve measures that limited his authority and that he would veto bills he regarded as inflationary. He vetoed defense and public-works appropriations despite their political appeal, and made the vetoes stick.

President Carter emphasized that he was reluctant to impose mandatory wage and price controls; instead, he appealed to all Americans to make sacrifices to slow the rate of inflation. He pledged thrift and austerity for his Administration and declared that the federal budget for 1980 would be a "very tight, very stringent" budget. See PRESIDENT OF THE UNITED STATES.

Personal Affairs. A report released by the White House on June 15 revealed that Carter earned almost $500,000 in 1977, including $236,458 in his combined salary and expense account, $114,283 from stock sales in a blind trust, $137,405 in royalties on his book *Why Not the Best?*, and interest from various bank accounts and insurance. His business losses of $306,272, presumably reflecting a poor peanut crop, offset his income, and his final tax payment was $48,152 in federal personal income taxes on a taxable income of $121,827. The President's assets were valued in 1977 at slightly less than $1 million.

In November 1978, it was revealed that the Carter family owed $2,328 in back property taxes and interest because of undervalued property and equipment. Jimmy Carter's share was $1,440.

The President, his wife, Rosalynn, daughter, Amy, and sons Chip and Jack vacationed in Idaho and Wyoming from August 21 to 30 and made a three-day, 71-mile (114-kilometer) trip down the middle fork of the Salmon River on a rubber raft. The presidential raft was equipped with telephone and radio communication, while a communications satellite, Strategic Air Command planes, and helicopters flew overhead. The President's party was followed by Secret Service agents, White House aides, reporters, and guides.　　Carol L. Thompson

In WORLD BOOK, see CARTER, JAMES EARL, JR.

CAT. America's most celebrated cat, Morris, the finicky feline who appeared in television cat-food commercials for 10 years, died on July 7, 1978. He was 17. Morris was discovered in 1966 in a Chicago animal shelter by pet handler Bob Martwick, who was looking for a cat for a TV commercial.

A controversy broke out in May over some 30 stray cats living in the basement of the United Nations (UN) Secretariat Building in New York City. The cats were said to be polluting and damaging stored documents. It was finally agreed that maintenance workers would catch the cats for members of the UN employees' animal rights club, who would try to find homes for them.

Tiki and Minet, mixed-breed cats, were cited for heroism by Delaware Governor Pierre du Pont IV in June. They roused their owner, Susan Dyson of Wilmington, after fire broke out in her house.

The Cat Fanciers' Association named Gr. Ch. Jama Kats Midnight Sun, a Persian male owned by Marlene Luyster of North Canton, Ohio, as Best Cat of the Year. Chosen Best Kitten was Gr. Ch. Jo-Le's Jet Set, a Persian male owned by Joseph and Carol Gianuzzi of Syracuse, N.Y. Best Alter award went to a Persian spay, Gr. Ch. and Gr. Pr. Nipawin Pipkin of Tabbyland, owned by Lawrence E. Filson of Potomac, Md.   Theodore M. O'Leary

In WORLD BOOK, see CAT.

CENSUS. The population of the United States was estimated at 219,874,966 on Jan. 1, 1979, according to the Bureau of the Census. During 1978, the population increased by 1.7 million – the result of 3.3 million births, 1.9 million deaths, and about 347,000 net immigrants.

The 1977 birth rate was 15.3 per 1,000 persons, up slightly from 14.7 in 1976. But at the same time, statistics indicate that women are delaying child-bearing longer now than a few years ago. Nonetheless, women under 35 report that they expect to have 2.1 children, on the average, during their lives.

The changing birth rate is altering the age structure of the population. In 1977, there were 6.4-million fewer children under 14 than in 1970. During the same period, the highest rate of population growth – 32 per cent – occurred among persons 25 to 34 years old, while the elderly population of 65 and over increased by 18 per cent. The median age of the population increased from 27.9 to 29.4 years.

The divorce rate was 5.1 divorces per 1,000 persons in 1977, compared with 5.0 divorces in 1976. Meanwhile, the marriage rate rose slightly from 9.9 marriages per 1,000 persons in 1976 to 10.1 in 1977, well below the peak of 11.0 in 1972.

For the first time in this century, nonmetropolitan areas grew faster than metropolitan areas during the 1970s – 1.2 per cent versus 0.8 per cent per year.

Fischetti © 1978 *Chicago Sun-Times*

"Good night, sweet prince, and flights of angels sing thee to thy rest!"

However, the farm population continued its slow, steady decline. There were 7.8 million living on farms in 1977, compared with 9.7 million in 1970.

The United States population increased by 13-million between 1970 and 1977, and 40 per cent of this growth was concentrated in California, Florida, and Texas. The rate of population growth during this time was highest in Alaska with 35 per cent; Nevada, 30 per cent; and Arizona, 29 per cent.

Work Force. The total U.S. work force in 1977, including the armed forces, passed the 100-million mark for the first time. Women made up 41 per cent of the civilian work force and accounted for 57 per cent of the increase since 1970.

Median family income, in constant dollars, was 3 per cent higher in 1976 than in 1975. The median family income in 1976 was $14,960. White families in 1976 had a median income of $15,540; blacks, $9,240; and Latin Americans, $10,260.

There were 24.5 million blacks in the civilian population in March 1977, 11.5 per cent of the total U.S. population. There were about 11.3 million Latin Americans, compared with 10.8 million in March 1974.   Manuel D. Plotkin

In WORLD BOOK, see CENSUS; POPULATION.
CENTRAL AFRICAN EMPIRE. See AFRICA.
CEYLON. See SRI LANKA.
CHAD. See AFRICA.

CHEMICAL INDUSTRY. Sweden in 1978 became the first country to legislate against fluorocarbon aerosol sprays because of concern that they might harm the atmosphere. The ban, passed on January 28, was to take effect on Jan. 1, 1979. In the United States, a federal ban cut off manufacture of aerosol products using fluorocarbons after Dec. 15, 1978.

Canada's National Health and Welfare Department said in October that it will allow cyclamates to be used to sweeten drugs, reversing a 1969 decision based on the suspicion that cyclamates cause cancer. Cyclamates are banned from food and soft drinks, but can be used as a table sweetener in Canada. They are banned from use in the United States.

The chemical industry in the United States operated at 85 per cent of capacity in 1978. Capital expenditures totaled $9.1 billion, up 10 per cent from 1977. Many large companies built cost-saving and energy-related projects, rather than adding to their capacity. United States chemical companies invested $2.6 billion for new plants and equipment overseas, up 11 per cent. The process industries, including paper, rubber, plastics, and nonferrous metals, invested $26.5 billion in U.S. plants in 1978, a 24 per cent increase over 1977.

Profits of most U.S. chemical manufacturers increased, with makers of housing and construction supplies leading the industry. Cement, forest-

World's largest fermenter is installed in March in new $76-million plant in Billingham, England. It will be used to produce protein to feed livestock.

products, and pharmaceutical companies did well. Fiber makers profited by reducing costs. Large manufacturers of industrial chemicals and synthetic materials had mixed results.

Health and Safety. The U.S. Environmental Protection Agency (EPA) issued a preliminary list of 269 chemicals as likely candidates for regulation as "potential occupational carcinogens." The American Industrial Health Council, representing 76 producers and users of industrial chemicals, claimed EPA chose the chemicals without sufficient review or analysis.

The EPA on February 15 restricted the sale of 2,000 pesticides containing 23 "potentially hazardous chemicals" to farmers and commercial users. EPA officials estimated that the pesticide industry would have to spend $4.5 million to relabel the products.

On June 7, the EPA proposed a ban on making and using polychlorinated biphenyls (PCB's), industrial chemicals that are linked to cancer and other diseases. All domestic manufacture of PCB had stopped voluntarily in 1977, but the Toxic Substances Control Act required the formal ban. Used by industries since 1929, PCB's have found their way into the environment and have contaminated fish in the Hudson River and the Great Lakes.

New Regulations. The U.S. Department of Labor's Occupational Safety and Health Administration (OSHA) on September 29 limited worker exposure to acrylonitrile, a liquid used in synthetic fibers and other plastics, to 2 parts per million (ppm) of air over an eight-hour period. Laboratory tests and surveys of exposed workers had linked the chemical to cancer. OSHA gave companies two years beyond the November 2 effective date to install equipment to meet the standard.

In the Courts. A $1-billion class-action lawsuit against 15 asbestos companies was filed in Los Angeles on October 27 on behalf of 5,000 workers at two shipyards. The plaintiffs said the companies concealed and distorted reports on the health dangers of asbestos. More than 1,000 lawsuits, claiming more than $2 billion, were filed against the asbestos industry by the end of 1978.

OSHA cut the allowable level of benzene in workplace air on February 2 from 10 ppm to 1 ppm. A federal appeals court in New Orleans voided the rule on October 5, saying it was based on old evidence that failed to show benefits related reasonably to the $500-million cost of compliance.

A federal judge in Lake Charles, La., issued a preliminary injunction on September 14 nullifying a ruling by the Consumer Product Safety Commission that perchloroethylene should be restricted because of a cancer risk. It is a solvent used in cleaning, household, and office products.   Frederick C. Price

See also ENVIRONMENT. In WORLD BOOK, see CHEMICAL INDUSTRY.

CHEMISTRY. Two West German chemists advanced the chemical theory of aromaticity in July 1978. Heinz A. Staab and François Diederich of the Max Planck Institute for Medical Research in Heidelberg synthesized kekulene, a large compound made up of 12 benzene rings arranged in a circle.

Benzene possesses *aromaticity* (extra stability caused by its planar system of adjacent double bonds of carbon atoms). The chemists wanted to learn whether kekulene also possessed aromaticity or whether it behaved as a polyolefin, a compound with many double bonds but no aromaticity.

Staab and Diederich synthesized kekulene by using recently developed reactions for the formation of carbon-carbon bonds via sulfur extrusion from dithia [3.3] phanes. Kekulene forms greenish-yellow crystals and is extremely insoluble in most solvents. To determine whether kekulene possessed aromaticity, the chemists used nuclear magnetic resonance (NMR) spectroscopy, a technique that measures the magnetic and electronic environments in a molecule. The extreme insolubility of kekulene made it necessary to measure the NMR spectrum 50,000 times, using automated scanning techniques and signal averaging. The results indicated that kekulene is an aromatic compound.

New Synthesis. A compound that eluded chemists for decades has been synthesized by chemists Charles L. Perrin and Thomas Arrhenius of the University of California, San Diego. Perrin and Arrhenius reported in August that they had obtained malonic anhydride, a highly strained four-membered ring, by reacting diketene and ozone at $-108.5°$ F. $(-78°C)$. At room temperature, malonic anhydride breaks up spontaneously into ketene $(CH_2=C=O)$ and carbon dioxide. The California researchers also synthesized the dimethyl derivative of malonic anhydride from a dimer of dimethylketene under the same conditions.

Optically Active Compounds. Ernest L. Eliel, Jorma K. Koskimies, and Bruno Lohri of the University of North Carolina in Chapel Hill reported in March that they prepared an almost 100 per cent yield of one optically active form of atrolactic acid methyl ester.

Optically active molecules differ in only their *chirality* or handedness – that is, they differ as your right hand differs from your left hand. In nature, usually only one optically active form of a molecule occurs. In molecules synthesized in the laboratory, both forms occur, usually in equal numbers.

Beginning with a 1,3-oxathiane, a cyclic, chiral compound containing four carbons, an oxygen, and a sulfur atom in its ring, the chemists used two reactions to transfer the handedness at the ring carbon to a new carbon group adjacent to the ring. Later reactions split off the new group and formed atrolactic acid methyl ester, almost all of which was of one optically active form. Eliel and his colleagues are applying this method to synthesizing some of the biologically most important compounds, the optically active amino acids.

NMR Imaging. Researchers reported advances in the use of NMR to obtain chemical images from inside the body. In April, a research team headed by Waldo S. Hinshaw of the University of Nottingham, England, reported making cross-sectional NMR images of the head and forelegs of a rabbit.

NMR uses electromagnetic fields to measure the magnetic moments in the nuclei of chemical elements. The fields present no known hazard to people. Hinshaw's NMR instrument measures the hydrogen atoms in the water present in tissue. It provides a two-dimensional map of water distribution.

NMR imaging has great potential for biological and clinical research. However, its development for use in medical diagnosis will take several years.

Nobel and Priestley. Peter Mitchell, 58, of the Glynn Research Laboratories near Cornwall, England, won the 1978 Nobel Prize for Chemistry for his work on energy transfer in living cells (see NOBEL PRIZES). Glenn T. Seaborg, 66, of the University of California, Berkeley, won the 1979 Priestley Medal of the American Chemical Society, the highest honor in U.S. chemistry. Seaborg was co-winner of the 1951 Nobel Prize for Chemistry.   Lawrence Verbit

In WORLD BOOK, see BENZENE; CHEMISTRY; SEABORG, GLENN THEODORE.

CHESS. Anatoly Karpov, 27, of Russia retained his world chess championship in 1978. He defeated Viktor Korchnoi, 47, a Russian defector now living in Switzerland, six games to five in a 32-game match in Baguio, the Philippines, that began on July 17 and ended October 17. It was the longest championship match in history, with 21 games resulting in draws. The purse, awarded in Swiss francs, was valued at $550,000 when the match began. At the end of the match, its value had climbed to $696,233.30 due to the loss in value of the dollar. Karpov received $432,645.80; Korchnoi got $263,587.50.

Tournament Theatrics. The contestants, each trying to gain a psychological edge, squabbled over such physical details as the flags flown and furniture used. Korchnoi charged that Russian parapsychologist Vladimir Zoukhar, a Karpov aide, was trying to muddle his thinking by long-distance hypnosis. Korchnoi enlisted the aid of two young Americans, members of Ananda Marga, an Indian religious sect, who instructed him on yoga.

Korchnoi won the right to challenge Karpov by defeating Boris Spassky of the Soviet Union, $10^{1}/_{2}$ to $7^{1}/_{2}$, in a match that ended on January 12 in Belgrade, Yugoslavia.

Computer Chess. British chess master David Levy defeated the champion of computer chess, Northwestern University's chess program, *Chess 4.7,* in Toronto, Canada, on September 4 by a score of

$3^{1}/_{2}$ to $1^{1}/_{2}$. Meanwhile, Bobby Fischer of the United States, who refused to defend his world championship in 1975 and had not played competitively in six years, went to Yugoslavia in October to make arrangements for a match with Yugoslav champion Swetozar Gligornic. Fischer is guaranteed $1 million, regardless of the outcome of the match, which is scheduled for March 1979.

Other Matches. Lubomir Kavalck of Washington, D.C., won first prize of $4,200 at the United States Open Chess Championship played from June 4 to 26 at Pasadena, Calif. He scored 10 points to 9 for runner-up James Tarjan of Los Angeles. Kavalck and Tarjan qualified as U.S. entrants in the 1979 interzonals, the next stage in the 1981 world championship competition. A third participant has yet to be selected. Walter Browne of Berkeley, Calif., U.S. champion since 1974, walked out of the tournament in a dispute over playing conditions, forfeiting his chance at the next world championship.

Arthur B. Bisguier of Rock Hill, N.Y., won the National Open Championship played from March 19 to 23 in Charleston, S.C. Rachel Crotto of Jamaica, N.Y., and Diane Saveride of Culver City, Calif., tied for first in the U.S. Women's Championship in June in Rochester, N.Y. Both qualified to participate in the women's interzonal tournaments of 1979.   Theodore M. O'Leary

In WORLD BOOK, see CHESS; HOBBY.

CHIANG CHING-KUO (1910-   ) was sworn in as president of the Nationalist Chinese government on Taiwan on May 20, 1978, filling a post that had been held by his father, Chiang Kai-shek, for 26 years. See TAIWAN.

Chiang was born in Chekiang Province in China and attended several Chinese schools before his father sent him to Russia in 1925 to study at Sun Yat-sen University in Moscow. He was not permitted to return to China because he had joined the Communist Youth Corps, so he worked at various agricultural and industrial jobs in Russia and married an orphaned Russian girl named Faina in 1935.

Renouncing his Communist affiliations, Chiang returned to China in 1937, joined the Kuomintang (Nationalist) Party, and became deputy commander of the army in Kiangsi Province. In early 1945, as World War II drew to a close, Chiang served as his father's personal representative at a conference in Moscow to work out details of the Yalta pact that specifically concerned China.

After the Communists conquered China in 1949, Chiang fled to Taiwan, where his father established the Nationalist government. Chiang took charge of the Nationalist secret police and directed youth and veterans' organizations. He served as minister of defense from 1965 to 1969, deputy prime minister from 1969 to 1972, and prime minister from 1972 to 1978. He has four children.   Foster Stockwell

CHICAGO, "the city that works," worked at putting its house in order in 1978. The city initiated a new voluntary school-desegregation program; began to revitalize its downtown Loop shopping area; and took steps to lure middle-income families back to the city.

Chicago's voluntary desegregation program, Access to Excellence, started on September 6. The program offered three special classical schools, an elementary language academy, preschool centers, advanced-placement programs, and other offerings to draw pupils from all parts of the city. By December 1, some 18,000 students were enrolled.

Minority-group members of the Board of Education opposed the program, contending that it would not be effective. Superintendent of Schools Joseph P. Hannon had refused to consider forced busing as an alternative to a voluntary desegregation plan. He maintained that the system, with a white enrollment of only 20 per cent, could not achieve full racial balance. The voluntary plan was established with a five-year goal of involving all students in integrated programs on at least a part-time basis.

Loop Renovation. Work began on converting the portion of State Street that runs through Chicago's downtown Loop shopping district into a pedestrian mall. Construction was also underway on a $150-million development of town houses, apartment buildings, and condominiums just south of the Loop. Both projects were designed to draw middle-income families back to the city.

On July 10, the City Council approved a $100-million mortgage plan to provide low-interest home loans of up to $80,000 for families with incomes of $40,000 or less. The mortgage funds would be backed by the sale of city bonds.

Inspection Shakeup. Four building department supervisors were convicted and 29 electrical inspectors were indicted in November, both groups on charges of taking kickbacks from contractors. The court action came 10 months after the Better Government Association and the *Chicago Sun-Times* operated a tavern with numerous building and electrical code violations and reported on how inspectors could be bribed to overlook the defects. In November, Mayor Michael A. Bilandic created a permanent agency to monitor city inspectors.

Other Developments. Richard G. Albrecht was appointed fire commissioner on April 5, and James E. O'Grady was confirmed as police commissioner on April 10. Chicago's last major afternoon daily newspaper, the *Chicago Daily News,* ceased publication on March 4. The city broke its snowfall record for one season with a total accumulation of 82.3 inches (209 centimeters).   James M. Banovetz

See also CITY. In WORLD BOOK, see CHICAGO.

State Street, the busiest street in Chicago's Loop, is limited to bus traffic as workers begin converting it to a mall in June.

Mr. Yuk, the new poison-warning symbol, draws an appropriate response.
The symbol replaces the skull and crossbones, which some children ignore.

CHILD WELFARE. United States legislators took steps in 1978 to deal with the continuing national problem of child exploitation and abuse. On January 24, the U.S. House of Representatives gave final approval to a bill making the interstate use of children for prostitution or pornography a federal crime. The bill had passed the Senate on Nov. 4, 1977. President Jimmy Carter signed it into law on February 6.

A four-year extension of the Child Abuse Prevention and Treatment Act of 1973 went into effect on April 24, 1978. Congress authorized the spending of $112.5 million through Sept. 30, 1981, for prevention and treatment programs, and made it possible for successful pilot projects to become ongoing operations. The same bill directed the Department of Health, Education, and Welfare (HEW) to set up a national adoption system to help find homes for children, and also called for an HEW study of "black-market" adoptions.

Two outstanding professional books published in 1978 were aimed at understanding and combating child abuse. They are *The Battered Child* (Helfer and Kempe, eds., University of Chicago Press) and *The Maltreatment of Children: A Comprehensive Guide to the Battered Baby Syndrome* (Selwyn Smith, M.D., University Park Press, Maryland).

Worldwide preparations were made for observing the International Year of the Child in 1979, as proclaimed by the United Nations General Assembly. National commissions to increase services to children were set up in more than 120 countries. See UNITED NATIONS (Close-Up).

Infant Mortality. The U.S. National Center for Health Statistics in July reported a "provisional" 1977 rate of 14 deaths per 1,000 live births, a decline of 7.9 per cent from 1976. But 14 nations still have lower infant-mortality rates than the United States, said a report issued in February by the Coalition for Children and Youth in Washington, D.C.

Stress and Children's Illness. Recent research indicates that family tension and conflict affect children both emotionally and physically. A study reported in July by the National Institute of Mental Health concluded that while family conflict will not cause a physical illness such as diabetes, it may make children so psychologically vulnerable that they cannot benefit from medical treatment.

The growing number of mothers working outside the home increased interest in the varied options for child day care. The Women's Bureau of the U.S. Department of Labor reported in January that the number of women workers more than doubled between 1940 and 1976, but the number of mothers working outside the home increased more than fivefold. The child-care options open to working mothers are discussed in a 1978 book, *Who Cares for the Baby?* (Glickman and Spring, New York, Schocken Books). The authors regard expansion of day-care facilities as inevitable, but they urge caution and emphasize that research has not yet demonstrated how a fundamental change in the way children are brought up will affect them or society.

Foster Homes. Many children remain in foster homes, some changing homes frequently, because they have not been released for adoption by their natural parents or because the agency involved cannot find an adoptive home for those who are "difficult to place" – older, handicapped, or members of a minority group. A report issued in May, using data collected between December 1975 and December 1976 on 25,000 children regularly in the care of 120 agencies in New York City, noted relatively little progress in solving this problem. About 20 per cent of these children were slated for adoption on both dates, and fewer than half of them were actually free for adoption. The report asked the cooperating agencies to find new ways to move more children from foster homes to adoptive homes when such a transfer is in the best interest of the child.

Speak Up for Children! is the name of a new program announced on October 2, the 50th anniversary of Child Health Day, by the American Academy of Pediatrics.   Frances A. Mullen

In WORLD BOOK, see CHILD WELFARE.

CHILDREN'S BOOKS. See LITERATURE FOR CHILDREN.

CHILE. President Augusto Pinochet Ugarte received nearly 75 per cent of the 4.5 million votes cast in a nationwide plebiscite held on Jan. 4, 1978. Pinochet called for the referendum five days after the United Nations had adopted a resolution condemning Chile for human rights violations.

The vaguely worded question put to the voters asked whether they supported Pinochet in "his defense of the dignity of Chile." The president had campaigned for a "yes" vote, declaring that it had "nothing to do with internal politics." But immediately after the results were in, he claimed it was an endorsement of all his policies, and indicated that no further vote would be needed for 10 years.

Protest Grows. In the days before the vote, members of the outlawed Christian Democrat Party, the Roman Catholic Church, and scores of young demonstrators protested the plebiscite. Air Force General Gustavo Leigh Guzman, a junta member, argued that the president had overstepped his authority in calling the plebiscite, and Leigh was backed by the controller general, an independent who declared the referendum unconstitutional. Pinochet removed the controller general and replaced him with one who ruled the vote constitutional.

State of Siege Ended. On March 9, Pinochet ended the state of siege under which he had ruled Chile since 1973, but a milder form of dictatorial rule under a state of emergency was left in force. On

President Augusto Pinochet Ugarte rejoices after Chileans endorsed his policies in a national referendum held in January.

April 19, he declared an amnesty for all prisoners held without trial under the state-of-siege laws, persons sentenced by military courts since 1973, and those whose prison terms had been commuted to exile. The act, which affected 2,071 persons, drew general praise from the United States Department of State, but a group of lawyers, many of them Christian Democrats, protested that the amnesty also forgave members of the secret police who had murdered or tortured victims.

The United States pressed Chilean authorities to cooperate in the investigation of the Sept. 21, 1976, bombing death of Orlando Letelier, a former Chilean foreign minister, in Washington, D.C. Under pressure, Chilean authorities on April 8 deported Michael V. Townley, an American who had lived in Chile since 1957. Townley, an agent of the dreaded Chilean secret police force – the National Intelligence Directorate (DINA) – pleaded guilty and admitted he had placed the bomb under Letelier's car. Subsequently, a Washington, D.C., grand jury indicted the former DINA chief, General Manuel Contreras Sepulveda, and two other DINA officers as well as four Cuban exiles living in the United States. The U.S. Department of Justice formally requested the extradition of the accused DINA officers. See COURTS AND LAWS.   Everett G. Martin

See also LATIN AMERICA (Facts in Brief Table). In WORLD BOOK, see CHILE.

CHINA, PEOPLE'S REPUBLIC OF

CHINA, PEOPLE'S REPUBLIC OF. The International Club in Peking, "at the demand of lovers of dancing," announced its first ball in 15 years in 1978. In November, China signed a $500-million contract to have Intercontinental Hotels, a United States chain, build seven hotels in major Chinese cities. Plans were also made to build a golf course in Peking for visitors from other lands. All 168 of Hans Christian Andersen's fairy tales were translated into Chinese, as were some of Mark Twain's works, and Radio Peking began broadcasting Western music for children. The Communist Party newspaper *People's Daily* published a reader's letter proposing that provincial leaders be "elected by the masses."

These were all fragments in the mosaic of Chinese life in 1978. It was a startlingly new pattern after the dozen years of turmoil, violence, and self-isolation that marked the Cultural Revolution and its aftermath. The change affected every field, from education to military strategy, from agriculture to opera. But perhaps the most significant change of all was the agreement between China and the United States to establish full diplomatic relations in 1979.

Pragmatic Leadership. The stamp of the remarkable 74-year-old Deputy Premier Teng Hsiao-p'ing, twice purged since 1967 and twice brought back to power, lay on all these changes. Although he was generally listed as third in the nation's high command – after 58-year-old Communist Party Chairman and Premier Hua Kuo-feng and 79-year-old Defense Minister Yeh Chien-ying – Teng appeared to be the real power in Peking. A pragmatist, Teng was determined to set China on the path to scientific progress and industrialization. His philosophy was expressed in a saying for which he was denounced during the Cultural Revolution, "It doesn't matter if the cat is black or white so long as it catches mice." See TENG HSIAO-P'ING.

While Mao taught that "to rebel is justified," the emphasis under Teng was on law and order. And though Mao insisted it was better to be red than expert, the stress in 1978 was on expertise.

The tight ideological shackles on culture were also eased. Scores of plays, operas, and films that were condemned during the Cultural Revolution as "bourgeois" now drew full houses. Suppressed books were published – as were works that could formerly be circulated only secretly. Many writers who had been exiled to the countryside or arrested during the Cultural Revolution were now honored.

Back to Textbooks. Changes in the educational system were among the most significant. Universities were expanded, and millions of young people sat for their first examinations in a dozen years. University admission was no longer confined to the children of ideologically deserving workers and peasants. Stu-

King Juan Carlos I and Queen Sophia of Spain become the first European monarchs to visit China as they arrive at the Peking airport in June.

dents, once required to do manual labor and study Mao's ideas, were now expected to apply themselves to textbooks. And, in a reversal of earlier practices, Peking began negotiations to send 10,000 students to universities in Japan and the West.

The changes ran into opposition, and a series of purges swept out thousands of party and government officials. The more important officials were denounced at mass rallies and arrested. Teng's October purge removed Wu Teh as mayor of Peking, though he retained his Communist Party Central Committee seat, and at least six provincial Communist Party secretaries. The purge was especially severe in the northeast and in the city of Shanghai, which had been the base for the "Gang of Four" – Mao Tse-tung's widow, Chiang Ching, and three radical Shanghai leaders, Chang Chung-chiao, Yao Wen-yuan, and Wang Hung-wen.

Modifying Mao. Coupled with the purge was a subtle and sustained campaign to modify Mao's doctrines. The official argument was that Lin Piao, once designated as Mao's heir, and the Gang of Four made the people believe Mao was infallible. Under their leadership, the *People's Daily* said in October, if an editor inadvertently crossed out Mao's name or one of his quotations, "it would be regarded as a major case of disrespect and bring trouble to the editor." But truth, Peking argued, is confirmed only by practice, not blind faith. "This," the party newspaper said, "calls for . . . removing [Mao's thought] from the pedestal set up by Lin Piao and the Gang of Four to fool the masses, [and] placing it on a scientific basis."

In action comparable to the Russian de-Stalinization campaign in the 1950s, Peking began to tell the nation that while some aspects of the Cultural Revolution were glorious, others involved wholesale injustice and brutality. It was a rare week that did not produce some harrowing report of the arrest and torture of engineers, scientists, party officials, and ordinary citizens who accidentally crossed the radicals in power between 1966 and 1976. In mid-November, it was indicated that hundreds of thousands of Cultural Revolution victims would be rehabilitated.

For six months in 1978, the *People's Daily* ran a discussion on the "true values of life," ranging from politics to love. The unusual action, which eventually involved 400,000 young people, began after a reader charged in a letter that the radicals had "robbed a whole generation of its youthful dreams."

The revised Constitution, published on March 7, ostensibly strengthened the rights of citizens to speak out and increased the powers of the National People's Congress. The limits of the new tolerance were tested in December when countless posters voiced public grievances and denounced heavy-handed officials.

The Boom. Teng put all emphasis on production rather than dogma. The ambitious goal was to make China a modern industrial state by the year 2000. The plans called for investing $350 billion in the economy by 1985, and building 120 major industrial projects, including 10 steel and iron complexes, eight coal mines, six trunk railways, and five key harbors. Similar plans were aired in China in 1958 when Mao launched his Great Leap Forward, a program that faltered in midair. But there were two essential differences this time – work started on many of the projects before the year ended, and China emerged from its isolation to turn to Japan and to the West for completed plants, technological know-how, and financial help.

The Japanese began building a $2-billion steel mill in Shanghai, West Germany signed a $4-billion deal to modernize China's coal mining, and four giant United States oil companies signed contracts to help China look for offshore oil. United States Secretary of Energy James R. Schlesinger, in November, offered to help China develop its energy reserves in joint enterprises. Indeed, China's plans laid the heaviest emphasis on oil and coal, because these exports would help to pay for the import of needed industrial plants.

China was entering a time of boom – and trade with Japan provided a striking illustration. In February, Tokyo and Peking signed a $20-billion two-way trade agreement. But after only seven months, Japan proposed that the amount be doubled.

The Farmers' Burdens. China suffered what was described as the worst drought in a century in 1978. But even more serious than the occasional calamity was the customary backwardness and inefficiency of Chinese agriculture. The *People's Daily* estimated in May that while a U.S. farmer needed three hours of labor to grow 1 acre (0.4 hectare) of wheat, the Chinese peasant needed 480 to 600 hours. In July, the government launched a campaign, "Lightening the Peasants' Burdens," to deal with such problems.

New Friends. No less startling than the changes at home were the changes in foreign policy. China and its long-loyal ally Albania angrily parted ways in July, after China accused the Albanian leader of pursuing an "anti-China course" and of sabotaging economic and military cooperation between the two countries. Relations with another ally, Vietnam, deteriorated to a state of near-war. There were clashes along the border, and China helped Cambodia in its bloody conflict with Vietnam. Vietnam and Albania had previously been the chief recipients of China's foreign aid, and were among its closest friends. Vice-Premier Teng disclosed that aid to Vietnam alone had amounted to $10 billion, and to Albania, $5 billion. Accounts by Chinese refugees fleeing their homes in Vietnam tended to substantiate charges by Peking that Hanoi had harassed them, confiscated their property, and forced many of them to "volunteer" to move to harsh, uninhabited areas in the countryside. See VIETNAM.

Delegates to China's National People's Congress adopted a new Constitution
in March that gives Chinese citizens the right to criticize the government.

But, as Peking saw it, Russia remained the deadliest foe, and the struggle with the Soviets dominated Peking's foreign policy and strategic thinking. Chairman Hua went to Yugoslavia, Romania, and Iran in August, while Teng made rare trips to Burma, Nepal, Thailand, Sri Lanka, and Singapore in an effort to find new friends in Southeast Asia. Peking signed a treaty of peace and friendship with Japan on August 12, and agreed to normalize relations with the United States on Jan. 1, 1979.

The decision was announced by both countries on December 15. Ambassadors would be exchanged on March 1, 1979. The crucial issue of Taiwan was settled by a U. S. decision to break diplomatic ties with Taiwan, and to end the mutual defense treaty. In return, Peking undertook to tolerate U. S. investments in Taiwan, and apparently promised not to use force in regaining control of the island. The surprise announcement ended what one senior United States official described as "a 30-year anomaly in international affairs." Teng was to visit Washington, D.C., early in 1979 to meet with President Jimmy Carter. Mark Gayn

See also ASIA (Facts in Brief Table). In WORLD BOOK, see CHINA.

CHRONOLOGY. See pages 8 through 16.

CHURCHES. See EASTERN ORTHODOX CHURCHES; JEWS AND JUDAISM; PROTESTANTISM; RELIGION; ROMAN CATHOLIC CHURCH.

CITY. A taxpayer revolt surged through United States cities in 1978, triggered by the June passage of Proposition 13 in California. That measure was calculated to reduce California's property taxes by 57 per cent, or nearly $7 billion, in the first year and impose stiff new restrictions on future tax increases. Similar limitations were enacted in Alabama, Idaho, Nevada, and Texas. See TAXATION (Close-Up).

Taxpayers in cities throughout the United States duplicated these measures, voting their disapproval of high taxes and extravagant public spending. Voters in Cleveland and Columbus, Ohio, rejected increased school tax levies on June 6 and, by doing so, imperiled scheduled school openings in the fall. Some 1,300 persons attended the annual town meeting in Kingston, Mass., on July 15 and rejected every proposed spending increase.

Other voters followed suit in the November 7 elections. Residents of Bernalillo County in New Mexico, which is made up mainly of Albuquerque and its suburban area, approved only $1.6 million of the $14.4 million requested in bond issues. San Diego voters placed new limits on government spending beyond those set by Proposition 13.

The impact of Proposition 13 was felt most severely in California, where cities and schools faced substantial budget cuts despite a $5-billion state-aid package passed by the California legislature in late June. However, the state's local officials were more worried by state restrictions on how they could use the funds. See LOS ANGELES-LONG BEACH; SAN FRANCISCO-OAKLAND.

Financial Affairs were in critical condition. Some cities saw their payrolls swell, felt pressure from striking public employees for larger pay raises, and had to continue to cope with urban blight. The U.S. Bureau of the Census reported on August 22 that the number of state, county, and municipal government employees increased 207 per cent to 12.6 million in the 25-year period ending in October 1977. Payrolls were up 842 per cent in the same period.

Alice M. Rivlin, director of the Congressional Budget Office (CBO), reported on February 3 that state and local governments were running a $13-billion surplus after operating at a $6-billion deficit in 1975, but that many cities were still in distress. On May 26, the Department of the Treasury released a list of 12,000 cities, counties, and towns that qualified as distressed areas. Most of the hard-pressed cities were located in the North and Northeast, but a CBO study released on September 10 noted that some Southern cities were similarly afflicted. Several cities in other countries, including Tokyo, also experienced severe financial problems during the year. See CLEVELAND; NEW YORK CITY.

Urban Policy. President Jimmy Carter's new urban policy, announced on March 27, called for the creation of a national development bank to provide investment subsidies for firms that locate in designated rural or urban distressed areas, guarantee $11-billion in loans for such firms, and coordinate $550-million in new economic-development grants. The plan also called for a $1-billion public works fund, a privately run youth-jobs program, tax credits for firms hiring the hard-core jobless, a $15-million fund for direct loans to neighborhoods for revitalization projects, and $150 million in social service grants.

Carter also proposed a revival of the current $1-billion countercyclical aid program that provides budget relief to cities with particularly high unemployment rates. He also recommended a $200-million state incentive program to provide rewards for states that deal with urban blight. The $1-billion program would funnel only $742 million in new funds into the cities in the first year. The remainder was to be rechanneled from existing programs.

The 95th Congress, however, left little of Carter's program intact. Among the major elements lost were the public works fund, the national development bank, the state incentive program, and the countercyclical aid plan. Cities could take some comfort in the extension of the Comprehensive Education and Training Act, which will generate some 660,000 new jobs and pour an additional $11-billion annually into the cities.

Municipal Strikes. Fire fighters played a leading role in a year of worldwide public-employee strikes. In Great Britain, the nation's 43,000 fire fighters walked off the job for nine weeks – from Nov. 14, 1977, to Jan. 16, 1978 – in an unsuccessful effort to secure pay raises in excess of the government's 10 per cent ceiling. The government mobilized 18,000 military personnel and 400 civil-defense workers into emergency fire squads.

The worst U.S. strike occurred in Memphis, Tenn., where fire fighters walked off the job twice. The first strike started on July 1, and the situation became serious the following evening when more than 350 fires raged throughout the city and led Mayor Wyeth Chandler to declare a state of emergency. The 1,400 strikers accepted a back-to-work order on July 3 but walked off the job again on August 14 to join the city's police, who went on strike on August 10. The National Guard was called out to keep order in the city, jammed with thousands of Elvis Presley fans commemorating the first anniversary of his death. The strike ended on August 18.

Twenty-two fire fighters in Normal, Ill., served 42-day jail terms when they refused to obey a back-to-work order during an eight-week strike that started on March 21. Half the force remained in jail while the other half manned the fire stations, changing places every 24 hours.

The National Guard was called in to provide protection during fire fighters' strikes in Louisville,

The new City Hall in Rochester, N.Y., a former federal building renovated at a relatively low cost, is dedicated on May 5.

Ky., and Manchester, N.H. Fire fighters also struck in Chattanooga, Tenn.; Wichita, Kans.; and Pascagoula, Miss.

Police officers struck in Cleveland; Wichita, Kans.; and Memphis. Sanitation workers walked out in New Orleans; Detroit; Philadelphia; Tuscaloosa, Ala.; and San Antonio, Tex. Transit workers struck in Detroit; Boston; St. Louis; Toronto, Canada; and in Tel Aviv and other Israeli cities.

Teachers walked out in Bridgeport, Conn.; Cleveland; Memphis; New Orleans; and Seattle. In Philadelphia, 19,500 nonuniformed municipal employees struck from July 14 to 21. A 24-hour strike by ground personnel disrupted air traffic at Rome's Leonardo da Vinci Airport on April 9. See also BOSTON; DETROIT; NEW ORLEANS; PHILADELPHIA; SAINT LOUIS; SEATTLE.

Regional Government. Voters in the tri-county Portland, Ore., metropolitan area approved the first multicounty, elected regional government in the United States on May 2. The new government – the Metropolitan Service District (MSD) – was scheduled to begin operations on Jan. 1, 1979. A chief executive officer and a 12-member council were elected on November 7.

The MSD will assume authority over regional planning, city-county plan coordination, solid waste planning and coordination, and operation of the Washington Park Zoo. The district also will handle the metropolitan aspects of sewage disposal, water supply, recreation, mass transit, flood control, cultural and sports facilities, local government boundary control, social services planning and coordination, corrections, and libraries.

Declining Growth. A Gallup Poll released on March 1 reported that more than one-third of America's urban residents would like to move out of their cities. The Bureau of the Census issued statistics in February indicating that the nonmetropolitan areas of the nation grew at a rate of 7.8 per cent between 1970 and 1976, compared with 4.7 per cent for the metropolitan areas.

Court Action. Court-ordered school desegregation has accelerated "white flight" and resulted in greater isolation of racial minorities in major U.S. cities, according to a Rand Corporation study released on August 22. Federal desegregation efforts suffered a setback on July 19 when U.S. District Court Judge John J. Sirica ruled that two recent congressional amendments preventing the Department of Health, Education, and Welfare from ordering school busing did not violate the equal-protection guarantees of the federal Constitution. The Sixth District Court of Appeals ordered school busing reinstated in Dayton, Ohio, on July 27, and the California Supreme Court refused to stop a busing program in Los Angeles on August 8.

The Supreme Court of the United States ruled on March 29 that city governments were not exempt from antitrust laws. Dissenters in the 5 to 4 opinion feared that the decision could impose "staggering costs" on municipalities, subjecting them to possible antitrust suits carrying triple damage penalties.

In other actions, the Supreme Court upheld a Maywood, Ill., requirement that municipal employees must live within the village boundaries; refused to review an Illinois Supreme Court decision that permitted Chicago to sue auto-rental companies for parking violations ticketed against their rental customers; and ruled that localities may ban commuter parking on their streets and impose other traffic restrictions to preserve the quality of life.

New Policies. Atlantic City, N.J., initiated legalized gambling when a $50-million casino-hotel opened on May 26 in an effort to restore the city's fading resort business. Innovative financing plans designed to encourage home ownership were adopted in Chicago; Denver; Evanston, Ill.; and Pueblo, Colo. The cities use tax-exempt revenue bonds to raise funds for home mortgages made to local residents at below-market rates of interest (see CHICAGO). Oak Park, Ill., started a municipally funded program that insured participating homeowners for up to 80 per cent of any loss suffered due to declining property values caused by changing racial or socioeconomic conditions. James M. Banovetz

In WORLD BOOK, see CITY and articles on cities.

Memphis firemen go on strike for better wages and working conditions in July. A court order forced them back to work after three days.

CIVIL RIGHTS showed some gains around the world in 1978, but generally the situation was bleak. This was illustrated in a United States Department of State report issued on February 9 on the observance of human rights in the 105 countries that receive U.S. aid or buy U.S. weapons. The report described widespread rights violations in all but a few non-Western countries.

In Rhodesia, Prime Minister Ian D. Smith and moderate black leaders agreed on March 3 that whites could have 28 of 100 seats in a new parliament, with a limited veto for a time. But the United States and Great Britain rejected the agreement, intended to transform Rhodesia peacefully into the independent black nation of Zimbabwe. The two Western powers believed that the agreement should include the Marxist Patriotic Front guerrilla forces engaged in an increasingly destructive war in Rhodesia against Smith's government. See RHODESIA.

President Ferdinand E. Marcos of the Philippines conducted a national election in April under martial law, but allowed few opportunities to the opposition. He proclaimed himself the winner and arrested demonstrators who accused the government of flagrant election frauds. See PHILIPPINES.

Attention also centered on the trials of Anatoly Shcharansky and other Russian dissidents. President Jimmy Carter condemned these trials as "an attack on every human being who believes in human freedom and is willing to speak for these freedoms or fight for them." He had to rebuke U.S. Ambassador to the United Nations Andrew Young, who said that there were "hundreds, perhaps even thousands, of political prisoners in the U.S." See RUSSIA.

Bakke Decision. In a long-awaited decision, the Supreme Court of the United States ruled on June 28, by a 5 to 4 vote, that Allan P. Bakke, a white man, must be admitted to the University of California School of Medicine, Davis. The justices reasoned that the school's affirmative-action program was too inflexible and unjustifiably discriminatory toward white applicants. The Supreme Court considered the medical school's program rigid because it set aside 16 of 100 places specifically for minority-group students. In September, six years after his original application, the 38-year-old Bakke entered the medical school.

On the same day, also by a 5 to 4 vote, the court affirmed the constitutionality of college admissions programs that give special advantage to blacks and members of other minority groups to counterbalance past discrimination. Early evaluations of these two decisions suggested that most affirmative-action programs, public and private, will continue.

Benjamin L. Hooks, executive director of the National Association for the Advancement of Col-

Civil rights leaders expressed mixed reactions after the U.S. Supreme Court issued its ruling on June 28 in the controversial Bakke case.

ored People (NAACP), called the Bakke decision a "clear-cut victory for voluntary affirmative action." Arnold Forster, the general counsel of the Anti-Defamation League of B'nai B'rith, said his organization was "comforted that, once and for all, the United States Supreme Court has held that racial quotas are flatly illegal." See SUPREME COURT OF THE UNITED STATES (Close-Up).

Other perennial educational issues remained prominent in civil rights developments. On April 24, the U.S. Fifth Circuit Court of Appeals in New Orleans rejected a student-assignment plan intended to desegregate schools in Dallas – a program previously viewed as a model for desegregation with minimal busing. The court found unacceptable the number of one-race schools under the plan that left more than 27,000 students in all-black schools, while busing 17,000 of 136,547 students in the district.

Black Civil Rights activity and debate centered on economic issues. Controversy erupted in January when the board of directors of the NAACP adopted an energy-policy statement endorsing deregulation of oil and natural gas prices and urging nuclear power development. Seen as an effort to broaden traditional civil rights activity by moving closer to private industry, the statement was attacked as a "sellout" by most other black civil rights organizations. In rebuttal, NAACP Board Chairman Margaret B. Wilson said that the energy policies rejected in the statement, including those of President Carter, called for a decline of economic activity. "Under slow growth, blacks suffer more than anyone else," Wilson said.

In a July 3 ruling, the Supreme Court suggested that it would continue to view quota systems in employment discrimination cases more receptively than the university admissions quotas rejected in the Bakke case. The court let stand a 1973 consent decree requiring the American Telephone and Telegraph Company to hire more blacks and women.

In August, the chairman of the Equal Employment Opportunity Commission (EEOC), Eleanor H. Norton, announced a new program, consisting of a series of major lawsuits, designed to end "patterns and practices" of discrimination in key businesses and industries across the United States. Previously, the EEOC acted on individual complaints, with an ever-expanding backlog of unresolved cases.

Women's Rights. A major development came in October when Congress extended the deadline for ratification of the Equal Rights Amendment by 39 months. The amendment, three states short of ratification, was due to expire in March 1979.

Intense controversy over abortion continued to divide various state legislatures. Broadened regulations announced by the U.S. Department of Health, Education, and Welfare on January 26 increased opportunities for poor women to obtain abortions under government funding.

The Supreme Court ruled on April 25 that, though women live longer than men on the average, an employer who charges women more than men to participate in a pension plan is committing illegal sex discrimination. In an October settlement of a class-action sex-discrimination suit, *The New York Times* agreed to try to place a certain percentage of women in various jobs, including top management.

The Press. The Supreme Court ruled on May 31 that police have the right to obtain a warrant and to make unannounced searches of private property, including newsrooms, in seeking criminal evidence. In August, a New Jersey Superior Court imposed severe fines on *The New York Times* and fines and a six-month jail sentence on reporter Myron A. Farber for his refusal to turn over his notes for possible use in the murder trial of surgeon Mario E. Jascalevich. The Supreme Court declined to act on appeal and Farber was jailed. When Jascalevich was found innocent, Farber was promptly freed.

On July 3, the Supreme Court ruled that the free-speech protection of the First Amendment does not bar the government from prohibiting radio broadcasting of words that are "patently offensive" but fall short of the constitutional definition of obscenity. The case grew out of a radio broadcast of a comedy album by George Carlin.   Louis W. Koenig

See also articles on individual countries; COURTS AND LAWS. In WORLD BOOK, see CIVIL RIGHTS.

CLEVELAND became the first United States city to go into default since the Great Depression when it could not pay off $15.5 million in short-term notes due Dec. 15, 1978. The default capped off a year that began with blizzards that caught the city with its snowplows in the repair shop. It was a year during which the city tried to oust its mayor, indicted most of its City Council, faced police and school strikes, and hovered on the brink of bankruptcy.

Cleveland's credit rating in the bond market was lowered by Moody's Investors Service and suspended by Standard & Poors Corporation, two influential financial rating services, in July. Both agencies criticized the city for its inability to provide reliable financial information.

A private accounting firm hired to audit the city's books disclosed in August a $52-million deficit in the city's treasury accounts.

Mayor Dennis J. Kucinich narrowly survived a recall election on Aug. 13, 1978, by a mere 236-vote margin out of some 120,000 votes cast. The campaign to recall Kucinich, the youngest mayor of a major United States city at 32, was spearheaded by City Council President George Forbes. Forbes and five other council members were indicted on felony charges on October 27.

Police Strike. In mid-July, Cleveland police refused to go on patrol alone in 14 high-crime housing projects. Kucinich fired 13 patrolmen, and

Cleveland's Mayor Dennis J. Kucinich and his wife, Sandy, celebrate his narrow victory in the special recall election on August 13.

was faced with a sympathy walkout by 2,000 members of the force on July 14. The next day the strike ended when the officers who had been fired were ordered reinstated by a court and the city agreed to two-man patrols in squad cars.

Troubled Schools. Public schools were almost forced to close on March 31 because there was no money to pay the school system's 11,000 employees. However, the Ohio Supreme Court on April 11 refused a Cleveland request to close the schools and allow teachers to collect unemployment compensation. The employees worked without pay until April 14, when the state of Ohio agreed to advance Cleveland $3 million.

After two school-revenue proposals were defeated on April 6 and June 6, the city was forced to borrow $21 million from the state to open the schools in September. Nevertheless, schools remained closed because about 15,000 employees were on strike, demanding their first pay raise in two years. Schools finally opened on October 16 after employees agreed to accept an 8 per cent salary increase.

Federally ordered school desegregation was again postponed. The city's school district did not have the funds to finance a program to bus about half of the city's 100,000 students. James M. Banovetz

See also CITY; EDUCATION. In WORLD BOOK, see CLEVELAND.

CLOTHING. See FASHION.

COAL will play a major energy role in the United States, according to the energy bill Congress passed on Oct. 15, 1978. New power plants and most new industrial plants will have to use coal to fire their boilers. Existing power plants will have to stop using natural gas by 1990, and the Department of Energy (DOE) may make them stop using oil by then. Other provisions of the bill specified that existing power plants may not burn more gas than they averaged between 1974 and 1976; if a utility did not use gas as a primary fuel in 1977, it may not switch to gas before 1990; and DOE may order industrial plants that can burn coal to use that fuel. See ENERGY.

Coal Conflict. President Jimmy Carter's drive for greater use of coal clashed with Environmental Protection Agency (EPA) policies in 1978. Acting under new clean-air legislation, the EPA in December 1977 proposed that utilities remove up to 90 per cent of the sulfur dioxide from all their fuels. Secretary of Energy James R. Schlesinger declared in May 1978 that environmental policymakers must lower their standards or jeopardize promising energy technologies, including solvent-refined coal, fluidized-bed combustion, and coal gasification. EPA lowered the target figure to 85 per cent in September.

A Department of Transportation report said in February that the existing transportation system, with minor modifications, could handle the shift from oil to coal that Carter's energy program called for. Major investments in equipment would be needed. See RAILROADS; TRANSPORTATION.

The longest coal strike in United States history ended in its 110th day on March 25, when the United Mine Workers and the Bituminous Coal Operators Association signed a three-year contract. See LABOR.

Anthracite Wastes. DOE financed the design and construction of a boiler system to remove energy from large piles of anthracite coal wastes. Almost 910 million cubic yards (700 million cubic meters) of these wastes in northeastern Pennsylvania hold the equivalent of 1 billion barrels of oil.

Environmental Project. The National Coal Policy Project, an association of environmentalists and industry leaders, released its first report, "Where We Agree," in February. The project was created in 1976 to resolve coal issues. For 13 months, representatives discussed transportation, air pollution, fuel utilization, conservation, and energy costs. They made more than 150 recommendations on such issues as location and pattern of development, coal-reserve quality and quantity, reclamation, water resources, and socioeconomic impacts. Georgetown University's Center for Strategic and International Studies served as a neutral sponsor.

Coal Gasification. Attacking the coal industry's refusal to supply it with data, the U.S. Federal Energy Regulatory Commission filed a motion on

State police escort a convoy of nonunion trucks in Norton, Va., in March during the 110-day coal strike, the longest in United States history.

COIN COLLECTING. The Nathan M. Kaufman collection, one of the most important coin collections in the United States, was auctioned off in Chicago in August 1978. Most of the 1,530 pieces were sold individually for a total of $2.25 million, $250,000 more than experts had estimated. The highest price at the Kaufman auction was $140,000 paid for an 1825 gold piece. One of two such coins in existence, the gold piece is dated with the number 5 stamped over the number 4. In contrast, a rare Kellogg gold piece, one of 13 known, brought only $115,000 – $5,000 less than was paid for one of the coins in 1975.

There were several other significant coin sales during the year. One of five known U.S. 1913 V Liberty nickels sold for $200,000, third highest price ever paid for a coin. A five-point British gold piece of 1839, valued in 1962 at from $600 to $900, sold for $12,000. A 1916 Mercury dime listed in 1977 price guides at $1,800 brought $4,400.

Prices for medals also went up. In New York City on June 17, a Philadelphia antique dealer paid a record $51,000 – $36,000 more than expected – for a gold medal awarded to Revolutionary War General "Mad Anthony" Wayne by the Continental Army. A set of 15 gold medals honoring prime ministers of Canada, issued by the privately owned Franklin Mint in 1971 and 1972 at $570, were listed in 1978 at $1,100 to $1,250.

October 1 to dismiss with prejudice what could be the nation's first commercial coal-gasification project. The project was put together by five companies – American Natural Resources Company in Detroit; Columbia Gas System, Incorporated, in Wilmington, Del.; Tenneco, Incorporated, and Transco Company in Houston; and People's Gas Company in Chicago.

In Other Countries. After missing its 1977 production target, Russia's coal industry continued to have trouble. Typical was its April 1978 output of 66.6 million short tons (60.4 million metric tons), about 110,000 short tons (100,000 metric tons) less than in April 1977. Problems included poor management and shortages of skilled labor, railroad cars, and modern mining equipment.

Israel completed plans to obtain coal for the power station it is building at Hadera, on the Mediterranean. Most of the 3.4 million short tons (3-million metric tons) per year would come from South Africa and Australia.

West Germany announced in June research-and-development grants of $290 million per year through 1981 to offset lagging investment in the coal market. Italy's electric-power agency started an emergency program to build coal-fired generating stations instead of nuclear stations. James J. O'Connor

See also MINES AND MINING. In WORLD BOOK, see COAL.

New U.S. dollar coin will feature suffragist Susan B. Anthony on its face and the *Apollo 11* landing on the moon on the reverse side.

New Coins and Medals. The House of Representatives gave final congressional approval on September 26 to a bill authorizing a new dollar coin that will bear the likeness of suffragist Susan B. Anthony. Anthony is the first woman to be pictured on a U.S. general-circulation coin.

Former President Gerald R. Ford struck the first of a series of medals on February 24 commemorating notable presidential events. Ford helped choose the subjects for the medals, which are being produced by the Franklin Mint. The first medal in the series depicted the inauguration of George Washington as President.

Gold Coins. The soaring price of gold stimulated interest in gold coins, which are said to afford both liquidity and relative safety in a period of inflation. Noting the worldwide popularity of the South African Krugerrand, a coin containing 1 troy ounce (31.1 grams) of gold, Congressman Steven D. Symms (R., Idaho) and Senator Jesse A. Helms (R., N.C.) introduced legislation in May that would require the U.S. government to sell part of the gold it plans to auction in the form of 1-troy-ounce and ¹/₂-ounce (15.5-gram) gold coins. United States residents purchased 1.1 million Krugerrands in 1977, and sales for the first quarter of 1978 equaled half of the 1977 total.   Theodore M. O'Leary

In WORLD BOOK, see COIN COLLECTING; GOLD.

COLOMBIA. Julio Cesar Turbay Ayala, a Liberal Party member, took office as president on Aug. 7, 1978. A formal political agreement between the Liberals and the Conservative Party expired with his election. The rival groups had agreed in 1957 to divide Cabinet posts and alternate the presidency as a means of ending the bloody interparty warfare that began in 1948 and over a 10-year period had claimed an estimated 100,000 lives, mostly in rural areas. See TURBAY AYALA, JULIO CESAR.

The election had been a hotly contested one, featuring name-calling and occasional violence rather than discussions of the issues. Drug traffickers on the northeast coast were widely reported to be financing candidates and buying votes. At one point in the campaigning, Turbay and his opponent, Conservative Party candidate Belisario Betancur, had indulged in campaign vilification. Betancur tried to link Turbay with drug smugglers; in a bit of irony, Turbay accused the Roman Catholic Church of intervening on Betancur's behalf when it urged voters to select the candidate with the most honest and effective solution to the nation's problems.

Terrorist Violence. Because of guerrilla activity during the campaign, about 200,000 troops were deployed nationwide to maintain order. On three occasions in January and February, the Colombian Revolutionary Armed Forces (FARC) terrorist

Rock-throwing students, angered by economic conditions, defy a policeman during demonstrations at the National University in Bogotá, Colombia, in May.

group killed at least eight soldiers in Santander Department. Another terrorist group, known as M-19, set off a series of bombs in Bogotá and appealed to the public to ignore the elections.

Police reported that 12 members of the Andreas Baader Brigade, a West German terrorist organization, had joined with a local group to blow up the Lufthansa airline office in Bogotá, on February 17. In March, the FARC sacked three rural towns; on April 20 they kidnapped the son of a rancher.

Other violence flared in May when a 12 per cent increase in mass-transit fares touched off month-long riots in Bogotá and five other cities. At least one policeman and five rioters were killed.

Drug "Crusade." On August 7, in a move that pleased the United States, Turbay vowed in his inaugural address to launch a "crusade" to halt drug traffic, particularly the growing shipments of marijuana that were creating hundreds of new-rich among smugglers in the northeast. On November 1 he barred air traffic over the Guajira Peninsula to try to stop the almost nightly flights of planes loaded with marijuana that operated secretly out of some 150 airstrips on the barren peninsula. Everett G. Martin

See also LATIN AMERICA (Facts in Brief Table). In WORLD BOOK, see COLOMBIA.

COLORADO. See STATE GOVERNMENT.

COMMON MARKET. See EUROPE.

COMMUNICATIONS. The United States Congress set out to form a new communications policy in 1978, and many people thought it was about time. The last major communications legislation was the Communications Act of 1934, which established the Federal Communications Commission (FCC) to regulate broadcast and wire communications.

Since then, communications technology has undergone a revolution. And by 1978, the FCC found itself regulating television, microwave communications, satellites, and electronic switching and transmission—technologies that did not exist in 1934.

The Communications Act of 1978, introduced in the House of Representatives in June, had three objectives—to encourage competition in communications wherever feasible; to regulate communications as little as possible; and to foster the widest application of communications technology.

After extensive hearings on the bill in the late summer and fall, legislators began to rewrite it. They planned to reintroduce it early in the 1979 session. The bill's sponsors insisted that its basic aims would remain unchanged and that more competition, with lessened regulation, would be the new order of the day in communications.

This was good news to *interconnect* companies, which sell switchboards, telephones, and other ter-

With telephones being sold in retail stores, manufacturers vie to lure buyers with fashionable styling and many special features.

minal equipment to users; and to specialized common carriers, which provide private-line telephone service over microwave links in competition with the Bell Telephone System's long-distance facilities. These companies came into existence in the late 1960s and early 1970s under FCC rulings, and multiplied and expanded as a result of increasingly liberal rulings by the communications agency and courts.

Bell Reorganized. Taking action to counter the competitive threat were the franchised telephone common carriers—American Telephone and Telegraph Company (A.T. & T.) with its 25 Bell System operating companies, and the 1,550 independent telephone companies. The Bell System underwent a massive reorganization in 1978 in an effort to gain marketing strength. It stepped up its "Phone Mart" program, establishing hundreds of retail outlets where customers could select telephones to carry home and plug in themselves. The Bell System began selling the outer shells of its decorator phones, but the working parts and maintenance remained Bell's property and responsibility.

Several independent telephone companies with considerably more regulatory leeway than Bell began selling phones and switchboards outright in competition with themselves, other telephone companies, and the interconnect firms. There was also a strong movement toward retail operations that were aimed primarily at residence customers. The General Telephone System, largest of the independents, set up the first of a projected network of business-communications centers to cater to the needs of commercial customers.

Business-Service Battle. The greatest competitive battle in communications is shaping up in the business-service arena. A.T. & T. asked the FCC to permit it to implement an Advanced Communications Service, a shared, switched-data communications network that will provide compatibility among many diverse terminals and computers. At stake is a share of the huge data-communications market, currently estimated at $5 billion and growing at a rate of 21 per cent annually.

With the explosive growth of information technology, a no man's land has emerged — the hazy area between computing and communications. International Business Machines Corporation (IBM) and the computer industry strove to contain A.T. & T. in the area of transmission, while A.T. & T. tried to restrict IBM and the computer industry to the office, factory, computer room, and communications center. That sector will be the major battleground of the future as the advancing technologies of computers and communications merge and two giants of American industry struggle to claim a major share of the market.   Leo S. Anderson

In WORLD BOOK, see COMMUNICATIONS; TELEPHONE.

COMMUNITY ORGANIZATIONS. The 150th anniversary of the birth of Jean Henri Dunant, founder of the International Red Cross and co-winner of the first Nobel Prize for Peace in 1901, was commemorated on May 8, 1978. The American Red Cross Board of Governors approved six-year corporate goals on May 21. The goals emphasize strengthening disaster and blood services; expanding community, health, and safety services; and examining international services for adequacy.

The Salvation Army provided emergency disaster relief during the major snowstorms that paralyzed sections of the eastern and midwestern United States in January and February. Workers set up shelters and mobile canteens where the need was greatest.

Emergency aid was provided in Oklahoma City, Okla., and parts of Florida that were hit by tornadoes in May. The Salvation Army also delivered food and clothing to more than 4,000 May flood victims in Tijuana and Ensenada, Mexico.

The Young Men's Christian Association (YMCA). About 9 million participants were registered in YMCA's in the United States alone in 1978, with millions more in 88 other countries around the world. In the United States, women made up 39 per cent of the membership. Family memberships were the fastest-growing segment of Y enrollment.

Health and physical education programs continued to be popular activities. The Y's heart programs were among its most important new contributions.

The Young Women's Christian Association (YWCA). The YWCA supported the Equal Rights Amendment (ERA) in 1978. The organization will not hold its national convention in states that have failed to ratify ERA or have rescinded ratification.

Postmastectomy group rehabilitation programs, designed to renew the physical and emotional strength of women who have undergone breast surgery, were established.

YWCA membership in the United States stood at 2.5 million in 1978; 350,000 men participated as associates.

Service Organizations. Kiwanis International reported its 1978 membership at nearly 300,000 in 7,300 clubs in 64 nations. Hilmar L. Solberg, an Appleton, Wis., advertising man, was elected president of Kiwanis International in June. He announced that the 1978 Kiwanis program "Rightstart" would aim at helping young people to understand basic social values.

Lions International elected Ralph A. Lynam of Alma, Mich., president in June. He called for an action program to help those with hearing and speech impairments. Lions International membership as of June 30 was 1,244,717 in 32,363 clubs throughout the world.

Rotary International elected Clem Renouf of Nambour, Australia, president in July. Membership exceeded 830,000 in more than 17,800 clubs in 154 countries. More than 1,400 students received Rotary Foundation grants for study in other countries.

Veterans Organizations. The American Legion and the Veterans of Foreign Wars successfully lobbied in Congress against President Jimmy Carter's attempts to modify veterans' preference for Civil Service jobs. Carter and the Civil Service Commission contended that women and minority group members were prevented from getting federal jobs because veterans get a five-point edge in the civil service examination.

With 13.3 million veterans of World War II in or nearing their 60s, Max Cleland, head of the Veterans Administration, announced a new program to train doctors in caring for elderly veterans with special medical needs.

The Board of Veterans Appeals announced on August 1 it would award benefits for service-connected disability to a retired U.S. Army man, Donald C. Coe of Tompkinsville, Ky., who claimed that his leukemia was caused by exposure to radiation at a Nevada nuclear weapons test in 1957. The ruling seemed likely to prompt other veterans to seek special benefits.   Virginia E. Anderson

In WORLD BOOK, see articles on the various community organizations.

COMOROS. See AFRICA.

CONGO (BRAZZAVILLE). See AFRICA.

CONGO (KINSHASA). See ZAIRE.

CONGRESS OF THE UNITED STATES. The overwhelmingly Democratic 95th Congress convened its second session on Jan. 19, 1978, and adhered to its middle-of-the-road course until it wearily adjourned in the early, predawn hours of October 15.

Despite its Democratic majorities, the 95th Congress clashed repeatedly with Democratic President Jimmy Carter. It granted fewer than half the President's requests. But the second session worked more cooperatively with the President, and he, in turn, set more realistic goals.

Members of both parties in the House and Senate proved sensitive to the conservative shift of the electorate and the popular revolt against bureaucracy and taxes. More than most Congresses in recent memory, the 95th was influenced by special-interest groups who lobbied intensely to influence the tax-reform and energy legislation finally passed in the last hours of the session.

Congressional Leaders. Vice-President Walter F. Mondale served in his constitutional role as president of the Senate. West Virginia's Robert C. Byrd was Senate majority leader, and Alan Cranston of California was majority whip. Howard H. Baker, Jr., of Tennessee served as minority leader, with Theodore F. Stevens of Alaska as minority whip. Senator Hubert H. Humphrey, Democratic senator from Minnesota and former Vice-President of the

United States, died on January 13 after a long illness. He had been the Senate's deputy president pro tempore.

Thomas P. (Tip) O'Neill, Jr., of Massachusetts was speaker of the House of Representatives. Democrats James C. Wright, Jr., of Texas and John Brademas of Indiana were majority leader and majority whip, respectively. For the Republicans, John J. Rhodes of Arizona was minority leader and Robert H. Michel of Illinois, minority whip.

The Budget. On January 23, President Carter sent Congress a $500.2-billion federal budget for fiscal 1979, beginning in October 1978. The budget included a $60.66-billion deficit and an appropriation of $117.8 billion for defense, 9.4 per cent higher than fiscal 1978.

In September, Congress adopted a target ceiling of $487.5 billion for the federal budget for fiscal 1979, with a projected deficit of $38.8 billion.

Foreign Affairs. Countering very vocal opposition, President Carter persuaded the Senate to approve two Panama Canal treaties. The Senate ratified the Panama Canal Neutrality Treaty on March 16, voting 68 to 32, and the Panama Canal Treaty by the same majority on April 18. According to the new treaties, the Panama Canal will be turned over to the Republic of Panama by the year 2000.

President Carter won final approval on May 15 for the simultaneous sale of jet fighter planes to Israel, Egypt, and Saudi Arabia despite Israel's protests that Saudi Arabia and Egypt were arming against it.

Congress also acceded to the President's request to end the embargo on arms sales to Turkey. President Carter signed the $2.8-billion International Security Assistance Act on September 26 that authorized him to end the embargo.

Congress passed a $9.1-billion appropriation for foreign aid on October 14, including the U.S. contribution of $1.8 billion to the International Monetary Fund lending pool.

Senator Barry Goldwater (R., Ariz.) filed suit on December 22 to preserve the U.S. defense treaty with Taiwan. Carter had announced on December 15 that the treaty would terminate when the United States established diplomatic relations with the People's Republic of China on Jan. 1, 1979.

Military Policy. Development of the B-1 bomber was halted at the President's request when Congress voted in February to withhold the use of $462 million in unused funds for B-1 bomber development. President Carter also vetoed a $37-billion military-weapons authorization bill on August 18 because it included $2 billion for a new nuclear-powered aircraft carrier he regarded as unnecessary. The House upheld his veto 206 to 191 on September 7. Then the President signed a $35.23-billion bill on October 20 that excluded funds for the nuclear-powered aircraft carrier.

The Economy, particularly the accelerating rate of inflation, caused widespread congressional concern and led to clashes with the President in 1978. On September 27, Congress passed a $10.2-billion public-works appropriation bill. As he had warned, the President vetoed the bill as inflationary on October 4, and the House sustained the veto on October 5. The President signed a $27-billion public-works appropriation bill on October 19 that included funding for the Department of Energy and a compromise, less-expensive public-works program that extends the Comprehensive Employment and Training Act (CETA) for four years at a cost of $11-billion.

The President signed a pallid version of the Humphrey-Hawkins "full employment" bill on October 26. This measure set national goals of 4 per cent unemployment and a 3 per cent inflation rate in five years.

The second session of the 95th Congress also passed legislation phasing out federal regulation of airline fares and routes; extended housing-aid programs; and authorized $51 billion for highway and mass-transit construction over a four-year period.

Social Legislation included an extension of the ban on federal funding for most abortions, as a rider on a $56-billion appropriations bill for the Department of Health, Education, and Welfare (HEW).

President Carter signed the HEW bill on October 18. He signed a bill on November 1 that granted $50-billion in aid to elementary and secondary schools over a five-year period, and another bill increasing the income limit from $15,000 to $26,000 on eligibility for federal loans for middle-income college students. Carter also signed a $5-billion Comprehensive Vocational Rehabilitation Act for the handicapped on November 6.

Energy Policy was debated for 18 months by the 95th Congress before it passed a compromise energy act in the last hours of the session on October 15. The Energy Act of 1978, signed by the President on November 9, will eventually save an estimated 2.25-million barrels of oil per day. It allowed gas prices to increase at prescribed rates over the next few years and ended price controls on new gas in 1985. See ENERGY.

Tax Reform. Congress also passed an act to cut taxes on October 15. Most of the $18.7 billion in tax cuts will benefit middle- and upper-income taxpayers. See TAXATION.

Mandatory Retirement. President Carter signed legislation on April 6 that amended the Age Discrimination in Employment Act, raising the age at which most workers could be forced to retire from 65 to 70. High-salaried business executives and — for the next three years — college professors were specifi-

South Korean rice broker Tong Sun Park, left, charged with bribing U.S. congressmen, confers with his attorney during House ethics hearings.

Muriel Humphrey, appointed to Senate term of her late husband, Hubert H. Humphrey, chats with Vice-President Mondale and Sen. Wendell R. Anderson.

cally excluded from the act's provisions. It abolished completely the mandatory retirement age for government workers. See LABOR.

Constitutional Amendments. A constitutional amendment allowing the 750,000 residents of the District of Columbia full voting representation in both houses of Congress was approved by the House on March 2 and by the Senate on August 22. The Equal Rights Amendment (ERA) was given a new lease on life when Congress extended the deadline for its ratification from March 22, 1979, to June 30, 1982. By the end of 1978, the ERA had been approved by only 35 states; three more must approve before ERA becomes the 27th Amendment to the Constitution. See CONSTITUTION OF THE UNITED STATES.

Conservation and Ecology. President Carter signed legislation on March 22 authorizing the expenditure of $90 million over three years for land acquisition and the protection of the Appalachian National Scenic Trail. On March 27, he signed an act adding to and protecting Redwood National Park in northern California. An act authorizing $26.5 million for fish and wildlife preservation on federal lands was signed on October 6. President Carter signed a controversial law on October 23 adding more than 1 million acres (405,000 hectares) to the Boundary Waters Canoe Area of Minnesota, declaring it a wilderness area, restricting the use of

motorboats and snowmobiles, and forbidding logging and mining in the area.

Congress also extended the Endangered Species Act for 18 months, adding a review procedure for evaluating public-works projects that threaten endangered species and providing a special expedited review of the Tellico Dam project. Work on the dam has been halted because it endangers the survival of the tiny snail darter fish. The President signed this legislation on November 10.

The President also signed into law on November 10 the most ambitious conservation program in U.S. history, authorizing an expenditure of $1.2 billion for more than 100 parks and conservation projects across the nation. See CONSERVATION.

In Other Action, the second session of the 95th Congress authorized $3 million for two White House conferences on the humanities and the arts and $1.65-billion in federal loan guarantees for New York City. Congress established world annual immigration quotas in 1978 by combining the quotas for Eastern and Western Hemispheres; made it easier for alien adopted children to enter the United States and become naturalized citizens; and restricted the legal immunity of personnel affiliated with foreign embassies in the United States. Congress also passed the Civil Service Reform Act and the Presidential Record Act, which made presidential papers public property. Congress also increased veterans' pensions.

Members of the United States Senate

The Senate of the first session of the 96th Congress consisted of 58 Democrats, 41 Republicans, and 1 Independent, when it convened in January 1979. Senators shown starting their term in 1979 were elected for the first time in the Nov. 7, 1978, elections (Senators Donald W. Stewart of Alabama and David L. Durenberger of Minnesota were elected on November 7 but were sworn into office on November 9 because they replaced Senators who had been appointed to serve only until the election). Those shown ending their current terms in 1985 were re-elected to the Senate in the same balloting. The second date in each listing shows when the term of a previously elected senator expires. For organizational purposes, the one Independent will line up with Democrats.

State	Term	State	Term	State	Term
Alabama		**Louisiana**		**Ohio**	
Donald W. Stewart, D.	1978—1981	Russell B. Long, D.	1948—1981	John H. Glenn, D.	1975—1981
Howell T. Heflin, D.	1979—1985	J. Bennett Johnston, Jr., D.	1972—1985	Howard M. Metzenbaum, D.	1977—1983
Alaska		**Maine**		**Oklahoma**	
Theodore F. Stevens, R.	1968—1985	Edmund S. Muskie, D.	1959—1983	Henry L. Bellmon, R.	1969—1981
Mike Gravel, D.	1969—1981	William S. Cohen, R.	1979—1985	David L. Boren, D.	1979—1985
Arizona		**Maryland**		**Oregon**	
Barry Goldwater, R.	1969—1981	Charles McC. Mathias, Jr., R.	1969—1981	Mark O. Hatfield, R.	1967—1985
Dennis DeConcini, D.	1977—1983	Paul S. Sarbanes, D.	1977—1983	Robert W. Packwood, R.	1969—1981
Arkansas		**Massachusetts**		**Pennsylvania**	
Dale Bumpers, D.	1975—1981	Edward M. Kennedy, D.	1962—1983	Richard S. Schweiker, R.	1969—1981
David H. Pryor, D.	1979—1985	Paul E. Tsongas, D.	1979—1985	H. John Heinz III, R.	1977—1983
California		**Michigan**		**Rhode Island**	
Alan Cranston, D.	1969—1981	Donald W. Riegle, Jr., D.	1977—1983	Claiborne Pell, D.	1961—1985
S. I. Hayakawa, R.	1977—1983	Carl M. Levin, D.	1979—1985	John H. Chafee, R.	1977—1983
Colorado		**Minnesota**		**South Carolina**	
Gary Hart, D.	1975—1981	David L. Durenberger, R.	1978—1983	Strom Thurmond, R.	1956—1985
William L. Armstrong, R.	1979—1985	Rudolph E. Boschwitz, R.	1979—1985	Ernest F. Hollings, D.	1966—1981
Connecticut		**Mississippi**		**South Dakota**	
Abraham A. Ribicoff, D.	1963—1981	John C. Stennis, D.	1947—1983	George S. McGovern, D.	1963—1981
Lowell P. Weicker, Jr., R.	1971—1983	Thad Cochran, R.	1979—1985	Larry Pressler, R.	1979—1985
Delaware		**Missouri**		**Tennessee**	
William V. Roth, Jr., R.	1971—1983	Thomas F. Eagleton, D.	1968—1981	Howard H. Baker, Jr., R.	1967—1985
Joseph R. Biden, Jr., D.	1973—1985	John C. Danforth, R.	1977—1983	James R. Sasser, D.	1977—1983
Florida		**Montana**		**Texas**	
Lawton Chiles, D.	1971—1983	John Melcher, D.	1977—1983	John G. Tower, R.	1961—1985
Richard B. Stone, D.	1975—1981	Max Baucus, D.	1979—1985	Lloyd M. Bentsen, D.	1971—1983
Georgia		**Nebraska**		**Utah**	
Herman E. Talmadge, D.	1957—1981	Edward Zorinsky, D.	1977—1983	Edwin Jacob Garn, R.	1975—1981
Sam Nunn, D.	1972—1985	J. James Exon, D.	1979—1985	Orrin G. Hatch, R.	1977—1983
Hawaii		**Nevada**		**Vermont**	
Daniel K. Inouye, D.	1963—1981	Howard W. Cannon, D.	1959—1983	Robert T. Stafford, R.	1971—1983
Spark M. Matsunaga, D.	1977—1983	Paul Laxalt, R.	1975—1981	Patrick J. Leahy, D.	1975—1981
Idaho		**New Hampshire**		**Virginia**	
Frank Church, D.	1957—1981	John A. Durkin, D.	1975—1981	Harry F. Byrd, Jr., Ind.	1965—1983
James A. McClure, R.	1973—1985	Gordon J. Humphrey, R.	1979—1985	John W. Warner, R.	1979—1985
Illinois		**New Jersey**		**Washington**	
Charles H. Percy, R.	1967—1985	Harrison A. Williams, Jr., D.	1959—1983	Warren G. Magnuson, D.	1944—1981
Adlai E. Stevenson III, D.	1970—1981	Bill Bradley, D.	1979—1985	Henry M. Jackson, D.	1953—1983
Indiana		**New Mexico**		**West Virginia**	
Birch Bayh, D.	1963—1981	Pete V. Domenici, R.	1973—1985	Jennings Randolph, D.	1958—1985
Richard G. Lugar, R.	1977—1983	Harrison H. Schmitt, R.	1977—1983	Robert C. Byrd, D.	1959—1983
Iowa		**New York**		**Wisconsin**	
John C. Culver, D.	1975—1981	Jacob K. Javits, R.	1957—1981	William Proxmire, D.	1957—1983
Roger W. Jepsen, R.	1979—1985	Daniel P. Moynihan, D.	1977—1983	Gaylord Nelson, D.	1963—1981
Kansas		**North Carolina**		**Wyoming**	
Robert J. Dole, R.	1969—1981	Jesse A. Helms, R.	1973—1985	Malcolm Wallop, R.	1977—1983
Nancy Landon Kassebaum, R.	1979—1985	Robert Morgan, D.	1975—1981	Alan K. Simpson, R.	1979—1985
Kentucky		**North Dakota**			
Walter Huddleston, D.	1973—1985	Milton R. Young, R.	1945—1981		
Wendell H. Ford, D.	1975—1981	Quentin N. Burdick, D.	1960—1983		

Members of the United States House

The House of Representatives of the first session of the 96th Congress consisted of 276 Democrats and 157 Republicans (not including representatives from the District of Columbia, Guam, Puerto Rico, and the Virgin Islands) with 2 seats vacant (because of deaths after the Nov. 7, 1978, election) when it convened in January 1979, compared with 285 Democrats and 146 Republicans, with 4 seats vacant, when the 95th Congress adjourned. This table shows congressional districts, legislator, and party affiliation. Asterisk (*) denotes those who served in the 95th Congress; dagger (†) denotes "at large."

Alabama
1. Jack Edwards, R.*
2. William L. Dickinson, R.*
3. William Nichols, D.*
4. Tom Bevill, D.*
5. Ronnie G. Flippo, D.*
6. John H. Buchanan, Jr., R.*
7. Richard C. Shelby, D.

Alaska
† Don Young, R.*

Arizona
1. John J. Rhodes, R.*
2. Morris K. Udall, D.*
3. Bob Stump, D.*
4. Eldon Rudd, R.*

Arkansas
1. Bill Alexander, D.*
2. Edwin R. Bethune, Jr., R.
3. J. P. Hammerschmidt, R.*
4. Beryl Anthony, Jr., D.

California
1. Harold T. Johnson, D.*
2. Don H. Clausen, R.*
3. Robert Matsui, D.
4. Vic Fazio, D.
5. John L. Burton, D.*
6. Phillip Burton, D.*
7. George Miller, D.*
8. Ronald V. Dellums, D.*
9. Fortney H. Stark, D.*
10. Don Edwards, D.*
11. Vacant
12. Paul N. McCloskey, Jr., R.*
13. Norman Y. Mineta, D.*
14. Norman Shumway, R.
15. Tony Coelho, D.
16. Leon E. Panetta, D.*
17. Charles Pashayan, Jr., R.
18. William M. Thomas, R.
19. Robert J. Lagomarsino, R.*
20. Barry M. Goldwater, Jr., R.*
21. James C. Corman, D.*
22. Carlos J. Moorhead, R.*
23. Anthony C. Beilenson, D.*
24. Henry A. Waxman, D.*
25. Edward R. Roybal, D.*
26. John H. Rousselot, R.*
27. Robert K. Dornan, R.*
28. Julian C. Dixon, D.
29. Augustus F. Hawkins, D.*
30. George E. Danielson, D.*
31. Charles H. Wilson, D.*
32. Glenn M. Anderson, D.*
33. Wayne Grisham, R.
34. Dan Lungren, R.
35. Jim Lloyd, D.*
36. George E. Brown, Jr., D.*
37. Jerry Lewis, R.
38. Jerry M. Patterson, D.*
39. William E. Dannemeyer, R.
40. Robert E. Badham, R.*
41. Bob Wilson, R.*
42. Lionel Van Deerlin, D.*
43. Clair W. Burgener, R.*

Colorado
1. Patricia Schroeder, D.*
2. Timothy E. Wirth, D.*
3. Ray Kogovsek, D.
4. James P. Johnson, R.*
5. Ken Kramer, R.

Connecticut
1. William R. Cotter, D.*
2. Christopher J. Dodd, D.*
3. Robert N. Giaimo, D.*
4. Stewart B. McKinney, R.*
5. William Ratchford, D.
6. Anthony J. Moffett, D.*

Delaware
† Thomas B. Evans, Jr., R.*

Florida
1. Earl Hutto, D.
2. Don Fuqua, D.*
3. Charles E. Bennett, D.*
4. William V. Chappell, Jr., D.*
5. Richard Kelly, R.*
6. C. W. Young, R.*
7. Sam M. Gibbons, D.*
8. Andy Ireland, D.*
9. Bill Nelson, D.
10. L. A. Bafalis, R.*
11. Dan Mica, D.
12. Edward J. Stack, D.
13. William Lehman, D.*
14. Claude D. Pepper, D.*
15. Dante B. Fascell, D.*

Georgia
1. Ronald Ginn, D.*
2. Dawson Mathis, D.*
3. Jack T. Brinkley, D.*
4. Elliott H. Levitas, D.*
5. Wyche Fowler, Jr., D.*
6. Newton L. Gingrich, R.
7. Lawrence P. McDonald, D.*
8. Billy Lee Evans, D.*
9. Ed Jenkins, D.*
10. Doug Barnard, D.*

Hawaii
1. Cecil Heftel, D.*
2. Daniel K. Akaka, D.*

Idaho
1. Steven D. Symms, R.*
2. George Hansen, R.*

Illinois
1. Bennett Stewart, D.
2. Morgan F. Murphy, D.*
3. Martin A. Russo, D.*
4. Edward J. Derwinski, R.*
5. John G. Fary, D.*
6. Henry J. Hyde, R.*
7. Cardiss Collins, D.*
8. Dan Rostenkowski, D.*
9. Sidney R. Yates, D.*
10. Abner J. Mikva, D.*

11. Frank Annunzio, D.*
12. Philip M. Crane, R.*
13. Robert McClory, R.*
14. John N. Erlenborn, R.*
15. Tom Corcoran, R.*
16. John B. Anderson, R.*
17. George M. O'Brien, R.*
18. Robert H. Michel, R.*
19. Thomas F. Railsback, R.*
20. Paul Findley, R.*
21. Edward R. Madigan, R.*
22. Daniel Crane, R.
23. Charles Melvin Price, D.*
24. Paul Simon, D.*

Indiana
1. Adam Benjamin, Jr., D.*
2. Floyd J. Fithian, D.*
3. John Brademas, D.*
4. J. Danforth Quayle, R.*
5. Elwood H. Hillis, R.*
6. David W. Evans, D.*
7. John T. Myers, R.*
8. H. Joel Deckard, R.
9. Lee H. Hamilton, D.*
10. Philip R. Sharp, D.*
11. Andrew Jacobs, Jr., D.*

Iowa
1. James Leach, R.*
2. Thomas J. Tauke, R.
3. Charles E. Grassley, R.*
4. Neal Smith, D.*
5. Tom Harkin, D.*
6. Berkley Bedell, D.*

Kansas
1. Keith G. Sebelius, R.*
2. James E. Jeffries, R.
3. Larry Winn, Jr., R.*
4. Dan Glickman, D.*
5. Robert Whittaker, R.

Kentucky
1. Carroll Hubbard, Jr., D.*
2. William H. Natcher, D.*
3. Romano L. Mazzoli, D.*
4. Marion Gene Snyder, R.*
5. Tim Lee Carter, R.*
6. Larry Hopkins, R.
7. Carl D. Perkins, D.*

Louisiana
1. Robert L. Livingston, R.*
2. Lindy Boggs, D.*
3. David C. Treen, R.*
4. Claude Leach, D.
5. Jerry Huckaby, D.*
6. W. Henson Moore, R.*
7. John B. Breaux, D.*
8. Gillis W. Long, D.*

Maine
1. David F. Emery, R.*
2. Olympia Snowe, R.

Maryland
1. Robert E. Bauman, R.*
2. Clarence D. Long, D.*

3. Barbara A. Mikulski, D.*
4. Marjorie S. Holt, R.*
5. Gladys N. Spellman, D.*
6. Beverly Butcher Byron, D.
7. Parren J. Mitchell, D.*
8. Michael Barnes, D.

Massachusetts
1. Silvio O. Conte, R.*
2. Edward P. Boland, D.*
3. Joseph D. Early, D.*
4. Robert F. Drinan, D.*
5. James Shannon, D.
6. Nicholas Mavroules, D.
7. Edward J. Markey, D.*
8. Thomas P. O'Neill, Jr., D.*
9. John J. Moakley, D.*
10. Margaret M. Heckler, R.*
11. Brian Donnelly, D.
12. Gerry E. Studds, D.*

Michigan
1. John Conyers, Jr., D.*
2. Carl D. Pursell, R.*
3. Howard Wolpe, D.
4. David Stockman, R.*
5. Harold S. Sawyer, R.*
6. Bob Carr, D.*
7. Dale E. Kildee, D.*
8. Bob Traxler, D.*
9. Guy Vander Jagt, R.*
10. Donald Albosta, D.
11. Robert Davis, R.
12. David E. Bonior, D.*
13. Charles C. Diggs, Jr., D.*
14. Lucien N. Nedzi, D.*
15. William D. Ford, D.*
16. John D. Dingell, D.*
17. William M. Brodhead, D.*
18. James J. Blanchard, D.*
19. William S. Broomfield, R.*

Minnesota
1. Arlen Erdahl, R.
2. Thomas M. Hagedorn, R.*
3. Bill Frenzel, R.*
4. Bruce F. Vento, D.*
5. Martin Sabo, D.
6. Richard Nolan, D.*
7. Arlan Stangeland, R.*
8. James L. Oberstar, D.*

Mississippi
1. Jamie L. Whitten, D.*
2. David R. Bowen, D.*
3. G. V. Montgomery, D.*
4. Jon Hinson, R.
5. Trent Lott, R.*

Missouri
1. William L. Clay, D.*
2. Robert A. Young, D.*
3. Richard A. Gephardt, D.*
4. Ike Skelton, D.*
5. Richard Bolling, D.*
6. E. Thomas Coleman, R.*
7. Gene Taylor, R.*

8. Richard H. Ichord, D.*
9. Harold L. Volkmer, D.*
10. Bill D. Burlison, D.*

Montana
1. Pat Williams, D.
2. Ron Marlenee, R.*

Nebraska
1. Douglas Bereuter, R.
2. John J. Cavanaugh, D.*
3. Virginia Smith, R.*

Nevada
† James Santini, D.*

New Hampshire
1. Norman E. D'Amours, D.*
2. James C. Cleveland, R.*

New Jersey
1. James J. Florio, D.*
2. William J. Hughes, D.*
3. James J. Howard, D.*
4. Frank Thompson, Jr., D.*
5. Millicent Fenwick, R.*
6. Edwin B. Forsythe, R.*
7. Andrew Maguire, D.*
8. Robert A. Roe, D.*
9. Harold C. Hollenbeck, R.*
10. Peter W. Rodino, Jr., D.*
11. Joseph G. Minish, D.*
12. Matthew J. Rinaldo, R.*
13. James A. Courter, R.
14. Frank J. Guarini, D.
15. Edward J. Patten, D.*

New Mexico
1. Manuel Lujan, Jr., R.*
2. Harold Runnels, D.*

New York
1. William Carney, R.
2. Thomas J. Downey, D.*
3. Jerome A. Ambro, Jr., D.*
4. Norman F. Lent, R.*
5. John W. Wydler, R.*
6. Lester L. Wolff, D.*
7. Joseph P. Addabbo, D.*
8. Benjamin S. Rosenthal, D.*
9. Geraldine A. Ferraro, D.
10. Mario Biaggi, D.*
11. James H. Scheuer, D.*
12. Shirley Chisholm, D.*
13. Stephen J. Solarz, D.*
14. Frederick W. Richmond, D.*
15. Leo C. Zeferetti, D.*
16. Elizabeth Holtzman, D.*
17. John M. Murphy, D.*
18. S. William Green, R.*
19. Charles B. Rangel, D.*
20. Ted Weiss, D.*
21. Robert Garcia, D.*
22. Jonathan B. Bingham, D.*
23. Peter A. Peyser, D.
24. Richard L. Ottinger, D.*
25. Hamilton Fish, Jr., R.*

26. Benjamin A. Gilman, R.*
27. Matthew F. McHugh, D.*
28. Samuel S. Stratton, D.*
29. Gerald Solomon, R.
30. Robert C. McEwen, R.*
31. Donald J. Mitchell, R.*
32. James M. Hanley, D.*
33. Gary Lee, R.
34. Frank Horton, R.*
35. Barber B. Conable, Jr., R.*
36. John J. LaFalce, D.*
37. Henry J. Nowak, D.*
38. Jack F. Kemp, R.*
39. Stanley N. Lundine, D.*

North Carolina
1. Walter B. Jones, D.*
2. L. H. Fountain, D.*
3. Charles Whitley, D.*
4. Ike F. Andrews, D.*
5. Stephen L. Neal, D.*
6. L. Richardson Preyer, D.*
7. Charles Rose, D.*
8. W. G. Hefner, D.*
9. James G. Martin, R.*
10. James T. Broyhill, R.*
11. Lamar Gudger, D.*

North Dakota
† Mark Andrews, R.*

Ohio
1. Willis D. Gradison, Jr., R.*
2. Thomas A. Luken, D.*
3. Tony P. Hall, D.
4. Tennyson Guyer, R.*
5. Delbert L. Latta, R.*
6. William H. Harsha, R.*
7. Clarence J. Brown, R.*
8. Thomas N. Kindness, R.*
9. Thomas L. Ashley, D.*
10. Clarence E. Miller, R.*
11. J. William Stanton, R.*
12. Samuel L. Devine, R.*
13. Donald J. Pease, D.*
14. John F. Seiberling, D.*
15. Chalmers P. Wylie, R.*
16. Ralph S. Regula, R.*
17. John M. Ashbrook, R.*
18. Douglas Applegate, D.*
19. Lyle Williams, R.
20. Mary Rose Oakar, D.*
21. Louis Stokes, D.*
22. Charles A. Vanik, D.*
23. Ronald M. Mottl, D.*

Oklahoma
1. James R. Jones, D.*
2. Michael L. Synar, D.
3. Wes Watkins, D.*
4. Tom Steed, D.*
5. Mickey Edwards, R.*
6. Glenn English, D.*

Oregon
1. Les AuCoin, D.*
2. Al Ullman, D.*
3. Robert B. Duncan, D.*
4. James Weaver, D.*

Pennsylvania
1. Michael Myers, D.*
2. William H. Gray III, D.
3. Raymond F. Lederer, D.*
4. Charles F. Dougherty, R.
5. Richard T. Schulze, R.*
6. Gus Yatron, D.*
7. Robert W. Edgar, D.*
8. Peter H. Kostmayer, D.*
9. E. G. Shuster, R.*
10. Joseph M. McDade, R.*
11. Daniel J. Flood, D.*
12. John P. Murtha, D.*
13. Lawrence Coughlin, R.*
14. William S. Moorhead, D.*
15. Donald L. Ritter, R.
16. Robert S. Walker, R.*
17. Allen E. Ertel, D.*
18. Doug Walgren, D.*
19. William F. Goodling, R.*
20. Joseph M. Gaydos, D.*
21. Donald A. Bailey, D.
22. Austin J. Murphy, D.*
23. William F. Clinger, Jr., R.
24. Marc L. Marks, R.*
25. Eugene Atkinson, D.

Rhode Island
1. Fernand J. St. Germain, D.*
2. Edward P. Beard, D.*

South Carolina
1. Mendel J. Davis, D.*
2. Floyd D. Spence, R.*
3. Butler C. Derrick, Jr., D.*
4. Carroll A. Campbell, Jr., R.
5. Kenneth L. Holland, D.*
6. John W. Jenrette, Jr., D.*

South Dakota
1. Thomas A. Daschle, D.
2. James Abdnor, R.*

Tennessee
1. James H. Quillen, R.*
2. John J. Duncan, R.*
3. Marilyn Lloyd, D.*
4. Albert Gore, Jr., D.*
5. William H. Boner, D.
6. Robin L. Beard, Jr., R.*
7. Ed Jones, D.*
8. Harold E. Ford, D.*

Texas
1. Sam B. Hall, Jr., D.*
2. Charles Wilson, D.*
3. James M. Collins, R.*
4. Ray Roberts, D.*
5. James Mattox, D.*
6. Phil Gramm, D.
7. Bill Archer, R.*
8. Bob Eckhardt, D.*
9. Jack Brooks, D.*
10. J. J. Pickle, D.*
11. Marvin Leath, D.
12. James C. Wright, Jr., D.*
13. Jack Hightower, D.*
14. Joe Wyatt, D.
15. Eligio de la Garza, D.*
16. Richard C. White, D.*
17. Charles Stenholm, D.

18. Mickey Leland, D.
19. Kent Hance, D.
20. Henry B. Gonzalez, D.*
21. Thomas G. Loeffler, R.
22. Ronald E. Paul, R.
23. Abraham Kazen, Jr., D.*
24. Martin Frost, D.

Utah
1. K. Gunn McKay, D.*
2. Dan Marriott, R.*

Vermont
† James M. Jeffords, R.*

Virginia
1. Paul S. Trible, Jr., R.*
2. G. William Whitehurst, R.*
3. David E. Satterfield III, D.*
4. Robert W. Daniel, Jr., R.*
5. W. C. Daniel, D.*
6. M. Caldwell Butler, R.*
7. J. Kenneth Robinson, R.*
8. Herbert E. Harris, D.*
9. William C. Wampler, R.*
10. Joseph L. Fisher, D.*

Washington
1. Joel Pritchard, R.*
2. Allan B. Swift, D.
3. Don Bonker, D.*
4. Mike McCormack, D.*
5. Thomas S. Foley, D.*
6. Norm Dicks, D.*
7. Michael E. Lowry, D.

West Virginia
1. Robert H. Mollohan, D.*
2. Harley O. Staggers, D.*
3. John M. Slack, D.*
4. Nick J. Rahall, D.*

Wisconsin
1. Les Aspin, D.*
2. Robert W. Kastenmeier, D.*
3. Alvin J. Baldus, D.*
4. Clement J. Zablocki, D.*
5. Henry S. Reuss, D.*
6. Vacant
7. David R. Obey, D.*
8. Toby Roth, R.
9. F. James Sensenbrenner, Jr., R.

Wyoming
† Richard B. Cheney, R.

Nonvoting Representatives

District of Columbia
Walter E. Fauntroy, D.*

Guam
Antonio Won Pat, D.*

Puerto Rico
Baltasar Corrada, D.*

Virgin Islands
Melvin H. Evans, R.

269

A Senator's Fleecy Flail

When Jason and the Argonauts set sail in search of the Golden Fleece in the Greek myth, they were looking for the skin of a magic ram. Its wool was made of pure gold. When Senator William Proxmire (D., Wis.) sallies forth on the floor of the United States Senate to present his monthly Golden Fleece Award, he often strikes pure political gold.

Proxmire began presenting the Golden Fleece in 1975 for the "biggest, most ridiculous, or most ironic example of wasting federal tax funds." The awards enrage many government officials and private researchers working under federal grants. But, as Proxmire well knows, they also delight the press and arouse public indignation. Besides enhancing his political image as a frugal cost cutter, the senator believes the awards help to inform the public of the myriad ways in which their tax money can be spent – or misspent.

Proxmire plays no favorites with his awards. In March 1978, one went to his own group, the United States Senate, for planning to spend $122-million on a third Senate office building that "would make a Persian prince green with envy." The appropriation represented a cost overrun of 154 per cent.

Awards to research projects account for only about one-fourth of the Golden Fleeces, but they arouse great resentment among scientists. The U.S. Department of Agriculture received the August 1978 award for research in which pregnant pigs walked on treadmills to lessen boredom and psychological stress. Then there was a $500,000 study by a Michigan psychologist on why rats, monkeys, and humans clench their teeth. "The government should get out of this monkey business," said Proxmire. That award brought a $6-million lawsuit by the researcher, but a federal court ruled that the senator was protected by congressional immunity.

Proxmire awarded the February Fleece to the National Aeronautics and Space Administration for supporting the search for extraterrestrial intelligence. Cornell University astronomer Frank Drake, a pioneer in the search, grumbled that the senator should be given an honorary membership in the "Flat Earth Society."

Commenting on an award for a $102,000 study of aggressive behavior in drunken sunfish, Proxmire suggested that this "fishy research" should not be swallowed "hook, line, and sinker by the American taxpayer."

Other research grants attacked by Proxmire included a study on how long it takes to cook an egg and a study on why inmates want to escape from prison. One of his favorites was a grant to an artist to film four mile-long rolls of crepe paper as they fell from an airplane.

But the senator reserves his greatest wrath for overspending, self-indulgent public servants, including the military. His July award went to Pentagon officials for spending more than $1.2 million a year for parties, trips, and other entertainment. The money was hidden in the defense budget under "Emergencies and Extraordinary Expenses."

One of his pet peeves is the use of Air Force planes for minor trips, at a cost of some $52 million a year. The chauffeured limousines used by many officials, and coveted by many more, also make him angry. One of the few "Awards of Merit" he has given went in March 1977 to Max Cleland, the triple-amputee administrator of the Veterans Administration who drives his own car to work. Proxmire figures this saves taxpayers $16,000 a year.

Though they are written in a breezy style, the awards are not frivolous, and administrators know it. Proxmire does his homework, and when he cites a bureaucratic bungle or boondoggle, he has the figures to prove his case. Also, he is chairman or member of a number of important committees, including the Senate Committee on Appropriations. Many of the award "winners" must face the senator in budget hearings, and they find that the fleece has a sharp sting.

Meanwhile, the hardworking, 63-year-old senator – who runs 5 miles (8 kilometers) from home to office every day – continues the awards. Indeed, Golden Fleeces may run in the Proxmire family. The senator's first grandson was born in August 1978. He was named Jason.   Edward G. Nash

Senator William Proxmire

A new Senate office building, destined to be one of the most luxurious in Washington, D.C., may eventually cost $200 million.

Hearings, Scandals, and Corruption. More members of the 95th Congress were investigated, reprimanded, or indicted than in any other Congress. At least 13 representatives and three senators were involved in some sort of scandal. The House Committee on Standards of Official Conduct (the ethics committee) worked throughout the year to uncover the facts in the alleged influence-buying activities of South Korea. South Korean lobbyist Tong Sun Park testified in Seoul in January that he gave $850,000 to U.S. officials between 1970 and 1975 to influence them in favor of South Korea.

Former Congressman Richard T. Hanna (D., Calif.) was sentenced to 16 to 30 months in prison on April 24 for his role in the scandal. The House reprimanded California Democrats John J. McFall, Charles H. Wilson, and Edward R. Roybal and a New Jersey Democrat, Edward J. Patten, for their involvement.

The House ethics committee also investigated charges of improper conduct against Pennsylvania Democrats Daniel Flood and Joshua Eilberg, and voted unanimously on September 13 to file charges against them. Both men were charged with breaking federal law and violating the rules of the House. Flood was indicted on charges of bribery and conspiracy on September 5. Eilberg was indicted on October 24 for accepting fees from his law firm while the firm was helping Hahnemann Hospital in Phila-

delphia to secure a federal grant for a hospital addition. Representative Charles C. Diggs, Jr., a Michigan Democrat, was convicted on October 10 and sentenced on November 20 to three years in prison for mail fraud and diversion of congressional employees' salaries to his personal use. Flood and Diggs were re-elected on November 7.

The Senate ethics committee on December 19 filed charges against Senator Herman E. Talmadge, a Georgia Democrat, for financial wrongdoing in his handling of expense claims and campaign contributions. The committee will hold a hearing into the matter, the first such proceeding since 1967.

On September 6, the House Assassinations Committee opened public hearings on the assassinations of President John F. Kennedy and civil rights leader Martin Luther King, Jr. The committee concluded on December 30 that both assassinations resulted from conspiracies.

Representative Leo J. Ryan (D., Calif.) was killed on November 18 by members of the People's Temple in Jonestown, Guyana. Ryan had gone to Guyana to investigate the activities of the cult, which included many Californians among its members. See LATIN AMERICA (Close-Up). Carol L. Thompson

See also PRESIDENT OF THE UNITED STATES; UNITED STATES, GOVERNMENT OF THE. In WORLD BOOK, see CONGRESS OF THE UNITED STATES.

CONNECTICUT. See STATE GOVERNMENT.

CONSERVATION. Legislation setting aside almost 100 million acres (40 million hectares) in Alaska for parks, wildlife refuges, scenic rivers, and national forests died in Congress on Oct. 14, 1978. President Jimmy Carter's Administration and conservation forces considered Alaskan wilderness preservation their top environmental priority. Supporters of the measure began looking for other ways to keep these lands from being opened to development.

The Administration proposed in 1977 to set aside 92.5 million acres (37.4 million hectares) of Alaskan federal lands. The House voted on May 19 to preserve 102 million acres (41.3 million hectares) as "national interest" lands. However, the Senate Energy and Natural Resources Committee voted to protect only 83 million acres (33.6 million hectares), and to reduce from 66 million to 36 million acres (27 to 15 million hectares) the area classified as wilderness, in which oil exploration, mining, and timber cutting would be prohibited. The Senate bill would also have opened parts of the Arctic National Wildlife Range to oil and gas exploration.

Senator Theodore F. Stevens (R., Alaska) and Secretary of the Interior Cecil D. Andrus tried to work out a compromise before Congress adjourned. Andrus said the effort failed because Senator Mike Gravel (D., Alaska) rejected a compromise "which recognizes the national interest as well as the state interest."

The protection provided by the Alaska Native Claims Settlement Act of 1971 expired on Dec. 18, 1978. The Carter Administration promised to protect the lands by executive action until Congress acts in 1979. Andrus withdrew 110 million acres (45-million hectares) from development for three years in November, under authority of the Bureau of Land Management Organic Act. This acreage included nearly all the land designated in the Administration bill. President Carter placed 56 million acres (23-million hectares) of the land in the National Park System on December 1, under authority of the Antiquities Act of 1906. The President's action protected the lands permanently by designating them national monuments.

Omnibus Park Bill. Congress authorized $1.3-billion on October 13 for the most expensive expansion and development of the National Park System in history. The bill authorized more than 100 projects in 44 states. The House passed the bill, 341 to 61, on July 12 after cutting $400 million from the original $1.7-billion price to win Administration support. The Senate passed the bill on October 13.

Projects range from national parks and seashores to historic sites and inner-city playgrounds. Adding Mineral King Valley near Fresno, Calif., to Sequoia National Park ended the controversy over Walt Disney Productions' plan to build a ski resort in the valley. The bill's most costly provision provided cities with more than $600 million in matching

The Siberian crane's future is in the hands of American and Russian conservationists working to prevent its extinction. Only 360 are left.

recreation grants. The bill ended a 10-year battle by providing $25 million to buy pine and marshland in New Jersey.

The bill killed the Tocks Island Dam project in Pennsylvania, which had threatened the Delaware River, one of the East's last free-flowing rivers. The 90,000-acre (36,000-hectare) Santa Monica National Recreation Area will give Los Angeles one of the largest urban recreational parks.

More Wilderness. President Carter signed a bill on February 24 that created 13 wilderness areas totaling 1.3 million acres (525,000 hectares) and expanded four others, in 10 Western states. The addition, the largest since the 1964 Wilderness Act passed, increased U.S. wilderness areas to 15.7 million acres (6.4 million hectares).

Carter signed legislation on March 27 adding 48,000 acres (19,000 hectares) to California's Redwood National Park. The park's 1968 boundaries did not protect the world's tallest trees from the effects of erosion caused by cutting down trees outside the park. Expansion opponents argued that 2,000 loggers would lose their jobs. The bill provided $40 million for workers who lost their jobs because of the expansion. They would receive the equivalent of their salaries for six years. Senator James G. Abourezk (D., S. Dak.) contended that the government should reimburse people when it takes their jobs. The bill authorized $359 million to buy land.

President Carter signed legislation on March 22 increasing federal spending to protect the Appalachian National Scenic Trail from $5 million to $30-million a year. Carter called the trail, which stretches from Maine to Georgia, "an important part of our national heritage."

Carter signed a bill on October 23 limiting motorboats and snowmobiles and banning logging and mining in the Boundary Waters canoe area on Minnesota's border with Canada. The bill ended a 10-year controversy over wilderness preservation in the 1-million-acre (405,000-hectare) area.

Endangered Species. The Supreme Court of the United States ruled, 6 to 3, on June 15 that a lower court was correct in halting the Tennessee Valley Authority's nearly completed $116-million Tellico Dam in Tennessee because the project threatened to destroy the only known habitat of the snail darter, a 3-inch (7.6-centimeter) fish. Chief Justice Warren E. Burger said that the Endangered Species Act of 1973 clearly shows that Congress viewed the values of endangered species as "incalculable."

The act directed federal agencies "to insure that actions authorized, funded or carried out by them" do not jeopardize an endangered species. On October 15, Congress extended the act for 18 months with an amendment calling for a Cabinet-level panel to arbitrate conflicts between projects and endangered species. The extension also called for an expedited review of the Tellico Dam. The Senate rejected a House amendment exempting the Tellico project.

In July, the United States Department of the Interior took the first animal off the endangered species list because the species had become extinct. The Tecopa pupfish, about 1 1/2 inches (3.8 centimeters) long, lived in small pools and thermal springs near Tecopa, Calif. About 30 years ago, builders of a bathhouse rechanneled some of the springs. The pupfish could not adapt. Biologists failed to find any pupfish during a recent search of 11 sites.

Whale Quotas. At an International Whaling Commission (IWC) meeting in London from June 26 through 30, the 1979 quota of bowhead whales for Alaskan Eskimos was increased to 18 landed or 27 struck. The previous quota, approved in 1977, was 12 landed or 18 struck. An Alaskan Eskimo delegation walked out of the meeting after contending they needed between 37 and 45 whales for subsistence and cultural needs. The United States persuaded the IWC in 1977 not to ban all bowhead killing, but to give the Eskimos a quota.

The IWC, under pressure from Japan and Russia, the main whaling countries, reduced by 5 per cent the number of whales to be killed in 1979.

The African Elephant. The U.S. Fish and Wildlife Service listed the African elephant, the largest living land mammal, as a threatened species on May 10. The agency said that, though there are now about 1 million African elephants, the growing demand for ivory and human encroachment on the elephants' habitat will endanger them if they are not protected.

Kenya banned the sale of wildlife trophies on March 12, to save wildlife. Kenya had lost more than half its elephants since 1970. According to Ellis Monks of the World Wildlife Fund in Kenya, closing souvenir shops will not stop all illegal killing of elephants, because most illegal ivory sales have been in bulk, to overseas customers, rather than in finished goods sold in shops. Monks said that wildlife species could recover if the government stopped the killing. Kenya's first comprehensive aerial survey of 20 species showed that only the black rhinoceros was in trouble – just 1,800 of these animals were left.

UN Lists U.S. Parks. The World Heritage Committee of the United Nations Educational, Scientific, and Cultural Organization, which met in Washington, D.C., in September, included Yellowstone National Park in Idaho, Montana, and Wyoming, and Mesa Verde National Park in Colorado among 12 sites on the first World Heritage list of natural or cultural areas. Yellowstone National Park, established in 1872, was the world's first national park. Mesa Verde National Park preserves prehistoric cliff dwellings and other remains of the Pueblo Indians' culture.   Andrew L. Newman

See also ENVIRONMENT. In WORLD BOOK, see CONSERVATION.

CONSTITUTION OF THE UNITED STATES. A constitutional amendment that would give the 700,000 District of Columbia residents voting representation in both houses of Congress was passed by the United States Senate on Aug. 22, 1978. The House of Representatives had approved the amendment on March 2. If ratified by 38 state legislatures, it would create two additional Senate seats, bringing the total number of senators to 102. It would add one or two representatives temporarily, but House membership would stabilize at 435 following the next congressional reapportionment.

Proponents of the Equal Rights Amendment (ERA), which would prohibit discrimination on the basis of sex, hoped to have it passed by three more state legislatures, thus putting it into law. They made a concentrated effort in Illinois, the only Northern industrial state still withholding ratification, but ERA was defeated by a narrow margin in that state's legislature in June.

Hope was offered ERA supporters, however, when the House approved an extension of its ratification deadline on August 15. Approved by the Senate on October 6, the deadline for ratification was extended by 39 months to June 30, 1982. Such an extension was unprecedented and was expected to be challenged in court.   Beverly Merz

In WORLD BOOK, see CONSTITUTION OF THE UNITED STATES; EQUAL RIGHTS AMENDMENT.

CONSUMER AFFAIRS. Prices rose to a painful point for many consumers in the United States in 1978. By October, the Consumer Price Index had reached 200.9 per cent of the 1967 level, almost 8.9 per cent above its January level. Although there were no national boycotts or major consumer protests, pressures increased for government action to stop the price rise.

According to a Louis Harris public opinion poll in October, the public favored price and wage controls by 58 to 35 per cent. During the same month, a coalition of labor, consumer, and other citizen groups was created to call attention to the 11.6 per cent increase in prices of four basic necessities: food, fuel, housing, and health care.

Anti-Inflation Program. On October 24, two weeks before the national elections, President Jimmy Carter announced an "anti-inflation program." He acknowledged that inflation had become "our nation's most serious economic problem," and that his Administration had "made no progress" on it.

He called for voluntary cooperation by all Americans to keep price increases generally down to 5.75 per cent and wage increases at 7 per cent or below. In an effort to gain support from organized labor, which belittled the President's plan in advance, he added a "wage-insurance" device. Under this proposal, groups of workers whose wages did not rise

more than 7 per cent would automatically become eligible for tax refunds equal to any price index increase above 7 per cent. However, the wage insurance plan would have to be approved by Congress before it could take effect. Carter also put a tighter lid on government spending, and ordered that government contracts above $5 million in 1979 be withheld from firms that did not comply with the wage and price limits. See ECONOMICS.

Many people doubted that the plan would work. The dollar fell further on international monetary exchanges, and the stock market went into a tailspin. Another adverse sign was a 0.9 per cent increase in wholesale prices in October, an annual inflation rate of more than 11 per cent. More than half of the increase was in food and fuel prices, which were largely exempted from the plan. Government-induced increases in bank rates brought mortgage rates above 10 per cent in many areas, a rate that many feared would depress housing sales.

Health-care costs drew special attention from the Administration, which noted that they had continued to rise about twice as fast as other living costs for several years. As a result, demands for national health insurance grew louder. But, rather than proposing a new federal program, the Administration chose to ask Congress to impose a 9 per cent ceiling on hospital cost increases that had averaged more than 15 per cent a year. Spirited lobbying by the medical community helped defeat the proposal in Congress. See HEALTH AND DISEASE.

Federal Legislation. Congress passed several new laws designed to provide greater consumer protection, but it failed to approve the bill that consumer affairs leaders wanted most – a new federal consumer agency. A watered-down version of the plan was defeated 227 to 189 in the House of Representatives on February 8 even though a Louis Harris poll reported that the public approved the idea by a 2 to 1 margin. Intensive lobbying by business groups, led by the U.S. Chamber of Commerce and the National Association of Manufacturers, was generally credited with being a decisive factor in the defeat.

Other consumer bills denied congressional approval included one to set a national system of "no-fault" automobile insurance and one to authorize all regulatory agencies to repay private citizens for the expenses of participating in government hearings and meetings.

Congress approved and President Carter signed bills dealing with cooperatives, bankruptcy, college expenses, and home insulation. A law signed by Carter on August 20 provided $300 million in seed money funds for a national cooperative bank, to help establish and expand cooperatives for low-income Americans.

A bankruptcy measure signed by Carter on November 8 set up a new system of federal courts. It also created a new category of consumer debtors and an

Safety Commission's Home-Hazard Index	
	Hazard Index
1. Bicycles and equipment	40.6
2. Stairs, ramps, and landings	23.5
3. Footballs and football gear	13.7
4. Baseballs and equipment	12.9
5. Playground equipment	12.5
6. Power lawn mowers	12.0
7. Skates, skateboards, and scooters	11.1
8. Swimming pools and equipment	11.1
9. Nonglass tables	11.0
10. Beds and bunk beds	9.7
11. Chairs, sofas, and sofa beds	8.3
12. Basketballs and equipment	7.8
13. Floors and flooring materials	7.4
14. Nails, carpet tacks, and thumbtacks	7.2
15. Architectural glass	6.3
16. Bathtubs and nonglass shower enclosures	5.8
17. Liquid fuels, kindling, and lighting products	5.5
18. Bleaches, dyes, and cleaning compounds	5.4
19. Cookware – metal, ceramic, and glass	5.1
20. Desks, cabinets, bookshelves, and racks	4.4

Bicycles rank as the most hazardous item
found around the home, according to a
Consumer Product Safety Commission survey.

alternative procedure to bankruptcy that allows repayment over an extended period of time.

Another law, signed on November 1, made government loans available to several million more college students. The family-income limit for these Basic Educational Grants was raised from about $16,000 to $26,000. Grants for low-income families were also increased substantially. See Section Two, How to Cope with Rising College Costs.

Homeowners gained special tax benefits in the omnibus energy law signed on November 9. The benefits included tax credits of 15 per cent on the first $2,000 spent for insulation and fuel conservation, and up to $2,200 in tax credits for solar- or wind-energy equipment. Exemption from the 4-cent federal excise tax on gasoline was granted for *gasohol* (gasoline containing 10 per cent or more alcohol), but special penalties were added for cars with low fuel efficiency.

In addition, public utilities were required to provide information on request, including names of local contractors, to customers who want to know how they can save fuel, how much they can save, and how to finance the costs. The law allowed customers to repay loans for such purposes on their monthly utility bills. Consumers also gained new rights to intervene in state regulatory proceedings and to seek court review, if desired.

Other federal laws included a customs-reform measure, increasing to $300 the amount of duty-free merchandise a traveler can bring back to the United States, and a bank-reform law that limited liability to $50 for the holder of a lost or stolen debit card, one used to withdraw money from automatic tellers.

Deregulation gained new impetus on many fronts. The principal effect of the energy bill approved by Congress on October 15 was to reduce federal controls on oil and gas industries. The net result will be higher prices in the years ahead. See Petroleum and Gas.

But deregulation efforts in other fields were expected to lower prices. Most dramatic were substantial reductions in airfares, following action by the Civil Aeronautics Board to relax federal restrictions and promote competition (see Aviation). By November, the Interstate Commerce Commission was pressed by other federal agencies and consumer groups to allow more competition by letting bus and train companies reduce fares. Lower prices for eyeglasses were expected when a Federal Trade Commission (FTC) rule ended restrictions on advertising eyeglasses in May.

Congress also blocked regulations that were opposed by various industry groups. Legislators temporarily delayed appropriation bills for the U.S. Department of Agriculture, the FTC, and the Food and Drug Administration after receiving complaints from representatives of the sugar, cereal, advertising, and funeral industries. The House voted itself veto authority over FTC actions at one point, but the effort failed when the Senate refused to go along with the legislation. Congressional hostility toward federal regulation of certain business groups was expected to increase in the 96th Congress, which was given a slightly more conservative tinge by the November election results.

The Firestone Recall. One of the more controversial regulatory actions was not vetoed, however – a massive recall of Firestone "500" steel-belted radial tires. In a bitter, prolonged battle ending on November 29, the Firestone Tire & Rubber Company agreed to recall some 13 million automobile tires at an estimated cost of $400 million (after taxes), after the government had ruled them unsafe. It was the largest tire recall in history. Auto recalls for safety defects reached a peak of 12.9 million in 1977 and continued at a high level in 1978.

Consumer issues were frequently debated in the election campaigns, particularly in New Hampshire. Republican Governor Meldrim Thomson, Jr., was unexpectedly beaten there by Democrat Hugh Gallen, a relatively unknown automobile dealer, largely because Thomson approved increasing electric utility rates to pay for the construction of a nuclear plant at Seabrook, N.H. The two candidates differed little on other matters.   Arthur E. Rowse

In World Book, see Consumer Protection.

COSTA RICA. See Latin America.

COURTS AND LAWS

COURTS AND LAWS. For the legal profession around the world, 1978 was a year of extraordinary contention and controversy. Several opportunities for orderly settlement of disputes under international law were lost, at least temporarily, because of a lack of credible enforcement mechanisms. In the United States, the legal profession came under critical attack by President Jimmy Carter and others for failing to live up to inherent responsibilities. A top American Bar Association (ABA) official, surveying the adverse publicity, called 1978 the "Year of the Lawyer."

Beagle Channel. On January 25, Argentina formally rejected an arbitration decision by a panel of five judges from the International Court of Justice that favored Chile in a long-standing dispute over ownership of three tiny, uninhabited islands. The islands are in the Beagle Channel, south of the Strait of Magellan, near the southern tip of South America. When the panel announced its decision, Chile pressed its advantage by claiming a 200-nautical-mile economic zone around the islands extending well into the Atlantic Ocean, and by expanding its proportional claim to Antarctica. Argentina responded on October 11 by calling up 500,000 army reservists and conducting blackout drills.

The prospect of war was tempered by the possibility of intervention by others. Chile feared Peru and Bolivia would seize the opportunity to press long-simmering border claims, and Argentina worried that Brazil might intervene. On December 22, Pope John Paul II announced that both countries had accepted his offer to mediate the dispute. See LATIN AMERICA.

Other International Disputes. In a surprise development, Turkish Prime Minister Bulent Ecevit reversed his previous position on March 11 and agreed to submit Turkey's long-standing dispute with Greece over mineral rights in the Aegean Sea to international arbitration. After serious criticism in Turkey, however, Ecevit reversed himself, announcing on April 25 that the International Court of Justice was not competent to rule on the dispute.

An Inter-American Court on Human Rights, to be based in San José, Costa Rica, gained approval on July 18 when Grenada became the 11th member of the Organization of American States (OAS) to ratify its Convention on Human Rights. The convention, proposed by the OAS in 1969, calls for a court calendar of about two weeks per year to hear civil liberties cases.

The Letelier Affair. United States and Chilean authorities became embroiled in an international legal incident stemming from the 1976 car-bomb murder of former Chilean Foreign Minister Orlando Letelier and his aide, Ronni K. Moffitt, in Wash-

Attorney General Griffin Bell, left, introduces Chief Justice Warren E. Burger, critic of trial lawyers, at American Bar Association convention.

ington, D.C. A federal grand jury in Washington indicted three Chileans and four Cuban exiles on August 1 on charges stemming from the murder. An American resident of Chile, Michael V. Townley, pleaded guilty on August 11 to conspiracy to murder Letelier, giving details of the crime. He was sentenced to at least 40 months in prison.

The indicted Chileans were high-ranking officials of the now-disbanded Chilean secret police force, and included General Manuel Contreras Sepulveda, brother-in-law and close associate of Chile's President Augusto Pinochet Ugarte. The United States asked Chile on September 20 to extradite the three, but the case was turned over to Chile's Supreme Court, which said that a secret, closed-door review lasting more than a year would be necessary before any extradition decision would be made.

Lawyers and Judges. Public criticism of the U.S. legal profession received national publicity. Chief Justice Warren E. Burger of the Supreme Court of the United States told the ABA on February 12 that as many as half of the nation's trial attorneys were incompetent. President Carter, addressing a bar meeting in Los Angeles on May 4, said lawyers had contributed heavily to unequal justice in the United States. ABA leaders, including President William B. Spann, Jr., defended the quality and competency of lawyers.

Major Trials. The year's most publicized trial ended in the acquittal on October 24 of surgeon Mario E. Jascalevich, charged in Bergen County, N.J., with the murder of three hospital patients by injections of curare, a muscle relaxant, in 1965 and 1966. During the trial, which began on February 27, Myron A. Farber, a reporter for *The New York Times*, was jailed twice on criminal contempt charges after he refused to turn over his notes on the Jascalevich case. The newspaper was fined $5,000 per day for supporting Farber. The newspaper paid about $285,000 and Farber spent 38 days in jail before the acquittal ended the confrontation.

In other celebrated trials, William and Emily Harris, Symbionese Liberation Army (SLA) founders, were sentenced in Oakland, Calif., in October to 10 years to life in prison. They pleaded guilty to the 1974 kidnapping of newspaper heiress Patricia Hearst. On June 13, David Berkowitz, the "Son of Sam" killer, received the maximum prison term for each of six murders in New York.

In a legal move said to be without precedent, the Department of Justice filed a court brief in November supporting a defense contention that the "Wilmington 10" civil rights activists might have been denied due process of law when they were convicted in North Carolina in 1971 of burning grocery stores during rioting a year earlier.   David C. Beckwith

See also CIVIL RIGHTS; CONSUMER AFFAIRS; SUPREME COURT OF THE UNITED STATES. In WORLD BOOK, see COURT; LAW.

CRIME. International political terrorism continued to bedevil governments around the world during 1978, but more sophisticated security measures and intergovernmental cooperation cut sharply into the violence. The year's most spectacular terrorist incident occurred in Cyprus on February 18 and 19.

After killing newspaper editor Youssef el-Sebai, a close associate of Egypt's President Anwar al-Sadat, to protest Sadat's peace initiatives, two Arab gunmen hijacked a Cyprus Airways DC-8 and flew around the Mediterranean area. When no country would grant asylum, the plane returned to Cyprus. Egypt flew a team of 74 commandos to Larnaca Airport on Cyprus. The Egyptian force began to storm the plane without permission from Cyprus, and Cypriot troops opened fire, killing 15 commandos in a one-hour battle. The hijackers then surrendered their 15 hostages unharmed.

To combat such crimes, Canada, France, Great Britain, Italy, Japan, West Germany, and the United States agreed on July 17 to end all flights to and from any country that refused to prosecute hijackers. See EUROPE (Close-Up).

White-Collar Crime. As the incidence of street crime leveled off in the United States, prosecutors turned their attention to bribery, fraud, tax evasion, and other white-collar crimes. Among those charged or convicted on corruption charges during the year were current or former ranking officials of more than a dozen major U.S. corporations.

Three top former Federal Bureau of Investigation officials, including onetime Acting Director L. Patrick Gray, were indicted on April 10 on civil rights conspiracy charges for having approved illegal break-ins and searches in 1972 and 1973 against the Weathermen group, a radical antiwar organization.

Several congressmen ran into serious trouble. Representative Joshua Eilberg (D., Pa.) was indicted on October 24 on conflict-of-interest charges involving payments from a federally financed hospital project. Representative Daniel J. Flood (D., Pa.) was indicted on September 5 for allegedly lying about payoffs and again on October 12 for conspiracy and bribery. Representative Charles C. Diggs, Jr., (D., Mich.) was convicted on October 7 on 29 counts of mail fraud and filing false congressional payroll data and was sentenced on November 20 to three years in prison. Representative Frederick W. Richmond (D., N.Y.) was indicted for soliciting a male policeman for sexual purposes on April 5; charges were dropped after Richmond agreed to seek psychiatric help. Voters re-elected Flood, Diggs, and Richmond.

Continuing a recent trend, crime incidence dropped in the United States, falling 2 per cent during the first nine months, compared with the same period in 1977. Violent crimes – rape, assault, murder, and robbery – rose 1 per cent, but property crimes – larceny, burglary, and auto theft – declined 3 per cent.

White-collar crime is the most costly to the U.S., says John Conyers, Jr. (D., Mich.), chairman of a House subcommittee studying the problem.

San Francisco Mayor George Moscone and Supervisor Harvey Milk were shot to death in the City Hall on November 27. Former City Supervisor Dan White was charged with the killings. See SAN FRANCISCO-OAKLAND.

Stanley Mark Rifkind, a computer expert, was accused in November of the complicated computer theft of $10.2 million from Security Pacific Bank in Los Angeles. Federal agents said Rifkind used most of the money to buy diamonds from Russia.

In December, six masked men stole more than $6-million in currency and jewelry from the Lufthansa Airlines cargo facility at New York City's Kennedy International Airport. It was the biggest cash robbery in U. S. history. In Cook County (Ill.), investigators uncovered 27 bodies of young men buried under or close to the home of John Wayne Gacy near Chicago in late December. Two other bodies found in a nearby river were associated with Gacy. At year's end, Gacy was under arrest for what appeared to be one of the worst mass murders in U.S. history.

London police broke up one of history's most successful forgery rings. Five men, known as the Hungarian Circle, were convicted on May 31 on charges of defrauding some 40 leading banks worldwide of more than $400 million over 15 years through counterfeit bank drafts.   David C. Beckwith

In WORLD BOOK, see CRIME; TERRORISM.

CUBA. Relations with the United States continued their slow thaw in 1978 despite angry exchanges over two major issues. One centered on Russia's involvement in Cuban defense strategy; the other involved Cuban troops in Africa. See AFRICA.

On February 14, a U.S. intelligence official charged that Soviet pilots flying MIG-23 fighter planes had taken over a large part of Cuba's aerial defense to free Cuban pilots for combat in Ethiopia. Although Cuba denied the charges, President Jimmy Carter ordered U.S. photo reconnaissance flights over Cuba to determine whether the MIG-23s had been modified to carry nuclear weapons. Such a modification would be a violation of the understanding between the United States and Russia concluded after the Cuban missile crisis in 1962. The invasion of Shaba province in Zaire by rebels based in Angola also brought an accusation from Carter on May 25 that "Cuba had known of the plans to invade and obviously did nothing to restrain them."

Castro Denial. In an emotional outburst to U.S. reporters accompanying two congressmen on a visit to Havana, President Fidel Castro Ruz declared on June 13 that Carter's charge "is not a half lie. It is an absolute, total, complete lie." Castro also disclosed that he had called the U.S. representative in Cuba to his office on May 17 to explain that he had tried to stop the invasion when he heard "rumors" of it.

Closer U.S. Contacts. Despite these charges, groups of U.S. citizens continued to visit Cuba, and the U.S. Coast Guard and the Cuban coastal service completed arrangements to establish radio links to avoid incidents in which small U.S. boats were seized when they strayed into Cuban waters. This agreement complemented the treaty concluded in December 1977, delineating the maritime boundaries between the two countries. When a group of U.S. mayors and their wives spent a week in Cuba in June, Castro indicated that he would be willing to meet with Carter, but that Carter must take the initiative.

The U.S. Department of State said on November 13 that U.S.-Cuban relations had improved because of some humanitarian gestures by Castro. These gestures included giving Cuban-American dual nationals the right to emigrate to the United States.

United States sources said that the cost to Russia of keeping the Cuban economy viable had risen to $5 million per day. Although Cuba claimed to have a sugar harvest of 8 million short tons (7.3 million metric tons), the second highest in its history, low world sugar prices forced the government to cancel the purchase of new industrial plants it had ordered in an effort to trim its import bill and ease its trade deficit.   Everett G. Martin

See also LATIN AMERICA (Facts in Brief Table). In WORLD BOOK, see CUBA.

CYPRUS. Greece and Turkey made slight progress toward ending the deadlock over a Cyprus settlement in 1978. Turkey offered a series of proposals to United Nations Secretary-General Kurt Waldheim on April 13, one of which would allow 35,000 Greek Cypriots to return to their homes and businesses in Varosha, the Greek area in the city of Famagusta.

The Turkish proposals were based on the principle of "an independent, nonaligned, bizonal, and bicommunal Federal State of Cyprus." Cyprus would have two separate legislatures. Cyprus President Spyros Kyprianou described the proposals as "totally inadequate." Waldheim visited Athens, Greece, on April 16 to discuss the proposals, but found the issue clouded by United States unwillingness to lift its arms embargo against Turkey. On July 24, Greece accepted the Turkish offer to let Greeks return to Famagusta, on condition that Turkey agree to peace talks on wider issues concerning Cyprus. The Turks agreed. On September 26, the United States lifted its arms embargo.

Egypt and Cyprus exchanged angry charges after Egyptian commandos landed at Larnaca airport on February 19 and stormed a jetliner to rescue hostages held by Arab terrorists. Cypriot forces fired on the commandos, killing 15 of them.   Kenneth Brown

See also GREECE; MIDDLE EAST (Facts in Brief Table); TURKEY. In WORLD BOOK, see CYPRUS.

Egyptian commandos rush plane at Larnaca airport in Cyprus in attempt on February 19 to free 15 hostages being held by two Arab terrorists.

CZECHOSLOVAKIA

CZECHOSLOVAKIA. President and Communist Party General Secretary Gustav Husak consolidated his position in 1978. He was rumored to be under pressure from the ultraconservative Presidium member from Slovakia, Vasil Bilak, but Russia demonstrated its support for Husak during Chairman Leonid I. Brezhnev's visit to Czechoslovakia from May 30 to June 2.

Czechoslovakia continued to harass members of the dissident Charter 77 movement, but the dissidents published a document in August denouncing the 1968 invasion of Czechoslovakia by Warsaw Pact forces. Members of Charter 77 met secretly with their Polish counterparts at the border in August to commemorate the invasion. Professor Jaroslav Sabata, a Charter 77 spokesman, was arrested in October because of the meeting.

Pope Paul VI appointed Frantisek Cardinal Tomasek archbishop of Prague on January 10, to try to normalize relations between the Roman Catholic Church and Czechoslovakia. The country had had no primate since the exiled Archbishop Josef Beran died in 1969. The Vatican set up an independent Slovak Roman Catholic church province.

President Husak visited West Germany in April for trade talks. Czechoslovakia agreed in April to limit its steel shipments to the European Community (EC or Common Market) to 735,000 short tons (667,000 metric tons) in 1978, compared with 806,000 short tons (731,000 metric tons) in 1976 and 635,000 short tons (576,000 metric tons) for the first nine months of 1977. This was Czechoslovakia's first agreement with the EC.

Economic Changes. Minister of Finance Leopold Ler announced on February 14 a three-year economic reorganization experiment affecting 150 industrial enterprises, 9 trading companies, and 21 research and development organizations. The total output of these enterprises is estimated at about $7.7-billion, 9 per cent of Czechoslovakia's gross national product, and they employ 487,000 persons, 14 per cent of the nation's work force.

Wages under the experiment would reflect quality of production rather than quantity. Standards for evaluating factories would include not only quantity, but also the proportion of new products and the degree of competitiveness in foreign trade. Prices would take quality into account.

For the year, industrial output increased by 4.8 per cent. Czechoslovakia obtained a seven-year, $150-million Eurocredit in March from a lending group that was led by Creditanstalt-Bankverein, an Austrian bank.
Chris Cviic

See also EUROPE (Facts in Brief Table). In WORLD BOOK, see CZECHOSLOVAKIA.

DAIRYING. See AGRICULTURE.

Czechoslovak President Gustav Husak speaks in Old Town Square in Prague during the Communist government's 30th anniversary celebration.

DALLAS-FORT WORTH. The Dallas school district's desegregation plan was rejected on April 24, 1978, by the United States Fifth Circuit Court of Appeals. In effect since 1976, the plan counted on 14 magnet schools with specialized programs to attract students of all races and bring about voluntary desegregation. However, the court noted that the district had bused only 17,000 of the city's 136,500 students and that 27,000 students still attended all-black schools.

School Issues. It was revealed in July that more than half of the 535 first-year teachers in the school system had failed a mental ability test designed for persons 13 years old and older. School administrators who took the test scored even lower, on the whole, than the teachers. The school district concealed the test results for three months, but released them after the Texas attorney general's office ordered that the scores be made public.

The question of separation of church and state in Dallas public schools was raised in July when candidates for the position of superintendent of schools complained that they had been questioned by school district trustees about their religious beliefs and practices. Dallas County District Attorney Henry Wade said such questioning was in violation of the Texas education code and took the matter to a grand jury. The grand jury had not released its recommendations by year-end.

Heat Wave. The Dallas-Fort Worth area sweltered under a record-breaking 18-day heat wave in July during which temperatures soared daily over 100° F. (38°C). At least 21 deaths were attributed to the heat, and countless persons were treated in area hospitals for heat-related maladies. Meteorologists blamed a high-pressure system over New Mexico and lack of movement in upper-air patterns for the torrid weather.

A Department of Labor report released on April 26 ranked Dallas as one of the least expensive large cities in which to live. The report said it would cost an average family of four $15,313 per year to live in moderate comfort in the Dallas area, more than 10 per cent less than the national average cost of $17,106. The same study showed that it would cost such a family $9,618 to sustain a minimum standard of living and $22,500 to maintain a higher-level life style. Living costs in the area rose 5.5 per cent in the 11-month period ending in April.

United States Secretary of Transportation Brock Adams recommended to Congress on May 8 that rail passenger service to Dallas-Fort Worth by the National Railroad Passenger Corporation (Amtrak) be discontinued. This was part of a proposal to reduce Amtrak operating costs by eliminating more than 8,000 miles (13,000 kilometers) of the 27,000-mile (43,000-kilometer) system.   James M. Banovetz

In WORLD BOOK, see DALLAS; FORT WORTH.

DAM. See BUILDING AND CONSTRUCTION.

The Reunion Tower in Dallas, a 50-story shaft capped by a geodesic sphere, dominates the city's skyline. The tower was completed in April.

DANCING

The world of ballet was astonished in 1978 by a dancer's unexpected decision to move from one company to another. Mikhail Baryshnikov announced the termination of his four-year association with the American Ballet Theatre (ABT) on April 26 and said he would join the New York City Ballet (NYCB) in July. He cited artistic reasons for the move, specifically the opportunity to work with choreographers George Balanchine and Jerome Robbins. Baryshnikov made his debut with NYCB in *Coppelia* on July 8, during the company's season in Saratoga Springs, N.Y. Its winter season at the New York State Theatre, beginning November 14, provided further evidence of Baryshnikov's adaptability to the rigors and modernity of the Balanchine style.

Amid the hullabaloo of the Baryshnikov announcement, NYCB found itself in unusual straits during its two-month New York spring season. Balanchine was recovering from a mild heart attack, which meant that the two new ballets he was slated to create were assigned to others. The long-awaited *Tricolore* was turned over to Robbins and two of the group's principal dancers. First performed on May 17, it was an artistic disaster. Many observers speculated that not even Balanchine could have made the commissioned Georges Auric score palatable. The second première, on June 8, was *A Sketch Book*, from the "pages" of Robbins and Peter Martins. Although the dances were obviously works in progress, critics saw much delightful material in them.

ABT's Big Production was *Don Quixote*, staged, ironically enough, by Baryshnikov. The ballet, which premièred on March 23 at the John F. Kennedy Center for the Performing Arts in Washington, D.C., is a modernization of the old Russian ballet. Its bubbling pace impressed critics more than its choreography. Baryshnikov's amazing virtuosity and comic energy in the role of Basil, the barber, were incontestable. Another noteworthy première was a ballet to music of Antonín Dvořák by Antony Tudor, introduced in December at the Kennedy Center.

Agnes de Mille, like Tudor, is a venerable choreographer who has not created many ballets in recent years. In 1978, De Mille offered a new work, *A Bridegroom Called Death*. The Joffrey Ballet mounted it on November 1 during an engagement at the New York City Center 55th Street Theater from October 18 to November 26. Continuing its policy of reviving historically important works, the Joffrey Ballet opened Sir Frederick Ashton's *A Wedding Bouquet* on October 18.

While the Joffrey Ballet and ABT boast a varied repertory, the Feld Ballet centers around Eliot Feld's work. This year found Feld in a Latin American mood. *La Vida* and *Danzon Cubano*, both set to Aaron Copland scores, incorporate Latin dance styles into the classical ballet vocabulary. The result is a kind of abstract character dance. Less ambitious and more successful was the all-American *Half Time* premièred on September 20 during the Feld Ballet's three-week stint at New York City's Public Theatre.

While Feld was poking fun at the American love of pompons and cheerleaders in *Half Time*, other companies were commemorating a more serious side of American life. A number of programs were devoted to the golden anniversary of modern-dance pioneer Doris Humphrey, who formed her first performing group in 1928. The Connecticut Dance Theatre gave all-Humphrey recitals in New England in October, as did the Arizona State University Dance Theater in the Southwest in November. The José Limón Dance Company, which Humphrey served as artistic adviser until her death in 1958, revived her *Passacaglia in C Minor* in December 1978. On December 20, at New York's City Center, the Limón company premièred *Suite for Erik*, a work by Murray Louis starring Erik Bruhn.

Two major trends may be noted in the world of dance. Modern-dance companies are beginning to build repertories upon the multichoreographer concept, and aging ballet dancers, such as Bruhn, are turning to nonballetic choreographers to inject their careers with new life. Another obvious example is Rudolf Nureyev, who also danced Murray Louis works in 1978.

Modern-Dance Companies that traditionally perform only the works of their founders — those of Martha Graham, Paul Taylor, and Merce Cunningham — had a busy year. The Graham dancers performed at the Metropolitan Opera House in New York City from June 26 to July 1, marking the first time the Met has produced modern dance. Graham created three new works, but the novelty of the Graham-Met marriage was paramount.

Taylor's group toured throughout the United States and also visited Russia from September 18 to October 15. Cunningham's tours were highlighted by five weeks in Massachusetts, premièring *Fractions* in Boston on February 26. A second première, the brilliantly virtuosic *Exchange*, was unveiled at New York's City Center on September 27.

Diplomatic Dancers. The changing political scene left a mark on dance activity. The National Ballet of Cuba, which has danced in Canada, made its U.S. debut on May 30, when it opened a two-week run at the Kennedy Center. Starring its founder, Alicia Alonso, the troupe brought a varied

American Ballet Theatre's vibrant *Don Quixote,* starring Gelsey Kirkland and Mikhail Baryshnikov, was the Russian dancer's last role with ABT.

The National Ballet of Cuba features Alicia
Alonso, its founder and director, in foreground,
as *Giselle* in its first United States visit.

repertory of classics and contemporary Cuban
works. The vivacity of the dancers proved most
appealing, though some critics found interest in the
modern ballets. The second diplomatic event involved the Performing Arts Company of the People's
Republic of China. Formed specifically for the U.S.
tour, the group offered selections from Peking Opera, the "revolutionary ballet" *Red Detachment of
Women*, folk dance, and instrumental numbers. The
extraordinary skill of the acrobats in the Peking

Opera excerpts was thrilling, but the rest of the
program struck many as a superficial hodgepodge.
After opening at the Met on July 5, the Chinese
group went on to the Kennedy Center; Wolf Trap
Farm Park in Virginia; Minneapolis, Minn.; Los
Angeles; and San Francisco.

Great Britain's Royal Ballet began a month-long
tour in Los Angeles on May 23 and moved on to
Houston and Chicago. Kenneth MacMillan's new,
full-evening *Mayerling* was the major novelty, but a
new *Sleeping Beauty* also provoked interest.

Classical ballet lost one of its all-time glittering
stars when Russian ballerina Tamara Karsavina
died in London on May 26.   Nancy Goldner

In World Book, see Ballet; Dancing.

DEATHS OF NOTABLE PERSONS in 1978 included those listed below. An asterisk (*) indicates the person is the subject of a biography in THE WORLD BOOK ENCYCLOPEDIA. Those listed were Americans unless otherwise indicated.

Adoula, Cyrille (1922-May 24), premier of the Republic of Congo (now Zaire) from 1961 to 1964.

Ahn, Philip (1906-Feb. 28), actor who appeared in more than 270 motion pictures, best known as Master Kan in the "Kung Fu" television series.

Allen, Clifford R. (1912-June 18), Tennessee Democratic congressman since 1975 who battled utilities and insurance companies for 30 years.

Allen, James B. (1912-June 1), Democratic senator from Alabama since 1968.

Baldwin, Faith (1893-March 18), who wrote more than 85 books, most of them light fiction. Her characters had money, morals, and good manners.

Barrie, Wendy (1912-Feb. 2), English-born actress who appeared in such films as *Dead End* and *The Private Life of Henry VIII* and later in TV commercials.

Begle, Edward G. (1914-March 2), mathematician who led the "new math" revolution in U.S. schools.

Bergen, Edgar (1903-Sept. 30), ventriloquist who brought laughter to the world for 59 years with his impudent, top-hatted dummy Charlie McCarthy.

Bertoia, Harry (1915-Nov. 6), Italian-born sculptor and designer who adapted the techniques of industrial metalwork to fine art.

***Best, Charles H.** (1899-March 31), Canadian physiologist who, as a medical student, helped Frederick G. Banting discover insulin in 1921.

Betz, Carl (1922-Jan. 18), stage, film, and television actor who won an Emmy for "Judd for the Defense."

Bieber, Margarete (1879-Feb. 25), German-born archaeologist and authority on Greek and Roman art whose many books include *Copies: A Contribution to the History of Graeco-Roman Sculpture*, published when she was 96.

Bliss, George W. (1918-Sept. 11), an investigative reporter for the *Chicago Tribune* who won three Pulitzer Prizes.

Bolin, Wesley (1909-March 4), governor of Arizona since October 1977, a long-time Democrat.

Borland, Harold G. (1900-Feb. 22), writer and naturalist whose editorials in *The New York Times* chronicled the seasons for 35 years.

Bostock, Lyman (1950-Sept. 23), outfielder with the Minnesota Twins and the California Angels.

***Boumediene, Houari** (1925?-Dec. 27), president of Algeria since 1965.

Boyer, Charles (1899-Aug. 26), French-born actor noted for his suave performances in such films as *Algiers* and *Barefoot in the Park*.

Braden, Spruille (1894-Jan. 11), assistant secretary of state from 1945 to 1947 and former ambassador to Colombia, Cuba, and Argentina.

Bradford, Alex (1927-Feb. 15), gospel singer, composer, and minister of the Greater Abyssinian Baptist Church in Newark, N.J., who won an Obie Award for his role in *Don't Bother Me, I Can't Cope.*

Bray, John R. (1879-Oct. 10), motion-picture producer who invented the animated-cartoon process.

Brel, Jacques (1929-Oct. 9), Belgian composer and singer, best known for the hit 1968 musical *Jacques Brel is Alive and Well and Living in Paris.*

Brown, General George S. (1918-Dec. 5), chairman of the Joint Chiefs of Staff from 1974 until he retired in June.

Brown, Zara Cully (1892-Feb. 28), film and TV actress who played Mother Jefferson in the TV series "The Jeffersons."

Busia, Kofi (1913-Aug. 28), prime minister of Ghana from 1969 to 1972.

Byron, Goodloe E. (1929-Oct. 11), Democratic congressman from Maryland since 1970.

***Catton, Bruce** (1899-Aug. 28), Civil War historian and writer. He won a Pulitzer Prize and the National Book Award in 1954 for *A Stillness at Appomattox.*

Cazale, John (1936-March 12), stage and screen actor, best known for his role as Al Pacino's weak older brother in *The Godfather.*

Chambers, Jack (John) (1931-April 13), Canadian artist, filmmaker, and writer.

Chase, Ilka (1905-Feb. 15), actress, writer, and TV personality whose films included *The Women* and *Now, Voyager.*

Chávez, Carlos (1899-Aug. 2), Mexican composer and conductor of Mexico's National Symphony Orchestra.

***Chirico, Giorgio De** (1888-Nov. 20), Greek-born artist who helped found the Metaphysical School in Italy in the early 1900s.

Clapper, Dit (Aubrey V.) (1907-Jan. 20), Canadian hockey player with the Boston Bruins from 1927 to 1947.

Clark, Earl H. (Dutch) (1906-Aug. 5), former quarterback and coach of the Detroit Lions and one of the 17 charter members of football's Hall of Fame.

***Clay, General Lucius D.** (1897-April 16), commander of U.S. forces in Europe from 1947 to 1949. He organized the Berlin Airlift during the Russian blockade in 1948.

***Conant, James B.** (1893-Feb. 11), organic chemist noted for his work on chlorophyll and hemoglobin. He was president of Harvard University from 1933 to 1953 and ambassador to West Germany.

Sir Robert G. Menzies, twice prime minister of Australia.

Ford C. Frick, a baseball commissioner.

Margaret Mead, a noted American anthropologist.

Daniel James, Jr., a U.S. four-star general.

*Cozzens, James G. (1903-Aug. 9), writer of such best-selling novels as *By Love Possessed* (1957) and the Pulitzer Prize-winning *Guard of Honor* (1948).

Crane, Bob (1928-June 29), actor who starred in the TV series "Hogan's Heroes" from 1965 to 1971.

Dailey, Dan (1915-Oct. 16), song-and-dance star of such Hollywood musicals as *My Blue Heaven.*

Daly, James (1918-July 3), Emmy-winning actor, who starred in the TV series "Medical Center."

Daly, Lar (1912-April 18), perennial Chicago candidate for public office since 1938 who campaigned in an Uncle Sam suit.

Daoud, Mohammad (1909-April 27), president of Afghanistan since 1977.

Davis, Abraham L. (1915-June 24), New Orleans Baptist minister who cofounded the Southern Christian Leadership Conference with Martin Luther King, Jr., in 1957.

Davis, Francis W. (1887-April 19), who invented the first power-steering unit for automobiles in 1926.

Diederichs, Nicolaas (1903-Aug. 21), president of South Africa since 1975.

Dupont, Clifford W. (1906-June 28), English-born lawyer who served as the first president of Rhodesia from 1970 to 1975.

*Du Vigneaud, Vincent (1911-Dec. 11), biochemist who won the Nobel Prize for Chemistry in 1955 for discovering a process for making synthetic hormones. He was chairman of Cornell University's Department of Biochemistry from 1938 to 1967.

Eames, Charles (1907-Aug. 21), architect who designed the popular molded-plywood Eames chair.

Norman Rockwell, a popular illustrator.

John D. Rockefeller III, head of the Rockefeller Foundation.

Golda Meir, prime minister of Israel.

Aram I. Khachaturian, a renowned Russian composer.

Eilers, Sally (1909-Jan. 5), actress who appeared in more than 40 films, starting with Mack Sennett's *The Goodbye Kiss* in the 1920s.

Etting, Ruth (1896-Sept. 24), *Ziegfeld Follies* singer and motion-picture star. The motion picture *Love Me or Leave Me* was based on her life.

Evans, Bergen (1904-Feb. 4), educator and authority on English who hosted the television show "Down You Go" in the 1950s.

Evans, Tolchard (1901-March 12), British songwriter of the 1930s whose hits included "Lady of Spain" and "Let's All Sing Like the Birdies Sing."

Fabian, Robert (1901-June 14), British detective who headed Scotland Yard's Flying Squad. His book *Fabian of the Yard* became the basis for a TV series.

Fields, Totie (1930-Aug. 2), raucous-voiced nightclub comedienne and television talk-show personality.

Fine, John S. (1893-May 21), Republican governor of Pennsylvania from 1951 to 1955.

Flanner, Janet (Genet) (1892-Nov. 7), journalist whose biweekly "Letter from Paris" appeared in *The New Yorker* magazine for more than 50 years.

Fontaine, Frank (1920-Aug. 4), comedian, best known for his TV performance as Crazy Guggenheim on "The Jackie Gleason Show."

Freeman, Don (1908-Feb. 1), illustrator and author of such children's books as *Norman the Doorman* and *The Circus in Peter's Closet.*

*Frick, Ford C. (1894-April 8), commissioner of baseball from 1951 to 1965. He was named to the National Baseball Hall of Fame in 1970.

Geer, Will (1902-April 22), versatile actor who won a 1975 Emmy Award for his role as the crusty grandfather in the television series "The Waltons."

Geller, Bruce (1930-May 21), writer who originated the "Mission Impossible" TV series.

Genn, Leo (1906-Jan. 26), British lawyer and actor. He was an assistant prosecutor at the Nuremberg trials after World War II and appeared in such films as *Snake Pit* and *Quo Vadis?*

Gilliam, Jim (Junior) (1928-Oct. 8), coach for the Los Angeles Dodgers since 1967 and an infielder for the Brooklyn Dodgers in the 1950s and 1960s.

Gödel, Kurt (1906-Jan. 14), Czech-born logician who, in 1931, formulated Gödel's theorem, which states that certain mathematical theories cannot be proved or disproved with the accepted method of mathematics.

Goff, Norris (1906-June 7), actor who played Abner, the bumbling shopkeeper, on the "Lum and Abner" radio show from 1931 to 1955.

Gordon, Joe (Flash) (1915-April 15), second baseman for the New York Yankees and Cleveland Indians from 1938 to 1950.

Gordon, John F. (1901-Jan. 6), president of General Motors Corporation from 1958 to 1965.

Gracias, Valerian Cardinal (1908-Sept. 11), Roman Catholic archbishop of Bombay since 1950 who became India's first cardinal in 1953.

Grant, Duncan J. (1885-May 10), Scottish artist and the last survivor of the Bloomsbury Group of British intellectuals of the early 1900s.

Greenwood, Charlotte (1891-Jan. 18), gangly comedienne who played Aunt Eller in the film *Oklahoma!* (1954), a part that was written especially for her by Oscar Hammerstein II.

*Halpern, Bernard N. (1904-Sept. 23), Russian-born French biologist and physician who discovered antihistamine drugs.

Hamada, Shoji (1894-Jan. 5), Japanese potter who was designated a national treasure by Japan in 1955.

Harrah, William M. (1911-June 30), multimillionaire founder of Harrah's, a Nevada-based gambling casino.

Hasselblad, Victor (1906-Aug. 5), Swedish inventor whose cameras were used on U.S. space flights.

Legacy of Two Popes

Pope Paul VI inherited another man's revolution. It is one thing to "open the windows" as his predecessor, Pope John XXIII, had done, but it is quite another to stand in the draft. The genius that set Vatican Council II in motion needed an equal in dexterity to manage the massive changes it wrought.

The underlying change was in the church as an organized society. The Roman Catholic Church went into Pope John's ecumenical council with lingering attitudes of immodest certainty. It emerged in Pope Paul's time as a "Pilgrim Church," unafraid to acknowledge that faith seeks understanding in history.

It fell to Pope Paul to integrate the far-reaching decisions of Vatican II into the ongoing life of a church unaccustomed to change, a church suddenly called upon to assimilate virtually overnight what should have taken place over five centuries.

Paul began well, decrying war before the United Nations General Assembly, extending the hand of friendship to the Protestant and Eastern Orthodox churches, patiently advancing new liturgical directives, and quietly reviving the structure of the church behind the Iron Curtain. He also internationalized the Cardinalate and the Curia.

After Vatican II, the traditional from-the-top-down process by which the church discerned its mission began to be modified by grass-roots assertiveness. The *fiat*, or decree, by which the business of the church was ordinarily conducted now found itself subject to scrutiny, if not veto. Power began to be decentralized. Authority of service became an alternative to authority of office. Pope Paul had to deal with an open church, one that realized that a "teaching church" implied a "listening church."

His first decade was marked by gale-force winds that rocked Peter's barque. Priests, brothers, and sisters left their formal religious commitments in unprecedented numbers, while new vocations dwindled. Mass attendance — always a touchstone of "practical Catholicism" in the United States — fell to 50 per cent, and the U.S. parochial school system, the

Paul VI (1897-1978)

John Paul I (1912-1978)

pride of its immigrant church, suffered cutbacks. The implementation of Vatican II was met with resistance by many, who objected to such things as the demise of the Latin Mass.

Humanae Vitae, the 1968 papal *encyclical* (letter to bishops) declaring artificial contraception morally unacceptable, focused the tensions of the post-Vatican II era. Pope Paul had sought the advice of experts, but in the end had gone against their consensus. His supporters defended his unpopular teaching as prophetic, cutting against a hedonistic grain in contemporary society that lulled the conscience of the faithful. Several theologians, however, formed a chorus of loyal opposition that challenged the encyclical in a manner unusual in its candor and in its media dissemination.

Perhaps realizing that the next pope would have to confront this cleavage, the conclave that gathered in the wake of Pope Paul's death on Aug. 6, 1978, chose a man with a pastoral touch, a man who had seen how abstract theology really works when applied to the concrete lives of believers. Pope John Paul I's supreme pastorate lasted only 34 days, until his death on September 28, but he was probably one of history's best-known pontiffs because of concentrated television exposure. He preferred informality to convention, and was a man of humor and anecdote. His style hinted at a welcome substance.

Paul VI and John Paul I left a church neither more secure nor safer, neither more peaceful nor more orderly, but a church more modest and less triumphant; more Christ-like and less worldly and wealthy; more conscious of its central apostolic mission and less cluttered by interference in secular affairs; more involved in growing global problems of justice and peace and less immersed in narrow politics; and more concerned with ecumenical "oneness in Christ" and less conscious about others acknowledging it. Above all, they left a church more ready to learn and less certain of teaching everyone everything, and more open to the Holy Spirit — the most fundamental openness of all.   Theodore M. Hesburgh

Herbert, Gregory (1947-Jan. 31), saxophone player with the rock group Blood, Sweat, and Tears.

Highet, Gilbert (1906-Jan. 20), Scottish-born educator who popularized Greek and Roman classics. Tapes of his popular 1950s radio program "People, Places, and Books" are still broadcast.

Homolka, Oscar (1898-Jan. 27), Austrian-born character actor, best known for his role in *I Remember Mama.*

Hornby, Albert S. (1898-Sept. 13), British lexicographer who compiled the *Oxford Advanced Learner's Dictionary of Current English.*

*Humphrey, Hubert H. (1911-Jan. 13), Democratic Vice-President of the United States from 1965 to 1969, elected to the Senate from Minnesota three times.

Hunter, Edward (1902-June 24), journalist and expert on psychological warfare who introduced the term *brainwashing* to the English language from the Chinese *hsi nao* (wash brain).

Ivy, Andrew C. (1893-Feb. 7), physiologist and former promoter of Krebiozen, a controversial drug for the treatment of cancer.

James, General Daniel, Jr. (Chappie) (1920-Feb. 25), former commander of the North American Air Defense Command and the first black to become a four-star general in the U.S. armed forces.

John Paul I, Pope (Albino Luciani) (1912-Sept. 28), who became head of the Roman Catholic Church on August 26. See Close-Up.

Karsavina, Tamara (1885-May 26), Russian-born ballerina with Les Ballets Russes de Diaghilev. She was the first ballerina to dance the Firebird and was the first ballerina doll in *Petrouchka.*

Kenny, Bill (1915-March 23), tenor with the Inkspots, whose hits included "If I Didn't Care" and "We'll Meet Again."

*Kenyatta, Jomo (1890?-Aug. 22), president of Kenya since its independence in 1964. He was once imprisoned by Great Britain as the leader of the bloody Mau Mau rebellion in Africa in the 1950s.

Kenyon, Dame Kathleen M. (1906-Aug. 24), British archaeologist who discovered the Biblical city of Jericho in 1952.

Ketchum, William M. (1921-June 24), Republican congressman from California since 1974.

*Khachaturian, Aram I. (1903-May 1), Russian composer best known for the ballet *Gayane* (1942), which included the fiery "Sabre Dance."

Kiernan, Walter (1902-Jan. 8), news commentator whose newspaper column "One Man's Opinion" was featured on radio from 1945 to 1969.

King, Cyril E. (1921-Jan. 2), governor of the U.S. Virgin Islands since 1974.

Kipnis, Alexander (1891-May 14), Russian-born singer with the Chicago Civic Opera and New York City's Metropolitan Opera, one of the great basses.

Koch, John (1909-April 19), realist painter, noted for his elegant representations of Manhattan life.

Krag, Jens O. (1914-June 22), prime minister of Denmark from 1962 to 1968 and 1971 to 1972.

Lear, William P. (1902-May 14), electrical engineer who designed the Lear Jet and invented the first practical automobile radio, the automatic pilot for aircraft, and the eight-track stereo cartridge.

Leibowitz, Samuel S. (1893-Jan. 11), Romanian-born lawyer whose defense in the 1930s Scottsboro Boys case led the Supreme Court of the United States to ban the exclusion of blacks from juries.

Light, Enoch (1906-Aug. 18), orchestra leader who pioneered in stereophonic recording with such disks as "Persuasive Percussion."

Lipton, Marcus (1900-Feb. 27), British Labour Party member of Parliament for 33 years whose unusual campaigns included a successful drive to have the sales tax removed from wrought-iron chastity belts.

*Lloyd, Selwyn (1904-May 17), British foreign secretary from 1956 to 1960 and speaker of the House of Commons from 1971 to 1976.

Lo Jui-ching (1907-Aug. 3), a member of China's Central Committee since 1977 and a veteran of the Long March of 1934.

MacArthur, John A. (1897-Jan. 6), billionaire who built the Bankers Life and Casualty Company by selling insurance door-to-door in 1935.

MacDiarmid, Hugh (Christopher M. Grieve) (1892-Sept. 9), Scottish poet and a founder of the Scottish National Party.

*Madariaga, Salvador De (1886-Dec. 14), Spanish novelist, historian, and diplomat whose many works included *The Genius of Spain* and *Anarchy or Hierarchy.* He said that "Man's most precious possession is the gift of thinking freely."

Mallowan, Sir Max (1904-Aug. 19), British archaeologist and the widower of writer Agatha Christie.

Martinson, Harry E. (1904-Feb. 10), Swedish poet and novelist who shared the 1974 Nobel Prize for Literature with Eyvind Johnson.

Mason, F. Van Wyck (1901-Aug. 28), author of 57 historical novels such as *Valley Forge, 1777* (1950) and numerous spy thrillers.

Matlock, Julian (Matty) (1909-June 14), jazz clarinetist with such big bands as Bob Crosby's Bobcats.

McCarthy, Joe (Joseph V.) (1887-Jan. 14), baseball manager who led the New York Yankees to eight American League pennants from 1931 to 1946.

Hubert H. Humphrey, a U.S. Vice-President.

Zara Cully Brown, an actress on "The Jeffersons" TV show.

James B. Conant, a noted educator.

Aldo Moro, who served five terms as premier of Italy.

McCoy, Colonel Tim (Timothy Fitzgerald) (1891-Jan. 29), cowboy movie star who was a World War I cavalry colonel and an Indian expert.

*****McGinley, Phyllis** (1905-Feb. 22), writer whose light verse won the Pulitzer Prize for Poetry in 1961.

McNamara, Maggie (1931-Feb. 18), star of the controversial film *The Moon Is Blue* in 1953.

*****Mead, Margaret** (1901-Nov. 15), anthropologist and social critic for more than 50 years whose many books included *Coming of Age in Samoa* (1928), which is now a classic in the field.

*****Meir, Golda** (1898-Dec. 8), Israeli politician, born in Russia, one-time schoolteacher in Milwaukee who served as prime minister of Israel from 1969 to 1974.

*****Menzies, Sir Robert G.** (1894-May 15), prime minister of Australia from 1939 to 1941, and from 1949 to 1966.

Mercader, Ramon (1914-Oct. 18), Spanish-born mystery man who murdered Leon Trotsky in Mexico in 1940.

Messerschmitt, Willy (1898-Sept. 15), German engineer who designed the fighter plane that spearheaded Adolf Hitler's air attack in World War II.

Metcalf, Lee (1911-Jan. 12), Democratic senator from Montana since 1961. He served in the U.S. House of Representatives since 1953.

Metcalfe, Ralph H. (1910-Oct. 10), Illinois Democratic congressman from Chicago since 1970 and a former Olympic track star.

Michaud, Herve J. (1912-June 5), Canadian Liberal senator from New Brunswick since 1968.

*****Mikoyan, Anastas** (1895-Oct. 21), president of Russia from 1964 to 1965 and a member of Russia's Politburo from 1926 to 1966 – the first of the old Bolsheviks to retire from his office with honor.

Montoya, Joseph M. (1915-June 5), Democratic senator from New Mexico from 1965 to 1976. He served on the Senate Watergate Committee in 1973.

Moon, Keith (1947-Sept. 7), star drummer of The Who, a British rock group.

Moore, Sir Henry Ruthven (1886-March 12), British admiral who won fame in the Battle of Jutland in World War I and in air-sea strikes off Norway in World War II.

*****Moreell, Admiral Ben** (1892-July 30), U.S. naval officer who organized the Seabees in 1942.

Moro, Aldo (1916-May 9), premier of Italy five times since 1963 and leader of the Christian Democratic Party. He was kidnapped and murdered by the Red Brigades terrorist group.

Morrison, Bret (1912-Sept. 25), radio actor who thrilled listeners to his show in the 1930s and 1940s with the sonorous opening, "Who knows what evil lurks in the hearts of men? The Shadow knows."

Moscone, George (1929-Nov. 27), mayor of San Francisco since 1975, who was known for his humanitarian approach to public office.

Mullin, Willard (1902-Dec. 21), sports cartoonist who created the Brooklyn Bum – a grizzled caricature of the Brooklyn Dodger baseball fan – in the 1930s.

Murphy, Robert D. (1894-Jan. 9), U.S. undersecretary of state from 1958 to 1959, a former ambassador to Belgium and Japan, and a troubleshooter for Presidents.

Nebel, Long John (John Zimmerman) (1911-April 10), host of radio's first all-night talk show, in New York City, for more than 20 years.

Nijinsky, Romola (1892-June 8), Hungarian dancer, widow and biographer of Russian dancer Vaslav Nijinsky.

Nikodim, Archbishop (Boris G. Rotov) (1929-Sept. 5), Russian Orthodox archbishop, one of the six presidents of the World Council of Churches.

Noble, Ray, (1908-April 3), British composer and orchestra leader whose hits included "Goodnight Sweetheart" and "The Very Thought of You."

Norrish, Ronald G. W. (1898-June 7), who shared the Nobel Prize for Chemistry in 1967 for his work on flash spectroscopy.

Oakie, Jack (Lewis Delaney Offield) (1903-Jan. 23), Hollywood motion-picture actor who appeared in more than 100 movies, including *The Great Dictator* (1940) with Charlie Chaplin.

Obolensky, Serge (1890-Sept. 29), Russian prince who became a New York City publicist and an international socialite.

Ó Dálaigh, Cearbhall (1911-March 21), president of Ireland from 1974 to 1976.

*****Paul VI, Pope (Giovanni Battista Montini)** (1897-Aug. 6), head of the Roman Catholic Church since 1963. See Close-Up.

Pei, Mario A. (1901-March 2), Italian-born linguist who made philology and etymology interesting to the general reader in such fascinating books as *The Story of Language* (1965).

Peterson, Ronnie (1944-Sept. 11), Swedish racing-car driver who participated in 100 Grand Prix races.

Porteous, George (1903-Feb. 7), lieutenant governor of Saskatchewan, Canada, since 1976.

Prima, Louis (1910-Aug. 24), gravel-voiced bandleader and jazz musician whose hit recordings included "Old Black Magic" in 1961.

*****Rattner, Abraham** (1895-Dec. 14), painter who was noted for his use of brilliant glowing color, rich texture, and symbolism using religious subjects and Biblical themes such as the Crucifixion and the Last Judgment.

Ray, Joie (1894-May 13), track star who set the world's indoor-mile record of 4 minutes 12 seconds in 1924.

Will Geer, a versatile stage and television actor.

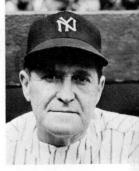

Joe McCarthy, who managed the Yanks.

Robert Shaw, a noted British author and actor.

Karl Wallenda, a high-wire walker.

Reynolds, Malvina (1900-March 17), songwriter who became famous in the 1960s for such songs as "What Have They Done to the Rain?" and "Little Boxes."

Rich, Lorimer (1891-June 2), architect who designed the Tomb of the Unknown Soldier in the National Cemetery in Arlington, Va.

Roberts, Gilbert (1899-Jan. 1), British engineer who designed Scotland's Firth of Forth Bridge.

Robson, Mark (1913-June 20), Canadian-born film director whose many movies included *Champion* (1949) and *The Inn of the Sixth Happiness* (1958).

*Rockefeller, John D. III (1906-July 10), director of the Rockefeller Foundation and oldest of the five grandsons of the founder of Standard Oil Company.

*Rockwell, Norman (1894-Nov. 8), illustrator whose scenes from small-town America graced some 360 *Saturday Evening Post* covers.

Rodden, Michael (1891-Jan. 11), Canadian athlete, first person to be elected to both the Canadian football and hockey halls of fame.

Romero, Juan de Jesús (1875-July 30), spiritual leader of the Taos Pueblo Indians who successfully campaigned for the restoration of the sacred Blue Lake and 40,000 acres (16,000 hectares) of land in New Mexico to the Pueblo.

Rosen, Pinhas (1887-May 3), German-born lawyer who helped establish Israel's judicial system. He was Israel's minister of justice from 1948 to 1961.

Rothermere, Viscount (Esmond Cecil Harmsworth) (1898-July 12), British publisher of London's *Daily Mail* and *Evening News*.

Rubicam, Raymond (1892-May 8), advertising executive who founded the Young & Rubicam advertising agency in 1923.

Ryan, Leo J. (1925-Nov. 18), Democratic congressman from California since 1973.

Sahlin, Donald G. (1928-Feb. 20), puppet maker who created hundreds of the Muppet characters for TV's "Sesame Street" and "The Muppet Show."

Shaw, Robert (1927-Aug. 28), British author and actor. His films included *A Man for All Seasons, The Sting,* and *Jaws,* and his novels include *The Man in the Glass Booth,* which became a play.

Shay, Dorothy (1921-Oct. 22), singer known as the "Park Avenue Hillbilly." Her hits included "Feudin', Fussin', and Fightin'."

*Siegbahn, Karl Manne Georg (1886-Sept. 26), Swedish physicist who won the Nobel Prize for Physics in 1924 for work on X-ray spectroscopy.

Silone, Ignazio (1900-Aug. 22), Italian author of the anti-Fascist novels *Bread and Wine* and *Fontamara.*

Smith, W. Eugene (1918-Oct. 5), photojournalist for *Time* and *Newsweek* magazines, best known for his book *Minamata* on the effect of mercury poisoning on a Japanese fishing village.

Sobukwe, Robert M. (1924-Feb. 27), South African nationalist leader who spent his last 18 years in prison or under other government restriction.

Steiger, William A. (1938-Dec. 4), Republican congressman from Wisconsin since 1966.

*Steinberg, William (1899-May 16), German-born orchestral conductor who was music director of the Pittsburgh Symphony Orchestra from 1952 to 1976.

*Stone, Edward Durell (1902-Aug. 6), architect who designed the Museum of Modern Art in New York City and the John F. Kennedy Center for the Performing Arts in Washington, D.C.

*Tunney, Gene (James Joseph) (1897-Nov. 7), world heavyweight boxing champion from 1926 to 1928 who defeated Jack Dempsey.

Utley, Clifton (1904-Jan. 19), television news reporter and anchor man for the National Broadcasting Company in the 1950s.

Venuti, Joe (1896-Aug. 14), Italian-born musician, the "father of the jazz violin," whose quartet The Blue Four introduced an innovative chamber-music sound to jazz in the 1920s.

Wallenda, Karl (1905-March 22), patriarch and founder of the Great Wallendas, the most famous troupe of high-wire walkers in circus history.

Warner, Jack L. (1892-Sept. 9), motion-picture producer who brought sound to feature films in 1927 with *The Jazz Singer* starring Al Jolson.

Warner, Sylvia Townsend (1893-May 1), English novelist and poet noted for her satiric social commentary and graceful style.

Wheelock, John (1886-March 22), poet and editor whose work spanned 60 years. He celebrated the richness of living in such books as *The Human Fantasy* (1911) and *By Daylight and in Dream: New and Collected Poems* (1970).

Whitehead, Commander Edward (1908-April 16), British businessman whose elegant beard and dry demeanor helped sell Schweppe's tonic water.

Wood, Peggy (1892-March 18), actress, star of the TV series "I Remember Mama" from 1949 to 1957.

Wrathall, John J. (1913-Aug. 31), English-born lawyer, president of Rhodesia since 1976.

Young, Gig (Byron Barr) (1917-Oct. 9), stage and screen actor who won an Oscar in 1969 for his role as the master of ceremonies in the motion picture *They Shoot Horses, Don't They?*

Youngdahl, Luther W. (1896-June 21), Republican governor of Minnesota from 1947 to 1951.   Irene B. Keller

DELAWARE. See STATE GOVERNMENT.

Jomo Kenyatta, first president of Kenya.

Wendy Barrie, an English-born film and TV actress.

Faith Baldwin, popular and prolific novelist.

Louis Prima, veteran jazz bandleader.

DEMOCRATIC PARTY lost ground in Congress in 1978 but kept control of both the House of Representatives and the Senate. The number of Democratic governors also declined, but the party still held a commanding majority of statehouses.

The party alignment of Congress was not substantially changed despite a Republican gain of three senators and 11 representatives. Democrats held a 59-41 advantage in the Senate and a 276-157 majority in the House, with two seats vacant because of death. Their edge in governorships was 32-18.

In the Senate, five liberal Democrats were defeated by more conservative Republican opponents. Senator Richard C. Clark of Iowa was upset by Roger W. Jepsen, a former lieutenant governor; in Colorado, Senator Floyd K. Haskell was ousted by Representative William L. Armstrong; Gordon J. Humphrey, a 37-year-old airline pilot, defeated veteran Senator Thomas J. McIntyre in New Hampshire; Senator Wendell R. Anderson was rejected by Minnesota voters, who put plywood manufacturer Rudolph E. Boschwitz in the seat; and in Maine, Senator William D. Hathaway was replaced by Representative William S. Cohen, a moderate.

In return, Democrats took two seats away from long-time incumbent Republicans. In Michigan, Carl Levin, former president of the Detroit City Council, beat Senator Robert P. Griffin, once the Republican whip. In Massachusetts, Representative Paul E. Tsongas defeated Senator Edward W. Brooke, the only black member of the Senate.

Seven other Democratic newcomers went to the Senate in November. They included former basketball star Bill Bradley, who won an easy victory in New Jersey; Donald W. Stewart, an Alabama liberal who was supported by organized labor; Howell T. Heflin, former chief justice of Alabama; David H. Pryor, former governor of Arkansas; Max S. Baucus, former member of the House from Montana; former Oklahoma governor David L. Boren; and former Nebraska Governor J. James Exon. Exon's victory marked the first time that two Democrats have represented Nebraska in the Senate. The other seat is held by former Omaha Mayor Edward Zorinsky.

In the House, the Democrats suffered a net loss of 11 seats. A total of 14 Democratic incumbents were defeated, including seven who were elected in 1974, the first post-Watergate election.

Also beaten was Representative John J. McFall of California, once the Democratic whip. McFall was reprimanded by Congress in October for accepting favors from Korean lobbyist Tong Sun Park.

Joshua Eilberg, a Pennsylvania Democrat indicted on conflict-of-interest charges, was defeated. Another Pennsylvania Democrat, Daniel J. Flood, also under indictment on corruption charges, was

President Jimmy Carter congratulates John C. White following his election as chairman of the Democratic National Committee in January.

re-elected, however, as was Michigan Democrat Charles C. Diggs, Jr., who was convicted on October 7 of taking kickbacks. Diggs won with 80 per cent of the vote.

Two Democratic women, Martha E. Keys of Kansas and Helen S. Meyner of New Jersey, were defeated. Two others, Geraldine A. Ferraro of New York and Beverly B. Byron of Maryland, were elected to the House for the first time.

Gubernatorial Races. California Governor Edmund G. (Jerry) Brown, Jr., scored a resounding victory, winning a second term by a margin of 1.3-million votes. Governor Hugh L. Carey kept New York under Democratic leadership despite strong opposition from Republican Perry B. Duryea.

Incumbent Democratic governors Rudy Perpich of Minnesota, Martin J. Schreiber of Wisconsin, and Robert W. Straub of Oregon were defeated by Republicans. In Texas, Republican William Clements beat Democratic Attorney General John L. Hill in a free-spending campaign. Clements became the first Republican governor of Texas in more than a century. Democrat Pete Flaherty, former mayor of Pittsburgh, lost in Pennsylvania to Richard L. Thornburgh, a former prosecutor who attacked scandals in the previous Democratic administration.

Democrats scored two upsets, however. John W. Carlin defeated Kansas Governor Robert F. Bennett, and Hugh J. Gallen ousted New Hampshire's archconservative Governor Meldrim Thomson, Jr. Conservative Democrat Edward J. King was elected governor in Massachusetts after defeating Governor Michael S. Dukakis in a primary contest. In Maryland, reformer Harry R. Hughes won by a landslide in another state plagued by official corruption.

Other Developments. John C. White of Texas was installed on January 27 as chairman of the Democratic National Committee. He succeeded Kenneth M. Curtis of Maine.

The Democrats revised a number of rules for choosing a presidential nominee on June 9. Under the 1976 rules, convention delegates were apportioned to any candidate who got 15 per cent of the vote in a state primary or caucus. The new rule will raise that figure to 25 per cent, making it harder for dissident contenders to get the nomination. Another new rule will forbid "open" primaries in Michigan, Wisconsin, and Montana, where non-Democrats had been allowed to vote in the past.

At a midterm conference in Memphis, Tenn., in December, Democrats voted 822 to 521 to support President Jimmy Carter's plans for an austere budget, despite liberal demands that he spare social programs from spending cuts. Senator Edward M. Kennedy of Massachusetts stirred speculation over his 1980 presidential intentions when he attacked Carter's budget. William J. Eaton

See also CONGRESS of the UNITED STATES; ELECTIONS. In WORLD BOOK, see DEMOCRATIC PARTY.

DENMARK voted on Nov. 17, 1978, to give home rule to Greenland, an 840,000-square-mile (2.2-million-square-kilometer) island with 48,000 inhabitants. Greenlanders will make their own choices on taxes, education, social security, and labor by 1981. They will take control of business and trade in 1984; and housing, health, and communications at a later date. Denmark will direct Greenland's defense and foreign relations. Greenland had been an integral part of Denmark since 1953.

A three-week political crisis in Denmark ended on August 30, when the Social Democrats and Liberals formed a coalition government. The two parties, rivals for 80 years, had the backing of 88 of the 179 members of the *Folketing* (parliament), one short of a majority. But support of right-center parties was expected to carry the government through the 2½ years before the next scheduled general election.

Prime Minister Anker Henrik Jorgensen said the coalition was formed to correct economic problems and stabilize the government. He immediately announced an economic program, including income, price, and profit controls; a 2 per cent increase in the value-added tax; and low-interest loans for exporters. Trade unions reacted with short strikes that closed shipyards and stopped public services.

Economic Trouble. Jorgensen had struggled since his election victory in February 1977 to cope with a balance-of-payments deficit nearing $4 billion, a huge national debt, and 200,000 unemployed. Despite a 1977 devaluation of the currency, output growth was sluggish in 1978. The Organization for Economic Cooperation and Development urged Denmark to adopt a monetary policy geared primarily to "protecting the foreign reserve position."

When Minister of Finance Knud Heinesen presented the finance bill on August 15, he said that unless fiscal policy was tightened, real private consumption would rise 4.5 per cent, income would go up 10 per cent, and consumer prices would increase 5 per cent. Heinesen asked for approval of foreign loans of $800 million in 1978 and $1.1 billion in 1979.

Port Blockade. Danish fishermen used their boats to block the entrance to Copenhagen harbor and five other ports on May 5 to protest reduced fishing quotas. About 2,000 fishermen marched to the Folketing to demand larger quotas. On May 12, the government offered $14 million in loans to help those hit by loss of traditional fishing grounds in the Baltic Sea. The grounds were lost when East Germany, Poland, Russia, and Sweden extended their fishing limits in 1977. North Sea cod fishermen had their cod quota cut in half on August 16, when they had almost reached the annual quota of 35,200 short tons (32,000 metric tons).

A referendum lowering the voting age from 20 to 18 passed on September 19. Kenneth Brown

See also EUROPE (Facts in Brief Table). In WORLD BOOK, see DENMARK.

A dental health specialist is surrounded by a model of the lower jaw and teeth as she talks to students in St. Louis about dental hygiene.

DENTISTRY. Proper matching of donors and recipients before transplanting teeth should improve the success rate, a United States Navy dental scientist suggested in March 1978. James E. Yaeger of the U.S. Naval Dental Research Institute in Great Lakes, Ill., reported on the results of a tooth-transplantation study in 30 rhesus monkeys at the annual meeting of the International Association for Dental Research in Washington, D.C. The animals were paired and classified on the basis of certain antigens, foreign proteins that cause the body to produce antibodies. Three teeth transplanted among animals that were fully matched for these antigens remained in position for the 18 months the study continued, while 27 per cent of the other transplants in the incompletely matched and nonmatched transplant pairs were lost. With more precise donor and recipient matching, the transplanting of teeth between individuals could possibly become a feasible clinical procedure, Yaeger predicted in his report.

Tooth Decay. The sweetener xylitol inhibited *caries* (tooth decay) when fed to rats in a laboratory study, according to investigators at Emory University Dental School in Atlanta, Ga. However, rats fed xylitol also ate less food and did not gain weight as fast as did animals on a normal diet. "It is possible that at least part of the caries reduction attributed to xylitol might be related to decreased feeding or to other factors," reported dental researchers Stephen Kreitzman and John Yagiela.

Dental researchers at the University of Maryland in Baltimore may have discovered why some individuals escape dental decay throughout their lives. "One possible explanation is that the bacteria which reside in the mouths of caries-free people are different from the oral bacteria of caries-active individuals," according to dental researcher Glenn E. Minah. A newly developed technique permits studies of the bacteria thought responsible for tooth decay and gum disease. Preliminary experiments at the University of Maryland with oral bacteria from caries-free persons and those with caries have revealed that the population of certain oral bacteria is remarkably stable, while others fluctuate. Another finding was that caries-free individuals consumed significantly less sugar than did those individuals with caries.

More Decay Protection. Children treated with a combination of five preventive techniques had 77 per cent less tooth decay than a control group that received only oral-hygiene instruction, University of Michigan dental researcher Robert A. Bagraman reported. The five preventive methods were cleaning the teeth, coating chewing surfaces with a plastic sealant, applying a fluoride gel, instruction in oral hygiene, and filling all decayed teeth.   Lou Joseph

In WORLD BOOK, see DENTISTRY; TEETH.

DETROIT

DETROIT. A wildcat strike by 1,350 city employees on Aug. 1, 1978, left 180,000 Detroit commuters stranded and piles of trash at the city's curbs. The trouble started when 375 bus mechanics and 250 clerical workers walked out to protest the city's mandatory overtime work policies. The strikers were joined by 650 sanitation workers and 75 civilians who man emergency telephone lines. Bus drivers and garbage-truck drivers then refused to cross the picket lines.

Wayne County Circuit Judge Myron Wahls ordered the strikers back to work on August 2, and Mayor Coleman A. Young threatened to fire any worker who refused to obey the court order. The strikers returned to their jobs on August 4 after being promised that none of them would be fired.

Police Ruling. Chief U.S. District Court Judge Frederick W. Kaess ruled on February 27 that the Detroit Police Department's affirmative-action promotion program was unconstitutional because it violated "the rights guaranteed to whites" under the 14th Amendment. The Detroit Police Officers Association filed a class-action suit in 1974 accusing the department of reverse discrimination. Promotions to sergeant had been divided equally between blacks and whites, regardless of the eligibility ranking of applicants. The court ordered that future appointments be made in strict accordance with ranking on the current eligibility list.

An internal investigation conducted by the department revealed that as many as 400 Detroit police officers and civilian employees might be guilty of welfare fraud. The findings were announced on September 28 by Police Chief William Hart.

Standard of Living. Living costs in the Detroit area rose 6.3 per cent between April 1977 and April 1978. The Department of Labor announced on April 26 that it would cost $10,400 per year for an average family of four to live at a minimum level of comfort; $17,427 to maintain a moderate standard of living; and $25,550 to live at the upper level in Detroit.

Republican National Committee members and about 100 of the party's county chairmen met in Detroit in July to study inner-city urban-renewal sites and social projects. According to a report issued on October 18 by the Federal Bureau of Investigation, Detroit had the 11th highest rate of violent crime among U.S. cities in 1977.

Detroit was classified as one of 10 "high need" cities in a report on social and urban problems in 39 cities released on September 10 by the Congressional Budget Office. The city was ranked as the nation's 18th most crowded city, with 1,130 persons per square mile (2.6 square kilometers), by the Department of Commerce.   James M. Banovetz

See also CITY. In WORLD BOOK, see DETROIT; MICHIGAN.

DICTIONARY. See Section Six, DICTIONARY SUPPLEMENT.

DISASTERS. The worst monsoon season in India's history caused devastating floods in northern and eastern sections of the country throughout the summer of 1978. About 2,000 persons died and property valued at $2 billion was destroyed between mid-June and mid-September. Approximately 32.5-million persons – 5 per cent of India's population – were affected.

Disasters that resulted in 10 or more deaths in 1978 included the following:

Aircraft Crashes
Jan. 1 – Bombay, India. An Air India jumbo jet carrying 213 persons exploded and plunged into the Arabian Sea shortly after take-off from Bombay airport. There were no survivors. It was the third worst disaster in aviation history.

Feb. 10 – Artigas, Uruguay. An Uruguayan Air Force transport plane making a commercial flight crashed during an emergency landing. All 31 persons aboard were killed.

Feb. 10 – Richland, Wash. All 17 persons aboard were killed when a Columbia Pacific Airlines twin-engine plane crashed and exploded shortly after take-off.

Feb. 11 – Cranbrook, Canada. A Pacific Western Airlines jet crashed while landing in a snowstorm, killing 41 passengers.

March 1 – Kano, Nigeria. Sixteen civilians and two air force crewmen were killed when a Nigerian Airways aircraft collided in midair with a Nigerian Air Force plane.

March 3 – Caracas, Venezuela. A government-owned twin-engine passenger plane fell into the Caribbean Sea shortly after take-off from the Caracas airport. All 47 aboard were killed.

March 16 – Sofia, Bulgaria. A Bulgarian airliner carrying 66 passengers and seven crew members crashed shortly after take-off. There were no survivors.

March 25 – Rangoon, Burma. A Burmese airliner exploded after take-off. All 48 aboard were killed.

June 27 – North Sea. A helicopter en route to an offshore oil rig plunged into the sea west of Norway, killing the 18 persons aboard.

Sept. 2 – Vancouver, Canada. Eleven persons, including nine Japanese tourists, were killed when a twin-engine Air West Airlines plane crashed into a yacht basin in Vancouver harbor.

Sept. 9 – Mexico City, Mexico. A twin-engine charter plane crashed and exploded in a mountainous area at the edge of the city. Nineteen of the 23 aboard were killed.

Sept. 14 – Manila, the Philippines. A Philippine Air Force plane, carrying members of President Ferdinand E. Marcos' security staff and journalists, crashed while trying to land in a thunderstorm. At least 32 persons were killed.

Sept. 25 – San Diego. A Pacific Airlines Boeing 727 collided with a small private plane and both crashed in flames into a heavily populated residential area. Of the 144 persons killed, 135 were aboard the jet, 2 were in the private plane, and 7 were on the ground. It was the worst air disaster in U.S. history.

Oct. 6 – Santiago, Chile. A U.S. Navy DC-6 crashed into a hill, killing all 18 persons aboard. It had been taking part in Operation Unitas, a joint naval training exercise involving the United States, Chile, and Peru.

Nov. 15 – Colombo, Sri Lanka. An Icelandic Airlines plane carrying Muslim pilgrims home from Mecca crashed on approach to the airport during a heavy thunderstorm, killing 202 persons.

Nov. 18 – Caribbean Sea. An Air Guadeloupe airliner plunged into the Caribbean between the islands of Guadeloupe and Marie Galante during a violent thunderstorm. Fifteen persons were killed.

Nov. 19 – Leh, India. An Indian Air Force transport plane carrying servicemen crashed while approaching the airport. All 77 aboard the plane and one man on the ground were killed.

Dec. 23 – Palermo, Italy. An Alitalia jet plummeted into the Tyrrhenian Sea, killing 108 persons.

Bus and Truck Crashes

Jan. 1 – Chaiyaphum, Thailand. A bus carrying New Year revelers collided with a truck 170 miles (270 kilometers) north of Bangkok, killing 25 persons and injuring 86.

Jan. 14 – Chainat, Thailand. A crash involving a hospital bus and a heavy truck killed 12 persons. The victims were missionaries and their families who worked in a hospital 120 miles (190 kilometers) north of Bangkok.

Feb. 10 – Near Allahabad, India. A bus carrying Hindu pilgrims returning from the Ganges River plunged into another river 65 miles (105 kilometers) from Allahabad, killing 53 persons.

Feb. 15 – Aguas Buenas, Puerto Rico. A school bus plunged off a narrow road into a 500-foot (150-meter) ravine, killing 11 students and injuring 30.

Feb. 27 – Shahdara, Pakistan. Twenty-two persons were killed and 90 were injured when a passenger bus and a train collided in northeast Pakistan.

March 21 – Near San Luis, Mexico. Two buses collided head-on, killing at least 30 persons.

May 4 – Pasto, Colombia. A tourist bus plunged over a precipice, killing 11 persons.

July 17 – Cairo, Egypt. A bus collided with a cement truck and plunged over a retaining wall into the Nile River. At least 56 persons were killed.

Aug. 4 – Eastman, Canada. A bus carrying handicapped people and volunteer assistants plunged into Lac d' Argent, 50 miles (80 kilometers) southwest of Montreal, Que., killing 41 persons. It was the worst bus accident in Canada's history.

Sept. 1 – Barranquilla, Colombia. A bus veered out of control on a bridge and plunged into a canal, killing at least 32 of the 68 persons aboard.

Sept. 4 – Vendrell, Spain. A bus carrying about 50 passengers hit a truck broadside in a heavy rainstorm in Tarragona province, killing 18 persons.

Oct. 1 – Basirhat, India. A bus, swerving to avoid a cow, overturned and tumbled into a flooded ditch, killing 88 persons and injuring 20.

Earthquakes

Jan. 14 – Izu Peninsula, Japan. An earthquake shook the crowded vacation area along Japan's Pacific coast, leaving 23 persons dead.

June 12 – Honshu Island, Japan. At least 27 persons were killed and about 1,100 injured when the strongest earthquake in 14 years rocked Japan's main island. The quake measured 7.5 on the Richter scale.

June 20 – Salonika, Greece. This city of 654,000 was devastated by an earthquake that killed 51 persons, most of whom were in buildings that collapsed.

Sept. 16 – Tabas, Iran. A powerful earthquake measuring 7.7 on the Richter scale leveled this oasis town, killing about 15,000 of its 17,000 residents. More than 10,000 inhabitants of surrounding villages also perished.

Dec. 15 – Southwest Iran. An earthquake severely damaged 17 villages near the town of Izeh. At least 42 persons were killed and 10 injured.

Explosions and Fires

Jan. 3 – Manila, the Philippines. Eleven worshipers died when fire broke out in a Buddhist temple.

Jan. 28 – Kansas City, Mo. Fire destroyed the historic Coates House hotel, and 20 persons were killed in the deadliest blaze in the city's history.

Wreckage litters a fire-scarred campsite in southern Spain. A gas truck explosion engulfed the area in flames, killing 250 persons, on July 11.

An investigator surveys the charred remains of a jet that collided with
a small private plane over San Diego on September 25, killing 144 persons.

June 10 – Borås, Sweden. A fire swept through a five-story hotel, killing 20 teen-agers who were celebrating their graduation from high school.

July 6 – Great Britain. Fire in two sleeping cars of a night train en route from Penzance to London killed 11 passengers.

July 9 – Manila, the Philippines. At least 11 persons were killed and 110 injured when fire broke out in a theater complex.

July 11 – San Carlos de la Rápita, Spain. A tank truck carrying liquid industrial gas overturned and exploded at a campsite on the Mediterranean coast, engulfing the campsite in flames. At least 250 campers were killed.

Nov. 26 – Greece, N.Y. At least 10 persons died when fire swept through a fully occupied Holiday Inn. Many of the victims were Canadian tourists.

Floods

March 20-25 – Mozambique. The worst flooding of the Zambezi River in this century caused at least 45 deaths and left 250,000 persons homeless.

July 9 – Afghanistan-Pakistan border. At least 122 persons perished in floods that followed torrential rains.

Aug. 3 – Central Texas. The Pedernales and Guadalupe rivers, swollen by 30 inches (76 centimeters) of rain in two days, flooded central Texas, killing 30 persons.

Aug. 3-6 – West Texas. Rain from the tropical storm Amelia gorged the Brazos River, producing floods throughout west Texas. Twenty-two persons were killed.

Aug. 18 – Acajutla, El Salvador. A gigantic wave spawned by an earthquake off the Pacific coast of Guatemala swept through the main port of El Salvador, killing at least 100 persons.

Sept. 13 – Arkansas and Southeast Texas. At least 11 persons were killed and hundreds were evacuated when heavy thunderstorms caused flooding.

Sept. 27 – Southeast Asia. The worst floods in 40 years surged through a four-nation region, leaving at least 111 persons dead. Vietnam and Thailand reported heavy casualties. Laos and Cambodia were also affected.

Hurricanes, Tornadoes, and Other Storms

Jan. 25-30 – Midwestern United States. A blizzard with winds up to 100 miles (160 kilometers) per hour dropped up to 31 inches (79 centimeters) of snow on Illinois, Indiana, Kentucky, Michigan, Ohio, and Wisconsin. An estimated 100 persons died in storm-related incidents.

Jan. 28-30 – Western Europe. Severe storms swept across Europe, bringing blizzards to northern Scotland; snow to the Italian Riviera; flash floods to Venice, Italy; and gale-force winds to Spain. Thirty-six persons were killed in accidents resulting from the storms.

Feb. 5-7 – Northeastern United States. An estimated 99 persons died when one of the worst winter storms in U.S. history hit the New England States and parts of New York.

Feb. 10 – Southern California. One of the most destructive storms ever to strike the region was blamed for the deaths of 25 persons. Hurricane-force winds and heavy rainfall caused mud slides and flash floods.

April 17 – Orissa, India. A tornado slammed through six villages, killing 500 persons.

April 17 – West Bengal, India. A tornado caused the deaths of at least 100 persons.

Aug. 7 – Swiss and Italian Alps. At least 23 persons were killed when storms brought torrential rains and freak blizzards to the Alpine region.

Aug. 25 – Manila, the Philippines. Tropical storms severely battered the northern Philippines, killing more than 50 persons.

Sept. 22 – Korea. Tropical storm Carmen dropped up to 24 inches (61 centimeters) of rain on some parts of Korea, causing 29 deaths.

Oct. 27 – Manila, the Philippines. Typhoon Rita pummeled Manila with winds up to 94 miles per hour (150 kilometers per hour). At least 20 were killed and 70,000 left homeless in the floods that resulted.

Nov. 25 – Sri Lanka. Nearly 500 persons perished in floods caused by the worst cyclone ever to hit Sri Lanka.

Shipwrecks

Jan. 25 – Pacific Ocean. The *Chandra Gupta,* an Indian freighter carrying wheat from Oregon to Iran and Sri Lanka, sank about 1,000 miles (1,600 kilometers) northwest of Hawaii. All 69 persons aboard were lost.

Feb. 17 – Off Korea. A freighter and two fishing boats capsized in stormy seas, drowning 23 persons. Twenty-two others were lost from seven other boats.

April 8 – Bay of Bengal. A boat carrying more than 200 passengers capsized about 300 miles (480 kilometers) northwest of Rangoon, Burma. More than 100 drowned.

April 18 – Bangladesh. A launch overloaded with 600 persons capsized in the Ghorautra River, 200 miles (320 kilometers) northeast of Dacca, drowning more than 100.

June 11 – Lake Témiscamingue, Canada. Twelve boys and a teacher, on an outing from a school in Ontario, died when their canoes capsized in a violent squall.

June 17 – Near Topeka, Kans. In the worst boating disaster in Kansas history, 15 passengers drowned when a small tornado capsized the showboat *Whipoorwill* on Lake Pomona during a dinner-theater performance.

Nov. 15-Dec. 2 – Off the coast of Malaysia. In a series of separate incidents, more than 330 Vietnamese refugees died when their crowded boats sank. The refugees had been refused admission by the Malaysian government.

Train Wrecks

Feb. 24 – Northern Argentina. A passenger train crashed into a trailer truck and derailed, killing 37.

Feb. 24 – Waverly, Tenn. A derailed tanker car loaded with liquid propane exploded, killing 21 persons.

April 14 – Budapest, Hungary. Sixteen persons were killed when an express train crashed into a station waiting-room.

April 15 – Near Bologna, Italy. A southbound express train collided head-on with a northbound local that had been derailed by a mud slide. At least 45 persons were killed.

Dec. 21 – Salamanca, Spain. A school bus and a locomotive collided at a railroad crossing, killing 27 children and one adult.

Other Disasters

Jan. 19 – Eastern India. A section of a bridge under construction 600 miles (965 kilometers) southeast of Delhi collapsed, killing some 70 workers.

Feb. 4-5 – French-Austrian Alps. Twenty-one skiers and vacationers were killed by avalanches.

April 27 – Willow Island, W. Va. A construction scaffold inside a power-plant cooling tower collapsed and fell about 170 feet (52 meters), and all 51 workers on the scaffold were killed.

May – Delhi, India. More than 200 persons died during a month-long heat wave. Temperatures ranged from 105°F. (40°C) to 110°F. (43°C) during the day, and remained above 90°F. (32°C) at night.

Mid-July – Texas. A heat wave, with 18 consecutive days of temperatures over 100°F. (38°C) and 41 days without rain, caused 21 deaths in the Dallas-Ft. Worth area.

July 24 – Cairo, Egypt. An apartment building scheduled for demolition collapsed, killing 42 persons.

Oct. 7 – Montevideo, Uruguay. A century-old apartment building collapsed in the city's downtown area, killing at least 17 persons. Beverly Merz

DJIBOUTI. See AFRICA.

DOG. For the first time, the Westminster Kennel Club on Feb. 14, 1978, named a Yorkshire terrier its best-in-show. It was the 33rd such award for Ch. Cede Higgens, owned by Mr. and Mrs. Charles Switzer of Seattle and shown by their daughter, Marlene Lutovsky. The terrier weighed 5½ pounds (2.5 kilograms) and was 10 inches (25 centimeters) long. There were 3,072 dogs entered in the show.

Top honor at the International Kennel Club show, held in Chicago on April 1 and 2, went to Ch. Kishniga's Desert Song, a borzoi owned by Richard Meen of Campbellville, Canada. The show drew 3,602 entries.

According to figures released in March, poodles held the largest number of American Kennel Club registrations done in 1977, as they have since 1960. Doberman pinschers replaced German shepherds as the second most popular breed. After shepherds, in order, were cocker spaniels, Irish setters, Labrador retrievers, beagles, dachshunds, miniature schnauzers, and golden retrievers.

Under the terms of New York City's Canine Waste Disposal Act, effective in August 1978, owners of the city's 1 million dogs were required to clean up after their pets in public places. Violators could be fined up to $100. Theodore M. O'Leary

In WORLD BOOK, see DOG.

DOMINICAN REPUBLIC. See LATIN AMERICA.

Ch. Cede Higgens, a Yorkshire terrier, becomes the first of his breed to win best-in-show honors at the Westminster Kennel Club dog show.

DREYFUSS, RICHARD (1947-   ), won the Academy of Motion Picture Arts and Sciences best actor award on April 3, 1978. He received the Oscar for his role in *The Goodbye Girl.*

Dreyfuss was born on Oct. 29, 1947, in Brooklyn, N.Y. His lawyer father and his mother were active in politics. The family moved to Los Angeles when he was 8, and Dreyfuss made his stage debut at the Westside Jewish Community Center at the age of 11.

He attended Horace Mann Elementary School and began acting at the Gallery Theater during his sophomore year at Beverly Hills High School. After several years of television acting, Dreyfuss appeared in 1973 in the play *Major Barbara* in Los Angeles. His performance brought him the role of Curt Henderson in the film *American Graffiti* in 1974.

A stage tour in *The Time of Your Life* followed, then Dreyfuss starred in the film *The Apprenticeship of Duddy Kravitz* in 1974. After refusing a part in *Jaws* three times, he finally agreed to play the young oceanographer, and his performance made him a star. He appeared next in *Close Encounters of the Third Kind* and in *The Goodbye Girl.*

Dreyfuss' awards include the Hollywood Foreign Press Golden Globe and the Los Angeles Film Critics Award. In 1977, he was named Harvard Hasty Pudding Man of the Year.   Marsha F. Goldsmith

DROUGHT. See WATER; WEATHER; Section Two, COLDER WEATHER AHEAD, UNLESS IT'S WARMER.

DRUGS. With 700 islands and 2,000 bays, almost like stepping stones into Florida, the Bahamas became a major avenue for smuggling cocaine and marijuana into the United States in 1978. Better policing by drug-enforcement agents in the United States and other countries had closed Mexico as a main supplier of marijuana and Jamaica as a distribution point for cocaine. At the same time, "white" heroin from Southeast Asia became a leading drug problem in six large American cities. The heroin—made from opium grown in Burma, Laos, and Thailand—challenged Mexican "brown" heroin for dominance in the drug markets in Baltimore, Detroit, Houston, Jersey City, Los Angeles, and San Francisco.

Thousands of farmers in India—the world's largest producer of opium, both legal and illegal—harvested the opium poppy in March under rigid police control. India's annual crop, about 1,200 short tons (1,100 metric tons) of opium, is exported for use in the legitimate manufacture of medicinal narcotics, such as codeine. The United States buys about 25 per cent of India's crop. The average yield is about 27 pounds of black opium gum per acre (5 kilograms per hectare), for which the farmer is paid $10 per pound (0.45 kilogram). It takes about 10 pounds (5 kilograms) of the gum to produce a pound of pure heroin, which has a wholesale value of about $50,000 in New York City.

Angel Dust. The National Institute on Drug Abuse identified the dangerous psychoactive chemical phencylidine (PCP or angel dust) as America's biggest drug problem. It estimated that about 7-million persons in the United States were using the drug, three times the number of heroin users and not far behind cocaine. A congressional hearing into the use of narcotics in the New York City school system heard testimony in August that angel dust had been used at least once by about 260,000 secondary school students in the city and state during 1978.

Saccharin and Sedatives. Saccharin and other artificial sweeteners do not increase the risk of bladder cancer, according to a study published on July 28 by Baltimore physicians Irving Kessler of the University of Maryland School of Medicine and J. Page Clark of Johns Hopkins University. They said that the relevance of animal tests to the development of cancer in human beings was unclear. In the meantime, Congress was still studying a controversial U.S. Food and Drug Administration (FDA) attempt in 1977 to ban saccharin. Starting on June 1, 1978, stores selling products containing saccharin or other artificial sweeteners had to post labels warning of possible hazards. Saccharin must be listed on the ingredient statements of foods that contain it.

On June 12, the FDA proposed restrictions on over-the-counter sales of daytime sedatives. The agency said that such sedatives might make users

Leaves painted on Coast Guard cutter *Dauntless* indicate how many times the ship has seized marijuana at sea in battle to end drug trade.

sleepy at times when drowsiness is dangerous and that they are ineffective in reducing nervous tension. Sedatives restricted would include such products as Compoz, Cope, Miles Nervine, Tranquim, and Quiet World. Nighttime sleep aids, some bearing the same brand names, would not be similarly restricted.

A panel of experts headed by J. Weldon Bellville of the University of California, Los Angeles, presented a report in July urging the FDA to require warning labels on aspirin packages and to stop manufacturers from claiming that aspirin provides effective arthritis or rheumatism relief. The 1,200-page report, the culmination of a four-year study, said that most of the 50,000 aspirin-based products are safe and effective for the temporary relief of pain, but are in no sense cures.

New Drugs. After decades of research, the FDA in early 1978 approved two potent enzyme products, urokinase and streptokinase, that remove life-threatening blood clots in the lungs. Massive blood clots in the lungs are a leading cause of death, killing some 200,000 Americans annually. Initially, the drugs will be stockpiled at 45 strategically located hospitals, so that they can be rushed to seriously ill patients who need them.   Mary E. Jessup

In WORLD BOOK, see DRUG; DRUG ABUSE; HEROIN; OPIUM; SACCHARIN.

EARTHQUAKE. See DISASTERS.

EASTERN ORTHODOX CHURCHES. The Ecumenical Patriarchate in Istanbul, Turkey, was a center of controversy throughout 1978. In February, a joint statement drafted by Archbishop Iakovos, head of the Greek Orthodox Church in North and South America, and Roman Catholic Cardinal William Baum of Washington, D.C., denounced the Turkish government as a "threat to the very existence of the Ecumenical Patriarchate." The statement was sent to President Jimmy Carter, but it was refuted by Metropolitan Meliton of Chalcedon, the ranking member of the Holy Synod of Constantinople, who declared that his church and the Turkish government can work out their differences without the "interference of foreigners."

In September, President Carter invited Archbishop Iakovos to join the official United States delegation attending the funeral of Pope John Paul I, but the Patriarchate forbade the archbishop to accept this invitation, saying it would be "against the interests of the Mother Church." Archbishop Iakovos subsequently submitted his resignation to the Holy Synod, but it was not accepted.

The Russian Orthodox Church in Moscow in May celebrated the 60th anniversary of the 1918 restoration of the office of patriarch, which had been abolished by the Russian Czar Peter the Great in the early 1700s.

Metropolitan Nikodim of Leningrad died of a heart attack on September 5 in Rome during a private audience in the Vatican with newly enthroned Pope John Paul I. He was considered one of the most influential leaders of the Moscow Patriarchate and architect of the Patriarchate's ecumenical policy. He was replaced by Russia's Metropolitan Anthony, formerly of Minsk and Byelorussia.

United States. The Third International Conference of Orthodox Theologians, sponsored by the Orthodox Theological Society in America, was held in August in Brookline, Mass. The main theme was the agenda of the forthcoming "Great and Holy Council" of Orthodox Churches. Virtually every speaker defended the need for a united Orthodox Church in America and for greater attention to the growing Orthodox dispersion in the Western Hemisphere.

In September, Maxim, the patriarch of Bulgaria, visited the United States, where some 10 parishes are under his jurisdiction. The Orthodox Church in America's Archbishop John (Garklavs) of Chicago and Minneapolis, Minn., retired on September 1. A diocesan convention unanimously nominated Archimandrite Boris Geeza as successor on October 2. He was only the fourth American-born Orthodox bishop to be consecrated in the Orthodox Church in America.   Alexander Schmemann

See also RELIGION. In WORLD BOOK, see EASTERN ORTHODOX CHURCHES.

ECONOMICS. There was almost unanimous agreement in the United States in 1978 that the primary problem facing the country was continued and growing inflation. But there was no such agreement on how to check the rise in prices. That spiral seriously hurt all Americans on fixed incomes; eroded the purchasing power of workers so that even substantial wage increases bought little, if any, more than their wages bought a year earlier; and contributed to a loss of confidence in the U.S. dollar.

The problem was not a new one. Since 1967, consumer prices had nearly doubled. They rose 11 per cent in 1974 and another 9 per cent in 1975. The rate dropped in 1976 to slightly less than 6 per cent, still a long way from satisfactory. It increased to slightly more than 8 per cent in 1978.

Measuring Inflation. When the prices of all goods and services were considered, rather than only those used by consumers, the 1978 price rise was slightly over 7 per cent, still significantly above the 5.2 and 5.8 per cent increases in 1976 and 1977, respectively. But this decade of rapidly increasing prices has made the use of figures expressed in current dollars almost meaningless.

As every consumer knows, what counts is not how many dollars one has but how much these dollars will purchase. So in measuring the progress of the U.S. economy, it is necessary to express the data in real terms – that is, the actual amount of goods and

Leaders of Canada, France, Great Britain, Italy, Japan, the United States, and West Germany meet at economic summit in July in Bonn.

services produced expressed in constant dollars. For example, the United States had a gross national product (GNP) in excess of $2 trillion ($2,000,000,-000,000) for the first time in history in 1978 — measured in current 1978 dollars. The American economy reached the $1-trillion level (also measured in prices as they stood at that time) in 1971, so it would appear that the American economy had nearly doubled in seven years. However, in *real terms* (measured in 1972 dollars to discount inflation) the growth was much less rapid. The 1971 GNP was $1,107,500,000,000 (measured in 1972 dollars), but by the same measure, the actual output of goods and services in 1978 was about $1,390,000,000,000 — only 25 per cent above the 1971 total.

The same effect can be seen in other commonly measured aspects of the economy. For example, there are at least two logical ways to measure profits. One method is to examine their relative share in the national income from period to period, and the other is to look at the absolute volume of profits corrected for the inflationary effects of the period. Thus, corporate profits before taxes in 1967 were $79.3-billion, or 12 per cent of the national income of $655.8 billion. In 1978, profits were estimated at $160 billion. But the national income had risen to $1.7 trillion, so the share of national income going to profits had really decreased to 9.4 per cent. If profits are measured in terms of purchasing power, the estimated $160 billion in corporate profits in 1978 shrinks to $81.2 billion in 1967 dollars, only slightly higher than profits were in 1967.

Employee compensation, looked at in exactly the same fashion, shows that 1967 salaries and benefits totaled $471.9 billion, or 72 per cent of the national income. In 1978, the total compensation of employees rose to about $1.29 trillion, or more than 75 per cent of the estimated national income. If the dollar changes are corrected for the shifting price levels, employee compensation in 1978 (measured in constant 1967 dollars) had risen to $657 billion, 39 per cent more than in 1967.

Labor's Share. It is clear that there has been a substantial increase in the share of the national income going to labor and a decline in the share going to profits. Much of this change came about because many more people have jobs now than in 1967. We can get a better picture of the individual worker's position by looking at the change in hourly earnings through the same period. The average hourly rate of pay in private nonagricultural occupations in 1967 was $2.68. By 1978, it had more than doubled — to $5.73. But when these current dollar rates are adjusted for the effects of price changes, it appears that the increase has been about 10 per cent. However, such an increase probably understates the net improvement in the well-being of most U.S. families. The substantial increase in the number of women employed over the past 10 years means that many families have two or more wage earners.

Employment and Production. Measured in terms that are not affected by price changes, the 1978 performance of the American economy was more than reasonably satisfactory. At year-end, about 94-million Americans were at work and the unemployment rate had dropped to 5.8 per cent. This was a full percentage point below the 1977 average, and employment was up by more than 3.5 million.

And, even better news, the average duration of unemployment continued to drop. Almost half the jobless were out of work for less than five weeks, and only about 20 per cent were out of work for more than 14 weeks. See LABOR.

The Federal Reserve System's index of industrial production was up 5 per cent, with durable manufactured goods leading the way. This reflected the surge in spending for plant and equipment, up 13 per cent. As in 1977, about 2 million new houses were started, and slightly more than 9 million cars were produced. See AUTOMOBILE; MANUFACTURING.

Because of high prices, nearly full employment, and a relatively rapid rate of economic expansion, imports flooded U.S. markets. Machinery and transport equipment and manufactured goods, most of it coming from Western Europe and Japan, surpassed oil imports as the biggest factor in an estimated

$30-billion deficit in the U.S. trade balance for 1978. The total deficit on current account – including services, investment income, tourism, and other nontangible transactions – was somewhat more than half that amount.

In Other Countries. Although prices in the United States were rising well above those of the industrial countries as a whole, there were exceptions. Italy experienced double-digit inflation running at a rate of about 12 per cent, and Denmark's rate was only slightly lower. Nevertheless, the excellent records of Switzerland with approximately a 1 per cent rate; West Germany with slightly more than 2 per cent; and Japan, Belgium, and the Netherlands with 4 per cent provided evidence that the price problem could be controlled in countries where money supplies were held down and governmental deficits limited.

But growth rates in Western Europe were generally somewhat lower than those in the United States. Industrial production was up about 2 per cent in West Germany, less than 2 per cent in Great Britain, and down in Italy. As usual, Japan increased its industrial output, but by somewhat less than the 7 per cent hoped for.

Almost the only news of economic performance in Russia, the largest industrial power after the United States, came through the annual comments that government officials made on economic progress

Economic Ups and Downs

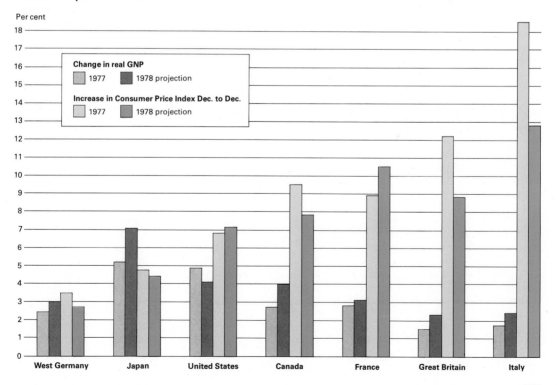

Per cent

	Change in real GNP	
	1977	1978 projection
	Increase in Consumer Price Index Dec. to Dec.	
	1977	1978 projection

West Germany   Japan   United States   Canada   France   Great Britain   Italy

and problems. They claimed in December that 1978 industrial production would be about 5 per cent over 1977 levels, compared with the planned increase of 4.5 per cent. But Western analysts pointed out that this would still leave Russia well behind the goals announced at the beginning of the five-year plan that ends in 1980.

Anti-Inflation Policy. Prodded by the spectacular decline of the U.S. dollar on foreign exchange markets and alarmed by the growing popular resentment of rising prices at home, President Jimmy Carter unveiled the Administration's anti-inflation policy on October 24. Carter asked labor and industry to accept voluntary wage-price guidelines for 1979. Essentially, the program called for a 7 per cent limit on wage increases, including fringe benefits, for those making $4 an hour or more, and asked that industry hold price increases to 0.5 per cent below the average increase in 1976 and 1977. Carter named Alfred E. Kahn, chairman of the Civil Aeronautics Board, as chairman of the Council on Wage and Price Stability, directing the anti-inflation drive.

Carter apparently was agreeable to further increases in interest rates, and this was confirmed on November 1 when the Federal Reserve Bank took the unprecedented action of increasing the discount rate – the rate at which it lends to member banks – by a full percentage point. This was part of a U.S. drive to boost the dollar's value in world markets.

Carter hoped that this program would gradually reduce the rate of inflation by holding down the most important element in costs and by reducing expectations that future price increases would be even greater than those in the past. Results were not expected to show up for six to nine months, and few experts believed that the program would be successful even then. By late December, the inflation rate had reached 8 per cent.

Among the first to show strong opposition to Carter's plan was George Meany, president of the American Federation of Labor and Congress of Industrial Organizations (AFL-CIO). Meany had long been an opponent of any sort of wage and price controls, but he said that he would prefer mandatory wage and price controls to Carter's voluntary program. He apparently believed that the ceiling on wage increases would be reasonably effective against labor but that the price-control aspects of the program would be so full of exceptions as to be meaningless. Labor seemed opposed to the guidelines.

By contrast, businessmen generally supported the Administration program, but they were confused as to how firms producing hundreds or thousands of products could effectively comply. They wondered if exceptions would be granted in cases where rising costs required larger price increases than those stipulated. To meet this problem, the plan's proponents decided that a secondary measure limiting profit margins to those of previous years might be used to keep price increases within the permitted margins, even though the price increase itself fell outside the guidelines.

Although the program was called "voluntary," there were indications that businesses that failed to keep their prices within the limits, or granted wage increases above the 7 per cent level, might lose government contracts or be subjected to such pressure as antitrust investigation. Early in December, inflation adviser Kahn even suggested that consumer boycotts of companies found guilty of noncompliance might be encouraged. Whether all the pressures the government might bring to bear against nonconforming companies fell within the proper limits of executive power was open to question.

A further indication of the difficulties with Carter's program came in early December when there were some shortages of premium unleaded gasoline. It appeared that shortages might become prevalent during the winter unless prices were allowed to rise to meet the heavy costs of producing this gasoline. Kahn seemed to be bending the rules when he suggested that wage-price guidelines might have to be relaxed with respect to energy. A 7 to 15 per cent increase in the price of imported oil seemed likely by early 1979 after the Organization of Petroleum Exporting Countries decided on December 17 to raise the price of its oil by 14.5 per cent in 1979.

Fear of Recession. Many economists and business analysts expressed concern late in the year that the high interest rates and expected reduced growth rates in the money supply would trigger a recession in 1979. Others predicted that there would simply be some reduction in the rate of economic expansion. A *recession* is defined as a period during which the GNP (measured in constant dollars) declines for two successive quarters – six months. Thus, even if the GNP rose at a rate of 5 per cent and inflation continued at the rate of 6 per cent or higher, it would be possible to experience *stagflation*, a condition in which economic activity declines while prices rise.

Most of these forecasters predicted, however, that if a recession developed, it would be relatively mild and brief. Most experts believed that a slowing of economic activity, or even a mild decline, would at least retard the inflation rate. But some expressed doubts that Congress and the Administration could, or would, resist pressures for new expansionary measures if unemployment continued to increase for six months. If this scenario should occur, Americans would again experience the sort of "stop-go" policy that contributed substantially to the recession of 1969-1970, the expansion of 1970-1973, and then again the 1973-1974 recession.

The problem centers around two aspects of American thinking about the economy. The first is the belief that the economy can sustain annual real growth of 3.5 to 4 per cent, and that fiscal and

Selected Key U.S. Economic Indicators

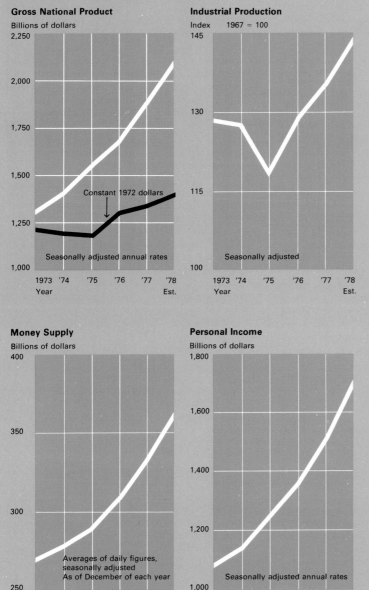

Gross National Product
Billions of dollars

2,250
2,000
1,750
1,500
1,250
1,000

Constant 1972 dollars

Seasonally adjusted annual rates

1973 '74 '75 '76 '77 '78
Year Est.

Industrial Production
Index   1967 = 100

145
130
115
100

Seasonally adjusted

1973 '74 '75 '76 '77 '78
Year Est.

Corporate Profits
Billions of dollars, after taxes

125
110
95
80
65

Seasonally adjusted annual rates

1973 '74 '75 '76 '77 '78
Year Est.

Money Supply
Billions of dollars

400
350
300
250

Averages of daily figures,
seasonally adjusted
As of December of each year

1973 '74 '75 '76 '77 '78
Year Est.

Personal Income
Billions of dollars

1,800
1,600
1,400
1,200
1,000

Seasonally adjusted annual rates

1973 '74 '75 '76 '77 '78
Year Est.

Consumer Price Index
Index   1967 = 100

200
175
150
125
100

All items

1973 '74 '75 '76 '77 '78
Year Est.

The most comprehensive measure of the nation's total output of goods and services is the *Gross National Product* (GNP). The GNP represents the dollar value in current prices of all goods and services plus the estimated value of certain imputed outputs, such as the rental value of owner-occupied dwellings. *Industrial Production* is a monthly measure of the physical output of manufacturing, mining, and utility industries. *Corporate Profits* are quarterly profit samplings from major industries.

Money Supply measures the total amount of money in the economy in coin, currency, and demand deposits. *Personal Income* is current income received by persons (including nonprofit institutions and private trust funds) before personal taxes. *Consumer Price Index* (CPI) is a monthly measure of changes in the prices of goods and services consumed by urban families and individuals. CPI includes selected goods and services All 1978 figures are *Year Book* estimates.

monetary policies can bring about that rate of growth. If, as most analysts suspect, the sustainable rate of growth is below that level, the policies adopted are certain to inject more dollars into the market place than can be absorbed without an increase in prices. Related, but distinct in the minds of political leaders, is the second belief of many Americans – that an unemployment rate above 4.5 to 5 per cent is less than full employment and should be corrected.

At such levels of unemployment, shortages of certain workers start to appear – especially skilled workers. Such shortages force wages up, which in turn increases costs. Rising costs are reflected in higher prices, and the net result is that in the next round of bargaining, labor asks for even higher wages to keep up with the rising cost of living.

The problem is intensified by the fact that many workers have cost-of-living clauses in their wage contracts so that every time prices increase, wages go up. Unless these increases are matched by increasing worker productivity, inflation simply gets worse.

Pecuniary Proposition. Despite the growth of consumerism in the last few years, citizens have seldom spoken more loudly than they did in California on June 6 when voters overwhelmingly adopted Proposition 13, which, in effect, cut property taxes drastically and reduced the property tax burden by more than 50 per cent. This controversial proposal had its greatest impact on local communities, which rely heavily on the property tax to support such activities as social services and the arts. In November, another crop of tax- and expenditure-cutting proposals was on the ballot in 16 states. Those of the Proposition 13 type passed in Idaho and Nevada, and other proposals to limit spending passed in Michigan, Arizona, Hawaii, and Texas. See TAXATION (Close-Up).

Just what effect these proposals might have on the economy is difficult to assess. However, it is apparent that even if socially popular programs are not reduced, there will be growing resistance to their expansion. Rising costs must be met either by increasing revenues (taxes) or by incurring deficits – the situation reveals the dilemma faced by any economy in a period of inflation.

European Monetary System. One unexpected result of the U.S. dollar's plunge in value was the formation of the European Monetary System (EMS) by countries of the European Community (EC or Common Market). The EMS was scheduled to begin on Jan. 1, 1979, but it was delayed by France because of a dispute about farm subsidies (see EUROPE). During the decline of the dollar, beginning in 1972, European countries had tried to keep their currencies relatively stable against one another so as to facilitate trade through stable exchange rates. The central banks in each country acted independently to maintain stability.

This became increasingly difficult as the dollar plunged steeply in 1978. In late November, the dollar had declined more than 13 per cent against the West German Deutsche mark, less than 10 per cent against the French franc, and just under 3 per cent against the Italian lira in one year. EMS plans called for establishing a fund that would make $32-billion available in short- and medium-term credits, so that EC countries could keep the value of their currencies within 2.25 per cent of a fixed value set in relation to other currencies in the EMS. Italy was promised that countries with especially weak currencies, such as the Italian lira, could join the system with the provision that 6 per cent would be the margin.

If the new system operates effectively, it could be a first step toward the creation of a common currency unit for all participating countries. This in turn would reduce uncertainty about relative costs and would encourage trade among the EMS nations. The impact of the new system on the dollar is uncertain. If the system succeeds, the dollar might drop further in value, particularly if inflation continues at a higher rate in the United States than in Europe.   Warren W. Shearer

See also Section One, FOCUS ON THE ECONOMY; INTERNATIONAL TRADE AND FINANCE. In WORLD BOOK, see ECONOMICS; GROSS NATIONAL PRODUCT; NATIONAL INCOME.

ECUADOR. In a nationwide referendum held on Jan. 15, 1978, voters approved a new Constitution under which the military government would surrender power to an elected civilian government at year's end. The charter called for a one-house legislature. It gave the vote to every adult, including illiterates. It also stipulated that the president would be limited to one five-year term.

Presidential elections were scheduled for July 16, but the legislative elections were not to be held until sometime in 1979. In the interim, the president and his Cabinet would rule as a civilian dictatorship.

Bucaram Blocked. The electorate's apparent presidential favorite was Asaad Bucaram, the former mayor of Guayaquil, who was head of a leftist coalition called the Concentration of Popular Forces (CFP). The junta, however, headed by Supreme Council President Alfredo Poveda Burbano, regarded Bucaram as a dangerous demagogue. The military had seized power in 1972 largely to prevent him from winning the presidential election scheduled that year.

On February 20, the military moved to block Bucaram's candidacy by passing an electoral decree stating that no one could be president whose parents were not Ecuadorean by birth. Bucaram's parents were born in Lebanon. The new law also decreed that no former president of Ecuador could run again, thus effectively eliminating two other candi-

Voters in Quito, Ecuador, shoulder their way past guards to approve a new Constitution in January, the first step on the way to ending military rule.

dates the military disliked, Carlos Julio Arosemana and José Velasco Ibarra.

Thwarted Again. Bucaram, thwarted in his presidential ambitions, then decided to run for deputy mayor of Guayaquil. Once again, the military blocked him by ruling that because he had been mayor once, he could not seek the office again. Bucaram then proposed that his wife seek the position, but the military produced yet another law requiring candidates to be university graduates.

Bucaram was apparently able to outmaneuver the junta, however, by putting up Jaime Roldos, his son-in-law, as the CFP's presidential candidate. In the July 16 election, Roldos polled 31 per cent of the votes, while conservative coalition candidate Sixto Duran Ballen polled 23 per cent. Because no candidate received a majority, a runoff was planned. On September 22, however, all the electoral college members resigned, charging that the election had been marred by massive fraud and recommending that it be annulled. Roldos immediately voiced his fears that it was all part of a plot to keep him out of a runoff, which he predicted he would win by a landslide.

The junta decided to hold a recount, however. It postponed a runoff until the legislative elections could be held at the same time.   Everett G. Martin

See also LATIN AMERICA (Facts in Brief Table). In WORLD BOOK, see ECUADOR.

EDUCATION. The Supreme Court of the United States ruled on June 28, 1978, that Allan P. Bakke must be admitted to the University of California School of Medicine at Davis. The court said in a 5 to 4 decision that the Davis affirmative-action program was unjustifiably biased against white applicants like Bakke. After he had been rejected twice by Davis, he sued, charging that he had been denied admission because 16 places had been reserved for minority-group candidates whose scores were lower than his. Despite ruling for Bakke, the high court held, in a second vote, that affirmative-action programs that consider race as one of many factors, but not as the sole determining factor, are permissible. See SUPREME COURT OF THE UNITED STATES (Close-Up).

Growing Problems. Proposition 13, the tax-cutting referendum passed by California voters in June, caused mounting concern among U.S. educators, who already faced acute economic pressures and declining enrollments. Officials feared that the schools might have to bear the brunt of the new austerity, because municipal governments would be reluctant to cut such essential services as sanitation, or police and fire protection.

In the November 7 national election, voters in 16 more states were asked to approve proposals either to cut taxes or limit spending. Although opposed by many educational groups, 80 per cent of the initiatives were passed. They were defeated in Colorado, Michigan, Nebraska, and Oregon. See STATE GOVERNMENT; TAXATION (Close-Up).

A number of school systems were financially hard-pressed. For example, teachers in Cleveland, Ohio, worked without pay for several weeks in the spring because the system ran out of money. Two school revenue proposals were defeated in April and June. A $21-million loan from the state allowed Cleveland schools to open on October 16, after a teacher strike was settled. See CLEVELAND.

The "back-to-basics" movement gathered momentum. While much of the movement's support came from those who are dissatisfied with the quality of public education, the call for a return to "the three R's" was also supported by those who see basic education, without frills, as a way to save money.

Other critics focused attention on testing as an instrument of quality control. Many state legislatures either imposed or considered competency-test programs at various grade levels, but particularly before high school graduation. In Florida, for instance, students must now pass a literacy test in order to receive a high school diploma. If they fail three times, they are awarded only a certificate of attendance. The United States Senate held hearings on the desirability of national test programs, but the U.S. Department of Health, Education, and Welfare (HEW) and a number of education groups opposed them as a threat to local control of education.

Aroused California teachers protest possible job losses after Proposition
13 forced a drastic cut in the state property taxes that support education.

About 15,000 of Chicago's 40,000 public school eighth-grade students spent part of their summer taking remedial reading courses. The Board of Education now requires that students entering high school read at least at the level of a beginning eighth grader. The national reading level for eighth graders is 8.5; in Chicago, it is 6.8. New York City school officials have also proposed tougher promotion standards at all public educational levels.

Inflation continued to raise the cost of education, especially at the college level. In response to complaints, particularly from middle-class voters, Senators Daniel P. Moynihan (D., N.Y.) and Robert W. Packwood (R., Ore.) introduced a bill that would allow tax credits for parents who pay college tuition bills. But the proposal died in Congress. See Section Two, How to Cope with Rising College Costs.

Acting on a promise made during his 1976 presidential campaign, President Jimmy Carter in April proposed the creation of a separate, Cabinet-level Department of Education, despite considerable opposition from the ranks of higher education, as well as from HEW Secretary Joseph A. Califano, Jr. The new department would take over all of HEW's Education Division; the educational responsibilities of HEW's Civil Rights Division; the Department of Housing and Urban Development's college housing program; the Department of Defense's overseas dependents' schools; and a number of other federal programs. It was estimated that the new department would have a budget of $17.5 billion and more than 23,000 employees.

Higher Education paid increasing attention to the undergraduate curriculum, in response to growing dissatisfaction with the easing of course requirements that resulted from the student rebellions of the 1960s. Although such academic reassessments had begun on many campuses, the process moved into the national limelight on May 2, when the Harvard University faculty approved the establishment of a core curriculum requiring students to enroll in certain courses. Students would also have to demonstrate competence in a foreign language, in mathematics, and in writing.

Total Enrollment in U.S. schools and colleges declined slightly for the sixth consecutive year, after almost three decades of constant growth. College enrollments continued to grow, but at a severely reduced rate of only 3 per cent — a trend expected to continue into the early 1980s.

Enrollment in public and private institutions at all levels dropped to 59.8 million in the fall of 1978 from 60.3 million in 1977. Elementary grades enrolled 32.6 million, with 28.8 million in public schools, compared with 29.4 million in 1977. High schools had a total enrollment of 15.6 million students, with 14.1 million in public high schools, down from 14.3-million in 1977.

Office of Education estimates placed higher education – colleges, universities, professional schools, and junior colleges – enrollment at a record 11.6-million, up about 300,000. Public colleges and universities, with an estimated 9.1 million, continued to grow at a faster rate than private ones, which gained only about 60,000 students.

The annual number of high school graduates has remained near 3.1 million for four years and little change was expected for 1978-1979. Colleges and universities were expected to confer a new high of 1 million bachelor's degrees, 67,000 first professional degrees, 347,000 master's, and 37,000 doctorates.

Education directly involved 63.4 million Americans in the fall of 1978, according to the Office of Education. In a population of about 220.8 million, this means that 3 persons out of every 10 participate in the educational process. Estimates based on Bureau of the Census data show that 92 per cent of all 5-year-olds; 99 per cent of 6- to 13-year olds; 94 per cent of 14- to 17-year-olds; and 30 per cent of 18- to 24-year-olds were enrolled in classes.

The Teachers. There were an estimated 3.3 million classroom teachers in 1978, and another 300,000 working as superintendents, principals, and supervisors. The total includes about 830,000 teachers in higher education, up 1 per cent. About 500,000 taught in the private sector.

The pupil-teacher ratio in public elementary and secondary schools has been declining in recent years. The ratio decreased from 23.7 students per teacher in 1967 to 19.9 to 1 in the fall of 1977. Critics of the schools' effectiveness cited the fact that more funds go to pay greater numbers of teachers, while children's achievements decline, as proof of lower teacher productivity and waste of public funds.

The average salary of teachers rose to $14,244 at all public school levels, and to $13,902 for elementary-school teachers, a gain of about 6.6 per cent over 1977. Averages ranged from Mississippi's $9,741 to Alaska's $21,109. The National Center for Education Statistics reported that faculty salaries in higher education rose an average of 5.2 per cent.

Teachers' Unions. Fierce competition continued between the two largest U.S. teacher organizations, the 1.8-million-member National Education Association (NEA) and the American Federation of Teachers (AFT), which had about 447,000 members. The two organizations took opposing positions on the creation of a separate Department of Education; the NEA lobbied hard for such a department and the AFT opposed it.

The 1978-1979 school year started with an apparent increase in the number of teacher strikes. Strikes in September affected more than 625,000 students in 13 states. At the same time, faculty walkouts at colleges and universities reached a new high. An estimated 170,000 students found their higher education curtailed.

Education Expenditures at all levels for 1978-1979 were estimated by the Office of Education at above $155 billion, an increase of $11 billion. However, that increase was only slightly above the rate of inflation, leaving education with a real gain of less than $1 billion. Elementary and secondary schools were expected to spend $100 billion. This left $55-billion for higher education. Public school and college expenditures were estimated at $127 billion, with those of privately controlled institutions running close to $28 billion.

State governments contributed $57.1 billion, or 36.8 per cent of the total; local governments, $43.3-billion, or 27.9 per cent; the federal government, $16.5 billion, or 10.6 per cent; and all other sources, $38.3 billion, or 24.7 per cent. National educational expenditures remained constant at about 8 per cent of the gross national product.

Student Achievement was under critical scrutiny, but the College Entrance Examination Board reported that the average verbal score on the Scholastic Aptitude Test (SAT) in 1978 held at the previous year's level of 429 – on a scale of 200 to 800 – for the first time since a steady decline began in 1963. Mathematical scores continued to slip, to a 468 average from 470 last year. During the 15-year decline that seriously concerned educational observers, the verbal scores slipped 49 points and the math scores dropped 34 points. "During the last three years, the decline in SAT scores has not been as precipitous as it was in the early 1970s," a College Board spokesman said. "However, it's impossible to predict whether the decline will be arrested, or whether we merely have a momentary pause."

Public Attitudes toward the schools were mixed. A teacher survey by the NEA indicated that an increasing number of pupils may receive lower and failing grades and may be held back to repeat a grade. This resulted from a reassessment of the policy of "social," or automatic, promotion under which most children were moved ahead regardless of their achievements. That policy was based on the belief that holding children back in a grade might do serious emotional damage.

More than two-thirds of those queried in the 10th annual Gallup Poll of the public's attitudes toward public schools favored promoting children only if they can pass the required tests. But an even larger majority favored special remedial classes in problem subjects rather than requiring students to repeat a year's work.

In response to the decline in student enrollment in language studies, President Carter appointed a 21-member President's Commission on Foreign Language and International Studies to make recommendations on how to increase public interest in foreign-language studies. Fred M. Hechinger

See also Section One, Focus on Education. In World Book, see Education.

EGYPT. President Anwar al-Sadat's sharing of the 1978 Nobel Peace Prize with Israel's Prime Minister Menachem Begin capped a year of decision and triumph for the Egyptian leader. Following his historic peace mission of November 1977, Sadat saw his efforts crowned with the September agreement at Camp David, Maryland, to pursue final negotiations for an Egyptian-Israeli peace treaty. The Egyptian People's Assembly ratified the pact by a 351-9 vote on October 12, underscoring Sadat's broad support. The peace negotiators themselves see-sawed until year's end without significant results. See MIDDLE EAST.

Domestic Opposition. A fourth political party, the New Wafd, was officially legalized in February by the Arab Socialist Union (ASU), Egypt's umbrella political organization. The original Wafd party dominated Egyptian political life from 1920 until the 1952 revolution. The New Wafd held 28 seats in the Peoples' Assembly. It promptly challenged the government to implement the principles of unity, socialism, and democracy embodied in the charter of the revolution.

Sadat faced some opposition from both the extreme right and the extreme left. He moved first against the rightists, whose Muslim conservatism represented a threat to the government. In January and February, two radical Muslim groups, *Jihad* and the Society for Repentance and Retreat from Sin, were banned for conspiracy to overthrow the government. Five members of the latter group were hanged for the 1977 murder of Minister of Religious Affairs Muhammad Hussein al-Zahabi.

In May, the left came under attack. A law restricting domestic criticism of government policies and banning Communists and avowed Marxists from holding public office was approved in a national referendum on May 21 and passed by the Assembly on June 1. Some 131 persons, including opponents of Sadat jailed since 1971, were affected by the law. The New Wafd and the leftist National Progressive Unionist Party disbanded in protest.

Responding to criticism, Sadat dissolved the ASU on July 22 and formed as its successor the National Democratic Party. Composed of his supporters, it held 305 of the 360 seats in the Assembly.

Other Problems. Egypt's critical social and economic problems remained unsolved. The population reached 40 million in January. With a birth rate of 2.5 per cent, inflation running at 25 per cent, urban unemployment at 12 per cent, and $3.2 billion in unpaid foreign debts, Egypt needed radical internal surgery as badly as foreign aid. But there were some positive developments. New oil strikes in the Gulf of Suez and a major natural gas field offshore near Abu Qir, discovered in July, would boost export earnings to $780 million.   William Spencer

See also MIDDLE EAST (Facts in Brief Table). In WORLD BOOK, see EGYPT.

During a busy and turbulent year, President Anwar al-Sadat led Egypt closer to a settlement with Israel and shared the Nobel Peace Prize.

ELECTIONS. California's adoption of a 57 per cent reduction in property taxes on June 6, 1978, was widely interpreted as the start of a tax revolt in the United States. The passage of Proposition 13 by a margin of nearly 2 to 1 fostered a more conservative climate for the November campaign.

The measure, put on the California ballot as a voters' initiative, rolled back existing property taxes by $7 billion and limited future increases to 2 per cent per year. It also required a two-thirds vote of the state legislature and local government boards to approve any new taxes.

Republicans were jubilant about the California vote, believing that their past advocacy of tax cuts and spending reductions would lead to victory in the November elections. Democrats, however, quickly became advocates of fiscal responsibility and neutralized most of the GOP advantage.

As a result, the Republicans made only modest gains in the midterm balloting, picking up 3 seats in the U.S. Senate and 11 in the House of Representatives, and increasing the ranks of GOP governors by 6. Democrats retained large majorities in the Senate (59-41), in the House (276-157, with 2 seats vacant because of deaths after the election), and among the governors (32-18).

After California adopted Proposition 13, several other states approved measures to cut property taxes, limit state spending, or restrict the growth of tax revenues. Idaho and Nevada set constitutional limits on property taxes; Arizona limited state spending to 7 per cent of its residents' total personal income; North Dakota slashed income taxes by 37 per cent; and Texas cut property taxes by $500 million and stipulated that state spending be proportional to economic growth. Only in Maryland and Nebraska were curbs on taxes or spending clearly rejected. See TAXATION (Close-Up).

The Republican Party failed nationally, however, in its efforts to bring about a one-third reduction in federal income taxes over the next three years, as provided in legislation sponsored by Representative Jack F. Kemp of New York and Senator William V. Roth, Jr., of Delaware, both Republicans. Despite the endorsement of top Republicans, the Senate and House rejected the big tax cut by large margins.

Other Issues. Taxes and spending were not the sole issues put before the electorate on November 7. Some 200 referendums, dealing with a variety of issues, were on the ballot in 38 states.

Voters bet against gambling in 1978. New Jersey refused to allow betting on jai alai, and Virginians turned down legalized parimutuel wagers at race tracks. Florida struck down a measure to allow casino gambling in Miami Beach and Hollywood.

The legal drinking age was raised from 18 to 19 in Montana, and from 19 to 21 in Michigan. Californians struck down Proposition 5, which would have banned smoking in a variety of public places.

Gay-rights issues prompted heated debates in a number of cities and states. Voters in Dade County, Florida, refused to reinstate a law barring discrimination against homosexuals that had been repealed in 1977. Seattle voters retained a law barring such discrimination, however, and Californians rejected a proposition to ban homosexuals from teaching in public schools.

The Senate Elections were a small disaster for liberal incumbents of both parties. Five liberal Democrats were defeated by more conservative opponents. Two mainstays of the small band of Senate Republican liberals were rejected by the voters. Democratic newcomers from the South, more moderate than their predecessors, also helped to modify the ideological shift to the right.

Among the liberal Democrats ousted from the Senate were Richard C. Clark of Iowa, William D. Hathaway of Maine, Floyd K. Haskell of Colorado, and Thomas J. McIntyre of New Hampshire. Senator Wendell R. Anderson and Robert Short lost as Minnesota handed seats once held by Hubert H. Humphrey and Walter F. Mondale to the GOP.

Senate seats yielded by liberal Republicans were taken by liberal Democrats, however. Senator Edward W. Brooke of Massachusetts was beaten by Representative Paul E. Tsongas; Robert P. Griffin of Michigan lost to Carl Levin; and Clifford P. Case of New Jersey was defeated in the primary. Democratic liberal Bill Bradley, former Rhodes scholar and professional basketball star, won Case's seat.

Victors in other Senate races included Nancy Landon Kassebaum, daughter of 1936 GOP presidential candidate Alfred M. Landon, a Kansas Republican; Thad Cochran, the first Republican elected from Mississippi since the Reconstruction era; and John Warner of Virginia, former secretary of the Navy and husband of film star Elizabeth Taylor.

The Governors' Races showed greater Republican gains. The biggest upset was scored by William Clements in Texas, the first GOP governor of that state in more than a century. He defeated John L. Hill, who had ousted incumbent Democratic Governor Dolph Briscoe in the primary.

Republicans were strongest in the Midwestern states, where they won eight of nine races. Incumbent James R. Thompson won a big victory in Illinois. GOP governors William G. Milliken, James A. Rhodes, and Robert D. Ray were returned to office in Michigan, Ohio, and Iowa, respectively.

Democrats kept a grip on the two largest states. Edmund G. Brown, Jr., won by a record margin in California, and Hugh L. Carey gained a second term in New York. They also did well in the East and West, and lost only one statehouse in the South — Tennessee.

In the House, Republicans picked up a net total of 11 seats, gaining three in California, two in

New senators include, *clockwise from upper left,*
basketball star Bill Bradley (D., N.J.,); Nancy
Landon Kassebaum (R., Kans.), daughter of Alf
Landon; and Thad Cochran, first Republican from
Mississippi since Reconstruction. Meanwhile,
Edward W. Brooke (R., Mass.), the only black
in the Senate, contemplates his defeat.

Pennsylvania, two in Texas, and one in Arkansas, Georgia, Illinois, Indiana, Iowa, Kansas, Kentucky, New Jersey, New York, South Carolina, Wisconsin, and Wyoming. Democrats, however, picked up two House seats in Florida and Michigan, and single seats in Connecticut, Maryland, South Dakota, and Washington.

Turnover in the House continued at a rapid pace, with 77 new members – 42 Democrats and 35 Republicans – elected. Nearly half of the members of the House have been elected since 1974.

Eight members of the House of Representatives ran for re-election after being reprimanded, indicted, or convicted of various charges. J. Herbert Burke, a Florida Republican found guilty of drunkenness; Joshua Eilberg, a Pennsylvania Democrat indicted on conflict-of-interest charges; and John J. McFall, a California Democrat reprimanded by the House in the Korean lobbying scandal, were defeated. Voters re-elected Charles C. Diggs, Jr., a Michigan Democrat convicted and sentenced to prison for taking kickbacks; Daniel J. Flood, a Pennsylvania Democrat indicted on federal bribery charges; and Frederick W. Richmond, a New York Democrat who pleaded guilty to a morals charge. Edward R. Roybal and Charles H. Wilson, California Democrats who were reprimanded for their involvement in the Korea lobbying scandal, were also re-elected.

Spending and Strategy. Heavy spending and sophisticated strategy were employed on a large scale in the 1978 elections. Spending set a record for midterm elections. Between $200 million and $250-million was spent on congressional and gubernatorial races. Lobbies and special interests provided up to $60 million, while parties spent about $30 million.

At least 20 Senate candidates spent $1 million or more, with victorious Republicans Jesse A. Helms of North Carolina and John G. Tower of Texas spending $3.6 million each to retain their seats. Expenditures of almost $2 million each failed, however, to win election for Democrats Robert Krueger of Texas and Robert Short of Minnesota.

Computer analysis was widely employed by candidates to interpret opinion polls, plan strategies, and raise campaign funds. By feeding the results of detailed opinion polls to computers, candidates could detect popular issues and plan their positions accordingly. Incumbents, in particular, used computers effectively in fund raising. Many used extensive, computer-compiled lists of constituents who were sympathetic to their positions.

Television advertising accounted for an average of 60 to 70 per cent of most candidates' expenditures, according to John Deardourff, a media expert who engineered eight successful campaigns in seven states.   William J. Eaton

See also DEMOCRATIC PARTY; REPUBLICAN PARTY. In WORLD BOOK, see ELECTION.

ELECTRIC POWER. See ENERGY.

ELECTRONICS. Semiconductor technology continued to be at the forefront of electronics development in 1978. The amount of circuitry that can be placed on a single tiny "chip" increased dramatically. Fujitsu Limited of Japan announced the first 65,536-bit dynamic random access memory (65k RAM). (A *bit* is the basic unit of information in digital computers.) The previous standard had been the 4k (4,096-bit) RAM. Other semiconductor manufacturers quickly followed suit with dynamic 65k RAM's.

Texas Instruments, Incorporated, of Dallas introduced a 16,384-bit (16k) static RAM in July. The previous standard had been a 4,096-bit 4k RAM. Static RAM's are faster and simpler than dynamic RAM's and they require fewer extra components in order to work. But each static memory cell has more circuitry than a dynamic cell, thus less memory capacity per unit area.

Mostek Corporation of Carrollton, Tex., introduced a 16k pseudostatic RAM in August that has dynamic cells for memory, and an on-chip refresh and counter circuit to boost the voltage level, which drops periodically because of capacitor leakage. Pseudostatic RAM's are smaller, but slower, than static RAM's.

The capacity of bubble-domain memory devices surpassed the previous 92,304-bit standard when Texas Instruments announced a *bubble memory* with a 250,000-bit capacity. Bubble memories are garnet chips in which certain atoms align themselves in cylindrical groups called *bubbles* when exposed to magnetic fields originated outside the chip. The presence or absence of a bubble represents a binary 0 or 1 in computer language.

International Business Machines Corporation (IBM) of New York City announced on May 9 that research scientists E. A. Giess and R. J. Kobliska had produced stable magnetic bubbles one-eighth the size of commercially available bubbles. Experiments with various combinations of chip materials and structures yielded stable bubbles as small as 0.4 micron (0.0000156 inch) in diameter. Commercially available bubbles are 3 to 5 microns in diameter.

New Machines. Weidner Communication Systems of La Jolla, Calif., introduced a translating machine in October that lets the operator make word choices and interpretations. Previous machines gave the operator no choice, providing only one translation for each foreign word or word group received. Many sentences resulting from these machine translations were wrong or hard to understand. The Weidner machine displays alternate translations on a video screen. The operator acts as an editor, selecting from the alternate translations and writing a sentence that reads well. For example, if the machine received the Spanish sentence, "*Pero Odense es mejor conocido por el más célebre de sus habitantes,*" it would display on the screen, "But

Odense is better known (by/for/through) the more famous (of/from) (his/her/your/its) inhabitants.'' The human translator operating the machine could then write, ''But Odense is better known for the most famous of its inhabitants.''

Texas Instruments introduced Speak and Spell, a device that gives children spelling and pronunciation drills disguised as games. Speak and Spell has a voice-synthesizer chip, enabling it to talk to the children. Also new is an electronic watch with a liquid-crystal analogue display.

Prices of 4-bit microprocessors fell to 99 cents each in quantity, an attractive price for manufacturers of kitchen blenders and laboratory testing and measuring equipment.

Electronic Mail. United States Postmaster General William Bolger said in November that the U.S. Postal Service (USPS) will conduct a $4-million, year-long test of an electronic mail-delivery system, beginning in 1979. If the test succeeds, USPS probably will build a $20-million system to serve three to 10 cities within three years. The final system would eventually cost approximately $2 billion and would serve 87 cities. Marilyn J. Offenheiser

In WORLD BOOK, see ELECTRONICS.

EL SALVADOR. See LATIN AMERICA.

EMPLOYMENT. See ECONOMICS; EDUCATION; LABOR; SOCIAL SECURITY; SOCIAL WELFARE.

ENDANGERED SPECIES. See CONSERVATION.

ENERGY. President Jimmy Carter signed into law a five-part national energy plan on Nov. 9, 1978, about 18 months after he submitted energy legislation to the United States Congress. Congress passed the compromise measure on October 15 after one of the longest legislative battles in years. The major provisions of the energy package included:

■ Gradual deregulation of newly discovered natural gas by 1985 and sizable price increases in the interim. Intrastate gas will be subject to federal price controls for the first time.

■ A mild energy-tax bill that will tax gas-guzzling cars starting in 1980. It provides tax credits for homeowners and businesses that install energy-saving weather protection, and gives various tax breaks to oil and gas producers.

■ A requirement that most electric power plants burn coal instead of oil or natural gas and, where feasible, that industrial plants do likewise.

■ A demand that state regulatory agencies consider new rate structures for utilities that promote energy conservation.

■ A series of general conservation measures, including a requirement that utilities offer information and arrange financing for residential users to install energy-saving insulation.

The law that emerged from Congress differed considerably from Carter's first energy proposals made in April 1977. Congress put less emphasis on forced conservation and more on providing incentives to expand fuel production.

Still, the energy program has significant conservation features that have the effect of thrusting Washington more deeply into decisions on power generation. Critics of the legislation, however, said that federal enforcement power is too diluted.

On the Supply Side, the year closed with ample reserves of fuel — oil, coal, uranium, and natural gas — in most parts of the world. The United States came through the year well, boasting an overabundance of ready-to-fire fuel at times. But some experts predicted a shortage of power plants for converting raw fuel into electricity, as power demands grow.

The first phase of the energy plan Carter submitted to Congress in 1977 sought to restrain energy demand on the residential, commercial, and transportation fronts. But it did little to promote the production of new forms of energy.

Carter and Secretary of Energy James R. Schlesinger then turned to the supply side of the problem in May. They sent Congress a preliminary set of ''energy-supply initiatives'' and promised a more comprehensive supply strategy by early 1979 to form the basis for the second phase of the energy plan.

For many, especially in the electric-utility industry, the supply initiatives were disappointing. They represented some federal funding increases, incentives for development of synthetic fuels, photovoltaic solar energy, wind-generated power, and small hydroelectric systems, but the $130 million that the Department of Energy (DOE) started spending on Oct. 1, 1978 – the start of fiscal 1979 – represented a sharp cutback from the $368-million package that DOE first proposed. The Office of Management and Budget (OMB) rejected the larger amount and insisted that DOE find the $130 million by cutting elsewhere in its budget. One of the cuts was $40-million taken from a program to improve the productivity and safety of light-water nuclear reactors. DOE picked up another $45 million for the supply initiatives by shifting funds from an aborted coal-conversion project. Another $51 million came by deferring spending on nuclear-waste-management facilities pending a nuclear-waste-disposal policy.

In announcing the supply initiatives, Schlesinger emphasized the importance of developing "a wide range of commercially viable new technologies" to help increase production of energy from domestic resources in the 1980s and beyond.

Environmental Requirements started a major debate in the energy area in September, after the Environmental Protection Agency (EPA) proposed stringent air-pollution standards for new power plants. To carry out the 1977 congressional amendments to the Clean Air Act that required new plants to use the "best available technology," EPA opted for systems that would reduce sulfur dioxide emis-

sions by 85 per cent, measured on a daily average basis, at all new coal-burning power plants.

DOE, which wants the nation to burn more coal, has been pushing for removal of 85 per cent of the sulfur dioxide measured on a monthly, rather than daily, average. The DOE proposal would call for only 40 per cent scrubbing for some coals. Utilities banded together in the Utility Air Regulatory Group favored a sliding-scale standard that would require only a 20 per cent sulfur dioxide reduction for low sulfur coals.

New Power Sources. DOE has been considering reactivating small hydroelectric plants or building new ones across the United States. In October, the Federal Energy Regulatory Commission simplified licensing procedures for such plants to speed approval for projects capable of generating up to 1,500 kilowatts (kw).

Global Marine Development, Incorporated, of Newport Beach, Calif., was selected by DOE to design, build, and operate the first experimental system for generating power with the ocean thermal-energy conversion concept (OTEC). The company will conduct tests off the coast of Hawaii, running polyethylene pipes almost $1/2$ mile (0.8 kilometer) into the ocean from a converted U.S. Navy tanker. Water pumped from that depth off Keahole Point is about 40° F. (22°C) colder than the

The "Sun Flag" flies over solar energy supporters as they celebrate Sun Day in Maine. Unfortunately, clouds obscured the sunrise they hoped to see.

surface water, and this temperature difference will drive the turbine-generator OTEC system. The warm surface water will be pumped through heat exchangers to evaporate a working fluid, such as freon or ammonia. The vapor will turn a power-generating turbine and then be cooled by the water drawn from the deep. The vapor will then liquefy, and the cycle will be repeated. This is an application of solar energy; the sun's heating of the ocean surface causes the difference in temperature.

Zinc chloride batteries were selected by DOE in October for testing in electric-utility load-leveling applications. Batteries that meet peak electric loads could reduce the need for new power plants. The batteries would be recharged at night when spare generating capacity is available.

Methane gas from landfill in California was pumped into pipelines in September by the Pacific Gas & Electric Company at the rate of 300,000 cubic feet (8,500 cubic meters) per day. Impurities are removed from the methane so that it can be mixed with other gas supplies and distributed to customers. The project's main goal is to examine the commercial feasibility of recovering methane gas – the main component of natural gas – from municipal solid wastes. Over 2,200 short tons (2,000 metric tons) of solid wastes from San Francisco and Mountain View are deposited at the landfill site each day. Methane forms underground as the buried waste decomposes.

Electric Utilities in the United States reported their peak demand grew only 1.4 per cent, and electric energy use was up 2.6 per cent in 1978, well below many forecasts. Widespread cool summer weather cut the national peak a full percentage point. Energy conservation and lack of industrial growth, coupled with the use of more efficient equipment, also made a sizable contribution.

There were no basic changes in residential energy use, simply adjustments and fine tuning. Appliances were being made more efficient and were slowly worked into existing stocks for use in America's 76-million households. Appliance shipments in 1978 were up 6 per cent to about 38 million units.

Nuclear Power. Government vacillation and the continued effectiveness of antinuclear groups in using the courts to delay construction and licensing slowed nuclear growth. Increased capital costs for nuclear units were also felt. There were no new orders for nuclear plants in 1978.

Utility executives continued to hold back on capital spending. At year's end they reported that total capability in 1978 came to 550 million kw, a 5.8 per cent increase from 520 million kw in 1977. Utilities generated 2.20 trillion kilowatt-hours (kwh) in 1978, an increase of 2.8 per cent from the 2.14 trillion kwh in 1977.   James J. O'Connor

See also COAL; PETROLEUM AND GAS. In WORLD BOOK, see ENERGY; ENERGY SUPPLY.

ENGINEERING. See BUILDING & CONSTRUCTION.

ENVIRONMENT. Many conservation activists in the United States viewed the 95th Congress as responsive to environmental concerns in 1978, especially in the ways it acted to preserve wilderness and parklands. "The environmental movement has never been in better shape," said Brock Adams, director of the Sierra Club's office in Washington, D.C., on October 22.

Some environmental leaders, however, feared that President Jimmy Carter's efforts to control inflation could hamper rigorous enforcement of environmental laws. Carter's complex plan to restrain wage and price increases, announced on October 24, called for the creation of a regulatory council to review proposed new regulations to try to keep down their costs. This proposal was viewed as stepping up White House pressures on the United States Environmental Protection Agency (EPA) to aid the fight against inflation by relaxing costly environmental regulations. While some environmentalists were willing to accept the objective of making antipollution regulations more cost effective, many feared the anti-inflation drive would be used increasingly to undermine the basic goals of environmental laws.

Sun Day. Tens of thousands of Americans took part in a coast-to-coast observance of Sun Day on May 3. A sequel to the 1970 Earth Day observance that sparked environmental legislation in the United States, Sun Day was organized to increase public awareness of the promise of solar energy.

President Carter declared that making solar power a primary energy source for the United States is "a cornerstone of this nation's energy policy." He directed the Department of Energy to reallocate $100 million from other programs to solar research. This brought the budget's solar-energy commitment to $600 million.

Carter expressed the hope that solar energy would meet half the United States energy needs by the year 2020. Representative Mike McCormack (D., Wash.), chairman of a House subcommittee on energy research, warned that solar energy has real limits in spite of its advantages. "It can't possibly relieve our heavy reliance on coal and nuclear energy to fill our energy needs to the end of the century," he said on May 3.

Offshore Oil Legislation. President Carter signed an amendment to the Outer Continental Shelf (OCS) Lands Act on September 18. The legislation was the first change in the law since its enactment in 1953.

The amendment mandated changes to improve environmental safeguards in offshore oil and gas development and to promote greater cooperation between the federal government and the states in planning OCS projects. Carter said the legislation provided the framework for a well-coordinated program to make use of OCS energy resources.

About 1.6 million barrels of oil pours into the Atlantic Ocean from the stricken supertanker *Amoco Cadiz*, fouling France's Brittany coastline.

Nuclear Power. The battle over which path the United States should follow in its development of nuclear power intensified during the year. Voters in Kern County, California, voted 2 to 1 on March 7 against the construction there of what might have been the world's largest nuclear power plant. Montana voters on November 7 approved imposing severe restrictions on new nuclear power plants.

Despite warnings that "the lights may go out in California in five years" unless nuclear energy is developed, California Governor Edmund G. Brown, Jr., predicted an "energy bonanza" in the state from other sources. Demonstrations by the Clamshell Alliance, a coalition of antinuclear groups, stopped construction of the controversial Seabrook nuclear power plant in New Hampshire several times. The Nuclear Regulatory Commission decided in August that the cooling system was environmentally acceptable and construction could be resumed.

The Energy Bill. The energy program approved by Congress on October 15, after an 18-month effort, was a radical change from the energy package that the President had asked for in April 1977. Carter's proposal was designed to encourage the production of coal. The bill finally passed emphasized gradually relaxing controls on natural gas prices to boost natural gas production. Environmentalists were split on many aspects of the complex legislation, but most welcomed the tax credits it provided for home insulation and for installing solar, geothermal, and wind equipment. Many conservationists viewed the other energy-conservation measures – such as a tax on gas-guzzling automobiles, utility pricing, and conversion of power plants from oil and natural gas to coal – as too weak to have a significant impact.

Sea Law Pact. The Seventh United Nations Law of the Sea Conference session concluded on September 16 with the delegates still deadlocked over seabed-mining issues. Elliot L. Richardson, the chief U.S. representative, again called for legislation that would permit U.S. firms to begin mining the ocean's rich mineral resources before an international agreement is concluded. Richardson added that the United States remained committed to a treaty.

The next conference session was scheduled for March 1979 in Geneva, Switzerland. Agreement has been reached on about 90 per cent of the issues involved, but the seabed deadlock was expected to delay a treaty until 1980.

Clean Air. The EPA proposed strict new rules on September 11 for cleaning up air pollution from coal-fired electric-utility plants. Its proposal would require power plants to install expensive scrubbers to remove 85 per cent of the sulfur-dioxide emission.

The Natural Resources Defense Council called the proposal "perhaps the most significant single rule-making action" that EPA will take under the

1977 amendments to the Clean Air Act. The Edison Electric Institute, an industry association, charged that the proposal would cost U.S. consumers $3.19-billion more for electricity in 1990 than would have been required under the industry's approach to the clean-air problem. EPA Administrator Douglas M. Costle conceded that the question of how to implement the 1977 legislation "has been a difficult one." He said the agency would continue to consider alternative recommendations before final regulations are adopted, probably in March 1979.

EPA wrestled for many months trying to resolve the conflicting pressures on how strict to make the new regulations. Some staffers feared that the full scrubbing standards that were being proposed would force utilities to shift from low-sulfur western coal to less expensive but dirtier eastern coal, because the costly scrubbers would be required in either case. The EPA was also under pressure from the U.S. Department of Energy for an interpretation of the 1977 legislation that would permit a varying standard for sulfur removal as long as sulfur dioxide emissions were kept below specified levels. Utility spokesmen contended that the final decision would indicate whether President Carter was willing to take tough action to control inflation.

The EPA on August 10 proposed relaxed water-pollution standards for 18 industries. Under 1977 amendments to the Clean Water Act, the EPA can review existing requirements for industrial controls on water pollution. Costle said the agency was studying how to adjust its regulations to reduce their inflationary impact.

Range Improvement. President Carter signed legislation on October 25 authorizing the U.S. Bureau of Land Management to spend more than $360 million over the next 20 years to improve 170 million acres (68 million hectares) of federal rangelands. The Administration supported the Public Rangelands Improvement Act of 1970 as necessary to ensure increased productivity of rangelands.

The legislation also authorized the bureau to kill excess wild horses and burros, if necessary, to protect the lands. Legislation enacted in 1971 protected wild horses and burros. The Humane Society opposed any slaughter of the free-roaming animals, but the National Audubon Society supported such action because the horses and burros were harming the habitat of other wildlife.

Massive Oil Spill. After ramming a reef off France's Brittany coast on March 17, the oil tanker *Amoco Cadiz* broke in two and spilled 1.6 million barrels of oil over 400 square miles (1,000 square kilometers) of ocean. The spill was the worst ecological disaster in French history.   Andrew L. Newman

See also CONSERVATION; ENERGY. In WORLD BOOK, see ECOLOGY; ENVIRONMENT; ENVIRONMENTAL POLLUTION.

EQUATORIAL GUINEA. See AFRICA.

ETHIOPIA won major military victories against secessionists in two key regions of the country in 1978. With Russian and Cuban help, the government regained control in the Ogaden region and in Eritrea province.

The Ogaden, in southeastern Ethiopia, borders on Somalia. Most of its inhabitants are Somali-speaking people, and Somalia has long claimed the right to annex the area. Somali troops joined Ogaden guerrillas in a major offensive in July 1977 to get control of the region. They had captured most of the Ogaden and cut Ethiopia's main shipping route to the sea, the Addis Ababa-Djibouti railroad, before their advance was checked.

The Counterattack. Ethiopia launched a counter-offensive in January 1978 with the aid of more than 10,000 Cuban troops and 1,000 Russian military advisers, as well as Russian tanks, armored vehicles, and fighter planes. With Soviet and Cuban assistance, Ethiopia gained the advantage. Somalia appealed to the United States and West Germany for military aid in January, but without success.

Ethiopian forces regained control of the strategic town of Jijiga on March 5, cleared the rail link to Djibouti, and reached the Somali border at several places. Ethiopia Provisional Military Government Chairman Mengistu Haile Mariam promised not to cross the border, but he warned that lasting peace depended on Somalia's renouncing its claims to the Ogaden. Somalia's President Mohamed Siad Barre pledged on March 9 to withdraw all Somali troops from Ethiopia. However, his government was thought to have continued to encourage guerrilla warfare against Ethiopian rule.

Victory in Eritrea. Following the victories in the southeast, government forces concentrated on ending the 17-year-old secessionist rebellion in the northern province of Eritrea. Like the Somalis in the Ogaden, the Eritreans are ethnically unrelated to most Ethiopians, and they are Muslim while the majority of Ethiopians are Christians. Eritrean nationalists controlled about 90 per cent of the province in May, including all but five of the major towns and cities. Without Eritrea, which borders on the Red Sea, Ethiopia would be landlocked.

The government launched an offensive in May. It had regained control of 27 major towns and cities by early August and occupied the province's capital, Asmara. By early December, Ethiopia had gained control of Keren, the last major town held by secessionists, and had eradicated all but a few minor remnants of resistance in the province.

Extended Drought resulted in poor harvests and famine. By November, 2 million persons were near starvation in central Ethiopia, and another 98,000 faced desperate food shortages in the north-central section of the country.   John D. Esseks

See also AFRICA (Facts in Brief Table.) In WORLD BOOK, see ETHIOPIA; SOMALIA.

EUROPE

Caged members are among 29 Red Brigades terrorists who were sentenced to prison terms in Turin, Italy, in June on a variety of charges.

Europe struggled throughout 1978 to emerge from the economic doldrums left from the 1976 recession. International discussions centered on measures to raise productivity, halt rising unemployment, and minimize inflation. The decline of the United States dollar against European currencies gave impetus to efforts to set up a better system for limiting currency fluctuations.

The European Community (EC or Common Market) unveiled in April a five-year plan for a monetary and economic union. The plan calls for tying the economies of the nine member countries more closely and for freer circulation of goods and services. The EC agreed on December 21 to membership for Greece by Jan. 1, 1981. Slow progress was made toward admitting Spain and Portugal.

Terrorism continued to be a major problem, and the Rome kidnapping and murder of Italy's former Prime Minister Aldo Moro by the Red Brigades terrorist group shocked the world. See CLOSE-UP.

French voters averted the threat of a leftist take-over in March elections, but Belgium, Denmark, Finland, Portugal, and Sweden had severe political crises. West Germany's coalition government was shaky in the face of 1979 general elections, and British Prime Minister James Callaghan decided to try to maintain his minority government until 1979. Spain adopted a new Constitution, ushering in Western-style democracy.

Economic Doldrums. Leaders of the seven major Western nations – Canada, France, Great Britain, Italy, Japan, the United States, and West Germany – held the fourth World Economic Summit on July 16 and 17 in Bonn, West Germany. They discussed ways to promote economic growth, cut unemployment, and save energy. A report by the Organization for Economic Cooperation and Development had forecast rising unemployment in 1979 in the West unless the growth rate was boosted above 3.25 per cent.

The comprehensive strategy agreed upon in Bonn sent the seven leaders home to seek the support of their governments and citizens for new policies. President Jimmy Carter had to persuade the United States to take steps to cut oil imports by 2.5 million barrels per day by 1985 and raise the price of oil in the U.S. to world levels by 1980. West German Chancellor Helmut Schmidt had to persuade his country to stimulate its economy by up to 1 per cent of the gross national product. Japanese Prime Minister Takeo Fukuda had to try to stick to the 7 per cent growth target to which he was already committed for 1978. The other leaders had to try to expand their nations' economies. See INTERNATIONAL TRADE AND FINANCE.

The seven leaders agreed to stop all flights to any country that gives sanctuary to aircraft hijackers, and they called on other governments to do the same.

Monetary System. The EC discussed setting up a European Monetary System (EMS) to stabilize currencies and fight inflation. EC leaders, meeting in July in Bremen, West Germany, studied a French-West German proposal. The countries would set up a fund from which they could draw to hold their currencies within specified ranges of value. West Germany and the countries linked to it in the present currency *snake* of jointly floating European currencies – Belgium, Denmark, Luxembourg, the Netherlands, and Norway – would continue to keep their currencies within 2.25 per cent of one another. Any other country that joined the monetary union would have to hold its currency within a specified range of the currencies of the snake members. The linked currencies would then fluctuate as a unit against the U.S. dollar.

West Germany and France differed on some details. West Germany favored a *parity grid* system in which each currency would be held within a specified range of every other currency. If one currency moved very far against another, the central banks of the two countries would intervene to keep the currencies within the specified range.

France favored a *basket* system – each currency would be held within a specified range of the average value of the other currencies. If a country's currency moved very far from the average, only that country's central bank would intervene.

West Germany and France announced on September 18 that they had agreed on details. Their representatives told EC finance ministers in Brussels, Belgium, that their compromise proposal would blend the parity grid and basket plans.

The EC leaders decided on December 4 and 5 to base the EMS on the parity grid, with all currencies staying within 2.25 per cent of each other. Italy's currency would be an exception. It would be allowed to deviate 6 per cent. Within the parity grid system will be an early-warning system, based on the basket, that will indicate when currencies are approaching the 2.25 per cent limit (6 per cent, in the case of Italy), and which currency is moving. The country out of line will be "presumed" to take steps to raise or lower its currency's rate. If two currencies fluctuate beyond 2.25 per cent of each other (6 per cent, in the case of Italy), then both countries will intervene.

Great Britain decided not to join the EMS on its scheduled starting date of Jan. 1, 1979. Ireland and Italy decided initially not to join, but changed their decisions later in December.

Britain said it would link the pound to the EMS, but would not join the EMS formally. Some British feared that joining the EMS might lead eventually to a devaluation of the pound, making British exports more expensive, thus increasing domestic unemployment. Ireland and Italy wanted more industrial-development grants and low-interest loans. Italy's government finally decided to join on December 12 and received parliamentary approval on December 13. Ireland's Prime Minister Jack Lynch said on December 15 that the government had decided to join after EMS countries agreed to grant Ireland $50 million in both 1979 and 1980 to help it meet problems of linking its pound to stronger currencies. The money is an addition to the $90-million per year for five years that the EC promised Ireland.

On December 29, France blocked the start of the EMS in a dispute over farm subsidies.

Uranium Dispute. A confrontation between the United States and the EC over American supplies of enriched uranium lasted from April to July. The difficulty arose because only France among the EC members would not yield to a U.S. request to renegotiate the terms of supply until after international talks are held on nuclear fuel-cycle evaluation. The talks may not take place until the end of

Terrorism In Europe

On Oct. 4, 1978, the *Daily Mirror,* published in London, reported demands for an investigation into the sudden and unexpected death on September 28 of Pope John Paul I. "Ordinary Italians, desperately worried over the country's slide into lawlessness and terrorism, are asking if something sinister could have taken place behind Vatican walls," wrote the *Mirror's* Rome correspondent. And a leading Rome newspaper stated that lack of a post-mortem on the pope's body raised "inevitable doubts."

Terrorism in the Vatican in the 1970s? Shades of the Borgias? Such reports passed almost unnoticed on a continent where every country—even tiny, neutral Switzerland—has recently had to cope with terrorism.

Violence is nothing new in Europe. And the argument over whether it takes violent measures to cure what ails society, or whether violence and intolerance cause society's ills, is far from ended. Religious persecution, the Spanish Inquisition, the British Bloody Assizes, are well documented in history. Present-day terrorism is perhaps more closely allied to the Nihilists in Russia in the mid-1800s, who wanted to destroy all authority.

The causes for terrorism in 1978 varied from country to country. Separatists seeking national "states" in Spain and Switzerland used it to press their claims. The Netherlands had to cope with immigrant South Moluccans demanding that their home islands be made a republic independent from Indonesia. Dutch marines had to storm a provincial administration building in Assen on March 14 to free 70 hostages held there for a day by three South Moluccan terrorists.

The country most at risk from a breakdown of law and order inspired by radical political factions was Italy, where the kidnapping and murder of former Prime Minister Aldo Moro shocked the world. The Red Brigades, an extreme left wing group founded in 1969 by Renato Curcio and others with the slogan "Carry the Battle into the Heart of the State," kidnapped Moro on March 16 in a bloody ambush that left his five bodyguards dead. They demanded the liberation of Communist prisoners and played

Kidnapped Aldo Moro

a cat-and-mouse game with security forces until May 9, when Moro's body was found in a stolen car.

Nor was Moro the only victim in Italy. Judges, magistrates, journalists, and industrialists were shot, most of them wounded in the legs, in city streets. By the end of September, kidnappers had seized their 30th Italian victim in 1978, a Florence businessman. Curcio was sentenced to 15 years in jail on June 23, and 28 other Red Brigades members were sent to prison for from three to 14 years.

West Germany has taken a firm stand on terrorists since the murder of industrialist Hanns-Martin Schleyer in September 1977 and the hijacking of a Lufthansa plane and subsequent prison suicide of terrorist Andreas Baader in October 1977. An antiterrorism operations center at Karlsruhe, led by federal prosecutor Kurt Rebmann, claimed to have disrupted terrorists' plans, damaged their organizations, and seized their arms.

Several members of the notorious Baader-Meinhof gang were arrested and returned to West Germany from other countries in 1978. The most notable among these was Gabriele Rollnick, arrested in Bulgaria. Another, Astrid Proll, found in London, where she worked under another name, also faces extradition. Nevertheless, West Germany's leaders talked of "a new breed of terrorists," probably financed by neo-fascists.

In the face of this growing threat, Europe showed a new spirit of international cooperation in 1978. Canada, Japan, and the United States joined France, Great Britain, Italy, and West Germany to deal with one form of terrorism on July 17. They agreed to boycott any nation that fails to extradite hijackers that land on its soil. The determination of each country not to submit to demands made under duress may show terrorists that their operations yield scant profit.

The wave of terrorism may recede, but it is doubtful if it can ever be totally eliminated. There will always be those persons who insist that they have the medicine to cure all of society's ills and that terror is the only way that they can get others to accept that medicine.   Kenneth Brown

Facts in Brief on the European Countries

Country	Population	Government†	Monetary Unit*	Foreign Trade (million U.S. $) Exports	Imports
Albania	2,794,000	Communist Party First Secretary Enver Hoxha; People's Assembly Presidium Chairman Hashi Lleshi; Prime Minister Mehmet Shehu	lek (9.8 = $1)	60	98
Andorra	36,000	The bishop of Urgel, Spain, and the president of France	French franc and Spanish peseta	no statistics available	
Austria	7,614,000	President Rudolf Kirchschlaeger; Chancellor Bruno Kreisky	schilling (14.1 = $1)	9,808	14,248
Belgium	9,914,000	King Baudouin I; Prime Minister Paul vanden Boeynants	franc (30.3 = $1)	37,457 (includes Luxembourg)	40,142
Bulgaria	8,941,000	Communist Party First Secretary & State Council Chairman Todor Zhivkov; Prime Minister Stanko Todorov	lev (1.2 = $1)	6,329	6,329
Czechoslovakia	15,161,000	Communist Party General Secretary & President Gustav Husak, Prime Minister Lubomir Strougal	koruna (11.1 = $1)	10,818	11,149
Denmark	5,161,000	Queen Margrethe II; Prime Minister Anker Henrik Jorgensen	krone (5.4 = $1)	10,117	13,239
Finland	4,783,000	President Urho Kekkonen; Prime Minister Kalevi Sorsa	markka (4.1 = $1)	7,670	7,603
France	54,040,000	President Valéry Giscard d'Estaing; Prime Minister Raymond Barre	franc (4.4 = $1)	63,560	70,498
Germany, East	16,716,000	Communist Party Secretary General & State Council Chairman Erich Honecker; Prime Minister Willi Stoph	mark (2.1 = $1)	11,361	13,196
Germany, West	62,827,000	President Walter Scheel; Chancellor Helmut Schmidt	Deutsche mark (1.9 = $1)	117,895	100,672
Great Britain	56,387,000	Queen Elizabeth II; Prime Minister James Callaghan	pound (1 = $1.94)	57,457	63,677
Greece	9,302,000	President Constantine Tsatsos; Prime Minister Constantine Karamanlis	drachma (34.5 = $1)	2,724	6,778
Hungary	10,710,000	Communist Party First Secretary Janos Kadar; President Pal Losonczi; Prime Minister Gyorgy Lazar	forint (19.5 = $1)	5,832	6,522
Iceland	221,000	President Kristjan Eldjarn; Prime Minister Olafur Johannesson	króna (307 = $1)	513	607
Ireland	3,280,000	President Patrick J. Hillery; Prime Minister Jack Lynch	pound (1 = $1.94)	4,396	5,378
Italy	57,618,000	President Alessandro Pertini; Prime Minister Giulio Andreotti	lira (833 = $1)	45,063	47,580
Liechtenstein	27,000	Prince Francis Joseph II	Swiss franc	no statistics available	
Luxembourg	371,000	Grand Duke Jean; Prime Minister Gaston Thorn	franc (30.3 = $1)	37,457 (includes Belgium)	40,142
Malta	331,000	President Anton Buttigieg; Prime Minister Dom Mintoff	pound (1 = $2.68)	289	513
Monaco	27,000	Prince Rainier III	French franc	no statistics available	
Netherlands	14,151,000	Queen Juliana; Prime Minister Andreas A. M. Van Agt	guilder (2.1 = $1)	43,703	45,616
Norway	4,120,000	King Olav V; Prime Minister Odvar Nordli	króne (5.2 = $1)	8,717	12,877
Poland	35,261,000	Communist Party First Secretary Edward Gierek; President Henryk Jablonski; Council of Ministers Chairman Piotr Jaroszewicz	zloty (19.9 = $1)	12,336	14,674
Portugal	8,832,000	President Antonio Dos Santos Ramalho Eanes; Prime Minister Carlos da Mota Pinto	escudo (47.6 = $1)	2,023	4,963
Romania	21,951,000	Communist Party General Secretary & President Nicolae Ceausescu; Prime Minister Manea Manescu	leu (5 = $1)	6,138	6,095
Russia	266,403,000	Communist Party General Secretary & Supreme Soviet Presidium Chairman Leonid Ilich Brezhnev; Council of Ministers Chairman Aleksey Nikolayevich Kosygin	ruble (1 = $1.46)	45,161	40,817
San Marino	21,000	2 regents appointed by Grand Council every 6 months	Italian lira	no statistics available	
Spain	37,210,000	King Juan Carlos I; Prime Minister Adolfo Suarez Gonzalez	peseta (71.4 = $1)	10,230	17,846
Sweden	8,327,000	King Carl XVI Gustaf; Prime Minister Ola Ullsten	krona (4.5 = $1)	18,823	19,566
Switzerland	6,584,000	President Hans Huerlimann	franc (1.7 = $1)	17,682	17,979
Turkey	44,100,000	President Fahri S. Koruturk; Prime Minister Bulent Ecevit	lira (25.3 = $1)	1,753	5,694
Yugoslavia	22,131,000	President Josip Broz Tito; Prime Minister Veselin Djuranovic	dinar (18.8 = $1)	5,254	9,634

*Exchange rates as of Dec. 1, 1978. †As of Dec. 31, 1978.

1979. The French relented, however; the EC said on July 10 it was ready to discuss adapting present arrangements for U.S. uranium supplies to bring them into line with the U.S. 1978 Nuclear Nonproliferation Act.

Steel Limits. The EC and the United States agreed in Brussels on May 26 to work for an international agreement that would deal with problems created by the world steel recession. The EC planned tougher sanctions against companies breaking minimum-price rules, in a bid to curb overproduction and limit stockpiling.

Experts told the EC that Europe's steel industry would lose another 100,000 jobs in the next two years—on top of 40,000 jobs lost since December 1975. The losses would reduce the work force to 720,000 persons. The EC asked steelmakers on September 13 to hold total production to 34 million short tons (31 million metric tons) in the final quarter of the year to prevent supply from overrunning demand and depressing prices further.

The Arms Gap. Russia and its Warsaw Pact allies continued to build up nuclear and conventional armaments and widened the gap with the North Atlantic Treaty Organization (NATO), the London-based International Institute for Strategic Studies (IISS) said on August 31. But the IISS added that the overall balance still makes military aggression in Europe unattractive for Russia. Russia would run incalculable risks, including nuclear escalation. The IISS said that Russia had deployed at least 370 new intercontinental ballistic missiles during the previous year and had added 7,000 tanks.

NATO members agreed on a defense plan for the next 15 years at a summit meeting in Washington, D.C., in May. The plan emphasized fighting capabilities in Western Europe.

NATO was split on how to react to Russian involvement in Africa. President Jimmy Carter said that the West "cannot be indifferent" to Russian and Cuban activities there. British Prime Minister Callaghan, however, said that Russia and Cuba were exploiting old regional and group tensions. "Let's not start off assuming this is an East-West matter in its origins," he said.

Disarmament Progress. The 31-country United Nations Committee on Disarmament made progress toward a treaty banning all nuclear-weapon tests. Members also agreed at a special session in Geneva, Switzerland, in June to rotate the chairmanship monthly. The United States and Russia had held the post jointly, but France said that it would take part if the chairmanship were shared with other countries.

The fifth year of force-reduction talks between NATO and the Warsaw Pact nations ended on October 25 with no agreement. Both sides agreed to reduce their armies to 700,000 persons, but they disagreed on how many troops Warsaw Pact nations would have to withdraw to reach that number.

Agricultural Issues. The EC resolved an old dispute with Great Britain concerning support prices paid to British farmers under the EC's Common Agricultural Policy. Great Britain wanted the EC to increase guaranteed prices 8.1 per cent. West Germany, the Netherlands, and Belgium had blocked an earlier British request to do so, but the EC granted the request in Brussels on January 31. The EC had difficulty in agreeing on prices to be paid to the EC's 8.5 million farmers. A May agreement after five months of haggling resulted in an average increase of 2.25 per cent in support prices.

A Fishing Dispute isolated Great Britain from its EC partners in January. The European Commission, the EC's executive branch, joined the eight other EC countries in refusing to accept the British demand for preferential access to waters between 12 and 50 nautical miles off the British coast. Britain vetoed a resolution drafted by the EC's agricultural ministers on January 30 and 31 in Brussels to control conservation, licensing, quotas, and patrols. The EC's existing fishing regulations expired on February 1, giving way to national regulations.

Britain then decided to fix herring quotas in British waters unilaterally. Minister for Agriculture and Fisheries John E. Silkin told EC ministers in Luxembourg on June 19 that Britain's demands were elementary justice. Then, on July 26, Great Britain asserted its right to veto EC fishing measures it judged harmful to its national interests. The commission told Silkin on August 22 that unilateral measures to protect herring stocks were unacceptable. The measures, enforced after August 21, reduced the permissible herring catch in the Irish Sea from 13,750 to 9,900 short tons (12,500 to 9,000 metric tons) in the 1978 season, and closed the area to all herring fishing after September 24. British fishermen may take up to 8,900 short tons (8,100 metric tons), leaving 1,000 short tons (900 metric tons) for boats from other EC countries.

European Parliament. EC leaders agreed on April 7 in Copenhagen, Denmark, to hold direct elections to the European Parliament in June 1979. National legislatures of member countries had chosen the previous parliaments.

Each country will decide how to elect its representatives to the 410-seat parliament. The most common methods of election in Europe are the proportional and first-past-the-post. In a proportional election, political parties are awarded seats according to the proportion of the popular vote each receives. A first-past-the-post election is made up of simultaneous elections for individual seats, as in the United States.

Talks With COMECON. An EC delegation told representatives of the Communist-bloc's Council for Mutual Economic Assistance (COMECON) in Moscow on May 30 that direct trade between the two groups was unlikely. Neither group formally

Russia's Leonid I. Brezhnev, left, arrives in Prague, Czechoslovakia, on May 30 for a four-day visit. With him is Czechoslovak President Gustav Husak.

recognizes the other. They discussed mutual recognition in November talks in Brussels.

Iceland's New Government. Iceland's Cabinet resigned on June 26 after suffering heavy losses in the general election the day before. The ruling coalition of the Independence and Progressive parties still had 32 of the 60 seats in the *Althing* (parliament), but the Progressives withdrew from the coalition. The Marxist People's Alliance and the Social Democrats won 14 seats each. The major election issue was inflation, running at 40 per cent.

The Progressives, Marxists, and Social Democrats formed a government on August 31 with Progressive Olafur Johannesson as prime minister. In reaching agreement with the other parties, the Marxist party dropped its demand to take Iceland out of NATO, and supported a devaluation of the króna.

The Iceland government announced drastic economic measures on September 10 – a wage freeze effective until Dec. 1, 1979; food subsidies based on living costs; a tax on currency sold in banks for travel; higher income taxes for middle-income earners; a 50 per cent increase in private property taxes; a 100 per cent increase in business property taxes; and increased duties on imported luxuries. Kenneth Brown

See also the various European country articles. In WORLD BOOK, see EUROPE; NORTH ATLANTIC TREATY ORGANIZATION (NATO).

EXPLOSION. See DISASTERS.

FAIRS AND EXPOSITIONS. More than 800 international trade fairs were held in 1978, 264 of them in the United States. Collectively, they displayed nearly every product made by human beings or machines. Sports and leisure-equipment fairs predominated among those held outside the United States. There were 50 such expositions. Next in interest were fashion events, with 40 held in other countries. The electronics industry, displaying everything from audio-visual material to the most sophisticated computer systems, hosted 30 shows overseas, a gain of eight over 1977.

More than 2,500 agricultural fairs were held in North America in 1978, some 50 of them in New York state. Typical was New York's Orange County Fair, which opened for a week on July 28 and combined competition and entertainment with the traditional display of livestock and prize agricultural products. Ox-pulling competitions tended to dominate at about 75 New England fairs, with the oxen divided into classes according to weight.

Frontier Days, a big 10-day rodeo, opened in Cheyenne, Wyo., on July 20. By the week's end, more than 150,000 visitors had arrived to view the festivities, which included some of the roughest and wildest rodeo events anywhere. The Owyhee Cattlemen's Association, one of the country's oldest, celebrated its 100th anniversary in the old mining town of Silver City, Ida. The association was formed in

1878 to protect ranchers from Indians. The celebration drew 2,000 visitors.

The 78th convention of the American Booksellers Association was held in Atlanta, Ga., in June. With an estimated attendance of 20,000, it was by far the largest book fair ever held by this group. Many British, Australian, Canadian, and Israeli publishers attended, bearing out the 1977 forecast that this event is becoming the English-language equivalent of West Germany's Frankfurt Book Fair.

Flea Markets. Across the United States, inflation-weary citizens turned flea markets into big business in 1978. Thousands of these street markets operated in parking lots, outside discount stores, in open fields, and at drive-in theaters, offering everything from shells and sponges to figurines, furniture, and appliances. One of the largest, in Houston, attracted 15,000 bargain hunters each weekend. Flea markets achieved enough respectability for the U. S. Economic Development Administration to fund a permanent one in Washington, D.C.

At the seventh annual International Hot Air Balloon Fair in Albuquerque, N. Mex., in October, the maximum number of 270 launching pads were filled for the first time. The biggest ballooning event in history, it attracted more than 250,000 spectators.

Caribbean Events. The 11th annual Caribbean Festival took place in New York City in September. Sponsors reported that 1,600 islanders from the United States and several Caribbean countries took part in the celebration, and an estimated 2 million persons enjoyed the dancing, food, a parade, and music by hundreds of bands.

Nearly 20,000 delegates from 145 countries went to the 11th International Youth Festival, which opened July 28 in Havana, Cuba. The group included 400 young people from the United States. The Cuban government used the occasion to make some political propaganda, but also organized block parties that enabled visitors to meet Cuban citizens.

Other Shows. The National Fancy Food and Confection Show held its 24th annual fair in July in New York City. An estimated 15,000 buyers worked their way through 200 displays of more than 4,000 products, including cheeses, sausages, beers and bottled waters, and an array of packaged foods.

The International Inventors Expo 78, which opened in New York City for three days on July 15, featured 178 participants. They displayed a variety of inventions ranging from a spokeless bicycle wheel to a game that combined lawn golf with Monopoly.

The National Arts and Antiques Show, one of America's largest, was held in New York City in October. More than 150 exhibitors attracted an audience of 75,000 persons who browsed and shopped their way through 6,000 years of art treasures and a photography exhibit.　　Lynn Beaumont

In WORLD BOOK, see FAIRS and EXPOSITIONS.

FARM MACHINERY. See MANUFACTURING.

FASHION took a dramatic turn midway through 1978. The casually loose, free-flowing silhouettes of the early part of the year suddenly slimmed down. There was a growing sense of structure. The paring away of volume meant sharper tailoring and a clearer definition of the figure. Broad shoulders loomed above belted waists, hip-rounding skirts, and pegged pants. The new shape was that of an isosceles triangle standing on its point as it tapered hemward from the extended shoulders. Shoulder pads were resurrected, as were the severe, tailored business suits and whimsical little tilted hats worn by 1940s and 1950s movie heroines. Sultry black dresses worn with elaborately rolled upswept hairdos, silver-fox boas, braceleted gloves, and spike-heeled sandals summed up the mood of nostalgic glamour.

The "Retro Look," as French fashionables called it, looked best when carried off with a touch of humor by young people dressed for disco dancing.

Also revived in 1978 were strapless tops, bust darts, midriff seams, drop-dead Hollywood-style shirring, cummerbunds, waist cinchers, obi wraps, and toreador-snug pants as designers zoomed in on the body. The new high visibility of the female form—in both skin-tight dresses and slits that revealed a lot of skin—started with the Paris fall collections and was later strengthened in United States and European ready-to-wear showings.

Many retailers were cool toward the new curvier clothes. Some considered them in bad taste, but the fashion industry was convinced that the narrow, sensuous silhouette was the next direction because women have been preoccupied with jogging and keeping fit. They were tired of hiding their hard-earned figures under layers of wraps.

Shoulders and Shape made their debut in the exaggerated and controversial collections of a new group of young influential designers. In Milan, Italy, Giorgio Armani and Gianni Versace sent models marching down the runways in militaristic, bold-shouldered outfits of leather and khaki. The Paris padding was provided by the gargantuan-shouldered topcoats of Claude Montana, Jean Claude de Luca, and Thierry Mugler. The fervent customer acceptance of pencil-slim separates by Americans Perry Ellis and Calvin Klein plus the daring tight-torso dresses of Karl Lagerfeld for Chloé pointed the way back to the body.

There was a resurgence of the complete costume, away from the sportswear concept, with jackets and skirts in matching or related fabrics meant to be worn together. A new selection of handsome coats included reefers, reversibles, and three-quarter or seven-eighth length garments tailored in melton, alpaca, and tweed.

Textures were mixed with abandon, the more varied the better—crunchy weaves with smooth flannels, leather with crepe de Chine, suede with satin, lace with snakeskin. Combinations of several neutral shades were jolted with an electric streak of color – violet, orange, or turquoise. Gold-shot chiffons, whisper-weight lamés, sequins and bugle beads added all-out dazzle to nights.

Menswear. The overall feeling was more relaxed with "unconstructed" jackets and a slouchier look somewhat reminiscent of the baggy styles of the 1930s. Tweeds dominated suits, jackets, and coats. The raglan-sleeve coat gained new adherence as opposed to the fitted coat. Trousers were flared less or not flared at all. Lapels, ties, and shirt collars narrowed. The single most important accessory was the scarf worn outside the jacket. Evening wear particularly reflected this scarf conceit – the silken, white, fringed scarf was everywhere.

The Coty Awards. Two Winnie awards for outstanding achievement were given in the women's category. Bill Atkinson won a Winnie for an inventive mix of colorings and patterns, and Charles Suppon was recognized for his offbeat treatment of texture on texture. Mary McFadden received the Return Award for her exotic evening dresses. Menswear designer Bill Kaiserman was given a special Hall of Fame citation. The men's fashion Winnie went to Robert Stock. Danskin and Head ski wear were given awards for creativity, as were Joan and David Halpern, shoe designers. Kathryn Livingston

In WORLD BOOK, see FASHION.

Multilayered outfits of classic wool and suede were favored by designer Bill Atkinson, 1978 Coty American Fashion Critics Award winner.

FEINSTEIN, DIANNE (1933-   ), became acting mayor of San Francisco on Nov. 27, 1978, following the assassination of Mayor George R. Moscone. On December 4, the Board of Supervisors selected her as mayor. She will serve until the end of 1979. See SAN FRANCISCO-OAKLAND.

Dianne Goldman Feinstein was born on June 22, 1933, in San Francisco. Her father was Jewish; her mother, Roman Catholic. In later life, Feinstein chose the Jewish faith. She attended the Convent of the Sacred Heart and Stanford University, where she earned a degree in history and political science.

While in college, Feinstein demonstrated acute political skills and, after graduation, she won a Coro Foundation fellowship that permitted her to spend a year as an intern in various city agencies in San Francisco.

In 1961, Feinstein was appointed to California's Women's Board of Terms and Paroles. Subsequently, she was named to a number of city boards and firmly established her reputation as a reformer and an environmentalist. She was elected to the Board of Supervisors of the County and City of San Francisco in 1969 and was elected board president three times.

Mayor Feinstein, a widow, has been married twice. Her first marriage, to lawyer Jack Berman, was dissolved. In 1962, she married Bertram Feinstein, who died in 1977. She has a daughter, Katherine Ann, by her first marriage. Paul C. Tullier

FIGUEIREDO, JOÃO BAPTISTA DE OLIVEIRA (1918-   ), was elected president of Brazil on Oct. 15, 1978. He succeeded Ernesto Geisel, who had decided not to run for re-election. Geisel's five-year term was to end on March 15, 1979. See BRAZIL.

Figueiredo was born in Rio de Janeiro on Jan. 15, 1918. His father, General Euclydes Figueiredo, became a national hero when he helped lead an unsuccessful revolt that sought to restore civilian rule in Brazil in 1932. At the age of 10, Figueiredo entered military school in Pôrto Alegre. Later he attended the junior officer's school and the army command and general staff school. He was a teacher during much of his army career, first in the cavalry and later in intelligence. He also served with the Brazilian military mission in Paraguay, the armed forces general staff, and the National Security Council. Eventually, he headed the Rio office of the National Information Service (NIS) and the military police force in São Paulo before being named chief of staff of the powerful Third Army of Pôrto Alegre. He served as chief of the NIS from 1974 to 1978, but he resigned from that post to run for the presidency.

Figueiredo married Dulce Guimaraes de Castro. They have two grown sons. His favorite sport is horseback riding, but he also enjoys playing chess. He is said to be a self-effacing man who avoids the limelight as much as possible. Paul C. Tullier

FINLAND. President Urho Kekkonen was re-elected to his fourth consecutive term in January 1978. The parties backing Kekkonen won 84 per cent of the vote.

On February 16, six days after an 8 per cent devaluation of Norway's monetary unit, the krone, Finland devalued the markka 8 per cent. Disagreement within the government led Prime Minister Kalevi Sorsa and his Cabinet to resign. A majority of the five-party center-left coalition favored the devaluation. But the Social Democrats wanted a smaller devaluation and other economic measures, and the Communists opposed devaluation. Sorsa continued in office and formed another coalition. But he faced Finland's worst economic crisis since the 1930s, with unemployment at about 8 per cent and low real income and domestic demand.

A July 20 agreement with Australia on safeguards cleared the way for Finland to import Australian uranium for its power plants. Finland would need Australian consent to enrich the uranium, to reprocess it for use as a fuel, or to export it to another country. Australia reserved the right to halt shipments if Finland violates International Atomic Energy Agency safeguards.   Kenneth Brown

See also Europe (Facts in Brief Table). In World Book, see Finland.

FIRE. See Disasters.

FISHING. Two world records for swordfish were set in Florida in 1978 as more anglers took their boats out for night fishing. Stephen Stanford of Miami landed a swordfish weighing 612 pounds 12 ounces (278 kilograms) on May 7, 1978, a new 80-pound (36-kilogram) line-class record. The fish was hooked off Miami at 2 A.M. and landed at 8 A.M. Mark Houghtaling of Miami set the second record May 21, landing a 196-pound (89-kilogram) broadbill swordfish on 20-pound (9-kilogram) line.

The records were among those certified during the year by the International Game Fish Association (IGFA), based in Fort Lauderdale, Fla. IGFA has been the official record-keeping organization for saltwater game-fish records since 1939. *Field and Stream* magazine transferred its freshwater record-keeping system to the IGFA in June. The IGFA started a freshwater fishing contest recognizing the three largest fish caught in each species category and said it would establish freshwater angling rules.

On March 14, armed game wardens of the Crow Indian Tribe closed the section of the Bighorn River in Montana that passes through their reservation after fishermen began fishing on the reservation.

California continued to lead in sales of fishing licenses in 1977 with 5.3 million sold. Michigan was runner-up with 1.6 million.   Andrew L. Newman

In World Book, see Fishing.

U.S. Coast Guardsman checks fishermen on Lake St. Clair on the Canadian border as fishing-zone dispute grows between Canada and U.S.

FISHING INDUSTRY. A heated dispute between Canadian and United States fishermen broke out in 1978. Canadians began to expel fishermen from the United States from Canadian fishing waters on June 4, and the United States retaliated in kind after negotiations between the two countries on a treaty setting maritime boundaries broke down.

President Jimmy Carter signed legislation on July 1 that authorized an interim agreement with Canada to allow fishermen from each country to resume traditional fishing patterns in the waters of the other while discussions continued. Carter said he hoped that "we can now immediately proceed to restore" reciprocal fisheries that have existed since the 1700s. Negotiations to resume reciprocal fishing, as well as to draft a maritime treaty, remained stalled in December. The "fishing war" created economic hardships for both U.S. fishermen and consumers. Since the best fishing grounds for such species as scallops are on the Canadian side of George's Bank, which lies off Cape Cod but within the 200-nautical-mile limit of both countries, the U.S. supply diminished and prices on the East Coast rose as much as 70 cents per pound (0.45 kilogram).

New Regulations. The 1977 Fishery Conservation and Management Act was amended, effective on August 29. The new provision allows fish-processing vessels of other countries to buy fish caught by U.S. fishermen within 200 nautical miles of the U.S. coast. But such fish may be bought only if American processors do not intend to process them. Reports from the National Marine Fisheries Service (NMFS) indicated that the first year of operation under the 1977 act was a success. Officials cited a modest increase in the United States catch and signs of vigor in the fishing industry. Orders for new fishing vessels and fishing gear increased significantly. Other nations paid $10 million to fish in the 200-nautical-mile zone in 1978; Japan paid the largest fee, $5.9 million.

Peruvian Anchovies came under that South American government's protection on February 11, when all catches were banned. Stocks of the fish have declined sharply since 1972, and the Marine Institute in Callao, Peru, warned early in 1978 that any further anchovy fishing before the schools have a chance to increase could ruin the Peruvian industry. Peru's catches of anchovies were processed primarily into cattle feed and oil for margarine.

Aquaculture in the United States may one day rival agriculture as a supplier of much-needed protein. About 5,000 food and nonfood corporations are now engaged in fish farming projects, and the number increases yearly. For example, the Coca-Cola Company plans to produce 33 short tons (30 metric tons) of shrimp in 1978 in its farm ponds off the Gulf of California. The Weyerhaeuser Company, known for forestry rather than fisheries, expects to harvest its first salmon crop from ocean pens in

A crabbing vessel being built for Alaskan waters reflects the hopes of fishermen encouraged by recent record prices for fish and shellfish.

1979. Union Carbide Corporation has been raising salmon in pens off Bremerton, Wash., for eight years, and officials predicted the pens will turn their first profit in 1978.

Porpoise Progress. Officials of NMFS said on September 1 that the tuna industry's performance in 1978 proves that the quota system on porpoise kills is workable. The fishermen in September predicted a possible record year in 1978 that would turn 1977's loss of $40 million to $70 million into a $100-million profit. Some fishermen attributed their success in holding down porpoise kills to their "good fortune" in catching many skipjack tuna, rather than yellow-fin tuna. They said that larger skipjack catches usually mean that fewer porpoises are netted accidentally because porpoises more often swim with the yellowfin.

The value of fish and shellfish landed by U.S. commercial fishermen during 1977 reached an all-time high of more than $1.6 billion, though the 5.3-billion pounds (2.4 billion kilograms) landed was down 4 per cent from 1976. The number of nonedible industrial fish caught decreased, while the catches of shrimp, crab, salmon, tuna, and flounder increased.   Andrew L. Newman

In WORLD BOOK, see FISHING INDUSTRY.
FLOOD. See DISASTERS.
FLORIDA. See STATE GOVERNMENT.
FLOWER. See GARDENING.

FOOD prices rose rapidly in the United States in early 1978, jumping 8 per cent from January to July. Although the rate of increase slowed after that, retail food prices for the year still averaged about 10 per cent above 1977. This double-digit inflation rate for food prices had been exceeded only twice in 25 years—increases of a little more than 14 per cent were recorded in 1973 and again in 1974.

Smaller supplies of a few key food products accounted for part of the price rise. Chief among those was beef, the mainstay of the American meat menu. Total production declined about 4 per cent from the previous year and was about 7 per cent below the record 1976 high. After several years of poor economic returns and adverse weather, cattlemen had reduced the size of their herds.

Pork supplies, which normally would have expanded to help fill the void left by smaller beef supplies, increased very little. Cold weather and disease during the winter, along with high costs for new production facilities, were the major causes. Poultry producers responded to the smaller beef supplies and higher meat prices by expanding broiler output some 7 per cent. But this was not enough to offset the beef reduction, and total meat and poultry production fell slightly below the 1977 level.

Bad Weather. The most dramatic example of short supply causing high prices occurred during the winter when excessive rains and flooding disrupted lettuce harvesting and planting in California. Retail lettuce prices skyrocketed in a matter of days when the crops could not be harvested.

But lettuce was not the only produce item to be affected by weather. Citrus supplies were smaller as a result of the freeze in Florida in early 1977, which affected the 1978 crop. Cold spring weather and poor pollination also reduced supplies of several noncitrus fruits and tree nuts. Then rains in California during the late summer turned a bountiful grape harvest into a shortage of raisins, driving their prices sharply higher late in the year.

Strong Consumer Demand undoubtedly also contributed to higher prices. Continued economic growth resulted in large employment gains. Rising wages also provided consumers with more purchasing power and increased demand. Higher prices for meats, fruits, vegetables, and convenience foods were at least partly attributable to this demand.

The demand for U.S. farm products in other countries was also strong. Led by large increases for grains, soybeans, and oilseed products, farm exports for the fiscal year ending in September reached $27.3 billion, 20 per cent above the previous year.

All of these factors contributed to a sharp upturn in average farm commodity prices. The farm value of domestically produced foods, which had remained steady since 1974 in the face of rising farm production expenses, rose nearly 17 per cent in 1978. Consequently, for the first time in four years, higher farm commodity prices contributed to higher retail food prices and, in turn, to the overall inflation rate.

While rising food prices contributed to increased inflation, general inflation also contributed to higher food prices. About 60 per cent of the total cost of an average market basket represents costs incurred after the commodities leave the farm. Such charges rose about 7½ per cent in 1978, mainly reflecting rising wages and energy and packaging costs.

Generic Labeling. One of the newest competitive tactics adopted by many food retailers was the introduction of *generic* food products—items with no trademark. During the spring of 1978, about 20 retail chains carried generic labels; by midsummer, the ranks had swelled to about 100 firms. Sometimes referred to as "no-frills" products, these items reportedly offer consumers savings because of cheaper ingredients, less advertising and promotion, and less expensive packaging and labeling.

Electronic Checkout. The use of electronic scanning devices at supermarket checkout counters continued to grow, but not as fast as expected. Only 309 scanning installations were reported by June, well below a widely circulated industry estimate that 7,500 installations would be in place by the end of 1975. Organized opposition by unions and consumer groups proved more widespread and effective than the industry had anticipated.

Per Capita U.S. Food Consumption, 1977–1978

	1977	1978
	Pounds (Kilograms)	
Milk and cream	289.4 (131.3)	288.9 (131.0)
Potatoes	119.8 (54.3)	125.4 (56.9)
Fresh vegetables	93.2 (42.3)	95.2 (43.2)
Sugar	95.7 (43.4)	93.2 (42.3)
Beef	93.2 (42.3)	89.0 (40.4)
Fresh fruits	81.2 (36.8)	80.4 (36.5)
Pork	56.7 (25.7)	56.7 (25.7)
Canned vegetables	52.9 (24.0)	53.0 (24.0)
Chicken	44.9 (20.4)	47.5 (21.5)
Eggs	34.5 (15.6)	34.6 (15.7)
Ice cream	17.7 (8.0)	17.7 (8.0)
Cheese	16.4 (7.4)	17.4 (7.9)
Canned fruits	20.0 (9.1)	17.2 (7.8)
Fish	12.8 (5.8)	12.9 (5.8)
Margarine	11.6 (5.3)	11.9 (5.4)
Frozen fruits and fruit juices	11.9 (5.4)	11.4 (5.2)
Frozen vegetables	10.3 (4.7)	10.9 (4.9)
Turkey	9.2 (4.2)	9.5 (4.3)
Coffee	6.9 (3.1)	7.3 (3.3)
Butter	4.4 (2.0)	4.6 (2.1)
Veal	3.2 (1.4)	2.5 (1.1)
Lamb and mutton	1.5 (0.7)	1.4 (0.6)
Tea	0.9 (0.4)	0.8 (0.4)

Source: U.S. Department of Agriculture.

Workers harvest lettuce in California's Salinas Valley in May. Heavy winter rains washed out much of the early crop, raising the prices to consumers.

Food Additives. The use of nitrates and nitrites in processing meats continued to be a source of scientific debate and public controversy. Scientists have known since the early 1960s that nitrite interacts with substances in meat to produce compounds that are generally considered to cause cancer. The U.S. Department of Agriculture issued proposals in April and May to reduce the levels of nitrite used in bacon. The agency also proposed to prohibit the use of nitrate- or nitrite-cured meat in baby foods.

The Department of Agriculture and the Food and Drug Administration issued a statement on August 11 making public the results of a Massachusetts Institute of Technology study on nitrites. The study suggests that nitrite produces cancer of the lymphatic system in test animals. While the study indicates that nitrites may pose a risk to human health, they also protect against the formation of botulism toxin, a deadly food poison. The issue was unresolved as the year ended; the two types of health risks will have to be weighed to provide maximum public protection.

On November 28, the Federal Trade Commission (FTC) proposed tough new standards for food advertisements. Among other changes, the FTC would curb the use of terms such as "organic" and "natural" and require supporting evidence for other advertising claims.   Larry V. Summers

See AGRICULTURE. In WORLD BOOK, see FOOD.

FOOTBALL. The Dallas Cowboys and Pittsburgh Steelers, two of the most successful teams of the decade, were the strongest teams in 1978, the National Football League's (NFL) longest and perhaps most troubled season. After the bowl games on New Year's Day 1979, the University of Alabama and the University of Southern California both claimed the college championship.

The NFL reshaped the professional game for television. The regular season, formerly 14 games per team, was lengthened to 16 games. The exhibition season, formerly six games per team, was reduced to four games. Two wild-card teams were added to the play-offs, so the six division champions were joined by four wild-card teams rather than two. Rules were changed to protect pass receivers and ease the job of pass blockers. Televised games were added on Sunday and Thursday nights.

The result, according to *Sports Illustrated,* was, "Too many games, too many flags, too few good teams, and only one real star — rookie running back Earl Campbell of the Houston Oilers." In addition, there were season-long controversies over officiating errors and, of all things, cheerleaders.

NFL Season. The six division winners were Pittsburgh (14-2), Dallas and the Los Angeles Rams (12-4), New England Patriots (11-5), Denver Broncos (10-6), and Minnesota Vikings (8-7-1). They were joined in the play-offs by the Miami Dolphins (11-5), Houston Oilers (10-6), and the Philadelphia Eagles and Atlanta Falcons (9-7).

The Washington Redskins won their first six games, then lost eight of their last 10. The St. Louis Cardinals, under their new coach, Bud Wilkinson, lost their first eight games, then won six of their last eight. The San Francisco 49'ers (2-14) suffered when injuries slowed O. J. Simpson, the legendary running back. Quarterback injuries decimated the Baltimore Colts (5-11) and Cincinnati Bengals (4-12). Age caught up with the Oakland Raiders (9-7).

The Play-Offs were extended one week to accommodate two Christmas Eve games among the wild-card teams. Houston upset Miami, 17-9, as Dan Pastorini passed for 306 yards despite bruised ribs, knee, elbow, and hamstring. Atlanta beat Philadelphia, 14-13, on two touchdown passes by Steve Bartkowski in the last five minutes. The rally was commonplace for Atlanta, which won six games in the last 90 seconds.

The American Football Conference (AFC) play-offs were held December 30 and 31. Houston upset New England, 31-14, as Pastorini passed for three touchdowns and Campbell ran for 118 yards. Pittsburgh routed Denver, 33-10, as Terry Bradshaw completed 10 passes to end John Stallworth. In the AFC final on January 7 at Pittsburgh, Bradshaw completed 11 of 19 passes for 200 yards and two touchdowns as the Steelers buried Houston, 34-5, in a sleet storm.

In the National Football Conference (NFC) play-offs, Dallas got by Atlanta, 27-20, though Dallas quarterback Roger Staubach missed the second half with a concussion. Los Angeles eliminated Minnesota, 34-10. In the NFC final at Los Angeles, the Cowboys beat the Rams, 28-0.

In Super Bowl XIII on January 21 in Miami's Orange Bowl, Bradshaw's record-breaking performance led the Steelers to a 35-31 victory over Dallas. He completed 17 of 31 passes for 318 yards and four touchdowns, both Super Bowl records.

Best Pro Player of the year may have been Campbell, the best college player of 1977. The 228-pound (103-kilogram) Houston rookie led the NFL with 1,450 yards rushing.

Fran Tarkenton of Minnesota, at age 37, led the league with 345 pass completions in 572 attempts. Other outstanding quarterbacks were Bradshaw of Pittsburgh (the leader in touchdown passes with 28), Staubach of Dallas, Jim Zorn of Seattle, and Gary Danielson of the Detroit Lions. Other offensive stars included running backs Wilbert Montgomery of Philadelphia and Terdell Middleton of Green Bay, and wide receivers Harold Carmichael of Philadelphia and Wesley Walker of the Jets.

The Officiating. Although the NFL added a seventh game official, penalty flags often seemed to fly everywhere. The fourth quarter of a Pittsburgh-Los Angeles game was marred by 15 penalties and took 68 minutes to play (30 minutes was the norm).

Standings in National Football Conference

Eastern Division	W.	L.	T.	Pct.
Dallas	12	4	0	.750
Philadelphia	9	7	0	.563
Washington	8	8	0	.500
New York Giants	6	10	0	.375
St. Louis	6	10	0	.375

Central Division	W.	L.	T.	Pct.
Minnesota	8	7	1	.531
Green Bay	8	7	1	.531
Detroit	7	9	0	.438
Chicago	7	9	0	.438
Tampa Bay	5	11	0	.313

Western Division	W.	L.	T.	Pct.
Los Angeles	12	4	0	.750
Atlanta	9	7	0	.563
New Orleans	7	9	0	.438
San Francisco	2	14	0	.125

National Conference Individual Statistics

Scoring	TDs.	E.P.	F.G.	Pts.
Corral, Los Angeles	0	31	29	118
Septien, Dallas	0	46	16	94
Ricardo, Detroit	0	32	20	92
Danelo, N.Y. Giants	0	27	21	90
Moseley, Washington	0	30	19	87

Passing	Att.	Comp.	Pct.	Yds.	TDs.
Staubach, Dallas	413	231	55.9	3,190	25
Manning, New Orleans	471	291	61.8	3,416	17
Danielson, Detroit	351	199	56.7	2,294	18
Tarkenton, Minnesota	572	345	60.3	3,468	25
Jaworski, Philadelphia	398	206	51.8	2,487	16

Receiving	No. Caught	Total Yds.	Avg. Gain	TDs.
Young, Minnesota	88	704	8.0	5
Galbreath, New Orleans	74	582	7.9	2
Rashad, Minnesota	66	769	11.7	8
Tilley, St. Louis	62	900	14.5	3
Foreman, Minnesota	61	396	6.5	2

Rushing	Att.	Yds.	Avg. Gain	TDs.
W. Payton, Chicago	333	1,395	4.2	11
Dorsett, Dallas	290	1,325	4.6	7
Montgomery, Philadelphia	259	1,220	4.7	9
Middleton, Green Bay	284	1,116	3.9	11
Riggins, Washington	248	1,014	4.1	5

Punting	No.	Yds.	Avg.	Longest
Skladany, Detroit	86	3,654	42.5	63
Jennings, N.Y. Giants	95	3,995	42.1	68
Blanchard, New Orleans	84	3,532	42.0	61
Green, Tampa Bay	100	4,092	40.9	61
D. White, Dallas	76	3,076	40.5	56

Punt Returns	No.	Yds.	Avg.	TDs.
Wallace, Los Angeles	52	618	11.9	0
Green, Washington	42	443	10.5	1
J. Thompson, Detroit	16	161	10.1	0
Harrell, St. Louis	21	196	9.3	1
Odom, Green Bay	33	298	9.0	0

Standings in American Football Conference

Eastern Division	W.	L.	T.	Pct.
New England	11	5	0	.687
Miami	11	5	0	.687
New York Jets	8	8	0	.500
Buffalo	5	11	0	.313
Baltimore	5	11	0	.313

Central Division	W.	L.	T.	Pct.
Pittsburgh	14	2	0	.875
Houston	10	6	0	.625
Cleveland	8	8	0	.500
Cincinnati	4	12	0	.250

Western Division	W.	L.	T.	Pct.
Denver	10	6	0	.625
Oakland	9	7	0	.563
Seattle	9	7	0	.563
San Diego	9	7	0	.563
Kansas City	4	12	0	.250

American Conference Individual Statistics

Scoring	TDs.	E.P.	F.G.	Pts.
Leahy, N.Y. Jets	0	41	22	107
Yepremian, Miami	0	41	19	98
Cockroft, Cleveland	0	37	19	94
Benirschke, San Diego	0	37	18	91
Sims, Seattle	15	0	0	90

Passing	Att.	Comp.	Pct.	Yds.	TDs.
Bradshaw, Pittsburgh	368	207	56.3	2,915	28
Fouts, San Diego	381	224	58.8	2,999	24
Griese, Miami	235	148	63.0	1,791	11
Sipe, Cleveland	399	222	55.6	2,906	21
Morton, Denver	267	146	54.7	1,802	11

Receiving	No. Caught	Total Yds.	Avg. Gain	TDs.
Largent, Seattle	71	1,168	16.5	8
Casper, Oakland	62	852	13.7	9
Swann, Pittsburgh	61	880	14.4	11
Mitchell, San Diego	57	500	8.8	2
Jefferson, San Diego	56	1,001	17.9	13

Rushing	Att.	Yds.	Avg. Gain	TDs.
Campbell, Houston	302	1,450	4.8	13
Williams, Miami	272	1,258	4.6	8
Harris, Pittsburgh	310	1,082	3.5	8
Van Eeghen, Oakland	270	1,080	4.0	9
Miller, Buffalo	238	1,060	4.5	7

Punting	No.	Yds.	Avg.	Longest
McInally, Cincinnati	91	3,919	43.1	65
Guy, Oakland	81	3,462	42.7	69
Andrusyshyn, Kansas City	79	3,247	41.1	61
Roberts, Miami	81	3,263	40.3	59
Ramsey, N.Y. Jets	74	2,964	40.1	79

Punt Returns	No.	Yds.	Avg.	TDs.
Upchurch, Denver	36	493	13.7	1
Moody, Buffalo	19	240	12.6	1
Harper, N.Y. Jets	30	378	12.6	1
E. Payton, Kansas City	32	364	11.4	0
Fuller, San Diego	39	436	11.2	0

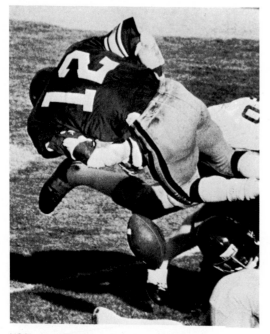

USC's Charles White dives over goal line without the ball, but officials awarded a touchdown in the 17-10 Rose Bowl victory over Michigan.

1978 College Conference Champions

Conference	School
Atlantic Coast	Clemson
Big Eight	Nebraska-Oklahoma (tie)
Big Sky	Northern Arizona
Big Ten	Michigan-Michigan State (tie)
Ivy League	Dartmouth
Mid-American	Ball State
Missouri Valley	New Mexico State
Ohio Valley	Western Kentucky
Pacific Ten	Southern California
Southeastern	Alabama
Southern	Furman-Tennessee (Chattanooga) (tie)
Southwest	Houston
Southwestern	Grambling
Western Athletic	Brigham Young
Yankee	Massachusetts

The Bowl Games

Bowl	Winner	Loser
Bluebonnet	Stanford 25	Georgia 22
Blue-Gray	Gray 28	Blue 24
Cotton	Notre Dame 35	Houston 34
Fiesta	Arkansas 10	UCLA 10 (tie)
Garden State	Arizona State 34	Rutgers 18
Gator	Clemson 17	Ohio State 15
Hall of Fame	Texas A & M 28	Iowa State 12
Holiday	Navy 23	Brigham Young 16
Independence	East Carolina 35	Louisiana Tech 13
Liberty	Missouri 20	Louisiana State 15
Orange	Oklahoma 31	Nebraska 24
Peach	Purdue 41	Georgia Tech 21
Pioneer	Florida State 35	Massachusetts 28
Rose	Southern California 17	Michigan 10
Shrine	East 56	West 17
Sugar	Alabama 14	Penn State 7
Sun	Texas 42	Maryland 0
Tangerine	North Carolina State 30	Pittsburgh 17

All-America Team (as picked by UPI)
Offense
Wide receiver—Kirk Gibson, Michigan State
Tight end—Kellen Winslow, Missouri
Tackles—Keith Dorney, Penn State; Matt Miller, Colorado
Guards—Greg Roberts, Oklahoma; Pat Howell, Southern California
Center—Dave Huffman, Notre Dame
Quarterback—Chuck Fusina, Penn State
Running backs—Billy Sims, Oklahoma; Charles White, Southern California; Ted Brown, North Carolina State
Placekicker—Matt Bahr, Penn State

Defense
Ends—Al Harris, Arizona State; Hugh Green, Pittsburgh
Tackles—Bruce Clark, Matt Millen, Penn State
Middle guard—Reggie Kinlaw, Oklahoma
Linebackers—Jerry Robinson, UCLA; Tom Cousineau, Ohio State; Bob Golic, Notre Dame
Defensive backs—Johnnie Johnson, Texas; Pete Harris, Penn State; Ken Easley, UCLA

Games were won and lost by questionable officiating. Oakland defeated San Diego on a last-play touchdown made possible by three forward fumbles on the same play. After the game, the players involved admitted that the fumbles were intentional. Pittsburgh beat the Cleveland Browns because a Pittsburgh fumble was wiped out when the officials said the ball was dead.

There was a clamor that the officials use television instant replay on controversial calls. During the exhibition season, the NFL experimented with a form of instant replay.

The Cheerleaders in the NFL did not really lead cheers, but instead performed dance routines. Twenty of the 28 teams used cheerleaders, dressed the young women in revealing costumes, and gave them such names as the Los Angeles Embraceable Ewes and the Chicago Honey Bears.

Then came all kinds of problems. Two Denver cheerleaders were arrested and charged with picking the pocket of an undercover policeman. The New Orleans Saints learned that their cheerleading leader was under arrest, charged with drug possession. When NFL teams heard that some cheerleaders had posed nude or near nude for *Playboy* magazine, they fired many of those involved. San Diego fired all its cheerleaders. New Orleans disbanded its group, and all other teams required their cheerleaders to agree in writing not to pose nude.

Canadian Football. The Edmonton Eskimos and Ottawa Rough Riders won the conference titles in the nine-team Canadian Football League (CFL). Edmonton and the Montreal Alouettes reached the Grey Cup championship game for the fourth time in five years, and Edmonton won the cup by upsetting Montreal, 20-13, on November 26 at Toronto, Ont.

Tony Gabriel, the Ottawa tight end, was voted the league's Most Valuable Player. He also was chosen as the top Canadian player for the fourth time. Mike Strickland of the Saskatchewan Roughriders led in rushing with 1,306 yards in 16 games.

The Colleges. Of the 144 teams playing major-college football, only Pennsylvania State University completed the regular season undefeated and untied. All Penn State needed to become national champion was a victory over Alabama in the Sugar Bowl at New Orleans. Instead, Penn State lost, 14-7, and the unofficial collegiate championship was decided – or undecided – at the polls.

The best won-lost-tied records during the regular season were: Penn State (11-0), Southern California (11-1), Alabama (10-1), Oklahoma (10-1), Michigan (10-1), Clemson (10-1), Jackson State (10-1), Georgia (9-1-1), and Grambling (8-1-1).

After the regular season, the polls by the Associated Press (AP) board of writers and broadcasters and the United Press International (UPI) board of coaches were identical for the first six places. Penn State was first, Alabama second, Southern California third, Oklahoma fourth, Michigan fifth, and Nebraska sixth.

The top six teams met in three bowls on Jan. 1, 1979 – Penn State against Alabama in the Sugar Bowl, Southern California and Michigan in the Rose Bowl at Pasadena, Calif., and Oklahoma versus Nebraska in the Orange Bowl at Miami.

Alabama beat Penn State by stopping Penn State twice on successive plays inside the Alabama 1-yard line. Southern California defeated Michigan, 17-10, the winning touchdown coming on a play on which Southern California running back Charles White apparently fumbled the ball before crossing the goal line. Oklahoma beat Nebraska, 31-24.

Alabama then claimed the national title because it had beaten the number-one team. Southern California claimed the title because it, too, had lost only once, and it had beaten Alabama.

The voters were confused. The final AP poll placed Alabama first, Southern California second, Oklahoma third, Penn State fourth, Michigan fifth, Clemson sixth, Notre Dame seventh, Nebraska eighth, Texas ninth, and Houston 10th. The final UPI ratings had Southern California first, Alabama second, Oklahoma third, Penn State fourth, Michigan fifth, Clemson and Notre Dame tied for sixth, Nebraska eighth, Texas ninth, and Arkansas 10th. The National Football Foundation and Hall of Fame voted its MacArthur Bowl to Alabama.

There was a disquieting note in the Gator Bowl on December 29 at Jacksonville, Fla. In the last two minutes, Charlie Bauman of Clemson intercepted a pass in front of the Ohio State bench, ensuring Clemson's 17-15 victory. An enraged coach Woody Hayes of Ohio State punched Bauman, and when an Ohio State player tried to restrain his coach, Hayes turned on him. The next morning, Ohio State fired Hayes, its highly successful coach for 28 years.

Top Players. Billy Sims, the Oklahoma tailback, won the Heisman Trophy as the outstanding college player. He narrowly defeated Chuck Fusina, the Penn State quarterback, in the voting. The Outland Trophy as the outstanding interior lineman went to Greg Roberts of Oklahoma.   Frank Litsky

FORD, GERALD RUDOLPH (1913-   ), the 38th President of the United States, enjoyed an active retirement in his new home in Palm Springs, Calif., in 1978. He traveled widely to promote Republican Party candidates and private business ventures.

In a departure from tradition, the former President contracted with the Franklin Mint, a private manufacturer of medallions and coins, to develop a series of 100 medals commemorating important events in the U.S. presidency. Ford struck the first medal on February 23 after making a personal appeal for sales in a form letter addressed "Dear Fellow American." According to his contract, the former President is to select the events and edit the text that accompanies each medal.

Business, Politics. In April, Ford filmed a television interview as part of a series of documentaries he has agreed to participate in under a five-year contract with the National Broadcasting Company.

The former President took an active role in Republican politics. He launched a speaking tour on June 5 in which he addressed 100 audiences in 157 days. Ford also converted his 1976 campaign committee into a "multi-candidate political action committee" in July. By doing so, he could parcel out excess campaign funds totaling $220,000 to Republican candidates of his choice and thereby increase his influence during the election year.

A "New" Betty Ford. Ford canceled a political tour in April because of his wife's illness. Betty Ford was admitted to Long Beach (Calif.) Naval Hospital on April 11 for treatment of alcoholism and addiction to the arthritis medication she had been taking for some time. She left the hospital on May 5.

Pleased with the success of her treatment, Betty Ford declared that she wanted "a nice new face to go with my beautiful new life," and underwent plastic surgery on September 14 to remove wrinkles from her face and neck. She made her next, much-photographed, public appearance on October 5 at a dinner honoring actor Fred Astaire.

Betty Ford's autobiography, *The Times of My Life,* was published in November by Harper & Row. The *Ladies' Home Journal* magazine bought the rights to publish excerpts of the book for an undisclosed sum in June. Later that month, Ballantine Books agreed to pay $1 million to publish the paperback version.

The Ford family moved into their new 15-room house overlooking the Thunderbird Country Club golf course in Palm Springs in March. The family celebrated daughter Susan's 21st birthday in Vail, Colo., on July 8. Her engagement to Charles F. Vance was announced in October. Vance is a Secret Service agent who was assigned to guard the Ford family.   Carol L. Thompson

See REPUBLICAN PARTY. In WORLD BOOK, see FORD, GERALD RUDOLPH.

FOREST AND FOREST PRODUCTS. A housing start rate of about 2 million units made lumber costs rise rapidly in the United States in 1978. In his April 11 anti-inflation message, President Jimmy Carter said that because lumber accounts for about 25 per cent of the cost of a new house, increased production and more efficient use of existing lumber output would relieve the situation somewhat. Carter's instructions to key agencies to develop plans for expanding timber harvests plunged his Administration into bitter conflict.

Agriculture versus Interior. The U.S. Department of Agriculture announced on May 30 that it was increasing the amount of timber to be harvested from national forests in the year ending September 30 from 11.5 billion board feet (27 million cubic meters) to 12.2 billion board feet (28 million cubic meters). United States Secretary of Agriculture Bob Bergland held out little hope for increased cutting on U.S. Forest Service land in the near future. He predicted Forest Service sales of about 12.5 billion board feet (29 million cubic meters) for 1978.

Secretary of the Interior Cecil D. Andrus criticized Bergland's approach and urged an annual harvest goal of 13.5 billion board feet (32 million cubic meters). The Council on Wage and Price Stability said that years of planning would be required before increased cutting curbed the up-

ward trend in housing prices. Conservation spokesmen vowed to resist more timber cuts. More than half the commercial-grade timber in the U.S. is in the national forests, which now supply more than 25 per cent of the annual softwood harvest.

The National Forest Products Association asserted on September 15 that an increase in wood supply from private lands is impossible in the near future. The association pointed out that the United States imports 26 per cent of its annual consumption of softwood lumber, and urged policies that would encourage self-sufficiency and enable the United States to seize market opportunities as the world demand for lumber rises.

Beetle Blight. United States Forest Service regional specialists warned on August 13 that forests in Colorado, Idaho, Montana, South Dakota, Utah, and Wyoming were being seriously blighted by a mountain pine beetle epidemic. In Yellowstone National Park, 200,000 acres (80,000 hectares) are under attack, and an estimated 600 million board feet (1.4 million cubic meters) of timber have been lost to beetles in the region since 1970. The outbreak became more severe because of overcrowded forests and the 1977 drought. Andrew L. Newman

In World Book, see Forest; Forest Products; Forestry.

FORT WORTH, TEX. See Dallas-Fort Worth.
FOUR-H CLUBS. See Youth Organizations.

Park rangers fell a damaged redwood tree in California's Smithe Redwoods State Preserve. Vandals had slashed several with a chain saw.

FRANCE. The ruling center-right coalition of Gaullists and Giscardians defeated the Union of the Left parties in 1978 national elections. After the second round of elections on March 19, the Gaullists had won 148 seats and the Giscardians 137. Total pro-government seats numbered 291. Among the 200 opposition seats, the Communists won 86; the Socialists, 103; and the Radicals, 10. President Valéry Giscard d'Estaing saw the victory as a vindication of his reform policy.

Prime Minister Raymond Barre had launched the government election program on January 7. Among 30 proposed measures, he offered a two-year moratorium on tax increases, bigger family allowances and pensions, shorter hours in heavy industry, 10,000 more police, and a wealth tax. The leftists did not announce an election strategy as the breach between Socialists and Communists widened. Giscard d'Estaing warned voters on January 27 that a leftist government would lead to economic chaos.

Leftist Accord. In the first round of voting, on March 12, the left won 48.4 per cent of the votes; the government, 46.5 per cent. For the second round of voting, the Communists agreed to support Socialists who had led Communists in the first round. The Communists and Socialists quickly produced a common program, offering raises of 37 per cent on basic wages and 50 per cent on family allowances. Faced with this agreement, the government coalition parties made their own agreement. Every voter thus had a choice between a leftist and a government candidate. The Union of the Left fell apart quickly after its second-round defeat. The Socialists and Communists blamed each other for the defeat.

Reappointed prime minister on March 31, Barre formed a Cabinet on April 5 that included almost all of the previous Cabinet members. Giscard told the new Cabinet on April 6 that its priorities must be economic recovery, international relations, and social progress.

In his first policy speech since the elections, Barre maintained on April 19 the need for economic stringency to combat inflation. He promised to try to cut unemployment, increase the wages of lower-paid workers, and extend collective bargaining between the state and professional organizations and unions. He pleased the opposition by pledging to consider a wealth tax and take measures against tax evaders.

Barre comfortably won a vote of confidence on April 20. On April 27 the government announced price increases ranging from 9 to 20 per cent for gas, electricity, transportation, and postage. Barre said the increases were the only way to reduce the national deficit.

Economic Difficulties. All was not plain sailing for the new government. Beginning June 18, Paris police staged a weeklong work slowdown to protest

Radicals bombed the Palace of Versailles, France, in June, wrecking three rooms and destroying paintings, furniture, and statues.

pay levels and working conditions. The slowdown was a signal for strikes in many industries throughout the country. On July 2, the government announced the third series of price increases since the election, covering coal, gas, gasoline, and rents.

Intervention in Africa. France sent troops to Zaire's Shaba province on May 19 to rescue French citizens caught in a local uprising. By May 22, with some 260 Europeans dead or missing, France was under heavy diplomatic pressure to withdraw. But the troops stayed in Africa for three more days, to the dismay of President Mobutu Sese Seko of Zaire. The intervention drew criticism. See ZAIRE.

Budget Approved. On August 28, President Giscard d'Estaing approved a 1979 budget that increased spending 14 per cent and provided for a $4.65-billion deficit. The Cabinet approved the budget on September 6, with a $3.45-billion deficit. At a July economic summit meeting in Bonn, West Germany, Giscard had promised to stimulate the French economy.

On December 29, France blocked the start of the European Monetary System in a dispute over farm subsidies. The system was scheduled to begin on Jan. 1, 1979. See EUROPE.

The government on September 21 outlined a plan to rescue the debt-ridden steel industry. The government would manage the industry and control its finances through three holding companies.

And in October, the government adopted a draft bill to help small and middle-sized companies facing bankruptcy. Banks and the government would select financially sound companies to control the poor companies. Those capable of survival would receive low-interest loans. Parliament still had to approve the measure.

Nuclear Sale Off. France decided on August 23 not to sell a nuclear-reprocessing plant to Pakistan, thus breaking a 1976 agreement. The plant not only would have reprocessed waste from Pakistan's nuclear power station, but also could have isolated enriched plutonium, key ingredient of atomic bombs.

Tanker Spill. The supertanker *Amoco Cadiz* broke up on rocks off the northern coast of Brittany on March 17. It spilled a record 1.6 million barrels of oil, fouling the coast and endangering the wildlife.

Holiday Chaos. Work slowdowns by French air-traffic controllers disrupted flights throughout Europe at peak vacation time. The slowdown, over pay, began on July 14. From August 2 to 11, the controllers resumed normal service, as they negotiated with the government. The slowdown resumed on August 11 and ended on August 21.   Kenneth Brown

See also EUROPE (Facts in Brief Table). In WORLD BOOK, see FRANCE.

FUTURE FARMERS OF AMERICA (FFA). See YOUTH ORGANIZATIONS.

GABON. See AFRICA.

GAMBIA. See AFRICA.

GAMES, MODELS, AND TOYS

GAMES, MODELS, AND TOYS. A variety of electronic games continued to captivate adults and older children in 1978. Public arcades equipped with electronic consoles gave their customers a chance to try large-scale games like Starship I, in which the player pilots a spacecraft and tries to destroy invaders from another galaxy. New models of video-game systems for home TV sets could be programmed by cartridge, allowing greater variety. One of these, the Atari Video Computer System, gave players a choice of six cartridges, each offering up to 50 variations, ranging from blackjack to basketball.

For the first time, electronic games that did not require the use of a TV receiver were widely available in the United States. They came in two basic forms—a small handheld unit and a large tabletop model. Among the most popular handheld games were Football, Auto Race, and Missile Attack. Tabletop games were designed to appeal to a broad range of interests. They included Chess Challenger and Electronic Backgammon as well as Merlin, an instrument that could be programmed to play tic-tac-toe or Ludwig van Beethoven's *Symphony No. 9.*

Star Wars toys, based on characters from the motion picture, were popular with children. Many such toys were bought with I.O.U. certificates issued during the 1977 Christmas season, when demand for Star Wars toys exceeded the supply.

Board Games. Fantasy games, based on mythology, popular fiction, and futurism, were played in a spirit of fun rather than competition. Many of these games had no winners and some were known to last as long as 18 months. War of the Ring, based on the book *The Lord of the Rings* by J. R. R. Tolkien, was among the most popular of these.

Financial games also commanded attention. Class Struggle, invented by Marxist scholar Bertrell Ollman, was designed to present the workings of capitalism from the worker's point of view. Tryopoly, marketed on a regional basis, was played with properties and businesses named for those actually in the area.

Skates and Skateboards. A revival of interest in roller skating that originated in California spread across the United States, with such entertainers as Cher, Linda Ronstadt, and Kate Jackson among the avid skaters. Roller rinks throughout the United States reported increased attendance; disco nights were especially popular on the East Coast.

The National Injury Information Clearing House reported in July that bicycles still topped the federal government's ranking of hazardous products. Skateboards jumped from 18th place to seventh in fiscal 1977, with 140,070 skateboard-associated injuries reported in 1977.   Theodore M. O'Leary

In WORLD BOOK, see DOLL; GAME; MARBLE; MODEL MAKING; TOY.

Ken Pyne in *Punch.* © *Punch*/Rothco

GARDENING. Weather conditions in most sections of the United States stimulated lusty growth of ornamental plants in 1978. But they also encouraged the spread of weeds, fungi, and insect parasites, keeping outdoor gardeners busy and affecting indoor gardens as well. Nonetheless, there was a drop in demand for insect- and fungus-control products, according to Jack Lang of Planters Aide Products Company in Melrose Park, Ill. He attributed this to "much better plant materials" coming from Florida growers and house-plant wholesalers.

Poisonous Plants, long a source of controversy between horticulturists and journalists who write about the dangers of such plants, were in the news. *The American Horticulturist,* a publication of the American Horticultural Society, quoted Robert F. Lederer, executive vice-president of the American Association of Nurserymen, as saying that "We can find no record for many years of a single registered fatality from being near, or from eating cultivated plant material." His authority was the National Clearing House for Poison Control Centers in Bethesda, Md. Also, the United States Consumer Products Safety Commission cited an Ohio State University-Society of American Florists research project indicating that test animals, even when given high doses of various parts of the poinsettia plant, usually considered poisonous, "showed no mortality, no symptoms of toxicity, and no changes

Swiss farmer Felix Merki displays his unusual
strawberry plot. The pot-towers increase the
berry yield and make the harvesting easier.

New Plants won eight All-America Awards –
five flowering plants and three vegetables. Silver
medals were given for "Dianthus Snowfire," a 6- to
8-inch (15- to 20-centimeter) cousin of the carnation
with single, fringed, pink-centered, fragrant
blooms; "Zinnia Cherry Ruffles," bearing ruffled
blossoms – crimson with a touch of blue – on 24- to
30-inch (61- to 76-centimeter) plants; and "Zinnia
Yellow Ruffles," similar to "Cherry Ruffles," but
with canary-yellow blooms. Bronze medals went to
"Zinnia Peter Pan," a 12- to 14-inch (30- to 36-
centimeter) plant with twisted, cream-colored petals; and "Zinnia Red Sun," an 18- to 24-inch (46- to
61-centimeter) plant with flat, scarlet petals. The
vegetables, all bronze-medal winners, were "Cucum-
ber Liberty," distinguished for its disease resistance;
"Tomato Floramerica," recommended for its
medium-height vines and disease tolerance; and
"Watermelon Sweet Favorite," selected for its
sweetness and 15- to 20-pound (7- to 9-kilogram)
striped fruit.

All-America rose selections were "Sundowner," a
fragrant, orange grandiflora; "Friendship," a fragrant, coral-rose hybrid tea rose; and "Paradise," a
ruby-red, shading to pink, hybrid tea.   Phil Clark

In WORLD BOOK, see FLOWER; GARDENING;
HYDROPONICS; PLANT.

GAS AND GASOLINE. See ENERGY; PETRO-
LEUM AND GAS.

GEOLOGY. H. Jay Melosh, professor of geology at
the California Institute of Technology, developed a
new theory in 1978 on how rocks deform. According
to his theory, the underlying behavior of landslides,
meteorite craters, earthquakes, and mountain ranges is similar, though they have different origins.

Previously, specialists studying rock behavior
chose the theory that seemed easiest to apply to the
kind of geologic structure under study. Sometimes
they likened the movement of rocks to that of a
viscous liquid, such as honey. In other cases, they
compared it to dry sand, in which resistance to
movement results from friction between the grains.

However, none of the available theories explained the behavior of giant landslides – the rapid
flow of broken rock down gentle slopes. The slides
move with considerable speed, traveling great distances in a few minutes. Among the largest observed
by geologists were slides that brought down 20-
million short tons (18 million metric tons) of rock
onto Sherman Glacier in Alaska after a 1964 earthquake, and a slide of 40 million short tons (36 million
metric tons) of rock in Madison Canyon, Montana,
following the 1959 Hebgen Lake earthquake. The
slides usually started on steep mountain slopes, but
many continued across gentle valley slopes less than
10 degrees in inclination.

A Flowing Mass. How the slides are able to travel
across areas without steep slopes was one of many

in dietary intake or behavior patterns." Many cultivated and wild plants contain poisons, but they were
largely evolved for protection against insects. Apparently, it is a question of the amount consumed,
and larger animals and humans would have to ingest
very large quantities of these plants to feel the effects
of the poison.

Hydroculture – growing plants in heavily fertilized water – grew in popularity as a result of improved methods and materials, though it is still not
as widely practiced in the United States as in Great
Britain. But on both sides of the Atlantic, more
effective fertilizers and improved growth mediums
have been developed for use in water.

The Gardening Boom continued, but the rate of
increase leveled off. Indoor trees, shrubs, and other
plants have become as essential as drapes and furniture to the décor of banks, restaurants, and other
businesses. The living-room tree is a fixture in both
city apartments and suburban houses. Community
gardens in urban areas expanded.

Seedling-pot size is an important factor in
vegetable-seedling growth, according to research at
the University of Illinois at Urbana-Champaign. In
a 1978 experiment, vegetables were seeded in 4-inch
(10-centimeter) and 2½-inch (6-centimeter) pots.
The smaller pots produced smaller plants, because
more limited amounts of nutrients and soil volume
were available for root growth.

unresolved problems geologist Barry Voight, a professor at Pennsylvania State University at State College, considered. Voight expanded his field studies to include a wide range of historic and prehistoric landslides. Then, under his editorial guidance, a worldwide group of experts compiled a two-volume study of rockslides and avalanches.

A pattern emerged from these studies, showing that a great rockslide is actually a flowing mass rather than a chaotic, bouncing mass. Such slides must contain rocks that move without being influenced by the pressure of other rocks above them. A theory of material behavior that explains such flow has long been known as *plasticity*.

Melosh's Work. Melosh extended the idea of plasticity to a wider range of geologic problems. Using a large digital computer, he compared theoretical models based on plasticity with real observations. Melosh then carried out similar computer comparisons of large meteorite craters with the pattern expected if the rocks within them were ideally plastic. The computed craters and the real craters agreed remarkably well. In particular, the central peaks of many meteorite craters on the moon turned out to be the places at which rock flows converge. Kenneth S. Deffeyes

See also PALEONTOLOGY. In WORLD BOOK, see GEOCHEMISTRY; GEOLOGY; GEOPHYSICS.

GEORGIA. See ATLANTA; STATE GOVERNMENT.

GERMANY, EAST. An experiment by Communist Party Secretary General and State Council Chairman Erich Honecker to accumulate foreign currency and decrease consumer unrest backfired in 1978. He opened "Intershops" throughout the country to sell luxury goods – from Scotch whisky at $7.09 to color-TV sets at $536 – while "Exquisit" shops sold higher-priced Western goods, including automobiles. The stores accepted only West German Deutsche marks, not East German marks. Because Honecker did not change East Germany's exchange regulations, most East Germans could get Deutsche marks only from friends or relatives in West Germany. But this created a privileged class of senior party officials, because rank-and-file party members are banned from contact with Westerners, and built up a vast black market.

Moreover, Intershops catered to foreign travelers and charged less than Exquisit shops. Price differences in imported food, tobacco, and liquor caused a May 1 protest by 300 persons in Wittenberg. And women at an electric lamp factory in East Berlin went on strike in January to demand payment of part of their wages in Deutsche marks, because the lamps they made were sold in West Germany.

Low Productivity. The economy continued to suffer from low productivity, inferior production, and outdated technology. A planned industrial investment of 2.1 per cent for 1978 – compared with 6

per cent in 1977 – was regarded as remarkably low, in view of the need to modernize. East Germany also had difficulty meeting its export targets to Russia, its most important trading partner.

Magazine Closed. East Germany barred the entry of a new correspondent of *Der Spiegel*, a West German news magazine, on January 4 after *Der Spiegel* printed an article saying there was an opposition group within the East German Communist Party. After a second article on the same subject, East Germany closed *Der Spiegel*'s East Berlin office on January 10.

Inter-German relations worsened on January 15, when East Germany refused to let Helmut Kohl enter East Berlin. Kohl is chairman of the West German Christian Democratic Union Party (CDU) and leader of the opposition in the *Bundestag* (Federal Diet).

A more hopeful sign was the June 23 start of negotiations on a proposed highway to link West Berlin with Hamburg, West Germany.

Military Training. East Germany's Protestant churchmen read a letter on June 25 protesting a government plan to introduce compulsory military training of 14- and 15-year-olds in schools. The training will bolster the activities of "voluntary" paramilitary youth groups. Kenneth Brown

See also EUROPE (Facts in Brief Table). In WORLD BOOK, see GERMANY.

GERMANY, WEST. A visit by President Jimmy Carter in July 1978 eased West Germany's relations with the United States. Causing the strains were U.S. pressure to boost the economy and West Germany's reluctance to declare outright support for the neutron bomb. Both sides tried to create an atmosphere of warm friendship during Carter's visit.

During an economic summit of Western leaders in Bonn on July 16 and 17, West Germany agreed to stimulate its economy. Accordingly, Chancellor Helmut Schmidt on July 28 announced a program that would add about $6.5 billion to the 1979 economy. Parliament approved a $7.8-billion program on November 24, and scheduled it to begin on Jan. 1, 1979. The opposition Christian Democrats increased the program's size by demanding larger tax cuts for business and higher child allowances. To finance the program, the value-added tax on goods was scheduled to increase from 12 to 13 per cent on July 1, 1979.

Shaky Government. The coalition of Social Democrats and Free Democrats faced defeat in February over antiterrorist measures. A small group of left wingers in Schmidt's Social Democratic Party threatened to vote against the government in the *Bundestag*, the house of parliament that passes laws. The disputed measures included allowing police to hold people up to 12 hours while establishing identity, setting up checkpoints in a terrorist attack, and

President Jimmy Carter's wife, Rosalynn, and daughter, Amy, visit a West German castle in July while he attends an economic summit meeting.

all workers. The union wanted a 5 per cent increase and gradual introduction of a 35-hour week.

The government made an international appeal in September for evidence of uninvestigated Nazi crimes so that it can begin proceedings before the statute-of-limitations deadline in 1979. The deadline has been extended twice.

The German Demographic Society reported on August 16 that the West German birth rate of 9.8 babies per 1,000 inhabitants per year was the lowest in Europe. At that rate, West Germany's current population of 62.8 million would drop to 40 million in 50 years.

Police shot and killed suspected terrorist Willy Peter Stoll in a Düsseldorf restaurant on September 6. Stoll was a major suspect in the 1977 kidnapping and murder of industrialist Hanns-Martin Schleyer. Stoll reportedly pulled a pistol when two policemen asked him for identification. Four other suspects in the case were flown out of Yugoslavia after a November 17 announcement that they would not be extradited to West Germany. In September, West Germany had refused to extradite to Yugoslavia several Croatian nationalists wanted as terrorists. West Germany termed the release of the four "a step backward in the international fight against terrorism." See EUROPE (Close-Up). Kenneth Brown

See also EUROPE (Facts in Brief Table). In WORLD BOOK, see GERMANY.

giving police greater search powers. Slightly watered-down measures passed on February 6, by one vote. Four Social Democrats voted against them.

The government played for time when divisions became apparent among the various parties over the neutron bomb. Christian Democrats favored the bomb to counter Russia's tank superiority. The Social Democrats, however, had ethical objections to a weapon that can kill people but leave buildings intact. The Free Democrats sat on the fence. Schmidt told the Bundestag on April 12 that the government would allow neutron bombs to be stored in West Germany.

Share prices in August reached their highest level in eight years. Only labor shortages held the building industry back. Volkswagenwerk sought ways to invest its soaring profits. Inflation remained under 3 per cent and unemployment continued at about 1 million. The country's five leading economic research institutes said in October that 1978 real growth would be between 3 and 3.5 per cent, partly because of the economic stimulus program.

Other Developments. Northwest Germany's first steel strike in 50 years began on November 28, when 37,000 members of the Industrie-Gewerkschaft Metall union struck nine plants. Management retaliated on December 1 by locking 29,000 workers out of eight other plants. Management had offered a 3 per cent wage increase and six weeks of vacation for

GHANA. General Ignatius Kutu Acheampong, Ghana's government leader since January 1972, was forced to resign in a coup d'état on July 5, 1978. Commanders of the army, police, and border guards were forced out at the same time. Lieutenant General Frederick William Kwasi Akuffo, who had been chief of defense and a member of Ghana's ruling Supreme Military Council, replaced Acheampong (see AKUFFO, FREDERICK WILLIAM KWASI). These changes followed many months of inflation, shortages, and antigovernment agitation.

Before the take-over, Acheampong had pledged to turn power over to an elected government in July 1979. His proposed "union government" plan called for direct election of a legislature and an executive president, the prohibition of political parties, and continuing military participation in government. Voters approved Acheampong's plan on March 30.

Akuffo concentrated on coping with Ghana's economic difficulties. Due to bad weather, production in the country's cacao industry, which accounts for more than half of Ghana's total export income, fell sharply during the year. The 1978-1979 cacao harvest was expected to be less than half of the 1964-1965 level. John D. Esseks

See also AFRICA (Facts in Brief Table). In WORLD BOOK, see GHANA.

GIRL SCOUTS. See YOUTH ORGANIZATIONS.
GIRLS CLUBS. See YOUTH ORGANIZATIONS.

GOLF. For the first time in a long while, the year's outstanding golfer was a woman – 21-year-old Nancy Lopez, playing her first full year on the women's tour in 1978. Among the men, Tom Watson won the most tournaments and most money, and Jack Nicklaus, Gary Player, Andy North, and John Mahaffey won the four major tournaments.

The Ladies Professional Golf Association (LPGA) staged the longest (38 tournaments) and richest ($3.4 million) of its 26 annual tours. It visited 18 states in the United States and Canada, Great Britain, Australia, and Japan.

Lopez won nine tournaments, five in a row. Jo Anne Carner, Pat Bradley, and Donna Caponi Young won three tournaments each, and Hollis Stacy captured the women's United States Open for the second straight year. Lopez earned $203,430, breaking Judy Rankin's 1976 record of $150,734. In her rookie year from July 29, 1977, to July 28, 1978, Lopez won $161,235, breaking the rookie record of $153,102 set by Jerry Pate in 1976 on the richer Professional Golfers' Association (PGA) tour for men.

The first two tournament victories for Lopez came in February at Sarasota, Fla., and March in Los Angeles. In May and June, she played five tournaments in six weeks and won them all – at Lutherville, Md.; Jamesburg, N.J.; New Rochelle, N.Y.; Kings Island, Ohio; and Rochester, N.Y.

Nancy Lopez cheers as she wins record fifth straight tourney at Rochester, N.Y., in June and breaks rookie earnings mark of $153,102.

At Kings Island, she won the LPGA championship by six strokes. At Rochester, she shot a record 32 on the front nine to make up five shots on the leader. Her streak ended when she finished 13th at Hershey, Pa., 15 shots behind Bradley, the winner.

After a victory in the European Open in Sunningdale, England, in August, Lopez missed two tournaments because of a sore upper right arm. After that, she played erratically, seemingly tired from all the demands on her time. She became the biggest attraction in women's golf since the late Babe Didrikson Zaharias. As Jim Cour of United Press International wrote, "She has given women's golf a lot of what Arnold Palmer brought to the men's tour two decades ago." See LOPEZ, NANCY.

PGA Tour. The men's tour comprised 42 tournaments worth $10,373,000, a record. Watson won five tournaments and Nicklaus, Player, and Andy Bean three each. Gil Morgan, an optometrist who played golf full-time, won the richest winner's purse ($100,000) in the World Series of Golf September 28 to October 1 at Akron, Ohio. Watson's earnings of $362,429 broke Johnny Miller's record of $353,021.

Nicklaus won his third British Open, beating unheralded Simon Owen of New Zealand by two strokes in July at St. Andrews in Scotland. Nicklaus, with a 72-hole score of 281, scored his 16th victory in one of the world's four major tournaments.

Nicklaus also had rough moments. He failed to qualify for the final 36 holes of the PGA championship after a first-round 79. Nicklaus was philosophical, saying, "It's better than an 80." Despite that round, Nicklaus seemed more relaxed all year. He played fewer tournaments, spending more time with his family.

Player, a 42-year-old South African, won his third Masters title. His final-round 74 gave him a total of 277, beating Watson, Hubert Green, and Rod Funseth by a stroke in April in Augusta, Ga., and making him the oldest Masters champion.

The 28-year-old North barely won the United States Open in June in Denver. He led by four strokes with five holes to play, then fell back. On the 18th hole, he saved the victory by blasting out of a bunker and sinking a 4-foot (120-centimeter) putt. That gave him a 285 and a one-stroke victory over Dave Stockton and J. C. Snead.

Mahaffey, Watson, and Pate tied at 276 in the PGA championship in August in Oakmont, Pa. Mahaffey won when he sank a 5-foot (150-centimeter) putt on the second hole in the sudden-death play-off. Before that, everything seemed to have gone wrong for the 30-year-old Mahaffey – collapses just short of victory in the 1975 and 1976 United States Opens, a deteriorating game, an injured elbow, a broken hand, and a broken marriage.   Frank Litsky

In WORLD BOOK, see GOLF.

GOVERNORS, U.S. See STATE GOVERNMENT.

GRAY, HANNA HOLBORN (1930-   ), became the 10th president of the University of Chicago on July 1, 1978. She is one of the first women to head a major United States university.

Gray was born in Heidelberg, Germany, on Oct. 25, 1930, to Hajo and Annemarie Holborn. Her father was a historian at the University of Berlin and her mother was a philologist. In 1934, the Holborns fled Nazi Germany, moving first to London and later to the United States.

At 15, Gray entered Bryn Mawr College in Pennsylvania. She received a bachelor's degree in history in 1950 and studied as a Fulbright scholar at Oxford University, England, in 1951 and 1952. She taught at Bryn Mawr in 1953 and 1954, then resumed her studies at Harvard University. She received a Ph.D. in history in 1957.

Gray was an instructor and assistant professor at Harvard from 1957 to 1960. She taught at the University of Chicago from 1961 to 1972, when she was appointed dean of Northwestern University's College of Arts and Sciences in Evanston, Ill. Gray served as the first woman provost of Yale University from 1974 until May 1977, when she was named the university's acting president.

Gray serves as a trustee for several educational institutions, including Bryn Mawr. She married Charles Gray, a law historian, in June 1954. They have no children.   Edward G. Nash

GREAT BRITAIN. Prime Minister James Callaghan surprised everyone in 1978 by deciding not to dissolve Parliament and call a general election. Despite losing his overall majority in the House of Commons in July when the 13 Liberals ended their alliance with his Labour Party (the so-called Lib-Lab pact), Callaghan had enough backing to stay in power at least until spring 1979.

Admitting that his government was more vulnerable to defeat without Liberal support, Callaghan tried to keep the friends he had and avoid making new foes by introducing an unusually bland autumn legislative program in November.

Callaghan's Gamble. The main item was a pledge to allow the Scots and Welsh to vote early in 1979 on proposals for limited autonomy. Callaghan calculated that his plan for elected assemblies in Edinburgh and Cardiff would be enough to prevent Scottish and Welsh Nationalists from joining the Conservatives on key votes. Two bills providing for directly elected assemblies in Scotland and Wales became law on July 31. The bills give the Scottish and Welsh people the right to decide in a 1979 referendum whether they want these assemblies.

But an amendment that could prove crucial was passed during the lengthy debate on the Scottish bill, to the government's great annoyance. A group of rebel antidevolutionist Labour members of Parliament (MP's), backed by the Conservatives, man-

aged to insert a clause stipulating that the whole legislative package would be dropped if less than 40 per cent of the Scottish electorate voted "yes" to the *devolution* (limited home rule) proposals. There were howls of protest from the Scottish Nationalist Party (SNP) MP's, for whom the assembly was to be a first step toward full independence.

However, Labour started to recover popularity in Scotland and held several seats in October by-elections – most of them at the expense of the Scottish Nationalists, who had been gaining ground. The SNP decline began when they failed to capture the Glasgow industrial suburb of Garscadden on April 13. Labour held it, though with a reduced majority. The SNP tide continued to ebb when Labour increased its majority on May 31 at Hamilton, south of Glasgow, with a swing toward Labour of 4.5 per cent. Labour held off another SNP challenge at Berwick and East Lothian on October 26.

The most intriguing question was whether Labour's growing popularity in Scotland would spread to England. Ironically, the collapse of the SNP vote was considered a good sign for the Conservatives, because in the last general election the SNP won the rural seats, virtually wiping out Conservative representation in Scotland. A swing away from the SNP would give Conservative leader Margaret Thatcher's party half a dozen seats.

British Prime Minister James Callaghan is greeted by Indian Prime Minister Morarji Desai during a January visit to New Delhi.

A huge crowd is on hand as Queen Elizabeth II and Prince Philip ride in an open coach during a birthday parade held for her in West Berlin on May 24.

Nevertheless, a Gallup Poll in late October indicated that perhaps Callaghan had gambled correctly in delaying the election. The poll showed Labour running 5½ points ahead of the Conservatives, a gain of more than 12 points over September.

One political career remained in limbo at year-end. Jeremy Thorpe, former Liberal leader, was ordered on December 13 to stand trial on charges of conspiracy to murder. Although he retained his seat in Parliament, his future was uncertain. His trial was expected to start in the spring of 1979.

The Economy. The government's counterinflation policy for the year beginning on Aug. 1, 1978, when the previous Phase Three policy expired, was published on July 21. The new program limited increases in earnings to 5 per cent and called for continued price restraint.

However, the policy quickly ran into trouble. Despite pleas from Chancellor of the Exchequer Denis Healey and Callaghan, who argued that inflation would soar again if wages were not controlled, both the Trades Union Congress (TUC) and the Labour Party's own annual conference rejected the 5 per cent pay limit.

Healey angrily retorted that free collective bargaining would simply put more money into the pockets of the members of powerful unions, such as the miners, railwaymen, and dockers, at the expense of their weaker brethren. He added that if wage deals got out of hand, the government would use other weapons, such as raising the income tax, in an attempt to curb inflation.

Labor Discontent characterized the autumn season, and Callaghan, having staked both his personal prestige and his party's re-election chances on the pay issue, desperately tried to sway the TUC away from its hostile line. But under pressure from tough, militant shop stewards, TUC leaders showed little inclination to compromise. Strike threats came from coal miners and municipal-service workers demanding 40 per cent pay increases. Power workers asked for 30 per cent raises, while Britain's 500,000 truckdrivers pushed for increases of 20 to 30 per cent.

A total of 57,000 Ford Motor Company workers went on strike in September after rejecting their company's pay offer, and the repercussions began to slow down Ford operations elsewhere in Europe. The British workers returned to work late in November after receiving a 16.8 per cent wage increase, but the government immediately imposed sanctions against Ford for exceeding the legal 5 per cent increase. The penalties, the first levied against an American-owned company, included withholding orders for Ford vehicles. On December 13, the Conservatives instigated a government vote against sanctions. Callaghan lost, and said the Ford sanctions would be lifted. The next day, he asked Parliament for a vote of confidence and won, 300 to 290.

Hospital engineers and supervisors struck, and after a month the walkout triggered charges that people were dying for lack of treatment. More than 60,000 patients waited for surgery, and 300 hospitals admitted only emergency cases. The only bright spot was a decision by Vauxhall auto workers to reject their shop stewards' call for a strike while negotiating new pay scales.

The government had come under fire in the House of Commons in February for compiling a blacklist of companies said to have given pay increases above the 10 per cent ceiling imposed under Phase Three. The government roused Opposition ire by withholding state contracts from such companies. From time to time, the Treasury published the number of firms against whom these sanctions had been taken. In early August, there were 74.

The 193-year-old *The Times* (London) suspended publication on November 30 for reasons similar to those that shut down *The New York Times* for three months earlier in the year. In both cases, workers objected to the introduction of new production technology that would put some employees out of jobs. The bitter British dispute was aggravated by the fact that management had to deal with the demands of nine unions that were represented by 65 bargaining units. The strike, which also affected *The Sunday Times* and the *Times Literary, Educational,* and *Higher Educational* supplements, was expected to take months to settle. See NEWSPAPER.

Frustration in Rhodesia. In cooperation with the United States, Britain continued trying to arrange a settlement in Rhodesia, but there were increasing signs that Anglo-American hopes were in vain. Foreign Secretary David Owen declared on March 22 that the "internal settlement" under which Rhodesia's Prime Minister Ian D. Smith and black African moderates had formed a multiracial "executive council" was illegal, because the new government did not represent black African opinion. Owen and U.S. Ambassador to the United Nations Andrew Young tried to bring together all the concerned factions, including the Patriotic Front guerrillas fighting from bases in Zambia and Mozambique. But the chances of such a conference appeared remote as the war spread and the atrocities and bitterness increased. See RHODESIA; SOUTH AFRICA.

Common Market. Britain acquired the reputation of being a difficult partner in its relations with the European Community (EC or Common Market). Differences between Britain and the rest of the EC over fishing rights in British waters went unresolved. At several acrimonious meetings, Britain, which controls the largest area of sea among the nine Common Market nations, pressed its right to impose strict quotas within a 200-nautical-mile limit to protect fish stocks. It accused some Common Market countries of overfishing in those areas.

John Silkin, minister of agriculture, fisheries, and food, also continued Britain's attack on the Common Market's common agricultural policy. He claimed it was producing high retail prices and periodic surpluses – "butter mountains and wine lakes."

As the year ended, Britain decided not to join the European Monetary System (EMS). The EMS was a joint proposal by France and West Germany that exchange rates among European countries should be fixed, partly as a step toward European unity but more probably to detach European currencies from the fluctuations of the U.S. dollar. Nine European heads of state met on December 5 in Brussels, Belgium, and Belgium, Denmark, France, Luxembourg, the Netherlands, and West Germany agreed to start the EMS. Ireland and Italy joined within two weeks, but Britain would not make a commitment for at least six months after the EMS was scheduled to begin in 1979.

Callaghan argued that the EMS would force countries with different economies into an economic straitjacket and limit their ability to adjust policies by making changes in exchange rates. Countries with a tendency toward high inflation, such as Britain, would see their exports priced out of the market and be forced to deflate their economy and raise unemployment. See EUROPE.   Ian Mather

See also EUROPE (Facts in Brief Table). In WORLD BOOK, see GREAT BRITAIN.

GREECE was troubled by the United States decision in 1978 to lift its arms embargo against Turkey. The embargo was imposed after Turkey's "unlawful" use of U.S. arms when it invaded Cyprus in 1974. A condition of lifting the embargo was that progress be made toward solving the Greek-Turkish dispute over Cyprus. The Greeks felt the U.S. decision could worsen its relations with Turkey and raise problems of peace and security in the area. See CYPRUS.

The quarrel with Turkey over control of the oil-rich Aegean Sea, as well as on the Cyprus question, was reflected in attitudes toward the North Atlantic Treaty Organization (NATO), of which both countries are members. In NATO military exercises held in May, the two countries staged separate national maneuvers in different parts of the Aegean. The maneuvers are usually combined.

The prime ministers of Greece and Turkey met in Montreux, Switzerland, on March 10 and 11 in an effort to settle their differences. Although they reported no progress, they agreed on further talks. Representatives of both governments met in Ankara, Turkey, in July to discuss air and surface rights in the Aegean Sea. The third round of talks ended on December 4, with little progress reported.

EC Membership. Prime Minister Constantine Karamanlis visited London; Brussels, Belgium; Paris; and Bonn, West Germany, in January, to try to speed up Greece's entry into the European Community (EC or Common Market). Karamanlis secured the agreement of European leaders to facilitate Greece's admission. In Brussels, EC foreign ministers agreed on February 7 to try to finish negotiations by the end of 1978, so that Greece could join by 1981. On July 27, the European Commission, which carries out EC policy, recommended to the Council of Ministers, the policy-making body, that the EC bring in most parts of the Greek economy over a five-year period and agriculture and industry over seven or eight years.

Cabinet Shuffle. Karamanlis appointed two liberals to his Cabinet on May 10 to broaden the base of his conservative New Democracy Party government. Constantine Mitsotakis was named minister of coordination and planning, and Athanasios Canellopoulos became minister of finance.

Trade Pact. Commerce Minister George Panagiotopoulos signed a trade agreement with Albania during a visit to Tiranë in March. He re-entered Greece through the Kakavia Pass, which had been closed for 38 years.   Kenneth Brown

See also EUROPE (Facts in Brief Table). In WORLD BOOK, see GREECE.

GRENADA. See LATIN AMERICA.

GUATEMALA. See LATIN AMERICA.

GUINEA. See AFRICA.

GUINEA-BISSAU. See AFRICA.

GUYANA. See LATIN AMERICA.

GUZMAN FERNANDEZ, SILVESTRE ANTONIO (1911-   ), was sworn in as the 77th president of the Dominican Republic on Aug. 16, 1978. Guzman, leader of the left-of-center Dominican Revolutionary Party, defeated Joaquin Balaguer, who had been backed by the military in his try for a fourth consecutive term as president.

President Guzman was born in La Vega on Feb. 12, 1911, the son of well-to-do parents. He attended public schools, and majored in agriculture at Dolores Morilla Normal School. After graduating in 1933, he operated his family estates, which included a cattle ranch and a coffee plantation. But he became concerned over the plight of workers and opposed dictator Rafael Leonidas Trujillo Molina.

After the assassination of Trujillo in 1961, Guzman joined the Dominican Revolutionary Party, which had been founded in exile by Juan Bosch. He assumed the party leadership when Bosch retired. During his 1978 campaign, Guzman emphasized that the party was not revolutionary, but that its members shared a common desire to drive the Balaguer regime from power.

Guzman and his wife, Renée, have a daughter, Sonia. Guzman also has a daughter, Lillian, by his first wife.   Paul C. Tullier

See also LATIN AMERICA (Facts in Brief Table). In WORLD BOOK, see DOMINICAN REPUBLIC.

HAITI. See LATIN AMERICA.

HANDICAPPED. The Department of Health, Education, and Welfare (HEW) on Jan. 13, 1978, issued regulations barring discrimination against the handicapped by United States government agencies and all federally funded projects. The rules, implementing Section 504 of the Rehabilitation Act of 1973, say that handicapped persons may not be "excluded from participation in, be denied the benefits of, or otherwise be subjected to discrimination under" any federally funded or assisted project because of a handicap. In addition, facilities must be designed to accommodate the handicapped persons served by some 30 federal agencies and all government-funded projects.

Problems for Schools. Major financial problems are developing for United States schools because of provisions in the Education for All Handicapped Children Act, which became effective in September 1977. Under the act, institutions were given three years to provide appropriate education to all qualified handicapped students. Failure to comply could mean loss of all federal funds.

Colleges were particularly hard hit. The law required that curbs, stairs, and other architectural barriers be eliminated or modified; elevators be installed; and lavatories be altered to serve the handicapped. Interpreters using sign language would have to be stationed beside lecturers to aid the

A New York City school bus driver helps a boy board a bus. New rules require that all public facilities be accessible to the handicapped.

deaf, and readers and recorded materials would have to be provided for blind students. "It is the right thing for us to be doing," said Zeddie Bowen, provost of Beloit College in Wisconsin. "But I don't think when they passed the law they realized all the problems that would be created."

David S. Latel, director of HEW's Office of Civil Rights, which is charged with enforcing the new law, told critics, "The regulations do not require the elimination of all architectural barriers. While a part or percentage of an institution's facilities must be accessible, there is no prescribed number or percentage that is required. The object is to make the programs of an institution accessible, not every classroom or dormitory room."

The new law also poses huge financial burdens for public school districts. State officials complain that the federal government is paying only 9 per cent of the extra costs that the law forces on the schools. More than 3.5 million youngsters have already been identified as eligible for handicapped services. The federal contribution, now $250 million, will rise sharply each year. But the states and local districts must bear the bulk of the fiscal load.

Air Safety. More than 1,500 blind people demonstrated outside Federal Aviation Administration (FAA) Headquarters in Washington, D.C., on July 5 against a ruling prohibiting blind passengers from carrying white canes aboard airplanes. The FAA defended the regulation, saying that canes could be a hazard if there is turbulence or an accident.

Representatives of seven organizations of the blind met with FAA Deputy Administrator Quentin S. Taylor, who said the agency would consider alternatives. Meanwhile the National Federation of the Blind filed a lawsuit against United Airlines, which forbids passengers to use white canes on their aircraft.

New Library. The Illinois Regional Library for the Blind and Physically Handicapped was dedicated in July. The library, on the near-west side of Chicago, is designed to serve the special needs of the handicapped and is also an eloquent work of architecture. The building is the work of architect Stanley Tigerman. See ARCHITECTURE.

James D. Jeffers, director of the Illinois Division of Vocational Rehabilitation and first executive director of the Architectural and Transportation Barriers Compliance Board, was recognized during Handicapped Week in May as Handicapped American of the Year by the President's Committee on the Employment of the Handicapped. In accepting the award, Jeffers said, "Disabled Americans are taking charge of their lives. We are being seen and heard and, as we do so, we are earning dignity, respect, and independence." Virginia E. Anderson

In WORLD BOOK, see HANDICAPPED.

HARNESS RACING. See HORSE RACING.

HAWAII. See STATE GOVERNMENT.

HEALTH AND DISEASE. The mysterious and deadly bacteria responsible for Legionnaire's disease was isolated and identified in Bloomington, Ind., on Aug. 11, 1978, after it killed three persons there. The disease was named for an outbreak that killed a number of delegates to an American Legion convention in Philadelphia in 1976. The Center for Disease Control in Atlanta, Ga., tracked the virus in Bloomington to a cooling tower at Indiana University and to a nearby creek.

Legionnaire's disease flared up again in September in the bustling garment district of New York City, killing two young men and sickening 118 other persons. City officials ordered streets and subway stations scoured; water towers treated with chlorine; and central air-conditioning units, which often play a role in the disease's spread, turned off temporarily. Federal officials said the New York City outbreak was one of at least 14 in the United States since 1965. But they stressed that Legionnaire's disease is no longer a mystery killer. The virus has been identified and can be treated with erythromycin, an antibiotic.

Heart Disease, the number-one killer in the U.S., claimed fewer lives in 1977 than in any year since 1963. Federal officials reported on October 24 that some 959,000 persons died of heart and blood-vessel disease in 1977. Great Britain and Australia also reported a decrease while Bulgaria, Czechoslovakia, Poland, Romania, and Sweden reported increases.

Cancer Research. The National Cancer Institute (NCI) changed policy in its fight against the second-greatest U.S. killer. Criticized because its costly "war on cancer" had not produced spectacular results, the institute said it would give top priority to projects started by various research groups rather than continuing to fund on a contract basis only projects developed and directed by the NCI.

A new test for prostate cancer, reported in January, could help save the lives of many of the 60,000 persons who develop this type of cancer each year in the United States. The test can detect prostate cancer before it spreads to other organs by measuring any marked rise in acid phosphatase, an enzyme produced by the prostate gland. Radioimmunoassay is another new early-warning technique for prostate cancer. By using a radioactive substance, scientists can detect small increases in phosphatase production. Radioimmunoassay is considered more sensitive than other tests, but also more expensive and time-consuming. The simpler test was endorsed in June for use in all routine medical examinations.

Pregnant women who took diethylstilbestrol (DES) to prevent miscarriage may, like their daughters, run a higher risk of developing cervical cancer, researchers reported in June. But two large-scale Boston studies had good news for DES daughters. Most of the lesions found in these women regressed and disappeared, and the risk of life-threatening cancer may not be as great as had been predicted.

Military veterans and civilians who witnessed a 1957 atmospheric nuclear test in the Nevada desert were found to have high cancer rates. On February 9, the U.S. Department of Defense set up toll-free telephone lines so that people who took part in the nuclear-testing program between 1946 and 1962 could find out whether they were exposed to dangerous amounts of radiation.

Six to 11 million U.S. workers may have breathed in dangerous amounts of asbestos while on the job, a federal research team reported in September. That exposure could lead to 67,000 cancer cases in the next 30 to 35 years. The study also concluded that the incidence of job-related cancers from cancer-causing substances is much higher than previously estimated, perhaps as high as 20 per cent of all cases. Besides asbestos, other such hazardous chemicals in the workplace include arsenic, benzene, chromium, iron oxide, nickel, petroleum distillates, and coal-tar pitch and coke-oven emissions.

Other Developments. A new Russian flu virus appeared in the United States in 1978, striking primarily at people under 25. Most older people were immune because they had developed antibodies from a similar flu strain that hit about 20 years earlier. Two other flu strains, A/Texas and A/Victoria, infected Americans of all ages.

The U.S. Food and Drug Administration issued strong warnings about liquid-protein diets after at least 40 deaths were traced to the near-starvation weight-loss technique. Followers of this fad diet consumed only liquid-protein preparations. Despite a continuing fascination with new ways to lose weight, Americans weighed an average of 14 pounds (6.3 kilograms) more in 1978 than they did 15 years before, according to the National Center for Health Statistics in Washington, D.C.

The Center for Disease Control reported that women over 27 who took birth-control pills for four or more years ran a risk at least 200 times normal of developing liver tumors. Women under 27 who took birth-control pills were 19 times as likely to develop the tumors.

National Health Insurance legislation again made a routine appearance before Congress. President Jimmy Carter outlined a set of principles for a health plan on July 29, including protection against catastrophic medical expenses, aggressive cost containment, and a continuing role for private insurers. Senator Edward M. Kennedy (D., Mass.) on August 28 broke with Carter and unveiled a new program supported by labor that would regulate health care tightly. Although hearings were conducted before Congress adjourned, a national health plan was still viewed as years away from reality. Dianne Rafalik Hales

See also DRUGS; MEDICINE; PUBLIC HEALTH. In WORLD BOOK, see CANCER; HEALTH.

HIGHWAY. See BUILDING AND CONSTRUCTION; TRANSPORTATION.

HOBBIES. The log of the *Enola Gay,* the plane that dropped the first atomic bomb on Hiroshima, Japan, during World War II, was sold for $85,000 on Nov. 14, 1978. The log, kept by the plane's co-pilot, Robert Lewis, brought the highest recorded price ever paid for a handwritten American document at an auction of items from the autograph collection of the late Phillip Sang, a Chicago businessman.

Its purchaser, Malcolm Forbes, Jr., also paid a record $32,000 for a Lincoln letter, for which the previous high was $20,000, at the same auction. At an auction of other items from the Sang collection on April 26, Forbes paid $70,000 for an expense account submitted by Paul Revere. At that auction, a Thomas Jefferson letter sold for $14,000, and a set of signatures of the signers of the Declaration of Independence brought $195,000.

The 1978 Hummel Plate proved so popular with collectors and investors that none of the plates was available at the usual United States outlets by September. Goebel Art, Incorporated, a West German firm, has been producing Hummel figurines for decades and began making and selling collectors' plates in 1971, smashing the mold at the end of each year. Although the 1978 plate originally carried a list price of $75, resale prices had reached $300 by the end of the year. The 1971 plate, originally priced at $25, went for more than $1,000 in 1978.

A Gutenberg Bible is auctioned off at Christie's in New York City in April. The Bible sold for $2 million, highest price ever paid for a book.

Collectors showed increasing interest in old mechanical banks. A 50-year-old tin bank in the form of a snake feeding coins to a frog brought $7,421 in London on May 26 – a world auction record. However, such banks have reportedly been bringing up to $10,000 in private sales.

Record Sales. A collection of duck decoys assembled by the late Stewart E. Gregory was expected to bring $160,000 at a July auction in Hyannis, Mass. However, sales totaled $240,000, including a record-tying single-item price of $10,500 for a Hudsonian curlew carved by John Dilley.

Antique-automobile collectors reported that the most-sought-after vehicles in 1978 were Model J and SJ Duesenbergs of the 1928-1937 era, 12- and 16-cylinder Cadillacs, and 12-cylinder Packards. A 1932 Cadillac V-16 sold for about $125,000 while a 1932 Duesenberg phaeton brought $250,000.

In March, New York City book dealer Hans P. Kraus sold a Gutenberg Bible to the Gutenberg Museum in Mainz, West Germany, for $1.8 million. Less than a month later, the state library in Stuttgart, West Germany, paid a dealer more than $2-million for another Gutenberg Bible. The dealer had bought it from the Episcopal Church General Theological Seminary in New York.   Theodore M. O'Leary

See also Coin Collecting; Stamp Collecting. In World Book, see Hobby.

HOCKEY. The Montreal Canadiens continued their domination of the National Hockey League (NHL) in the 1977-1978 season. They had the best record during the regular season, and at one point went 28 games without defeat. Then they won the Stanley Cup by taking 12 of their 15 play-off games.

During the regular season, each of the 18 teams played 80 games from October to April. The division champions were the Canadiens, Boston Bruins, New York Islanders, and Chicago Black Hawks.

Twelve teams advanced to the play-offs, but none could threaten the Canadiens. Montreal beat Detroit 4 games to 1, the Toronto Maple Leafs in four straight games, and Boston by 4 games to 2. Thus, the Canadiens won the Stanley Cup for the third consecutive year and the 21st time overall.

But the Canadiens were not complacent. Coach Scotty Bowman said, "We're a good team, but we've had it pretty easy the last few years." And goalie Ken Dryden said, "We're not machines. We're humans sometimes, too."

Despite Dryden's disclaimer, the Canadiens often played with the efficiency of machines. Right wing Guy Lafleur won the Art Ross Trophy as scoring champion for the third straight year and the Hart Trophy as the league's Most Valuable Player for the second straight year. Dryden and Michel Larocque won the Vezina Trophy for goaltending; Bob

Jubilant members of the Montreal Canadiens hoist the Stanley Cup after beating the Boston Bruins to win their third consecutive NHL title.

Gainey, the first Frank Selke Award as the best defensive forward; and Larry Robinson, the Conn Smythe Trophy as most valuable in the play-offs.

After the play-offs, the Bronfman family sold the Canadiens to Molson Breweries for $20 million and their long-term lease to the Montreal Forum for millions more. Later, Sam Pollock, the general manager who built the team, retired.

Other Awards. The Canadiens left a few honors for others. New York Islanders won the Norris Trophy for the best defenseman (Denis Potvin) and the Calder Trophy for Rookie of the Year (Mike Bossy). Butch Goring of Los Angeles received the Lady Byng Trophy for sportsmanship and the Bill Masterton Memorial Trophy for perseverance.

The all-star team consisted of Dryden in goal, Brad Park of Boston and Potvin on defense, Bryan Trottier of the Islanders at center, and Clark Gillies of the Islanders and Lafleur at wing. Lafleur led the league in scoring (132 points in 78 games), goals (60), and game-winning goals (12). Trottier had the most assists (11). Bossy scored 53 goals, a rookie record.

In the WHA. The World Hockey Association (WHA) again struggled for recognition and solvency. Although it made progress, it fell short of its goals.

The eight teams played 80 games each in one division. Each played against Russian and Czechoslovak teams, the games counting in the standing.

Standings in National Hockey League

Clarence Campbell Conference

Lester Patrick Division	W.	L.	T.	Points
New York Islanders	48	17	15	111
Philadelphia	45	20	15	105
Atlanta	34	27	19	87
New York Rangers	30	37	13	73
Conn Smythe Division				
Chicago	32	29	19	83
Colorado	19	40	21	59
Vancouver	20	43	17	57
St. Louis	20	47	13	53
Minnesota	18	53	9	45

Prince of Wales Conference

James Norris Division	W.	L.	T.	Points
Montreal	59	10	11	129
Detroit	32	34	14	78
Los Angeles	31	34	15	77
Pittsburgh	25	37	18	68
Washington	17	49	14	48
Charles F. Adams Division				
Boston	51	18	11	113
Buffalo	44	19	17	105
Toronto	41	29	10	92
Cleveland	22	45	13	57

Scoring Leaders	Games	Goals	Assists	Points
Guy Lafleur, Montreal	78	60	72	132
Bryan Trottier, N.Y. Islanders	77	46	77	123
Darryl Sittler, Toronto	80	45	72	117
Jacques Lemaire, Montreal	76	36	61	97
Denis Potvin, N.Y. Islanders	80	30	64	94
Mike Bossy, N.Y. Islanders	73	53	38	91

Leading Goalies	Games	Goals against	Avg.
Ken Dryden, Montreal	52	105	2.05
Michel Larocque, Montreal	30	77	2.67
Montreal Totals	82	183	2.29
Bernie Parent, Philadelphia	49	108	2.22
Wayne Stephenson, Philadelphia	26	68	2.75
Rick St. Croix, Philadelphia	7	20	3.04
Philadelphia Totals	80	200	2.50

Awards
Calder Trophy (best rookie)—Mike Bossy, N.Y. Islanders
Hart Trophy (most valuable player)—Guy Lafleur, Montreal
Lady Byng Trophy (sportsmanship)—Butch Goring, Los Angeles
Norris Trophy (best defenseman)—Denis Potvin, N.Y. Islanders
Art Ross Trophy (leading scorer)—Guy Lafleur, Montreal
Conn Smythe Trophy (most valuable in Stanley Cup)—
  Larry Robinson, Montreal
Vezina Trophy (leading goalie)—
  Ken Dryden, Michel Larocque, Montreal
Bill Masterton Trophy (perseverance, dedication to hockey)—
  Butch Goring, Los Angeles

Standings in World Hockey Association

	W.	L.	T.	Points
Winnipeg	50	28	2	102
New England	44	31	5	93
Houston	42	34	4	88
Quebec	40	37	3	83
Edmonton	38	39	3	79
Birmingham	36	41	3	75
Cincinnati	35	42	3	73
Indianapolis	24	51	5	53

Scoring Leaders	Games	Goals	Assists	Points
Marc Tardif, Quebec	78	65	89	154
Real Cloutier, Quebec	73	56	73	129
Ulf Nilsson, Winnipeg	73	37	89	126
Anders Hedberg, Winnipeg	77	63	59	122
Bobby Hull, Winnipeg	77	46	71	117
Andre Lacroix, Houston	78	36	77	113
Robbie Ftorek, Cincinnati	80	59	50	109
Kent Nilsson, Winnipeg	80	42	65	107
Gordie Howe, New England	76	34	62	96
Mark Howe, New England	70	30	61	91

Leading Goalies	Games	Goals against	Avg.
Al Smith, New England	55	174	3.22
Louis Levasseur, New England	27	91	3.30
New England Totals	80	265	3.24
Joe Daley, Winnipeg	37	114	3.30
Gary Bromley, Winnipeg	39	124	3.30
Markuss Mattsson, Winnipeg	10	30	3.52
Winnipeg Totals	80	268	3.32
Ernie Wakely, Houston	51	166	3.24
Lynn Zimmerman, Houston	20	84	4.32
Wayne Rutledge, Houston	12	47	4.45
Houston Totals	80	297	3.66

Awards
Most Valuable Player—Marc Tardif, Quebec
Scoring Champion—Marc Tardif, Quebec
Best Defenseman—Lars-Erik Sjoberg, Winnipeg
Best Goaltender—Al Smith, New England
Rookie of the Year—Kent Nilsson, Winnipeg
Most Gentlemanly Player—Tom Webster, New England
Coach of the Year—Bill Dineen, Houston
AVCO Cup Play-Off Most Valuable Player—
  Bob Guindon, Winnipeg

Six teams advanced to the Avco Cup play-offs. The Winnipeg Jets, who had the best regular-season record, won the play-offs, beating the New England Whalers in four straight games in the finals.

Marc Tardif of the Quebec Nordiques led in scoring (154 points in 78 games) and goals (65) and tied with Ulf Nilsson of Winnipeg for first in assists (89). Tardif was voted Most Valuable Player.

Winnipeg had the league's best line in Bobby Hull, the former NHL star, and Nilsson and Anders Hedberg, both from Sweden. When the contracts of Nilsson and Hedberg expired after the season, they signed with the New York Rangers of the NHL. They received about $475,000 each per year for two years. According to their Winnipeg contracts, Winnipeg could have kept them by offering $25,000 less. But Winnipeg, though making a profit, did not think it could afford such high contracts.

The Houston Aeros of the WHA went out of business when their new owners refused to assume the debts of the previous ownership. The WHA was reduced to six teams in December when the Indianapolis Racers folded. The Minnesota North Stars and Cleveland Barons of the NHL merged.

Hockey lost two of its greatest stars in November, when Hull and Black Hawks defenseman Bobby Orr announced they were retiring. Frank Litsky

In WORLD BOOK, see HOCKEY.

HONDURAS. See LATIN AMERICA.

HORSE RACING. Affirmed came out of the West in 1978, where he won the Santa Anita and Hollywood Derbies, to become the United States 11th Triple Crown winner. Alydar, whose preparation included victories in Florida in the Flamingo Stakes and Florida Derby, was favored for the Kentucky Derby, first of the Triple Crown events, but finished second in that race and the next two in the series for 3-year-olds.

Bred and owned by Louis E. Wolfson's Harbor View Farm, Affirmed won the Kentucky Derby at Churchill Downs on May 6, the Preakness at Pimlico on May 20, and the Belmont Stakes at Belmont Park on June 10. He was the second horse in a row to triumph in the trio of races.

The 1977 Triple Crown winner, Seattle Slew, overcame a near-fatal illness and an injury during the first half of 1978 to prove himself a top handicap competitor. He won the Marlboro Cup on September 16 and the Woodward Handicap on September 30, both at Belmont Park. Affirmed finished second to Seattle Slew in the Marlboro, the first time two Triple Crown winners met in competition.

Exceller narrowly beat Seattle Slew in the Jockey Club Gold Cup at Belmont Park on October 14 to challenge for Horse-of-the-Year honors. Earlier in the year in California, Exceller won the San Juan Capistrano, Hollywood Invitational, Sunset Handicap, and Hollywood Gold Cup. A 5-year-old, he

ranks fourth on the all-time list of leading thoroughbred money earners.

Forego, Horse of the Year in 1974, 1975, and 1976 and champion older horse in those years and in 1977, was retired on July 10 at the age of 8. He won 34 of 57 races and earned $1,938,957 to be the second leading earner of all time after Kelso ($1,977,896).

Spectacular Bid dominated the 2-year-olds with victories including the Laurel Futurity at Laurel, Md., which he won on October 28 in track-record time of 1 minute 41 3/5 seconds for 1 1/16 mile.

Horses trained by Lazaro S. Barrera, which included Affirmed, earned more than $3 million, a world record. Jockey Darrel McHargue broke Steve Cauthen's earnings mark, winning $6,155,153.

Harness Racing. The richest race in the history of both standardbred and thoroughbred racing was the $560,000 Meadowlands Pace run at The Meadowlands in New Jersey on August 3. The market for standardbred yearlings sold at auction broke all records. A yearling colt by leading sire Meadow Skipper brought a record bid of $385,000 on October 5 at the Tattersalls sale in Lexington, Ky.

Quarter Horse Racing. Two-year-old colt Moon Lark won the $1.28-million All-American Quarter Horse Futurity at Ruidoso Downs, N. Mex., in September. First money was $437,500. Jane Goldstein

In WORLD BOOK, see HARNESS RACING; HORSE RACING.

Major Horse Races of 1978

Race	Winner	Value to Winner
Belmont Stakes	Affirmed	$110,580
Canadian International Championship	Mac Diarmida	111,180
Epsom Derby (England)	Shirley Heights	177,140
Grand National Steeplechase (England)	Lucius	73,100
Irish Sweeps Derby	Shirley Heights	140,325
Jockey Club Gold Cup	Exceller	193,080
Kentucky Derby	Affirmed	186,900
King George VI & Queen Elizabeth Diamond Stakes (England)	Île de Bourbon	186,900
Marlboro Cup Handicap	Seattle Slew	180,000
Preakness	Affirmed	136,200
Prix de l'Arc de Triomphe (France)	Alleged	275,000
Prix du Jockey-Club (French Derby)	Acamas	195,652
Santa Anita Handicap	Vigors	180,000
Washington D.C. Int'l.	Mac Diarmida	120,000
Woodward Handicap	Seattle Slew	97,800

Major U.S. Harness Races of 1978

Race	Winner	Value to Winner
Cane Pace	Armbro Tiger	$ 72,592
Hambletonian	Speedy Somolli	120,640
Little Brown Jug	Happy Escort	49,492
Meadowlands Pace	Falcon Almahurst	210,000
Roosevelt Int'l.	Cold Comfort	100,000
Woodrow Wilson Pace	Scarlet Skipper	240,625
Yonkers Trot	Speedy Somolli	116,797

HOSPITAL. Spurred by the threat of proposed legislation that would put a 9 per cent ceiling on cost increases, hospitals in the United States struggled in 1978 to hold the line on spending. For the first six months they succeeded, reducing the hospital inflation rate to 12.9 per cent from 15.8 per cent in early 1977. But then costs began to accelerate again.

The 95th Congress, which considered a cost-containment bill that would have mandated a maximum cost, agreed to let hospitals set up a voluntary effort. Organized by the American Hospital Association, the American Medical Association, and the Federation of American Hospitals, the program's goal was to reduce hospital spending by 2 percentage points in 1978 and in 1979. Hospitals ordered job freezes, pressured suppliers into delaying price hikes, and begged patients to be "sensible" about malpractice suits.

Other Serious Problems included an average daily occupancy rate of only 75 per cent in 1978. The U.S. Department of Health, Education, and Welfare (HEW) set 80 per cent as the minimally acceptable occupancy rate for acute-care beds. Estimating the cost of building and support services for one hospital bed at $100,000, with annual maintenance costs of $60,000, HEW called for a maximum of four beds per 1,000 persons in the area serviced by a hospital. The agency estimated the waste resulting from unused hospital beds at $2 billion a year.

In a ruling of national significance, the Arizona Supreme Court held in February that a private community hospital may require a physician to carry malpractice insurance as a condition for granting him staff privileges. Stating that a hospital has the "right to protect itself and its patients," the court said that the requirement of malpractice coverage was not "unlawful, arbitrary, or capricious."

Hospitals in Florida, Minnesota, Ohio, and Texas reported "scares" related to ethylene oxide, a toxic and highly explosive gas that may produce cancer. A special occupational-hazard review by federal authorities revealed that an estimated 100,000 hospital workers may be exposed daily to the gas, which is used to sterilize delicate medical instruments.

Fire Safety Check. Some of the most prestigious hospitals in the United States were ordered to modernize their facilities to meet new fire and safety standards or lose their accreditation. HEW's Bureau of Health Insurance sent inspectors to check hospital construction features.

The European concept of the *hospice*, a place to provide physical and emotional support for terminally ill people, gained greater acceptance in the United States. A newly formed National Hospice Organization held its first meeting in Washington, D.C., in October. Hospices are designed to give the humanistic and comprehensive care for the dying that conventional hospitals cannot. Dianne Rafalik Hales

In WORLD BOOK, see HOSPITAL.

HOUSING. The United States housing industry enjoyed a record year in 1978 as home prices, interest rates, housing starts, and home sales reached new heights. Demand for home ownership remained strong, with increasing numbers of young home buyers purchasing as a hedge against inflation.

The median price of a new house reached $56,600 in August, 16 per cent above the previous year's price, according to a U.S. Bureau of the Census report issued on November 8. The price represented a 140 per cent increase over the 1970 median of $23,500.

The average effective interest rate on conventional mortgages for new homes continued its record climb, reaching 9.84 per cent in October. Actual mortgage rates, however, had already reached the 10 per cent level in some metropolitan areas during the spring. The U.S. Department of Housing and Urban Development (HUD) raised the interest rate on federally guaranteed mortgages to 8.75 per cent on February 27.

Construction Boom. Higher prices failed to halt the boom in housing construction. Despite a slow beginning, housing starts for the year were estimated at close to the 2-million record set in 1977. Although housing starts fell 29 per cent in January – the largest single monthly decline on record – because of severe winter weather and remained off in

Artemas Cole in *The Wall Street Journal*

"They're not as young as they look . . . they have a 4¹/₂% mortgage!"

February, they accelerated by a record 31.8 per cent in March and remained at high levels for the remainder of the year.

Home resales hit their highest rate ever – a seasonally adjusted 4.1 million units – in August, according to a survey released in October by the National Association of Realtors. The report also noted that the median price of such homes had passed the $50,000 mark for the first time.

The mobile-home industry claimed to be recovering from its slump and estimated production at from 290,000 to 307,000 units in 1978. Production was still down considerably from its peak year of 1972, when 576,000 units were built.

Discrimination in Housing. A report released on July 31 by the National Urban Coalition blamed housing rehabilitation for the displacement of the poor by middle-income families in many urban neighborhoods. The study covered rehabilitation in 65 neighborhoods of 44 cities and claimed that too little effort was being made to deal with the effects of displacement upon lower-income groups.

A nationwide survey conducted by HUD reported in April that blacks still face a 75 per cent chance of encountering discrimination when looking for rental housing and a 62 per cent chance of discrimination when trying to buy a home. The survey showed that the incidence of discrimination in home sales was four times higher in the North Central States than in the South or West and lowest in the Northeast. Discrimination in rental practices was about the same throughout the United States.

The Federal Home Loan Bank Board (FHLBB) issued regulations on May 18 prohibiting federally chartered savings and loan associations from *redlining* – refusing to make loans on houses because they are old or located in inner-city neighborhoods. Lending institutions were also required to register all loan applications.

Mortgages. The 12,600 federally chartered credit unions in the United States were authorized to offer their customers 30-year mortgage loans starting on May 8. Previously they were not allowed to make loans for more than 10 or 12 years, which virtually excluded them from the home-mortgage market.

The FHLBB released a study on January 12 calling for more flexible mortgage arrangements to better serve the needs of the young and the elderly. In July, the board proposed four types of variable-rate mortgages – graduated-rate mortgages, with interest rates that increase over time; standard variable-rate mortgages, in which the interest rate could be adjusted to reflect general market conditions; rollover mortgages, now commonly used in Canada, in which long-term loans are refinanced at regular intervals; and reverse-annuity mortgages, which would allow retired people to borrow money against the equity in their homes.   James M. Banovetz

In WORLD BOOK, see HOUSE; HOUSING.

HOUSTON. Studies released in 1978 indicated that Houston's building boom was continuing unabated. The National Association of Home Builders reported in May that Houston ranked second only to Chicago as the largest United States producer of housing for the period from 1969 to 1978, erecting an estimated 403,200 units during that decade.

Houston and Chicago also led the nation in new housing during the first half of 1978. Both cities registered more than 15,000 new units, according to statistics released by the F. W. Dodge Division of McGraw Hill Publications Company on August 23.

The U.S. Bureau of the Census reported in November that Houston's population had grown by 13.5 per cent, to an estimated 1,455,046 persons, between 1970 and 1976. The report cited the annexation of unincorporated suburbs, which increased Houston's area by 50 per cent in 15 years, as a significant cause of the city's population increase.

Quality of Life. Houston shared fourth place with New York City on the Environmental Protection Agency's (EPA) list of cities having the highest ozone pollution level. The EPA recommended in a study released in July that the city's many chemical and petroleum plants use more effective emissions-control devices and that vehicle traffic be reduced 20 per cent.

Living costs rose 8.3 per cent in Houston during the 11-month period ending in June 1978 – a high rate for major U.S. cities. However, living was still relatively inexpensive in Houston. A U.S. Department of Labor report issued on April 26 indicated that it cost an average family of four $15,488 to maintain a middle-level standard of living in the Houston area, 9.5 per cent below the national average.

Police Problems. Houston's assistant police chief, Carrol Lynn, was on trial at year-end on charges of obstructing justice in connection with an alleged $45,000 bribery scheme. Houston's police department, already under fire from the city's black and Mexican American communities over alleged police brutality, received further criticism from minority groups in April when U.S. District Court Judge Ross Sterling rejected a Department of Justice motion challenging the lenient sentences given to three former Houston policemen who were convicted in the 1977 death of a young Mexican American prisoner.

Other Developments. The 1974 conviction of Elmer Wayne Henley for the killings of 27 men in the Houston area was overturned by the Texas Court of Criminal Appeals on December 20 and sent back to the San Antonio Court that tried him.

Houston became a link in Pan American World Airways' international service on July 1. The airline began using Houston Intercontinental Airport for flights to London.   James M. Banovetz

See also CITY. In WORLD BOOK, see HOUSTON.

HUNGARY expanded relations with the West and increased industrial production in 1978. The Congress of the United States granted Hungary most-favored-nation status on May 5, and the United States and Hungary agreed tentatively to reduce duties on $6 million in bilateral trade during trade negotiations in Geneva, Switzerland, in November.

Hungary revalued its monetary unit, the forint, against Western currencies on November 11. The currencies of Austria, Belgium, Luxembourg, the Netherlands, and West Germany went up 6 per cent in relation to the forint. The Swiss franc went up 8 per cent, and the forint's value increased 5 per cent in relation to the U.S. dollar.

Hungary and Austria agreed on May 5 to abolish visas for travel between the two countries as of Jan. 1, 1979. Travel rules issued in October let Hungarian refugees and their relatives in Hungary visit one another without special permission, beginning Jan. 1, 1979. The ministry of the interior in October relaxed regulations for issuing passports for travel to the West, also effective Jan. 1, 1979. Early in 1978, five intellectual critics of the regime, including sociologist and former Prime Minister Andras Hegedüs, were allowed to leave Hungary for a temporary stay in the West.

Industrial Production increased 6.4 per cent in the first half of 1978, compared with the first half of 1977. Pharmaceutical output increased 19 per cent; precision engineering, 15 per cent; and telecommunications and electronics, 10 per cent.

A factory licensed to manufacture Levi Strauss blue jeans opened in Budapest in August. The Eaton Corporation of Cleveland agreed in September to buy $300 million in truck axles from the Raba Enterprise in Györ. The Council for Mutual Economic Assistance investment bank granted Hungary's aluminum industry a $1.9-billion credit in September.

Subsidies to End. The Communist Party Central Committee decided on April 20 to phase out most price subsidies for consumer goods over two years. Subsidies accounted for $7 billion of Hungary's 1977 budget of $20 billion. The heavy taxes on excess profits, which financed the subsidies, also were to be phased out. Officials hoped the public would accept the expected price increases, because some wages also would be increased.

St. Stephen's crown, Hungary's national symbol, was returned on January 6 by a U.S. delegation led by Secretary of State Cyrus R. Vance. The crown, along with a gold-embroidered royal mantle, a sword, a scabbard, a scepter, and an orb, had been in the United States since World War II.   Chris Cviic

See also EUROPE (Facts in Brief Table). In WORLD BOOK, see HUNGARY.

The Crown of St. Stephen, symbol of Hungarian national pride, held in the United States for 33 years, is returned to Budapest by a U.S. delegation.

HUNTING. Lynn A. Greenwalt, director of the United States Fish and Wildlife Service, declared on March 29, 1978, that he wanted to stop any movement aimed at ending hunting or fishing in national wildlife refuges. Greenwalt's statement supporting hunting was included in a task-force report on the national refuge system. That report suggested that some forms of hunting, trapping, and fishing in the refuges were contrary to the system's purpose.

John Grady, executive vice-president of the Defenders of Wildlife, a conservation organization, said Greenwalt's request for public comment on the task-force report was absurd. "Greenwalt's already made up his mind," he said. Sportsmen, who have often criticized what they considered antihunting positions taken by the Fish and Wildlife Service, generally welcomed Greenwalt's statement that hunting is a legitimate recreational use of refuges.

Lead Shot. Waterfowl hunters using other than 12-gauge shotguns were permitted to use lead shot in steel-shot zones during the 1978 fall hunting season. In a proposal published on June 29, however, the Fish and Wildlife Service indicated that nontoxic steel shot would be required in all gauges in designated zones beginning in 1979. The service estimates that ingesting spent lead pellets causes the deaths of about 2 million waterfowl annually.

Many hunters supported a rider in the Department of the Interior appropriations bill that would have banned enforcement of steel-shot rules. Under pressure from conservationists, a House-Senate Conference Committee changed the rider on September 29 to permit enforcement if state authorities agreed. Fish and game commissioners in most states gave their approval.

Other Developments. Secretary of the Interior Cecil D. Andrus, at the Third Annual Waterfowl Symposium in New Orleans on January 27, said that U.S. sportsmen have a major stake in decisions made in Congress classifying federal lands in Alaska. "If we have the vision to protect the vital ecosystems of Alaska, we will be maintaining a life-giving reservoir to support a rich array of wildlife for decades and centuries to come," Andrus said.

The Alaska Lands legislation was not passed by Congress. Some sportsmen objected to provisions of the bill as passed by the House giving subsistence hunters and fishermen priority in taking fish and game and setting aside large areas of lands for national parks in which hunting would be banned.

Andrus said on April 17 that he opposes the concept of a federal hunting license, though he thought some states charge too much for nonresident hunting licenses. Andrus said he believed most state fish and game departments were doing a good job. "Management of fish and game should be at the state level and not in the hands of a massive federal bureaucracy," he said.   Andrew L. Newman

In WORLD BOOK, see AMMUNITION; HUNTING.

ICE SKATING. Eric Heiden of Madison, Wis., in 1977 became the first speed skater to win the world overall, sprint, and junior championships in one year. In 1978, he won the three titles again. His younger sister, Beth, became a world champion, too.

Eric Heiden was a 19-year-old sophomore at the University of Wisconsin. He stood 6 feet 1 inch (185 centimeters) and weighed 165 pounds (75 kilograms), with thighs so thick that they rubbed together when he walked. Strong thighs are the most important physical asset of a speed skater. Beth was an 18-year-old freshman at Wisconsin, 5 feet 1 inch (155 centimeters) and 90 pounds (41 kilograms).

The Winners. The world-championship season started with the junior championships on February 4 and 5 in Montreal, Canada. Eric won all four men's races and Beth won all four for women.

In the sprint championships on February 11 and 12 at Lake Placid, N.Y., Eric won three of the four races for men. In women's competition, Lyubov Sadchikova of Russia took two races; Beth Heiden, one; and Kim Kostron of St. Paul, Minn., one. Sadchikova won the title. Beth Heiden was second.

The men's overall championship, the most important of the three, was skated on February 25 and 26 at Göteborg, Sweden. Eric won three races (500, 1,500, and 5,000 meters) and was fifth in the other (10,000 meters).

Tatiana Averina of Russia won two of the four races and the women's overall title on March 4 and 5 at Helsinki, Finland. Sylvia Burka of Winnipeg, Canada, in sixth place, was the leading North American.

Figure Skating. Charles Tickner of Littleton, Colo., who used self-hypnosis to build confidence, won the men's world title in March in Ottawa, Canada. Anett Poetzsch of East Germany took the women's title, with defending champion Linda Fratianne of Northridge, Calif., second. The 24-year-old Tickner rallied with a strong free-skating routine. Poetzsch, the 17-year-old European women's champion, built an early lead and held off superior free skaters. Tickner and Fratianne had retained their United States titles in February.

Fratianne was a shy high school senior, 5 feet 1 inch (155 centimeters) tall and weighing 95 pounds (43 kilograms). Her free-skating routine, while competent, lacked spark.

The world pairs champions for the sixth straight year were Alexander Zaitsev and Irina Rodnina, husband and wife, of Russia. Rodnina won the title four straight years with Alexsei Ulanov before she teamed with Zaitsev. Tai Babalonia of Mission Hills, Calif., and Randy Gardner of Los Angeles won their third consecutive American pairs title.   Frank Litsky

In WORLD BOOK, see ICE SKATING.

ICELAND. See EUROPE.

IDAHO. See STATE GOVERNMENT.

ILLINOIS. See CHICAGO; STATE GOVERNMENT.

IMMIGRATION. President Jimmy Carter approved an interim refugee policy concerning Vietnamese and other Indochinese immigrants on March 30, 1978. The new policy would permit entry into the United States of all "boat people" – Vietnamese refugees who fled their country in small fishing boats and have been refused entrance to other nations. It would also admit all Indochinese with close personal or political ties to the United States who are currently in refugee camps. The policy was expected to admit an additional 25,000 Indochinese within the first year. These procedures would remain in effect until new long-term refugee legislation is enacted.

The wholesale expulsion of Haitian immigrants from the Bahamas in June brought hundreds to Florida. Although Haitians had been entering the United States in a steady stream since President Carter relaxed deportation regulations in November 1977, record numbers began arriving in June. Many of the refugees claimed to be seeking political asylum, but immigration officials suspected that most of them were actually looking for work.

A study released by the U.S. Department of State in April revealed that, since 1965, Latin America and Asia have provided the greatest number of immigrants to the United States. The report indicated that the number of immigrants from Asia, particularly from the Philippines, South Korea, India, and China, has been growing at a much faster rate than the number from Latin America.

Illegal Immigration. Leonel J. Castillo, commissioner of immigration and naturalization, reported that experts estimated the number of illegal immigrants to the United States at 3 million to 5 million annually, but he cautioned that such estimates may not be extremely reliable. Nearly 90 per cent of the illegal aliens apprehended were Mexicans.

Castillo estimated that organized smuggling rings brought in as many as 25 per cent of all illegal aliens. These networks were thought to be bringing aliens through Mexico from as far south as Ecuador.

New Identification Measures. The U.S. Immigration and Naturalization Service issued a new identity card for resident aliens. It contains a special code that will enable immigration officers to determine whether the cardholder is actually the person described on the card.

The Social Security Administration took steps to prevent the issuance of Social Security cards to illegal aliens. The agency's new rules require applicants to submit documentary evidence of citizenship or alien status.   William J. Eaton

In WORLD BOOK, see IMMIGRATION AND EMIGRATION.

INCOME TAX. See TAXATION.

More than 1,200 persons become United States citizens in the largest naturalization ceremony in over 25 years on May 23 in New York City.

INDIA. At least on paper, 1978 should have been a good year for India. Most of the harsh decrees enforced by former Prime Minister Indira Gandhi during the emergency period that lasted from 1975 to 1977 had been repealed, and nearly all of the 160,000 prisoners had been freed. The forced sterilization of millions of men, directed by Gandhi's son, Sanjay, had ended. The press was free once again. Inflation had been contained, and India enjoyed the best harvest in history.

Desai's Woes. But 1978 is more likely to be remembered as a year of disastrous discord within Prime Minister Morarji Desai's Janata Party. Hastily organized early in 1977 to unseat Gandhi, the party soon began to fall apart because of internal dissension. Home Minister Charan Singh was forced out of office in June 1978 in a dispute with his rivals. Along with him went Health Minister Raj Narain, who defeated Mrs. Gandhi in the 1977 elections. Throughout the summer, go-betweens tried to arrange a truce. But the crisis deepened when Desai resisted demands for an investigation of the business dealings of his son, Kanti. At the same time, the son of another Janata leader, Defense Minister Jagjivan Ram, became embroiled in a pornography scandal.

While the wrangling went on, Janata campaign promises went unfulfilled. Urban unemployment remained at about 20 million, and millions of landless peasants and seasonal workers continued to lead a hungry existence. Violence returned to factories, streets, and university campuses. Hundreds were killed in clashes with the police, and some universities were ordered closed. As labor unrest spread, workers occupied a few plants and police were called to eject them. In early April, the army had to halt bloody fighting in two southern cities.

But even worse was the conflict between the *Harijans*, or untouchables, and members of the higher castes in the backward and populous Bihar state. The trouble began when the state's chief minister, himself a low-caste Hindu, decreed that an additional 26 per cent of state civil service jobs would be reserved for the underprivileged castes, on top of 24 per cent reserved for the untouchables. At least 15 persons were killed and hundreds were injured in village clashes, many provoked by resentful members of the higher castes. Desai's critics said he had failed to deal with the problems because he was putting his most vigorous efforts into his campaign for total prohibition of alcoholic beverages by 1981.

Indira Gandhi's Return. With her Congress Party decimated in the March 1977 election, Gandhi made a spectacular recovery in 1978. To be sure, trouble continued to pursue her. Her son, Sanjay, faced criminal charges. The Shah Commission, appointed to investigate excesses committed during the emergency period, reported in May that Gandhi's government had engaged in illegal acts, widespread repression, and systematic violation of human rights.

Charan Singh and his allies pressed for legal action against Gandhi, but she had regained enough power to make such steps politically dangerous. In January, Gandhi's followers quit the Congress Party to form the Congress-I Party (the I is for Indira). Thanks mainly to defections from the rival wing, Congress-I was recognized on April 12 as the official opposition party in Parliament. In November, Gandhi was elected in the friendly southern state of Karnataka. However, Parliament took away her seat on December 19 and ordered her jailed for contempt of Parliament for blocking a probe of her son's business dealings in 1975. The action triggered violent protests by her supporters. She was released from jail on December 26 and vowed another political comeback.

Killer Floods. Heavy monsoon rains caused catastrophic floods across India's northern states in July and August. At least 1,500 deaths were reported, with the highest toll in West Bengal, and some 40 million persons were affected. In the wake of these floods came epidemics of cholera and malaria. Although millions of acres of cultivated land were inundated, the government insisted that only 3-million short tons (2.7 million metric tons) of grain were lost and that India would still have a bumper crop.   Mark Gayn

See also ASIA (Facts in Brief Table). In WORLD BOOK, see GANDHI, INDIRA PRIYADARSHINI; INDIA.

INDIAN, AMERICAN. A band of militant Indians and their supporters, a total of almost 3,000 persons, marched on Washington, D.C., in July 1978 to protest what they charged was anti-Indian legislation pending in Congress. The Indians called their demonstration The Longest Walk. It was a 3,000-mile (4,800-kilometer) trek that began on Alcatraz Island in San Francisco Bay on February 11. The Indians set up tepees near the Washington Monument and staged rallies and ritual ceremonies during their nine days in the capital.

Some of the leaders of The Longest Walk were members of the American Indian Movement (AIM), the group that had seized and vandalized the Bureau of Indian Affairs (BIA) headquarters in 1972. To avoid similar violence, the Department of the Interior spent $300,000 to provide food, shelter, and security for the Indians during their stay.

Concern Voiced. From April 12 to 15, leaders of more than 120 tribes met at the Navajo Nation's headquarters in Window Rock, Ariz., to set up a new coordinating group to deal with what they saw as waning support for Indian causes in Congress, the White House, and the courts. The new group, the Native American Treaty Rights Organization, had the support of two important activist groups – AIM and the National Council of Indian Youth.

Among the signs of lessening support cited by the Indians was the 6 to 2 decision of the Supreme Court of the United States on March 6 that denied to Indian tribal courts the power to prosecute non-Indians for crimes committed on Indian reservations. Some 34 Indian tribes had claimed authority over non-Indians on their reservations as part of the tribal self-government system. They also expressed concern over the influence of the Interstate Congress for Equal Rights and Responsibilities, an organization seeking to end the trustee status of Indians.

Indian scholars and activists meeting in Sun Valley, Ida., on July 9 accused President Jimmy Carter of quietly favoring a policy of terminating the federal government's protective relations with Indian tribes. Alvin M. Josephy, Jr., who prepared Indian policy papers for previous administrations, said that the Carter proposal to remove educational programs from the Bureau of Indian Affairs and place them in a proposed new Department of Education, was a prelude to the eventual dismantling of the bureau.

Land Settlements. An agreement clearing the way for settlement of the claims of the Passamaquoddy and Penobscot tribes to 12.5 million acres (5-million hectares) in Maine was announced by the White House on October 17. The agreement provides for a federal cash payment of $27 million plus $10 million that the tribes could use to purchase 100,000 acres (40,000 hectares) of timberland.

American Indians march in Washington, D.C., in July during nine days of demonstrations against bills they oppose that are pending in Congress.

The Canadian government and the Inuit (Eskimos) of the Western Arctic signed an agreement on October 31 giving the Inuit ownership of 37,000 square miles (96,000 square kilometers) of oil-rich land in the Mackenzie River Delta and in the Beaufort Sea region. The Inuit also received a $45-million settlement.

President Carter signed legislation on September 30 under which the Narragansett Indians of Rhode Island would receive $3.5 million to buy 900 acres (360 hectares) in Charlestown, R.I The state of Rhode Island would contribute another 1,000 acres (400 hectares).

Energy Resources. The Council of Energy Resource Tribes (CERT), a group of 25 Indian tribes whose land includes a huge share of the energy resources in the Western states, announced on February 14 that the tribes would refuse to lease their resources unless they received more federal technical assistance. CERT claimed that member tribes own 70 billion short tons (64 billion metric tons) of coal and about half of America's uranium. An estimated 16 per cent of the nation's total energy resources are owned by Indians. The Department of Energy announced on September 14 that it was awarding CERT $1.99 million for use in energy-resource development.   Andrew L. Newman

In WORLD BOOK, see INDIAN, AMERICAN.

INDIANA. See STATE GOVERNMENT.

INDONESIA, on the surface, seemed prosperous and its people content in 1978. The rice harvest of 18.3 million short tons (17.5 million metric tons) was the best in five years. The inflation rate had slowed to less than 10 per cent. Back in 1975, the national treasury had to be drained to pay off $1.5 billion in bad debts incurred in an orgy of borrowing by the giant state-owned Pertamina oil conglomerate. Thanks to tighter management, President Suharto could tell the nation in 1978 that the treasury had $2.6 billion in foreign exchange.

But there were disturbing signs behind this pleasing facade. Indonesia was nowhere near self-sufficiency in rice, and the nation's birth rate far outpaced the growth in rice yield. The income from oil and gas, which accounted for 70 per cent of the foreign-exchange earnings, remained static.

The National Ills. Far more serious than these problems, however, were the national ills for which no cures were being provided. In 1978, Indonesia remained a nation in which 60 per cent of the 152.5-million inhabitants were undernourished, with a daily protein intake below the 40-gram (1.4-ounce) minimum requirement set by the United Nations Food and Agriculture Organization. One of every five children born in Indonesia in 1978 was not expected to live beyond 1983. About 35 per cent of the rural workers and 20 per cent of the urban workers were unemployed or underemployed.

New Scandals. Indonesia's problems could be blamed in part on poor government, dominated by the military, and corruption that was startling even by Asian standards. In 1978, the nation was treated to revelations of a series of scandals, one of which saw 14 police generals charged with misappropriating $11.5 million in three years. Foreign firms doing business in Indonesia reluctantly admitted giving huge payoffs to the generals. And Indonesian banks were shown to have as much as $1.7 billion in overdue or uncollectable loans – many of them given to cronies on orders of top leaders.

Despite student demonstrations, Suharto easily won re-election to a third 5-year term on March 22. He reorganized the Cabinet, naming three "super-ministers" – two of them generals – each in charge of a cluster of ministries. He also decreed a "civilianization" of the ruling Sekber Golkar party. Critics saw it as a meaningless gesture because retired generals often replaced active officers in the party's leadership. Suharto was made chairman of the powerful Golkar "advisory" board in October. Suharto released about 20,000 prisoners held without trial after the attempted coup d'état by army officers in 1965. By the end of the year, the number of persons under detention was officially put at around 9,000, including many intellectuals. Mark Gayn

See also ASIA (Facts in Brief Table). In WORLD BOOK, see INDONESIA.

INSURANCE. The property and casualty insurance business in the United States enjoyed good financial results during 1978. Underwriting profits were expected to exceed $1 billion for the year, while investment income posted excellent earnings of $3.4-billion for the first six months. Financial analysts projected good results for the year, barring an unforeseen catastrophic loss. Premiums reached $36.2 billion by July, a 13 per cent rise over the same period in 1977. The industry's 1977 income reached $71.6 billion, substantially more than the $66 billion that had been predicted. Total premiums for 1978 were estimated at more than $80 billion.

To a large extent, the increase in premiums must be attributed to higher rates in 1976 and early 1977. Profits and greater capital and surplus resulted from a combination of higher rates, a somewhat moderating trend to claims, and no catastrophes. Industry analysts became pessimistic late in 1978 about the future, because inflationary pressures appeared to be on the verge of overtaking rate increases.

Inflation was also responsible for increases in automobile repair costs. The estimated cost of replacing a totally demolished standard automobile went from $21,471 in 1977 to $23,400 in 1978. Other cost statistics, compiled by the Alliance of American Insurers, showed the average loss payment for an auto collision rose 11 per cent in 1978. Physicians' services cost 9.2 per cent more and hospital-room charges were up 11.3 per cent, while the average cost of auto insurance rose only 6.5 per cent.

Despite fiscal improvements in 1977 and 1978, insurance brokers and agents in large metropolitan areas still found it difficult to place automobile and fire insurance for their customers. They had to use Automobile Assigned-Risk plans and Free Access to Insurance Requirements (FAIR) plans, with rates generally higher than those in the voluntary market. An amendment designed to overcome this price discrepancy was signed by President Jimmy Carter in October. Introduced by Representative Elizabeth Holtzman (D., N.Y.), it prohibits FAIR plans from charging higher rates than those set for essential-property coverage in the voluntary market. In states that failed to comply by Jan. 31, 1979, companies could not buy federal riot reinsurance.

No-Fault Insurance. For the fourth consecutive year, the House Commerce Subcommittee in August killed any chance of enacting a federal no-fault standards bill by voting 22 to 19 against reporting the bill to the floor. A Senate version of the bill, which would have established minimum state standards, had been approved by the Senate Commerce Committee but was not sent to the floor pending House action. Subcommittee Chairman Bob Eckhardt (D.,Tex.), chief sponsor of the House bill, said he would try again in 1979.

No state adopted no-fault laws in 1978. However, the supreme courts of Pennsylvania and Michigan upheld the constitutionality of the laws in those states. The Michigan Supreme Court, ruling on June 8, also said that the manner in which no-fault coverage rates were set was "constitutionally inadequate," and gave the state 18 months to make rates fair and equitable to all citizens. In order to further limit law suits arising from auto accidents, Florida enacted a reform bill, effective on Jan. 1, 1979, to make it more difficult for accident victims to sue. But it calls for higher mandatory personal-injury protection limits. Pennsylvania Governor Milton J. Shapp vetoed a $100,000 limit per victim on no-fault medical coverage.

Other Developments. An Insurance Exchange that may become an American rival of Lloyd's of London was set up in New York in 1978. It resulted from a recent law designed to create an insurance free-trade zone limiting rate and policy regulation on large risks. A National Association of Insurance Commissioners' task force recommended on September 19 that automobile-insurance rates should not be based on a driver's age, sex, or marital status, saying that such factors constitute "unfair discrimination." A rate structure following the new guidelines would, among other things, relieve the insurance burden of young urban males, who now have to pay the highest premiums. Emanuel Levy

In WORLD BOOK, see INSURANCE; NO-FAULT INSURANCE.

INTERIOR DESIGN. Furniture and home-fashions manufacturers, aware of changing consumer life styles and increased mobility and incomes, offered Americans selections with style and versatility in 1978. Sleek, clean lines and an uncluttered appearance highlighted contemporary furniture made of wood, chrome, aluminum, acrylics, and glass.

Retailers offered an extensive selection of knockdown, or ready-to-assemble, furniture, which made it possible to furnish a room or an entire home immediately. Such furniture included upholstered sofas, chairs, tables, bookcases, beds, and storage systems. Packed by the manufacturers with complete assembly instructions, this furniture can be taken home upon purchase, doing away with delivery costs or delays. The handsome ready-to-assemble furniture, available in oak, ash, pine, and other natural woods, and in combinations of man-made materials and fibers, was so popular that 1978 sales were estimated at $350 million.

"High Tech" was an avant-garde decorating trend that carried the streamlined look to an extreme, putting industrial materials and hardware to use in the home. Increasing numbers of people considered such functional furnishings as wire storage cubes and movers'-pad-covered couches a logical follow-up to butcher-block tables and track lighting systems.

Another readily accepted innovation was the platform-base bed. Fully upholstered platforms, covered in a variety of fabrics from denim to velvet, served as bases for mattresses, and the look was completed with colorful, designer-inspired linens and coverings.

Area rugs in sparkling colors such as emerald green, terracotta, and crisp blues were popular, used on backgrounds of earth tones. Manufacturers offered "wardrobes" of rugs in various shapes, sizes, colors, and fibers to meet the needs of every room.

Important trends at the 18th Italian Furniture Exhibition, held in Milan in September, included off-white textured, striped, and patterned fabrics.

"Complete packages" of furniture for the living room, dining room, or bedroom were shown at the Southern Furniture Market in High Point, N.C., in October. These collections included such basic pieces as sofa, love seat, and chairs, plus correlated tables, lamps, and decorative accessories.

New Subtlety was evident in upholstery fabrics featuring soft colors in prints and delicate patterns. The strong, bold look of past seasons was replaced with pinks, plums, and earth tones and a resurgence of blues and beiges. Cotton prints were highlighted along with olefin-fiber solid colors, jacquards, and velvets. The emphasis was on elegance.

Decorative accessories, wall plaques, clocks, and collections continued the trend toward museum reproductions. Ceramics imported from Europe and Asia were also featured. Pop-culture motifs, such as comic-book personalities like Wonder Woman and Superman, brightened many rooms.

Growing Sales. The industry enjoyed a prosperous year in 1978 with 15 manufacturers reporting annual sales of more than $100 million. Three of these companies—the Mohasco Corporation, Bassett Furniture Industries, and Broyhill Furniture Industries—reported sales of over $200 million.

Economists projected continued growth into the 1980s. Thomas E. Swanstrom, manager of economics and sales forecasting for Sears, Roebuck and Company, predicted that people 25 to 35 years old will make up nearly 20 per cent of the U.S. population by 1985. He described this segment as "an educated, affluent, stable group whose life focus is on establishing careers and forming families."

The 1978 Trailblazer Award of the National Home Fashions League went to Vesta V'Soske, who pioneered hand-tufted rug-making techniques.

Federal Regulation. In response to hearings conducted by the Consumer Products Safety Commission, the Upholstered Furniture Action Council began a voluntary program to manufacture upholstered furniture that resists ignition by burning cigarettes. The Federal Trade Commission's Bureau of Consumer Protection recommended that manufacturers of upholstered furniture, slipcovers, carpets, and rugs attach care labels.   Helen C. Schubert

In WORLD BOOK, see INTERIOR DECORATION.

INTERNATIONAL TRADE AND FINANCE. The world economy continued generally prosperous in 1978 despite a few trouble spots. Moderate growth of production and incomes was common, and world trade continued to expand. The decline in the value of the United States dollar against most of the other major currencies was the most striking event of the year. Two factors caused the decline—the continuing huge deficit in U.S. foreign trade, with 1978 imports exceeding exports by about $30 billion, and a U.S. inflation rate that was a little higher than that in most other industrial countries.

For Americans, the declining dollar meant higher prices for imported goods and soaring foreign-travel costs. In other countries, the drop in the dollar brought some benefits. As U.S. goods became cheaper, exports—and jobs with them—expanded.

Much of the alarm about the declining dollar came from other countries, which feared a drop in their exports to the United States—or at least felt the need to shave prices and profits in order to keep their American markets. The leaders of other countries were also concerned that the instability of the world's "key currency" threatened the orderly expansion of world trade and investment. This view was supported by the continued sluggishness of private investment in new plants and equipment in Europe and Japan. When the dollar's decline accelerated in October, President Jimmy Carter announced measures on November 1 to halt the slide. These included mobilization of up to $30 billion in foreign currencies, mainly through borrowing, to use in exchange trading to support the dollar. The dollar then recovered somewhat. In December, the U.S. Treasury began the sale of about $1.58 billion in large-denomination notes in West Germany.

Floating Currency exchange rates, which have existed since the early 1970s, caused the dollar's movements against individual countries to vary widely. For example, the dollar rose against the Canadian dollar and against the currencies of some important developing countries, such as Brazil. By far the largest declines occurred against the Japanese yen and Swiss franc – about 40 per cent from early 1977 to late 1978. The dollar dropped 20 per cent against the West German Deutsche mark and the cluster of jointly floating European currencies.

By the end of 1978, the sharp change in currency rates was reflected in better U.S. foreign-trade performance. The excess of imports over exports in August and September was only half the average monthly trade deficit of almost $3 billion in the first five months of the year. Oil imports continued at a rate of about $40 billion for the year, somewhat lower than in 1977 because Alaskan oil became available for the first time. The big improvement came in manufactured goods, where trade, heavily

in deficit early in the year, swung into a modest surplus by late summer.

World Trade, measured by the volume of goods shipped, grew only about 5 per cent, due partly to the sluggishness of the industrial economies. The European economies grew about 2 to 3 per cent for the second consecutive year, only about half as much as was customary earlier. Unemployment continued relatively high, particularly among young jobseekers, but the situation did not worsen significantly. The story was similar in Japan, where growth was about 5 per cent, also just half of normal. Only the United States showed marked improvement on the job front, with unemployment dropping to about 6 per cent of the labor force in a year of fairly good growth. However, the U.S. inflation picture was worse than that of other industrial nations.

At the economic summit of the West's seven leading industrial countries – held in July in Bonn, West Germany – Japan and West Germany pledged to stimulate their economies. These key economies were expected to grow a little faster in 1979.

Freer Trade was a prime topic at the annual meeting of the World Bank and the International Monetary Fund (IMF) in September. Robert S. McNamara, president of the World Bank, warned that "throughout the industrialized nations, the trend toward protectionism is gathering momen-

Lansky in *San Diego Union*

Japanese and European representatives greet special U.S. delegate Robert Strauss, center, at General Agreement on Tariffs and Trade conference.

tum." This threatens particularly the prospects of developing countries that are competing in exporting manufactured goods. McNamara cited several cases where existing restrictions on imports from such countries were tightened. However, weighed against the total volume of world trade, these restrictions were still comparatively minor. In fact, world exports topped $1 trillion for the first time in 1977.

Whether the world could continue along the road to gradually freer trade and reduced barriers hung on the outcome of the General Agreement on Tariffs and Trade negotiations taking place in Geneva, Switzerland. These negotiations have been proceeding slowly among nearly 100 nations since 1974. At year's end, final agreement had not been reached. The U.S. authority to negotiate, granted by Congress in 1974, was to expire at the end of 1979.

In its 1978 annual report, the World Bank noted the remarkable ability of many of the so-called middle-income countries, such as Brazil, Malaysia, and South Korea, to cope with the storms of the world economy and continue to advance. In 1977, the report stated, "the developing countries as a whole continued to outpace the industrialized countries in terms of economic growth." However, there remains the grave problem, termed "absolute poverty" by McNamara, that continues to afflict at least half a billion persons in countries where populations continue to rise faster than production.

The Petrodollar Problem, which caused much alarm in the early 1970s, eased further in 1978. The problem concerns the large trade and balance-of-payments surplus of a handful of oil-producing countries. After reaching a peak of more than $60-billion in 1974, the surplus of the members of the Organization of Petroleum Exporting Countries probably dropped to less than $20 billion in 1978 as they spent more of their earnings on imports of industrial equipment and consumer goods.

A few countries – such as Peru, Portugal, Turkey, Zaire, and Zambia – had difficulty paying their large debts in 1978, but in general the debt problem remained manageable. The IMF again played an important role, lending some of its own funds to countries in difficulty and, more important, requiring economic reforms that opened the way for private lending. The IMF's resources were augmented by the new $10-billion "Witteveen facility," named for IMF's former Managing Director H. Johannes Witteveen. The facility, a special lending plan for nations whose balance of payments continues to show deficits, went into operation after approval by the Congress of the United States on September 22.   Edwin L. Dale, Jr.

See also ECONOMICS; Section One, FOCUS ON THE ECONOMY. In WORLD BOOK, see INTERNATIONAL TRADE.

IOWA. See STATE GOVERNMENT.

IRAN. Shah Mohammad Reza Pahlavi struggled throughout 1978 to save his throne, but his efforts failed to stem the violent protest. As the year ended, bloody rioting rocked the nation. The shah imposed a military government in November, but it failed to quiet the protest, and a civilian government headed by Shahpour Bakhtiar replaced it on Jan. 6, 1979.

An unlikely combination – right wing ultraconservative *mullahs* (religious leaders) and left wing students, professors, and intellectuals – spearheaded opposition to the shah. The mullahs condemned modernization plans that might undermine traditional Muslim beliefs. The student-intellectual coalition opposed a government that banned political parties and used Savak, the secret police, to suppress dissent. They were supported by a middle class dissatisfied with heavy military expenditures at the expense of development, and 50 per cent inflation.

The Demonstrations and riots began in Teheran in January and spread quickly to other cities. The protesters demanded land reform, abolition of women's rights, and a strict adherence to the Koran.

There were more riots in May and again from August through December. On August 21, the unrest took an ugly turn when someone, presumably a fanatic objecting to the showing of films from the West, set fire to a movie house in Abadan, killing 377 persons. By late December, more than 1,500 persons had been killed in riots. Oil-field workers went on strike on October 1, crippling the economy with a walkout that cost Iran $60 million a day. Strikes and violent demonstrations continued in December, bringing the country to a standstill.

Too Little? Too Late? After each wave of demonstrations and riots, the shah made concessions. He granted a partial amnesty for political prisoners and introduced a code of conduct that prohibited members of the royal family from holding office. He sacked public officials and arrested 14 prominent officials, including the Savak chief and the shah's long-time adviser, former Prime Minister Amir Abbas Hoveyda. He agreed to allow political parties to organize when the situation returned to normal.

The shah canceled an order for 70 Grumman F-4 fighter planes on October 24 and said he would use the funds for social programs. Government workers were given a 15 per cent pay raise. But violence persisted. The military and police remained loyal, but it was not clear whether the shah's liberalization efforts had come in time to save his throne.

A major earthquake in eastern Iran in September added to the country's problems. About 25,000 persons were killed, including almost the entire population of the city of Tabas.　　William Spencer

See also MIDDLE EAST (Facts in Brief Table). In WORLD BOOK, see IRAN.

Rioters burn bank furniture in downtown Teheran during an antigovernment demonstration in November. Similar riots hit several other Iranian cities.

IRAQ. The ruling Baath Party ended, at least temporarily, its intermittent 12-year rivalry with Syria's Baath leadership in October 1978, following a visit by Syria's President Hafiz al-Assad. Assad and Iraqi President Ahmad Hasan al-Bakr announced on October 25 that they had agreed on a joint Iraqi-Syrian military command to oppose the Egyptian-Israeli peace talks and develop a common Arab front against Israel. At the same time, a joint steering committee was formed to oversee the economic, political, and cultural integration of the two Arab neighbors. The renewed friendliness was a move away from Iraq's self-imposed isolation from both Egypt and the Arab rejectionist bloc that opposes Egypt's peace moves.

Internal Purges. The Iraqi Baath Party faced some internal challenges to its leadership. It carried out a series of purges in April and May in an attempt to consolidate its authority. The purges, directed by Deputy Chairman Saddam Hussein al-Takriti, were aimed at the civil service, the diplomatic corps, and the Iraqi Communist Party (IPC) as well as the Baath Party itself. About 1,000 civil servants and several hundred party members were dismissed for exploiting their positions for personal gain. Then, 41 Iraqi ambassadors were retired because they were either inefficient or lacked strong party loyalty.

The IPC was the last group to be affected by the purges. It had joined the Baath and the Kurdish Democratic Party in a National Progressive Front after a 1976 reconciliation. But the honeymoon was brief. In May, Saddam Hussein al-Takriti announced the discovery of a Communist plot in the armed forces. Some 1,000 Communists were arrested, and a government spokesmen confirmed that 21 IPC leaders were executed. Following the executions, a government decree made the death penalty mandatory for anti-Baath conspiracies.

Kurdish areas remained relatively quiet. Some guerrilla resistance, however, followed the government's relocation of about 28,000 Kurdish villagers from their mountain homes in border areas to lowland villages built for them.

Birthday Gifts. The Baath Party celebrated its 10th year in power by completing a number of development projects. These included a $155-million natural gas bottling plant and a local gas industry project in Basra, a bridge over the Tigris River, three centralized cattle-breeding and dairy farms, a $41-million cement plant at Al Fallujah, and a $99-million oil refinery at Doura. The first bridge over the Shatt al Arab estuary, 2,500 feet (760 meters) long, was dedicated on August 2. At midpoint in Iraq's 1976-1980 development plan, it was clear that the goal of a per-capita income increase from the present $1,280 to $2,000 was well within reach.   William Spencer

See also MIDDLE EAST (Facts in Brief Table). In WORLD BOOK, see IRAQ.

IRELAND experienced less violence in 1978, but the year began with a political bombshell. In an interview on Irish radio on January 8, Prime Minister Jack Lynch mentioned the unmentionable – Irish unification and the withdrawal of British troops from Northern Ireland. Lynch argued that Great Britain should encourage Irish unity and reconsider the "negative guarantees" under which Britain pledged that Northern Ireland will remain part of the United Kingdom until a majority in the North wishes otherwise.

Lynch's remarks on this subject and on *devolution* (limited home rule) wrecked talks between politicians in Britain and Northern Ireland. Lynch was also widely attacked in Britain for appearing to give new heart to the Irish Republican Army (IRA), and relations between London and Dublin cooled. However, Lynch remained popular at home. A Gallup Poll on May 9 showed strong support in the Republic of Ireland for his radio comments, with 34 per cent being in favor and another 35 per cent taking a stronger line in demanding a date for a British pullout from Northern Ireland.

The Economy. Ireland continued to be one of the most enthusiastic members of the European Community (EC or Common Market) and a major beneficiary of its grants. Irish industrial growth almost doubled the average for Common Market countries and was well over twice that of Great Britain, while investment and productivity continued to rise. In a flush of self-confidence, Prime Minister Lynch abolished *domestic rates* (private property taxes), taxes on wealth, and road-fund licenses on compact cars while cutting income tax. Much of the expansion was based on the use of two institutions, the Industrial Development Authority and the Irish Export Board, which give discriminatory relief of up to 100 per cent to export industries. Farm incomes also rose rapidly, partly because continental markets are now open to Irish beef and lamb and partly because of regional EC grants. Ireland decided to join the European Monetary System, after initial reluctance. See EUROPE.

Human Rights. A long-running legal battle between Great Britain and Ireland ended on January 18 when the European Court of Human Rights ruled that between August and October 1971, Britain had allowed its forces to use interrogation techniques that amounted to "inhuman and degrading treatment."

In an unprecedented statement issued in April, the Roman Catholic bishops in Ireland relaxed their opposition to legalizing contraceptives, clearing the way for legal sale. While birth control devices are morally wrong, they said, it does not necessarily follow from this that the state is bound to prohibit the sale of contraceptives.   Ian Mather

See also GREAT BRITAIN; NORTHERN IRELAND. In WORLD BOOK, see IRELAND.

ISRAEL and Egypt agreed to a framework for a peace treaty in Camp David, Maryland, summit talks that ended on Sept. 17, 1978. The pact provided that the two nations would conclude a peace treaty within three months, but, by year's end, no peace settlement had been reached (see MIDDLE EAST). The *Knesset* (parliament) ratified the Camp David accord on September 28. The accord strengthened domestic support for Prime Minister Menachem Begin and his Likud Party. Sharing the Nobel Peace Prize with President Anwar al-Sadat of Egypt also added to Begin's popularity (see NOBEL PRIZES).

But most Israelis still distrusted Arab intentions and were concerned over Israeli security. The key issue of Jewish settlements on the West Bank and the occupied Sinai hampered the domestic consensus as well as negotiations with Egypt. The government approved four new West Bank settlements on January 10 and then halted work on them until April. To placate militants of the *Gush Emunim* (Faithful Bloc), who advocate Jewish settlement in the occupied areas, the government allowed them to establish an archaeological camp on the site of Biblical Shiloh. However, the camp was quickly turned into a settlement. Begin's difficulties were compounded by a dispute between Defense Minister Ezer Weizman, who favored limiting settlements to two or three urban areas, and Agriculture Minister Ariel Sharon, an advocate of large-scale Jewish expansion in small villages throughout the occupied territories.

Partly to counter Gush Emunim militance and to pressure the government to seize what seemed to many Israelis the best chance for peace in 30 years, *Shalom Akhshav* (Peace Now), a nonpartisan organization, was formed in Haifa in March. The group organized demonstrations.

Lebanon Invaded. Effective border defenses and efficient public security kept internal terrorist incidents to a minimum. The glaring exception was a seaborne raid by Palestinian commandos on March 11, in which a bus was hijacked. Thirty-seven persons were killed and 82 injured, including the terrorists, in a shoot-out on the main Haifa-Tel Aviv highway. On March 14, Israeli troops invaded and occupied southern Lebanon in an attempt to root out guerrilla bases. The Israelis pulled out on June 13. See LEBANON.

Arab Benefits. The drive to end 30 years of isolation under siege also produced some positive steps to improve the status of Israel's Arab population. On March 30, the Israel Land Administration paid Arab families in Galilee $9 million for lands expropriated after the 1967 Six-Day War.

In Jerusalem, a new city plan allocated 115 acres (47 hectares) of land in the Arab sector for day-care

Prime Minister Menachem Begin, home after the Camp David conference, gets traditional hero's welcome in Jerusalem—wine and a twisted loaf of bread.

Israeli soldiers carry a Gush Emunim settler from a West Bank encampment after a right wing protest against the Camp David agreements.

20 per cent in such necessities as fuel, gasoline, and electricity. Basic price subsidies on such food items as bread, milk, sugar, and salt expired on November 1 but were continued on a temporary basis, averting the threat of further increases.

Production Increases partially offset those problems. Production at the offshore Alma oil field in occupied Sinai increased to 70,000 barrels per day, 40 per cent of domestic oil requirements. Tourism brought in $461 million. Expanded agricultural production in the kibbutzes and new farms, using advanced irrigation techniques in the Dead Sea and Negev areas, began to show significant results as more land was cultivated. Industry also gained. Petrochemical products sales rose 33 per cent. United States economic aid also brightened the picture somewhat. In early December, the United States agreed to give Israel $785 million in grants and loans for the year ending Sept. 30, 1979. But a real economic breakthrough depended on peace with Egypt, however devoutly Israelis wished for prosperity through their own efforts.

Golda Meir, prime minister of Israel from 1969 to 1974 and one of the 25 signers of Israel's Declaration of Independence in 1948, died on December 8. She was 80 years old.   William Spencer

See also EGYPT; MIDDLE EAST (Facts in Brief Table); NAVON, YITZHAK. In WORLD BOOK, see ISRAEL.

centers, clinics, schools, and other badly needed facilities. The land previously had been allocated for Jewish housing. And in November, the first group of Israeli Muslims was permitted to make the pilgrimage to Mecca in Saudi Arabia.

On the West Bank, Israel established about 25 vocational training centers to provide skilled-trades training. More than 3,000 Arabs graduated from the program.

Economic Woes. The high cost of military preparedness along with inflation, a decline in purchasing power, and other factors blunted the austerity program initiated in 1977 and continued to slow economic development. The Knesset approved a budget in January that allocated $3.5 billion, 33 per cent of the total, for defense spending.

One consequence of inflation was labor unrest. Strikes occurred with increasing frequency, the longest being a 10-week walkout that began in January by merchant seamen and paralyzed the Israeli tanker fleet. Teachers, journalists, radio and television technicians, postal employees, and others went on strike during the year, and each strike shut down some sector of the economy. In October, the government settled back-to-back postal walkouts with a 7.5 per cent wage increase and later approved a 12.9 per cent cost-of-living adjustment for all salaried government workers. But the adjustments were largely canceled by price increases averaging

ITALY was staggered by a series of crises in 1978, including the resignation of its government and president and the kidnapping and murder of a former prime minister, Aldo Moro.

Prime Minister Giulio Andreotti's minority Christian Democratic government was shaken on January 4 when the Communist Party called for its replacement by an emergency coalition that would include Communists. Andreotti resigned on January 16, after the Communists, Socialists, and Republicans withdrew support. After negotiations, the three parties and the Social Democrats decided on March 8 to support a new Christian Democrat minority government with Andreotti as prime minister.

The government's decision to enter the European Monetary System (EMS) caused a break with the Communists. On December 12, Andreotti proposed that Italy join EMS. Parliament approved the proposal on December 13, with the Communists voting against it and the Socialists abstaining. Both parties said that entering would commit Italy to economic austerity without parliamentary debate. The EMS was scheduled to begin on Jan. 1, 1979, but a farm-subsidy dispute delayed it. See EUROPE.

The Communists renewed their call for Cabinet seats on December 20. Communist Party leader Enrico Berlinguer said the government had not kept the March agreements with the other parties and that his party would take a tough position in the economic austerity debates scheduled for Parliament in January 1979.

President Resigns. Giovanni Leone resigned as president on June 15, six months before his seven-year term expired. He had been accused of financial and tax irregularities. Parliament and regional representatives elected Alessandro Pertini, 81, on July 8, on the 16th ballot. See PERTINI, ALESSANDRO.

Former Prime Minister Killed. Aldo Moro, 61, five times prime minister and a favored candidate for president, was kidnapped from a car in Rome on March 16. His captors, the Red Brigades, a leftist terrorist group, killed Moro's five bodyguards. The Red Brigades said that Moro would have a trial by a "people's court." The government refused to negotiate for Moro's freedom. His body was found in a stolen car in central Rome on May 9. Corrado Alunni, said to be the Red Brigades' leader, was sentenced on September 20 to 12 years in prison for illegal possession of firearms. See EUROPE (Close-Up).

Abortion Legalized. On May 18, Parliament passed a law allowing women over 18 years old to obtain an abortion virtually on demand in the first 90 days of pregnancy. Kenneth Brown

See also EUROPE (Facts in Brief Table). In WORLD BOOK, see ITALY.

IVORY COAST. See AFRICA.

JAMAICA. See WEST INDIES.

JAPAN and China signed a treaty of peace and friendship on Aug. 12, 1978. The signing in Peking, China, came after four years of negotiations and six years after they established diplomatic relations. The treaty provides that Japan and China will develop relations of "perpetual peace and friendship," settle all disputes by peaceful means, and "refrain from the use or threat of force in their relations." The two governments also pledged to promote economic and cultural relations and to encourage exchanges between their citizens.

A key provision of the new treaty states that neither country shall seek political domination in the Asia-Pacific area and that each will oppose efforts by any other country or group of countries to dominate the area. This provision had stood in the way of concluding the treaty for many months. Japan was concerned over its obviously anti-Russian implications. China finally accepted a separate provision suggested by Japan that the treaty will not affect the relations of either country with any third country. Although this provision allayed Japanese concern, it did not satisfy Russia, which labeled the treaty anti-Soviet and "fraught with tremendous danger."

Trade Pact. The Chinese government and a group of private Japanese industrialists signed an eight-year trade agreement on February 16 calling for each country to sell $10 billion of selected products to the other. In the first five years, Japan will sell China industrial plants and technology, including three large steel mills valued at from $7 billion to $8 billion. During the same period, China will sell Japan about 350 million barrels of oil and more than 9 million short tons (8 million metric tons) of coal at prices to be determined later. Trade between the two countries totaled $3.5 billion in 1977, almost 15 per cent more than in 1976, with Japan enjoying a trade surplus of $400 million.

Efforts to conclude a Japanese-Russian peace treaty continued to be stalled over Japan's demand that the Soviet Union return four of the southernmost islands in the Kuril chain that Russia occupied after World War II. In January 1978, Russia proposed a treaty of "good neighborliness and cooperation," apparently to counter the Japan-China treaty then in negotiation. But Japan notified the Soviets in September that such a treaty could not be considered unless Moscow agreed to return the disputed islands.

Japanese trade with Russia continued to grow, however. It reached $3.36 billion in 1977, and Japan enjoyed a favorable balance of $512 million. Economic relations centered on joint exploitation of natural resources in Siberia. In May, Japanese, Russian, and U.S. planners agreed on a contract calling for a joint Japanese-American investment of nearly $4 billion in a natural gas project in the Yakutsk area of Siberia.

Demonstrators are engulfed by flames from a firebomb during protests at Tokyo's new Narita airport, which finally was opened on May 21.

U.S. Relations. The U.S. dollar plunged to a rate of 176 yen to $1 in October 1978, a decline of 30 per cent during the year, and economic relations with the United States continued to be a matter of serious concern. Prime Minister Takeo Fukuda visited Washington, D.C., in May to confer with President Jimmy Carter on Japanese and U.S. roles in world affairs. Both with the President and in meetings with other officials, Fukuda emphasized world economic problems. He declared that Japan was determined to reduce its very large trade surplus, increase its rate of economic growth to encourage imports, and limit such exports as automobiles, steel, and color television sets. In 1977, the Japanese trade surplus with the United States was $9 billion.

Representatives of the two governments agreed on January 13 in Tokyo on a comprehensive program to bring their trade more in balance. The Japanese agreed to substantially lower trade barriers to U.S. imports. A 140-person U.S. trade delegation, led by Secretary of Commerce Juanita M. Kreps, arrived in Japan on October 2 to explore means of further reducing the trade imbalance.

Growth Rate. Late in 1977, the government announced a target of 7 per cent in real economic growth for fiscal 1978. This was designed to stimulate the economy so it could absorb more imports, thus reducing Japan's 1977 overall $14-billion trade surplus. Growth figures for the July-September quarter, however, indicated the 7 per cent would not be reached. The rate of economic growth for fiscal 1977 was 5.4 per cent, short of the planned 6.7 per cent. At a seven-nation economic summit conference held in July in Bonn, West Germany, Fukuda pledged to achieve the 7 per cent growth rate. On September 3, he announced a major program, including more than $13 billion in public-works spending, to attain the goal.

Other Developments. Tokyo's new international airport at Narita was finally opened to traffic on May 21 after seven years of opposition, often violent, by local farmers and radical extremists. The opening, originally scheduled for March 30, was postponed because control tower equipment was wrecked four days earlier in a violent attack by protesters.

To everyone's surprise, Fukuda lost the first-round election for the presidency of the ruling Liberal Democratic Party, on November 27, and withdrew from a run-off election. This ended his two-year reign as prime minister. He was replaced by the party's secretary-general, Masayoshi Ohira, a long-time rival. See OHIRA, MASAYOSHI.

In 1977, life expectancy reached 77.9 years for females and 72.7 for males, making Japan the nation with the longest life span in the world. The number of crimes increased 6.3 per cent during the first six months of 1978.　　　　　　　　　　John M. Maki

See also ASIA (Facts in Brief Table). In WORLD BOOK, see JAPAN.

JEWS AND JUDAISM. The Israeli Ministry of Absorption said in May that up to 1,000 Jews per month would be allowed to emigrate to Israel from Russia throughout 1978. Not all of the Jewish emigrants from Russia were settling in Israel, however. Leon Dulzin, chairman of the World Zionist Organization, said on May 30 that nearly 60 per cent of the Jewish emigrants chose destinations other than Israel. According to the Hebrew Immigrant Aid Society in New York City, 6,484 Russian Jews settled in the United States between January and July, compared with 6,776 for all of 1977.

Russian Jewish Dissidents continued activities that brought arrest and imprisonment. Among those whose trials and sentences generated widespread international condemnation were Vladimir Slepak, Ida Nudel, Anatoly Shcharansky, and Alexander Ginzburg. See RUSSIA.

There were some signs of hope. Four Russian students were reportedly attending the Jewish Theological Seminary in Budapest, Hungary, and one of these, Adolf Shayevich, was scheduled to return to Moscow as the first ordained rabbi in more than a generation. Also, Sholom Kleinman, president of the Moscow Synagogue, reported in a telephone conversation on January 12 that Soviet Jews received 505 short tons (458 metric tons) of flour to bake Passover matzoth during 1977, an increase over

Rabbis handcuff themselves to the White House fence in May to protest the decision to sell U.S. fighter planes to Arab nations.

the amount of flour allotted in 1976, at prices lower than those of the previous year.

Former Nazis became a major concern for Jews. A group of jurists, meeting in Philadelphia on January 17, formed the Holocaust Committee of Concerned Judges and Lawyers to disseminate information on ex-Nazis living in America and to coordinate community action against them. The U.S. Immigration and Naturalization Service reported on March 9 that it was investigating 169 cases in which persons allegedly entered the United States illegally and became citizens after concealing their part in Nazi war crimes.

Both the Senate and the White House acted to establish permanent memorials to victims of the mass Nazi extermination of Jews before and during World War II, known as the Holocaust. Senator Wendell R. Anderson (D., Minn.) introduced a bill in April to create such a remembrance, and on May 1, President Jimmy Carter appointed a special commission to make recommendations.

Skokie, a Chicago suburb with a large Jewish population that includes 7,000 concentration-camp survivors, the largest number in the United States, became a focus for controversy when a group of neo-Nazis threatened to march there. The American Civil Liberties Union defended the Nazis' constitutional right to march after Skokie city officials sought a court order forbidding the demonstration. The controversy ended in June when the Nazis canceled their march.

Religious Education. For the first time, the government of Israel in May granted full recognition to a religious school sponsored by a non-Orthodox synagogue. The school, sponsored by a Conservative synagogue in the Givat Shapiro section of Jerusalem, received official approval from Minister of Education and Culture Zevulun Hammer after weeks of strife. Some groups vehemently opposed the break with the previous policy of granting recognition only to Orthodox religious schools.

The World Zionist Congress passed a resolution in February calling for full equality of the Reform and Conservative movements in its affairs. While the resolution does not bind the Israeli government, it puts increased pressure on Israel to grant formal religious pluralism. The Congress is the official conveyor of Jewish culture and religion. Like the state of Israel, it has been dominated for many years by Orthodoxy.

World Population. The *American Jewish Year Book* reported the 1977 world Jewish population at 14,259,525, an increase of 115,000 over 1976. The United States had the single largest Jewish population with 5,775,935. The second largest Jewish population was in Israel – 3,095,000. The third largest was in Russia – 2,678,000.   Judah Graubart

See also ISRAEL; MIDDLE EAST. In WORLD BOOK, see JEWS; JUDAISM.

JOHN PAUL I (1912-1978) was elected pope of the Roman Catholic Church on Aug. 26, 1978; he died on September 28, after only 34 days as pontiff. He was the first pope to take two names, choosing the names of his two immediate predecessors, John XXIII and Paul VI. Pope John Paul I succeeded Pope Paul VI, who died on August 6. Unlike his most recent predecessors, the new pope had never been a Vatican diplomat, though he could speak French, German, and some Slavic dialects. See DEATHS OF NOTABLE PERSONS (Close-Up); ROMAN CATHOLIC CHURCH.

John Paul I was born Albino Luciani on Oct. 17, 1912, in Forno di Canale in the mountains of northeastern Italy near the Austrian border. His father worked several years in Switzerland, then worked in a glass factory on the island of Murano in the Venetian lagoon.

Luciani studied in seminaries in Feltre and Belluno, specializing in philosophy as well as theology. He was ordained a priest in 1935, and continued his studies at the Pontifical Gregorian University in Rome. Luciani then taught religion in a Belluno public school. During World War II, he lectured at a Belluno seminary.

Luciani was named bishop of Vittorio Veneto in 1958 and became patriarch of Venice in 1969. He was appointed a cardinal by Pope Paul VI four years later, in 1973.   Foster Stockwell

JOHN PAUL II (1920-   ), a Pole, was elected pope of the Roman Catholic Church on Oct. 16, 1978, succeeding John Paul I, who died on September 28. John Paul II is the first pope from Eastern Europe, the first non-Italian elected since 1522, and, at 58, the youngest pope chosen since 1846.

Karol Wojtyla – who took the name John Paul II after his election as pope – was born on May 18, 1920, at Wadowice, Poland. The son of working-class parents, he worked in a chemical factory while he was attending high school and college. He was ordained a priest in 1946 and studied two years at the Angelicum in Rome, where he received a doctorate in philosophy. He then earned a doctorate in theology in Kraków. He became auxiliary bishop of Kraków in 1958, archbishop in 1964, and cardinal in 1967.

A scholar and philosopher, the new pope was once an amateur actor and a poet. He has also written several books and about 300 articles on a variety of topics. During Vatican Council II, he favored religious liberty. He attended all of the bishops' synods held after the Vatican Council and was a member of three Vatican congregations – clergy, Catholic education, and sacraments and divine worship.

John Paul II likes to ski, swim, climb mountains, camp, and play table tennis.   Foster Stockwell

See also DEATHS OF NOTABLE PERSONS (Close-Up); JOHN PAUL I; ROMAN CATHOLIC CHURCH.

King Hussein marries American Elizabeth Halaby in June in Amman. Jordan's
chief justice reads verses from the Koran in a brief Muslim ceremony.

JORDAN. King Hussein I married for the fourth
time on June 15, 1978. The new bride, Elizabeth
Halaby, daughter of former Pan American Airways
Board Chairman Najeeb Halaby, changed her name
and faith with the ceremony, becoming Noor al-
Hussein (Light of Hussein) and a Muslim. The king
immediately made her his queen. Hussein also
changed the royal succession, placing Prince Ali, his
2-year-old son by the late Queen Alia, next in line
after the king's brother, Prince Hassan.

Fence Sitting. Hussein spent most of the year
sitting on the fence about the Egyptian-Israeli peace
negotiations. He continued to support the "legitimate" rights of the Palestinians and the establishment of a Palestinian state, but at the same time he
encouraged Egypt's President Anwar al-Sadat's initiatives. When Israel attacked guerrilla bases in
South Lebanon in March in retaliation for a guerrilla assault in Israel, Hussein urged Arab solidarity in
the face of "common danger." See MIDDLE EAST.

Fears of a possible threat from both Israel and the
Arabs opposing Israeli-Egyptian peace talks prompted Hussein to organize a Consultative National
Assembly to replace the Chamber of Deputies,
which was dissolved in 1974. The Assembly took
office on April 16. Its 60 members, including 3
women, 3 Cabinet ministers, and 13 Palestinians,
were appointed for a two-year term. Since political
parties are prohibited, observers saw it as a forum for
public opinion as well as an advisory council for
Cabinet-sponsored legislation.

Boon from Beirut. Jordan's economy continued
to benefit from the plight of war-wracked Lebanon.
The Amman Stock Exchange opened in January,
the third such agency in the Arab world. Although
trading was limited to shares in companies with
Jordanian majority ownership, the volume of trade
quickly surpassed that of the Beirut exchange.

Jordan's potash industry, the country's major
source of international earnings, got a big boost in
June when Libya and the World Bank loaned $70-
million and $25 million, respectively, to expand
production. The main effort would be the construction of diked evaporating ponds on 25,000 acres
(10,000 hectares) near the Dead Sea, the source of all
of Jordan's potash. Using solar energy, a system of
pipe collectors would draw the brine from the Dead
Sea to the ponds, where the water would be evapo-
rated and potash extracted. With annual production
estimated at 1.3 million short tons (1.2 million metric
tons), the project would make Jordan a major world
supplier.   William Spencer

See also MIDDLE EAST (Facts in Brief Table). In
WORLD BOOK, see JORDAN.

JUDAISM. See JEWS AND JUDAISM.

JUNIOR ACHIEVEMENT. See YOUTH ORGANI-
ZATIONS.

KANSAS. See STATE GOVERNMENT.

KEATON, DIANE (1946-   ), won the Academy of Motion Picture Arts and Sciences best actress award on April 3, 1978. She won the Oscar for her performance as the heroine in *Annie Hall.*

Born Diane Hall on Jan. 5, 1946, in Santa Ana, Calif., Keaton adopted the maiden name of her mother, a former "Mrs. Los Angeles." Her father heads a firm of consulting engineers.

Keaton attended Santa Ana schools, studied at Santa Ana College, and graduated in 1968 from the Neighborhood Playhouse School of the Theater in New York City. Later that year, she made her professional debut in the Broadway production of *Hair.* Her friendship with Woody Allen began when they co-starred in the stage comedy *Play It Again, Sam.* Keaton's first film was *Lovers and Other Strangers* in 1971. She appeared with Allen in the film version of *Play It Again, Sam* and in *Sleeper, Love and Death,* and the somewhat autobiographical *Annie Hall.* See ALLEN, WOODY.

Keaton switched to dramatic roles as Al Pacino's wife in both *The Godfather* and *Godfather II* and as the star of *Looking for Mr. Goodbar.* Then she appeared in the film *Interiors,* directed by Allen.

Keaton, who spends so much time in front of the camera, relaxes by getting behind it. Her favorite hobby is photography.   Marsha F. Goldsmith

KENTUCKY. See STATE GOVERNMENT.

KENYA. Jomo Kenyatta, president since 1964 and the country's dominant political personality since the early 1950s, died on Aug. 22, 1978. Under his leadership, Kenya enjoyed a political stability and prosperity unknown to most other African countries.

The transition went smoothly. Daniel T. arap Moi, vice-president since 1967, became acting president. Then the country's sole political party – the Kenya African National Union – elected him president on October 6. See MOI, DANIEL T. ARAP.

The government withdrew on June 30 from the East African Community (EAC), which linked Kenya with Tanzania and Uganda. At one time, the EAC nations had a common currency, customs union, transportation service, and school system.

The Ethiopian-Somali war over control of the Ogaden region threatened to jeopardize Kenya's relations with the United States. Communist nations gave Ethiopia aid, and Somalia appealed for U.S. military assistance. But Kenya warned in March that any such aid might result in the closing of Kenya's Indian Ocean ports to U.S. warships. Kenya opposed strengthening Somalia because of a long-standing border dispute.   John D. Esseks

See also AFRICA (Facts in Brief Table); ETHIOPIA; SOMALIA. In WORLD BOOK, see KENYA.

KIWANIS INTERNATIONAL. See COMMUNITY ORGANIZATIONS.

Daniel T. arap Moi, right, who became president of Kenya following the death of Jomo Kenyatta on August 22, chats with Attorney General Charles Njonjo.

KOCH, EDWARD I. (1924-   ), took office as mayor of New York City on Jan. 1, 1978, and assumed the responsibility of trying to reduce that city's enormous debts. He made good on a campaign promise to hold down costs by adopting a firm stance in contract negotiations with municipal workers' unions. The terms of the new contracts, which went into effect on July 1, held the average wage increase to 8 per cent over two years. See NEW YORK CITY.

Koch was born in New York City on Dec. 12, 1924. The son of Polish immigrants, he moved with his parents to Newark, N.J., where he helped his father run a hatcheck concession in an uncle's catering hall. He graduated from Southside High School in Newark and attended City College of New York. After a European tour of duty with the United States Army in World War II, Koch received his law degree from New York University in 1948. He was admitted to the bar the following year.

Entering private law practice, Koch soon became involved in New York City politics. A charter member of the maverick Village Independent Democrats, he was that organization's successful candidate for a City Council seat in 1966. He was elected to Congress in 1968. During his four terms in the House, Koch became one of the most effective legislators in his delegation, compiling a liberal voting record but collaborating frequently with conservatives to get measures passed.   Beverly Merz

KOREA, NORTH. The failure of the nation's ruling Communist party, the Korean Workers' Party, to hold its sixth national congress in 1978 and the unexplained disappearance of Kim Chong-il indicated political troubles inside the tightly closed country. Kim, the 38-year-old son of President Kim Il-song, had been designated the "sole successor" to his father, but he was seriously injured in an assassination attempt, according to reports. The campaign to publicize Kim stopped early in 1978; his assailants were reported to have been executed.

The attack on Kim reflected tension over presidential policies that have kept North Korea's economy oriented toward military preparations at the cost of civilian development. Income per capita is lower than in South Korea. The United States Central Intelligence Agency (CIA) estimated North Korea's foreign debt at $2.4 billion.

South Korea on June 23 proposed a joint Cabinet-level committee to promote trade "in an attempt to establish the basic groundwork for peace and eventual reunification of the divided nation." North Korea immediately rejected the move, saying the idea "does not even deserve a passing notice."

Relations with China improved in May when North Korea became the first country to be visited by China's Premier Hua Kuo-feng.   Henry S. Bradsher

See also ASIA (Facts in Brief Table). In WORLD BOOK, see KOREA.

KOREA, SOUTH. The National Conference for Unification, an electoral college, re-elected President Chung Hee Park to a fourth 6-year term on July 6, 1978. As chairman of the conference, Park made a brief speech before the balloting, emphasizing the importance of political stability and continued economic prosperity as the only answers to a military threat from North Korea.

Park was the only candidate. All opposition leaders had been placed under house arrest before the vote to prevent rival candidacies. The former leader of the opposition New Democratic Party, Kim Dae Jung, quit that party on March 29. He complained that the party had failed to oppose the government's harsh treatment of student dissidents. But, the New Democratic Party scored sharp gains in parliamentary elections on December 13.

In its annual report to the United States Congress on human rights, the United States Department of State said there had been some improvement in South Korea. Some dissidents were arrested when they demonstrated in Seoul on February 17 to deny this statement. They and others were released by a general amnesty in December. On April 10 and 11, pro-government demonstrators protested a reported admission by former U.S. Ambassador William J. Porter that the United States had bugged Blue House, Park's official residence.

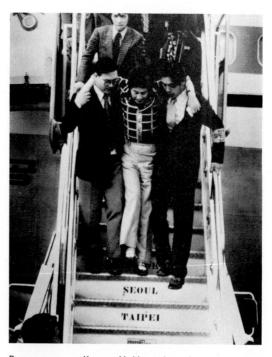

Passengers on a Korean Air Lines plane shot down when it flew over Russian territory arrive in Tokyo. Two persons were killed.

Troop Withdrawal. On April 21, President Jimmy Carter announced a slowdown in the projected withdrawal of U.S. troops from South Korea. Instead of 6,000 troops leaving by the end of 1978, as the President had proposed in 1977, only 800 troops and 2,600 support personnel would be withdrawn. The change was made when Carter thought Congress might not grant his request for the transfer to South Korea of military equipment worth $800-million that would be left behind by U.S. troops and for $275 million in credits to buy other armaments. Congress approved these requests on September 12, after receiving assurances from Carter that he would report on the Korea situation before further troop withdrawals were made.

United States Secretary of Defense Harold Brown announced on February 12 that at least 12 additional U.S. Air Force jet fighters would be stationed in South Korea to offset troop withdrawals. On July 27, Brown pledged "prompt and effective support" if the country were attacked.

Airplane Incident. A South Korean airliner flying across the Arctic from Paris to Seoul strayed over Russia's heavily militarized Kola Peninsula on April 20. Russian fighters fired on the plane, killing two of the 110 persons on board. The plane crash-landed on a frozen lake 280 miles (450 kilometers) south of Murmansk. Because Russia and South Korea have no diplomatic relations, the United States and Japan helped repatriate the passengers, but the pilot and navigator were released only after they had admitted violating Russian air space. The plane's co-pilot blamed failure of navigational equipment for the incident. Still, there were signs of a slow improvement in Russian-South Korean relations, possibly as a result of North Korea's support for China in the Russian-Chinese dispute (see CHINA).

Economic Growth continued despite inflation and trade problems. The U.S. Central Intelligence Agency (CIA) reported that South Korea's foreign debt was $8.8 billion, but it called this manageable. The country has "easy access to international financial markets," the CIA said.

Inflation, estimated at 27 per cent in 1977, was still a problem in 1978, when poor weather hurt crops and pushed up farm prices. The Korean Traders Association reported that Korea had an average annual increase in wages of 33.3 per cent between 1975 and 1977, compared with 11.7 per cent in Taiwan and 11.3 per cent in Japan.

The government announced that the expanding industrial base would be used in 1979 to increase self-reliance in military equipment. A parade on October 1, marking the 30th anniversary of the founding of the country's armed forces, displayed weapons made in South Korea.　　Henry S. Bradsher

See also ASIA (Facts in Brief Table). In WORLD BOOK, see KOREA.

KUWAIT. See MIDDLE EAST.

KYPRIANOU, SPYROS ACHILLES (1932-　　), who became the acting leader of Cyprus on the death of Archbishop Makarios III in August 1977, won a five-year term as president of Cyprus on Jan. 26, 1978, after the opposition failed to name a candidate to run against him. See CYPRUS.

Kyprianou was born in Limassol, Cyprus, on Oct. 28, 1932, one of nine children of a successful businessman. After early schooling in Cyprus, he studied at the City of London College and received a law degree from Gray's Inn in London. He was admitted to the bar in England in 1954.

Early in the 1950s, Kyprianou became the London representative for Ethnarchy, a national council of Cypriots who sought independence from Great Britain. Ethnarchy was headed by Archbishop Makarios, then in exile. Kyprianou later returned to Cyprus, and became foreign minister in August 1960 after Cyprus gained independence from Britain. He held that post until 1972.

Kyprianou returned to politics in 1976, with the archbishop's approval. He formed the National Democratic Front Party, composed of Socialists and other leftists, which won 21 of 35 seats in the House of Representatives in elections that year. He was president of the House of Representatives when Makarios died.

Kyprianou married Mimi Pagathrokliton in England in 1956. They have two sons.　　Foster Stockwell

LABOR. Although the unemployment picture in the United States continued to brighten, workers felt the effects of escalating inflation in 1978. The revised Bureau of Labor Statistics (BLS) Consumer Price Index (CPI) for wage earners and clerical workers (CPI-W) rose 8.8 per cent during the year ending in October, while a new CPI for all urban consumers (CPI-U) – which covers about 80 per cent of the population – rose 8.9 per cent. The CPI increased by 4.8 per cent in 1976 and 6.8 per cent in 1977.

The real average weekly earnings of production workers in the nonfarm economy declined 0.6 per cent during the first 10 months of 1978, as the 8.8 per cent rise in the CPI-W more than offset the 8.1 per cent rise in average weekly earnings. Adding the 3 per cent average increase in Social Security and federal income tax rates for a married worker with three dependents resulted in a 3.3 per cent overall decline in spendable earnings.

The job market afforded better news, however. Total employment rose 3.3 million, to more than 95.7-million for the year ending in October. The October jobless rate of 5.8 per cent was well within the unemployment rate range for the year, with a high in January of 6.3 per cent, and a low of 5.7 per cent in June. The unemployment rate continued to decline steadily after reaching a high of 8.5 per cent in 1975.

Anti-Inflation Efforts were intensified on October 24 when President Jimmy Carter called on "all

United Mine Workers President Arnold R. Miller talks to reporters in
March after his union ratified a new contract, ending a 110-day coal strike.

employees to limit their wage increases to a maximum of 7 per cent a year." The 7 per cent ceiling was
to include all fringe benefits as well as expected
cost-of-living raises (assuming a 6 per cent inflation
rate). The plan exempts those earning under $4 an
hour—about one-fourth of full-time workers—
while allowing higher settlements where there are
productivity increases, or, if necessary, to maintain a
historical "tandem" relationship with a group that
settled before October 24.

A "real-wage insurance" provision, which needed
congressional approval, would offer a tax rebate to
any worker conforming to the 7 per cent guide if the
CPI rises over 7 per cent.

The program was not mandatory, but the government could apply sanctions against violators
through its power over contract awards and import
restrictions, and as a major purchaser of goods and
services. Carter named Alfred E. Kahn, former
chairman of the Civil Aeronautics Board, to lead the
anti-inflation drive as chairman of the Council on
Wage and Price Stability.

Collective Bargaining in the first nine months of
1978 resulted in average wage increases of 7.7 per
cent during the first year of the new contracts and 6.5
per cent over the life of the major agreements. The
1978 data, which exclude possible gains under
"cost-of-living" escalator clauses, covered some 2-
million workers.

Primarily because of a lengthy strike by 160,000
bituminous coal miners, and as many as 330,000 rail
workers who honored picket lines by 20,000 Norfolk
and Western Railway employees, idleness resulting
from labor-management disputes in the first nine
months of 1978 reached the highest level since 1974.
There were 32.6 million days of idleness, compared
with 24.3 million and 29.7 million during comparable periods in 1977 and 1976, respectively. Two
other strike statistics, however—the number of work
stoppages and the number of workers involved—
were lower than in recent years.

The Coal Settlement. A series of wildcat strikes
by United Mine Workers of America (UMW) members in the summer of 1977 over unsatisfied grievances had left the union's health and retirement
funds depleted, resulting in a cutoff of benefits. As a
result, the UMW sought to restore and guarantee
the health-benefit funds, and to gain the right to
strike over local grievances when negotiations to
replace the expiring contract began. The Bituminous Coal Operators Association (BCOA) proposed
instead to improve labor "stability" by fining wildcat strikers, and to toughen up productivity and
attendance requirements.

Before a final settlement on March 25, 1978,
ended the 110-day strike, the UMW rank and file
rejected two accords, including one reached on
February 24 that had been approved 25 to 13 by the

UMW bargaining council. That accord had followed a UMW settlement with the Pittsburgh and Midway Coal Mining Company on February 20, and was achieved through the intervention of Secretary of Labor F. Ray Marshall and the Federal Mediation and Conciliation Service.

After the miners rejected that agreement on March 5, President Carter invoked compulsory back-to-work provisions of the Taft-Hartley Act on March 6, citing his responsibility to "protect the health and safety of the American public." The back-to-work order, obtained on March 9, was largely ignored, however.

On March 24, UMW miners voted to ratify another tentative contract reached on March 14. Most miners did not return to work until early April, however, as 19,000 miners honored picket lines set up by 10,000 UMW mine-construction workers on March 27. The construction workers returned on April 5 after ratifying a settlement patterned after the miners' pact.

The three-year coal settlement raised wages by $1 an hour the first year, with an additional 70 cents per hour in the second and third years. The 70 cents included a 30-cent "cost-of-living" increase that was not tied to any changes in the BLS-CPI.

The new contract also raised pensions by up to $13.50 per month for the first 10 years of service to a top of $15 per month for each year of service over 30 years. Payments were guaranteed, and the $275 per month for those retiring prior to 1976 was effective at once, instead of in steps. The maximum sum deductible from medical benefits was reduced from the $700 negotiated earlier to $200. A "labor-stability" clause that would have called for dismissal of wildcat-strike leaders was dropped.

Postal Bargaining also illustrated rank-and-file restiveness, and required the intervention of a third party. A three-year arbitration award for some 570,000 postal workers, issued on September 15 by arbitrator James J. Healy of Harvard University, averted a tie-up of the U.S. mail.

The award raised wages by $500 in July 1978 and July 1980, with 3 per cent due in July 1979. In addition, postal workers gained layoff protection for their "work lifetime" as opposed to only for the duration of the contract. The parties agreed to arbitration after a 15-day negotiating effort failed.

Railroad Bargaining focused on the long-smoldering crew-size issue, as the nation's financially ailing railroads sought to cut costs. Although settlements were reached on July 21 with five unions, bargaining continued with eight other unions to replace contracts that had expired on Dec. 31, 1977. By late December, agreements had been reached for some 400,000 rail workers, with the 100,000-member Brotherhood of Railway and Airline Clerks and the 2,500-member Train Dispatchers the only holdouts.

The 39-month agreements raised wages 14 per cent over the term, with 3 per cent retroactive to April 1; semiannual cost-of-living adjustments were continued; and vacation, medical, and dental benefits were improved.

A similar settlement between the United Transportation Union (UTU) and the Consolidated Rail Corporation (Conrail) also resolved the crew-size issue by reducing the number of brakemen to one on freight runs of 70 cars or less. In return, UTU members were to receive $4 for each run as part of a reduced crew, Conrail agreed to contribute to a special "productivity fund" for each such operation, and any work-force reductions were to be accomplished through attrition.

Newspaper Strikes. A three-month strike by pressmen against New York City's major newspapers ended on November 6 after agreement on six-year contracts by the Pressmen's Union with *The New York Times* and the *Daily News*. The *New York Post* resumed publication on October 5 after agreeing to abide by the terms of any future settlement. The strike was precipitated on August 9 after the dailies unilaterally published new work rules that would lead to an attrition program that the pressmen claimed would eliminate half of their jobs.

Although eight other unions struck with the pressmen, the newspapers were forced to shut down only

Chicago and North Western railroad workers picket during a brief strike that disrupted Chicago commuter service in September.

because the deliverers' unions joined the walkout. The settlement provided for an increase of $68 a week over three years, with subsequent negotiations over wages for the second half of the six-year period. The agreement also guaranteed the jobs of all 1,508 union pressmen over the six years, with staff reductions being attained through attrition or incentives for workers to retire.

Other Settlements. Some 200,000 workers employed by fiscally troubled New York City finally received wage increases, and a three-year settlement covered 76,000 Pennsylvania state employees. However, in the wake of Proposition 13, Governor Edmund G. Brown, Jr., vetoed a 2.5 per cent raise approved by the legislature for 200,000 California state workers. Municipal workers struck in a number of U.S. cities, but, on the whole, received only modest increases in wages and benefits for their efforts. See CITY; TAXATION (Close-Up).

Safety Measures. The Department of Labor's Occupational Safety and Health Administration (OSHA) announced extensive new regulations on November 13 to protect an estimated 1 million workers from lead poisoning. OSHA cited the dangers caused by lead exposures as "irreversible kidney disease or anemia" with the "risk of damage to the central nervous system and possible sterility." The lead industry immediately challenged the new rules as too costly and in violation of the President's anti-inflation program, and filed a petition for a review of the standard with the Fifth U.S. Circuit Court of Appeals in New Orleans.

That same New Orleans court on October 5 set aside OSHA's new permanent standard on exposure to benzene on the grounds that the agency failed to show a "reasonable relationship" between the estimated costs for companies to comply and anticipated benefits.

President Carter signed the Black Lung Benefits Reform Act of 1977 on March 1. The legislation removed some eligibility restrictions that had prevented many miners suffering from the disease from getting benefits.

Federal Reforms. Carter signed the Civil Service Reform Act of 1978 on October 13. The legislation streamlined the processes for disciplining and dismissing incompetent, unproductive workers; made pay raises for supervisors in grades GS-13 to GS-15 subject to the quality of their performance; created a Senior Executive Service for some 9,000 senior officials (grades GS-16 to GS-18) under which performance would determine wage increases or demotions; and provided protection from retaliation for those who report wrongdoing by their agencies. The bill also facilitated the handling of contract impasses, mandated the arbitration of grievances,

Striking newspaper guild members try to block the delivery in June of editions of the *Daily News* produced by nonunion workers in New York City.

and created a Federal Labor Relations Authority similar to the National Labor Relations Board (NLRB) in the private sector.

Two measures to increase flexibility in the federal work force were enacted. One allows federal agencies to alter the traditional five-day, 40-hour workweek; the other requires most federal agencies to establish part-time job programs at all grade levels.

Another measure eliminated the retirement age of 70 that was applied to most federal employees. The legislation amended the Age Discrimination in Employment Act of 1967 and raised from 65 to 70 the age at which state and local governments and employers in the private sector can force employees to retire. See OLD AGE.

Employment Changes. Preliminary BLS estimates of major employment changes in 1978 are summarized in the table below:

	1977	1978*
	(in thousands)	
Total labor force	**99,534**	**102,147**
Armed forces	2,133	2,117
Civilian labor force	97,401	100,030
Total employment	90,546	93,973
Unemployed	6,855	6,057
Unemployment rate	7.0%	6.1%
Change in real weekly earnings (Workers with 3 dependents— Private nonfarm sector)	-0.3%	-3.3%†
Change in output per man-hour (Total private economy)	+1.3%	+0.7%‡

*January to September average, seasonally adjusted, except for armed forces data.
†For 12-month period ending Sept. 30, 1978.
‡Third quarter of 1978, compared with third quarter of 1977.

Union Developments. Organized labor continued its nationwide boycott of J. P. Stevens & Company products. The Amalgamated Clothing and Textile Workers union saw "little cause for celebration" when the textile firm on April 28 agreed to stop allegedly illegal labor practices and the NLRB dropped its suit against the firm.

In other union developments, United Farm Workers of America President Cesar Chavez announced on January 31 that his union was ending its boycott of table grapes, iceberg lettuce, and Gallo wines; the Department of Labor sued Teamsters President Frank A. Fitzsimmons and other officials for alleged pension fund mismanagement on February 1; and Joseph P. Tonelli, former president of the United Paperworkers International Union, was sentenced to three years in prison for embezzling union funds. Leon Bornstein

See also COAL; CONGRESS OF THE UNITED STATES; ECONOMICS; POSTAL SERVICE, UNITED STATES; PRESIDENT OF THE UNITED STATES. IN WORLD BOOK, see LABOR; LABOR FORCE.

LAOS. This tiny state of 3½ million persons suffered through yet another year of unrest, short rations, and calamity in 1978. After two years of severe drought, the government said that there was only enough grain to feed the nation until March 1978 and that an additional 367,000 short tons (333,000 metric tons) of cereals would be needed to provide food until the next harvest. If no aid came, Laos would face famine. Help did come, in part from the United States, but it was not enough.

The spring and summer weather was kind, and the government in Vientiane said that "young rice plants looked healthy and beautiful." But heavy rains began on August 10 and continued for more than a month. In Champassak province, the heart of the rice country, 90 per cent of the fields were flooded. Other provinces on the Mekong River Delta fared little better.

Many Die. Many hundreds of Laotians died, thousands of head of cattle drowned, and stored food was washed away by the rains. "As a result," the government said, "our people will face difficulties and starvation, as they did in 1977. The difficulties anticipated in the coming season will be even worse." Because the floods hit areas that had endured two years of drought, the suffering was expected to be severe and to "limit the ability of the government to fight the enemy and maintain public security and order."

Guerrillas Active. There was good reason for concern. Although an estimated 40,000 Vietnamese troops were encamped in Laos, anti-Communist guerrillas operated in much of the countryside and made the few major roads unsafe, especially at night. Knowledgeable Western observers said that the farmers were disenchanted with the Communist regime, the low prices paid for their rice, and collectivization policies.

Aid from its patron, Vietnam, kept Laos going. Some observers described the country as "Hanoi's satellite." But Laos also found itself an arena in which Russia and China pressed their feud. The Chinese continued to extend the web of strategic highways across the country. The Laotian government in Vientiane, however, made it clear that its heart lay with Hanoi and Moscow. Russia had an estimated 1,500 specialists in Laos helping to restore the nation's transport system, fly its planes, and build a large airport on the Plain of Jars.

Relations with the West were less cordial. Laos ordered French diplomats to leave the country in August, charging them with "defamatory propaganda" and "aiding and abetting young Laotian intellectuals and technicians" to flee the country and "backing Laotian traitors" in France and Laos. Other missions in Vientiane had already sharply reduced their personnel. Mark Gayn

See also ASIA (Facts in Brief Table). In WORLD BOOK, see LAOS.

LATIN
AMERICA

Territorial conflicts between neighboring countries created tensions in the region during 1978. On January 18, Peru charged that Ecuador had attacked one of its garrisons in the Amazon jungle. Ecuador claimed the Peruvian base was on ground that Peru seized by force in an undeclared 10-day war in 1941. Ecuador had never recognized the validity of an international protocol signed in Rio de Janeiro, Brazil, in 1942 that delineated the boundary.

Ecuador denied the charge, and Supreme Council President Alfredo Poveda Burbano telephoned Peruvian President Francisco Morales Bermudez Cerrutti, arranging to have their chiefs of staff meet in Quito, Ecuador, on January 20. The meeting ended in declarations of mutual friendship.

Rival Claims. Guatemala's claim to control over Belize, a British dependency in Central America, continued to delay independence for Belize. Guatemala's President Kjell Eugenio Laugerud Garcia reaffirmed on February 24 that his country sought complete control over Belize, which blocks Guatemala's landlocked El Petén province from access to the Gulf of Honduras and the Caribbean Sea. However, Laugerud indicated that he might accept a part of Belizean territory as a final settlement with Great Britain.

That solution had been proposed earlier by the British, but Premier George Price of black, English-speaking Belize had refused on January 24 to cede any territory to the Spanish-speaking Guatemalans. The British proposal, he declared, called for Belize to cede 300 square miles (780 square kilometers) of land and 700 square miles (1,800 square kilometers) of sea at its southern end to Guatemala. Price also pointed out that the area is larger than some of the independent countries of the Caribbean and that Exxon Corporation was drilling in the ocean area for oil.

On June 2, Premier Price and Dean Lindo, leader of the opposition party, joined forces to keep the issue out of politics, and both swore not to give up any territory. Observers said that other black, English-speaking nations in the Caribbean supported their position. Conversely, Guatemala drew no support from the Spanish-speaking countries, leaving it isolated in the region.

Guatemala nonetheless continued to demand a piece of Belizean territory, a joint Guatemalan-Belizean military staff, and a measure of control over Belizean foreign policy. Great Britain offered to give Guatemala a free port in Belize and to construct a road to El Petén province that would provide an outlet to the Caribbean. Guatemala refused the offer, however, declaring it would try to negotiate directly with Belize.

Bolivia-Chile Dispute. Bolivia broke off diplomatic relations with Chile on March 17, claiming that negotiations for a Bolivian corridor to the sea across Chile's northern desert had come to a standstill. Bolivia had lost its seacoast to Chile in the 1879 War of the Pacific — at the same time Chile had seized Peru's copper-and-nitrate-rich northern desert region. Both sides had hoped to mark the 100th anniversary of the war's end by opening an outlet to the sea for Bolivia. However, the treaty ending the war had also given Peru veto power over any disposition of its former territory. Several proposals had been advanced, and all were refused by Bolivia, Peru, and Chile.

Chile Versus Argentina. The region's most serious territorial confrontation in 1978 was between Chile and Argentina. It involved ownership of the tiny islands of Lennox, Nueva, and Picton, which lie in the Beagle Channel just below Tierra del Fuego at the southernmost tip of South America. Both nations have claimed sovereignty over the virtually uninhabited islands for more than a century.

The dispute nearly reached open warfare in 1978 after the International Court of Justice at The Hague in the Netherlands awarded all three islands to Chile. The two countries had agreed to binding arbitration in a treaty that was signed in 1902, but arbitration was not set in motion until after a second treaty, signed in 1971 between the two countries, restated the principle that the findings would be binding on both sides.

The court had deliberated for six years before announcing its decision on May 2, 1977. At that time, both sides had been given nine months to comply with the findings. But Argentina rejected the court's decision on January 25, charging that it was "against international law." Earlier in January, Chilean newspapers had reported that Argentine naval and army units were on maneuvers in the vicinity of the islands. Other sources claimed, however, that Chile had actually moved its forces into the area sometime earlier.

Chile's President Augusto Pinochet Ugarte and Argentine President Jorge Rafael Videla met twice to discuss the issue. On February 20, they agreed to hold a series of talks that would ultimately result in a decision by November 2. Chile said it would not discuss the validity of the court's decision, however, pointing out that both sides had agreed to accept it as binding. This point was reaffirmed in a court

Flag-waving Panamanians celebrate ratification of treaties by the U.S. Congress in April that give Panama control of the canal on Dec. 31, 1999.

Guerrilla leader "Zero" leaves Nicaragua in
August after his Sandinista rebel forces
failed to topple the Somoza government.

communication to both sides, dated March 8, which said that the nine-month compliance period "was not intended as a period within which [either party] could decide whether or not they would accept the award." Argentine officials declared, nevertheless, that they would never relinquish their sovereignty in the Beagle Channel.

Several aspects of the issue agitated the Argentines. The most important one was that during the time the arbitration panel had been deliberating, the international practice concerning offshore territories was changed by the United Nations Law of the Sea Conference. Under the new concept, Chile might now lay claim to all ocean territory 200 nautical miles from the islands. In January, Chile appeared to do just that. It published a map that not only claimed a portion of the Atlantic Ocean, but also widened its claim in Antarctica based on the position of the disputed islands. The claims violated a principle that had been a cornerstone in the peaceful relations between the two countries – namely, that Argentina was solely an Atlantic Ocean power and that Chile was solely a Pacific Ocean power. An additional cause of friction was the possibility that the area in contention might contain rich petroleum deposits.

When the November 2 deadline passed without an agreement, many Argentines – inflamed by fiery political rhetoric – expected an outbreak of war.

However, a joint communiqué issued by the two nations talked vaguely about economic integration and cooperation in the far south and made no mention of the sharp differences. On December 23, both countries agreed to accept as a mediator Antonio Cardinal Samoré, an Italian member of the Vatican Curia appointed as a peace envoy by Pope John Paul II.

Other Actions. The General Assembly of the Organization of American States (OAS) convened in Washington, D.C., on June 21. United States President Jimmy Carter, in an opening address, indicated that U.S. policy toward Latin America was still focused mainly on human-rights issues. He mentioned no specific nations as violators, but, as he spoke, various delegations were given copies of reports by the OAS Inter-American Commission on Human Rights charging flagrant abuses by Paraguay and Uruguay and less serious violations by Chile. In March, President Carter, accompanied by his wife, Rosalynn, and his daughter, Amy, visited Venezuela and Brazil.

Nicaragua experienced a year of strikes and open warfare between army troops and left wing guerrillas. The disturbances were touched off by the January 10 murder of a newspaper editor, and the objective was to topple the government of President Anastasio Somoza Debayle. See NICARAGUA.

Economic Strain. A report issued during the year by the Inter-American Development Bank indicated that Latin American countries were still staggering under the impact of the quadrupling of world oil prices in 1973. Growth in the area's overall economy remained below 5 per cent a year.

Economic difficulties caused members of the Caribbean Common Market (Caricom) to abandon plans to establish joint development projects in several areas. The projects included a regional aluminum smelter, a regional food corporation, and a collectively owned shipping firm.

Jamaica and Guyana were suffering acute balance-of-payments deficits and could not make any financial commitments to the projects. Restrictive barriers adopted by both nations to curtail imports also hurt the spirit of free trade Caricom was trying to encourage. Guyana became the center of world attention in November when some 900 members of a religious cult committed suicide or were murdered at Jonestown (see Close-Up).

At Venezuela's instigation, a special $122-million fund was set up within the World Bank to provide economic relief for Caribbean countries with financial problems. On July 3, the foreign ministers of Bolivia, Brazil, Colombia, Ecuador, Guyana, Peru, and Venezuela plus the prime minister of Surinam signed the Treaty of Amazonian Cooperation at ceremonies in Brasília, the capital of Brazil. The treaty set up a cooperative Amazon River Basin development program, with all the nations sharing the river system. Venezuelan Foreign Minister Simon Alberto Consalvi declared in the principal speech at the ceremony that "up until a short time ago, Amazonia was a vacuum, the aggregate of the farthest part of our backyards, an impenetrable green cape that separated rather than united us. We have now created the instrument to turn Amazonia into a fertile field for cooperation."

The Amazon Pact, as it was known, was the result of a Brazilian initiative to ensure that all the nations involved shared in the development of the region and that the environment was protected. Previously, the smaller nations surrounding Brazil had been fearful of its dominance in the area. The pact represented Brazil's first attempt to ease these fears

and to cooperate with its smaller, Spanish-speaking neighbors.

President Carter's Visit to Venezuela and Brazil in March was a good-will venture. The President's stopover in Venezuela on March 28 and 29 reaffirmed the cordial relations that had existed between Carter and Venezuelan President Carlos Andres Perez. By contrast, the President received a correct but chilly welcome on his arrival in Brasília on March 29. The welcome reflected the Brazilians' hard feelings toward Carter's criticism of their human-rights record and his attempts to dissuade West Germany from fulfilling its agreement to ship Brazil a breeder reactor to produce plutonium for nuclear power generation.

Facts in Brief on Latin American Political Units

Country	Population	Government†	Monetary Unit*	Foreign Trade (million U.S. $)	
				Exports	Imports
Argentina	26,729,000	President Jorge Rafael Videla	peso (909 = $1)	5,652	4,162
Bahamas	235,000	Governor General Gerald C. Cash; Prime Minister Lynden O. Pindling	dollar (1 = $1)	2,423	2,858
Barbados	251,000	Governor General Sir Deighton Harcourt Lyle Ward; Prime Minister J. M. G. Adams	dollar (2 = $1)	96	275
Belize	158,000	Governor Peter Donovan McEntee; Premier George Price	dollar (2 = $1)	65	93
Bolivia	6,268,000	President David Padilla Arancibia	peso (20 = $1)	446	558
Brazil	120,593,000	President Ernesto Geisel	cruzeiro (20 = $1)	12,120	13,257
Chile	11,011,000	President Augusto Pinochet Ugarte	peso (33.2 = $1)	2,190	2,367
Colombia	26,289,000	President Julio Cesar Turbay Ayala	peso (35.7 = $1)	2,433	1,880
Costa Rica	2,181,000	President Rodrigo Carazo Odio	colón (8.6 = $1)	805	1,013
Cuba	10,020,000	President Fidel Castro Ruz	peso (1 = $1.31)	3,573	4,066
Dominican Republic	5,287,000	President Silvestre Antonio Guzman Fernandez	peso (1 = $1)	794	793
Ecuador	7,846,000	Supreme Council President Alfredo Poveda Burbano	sucre (25 = $1)	1,229	1,508
El Salvador	4,510,000	President Carlos Humberto Romero	colón (2.5 = $1)	959	950
Grenada	98,000	Governor General Paul Scoon; Prime Minister Sir Eric M. Gairy	dollar (2.7 = $1)	12	24
Guatemala	6,820,000	President Fernando Romeo-Lucas Garcia	quetzal (1 = $1)	760	839
Guyana	863,000	President Raymond Arthur Chung; Prime Minister Forbes Burnham	dollar (2.6 = $1)	269	363
Haiti	4,884,000	President Jean-Claude Duvalier	gourde (5 = $1)	79	121
Honduras	3,539,000	Military Junta President Policarpo Paz	lempira (2 = $1)	504	575
Jamaica	2,171,000	Governor General Florizel Glasspole; Prime Minister Michael Norman Manley	dollar (1.6 = $1)	746	861
Mexico	69,018,000	President Jose Lopez Portillo	peso (22.7 = $1)	4,123	5,487
Nicaragua	2,454,000	President Anastasio Somoza Debayle	córdoba (7.1 = $1)	633	721
Panama	1,885,000	President Aristides Royo; National Guard Commander Omar Torrijos Herrera	balboa (1 = $1)	253	861
Paraguay	2,784,000	President Alfredo Stroessner	guaraní (126 = $1)	274	301
Peru	17,896,000	President Francisco Morales Bermudez Cerrutti; Prime Minister Oscar Molina Pallochia	sol (142.8 = $1)	1,564	1,880
Puerto Rico	3,421,000	Governor Carlos Romero Barcelo	US $	3,735	5,933
Surinam	481,000	President Johan H. E. Ferrier; Prime Minister Henck A. E. Arron	guilder (1.8 = $1)	277	262
Trinidad and Tobago	1,120,000	President Ellis Emmanuel Innocent Clarke; Prime Minister Eric E. Williams	dollar (2.4 = $1)	2,174	1,862
Uruguay	2,820,000	President Aparicio Mendez Manfredini	peso (6.5 = $1)	546	587
Venezuela	13,446,000	President Carlos Andres Perez	bolivar (4.3 = $1)	9,548	9,810

*Exchange rates as of Dec. 1, 1978. †As of Dec. 31, 1978.

Death in Guyana's Jungle

The horrifying end of the People's Temple, a California-based religious cult, left the world in shocked disbelief in November 1978. Congressman Leo J. Ryan (D., Calif.) and four other Americans were shot to death on November 18, and 911 men, women, and children—including cult leader Jim Jones—died soon after in a stunning orgy of suicide and murder at Jonestown, Guyana.

Jones, a preacher who allegedly came to believe he was God, had moved most of his cult from its San Francisco headquarters to a large jungle commune called Jonestown in 1977. Conflicting reports drifted back to California. Some said the cult offered new hope to its followers; others told bizarre tales of torture and "brainwashing." Ryan went to Jonestown in November with a party of aides and newsmen to investigate.

Ryan, three newsmen, and one cult defector were murdered as they were boarding a plane to leave Jonestown.

Two other members of the party, lawyers Charles Garry and Mark Lane, were still at Jones's camp when the man his followers called "Dad" decided it was time for his entire "family" to die.

Tubs of cyanide-laced fruit drink were prepared, and Jones and his people apparently fed it to the children, drank it themselves, or had it forced upon them. Garry, Lane, and a few others fled; the rest fell dead.

As the horrible story unfolded, 911 bodies were flown to the United States for disposition. Guyanese authorities held Larry Layton, a cult member, on charges of murder, and the Federal Bureau of Investigation prepared to arrest several other persons. A tape recording of events on Jonestown's last grisly night was found in the commune. But no one could explain how the People's Temple, champion of service to the poor, came to deal in death.

Marsha F. Goldsmith

The poison tub

Nothing substantive was accomplished during the trip, but Carter did manage to smooth relations between the two countries, keeping all references to their differences low-key. On his final day in the country, however, Carter visited in Rio de Janeiro with six prominent civilians who were frequently critical of the Brazilian military regime. Among them was Paulo Evaristo Cardinal Arns, Roman Catholic archbishop of São Paulo, who has publicly condemned the Brazilian government for its violations of human rights. Arns's office said Carter had given him a handwritten letter for delivery to a Pentecostal minister who had been arrested by police in São Paulo.

Pressure from President Carter was credited with forcing the Dominican Republic armed forces to accept the results of the election held on May 16 in which incumbent President Joaquin Balaguer lost to Silvestre Antonio Guzman Fernandez. The armed forces, which supported Balaguer, had interrupted the vote count for a 30-hour period on May 17 and 18, arousing U.S. fears that the military were trying to steal the election. See GUZMAN FERNANDEZ, SILVESTRE ANTONIO.   Everett G. Martin

See also articles on the various Latin American countries. In WORLD BOOK, see LATIN AMERICA and articles on the countries.

LAW. See CIVIL RIGHTS; COURTS AND LAWS; CRIME; SUPREME COURT OF THE UNITED STATES.

LEBANON. A dismal succession of battles, unsuccessful cease-fires, and murders kept Lebanon in turmoil throughout 1978. The instability, marked at times by clashes as violent as those of the 1975-1976 civil war, hampered recovery and risked setting off a wider conflict involving other Arab nations and Israel.

A truce among the various Lebanese factions that had held, at least nominally, for about three months collapsed early in January. Christian militiamen fought Syrian troops of the Arab peacekeeping force and Palestinian guerrillas. A declaration issued on January 21 by the Lebanese Front, a coalition of Maronite Christian leaders, demanded the right of each community to govern its own affairs, a position opposed by President Elias Sarkis.

Israel Invades. The conflict spread to southern Lebanon in February as Christian rightists battled Palestinian guerrillas. After Palestinians captured a key Christian village near the Israeli border and a Palestinian landing party hijacked an Israeli bus near Haifa on March 11, a raid in which 37 Israelis were killed, Israel invaded Lebanon on March 14 and 15. The Israelis caused about 400 casualties.

With Israel occupying Lebanon as far north as the Litani River, the Lebanese conflict shifted northward. Syrian units fought major battles in early April with Christian Falangists, one of two Christian right wing groups. Prime Minister Salim Ahmad al-Huss resigned on April 19, saying that the public interest demanded a new government. But no replacement was forthcoming, and Sarkis reappointed him in May.

The Fighting Increases. Israeli forces completed a two-phase withdrawal from Lebanon on June 13, turning over major posts to Christian militia units rather than the United Nations Interim Force in Lebanon. At about the same time, Falangists attacked supporters of former President Sleiman Frangie, also Christians, and murdered Frangie's son Tony and his family. The Frangie clan retaliated with a raid on Falangist headquarters.

The worst fighting since 1976 broke out in Beirut in July. It pitted the Arab peacekeeping force against the Falange. Shelling completely shut down Beirut's port, which had begun to recover its economic importance. In October, Sarkis issued an ultimatum to the Arab force to draw up a plan to disarm all private armies and prohibit armed action by Palestinians on Lebanese soil. On November 15, the Arab force submitted a plan, but the Lebanese Cabinet could not agree to accept it.

The economic scorecard for the three-year civil war showed estimated losses of $2.45 billion in building damages, $1 billion in commercial property, and $512 million in other investments.   William Spencer

See also MIDDLE EAST (Facts in Brief Table). In WORLD BOOK, see LEBANON.

LÉGER, JULES (1913-   ), completed his fifth and final year as governor general of Canada in 1978. On December 7, Edward Schreyer, formerly premier of Manitoba, was named to succeed him.

In spite of the stroke that has handicapped him, Governor General Léger carried out an active round of functions. He and his wife, Gabrielle, welcomed Queen Elizabeth II, Prince Philip, and two of their children, Andrew and Edward, as they arrived in Canada on July 26, to attend the XI Commonwealth Games in Edmonton, Alta. Prince Andrew later visited Government House in Ottawa, Ont. The Légers spent the first two weeks of August touring western Canada. They visited British Columbia to celebrate the bicentennial of Captain James Cook's landing and went to Alberta to participate in the closing ceremonies of the Commonwealth Games. From August 20 to 25, the Légers visited the mammoth James Bay hydroelectric power installation in northern Quebec and went on to Frobisher Bay on Baffin Island.

Among awards the governor general presented to Canadians for achievements in various fields was one investing hockey star Bobby Hull as an Officer of the Order of Canada.   David M. L. Farr

See also CANADA. In WORLD BOOK, see LÉGER, JULES.

LESOTHO. See AFRICA.

LIBERIA. See AFRICA.

LIBRARY. The unprecedented 1978 taxpayer revolt against government spending left United States libraries with mixed financial prospects. Prior to the passage in June of California's Proposition 13 to limit property taxes, library construction and renovation was stimulated by local and state support plus such federal aid as revenue sharing, Comprehensive Employment and Training Act (CETA) funds, and other programs.

For instance, the Dallas Public Library received a $4.9-million Public Works Employment Act grant to help cover the costs of building a new central research library. The National Endowment for the Humanities offered a $500,000 challenge grant, to be matched by private donations, for materials to stock the new building. The Newport Beach Public Library in California received $419,000 to build and stock the Newport Center Branch Library.

Energy saving and new building designs received more emphasis during 1978. The Stark County District Library in Canton, Ohio, received $4.6-million in federal public works funds to build a pyramid-shaped building that will depend on solar energy to furnish much of its heating and cooling needs. The Bridgewater Free Library in New York completed construction of a new prefabricated building. The carpeted, fully insulated, 1,200-square-foot (111-square-meter) library cost only $16,600, including furnishings.

Academic Libraries. California Polytechnic State University in Pomona announced plans to build a $10.6-million library with room for 500,000 volumes to replace its crowded 1947 building.

Perhaps in anticipation of a full-fledged taxpayer revolt, substantial private gifts to libraries appeared to be on the increase. In New York City, the Vincent Astor Foundation offered a $5-million challenge grant to help the New York Public Library.

Library Freezes. The Library of Congress announced plans to "freeze" its card catalog. After Jan. 1, 1980, the library will rely on automated data for access to its collections.

In another type of freeze, some 37,000 books in Yale University's Beinecke Rare Book and Manuscript Library in New Haven, Conn., were protected from book-eating insects by a new deep-freeze technique. The books were placed in a blast-freezer chamber, 300 at a time, and frozen at -20° F. (-29°C) for three days. This method kills beetles and other insects nesting in books and is safer and more practical than traditional fumigation.

Library Meetings. The Canadian Library Association's annual conference was held in Edmonton, Alta., from June 15 to 20. The 97th American Library Association annual conference was also held in June in Chicago.   Robert J. Shaw

See also AMERICAN LIBRARY ASSOCIATION; CANADIAN LIBRARY ASSOCIATION. In WORLD BOOK, see LIBRARY.

LIBYA. Head of government Muammar Muhammad al-Qadhaafi continued his strong commitment to the Palestinians and other Third World causes in 1978. Qadhaafi opposed Egyptian President Anwar al-Sadat's peace overtures to Israel and attended summit meetings of the Arab "rejectionist front." But Libya reconciled its differences with Sudan, whose President Muhammed Nimeiri supported Sadat. Libya closed the training camps it had set up as bases for Nimeiri's political opponents.

Chad broke off diplomatic relations on February 6, charging Libya with supplying funds and arms to Frolinat, the Chad rebel movement, and with illegal occupation of a strip of Chad's territory thought to contain uranium. The two countries agreed to restore relations on February 18; and Libya mediated a cease-fire between regular Chad forces and Frolinat on February 22, but it did not hold. On July 22, Chad President F. Malloum Ngakoutou Bey-Ndi accused Libya of trying to partition his country and took the issue to the Organization of African Unity for arbitration.

Part II of the *Green Book,* Qadhaafi's blueprint for the Libyan revolution, was published on February 5. It describes the economic and social elements in Qadhaafi's "Universal Third Doctrine," a program designed to establish a political system that effectively gives power to the people. The General People's Congress, the supreme legislative body, passed laws in May introducing compulsory military service for Libyan males between 18 and 35 years of age and limiting private property ownership to one house and lot, except for commercial property. Administrative control by committees of employees in businesses and government agencies continued.

Economic Development. Because of its vast wealth and freedom from prior obligations, Libya could afford to experiment and support revolutionary causes without jeopardizing its economic development. The revised five-year-plan approved in January increased development expenditures by 23 per cent to $31.9 billion.

Foreign Aid. Libya funded the largest part of the Palestine Liberation Organization's budget and such other causes as the Canary Islands independence movement.

Jordan received $70 million for potash-plant expansion in May. Libya postponed until 1983 repayment by Turkey of $15 million in debts and doubled the number of Turkish workers in Libya. A similar agreement was made with Malta. William Spencer

See AFRICA (Facts in Brief Table). In WORLD BOOK, see LIBYA.

LIECHTENSTEIN. See EUROPE.

LIONS INTERNATIONAL. See COMMUNITY ORGANIZATIONS.

President Mohamed Siad Barre of Somalia, left, arrives in Libya on March 1 to ask General Muammar Muhammad al-Qadhaafi, right, for aid against Ethiopia.

LITERATURE. There was a remarkable flood of first-rate novels and collections of short stories from the younger generation of American writers in 1978. For the first time in years, American fiction was as rich, innovative, and powerful as that coming from other countries, and its future seemed assured.

This was especially encouraging in a year that saw considerable controversy over the mergers of publishing houses and their acquisition by huge corporations. Some observers feared a decline in the number of serious novels, which tend to do poorly at the cash register. See PUBLISHING.

The variety from young writers was as astonishing as the quantity. The huge family novel made a comeback in David Plante's *The Family,* the story of a French-Canadian home in Rhode Island; Julia Markus' Jewish-oriented *Uncle;* and Susan Fromberg Schaeffer's Galsworthian saga of a New England family, *Time in its Flight.* Mary Gordon's *Final Payments,* the affecting and powerful tale of a young woman's caring for her dying father, was the year's finest first novel.

Another excellent first novel was *Appalachee Red,* by Raymond Andrews, a complex, allusive, and wryly ironic story of the tangled relationships between blacks and whites in the 20th century. Two novels of Vietnam, James Webb's *Fields of Fire* and Tim O'Brien's *Going After Cacciato,* were fine examples of the surreal war reportage that has marked the best fiction to emerge from the Vietnam War.

The American tendency to violence was explored in the remarkable *The World According to Garp* by John Irving, a sometimes melodramatic and often powerful novel that was a considerable best seller. Paul Theroux' *Picture Palace* was a scathing parody of the world of art photography.

Women novelists made especially strong strides. There was excellent work from Rita Mae Brown *(Six of One);* Rosellen Brown *(Tender Mercies);* and Maria Katzenbach *(The Grab,* another superb first novel). Slightly older authors also turned in first-class fiction, notably Alice Adams *(Listening to Billie),* Joyce Carol Oates *(Son of the Morning),* Diane Johnson *(Lying Low),* and Gail Godwin *(Violet Clay).*

The Old Hands were also busy. John Updike's *The Coup* was a passionate double satire of America and Africa. *The Stories of John Cheever* was a landmark in a distinguished writer's career, as was Irwin Shaw's *Short Stories: Five Decades.* The posthumously published *Whistle* added to James Jones's luster as a war novelist. Two months after his novel *Shosha* appeared, Isaac Bashevis Singer won a richly deserved Nobel Prize (see NOBEL PRIZES).

There were also satisfying novels from Thomas McGuane, Don DeLillo, Wilfrid Sheed, Hubert Selby, Jr., Frederick Manfred, Ward Just, Ernest J. Gaines, Russell Banks, and Thomas Williams, among others too numerous to list. James Miche-

© Thomas Victor

Mario Puzo, author of the 1978 best seller *Fools Die,* awaits a return on the tennis court at his home on Long Island, N.Y.

ner's *Chesapeake,* Mario Puzo's *Fools Die,* and Herman Wouk's *The Winds of War* were popular successes.

There was less fiction from other countries, but it was of high quality. Great Britain contributed Doris Lessing's *Stories,* V. S. Pritchett's *Selected Stories,* and Iris Murdoch's *The Sea, The Sea.* From Ireland came Sean O'Faolain's *Selected Stories.*

Latin America sent the Colombian Gabriel Garcia Marquez' *Innocent Erendira and Other Stories* and Peruvian Mario Vargas Llosa's comic *Captain Pantoja and the Special Service.* George Konrad's dense, brilliant *The City Builder* was translated from the Hungarian, and Peter Handke's *The Left-Handed Woman* enhanced the reputation of the Austrian radical. Poland was represented by *Sanatorium Under the Sign of the Hourglass,* by Bruno Schulz, a Polish Jew who was murdered by the Nazis in 1942. Günter Grass's *The Flounder* was perhaps the West German novelist's finest work.

Biography, an always reliable genre, enjoyed a productive year, especially in lives of British writers. Angus Wilson's *The Strange Ride of Rudyard Kipling* and Lord Birkenhead's long-suppressed *Rudyard Kipling* resurrected the reputation of the great English imperialist. P. N. Furbank began a long-needed reassessment in *E. M. Forster: A Life.* Victoria Glendinning turned in the fine *Elizabeth Bowen.* George D. Painter offered the first in what promises

General Douglas MacArthur, shown wading ashore triumphantly in 1944 in the Philippines, was the subject of William Manchester's biography.

to be a magisterial multivolume biography of *Chateaubriand.* Deirdre Bair's *Samuel Beckett* was a solid life of the complex Irish playwright.

Closer to home, *What Is an Editor? Saxe Commins at Work,* by Dorothy Commins, and *Maxwell Perkins: Editor of Genius,* by A. Scott Berg, were excellent biographies of two giants of publishing.

Political biographies were few, and of these, the controversial and partisan *Robert Kennedy and His Times* by Arthur M. Schlesinger, Jr., was the most notable. William Manchester wrote the massive, masterful, and evenhanded *American Caesar: Douglas MacArthur, 1880-1964.*

Other good American biographies were James Thomas Flexner's *The Young Hamilton,* Irving H. Bartlett's *Daniel Webster,* and Paula Blanchard's *Margaret Fuller.*

Autobiography. Three significant memoirs were written by American journalists. Theodore H. White's *In Search of History* was a runaway best seller. *On Becoming American,* by Ted Morgan, was an engaging and popular tale of a former French count's Americanization. *The New York Times* columnist Tom Wicker's *On Press* offered cogent commentary on his profession in America.

There were some interesting if not particularly important literary autobiographies: Alfred Kazin's *New York Jew* and Stephen Spender's *The Thirties and After* were among them. Arthur Koestler's *Janus: A Summing Up* was another leader in this category.

Important political autobiographies came from the West German Willy Brandt *(People and Politics: The Years 1960-1975)* and the French father of the Common Market, Jean Monnet *(Memoirs).*

Adding to the groaning Watergate shelf were two long-awaited and notably self-serving memoirs, *RN: The Memoirs of Richard Nixon* and *The Ends of Power,* by H. R. Haldeman, Nixon's former White House chief of staff.

One very affecting memoir was *A Place for Noah,* journalist-screenwriter Josh Greenfeld's journal of life with his brain-damaged son. It was also a powerful indictment of society's failure to deal with mentally handicapped children.

Letters. There were some excellent collections of literary correspondence. Among them: *The Selected Letters of Conrad Aiken,* edited by Joseph Killorin; *Selected Letters of John O'Hara,* edited by Matthew J. Bruccoli; *Collected Letters of Thomas Hardy: Vol. I, 1840-1892,* edited by Richard Little Purdy and Michael Millgate; and *Tolstoy's Letters: Vol. I, 1828-1875* and *Vol. II, 1880-1910,* edited by R. F. Christian.

The three-volume *Letters of Sidney and Beatrice Webb,* edited by Norman MacKenzie, shed new light on the lives of the British social scientists and political activists.

Among personal journals, *Final Entries 1945: The Diaries of Joseph Goebbels,* edited by Hugh Trevor-Roper, revealed much about the twisted mind of Adolf Hitler's propaganda minister. *Cosima Wagner's Diaries: Vol. I, 1869-1877,* edited by Martin Gregor-Dellin and Dietrich Mack, was an enormous repository of the household lives of the composer Richard Wagner and Cosima, once his lover and then his wife. *Linotte: The Early Diaries of Anaïs Nin* was another brick in the growing posthumous edifice of the pioneer feminist writer.

Virginia Woolf's life and work is practically a genre by itself, and three important books were added to it in 1978: *The Letters of Virginia Woolf: Vol. III, 1923-1928,* edited by Nigel Nicolson and Joanne Trautman; *The Diary of Virginia Woolf: Vol. II, 1920-1924,* edited by Anne Olivier Bell; and a feminist-oriented biography, *Woman of Letters: The Life of Virginia Woolf,* by Phyllis Rose.

Criticism and Literary History. Susan Sontag applied her considerable intellect to *On Photography,* a landmark in the history of arts criticism, as well as *Illness as Metaphor,* a profound essay on the way we perceive such diseases as tuberculosis and cancer in our literature. Cleanth Brooks, another distinguished critic, wrote *William Faulkner: Toward Yoknapatawpha and Beyond.* The novelist William H. Gass offered fascinating essays on the nature of language in *The World Within the Word.* Political scientist Hannah Arendt's posthumous *The Life of the Mind: Vol. I, Thinking; Vol. II, Feeling,* was a monument of its kind.

Malcolm Cowley, the aged and august dean of American critics, proved his mind still nimble and provocative in—*And I Worked at the Writer's Trade: Chapters of Literary History, 1918-1978.* The massive intelligence of the German critic and thinker Walter Benjamin, who died in 1940, was brought to contemporary readers in his *Reflections* and *The Origin of German Tragic Drama,* both very difficult but important and original works.

Science and Social Science. An unusual contribution to this genre was Norbert Elias' *The Civilizing Process: The History of Manners,* an amusing yet profound study of the habits of our civilization.

More immediately significant were two important and troubling volumes on a fundamental social concern, *Criminal Violence, Criminal Justice,* by Charles E. Silberman, and *Discipline and Punish: The Birth of the Prison,* by France's Michel Foucault. Both offered deeply pessimistic views on crime and punishment.

The sociologist Christopher Lasch found much worth preserving in the American family in *Haven in a Heartless World.* Robert Coles, the psychiatrist, added two volumes to his distinguished "Children of Crisis" series: *Vol. IV, Eskimos, Chicanos, Indians,* and *Vol. V, Privileged Ones: The Well-Off and the Rich in America.*

Contemporary Affairs and History. The checkered history of communism came under scrutiny in several important books. Alexander Solzhenitsyn completed the third and final volume in his massive study of Russian repression, *The Gulag Archipelago 1918-1956,* and François Ponchaud explored another kind of communist repression, genocide, in *Cambodia: Year Zero.*

Vivian Gornick turned out an affecting oral history of idealism and disillusionment in *The Romance of American Communism,* and David Caute ably surveyed a sorry period of American history in *The Great Fear: The Anti-Communist Purge under Truman and Eisenhower.*

One of the sharpest continuing post-World War II issues has been whether Alger Hiss, a former high official in the U.S. Department of State, committed perjury when he declared before a congressional committee that he was never a Communist spy. Historian Allen Weinstein declared him guilty in the closely reasoned but still controversial *Perjury: The Hiss-Chambers Case.*

To date, most scholarly studies of the American involvement in Vietnam have condemned the U.S. government, but Guenter Lewy's provocative *America in Vietnam* took the opposite side. He contended that though U.S. involvement in the war was unwise, there was no American guilt for atrocities in

The paperback historical novels of John Jakes, which form a running history of the United States, have become runaway best-sellers.

which the North Vietnamese and the Viet Cong were not equally deserving of blame.

Two important works on the early history of the United States were published. The gifted polemicist Garry Wills wrote a brilliant essay on the ideas that shaped Thomas Jefferson's mind, *Inventing America: Jefferson's Declaration of Independence*, and Philip Greven explored *The Protestant Temperament: Patterns of Child Rearing, Religious Experience, and the Self in Early America*.

From Barbara W. Tuchman came the immensely readable popular history *A Distant Mirror: The Calamitous Fourteenth Century*, which immediately went on best-seller lists. Another distinguished popular history was Christopher Hibbert's account of the Sepoy Rebellion, *The Great Mutiny: India 1857*.

Important contributions to the time-honored genre of muckraking were two books on James R. Hoffa and his powerful union – *The Teamsters*, by Steven R. Brill, and *The Hoffa Wars*, by Dan E. Moldea. *The Mind Stealers* by Samuel Chavkin and *Mind Control* by Peter Schrag explored the growing threat of behavior control. Henry Kisor

See also AWARDS AND PRIZES (Literature Awards); CANADIAN LITERATURE; LITERATURE FOR CHILDREN; POETRY. In WORLD BOOK, see LITERATURE.

LITERATURE, CANADIAN. See CANADIAN LIBRARY ASSOCIATION; CANADIAN LITERATURE.

LITERATURE FOR CHILDREN. Sales of paperback books for children went up 33 per cent in the first half of 1978, compared with the same period in 1977, while hard-cover sales increased only 3 per cent. The increasing popularity of paperbacks undoubtedly means that the trend toward publication of titles only in paperback will continue. The predicted decrease in full-color printing due to rising costs also became more apparent. There was a noticeable increase in picture books illustrated in only one or two colors. Several children's books have been dramatized for afternoon television, and this trend may encourage authors to write with TV production in mind. Some outstanding 1978 books were:

Picture Books

John Brown, Rose and the Midnight Cat, story by Jenny Wagner, illustrations by Ron Brooks (Bradbury). Winner of the 1974 Best Australian Picture Book of the Year Award, this is the story of Rose and her dog, John Brown, who has taken care of her since her husband died, and what happens when the Midnight Cat appears. Lovely colored pen-and-ink drawings add much to the mood and characterization. Ages 3 to 7.

Cloudy with a Chance of Meatballs, by Judith Barrett, illustrated by Ron Barrett (Atheneum). This is a funny story about the town of Chewand-swallow that gets its weather – all food – three times a day. The humorous illustrations show what happens when the town's formerly pleasant and predictable weather takes an unexpected turn for the worse. Ages 4 to 8.

Grasshopper on the Road, an I Can Read Book, by Arnold Lobel (Harper). Beautiful soft pictures in rose and green show Grasshopper as he takes his walk, meeting a Good Morning Club of beetles, a mosquito in a rowboat, and various other insects. Ages 4 to 8.

The Stupids Have a Ball, by Harry Allard and James Marshall (Houghton). When their two children bring home straight-F report cards, Mr. and Mrs. Stupid say proudly, "That's hard to do!" and decide to give a costume ball to celebrate. The humor in text and illustrations should delight the 4- to 9-year-olds.

We're Going to Have a Baby, by Doris and John Helmering, illustrated by Robert Cassell (Abingdon). When his parents tell 4-year-old Jimmy they are going to have a baby, he does not know whether to be glad or mad, scared or sad. A wise neighbor tells him there probably will be times when he is each of those things. This book is an attractive introduction to the situation for an expectant sibling. Ages 4 to 8.

Time to Get Out of the Bath, Shirley, by John Burningham (Crowell). While her mother is talking about such things as picking up clothes, Shirley is mentally riding horseback down the bathtub drain to a magical land of knights and jousting. On the left page, the mother is portrayed in the real setting; on the right, Shirley in her imagined one. Ages 4 to 8.

We Came A-Marching – 1, 2, 3, by Mildred Hobzek, illustrated by William Pene du Bois (Parents'). This little verse gives the reader a chance to learn to count (and how to pronounce) 1, 2, 3, in 12 different languages. The three marching figures who appear in the full-color illustrations have several small adventures. Ages 4 to 8.

Bunches and Bunches of Bunnies, by Louise Mathews, illustrated by Jeni Bassett (Dodd). Dozens of appealing little bunnies busy with a variety of activities give a counting book personality and charm. The illustrator is a talented 17-year-old. Ages 4 to 8.

The Simple Prince, by Jane Yolen, illustrated by Jack Kent (Parents'). An easy-to-read story about a prince who tires of pomp and circumstance and decides he wants to lead the simple life. He discovers it is not as easy as he thought it would be. Cartoon-style pictures add humor and flavor to this enjoyable story. Ages 4 to 7.

The Wounded Wolf, by Jean Craighead George, pictures by John Schoenherr (Harper). Naturalist-author Jean George tells the story, based on an observed incident, of a wolf helping to save the life of a wounded member of its pack. Sketches catch the mood of the event. Ages 4 to 8.

Noah's Ark, illustrated by Peter Spier, won the 1978 Caldecott Medal for the most distinguished picture book for children.

The Girl Who Loved Wild Horses, by Paul Goble (Bradbury). This story of an Indian girl who goes off to join the wild horses and is transformed into a horse is told as though it were an Indian legend. The beautiful illustrations convey an authentic feeling of Indian art and are filled with many details of half-hidden woodland animals, flowers, and birds. Ages 5 to 7.

Old Tiger, New Tiger, by Ronald Roy, illustrated by Pat Bargielski (Abingdon). When the old tiger grows blind and weak, the monkeys are very happy until a wise monkey points out that a new tiger will come when the old one dies. How the wise monkey solves the problem for the monkeys and the old tiger is shown in text and two-color pictures. Ages 5 to 8.

Hickory, by Palmer Brown (Harper). Hickory, a young mouse, moves from the farmhouse to the meadow, and a grasshopper becomes his friend there. The story ends as the two friends are trying to hurry south to get away from the coming winter's cold weather, which will spell the end for the grasshopper. Colored pen-and-ink drawings add much to this gentle story. Ages 6 to 9.

Hot Cross Buns And Other Old Street Cries, chosen by John Langstaff, illustrated by Nancy Winslow Parker (Atheneum/McElderry). These old cries of street peddlers, delightfully illustrated in an 18th-century setting, have simple treble indications of the original melodies of the chants with occasional notations on how they might be combined or sung as a round. Age 8 and up.

Things to Do

Messages: Sending and Receiving Them; Cover-ups: Things to Put on Yourself; Constructions: Big Things to Make; Smells: Things to Do with Them; and *Exploring: Getting to Know Your World* are five paperbacks, written and produced by McPhee Grible Publishers (Penguin). They should be just the thing for the child who is always asking, "What can I do?" They include projects and experiments to sharpen one's observation and instructions for constructing a variety of things. Age 8 and up.

Antique Paper Dolls 1915-1920, edited by Arnold Arnold (Dover); *Antique Paper Dolls: The Edwardian Era,* as produced by the Imagerie Pellerin at Epinal (Dover); and *Fashion Paper Dolls from "Godey's Lady's Book" 1840-1854,* by Susan Johnson (Dover). All three of these paperbacks should be a delight to children who love paper dolls and are fascinated by the clothes of the past. Age 6 and up.

Learning and Going Places

Zero Is Not Nothing, Young Math Book by Mindel and Harry Sitomer, illustrated by Richard Cuffari (Crowell). This interesting book develops the concept of zero through text and illustrations in a way that should be intriguing for the 6- to 9-year olds.

Tyrannosaurus Rex, by Millicent Selsam (Harper). Illustrated with photographs of the expedition, this is the story of the discovery and unearthing of the first *Tyrannosaurus Rex* fossil; there is also a brief section on some other kinds of dinosaurs that lived at the same time as *Tyrannosaurus*. The book is an authoritative account with detailed information. Ages 8 to 10.

Modern Auto Racing Superstars, by Ross R. Olney (Dodd). This high-interest, low-vocabulary book should attract readers much older than its fourth-grade reading level would imply. Stories about seven of racing's best-known superstars include accounts of some of their greatest races and show photographs of cars and drivers. Age 9 and up.

Trucks, Trucking, and You, by Hope Irvin Marston (Dodd). This book gives a look at diesel and gasoline engines, interviews with real truckers, jobs associated with trucking, rescue operations that truckers have arranged, and a glossary of CB and truckers' jargon. There are many photographs of all types of trucks. Age 10 and up.

The Bakery Factory: Who Puts the Bread on Your Table, by Aylette Jenness (Crowell). An interesting firsthand account of a visit to a bakery, with photographs and descriptions of the production process and interviews with some of the workers. Projects and recipes are included. Age 10 and up.

By the Seat of Their Pants: The Story of Early Aviation, by Phil Ault (Dodd). A fascinating account of some early stunt fliers, their hair-raising performances, and landmark flights up to World War II, with numerous photographs. Age 12 and up.

On the Ice in Antarctica, by Theodore K. Mason (Dodd). This description of a trip to the South Pole is accurate and vivid in text and photographs. The reader learns how things are, and also how things were on the exciting and hazardous expeditions of the past. Age 12 and up.

State Flowers, by Anne Ophelia Dowden (Crowell). By one of America's leading botanical illustrators, this book has a beautiful full-color painting of each state flower and a one-page description of the flower and its connection with the state. The official statute making it the state flower is also given. All ages.

Fiction

A Mitzvah Is Something Special, by Phyliss Rose Eisenberg, illustrated by Susan Jeschke (Harper). Lisa learns about mitzvahs from her two grandmas, and though at first she thinks the two are very different, she finds out they have a big thing in common—they both love Lisa. Ages 5 to 9.

The Practical Princess and Other Liberating Fairy Tales, by Jay Williams, illustrated by Rick Schreiter (Parents'). Princesses who figure out how to rescue themselves from dragons, or help likable but not very bright princes to carry out their quests, give this collection of fairy tales an unexpected and humorous twist. Age 7 and up.

A nature book, *The View from the Oak: The Private Worlds of Other Creatures,* by Judith and Herbert Kohl, won a National Book Award.

The Forbidden Forest, by William Pène du Bois (Nordstrom/Harper). This is the tall tale of how a man, a kangaroo, and a bulldog defeated the Germans and ended the Great War. Magnificent full-color pictures by this famous author-illustrator show all the exciting action. Age 7 and up.

The Lost Umbrella of Kim Chu, by Eleanor Estes, illustrated by Jacqueline Ayer (Atheneum/McElderry). Kim Chu takes a very special umbrella, which had been awarded to her father, to the library, where it disappears. Kim Chu's adventures in searching for the umbrella are related with an understanding of a child's way of looking at things. Ages 7 to 12.

Conquista!, by Clyde Robert Bulla and Michael Syson, illustrated by Ronald Himler (Crowell). This account of a young Indian boy's reaction when he meets his first horse, an animal escaped from Coronado's train, portrays the fear and awe of such an encounter. Ages 7 to 10.

The Men from P.I.G. and R.O.B.O.T., by Harry Harrison (Atheneum). This has two funny science-fiction adventures, set in the far-distant future and complete with all the technology, adventure, excitement, and humor the reader could desire. Age 10 and up.

When the City Stopped, by Joan Phipson (Atheneum/McElderry). Through a series of mishaps, Nick and his little sister find themselves alone when strikes begin that turn the city into a nightmare. They have numerous adventures as they try to make their way to the country. Ages 10 to 14.

The Bassumtyte Treasure, by Jane Louise Curry (Atheneum/McElderry). Events from the time of Mary, Queen of Scots, become intermeshed with the present when Small Thomas returns to the English home of his ancestors and remembers the riddle his grandfather had taught him. Ages 10 to 14.

Star Lord, by Louise Lawrence (Harper). Rhys and his dog, Blod, find and hide an injured pilot, a star lord from another world after a mysterious crash. The family helps return the pilot to his own world, but at a terrible price he can only partially repay. Age 12 and up.

The View Beyond My Father, by Mabel Esther Allan (Dodd). Mary Angus is blind and she feels that her family, particularly her dominating father, treat her as though her blindness makes her stupid as well. The story tells about an operation that helps Mary Angus regain partial sight, and the new friends who help her find her freedom. Age 12 and up.

C. C. Poindexter, by Carolyn Meyer (Atheneum/McElderry). C. C. is 15 years old, 6 feet 1 inch (185 centimeters) tall, and still growing. She feels unsure of herself as she tries to adjust to her parents' divorce, goes with her aunt to a feminist rap session, and dreams of joining a commune. The book presents an appealing protagonist. Age 12 and up.

Shadow of a Ghost, by Constance Leonard (Dodd). When Kathy discovers an old slipper and finds there is a curse connected with it, she is determined to set things right. Her journey involves her in suspense-filled encounters with an old house, a ghost, and a murderer. Age 13 and up.

Awards in 1978 included:
American Library Association Children's Service Division Awards: The *Newbery Medal* for "the most distinguished contribution to American literature for children" was awarded to Katherine Paterson for *Bridge to Terabithia;* the *Caldecott Medal* for "the most distinguished American picture book for children" went to artist Peter Spier for illustrating *Noah's Ark.*

The winner of the National Book Award for Children's Literature was Judith and Herbert Kohl's *The View from the Oak: The Private Worlds of Other Creatures.*

The 1978 *Hans Christian Andersen Medals* were awarded to writer Paula Fox and illustrator Svend Otto. The medals are given every two years to an author and an illustrator for the body of their work for children.   Lynn de Grummond Delaune

See also CANADIAN LITERATURE; LITERATURE; POETRY. In WORLD BOOK, see LITERATURE FOR CHILDREN.

LIVESTOCK. See AGRICULTURE.

LONG BEACH, CALIF. See LOS ANGELES-LONG BEACH.

LOPEZ, NANCY (1957-   ), became the sensation of 1978 as a rookie on the Ladies Professional Golf Association (LPGA) tour. She won nine tournaments and $203,430 in prize money during the year, beginning with a record five consecutive tournament victories. She earned $161,235 during her rookie year, which ended in July, a record for both male and female first-year pros, and was named Rookie of the Year and Golfer of the Year.

Her dominating play and friendly personality quickly attracted large followings. Her gallery became known as "Nancy's Navy," recalling Arnold Palmer's loyal rooters, "Arnie's Army."

Lopez was born in Torrance, Calif., on Jan. 6, 1957, and grew up in Roswell, N. Mex. She began playing golf there at 7, following her father around a public course. Domingo Lopez, owner of an auto-body repair shop, gave her the only golf lessons she ever had and quickly recognized her talent. Her mother, who died in 1977, sewed Lopez' golf outfits, and the family saved money during the winter to finance her trips to golf tournaments.

Lopez won the national girls' junior title in 1972 and 1974, played on her high school's state champion boys' team, and entered her first U.S. Women's Open at 16. She then accepted a University of Tulsa athletic scholarship and won 14 of 18 college tournaments. Lopez quit college after two years and became a professional in July 1977.   Joseph P. Spohn

LOS ANGELES-LONG BEACH. A massive busing program to achieve school integration in Los Angeles began on Sept. 12, 1978, despite a white boycott reportedly involving as many as 13,000 students. The integration plan, approved on January 3, called for busing about 65,000 students in grades four through eight.

The California Court of Appeals had ordered the program delayed indefinitely on September 1, pending further court hearings. The California Supreme Court overruled that action on September 6.

Although the integration program was termed a success in the opening days of school, the court-appointed referee, Monroe E. Price, reported on October 10 that too few white students had enrolled in minority schools to achieve real integration. Many of the white students scheduled for busing had transferred to magnet schools or private schools.

Belt Tightening. Voter approval of Proposition 13, the California referendum calling for property-tax reductions, led Los Angeles County officials to announce on June 7 that 37,000 of the county's 73,000 employees would be laid off. Mayor Thomas Bradley said that the city would fire 8,300 municipal employees, including 1,080 uniformed police officers, and school officials canceled summer-school programs. The severity of the cutbacks was reduced, however, when the state approved a $5-billion relief program and prohibited police and fire cutbacks.

A road grader clears mud from the streets to free cars and trucks after heavy rains flooded the suburban area north of Los Angeles in February.

By November 20, Los Angeles' reserve fund, used for unforeseen fiscal emergencies, had dropped to $943,318, its lowest level in 17 years. The previous low was about $3 million. The city was saved from crisis by the state's assistance and the transfer of a $65-million budget surplus to the reserve fund.

Flood and Fire. Torrential rains and hurricane-force winds tore through southern California on February 11, leaving more than seven persons dead, causing $22.6 million in property damage, and forcing officials to close the Los Angeles and Long Beach ports.

A brushfire on October 23, touched off by an arsonist, consumed more than 25,000 acres (10,000 hectares) of brush and ranch land as well as a number of elegant homes in the Malibu Beach area.

Bradley signed a contract designating Los Angeles as host of the 1984 Summer Olympic Games on October 20. It provided that the U.S. Olympic Committee and the local organizing committee protect the city against financial liability for the games. See OLYMPIC GAMES.

The Board of Airport Commissioners approved an $89.1-million system of roadways, busways, and parking structures for Los Angeles International Airport on October 23.   James M. Banovetz

See also CITY; TAXATION (Close-Up). In WORLD BOOK, see LONG BEACH; LOS ANGELES.

LOUISIANA. See NEW ORLEANS; STATE GOV'T.

LUCAS GARCIA, FERNANDO ROMEO-(1924-), was sworn in as president of Guatemala on July 1, 1978. He succeeded Kjell Eugenio Laugerud Garcia, who was prevented by the Constitution from succeeding himself.

Lucas was born in San Juan, Chamelco, on July 14, 1924. He attended public schools in Cobán and graduated with honors from the Escuela Politecnica. He entered military service and eventually became a brigadier general. Over a 20-year period, he held various government positions, serving from 1975 to 1977 as defense minister under President Laugerud.

The new president is known for his ability to create harmonious relationships between disparate groups. In 1977, he played a dominant role organizing a center-right coalition comprised of the Revolutionary Party, the Democratic Institutional Party, and the Organized Arañista Central Party. It was as the coalition's candidate that he ran for the presidency. Because Lucas obtained less than 50 per cent of the votes cast in the election, held on March 5, he had to be declared president-elect by the Congress on March 13.

Lucas Garcia is a bachelor. He enjoys good conversation and good food. His favorite hobbies are cattle raising and farming.   Paul C. Tullier

See also GUATEMALA.

LUMBER. See FOREST AND FOREST PRODUCTS.

LUXEMBOURG was chosen in 1978 as the home of the European Parliament, the advisory body of the European Community (EC or Common Market). Under a 1965 decision, the European Parliament had previously met in Luxembourg and Strasbourg, France.

In 1979, the EC Parliament will expand from 198 members to 410. It will need three assembly halls and 300 more offices. Brussels, Belgium, where committee meetings have been held for several years, was a strong contender for the site. Luxembourg offered to lease a $120-million building for $12 million a year. On February 14, French President Valéry Giscard d'Estaing supported Luxembourg's bid and clinched the deal.

Luxembourg conservatives did not send a delegation to the first meeting, in April, of the European Democratic Union, an international group of center and center-right parties that will cooperate in the first direct elections to the EC Parliament. They considered the union an undesirable competitor to a similar group, the European People's Party.

Luxembourg's currency, tied to Belgium's, remained strong. Receipts of the financial sector, including more than 90 banks, helped keep the balance of payments positive.   Kenneth Brown

See also EUROPE (Facts in Brief Table). In WORLD BOOK, see LUXEMBOURG.

MADAGASCAR. See AFRICA.

MAGAZINE advertising revenues in the United States set a record in 1978, surpassing $2 billion, according to the Magazine Publishers Association (MPA). The number of advertising pages increased 8 per cent.

The Audit Bureau of Circulation in Chicago estimated circulation of consumer and farm publications for the first six months of 1978 at 267 million, up 4 per cent from 1977. Circulation continued to provide 45 per cent of magazine revenues in 1978.

The New *Life*. A highlight was the reintroduction of *Life* on September 25. *Life* premièred as a weekly in November 1936 and ceased publication in December 1972. Reasons for its decline were competition from television, and the combined effect of high postal costs and extremely large circulation. *Life* returned as a monthly, with a price of $1.50, aiming more for single-copy sales than subscriptions.

Publisher Charles A. Whittingham said in November that the April 1979 issue's guaranteed circulation would be 1 million, with no increase in advertising cost per reader. Guaranteed circulation of the October 1978 issue was 700,000, but 1 million copies were sold.

New Magazines. Of the 325 magazines introduced in 1978, three were about running. World Publications, publisher of *Runner's World,* in April introduced *On the Run,* a biweekly for runners and joggers; and *Marathoner,* a quarterly for runners of marathons and longer races. New Times Publishing Company introduced *The Runner,* a monthly for all runners, in September. *Vital,* a health magazine published by Bart Clayton, Incorporated, began bimonthly publication in September. It provides facts and opinion for people from 18 to 45 years old. Penthouse International Limited introduced *Omni,* a monthly of science fact and fiction, in October. Subjects include space colonization, paranormal psychology, radio astronomy, and film and book reviews.

Working Mother was introduced by the McCall Publishing Company on August 29, five days before Working Mother's Day was celebrated in at least 45 states—a holiday suggested by McCall. The second issue was scheduled for March 1979, after which the magazine was to appear bimonthly. *Working Mother* is aimed at working mothers with children under 18. *Ambiance* was launched in February and will be issued 10 times a year by LaLinea USA Publications, Incorporated.

Major Business Ventures. Filipacchi Publications, led by French publisher Daniel Filipacchi, bought Popular Publications and announced plans in March to bring back *Look* magazine. Gruner & Jahr AG of Hamburg, West Germany, bought Parents' Magazine Enterprises, Incorporated, in April. The acquisition included eight magazines,

The new *Life* is launched in October as a monthly magazine with more pictures than its weekly predecessor, which folded in 1972.

among them *Parents' Magazine,* with a circulation of 1.5 million. Financially ailing *More* magazine merged with the *Columbia Journalism Review* in July. James B. Adler claimed he lost more than $300,000 publishing *More.* John J. Veronis sold the four-year-old *Book Digest* to Dow Jones & Company for about $10 million.

Publisher George A. Hirsch said on November 15 that *New Times* would cease publication at the end of 1978. He cited lack of reader interest in "investigative reporting, social issues, or public affairs" as reasons for the five-year-old magazine's demise.

National Magazine Awards in 1978 went to *Architectural Digest* for visual excellence, *Esquire* for essays and criticism, *Mother Jones* for public service, *Newsweek* for service to the individual, *The New Yorker* for both fiction and reporting excellence, and *Scientific American* for specialized journalism. The awards are sponsored by the American Society of Magazine Editors and administered by the Columbia University Graduate School of Journalism through an MPA grant.

Richard E. Deems, chairman of Hearst Magazines, received the 1978 Henry Johnson Fisher Award, the industry's top honor.   Gloria Ricks Dixon

In WORLD BOOK, see MAGAZINE.

MAINE. See STATE GOVERNMENT.

MALAWI. See AFRICA.

MALAYSIA. Racial tension between Malays, who make up 45 per cent of the country's population, and Chinese, who make up 35 per cent, troubled Malaysia in 1978. About 1,200 Chinese businessmen denounced government policies favoring the Malays in March. They complained of being pushed out of many trades in favor of Malays, of being denied public service jobs, of quotas that sharply limited their access to schools, and of being refused land for mining or agriculture.

The racial divisions left a heavy imprint on July elections. Predictably, the United Malays National Organization of Prime Minister Datuk Hussein Onn re-emerged as the strongest party. Onn's National Front, which also includes the Malaysian Chinese Association (MCA), again won a heavy majority in Parliament. But the resentful Chinese strongly supported the predominantly Chinese Democratic Action Party (DAP). The National Front received only slightly more than 50 per cent of the vote, and the DAP had nearly 21 per cent.

The increased flow of oil from new wells off the east coast helped the nation's economy.   Mark Gayn

See also ASIA (Facts in Brief Table). In WORLD BOOK, see MALAYSIA.

MALDIVES. See ASIA.

MALI. See AFRICA.

MALTA. See EUROPE.

An assortment of political posters greets Malaysian voters in Kuala Lumpur during July elections that returned the National Front to power.

MANITOBA. Premier Sterling R. Lyon and his Progressive Conservative administration adopted a policy of restraint in 1978, an approach that brought it into conflict with unions and civil servants. The speech from the throne at the opening of the new session on March 16 announced a small reduction in Manitoba's basic income tax and small-business tax. Priority was given to new legislation in the family-law field.

The budget of April 10 proposed further tax reductions, including acceptance of the federal government's offer to compensate the provinces for a temporary reduction in provincial sales taxes. Expenditures of $1.65 billion were expected, leaving a deficit of $114 million. When the legislature recessed on July 21, 60 bills had been approved in the longest legislative proceedings in Manitoba's history.

The province agreed on March 17 to compensate five Indian tribes in northern Manitoba for land flooded by a power project on the Nelson River. The Indians received four acres (1.6 hectares) of Crown land for every acre (0.4 hectare) of reserve land made unusable by the power project. The agreement was reached after several years of negotiation among all those concerned – the Indians, the federal government, and the previous New Democratic Party administration.   David M. L. Farr

See also CANADA. In WORLD BOOK, see MANITOBA; PRAIRIE PROVINCES.

MANUFACTURING. Even with the threat of rising inflation hanging over the United States in 1978, the strength of U.S. manufacturers' September and October orders indicated that the economy was speeding up rather than slowing down. As the year ended, the rate of factory utilization approached the 1974 peak period, when there was not enough plant capacity to meet demand, and purchasing agents began to complain of spot shortages of materials and parts.

These positive factors seemed to belie the pessimists' gloom, even though it was still too early to tell what effect President Jimmy Carter's anti-inflation program of voluntary wage-price standards would have on the economy. See ECONOMICS.

Nevertheless, encouraging signs abounded. New factory orders for durable goods rose a healthy 6.3 per cent in October to a seasonally adjusted $77.2-billion, following a rise of 1.5 per cent in September and 9.8 per cent in August. Department of Commerce October figures showed durable goods registering the most backlog orders since the 3.6 per cent rise in March 1973. New orders for nondefense capital goods, considered a barometer of future plant and equipment spending, rose a strong 10.1 per cent in October, to an adjusted $22.2 billion, after moving up 4.2 per cent in September. The steady rise in new orders outpaced shipments. As a result, order backlogs in October were $220.4 bil-

lion, an exceptional increase of $6.8 billion in one month, and an awesome $41.5 billion over the year.

Industrial Production in October increased by 0.5 per cent for the second consecutive month, to 148.4 per cent of the 1967 average, up 6.8 per cent from a year earlier, according to the Federal Reserve Board (Fed). The rise trailed the 0.7 per cent average increase of the prior three months, reflecting a slowdown in economic growth. The Fed also reported that U.S. factories in October operated at their highest rate since September 1974, at a seasonally adjusted 85.3 per cent of capacity. This reflected the rise in new orders and the growing backlogs. Factories operated at only 82.9 per cent of capacity in October 1977. Most important, the rate of operating capacity rose throughout 1978. Primary processing industries ran at the high rate of 87.7 per cent of capacity.

Shortages of materials and parts once again became part of the industrial scene, as they did in 1973-1974. At the start of the fourth quarter of 1978, products in short supply included printing paper; finished lumber; household furniture; antifreeze chemicals; printed circuit boards; electric motors; clothing fabrics such as wool, some cotton blends, and synthetics; building materials; and some industrial products made of aluminum, titanium, steel, and nickel alloys.

Hundreds of television picture tubes dry out on a conveyor in the 1-million-square-foot (93,000-square-meter) Sylvania plant in Ottawa, Ohio.

Pennsylvania Governor Milton J. Shapp admires the first U.S.-built
Rabbit to roll off the assembly line at Volkswagen's New Stanton plant.

Plant and Equipment Outlays rose to an estimated $156 billion, up from $136.5 billion in 1977. That modest increase and the equally small increase to $171.4 billion estimated for 1979 could mean a continued stretchout of both deliveries and shortages.

Output per man-hour rose at an annual rate of 3.4 per cent in the third quarter of 1978, following a rise of only 1.2 per cent in the second quarter and a decline of 4.5 per cent in the first quarter. The gain in manufacturing was most impressive throughout the year. Output rose sharply in the second and third quarters, bringing the increase for the first nine months to 3 per cent.

Labor Developments. Unemployment dropped to 5.8 per cent in October, its lowest rate since the 5.7 per cent in June. The number of persons employed rose to about 96 million. Strike activity was at a four-year high in the first nine months of 1978, causing 32.6 million lost working days. Shortages of skilled and semiskilled workers became common. Manufacturers searched for machinists, tool and diemakers, electricians and electronic technicians, loom fixers and weavers, sewing-machine operators, and keypunch operators. Engineers, who experienced a post-Vietnam War slump, were again in demand in 1978.

New Technology. American Telephone and Telegraph Company (A.T. & T.) installed optical transmission, or *lightwave*, communications systems for five of its telephone companies. Such a system uses glass threads, rather than copper wire, to transmit phone calls. Sound pulses are sent by laser beam through hollow, hairlike glass threads, or fibers, made by Corning Glass Works. Bundled into cables of various thicknesses, these glass fibers do not offer speedier communication than copper, but they make possible the transmission of more phone calls in a given amount of space. A.T. & T. spokesmen claim that glass-fiber cable "the size of an index finger" can do the job of copper cable that is "the size of a forearm." The lightwave communications system was installed in the five phone companies after the equipment underwent an 18-month trial in downtown Chicago. It was used as a 1.5-mile (2.4-kilometer) link between two Illinois Bell Telephone Company switching stations and an office building.

International Business Machines Corporation (IBM) introduced a family of computer products that feature advanced electronic memory circuits and are designed for use in networks of equipment that share information and data-processing tasks. The IBM 8100 system includes processors in two models with a variety of memory sizes and associated new display printing and data-storage units. The processors can be linked to each other or to another computer for distributed data processing. One of the new computers will incorporate very small electronic parts that can store and randomly recall 64,000 *bits*, or basic units, of information on a single crystal wafer. Most other new computers use 16,000-bit memory elements. See ELECTRONICS.

The Black Clawson Company of Middletown, Ohio, a manufacturer of paper-disposal equipment, developed a means of separating steel, concrete, and other foreign matter found in bales of wastepaper. The method, which is protected by 17 patents, mixes the waste materials with water, then shreds the resulting mixture into 1-inch (2.5-centimeter) particles and separates them according to material. Recovered metals and glass are set aside for sale as scrap, and the remaining particles are fed into huge boilers and burned. The resulting steam is used to turn turbogenerators to produce salable electricity.

Stanford R. Ovshinsky, a controversial scientist-inventor who developed a new class of low-cost electronic materials in 1968, claimed that one of these materials could be used to convert sunlight into electricity at prices low enough for the average home. He said the solar-cell material—an alloy of silicon, fluorine, and hydrogen made by starting with silicon tetrafluoride—will convert at least 10 per cent of the sunlight that strikes it into electricity. The inventor said that sheets of solar cells could be ready for use within five years.

Machine Tool orders reached a record level in October. There were no signs that buyers were scaling back orders because of higher interest rates and the possibility of a slowdown in 1979. October orders for the tools used to shape and form most metal parts totaled $414 million, up 24 per cent from $334.7 million in September and 73 per cent above October 1977. Though many manufacturers planned to step up production schedules, deliveries of some machines were put off until 1980.

The long wait for U.S.-built machines made the machine-tool industry vulnerable to competition from imports. For the first 10 months of the year, orders reached $3.5 billion, compared with $2.4-billion in 1977. Total industry backlogs stood at $3.26 billion on November 1, 59 per cent higher than in 1977.

Other Products. The National Electrical Manufacturers Association (NEMA) estimated that shipments of electrical products hit a record $85.1-billion, 7.4 per cent over the 1977 record. Electronics and communications equipment, the largest category, rose 5.9 per cent to $29.8 billion. Consumer products and industrial equipment, the next largest product categories, rose 7.6 per cent and 6.5 per cent, respectively, from $15.7 billion to $16.9 billion and from $12.3 billion to $13.1 billion. NEMA noted that in the 10-year period from 1968 to 1978, total industry shipments more than doubled, from $41.6-billion to an estimated $85.1 billion.

A giant pulp mill, towed 15,000 miles (24,000 kilometers) from Japan, was scheduled to go into operation in the Brazilian wilderness in 1979.

Through September, 22.6 million passenger, truck and bus, and farm-implement tires were shipped, compared with 20.9 million in 1977. Industry sources estimated that radial tires accounted for 50 per cent of all U.S. auto-tire shipments for the first time. In radial tires, the cords are laid at a 90-degree angle to the line of travel, for better handling and durability. Goodyear Tire & Rubber Company, the industry's radial leader, began delivering radials from a recently expanded plant in Gadsden, Ala. To maintain its leadership, Goodyear announced plans to build a $75-million tire technical center in Akron, Ohio. Production was expected to start in 1979 at a $180-million plant under construction in Lawton, Okla.

The General Tire & Rubber Company joined with Caterpillar Tractor Company to develop a vehicle tire for highway use that is similar to the ones Caterpillar developed for earth-moving machines. The new tire, looking somewhat like a reinforced inner tube, is basically an oval hose that fits around the wheel. It has a single ply, which eliminates friction between the plies as the tire rolls and lowers heat build-up and rolling resistance.

Not all tires were rolling smoothly. In November, the Firestone Tire & Rubber Company recalled some 13 million possibly unsafe steel-belted radials. See CONSUMER AFFAIRS. George J. Berkwitt

In WORLD BOOK, see MANUFACTURING.

MARGARET, PRINCESS (1930-   ), sister of Queen Elizabeth II of Great Britain, divorced the Earl of Snowdon, Antony Armstrong-Jones, on May 24, 1978, after 18 years of marriage. The couple had separated in 1976. She retained custody of their two children. Despite the divorce, which was the first in the immediate royal family since Henry VIII broke off his marriage with Anne of Cleves in 1540, Margaret remains sixth in line of succession to the British throne.

Margaret was born on Aug. 21, 1930, at Glamis Castle in Scotland, the second daughter of Prince Albert and Lady Elizabeth Bowes-Lyon, the Duke and Duchess of York. She spent her early childhood at Glamis. Her father became King George VI in 1936.

Her romantic life created a sensation in 1953. A romance with Group Captain Peter Townsend of the Royal Air Force attracted great attention because Townsend was divorced, and the Church of England forbids the remarriage of divorced persons. Margaret formally ended their relationship in 1955. Princess Margaret lives in London's Kensington Palace. Edward G. Nash

MARINE CORPS, U.S. See ARMED FORCES.

MARYLAND. See BALTIMORE; STATE GOV'T.

MASSACHUSETTS. See BOSTON; STATE GOV'T.

MAURITANIA. See AFRICA.

MAURITIUS. See AFRICA.

McDERMOTT, DENNIS (1921-   ), became president of the Canadian Labour Congress (CLC) on April 6, 1978. His election capped a 30-year career in the trade-union movement.

McDermott was born in England. He joined the Royal Navy at the age of 17 and served aboard destroyers for nine years, including all of World War II. In 1947, he emigrated to Canada.

While working as a welder at the Massey-Ferguson, Incorporated, farm implement plant in Toronto, Ont., McDermott joined the United Automobile Workers (UAW) in 1948. He quickly became intensely involved in union activity. "I soon found out that the UAW was more than a bargaining tool to get people raises, but a powerful force spearheading social reform," he said later.

In 1954, McDermott became a full-time UAW organizer; in 1960, subregional director. He was named Canadian director in 1968 and international vice-president in 1970. McDermott was general vice-president of the CLC from 1968 to 1978.

As concerned with individual rights as he is with labor issues, he is a member of the Canadian Civil Liberties Association and was an executive of the Toronto Labour Committee for Human Rights.

McDermott and his wife, Claire, live in an art-filled home in Agincourt, a suburb of Ottawa, Ont. The hard-driving labor leader relaxes by painting in the abstract expressionist style. Marsha F. Goldsmith

McINTOSH, C. IRWIN (1926-   ), became Canada's youngest lieutenant governor when he was sworn into office in Saskatchewan on Feb. 22, 1978. He succeeded George Porteous, who died on February 7.

Cameron Irwin McIntosh was born in North Battleford, Sask., on July 1, 1926. He attended elementary and high school in North Battleford and Ottawa, Ont., and studied at the University of Saskatchewan.

McIntosh served as editor of the *North Battleford News* from 1952 to 1954, when he joined the *North Battleford News-Optimist*. He became publisher of the *News-Optimist* in 1971. In 1977, he became publisher of *Western Canada Outdoors*.

Long active in civic affairs, McIntosh was a member of the North Battleford School Board for 16 years and served as its chairman. He was also president of the North Battleford Chamber of Commerce and of the Saskatchewan Travel Association.

McIntosh enjoys skiing and was president of the Battlefords Ski Club, first chairman of Table Mountain Regional Park, vice-president of the Saskatchewan Ski Association, and editor of the *Sakatchewan Ski Journal*.

McIntosh and his wife, the former Barbara L. Aylesworth, have three children. They live in North Battleford, where McIntosh is an elder of St. Andrew's Presbyterian Church. Marsha F. Goldsmith

MEDICINE. The world's first "test-tube baby," Louise Joy Brown, was delivered by Caesarean section in Oldham, England, on July 25, 1978, amid worldwide publicity and furor over the implications. Gynecologist Patrick C. Steptoe and physiologist Robert G. Edwards, who had been experimenting with laboratory fertilization for more than 10 years, successfully removed an egg from one of Lesley Brown's ovaries, placed it in a laboratory culture, and fertilized it with sperm from her husband, John. When the fertilized egg reached the stage when it normally would travel along the Fallopian tubes to the uterus, it was inserted into Lesley Brown's uterus. See BIOLOGY (Close-Up); Section One, FOCUS ON SCIENCE.

An Indian medical team announced the birth of a second test-tube baby in October. In the United States, where a physician was successfully sued for aborting a 1973 attempt at laboratory fertilization, the Ethics Advisory Board of the National Institutes of Health sponsored public forums to debate the merits of supporting research on this technique.

Another form of reproduction – *cloning,* or using genes from any cell to create an offspring – dominated headlines in March when New York City science writer David Rorvik claimed that an elderly millionaire had successfully cloned a living baby. Scientists around the world criticized Rorvik's book *In His Image.* They argued that cloning, while not impossible, was unfeasible for present-day genetics.

Insulin Study. The need for insulin in adult diabetics was challenged by the University Group Diabetes Program, a federally funded research team that studied more than 1,000 adult diabetics for nine to 11 years. The team reported in July that there is no evidence that insulin prevents or retards progressive damage to blood vessels, the main cause of blindness, heart attacks, disability, and death in diabetics. One of the main reasons insulin is given to adult diabetics is to prevent such damage. Most diabetics who need insulin to prevent life-threatening comas have juvenile – rather than adult-onset – diabetes.

Heart Surgery. The debate over the merits of coronary by-pass surgery, an expensive procedure, raged throughout 1978. In cardiac by-pass surgery, lengths of vein are taken from a patient's limb and stitched to the aorta and coronary arteries to by-pass blockages. Cardiovascular surgeons continued to challenge a 1977 Veterans Administration (VA) study that showed similar survival rates among patients who had undergone such surgery and those who had been treated only with medication. The chief of cardiology at the VA Hospital in Hines, Ill., challenged the findings, reporting a mortality rate of 32 per cent for patients treated with medication and only 14 per cent for those treated by surgery.

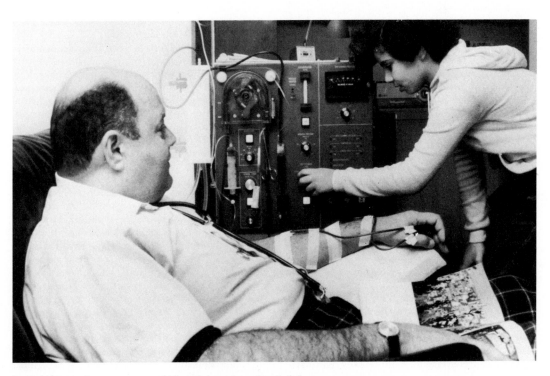

Some kidney patients can now avoid hospital care by using dialysis machines installed in their homes to cleanse the blood of impurities.

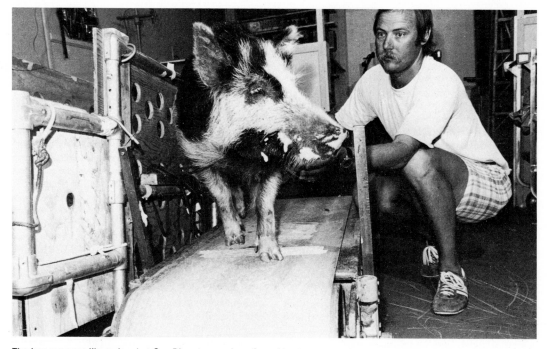

The hog may not like to jog, but San Diego researchers force him to go 5 miles (8 kilometers) a day to see how exercise affects heart disease.

Noted heart surgeon Denton Cooley reported that 9,061 patients undergoing surgery at the Texas Heart Institute in Houston had done "significantly better" than the VA's sample. During the year, Cooley performed his first heart transplant since 1969, and implanted an artificial heart and later transplanted both a heart and a kidney. The heart functioned well, but the patient died of kidney, lung, and liver failure 21 days later.

A Swiss technique for opening up a blocked cardiac artery by inserting a balloon and inflating it so that it forces the obstructing plaque against the arterial wall was used successfully on three dozen patients in the United States in 1978. Surgeons estimated that this procedure, known as percutaneous transluminal coronary angioplasty, could be used in 10 to 15 per cent of heart patients who otherwise would need the by-pass operation.

Anturane, a drug formerly used only for gout, may also help heart patients. A study released in February of 1,475 heart-attack victims at 26 U.S. and Canadian medical centers showed that those taking Anturane had a death rate almost 50 per cent lower than the control group. Even more dramatic was the 57 per cent reduction in sudden coronary deaths among Anturane users.

Simple aspirin, taken five times daily, can halve the chances of stroke for high-risk men, but not for women, Canadian researchers reported in March.

Two research teams monitored 76 patients. Their report confirmed similar findings in a smaller, two-year study at the University of Texas in Austin.

A congenital heart defect in which the pulmonary artery and the aorta are transposed, usually fatal within the first year of life, can be corrected surgically in the first three months after birth, researchers at the University of California, San Francisco, reported in May. The key to surgical success is a technique called deep hypothermia that lowers an infant's body temperature until the child enters a state of suspended animation, during which the surgeons can operate more safely and precisely.

Clinical Tests. Cancer researchers in Houston and Palo Alto, Calif., began testing interferon, an antivirus substance normally produced in the body. The tests were to be conducted on 100 to 150 patients with six different kinds of tumors. Interferon, which is difficult and expensive to obtain, has proven highly successful in treating animal tumors. In a Swedish test, bone-cancer patients who received it had a three-year survival rate of 70 per cent, compared with 10 to 20 per cent for patients treated surgically. Interferon is believed to be nontoxic.

Clinical trials for Laetrile, the controversial cancer drug derived from apricot pits, were approved by the National Cancer Institute (NCI) on September 27. A federal court ruled earlier that terminally ill cancer patients could procure injectable Laetrile for their personal use, and 17 states legalized its use as a cancer medication. The NCI, estimating that 70,000 to 75,000 Americans have used Laetrile, planned a $250,000 testing program of 300 patients with advanced, untreatable tumors.

The U.S. Food and Drug Administration (FDA) on October 24 approved the first injectable drug for the treatment of herpes simplex virus encephalitis, a dangerous infectious disease. The drug, Vidarabine, was heralded by the FDA as "a major development in medicine."

The Epilepsy Foundation of America in March won its long campaign for FDA approval of valproic acid, a drug similar to sodium valproate. More than 200,000 Europeans had been reported helped by the drug, which was banned in the United States.

Crib Deaths. California Department of Health researchers in Berkeley in June identified an unusual form of botulism as one cause of sudden death in infants. The evidence showed that at least some babies who die of the mysterious affliction called crib death may be victims of an infectious disease. It also suggested that some of these infant deaths may eventually be preventable. The researchers reported that they had isolated the bacterium, *Clostridium botulinum,* from the digestive tracts of 10 babies among 211 victims of crib death.   Dianne Rafalik Hales

See also DRUGS; HEALTH AND DISEASE; PUBLIC HEALTH. In WORLD BOOK, see MEDICINE.

MENTAL HEALTH. In its final report in April 1978, President Jimmy Carter's specially appointed Commission on Mental Health estimated that 15 per cent of the population of the United States is affected by mental disorders in any given year. Of these, only 3 per cent receive care in specialized mental health facilities. More than 9 per cent of the population – 60 per cent of those estimated to have mental disorders – receive treatment only in primary-care out-patient facilities.

President Carter's wife, Rosalynn, played an active role in the commission's deliberations, which gave top priority to children, adolescents, rural residents, minority groups, the elderly, and chronic mental patients discharged from state hospitals. Noting that all proposed national health-insurance plans exclude mental health care, the commission argued for insurance coverage on the grounds that mental and physical health are inseparable.

As major objectives, the commission called for the enlistment of mental health specialists to work in areas of severe shortage; an increase in the number of qualified personnel from minority groups in mental health programs; and the rebuilding of research capacity in mental health facilities, including research on drug and alcohol abuse. The commission also recommended special funding for education in mental health principles for students in nursing and other aspects of health care.

Treatment Advances. Two research groups reported success in treating tardive dyskinesia, one of the most serious side effects of antipsychotic medications. This incapacitating disorder causes the victim's limbs and body to jerk uncontrollably, the face to contort, and the tongue to dart in and out of the mouth. Researchers at Stanford University in California reported in September that treatment with choline, an amino acid derivative found in many common foods, including eggs, fish, and poultry, produced good results. Columbia University researchers in New York City successfully experimented with low doses of the sedative reserpine and another drug still in experimental development. Tardive dyskinesia, previously considered irreversible, affects up to 40 per cent of all psychotic patients on long-term treatment with strong tranquilizers.

Researchers at the University of Chicago and New York University achieved some success in separate studies in treating schizophrenia with medications that once were thought to worsen rather than alleviate symptoms of this disease. The New York University group used L-dopa, a brain chemical messenger that the body converts into the hormone dopamine. The Chicago researchers reported that the drug apomorphine, which also increases dopamine in the brain, produced good results in half of the patients in their studies.

European researchers reported in January that vasopressin, a hormone that regulates water in the body, restored memory function in depressed and psychotic patients and in elderly people. They said the research subjects recalled long-forgotten incidents after inhaling vasopressin. Two U.S. teams also experimented with vasopressin, and the National Institute of Mental Health in Washington, D.C., announced in July it would conduct a two-year trial on 54 patients with severe mental disorders, including schizophrenia.

Pain Relief. University of California, San Francisco, researchers told the Second World Congress on Pain in Montreal, Canada, in August that placebos such as sugar pills relieve pain by triggering events in the brain that release endorphins, the body's natural painkillers, which appear to act like morphine. Placebos relieve pain in one-third of the patients who receive them, researchers said.

Researchers at Massachusetts General Hospital in Boston, in June, challenged the theory that Down's syndrome, a severe form of retardation that is present at birth, is associated with the age of the child's mother. Researchers found that the mothers of most infants born with Down's syndrome are under 35, the age usually associated with greater risk. They also theorized that the father might be the source of the extra chromosome that causes Down's syndrome.   Dianne Rafalik Hales

See also DRUGS; PSYCHOLOGY. In WORLD BOOK, see DOWN'S SYNDROME; MENTAL HEALTH.

METRIC SYSTEM

METRIC SYSTEM. The 13 members of the new United States Metric Board, confirmed by Congress on March 21, 1978, may well end their terms of office by wishing the nation's Founding Fathers had listened to Thomas Jefferson. About 200 years ago, Jefferson suggested that the United States adopt a scheme of weights and measures based on the decimal, or metric, system. Nearly every other country has since done that, but the United States has maintained its hodgepodge of feet, gallons, inches, ounces, pints, pounds, and quarts. At present, the only other totally nonmetric countries are Borneo, Brunei, Liberia, and Yemen (Aden).

The Metric Board is charged with deciding whether the U.S. government will actively promote a national switch to the metric system or maintain a neutral position. The board is also to "coordinate the voluntary conversion to the metric system." Congress gave the board no enforcement powers, however, and delays in establishing the board by Presidents Gerald R. Ford and Jimmy Carter indicated that metric conversion had a low priority.

Weather and Maps. Some federal agencies have tried to metricate on their own. One early decision confronting the Metric Board was how to proceed with metrication of weather information. The National Weather Service submitted a plan for issuing public weather reports in metric units, beginning gradually in 1979. Starting in June of that year, the Weather Service proposed to report temperatures in degrees Celsius as well as Fahrenheit, and then switch to only Celsius in September 1979.

The U.S. Geological Survey, an agency of the Department of the Interior, has started to produce maps with contour lines and elevations given in meters instead of feet. It has published one metric map of an area in North Dakota.

GAO Study. A two-year study released in October by the General Accounting Office (GAO), an investigatory arm of Congress, said Americans appear to be blundering into "unwarranted" metric conversion because they believe it is inevitable, though many will not benefit from the switch. The GAO found that 42 per cent of the small businesses and 23 per cent of the general public believed conversion is mandatory. According to the GAO, the Metric Conversion Act of 1975 does not commit the United States to metric conversion. But the resulting "inevitability syndrome generates an atmosphere of conversion to the metric system that appears to be unwarranted," GAO concluded.

A principal argument for using the same measurement system as the rest of the world has been the prospect for larger U.S. exports. But the GAO ridiculed this belief. "GAO found no evidence to show that the nation's trade would be significantly affected by converting to the metric system," the agency said.   Foster Stockwell

In WORLD BOOK, see METRIC SYSTEM.

MEXICO. Workers' dissatisfaction with the government's austerity program touched off a wave of strikes led by independent left wing unions in 1978. It was the first serious challenge to the dominant role of the Confederation of Mexican Workers (CTM), which represents about 2 million of Mexico's 18-million workers and which is affiliated with the Institutional Revolutionary Party (PRI) that has ruled Mexico since 1929.

To block the challenge to the CTM, the government used the police and the army to break up strike activities by the independent unions. In June, security forces arrested 100 strikers at La Caridad copper mine in northern Mexico, where construction workers were trying to break away from the CTM. In July, Mexico City's general hospital refused to recognize an independent union, and police arrested 140 strikers.

Other independent union groups were reported to be forming in the steel, film, automobile, and telephone industries. The increasing dissatisfaction with the CTM was seen by some observers as a significant threat to President Jose Lopez Portillo's efforts to revive the economy and strengthen the peso. In his state of the nation address on September 1, the president said the independents were "minority" movements and declared that they would continue to be suppressed.

Mauldin in *Chicago Sun-Times*
New Deal

Unemployment Problems. The government's austerity program had been instituted to control an inflation rate of 16 per cent. But it began to come under fire after a 10 to 15 per cent raise in the minimum wage became effective on January 1. A month after the wage hike, price controls were lifted on more than 100 food items and services. Prices on some items immediately shot up as much as 40 per cent. Statistics released on February 26 showed that 53 per cent of the work force was either unemployed or underemployed and that the 3.6 per cent population growth rate was outstripping the 2.8 per cent economic growth rate achieved in 1977. The unemployment problem was even more acute because Mexico has no welfare programs and no unemployment compensation. Observers said that the government expected the unemployed to survive by illegally entering the United States to do seasonal work.

Political Reforms. Lopez Portillo continued his program of allowing more opposition politicians to function. The Mexican Communist Party, the Socialist Workers' Party, and the conservative Mexican Democratic Party were allowed to register as officially recognized parties and to run candidates in the 1979 congressional elections. To continue as recognized parties, however, each must get at least 1.5 per cent of the total votes cast in two successive elections. This action brought the number of opposition parties to six, none of which was considered a threat to the PRI. The president's reform also includes enlarging the Chamber of Deputies from 300 members to 400. The new seats would be distributed proportionately among opposition parties that won less than 60 seats each.

The Oil Reserves. President Lopez Portillo disclosed in his September 1 state of the nation speech that Mexico's proven oil and gas reserves were probably 37 billion barrels. Previously, the reserves had been estimated at 14.7 billion barrels. He said that possible reserves were 200 billion barrels.

United States attempts to buy Mexican natural gas were frustrated in 1978. The United States contended that Mexico's asking price of $2.60 per 1,000 cubic feet (28 cubic meters) was too high. It was also reported that the Mexican Congress opposed selling any gas to the United States. Lopez Portillo said that, "Selling our gas for a lesser price would be equal to burning it."

Fortune magazine estimated that Mexico would be producing 2.2 million barrels of oil per day by 1982 and exporting half of it to earn about $8.2-billion per year. The income, Lopez Portillo stressed in an interview in August, would not be wasted. "It will be earmarked for already established national priorities. Others won't be invented just because these resources exist."   Everett G. Martin

See also LATIN AMERICA (Facts in Brief Table). In WORLD BOOK, see MEXICO.

MICHIGAN. See DETROIT; STATE GOVERNMENT.

Mexican officials examine a huge 15th-century Aztec bas-relief found in February by repair crews digging up a street in Mexico City.

MIDDLE EAST

The search for peace brought President Anwar al-Sadat of Egypt and Prime Minister Menachem Begin of Israel the Nobel Prize for Peace in 1978. But peace still lay just beyond their grasp as the year ended. More than a year after Sadat's historic journey to Jerusalem, the two nations still grappled with the details of a peace accord that would end the 30-year state of war between them and perhaps bring stability to the Middle East.

President Jimmy Carter brought Sadat and Begin together at the Camp David presidential retreat in Maryland and kept them there until they fashioned a framework for peace. Carter continued his efforts to close the remaining gap, prodding here, suggesting there, and, above all, keeping the lines of communication open between the two states.

Despite deep Egyptian and Israeli desires for a peace that would permit rapid economic and social development, there were many times during the year when a treaty seemed beyond reach. The initial euphoria generated by Sadat's November 1977 Jerusalem visit and Begin's positive response dissipated quickly in 1978. Sadat abruptly recalled the Egyptian delegation to the Israeli-Egyptian joint Political Committee sessions on January 18, the day after its first meeting. Months of indecisive maneuvering followed, with the United States engaging in shuttle diplomacy in order to keep negotiations going and reconcile divergent viewpoints. The United States "honest broker" image as the only disinterested power acceptable to both Egyptians and Israelis was enhanced in May when the U.S. Senate, by a 54 to 44 vote, approved the Administration proposal to sell jet military aircraft to Saudi Arabia and Egypt as well as to Israel.

A U.S.-Israeli Rift became apparent when President Carter declared his support for the legitimate rights of the Palestinian people in a May speech. A subsequent Begin proposal for limited interim autonomy for the West Bank and the Gaza Strip was rejected by Egypt. The Israeli government's hardline policy on Jewish settlements in the occupied territories, though rooted in domestic political considerations, created a further obstacle to peace. Carter's irritation with Israel's refusal to soften its position was evident on a number of occasions during the year.

In July, Sadat submitted a six-point peace plan to U.S. Vice-President Walter F. Mondale for transmittal to Israel. The plan called for a transitional five-year period for the West Bank and Gaza during which time Egypt, Jordan, Israel, and the Palestinian people would establish a timetable for Israeli withdrawal, election of Palestinian representatives,

United Nations (UN) participation in the transfer of power, and an end to Jewish settlement in the territories.

Camp David. The United States sponsored a secret meeting of the Egyptian and Israeli foreign ministers at Leeds Castle in Great Britain in July, but the talks failed to bridge the gap between the two. The meeting was held under tight security because of threats by Palestinian extremist groups. But the deadlock was finally broken by President Carter. Staking U.S. prestige on the outcome, he invited Sadat and Begin to a closed-door September summit conference at Camp David. After 13 days of grueling negotiations and, reportedly, 23 different drafts, the Israeli and Egyptian leaders agreed on a framework for a permanent peace treaty on September 17. Again peace seemed to be just around the corner; Israelis began signing up for tours to Egypt, and Egyptians danced in the streets when the accords were ratified by the People's Assembly.

The Camp David accords bound both countries to comply with specific UN resolutions. Israel agreed to return the Sinai Peninsula to Egypt, including oil fields developed by Israeli technology and two vital airfields. Israel would terminate its administration of the West Bank and Gaza, except in limited areas for security purposes, and would share responsibility for the territories with Egypt, Jordan, and the Palestinian people for a five-year transitional period, after which authority would revert to an autonomous elected Palestinian council. In addition, Egypt and Israel agreed to terminate economic boycotts, to provide mutual protection for citizens with due process of law, and to renounce force to settle disputes. Finally, the Camp David framework would become the basis for a formal peace treaty to be signed within three months.

Unresolved Issues. But the accords left certain issues unresolved. The major one was that of linkages between the recovery of Egyptian territory and determination of a just territorial allocation to the Palestinians. Linkage was vital to Egypt. Without it, Egypt stood accused by other Arab nations of signing a separate peace agreement with Israel. For Israel, the future of the West Bank was bound up with Jewish settlements and Biblical "rights," with secure borders, control of Jerusalem, and other matters equally vital to the future of the Jewish nation.

As the three-month deadline for treaty signature came and went, talks were stalled over Egypt's insistence on a specific timetable for granting autonomy to the West Bank and Gaza, and Israel's equally adamant refusal to set a timetable. The peacemak-

A Civil War cannon at Gettysburg adds sense of urgency to Camp David peace talks, temporarily halted so participants could tour the battlefield.

ing process still seemed irreversible, but semantic differences were clearly getting in the way. See EGYPT; ISRAEL.

Other Arab Nations. The Egyptian-Israeli negotiating process effectively nullified Arab cooperation against the common enemy. The "Resistance and Confrontation States" — Algeria, Libya, Syria, and Yemen (Aden), plus the Palestine Liberation Organization (PLO) — met in Algeria in February and reiterated their declaration of no compromise or negotiation with Israel. But the front was weakened by the absence of Iraq, though the Iraqi government denounced the Sadat peace initiatives separately.

Reconciliation between the Baathist regimes of Syria and Iraq came in October, mainly because of their common economic problems. But a second summit conference of the confrontation states held in late October in Iraq could produce only a weak condemnation of Egypt. A $1-billion war chest supposedly established to help overthrow Sadat mysteriously turned into an aid package for the hard-pressed Egyptian economy.

Trouble in the Yemens. With Iraq and Syria friends for the moment, the principal Arab conflict involved the two Yemen regimes. On June 24, Command Council Chairman Ahmed al-Ghashmi, head of the moderate-conservative government of Yemen (Sana) was killed by a bomb hidden in the briefcase of a Yemen (Aden) envoy who allegedly was on a mission to discuss plans to merge the two Yemens. Sana authorities accused Aden of complicity and complained to the Arab League, which expelled the Marxist Aden regime from membership in the league.

Ghashmi's murder set off a power struggle within the Aden government that ended with the arrest and execution of Presidential Council Chairman Salim Ali Rubayya on June 26. Prime Minister Ali Nasir Muhammad briefly assumed the presidential office after a bloody struggle. On December 27, Abdul Fatah Ismail, secretary-general of the Yemeni Socialist Party, was elected president. Meanwhile, a four-member Presidential Council in Yemen (Sana) elected Colonel Ali Abdallah Salih president, the nation's third head of state in 18 months.

Afghan Coup. Another bloody coup d'état at the eastern end of the region overthrew the government of President Mohammad Daoud in Afghanistan on April 27. Daoud was killed in the fighting. The Afghan coup pitted the educated elite and elements of the Russian-trained army against powerful, conservative tribal families, notably the former royal clan to which Daoud belonged. The new government, headed by Revolutionary Council President and Prime Minister Noor Mohammad Taraki, was described as Communist, but it pledged democratic

Firemen put out fire after Israeli bus hijacked by Palestinian terrorists exploded on the outskirts of Tel Aviv, killing 37 persons and injuring 76.

Facts in Brief on the Middle East Countries

Country	Population	Government†	Monetary Unit*	Foreign Trade (million U.S. $) Exports	Imports
Bahrain	294,000	Amir Isa bin Sulman Al Khalifa; Prime Minister Khalifa bin Salman Al Khalifa	dinar (1 = $2.59)	1,821	2,030
Cyprus	660,000	President Spyros Kyprianou	pound (1 = $2.76)	318	620
Egypt	40,619,000	President Anwar al-Sadat; Prime Minister Mustafa Khalil	pound (1 = $2.56)	1,726	4,823
Iran	37,019,000	Shah Mohammad Reza Pahlavi; Prime Minister Shahpour Bakhtiar	rial (69.4 = $1)	24,250	13,750
Iraq	12,667,000	President Ahmad Hasan al-Bakr	dinar (1 = $3.44)	9,664	4,052
Israel	3,809,000	President Yitzhak Navon; Prime Minister Menachem Begin	pound (18.9 = $1)	2,959	4,663
Jordan	3,077,000	King Hussein I; Prime Minister Mudhar Badran	dinar (1 = $3.35)	249	1,276
Kuwait	1,257,000	Emir Jaber al-Ahmad al-Jaber Al-Sabah; Crown Prince & Prime Minister Saad al-Abdullah al-Salem Al-Sabah	dinar (1 = $3.68)	9,828	4,478
Lebanon	3,649,000	President Elias Sarkis; Prime Minister Salim Ahmad al-Huss	pound (2.9 = $1)	646	1,545
Oman	865,000	Sultan Sayyid Qaboos bin Said Al Bu Said	rial (1 = $2.89)	1,332	1,110
Qatar	104,000	Amir & Prime Minister Khalifa bin Hamad Al-Thani	riyal (3.9 = $1)	2,245	846
Saudi Arabia	10,091,000	King & Prime Minister Khalid ibn Abd al-Aziz al-Saud	riyal (3.4 = $1)	41,164	17,412
Sudan	19,600,000	President & Prime Minister Gaafar Muhammed Nimeiri	pound (1 = $2.50)	661	1,060
Syria	8,375,000	President Hafiz al-Assad; Prime Minister Muhammad Ali al-Halabi	pound (4 = $1)	1,063	2,672
Turkey	44,100,000	President Fahri S. Koruturk; Prime Minister Bulent Ecevit	lira (25.3 = $1)	1,753	5,694
United Arab Emirates	252,000	President Zayid bin Sultan al-Nuhayan; Prime Minister Maktum ibn Rashid al-Maktum al-Falasa	dirham (3.9 = $1)	8,688	5,662
Yemen (Aden)	1,910,000	President Abdul Fatah Ismail	dinar (1 = $2.90)	249	414
Yemen (Sana)	7,476,000	President Ali Abdallah Salih; Prime Minister Abdulaziz Abdul Ghani	rial (4.6 = $1)	11	1,040

*Exchange rates as of Dec. 1, 1978. †As of Jan. 6, 1979.

reforms, set up a constitutional commission, and approved the formation of political parties. Although Taraki signed a 20-year treaty of friendship and cooperation with Russia on December 5, there were indications that the new Afghanistan government would not become a disruptive force. See AFGHANISTAN; TARAKI, NOOR MOHAMMAD.

Turmoil in Iran. The same could not be said of Iran, where Shah Mohammad Reza Pahlavi faced the sternest test of his authority in 25 years. Religious leaders opposed the shah's economic and social reform programs, and educated Iranians opposed his unwillingness to allow a multiparty political system to develop. But the extent and depth of public resentment was unexpected.

Despite widespread violence throughout the year, the shah seemed to have the situation under control until November. The army remained loyal, so the shah introduced certain reforms designed to satisfy critics. He extended amnesty to political prisoners, and several thousand of his opponents were released from jail. He curtailed the powers of the dreaded Savak, Iran's secret police, and dismissed its director. Other reforms included a code of conduct for the royal family that forbade its members from holding public office. The government began to weed out corruption, and several prominent business and government leaders, including former Prime Minister Amir Abbas Hoveyda, were arrested on charges

of profiteering. But the reforms did not ensure that the shah could keep his throne.

He gave up on civilian government on November 6, and imposed martial law. He replaced Prime Minister Jafar Sharif-Emami, a moderate with ties to the religious leaders, with an all-military Cabinet headed by General Gholam Reza Azhari. The new Cabinet pledged to restore public security and fight corruption. Four hundred more political prisoners were released, leaving only 300 "hard-core terrorists" behind bars. But neither religious nor student-leftist groups were satisfied with the reforms. The oil industry was almost completely shut down by strikes, and this had a devastating effect on the economy. On Jan. 6, 1979, a new civilian prime minister, Shahpour Bakhtiar, took office, and it was clear that the shah was no longer in control of his own destiny or that of his country. See IRAN.

PLO Infighting. The PLO also experienced considerable dissension. Its various factions directed more violence against one another than against the vigilant Israelis. The loss of most of their guerrilla bases and equipment when Israel invaded southern Lebanon in March practically eliminated the PLO as a threat to Israeli security.

Palestinian-Arab terrorism turned inward, against its own operatives. Said Hammami, the PLO representative in London and a confidant of PLO leader Yassir Arafat, was murdered on January 4 by

403

an Arab gunman. Palestinian gunmen killed Egyptian editor Youssef el-Sebai, a close friend of Sadat's, in Nicosia, Cyprus, in February, and took PLO members hostage in their escape attempt.

Evidence of even greater disarray in the Palestinian leadership developed in July. The PLO representative in Kuwait was murdered, and several persons, including a French police officer and Iraqi guards, were killed in a shoot-out at the Iraqi Embassy in Paris. Ezzedine Kalak, the chief PLO representative in Paris, was shot by pro-Iraqi Palestinians. At the same time, clashes between Palestinian factions in Lebanon added to the bloody fighting in that strife-ridden country. See LEBANON.

Economic Problems. Uncertainty over a political settlement had an adverse effect on the Middle East's economic development. Nearly $6 billion in economic projects supported or initiated by the new Arab Economic Unity Council was stalled pending a peace settlement, while economic boycotts of Egypt by the confrontation states also cut down the funding flow within the region. An encouraging development came on November 1 when the European Community (EC, or Common Market) and eight Arab states signed agreements giving the Arab nations associate status and preferred access for their products in EC markets.　　　　William Spencer

In WORLD BOOK, see MIDDLE EAST and individual country articles.

MILLER, G. WILLIAM (1925-　　　), was sworn in as chairman of the Board of Governors of the Federal Reserve System on March 8, 1978. Then chairman of Textron, Incorporated, a multinational conglomerate, Miller was questioned at great length by members of the U.S. Senate Committee on Banking, Housing, and Urban Affairs about the Iranian dealings of a Textron subsidiary.

George William Miller was born in Sapulpa, Okla., on March 9, 1925. He grew up in Borger, Tex. A 1945 graduate of the U.S. Coast Guard Academy, he served in the Pacific and in China. He attended law school at the University of California, Berkeley, where he edited the law review and graduated in 1952 at the top of his class.

Miller practiced law in New York City until he joined Textron as assistant secretary in 1956. He became company president in 1960, assumed additional duties as chief executive officer in 1968, and was elected chairman of the board in 1974.

At the time of his appointment, Miller was also serving as a director of the Federal Reserve Bank of Boston. He had been active in several government and private organizations aimed at increasing the national employment rate, including the National Alliance of Businessmen and the President's Committee for HIRE.

Miller married Ariadna Rogojarski in 1946. He enjoys golf, squash, and sailing.　　　　Beverly Merz

MINES AND MINING. Australia cleared the way in 1978 to mine and export uranium. Parliament passed six bills on May 31 to provide environmental protection of mine sites, land rights for the Aborigine owners of the sites, and nuclear safeguards. Australian mining companies would be able to sign export contracts with firms in other countries, subject to approval by the minister of national resources and overseas trade. Australia had imposed an embargo on uranium exports in 1972.

The government and representatives of Northern Territory Aborigines agreed on August 25 on uranium royalties of 4.25 per cent for the Aborigines. The royalty agreement was seen as the last major obstacle to uranium mining. The mining companies were eager to begin work on the Ranger project near the East Alligator River before the rainy season began in November. But a dispute about who would pay the royalties and the Aborigines' reluctance to sign an agreement caused a postponement until the end of the rainy season in April 1979.

China ordered 1.5 million short tons (1.4 million metric tons) of Australian iron ore in September for 1979 delivery from the Mount Newman group, a consortium of five companies from Australia, Great Britain, Japan, and the United States. The ore increased China's share of Australia's iron-ore exports from 3 to 5 per cent.

Coal Strikes. In the United States, a coal strike ended in its 110th day on March 25. President Jimmy Carter then reaffirmed his intention to name a commission to study the industry's problems of health, safety, and productivity. See LABOR.

In Peru, 45,000 mineworkers ended a 35-day strike on September 8, after the government surrounded mine areas with troops, cut off food supplies, and authorized the mining companies to fire strikers. The strike threatened Peru's arrangement of an International Monetary Fund loan to help Peru out of its economic crisis. Peru had expected mineral exports to account for half of its foreign-exchange earnings in 1978. The country lost at least $2 million a day during the strike. The strikers' main demand was the reinstatement of 320 dismissed workers whom the Peruvian government called leftist agitators.

Copper Dips. United States copper producers pressed for import quotas while excessive foreign production decreased. Causing the decrease were the Peruvian strike, the flight of immigrant miners from Zambia, and fighting in Zaire's copper-rich Shaba province. See ZAIRE; ZAMBIA.

Brazil pushed ahead with the construction of its $783-million Cariba copper open-pit and underground mining project at Jaguarrari, 300 miles (480 kilometers) northwest of Salvador in Bahia.

In the tin-rich belt of Southeast Asia, high-grade reserves declined, and prospects for major finds were bleak. Prompted by high prices, government and industry turned their attention to reserves in the seas off Thailand, Indonesia, and Malaysia.

The Supreme Court of Canada on October 3 declared that Saskatchewan's system of prorating potash production and fixing minimum prices was unconstitutional. The court ruled the practice beyond a province's powers because potash is an export resource. Prorating began in 1969 when demand was weak and prices were depressed. The price-and-demand situation changed in 1974. Saskatchewan's potash fields are the largest in the world.

Congress Acts. President Carter signed a bill on August 20 increasing from 3 per cent to between 4.5 and 5.5 per cent the finance charge on government loans designed to help states cope with the impact of mining. Although the loan program had been approved in 1976, the federal government had not made the loans available because of the low rate.

The House of Representatives passed a bill on July 26 to set up a government system to allow U.S. companies to mine copper, nickel, manganese, and cobalt nodules from the Pacific Ocean floor. The Carter Administration supported the bill to pressure the United Nations (UN) Law of the Sea Conference into reaching agreement on the subject. The bill did not reach the U.S. Senate floor. The UN conference's seventh session closed in September with no agreement. See OCEAN. *James J. O'Connor*

In WORLD BOOK, see MINING.

MINNEAPOLIS-ST. PAUL. Redevelopment efforts made major gains in both Minneapolis and St. Paul in 1978. Minneapolis approved a four-block extension of Nicollet Mall and laid plans for developing the downtown Loring Park district. St. Paul received a $4.8-million grant from the Department of Housing and Urban Development (HUD) for the development of a downtown shopping mall.

The Minneapolis City Council unanimously approved a $2-million, four-block extension of Nicollet Mall on March 30 with provisions to allow nonprofit organizations to locate there. The Loring Park developers announced on March 17 that the Hyatt Hotel Corporation had agreed to manage and help finance a 540-room luxury hotel and trade mart in the district. The Minnesota Supreme Court helped the project on March 28 when it rejected objections to municipal construction of a 750-car parking ramp with 30,000 square feet (2,800 square meters) of exhibit space adjacent to the proposed hotel.

The St. Paul grant, awarded on April 5, was one of the first such urban-development grants made by HUD. It was slated to help build the Seventh Place Galleria, a three-level, glass-enclosed shopping mall covering an entire downtown block.

Hundreds of people made a pilgrimage to the Twin Cities on January 16 for the burial service of former U.S. Vice-President Hubert H. Humphrey. President Jimmy Carter signed a bill on April 27 authorizing a $5-million federal grant to help found the Hubert H. Humphrey Institute of Public Affairs at the University of Minnesota.

Living Costs in the Twin Cities area rose 7.7 per cent during the 11-month period ending in June, while food costs rose 6.1 per cent in the year ending in May. A Department of Labor report issued on April 26 noted that an average family of four would require $17,813 per year, or 4 per cent more than the national average, to live in middle-class comfort in the area.

Gay Rights. Voters repealed St. Paul's four-year-old gay-rights law on April 25 by a 5 to 3 margin and defeated a homosexual candidate for one of seven city council seats. The initiative deleted provisions in the city's human-rights ordinance prohibiting discrimination in housing, employment, education, and public accommodations on the basis of "sexual or affectional preference." In Minneapolis, Hennepin County Judge Robert Schumacher ruled on the same day that men seeking to join Big Brothers, a program for fatherless boys, may be asked if they are homosexual. *James M. Banovetz*

See also CITY. In WORLD BOOK, see MINNEAPOLIS; SAINT PAUL.

MINNESOTA. See MINNEAPOLIS-ST. PAUL; STATE GOVERNMENT.

MISSISSIPPI. See STATE GOVERNMENT.

MISSOURI. See ST. LOUIS; STATE GOVERNMENT.

MOI, DANIEL T. ARAP (1924-   ), was installed as the second president of the Republic of Kenya on Oct. 14, 1978, four days after his election to the office. As Kenya's vice-president, he had served as interim president since the death of Jomo Kenyatta on August 22. See KENYA.

Daniel Torotich arap Moi was born in Kenya's Rift Valley province, the son of farmers. He was educated at a primary school run by the British colonial government. Moi taught school after graduating from Tambach Teacher Training College in 1945. He also served as assistant principal of the college from 1949 to 1954.

Moi was one of only six Africans appointed by the colonial government in 1955 to serve in the Kenya National Assembly. As a member of the Assembly, he campaigned relentlessly for African suffrage – a goal that was realized in 1957. Moi also took part in the constitutional conferences that led to Kenya's independence in 1963.

In Kenya's early days as a republic, Moi was a leader of the opposition party, the Kenya African Democratic Union. He disbanded the party in 1964 and joined the majority party, the Kenya African National Union. Kenyatta appointed him vice-president in 1967 as a reward for his loyalty.

Moi is a shrewd politician, but less colorful and domineering than Kenyatta. He was expected to concentrate on economic development. *Beverly Merz*

MOLINA PALLOCHIA, OSCAR (1921-   ), was sworn in as prime minister of Peru on Jan. 31, 1978. At the same time, he became minister of war and commander of the army. The 56-year-old army general replaced General Guillermo Arbulu Galliani, who, along with 14 other senior army officers, had retired the preceding day after completing 35 years of service. See PERU.

Molina Pallochia was born in Lima, Peru, on Sept. 27, 1921. He became interested in a military career at an early age. Encouraged by his parents, he enrolled at the Lima Institute, from which he graduated in 1939. He entered the Lima Military Academy at Chorrillos in that same year, and joined the Peruvian Army as a second lieutenant in 1944 after completing his training. Subsequently, he served at various army installations in Peru. His rise through the ranks was rapid, and in 1976 he was named chairman of the Joint Chiefs of Staff of the Armed Forces, a position he held at the time he was named prime minister. One of his tasks as prime minister would be to initiate procedures to replace the ruling military junta with a democratic government.

The new prime minister enjoys a reputation as a calm, intellectual man who shuns publicity and oratory. He is married to the former Beatriz Galvez Almeida. They have six children.   Paul C. Tullier

MONACO. See EUROPE.

MONDALE, WALTER FREDERICK (1928-   ), 42nd Vice-President of the United States, reshaped the traditional role of his office to become one of President Jimmy Carter's most active and trusted advisers in 1978. Mondale was active in the everyday administration of government, in diplomacy, as liaison to Congress, and as a party leader.

President Carter asked Mondale to assume the responsibility for virtually all other activities of the government while the President took charge of the Middle East peace negotiations at Camp David, Maryland, in September. Mondale was also called to Camp David to take part in a negotiating session during the final days of the conference.

Political Ambassador. In a "listen and learn" political tour in January, Mondale visited seven Western states – Colorado, Idaho, Montana, Nevada, New Mexico, Utah, and Washington. He conferred with leaders of the large southwest Indian tribes in Albuquerque, N. Mex., on January 10, and met with 13 western Democratic governors in Reno, Nev., on January 13.

Mondale left for a diplomatic visit to the Far East on April 29. He made a 12-day tour of the Philippines, Thailand, Indonesia, Australia, and New Zealand to reassure those nations of continuing United States interest in their political and economic problems. In Manila, Mondale signed four agree-

Vice-President Walter F. Mondale leaves a peace message at the Wailing Wall in Jerusalem on June 30 while making an official visit to the Middle East.

ments with President Ferdinand E. Marcos on May 3 to provide about $41 million in U.S. aid to the Philippines.

Diplomatic Emissary. Vice-President Mondale also served as President Carter's deputy to the special United Nations General Assembly session on disarmament in May. In a formal address to the Assembly on May 24, Mondale reaffirmed the United States commitment to completing strategic arms limitation talks (SALT) with Russia. Mondale charged, however, that the Soviet Union was hampering negotiations by escalating missile deployment in Europe and by expanding naval operations in the Indian Ocean.

Mondale traveled to the Middle East in June, carrying letters from President Carter to Israeli and Egyptian leaders urging a speedy resumption of peace talks. He conferred with Israeli Prime Minister Menachem Begin on July 2 and persuaded Begin to have Israeli Foreign Minister Moshe Dayan meet with Egypt's Foreign Minister Muhammad Ibrahim Kamel in London on July 18 and 19. Mondale stopped in Alexandria on July 3 to receive Egypt's proposed peace plan and its pledge to participate in the London conference. Carol L. Thompson

In WORLD BOOK, see VICE-PRESIDENT OF THE UNITED STATES.

MONGOLIA. See ASIA.

MONTANA. See STATE GOVERNMENT.

MORIAL, ERNEST NATHAN (1929-   ), became mayor of New Orleans on May 1, 1978, the first black to be elected to that post. He was elected on Nov. 12, 1977. It was the latest in a series of firsts for Morial. In 1954 he became the first black to graduate from Louisiana State University Law School, and in 1967 he was the first black elected to the Louisiana House of Representatives in this century. He is a Democrat.

Morial was born on Oct. 9, 1929, the youngest of six children of French-speaking, middle-class parents in New Orleans. His father, Walter, was a cigar maker, and his mother, Leonie, a tailor. Morial attended public and parochial schools in New Orleans and graduated from Xavier University of Louisiana in 1951 before attending Louisiana State University's law school.

After serving for two years with the U.S. Army intelligence service, Morial began doing legal work on behalf of the civil rights movement. He was president of the New Orleans chapter of the National Association for the Advancement of Colored People from 1962 to 1965, when he became assistant U.S. attorney in New Orleans.

He served one term, then was appointed a juvenile court judge. In 1972, Morial became a judge in Louisiana's Fourth Circuit Court of Appeals and served until he ran for mayor. Foster Stockwell

See also NEW ORLEANS.

MOROCCO. King Hassan II played an important behind-the-scenes role in Arab-Israeli peace negotiations and mediated a number of African problems in 1978. About 1,700 Moroccan troops were airlifted to Shaba province, Zaire, in June to aid the Zairian government against a renewed rebellion there. About 6,000 troops were stationed in Mauritania, Morocco's Saharan partner, after a military coup d'état ousted the government there in July.

These efforts and the high cost of the campaign against Polisario, the guerrilla movement fighting for independence in the former Spanish Sahara, put a severe strain on the Moroccan economy. Nevertheless, the 1977 "pact of reconciliation" between Hassan and his political opponents held firm. The National Assembly was given responsibility for budget approval and legislation, though all bills must be screened by a committee composed of members of previous royalist cabinets.

To deal with economic strains, Hassan announced a 20 per cent cut in imports and a ban on imports of all luxury items in June. Phosphate production increased to 20 million short tons (18 million metric tons), but world phosphate prices declined. Continued drought also hurt the economy. But in October, Hassan announced the discovery of big new oil deposits. The site was not identified. William Spencer

See also AFRICA (Facts in Brief Table); ALGERIA.

In WORLD BOOK, see MOROCCO.

MOTION PICTURES. The American motion picture industry continued to flourish in 1978. Several U.S. films were added to the roster of record-breaking blockbusters that have revived a once-flagging movie industry since 1972, the year of *The Godfather.* There seemed no doubt that 1978's total domestic gross would be an all-time high of about $2.75 billion, surpassing 1977's record $2.3 billion gross by some 16 per cent. Only about one-fifth of this increase was due to inflated ticket prices. It was clear there had been a substantial rise in movie attendance, with the number of weekly admissions averaging 25 million for 1978, some 2 million per week above the previous year.

The Youth Market was the key factor in this growth, with 12- to 18-year-old moviegoers enthusiastically responding to the industry's determined courtship. Still reaping the profits of 1977's phenomenally successful *Star Wars,* which in 1978 became the highest-grossing film of all time, Hollywood hoped to capitalize further on the evident interest in such youth-oriented films. In 1978, it gave the 12- to 18-year-olds films not only with plots and characters intended to arouse their interest, but also with stars who had already won a large teen-age following. The strategy was clearly effective.

The combined earnings of the two highest-grossing movies—*Saturday Night Fever* and *Grease*—reached some $250 million and accounted

Television star John Travolta sings and dances in *Grease*, film version of the long-running Broadway show that features music of the 1950s.

for as much as 10 per cent of the year's total revenues. Although vastly different in quality, both films focused explicitly on teen-age culture and took advantage of the young audience's intense absorption in popular music. *Saturday Night Fever* touched on the current disco craze, and *Grease* cashed in on a revival of interest in 1950s rock and roll. Moreover, both films featured television's John Travolta.

In making his movie debut in *Saturday Night Fever*, Travolta proved that he was not only a dazzling musical entertainer, but also a surprisingly sensitive actor. Indeed, his performance as a 19-year-old Brooklyn hardware-store clerk who finds release from his dreary existence in dancing at a local disco palace, won Travolta an Academy Award nomination and, together with John Badham's fine direction and Norman Wexler's perceptive script, helped to make the film a penetrating study of the frustrations of contemporary blue-collar youth. However, it was the movie's music and dancing rather than its serious substance that seemed to excite the young audience, who otherwise were attracted to only the most lightweight fare.

Grease, an adaptation of the long-running Broadway show, was a thoroughly frivolous work. Dealing with the manners and mores of high-school students during the 1950s, this film's vision of teen culture was emphatically simplistic, with a boy-meets-girl, boy-loses-girl, boy-gets-girl plot that seemed to derive more from comic strips than from an accurate observation of the period it purported to parody.

The Comedies. Like *Grease*, another of the year's huge successes, *National Lampoon's Animal House*, offered a comic vision of school life. Here, however, the setting was college, the time was the 1960s, and the jokes were decidedly more irreverent. *Animal House* received an R rating, which, though suggesting that those under 17 not be permitted into theaters without an accompanying adult, apparently did more to attract young audiences than to keep them away. *Animal House* emerged as the sleeper of the year, a cult film among the young that, produced for under $3 million, grossed more than $60 million in the United States and Canada alone.

Though *Animal House's* vulgar undergraduate humor obviously accounted for much of its appeal, the fact that the film starred John Belushi, a featured member of the cast of television's *Saturday Night Live*, also was crucial. This program has a large teen-age viewing audience. Significantly, Chevy Chase, a young comedian who had also appeared on *Saturday Night Live*, starred in another box-office winner, *Foul Play*.

Recording stars also proved strong box-office attractions with teen-agers. *Up in Smoke*, a low-budget, amateurish spoof on marijuana smoking, featured comic recording artists Cheech and Chong and grossed more than $20 million in its first month.

The Thrillers. Much as comedies and musicals reflected the domination of the youth market, so did the year's thrillers. *Jaws 2* had its great white shark launch attacks on a band of vacationing youngsters; *Damien – Omen II* re-introduced a 13-year-old satanic villain; and Brian De Palma's *The Fury* dealt with the telekinetic powers of two terrifying adolescents. Although none of these thrillers did anywhere as well either critically or commercially as *Grease* or *Saturday Night Fever*, *Jaws 2* and *Omen II* enjoyed significantly higher box-office grosses than the thrillers that featured older protagonists, such as *The Boys from Brazil, Death on the Nile, The Eyes of Laura Mars*, and *Coma*. Still, the presence of youthful stars or subjects was not sufficient to ensure the popularity of all such films. *Sergeant Pepper's Lonely Hearts Club Band, American Hot Wax, I Wanna Hold Your Hand*, and *FM* – all directed at the youthful audience – proved disappointing at the box office.

If not all the youth-oriented movies were successful in 1978, neither were all the successful movies youth oriented. Some of the top moneymakers displayed the same lightness and triviality as the youth films, however. *Hooper*, directed by Hal Needham and starring Burt Reynolds, grossed some $40 million in the United States, though it was a slapstick comedy about the crashes, jumps, and death dives performed by Hollywood stuntmen. *Heaven Can Wait*, which earned more than $70 million, was a slight if amiable comedy with Warren Beatty as a football player who, having died before his time, finds himself searching for a new body in which to live out his allotted years.

Film Recycling. Significantly, *Heaven Can Wait* was a remake of a 1941 movie, *Here Comes Mr. Jordan*. As such, it signaled another discernible trend in American movies – the tendency to recycle proven properties through sequels, remakes, and adaptations. Aside from *Heaven Can Wait, Jaws 2*, and *Omen II*, the year saw the release of still another adventure of the bungling Inspector Clouseau, *The Revenge of the Pink Panther*. There was also *The Wiz*, a $30-million remake of *The Wizard of Oz*. Adapted from the Broadway musical, it featured an all-black cast with singer Diana Ross as a 25-year-old Dorothy. And there was *International Velvet*, a sequel to the 1944 Elizabeth Taylor classic about a girl and her horse.

The recycling trend certainly was not new, and neither was the tendency of several 1978 movies to take women as their subject. What was noteworthy about these films – which included Paul Mazursky's buoyant comedy, *An Unmarried Woman;* Woody Allen's intensely serious study of family relationships, *Interiors;* and Claudia Weill's understated, low-budget feature, *Girlfriends* – was their exceptional quality. All were intelligent, insightful, and highly sensitive works. They were graced, as well, by outstanding performances, most impressive of which

was Jill Clayburgh's as the title character in *An Unmarried Woman*. Considering their subject matter and tone, all did fairly well commercially.

In Other Countries. Although there were more hits than misses for the U.S. movie industry, this was not the case for movies made abroad. Italy, Japan, Spain, and West Germany all reported significant declines in both production and movie attendance. And while the industry was healthier in both France and England, U.S. films dominated the box office in these countries just as they did all over the world. Moreover, if foreign films found themselves trailing U.S. products at home, they were even less successful when competing for the American market. Not only were Americans importing fewer films than they had in recent years, but those films from abroad that did find U.S. distributors had little commercial success.

Part of the problem seemed to lie in the fact that these films, which generally dealt with mature characters and themes, were unable to attract America's growing youth market. In addition, most of the motion pictures made in Europe and Japan seemed inferior. In the past, American audiences could turn to imports for substance and seriousness, but many of the new films seemed just as trivial as their U.S. counterparts – if not more so. And the great European filmmakers of the 1950s and 1960s, such as François Truffaut, Jean-Luc Godard, Federico Fel-

Superman, a movie about the popular comic-strip crusader for justice, attracted big audiences when it opened in theaters in late December.

409

lini, Michelangelo Antonioni, and Claude Chabrol, produced nothing in 1978 or turned out inferior works.

Unfortunately, it was not only the European art film that foundered in 1978. In America as well, failure seemed to confront nearly all attempts at serious filmmaking. Robert Mulligan's study of blue-collar life, *Bloodbrothers*, emerged as a sentimental and melodramatic picture. Robert Altman's *A Wedding*, if less pretentious than his recent *3 Women*, seemed even more pointless. *Coming Home*, Hal Ashby's study of the effects of the Vietnam War, seemed contrived and heavy-handed, its only authentic achievement being Jon Voight's brilliant performance as a paraplegic veteran. And the year's most ambitious film, Terrence Malick's *Days of Heaven*, though filled with prodigiously beautiful images, lacked dramatic and thematic force.

The failure of *Days of Heaven* was especially significant. Malick's emphasis on form at the expense of content reflected a widespread trend in contemporary filmmaking, and one that seemed to point to the decline of film as art.　Joy Gould Boyum

See also ALLEN, WOODY; AWARDS AND PRIZES (Arts Awards); DREYFUSS, RICHARD; KEATON, DIANE; TRAVOLTA, JOHN. In WORLD BOOK, see MOTION PICTURE.

MOZAMBIQUE. See AFRICA.

MUSEUM. Museums throughout the world celebrated the first annual International Museum Day on May 18, 1978. Events included festive openings of exhibitions and new galleries, behind-the-scenes tours, lectures, and demonstrations.

An exhibition from Italy, "Pompeii A.D. 79," toured United States museums with more than 300 archaeological specimens vividly revealing life in the doomed Roman city. The show drew about 400,000 persons to the Museum of Fine Arts in Boston, then moved to the Art Institute of Chicago and the Dallas Museum of Fine Arts. More than 700 works of art from East Germany were loaned for "The Splendor of Dresden: Five Centuries of Art Collecting," an exhibition that opened at the National Gallery of Art in Washington D.C., then went to the Metropolitan Museum in New York. The Brooklyn (N.Y.) Museum launched a long-term scientific expedition to record fully the ancient remains in the Valley of the Kings in Egypt and develop methods for preserving them in place. The museum also helped to spearhead an international fund-raising campaign to rehabilitate the Cairo Museum and build a small museum to house and preserve the solar boats of King Khufu, also known as the pharaoh Cheops.

Government Funds. The newly established National Institute of Museum Services of the U.S. Department of Health, Education, and Welfare

The 2,000-year-old Temple of Dendur, a gift from Egypt to the U.S., opened to the public in September in New York City's Metropolitan Museum of Art.

made its first grants, totaling $3.5 million, to help hard-pressed museums meet essential operating expenses in 1978. The Federal Council on the Arts and the Humanities appointed a working group on federal museums policy to help coordinate the grant programs of the various federal agencies now offering financial aid to museums. The American Association of Museums and the Association of Art Museum Directors urged continued diversity and growth in government support. In Great Britain, Parliament increased museum grants by 27.8 per cent.

New Buildings and Exhibits. The National Gallery of Art opened its East Building on June 1. The impressive $94-million structure, designed by architect I.M. Pei, was a gift from the children of Andrew W. Mellon, the gallery's founder. See PEI, I.M.

In New York City, the Metropolitan Museum of Art built a glass wing to exhibit the ancient Temple of Dendur, a gift from Egypt to the American people. The first public museum, the Ashmolean Museum in Oxford, England, installed part of its 17th-century founder's collection in its new Tradescant Room. The exhibit included a deerskin mantle worn by the American Indian chief Powhatan, father of Pocahontas. Celebrating its 900th year, the Tower of London built a sunken gallery to display a pictorial exhibit of its history.

Museum Losses. Fire destroyed most of the San Diego Aero-Space Museum and its important collections in February. Old motion-picture film stored at the George Eastman House, an international museum of photography in Rochester, N.Y., caught fire in May. Flames demolished four outbuildings at an estimated $4-million loss. Fire swept through the glass-and-concrete Museum of Modern Art in Rio de Janeiro, Brazil, in July. More than 1,000 works of art – 80 per cent of the collection – were ruined.

A vandal slashed and ripped to pieces a large painting by the baroque French painter Nicolas Poussin in London's National Gallery. The National Museum of Man in Ottawa, Canada, closed the condemned building containing its historical collections and moved to temporary, but safer, quarters.

The Art Institute of Chicago discovered in late December that three paintings by French impressionist Paul Cézanne had been stolen from a storeroom. The paintings, valued at $3 million, had been stored during a hall renovation. Seventeenth-century Dutch paintings worth more than $1 million were taken from San Francisco's Michael H. DeYoung Museum just before Christmas.

United States museums began emphasizing participation by handicapped visitors in activities for the general public instead of providing separate programs. New regulations required that museum programs receiving federal grants be accessible to the handicapped.   Ralph H. Lewis

See also VISUAL ARTS. In WORLD BOOK, see MUSEUM.

MUSIC, CLASSICAL. The struggle against zooming costs and inflation continued in 1978. The concern increased as California's tax-cutting Proposition 13 started a nationwide movement to curb government spending. See TAXATION (Close-Up).

"If the California pattern becomes a national pattern, then the arts are going to be in deep trouble," pollster Louis Harris, who is chairman of the American Council for the Arts, predicted. When budgets are cut, Harris said, the arts will find it increasingly difficult to compete with education, welfare, and other "musts."

The budget crunch was a major area of discussion at the American Symphony Orchestra League convention in Chicago in June. President Beatrice Vradenburg of the Metropolitan Orchestra Managers Association urged "eyeball-to-eyeball contact" with legislators.

When the American Council for the Arts met in June, participants heard jazz musician Billy Taylor urge that the individual artist not be forgotten. "There is no deficit funding, no fund-raising benefit for the artist – unless he or she is sick, or dead. Is it unreasonable for the individual to ask for what the organization is already receiving?"

Money pressures led to more fund-raising activities, such as marathons, auctions, and special benefit concerts. But the Florida Philharmonic failed to meet a final season payroll in May. And musicians with the National Symphony Orchestra in Washington, D.C., went on strike in September, delaying the season's start while negotiators sought a pay scale that was satisfactory to musicians and achievable by management.

Musical Chairs. Orchestras in the United States underwent a lively round robin of conductor-moving. Antal Dorati took over the Detroit Symphony. Leonard Slatkin was named conductor of the St. Louis Symphony, and Neville Marriner will take the podium of the Minnesota Orchestra. Brian Priestman moved from Denver to Florida and was replaced by Gaetano Delogu.

But the two biggest changes involved New York City and Los Angeles. The personable, energetic Zubin Mehta moved from the Los Angeles Philharmonic to the New York Philharmonic, where he is expected to follow more closely the freewheeling style of Leonard Bernstein than did his predecessor, the coolly avant-garde Pierre Boulez. Los Angeles, temporarily stung by the loss of Mehta, rebounded by snaring Carlo Maria Giulini.

On the Road. Touring orchestras included the Toronto Symphony, which went to Japan in January; the New York Philharmonic, to Japan and Korea in June and to South America in September; the Cleveland Orchestra, to Asia in September; and the Chicago Symphony, to Europe in September. The Denver Symphony made a train tour of Wyoming and Idaho in late summer.

Denver's Boettcher Concert Hall has seats on all sides of the orchestra.
Ceiling reflector disks and a vault below the stage aid fine acoustics.

For the Denver orchestra, the big event of the year occurred in March, with the opening of its spectacular circular concert hall in which the stage is surrounded by more than 2,700 seats. Heralding the hall was a new composition, John Green's *Mine Eyes Have Seen: Symphony Parallels and Contradictions for Orchestra* with jazz combo, organ, and synthesizer tossed in for good measure.

New Works. Major compositions introduced by U.S. orchestras during 1978 included Easley Blackwood's *Symphony No. 4* (Chicago); Joaquin Rodrigo's *In Search of the Beyond* (Houston, in honor of that city's aerospace role); William Kraft's *Andirivieni* for tuba (Los Angeles); Stanislaw Skrowaczewski's *Saxophone Concerto* (Minnesota); Henri Dutilleux' *Timbres, espace, mouvement* (National Symphony); Samuel Barber's *Third Essay* and Jacob Druckman's *Viola Concerto* (New York); and Ned Rorem's *Sunday Morning* (Philadelphia).

Orchestras also programmed heavily in the choral, vocal, and operatic repertoire to attract audiences and attention. Ludwig van Beethoven's *Ninth Symphony* remained a heavy favorite with performances in Atlanta, Baltimore, Denver, Kansas City, Los Angeles, and Pittsburgh. His *Missa solemnis* was heard in Denver, Minnesota, and New York, and *Fidelio* in Kansas City and Indianapolis. Requiems were big: Giuseppe Verdi's in Rochester, N.Y., and Washington, D.C.; Hector Berlioz' in Dallas and

San Francisco; Gabriel Fauré's in Boston; Wolfgang Amadeus Mozart's in Toronto, Canada; Johannes Brahm's *German Requiem* in Chicago; and Benjamin Britten's *A War Requiem* in Cleveland. Sir Edward Elgar's *The Dream of Gerontius* (Houston); Arthur Honegger's *Joan of Arc at the Stake* (Cleveland) and *King David* (Milwaukee) were among other works programmed.

The 150th anniversary of Franz Schubert's death brought a number of his works to orchestra repertories, particularly in Detroit; Toronto, Canada; and Washington, D.C. But perhaps the most unusual program was a Shakespearean series in Dallas featuring music inspired by the Bard, including Felix Mendelssohn's *A Midsummer Night's Dream*, Vincenzo Bellini's *Capuletti e Montecchi*, Otto Nicolai's *Merry Wives of Windsor*, and Sergei Prokofiev's *Romeo and Juliet*.

Unusual Operas. It was a year for interesting programs in opera, too. Perhaps most encouraging were the fledgling opera companies' attempts to stage the unusual, rather than just the staples of the repertoire. For example, the Virginia Opera Association, in its third full season, offered the U.S. première of Thea Musgrave's *Mary, Queen of Scots*; and the schedule of the Opera Theatre of St. Louis consisted of Giacomo Puccini's *La Bohème*, Vincente Martin y Soler's *Tree of Chastity*, Britten's *Albert Herring*, and Gimi Beni's *Forever Figaro*.

The Opera Company of Boston did Verdi's *Stiffelio*, and the New York Amato Opera produced his *Oberto* in, surprisingly, its U.S. première. From the Colorado Opera Festival – with George Frideric Handel's *Xerxes* in its first professional. U.S. production – to the Handel Festival at Washington's John F. Kennedy Center for the Performing Arts with *Poro* in its first U.S. staging; from Stephen Oliver's *The Duchess of Malfi* at Santa Fe to Grigori Frid's *Diary of Anne Frank* at Syracuse University, both American firsts, there was great departure from the norm.

New Operas added to the excitement. In late November, Chicago's Lyric Opera presented *Paradise Lost* by Krzysztof Penderecki. Great Britain's Harrogate Festival introduced Wilfred Joseph's *Through the Looking Glass and What Alice Found There* in August. In July, Munich, West Germany, premièred *Lear*, written by Aribert Reimann and performed by baritone Dietrich Fischer-Dieskau.

April was a big month for world premières. John Eaton's *Danton and Robespierre*, a French revolutionary piece reflected in the light of our age, was seen at Indiana University in Bloomington. The Minnesota Opera offered Robert Ward's *Claudia Legare*, Henrik Ibsen's *Hedda Gabler* transplanted to the post-Civil War South. The Guelph, Canada, Spring Festival had the Charles Wilson-Eugene

A spectacular set highlights a revival of Richard Strauss's opera *Die Frau ohne Schatten* at the Metropolitan Opera in New York City.

Benson *Psycho Red*. In Stockholm, the latest work of György Ligeti, *The Ballad of the Grand Macabre*, told of a fantasy world in which a plot to destroy the earth is very simply circumvented when the culprits are tempted to drink too heavily and fall asleep.

But perhaps the most unusual première was that of *Gabriella di Vergy* in London. The work was written almost 150 years ago by Gaetano Donizetti and was only recently discovered.

People In the News. Composer-conductor André Previn and playwright Tom Stoppard collaborated on a play with music, *Every Good Boy Deserves Favor*. It is about a man who thinks he owns an orchestra and because of such thinking is put in a Russian insane asylum. There he creates discomfort for his cellmate, whose coughing, he charges, spoils the music. The audience hears the music along with the "mad" one. It was performed by Previn's Pittsburgh Symphony and actors John Wood and Eli Wallach.

Mstislav Rostropovich, the famed cellist-conductor, and his wife, soprano Galina Vishnevskaya, were stripped of their citizenship by the Russian government. They were charged with acts overseas "harmful to the prestige of the Soviet Union." Kirill Kondrashin, conductor of the Moscow Philharmonic, sought refuge in the Netherlands on December 4, after appearing as a guest conductor with the Concertgebouw orchestra in Amsterdam. He said that Russia was stifling his artistic freedom.

Baritone Simon Estes became the first black man to star at the Bayreuth Festival in West Germany. He played the title role in Wagner's *Flying Dutchman*. Soprano Marian Anderson was awarded the Congressional Gold Medal by President Jimmy Carter in a White House ceremony. Americans Nathaniel Rosen and Elmar Oliveira won top awards in cello and violin, respectively, in the prestigious Tchaikovsky Competition in Moscow.

Gold Baton Awards went to Composer Aaron Copland for contributions to American musical life and to the Exxon Corporation for support of the performing arts. The National Opera Institute, in a special series of awards, honored Texaco Incorporated for its broadcast sponsorship for 37 years of Metropolitan Opera; composer Gian Carlo Menotti for founding his two Spoleto Festivals – in Italy and South Carolina; the San Francisco Opera for presenting the first U.S. productions of major 20th-century operatic works; and Peter Herman Adler for his pioneering efforts in the production of televised opera.

Perhaps an "Adventure of the Year" award should have gone to Ron Hayes, a young man who took a string quartet, a couple of wind players, and 24 listeners down the rapids of the Colorado River to hold concerts under the sky in the Grand Canyon. For the person who has tried just about every kind of vacation, here is something different.　Peter P. Jacobi

In WORLD BOOK, see MUSIC.

MUSIC, POPULAR

MUSIC, POPULAR. By far the most successful popular music group of 1978 was the Bee Gees—Barry Gibb and his younger twin brothers Robin and Maurice. These singers, born in England and reared in Australia, released a sound-track album from the motion picture *Saturday Night Fever* late in 1977, and it sold almost 30 million copies.

The Bee Gees headed a list of performers whose scores contributed to such music-oriented films as *American Hot Wax, The Buddy Holly Story, Thank God It's Friday, The Last Waltz,* and *I Wanna Hold Your Hand.* See Close-Up.

Record Events. "Cal Jam II," a one-day concert held in Ontario, Calif., on March 18 drew the top paying audience in the history of American rock music to the Ontario Speedway. About 250,000 listeners heard diverse aspects of popular music represented by Aerosmith, Foreigner, Santana, Heart, Ted Nugent, Bob Welch, and Dave Mason.

The blending of country music with pop-rock ingredients and melodic nonrock arrangements helped generate a crossover—country to rock—success story. Led by Dolly Parton, this movement gained popularity in the big cities as well as in the rural areas traditionally associated with country music. Parton, with her inclination toward a pure pop-ballad style, and Willie Nelson, a ragged-sounding "renegade" who blended country with

rock, became popular all over the United States as radio stations became more willing to broadcast a variety of music styles.

Discothèque Music was also helped by this liberalized radio policy. Disco music was also heard in an increasing number of clubs around the country, though New York City remained a focal point for the most imaginative developments. Disco patrons bought the records they danced to and created an expanded market for single records. Some of these became *platinum singles*—that is, they sold 2 million copies. Among the 1978 platinum artists were Andy Gibb, the Bee Gees, John Travolta, Olivia Newton-John, Debby Boone, and Queen.

Other Performers. The first anniversary of Elvis Presley's death, on August 16, produced an outburst of radio-show tributes, memorial concerts, and a fan-club convention in Las Vegas, Nev. RCA continued to issue a number of Presley albums.

Nostalgia accounted for the reissue of several Beatles albums. This trend resulted partly from the release of a sound-track LP from *Sgt. Pepper's Lonely Hearts Club Band,* a motion picture with music featuring the Bee Gees and Peter Frampton. The film whetted the public's appetite for the original "Sgt. Pepper" album by the Beatles.

Johnny Mathis, a long-established, middle-of-the-road popular-song stylist, whose recording ca-

Recordings by the Bee Gees—Maurice, Robin, and Barry Gibb—were five of the Top Ten hits in March. "Night Fever" and "Stayin' Alive" headed the list.

The Sound Of Money

Forget about basketball, baseball, and the other professional sports that pay their stars six-figure salaries. Forget about chairmen of large corporations and their salaries and stock options. In 1978, the sound of money belonged to the sound of recordings.

Disk stars – particularly songwriter-producer-performer stars such as the Bee Gees, former Beatle Paul McCartney, and Stevie Wonder – were making more money than were superstars in any other area of show business. Marlon Brando's $4-million-a-picture fee was, comparatively speaking, chicken feed – as was Muhammad Ali's $3.5-million take from his February bout with Leon Spinks. Disk star Stevie Wonder's guarantee from Tamla-Motown Records was $13 million in artist royalties. He earned additional millions from his publisher-songwriter royalties and stage performances. And Stevie Wonder was but one among many.

Such superincomes came largely from supersales. Unit record sales in 1977 were 698.2 million – 18 per cent higher than in 1976. Record albums alone accounted for $2.2 billion in 1977. Sixty-eight LP's became *platinum records* – a recording-industry designation for any album that sells a million or more copies. At least 24 platinums were multimillion sellers, including Fleetwood Mac's "Rumours," which sold a staggering 9-million copies in the United States alone. The late Elvis Presley and Kiss – a far-out rock group – each had three platinum LP's. Barry Manilow, Barbra Streisand, Linda Ronstadt, Shaun Cassidy, Kansas, Neil Diamond, James Taylor, Ted Nugent, and Bob Seger had two each.

Total worldwide sales in 23 countries reached an incredible $8.6 billion in 1977, with the United States as the front-runner, followed by Japan, West Germany, Russia, and Great Britain. The U.S. share of the financial pie was a phenomenal $3.5-billion – a figure 28 per cent higher than that of 1976. According to the Recording Industry Association of America (RIAA), dollar volume would soar even higher in 1978.

The industry's overall receipts dwarfed the box-office take of the legitimate theater; it outstripped motion-picture industry receipts by almost a cool billion; and professional sports weren't even in the running. And, although official RIAA figures for 1978 would not be compiled until 1979, key industry sources were confident that skyrocketing sales would make 1978 the best year in history.

As of October 1978, the all-time best-selling album was "Saturday Night Fever," the sound-track LP from John Travolta's smash box-office film, produced by Robert Stigwood on the RSO label. The two-record set, which cost $12.98, sold more than 23 million copies in the United States and abroad. Singles from the album, including "Night Fever," "Stayin' Alive," and "More Than A Woman," were also best sellers around the world in 1978. And, during the summer, "Grease" – another movie sound-track album produced by Stigwood on his RSO label – became an international hit, largely because of its stars, Travolta and Olivia Newton-John. Nor did an upsurge in the popularity of the newer stars entirely displace the older ones. Singles and albums by the late Elvis Presley were on the best-seller charts throughout 1978. In the year following Presley's death in August 1977, an estimated 200 million of his records were sold, giving him a grand total of 850 million sales.

Heretofore, it was assumed that buyers of contemporary music such as rock and soul – 62 per cent of all disk sales – stopped buying when they reached their 20s. However, according to three separate studies, the largest group of record buyers today is not teen-aged. Young adults in their 20s account for 36 per cent of sales; over-30s, about 40 per cent; and teen-agers, less than 25 per cent.

The recording industry had indeed come a long way from its beginnings as a simple cylindrical tinfoil device that Thomas A. Edison invented in 1877 after investing about $18 in labor and material. For the industry as a whole, the world in 1978 had become one gigantic loudspeaker that poured forth a universal sound. Only the distant planets were as yet unaffected.   June Bundy Csida

A browsing record buyer

reer had been in a slump, enjoyed rejuvenation as a result of a duet recorded with a relatively unknown singer, Deniece Williams. The tune, "Too Much Too Little Too Late," also produced a hit album of the same name and was followed by another collaboration, "That's What Friends Are For."

The Classical Field received a major boost from the abundance of "space" movies, which led to a recording by Zubin Mehta and the Los Angeles Philharmonic of an album of themes from *Star Wars* and *Close Encounters of the Third Kind.* The orchestra performed these compositions at such large amphitheaters as the Hollywood Bowl.

Bruce Springsteen, back after an absence of two years, produced what was considered by many experts to be a definitive rock album, "Darkness on the Edge of Town." Not long after its release, it was registered by the Recording Industry Association of America as a platinum album, indicating sales of 1 million copies.

At year's end, Billy Joel was the most popular male singer in the United States. Two albums, "The Stranger" and "52nd Street," together sold 6 million copies in the United States alone in 1978.

Other leading performers were Steely Dan, who created a mildly jazz-flavored instrumental sound with their platinum album "Aja," and Bonny Tyler, a husky-voiced British singer who became one of Great Britain's most fashionable musical exports. Gerry Rafferty, with an album called "City to City," and Michael Johnson, in an album bearing simply his name, both represented a relatively soft vocal style. Patti Smith, one of the few survivors of 1977's "new wave" movement, which died out in the United States for lack of talent, became a surprising favorite on Top 40 radio. Frankie Valli, separated from the Four Seasons, emerged as a solo vocalist with the title tune from the motion picture *Grease,* which in October became the number-one soundtrack album.

Andy Gibb endeared himself to young listeners with his simple, basic vocal style. David Gates, the former lead singer with Bread, also had substantial individual success. Kenny Loggins and Jim Messina went their own way, and Loggins' album "Night Watch" rose high on the charts.

The Jazz Scene. Jazz enjoyed one of the most prestigious evenings of its eventful career on June 18 when President Jimmy Carter invited more than 30 musicians to perform a miniature history of jazz on the lawn at the White House. The President lauded jazz as the art form born in America. The concert included performances by 95-year-old ragtime pianist Eubie Blake; saxophonists Benny Carter, Stan Getz, and Illinois Jacquet; and pianists Dick Hyman, McCoy Tyner, Herbie Hancock, Chick Corea, and Mary Lou Williams.

Another jazz pioneer celebrated an anniversary on January 17. Benny Goodman and his orchestra

Versatile performer Donna Summer, whose 1978 hit song was "MacArthur Park Suite," has sung on records, television, film, and stage.

played a concert at Carnegie Hall in New York City, where they had broken the classical-music-only rule 40 years earlier, on Jan. 16, 1938. Vibraphonist Lionel Hampton and singer Martha Tilton were the only original band members to appear in 1978.

The first annual Women's Jazz Festival was staged in March in Kansas City, Kans., to salute the role of female performers in jazz. It featured pianists Marian McPartland and Mary Lou Williams, singer Betty Carter, and the big band led by pianist Toshiko Akiyoshi and her husband, saxophonist Lew Tabackin.

A tendency toward a return to acoustic jazz and away from electronic fusion sounds was noted in 1978. Irakere, a group from Havana, Cuba, came to New York City, played in the Newport Jazz Festival, and made an LP for CBS. The band played a mixture of jazz, rock, and Afro-Cuban rhythms.

Stan Kenton returned to the music scene in January after a serious illness, but broke up his band in August. He said he hoped to resume playing in 1979. Don Ellis also disbanded his group because of illness. Other big-band veterans such as Count Basie, Woody Herman, and Mercer Ellington — leading the orchestra he inherited from his father — remained popular.　　Leonard Feather and Eliot Tiegel

See also AWARDS AND PRIZES; RECORDINGS. In WORLD BOOK, see JAZZ; POPULAR MUSIC; ROCK MUSIC.

NABER, JOHN (1956-   ), the United States swimmer who won four gold medals and one silver at the 1976 Olympic Games in Montreal, Canada, was awarded the James E. Sullivan Memorial Award in February 1978. The award is presented annually by the Amateur Athletic Union (AAU) to the outstanding amateur athlete in the United States on the basis of character and achievements the previous year.

Naber set world records in the Olympic 100-meter and 200-meter backstroke events. He also swam on U.S. Olympic relay teams that set world records in Montreal in the 400-meter medley relay and the 800-meter free-style relay.

Naber won his first national title in 1973 at the AAU's short-course swimming championship in Cincinnati, Ohio. His first world record was in the 100-meter backstroke at the 1976 U.S. Olympic Trials in Long Beach, Calif.

When Naber retired from competitive swimming in 1977, he had set 16 records and still held the world marks in both the 100- and 200-meter backstroke. His 200-meter backstroke time of 1 minute 59.19 seconds broke the so-called 2-minute barrier. During his career, Naber won 15 AAU titles and 10 National Collegiate Athletic Association titles.

John Naber was born on Jan. 20, 1956, in Evanston, Ill. After graduation from the University of Southern California in 1977, he joined Walt Disney Productions as a marketing trainee.   Madelyn Krzak

Namibia – African Storm Center

NAMIBIA suffered a setback in its struggle for independence on Sept. 20, 1978, when South Africa rejected a United Nations (UN) election plan as part of its transition to independence. Formerly called South West Africa, Namibia has been ruled by South Africa since 1920 and was scheduled to become independent during 1978.

The major obstacle to independence was a dispute between South Africa and Namibian black nationalists over the conduct of elections leading to independence. The South West Africa People's Organization (SWAPO), the strongest political party representing Namibia's black majority, insisted on outside supervision of the elections and the prior withdrawal of all South African troops.

South Africa had been fighting SWAPO guerrillas for control of Namibia for more than 10 years, and feared that, once in power, SWAPO would permit black nationalist guerrillas from South Africa to use Namibia as a base. The two have a common border.

UN Intervention. Representatives of the five Western members of the UN Security Council – Canada, France, Great Britain, the United States, and West Germany – drafted a plan for UN-supervised elections. The plan called for a cease-fire, reduction of South African troops in Namibia from about 18,000 to 1,500, and confinement of SWAPO and South African forces during the election campaign. South Africa accepted this formula on April 25, SWAPO agreed on July 12, and the proposal was endorsed by the UN Security Council on July 27.

A 50-member UN transition team arrived in Namibia on August 6. It recommended that a 7,500-member peacekeeping force be deployed and elections scheduled for April 1979. South Africa rejected this plan on September 20, however, because it felt that the large size of the UN force as well as the long period before the elections would increase the chance of a SWAPO victory. South Africa decided instead to hold elections in December for an assembly to draft Namibia's constitution.

The Election. UN representatives went to South Africa in mid-October to try to persuade South African leaders to accept the UN plan. The leaders agreed to allow UN supervision of future elections, but insisted on holding the interim elections from December 4 to 8. SWAPO boycotted the elections, allowing the Democratic Turnhalle Alliance (DTA), the South African-backed party, to win 82 per cent of the vote. The DTA, a coalition of moderate blacks, persons of mixed race, and whites, lost its most influential black leader when Clemens Kapuuo was assassinated in March.   John D. Esseks

See also AFRICA (Facts in Brief Table); SOUTH AFRICA; UNITED NATIONS (UN). In WORLD BOOK, see SOUTH WEST AFRICA.

NATIONAL DEFENSE. See ARMED FORCES.

NAVON, YITZHAK (1921-   ), was inaugurated as the fifth president of Israel on May 29, 1978. Navon is the first member of the Sephardic community — Jews of Spanish, Portuguese, or Middle Eastern origin — to serve in the post.

Navon was born on April 19, 1921, the son of Yosef and Miriam Navon. His father, a teacher and scribe, was a member of a distinguished Sephardic family that has lived in Jerusalem for almost 300 years. Navon studied Arabic and Hebrew literature at the Hebrew University of Jerusalem. He served from 1946 to 1948 as head of the Arab Department of Haganah, the outlawed Jewish militia group active in the Israeli struggle for independence.

After Israel came into existence in 1948, Navon served in several diplomatic posts, and he was an aide to Prime Minister David Ben-Gurion from 1952 to 1963. From 1963 to 1965, he served in the Education and Culture Ministry as chief of the Department of Culture. Navon was elected to the *Knesset*, Israel's parliament, in 1965. He remained in the Knesset until his election as president.

Navon has written short stories and a prize-winning play. He and his wife, Ophira, live in Jerusalem with their two children.   Edward G. Nash

NAVY. See ARMED FORCES.

NEBRASKA. See STATE GOVERNMENT.

NEPAL. See ASIA.

NETHERLANDS. The center-right minority coalition government of Prime Minister Andreas A.M. Van Agt faced revolts in 1978 over spending cuts and its neutron-bomb policy.

A \$5.8-billion plan to stimulate investment went into effect in August, while Parliament considered plans to cut spending by \$4.5 billion over three years. Public employees struck on June 22 over a plan to keep their pay 1 per cent below that of workers in the private sector. Buses, streetcars, and trains stopped running, and electricity and gas supplies were reduced. On June 26, some 60,000 public employees marched to Parliament to demonstrate. The largest trade-union federation criticized the plans because they lacked details on creating jobs. The unions were also angry about the lack of progress on reforms. The previous government had promised worker participation in management and a program of sharing excess profits, in return for wage restraint.

Neutron Bomb. Minister of Defense Roelof Kruisinga resigned on March 4 because the Cabinet did not oppose production of the neutron bomb. Parliament adopted a motion opposing the bomb on March 8. Several members of Van Agt's Christian Democrat Party voted with the Socialists and Democrats '66. Van Agt wanted to remain uncommitted on the bomb. Some 50,000 persons paraded through Amsterdam on March 19 to demonstrate against the

Armed police check a South Moluccan's credentials in Assen, the Netherlands, at the June trial of three South Moluccan terrorists.

neutron bomb. The demonstration ended a two-day rally attended by people from 28 countries.

Folkerts Extradited. The Supreme Court ruled on May 8 that suspected West German Red Army Faction terrorist Knut Folkerts could not be extradited to West Germany in connection with the 1977 kidnapping and murder of industrialist Hanns-Martin Schleyer. The court cited the political nature of the offense. A lower court ruled on September 7 that he could be extradited in connection with the 1977 bombing of a government building in Karlsruhe, West Germany. He was extradited on October 17, apparently because he and two other imprisoned terrorist suspects went on a hunger strike. Folkerts was scheduled to return to the Netherlands for a court hearing on his appeal of the September 7 extradition decision.

Moluccan Siege. Marines stormed the provincial administration building in Assen on March 14 to free 70 hostages held by South Moluccan terrorists who want their home islands to be independent of Indonesia. The siege came as the government was talking with Moluccan leaders, preparing a program that would improve housing, education, and employment prospects for Moluccans living in the Netherlands. Kenneth Brown

See also EUROPE (Facts in Brief Table). In WORLD BOOK, see NETHERLANDS.

NEVADA. See STATE GOVERNMENT.

NEW BRUNSWICK. Premier Richard B. Hatfield's Conservative administration won its third consecutive term in a provincial election on Oct. 23, 1978, though it lost three seats to the Liberal opposition. In 1974, the Conservatives won 33 seats in the 58-seat legislature to the Liberals' 25. The recent election brought the standing to 30-28, each party gaining about 44 per cent of the popular vote.

The Liberals campaigned under Joseph Daigle, chosen on May 6 to succeed Robert Higgins, who resigned when his charges of government interference in a 1973 police investigation were found by a judicial inquiry to be unwarranted. Daigle was the second Liberal leader to be chosen from among the French-speaking Acadians in the province.

A budget revealed on April 4 that the Hatfield government had been forced to go back on a 1974 election promise that it would not raise taxes. A sales tax on building materials was reintroduced and taxes on cigarettes and tobacco were raised. The budget forecast a deficit of $95.2 million on total spending of $1.44 billion, which included $180.8-million for capital projects. The legislature passed 70 bills in 16 weeks of debate. David M. L. Farr

See also CANADA. In WORLD BOOK, see NEW BRUNSWICK.

NEW HAMPSHIRE. See STATE GOVERNMENT.
NEW JERSEY. See NEWARK; STATE GOV'T.
NEW MEXICO. See STATE GOVERNMENT.

NEW ORLEANS. Ernest N. Morial, the first black mayor of New Orleans, was sworn in on May 1, 1978. In his inauguration speech, the new mayor told listeners that the city's white majority need not fear reverse discrimination. He promised to run a "colorless" office.

Morial, a civil rights activist, defeated a large field of candidates, both black and white. He succeeded Moon Landrieu, who had often served as a spokesman for big-city mayors. See MORIAL, ERNEST N.

City Workers Strike. The city's 328 garbage collectors walked out on July 18 to protest a shortage of garbage trucks in good repair. The strike ended on July 21 after Morial threatened the workers with disciplinary action.

New Orleans' 4,200 teachers failed to show up for the opening day of school on August 30 after the United Teachers of New Orleans voted to strike rather than accept a 4 per cent pay increase. The teacher's union had asked for a 9 per cent increase.

Police patrolled the city's 140 public schools during the walkout to prevent harassment of substitute teachers and supervisors who kept some of the schools open. The strike ended after the union and the school board reached a settlement on September 11 allowing for a 7 per cent increase.

Flood Disaster. The New Orleans metropolitan area was declared a disaster area by President Jimmy

Ernest N. Morial, first black mayor of New Orleans, right, greets his predecessor, Moon Landrieu, at the inauguration on May 1.

Carter after the region was hit by almost 10 inches (25.4 centimeters) of rain on May 3. The storm, which produced the city's worst flooding in 51 years, caused six deaths and an estimated $160 million in property damage. Swollen floodwaters were 5 feet (1.5 meters) deep on some roadways.

Economy and Population. New Orleans had a 7.6 per cent unemployment rate at midyear, but residential construction in the city was up 13 per cent during the first five months of 1978. A report released on November 18 by the U.S. Bureau of the Census indicated that the city's population fell 2.1 per cent during the period from 1970 to 1976, and that New Orleans dropped from 19th to 20th place on the list of the most populous U.S. cities. A census report released earlier in the year indicated that New Orleans was the nation's 37th most crowded city, with 556 persons per square mile (215 per square kilometer).

The Amtrak board of directors agreed on December 13 to take over operation of the *Southern Crescent,* one of the few remaining old-fashioned luxury trains, from the Southern Railway Company. The *Southern Crescent,* which runs between Washington, D.C., and New Orleans, had lost some $36 million since 1971.
James M. Banovetz

See also CITY. In WORLD BOOK, see NEW ORLEANS.

NEW YORK. See NEW YORK CITY; STATE GOV'T.

President Jimmy Carter waves to New Yorkers after
signing a bill that authorizes $1.65 billion in
federal loan guarantees for the city on August 8.

NEW YORK CITY received help in its continuing effort to stave off bankruptcy when President Jimmy Carter signed a bill on Aug. 8, 1978, to give the city $1.65 billion in federal loan guarantees over four years. The measure, which included permission to use $325 million of the authorization for short-term cash needs during the first six months it is in effect, was enacted to replace a direct federal loan program that expired on June 30. During signing ceremonies held on the front portico of New York City Hall, President Carter said that if the city fulfills its commitments, the new guarantee program "will not cost the taxpayer a cent."

Balancing the Budget. Mayor Edward I. Koch, who took office on January 1, made his first budget proposal to the New York City Council on April 26. The budget, approved on June 28 for the fiscal year beginning on July 1, called for austerity in spending and a reduction of about 3,000 city jobs. The $13.5-billion budget, which depended on federal and state funds to supply about half of its revenue, developed a $149-million operating deficit in September when a sizable cutback in federal and state aid was projected. In an attempt to cut spending, Koch ordered a freeze on the hiring and promotion of city employees.

The new budget represented the first stage of a four-year plan to achieve a balanced budget in 1982 by eliminating up to 24,000 city jobs and reducing

municipal services. New York City needs a balanced budget to restore its credit rating, which has been revoked since 1975.

A Newspaper Strike, which took two of New York City's major newspapers out of circulation for almost three months and a third for two months, began on August 9 as a protest over management plans to reduce the number of pressmen. Although the *New York Post* resumed publication on October 5, after agreeing to accept whatever settlement was reached, *The New York Times* and the *Daily News* did not resume publishing until November 6. The *Daily News* had also been off the stands from June 13 to 17, during a strike by The Newspaper Guild, a union of editorial workers and other newspaper employees. See NEWSPAPER.

A report issued by the Bureau of the Census in December estimated that New York's population had fallen to its lowest level since 1930, reaching 7,312,181. The city's population stood at 6,930,446 in 1930, but had risen to 7,895,563 by 1970.

New Yorkers weathered the heaviest snows in 31 years, with a total accumulation for the season of over 50 inches (75 centimeters). Severe storms dumped 13.6 inches (34 centimeters) of snow on January 20 and 17.7 inches (45 centimeters) on February 6-7.
James M. Banovetz

See also CITY. In WORLD BOOK, see NEW YORK CITY.

NEW ZEALAND voters re-elected the National Party government, but by only a slight margin, on Nov. 25, 1978. The result was a vote of diminished confidence in Prime Minister Robert D. Muldoon's National Party government policy of reducing inflation in spite of increasing unemployment. In October, the inflation rate was 11 per cent, and there were 40,000 unemployed.

The budget presented on June 1 was intended to stimulate economic activity. It reduced taxes for lower-income workers. It also provided farmers with cash payments per head of sheep and cattle and gave them further help with minimum prices. Funds for education, health, the arts, and social welfare were increased.

Foreign Relations. Trade with the European Community (EC or Common Market) and Japan was a problem. The EC's refusal to buy more of New Zealand's butter and cheese, and fears about future EC decisions on sheep meat, caused concern.

Relations with Japan were strained after the crew of a Japanese trawler was arrested on January 25 for using fishing nets with undersized mesh in New Zealand's commercial fishing zone. On March 11, Prime Minister Muldoon accused Japan of "imperialism" for seeking to sell Japanese goods in New Zealand without buying any products, especially New Zealand beef. But by June 30 the two governments had concluded a trade agreement.

New Zealand and Australia agreed on March 19 to consult more closely on international legal matters and to coordinate the development of new industries in the two countries. They will set up a New Zealand-Australia Foundation and exchange visits of officials and parliamentary delegations.

Domestic Disputes included opposition to the restrictive abortion legislation passed in 1977. After several calls for repeal, amendments to the law were introduced in Parliament on May 17.

New Zealand's Family Proceedings Bill, introduced in Parliament on October 6, made the breakdown of marriage the sole ground for divorce. It also introduced new provisions for maintenance of wives and children.

A Human Rights Commission began investigating and mediating cases of discrimination and invasion of privacy on September 1. The commission also investigated complaints against trade unions and professional and trade associations.

New Zealand suffered a net loss in population of 42,116 by migration in the year ended March 1978, compared with 33,690 in 1977 and 17,862 in 1976. A former New Zealander, Naomi James, returned in triumph to Dartmouth, England, on June 8 after breaking Sir Francis Chichester's 1967 record for a solo round-the-world sailing voyage by two days. James made the trip in 272 days.   J. D. B. Miller

See also ASIA (Facts in Brief Table). In WORLD BOOK, see NEW ZEALAND.

NEWARK. Kenneth A. Gibson won a third term as mayor of Newark on May 9, 1978. Campaigning for another four-year term, Gibson used the theme "He put it all together" and symbolized his effort with a picture of black and white hands clasping. Gibson became the first black mayor of a major Northeastern industrial city when he was first elected to the office in 1970. He became the first black person to be elected president of the U.S. Conference of Mayors in 1976.

Quality of Life. Newark was named the neediest of 39 cities surveyed by the Congressional Budget Office in a study of urban problems released on September 10. The study was based on a composite index of social need derived from unemployment and per capita income data. Most of the largest U.S. cities were among those surveyed.

Newark was also listed as one of the nation's most rapidly shrinking cities in a U.S. Census Bureau report released on November 18. The bureau estimated Newark's 1976 population at 331,495, down 13.2 per cent from 1970. Only eight other U.S. cities suffered a more severe population loss.

Living costs for the overall Newark population rose only 5.5 per cent during the year ending in June 1978. Wage earners and clerical workers fared even better – their living costs rose only 4.9 per cent during the year ending in May. Food costs, though, rose 10 per cent in the latter period.

Residential construction in the area for the first five months of the year was 21.7 per cent above that for the same period in 1977. Construction started on 1,848 units during that period.

Other Developments. Construction began on a new 26-story, $65-million headquarters for the Public Service Electric and Gas Company. The new building will be the first significant addition to Newark's skyline in 20 years.

A Civil Aeronautics Board judge ruled on August 23 that World Airways, a West Coast charter airline, should be allowed to make low-cost, scheduled flights between Newark and the California cities of Oakland and Ontario-Long Beach. The airline also proposed eliminating the airport ticket counters for the flights and utilizing, instead, the Ticketron system for selling seats on the flights.

Newark was hit with two crippling snowstorms early in the year. The first came on January 20, dropping more than 1 foot (30 centimeters) of snow on the city and forcing schools, businesses, and Newark's airport to close. The second storm, on February 6 and 7, dumped record snows on the area.

Twenty wildcat strikers at the New York Bulk and Foreign Mail Center in New Jersey were fired on July 23 after they failed to obey an injunction issued by a U.S. District Court ordering them back to work. They were protesting a contract proposal made by the U.S. Postal Service.   James M. Banovetz

See also CITY. In WORLD BOOK, see NEWARK.

NEWFOUNDLAND continued to attract world attention in 1978 because of the hunting of baby seals on the rugged ice fields of the Labrador coast. An important source of income to local residents, the hunt was condemned by a 1977 United States congressional resolution. Congressman Leo J. Ryan (D., Calif.) visited the hunt in March and became engaged in a heated altercation with Newfoundland's Rural Development Minister John Lundrigan. Lundrigan suggested that American attention should be directed to the Pribilof Islands off Alaska, where the United States permits the slaughter of 30,000 to 40,000 seals.

Two members of Premier Frank Moores's cabinet resigned on August 7 after they were linked with alleged wrongdoing in the handling of Public Works Department contracts. A judicial inquiry was set up to look into works-department spending.

The legislature erupted in a stormy session on May 12 when 12 members of the Liberal opposition were expelled from the house for three days for accusing Moores of providing misleading information concerning government building contracts.

The budget of March 17 saw the provincial sales tax increased to 11 per cent, the highest rate in Canada. Unemployment in the province was twice the national average. David M. L. Farr

See also CANADA. In WORLD BOOK, see NEWFOUNDLAND.

The *Chicago Daily News* ends its 102-year career with the March 4, 1978, editions. Its demise left the Windy City with no afternoon newspaper.

NEWSPAPER. Labor disputes and unfavorable court decisions tormented the United States newspaper industry in 1978. New York City's three major dailies, *The New York Times,* the *New York Post,* and the *Daily News,* stopped their presses for 88 consecutive days when more than 1,500 pressmen began picketing their plants on August 9. *Post* publisher Rupert Murdoch scooped his competitors by tentatively settling two weeks ahead of them and briefly introducing a Sunday edition. Final contracts guaranteed the pressmen their jobs — jeopardized through new technology — and gave publishers the right to reduce employee ranks through attrition.

At least 20 strikes and lockouts plagued other papers across the United States. Employee walkouts also shut down papers in Canada, England, and West Germany. At year-end, the Montreal *Star* had not published since June 13, and the Vancouver *Sun* and *Province* had been out since November 1. *The Times* of London announced on November 30 that it would suspend publication until early 1979, or until solid labor agreements could be reached.

Court Rulings. The Supreme Court of the United States shocked the newspaper world on May 31 by ruling, 5 to 3, that police could conduct court-approved searches of newspaper offices. The case arose from a police search of the *Stanford Daily,* the Stanford University student newspaper, in 1971.

New York Times reporter Myron A. Farber made headlines when he refused to give his notes to the court during the murder trial of Mario Jascalevich, a New Jersey physician charged with giving five patients overdoses of curare. Farber's investigative series led to Jascalevich's indictment. Farber served 38 days in jail and *The New York Times* paid $285,000 in fines for failure to obey the court order. Jascalevich was found innocent on October 24.

Closings, Mergers, and Sales. The 102-year-old evening *Chicago Daily News* closed its doors on March 4 after collecting 15 Pulitzer Prizes. The *New York Trib,* which began morning publication on January 9, disappeared from newsstands in April.

Only 42 dailies changed hands, but more than 130 nondaily newspapers did. Gannet Company Incorporated agreed on May 8 to merge with Combined Communications Corporation in a $370-million stock-exchange transaction. In January, Gannett took over the *Wilmington* (Del.) *News Journal* for $60 million in cash. Time Incorporated bought the *Washington Star* from Joe L. Allbritton in February for a reported $20 million.

United States readers spent more than $4 billion for daily and Sunday newspapers in 1977, boosting circulation figures to 62 million during the week and 52 million on Sundays. Advertising revenues climbed to $9 billion during the first nine months of 1978, up 15.1 per cent. Celeste H. Huenergard

In WORLD BOOK, see JOURNALISM; NEWSPAPER.

NICARAGUA suffered through a year of rioting, general strikes, and open warfare between guerrillas and government troops in 1978. The murder on January 10 of Pedro Joaquin Chamorro, an opposition newspaper editor, touched off the violence, which was aimed at ousting President Anastasio Somoza Debayle. Somoza finally bowed to international pressure on November 30 and agreed to a national plebiscite to decide his future.

Somoza had steadfastly refused to resign throughout the year. In March and April, the turmoil mounted. About 80 per cent of Nicaragua's students went on strike, occupying 48 churches and 50 schools. Then, on August 22, members of the Sandinista National Liberation Front touched off an even more violent round of clashes by capturing the National Palace in Managua while the Chamber of Deputies was in session and holding 1,500 hostages. They got a $500,000 cash ransom, the release of 59 political prisoners, and safe conduct to Panama.

In September, guerrillas and armed youths seized the towns of León, Chinandega, and Esteli. Somoza's troops recaptured them, but the business districts were in ruins. Everett G. Martin

See also LATIN AMERICA. In WORLD BOOK, see NICARAGUA; SOMOZA.

NIGER. See AFRICA.

NIGERIA drafted a new Constitution in 1978 that provides for a nationally elected president, an independent judiciary, a 450-member House of Representatives, and a 95-member Senate. To ensure that future presidents have broad national support, the new Constitution requires that the winning candidate receive both a majority of the total vote cast and 25 per cent of the vote cast in at least 13 of Nigeria's 19 states.

The Federal Military Government (FMG) reaffirmed its pledge to hand power over to elected officials by Oct. 1, 1979. In preparation for the 1979 elections, the FMG in September lifted a 12-year ban on political parties. By September 22, three parties had formed.

United States President Jimmy Carter visited Nigeria from March 31 to April 3. Carter met with Nigerian head of state Olusegun Obasanjo, who asked the United States to prohibit new investments in South Africa.

A serious decline in oil earnings, Nigeria's major source of investment capital, early in the year jeopardized the completion of many projects. On March 31, Obasanjo announced policies designed to lessen Nigeria's dependence on oil and to concentrate on manufacturing and agriculture. John D. Esseks

See also AFRICA (Facts in Brief Table). In WORLD BOOK, see NIGERIA.

Nigerian workers examine a sample of crude oil taken from a well off the coast. Nigeria ranks among the world's leading suppliers of oil.

NIXON, RICHARD MILHOUS (1913-   ), returned to public life in 1978 after living in seclusion at his estate in San Clemente, Calif., since his resignation from the presidency of the United States in 1974. Nixon celebrated the publication of his memoirs, continued his legal battle over possession of the Watergate tapes, appeared at public and political events, traveled abroad, and demonstrated that he was still a controversial figure.

Nixon held a party to mark the publication of *RN: The Memoirs of Richard Nixon* in May. The book, Nixon's account of his presidency, remained on national best-seller lists for months. Excerpts from the book appeared in *Newsweek* and *The New York Times* and other newspapers.

In September, Nixon signed a contract with Warner Books, the publisher that paid $2 million for world-distribution rights to his memoirs, to write another book for publication late in 1979. At his first press conference in more than four years, he said the new book would deal with America's role in the world during the rest of the century.

Fight for the Tapes. The Supreme Court of the United States ruled on April 18 that recording companies have no constitutional right to reproduce and sell the Nixon tapes dealing with the Watergate scandal. The court also said that anyone wanting sound reproductions of the tapes could apply to the General Services Administration (GSA) for permission, in accordance with the Presidential Recordings Act of 1974. The decision applied only to the 30 tapes of 22 hours of White House conversations that were played at the Watergate trial. Nixon continued to challenge the GSA in the courts, demanding the tapes as his personal possessions.

Ending His Seclusion, Nixon left San Clemente several times in 1978. He was in Washington, D.C., for the first time in 3½ years to attend memorial services for Senator Hubert H. Humphrey on January 15. He delivered his first public speech since leaving office near Hyden, Ky., on July 2, at the dedication of a recreation center named in his honor.

Nixon also visited England and France in late November. He appeared on French television and spoke at Oxford University in England, where he vowed to "speak out on the great issues affecting the world." Several hundred students, including scores of Americans, threw eggs and tried to drown out his remarks. Ten students were arrested.

Nixon also hosted two large gatherings at his home – a reception for 273 former Vietnam prisoners of war in May and a $250-per-person fundraising party for Orange County, California, Republicans in July.   Carol L. Thompson

See also LITERATURE. In WORLD BOOK, see NIXON, RICHARD MILHOUS; WATERGATE.

Former President Richard M. Nixon visits Hyden, Ky., in July in one of his first formal public appearances since his resignation in 1974.

NOBEL PRIZES for peace, literature, economics, and various sciences were awarded in 1978 by the Norwegian *Storting* (parliament) and the Royal Academy of Science, the Caroline Institute, and the Swedish Academy of Literature, all in Stockholm, Sweden.

Peace Prize was shared by Egypt's President Anwar al-Sadat, 60, and Israel's Prime Minister Menachem Begin, 65, for their negotiations to end the Arab-Israeli conflict. The Nobel committee said in its citation that it "wishes not only to honor actions already performed in the service of peace, but also encourage further efforts to work out practical solutions which can give reality to those hopes of a lasting peace as they have been kindled by the agreements." The committee also praised President Jimmy Carter's "great role" in the negotiations.

Literature Prize was awarded to Isaac Bashevis Singer, 74, a Polish-born American who lives in New York City and still writes in his first language, Yiddish. The novelist and short-story writer, whose portraits of a bygone life in prewar Poland have won him a wide audience, has published English translations of eight novels – his most recent is *Shosha* – seven short-story collections, and 11 children's books. He was cited for his "impassioned narrative art which, with roots in Polish-Jewish tradition, brings universal human conditions to life."

Economics Prize went to Herbert A. Simon, 62, a professor of economics at Carnegie-Mellon University in Pittsburgh. He has done work in statistics, applied mathematics, and business administration and is the author of the classic business text *Administrative Behavior* (1947). He was cited for his pioneering work in challenging the traditional economic theory that businesses seek to maximize profits or satisfaction while consumers tend to maximize their personal satisfaction. Simon says that such behavior is not possible. Individuals and organizations cannot know what decision will maximize their profits or satisfaction and can only make the best choice for the immediate circumstances. He labeled such behavior "satisfying."

Chemistry Prize was given to Peter Mitchell, 58, a researcher at Glynn Research Laboratories near Cornwall, England. He received the award for his explanations of how animals and plants convert nutrition into useful energy. Mitchell has pursued the precise chemical reactions involved in moving nutrients into cells for 20 years.

Physics Prize was shared by two U.S. scientists and a Russian. The Americans, Arno A. Penzias, 45, and Robert W. Wilson, 42, both work at the Bell Telephone Laboratories in Holmdel, N.J. They were cited for their 1965 discovery of the so-called cosmic microwave background radiation while testing a radio telescope and receiver system in support of satellite communications development. They showed that this radiation was heat remaining from

Polish-born Isaac Bashevis Singer, who writes short stories and novels in Yiddish, won the 1978 Nobel Prize for Literature.

the "big bang" of some 15 billion years ago. Their discovery helped to confirm the big bang theory of the creation of the universe. The Russian, Peter Leonidovich Kapitza, 84, long considered one of the world's most eminent physicists, was honored for his pioneering work in atomic and space science. He once worked with Sir Ernest Rutherford in Cambridge, England, where he discovered superfluidity in liquid helium and a number of magnetic effects in other elements. Kapitza achieved worldwide fame when he refused Russian dictator Joseph Stalin's request that he help develop atomic weapons for Russia.

Physiology or Medicine Prize also went to three people – microbiologist Daniel Nathans, 49, and Hamilton O. Smith, 47, of Baltimore's Johns Hopkins University Medical School; and Werner Arber, 49, of the University of Basel in Switzerland. The Americans were cited for their work with restriction enzymes, special molecules that trigger chemical reactions in genes. Arber discovered these enzymes. Restriction enzymes act as "chemical knives," cutting genes into clearly defined fragments so that scientists can study their nature.   Foster Stockwell

In WORLD BOOK, see NOBEL PRIZES.

NORTH ATLANTIC TREATY ORGANIZATION (NATO). See EUROPE.

NORTH CAROLINA. See STATE GOVERNMENT.

NORTH DAKOTA. See STATE GOVERNMENT.

NORTHERN IRELAND. Violence decreased in 1978, but the province was no nearer a long-term solution of its troubles. There were 591 shootings during the first nine months of the year, compared with 1,081 in 1977 and 10,628 at the height of the troubles in 1972. Sixty-seven persons were killed, compared with 112 in 1977 and 296 in 1976.

Great Britain's Secretary of State for Northern Ireland, Roy Mason, claimed on March 6 that the Irish Republican Army (IRA) was "operating in isolation and shunned by the vast majority of the people of Northern Ireland." Despite the security successes of the British Army and the Royal Ulster Constabulary (RUC), however, the IRA showed it was still dangerous. It claimed responsibility when a firebomb gutted the La Mons restaurant in Belfast's outskirts on February 17, killing 12 persons.

Sophisticated weaponry and military equipment continued to reach the IRA. The RUC confirmed on January 19 that U.S.-made M60 machine guns were used in an attack on two police vehicles. Sources in Belfast said in September that the IRA had acquired "electronic binoculars," military night-vision devices, stolen from a U.S. National Guard armory in Massachusetts.

Peace Talks designed to lead to *devolution* (home rule) began on Dec. 7, 1977, between the British government and representatives of the province's main political parties. But the talks halted abruptly on January 8, when Prime Minister Jack Lynch of the Republic of Ireland stated on radio that he had been assured by British Prime Minister James Callaghan that there would be no devolution without power-sharing on an equal basis between Ulster's Protestant and Roman Catholic communities.

Meanwhile, Secretary of State Mason held separate meetings with members of Northern Ireland's four main political parties. On April 19, Prime Minister Callaghan announced that the British government had accepted recommendations to increase the number of Ulster members of the British Parliament (MP's) from 12 to 17 after the next general election. As Callaghan's minority Labour government struggled on into the winter, the Ulster MP's met to discuss ways of minimizing their differences so as to extract the greatest concessions from the Labour Party in return for their votes in the House of Commons.

Memorial Ceremonies marking the 10th anniversary of various events starting the Irish troubles took place during 1978. On one occasion, Protestants and Catholics clashed in Londonderry on October 8 during demonstrations on the anniversary of the first civil rights march.   Ian Mather

See also EUROPE (Facts in Brief Table). In WORLD BOOK, see NORTHERN IRELAND.

Masked Irish Republican Army gunman armed with a U.S.-made M60 machine gun mans a roadblock during a parade in January in Londonderry.

NORTHWEST TERRITORIES. The first land-claim settlement with an Inuit (Eskimo) group in the Northwest Territories was signed on Oct. 31, 1978, by Indian Affairs Minister Hugh Faulkner and Sam Raddi, president of the Committee for the Original People's Entitlement (COPE). Ottawa agreed to pay $45 million to about 2,500 Inuit in the western Arctic over the years 1981 to 1994. The Inuit also received ownership with surface and subsurface rights to 4,200 square miles (10,900 square kilometers) surrounding six communities, and surface rights over an additional 32,000 square miles (82,900 square kilometers) of territory. In return, the Inuit group agreed to give up Aboriginal rights over 168,000 square miles (435,000 square kilometers) of land. COPE land is located in the Mackenzie River Delta adjoining the Beaufort Sea, where there has been oil and gas exploration.

Radioactive pieces of Cosmos 954, a Russian satellite, fell to earth near Great Slave Lake in January. Canadian authorities said the government would ask Russia to pay the costs of the search for radioactive material, estimated at $5 million.

The Arctic, the first bulk freighter in the world with icebreaking capabilities, was launched in June in Ontario. The 28,000-ton vessel will be used to transport mineral ores to Europe.   David M. L. Farr

See also CANADA. In WORLD BOOK, see NORTH-WEST TERRITORIES.

Gigantic oil-drilling platform heading for a North Sea site will help Norway deal with its towering international payments deficit.

NORWAY took steps against high inflation and a high foreign debt in 1978. It started the year with a foreign debt greater than 14 per cent of its gross national product (GNP). High wages had made exports fall, while antirecession measures had stimulated home demand, increasing imports. North Sea oil revenues were lighter than anticipated.

The government imposed a program on January 28 and 29 to discourage installment buying and bank loans and encourage savings. The government devalued its monetary unit, the krone, by 8 per cent against the other countries in the European *snake* (joint currency float) on February 10. After December discussions of a new European monetary system, Norway withdrew from the snake.

On September 15, the government froze prices and wages until 1980. A government policy statement said that private consumption must not grow; spending on schools, roads, hospitals, social reform, and pollution control will be postponed; state aid to industry will become more selective; only the lowest-paid workers can expect an increase in real disposable income over the next few years; and aid to developing countries will remain at 1 per cent of the GNP. The 1979 budget presented on October 5 anticipated a 0.5 per cent increase in non-oil and shipping revenues, no increase in private consumption, a small increase in public spending, and a doubling of the 1.3 per cent unemployment rate.

Swedish Partnership. The government agreed tentatively on May 22 to buy an interest in a new company that would own AB Volvo, Sweden's largest industrial firm and automaker. The company would have the right to search for North Sea oil and would establish industrial facilities in Norway. The two countries signed the agreement December 8.

Fisheries Pact. Norway and Russia signed a fisheries agreement on January 11, covering a 26,000-square-mile (67,000-square-kilometer) area in the Barents Sea. The pact lets other countries' trawlers fish in the area, subject to quotas fixed by Norway and Russia. The quota of Arctic cod for other countries in the Barents Sea was set for 1978 at 143,000 short tons (130,000 metric tons), of which 22,000 short tons (20,000 metric tons) may come from the disputed area. On March 2, Norway agreed with the European Community (EC or Common Market) on reciprocal fishing rights. Norwegians were allowed to take 324,000 short tons (294,000 metric tons) in EC waters in 1978. The EC quota in Norway's zone was 447,000 short tons (406,000 metric tons).

Russian merchant ships strained international relations by stopping in Norwegian waters. International law lets them pass through these waters, but forbids them to stop.   Kenneth Brown

See also EUROPE (Facts in Brief Table). In WORLD BOOK, see NORWAY.

NOVA SCOTIA. Premier Gerald A. Regan's Liberal administration, in power for eight years, was defeated by the Conservatives under John Buchanan in an election on Sept. 19, 1978, that surprised most observers. Conservative strength jumped from 12 to 31 seats in an expanded 52-seat chamber. The Liberals fell from 30 to 17 seats, and the New Democratic Party gained 1 seat to take 4. Four of Regan's ministers were defeated. There was little difference between Liberal and Conservative platforms, but the Conservatives undoubtedly benefited from the antigovernment mood expressed by voters across Canada. High electricity charges to consumers also hurt the Regan government. Buchanan, a Halifax lawyer, was sworn in on October 5.

Before the election, an active 12-week legislative session approved 84 bills. The budget, presented on March 3, estimated expenditures at $1.35 billion. After taking office, the Buchanan government disputed the former government's report of finances.

Federal and provincial governments agreed on January 23 to create and finance a Maritime Energy Corporation to study energy projects in the Atlantic area, including harnessing the extraordinary tides of the Bay of Fundy. David M. L. Farr

See also CANADA. In WORLD BOOK, see BAY OF FUNDY; NOVA SCOTIA.

NUCLEAR ENERGY. See ENERGY.

NUTRITION. Researchers at General Mills, Incorporated, in Minneapolis, Minn., noted in 1978 that the healthfulness of food has become an increasingly important concern of consumers. However, the traditional interests in cost, convenience, and taste are still important to them. The group, headed by G. Burton Brown, assistant director of marketing research, reached this conclusion after correlating 32 nutritional studies made by government agencies, industry, and educational institutions.

The typical shopper scored more than 50 per cent in one survey carried out by the Food and Drug Administration to assess the consumer's nutritional knowledge. A Department of Agriculture study showed similar results, though only 3 per cent of those polled answered all the questions correctly. Consumers scored highest on questions about food handling and storage, the four major food groups, and the function of nutrients in the milk and meat food groups. They were less knowledgeable about individual variations in nutritional needs and the nutrients contained in fruits, vegetables, and cereals.

The major concern of those polled in all the surveys was food additives. Many consumers appeared to believe additives decreased nutritional value of food.

The data showed that 50 per cent of parents check nutrient labels on packaged food, though the overall

Sidney Harris in The Wall Street Journal

"Two breakthroughs—imitation eggs made of
soybeans and imitation soybeans made of eggs."

consumer average was only 30 per cent. Protein ranked as the most desirable nutrient. Carbohydrates—especially starchy and sweet foods—ranked lowest.

Diet and Cancer. Ernest L. Wynder, president of the American Health Foundation, said in June that as many as half of all male cancer cases and one-third of those in women may be linked to nutrition. He told the third national conference on nutritional factors in cancer, sponsored by the National Cancer Institute and the American Cancer Society, that diets high in meat fats, for example, are correlated epidemiologically to cancers of the colon and rectum. High alcohol intake increases the risk of upper respiratory and digestive-tract cancers. Other researchers believe that the increased intake of foods high in vitamin C has led to the decline of stomach cancer among Americans.

The researchers downplayed food additives as cancer-causing agents. They believe that the overall American diet—high in fat, meat, and especially excess calories—plays a more important role in the incidence of cancer.

Ideal Weights. Although scientists generally accept the figures for ideal weight developed by insurance actuaries, Reubin Andres, clinical director of the National Institute of Aging in Bethesda, Md., has reinterpreted this data. In an April 1978 paper reviewing the development of the ideal weights, Andres noted various problems. His most significant criticism was the lack of standardization in insurance company methods of collecting data. Using better-controlled health studies made in Framingham, Mass.; Baltimore; Chicago; and Alameda, Calif., he concluded that mortality may actually be lower at weight levels higher than those suggested by insurance companies. Andres suggested that the tables currently in use may recommend body weights 10 per cent lower than the ideal for most age groups. Thus, weight reduction may actually result in poorer health for some individuals if it is overdone. However, the evidence still emphasizes the harmful effects of gross obesity.

Trace Elements. Knowledge of how trace elements function in the body is increasing. For example, researchers have accumulated evidence that acrodermatitis enteropathica, a rare genetic disease, is caused by a failure to absorb zinc from the intestinal tract. Nutritionist Lucille S. Hurley and associates at the University of California, Davis, found in August that zinc from human milk is absorbed better than zinc in cow's milk because human milk contains a special protein. Infants suffering from acrodermatitis enteropathica cannot maintain adequate amounts of zinc in their bodies if cow's milk is their major zinc source.   Paul E. Araujo

See also FOOD. In WORLD BOOK, see DIET; FOOD; NUTRITION.

OAKLAND. See SAN FRANCISCO-OAKLAND.

OCEAN. The United Nations (UN) Law of the Sea Conference held two meetings in 1978, but failed to reach agreement. The conferees met in Geneva, Switzerland, from March 28 to May 19 and in New York City from August 21 to September 16. The 158-country group disagreed on the proposed Seabed Authority, which would regulate deep-sea mining. The United States and other industrial nations wanted a veto over Seabed Authority decisions. Other countries wanted majority rule.

Delegates from developing countries strongly opposed a bill passed by the United States House of Representatives on July 26 that would allow American mining companies to start deep-seabed operations before the UN group settles its differences. A spokesman for the Group of 77, representing 119 developing countries, said the U.S. bill would break international law because it would violate two UN General Assembly resolutions. Chief U.S. negotiator Elliot L. Richardson said the bill was a necessary interim measure because companies needed a legal framework to continue deep-sea mining research. The bill did not reach the U.S. Senate floor.

Deep Sea Drilling Project scientists aboard the drilling ship *Glomar Challenger* discovered new data about the geologic evolution of the north Philippine Sea during a 51-day mission that ended on January 31. Their data indicate that part of the northwestern Philippine Sea floor in the Daito Ridge and Basin region stood above sea level 40 million to 50 million years ago. Since then, the region has drifted northward while expanding eastward and subsiding to 4,000 feet (1,200 meters) below sea level.

A later mission, in the Mariana Trench near Guam, provided the major surprise of the cruise. Models of the *subduction* process, in which oceanic plates are thrust beneath the continents on island arcs, had called for pieces of the Pacific Ocean floor to be pushed into the western side of the trench. Adding these pieces should have enlarged and uplifted the region. Instead, the evidence indicates that the region near the trench has sunk, even though some rocks from the deepest holes may have been part of the Pacific plate. This suggests that the subduction process in the Mariana Trench is smoother than expected, with the Pacific plate adding little material.

Chemical Sampling. Six years of field work for the most comprehensive chemical sampling of the oceans ever undertaken ended in May. The Geochemical Ocean Section Study (GEOSECS) is part of the International Decade of Ocean Exploration program. GEOSECS has involved scientists from Belgium, Canada, France, India, Italy, the United States, and West Germany. Since 1972, the research vessel *Melville* from the Scripps Institution of Oceanography and the *Knorr* from Woods Hole Oceanographic Institution have covered the Atlantic, Indian, and Pacific oceans.

Scientists from the National Oceanic and Atmospheric Administration aboard the ship *Oceanographer* found that industry's first harvest of manganese nodules from the ocean floor caused no serious problem for marine ecosystems. The *Oceanographer* returned to Seattle on June 7 after monitoring a mining test 865 nautical miles southeast of Hawaii.

Natural gas was discovered in the Baltimore Canyon area off New Jersey in August by a drilling group composed of Texaco, Incorporated; Getty Oil Corporation; Sun Oil Company; Allied Chemical Corporation; Transco Exploration Company; and Freeport Oil. The well, drilled in 432 feet (132 meters) of water, flowed gas at a rate of 7.5 million cubic feet (0.21 million cubic meters) per day.

The largest oil spill in history occurred off the Brittany coast of France when the *Amoco Cadiz,* laden with 1.6 million barrels of oil, ran aground and broke up on March 17. On June 26, the United States orbited *Seasat-A,* a satellite to provide data on ocean currents, temperatures, storms, winds, wave heights and spacing, and ice fields. *Seasat-A* went dead on October 9, just two days after the United States and the European Space Agency agreed to provide its data to the European Seasat Users Research Group.   Arthur G. Alexiou

See also GEOLOGY. In WORLD BOOK, see DEEP SEA DRILLING PROJECT; OCEAN.

OHIO. See CLEVELAND; STATE GOVERNMENT.

OHIRA, MASAYOSHI (1910-   ), secretary-general of the ruling Liberal-Democratic Party, became prime minister of Japan on Dec. 7, 1978. He succeeded Takeo Fukuda, who resigned on November 27 after losing an election for the party presidency. Ohira had long been a political adversary of Fukuda within the party. See JAPAN.

Born on March 12, 1910, Ohira was the son of a farmer in Kagawa prefecture on Shikoku island in southwestern Japan. His father died when Ohira was 16 years old, and Ohira had to do farm work to help support the family. By concealing his studies from his family, he prepared for and passed the 1933 entrance examinations for Tokyo University of Commerce, now known as Hitotsubashi University. While in school, he became a Christian, joining the Salvation Army.

Ohira joined the finance ministry in 1936, serving there until the late 1950s. He then served on the staff of Prime Minister Hayato Ikeda from 1960 to 1964, helping to prepare Ikeda's successful "income-doubling plan" and becoming chief Cabinet secretary. He served as foreign minister from 1962 to 1964, minister of international trade and industry from 1968 to 1970, foreign minister from 1972 to 1974, and finance minister from 1974 to 1976.

Ohira is an avid reader. He lists golf as one of his favorite pastimes.   Foster Stockwell

OKLAHOMA. See STATE GOVERNMENT.

OLD AGE. President Jimmy Carter signed a bill on April 6, 1978, raising the mandatory retirement age from 65 to 70 for most employees, effective Jan. 1, 1979. For university teachers who have full tenure, the effective date is July 1, 1982. For an employee under a mandatory retirement agreement reached by collective bargaining, the effective date is the contract-expiration date or Jan. 1, 1980, whichever comes first.

The law also eliminated the age limit of 70 years for federal employees, effective Sept. 30, 1978. It did not change mandatory retirement ages for employees in high-risk jobs, nor did it change voluntary early-retirement plans. But it allows forced retirement at 65 of corporate executives and policy-makers eligible for pensions of at least $27,000 per year.

United States Secretary of Health, Education, and Welfare Joseph A. Califano, Jr., announced proposed regulations controlling age discrimination on November 30. The rules would end many forms of discrimination, but would allow such "age distinctions" as favorable tax or utility treatment or age limits on persons seeking driver's licenses.

Representative Claude D. Pepper (D., Fla.), chairman of the House Select Committee on Aging, charged on November 27 that U.S. elderly were paying about $1 billion a year in premiums for health-insurance policies they do not need. Many elderly eligible for Medicare also buy supplementary insurance, and are sold extra policies, though the fine print denies payment from more than one supplementary policy. The committee opened hearings on insurance abuses on November 28.

Budget Challenge. Califano told the American Academy of Political and Social Science on April 9 that the growth of the elderly population is challenging the system that supports them. Spending on Medicaid, Medicare, food stamps, housing subsidies, insurance, and pensions totaled $112 billion, or 24 per cent of the 1978 federal budget – 5 per cent of the gross national product (GNP). Califano said that by the year 2025, this could grow to $635 billion, or 40 per cent of the budget – 10 per cent of GNP.

Old and Poor. Califano told the Senate Committee on Aging on July 17 that 25 per cent of Americans over 65 years old had incomes less than 25 per cent above the poverty level, and that 1 in 7 was below the line.

The committee's annual report revealed on May 6 that Social Security accounted for half the income of 70 per cent of its beneficiaries. The report said also that the number of Americans over 65 grew 18 per cent between 1970 and 1977, while the total United States population grew 5 per cent. Seventy-five per cent of Americans reach 65. Among the elderly, 9 per cent are functionally illiterate; 8 per cent are college graduates; and 50 per cent did not finish one year of high school.   Jay Myers

In WORLD BOOK, see OLD AGE.

OLYMPIC GAMES. The International Olympic Committee (IOC), meeting on May 18, 1978, in Athens, Greece, awarded the 1984 Olympic Games to Los Angeles, the only bidder. The contracts were signed on October 12, after bitter negotiations.

Historically, the IOC has required the host city to accept financial liability for the Olympics. The Los Angeles City Council, fearing a deficit like that suffered by Montreal, Canada, in 1976, refused to accept such liability. When it appeared that the IOC would revoke its award, the United States Olympic Committee (USOC) persuaded all parties to accept two contracts. One, between the IOC and Los Angeles, required Los Angeles to stage the Olympics. The other, signed by the IOC, the USOC, and the nongovernmental, nonprofit Los Angeles Olympic Organizing Committee, placed financial responsibility on the USOC and the organizing committee.

The 1980 Summer Olympics were scheduled for Moscow, but many people called for a boycott because of Russia's suppression of individual freedoms. The 1980 Winter Olympics were scheduled for Lake Placid, N.Y.

The new Amateur Sports Act, which restructured U.S. amateur sports, passed by Congress in October, made the USOC overseer of U.S. programs in the 28 Olympic sports. *Frank Litsky*

In WORLD BOOK, see OLYMPIC GAMES.

OMAN. See MIDDLE EAST.

ONTARIO. The minority Progressive Conservative government of Premier William G. Davis backed away from a proposed 37.5 per cent increase in premiums for the Ontario Health Insurance Plan in April 1978, narrowly averting a provincial election. Provincial Treasurer Darcy McKeough proposed the steep increase in his budget of March 7, basing his decision on the user-pay principle. The opposition attacked the raise as unfair because it imposed an equal burden on rich and poor.

The government reduced the increase to 18.75 per cent on April 25, saying it would recover the revenue by increasing other taxes. With 58 seats in a house of 125, the Conservatives had been in a minority position since the 1975 elections. McKeough resigned in August, and Frank Miller succeeded him.

Premier Davis made it plain that he would not make French an official language in Ontario. A bill to do this, which was approved by a majority in the legislature in June, was killed by the Conservative cabinet. The premier explained that the government was working steadily to improve French-language services in schools, courts, and health facilities.

The New Democratic Party, with 33 members, elected Michael Cassidy, a financial journalist, its new leader on February 5. *David M. L. Farr*

See also CANADA. In WORLD BOOK, see ONTARIO.

OPERA. See MUSIC, CLASSICAL.

OREGON. See STATE GOVERNMENT.

PACIFIC ISLANDS. Decolonization of the Pacific came closer in 1978. Two more British territories became independent, and islanders voted in a referendum to determine the future political status of the United Nations (UN) Trust Territory of the Pacific Islands (Micronesia), administered by the United States. But in the British-French New Hebrides, difficulties posed by the influential Vanuaaku Party slowed plans for granting independence to the 100,-000 New Hebrideans in 1980.

New Nations. The Gilbert Islands, which will become independent in July 1979 as Kiribati, and tiny, isolated Pitcairn Island were the only British dependencies left in the Pacific after the Solomon Islands gained independence on July 7 and Tuvalu on October 1. The Solomons, which became a British protectorate in 1893, make up a richly endowed archipelago with a population of nearly 200,000 people, most of them Melanesians. Its leaders at independence were Governor General Baddeley Devesi and Prime Minister Peter Kenilorea. Tuvalu, comprising nine atolls scattered over 125,000 square miles (323,700 square kilometers) of sea, was formerly the Ellice Islands in the Gilbert and Ellice Islands Colony. With a land area of only 12 square miles (31 square kilometers), it is one of the world's smallest nations. Most of its 6,000 citizens are Polynesians. Copra is the only export, but sever-

Prime Minister Peter Kenilorea beams as he displays his country's flag. The Solomon Islands joined the United Nations in September.

al hundred Tuvaluans work as seamen and in the fast-diminishing phosphate deposits of Ocean Island and Nauru. Fishing is considered Tuvalu's best hope for the future. Great Britain has promised Tuvalu substantial aid until 1980, and Prime Minister Toalipi Lauti hopes for support from other countries.

Electoral Corruption. The Cook Islands government led by Prime Minister Sir Albert Henry was removed from office on July 24 following an unprecedented court ruling by the country's chief justice. After an inquiry into charges by the rival Democratic Party, the judge ruled that Henry and seven other members of his Cook Islands Party were elected in March as a result of "unlawful conduct of monumental dimensions." Henry was found to have spent 2.8 per cent of the country's budget (about $300,000) to fly in former islanders now living in New Zealand to vote for his party's candidates. The judge said he could imagine "no greater perversion of representative democracy" and declared the election invalid.

The judge, who also serves as queen's representative, awarded the Democrats the eight seats, giving them 15 seats in the 22-member Legislative Assembly. Their leader, Tom Davis, was then sworn in as prime minister.

Border Incidents. Hundreds of Melanesians from Irian Jaya, the Indonesian half of the island of New Guinea, fled across the border into Papua New Guinea (PNG) in 1978. Many belong to a separatist movement that opposes Indonesia's takeover of their country in 1963 and the subsequent immigration of thousands of Indonesians. The refugees, some pursued by Indonesian planes or troops, created a delicate diplomatic problem for the PNG government. Although desiring to remain on good terms with Indonesia, the PNG government was well aware that its own people looked on the separatists as "Melanesian brothers" and "freedom fighters" rather than as rebels. The government's solution was to act compassionately toward the separatists as refugees, while refusing to allow them to use PNG soil as a base for attacks on Indonesians in Irian Jaya.

Micronesia Referendum. The Caroline Islands ratified a proposed constitution for a federated state of Micronesia in association with the United States in July, but the Marshall and Palau islands rejected the proposal, preferring to seek separate status. Because the Mariana Islands voted in 1975 to join the United States as a commonwealth, the vote raised problems of political fragmentation in the area and prompted a suggestion that the Trust Territory of the Pacific Islands should join Guam and American Samoa to form the 51st state of the United States. Also in the Marshalls, 137 Bikinians were evacuated in August from their atoll, which is still radioactive from atomic tests.   Robert Langdon

In WORLD BOOK, see PACIFIC ISLANDS.

PAINTING. See VISUAL ARTS.

PAKISTAN. Men were hanged before huge crowds, and journalists and political activists were publicly flogged in Pakistan in 1978. Pakistan People's Party (PPP) supporters, protesting the continued detention of their leader, former Prime Minister Zulfikar Ali Bhutto, set themselves on fire in busy streets. Meanwhile, the nation's new strongman, President Zia-ul-Haq, who arrested Bhutto in a coup d'état on July 5, 1977, kept the country guessing as to when he would allow often-promised elections, or whether he intended to remain the country's military dictator.

Bhutto's Shadow. General Zia's plans were heavily influenced by the fate of Bhutto. Accused of a 1974 murder and sentenced to death in March 1978, Bhutto spent most of the year in jail. His appeal was still being considered by a hostile Supreme Court in December.

Bhutto may have been the nation's most hated man in 1977. Neither the police nor the troops he sent into the streets could halt riots against his government led by the Pakistan National Alliance (PNA), which accused him of rigging the 1977 election. A year later, he had become by far the most popular leader in the country. Observers agreed that Bhutto could easily win the next election if it were conducted fairly. Despite repression – as many as 10,000 PPP activists were reportedly jailed and scores were flogged – the PPP remained alive, and its survival lay at the heart of Zia's dilemma. He could not permit elections that would bring victory to Bhutto – and certain court martial to himself. But Zia's refusal to allow the elections created a deep sense of public unease.

A Cabinet of Talents. President Fazal Elahi Chaudhry resigned in September because the military failed to honor its pledge to hold early elections. Zia had himself installed as president, while retaining the post of chief martial law administrator. Without becoming prime minister, he also presided over a Cabinet of bureaucrats and obscure Muslim politicians which he called "a Cabinet of talents." He finally persuaded some PNA leaders to join the Cabinet in August. Other leading anti-Bhutto politicians stayed out of the Cabinet, however, demanding elections.

Ailing Economy. The political uncertainty was reflected in the economy. Although Zia had offered them rich incentives and denationalized some industries Bhutto had nationalized, rich investors in Karachi and Lahore and those from other lands were reluctant to invest in new plants and equipment. Zia's "austerity" budget, announced in June, relied for 26 per cent of its revenues on foreign aid, which was slow in coming. The difficulties were heightened by a poor wheat harvest, necessitating costly imports. There were many shortages, from cigarettes to cement.   Mark Gayn

See also ASIA (Facts in Brief Table). In WORLD BOOK, see PAKISTAN.

PALEONTOLOGY. The discovery of a nest of baby dinosaur fossils in Montana on July 29, 1978, lent support to the controversial theory that dinosaurs were warm-blooded animals related to birds, rather than cold-blooded reptiles. Baby dinosaur bones are extremely rare, and these specimens may represent the young of a new genus of duckbilled dinosaurs of the family *Hadrosauridae.*

The fossils were found on a barren hillside near Choteau, Mont., by paleontologist Jack Horner, assistant curator of the Princeton University Natural History Museum in New Jersey, and his assistant Bob Makela, a Rudyard, Mont., high school science teacher. Horner had spent seven summers hunting for dinosaur fossils in Montana.

Rare Find. Until Horner's discovery, the best specimen of a baby dinosaur found in North America, was a piece of a small skull found in Alberta, Canada, in 1955. Horner's discovery came with the help of Marion Brandvold, owner of a small rock shop in Bynum, Mont., near Great Falls. Horner identified some fossil bones for her, and she showed him a small box of weathered bones that he instantly recognized as the limb bones of a baby duckbilled dinosaur. The bones were about one-tenth the size of an adult.

A few days later, Horner and Makela went to the spot where Brandvold had found the bones, on a

Paleontologist Jack Horner begins the massive task of assembling the jumbled pile of rare baby dinosaur bones that he found in Montana.

ranch about 60 miles (100 kilometers) west of Great Falls. What they found surpassed their wildest expectations. There were thousands of bones in what once had been a small pit 4 feet (1.2 meters) deep and 6 feet (1.8 meters) across. The bones were encased in green mudstone that filled the pit and contrasted with the surrounding brown mudstone. Apparently the pit had been a nest, and the baby dinosaurs had been huddled together in it when they were killed and buried by a flash flood of an ancient river.

Adult Found. A short distance from the nest, Horner discovered the skull and several bones of an adult duckbilled dinosaur of a previously unknown genus. Could this adult have been a relative of the baby dinosaurs, perhaps even a parent? Horner must study and compare the bones carefully to answer that question. Both the babies and the adult duckbill were found in what is known geologically as the Two Medicine Formation, a strata of rock dated to about 75 million years ago.

Horner has begun the slow and painstaking process of piecing the bones together into whole skeletons at Princeton. He says the number of *tibia* (leg bones) in the find indicates that there are skeletons of 15 baby dinosaurs. Almost all the bones are broken, some into dozens of pieces. The task of reassembling them can be compared to putting together 15 large jigsaw puzzles of the same picture, each cut into hundreds of pieces in a different pattern. To make the process even more difficult, some pieces are missing.

So far, Horner has assembled the foot and hind leg of one baby dinosaur. When the skeleton is completed, he estimates, it will stand 15 inches (38 centimeters) high and be 30 inches (76 centimeters) long. A typical adult duckbill was 30 to 40 feet (9 to 12 meters) long and weighed 3 to 4 short tons (2.7 to 3.6 metric tons).

Age of Babies. Horner would like to know how old the young dinosaurs were when they died. Since little is known of dinosaur growth rates, he may never determine their age. But one thing is certain – the animals had hatched before death. Their teeth show signs of being slightly worn, so they must have been feeding.

The discovery of the baby duckbills shows that at least some dinosaurs behaved differently from living reptiles. Because the dinosaurs had hatched and were feeding, but still died together in a nest, Horner is sure that at least one of their parents must have cared for them, probably for as long as several months. In contrast, reptiles care for their young for only a few hours after they hatch. The evidence of long-term parental care shows that these dinosaurs behaved more like birds and mammals than living reptiles.   Ida Thompson

See also GEOLOGY. In WORLD BOOK, see DINO-SAUR; FOSSIL; PALEONTOLOGY.

Crowd cheers former President Arnulfo Arias (in sunglasses) as he returns from exile under amnesty granted by Panama's General Omar Torrijos.

PANAMA. Chief of the Government Omar Torrijos Herrera and United States President Jimmy Carter formally concluded the Panama Canal treaties in Panama City on June 16, 1978. Then Torrijos surprised his supporters and opponents alike when he declared on September 1 that he would not accept the presidency of Panama. It had been widely assumed that Torrijos' selection as president was assured because he controlled the new 505-member National Assembly of Community Representatives, which had been elected on August 6 and which was to choose a new president.

Torrijos, in refusing the presidency, declared that it was time for him "to go back to the barracks." A close associate explained that Torrijos did not like the ceremonial duties of the office. "He doesn't like to deal with details, or meet with ambassadors or businessmen." In his place, Torrijos nominated Aristides Royo, his education minister, who was elected on October 11. See ROYO, ARISTIDES.

Torrijos Still Powerful. As commander of the National Guard, Panama's army, Brigadier General Torrijos remained the most powerful man in the country. Still, it was not thought that Royo would be a mere figurehead with no executive power, as was his predecessor, Demetrio Lakas. Some observers feared that Royo, who had full executive powers, might set a leftist course for the nation. However, Royo declared in a speech to labor leaders shortly after his election that "our revolutionary process is not a socialistic one."

Arias Returns. On April 18, Torrijos declared an amnesty for political exiles, and former President Arnulfo Arias returned on June 10 after 10 years in exile to address a rally of 100,000 persons in a denunciation of the Panama Canal treaties. Arias also denounced Panama's high taxes, soaring food prices, economic stagnation, and alleged corruption in the Torrijos government. It was the largest antigovernment demonstration in 10 years, and it was followed by several antitreaty protests by students, including one on June 14 at the University of Panama that left two students dead and another 18 wounded.

The rioting caused the government to take strong security measures to protect President Carter when he arrived to exchange the treaty ratification instruments in public ceremonies held on June 16. The 20-minute function was attended by about 4,000 guests, including 16 members of the United States Congress. Later in the day, Carter addressed a crowd of 200,000 persons, most of them farmers, government workers, and schoolchildren bused in by the government from all parts of the country. See CONGRESS OF THE UNITED STATES. Everett G. Martin

See also LATIN AMERICA (Facts in Brief Table). In WORLD BOOK, see PANAMA; PANAMA CANAL ZONE.

PAPUA NEW GUINEA. See ASIA.

PARAGUAY. Alfredo Stroessner began his 25th year as president on Aug. 15, 1978, when he was inaugurated to a new five-year term. He won 89 per cent of the votes against only token opposition in an election held on February 12. He has been in office longer than any other dictator in Latin America.

Stroessner's inauguration was marked by three days of festivities, including the largest military parade in the country's history. It was believed the parade was held to show that Paraguay was still well armed despite the cutoff in United States military aid that followed criticism by President Jimmy Carter's Administration of Stroessner's poor record on human rights. A *Te Deum* religious service in the Roman Catholic cathedral, presided over by the archbishop of Asunción, was interpreted as a move for reconciliation between the Stroessner regime and the Roman Catholic Church – a relationship strained by the arrests of several priests in the past.

Human Rights. Under U.S. pressure, Stroessner had improved the human rights situation in Paraguay. In 1977, a total of 300 prisoners were released; on Sept. 19, 1978, it was reported that only 15 political prisoners were still in jail. On May 5, the state of siege in force since 1947 was lifted in all parts of the country except Asunción, the capital.

German Acosta Caballero, a lawyer and president of the opposition Liberal Party, was quoted in October as saying that human rights "are not chemically pure in the country, but it is evident that there is not an absolute denial of them." Domingo Laino, vice-president of the Authentic Radical Liberal Party, a faction not recognized by the government, credited Carter's human rights policy for "the liberation of almost 90 per cent of the political prisoners." Stroessner, however, made it clear that he would not countenance any effective political opposition. He exiled Carlos Pastore, a leader of the Liberal Party, on September 29 for trying to organize an opposition front. Other politicians were warned that they, too, would be exiled if they attempted anything similar.

Laino Incident. Laino became the center of a bitter exchange between the Stroessner government and the United States after he was arrested on July 7 for allegedly associating with the extreme left. The day before, Laino had returned from Washington, D.C., where he denounced Stroessner before the Inter-Commission on Human Rights, an agency of the Organization of American States.

United States Ambassador Robert E. White visited Laino's wife after his arrest to express his "condolences," prompting the government to accuse White of interfering in the internal affairs of Paraguay. Laino was released on August 8 after a judge declared the government had presented insufficient evidence of his "extremist" connections. Everett G. Martin

See also LATIN AMERICA (Facts in Brief Table). In WORLD BOOK, see PARAGUAY.

PARENTS AND TEACHERS, NATIONAL CONGRESS OF (PTA), spent much of 1978 on a drive to defeat the Tuition Tax Credit Act of 1977. The PTA and 39 other concerned groups formed the National Coalition To Save Public Education, and claimed victory when the bill was defeated in the United States Senate in August. Lobbying against the bill began after the PTA opened its Office of Government Relations in Washington, D.C., in 1977.

An Urban Advisory Task Force was formed to deal with the problem of human deterioration in U.S. cities and its effect on the quality of urban education. In addition, the PTA undertook a project in cooperation with Cornell University to create national policies on child and family development.

As part of its Comprehensive School Community Health Education project, the PTA held its first national conference on health education in January. The association also continued its battle against offensive television programming. The PTA said that violence has been reduced, but that sexually oriented programming has replaced violent shows. Another phase of the project, the development of a public school curriculum in TV-viewing skills, is underway. Virginia E. Anderson

In WORLD BOOK, see NATIONAL CONGRESS OF PARENTS AND TEACHERS; PARENT-TEACHER ORGANIZATIONS.

The PTA television commission reports that *Little House on the Prairie, Wonderful World of Disney,* and *60 Minutes* are among the 10 best TV shows.

PEI, I. M. (1917-), the architect who designed the new East Building of the National Gallery of Art in Washington, D.C., received widespread acclaim when the facility was opened to the public on June 1, 1978. Built on a difficult, irregularly shaped plot of land, Pei's addition to the museum is a study of acute angles and vast open spaces. It was hailed as a masterpiece of architecture.

Ieoh Ming Pei was born on April 26, 1917, in Canton, China. The son of a prosperous bank executive, he moved with his family to Shanghai, where the building boom of the 1930s stimulated his interest in architecture. He came to the United States in 1935, earning a bachelor's degree from Massachusetts Institute of Technology in 1940 and a master's degree from Harvard University in 1946.

As a young architect, Pei was associated with real estate developer William Zeckendorf, becoming an expert in multilevel-housing design and urban planning. In 1955, he formed I. M. Pei & Partners. His company has designed a number of notable buildings throughout the world. Pei was elected chancellor of the American Academy of Arts and Letters in December. He is only the second chancellor to be elected from the visual arts.

Pei married Eileen Loo in 1942. They have three sons and a daughter.   Beverly Merz

PENNSYLVANIA. See Philadelphia; State Government.

PERSONALITIES OF 1978 included the following newsmakers:

Bailey, Pearl, the irrepressible entertainer, enrolled at Georgetown University in Washington, D.C., on January 16 at the age of 58. Her classes included French, Islamic civilization and religious thought, Egyptian art, and philosophy. Bailey assured friends that she was seriously preparing for a teaching career. "I want to be ready if life calls on me," she said.

Berlin, Irving, composer of "God Bless America" and hundreds of other songs, celebrated his 90th birthday on May 11. On June 4, he received the Lawrence Langner Award for distinguished lifetime achievement in the theater. The citation read, "His songs are a proud and permanent expression of the buoyancy and optimism of our American heritage."

Black, Shirley Temple, Depression-era darling turned diplomat, celebrated her 50th birthday on April 23. "I had an enchanted childhood, a magic childhood, with great memories," the onetime child star of motion pictures recalled, "but I don't want to live in the past, and I don't live in the past." The mother of three children, she served as ambassador to Ghana and representative to the United Nations (UN) under President Richard M. Nixon and chief of protocol under President Gerald R. Ford.

Brynner, Yul, actor who gained fame for his film portrayal of the king of Siam, spoke on April 11 as honorary president of the Second World Romany Congress in Geneva, Switzerland. Brynner, whose mother was a Romanian gypsy, told gypsies from 25 nations that he would ask Kurt Waldheim, secretary-general of the UN, to back a proposal to recognize gypsies as a separate national minority.

Caroline, Princess, 21, of Monaco, was married to French businessman Philippe Junot, 38, on June 29 in the Grimaldi Palace by Monsignor Gilles Barthe, bishop of Toulon and Fréjus. Bishop Barthe had baptized Princess Caroline and officiated at the wedding of her parents, Prince Rainier III of Monaco and the former actress Grace Kelly, 22 years earlier. The newlyweds honeymooned in Tahiti.

Eisenhower, Jennie, was born to the former Julie Nixon and her husband David Eisenhower, grandson of President Dwight D. Eisenhower, on August 15 in San Clemente, Calif. The baby is the first grandchild for former President and Mrs. Richard M. Nixon.

Evitt, Ardath, 74, a Paris, Ill., grandmother, early in August apparently became the oldest woman to make a parachute jump. Evitt said she "got the bug" from her grandson, a sky diver.

Felderbaum, Moshe (Chico), 34, an Edmonton, Canada, real estate developer, won the richest backgammon tournament ever held, the first Amateur Backgammon Championship in Las Vegas, Nev., on January 29. He beat out 651 competitors to win the $180,000 first prize.

Ford, Steve, 21, son of former President Ford, became a Rough Rider. He performed as a calf roper and served as chief public spokesman for the Los Angeles Rough Riders rodeo team.

Galbraith, John Kenneth, economist, author, and diplomat, was awarded the Noble Prize by the Association for the Promotion of Humor in International Affairs (APHIA) for his "North Dakota Plan." APHIA, founded by three Americans in Paris, believes that "humor must be taken seriously." Harvard Professor Galbraith proposed solemnly that all national borders be redrawn to the shape and size of North Dakota, thus creating "straight, unmistakable frontiers which would cut right through every animosity, however cherished."

Gould, Gordon, physicist and vice-president of Optelecom Incorporated, in Gaithersburg, Md., was named Inventor of the Year by the Association for the Advancement of Invention and Innovation. He was honored for a patent, issued in October 1977, that covers optically pumped laser amplifiers. He has other laser patents pending.

Graham, Calvin, 48, of Fort Worth, Tex., a World War II veteran, finally received his campaign ribbons and an honorable discharge from the U.S. Navy. Even though he was wounded in the Battle of Guadalcanal in 1942, Graham was discharged without honors or benefits after the Navy discovered he had lied about his age when he enlisted at 12.

Wedding bells rang in May for Donny Osmond and Debra Glenn, *top left*, and Henry Winkler and Stacey Weitzman, *left*. Monaco's Princess Caroline wed Philippe Junot in June, *top*, and Christina Onassis married Sergei Kauzov in August, *above*.

437

Hart, Michael, 46, professor of astrophysics at Trinity University in San Antonio, Tex., and also a lawyer and chess master, believes he can name the all-time movers and shakers, and he wrote a book to prove it. *The 100. A Ranking of the Most Influential Persons in History* is just what its title implies. "Such a group of exceptional people, whether noble or reprehensible, famous or obscure, flamboyant or modest, cannot fail to be interesting; they are the people who have shaped our lives and formed our world," Hart said. Muhammad, the Prophet of Islam, is number one on Hart's list, and physicist Niels A. Bohr is ranked 100th; Jesus Christ (3); Karl Marx (11); Sigmund Freud (32); Voltaire (79); and 94 others furnish the basis for a pleasant evening of raging controversy.

Hope, Bob, entertainer and friend of soldiers and commanders in chief, celebrated his 75th birthday on May 29 and was honored at two days of festivities in Washington, D.C. With his wife, Dolores, at his side, Hope was honored by the House of Representatives, receiving an engraved plaque commending him for "enhancing national unity with unfailing commitment and humor." A gala benefit party at the John F. Kennedy Center for the Performing Arts, which President and Mrs. Jimmy Carter attended, was a benefit for the United Service Organization (USO), a favorite Hope charity. Parts of the gala were taped for a three-hour NBC television special, *Happy Birthday, Bob.* See also Section Two, WHERE THERE'S HOPE, THERE'S LIFE.

Horowitz, Vladimir, the world-renowned pianist, played a concert at the White House on February 26 to mark the 50th anniversary of his American debut. He had entertained there once before – on Jan. 8, 1931, Horowitz played for Herbert Hoover.

Johnston, Albert Sidney, accused of aiding the Confederate cause while commanding the United States Department of the Pacific in 1861, was cleared of all charges 117 years later – on Jan. 10, 1978. California Supreme Court Judge Harry W. Low heard witnesses in San Francisco's Court of Historical Review attest to Johnston's loyalty and ruled in his favor.

Korbut, Olga, 22, the pert Russian gymnast whose performance at the 1972 Olympic Games in Munich, West Germany, inspired a generation of little girls, was married on January 7 in the Minsk Wedding Palace to Leonid Bortkevich, 27, a pop singer. Korbut is now a gymnastics coach.

Laker, Freddie, 55, founder of Skytrain transatlantic economy flights, was on Cloud Nine after his name appeared on the Queen's Birthday Honours List. Queen Elizabeth II knighted the man who fought for six years to create Skytrain, and Sir Freddie was magnanimous in his moment of glory: "This shows the British spirit shining through," he said. "It shows the government is pleased with what we have achieved."

Miss Baker, 21 years old on June 22, was the guest of honor at a bang-up party given by the Alabama Space and Rocket Center in Huntsville, where she works. But it didn't compare with the blast that launched her career. Miss Baker, a squirrel monkey then 2 years old, became a space pioneer on May 28, 1959, when she rode a Jupiter rocket on a suborbital journey at 10,000 miles (16,000 kilometers) per hour. Now she and her mate, George, live quietly at the Marshall Space Flight Center where the Jupiter was built.

Napoli, Salvatore, 101, achieved a long-cherished ambition on June 16 when he became a United States citizen. Napoli learned only recently that his inability to read and write English was no longer a bar to naturalization. A law passed in 1952 waived the literacy requirement for anyone more than 50 years old who had lived in the United States since 1930. Napoli came to America from Calabria, Italy, in 1920.

Nyad, Diana, 28, long-distance swimmer, made a brave attempt at swimming from Cuba to Florida on August 13. A combination of ill winds, adverse currents, jellyfish, and fatigue defeated her after she spent almost 42 hours in the water.

Onassis, Christina, 27, who inherited a Greek shipping fortune, was married in Moscow on August 1 to Sergei Kauzov, 37, a former Russian merchant marine official. Kauzov was job hunting. He had to give up his post because Soviet officials may not have foreigners as wives. The bride remained calm. "I've been accustomed to having everything all my life," she said, "but I don't think there will be any great difficulties."

Palma, Emilio, became famous at birth because he is the first child born in Antarctica. Emilio was born to Maria Silva and her husband, Captain Jorge Emilio Palma, commander of the Argentine Army's Esperanza Base in Antarctica, on January 7.

Percival, John, a British Broadcasting Company (BBC) producer, conceived an exciting experiment in recreating the historic past. In April, 10 young men and women volunteers completed a year of living like the Iron Age Celtic tribes in Shaftesbury, England, about 2,200 years ago. Their day-to-day existence in a "round house" of thatch, wattle, and daub was documented once a week for a BBC series, but otherwise the group was left on its own to farm, forge tools, cook, weave, and generally get along with no modern conveniences. The volunteers enjoyed the experience, citing especially "the development of mutual support and dependence and the peace of the countryside."

Poenisch, Walter, a retired baker from Ohio, went swimming in Cuba to celebrate his 65th birthday on July 11 and left the water 33 1/2 hours later at Little Duck Key, Florida. Poenisch said he made the swim to try to foster "peace and better relations" between Cuba and the United States.

Darers of
The Dream

Quests for the new, the unique, the desired, are as old as humanity itself. Some quests are spiritual, like King Arthur's knights seeking the Holy Grail. Many are mundane, like Christopher Columbus' search for a new route to the Indies. A few are even frivolous, like Ponce de Léon's attempt to find the legendary Fountain of Youth. But some quests are undertaken for the reason George Leigh Mallory gave for climbing Mount Everest – "Because it is there."

In 1978, an intrepid Japanese explorer, Naomi Uemura, twice traversed some of the world's roughest terrain alone. He reached the North Pole on April 30, after a 57-day, 477-mile (767-kilometer) trek from Ellesmere Island, Canada. After a brief rest, he set off to cross the icy length of Greenland. Again accompanied only by husky dogs, Uemura finished this 103-day, 1,660-mile (2,670-kilometer) journey on August 22. Although he collected snow, ice, and air samples for scientific study, Uemura undertook his expeditions primarily for the sake of adventure.

The Arctic trips were the most recent accomplishments of Uemura's singular career. Possibly believing that he travels fastest who travels alone, he has rafted 4,000 miles (6,400 kilometers) down the Amazon River by himself and made the longest one-man dog-sled trip–7,500 miles (12,-000 kilometers) from Greenland to Alaska.

Uemura has also climbed alone to the top of the highest mountains on four continents: Mount Kilimanjaro in Africa, Mont Blanc in Europe, Mount Aconcagua in South America, and Mount McKinley in North America. He scaled Mount Everest in Asia with the first Japanese group to make the ascent, but the last feat was not his favorite. Insisted Uemura, with all the fervor of a 5-year-old, "Sharing a project means sharing the satisfaction from it. I want to do a project all by myself."

The urge to act individually in an increasingly group-oriented society is characteristic of those who dare to try what seems impossible. Three self-directed men, each the president of his own company, gained worldwide

Double Eagle II

fame on August 17 for an unprecedented achievement. Ben Abruzzo, Maxie Anderson, and Larry Newman of Albuquerque, N. Mex., made the first manned transatlantic balloon flight in *Double Eagle II*. The helium-filled, black-and-silver balloon carried them from Presque Isle, Me., to Miserey, France, in 137 hours 18 minutes, setting distance and time records.

The French gave them a spirited welcome, and they were guests at the American Embassy in Paris. There, Newman won the privilege of sleeping in a bed once occupied by the first solo transatlantic flier – Charles A. Lindbergh, the "Lone Eagle."

Women, too, feel the desire "to come down off this feather-bed of civilisation," as Robert Louis Stevenson phrased it, and test their mettle in the wide, wild world. Robyn Davidson, who crossed the Australian desert alone in 1977, expressed this feeling. "I like the freedom inherent in being on my own," she said, "and I like the growth and learning processes that develop from taking chances."

Two swimmers took their chances with the Atlantic Ocean on Aug. 13, 1978. American Diana Nyad left from Cuba and England's Stella Taylor began at the Bahamas, each headed for Florida, but neither could complete the swim. After struggling for almost two days against adverse winds and currents, beset by sharks and jellyfish, each had to admit defeat. But that did not end the quest. On September 29, Taylor tried – and failed – again.

An Englishwoman who reached her goal was Naomi James, who sailed the 53-foot (17-meter) *Express Crusader* into Dartmouth harbor on June 8. Despite meeting heavy weather and capsizing once, she made a solo round-the-world voyage in record time – 30,000 miles (48,000 kilometers) in 272 days.

Adventurers do not give up. Like fairy-tale heroes and heroines, they pursue their quests through briar and flame. Perhaps that is why they are admired so and held in such awe – they rekindle one's wonderful childhood faith in achieving "the impossible dream." Marsha F. Goldsmith

Point, Marie-Louise (Mado), widow of Fernand Point, France's most illustrious 20th-century chef, celebrated her 80th birthday in October at what was undoubtedly the gastronomic "fête of the century." Eight three-star chefs who had trained at Point's extraordinary Restaurant de la Pyramide in Vienne prepared an open-air feast at a government-owned château near Grenoble. Guests dined for hours on dozens of delightful dishes, and the guest of honor received a medal from Minister of Youth, Sports, Leisure, and Tourism Jean-Pierre Soisson, who declared that gastronomy brings "more foreign currency into France than any other activity."

Rosenfeld, Eric, 20, a student at Brown University in Providence, R.I., and other "carrottops" banded together to campaign against just such nicknames and stereotypes. Their group, called Redheads Are Special People, has a constitution, a newsletter, and about 40 members.

Rosenthal, Merilyn Carol, 22, was the first blind woman to be accepted as a Harvard Law School student. A Rutgers University honors graduate, she was one of four outstanding blind college students honored by President Jimmy Carter at a White House ceremony in May. The others, who will also go on to law school, were John Britt DeLuca of Duke University, Harry John Miller of Arizona State University, and Christopher John Palano of Clark University.

Stuart, Harry, 60, an American Airlines captain, invited 100 friends on a special charter flight to mark the end of his career. "Friends have always asked me, 'What goes on in the cockpit?' so I thought I would let them see for themselves before I retire," he explained. On the two-hour round trip between New York City's Kennedy International Airport and Burlington, Vt., guests enjoyed lunch, visited the cockpit, and cheered their highflying host.

Thomas, Ben, of Girard, Ohio, has been playing golf for seven years without being able to eye his shots. On his 1978 spring vacation in South Carolina, Thomas accomplished something his partners said you had to see to believe — the legally blind golfer scored a hole in one.

Washington, George, surveyor, planter, and first President of the United States, got a posthumous promotion. To make it absolutely clear that Washington is the U.S. Army's senior general, Clifford L. Alexander, Jr., secretary of the Army, signed a routine order in March promoting the "Father of His Country," who died in 1799, to rank of general of the armies of the United States as of July 4, 1976.

Zzyzzx, Hero, 31, is listed last in the Madison, Wis., telephone directory and just about everywhere else. Children, drunks, and jokers love to dial the last name in the book at all hours, but Zzyzzx says he does not have an unlisted number because young ladies also are apt to call and "once in a while you get a pleasant chat with somebody." Marsha F. Goldsmith

PERTINI, ALESSANDRO (SANDRO) (1896-   ), a Socialist, was sworn in as Italy's president on July 9, 1978. He succeeded Giovanni Leone, who resigned amid charges of corruption. See ITALY.

Sandro Pertini was born on Sept. 25, 1896, in Stella, near Savona, Italy. The son of well-to-do parents, he received a university education in law and political science. He served as an army lieutenant during World War I. Following the war, he joined the Socialist Party and entered politics. Pertini was arrested and held in jail for eight months in 1925 by the newly formed Fascist government on a charge of "inciting to class hatred and insulting the Senate." With two companions, he engineered the escape from prison in 1926 of Filippo Turati, a prominent Socialist leader. The four fled to France, where Pertini eventually became a volunteer radio broadcaster, beaming anti-Fascist programs to Italy from Nice.

After returning to Italy in 1929 to join the anti-Fascist underground movement, Pertini was sent to prison for 11 years after an unsuccessful attempt to assassinate dictator Benito Mussolini. Pertini was released in 1943, then arrested again. He escaped in October 1943 and rejoined the underground.

After World War II, Pertini was a member of the Constituent Assembly and president of the Chamber of Deputies for seven years. Foster Stockwell

PERU. Inflation, a crushing foreign debt, and the consequences of the military government's general economic mismanagement continued to dominate events in Peru in 1978. An investigating team from the International Monetary Fund (IMF) reported in March that the government was not implementing an austerity program mutually agreed on in 1977 in return for IMF loans. Consequently, the IMF refused the next credit installment. A committee representing some 200 commercial bank creditors simultaneously declared that the banks would also refuse to make further loans to refinance Peru's $8.2-billion foreign debt.

The government, confronted with debt payments that would absorb 56 per cent of its export income, faced default. Hastily, it announced a series of tough retrenchment measures on May 11, including a 7 per cent devaluation of the country's monetary unit, the sol, and tax increases of up to 50 per cent. On May 15, it reopened negotiations with the IMF. At the same time it announced a 70 per cent increase in the price of gasoline, a 50 per cent increase in urban transport fares, and sharp rises in prices of food staples that had been subsidized previously to help the poorer classes.

Civil Unrest. Public reaction demonstrated the junta's political problem in enforcing the IMF's terms. The public was incensed at the sacrifices it was being forced to make. Rioting broke out in several cities, and the Communist-controlled General Confederation of Peruvian Workers called a two-day general strike on May 22 that tied up Lima and brought troops into the streets.

About 100,000 primary and secondary school teachers struck from May 8 to July 27 for higher wages, and miners began a 35-day strike on August 4 that cost the country $70 million in mineral exports. The government had to cancel plans to fire 30,000 public employees after they struck on September 6.

The Election. Despite the unrest, the election for a 100-member Constituent Assembly was held on June 18. The Assembly was to write a constitution in preparation for a return to civilian rule, promised by President Francisco Morales Bermudez for 1980.

The center-left American Popular Revolutionary Alliance won 37 seats, and the conservative Popular Christian Party won 25 seats, but the surprise was the strong showing of five extreme left parties that won 30 seats.

Under a new civilian economic team, the government in August reached a less stringent agreement with the IMF on a $220-million line of credit extended over 30 months, and narrowly missed default when foreign banks postponed debt payments of $185 million until Jan 1, 1979.   Everett G. Martin

See also LATIN AMERICA (Facts in Brief Table). In WORLD BOOK, see PERU.

PET. See CAT; DOG.

PETROLEUM AND GAS. The world's oil supply should last 60 to 90 years at current consumption rates, according to a United States Central Intelligence Agency (CIA) report released in September 1978. The study reversed the CIA's earlier view that proven oil reserves would show signs of depletion by the 1980s. The CIA study, prepared by the RAND Corporation, asserted that even if oil demand increased and supplies decreased quickly, energy requirements could be met through further conservation and proven techniques for squeezing more oil from existing reserves. RAND estimated current world oil supplies at 1.7 to 2.3 trillion barrels.

Motorists in the United States consumed gasoline at a record rate of 8 million barrels per day (bpd) in July – 7.7 per cent more than in the same month in 1977. Total U.S. gasoline consumption for the first seven months of 1978 was up 3.7 per cent, according to the American Petroleum Institute (API). The increase almost equals the 4 per cent annual gains common before the 1973 Arab oil embargo. It is far greater than can be explained by the increase in the number of cars on the road. And it is surprising because it has occurred despite five years of government efforts to hold gasoline consumption down through such measures as the speed limit of 55 miles (88 kilometers) per hour, and public-awareness campaigns. The price jump during the embargo had also been expected to force conservation.

Shortages Again? Now, with consumption higher than ever, some energy planners question the effectiveness of any policy – short of rationing – to reduce gasoline use. Motorists may soon have trouble finding enough gasoline. For while there is plenty of crude oil available for making gasoline, there could be a shortage of gasoline-producing facilities. On December 1, Shell Oil Company announced that it would ration gasoline supplies to its dealers, in part because of maintenance work at some of its manufacturing facilities. Several other companies announced similar plans.

Despite the 1978 surge in consumption, government energy planners still expect gasoline demand to grow more slowly in coming years. That is partly because automobile manufacturers are being forced to increase the gasoline mileage of new cars. Regulators are also considering decontrolling the price of gasoline, which would force up pump prices.

Reusing Motor Oil has never caught on in the United States as it has in other countries. Only a scant 10 per cent of the estimated 1.2 billion gallons (4.5 billion liters) of motor oil sold annually is now refined again after it is used. Most used motor oil is mixed with fuel to be burned, used to coat dusty roads, or simply dumped by do-it-yourself oil changers. However, a combination of federal and state initiatives may radically change that.

The government has been a major barrier to re-refining oil in the United States. The Federal Trade Commission (FTC) ruled in 1965 that all such oil must be labeled "made from previously used oils." Consequently, "there's a stigma attached to re-refined oils," says Emil A. Malick, special projects director for Phillips.

The FTC decision followed Department of Defense studies that showed it was too expensive and time-consuming to test re-refined oil to certify its quality. But the Defense Department is now working with the National Bureau of Standards to develop less expensive tests.

If the FTC lifts its labeling requirement, re-refined-oil base stock could be used in top-of-the-line motor oils sold by major refiners. In tests made several years ago, "We determined that we can economically produce specification motor oil using re-refined oil," said George S. Kent, manager of product commercialization for Chevron U.S.A., Incorporated, a subsidiary of Standard Oil Company of California. "The only thing standing in our way is labeling requirements." The Department of Energy (DOE) spent $400,000 in 1978 on re-refining research.

Other Nations. The Philippines laid plans in 1978 to reduce its dependence on imported oil from 95 per cent to 78 per cent. The current oil-exploration program and the discovery of offshore oil deposits have been encouraging. The wells, operated by Cities Service Corporation, caused the government

Russian workers weld pipe at a drilling site, battling the cruel climate of western Siberia to tap extensive oil and gas deposits in the area.

to raise its offshore production estimate from 21,000 to 40,000 bpd.

Canada's crude supply and demand outlook was bright. The government's action in moving crude-oil prices toward world levels helped the Canadian supply picture markedly. Higher wellhead prices spurred oil and gas exploration, resulting in more discoveries, particularly of gas. The Canadian Petroleum Association argued strongly in June for gas exports to the United States, and the National Energy Board of Canada held hearings on the matter in October.

Mexico made headlines again in 1978 with news of its growing oil reserves. A fresh look at its potential capacity in September estimated production at 3.25-million bpd of crude oil by 1985. This is 25 to 30 per cent of the projected U.S. daily import level, according to a DOE estimate. The United States imported 83 per cent of Mexico's oil exports in 1977, clearly making future policy toward Mexico crucial to the U.S. supply. Production above 2.5 million bpd would put Mexico fifth in world production, after Russia, Saudi Arabia, Iran, and the United States. By the year 2000, Mexico could replace Saudi Arabia as the world's leading oil exporter.

National Economic Research Associates, Incorporated, stated in a mid-September report that Mexico would have more gas and oil than it could use if its natural gas production reached 10 billion

cubic feet (280 million cubic meters) per day and if oil production reached 2 million bpd by 1980. With Mexico's domestic use at 5 billion cubic feet (140-million cubic meters) per day, there would be another 5 billion cubic feet to be disposed of. Mexico was so confident that the United States would be willing to buy all the gas it had to offer that it was installing a large pipeline up Mexico's east coast from the Reforma fields to the border. For the time being, the pipeline will be used to supply Mexican industry along its route. One gas line originally intended to supply the United States is now slated to stop at Monterrey, in northeastern Mexico.

The first shipments of liquefied natural gas (LNG) began arriving at a new offshore terminal near Cove Point, Md., in March. The gas is being sold to a subsidiary of El Paso Gas Company by Sonatrach, which is the Algerian state petroleum organization. See ALGERIA.

New Refinery Construction continued through 1978 around the world, even though European refiners, already operating at a loss, were considering further plant shutdowns. Much of the new capacity is to serve the same European markets that produced financial losses in 1977.

Saudi Arabia currently has the most unused producing capacity. The Saudis reduced production from 8.9 million bpd to 6.5 million, to avoid a market glut. Existing facilities could have handled 11 million bpd. Iran's oil production ran about 6.7 million bpd until political turmoil crippled production in November and December. See IRAN.

U.S. Imports Drop. A July report from the API indicated that U.S. oil imports fell 10.5 per cent in the first 10 months of 1978. The drop was attributed to increased domestic production, particularly in Alaska's North Slope. Imports averaged 7.9 million bpd, down from 8.8 million bpd in the same period of 1977. Late in the year, imports began to creep up. Nevertheless, as the year closed, a Harvard economist suggested – perhaps with tongue in cheek – that a practical energy policy might be to buy foreign oil, especially from Saudi Arabia, while keeping untapped reserves in the United States as a future source of supply. He suggested that economics would favor the purchase and use of foreign supplies while building up U.S. reserves.

Members of the Organization of Petroleum Exporting Countries (OPEC) decided at a December meeting in Abu Zaby to raise oil prices by a total of 14.5 per cent in 1979. The hike would come in four stages, with an initial January rise of 5 per cent. By Oct. 1, 1979, OPEC oil would cost $14.54 a barrel, compared with 1978's $12.70. Several days later, Mexico indicated that it would follow OPEC's lead in pricing its oil. James J. O'Connor

See also ENERGY. In WORLD BOOK, see PETROLEUM; GAS (Fuel).

PHILADELPHIA. The firing of Philadelphia's United States attorney, David W. Marston, by U.S. Attorney General Griffin B. Bell on Jan. 20, 1978, created an uproar in the city and became a source of embarrassment to President Jimmy Carter. Marston, a Republican, was dismissed while investigating official corruption involving Democratic officeholders. Although President Carter would have routinely replaced Marston with a Democrat, he had been urged to speed up the process by Representative Joshua Eilberg, one of those under investigation. Carter denied that he had any knowledge of the investigation when he ordered Marston's removal. Marston was replaced by Peter F. Vaira on March 23. Eilberg was indicted in October on charges that he profited illegally from involvement in a federal contract for construction of a hospital. He was defeated in the November election.

Voters on November 7 rejected an amendment to the city's charter that would have permitted Mayor Frank L. Rizzo to serve a third term. Rizzo's current term expires in January 1980.

Workers Walk Out. Some 19,500 city employees, including garbage collectors and prison guards, struck on July 14 demanding higher wages and protection from layoffs. A court order issued on July 16 classified some of the workers as "essential" and forbade them to strike. Workers returned to their jobs on July 21 after accepting a contract that called for a 7 per cent pay increase and provisions for layoffs required by budget cuts.

Philadelphia's 13,000 public-school teachers established picket lines on September 1, but contract issues were resolved in time for schools to open on September 11. Teachers in Philadelphia's school system, the nation's fourth largest, received no pay increase in the first year of the new contract, but were to get 15 per cent increases in the second year.

The MOVE Incident. One policeman was killed and six policemen and five firemen were wounded on August 8 when police stormed a dilapidated house where members of a revolutionary group called MOVE had barricaded themselves. Two MOVE members were wounded in the action. Police had spent 50 days trying to starve out the radicals, who defied court orders to vacate the building because of health and fire-code violations.

Environmental Lawsuits. The U.S. Department of Justice filed two water-pollution suits against the city on May 24. One charged the city with violating the Clean Water and Ocean Dumping Act and with failure to upgrade its sewage-disposal plants, which discharge inadequately treated wastes into the Delaware River. The second charged the city with violating its ocean-dumping permit by dumping more than the monthly limit of sludge. James M. Banovetz

See also CITY. In WORLD BOOK, see PHILADELPHIA.

PHILIPPINES. President Ferdinand E. Marcos took the additional title of prime minister on June 12, 1978, when an Interim National Assembly was inaugurated. Marcos' action merged the presidential and parliamentary systems of government for an unspecified period. As prime minister he could veto Assembly bills, but his veto could be overridden by a two-thirds vote. But as president he retained the power to rule by martial law decree.

Of the Assembly's 200 members, 165 were elected on April 7 and the rest were appointed. The elections were controversial. Just before the voting, opponents staged the largest antigovernment demonstrations in Manila since Marcos declared martial law in 1972, to protest alleged intimidation and interference. Marcos' New Society Movement won, but the opposition People's Force Party charged fraud and other irregularities. In Manila, Marcos' wife, Imelda, headed a ticket that won all 21 Assembly seats from a ticket headed by an imprisoned former senator, Benigno S. Aquino, Jr. Protests against Manila election results ended in the arrest of some leading government foes.

As a result of the election complaints, the government on May 26 postponed municipal and provincial voting indefinitely, saying it was doubtful the nation could "endure another election."

The New Assembly became the first legislative body since 1972. Marcos told the inaugural session

President Marcos' regime won the Philippines'
first general election since 1972 in April,
but foes charged harassment and vote fraud.

that martial law would continue during a long transition from his authoritarian form of government, but he would "enlarge the democratic dialogue among all sectors of society."

Imelda Marcos became a member of the 27-person Cabinet sworn in on June 11. A movement later developed, apparently with some official support but not necessarily with her husband's blessing, to have her named deputy prime minister. The deputy would be considered Marcos' likely successor.

Another member of the Marcos family, daughter Imee, became prominent as a leader of a movement against allowing the United States to continue to use air and naval bases in the Philippines. However, Marcos agreed with visiting U.S. Vice-President Walter F. Mondale on May 4 that the United States should have continued unhampered use of the main U.S. military bases in East Asia. Negotiations to settle their status dragged on through the year.

Communist Relations. The Philippines continued normalizing its relations with Communist countries, receiving visits by senior government officials from Cambodia, China, Russia, and Vietnam. But the government could not quell either the Communist New People's Army guerrilla war or a larger rebellion by an estimated 20,000 Muslim guerrillas in the southern islands.   Henry S. Bradsher

See also ASIA (Facts in Brief Table). In WORLD BOOK, see PHILIPPINES.

PHOTOGRAPHY showed few big technical advances in 1978, but there were many improvements in products and processes. The biennial *photokina* (World's Fair of Photography), held in Cologne, West Germany, in September, previewed several important trends in cameras, lenses, and darkroom materials and equipment.

One such trend was exemplified by the Canon A-1, a 35-millimeter (mm) single-lens reflex camera, which offered one manual and five automatic methods of controlling exposure. The user can select either lens opening or shutter speed; then the camera's electronic circuits automatically supply the other exposure component. The camera also provides for manual setting of both speed and aperture and three other methods of exposure. Multiautomatic models from other manufacturers included two 35-mm reflex cameras with built-in motorized film winding.

Compact Cameras. Pocket-sized 110-format cameras appeared with many features similar to those of 35-mm models. For example, a tiny Pentax single-lens-reflex camera had interchangeable lenses, its own electronic flash, and a detachable motor winder. From Agfa came the first compact camera with a built-in motor winder. Telephoto pictures could be made with a 110 camera combined with a 7X20 binocular.

Another interesting trend was the return of many

Firemen battle to preserve irreplaceable prints at a $4-million fire that struck the International Museum of Photography in Rochester, N.Y., in May.

small range-finder or scale-focusing 35-mm cameras. Electronic circuitry combined with good, fast, inexpensive lenses made these cameras versatile as well as compact. Compact 35-mm range-finder cameras with automatic focusing were also on the increase.

Instant Photography. Two new "instant" cameras featured automatic focusing based on the subject's reflection of ultrasonic sound waves. Other instants included view cameras for professional photographers. And many conventional view cameras offered accessory backs to use with 8-by-10-inch (20-by-25-centimeter) instant film.

Videotape recorders appeared to rival 8-mm movie cameras for amateur filmmakers. These, along with small home-use TV cameras, can do many of the same things as 8-mm movies, and the results are available instantly, without processing. Still, a number of new Super-8 sound cameras and matching projectors were also shown. Some new projectors accepted all three 8-mm formats— Standard 8, Super 8, and Single 8.

New Materials to simplify photography appeared in 1978. Eastman Kodak Company and Minnesota Mining and Manufacturing Corporation (3M) announced 400-ASA-speed color slide films (800-speed with special processing). The Kodak film is available in 120-size rolls as well as 35-mm. Agfa marketed a 400-ASA color-print film,

and Fuji Photo Film Company of Japan a 400-ASA black-and-white film.

New printing papers included a fiber-based material from Ilford that differed from the common plastic-coated types. Two Cibachrome color papers were also introduced that offered better color and reduced contrast for printing directly from slides.

Hobby photography, especially color photography including darkroom work, continued to grow in popularity. Accessories to simplify color work, such as analyzers and kits of processing chemicals, were welcomed by hobbyists.

Holography, a form of three-dimensional photography, continued to gain importance as an industrial and scientific tool. As an experimental artist's medium, it rated its own museums in Chicago and New York City.

Collectors of fine art photography paid thousands of dollars for some individual prints. Because of the prints' value, research on photo preservation increased. For the first time, the United States issued a commemorative stamp to honor photography.

Photographers who died in 1978 included Victor Hasselblad, inventor of the camera the *Apollo* astronauts used on the moon; Marion Palfi, a photojournalist concerned with social problems; W. Eugene Smith, an outstanding photojournalist; and Otto Steinert, a European teacher and editor. Kenneth Poli

In WORLD BOOK, see CAMERA; PHOTOGRAPHY.

PHYSICS

PHYSICS. The Kosterlitz-Thouless theory of superfluid density and the Weinberg-Salam theory of the electromagnetic and weak forces received experimental support in 1978.

Measuring Superfluidity. When helium is cooled to a critical temperature several degrees above absolute zero, part of it suddenly becomes a *superfluid,* a very thin film that can flow through tiny channels at high velocities with little or no resistance. Physicists J. Michael Kosterlitz and David J. Thouless of the University of Birmingham in England proposed a theory in 1973 that predicts superfluid density. The theory treats the film as a collection of microscopic whirlpools moving freely through the liquid. As the temperature is lowered to the critical point, some whirlpools pair up with others rotating in the opposite direction, and part of the film becomes a superfluid.

David J. Bishop and John D. Reppy of Cornell University in Ithaca, N.Y., in June published experimental data for density agreeing with the theory. They coated a long, thin, plastic sheet with a film of liquid helium one or two molecules thick, then rolled up the sheet like a jellyroll and attached it to the end of a rod. Then, they rotated the rod back and forth rapidly. The whole system oscillated at its resonant frequency. Above the critical temperature, the film stuck to the sheet. When the scientists lowered the temperature to the critical value, superfluid suddenly formed that did not follow the motion of the sheet. This reduced the mass of the oscillating system, increasing resonant frequency slightly. The change in period (seconds per cycle) was only a few billionths of a second. The scientists used this number to calculate a value of superfluid density very close to the value predicted by the theory.

The Kosterlitz-Thouless theory is especially exciting because it might apply to many other areas of physics, including surface roughness and properties of liquid crystals.

Parity Violation. The experiment supporting the Weinberg-Salam theory depended on electron *spin* (angular momentum). An electron that spins clockwise as it moves forward is called *right-handed.* If it spins counterclockwise, it is *left-handed.* The laws of electrodynamics require that forces acting on electrons be independent of whether the electrons are left- or right-handed. Thus, if electrons struck an atomic nucleus, one would expect that left- and right-handed electrons would scatter with equal probability. *Parity* (equality) would be conserved.

In August, physicists from Switzerland, West Germany, and the United States announced the results of an electron-scattering experiment in which parity was not conserved. At the Stanford Linear Accelerator in Palo Alto, Calif., the scientists produced electrons of controlled handedness. Then they accelerated the electrons to extremely high energies and made them interact with atomic nuclei. Surpris-

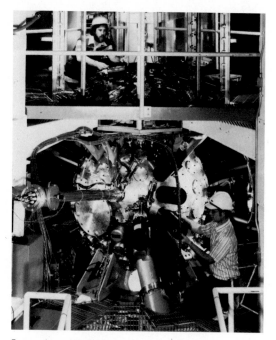

Researchers at Lawrence Livermore Laboratory in California get the world's most powerful laser, with 30 trillion watts of optical fire, ready for use.

ingly, left-handed electrons tended to scatter more often than right-handed ones. The effect was minute – involving differences of only one hundredth of 1 per cent or so – but parity was definitely violated.

An explanation for this parity violation can be found in a theory proposed in the 1960s by physicists Steven Weinberg of Harvard University in Cambridge, Mass., and Abdus Salam of the International Center for Theoretical Physics in Trieste, Italy. Their theory seeks to unify the electromagnetic force and the weak nuclear force. It predicts that the weak force should produce a small parity violation of exactly the magnitude observed.

Experiments on atomic decay failed to find the parity violation. However, the theory explained results of earlier experiments involving only the weak interaction. The explanations and the electron-scattering experiment make physicists confident that the theory can explain weak and electromagnetic forces in a unified framework.

Chinese Synchrotron. A 10-member delegation from the Institute of High-Energy Physics in Peking, China, visited the United States for three months to discuss China's plan to build a proton synchrotron of 30 to 50 billion electron volts capacity in five years. Thomas O. White

In WORLD BOOK, see PARITY; PARTICLE ACCELERATOR; PHYSICS.

PITTSBURGH. Allegheny County voters rejected a new governmental structure for the county by a 3-to-1 margin on Nov. 7, 1978. Neither political party took an official stand on the proposal, but most local political officials opposed it.

The proposal sought to replace the three existing county commissioners with an elected county executive officer and a nine-member county council elected by districts. It also would have eliminated the posts of eight elected administrative officers.

Proponents of the change argued that the new government would offer blacks more representation in the county's government, eliminate control over the county by "downtown" interests, base county appointments on merit rather than on patronage, and make it possible for Republicans to win some county offices. Opponents argued that the new government would increase costs and that the election of board members by district would lead to increased political conflict in each district.

School Busing. A suit was filed on October 23 to require Pittsburgh school officials to provide parochial school pupils with daily transportation to school. A 1972 state statute required public school districts to provide busing for parochial-school children living within 10 miles (16 kilometers) of their boundaries, but Pittsburgh has refused to comply with the law. Officials contend that it would cost the district more than $320,000 per year to transport the estimated 2,000 parochial-school children in the 10-mile zone. Pittsburgh's charge that the state law was unconstitutional was rejected by the Commonwealth Court in 1977.

Quality of Life. Pittsburgh lost 13.7 per cent of its population between 1970 and 1976, according to a U.S. Census Bureau report released on November 18. Only five of the nation's 40 largest cities suffered a larger decline. U.S. Department of Commerce figures ranked Pittsburgh 27th in the nation in terms of population density with 762 persons per square mile (294 persons per square kilometer).

Living costs rose 7.4 per cent during the 11-month period ending in June. Food costs rose by 8 per cent during the year ending in May. The U.S. Department of Labor reported on April 26 that living costs for an average family of four in the Pittsburgh area were slightly below the national average, with an annual income of $16,516 required for such a family to live on a middle-income budget.

Pittsburgh opened its Great House Sale lottery on May 20 in the hope of selling 32 dilapidated homes on the city's north side. Participation in the lottery was free, but winners had to pay $100 per home.

Pittsburgh's air, once notorious for its pollution, was canned and sold for $5.60 per six-pack as a collector's item during the year. Over 6,000 cans were reported sold during the first two weeks of marketing.   James M. Banovetz

See also CITY. In WORLD BOOK, see PITTSBURGH.

POETRY in 1978 was highlighted by crowning editions from a cluster of celebrated American poets. The *Collected Poems* of Howard Nemerov, which addressed the depths and "comprehensive silence" of the human landscape, won the Pulitzer Prize and the National Book Award for poetry.

Other major career achievements were Allen Tate's *Collected Poems: 1919-1976*, a proven and ironic body of work; the metaphysical visions of A. R. Ammons' *Selected Poems: 1951-1977*; and *New Collected Poems* from the venerable Robert Graves. Karl Shapiro's *Collected Poems: 1940-1978* presented unconventional verse stylings within the "context of sorrow." Robert Penn Warren's *Selected Poems: 1923-1975* provided an overview of the dramatic verse skills of one of America's most diverse men of letters.

Archibald MacLeish won the 1978 National Medal for Literature. British poet John Heath-Stubbs and Polish poet Czeslaw Milosz were honored for their international contributions to poetry.

Important Translations included *The Penguin Book of Zen Verse* by Lucien Stryk and Takashi Ikemoto; Galway Kinnell's rendering of *The Poems of François Villon;* and Howard Norman's *The Wishing Bone Cycle: Narrative Poems from the Swampy Cree Indians*, a rare and valuable look at native American poetry.

Russian poet Andrey Voznesensky, at a reading in Moscow in May, reads lines from a new work lamenting the problems of Russia and America.

Significant New Works. Canadian poet Margaret Atwood's *Selected Poems* offered fresh perspectives on nature and history. In *Images of Kin*, Michael Harper displayed a keen sense of political and personal event. Adrienne Rich's *Dream of a Common Language* stressed the "drive to connect" in women-to-women relationships. *The Mayan Poems* from James Schevill showed modern arrogance in conflict with ancient spirituality.

Bin Ramke articulated themes of loss and redemption in *The Difference Between Night and Day*, the most significant Yale Younger Poets' selection in a decade. Impressive work from other young poets included the delicate lyricism of Ira Sadoff's *Palm Reading in Winter*, and Alfred Corn's *A Call in the Midst of the Crowd*, which exhibited a dense, intricate voice.

Also notable were Vern Rutsala's *The Journey Begins*, a deeply introspective work; *To a Blossoming Pear Tree* by James Wright; Anthony Hecht's skillful *Millions of Strange Shadows*; *A Private Signal* by Barbara Howes; Diane Wakoski's *The Man Who Shook Hands*, which mourned love's dilemmas and losses; *A Full Heart*, an abundant book from Edward Field; and *The Retrieval System*, Maxine Kumin's view of separation from friends and family. Bill Knott's *Selected and Collected Poems* was judged best small-press poetry volume of the year.   G. E. Murray

In WORLD BOOK, see POETRY.

Huge coal excavator helped boost Poland's industrial output, partially offsetting shortfalls in meat and grain production.

POLAND struggled with dissidence, economics, and human rights problems in 1978. The Polish Writers' Union openly criticized state censorship in April and elected four prominent dissidents to its board of governors. More dissident publications appeared.

The Polish Social Self-Defense Committee, a dissident group, met secretly at the Czech border with the Charter 77 dissident group from that country in August to commemorate the 1968 invasion of Czechoslovakia by Russian-bloc countries.

Poland's Roman Catholic bishops issued a pastoral letter on September 17 denouncing censorship as a "weapon of totalitarian regimes," protesting the small number of catechisms permitted to be published, demanding more paper for independent Catholic publications, and demanding access to state-controlled radio and television for religious broadcasts.

The Polish Pope. Karol Cardinal Wojtyla, archbishop of Kraków, was elected pope on October 16 and became Pope John Paul II. Poland's President Henryk Jablonski attended the pope's installation in Rome on October 22. Polish radio and television, breaking with precedent, carried the installation live. More than 1,000 Polish pilgrims were allowed to go to Rome for the installation on special planes provided by the government. See DEATHS OF NOTABLE PERSONS (Close-Up); JOHN PAUL II; ROMAN CATHOLIC CHURCH.

Price Increases. After a March Central Committee meeting on agriculture and food supply problems, beef, veal, and pork prices paid to private farmers were raised. Polish farmers had struck in three provinces against an old-age-pension plan introduced in January. Poland failed by 440,000 short tons (400,000 metric tons) to reach its 1978 goal for meat.

Retail meat prices increased on June 1. The new prices ranged from 88 cents per pound (0.4 kilogram) for pork to $1.65 per pound for prime beef.

Poland boosted the price of alcoholic beverages 23 to 30 per cent on May 28 in an effort to decrease alcoholism. Gasoline prices increased on March 20 from $1.48 to $1.75 per gallon (3.8 liters).

Poland expected a poor grain harvest for the fifth consecutive year. It produced 23.7 short tons (21.5 metric tons), only 80 per cent of its needs.

Industrial output in the first half of 1978 increased 6.2 per cent, compared with the first half of 1977. Production fell short of the target in ships, refrigerators, plastics, synthetic fibers, furniture, and woolen textiles. Power shortages caused production delays.

Poland announced a plan in December to transfer 30,000 office administrators to other work in 1979, to get rid of superfluous bureaucrats.   Chris Cviic

See also EUROPE (Facts in Brief Table). In WORLD BOOK, see POLAND.

POLLUTION. See ENVIRONMENT.

POPULATION throughout the world was estimated at an all-time high of 4.365 billion persons on Dec. 31, 1978. By continuing to increase at the current 2 per cent annual rate, it will reach 6 billion by the year 2000.

Most of this growth will occur in what the United Nations (UN) calls the "developing" sector. The population of the "developed" sector – Europe, North America, Russia, Japan, temperate South America, Australia, and New Zealand – totaled 1.161 billion in 1978. In this group, prevailing low birth rates are moving toward a balance with death rates. The current growth rate of 0.8 per cent per year will double the population in about 100 years. Five countries in this sector with a total population of 156 million have already reached zero population growth.

In the developing sector, however, which comprises the rest of the world, population now totals about 3.2 billion. By the year 2000, it is expected that 4 out of every 5 people in the world will be living in this sector, mostly in Asia, Africa, and Latin America. Traditional high birth rates remain the rule in this sector, and these, coupled with continuing declines in death rates, are causing the rate of population growth to increase. The current growth rate of 2.4 per cent per year will double the population in this sector in 29 years to 6.4 billion and compound the already severe problem of feeding the burgeoning masses.

Study Released. The Environmental Fund of Washington, D.C., included in its *Population Estimate for 1978* a "per capita food index" that combines calories (energy) and protein (body-building and growth components). The index was instituted to measure the levels of nutrition that exist throughout the world.

In the developed countries, the per capita food index averaged 3.3 units. But in the developing world, the overall average per capita index was 1.2 units – the approximate equivalent of one U.S. meal per day. The index was 1.0 or less in 27 of the developing countries, including India. Three countries that are at the bottom of this inverted food pyramid – Liberia, Libya, and Mozambique – have indices of 0.7 and 0.6.

The UN Children's Fund (UNICEF) noted in late 1978 that "a whole generation of children are so hungry that they run the risk of being scarred for life by the effects of semistarvation and malnutrition – disease, blindness, mental retardation, stunted growth – unless massive emergency and long-range aid can be provided now." In many parts of Africa, almost every child under 5 suffers some protein malnutrition. It is estimated that more than half of all childhood deaths in Latin America are related to malnutrition.   Robert C. Cook

See also CENSUS, UNITED STATES. In WORLD BOOK, see POPULATION.

PORTUGAL struggled with inflation and debt problems that felled two governments in 1978. Prime Minister Mario Alberto Nobre Lopes Soares, ousted in December 1977, formed a new government on Jan. 26, 1978. He was dismissed on July 27. Alfredo Nobre da Costa succeeded him on August 28, but he was ousted on September 14. Carlos Mota Pinto then became prime minister on October 25.

Soares' Socialist-led coalition and the rightist Social Democratic Center (CDS) Party agreed on January 19 to pass an austerity program demanded by the International Monetary Fund (IMF) and 13 industrial nations from which Portugal sought $800-million in loans. The program aimed at cutting Portugal's $4.3-billion debt and reducing inflation to an annual rate of 20 per cent. It called for moderate domestic growth, higher taxes, lower subsidies, export promotion, investment in labor-intensive enterprises to reduce the 12.5 per cent unemployment rate, and a 20 per cent ceiling on wage increases to match the inflation rate.

Parliament approved a program of tax and price increases, import and credit restrictions, and restraints on welfare benefits on February 12. And on April 13 it approved a budget increasing sales taxes on nonessential consumer goods from 12 to 30 per cent; income taxes, 10 to 15 per cent; bus fares, 50 per cent; and rail fares, 20 per cent.

Also in April, Soares announced a 50 per cent hike in electricity and transportation costs; increases of 26.6 per cent in the minimum wage of industrial workers and 22 per cent in pension benefits; and 20.6 per cent price increases for many foods. Soares was dismissed on July 27 after his refusal to fire the minister of agriculture cost his coalition support of the CDS.

Alfredo Nobre da Costa succeeded Soares, forming a Cabinet of nonpartisan technicians chosen for their economic, commercial, and industrial competence. Soares charged that Da Costa's appointment defied the 1976 national elections, in which the Socialists won a plurality. The Communists and other leftists objected to Da Costa because he had headed large state and private companies under the right wing dictatorship ousted in 1974. Da Costa's government fell on September 14.

Mota Pinto. President Antonio Dos Santos Ramalho Eanes appointed law professor Mota Pinto as prime minister on October 25. A political independent, Mota Pinto is a former leader of the Social Democrats' parliamentary delegation and former minister of commerce. He took the oath of office on November 23, with a nonpartisan Cabinet of seven lawyers, four engineers, two army officers, an economist, and an agronomist. The Mota Pinto Cabinet survived a Communist motion to reject the government in December.   Kenneth Brown

See also EUROPE (Facts in Brief Table). In WORLD BOOK, see PORTUGAL.

POSTAL SERVICE, UNITED STATES. William F. Bolger became postmaster general on March 1, 1978. Bolger, who rose through the service's New England offices to become deputy postmaster general in 1975, succeeded Benjamin F. Bailar, who resigned.

Bolger took office in the midst of both good and bad news. The Postal Service reported on February 3 that its annual deficit had dropped to $687 million for the fiscal year that ended on Sept. 30, 1977, from $1.1 billion in fiscal 1976. But on May 29, the agency raised the price of postage on first-class letters from 13 cents to 15 cents. Newspaper, magazine, and parcel postage rates were also increased.

Strike Threat. After repeated threats of an illegal mail strike, the Postal Service concluded wage negotiations affecting 570,000 employees two months behind schedule. The Postal Service and postal unions reached a tentative agreement on July 21, but postal workers rejected it and threatened to walk out unless negotiations were reopened. The unions and the Postal Service agreed on August 28 to bargain for 15 days and turn to arbitration if they had not reached a settlement. Negotiations failed to produce a contract, so mediator-arbitrator James J. Healy, professor of labor relations at the Harvard Business School, issued a decision in September that sweetened pay increases over the July 21 agreement and provided a lifetime job guarantee for postal workers. Wages would rise 21.3 per cent over the three-year contract period and average annual pay would increase from $16,070 in late 1978 to $19,942 by 1981.

Electronic Innovations. The Postal Service announced on September 13 that it planned to introduce a nine-digit ZIP Code to speed electronic mail sorting by early 1981. The new code will replace the existing five-numeral ZIP Code used since 1963. The added digits will allow electronic reading machines to sort mail by carrier routes and city blocks.

A one-month operational test of a system of international electronic mail was scheduled to take place in February 1979. The Postal Service and the Communications Satellite Corporation worked together to develop nearly instantaneous facsimile transmission linking New York City and Washington, D.C., with points in five or six other countries.

The Postal Service on September 8 asked the Postal Rate Commission to approve an already functional form of electronic mail transmission for high-volume customers. Electronic Computer Originated Mail would be similar to the Western Union Telegraph Company's Mailgrams, but would cost 25 to 50 per cent less – 30 cents to 55 cents per message. Delivery anywhere in the United States would be assured within two days.   William J. Eaton

In WORLD BOOK, see POST OFFICE; POSTAL SERVICE, UNITED STATES.

Postmaster General William F. Bolger shows a model of the satellite to be tested in international electronic message service.

PRESIDENT OF THE UNITED STATES. Jimmy Carter struggled to control his own party in Congress and to stem the tide of inflation without plunging the nation into recession in 1978. His rating in public-opinion polls fell early in the year, then rose dramatically after his diplomatic success at Camp David, Maryland, in September.

On December 15, in a brief television announcement, he said that the United States and China would establish normal diplomatic relations on Jan. 1, 1979. See CHINA, PEOPLE'S REPUBLIC OF.

Relations with Congress. President Carter and the Congress controlled by his own Democratic Party clashed repeatedly, largely because the President vetoed legislation he regarded as inflationary. The second session of the 95th Congress sent the President 545 bills to sign. He vetoed 17 of them, 13 by pocket veto after the session ended.

In his State of the Union message on January 19, the President asked Congress for an effective energy program, tax reduction and reform, a new Department of Education, and Senate ratification of the Panama Canal treaties. On January 23, he proposed a $500.2-billion budget for fiscal 1979, with an estimated deficit of $60.6 billion. His budget earmarked $117.8 billion for defense, 3 per cent more than the 1978 defense budget.

The President pledged on October 24 that the fiscal 1980 budget would include a declining deficit,

Visiting France in January, President Carter tours Omaha Beach with French
President Giscard d'Estaing. Allied troops landed there during World War II.

first estimated at $30 billion then revised to $42.5-
billion. Despite his efforts to economize, he declared
that the 1980 budget would include an increase in
U.S. military spending in Europe.

President Carter refused to sign two major bills
that he considered inflationary. He vetoed a $37-
billion defense authorization bill on August 17
because it contained funds for a $2-billion nuclear-
powered carrier he deemed unnecessary. The House
sustained this veto on September 7. On October 5,
Carter vetoed a $10.2-billion public-works bill that
included six water projects not approved by the
President. The House sustained that veto later the
same day. See CONGRESS OF THE UNITED STATES.

Although Congress passed a five-part energy
program just before it adjourned on October 15, the
program was a compromise representing a much
weaker plan than Carter had originally proposed.
See ENERGY.

Inflation Continued as the nation's number-one
problem, and the President pleaded with Congress
and the American people for voluntary restraint to
keep wages, prices, and government spending from
spiraling. On January 20, in his annual economic
message to Congress, he urged voluntary guidelines
on price and wage increases. On April 11, addressing
the American Society of Newspaper Editors, he
declared that the government, industry, and labor
must "sacrifice for the common good" to fight

inflation, and he proposed that federal white-collar
salary increases be held to 5.5 per cent. On August
31, he told Congress that 1978 pay increases for
federal civilian and military employees would be
held to 5.5 per cent.

On September 20, speaking at the United Steelworkers Convention in Atlantic City, N.J., the President said he expected to announce "tough" anti-
inflation guidelines and again asked for sacrifices
from all Americans. Then on October 24, he announced to a nationwide television audience voluntary wage-price guidelines, pledging to cut federal
spending, place a partial freeze on federal hiring,
and reduce federal spending.

President Carter appealed to labor to accept a
ceiling of 7 per cent per year on wage and benefit
increases and asked industry to hold price increases
to 0.5 per cent less than their average in 1976-1977.
He also asked Congress to allow a tax rebate for
workers observing the guidelines if inflation rises
more than 7 per cent in 1979.

The President also acted to stem the decline of the
dollar, which reached record lows against the Japanese yen and the West German Deutsche mark in
late October. He declared on November 1 that the
United States would intervene "massively" in world
currency markets and issued $10 billion in U.S.
securities valued in West German Deutsche marks,
Japanese yen, and Swiss francs that would be used to

buy up dollars if the dollar's slide continued. He also announced that the Department of the Treasury would increase its sale of gold from government gold stocks to $1.5 billion per month beginning in December. In addition, the Federal Reserve System raised its discount rate a full percentage point to 9.5 per cent. The rate had not been raised so sharply since 1933. The Federal Reserve System also tightened reserve requirements for member banks, thus decreasing the supply of available credit. See ECONOMICS.

Military Policy. The President made several important decisions on defense in 1978, in addition to vetoing the $37-million weapons measure. In February he persuaded Congress not to allow $462 million in unused funds to be used to develop the B-1 bomber, a weapon he had rejected in 1977. On April 7, he announced that he had "decided to defer the production" of the controversial neutron bomb, a high-radiation warhead designed to kill enemy personnel with minimal damage to buildings and equipment. On September 29, the President approved a general upgrading of the United States civil defense system at an estimated cost of $2 billion over a five-year period. See ARMED FORCES.

Labor Policy. Labor troubles plagued the United States in 1978. President Carter declared on February 11 that the coal strike, then 68 days old, had caused a state of emergency in Ohio. He asked the miners and industry representatives on February 14 to resume negotiations, then invoked the compulsory back-to-work sections of the Taft-Hartley Act on March 6, after miners rejected a tentative agreement reached on February 24. His order was defied, but the miners finally ratified a new contract on March 24.

A rail strike beginning on September 26 involved 44 railroads and affected two-thirds of the rail traffic in the United States. On September 28, President Carter invoked the emergency powers of the National Railway Labor Act, forcing the strikers back to work for 60 days. Agreements with most of the rail workers concerned were reached by late December. See LABOR.

Administrative Activities. President Carter signed an executive order on January 24 reorganizing the administration of foreign intelligence activities and curbing the powers of intelligence agencies. In subsequent orders, he told federal agencies to write their regulations in "plain English," and revised classification procedures for government documents. At a town meeting in Fairfax, Va., on August 3, the President discussed his proposals to change the Civil Service to reward "dedication and excellence." He signed the Civil Service Reform Act on October 13.

The President was criticized early in 1978 for his dismissal of David Marston, federal district attorney in Philadelphia and a Republican. However, a

Department of Justice investigation completed on January 24 reported that neither the President nor Attorney General Griffin B. Bell was "guilty of improper conduct" in replacing a Republican with a Democratic district attorney. The President told a news conference on January 30 that the Marston dismissal was a "routine matter."

Far more serious charges involved corruption in the General Services Administration (GSA), the government's purchasing agency. The White House revealed on September 7 that the President had asked his friend and unofficial adviser, Georgia attorney Charles Kirbo, to monitor the continuing investigation of corruption in the GSA. The case promised to be one of the most serious ever involving a federal agency. See UNITED STATES, GOVERNMENT OF THE.

Camp David. President Carter took the initiative in getting Egypt and Israel to resume negotiations that might lead to a peace treaty and a general Middle East settlement. The White House announced on February 14 that the President had approved the $4.8-billion sale of advanced military warplanes to Egypt, Israel, and Saudi Arabia in a package deal to maintain the military balance of power in the Middle East. The move was widely interpreted as pressure on Israel to force its withdrawal from occupied territories.

President Jimmy Carter chats with predecessors Gerald Ford and Richard Nixon prior to memorial rites for Senator Hubert H. Humphrey in January.

One of the first women admitted to the White House honor guard, Navy E-2 Cathey Behnke shares a laugh with President Carter and his guests.

When negotiations between Egypt and Israel foundered, President Carter invited Israeli Prime Minister Menachem Begin and Egyptian President Anwar al-Sadat to a September meeting at his secluded Camp David presidential retreat. At that 13-day meeting, sequestered from the press, Begin and Sadat, monitored and occasionally prodded by President Carter, finally agreed on a framework for a peace settlement. This personal triumph for President Carter was announced to the world on September 17. Many disagreements between Egypt and Israel surfaced in the months that followed, and the other Arab states remained intransigent. But Carter's personal diplomacy at Camp David had brought peace closer to the Middle East in 1978 than anyone dreamed possible. See MIDDLE EAST.

Foreign Policy. The President's decision to establish diplomatic relations with China disturbed some members of Congress because it included the breaking of diplomatic ties with Taiwan.

In a major diplomatic triumph, President Carter gained congressional approval of the two Panama Canal treaties, despite vocal opposition in the United States. In accordance with the treaties, Panama will assume control over the canal in the year 2000. The treaties provided safeguards for the canal's neutrality and defense. President Carter and Panama's Chief of Government Omar Torrijos Herrera signed the treaties in Panama on June 16.

The President took a firm line toward Russia and Cuba. He warned the Soviet Union on March 17 that its military build-up threatened U.S.-Russian strategic arms limitation talks and said that the United States was prepared to increase its military arsenal if necessary. On May 5, the President revealed that he had warned Supreme Soviet Presidium Chairman Leonid I. Brezhnev about Russian and Cuban involvement in Africa.

Opening a North Atlantic Treaty Organization (NATO) meeting in Washington, D.C., on May 30, the President declared that the United States could not remain "indifferent" to Soviet and Cuban interference in Africa, or to Russia's military build-up in Europe.

The President also charged on May 25 that Cuba's Premier Fidel Castro Ruz was aiding the rebel invasion of Zaire. Castro denied the charge.

President Carter continued to criticize human-rights violations. On April 21, he labeled Cambodia "the worst violator of human rights in the world today." He also spoke out against the Russian trials of dissidents. Nonetheless, the President declared in May that he was committed to an arms pact with the Soviet Union.

On April 21, the President announced that he would withdraw one U.S. combat battalion from South Korea in 1978, but the other two scheduled for withdrawal at the same time would remain in Korea until 1979. It was revealed on September 21 that the President was extending the U.S. trade embargo against Vietnam. He ended the arms embargo against Turkey on September 26.

The President's Travels took him to three continents. During a nine-day trip to seven countries, he conferred with Jordan's King Hussein I on January 1; addressed India's Parliament in New Delhi on January 2; and met with leaders in Saudi Arabia the following day. Carter conferred with President Sadat in Aswan, Egypt, on January 4, then flew to France. He visited NATO headquarters in Brussels, Belgium, on January 6.

From March 28 to April 3, the President visited Venezuela, Brazil, Nigeria, and Liberia to strengthen U.S. relations with developing nations.

He went to Bonn, West Germany, on July 13 to confer with West German Chancellor Helmut Schmidt before an economic summit meeting with British, Canadian, Italian, French, West German, and Japanese leaders and a representative of the Executive Commission of the European Community (EC or Common Market).

The President also traveled in the United States. He made a four-state Western tour in May, and he campaigned in 22 states for Democratic candidates before the November elections.   Carol L. Thompson

See also CARTER, JAMES EARL, JR.; ELECTIONS. In WORLD BOOK, see PRESIDENT OF THE UNITED STATES; CARTER, JAMES EARL, JR.

PRINCE EDWARD ISLAND. A political era ended on Sept. 18, 1978, when Premier Alexander B. Campbell resigned after 12 years in office. Campbell's Liberal government had won a narrow victory in an election on April 24, but Liberal standing was cut from 26 to 17 seats in the 32-seat legislature. The Conservative opposition increased its strength from 6 to 15 seats. The Liberals' edge fell to 1 seat when Campbell dramatically announced his resignation from politics. The fact that the Liberals needed to appoint a speaker from their ranks further weakened their ability to govern.

The party caucus chose former Finance and Education Minister Bennett Campbell – no relation to the former premier – to be the Liberal leader and new premier on December 9. Following an election upset in Nova Scotia, Prince Edward Island had the only Liberal government among the provinces.

A five-week session of the legislature followed the election. Most of the 25 bills passed were housekeeping measures. Rent control formed part of the package. A budget presented on June 15 indicated a deficit of $3.2 million in spite of the government's drawing on an investment account to augment its revenues. Expenditures of $265.6 million were forecast, taking into account reductions in spending by 15 departments. David M. L. Farr

See also CANADA. In WORLD BOOK, see PRINCE EDWARD ISLAND.

PRISON. The population of United States correctional facilities continued to increase in 1978, but at a slower rate than during the previous five years. Figures released by *Corrections Magazine* in June indicated that state and federal prisons housed 294,896 inmates in early 1978, up 5 per cent from the 281,439 of 1977.

During the year, the Supreme Court of the United States clarified a number of important prison-administration issues. On February 22, the Supreme Court ruled, 7 to 2, that wardens who confiscated or neglected to mail inmate letters enjoyed a limited immunity from civil suit. In an 8 to 1 decision on June 23, the justices confirmed that a federal judge could single out a particular condition in a state prison as unconstitutional and order it corrected. And on June 26, by 4 to 3, the court held that the news media had no greater right of access to jails than the general public.

Prison Reform was mandated by 1978 court rulings. A federal judge ruled on April 19 that "boxcar" cells used for solitary confinement at the Marion, Ill., federal penitentiary constituted cruel and unusual punishment; the cells were 6 feet 6 inches (198 centimeters) wide and 8 feet (244 centimeters) long. Strip-frisk searches at New York's Great Meadow Correctional Facility were declared illegal by another federal judge on April 22. The U.S. Court of Appeals for the District of Columbia

ruled on July 12 that if an escaped prisoner could prove he fled because of intolerable conditions, and not merely to gain his freedom, he could be acquitted of escape charges.

A Tennessee chancery court judge on January 30 ordered an overcrowded state prison building at Nashville closed. It marked the first time that a state, rather than a federal, court shut down part of a substandard corrections facility.

Prison Riots. Bureau of Prisons investigators launched an inquiry on April 10 into a series of nine inmate murders in 18 months at the penitentiary in Atlanta, Ga. A 10th prisoner was knifed to death on September 21. A riot at the Pontiac, Ill., State Penitentiary on July 22 resulted in the stabbing deaths of three guards and the wounding of three others; fire damage during a four-hour inmate rampage was estimated at $2.5 million. The Pontiac facility, designed for 600 prisoners, held 2,000.

The most serious prison disturbance of 1978 occurred at Villa DeVoto Prison near Buenos Aires, Argentina, on March 14, when 55 convicts were killed and 78 injured during a riot. The facility held 4,000 prisoners, about 1,500 more than it was built to house. David C. Beckwith

In WORLD BOOK, see PRISON.

PRIZES. See AWARDS AND PRIZES; CANADIAN LIBRARY ASSOCIATION; CANADIAN LITERATURE; FASHION; NOBEL PRIZES.

PROTESTANTISM. The World Council of Churches (WCC), to which most Protestant and Eastern Orthodox denominations belong, was a center of controversy in 1978. The Switzerland-based organization in August sent $85,000 from its "program to combat racism" to the Patriotic Front of Zimbabwe, a Rhodesian guerrilla group headed by Robert Mugabe and Joshua Nkomo.

This move was controversial for a variety of reasons. Conservatives had consistently attacked the WCC for favoring Third World revolutionary groups. In Rhodesia, which would be called Zimbabwe under black rule, Bishop Abel Muzorewa and Ndabaningi Sithole, the two most important moderate black leaders, were members of the coalition government against which the Patriotic Front was fighting a guerrilla action. They were thus temporarily linked with Prime Minister Ian D. Smith's white-minority government in its moves toward "one-man, one-vote" rule. The WCC support for the guerrillas was seen as undercutting the moderate approach of these black African churchmen.

Worse, from the viewpoint of WCC critics, the grant came shortly after guerrilla forces allegedly murdered 20 white missionaries and members of their families at the Emmanuel mission school of Lumba. While these deaths were few compared to the large number of blacks killed in guerrilla actions, the incident caused new uneasiness and resentment

Anglican women priests and a bishop leave
the Lambeth Conference after it voted to let
national churches decide on ordaining women.

among North American Protestants. Although the WCC designated the funds for humanitarian purposes, critics argued that the $85,000 gift released other funds for military action.

The All-Africa Conference of Churches, which met in Togo in February, also experienced controversy. The conference, a WCC experiment in regional ecumenism, debated what critics called the "scandalous and adulterous" conduct of its general secretary, Burgess Carr of Liberia, who took a sabbatical leave that may mark the end of his leadership. Carr said that the charges were only an effort to discredit the often controversial All-Africa Conference of Churches and its political activities.

The Anglican Church was beset by controversy over the ordination of women priests. At the once-a-decade Lambeth Conference in August in Canterbury, England, bishops from throughout the world voted 316 to 37 to let each national church decide whether to ordain women. The Church of England voted no when the issue came before its annual conference in November.

American Protestants enjoyed relative prosperity. Many of the more conservative churches continued to grow, and some mainline Protestant groups cheered themselves with the idea that their decade-long decline had "bottomed out." Individualized Christianity, symbolized by radio evangelists and best-selling books on the "born again" theme,

was in a boom period. See Section Two, How Real Is America's Religious Revival?

But U.S. Protestantism also had its share of controversy. Denominational battles had raged over the question of ordaining homosexuals. Many churches evaded or postponed taking a position on the issue. The largely southern Presbyterian Church in the United States and the United Methodist Church took relatively critical stands in 1976. But an appeal for "definitive guidance" by the Presbytery of New York forced the United Presbyterian Church to render its decision. Emotions ran high during months of preparation for the General Assembly in San Diego in May; the issue of homosexuality came to be tied to tensions that threatened Presbyterian unity.

After prolonged debate, the Assembly voted 12 to 1 to urge the church to continue ministering to homosexuals, but found homosexual practice to be incongruent with Biblical teaching. The majority said the church should not sanction the homosexual style of living by making it exemplary in the ministry. The delegates claimed to see homosexuality as a sin no worse than greed or pride, but many Presbyterians who had not attended the assembly were more agitated over this issue than over other "sins." The San Diego vote was a setback to those who advocated more positive Protestant recognition of homosexuality. The Episcopal Church, traditionally more tolerant on the subject, faced a divisive struggle over the controversy during its 1979 general convention.

Following the momentum created in Dade County, Florida, in 1977 when entertainer Anita Bryant led fundamentalists to oppose "homosexual rights" ordinances, militantly conservative Protestants helped form coalitions against such rights in successful voting tests in Wichita, Kans.; St. Paul, Minn.; and Eugene, Ore. Such intrusions into electoral and legislative realms by conservatives reversed their stand on social action a decade earlier. In the late 1960s, these same conservative Protestants often critized moderate or liberal clergy who publicly supported civil rights or dissent against the Vietnam War. Now, while liberal Protestants were relatively quiet, conservatives demanded legislation against homosexuality, pornography, the Equal Rights Amendment, and liberalized abortion laws.

Crowded Seminaries. Although the mainline churches seemed passive as they recovered morale and a sense of mission, their young people signaled confidence in the future by entering the ordained ministry in increasing numbers. So large was the enrollment in various divinity schools in 1978 that a study based at the Hartford Seminary Foundation in Connecticut and Duke Divinity School in Durham, N.C., began to project problems of overcrowding in the ministerial ranks. If the rate of growth in seminaries continued while denominations declined or grew only slightly, the study predicted, Episcopalian, Presbyterian, and even prospering Southern Baptist ranks would have as many clerics as laity early in the next century. There were more than 9,000 Southern Baptist students enrolled in seminaries in 1977.

While the Mormons—members of the Church of Jesus Christ of Latter-day Saints—have tenuous relations with orthodox Protestants, the denomination's roots are in American Protestantism. The Mormons made headlines on June 9, when President Spencer W. Kimball announced a new revelation—something allowed for from the beginning in this church's teaching. As "prophet, seer, and revelator," he announced that "all worthy males" may enter the priesthood, which is the normal rank for men in Mormonism. Blacks had previously been denied this office and some "heavenly benefits" that went with it. The first black to be named a priest was Joseph Freeman, a Salt Lake City telephone company employee. He was ordained an elder on June 11.

Lay Congress. In more conventional Protestantism, a celebrated Congress of the Laity, organized by the Howard Butt Foundation in February, symbolized a new cordiality between evangelical and mainline Protestant and Catholic lay people, along with a new willingness to take faith into business and public life. Former President Gerald R. Ford and his wife, Betty, hosted the meeting.

Theological breaches remained, however. In October, some Protestant conservatives launched a 10-year, $10-million drive to promote the teaching that the Bible is free from error. They were motivated by their awareness that other, if equally conservative, views of Biblical authority now predominated in some evangelical seminaries.

Electronics. The February meeting of the National Religious Broadcasters Association heard its executive director, Ben Armstrong, cite the "electronic church" as a rival for loyalty to the local church. Armstrong referred to the 325-station network of evangelistic radio and television stations, which grew during the year at a rate of one station a week and launched satellite broadcasting late in the year. Celebrity preachers such as Oral Roberts, Robert Schuller, Rex Humbard, and Jerry Falwell built up "parachurch" or "quasidenominational" followings. The top 12 such enterprises each raised from $20 million to $70 million during the year.

The most controversial area of evangelistic outreach was the effort to convert Jews. The Lutheran Church—Missouri Synod, for example, was forced by criticism to withdraw evangelistic literature that reproduced racial stereotypes of Judaism. The synod did not step back, however, from its new alliance with the Jews for Jesus, an aggressive missionary group.   Martin E. Marty

See also RELIGION. In WORLD BOOK, see PROTESTANTISM and articles on Protestant denominations.

PSYCHOLOGY. Two experiments showed in 1978 that experience can markedly change the normal response to two different kinds of reproductive behavior that were previously regarded as purely instinctive. The male sex function and maternal care have often been regarded as changeable only by genetic alteration. Psychologists conducted the experiment on male sex function on male rats. The study on maternal care was made on female gorillas.

Rat Study. Psychologists Dennis W. Twiggs, Herbert B. Popolow, and Arnold A. Gerall of Tulane University in New Orleans showed that the sexual behavior of male rats that suffered damage to specific areas of their brains prior to puberty differed distinctly from the behavior of rats that suffered the same damage after they became adults. The behavioral differences could be linked only to learning experience.

Psychologists and neurologists have known for many years that certain kinds of brain damage cause more conspicuous deficits in adults than in infants and juveniles. They theorized that certain functions can be carried out equally well in early life by more than one brain region, so if one region is damaged another part of the brain will take over its functions. In later life, however, such developmental processes as experience confine each function to a specialized region. When brain damage occurs after specialization has taken place, there is a loss of function in the behavior controlled by the damaged area. But no one suspected until the Tulane experiment that the same theory applied to such instinctive functions as sexual behavior.

The psychologists concentrated on the medial preoptic area (MPA), a very small assemblage of nerve cells that lies deep within the brain. They found that male sexual behavior is greatly impaired if this area of the brain is destroyed by disease in human beings or by experimental surgery in animals. When the MPA in adult male rats, cats, dogs, monkeys, or human beings is damaged, sexual behavior is permanently and irreversibly damaged.

The Tulane team's experiment indicated that rats suffering MPA damage prior to puberty were normal in sexual behavior after they became adults. But, as expected, comparable damage in adult rats caused severe deficiencies in mating behavior.

Moreover, the investigators proved that the social experience enabled rats with MPA damage suffered prior to puberty to function sexually. Young rats with MPA damage that were raised in solitary cages and had no social experience did not mate normally as adults. Since juveniles play much more than do adults, the investigators speculated that play provides the experience that rats with pre-adolescent MPA damage need in order to develop normal sexual functions.

Gorilla Motherhood. Behavioral Scientist Ronald D. Nadler of the Yerkes Regional Primate

Research Center at Emory University in Atlanta, Ga., studied maternal abuse and the neglect of infant gorillas by caged mothers. The great apes, and especially gorillas, have a deserved reputation for low reproductive output in captivity. One principal problem has been that even when gorillas reproduce, the mothers refuse to care for their infants. Nadler found that only 10 of 30 gorillas that gave birth to normal babies for the first time took care of their offspring. He reported that seven of the 10 good mothers lived with other mothers or with their mates when the babies were young, while 87 per cent of those who were caged alone neglected or abused their babies.

When Nadler established a compatible social group of three females and a male, all three females took excellent care of their first-born infants.

Family sociologists and psychologists have shown interest in this gorilla study. "A lot of things contribute to human child abuse," Roy Kern of Georgia State University in Atlanta commented, "but I'm inclined to think that the abuse we have been hearing so much about recently is indeed related to the loneliness experienced by today's young mothers." Nadler hopes his findings will provide a key to understanding the relevance of social companionship to maternal behavior in humans.   Robert W. Goy

See also MENTAL HEALTH. In WORLD BOOK, see PSYCHOLOGY.

PUBLIC HEALTH. Secretary Joseph A. Califano, Jr., of the United States Department of Health, Education, and Welfare (HEW) launched an all-out, $23-million war on smoking in 1978, and several states left it to voters to decide whether nonsmoking areas should be required in public places. Califano described smoking, which has increased among women and teen-agers and decreased slightly among men, as "the nation's primary preventable cause of death."

The National Cancer Institute in Bethesda, Md., reported in October that lung cancer, the deadliest of the three most common cancers, has increased dramatically among women since 1973. Cancer cases generally have increased 1 to 2 per cent per year since 1970, the institute's five-year study indicated, but lung cancer rose 8 per cent per year among white women and 10 per cent among black women.

Controversy flared in 1978 over whether a "tolerable-risk" cigarette could be developed. While the American Cancer Society argued that there is no such thing as a safe cigarette, epidemiologic studies demonstrated that smokers of low-tar, low-nicotine cigarettes have a lower incidence of lung cancer. The incidence, however, is not as low as among nonsmokers. A 14-year study that was financed by six tobacco companies found that cigarette smoking may cause lung and heart disease and ulcers.

Alcoholism Increasing. HEW's National Institute on Alcohol Abuse and Alcoholism reported in October that an estimated 10 million Americans are problem drinkers or alcoholics, and that as many as 205,000 deaths each year can be traced to alcohol abuse. Some 3.3 million teen-agers from 14 to 19 years old also have drinking problems, the report said. Alcohol was indicated as a cause in up to one-third of all suicides, half of all murders, half of all traffic deaths, one-fourth of other accidental deaths, and thousands of birth defects.

Smallpox, Cholera, and the Flu. Virtually extinct around the world, smallpox caused one death in England in September; an Englishwoman apparently contracted the virus while working in a laboratory. The World Health Organization (WHO) said that such virus labs have become the last major source of smallpox danger, and recommended that only five major centers be allowed to store the virus for research purposes.

WHO also reported a drop in the number of cholera cases in 1977, but added that the disease had spread to 34 countries, as compared with 25 in 1976. Most alarming was its spread to the Pacific Islands and to countries in Africa and the Middle East that had no cholera for years.   Dianne Rafalik Hales

See also HEALTH AND DISEASE; MEDICINE. In WORLD BOOK, see HEALTH; PUBLIC HEALTH; SMOKING.

PUBLISHING. The merger trend in the United States publishing industry came under scrutiny in 1978 as antitrust enforcement agencies investigated its effects on freedom of expression. The U.S. Department of Justice sued CBS Inc. in June, calling for CBS to dispose of Fawcett Publications. Western Pacific Industries voluntarily sold back $10 million of its stock in Houghton Mifflin Company in July, two months after the purchase. And the Federal Trade Commission continued its inquiry into Doubleday & Company's 1976 acquisition of the Dell Publishing Company.

In September, Harper & Row acquired J.P. Lippincott by merger for an estimated $15 million. The Scott & Fetzer Company in August purchased World Book–Childcraft International, Inc., from Field Enterprises, Incorporated.

Foreign Publishers entered the U.S. book field in 1978. W. H. Smith and Sons Limited of London, Great Britain's largest publishing house, set up shop under the imprint of Mayflower Books. Methuen, Incorporated, became the only Canadian publisher in the United States when it opened a firm in New York City. And France's largest publisher, the Hachette Group, announced plans in July to enter the American market. The Oxford University Press celebrated 500 years of publishing in Oxford, England, with ceremonies throughout the world.

The Supreme Court of the United States decided

Oxford University Press officials blow out the candles as an exhibition
marking the press's 500th anniversary opens in March in New York City.

on May 23 that children should not be considered in determining community obscenity standards for published works and films.

Book Sales recorded healthy increases during the first six months of 1978. Hard-cover sales were up 17 per cent; mass-market paperbacks, 11 per cent; and trade paperbacks, 15 per cent.

New American Library handed over a record $2.55 million for the paperback rights to Mario Puzo's new novel, *Fools Die*. Harper & Row claimed a publishing first when it simultaneously introduced *The Azanian Assignment* throughout the English-speaking world under one imprint. Fawcett Books paid the highest price ever for nonfiction paperback rights – $2.25 million for *Linda Goodman's Love Signs*. James Michener's *Chesapeake* soared to the number-one spot on *The New York Times* best-seller list just one week after it hit store counters in July. Other best-sellers of the year included *Bloodline* and *The Thorn Birds*.

A Gallup Poll commissioned by the American Library Association reported that 1 out of 3 American adults reads a book or more per month. According to the study, 50 per cent of those surveyed read fiction; 35 per cent, nonfiction; and 7 per cent, how-to books. Celeste H. Huenergard

See also CANADIAN LITERATURE; LITERATURE; NEWSPAPER; POETRY. In WORLD BOOK, see BOOKS; PUBLISHING.

PUERTO RICO. Preoccupation with the island's future relationship with the United States intensified in 1978. Three factions pressed their views: The New Progressive Party (NPP) favored statehood; the Popular Democratic Party (PDP) wanted to retain commonwealth status; the Puerto Rican Independence Party favored independence.

Former Governor Rafael Hernandez Colon precipitated a crisis within the powerful PDP on July 21 by resigning as its president, a position tantamount to nomination for the governorship in the 1980 elections. Party members had hoped that Hernandez Colon's popularity would help sweep the PDP back into office and displace the pro-statehood NPP, which controls the governorship and the legislature.

The PDP crisis was heightened in October, when a pro-statehood faction took control of the party in an election of delegates to a November convention. The delegates selected would in turn attend the U.S. Democratic Party Convention in 1980.

Pro-independence Puerto Rico Socialist Party members continued to wage a campaign of violence. Two of its members were killed on July 25 after police discovered them trying to sabotage communication towers in Villalba. Paul C. Tullier

See also LATIN AMERICA (Facts in Brief Table). In WORLD BOOK, see PUERTO RICO.

PULITZER PRIZES. See AWARDS AND PRIZES.

QATAR. See MIDDLE EAST.

QUEBEC. The Parti Québécois (PQ) government of Premier René Lévesque revealed in 1978 that its promised referendum would be used to gain a mandate to negotiate "sovereignty-association" for Quebec with the rest of Canada. The PQ said it would not try to gain independence and then negotiate an association. "We don't want to break, but to transform radically, our union with the rest of Canada," Lévesque told the Quebec National Assembly in October. The PQ's objective was to win full equality with Canada. This would mean that Quebec would levy its own taxes and enact laws relating to its own territory. A referendum bill was passed in June, but the vote was not expected to take place before the end of 1979.

Quebec's provincial Liberal Party chose Claude Ryan as its new leader on April 15. Ryan, the influential editor of a Montreal newspaper and a federalist committed to major changes in Canada's constitutional structure, has been called "the conscience of Quebec" because of his moral standing and integrity. A by-election on July 5, the first since the PQ victory in late 1976, saw a Liberal candidate elected to Quebec's National Assembly. The PQ held 71 seats in a house of 110.

Finance Minister Jacques Parizeau's budget, brought down on April 18, forecast a $1-billion deficit for 1978-1979. It increased taxes for higher income earners and reduced them for middle- and low-income groups. Responding to the federal budget of eight days earlier, Parizeau removed the 8 per cent tax on clothing, shoes, furniture, and hotel rooms for 50 weeks ending March 31, 1979.

Leaving Quebec. Policyholders of the Sun Life Assurance Company of Canada voted on January 6 to move company headquarters to Toronto, Ont. The company claimed that new laws on the use of French in business and education would limit the company's ability to hire qualified personnel. Some operations would continue in Montreal, where the company was located for 108 years. The Royal Trust Company, one of Canada's largest, also moved some operations and, in a corporate reorganization, set up an office in Calgary, Alta., to handle all business outside Montreal.

Stores Closed. But the event that probably proved most upsetting to the average French-speaking citizen of Montreal was the closing in February of Dupuis Frères department stores, which had stood for more than 100 years as an exception to English-language domination in Quebec business and commerce. A variety of factors combined to end the retail establishment and put 700 persons out of work, with unemployment in Canada at its highest level since the Great Depression.   David M. L. Farr

See also CANADA; McDERMOTT, DENNIS. In WORLD BOOK, see QUEBEC.

RACING. See AUTOMOBILE RACING; BOATING; HORSE RACING; SWIMMING; TRACK AND FIELD.

RADIO made broadcasting history on Feb. 8, 1978, when the United States Senate permitted the first live radio – but not television – coverage of a floor debate. Discussion of the controversial Panama Canal treaties was aired briefly by the National Broadcasting Company (NBC) and the Columbia Broadcasting System (CBS). However, National Public Radio gave the debate gavel-to-gavel coverage for three days. The U.S. House of Representatives opened its day-to-day operations to live radio coverage on June 12, and, in England, the British Broadcasting Corporation aired its first broadcast from the House of Commons on April 3, 1978.

Broadcast Formats changed little in 1978. The most popular U.S. disk-jockey programming featured contemporary rock music. Lush, beautiful music was second, followed by middle-of-the-road and country music.

Radio's newest "contemporary" music format was disco, rock-rhythm records introduced for dancing in discothèques. WKTU-FM in New York City and KUTE-FM in Los Angeles, formerly low rated, became the number-two stations in their respective markets when they adopted adult disco formats.

The *CBS Radio Mystery Theater*, commercial network radio's only dramatic series in 1978, celebrated its fifth successful year. In October, CBS announced plans for a second series, *The Sears Radio Theatre*, scheduled to start on Feb. 5, 1979.

Government Regulation. The Supreme Court of the United States in July upheld a 1975 Federal Communications Commission (FCC) ruling that WBAI-FM in New York City had violated FCC rules by playing an "indecent" comedy album. Thus, the Supreme Court reversed a 1977 opinion by the U.S. Court of Appeals overturning the FCC ruling. By so doing, the Supreme Court reinforced the FCC's power to issue sanctions against "patently offensive" language on radio or TV.

The 48-year-old Mutual Broadcasting System in April bought its first owned and operated station, WCFL-AM, from the Chicago Federation of Labor and Industrial Union Council for $12 million.

Minority Ownership. President Jimmy Carter's Administration launched a wide-ranging program in April to increase ownership of radio and TV stations by minorities. Unity Broadcasting, the National Black Network, purchased WSAS-AM-FM in Philadelphia in October from Max M. Leon, Incorporated, for about $5 million. By the end of the year, blacks owned more than 50 radio stations, including WYCB-AM in Washington, D.C.; KCBS-FM in San Francisco; and KKTT-AM and KUTE-FM in the Los Angeles area.

The FCC began a formal inquiry on September 14 into the merits of five AM stereo-transmission systems. Due to technical complications, the inquiry was expected to be a long one.   June Bundy Csida

In WORLD BOOK, see RADIO.

RAILROAD systems in the United States ran into financial difficulty in 1978, struggling with strikes and increasing costs. Consolidated Rail Corporation (Conrail), the government-financed Northeastern line, obtained more federal funding and asked to free itself of Interstate Commerce Commission (ICC) regulation. President Jimmy Carter's Administration agreed that railroads should become more profitable without massive federal aid and promised rail-deregulation legislation for early 1979.

The Association of American Railroads (AAR) said U.S. railroads lost $43.1 million in the first nine months of 1978, compared with a $164.8-million profit in the first nine months of 1977. The railroads earned $28.2 million in the third quarter of 1978, compared with a $23.6-million deficit in the third quarter of 1977. Freight traffic increased 4.7 per cent through early December.

Operating revenues reached $15.9 billion in the first nine months, up 7.2 per cent. The ICC approved freight-rate increases of 2 to 4 per cent in June, and 6.6 per cent more in December. The industry had sought 8.1 per cent. A 110-day coal strike hurt railroads financially early in the year, and a 4-day industry-wide strike occurred at the end of an 82-day railway-clerks' strike that was called against the Norfolk & Western Railway and that came to an end on October 1.

Railroad cars are strewn like dominoes along track near Rochester, N.Y., after 40 cars of a train derailed in February.

Conrail Loss Up. Conrail lost $325.4 million in the first nine months of 1978, 12 per cent more than in the first nine months of 1977. Conrail Chairman Edward G. Jordan said in February that the system would need more time and more federal money than the government had predicted to turn its big losses into a profit. Congress authorized $1.2 billion in addition to previously approved funds of $2.1 billion. But Conrail said in November that it could not make a profit unless Congress freed it of ICC regulation.

Conrail reached an agreement in September with the AFL-CIO United Transportation Union, reducing the crew size on nearly all of its freight trains and ensuring that it would have one contract with uniform work rules by Sept. 1, 1979, instead of the 43 contracts inherited from its predecessor railroads. Jordan said the agreement would help Conrail "substantially achieve" its goal of saving $500 million over five years through collective bargaining and consolidating agreements.

Changes Asked. The U.S. Department of Transportation said in October that railroads might need $16 billion in federal financing over 10 years unless ICC regulation were rolled back, truckers charged more for using highways, and barge lines charged for using waterways.   Albert R. Karr

See also TRANSPORTATION. In WORLD BOOK, see RAILROAD.

RECORDINGS. Record and tape sales in the United States continued to soar in 1978, breaking the 1977 industry record of $3.5 billion and the $1.06-billion record for cassettes and eight-track cartridges alone.

For the first time, record companies could not meet the demand. As the sales pace accelerated during the fall, record pressers warned that there could be delays in meeting orders, not only for high-demand products, but also for the established records that are the mainstay of the industry. As a consequence, CBS Inc., which already makes most of its records, arranged to build a $50-million disk-and-tape plant in Carrollton, Ga.

Warner Communications Incorporated announced in October that it will build U.S. plants to make disks and tapes for its three United States record companies — Warner, Atlantic, and Elektra/Asylum/Nonesuch. Warner presently buys the disks and tapes. The first plant will be built in Olyphant, Pa., near a record-pressing plant Warner agreed to buy.

For the first time in the 20-year history of the Grammy Awards, two songs tied for best of the year: "Evergreen," by Barbra Streisand and Paul Williams, from the film *A Star Is Born;* and "You Light Up My Life," by Joe Brooks.

The Supreme Court of the United States ruled on April 18 against the release of the White House tape

Fleetwood Mac won the Grammy Award for best album with "Rumours," at the National Academy of Recording Arts and Sciences ceremony in Los Angeles.

Smiles lit up the faces of Debby Boone, father Pat, and mother Shirley in February when Debby received a Grammy Award as best new artist.

recordings of former President Richard M. Nixon. Warner Bros. Records wanted to produce a two-record set of the voices of Nixon and his aides as heard in the courtroom during the Watergate trials.

Hot Albums. Sales by pop artists reached astronomical levels. The Peter Frampton album, "Frampton Comes Alive," sold 13 million copies worldwide and "Saturday Night Fever" about 30 million. The sound-track album of *Grease* sold 10 million copies in the United States. Turning out million-selling LP's were the Bee Gees, Boston, the Eagles, Fleetwood Mac, Foreigner, and Barry Manilow. See MUSIC, POPULAR (Close-Up).

RCA Records released the first stereo recording of Sergei V. Rachmaninoff's *Third Piano Concerto* by Vladimir Horowitz, recorded in New York City's Carnegie Hall in January during his first performance with an orchestra in 25 years.

Fancy Disks. Two more kinds of LP's, picture disks and colored vinyl, became popular. Picture disks have the artwork of the album cover imprinted on them and cost from $13 to $15. Small companies were the first to start producing these disks. Larger companies followed suit, planning picture disks for Linda Ronstadt, Rod Stewart, and the Brothers Johnson.   Leonard Feather and Eliot Tiegel

See also MUSIC, CLASSICAL; MUSIC, POPULAR. IN WORLD BOOK, see PHONOGRAPH.

RED CROSS. See COMMUNITY ORGANIZATIONS.

RELIGION. President Jimmy Carter surprised his fellow "born-again" Christians at a widely publicized annual prayer breakfast in January 1978 in Washington, D.C., by asking them to join with him in thanking God for the faith of Egypt's President Anwar al-Sadat and Israel's Prime Minister Menachem Begin. To some conservative Protestants who ordinarily cast wary eyes on the faiths of Islam and Judaism, this presidential outlook seemed unnecessarily compromising. Yet, as the year went on, it became clear that Carter had been extremely perceptive about the part that faith would play in peace negotiations between the two Middle East leaders, perhaps the most important news story of the year. See MIDDLE EAST.

After the Camp David, Maryland, meeting in September, millions of Americans found their Sunday-evening television programs interrupted by a broadcast from the East Room of the White House. Carter, Sadat, and Begin greeted assembled dignitaries and the watching world with smiles that symbolized friendship and reconciliation between nations. All three acknowledged that differing religious interpretations had contributed both to the problems and to the agreements.

The reconciling aspect of religion appeared rarely elsewhere in world affairs. In Guyana a group of Christians, most of them from the United States and organized into a commune, evidently committed mass suicide at the behest of their leader, Jim Jones of the People's Temple of California (see LATIN AMERICA [Close-Up]). Ethnic factions wearing religious labels brought Lebanon to the edge of destruction. Syrian peacekeeping forces, usually identified as Muslim, fought belligerent right wing Christian forces, and the Jews of Israel sided with the Lebanese Christians. See LEBANON.

Islam's Problems. The Arab world saw Iran torn apart by religious differences. Factions within Islam were responsible for the conflict. A spectrum of discontented people, one that united conservative Shiite Muslims with Marxist university students, rebelled against Shah Mohammad Reza Pahlavi. The leaders of the Shiite Muslims, a sect to which 9 out of 10 Iranians belong, added their protests to those who disagreed with the shah's economic policies or charged that he was repressive. They claimed he had excluded religion from affairs in Iran, and charged that he was too lenient toward pornography, prostitution, and gambling. Their leading scholar, Ayatollah Shariat Madari, counseled nonviolence, but the dissenters launched violent attacks that threatened the unity of Iran and the survival of the shah's regime. See IRAN.

A variety of Islam in the United States underwent major changes. The World Community of Islam in the West, popularly known as the Black Muslims and not regarded as orthodox by most other Muslims, was surprised by the resignation in September

U.S. Church Membership Reported for Bodies with 150,000 or More Members

African Methodist Episcopal Church	1,950,000
African Methodist Episcopal Zion Church	1,083,391
American Baptist Association	1,350,000
American Baptist Churches in the U.S.A.	1,304,000
The American Lutheran Church	2,390,076
The Antiochian Orthodox Christian Archdiocese of North America	152,000
Armenian Church of America, Diocese of the (including Diocese of California)	326,500
Assemblies of God	1,283,892
Baptist Missionary Association of America	218,361
Christian and Missionary Alliance	152,841
Christian Church (Disciples of Christ)	1,256,849
Christian Churches and Churches of Christ	1,044,842
Christian Methodist Episcopal Church	466,718
Christian Reformed Church in North America	210,088
Church of God (Anderson, Ind.)	171,947
Church of God (Cleveland, Tenn.)	377,765
The Church of God in Christ	425,000
The Church of God in Christ, International	501,000
The Church of Jesus Christ of Latter-day Saints	2,486,261
Church of the Brethren	177,534
Church of the Nazarene	455,648
Churches of Christ	2,500,000
Conservative Baptist Association of America	300,000
The Episcopal Church	2,818,830
Free Will Baptists	216,831
General Association of Regular Baptist Churches	235,918
Greek Orthodox Archdiocese of North and South America	1,950,000
Jehovah's Witnesses	554,018
Jewish Congregations	5,775,935
Lutheran Church in America	2,967,168
The Lutheran Church-Missouri Synod	2,673,321
National Baptist Convention of America	2,668,799
National Baptist Convention, U.S.A., Inc.	5,500,000
National Primitive Baptist Convention, Inc.	250,000
Orthodox Church in America	1,000,000
Polish National Catholic Church of America	282,411
Presbyterian Church in the United States	869,693
Progressive National Baptist Convention, Inc.	521,692
Reformed Church in America	351,438
Reorganized Church of Jesus Christ of Latter Day Saints	186,414
The Roman Catholic Church	49,836,176
The Salvation Army	396,238
Seventh-day Adventists	522,317
Southern Baptist Convention	13,078,239
Unitarian-Universalist Association	180,240
United Church of Christ	1,785,652
The United Methodist Church	9,785,534
United Pentecostal Church, International	420,000
The United Presbyterian Church in the U.S.A.	2,561,234
Wisconsin Evangelical Lutheran Synod	401,489

*Majority of figures are for the years 1977 and 1978.

Source: National Council of Churches, *Yearbook of American and Canadian Churches* for 1979.

of Wallace D. Muhammad, who became leader of the movement after the death of his father Elijah Muhammad in 1975.

World Buddhism saw many setbacks and few recoveries. New Buddhist groups kept establishing themselves in Japan at the expense of the older Buddhist institutions. Buddhist leader Tich Man Giac failed to attract much attention to the plight of those persecuted for their religious beliefs in Vietnam. Letters from Prince Norodom Sihanouk, the once-exiled king and Buddhist leader of devastated Cambodia who had since returned to that country, praised the very regime that was suppressing Cambodian Buddhism. In Thailand, Communists attacked the majority Buddhist religion, while the growth of Hindu Tamil minorities threatened to overtake Buddhism's privileged position there. Only in North America did the Buddhists, though a tiny community, gain strength. They survived in a number of centers in California and Colorado, in mountain areas, and around university campuses. Despite their gains, however, they could not compensate for the losses that Buddhism was experiencing in a changing world. Martin E. Marty

See also EASTERN ORTHODOX CHURCHES; JEWS AND JUDAISM; PROTESTANTISM; ROMAN CATHOLIC CHURCH. In Section Two, see HOW REAL IS AMERICA'S RELIGIOUS REVIVAL? In WORLD BOOK, see RELIGION and articles on the various religions.

REPUBLICAN PARTY made a modest political comeback in 1978, gaining three seats in the United States Senate, adding 11 in the House of Representatives, and increasing the number of GOP governors by six. The increase was not as great as Republican strategists had expected and was smaller than the party out of power usually achieves in years when a President is not being elected. But the modest gains turned Congress in a slightly more conservative direction and advanced Republican prospects somewhat for the 1980 balloting.

There was reason for GOP optimism in the overall Senate results. Twenty Republicans were elected to the Senate, more than in any year since 1952, though Democrats still retained a 59-41 majority. Some veteran Republicans were defeated, however. In the liberal wing of the party, four-term incumbent Clifford P. Case of New Jersey lost a primary contest, and Edward W. Brooke of Massachusetts, the only black member of the Senate, failed in his re-election bid amid controversy over his divorce. Senator Robert P. Griffin of Michigan, once the GOP whip, was rejected in his quest for a third term.

Republicans won two Senate races in Minnesota, a Democratic stronghold for 20 years, with victories by David Durenberger, a lawyer, and Rudolph E. Boschwitz, a plywood manufacturer. They took over seats once held by Hubert H. Humphrey and Vice-President Walter F. Mondale.

New Senate Faces. Nancy Landon Kassebaum, daughter of the 1936 Republican presidential candidate, Alfred M. Landon, won the Senate race in Kansas. Other Senate victors were former Representatives William S. Cohen of Maine and Larry S. Pressler of South Dakota.

GOP conservatives defeated more liberal Democratic incumbents in three races. In Iowa, Roger Jepsen upset Richard C. Clark; former Congressman William L. Armstrong defeated Senator Floyd K. Haskell in Colorado; and airline pilot Gordon Humphrey ousted veteran Democratic Senator Thomas J. McIntyre in New Hampshire.

Thad Cochran became the first Republican elected to the Senate from Mississippi by popular vote in more than 100 years. Cochran benefited when an independent black candidate, Charles Evers, split the Democratic vote.

Virginia voters elected John W. Warner, former Navy secretary and husband of film star Elizabeth Taylor, as their new Republican senator. Republican Alan K. Simpson won the Wyoming Senate seat that had been vacated by his father, Milward L. Simpson, 12 years ago.

In the House, Republicans picked up 11 seats in the election but still trailed Democrats by a margin of 276 to 157, with 2 seats vacant because of death. The GOP picked up three seats in California and

Jesse Jackson of Operation PUSH, left, talks with GOP National Chairman William E. Brock before addressing the National Committee.

two each in Pennsylvania and Texas. But they failed to capitalize on the record number of seats left open by the retirement of Democratic incumbents.

The Governors' Races gave Republicans more to cheer about, raising the number of statehouses under GOP control from 12 to 18. Richard L. Thornburgh, a former federal prosecutor who once held a high post in the Department of Justice, scored a big gain for the GOP when he was elected governor of Pennsylvania. He defeated Pete Flaherty, former mayor of Pittsburgh. In Texas, Republican William L. Clements, seeking his first political office, won an upset victory to become the first GOP governor of the Lone Star State in more than 100 years.

Republicans won eight of nine governors' races in the Midwest, paced by a big re-election triumph by Illinois Governor James R. Thompson, a possible presidential contender in 1980 or later. Former Representative Albert H. Quie won easily in Minnesota, and former university Chancellor Lee Sherman Dreyfus swept Wisconsin by invoking the memory of Progressive Republican Robert M. LaFollette, Jr. Former Representative Charles Thone recaptured the statehouse in Nebraska for the GOP.

Lamar Alexander, a 38-year-old attorney, won the governor's race in Tennessee; Oregon State Senator Victor Atiyeh defeated Democratic incumbent Robert W. Straub; and Nevada Attorney General Robert List took the governor's chair from Democrat Mike O'Callaghan. Attorney General William J. Janklow became the first Republican governor in South Dakota in eight years.

Thompson's victory and the re-election of incumbents William G. Milliken in Michigan and James A. Rhodes in Ohio gave the GOP added strength in major states for 1980. Other victorious incumbents were Jay S. Hammond of Alaska, Richard A. Snelling of Vermont, and Robert D. Ray of Iowa.

Other GOP Developments. On August 2, Representative Philip M. Crane of Illinois announced his candidacy for the party's presidential nomination in 1980, the first Republican to do so. Crane, 47, is a conservative first elected to Congress in 1969.

Under Chairman William E. Brock III, the Republican National Committee began efforts to increase GOP support among traditionally Democratic blacks. Jesse L. Jackson, chairman of Operation PUSH, who addressed the Republican National Committee on January 20, urged support of progressive legislation if the party wanted to attract black votes. At the Republican Governors' Conference in Williamsburg, Va., in November, the newly elected governors urged the party to concentrate on attracting groups that traditionally align with the Democrats—minorities, union members, and urban ethnic groups.   William J. Eaton

See also CONGRESS OF THE UNITED STATES; ELECTIONS. In WORLD BOOK, see REPUBLICAN PARTY.

RETAILING reported a big gain in 1978 sales in the United States, but much of it was due to inflation. Most of the big chains reported that November sales were more than 10 per cent better than in the previous year. One exception was Sears, Roebuck and Company, the giant of the industry, which had a 6.4 per cent drop, the third in as many months. Sears executives said the decline resulted from a change in marketing policy and was only temporary.

Consumers bought freely but not extravagantly in 1978, showing a preference for quality merchandise. However, profits gained only slightly because costs rose unabated. Higher payrolls, high interest rates, and energy and other overhead costs led managements to press for expense reductions.

Retail construction was on the upswing, nevertheless, despite zooming building costs. Total square footage of retail space increased substantially—Sears, The May Company, and Macy's doubled their 1977 dollar investments in new stores in 1978.

Mergers and Sales continued to make news. Carter Hawley Hale Stores, Incorporated, purchased the 15 John Wanamaker stores in the Philadelphia area as well as the 26 Thalheimer units headquartered in Richmond, Va., adding about $240 million to sales. Marshall Field & Company bought Hess's of Allentown, Pa., with its 11 branches. The Younkers Department Stores of Des Moines,

Cost-conscious consumers turned in growing numbers to generic household supplies and foods to try to beat inflation's steady rise.

Iowa, were sold to Equitable of Canada. France's Apache-Willot group was completing negotiations for purchase of the E. J. Korvette stores in the Eastern United States.

Merchandising reflected public response to the motion picture *Saturday Night Fever,* as disco fashions swept the country. Some 13 million smoke alarms were sold in 1978. Americans still responded to novelty items, buying over 2 million "Pet Screws" at $5.95 each. The Neiman-Marcus Christmas catalog, famed for unusual items, offered a candy replica of the game of Monopoly for $600.

Designer names such as Halston and Pierre Cardin loomed more important than ever in fashion apparel and accessories, often dwarfing the names of well-known brands and manufacturers.

Sales in exercise and physical fitness classifications boomed, especially in jogging suits and shoes. Food processors, microwave ovens, and other kitchen items were in demand, as were video recorders and stereo components.

A survey by the National Retail Merchants Association revealed that 84 per cent of department stores and 52 per cent of specialty stores were using some form of electronic system to register sales and control inventory. Joseph R. Rowen

In WORLD BOOK, see RETAILING.

RHODE ISLAND. See STATE GOVERNMENT.

RHODESIA installed a biracial transitional government on March 21, 1978. The new regime was to lead in transferring power to Rhodesia's black majority by the end of the year, but it ran into strong opposition.

The new government was headed by a Council of State composed of Prime Minister Ian D. Smith and three black leaders, Bishop Abel Muzorewa, Ndabaningi Sithole, and Chief Jeremiah Chirau. The council's chairmanship rotated among Smith, representing Rhodesia's 260,000 whites, and the three black leaders, representing some 7 million blacks. These men appointed one black and one white to head each ministry in the Council of Ministers.

The Transition Agreement, signed on March 3, set the form of government and established objectives. A new constitution was to be drafted, and parliamentary elections in which all Rhodesians over 18 years of age could vote were scheduled for December 31. The agreement also provided job security for white civil servants; "adequate compensation" for any expropriation of property; and 28 per cent of the seats in Parliament for whites—enabling whites to veto constitutional amendments affecting those safeguards.

The Opposition. But the transitional government made only limited progress. The black members appealed for a cease-fire in the six-year civil war

Bishop Abel Muzorewa, left, and Prime Minister Ian D. Smith sign accord in March to form an interim government of both blacks and whites in Rhodesia.

between the government and black guerrillas, but instead the war escalated. During September, an average of 26 persons died each day as a result of the war, compared with eight per day in the spring. Most of the guerrillas were loyal to Joshua Nkomo and Robert Mugabe, who had formed a loose alliance called the Patriotic Front and claimed to have 40,000 guerrilla fighters, most of them operating from neighboring Zambia and Mozambique.

Nkomo and Mugabe repeatedly denounced the transitional regime and rejected its cease-fire offer. The United States, the United Nations Security Council, and most African countries also opposed the interim regime and the settlement it represented.

All four members of the Council of State visited Washington, D.C., in October at the invitation of 27 U.S. senators in an unsuccessful effort to obtain U.S. recognition for their government and end the U.S. trade embargo. The economic sanctions contributed to a projected budget deficit of about $378 million for fiscal 1978.

The interim government on November 16 finally postponed elections for black-majority rule until April 1979. The draft constitution was published on Jan. 2, 1979, and was to be voted on by whites on January 30. If approved, it would take effect after the April election.   John D. Esseks

See AFRICA (Facts in Brief Table). In WORLD BOOK, see RHODESIA.

ROGERS, HARRY G. (1931-   ), became Canada's first comptroller general on April 2, 1978. The government established the post following recommendations made by Auditor General J. J. Macdonell. The comptroller reports to the president of the treasury board, and it is responsible for assessment and improvement of the government's financial-management programs.

Rogers was born in Toronto, Ont., on April 24, 1931. He attended Barrie Collegiate Institute in Barrie, Ont., and graduated with honors from the University of Western Ontario in 1954 with a degree in economics and political science.

In 1955, Rogers joined the Ford Motor Company of Canada and after two years was assigned to international operations. He held executive finance positions in Singapore, South Africa, and the United States, then served as general manager of Ford's operations in Japan from 1967 to 1969.

Rogers went to work for the Xerox Corporation in 1969. He became manager of international financial operations in 1972, and vice-president for finance of Xerox of Canada Limited in 1973. In September 1977, he was made vice-president for operations, and held that position when he was appointed comptroller general of Canada.

Rogers and his wife have six children. In his leisure time, he enjoys playing the piano and cross-country skiing.   Marsha F. Goldsmith

ROMAN CATHOLIC CHURCH. The deaths of two popes and the election of a third, all within a 71-day period, overshadowed all other events for Roman Catholics in 1978. The ailing Pope Paul VI, 80, succumbed to a heart attack at his summer home, Castel Gandolfo, on August 6. His successor, Pope John Paul I, was found dead in bed in his Vatican apartment on September 28, only 34 days after his election. On October 16, the College of Cardinals elected Karol Cardinal Wojtyla of Kraków, Poland, to the papacy. He was the first non-Italian pontiff to reign since Adrian VI of the Netherlands in 1522. He took the name of John Paul II.

Pope Paul will be especially remembered as an ecumenist who brought Catholic-Protestant and Catholic-Orthodox relations to a new level of Christian fellowship and implemented the reforms of Vatican II. John Paul I announced the day after his election that he intended to dedicate his prayerful attention "to everything that would favor union of the Christian churches." And John Paul II, speaking to representatives of other Christian churches on October 22, said, "A good part of the journey has already been traveled, but we must not stop before having realized that unity which Christ revealed for His church and for which He prayed." See DEATHS OF NOTABLE PERSONS (Close-Up); JOHN PAUL I; JOHN PAUL II.

The Ecumenical Movement made notable progress during the year. The Anglican-Roman Catholic consultation announced on Dec. 28, 1977, that the group had discovered a substantial unity of faith between the two churches after 12 years of dialogue.

In September 1978, Catholic and Lutheran theologians completed five years of talks on papal infallibility. Warren Quanbeck, a Lutheran participant, said that the two groups had reached agreement on the indefectibility of the church, but that "Lutherans are unable to see how we can speak of infallibility of a doctrine or a person or an office." The 9,000-word statement issued by the participants in October said, in part: "This, to be sure, is not yet full agreement. Catholics, as well as many Lutherans, regret the absence in Lutheranism of a universal *magisterium* [effective whole church], while Lutherans, as well as many Catholics, believe that the doctrine and the practice of papal teaching authority and infallibility are not yet sufficiently protected against abuses."

An international group of Catholic, Lutheran, and Reformed theologians came closer to agreement on marriage. Their differences concerned the sacramental nature and indissolubility of marriage. The Vatican Secretariat for Promoting Christian Unity and the Lutheran World Federation released a document in October stating that "Romans and Lutherans together confess a real and true presence of the Lord in the Eucharist." The text noted differences in theological statements on the mode and duration of the "real Presence," but stated that "these two positions must no longer be regarded as divisive contradictions."

Catholic-Jewish dialogue also made a few gains. There was a growing realization on the part of Christians that the dialogue is contributing to self-understanding and an awareness that anti-Semitism is in some measure a problem arising from centuries of Christian teaching of contempt for Jews.

Ordination of Women. The demand for ordination of women to the Catholic priesthood continued to gain momentum. Although the Vatican Sacred Congregation for the Doctrine of the Faith spoke against such ordinations in 1977, the Catholic Theological Society of America declared on June 10, 1978, that there is a consensus in its task force that arguments based on apostolic practice and tradition do not settle the issue, nor can reasons adduced from the Old Testament be supported by scholarship.

Louis Ligier, professor of sacramental theology at the Pontifical Gregorian University in Rome, said in April, however, that ordaining women at this time would create an ecumenical problem for other churches and that one Christian church should not introduce customs that would make friendly relations impossible. The Lambeth Conference of Anglican Bishops of the world, meeting in London from July 23 to August 13, approved a resolution allowing Anglican communions to make their own decisions concerning the ordination of women priests. But the Church of England decided in November against allowing the ordination of women.

Social Issues. Spanish-speaking persons in the United States continued to receive help from the Roman Catholic Church in their difficulties with employers and the government. Some Catholic leaders advocated amnesty for illegal aliens facing deportation in order to keep families together. Monsignor George Higgins of the National Conference of Catholic Bishops in Washington, D.C., said that many illegal aliens are victims of an oppressive economic system in their own country and of discriminatory United States legislation.

Some conservative Catholics have long tried to discourage social and political activity by religious communities. But, in July, the Vatican Congregation for Religious commended those religious involved in such activity. The Leadership Conference of Women Religious and the Conference of Major Superiors of Men told the Vatican Congregations dealing with this question that "Many major superiors will attest that the critical problem is not too much socio-political involvement. Quite the contrary; it is the continuing indifference of religious to the call of Paul VI, Vatican II, and the synods to concern themselves with justice in the world."

About 100,000 mourners, including world dignitaries, attend funeral services for Pope Paul VI in St. Peter's Square in Rome on August 12.

Pope John Paul II, the former Cardinal Wojtyla, bishop of Kraków, Poland, prays during his investiture service in St. Peter's Square in Rome.

The Catholic Charismatic movement was more alive than ever in 1978. Some 22,000 Catholics attended the National Charismatic Conference at Notre Dame University in Indiana on August 20. Although charismatics are often criticized for a preoccupation with "signs and wonders," the conference theme was "evangelization." The national service committee of the movement said in March that there is no unique approach to leadership roles in charismatic prayer groups, but "most communities believe that a pattern of governance by elders who are men is the one that corresponds best to the New Testament pattern and is therefore the one to be followed." See Section Two, How REAL IS AMERICA'S RELIGIOUS REVIVAL?

Marriage and Family. The bishops of the United States, meeting in Chicago in May, issued a "Plan of Pastoral Action for Family Ministry" designed to raise Catholic consciousness of the sacramental nature of marriage and the problems facing couples and families. Catholic leaders also joined with other church leaders in a statement expressing concern that pressure groups might use the 1979 White House Conference on Families for manipulative purposes unfavorable to family life. Reportedly, the appointment of Patricia Fleming, a divorced woman, as executive director of the conference, stirred a storm of protest that led to her resignation in January. The conference was postponed until 1981.

Catholic participation in the anti-abortion movement continued to be strong. The National Right to Life Committee, which includes Catholics, declared its intention to continue its national crusade for a right-to-life amendment to the U.S. Constitution. The U.S. Catholic Conference continued to oppose allowing medical payments for abortion.

Interest grew in ministry to divorced Catholics, a ministry pioneered by Father James Young. James Provost, president of the Canon Law Society of America, pointed out at the North America Conference on Divorced and Separated Catholics at Notre Dame University in July that those who have married a second time without church sanction are not excluded from reconciliation with the church.

Membership. According to the Official Catholic Directory, there were 58,485 priests in the United States in 1978, compared with 58,301 in 1977. The total Catholic population increased to 49,836,176 in 1978 from 49,325,752 in 1977. The number of nuns dropped to 129,391 from 130,804 in 1977. Catholic high school enrollment was 869,268 in 1978, compared with 890,062 in 1977, and the number of students in Catholic elementary schools dropped to 2,402,778 from 2,478,229 in 1977. There were 78,598 converts to Catholicism in 1978, compared with 79,627 in 1977.   John B. Sheerin

In WORLD BOOK, see ROMAN CATHOLIC CHURCH.

ROMANIA openly backed away from its Warsaw Pact partners on Nov. 25, 1978, when Communist Party General Secretary and President Nicolae Ceausescu revealed that he had opposed an increase in military spending approved by the other six partners at a summit meeting in Moscow that week. "It would be a big mistake . . . to intensify arming, since this would be a particularly heavy burden on our countries," he said. He convened a special two-day session of Romania's Communist Party Central Committee on November 29, gaining its support for his action. In his opening speech, part of which was later televised, Ceausescu said, "We are an independent Romania and we will always remain an independent Romania." But he took no action to remove Romania from the Warsaw Pact.

Chinese Premier Hua Kuo-feng visited Romania in August against the background of strong Russian denunciation of Chinese "meddling" in the Balkans. Romania conducted maneuvers on the Danube River close to Russia in September. Russia's Foreign Minister Andrei A. Gromyko paid a visit in October, which was interpreted as a move against China.

Personnel Changes. General Ion Pacepa, deputy head of intelligence and a close friend of Ceausescu, defected to the United States in August. As a result, Minister of the Interior Teodor Coman, two other ministers, two ambassadors, and several other officials were dismissed in September.

A March government reshuffle affected 23 ministers and senior Communist Party officials. A provincial party secretary and a local vice-chairman were dismissed in November for taking bribes and building villas with the proceeds. The government banned the ownership of private family houses.

A New Plan for the economy was unveiled on March 23, calling for profit sharing, a greater share in decision making for workers, and less central control of industry. State-owned enterprises could spend up to 25 per cent of their profits on imports that would increase production for export, improve product quality, or provide new technology. The plan was aimed at increasing production, especially of export goods.

Industrial output increased 9.9 per cent in the first half of 1978, compared with the first half of 1977. Investment increased 17.5 per cent.

Romania received a credit of 300 million Eurodollars on October 3 from a group led by Barclay's Bank International Limited of London. Romania agreed in October to buy two nuclear reactors worth $800 million each from Canada, then doubled the order in December. Chris Cviic

See also EUROPE (Facts in Brief Table). In WORLD BOOK, see ROMANIA.

ROTARY INTERNATIONAL. See COMMUNITY ORGANIZATIONS.

ROWING. See SPORTS.

ROYO, ARISTIDES (1940-   ), was sworn in as president of Panama on Oct. 11, 1978. Elected by the 505-member National Assembly, Royo replaced Demetrio B. Lakas, a figurehead president who served throughout Omar Torrijos Herrera's 10-year reign as chief of the government. Royo was favored by Torrijos, and was expected to wield considerably more influence over Panama's affairs than did his predecessor. See PANAMA.

Aristides Royo was born on Aug. 14, 1940, in La Chorrera, Panama. After completing his early education, he studied law at the University of Salamanca in Spain and the University of Bologna in Italy.

Returning to Panama in 1965, Royo became secretary-general in the office of Panama's attorney general, a position he held until 1968. He served on the commissions that drafted the nation's new penal code and the 1972 Constitution. Royo was appointed minister of education in 1973 and also led his nation's six-member delegation in negotiating the Panama Canal treaties with the United States.

Royo is generally considered a liberal in political and social issues. During his six-year term as president, he has said, he will support freedom of speech, strengthen the National Assembly, and redefine the role of the judicial branch of government. Royo also hopes to broaden the influence of Panama's business community in national affairs. Beverly Merz

RUBBER. See MANUFACTURING.

RUSSIA continued its arms-control negotiations with the United States, its crackdown on domestic dissidents, and its political and military involvement in Africa during 1978. Soviet rivalry with China became more intense in Asia and Eastern Europe.

SALT Talks. The United States and Russia resumed their pursuit of SALT 2, the strategic arms limitation treaty, on January 9 in Geneva, Switzerland. Russia strongly opposed the neutron bomb, a weapon that would kill people while leaving buildings and weapons intact. United States President Jimmy Carter had asked in July 1977 that the neutron bomb be produced, but on April 7, 1978, he announced that he had decided to defer it. He said the ultimate decision on producing the bomb would be affected by the restraint the Soviet Union showed on its arms programs and troop movements affecting U.S. security. On October 8, he decided to authorize production of the bomb's main components.

By the beginning of November, both sides were reported to have agreed on the central issue, limiting their strategic arsenals to 2,250 nuclear weapons systems until 1985 or later. Four main issues remained unresolved – limits on warheads, the U.S. cruise missiles, the Russian Backfire bomber, and the timing of weapons reductions.

Dissidents Punished. Russia deprived civil rights advocate General Pyotr G. Grigorenko and cellist

Russia's gasoline prices were nearly doubled in March, causing residents like this Muscovite to fill up the tank more carefully than ever.

and conductor Mstislav Rostropovich of their citizenship in March. Rostropovich had been out of Russia since 1974. He became music director and conductor of the National Symphony Orchestra in Washington, D.C., in 1977. Physicist Yuri Orlov, chairman of an unofficial committee of intellectuals set up to monitor Russia's compliance with the 1975 Helsinki Agreement (an accord to promote human rights), was sentenced on May 18 to seven years imprisonment followed by five years of internal exile. Two members of a Helsinki monitoring group in Georgia received three-year prison sentences on May 19, to be followed by two years of internal exile. Alexander Ginzburg, manager of a fund for Russian political prisoners, was sentenced to eight years in prison on July 13, and on July 14, Jewish activist Anatoly Shcharansky received three years in prison and 10 in a forced labor camp for espionage.

In retaliation, President Carter canceled the sale of a Sperry Univac computer to Russia, and made sales of oil-production equipment to Russia subject to federal licensing. The United States canceled a session of the U.S.-Russian committee on scientific and technological cooperation on July 26.

Americans Harassed. A Russian court found reporters Harold Piper of the *Baltimore Sun* and Craig Whitney of *The New York Times* guilty of libeling Soviet television and ordered them to pay a fine and publish a retraction. The two reported a Russian dissident's statement that another dissident had given a false confession on television. Whitney paid both fines on August 4, and on August 18 the Russian court said the retractions would not be necessary. Francis J. Crawford, Moscow representative of International Harvester Company of Chicago, left Russia on September 8 after receiving a five-year suspended sentence for breaking currency laws. He had denied the charge. After visiting Supreme Soviet Presidium Chairman Leonid I. Brezhnev in September, U.S. Senator Edward M. Kennedy (D., Mass.) said he thought that Russia would let 18 Jewish families emigrate. Professor Sergei Polikanov, a nuclear physicist and a member of the Helsinki monitoring group, was allowed to leave with his wife and daughter on October 10. Professor Venyamin Levich, a scientist who had applied to emigrate in 1972, received permission to leave on October 23 and left the country on November 30. In the first six months of 1978, 11,481 Jews were allowed to emigrate.

African Activities. Cuban troops and Russian advisers helped Ethiopia stage two successful counteroffensives in February that drove Somali forces from the Ogaden area of Ethiopia. In March, Russia and Cuba also helped Ethiopia in its war with Eritrean secessionists. President Carter's national

Siberia's New Artery: the Baykal-Amur Mainline Railway

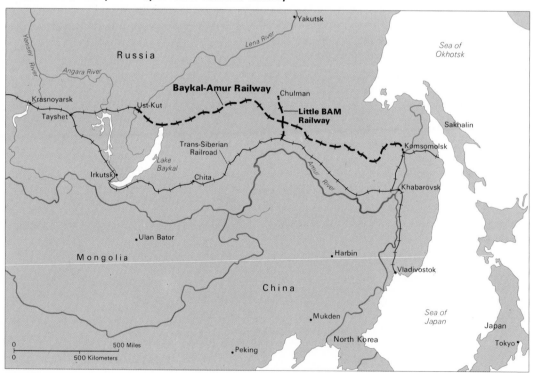

Friends gather around Irina Orlov after the Moscow trial at which
her dissident physicist husband, Yuri, received a 12-year sentence.

security adviser, Zbigniew Brzezinski, on May 28
blamed the Soviet Union and Cuba for an invasion
of Zaire earlier that month by Shaba rebels based in
Angola. Cuba and Angola denied involvement, and
Russia's foreign ministry said that Western help for
the Zairian government was imperialistic, so Russia's support for wars of liberation in Africa was
compatible with East-West détente.

Policy in Asia. Brezhnev warned the United
States against playing the "China card" in a June 25
speech in Minsk, and called U.S. collaboration with
China against Russia "short-sighted."

United States Secretary of State Cyrus R. Vance
said on December 17 that the U.S. decision to
establish diplomatic relations with China on Jan. 1,
1979, did not surprise Russia. Vance said he thought
it would not affect the SALT talks.

Russia reacted to the August visit to the Balkans
and Iran by Premier Hua Kuo-feng of China with
an anti-Chinese propaganda campaign. Russian
media denounced the August 12 signing of a treaty
of peace and friendship by China and Japan.

In Europe. Brezhnev made state visits to West
Germany and Czechoslovakia in May. In October,
Russian-bloc party secretaries met in Budapest,
Hungary. Foreign Minister Andrei A. Gromyko
paid an unannounced visit to Romania as part of a
Russian drive for closer military collaboration and
integration within the Warsaw Pact.

Other Developments. Fyodor D. Kulakov, 60,
secretary of the central committee, a member of the
Politburo, and a possible successor to Brezhnev, died
on July 16. Former President Anastas Mikoyan, 82,
the last surviving old Bolshevik leader, died on
October 21. Russian Orthodox Metropolitan Nikodim, archbishop of Leningrad, died during an audience with Pope John Paul I in Rome on September 5,
and Metropolitan Antoni of Minsk and Byelorussia
succeeded him on October 10.

Konstantin U. Chernenko, a national party secretary, was elected a full member of the Politburo on
November 27. Leonid Zamyatin, director general of
the news agency Tass, was appointed head of a
Central Committee department in March. Vladimir
Khatuntsev, deputy head of Tass since 1960, was
appointed director general on July 13.

Russian cosmonauts Vladimir Kovalyonok and
Aleksander S. Ivanchenko returned to earth on
November 2 after setting an endurance record of 139
days in space. See SPACE EXPLORATION.

A Record Grain Harvest of 259 million short tons
(235 million metric tons), well above the previous
record of 247 million short tons (224 million metric
tons) in 1976 and even further above the 1977
harvest, was announced in November. Russia raised
the prices of farm produce effective Jan. 1, 1979,
by 9 to 38 per cent. The increase would cost the
state $4.5 billion per year. Farm debts of $10 billion

471

were to be written off and loan payments totaling $6-billion were deferred.

State Planning Chairman Nikolai K. Baibakov said on November 29 that overall industrial output for 1978 would be up 5 per cent over 1977, compared with a planned increase of 4.5 per cent. He said heavy industrial production, planned for a 4.7 per cent increase, would be up 5.3 per cent; and labor productivity, planned for a 3.8 per cent increase, would be up 3.6 per cent. Baibakov said oil output would be 572.5 million short tons (519.4 million metric tons) in 1978, compared with a planned 575-million short tons (522 million metric tons); and that coal output would be 729 million short tons (661-million metric tons), compared with a planned 746-million short tons (677 million metric tons).

Railway Construction crews worked on the 300-mile (480-kilometer) western segment of the 2,000-mile (3,200-kilometer) Baykal-Amur Mainline (BAM) across eastern Siberia. Completion date for the $15-billion BAM is 1983. The western segment will include 18.1 miles (29.1 kilometers) of tunnels.

A Central Committee meeting in August noted shortcomings in engineering-industry technical standards. Russia's hard-currency deficit was estimated at $2.5 billion to $3 billion in 1978. Chris Cviic

See also EUROPE (Facts in Brief Table). In WORLD BOOK, see RUSSIA.

RWANDA. See AFRICA.

SAFETY. The need for greater consumer protection and the burden of added manufacturing costs imposed by government safety regulations continued to spark controversy in the United States in 1978. Some manufacturers complained that federal agencies were going too far, while other critics charged that they did not go far enough to protect unsuspecting buyers.

Congressional investigators working for the U.S. House Commerce Committee's Oversight Subcommittee criticized the Consumer Product Safety Commission in August. They charged that the commission had failed to protect the public against "chronic hazards," such as clothing treated with cancer-causing chemicals. The investigators specifically cited the commission's mishandling of the threat raised by the use of Tris, a fire-retardant chemical applied to children's sleepwear that has proved carcinogenic. The investigators declared that the agency moved too slowly and inadequately to safeguard the public.

In November, President Jimmy Carter announced a new policy that promised to "eliminate needless regulations" and to establish procedures that would minimize the inflationary impact of government regulations. Carter established a regulatory council, with representatives from all federal regulatory agencies and departments, to study the economic impact of proposed new regulations.

Also in November, the Occupational Safety and Health Administration revoked 928 job-safety standards that it considered "unneeded or unrelated to job safety and health." Among the rules eliminated was one requiring open-front toilet seats, and 321 standards applying to barrel making, bakery equipment, and laundry machinery and operation.

Accidental Deaths and Death Rates

| | 1977* | | 1978* | |
	Number	Rate†	Number	Rate†
Motor Vehicle	48,000	22.2	50,700	23.3
Work	12,700	5.9	12,800	5.9
Home	24,200	11.2	23,500	10.8
Public	22,000	10.2	21,400	9.8
Total**	102,500	47.4	104,000	47.7

*For the 12-month period ending August 31.

†Deaths per 100,000 population.

**The total does not equal the sum of the four classes because *Motor Vehicle* includes some deaths also included in *Work* and *Home*.

Source: National Safety Council estimates.

Tire Recall. The government and the Firestone Tire & Rubber Company of Akron, Ohio, reached an agreement in October under which the company recalled about 13 million passenger-car tires, the largest and perhaps the most costly recall in history.

Congressman John E. Moss (D., Calif.) examines a blown tire during hearings that resulted in the recall of 13 million steel-belted radials.

The company, in effect, agreed to replace free of charge Firestone 500's, and certain other Firestone steel-belted radials that were manufactured and purchased within certain dates. The government had charged that Firestone 500 blowouts or other failures had caused 41 deaths and 65 injuries.

The Consumer Product Safety Commission voted in October to ban the sale of thousands of toys, intended for children under the age of 3, that are small enough or have parts small enough to be swallowed or choked on. Final approval of this ban is not expected until about March 1979, and its effective date would come six months to a year after that. Meanwhile, the Toy Manufacturers of America set up voluntary standards similar to those proposed by the commission.

Highway Safety. The National Safety Council and others urged the government to give budget priority to funding highway-safety programs relating to the causes of accidents. The council said such programs should concentrate on alcohol and the driver; vehicle accidents involving pedestrians; early voluntary adoption of such passive restraints as airbags, prior to their federally mandated installation in 1984-model automobiles; and continued enforcement of the national speed limit of 55 miles (89 kilometers) per hour.   Vincent L. Tofany

In WORLD BOOK, see SAFETY.

SAILING. See BOATING.

SAINT LOUIS. Gordon D. Schweitzer was sworn in as civil sheriff of the city on Dec. 17, 1978. He replaced Benjamin L. Goins, who was convicted of federal charges of corruption and income tax evasion in July. Despite his conviction, Goins refused to step down, even after Mayor James F. Conway called for his resignation. He was removed from office by the Missouri Supreme Court on November 9, and Schweitzer was chosen to replace him in a special election.

Goins had also refused to abandon his pursuit of the Democratic nomination for a U.S. House of Representatives seat, but incumbent William L. Clay soundly defeated him in the August 8 primary. Clay and Goins, both black, had disagreed over issues affecting the city's black community.

Quality of Life. An ongoing preventive health program tested 12,530 St. Louis children for lead poisoning in 1978 — most of them from underprivileged families in older neighborhoods. Nearly 20 per cent had high lead levels and required medical attention or further tests.

Food costs rose 9.7 per cent in the area during the year ending in May, while the overall cost of living rose 7.5 per cent during the same period. A Department of Labor report suggested on April 26 that area living costs were less than the national average. The report indicated that an average family of four would need an annual income of $16,377, 4.3 per cent below the national average, to live in moderate comfort.

A Congressional Budget Office study released on September 10 placed St. Louis on its list of "high-need cities," indicating that the city had relatively severe socioeconomic problems. A Bureau of the Census report released in November indicated that the St. Louis area lost 16.5 per cent of its population between 1970 and 1976.

Museum Thefts. Four valuable sculptures were stolen from the St. Louis Museum of Art on January 21. The museum's chief of security resigned and two guards who were on duty at the time were dismissed.

In a similar theft on February 20, three bronze pieces, *Eustache de St. Pierre, Jean D'Aire,* and *The Clenched Hand,* were stolen. All were works of French sculptor Auguste Rodin, executed in 1885 and 1886. Their combined value was estimated at more than $100,000.

A moderate earthquake, registering 3.5 on the Richter scale, shook the St. Louis area briefly on September 20. The tremor cracked plaster and broke windows in some homes, but no injuries were reported. About 100,000 commuters were stranded on May 11 when bus drivers and mechanics staged a one-day wildcat strike.   James M. Banovetz

See also CITY. In WORLD BOOK, see SAINT LOUIS.

SALVATION ARMY. See COMMUNITY ORGANIZATIONS.

SAN FRANCISCO-OAKLAND. San Franciscans were stunned by the slayings of Mayor George Moscone and Supervisor Harvey Milk on Nov. 27, 1978. Former Supervisor Dan White surrendered to police and was charged with the murders.

White had resigned his office on November 10 because of its low salary, then asked to be reappointed, but Moscone had refused his request. Moscone was shot less than an hour before he was scheduled to announce the appointment of White's successor. Milk was the first avowed homosexual to be elected to the city's Board of Supervisors. White had opposed homosexual causes.

On December 4, the Board of Supervisors, San Francisco's legislative body, elected its president, Dianne Feinstein, to finish Moscone's unexpired term. See FEINSTEIN, DIANNE.

Area residents were also shocked by the mass suicides and murders of members of the People's Temple in Jonestown, Guyana, which began on November 18. The cult was based in San Francisco. See LATIN AMERICA (Close-Up).

Legislation Passed. Discrimination against homosexuals was outlawed in San Francisco when the Board of Supervisors voted 10 to 1 on April 3 to ban such discrimination in employment, housing, and public accommodations.

Passage of California's Proposition 13 property-tax referendum left San Francisco unable to provide

Carrying candles, grieving San Franciscans gather at City Hall after Mayor George Moscone and Supervisor Harvey Milk were murdered.

police, fire, and clean-up support for the city's July 4 fireworks display, so the event was canceled. Oakland raised its business gross-receipts tax from 90 cents to $14 per $1,000 gross receipts, in an effort to recoup lost revenues. See TAXATION (Close-Up).

City Strikes. Oakland bus drivers ended a two-month strike on January 28, when union strike benefits ended. The strike had forced 100,000 passengers to find other means of transportation.

Cable-car gripmen staged a two-day wildcat strike in November to protest faulty equipment on the system. Thirteen persons were injured earlier in an accident on the California Street line.

Forty-two picketing postal workers at the San Francisco Bulk Mail Center were fired on July 23 for taking part in a wildcat strike to protest a contract offered by the United States Postal Service.

Art Bequest. John D. Rockefeller III bequeathed his $10-million American collection of art, consisting of nearly 200 works ranging from the 17th to the 20th century, to the Fine Arts Museum of San Francisco. Rockefeller, killed on July 10 in an automobile accident, said in his will that he believed there was a greater need for the collection in the Western U.S. than in the East.   James M. Banovetz

See also CITY. In WORLD BOOK, see OAKLAND; SAN FRANCISCO.

SAN MARINO. See EUROPE.
SÃO TOMÉ AND PRÍNCIPE. See AFRICA.

SASKATCHEWAN. Premier Allan Blakeney, who heads Canada's only New Democratic Party (NDP) government, won a resounding vote of confidence in an election on Oct. 18, 1978. The NDP government, in office since 1971, won 44 of the 61 seats in the assembly, up from 39. The Conservatives also made gains, going from 11 to 17 seats. These advances were registered at the expense of the Liberal Party, which had formed the government only seven years earlier. It lost all its seats.

Blakeney campaigned on the need for more secure provincial control of natural resources, challenged by an October 3 Supreme Court of Canada ruling that Saskatchewan's prorating of potash production was unconstitutional.

Blakeney continued with his plans to purchase majority government ownership in the potash industry. He acquired control of two more mines in January, giving the Potash Corporation of Saskatchewan (PCS) control of 40 per cent of the province's production capacity. When expansion plans are completed at two PCS plants, the government's share will be almost 50 per cent.

The budget of March 7 reduced personal income taxes and lowered compulsory automobile-insurance rates. A $44-million deficit was projected on a budget of $1.7 billion.   David M. L. Farr

See also CANADA; McINTOSH, C. IRWIN. In WORLD BOOK, see SASKATCHEWAN.

SAUDI ARABIA played the role of honest broker in Arab disputes over the Egyptian-Israeli peace negotiations in 1978. Saudi officials moved from one capital to another, trying to knit the Arab states into a common front without making a total commitment to Egypt's peace moves. At the same time, the Saudi government carefully nurtured its ties with the United States.

The government decided on January 9 to hold oil prices at $12.70 per barrel through 1978. It also reduced oil production from 8.9 million barrels per day to 6.5 million, to avoid oversupply and consequent price cuts. See PETROLEUM AND GAS.

The economy remained generally healthy. On July 1, the Saudi riyal became the first Arab currency to be included in the "basket of currencies" used by the International Monetary Fund in determining the value of Special Drawing Rights.

The first motor-vehicle assembly plant in Saudi Arabia opened in Jidda in April. It will assemble 6,500 units per year. Construction began in September on two 750-mile (1,200-kilometer) pipelines to carry oil and natural gas across the Arabian Peninsula.   William Spencer

See also MIDDLE EAST (Facts in Brief Table); Section Two, SAUDI ARABIA: ALLAH'S WILL AND OIL WELLS. In WORLD BOOK, see SAUDI ARABIA.
SCHOOL. See CIVIL RIGHTS; EDUCATION; Section One, FOCUS ON EDUCATION.

Baby rhesus monkeys huddle together during study on parental deprivation. India's decision to ban export of the monkeys threatens such research.

SCIENCE AND RESEARCH. The status of science in Communist countries was the center of much debate in the world's scientific community during 1978. Several international scientific organizations issued statements deploring governmental restraints on scientific investigation in Russia and the arrest of several Russian scientists for alleged antigovernment activities.

The United States National Academy of Sciences (NAS) decided on a policy of public protest in its effort to aid scientists in Russia who suffer political persecution. When Russian physicist Yuri F. Orlov was sentenced to seven years in prison in May on charges of defaming the state, the NAS responded with strongly worded criticism of the Russians. At least four scientific delegations from the United States canceled visits to Russia, as did Secretary of Health, Education, and Welfare Joseph A. Califano, Jr. Orlov, a high-energy physicist, headed an unofficial group that monitored Russia's compliance with the human rights portion of the Helsinki agreements of 1975.

In China, the government adopted a general relaxation of controls on scientific research. The move was part of a massive drive to modernize its scientific establishment and to remove mind-numbing political interference that China concedes has kept it scientifically backward. Deputy Prime Minister Fang Yi, in presenting a draft for an eight-year scientific-development program to a national conference of scientists, said in March that the country was 15 to 20 years behind world standards in many areas.

U.S. Science Budget. Basic research received an 11 per cent increase in the United States budget for fiscal 1979 (Oct. 1, 1978, to Sept. 30, 1979) that President Jimmy Carter sent to Congress in January. The President requested about $27 billion for research and development – $3.6 billion for basic research, $6.3 billion for applied research, and $17.2-billion for development.

"I am determined to maintain our nation's leadership role in science and technology," Carter declared in his State of the Union message. He also stressed the importance of science to the nation's economic well-being, national security, and ability to solve domestic problems.

Gene-Splicing Bill. The U.S. Congress was unable to agree on legislation to regulate the controversial and important recombinant-DNA, or gene-splicing, research. This research technology involves inserting genes from other organisms into bacteria to endow them with new properties. Almost all scientists agree that the new gene-splicing technique constitutes a powerful research tool with extraordinary potential, but some critics have charged that there are also potential dangers. Potentially dangerous disease-causing organisms have been cited among the risks. New vaccines and important biological products have been cited among the possible benefits.

A key issue in the legislation that came before the House Commerce Committee's Subcommittee on Health and Environment was the question of whether federal law should pre-empt local laws and ordinances regarding gene-splicing. Environmentalists objected strongly to federal pre-emption.

Monkey Ban. Hundreds of biomedical research projects were threatened by India's decision to ban further export of rhesus monkeys after April 1. India was the world's largest supplier of these monkeys, which are used in many kinds of research. In 1977, U.S. scientists used about 12,000 rhesus monkeys. Nearly all of them were imported from India, where they were trapped in the wild. Several neighboring countries, such as Bangladesh, Nepal, and Pakistan, also export rhesus monkeys, but they do not have enough of these animals to replace the Indian supply.

The Indian ban is believed to have resulted from pressure by a U.S.-based animal-welfare group on India's sympathetic Prime Minister Morarji Desai, a Hindu who opposes the killing of animals on religious grounds. The U.S. group said some of the animals were used in military-weapons testing.

Solving Mysteries. Science historians came a step closer to solving the mystery of the Piltdown man, a fossil skull discovered between 1908 and 1912 in an English gravel pit. Hailed as the "missing link" suggested by Charles R. Darwin's still controversial theory of evolution, the skull was accepted as genuine by almost all experts at that time. Radiocarbon tests proved in 1955 that the skull was a hoax, but the prankster was not identified. The new suspect is William J. Sollas, a former professor of geology at Oxford University in England. A tape recording made by his successor, released posthumously, suggests that Sollas contrived the hoax to fool and discredit a professional colleague whom he disliked, but that he refrained from admitting the trickery when he found that others were taken in by it.

The mystery of the disappearance of Albert Einstein's brain, which he had bequeathed to research, was solved by two reporters working for the *New Jersey Monthly*. They discovered the brain in a preservative jar in Wichita, Kans. The owner of the jar, Thomas Harvey, a pathologist at the hospital where Einstein died in 1955, said that he had not published his findings on the brain because he had more work to do. But so far, he said, all measurements of the brain were within normal limits for a man of Einstein's age.   Nicholas Wade

See also the various science articles. In Section One, see FOCUS ON SCIENCE. In WORLD BOOK, see RESEARCH; SCIENCE.

SCOTLAND. See GREAT BRITAIN.
SCULPTURE. See VISUAL ARTS.

SEATTLE became the first major United States city to adopt voluntarily a mandatory busing program to achieve racial integration in its schools. The school board adopted the plan on March 8, 1978, and it operated throughout the year despite statewide opposition and defeat in the November 7 election.

The Seattle plan called for the mandatory busing of approximately 10,000 of the district's 58,000 pupils. Integration of junior and senior high schools was to be accomplished through changes in the district's "feeder patterns." The program proceeded without demonstrations, violence, or publicity. Implementation of the plan had been delayed for 17 days when Seattle's teachers went on strike on September 6 in a contract dispute.

Busing Opposition. Opponents of the busing program gathered about 180,000 signatures throughout the state to put the busing question on the November 7 general election ballot, and Washington voters approved a proposal prohibiting state school districts from assigning pupils to any but the nearest neighborhood school. This in effect dismantled the Seattle integration program.

Confronted with an apparent legal conflict between federal law, which requires school integration, and the new state law, the Seattle school board filed suit in federal court, challenging the new state law. The school busing program continued pending the outcome of the litigation.

On another November election issue, Seattle voters refused to repeal an ordinance that guarantees rights to homosexuals.

Economic Boom. The area's economy received a major boost in July when United Airlines awarded a $1.6-billion contract to the Boeing Company in Seattle and nearby Everett for 30 new 767 twinjets and thirty 727-200 trijets. In August, British Airways and Eastern Airlines ordered 757 models for $1-billion; in November, American Airlines and Delta Air Lines placed orders totaling $1.9 billion. To fill these orders, Boeing estimated that it would need to increase its work force by 64,000 employees.

Increases in tourism and the plane orders, plus expanded port operations caused by the Alaskan pipeline construction and greater trade with the Far East, boosted Seattle employment by some 44,000 jobs in the year ending in June. Residential construction was up 25 per cent, and nonresidential building was up 78 per cent during the first five months of the year.

However, living costs rose 9.8 per cent in the year ending in April. Food costs alone increased by a staggering 12.5 per cent during the same period. A Congressional Budget Office study released on September 10 labeled Seattle as a "low-need city" on its "composite measure of social need." James M. Banovetz

See also CITY. In WORLD BOOK, see SEATTLE.
SENEGAL. See AFRICA.
SEYCHELLES. See AFRICA.

SHIP AND SHIPPING. Lloyd's Register of Shipping counted 2,007 merchant vessels under construction throughout the world on Sept. 30, 1978, off 6 per cent from the previous September. Orders, including ships being built, fell to 3,151 from 3,717. Tonnage of vessels on order plummeted to a 13-year low of 28.1 million gross tons, off 33 per cent from September 1977, because of the world oversupply.

United States shipbuilders held orders of about $13 billion. The Maritime Administration reported commercial-vessel orders valued at $3.1 billion on September 30, down from $3.9 billion a year earlier. Some 48 ships were scheduled for completion by 1982, compared with 65 vessels in 1977.

A U.S. federal bankruptcy judge ordered Pacific Far East Line to liquidate on August 2, after the Maritime Administration foreclosed on four of the company's ships. In January, a bid by Farrell Lines, Incorporated, to acquire American Export Lines, a unit of American Export Industries Incorporated, was accepted in bankruptcy court.

U.S. Navy Contracts helped keep shipyards afloat. The Navy order book rose about 32 per cent to $9.9 billion, a figure that reflected the Shipbuilders Council of America's new method of showing only uncompleted work. New orders included nine guided-missile frigates, two *Trident* nuclear submarines, and one guided-missile destroyer.

The Navy agreed to settle shipbuilding contract claims by the Tenneco, Incorporated, subsidiary, Newport News Shipbuilding & Dry Dock Company; General Dynamics Corporation; Litton Industries, Incorporated; and a Lockheed Corporation subsidiary. The agreement resolved such issues as the Navy's obligation to reimburse shipbuilders when it changed construction plans.

The Maritime Commission escalated its attack on illegal shipping rebates, assessing $6.1 million in penalties against United States, Japanese, and Israeli ocean lines, and penalizing many of their customers. Some U.S. lines also paid court fines for rebating. President Carter vetoed legislation in November to increase the Maritime Commission's authority to crack down on rebates by foreign carriers, deciding instead to work with other nations to stop the practices. But the President signed a bill increasing the commission's power to reject rate cuts by lines controlled by other countries, as concern spread over Russia's rate trimming. A U.S.-Russian agreement in September boosted the grain-shipping rate from $16 to $18.25 per long ton.　　Albert R. Karr

See also TRANSPORTATION. In WORLD BOOK, see SHIP.

SHOOTING. See HUNTING; SPORTS.

SIERRA LEONE. See AFRICA.

SIKKIM. See ASIA.

The *Princess Anne*, world's largest hovercraft, can carry 416 passengers and 60 cars in English Channel service between Great Britain and France.

SILVERMAN, FRED (1937-   ), became president of the National Broadcasting Company (NBC) and one of the highest paid executives in television history in June 1978. His salary was said to be about $1 million a year. The appointment capped a television programming career that earned him a reputation as a popular-programming genius. He introduced such hit series as "Happy Days," "Charlie's Angels," "Kojak," and "M*A*S*H."

Silverman was born in September 1937 in New York City. He received a bachelor's degree from Syracuse University in New York in 1958 and a master's degree in television and theater arts from Ohio State University in Columbus in 1959. His thesis, an analysis of American Broadcasting Company (ABC) TV programming during the 1950s, came to the attention of Columbia Broadcasting System (CBS) executives and eventually led to Silverman's first major television job.

Silverman became director of CBS daytime programs in 1963. He became vice-president of programming in June 1970. In 1975 Silverman moved to ABC with responsibility for all network programming. During his years there, ABC moved from third to first place in the ratings.   Edward G. Nash

SINGAPORE. See Asia.

SKATING. See Hockey; Ice Skating; Section Five, Ice Skating.

SKIING. Americans made major gains in international skiing during 1978. But the most successful skiers were still Europeans — Ingemar Stenmark of Sweden among the men and Hanni Wenzel of Liechtenstein and Annemarie Proell Moser of Austria among the women. See Stenmark, Ingemar.

Stenmark and Moser won two gold medals each in the world championships, and Stenmark captured the men's World Cup for the third consecutive year. Wenzel won the women's World Cup.

Phil Mahre of White Pass, Wash., finished second in the World Cup standing, the highest by an American man since the competition began in 1967. American women placed 5th, 13th, 15th, 18th, and 21st, their best overall showing since 1969. In the Nation's Cup standing, which combined men's and women's performances, the Americans finished third behind Austria and Switzerland.

The World Cup competition ran from December to March in Europe and the United States, with 23 races for men and 23 for women. The new rules supposedly favored the all-around skier rather than the specialist, but 21-year-old Stenmark, who never skied the downhill, still won.

The 20-year-old Mahre won a slalom at Chamonix, France; a giant slalom at Stratton, Vt.; and a parallel slalom at Arona, Switzerland. His twin brother, Steve, won a slalom at Stratton. Ken Read

Hanni Wenzel of Liechtenstein exhibits the championship form that won the World Cup women's skiing title for her in 1978.

of Calgary, Canada, won a downhill at Chamonix and finished 11th for the season.

Wenzel, 21, won the women's overall title with 154 points to 147 for Moser. Moser lost 20 points when she was disqualified after finishing second in a giant slalom at Val d'Isere, France. Her ski suit failed a test that meant the fibers were too tight and would help her ski at dangerous speeds.

In the world championships at Garmisch-Partenkirchen, West Germany, Stenmark won the men's slalom and giant slalom; Josef Walcher of Austria the downhill; and Andreas Wenzel of Liechtenstein, Hanni's 19-year-old brother, the combined. Women's winners were Moser in downhill and combined, Lea Soelkner of Austria in slalom, and Maria Epple of West Germany in giant slalom.

The only U.S. medalist was Pete Patterson of Sun Valley, Ida., third in the men's combined. Cindy Nelson of Lutsen, Minn., was fifth in the world downhill and fifth in the World Cup standing.

In the World Nordic Championships at Lahti, Finland, East Germany and Sweden each won two of the seven men's events and Finland took two of the three women's events.

Professional. The North American circuit consisted of 27 races with $550,000 in prizes. André Arnold, a 22-year-old rookie from Austria, led in victories (12) and earnings ($92,883).   Frank Litsky

In WORLD BOOK, see SKIING.

Argentine team captain Daniel Passarella shows trophy to happy fans after Argentina beat the Netherlands, 3-1, in World Cup soccer final.

SOCCER. The World Cup competition – sort of a quadrennial World Series, Super Bowl, Grey Cup, and Kentucky Derby rolled into one – highlighted soccer in 1978. Sixteen nations competed from June 1 to June 25 in Argentina, and Argentina won.

After two years of regional eliminations, the final field was reduced to Argentina as host, West Germany as defending champion, and 14 other nations. The first round consisted of four round-robin tournaments of four teams each. Two teams from each group advanced and two were eliminated.

The survivors were Argentina, Italy, Poland, West Germany, Austria, Peru, the Netherlands, and Brazil. France, Tunisia, Spain, Sweden, Scotland, Iran, Hungary, and Mexico were eliminated.

The second round had two groups of four teams each, with the group winners advancing to the cup final. The Netherlands won Group A from Italy, Austria, and West Germany. Argentina and Brazil waged a close fight for the Group B title, with Poland and Peru eliminated.

Argentina and Brazil were tied for first on the final day of the second round. If they remained tied, the team with the better goal differential (goals scored versus goals allowed) would advance to the final.

On the afternoon of June 21, Brazil defeated Poland, 3-1. That meant Argentina would have to defeat Peru by at least four goals that night or Brazil would gain the final. Argentina did it, winning 6-0.

The final attracted a sellout crowd of 75,000 to River Plate Stadium in Buenos Aires. The game matched the disciplined and accurate European game played by the Netherlands against the virtuoso, effervescent South American game played by Argentina. Argentina won, 3-1, as Mario Kempes scored two goals in a 30-minute overtime.

There were wild celebrations in Argentina that night and considerable job and school absenteeism the next day. The patriotism pleased Argentina's military government, but few people outside Argentina thought the winning team was exceptional. As Rud Krol, a Dutch player, said, "Argentina is a good team, but if they were not playing at home they would not be champions."

The United States did not have enough good players to form a strong team. It played a series against Mexico and Canada, with two teams to advance. Mexico and Canada advanced, and Mexico eventually gained a World Cup berth but was eliminated in the first round.

U.S. Pro. The North American Soccer League (NASL) expanded in 1978 to 24 teams, selling franchises at $1 million each to Colorado, Detroit, Houston, Memphis, New England, and Philadelphia. Four established teams moved – Connecticut to Oakland, Calif.; Las Vegas to San Diego; Hawaii to Tulsa, Okla.; and St. Louis to Anaheim, Calif. Stability was a major problem.

Each team played 30 games from May to August. Then 18 of the 24 teams advanced to the play-offs. In the final on August 23 in East Rutherford, N.J., the Cosmos, defending champions, beat the Tampa Bay Rowdies, 3-1, before a crowd of 74,901. The Cosmos' season opener in the same stadium drew 71,219, an NASL regular-season record.

In attendance, salaries, and renown, the Cosmos (formerly the New York Cosmos) were in a world of their own. Even though Pelé of Brazil, the greatest star in soccer history, had retired, they still had such international players as Franz Beckenbauer of West Germany, Giorgio Chinaglia of Italy, Carlos Alberto of Brazil, and Dennis Tueart of England. Their average attendance exceeded 47,000. At the other extreme, Memphis averaged 4,000. The league average was 13,000, down 4 per cent.

In the ASL. The 10-team American Soccer League (ASL) averaged 2,630 spectators per game. The New York Apollo defeated the Southern California Skyhawks, 1-0, in the championship game.

In Europe. Liverpool of England won its second straight European Champions Cup and Anderlecht of Belgium took the European Cup Winners Cup. In England, Nottingham Forest won the first-division title and League Cup, and Ipswich upset Arsenal, 1-0, for the Football Association Cup.   Frank Litsky

In WORLD BOOK, see SOCCER.

SOCIAL SECURITY financing remained an unsettled issue in America in 1978, despite the sweeping legislation enacted in December 1977. Congressman Al Ullman (D.,Ore.), chairman of the House Ways and Means Committee, said the legislation "was designed to solve the problems of that system for at least the next 25 years. . . . However, this bill is not the last word on the subject. I am hopeful that before long we can take a broad look at all aspects of the Social Security program."

There were other unresolved issues that Congress debated during the year. These included the extension of mandatory coverage to federal civilian employees, members of Congress, and state and local government employees; revising the criteria for disability benefits, which have been climbing at a 21 per cent annual rate for five years; and the consideration of sexist distinctions that discriminate against women. The relationship of old-age benefits to other earnings by the elderly was another unresolved issue. There was strong sentiment in the Congress to let Social Security pensioners earn as much as they can by working without losing their benefits.

Congress considered various proposals to resolve these issues, such as an outright reduction or postponement in the payroll tax for Social Security, reducing benefits by raising the age for eligibility to 68, earmarking a new crude-oil tax to pay for a cut in

Jim Morin in *Richmond Times-Dispatch*

Social Security payroll taxes, and removing disability insurance and Medicare from the system and financing them with general revenue. But all these proposals were rejected, and Congress finally decided on an income-tax cut to partially offset the increase in the Social Security payroll tax.

Advisory Council. On February 26, Health, Education, and Welfare (HEW) Secretary Joseph A. Califano, Jr., announced a new Advisory Council on Social Security. The council will review all aspects of the Social Security program, including the status of Social Security trust funds, to determine their scope of coverage and adequacy of benefits.

"Past administrations and Congresses have held the work of past councils in high regard, but this may be the most important Advisory Council in the history of the program," Califano said. The council scheduled six days of hearings for Detroit; Los Angeles; New Orleans; Miami, Fla.; and Washington, D.C. It is to issue its report on Oct. 1, 1979.

New Administrator. Stanford G. Ross, a former White House aide to President Lyndon B. Johnson, was appointed on August 24 to be the new Social Security commissioner. He succeeded James Cardwell, who retired in 1977. The Social Security Administration is HEW's largest agency, with a budget of $107 billion during the fiscal year ending Sept. 30, 1978.   Virginia E. Anderson

In WORLD BOOK, see SOCIAL SECURITY.

SOCIAL WELFARE. President Jimmy Carter's comprehensive welfare-reform program failed to pass Congress in 1978. Key Democrats, such as House Ways and Means Committee Chairman Al Ullman (Ore.) and Senate Finance Committee Chairman Russell B. Long (La.), balked at the nearly $20-billion increase in costs over the current welfare system. Concerned congressmen tried to devise a more modest program. Congressional interest centered around four aspects of Carter's original proposal. These were:

■ Establishment of a national benefit level to eliminate the wide fluctuations in benefit levels that prevail from state to state. For instance, the high for a family of four is $6,132 in New York City and the low is $2,556 in Mississippi.

■ Extension of welfare coverage nationally to families headed by unemployed fathers. Nearly half the states now refuse such coverage, creating pressure that drives families apart.

■ Creation of a job program to provide training and jobs at reasonable wages and give welfare recipients some hope for the future.

■ Offering of fiscal relief for cities and states that now find welfare costs a heavy burden.

Bills including various combinations of these elements were introduced in the House of Representatives and the Senate. But Congress adjourned without taking action on welfare reform.

Computer Study. United States Secretary of Health, Education, and Welfare (HEW) Joseph A. Califano, Jr., announced that the government would begin comparing computer tapes of 110-million wage earners who pay Social Security taxes with names on welfare rolls to weed out welfare cheaters and reduce bureaucratic waste.

Califano predicted that the project would help restore public confidence in the welfare system by "getting the welfare rolls down to those people who are entitled to be on them." The new program is an expansion of Project Match, launched in 1977, which compared HEW's Washington, D.C., payroll with local welfare rolls.

The National District Attorney's Association criticized the program, saying that Project Match had uncovered few welfare cheaters. The organization also criticized Califano's policy of having the states prosecute most of the cheaters.

AFDC Errors. The rate of error in the largest U.S. welfare program, Aid to Families with Dependent Children (AFDC), declined from 16.5 per cent in 1973 to 8.6 per cent in 1978, according to HEW statisticians. But Califano declared that the rate must be reduced even more. He noted new incentives that now exist. Under Social Security amendments signed by President Carter on Dec. 20, 1977, states that reduce the error rate to specified levels will share the savings with the federal government.

Califano announced Project Responsibility on July 19, a plan to intensify efforts to find missing fathers of children on welfare and to make the parent pay child support. He said he hoped the program would double the collection rate to $1 billion annually by Sept. 30, 1979, the end of fiscal 1979.

Project Responsibility stems from the Child Support Enforcement Program enacted in 1975 to help states locate absent parents, establish paternity, and obtain child support. This federal-state partnership has had considerable success. From Aug. 1, 1975, to March 31, 1978, states collected $1.1 billion on behalf of AFDC families. Collections have increased each year. Califano promised to ensure that the rights of all parties are protected.

A Family Study directed by University of Pennsylvania sociologist Samuel Z. Klausner, and announced in July, concluded that traditional economic incentives are not the answer to improving the lot of welfare families, and that welfare policies should be reoriented around family and church ties. The researchers found that most welfare recipients constitute a subculture set apart from the rest of society.

The report also indicated that the vast majority of welfare mothers who avoid working outside the home do so because of a deeply embedded belief that a mother's place is with children, not to shirk work or because they are untrained.   Virginia E. Anderson

In WORLD BOOK, see FOOD STAMP PROGRAM; POVERTY; WELFARE.

SOMALIA. Eight months of warfare between Somali and Ethiopian troops came to an end in March 1978. The two countries fought for control of the Ogaden region in southeastern Ethiopia, which borders on Somalia. Most Ogaden inhabitants are ethnic Somalis.

Somalia committed most of its 32,000-member army to aiding secessionist guerrillas in the Ogaden who were fighting to join the territory to Somalia. The secessionists were successful in the beginning, but Ethiopia launched a successful counteroffensive in late January with Russian and Cuban help. See ETHIOPIA.

Aid Sought. Before the conflict with Ethiopia, Somalia relied on Russia for most of its military aid and supplies. However, Russia stopped arms shipments in October 1977 because Somalia invaded the Ogaden. At the same time, Russia stepped up its aid to Ethiopia.

Somalia's President Mohamed Siad Barre appealed in vain to the United States and other Western powers for military aid in mid-January and early February. Western governments withheld aid, however, because they viewed Somalia as the aggressor against Ethiopia.

Siad Barre announced the withdrawal of his troops from Ethiopia on March 9. The United States expressed a willingness to supply arms to help rebuild the Somali forces, which had been severely reduced during the fighting, but only if Somalia would pledge not to assist guerrillas operating against Ethiopia. Siad Barre refused to give such assurances, and military aid talks were suspended. However, the United States promised $7 million in food and other supplies for the refugees who had fled to Somalia from the Ogaden. United States aid was administered over six months, beginning in April.

Kenya's pro-Western government strongly opposed the proposed U.S. military assistance to Somalia. It warned the United States in April that it might close Kenyan ports on the Indian Ocean to U.S. warships in retaliation. Like Ethiopia, Kenya has land bordering on Somalia, and most of the people there are ethnic Somalis. Kenya feared a Somali invasion to gain control of the territory.

Attempted Coup. Dissident army officers and soldiers, dissatisfied with Siad Barre's conduct of the Ogaden war and fearing that he was planning an invasion of Kenya, tried to overthrow the government on April 9. Twenty persons died in the rebellion, which lasted only a few hours before it was put down by loyalist troops.

Sixty-six persons were tried in September for staging the rebellion, and 17 of them were executed in public on October 26. Jail terms ranging from three to 30 years were handed down to 36 others, and 21 were acquitted. 　　　　　John D. Esseks

See also AFRICA (Facts in Brief Table); In WORLD BOOK, see ETHIOPIA; SOMALIA.

SOUTH AFRICA shuffled its top leadership in 1978. Balthazar Johannes Vorster, prime minister since 1966, resigned on September 20 because of poor health. Pieter Willem Botha was chosen to succeed Vorster on September 28 by a caucus of the National Party, which has controlled South Africa's white-minority government since 1948. See BOTHA, PIETER WILLEM.

Botha's principal opponent for the premiership was Cornelius P. Mulder, minister for plural relations and development, the official responsible for policy regarding the country's blacks, about 70 per cent of the population. However, Mulder resigned from the Cabinet on November 7 after a judicial investigation linked him with covert financial dealings. Mulder's ministry had reportedly used at least $15 million in secret government funds to finance a newspaper and a magazine in an attempt to influence public opinion in favor of *apartheid* (racial segregation). Botha appointed Pieter Koornhof, a moderate on race relations, to succeed Mulder.

Independence for Venda. Before leaving office, Mulder announced that Venda, a black homeland in the northeast bordering on Rhodesia, would be given political independence by the end of 1979. The National Party's program for the "separate development" of races calls for distributing South Africa's black population among nine tribal states and even-

Pieter Willem Botha meets the press after he is chosen to succeed Balthazar Johannes Vorster as prime minister of South Africa on September 28.

tually giving them formal political independence. The nine cover 13 per cent of the country's area.

UN Plan. South Africa rejected a plan for United Nations (UN) supervision of pre-independence elections in Namibia (South West Africa) on September 20. The territory has been administered by South Africa since 1920. Vorster said the UN plan would have favored the South-West Africa People's Organization (SWAPO), a black nationalist movement fighting South African rule in Namibia.

The South African government conducted its own elections in Namibia from December 4 to 8 despite UN protests. The elections, which were boycotted by SWAPO, were won overwhelmingly by the Democratic Turnhalle Alliance (DTA), whose candidates won 41 of the 50 seats in the constitutional assembly. The DTA is a coalition of whites and moderate blacks, backed by South Africa. It pledged to end racial discrimination. See UNITED NATIONS.

South Africa's president since 1975, Nicolaas Diederichs, died on August 21. Vorster was elected to succeed him.   John D. Esseks

See also AFRICA (Facts in Brief Table); NAMIBIA. In WORLD BOOK, see SOUTH AFRICA.

SOUTH AMERICA. See LATIN AMERICA and articles on Latin American countries.

SOUTH CAROLINA. See STATE GOVERNMENT.

SOUTH DAKOTA. See STATE GOVERNMENT.

SOUTH WEST AFRICA. See NAMIBIA.

Female astronauts—from left, Margaret Seddon, Anna Fisher, Judith Resnik, Shannon Lucid, Sally Ride, and Kathryn Sullivan—begin training.

SPACE EXPLORATION. Russian cosmonauts set a space-endurance record on Nov. 2, 1978, when Vladimir Kovalyonok and Aleksander S. Ivanchenko returned to Earth after 139 days in space. They broke the record set on March 16, 1978, when Yuri V. Romanenko and Georgi M. Grechko landed safely in Russia after 96 days in space. Both teams of cosmonauts spent their time aboard the space station *Salyut 6,* launched on Sept. 29, 1977.

Vladimir Remek, a Czechoslovak and the first space traveler not from the United States or Russia, also spent time aboard *Salyut 6.* Kovalyonok and Ivanchenko docked *Soyuz 29* on June 17. Polish jet pilot Miroslaw Hermaszewski and veteran cosmonaut Pyotr I. Klimuk, in *Soyuz 30,* joined them on June 28 and returned to Earth on July 5. United States astronauts remained on the ground during the year, and Kovalyonok and Ivanchenko surpassed their record of 937 man-days in space on August 2.

Skylab Falling. The U.S. National Aeronautics and Space Administration (NASA) adjusted the decaying orbit of the *Skylab* space station in June, July, and November to keep the station from falling into the atmosphere. NASA controllers had hoped *Skylab* would stay in orbit until March or April 1980, when astronauts from the space shuttle might be able to attach rockets to bring it down in the ocean. But NASA abandoned the idea on December 18, "because of the limited potential for success." After

entering the atmosphere, Skylab will scatter about 25 short tons (23 metric tons) of debris along a path 3,000 miles (4,800 kilometers) long and 50 to 100 miles (80 to 160 kilometers) wide. NASA said that 75 per cent of *Skylab's* flight path is over water, and that the debris will be less dangerous than meteorites.

The first shuttle, with its fuel tanks and rockets, underwent vibration tests at Marshall Space Flight Center in Huntsville, Ala., in 1978. Engine problems forced NASA to reschedule its first manned orbital flight for September 1979.

New Astronauts reported to the Lyndon B. Johnson Space Center in Houston on July 10 to begin two years of training and evaluation. The 35 recruits included six women, three blacks, and one Japanese American. A shuttle scheduled for the early 1980s will carry *Spacelab,* a fully equipped scientific laboratory being developed and financed by 10 European nations. Scientist-astronauts Owen K. Garriot, a *Skylab* veteran, and rookie Robert A. Parker will fly this *Spacelab 1* mission. Four nonastronauts, including one woman, will work on *Spacelab 2.* Two of these *payload specialists* will fly in the laboratory in space, and two will operate support equipment on earth.

Six astronauts received the first Congressional Space Medals of Honor on October 1, during NASA's 20th anniversary celebration—Neil A. Armstrong; Frank Borman; Charles Conrad, Jr.;

John H. Glenn, Jr.; Virgil I. Grissom (posthumously); and Alan B. Shepard, Jr.

Venus Probes. The United States launched two unmanned spacecraft to Venus in 1978. *Pioneer Venus 1* left on May 20 and went into orbit around Venus on December 4. *Pioneer Venus 2,* launched on August 8, sent five probes into the Venusian atmosphere on December 9. All the instruments worked perfectly, collecting data on the planet's atmosphere. See ASTRONOMY.

Cosmos Falls. Russia's *Cosmos 954,* a nuclear-powered naval reconnaissance satellite, broke up in the atmosphere on January 24 and scattered radioactive debris over a large area near Great Slave Lake in northwestern Canada. Radiation and falling metal produced no known injury to people.

The United States launched *Seasat-A,* an unmanned, ocean-monitoring satellite, on June 26. An apparent short circuit shut down communications on October 9. NASA shut down its *Viking* satellite on July 25, 1978, after 706 orbits of Mars.

President Jimmy Carter released a statement on space policy for the next 10 years on October 11. It emphasized unmanned scientific exploration and practical applications of present technology and rejected space colonization, space manufacturing, and satellites to collect solar energy that could be converted to electricity.   William J. Cromie

In WORLD BOOK, see SPACE TRAVEL.

SPAIN granted limited political autonomy to several regions and adopted a new Constitution in 1978. Rioting and terrorism continued, however.

Two royal decrees on January 2 granted the Basques limited autonomy. On January 18, the Ministry of the Interior legalized the Basque Revolutionary Party, an offshoot of the military separatist organization Basque Homeland and Liberty.

A royal decree gave pre-autonomy to the Basque General Council on July 16 as a first step toward a regional Basque government. Additional Basque control over agriculture, industry, commerce, and planning was promised.

On June 30, Spain granted provisional autonomy to the Balearic Islands; the central Castile region, except Madrid; and the Estremadura area next to Portugal. The grants brought to 10 the number of regions with limited autonomy.

New Constitution. The Chamber of Deputies approved and sent to the Senate on July 21 a proposed constitution that would abolish the death penalty and the state religion, grant full rights to 18-year-olds, allow divorce and abortion to be legalized, and let regions have their own flags and official languages. The official national flag and language would be Spanish. The Senate ratified the proposed constitution on October 31. It was approved by a margin of 11 to 1 in a national referendum on December 6 and signed by King

Juan Carlos I on December 27. On December 29, Prime Minister Adolfo Suarez Gonzalez dissolved Parliament and set an election for March 1, 1979.

Pamplona Riots. The streets of Pamplona were deserted and littered with fire-gutted automobiles and rubble after the annual running-of-the-bulls festival ended in riots on July 8. One man was shot in the bull ring when Basque youths stoned riot police. A youth was killed on July 11 during a Basque protest outside a police station in San Sebastian. Basques temporarily cut off access to France by bombing rail lines and barricading roads.

Security police went on a rampage, firing smoke grenades into homes and shops and smashing windows in the San Sebastian industrial suburb of Renteria on July 13. The police, not used to working for a democratic government after years of a dictatorship, resented the soft line taken with demonstrators. A police platoon was arrested pending an investigation.

Economic Woes. Suarez Gonzalez replaced his Cabinet's major economic officials on February 24. Spain's economy was at its lowest point since the late 1930s with high unemployment, a high balance-of-payments deficit, and a high foreign debt. The International Monetary Fund granted Spain credits of $295 million.   Kenneth Brown

See also EUROPE (Facts in Brief Table). In WORLD BOOK, see BASQUE; SPAIN.

SPINKS, LEON (1954-   ), stunned the boxing world on Feb. 15, 1978, by defeating Muhammad Ali to win the heavyweight boxing championship. But the World Boxing Council withdrew its recognition of him as champion, and he held the World Boxing Association version of the title only seven months. Ali regained the title on September 15 by winning a unanimous decision in New Orleans.

Spinks was fighting only his eighth professional fight when he scored his stunning upset, winning a split decision in Las Vegas, Nev., in what was supposed to be only a warm-up match for Ali. That fight brought Spinks about $300,000, and he earned $3.7 million in the rematch. See BOXING.

Leon Spinks was born in a St. Louis slum, the oldest of seven children. He started boxing at the age of 15 and left home at about the same time "to give more room to the rest of my family." He continued to box during a four-year term in the United States Marine Corps. Spinks fought in 185 amateur bouts. Before becoming a professional in 1977, he won a bronze medal at the World Boxing Championships in Cuba and a silver medal at the Pan American Games in Mexico City, Mexico, in 1975, and the gold medal for light-heavyweights in the 1976 Olympic Games in Montreal, Canada. His brother Michael also won an Olympic Games gold medal in 1976 as a middleweight.   Joseph P. Spohn

In WORLD BOOK, see ALI, MUHAMMAD; BOXING.

SPORTS. Many phases of the United States sports world were bigger and sometimes better in 1978. Professional football played its longest regular season (16 games instead of 14) and its longest play-offs (involving 10 teams instead of eight). College football realigned to give the more important teams more control over their destinies and income. Major-league baseball attracted more than 40 million spectators, the most in history. Amateur sports received a boost when the federal government voted $16 million to the United States Olympic Committee, partly to build and run sports-training centers. Boxing, which attracted strong periodic attention with one world heavyweight champion, found itself with two. Thoroughbred horse racing, which turned up a triple-crown champion in 1977, had another one in 1978.

Television played an increasingly important role. The World Series, Super Bowl, and a Muhammad Ali-Leon Spinks heavyweight title fight drew more than 80 million television viewers each. Under four-year contracts, television networks were paying $656 million to professional football, $118 million to college football, $92.8 million to baseball, and $74-million to professional basketball. The networks televised more boxing and more horse racing.

More women were able to take part in more sports because the federal Title IX regulation forbids sexual discrimination by colleges receiving federal funds. In December, the government acted to "clarify" sex bias rules so that colleges and universities will spend equally for men and women athletes. Professional women athletes received more attention because of the success of Nancy Lopez in her first full year on the golf tour. See GOLF; LOPEZ, NANCY.

There were world championships in many sports, notably in soccer. Argentina won the World Cup (see SOCCER). Illegal use of drugs turned up at some of these championships. Disqualified athletes included a Russian swimmer and Austrian, East German, and Polish cyclists.

The international federations in gymnastics and track and field admitted China and, at China's insistence, expelled Taiwan. At year's end, China belonged to 11 international federations while Taiwan belonged to 15.

Among the Winners in 1978 were:

Curling. The United States defeated Norway, 6-4, in the final of the world championship on April 2 in Winnipeg, Canada. The U.S. rink was headed by Bob Nichols of Superior, Wis. The Sandy Robarge rink of Wausau, Wis., won the United States women's title.

Fencing. Russia won three and Hungary two of the eight titles in the world championships in July in Hamburg, West Germany. Russia gained the team title for the 16th straight year. Three Americans – Peter Schifrin of San Jose, Calif., in épée, and John Nonna of New York City and Mike Marx of Portland, Ore., in foil – reached rounds of 32.

Rowing. East Germany again dominated the world championships, winning eight of the 14 men's and women's events in November on Lake Karapiro in New Zealand.

More than 4,200 runners start the 82nd Boston Marathon. Bill Rodgers of Melrose, Mass., won the race in 2 hours 10 minutes 13 seconds.

The United States won only one silver and one bronze medal, both by women. The best college eights were Syracuse and Washington.

Shooting. The United States dominated the world championships, held from September 24 to October 4 in Seoul, South Korea, winning 18 of the 52 gold medals. The winners included Lones Wigger of Carter, Mont., in free rifle, three position; David Kimes of Monterey Park, Calif., in standard rifle; and Wanda Jewell of Fort Benning, Ga., in women's air rifle.

Weight Lifting. Russia won six of the 10 titles in the world championships in October at Gettysburg, Pa. Jurgen Heuser of East Germany took the super-heavyweight title, ending the eight-year reign of Vassili Alexeev of Russia. The 352-pound (160-kilogram) Alexeev withdrew from the competition after he pulled a tendon in his right hip while trying to lift 529 pounds (240 kilograms) on his first clean and jerk.

Wrestling. Leroy Kemp of Canton, Ohio, in the 163-pound class of free-style, was the only United States winner in the world championships. Russians won six of the 10 individual titles in free-style and six of the 10 in Greco-Roman and retained both team titles. Russia also won the World Cup for the sixth time in the six-year history of that competition.

Other Champions. *Archery,* world champions: men, Darrell Pace, Cincinnati; women, Anna Marie Lehmann, West Germany. *Badminton,* world champions: men, Liem Swie King, Indonesia; women, S. Ng, Malaysia. *Biathlon,* world champions: 20-kilometer, Odd Lirhus, Norway; 10-kilometer, Frank Ullrich, East Germany. *Billiards,* world pocket champions: men, Ray Martin, Fair Lawn, N.J.; women, Jean Balukas, Brooklyn, N.Y. *Bobsledding,* world champions: four-man, Horst Schonau, East Germany; two-man, Erich Scharer, Switzerland. *Canoeing,* U.S. 500-meter champions: canoe, Roland Muhlen, St. Charles,

Ill.; men's kayak, Steve Kelly, Bronx, N.Y.; women's kayak, Leslie Klein, Hadley, Mass. *Casting,* world all-around champion: Steve Rajeff, San Francisco. *Court tennis,* U.S. open champion: Jimmy Burke, Philadelphia. *Cricket,* World Series: West Indies. *Croquet,* U.S. champion: Richard Pearman, Bermuda. *Cross-country,* U.S. champions: AAU men, Greg Meyer, Boston; AAU women, Julie Brown, Northridge, Calif.; NCAA, Alberto Salazar, Oregon; AIAW, Mary Decker, Colorado. *Cycling,* world champions: men's pro road, Gerrie Knetemann, the Netherlands; women's road, Beate Habetz, West Germany; men's pro sprint, Koichi Nakano, Japan; women's sprint, Galina Zareva, Russia. *Darts,* U.S. champion: John Zimnawoda, Baltimore. *Equestrian events,* world champions: jumping, Gerd Wiltfang, West Germany; three-day, Bruce Davidson, Unionville, Pa. *Field hockey,* World Cup champion: Pakistan. *Gymnastics,* world champions: men's all-around, Nikolai Andrianov, Russia; men's floor exercises, Kurt Thomas, Terre Haute, Ind.; women's all-around, Elena Mukhina, Russia; women's uneven parallel bars, Marcia Frederick, Springfield, Mass. *Hang gliding,* world champion: Malcolm Jones, Tampa, Fla. *Horseshoe pitching,* world champions: men, Walter Williams, Chino, Calif.; women, Opal Reno, Lucasville, Ohio. *Judo,* AAU open champions: men, Michinori Ishibashi, Fort Worth, Tex.; women, Barbara Fest, Salem, Mass. *Karate,* AAU advanced champions: men, Domingo Llanos, Haverstraw, N.Y.; women, Ellen Beal, Barrington, N.H. *Lacrosse,* U.S. college champion: Johns Hopkins. *Lawn bowling,* U.S. champion: Skippy Arculli, Nutley, N.J. *Luge,* world champions: men, Paul Hindgartner, Italy; women, Vera Sosulya, Russia. *Modern pentathlon,* world champions: men, Pavel Lednev, Russia; women, Wendy Norman, Great Britain. *Motorcycling,* U.S. Grand National champion: Jay Springsteen, Lapeer, Mich. *Parachute jumping,* world overall champions: men, Nikolai Usmayev, Russia; women, Cheryl Stearns, Scottsdale, Ariz. *Polo,* U.S. open champion: Abercrombie and Kent, Oak Brook, Ill. *Racquetball,* U.S. champions: men, Marty Hogan, St. Louis; women, Shannon Wright, San Diego. *Racquets,* U.S. champion: William Surtees, New York City. *Rodeo,* U.S. all-around champion: Tom Ferguson, Miami, Okla. *Roller skating,* world champions: men, Thomas Nieder, West Germany; women, Natalie Dunn, Bakersfield, Calif. *Roque,* U.S. champion: Jack Green, Long Beach, Calif. *Rugby,* British Isles, Rugby Union, International champion: Wales. *Sambo,* U.S. unlimited champion: Chris Dolman, the Netherlands. *Shuffleboard,* U.S. summer champions: men, Charles Bone, Muscatine, Iowa; women, Dorcas Donelson, Carey, Ohio. *Sled-dog racing,* world champion: Eugene Corbin, Quebec City, Canada. *softball,* U.S. fast-pitch champions: men, Billard Barbell, Reading, Pa.; women, Raybestos Brakettes, Stratford, Conn. *Squash racquets,* U.S. champions: men, Mike Desaulniers, Montreal: women, Gretchen Spruance, Wilmington, Del. *Squash tennis,* U.S. champion: Pedro Bacallao, New York City. *Surfing,* U.S. champions: men, Tim Briers, Central Florida; women, Mary Ann Hayes, Central Florida. *Synchronized swimming,* world champion: Helen Vandenburg, Calgary, Canada. *Table tennis,* U.S. champions: men, Norio Takashima, Japan; women, Hong Ja Park, South Korea. *Tae kwon do,* world champion: Canada. *Team handball,* U.S. open champion: Air Force Academy. *Trampoline,* U.S. champions: men, Stuart Ransom, Memphis, Tenn.; women, Leigh Hennessey, Lafayette, La. *Volleyball,* world champions: men, Russia; women, Cuba. *Water polo,* world champion: Italy. *Water skiing,* United States overall champions: men, Ricky McCormick, Winter Haven, Fla.; women, Deena Brush, West Sacramento, Calif.   Frank Litsky

See also articles on the various sports; Section One, FOCUS ON SPORTS. IN WORLD BOOK, see articles on the various sports.

SRI LANKA. Six university campuses exploded in angry demonstrations in February 1978. The government, fearful of a repetition of the 1971 student riots, ordered the universities closed, but the unrest grew, and by May the army was called out to maintain order. Parliament then passed legislation "to prevent Sri Lanka from becoming another Chicago," as Justice Minister K. W. Dewanayagam put it. The bill permitted preventive detention of dissidents for up to a year.

Two Causes lay behind the turmoil. Some 1.4-million people, or more than 20 per cent of the work force, were out of work. The problem was especially severe among the young. The poor, and even the middle class, were hurt by soaring prices, shortages, and the abandonment of the old weekly ration of one free pound (0.45 kilogram) of rice per person for roughly half the population.

The second cause was the continuing demand for independence by 1.8 million Tamils, concentrated in northern and eastern Sri Lanka. Another million or so are recent arrivals from India. Most of them work on tea and rubber plantations. The Tamil United Liberation Front had become the main opposition party, with 20 seats in the 168-seat National State Assembly. But the party was divided, with young militants defying the more cautious older leaders. An outlawed underground group, the Tamil Liberation Tigers, sabotaged Air Ceylon's only operational jet on September 7.

Prisoners Freed. Junius Jayewardene, whose United National Party took 139 seats in the July 1977 election, gave up the premiership on February 3 to become president, with vastly enhanced powers. One of his first acts was to release political prisoners, including Moscow-trained Marxist Rohana Wijaweera, who led a bloody youth rebellion in 1971. Jayewardene also set up a commission to investigate alleged misdeeds committed by former Prime Minister Sirimavo Bandaranaike.

Jayewardene reversed many of Bandaranaike's socialist policies, established during her seven years in office. Once again, investors from other countries were tempted to invest in Sri Lanka's economy. While the tea plantations, nationalized by Bandaranaike, remained in government hands, the Jayewardene regime greatly improved their management. Efforts were also made to streamline the unwieldy bureaucracy. With tea and rubber prices rising in world markets, Sri Lanka's income went up. But resources were strained to pay $350 million a year for imported food, and half the population still lived below the poverty line.

Disaster struck Sri Lanka twice in November. An airliner crashed there on November 15, killing more than 200 passengers, and a fierce cyclone killed nearly 500 a week later.   Mark Gayn

See also ASIA (Facts in Brief Table). IN WORLD BOOK, see SRI LANKA.

STAMP COLLECTING. Four commemorative stamps were issued by the United Nations (UN) on March 31, 1978, to mark the near elimination of smallpox threats throughout the world. The worst form of this disease – the smallpox that kills, blinds, and maims – has been almost completely wiped out. The stamps honor the 10-year eradication program that the World Health Organization (WHO) started in 1967.

The four commemoratives consist of 13-cent and 31-cent stamps depicting an enlargement of a smallpox virus and 80-centime and 1.10-franc stamps showing two globes, one outlining areas that once were infected with smallpox and the other showing a smallpox-free world. The first two stamps are for use at WHO's New York City headquarters; the others, for UN headquarters in Geneva, Switzerland.

Togo and Lesotho also issued stamps to commemorate smallpox eradication, and it is expected that other countries will eventually do the same. Togo put out four stamps featuring Edward Jenner, the English physician who experimented with cowpox vaccine as a cure for smallpox, and showing children being vaccinated. One of Lesotho's stamps shows Jenner vaccinating a child; the other, the head of a child against a background of the WHO emblem.

Nondenominational U.S. Stamp. For only the third time in its history, the United States Postal Service issued a nondenominational stamp. It met needs created when the first-class postage rate was increased, on May 29, from 13 to 15 cents per ounce. Known as the "A" stamp, the nondenominational issue was printed in 1975 and 1976 in expectation of higher rates. Collectors were given until July 15 to acquire first-day-of-issue cancellations. The two earlier nondenominational stamps were issued by the Postal Service in 1975 to commemorate Christmas.

Accompanying the "A" stamp was a nondenominational postal card to meet the new 10-cent rate. The card honored John Hancock, the first signer of the Declaration of Independence. On May 19, the first day of issue, the cards were sold only in Quincy, Mass., Hancock's hometown. Postal officials reported that 5,500 of the nondenominational cards were purchased within two hours.

Another unusual U.S. stamp was an experimental diminutive 13-cent issue depicting an Indian-head penny. The stamp was placed on sale on January 11, and was designed partly to save paper costs. It measured only 1/2 by 2/3 of an inch (12.7 by 16.8 millimeters). Although some users found it difficult to handle, a survey by the Postal Service indicated a favorable reaction. Of the 2.8 million miniature stamps purchased by those surveyed, 37 per cent were bought by collectors.

Record Price. The celebrated 1918 U.S. airmail stamp with an inverted center brought a record price of $72,500 at the Rarities of the World sale in April conducted by the Robert A. Siegel Auction Galleries of New York City. In a little more than two hours, 324 lots of stamps brought $1,348,600. That topped by more than $200,000 the previous record for a single auction session. The Siegel Galleries' Baker Postal History collection auction, also in April, saw $50,000 paid for a U.S. "Overland via Marseilles" cover. It was the highest price ever paid for any U.S. cover.

Readers of *Linn's Stamp News* voted in 1978 that the Butterflies block of four was the most popular U.S. stamp issued in 1977. The Conserve Energy pair was voted the worst U.S. stamp, followed by the Talking Pictures and Peace Bridge issues. The last two were also voted the least necessary.

The Postal Service adopted an innovative reservation system to help collectors purchase one of the most popular issues of the year, the CAPEX 78 souvenir sheets. The sheets of eight 13-cent stamps, depicting four birds and four animals native to the border between the United States and Canada, were issued as a U.S. tribute to the Canadian Philatelic Exhibition, held in Toronto, Ont., in June. Collectors could reserve desired quantities of the sheets at any of the 248 U.S. philatelic centers. Thirty days after the July 28 deadline, collectors could pick up and pay for the stamps.   Theodore M. O'Leary

In WORLD BOOK, see STAMP COLLECTING.

Commemorative stamp honors Harriet Tubman, a leader of the "underground railroad" that helped slaves flee to freedom before the U.S. Civil War.

STATE
GOVERNMENT

Pocketbook issues ranging from property-tax cuts to spending limits preoccupied state officials and citizens of the United States in 1978. The action began in California's June 6 primary election, in which voters approved Proposition 13, an initiative reducing their property taxes nearly 57 per cent.

Economists predicted local governments and school districts in California would immediately lose $7 billion in revenue. To offset the loss, the legislature drew on a budget surplus to provide $5 billion in direct state aid to relieve local governments and schools, and set aside another $900 million for loans. The relief measures and an $800-million budget cut were not expected to prevent a $4.9-billion state government surplus from accumulating by the end of fiscal 1979. Governor Edmund G. Brown, Jr., froze the hiring of state employees on June 6. Brown signed a $14.73-billion state budget on July 6. The budget was down $10.6 million from the year before.

Proposals for widespread tax cuts or spending limits on state governments appeared on the November 7 ballots of at least 12 states. Several legislatures enacted tax-relief measures. California cut income taxes by $1 billion. Wisconsin provided tax credits totaling $105.8 million, including a property-tax credit of 10 per cent for homeowners. Colorado reduced taxes by $64 million and tied income taxes to the inflation rate recorded by the Consumer Price Index – an action duplicated in other states. Minnesota lawmakers passed a $100-million tax-relief package. Vermont repealed the 9 per cent income tax surcharge. Connecticut repealed the 2.5 per cent tax on business equipment and provided $12.9 million in tax-relief grants to cities and towns. Maine taxpayers will receive nearly $20 million in tax relief, and Mississippi increased its maximum standard deduction from $750 to $1,000 for individual taxpayers. See ELECTIONS; TAXATION (Close-Up).

Gambling. Voters in New Jersey, which opened its first state-controlled casinos in Atlantic City in May, refused to approve a constitutional amendment permitting betting on jai alai. Virginia voters rejected parimutuel betting on horse races, and Florida voters decisively turned down gambling casinos for the Miami Beach area. A district appeals court in Illinois overturned a state ban on race-track messen-

ger services on April 20, but the Illinois Supreme Court overruled the appeals court and reinstated the ban on July 14. A similar ban has been challenged in the Kentucky courts. In Delaware, the process for a constitutional amendment permitting jai alai bets began when the Delaware Supreme Court questioned the legality of the 1977 jai alai wagering law.

New Constitution. Although it did not receive national attention, Tennessee's passage of a new constitution in March probably was the voters' first response to pocketbook issues. The constitution requires that expenditures from state taxes not grow faster than the state's economy. Because the restriction applies only to state taxes, it covers about two-thirds of the state budget. The legislature must decide how to measure economic growth.

Women's Rights. The proposed Equal Rights Amendment (ERA) got a new lease on life on October 6 when the U.S. Senate extended the deadline for its ratification from March 22, 1979, to June 30, 1982. The House had voted for the extension on August 15. States were not permitted to rescind their previous votes for ratification. At the beginning of 1978, 35 states had approved the ERA. Three states – Idaho, Nebraska, and Tennessee – had rescinded. The Constitution requires ratification by 38 states.

Kentucky rescinded on March 16, but the lieutenant governor, in the absence of the governor, vetoed the rescission on March 20. The Illinois House of Representatives refused to ratify the ERA on June 7 and June 22.

Missouri sued the National Organization for Women (NOW) on February 28, charging it with violating antitrust laws and seeking an injunction against NOW's support of convention boycotts of states that have not ratified the ERA. Nebraska sued NOW on March 3. The Miami Beach Tourist Development Authority said in December that the boycott would cost the city at least $14 million in lost 1979 convention revenues.

Abortion Regulation and Funding was the most controversial health-and-welfare issue in 1978. Most states imposed regulations at least as stringent as the federal guidelines: Federal funds may be used for abortions if the woman's life is endangered, or if two doctors agree that the pregnancy would seriously impair her physical health, or if the pregnancy was the result of a promptly reported case of rape or incest. Continuing to fund abortions for poor women regardless of circumstances were Alaska, Colorado, Hawaii, Idaho, Maryland, Michigan, New York, North Carolina, Oregon, Virginia, Washington, and West Virginia. Court injunctions caused several states to continue the funding.

Legislatures overrode governors' vetoes of restrictions on abortion funding in Illinois, Massachusetts, and Pennsylvania. Michigan Governor William G. Milliken vetoed such legislation twice in 1978.

Howard Jarvis led the fight for Proposition 13, which cut California property taxes by 57 per cent. The state's voters approved it on June 6.

Selected Statistics on State Governments

State	Resident population(a)	Governor	House (D)	House (R)	Senate (D)	Senate (R)	State tax revenue(c)	Tax revenue per capita(d)	Public school enrollment 1977–78(e)	Public school expenditures per pupil in average daily attendance 1977–78(f)
Alabama	3,742	Forrest H. James, Jr. (D)	101	4	35	0	$ 1,589	$ 425	762	$1,281
Alaska	403	Jay S. Hammond (R)	24	15(g)	9	11	563	1,397	90	3,341
Arizona	2,354	Bruce E. Babbitt (D)	18	42	14	16	1,307	555	514	1,436
Arkansas	2,186	Bill Clinton (D)	94	6	35	0	926	424	459	1,193
California	22,294	Edmund G. Brown, Jr. (D)	50	30	26	14	15,019	674	4,289	1,674
Colorado	2,670	Richard D. Lamm (D)	27	38	13	22	1,212	454	562	1,649
Connecticut	3,099	Ella T. Grasso (D)	104	47	26	10	1,550	500	616	1,914
Delaware	583	Pierre S. du Pont IV (R)	21	20	13	9	450	771	118	2,138
Florida	8,594	Robert Graham (D)	88	32	27	13	3,764	438	1,536	1,594
Georgia	5,084	George Busbee (D)	159	21	52	4	2,189	431	1,090	1,189
Hawaii	897	George R. Ariyoshi (D)	42	9	18	7	755	841	172	1,963
Idaho	878	John V. Evans (D)	20	50	16	19	416	474	201	1,206
Illinois	11,243	James R. Thompson (R)	89	88	32	27	5,774	514	2,180	2,058
Indiana	5,374	Otis R. Bowen (R)	46	54	21	29	2,455	457	1,144	1,449
Iowa	2,896	Robert D. Ray (R)	44	56	23	27	1,402	484	589	2,002
Kansas	2,348	John Carlin (D)	56	69	19	21	1,051	448	446	1,682
Kentucky	3,498	Julian M. Carroll (D)	78	22	29	9	1,842	527	697	1,294
Louisiana	3,966	Edwin W. Edwards (D)	101	4	38	1	1,980	499	839	1,481
Maine	1,091	Joseph E. Brennan (D)	77	73	13	19	527	483	246	1,522
Maryland	4,143	Harry Hughes (D)	125	16	40	7	2,404	580	837	2,100
Massachusetts	5,774	Edward J. King (D)	130	30	37	7	3,301	572	1,165	2,137
Michigan	9,189	William G. Milliken (R)	70	40	24	14	5,326	580	2,036	1,975
Minnesota	4,008	Albert Quie (R)	67	67	48	19	2,759	688	836	1,962
Mississippi	2,404	Cliff Finch (D)	117	3	50	2	1,094	455	502	1,220
Missouri	4,860	Joseph P. Teasdale (D)	117	46	23	11	1,784	367	931	1,425
Montana	785	Thomas L. Judge (D)	64	36	24	26	338	431	169	1,906
Nebraska	1,565	Charles Thone (R)	49 (h) (unicameral)				680	435	306	1,526
Nevada	660	Robert F. List (R)	26	14	15	5	391	592	143	1,526
New Hampshire	871	Hugh J. Gallen (D)	169	231	11	13	240	276	175	1,366
New Jersey	7,327	Brendan T. Byrne (D)	54	26	27	13	3,440	469	1,421	2,333
New Mexico	1,212	Bruce King (D)	41	29	33	9	761	628	282	1,476
New York	17,748	Hugh L. Carey (D)	87	63	25	35	10,934	616	3,230	2,527
North Carolina	5,577	James B. Hunt, Jr. (D)	106	14	45	5	2,608	468	1,182	1,343
North Dakota	652	Arthur A. Link (D)	29	71	14	36	310	475	125	1,518
Ohio	10,749	James A. Rhodes (R)	62	37	18	15	4,135	385	2,182	1,581
Oklahoma	2,880	George Nigh (D)	75	26	38	9	1,315	457	594	1,461
Oregon	2,444	Victor Atiyeh (R)	34	26	23	7	1,159	474	473	1,929
Pennsylvania	11,750	Richard L. Thornburgh (R)	100	102	27	23	6,266	533	2,129	2,079
Rhode Island	935	J. Joseph Garrahy (D)	84	14	43	4	458	490	167	1,840
South Carolina	2,918	Richard W. Riley (D)	108	16	43	2	1,364	468	621	1,340
South Dakota	690	William J. Janklow (R)	24	48	11	24	224	324	144	1,385
Tennessee	4,357	Lamar Alexander (R)	60	38	20	12	1,704	391	878	1,209
Texas	13,014	William Clements (R)	131	19	27	4	5,390	414	2,843	1,352
Utah	1,307	Scott M. Matheson (D)	25	50	10	19	606	464	317	1,363
Vermont	487	Richard A. Snelling (R)	68	80	10	20	234	480	103	1,550
Virginia	5,148	John N. Dalton (R)	76	21	35	5	2,336	454	1,082	1,560
Washington	3,774	Dixy Lee Ray (D)	49	49	29	20	2,448	649	776	1,951
West Virginia	1,860	John D. Rockefeller IV (D)	74	26	26	8	981	527	401	1,374
Wisconsin	4,679	Lee S. Dreyfus (R)	60	39	21	12	3,089	660	918	(i)
Wyoming	424	Ed Herschler (D)	20	42	11	19	289	683	92	2,007

(a) Numbers in thousands, provisional estimates as of July 1, 1978
  (Bureau of the Census)
(b) As of Dec. 31, 1978
(c) 1978 preliminary figures in millions (Bureau of the Census)
(d) 1978 preliminary figures in dollars (Bureau of the Census)
(e) Numbers in thousands, fall, 1977 (U.S. Office of Education)
(f) Number in dollars, 1977–78 (U.S. Office of Education)
(g) 1 Independent
(h) Nonpartisan
(i) Not available. Expenditures for 1976-77 were $1,743

Special circumstances regulated abortions in some states. Tennessee required informed consent, an Oklahoma measure regulated facilities and set guidelines on abortions, an Illinois law required local schools to teach alternatives to abortion in family-hygiene and sex-education courses, and a Kentucky law required insurance policyholders to obtain optional insurance riders for coverage of elective abortions. At least 13 states have called for a U.S. constitutional convention to consider the abortion issue.

A federal appellate court in April overturned an Illinois law prohibiting an abortion on a woman under 18 without her parents' or husband's consent. A federal appellate court overturned a Missouri law in September requiring physicians to tell women they would lose custody of any child born during an attempted abortion. A federal district court delayed a stringent abortion law that was to go into effect in Louisiana in September.

Educational Competency. Florida conducted the nation's first experiment in requiring educational-competency testing for high school graduation. Florida's chapter of the National Association for the Advancement of Colored People charged that a higher proportion of blacks than whites failed the tests because the tests were culturally biased against blacks.

At least 11 states required students to pass literacy tests for high school graduation. Another 24 states set minimal competency standards, but not as graduation requirements. Arizona, California, Florida, and Maryland have competency standards for grade promotion. Oregon requires competency assessment for graduation, but lets local school districts set the standards and procedures.

A 1978 pilot competency-based test in Kansas focused on reading and mathematics. The legislature will decide whether the test should be established statewide. See EDUCATION.

Death Penalty. On May 2, the New York State Senate failed by one vote to override Governor Hugh L. Carey's veto of a bill to restore capital punishment. The bill would have replaced the mandatory death-penalty law that the New York State Court of Appeals struck down in November 1977. It would have allowed, but not required, juries to impose capital punishment in specified cases.

On March 3, New Jersey Governor Brendan T. Byrne *pocket-vetoed* a bill — left it unsigned after legislative adjournment — to institute the death penalty. Maryland's Acting Governor Blair Lee III signed into law on March 10 a bill allowing capital punishment for 10 types of first-degree murder. Maryland became the 33rd state to restore the death penalty since the U.S. Supreme Court voided all such laws in 1972.

Alabama's Supreme Court affirmed the state's 1975 death-penalty law by upholding the conviction

Singer Steve Lawrence throws the first dice to initiate legal gambling in Atlantic City, N.J., as Governor Brendan T. Byrne, left, looks on.

of two men sentenced under that law. The Supreme Court of the United States struck down Ohio's death-penalty law on July 3 and declined to review decisions voiding capital-punishment statutes in New York and Pennsylvania. On October 16, the court declined to review an appeal seeking to restore the New York law.

Church and State. The New York State Board of Regents on February 22 denied an application by Sun Myung Moon's Unification Theological Seminary to become a state-chartered, degree-granting institution. The board said the seminary "did not meet academic standards, has made deceptive claims, and had a questionable financial structure." The U.S. Supreme Court on March 24 stayed an appeals court decision that would have let New Hampshire's Governor Meldrim Thomson, Jr., carry out a proclamation ordering all flags outside state office buildings lowered to observe Good Friday. The court voided a Tennessee law on April 19 excluding the clergy from public office.

A federal court in December declared unconstitutional Utah state and local practices of granting public school academic credit for seminary classes on the Bible and the practice of using seminary attendance to satisfy public school attendance requirements.   Ralph Wayne Derickson

In WORLD BOOK, see STATE GOVERNMENT and articles on the individual states.

STEEL INDUSTRY. By the end of September 1978, United States steelmakers were overcoming some of the difficulties that had afflicted the industry. There were signs that a fragile harmony with the Administration of President Jimmy Carter was about to pay dividends in fewer imports and better earnings.

Import Curbs. Despite Carter Administration plans to curb steel imports, steel continued to enter the United States at a staggering rate in early 1978 – up 80 per cent from the year before. The pace slowed later, then rose again to about 1.9 million short tons (1.7 million metric tons) in August. However, domestic production, slowed by a severe winter and a long coal strike, began to gain ground.

Production and Prices. Steel output by the middle of November stood at 120 million short tons (109-million metric tons), with weekly operating rates at 89.5 per cent of capacity. This was a gain over the 1977 output for the same period of 110.5 million short tons (100 million metric tons).

Preliminary figures released in December by the International Iron and Steel Institute indicated that worldwide steel production set a record in 1978 of 712.5 million metric tons (785.4 million short tons). The previous record was 708.8 million metric tons (781.3 million short tons) in 1974.

Early in April, most of the major U.S. steel producers responded to government urging to keep down the rate of inflation by limiting their price increases to $5.50 per short ton (0.9 metric ton) on most products. However, a possible additional price increase of up to 7 per cent was forecast by Edgar B. Speer, chairman of United States Steel Corporation. Speaking at the annual meeting of the American Iron and Steel Institute in New York City in May, Speer said that the industry's survival depended on the construction of new mills, citing his company's projected construction of a new mill in Conneaut, Ohio, for which large cash flows would be needed. He predicted an annual growth of 2.4 per cent in domestic steel demand for the rest of the century, boosting U.S. demand for finished steel to about 180-million short tons (163 million metric tons) annually by the year 2000.

Government Aid. In April, the U.S. Department of Commerce launched a loan-guarantee program intended to generate more than $500 million in private financing to help the steel industry modernize plants and install pollution-control equipment. The federal assistance aimed at medium-sized companies that produce at least 250,000 short tons (227,000 metric tons) of steel per year. Such companies have experienced serious financial difficulties.

The first union-sanctioned strike in 50 years hit the ailing West German steel industry on November 28. The steelworkers demanded a shorter workweek and higher wages. The industry was operating at only 65 per cent of capacity.   Mary E. Jessup

In WORLD BOOK, see IRON AND STEEL.

STENMARK, INGEMAR (1956-   ), won the World Cup men's skiing title for the third consecutive year and also decisively took both the slalom and giant slalom in the World Alpine Ski Championships in 1978. His performance earned him ranking as the best male skier in the world. The men's World Cup competition consisted of 33 slalom, giant slalom, downhill, and combined events staged in eight European countries. Stenmark amassed a total of 150 points, 34 more than his nearest competitor, Phil Mahre of White Pass, Wash. See SKIING.

The son of a former Swedish skier, Stenmark still lives in Tarnaby, a village about 60 miles (97 kilometers) south of the Arctic Circle. He began skiing there when he was 5 years old, won his first race when he was 7, and quit school at 16 in order to devote all his time to skiing.

Stenmark is a shy bachelor who shuns parties and publicity, preferring to be by himself. He is said to spend his summers at Tarnaby fishing, running, bicycling, and walking a tightrope stretched between two trees to improve his balance.

Stenmark has great strength, and doctors who tested him say he is one of the strongest men in Sweden. His unique skiing style utilizes his great leg strength. Most skiers use a bobbing, up-and-down motion. Stenmark holds his head and body still, but stretches his legs out and pulls them in in a pistonlike manner.   Joseph P. Spohn

STOCKS AND BONDS. Stock prices in the United States trended upward for the first nine months of 1978, just about recouping a 20 per cent loss from the 1976 peak. Corporate profits, which had been in the doldrums earlier, rose strongly, up 21 per cent over the previous year in the third quarter. But inflation, the declining value of the dollar in other countries, rising interest rates, and slowed real growth were strong damping influences. In 12 successive sessions in October, the stock market experienced one of its steepest declines ever, with the Dow Jones average of 30 blue-chip industrial stocks tumbling 105 points to 792 on October 31.

Announcement of President Jimmy Carter's anti-inflation program in October did not slow the decline. The program recommended voluntary price-wage guidelines. Partly because of negative reactions in the stock and foreign exchange markets, the Administration took a series of bold steps on November 1 to bolster the sagging dollar and hold down inflation. The Department of the Treasury and the Federal Reserve Board arranged a standby credit of $30 billion to buy dollars in exchange markets. The Federal Reserve System raised required-reserve ratios on large certificates of deposit and increased the discount rate from an already record level of 8.5 per cent to 9.5 per cent. The discount rate is the fee member banks pay when they borrow from Federal Reserve banks.

Stocks Waver in 1978

Dow Jones industrial averages

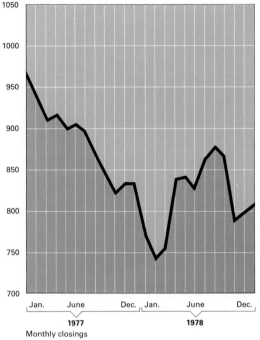

Monthly closings

currency values rose rapidly against the dollar, and they enjoyed comparatively low interest rates in their credit markets.

Canada slated a $750-million bond issue in the United States in 1978, its first in a decade. The proceeds were to be used to finance part of its balance-of-payments deficit. The U.S. government had a budget deficit of nearly $50 billion in fiscal 1978. About $20 billion was financed by issuing money, the balance by interest-bearing securities.

U.S. Investments in plants and equipment picked up somewhat in 1978, but remained low compared with earlier periods of economic expansion. One reason was that inflation raised taxes – for example, by distorting the market value of inventories. To some extent, inflation and the declining value of the dollar encouraged foreign investment in the United States. Japan's investments grew most rapidly, but they still amounted to less than half the amount of U.S. investments in Japan. Despite much publicity to the contrary, direct investment in the United States by the Organization of Petroleum Exporting Countries (OPEC) was only 1 per cent of the total. Most of the OPEC investment was in portfolio securities. Canada, Great Britain, and the Netherlands remained the major sources of direct investments in the United States.   William G. Dewald

See also ECONOMICS. In WORLD BOOK, see BOND; INVESTMENT; STOCK, CAPITAL; STOCK EXCHANGE.

The Stock Market responded on November 1 with a 4 per cent increase in prices, according to Standard and Poor's index of 500 common stocks, and a 35-point advance in the Dow Jones industrial stocks index – an unprecedented one-day increase. Fifty million shares were traded on the New York Stock Exchange, the seventh largest trading day in its history. For the year as a whole, 8.3 billion shares were traded on the New York Stock Exchange, which represented more than all other exchange and off-exchange transactions combined. The Dow ended the year at 805.0, after peaking at 909.9 on September 8.

Comparable fireworks were observed in foreign exchange markets. After two months of persistent declines, the value of the dollar exploded on November 1, gaining 7.5 per cent against the Swiss franc, 7 per cent against the West German Deutsche mark and French franc, and 5 per cent against the British pound and Japanese yen in hectic trading.

Bond Yields. In 1978, long-term government-bond yields rose to about 9 per cent in the United States and Canada even as inflation rates were accelerating to nearly the same level. In contrast, the long-term government-bond rate in Switzerland drifted down to not much over 2 per cent. The inflation rate in Switzerland remained at about 1 per cent a year. Other countries with low inflation rates, such as Japan and West Germany, found that their

SUDAN. President and Prime Minister Gaafar Muhammed Nimeiri and his political opponents agreed to reconcile in the interests of national unity in 1978. The opposition leaders formally disbanded the National Front on April 2. It was formed in 1976 by leaders of the Umma and Khatmiya parties and the supranational Muslim Brotherhood, which went into exile in Libya after an unsuccessful coup d'état attempt. The Front had been receiving Libyan funds and military equipment. The three leaders, Sadik al-Mahdi of Umma, Ali Mirghani of Khaimiya, and Sharif Hussein al-Hindi of the Brotherhood, were all former ministers who had long been associated with Sudanese nationalism.

The agreement pledged them to accept the Sudanese Socialist Union (SSU) as the only legal political organization and the Constitution as the law of the land. National Front training bases in Libya were closed and the equipment turned over to the Sudanese defense forces.

For his part, Nimeiri reorganized the government. He formed a 31-member Central Committee, which included opposition leaders, to direct SSU political activity. The former party leaders were also appointed to the Council of Ministers when it was reorganized on July 29. Nimeiri gave up the position of minister of national economy, which he had held since early 1977, but retained personal control over the ministry of defense.

The non-Muslim southern region, long dominated by the Muslim north, was reorganized to give it greater autonomy. A southern regional People's Assembly was elected in February to supervise regional development. Joseph Lagu, commander of the Anyanya Rebel Forces in the Sudanese civil war during the 1960s, was elected head of the Assembly's 15-member executive council. All political prisoners were also released.

Economic Development. Its new political unity enabled the Sudan to concentrate on economic development and closer relations with Egypt, its partner in the federated Sudanese-Egyptian Arab state. Joint urban-area development was approved in February for Egypt's Aswan province and Sudan's northern province. Customs duties, passports, and travel permits between the two countries were eliminated in August.

Sudan's potential as a major agricultural producer was underscored by new projects. One of the largest would develop cattle ranches on 500,000 acres (200,000 hectares) of land in central Sudan, enabling the country to become self-sufficient in meat and sell to the Middle East. Equally encouraging was the discovery of oil in southwestern Sudan. If commercially profitable, the reserves could solve Sudan's oil problem.   William Spencer

See also AFRICA (Facts in Brief Table). In WORLD BOOK, see SUDAN.

SUPREME COURT OF THE UNITED STATES

left many observers puzzled in 1978, partly because of splintering of the "Nixon bloc." It reversed two apparent trends of the 1970s – toward strengthening the hand of prosecutors and encouraging free expression – during the term that ended in July. Badly split opinions were prevalent, as typified by what amounted to a 4-1-4 split in the year's most publicized case, *Regents of the University of California v. Bakke* (see Close-Up; Section One, FOCUS ON EDUCATION).

A survey by *The New York Times* indicated that the four justices appointed to the high court by President Richard M. Nixon voted together only 36 per cent of the time in 1978; the four had voted as a unit in 67 to 75 per cent of the court's decisions over the previous five years. One effect of the split was a noticeable shift in criminal-case outcomes. In the 1978 term, defendants won 55 per cent of criminal cases; in the previous five terms, the majority sided about 65 per cent of the time with the prosecution.

In an important ruling on July 3, the Supreme Court held that a defendant must be allowed to air a wide array of mitigating factors, including data on his record, character, and case circumstances, before being subjected to the death penalty. The decision apparently requires new capital punishment laws in at least 20 states and makes wholesale resumption of capital punishment unlikely.

In a June 26 decision, the court gave defendants the right to challenge search warrants when law-enforcement authorities are reasonably suspected of using false statements to obtain them. And the court unanimously declared on March 21 that a criminal jury must have at least six members, invalidating an obscenity conviction by a five-member Georgia jury. But the court refused several opportunities to cut back on police wiretapping powers. It said that the number of conversations overheard under a court order need not be limited if a reasonable basis existed for listening to everything. It also said federal courts can order local telephone companies to install surveillance equipment on the basis of the same evidence required to obtain a search warrant.

The Environment. The court was equivocal toward environmental matters. In *Tennessee Valley Authority v. Hill*, a controversial case decided on June 15 by a 6 to 3 vote, it ordered the $116-million Tellico Dam project halted because tiny snail darter fish living in the river had been officially classified as an endangered species. In approving on June 26 New York City's ban of office construction above Grand Central Station, the court supported use of local police and zoning power to protect historic landmarks throughout the nation.

But the court also issued several rulings that displeased environmentalists. One decision reduced federal judges' ability to delay nuclear power projects, another denied states the right to ban oil supertankers from their waters, and a third struck down a state attempt to ban the import of wastes.

The Media. Many commentators interpreted a series of Supreme Court rulings as restricting freedom of expression and interfering with reporters' ability to gather and report news. In *Zurcher v. Stanford Daily*, decided by 5 to 3 on May 31, the court permitted police searches of news offices under a search warrant for evidence about third parties without prior hearing or any other previous notice.

The court also forbade newspapers to acquire new broadcast stations in their home locations, refused to allow broadcasts of President Nixon's White House tape recordings, declared that reporters have no more right of access to jails and other public facilities than the general public, and permitted government prohibition of so-called dirty words on the airwaves – words that are indecent or offensive even if not legally obscene. In one decision broadening the right of free expression, the justices held, by 5 to 4 on April 26, that corporations can spend unlimited advertising dollars to influence referendum votes.

Immunity. Two 1978 rulings broadened the ability of people alleging civil rights violations to sue for damages. On June 29, the court removed the absolute immunity from civil suit previously enjoyed by federal officials, holding that top officers charged with constitutional violations should have only qualified protection from suits. Another ruling reversed a

The Bakke Decision

According to advance billing, it was the most important racial case since *Brown v. Board of Education of Topeka* outlawed racial segregation in public schools in 1954. It was expected to indicate just how much special help could be accorded racial minorities and women to remedy America's long, pervasive history of discrimination.

As the Supreme Court of the United States pondered *Regents of the University of California v. Bakke,* which had been briefed and argued in 1977, the nation's press focused extraordinary attention on the case as a symbol of backlash against "reverse discrimination," the perceived penalization of whites in schooling and other situations to allow the disadvantaged to catch up.

However, the court's decision, announced on June 28, 1978, was hardly the decisive action that had been expected. The court split, 4 to 4, on the two key issues, leaving Justice Lewis F. Powell, Jr., to cast the deciding vote, and Powell tilted once in each direction. The court judged the racial quota system for minority admissions at the School of Medicine of the University of California, Davis, was unacceptable, and ordered Allan P. Bakke, a white, admitted. But the court also approved educators' consideration of race as a factor in deciding who can be admitted — a clear green light to more carefully drawn affirmative-action programs.

Bakke, an aerospace engineer and father of two, had earned a technical degree and a U.S. Marine Corps captaincy before belatedly deciding to become a doctor. When he first applied in 1972, medical schools turned the 32-year-old Bakke down. But at Davis, he later learned, 16 of 100 entering places in the medical school were specifically set aside for minorities, and all the applicants admitted under that program had lower test scores than he did. After a second rejection in 1973, Bakke sued. Two California courts agreed that he had been a victim of racial discrimination.

A Supreme Court majority, including Powell, John P. Stevens, Potter Stewart, William H. Rehnquist, and Chief Justice Warren E. Burger, held that Bakke had been illegally excluded because of his race. Powell based his judgment on a broad reading of the 14th Amendment to the Constitution, which guarantees equal protection of the laws for all. The other four justices cited narrower grounds — Title VI of the 1964 Civil Rights Act, prohibiting federally funded schools from discriminating because of "race, color, or national origin."

Burger, Stevens, Rehnquist, and Stewart refused to go any further, saying that Title VI considerations concluded this case. But Powell, backed by Justices William J. Brennan, Jr., Thurgood Marshall, Harry A. Blackmun, and Byron R. White, proceeded to issue a limited endorsement of affirmative-action plans — at least in academic admissions. Powell said race constitutionally can be taken into account in achieving educational diversity. The other four justices argued for even greater latitude in minority admissions.

Although Bakke himself was finally admitted to the School of Medicine at Davis in September at the age of 38, the decision produced only minor adjustments in U.S. race-relations policies. Many universities abolished separate-track admissions committees for minority or disadvantaged applicants, but most achieved similar end results by ordering consideration of such factors in the admissions process.

Officials cautioned that the Bakke case would not have significant impact on executive orders and agency rulings requiring affirmative action in employment. The legality of those steps was far from settled. After some maneuvering, the Supreme Court agreed, in December, to tackle another "reverse discrimination" problem arising from a case involving Brian F. Weber, a white laboratory technician in Gramercy, La. He was denied admittance to a company training program because the management had agreed to ignore seniority and instead promote whites and blacks in equal numbers. The prospect of a definitive ruling, following the tentativeness of the Bakke decision, was not universally welcome. "This is so explosive an area," said one lawyer, "that the court may again be tempted to vagueness."

David C. Beckwith

Allan P. Bakke

1961 decision and established that municipalities and local governments could be sued for civil rights incursions. But the court protected judges and quasi-judicial officers. In a case involving an Indiana judge who authorized sterilization of an allegedly promiscuous 15-year-old girl, the court ruled in March that the judge was immune from civil suit even though he had no apparent legal authority for his action and had failed to provide the girl with legal representation, a hearing, or any notice.

Women won two notable sex-discrimination cases. One forbade employers from stripping seniority from female employees taking pregnancy leave. The court ruled on April 25 that employers cannot charge women more in pension payments because women are likely to live longer than men.

Other Key Decisions included:
- A 5 to 3 ruling on May 23 that warrantless work-area inspections by the Occupational Safety and Health Administration were illegal.
- An 8 to 0 ruling on March 21 that public school students suspended without a hearing could collect no more than nominal damages, or $1, unless they could prove that they had been harmed by the suspension.   David C. Beckwith

See also COURTS AND LAWS. In WORLD BOOK, see SUPREME COURT OF THE UNITED STATES.

SURINAM. See LATIN AMERICA.

SWAZILAND. See AFRICA.

SWEDEN. The country's first non-Socialist government in 44 years resigned on Oct. 5, 1978, over Cabinet differences on nuclear energy policy. Prime Minister Thorbjorn Falldin and his antinuclear Center Party colleagues could not persuade their Moderate (rightist) and Liberal partners to put the issue of fueling two nuclear power reactors to a referendum. All parties agreed to wait until rock drilling showed whether nuclear waste could be stored safely. But differences arose over interpretation of the agreement. The Center Party had campaigned on an antinuclear platform in 1976, promising to halt nuclear development and close nuclear power plants in Sweden by 1985.

Ola Ullsten, head of the Liberals, succeeded Falldin on October 13. He was Falldin's deputy prime minister and minister for international development. Ullsten said he would prepare legislation on unemployment, the economy, and energy, and would work for "tighter control" over nuclear power plants. He said the change of government improved the coalition's chance of retaining power in the September 1979 election, because the three parties were no longer bickering. See ULLSTEN, OLA.

Road to Recovery. A start was made on the long road back to solvency after the 1975-1976 recession. Foreign trade in the first quarter showed a surplus of $263 million, compared with a loss of twice that sum in the same period of 1977. Exports rose 11 per cent,

King Carl XVI Gustaf of Sweden dances with Uzbek woman in Samarkand, Russia, during a royal visit to the Soviet Union in June.

and imports fell 5 per cent. Unemployment was down to 92,000, or 2.2 per cent of the work force, from 110,000 in January.

Presenting his budget on January 10, Falldin warned that a growth rate like that of the previous seven years would make it difficult to secure increased welfare for the elderly and higher living standards for production workers. The 1978-1979 budget called for a deficit of $7 billion, with state borrowing continuing at $2 billion per year.

Aerosol Ban. On January 23, Sweden became the first country to enact legislation against most aerosol sprays because they may harm the atmosphere. The ban, scheduled to take effect on Jan. 1, 1979, covers hair sprays, deodorants, air fresheners, insecticides, waxes, and other sprays using freon. Medicinal sprays, such as those used by asthma victims, are exempt. The legislation was based on data produced by the U.S. National Academy of Sciences.

Auto Agreement. AB Volvo, Sweden's largest industrial company and automaker, agreed tentatively on May 22 to sell 40 per cent of its stock to Norway's government or private Norwegian investors. The two countries concluded the agreement on December 7 as part of a 20-year economic pact involving Norway's crude oil and refined products and Sweden's technology and timber.   Kenneth Brown

See also EUROPE (Facts in Brief Table). In WORLD BOOK, see SWEDEN.

SWIMMING. With 15-year-old Tracy Caulkins of Nashville, Tenn., leading the way, American women again became the best in the world in 1978. Americans won nine of the 14 gold medals for women in the third world championships in August in West Berlin. Thus ended East Germany's five-year domination.

The American men, for years the best in the world, ruled again. They won 11 of the 15 titles and 20 of a possible 27 medals. And they did it even though Brian Goodell of Mission Viejo, Calif., winner of two free-style gold medals in the 1976 Olympic Games in Montreal, Canada, was absent because of illness. His teammate, 17-year-old Jesse Vassallo, won the 400-meter individual medley and 200-meter backstroke.

A Positive Attitude. Since 1973, when the East German women dominated the first world championships, the American women had lived in fear of them. This time, there was no fear. As Linda Jezek of Los Altos, Calif., said, "This was the first time we had a positive attitude."

No one had a more positive attitude than Caulkins, a calm, slim girl of 5 feet 8 inches (170 centimeters) and 117 pounds (53 kilograms) who wears glasses and braces. She won five gold medals in individual medley, butterfly, and relays and a silver medal in breaststroke. Before that, she won seven gold medals in the Amateur Athletic Union (AAU) national short-course championships, seven in the AAU national long-course championships, four in the American-Russian short-course meet, four in a women's international meet at Providence, R.I., and six of the 12 individual races in the Seventeen Meet of Champions at Mission Viejo.

Jezek took both world backstroke titles, setting a record in the 200-meter event, and won all four American backstroke titles for the third straight year. The other American women who won world titles were Joan Pennington and Cynthia Woodhead. American men who won included Mike Bruner, Joe Bottom, Bob Jackson, Nick Nevid, David McCagg, and Bill Forrester.

Why did the East German women do badly? "If we knew exactly what we did wrong, we wouldn't have done it," said Rudolf Schramme, the East German coach.

Swimmers – most of them Americans – set world records during the year in 13 of the 15 events for women and four of the 16 for men. The most prolific record breaker was 15-year-old Tracey Wickham of Australia, who bettered the women's free-style marks for 400, 800, and 1,500 meters.

Diving. Irina Kalinina of Russia won both women's world diving titles. The men's champions were Phil Boggs of Ann Arbor, Mich., off the 3-meter board and 18-year-old Greg Louganis of El Cajon, Calif., off the 10-meter platform.   Frank Litsky

In WORLD BOOK, see DIVING; SWIMMING.

SWITZERLAND voted in four referendums, its traditional way of making decisions, in 1978. The Swiss rejected on February 26 a proposal to reduce the retirement age for men from 65 to 60, and for women from 62 to 58. They rejected on May 28 a proposal to ban automobile travel on the second Sunday of each month; a plan to introduce daylight-saving time; a parliament-approved compromise on abortions; and government subsidies for university research. They approved a small increase in bread prices.

In a September 24 referendum, 82.3 per cent of the voters approved the establishment of a new *canton* (state), Jura, in the mountainous area next to France. The people of Jura are French-speaking Roman Catholics. Jura had been combined with the canton of Bern, whose people are German-speaking Protestants.

The Swiss on December 3 rejected a plan to create a national police force – a 200-member antiterrorist squad and a 1,000-member special-security unit. Switzerland has no federal law-enforcement agency.

The National Bank took measures on October 1 to reduce the Swiss franc's high rate of exchange. The bank, with United States help, promised a policy of major interventions in the foreign-exchange market.   Kenneth Brown

See also EUROPE (Facts in Brief Table). In WORLD BOOK, see SWITZERLAND.

SYRIA. Ten years of bitter and often bloody feuding between the rival Syrian and Iraqi Baath Party regimes ended, at least for the foreseeable future, in October 1978. Following President Hafiz al-Assad's visit to Iraq – his first since 1973 – he and Iraqi President Ahmad Hasan al-Bakr signed a "National Charter for Joint Action" on October 26. Although certainly motivated by the desire for a common front against the Camp David Israeli-Egyptian accords, the charter stressed Syrian-Iraqi cooperation toward the vaguer goal of Arab unity. A 14-member joint political organization was formed.

Following the agreement, Syria reopened its border with Iraq, civil air flights between Damascus and Baghdad were resumed, and the Syrian trade center in Baghdad was reactivated. On October 29, service was restored on the Syrian section of the rail line linking European cities with Baghdad.

Earlier, the Syrian Baath Party marked the 15th anniversary of the March 1963 coup d'état that had brought it to power. Assad, the sole survivor of the coup leaders, was re-elected for a second seven-year term beginning March 12. He was the only candidate nominated by the party and received 99.6 per cent of the popular vote. A new Cabinet was headed by Prime Minister Muhammad Ali al-Halabi, speaker of the People's Assembly. The Cabinet ministers included 18 Baathists, 8 Independents, 4 Arab Socialist Party members, and 2 Communists.

Assassins Strike. Although Assad and the Baath remained fully in control, continued factional rivalries in the leadership hampered the party in its efforts to achieve "Unity, Freedom, and Socialism." A series of assassinations of prominent members of Assad's minority Alawi Muslim community culminated in March with the murder of Ibrahim Naama, his relative. The head of Syrian Security services, General Naji Jamil, a member of the majority Sunni Muslim community, was dismissed for failure to uncover the group responsible for the murders; they were alleged to be financed by Iraq.

The installation of the last group of generators for the Euphrates Dam on March 30 was expected to revolutionize Syrian agricultural production by bringing 1.58 million acres (640,000 hectares) of arid land under irrigation. But the discovery in May of large gypsum deposits in the soil dampened optimism. The water-soluble gypsum caused the soil to give way as new irrigation canals were dug. The problem had not been foreseen by Soviet experts called in to advise on the project.

In January, Syria and Libya signed an agreement to form a joint investment company with a capitalization of $100 million. The agreement also called for cooperation by the two nations in industry, trade, and agriculture.   William Spencer

See also MIDDLE EAST (Facts in Brief Table). In WORLD BOOK, see SYRIA.

TAIWAN. Chiang Ching-kuo became president of the Nationalist government of Taiwan on May 20, 1978. He replaced Yen Chia-kan, who had succeeded Chiang's father, Chiang Kai-shek, who died in 1975. Chiang Ching-kuo had effectively administered Taiwan since 1972 as premier and has headed the Kuomintang Party, the controlling political organization, since 1975. See CHIANG CHING-KUO.

Chiang was 68 years old when elected on March 21 to a six-year term as president. He was chosen without opposition by the National Assembly, which is made up mostly of representatives elected in mainland China in 1947.

A Taiwanese leader, Shieh Tung-min, 72, was elected vice-president. Previously the provincial governor of Taiwan, Shieh became the highest-ranked native Taiwanese, but he had little real power. Chiang was succeeded as premier by Sun Yun-hsuan, a former minister of agriculture.

In a National Day speech on October 10, Chiang said it was clear "that our country is moving ahead, that we have made progress in social development, and that the combat capability of our armed forces is increasing. These facts are incontrovertible evidence of the promising future of our country and people."

Future Uncertain. The future was worrisome, however, because United States President Jimmy Carter announced on December 15 that the United States would establish normal diplomatic relations with mainland China on Jan. 1, 1979, and end diplomatic recognition of Taiwan. Carter said, however, that the United States would continue "cultural, commercial, and other unofficial relations" with Taiwan, including the sale of "selective defense weaponry." See CHINA, PEOPLE'S REPUBLIC OF.

The United States in June had rejected Taiwan's request to buy 60 F-4 Phantom jet fighter-bombers. Officials in Washington said they were following a long-standing policy of selling Taiwan only defensive weapons, and that F-4s could be used to bomb the mainland. The United States offered, instead, to permit the purchase of Israeli-made Kfir fighters with U.S. engines, but Taiwan rejected them. Then, in November, the United States offered to sell Taiwan 48 more F-5E lightweight fighters.

The Economy. Taiwan revalued its currency 5 per cent higher against the U.S. dollar on July 10, showing the country's economic strength and helping to relieve inflationary pressures. Import curbs were eliminated so that inflation would be held down by the availability of more low-priced goods, most of them from Japan. The Council for Economic Planning and Development announced in October that Taiwan's gross national product had grown 8.4 per cent in 1977 in real terms. In the first half of 1978, exports rose 34 per cent.   Henry S. Bradsher

See also ASIA (Facts in Brief Table). In WORLD BOOK, see TAIWAN.

TANZANIA. Troops from neighboring Uganda on Oct. 30, 1978, invaded a 710-square-mile (1,840-square-kilometer) section of northwestern Tanzania bounded by Lake Victoria on the east, Rwanda on the west, and Uganda on the north. Some 3,000 Ugandan troops crossed the border and quickly advanced to the Kagera River, 18 miles (29 kilometers) to the south. Uganda's President Idi Amin Dada announced on October 31 that his government had annexed all the land up to the Kagera. Amin said Uganda invaded because Tanzania used the territory as a base for infiltrating guerrillas opposed to his rule into Uganda.

Tanzania's government, under President Julius K. Nyerere, had never recognized Amin as the president of Uganda.

Amin was pressured in early November by other African governments and by Russia, his principal arms supplier, to withdraw his troops. He offered to withdraw on November 8 in return for Tanzania's pledge not to invade Uganda or assist exiles trying to overthrow his government. Tanzania refused to give such assurances and publicly pledged to work for Amin's ouster. By November 11, it had mobilized about 8,500 troops for a counteroffensive. On November 14, Amin announced his unconditional withdrawal.   John D. Esseks

See also AFRICA (Facts in Brief Table); UGANDA. In WORLD BOOK, see TANZANIA.

TARAKI, NOOR MOHAMMAD (1918?-   ), was named prime minister of Afghanistan and chairman of its ruling Revolutionary Council on April 30, 1978. Troops led by air force Colonel Abdul Qadir overthrew President Mohammad Daoud in heavy fighting in Kabul, the capital, on April 27 and 28. The new government is considered more pro-Russian than Daoud's. See AFGHANISTAN.

Noor Mohammad Taraki was born into a sheep-herding family in the rugged country west of Kabul. Little is known of his education, but he speaks English and describes himself as a journalist and novelist. He became a junior official in the ministry of information in 1940, was deputy director of Radio Kabul from 1941 to 1942, and served with the official Bakhtar News Agency from 1942 to 1944. From 1944 to 1947, he worked in the ministry of public works, then transferred to the ministry of agriculture until 1950. He was director general of publications in the ministry of press and information in 1950 and 1951, then returned to the Bakhtar News Agency as editor in chief. In 1953, while serving as press attaché at the Afghan Embassy in Washington, D.C., Taraki resigned to protest government policies and returned to Afghanistan.

Taraki worked for the United States Embassy in Kabul in 1953. He emerged in the 1960s as leader of the pro-Russian Khalq (Masses) Party, which took power in the 1978 coup d'état.   Edward G. Nash

TAXATION became a major issue in the United States in 1978. Growing taxpayer anger over steadily rising U.S. taxes led both Democratic and Republican politicians to campaign for lower taxes and decreased government costs. Yet, the second session of the 95th Congress did not pass a comprehensive tax-reform bill, despite pressure from President Jimmy Carter.

Instead, Congress passed a compromise $18.7-billion tax-cut bill on October 15, in the closing hours of the session, and the President signed it with misgivings on November 6. Most of the changes were effective for tax years beginning in 1979. The act included an increase in the "earned-income credit" to a maximum of $500 for the working poor, and made partial credits available to some families earning up to $10,000. The personal exemption for each taxpayer and each dependent was raised from $750 to $1,000; the standard deduction was increased; and some reductions in tax rates were scheduled. Taxpayer deductions for state and local gasoline taxes were eliminated.

Most of the tax breaks went to middle- and upper-income taxpayers. The "minimum tax" designed to prevent high-income investors from avoiding taxes altogether was diluted, and a hefty $2.2-billion cut in capital gains taxes primarily benefited well-to-do taxpayers with annual incomes of more than $50,000. Homeowners over age 55 were offered

a once-in-a-lifetime chance to sell the house they are living in and pocket the first $100,000 of profit tax free. Reductions in corporation taxes totaled $3.7-billion.

Most of the President's suggestions for tax reform were rejected. The proposal for a college-tuition tax credit, opposed by the President, was also defeated.

The average taxpayer would pay higher taxes in 1979, in any event, because a 7 to 10 per cent inflation rate would push many taxpayers into higher income brackets and because rising Social Security taxes would take a bigger bite from everyone's paycheck. The Social Security payroll tax will increase $8.5 billion in 1979. Changes in personal income tax rates will apply to 1979 incomes, and the differences will be noticed in 1979 take-home pay and in the tax returns filed in April 1980.

High-Income Taxpayers. In September, the Department of the Treasury released the results of a study of tax returns revealing that few high-income Americans avoid paying taxes altogether. Nonetheless, in 1976 about 500 persons with annual incomes of $200,000 or more paid virtually no taxes. The number of Americans in that income bracket who paid no tax whatsoever had declined from 215 in 1975 to 89 in 1976.

Federal Tax Receipts. In the fiscal year that ended on Sept. 30, 1978, federal tax collections totaled $399.8 billion. Individual income and employment tax receipts totaled $310.3 billion; corporation taxes, $65.4 billion; estate and gift taxes, $5.4-billion; and excise taxes, $18.7 billion.

The Internal Revenue Service (IRS) reported in February that the simplified 1978 federal tax forms cut down the number of mistakes made by taxpayers. In 1978, the IRS computer was expected to pick at least 5 million tax returns "with audit potential" out of some 88 million returns, and about 2 million of those returns would be audited – most of them from high-income taxpayers and those whose deductions were higher than the average deductions in their income bracket.

State and Local Taxes. Local governments in the United States have been spending almost $34 billion a year, one-third of which has traditionally been raised by taxing property owners. Protesting rising taxes in 1978, California passed Proposition 13, a property-tax limitation amendment, on June 6. See Close-Up.

Massachusetts passed legislation banning rapid increases in residential property taxes; Texas reduced property taxes some $500 million; and Idaho and Nevada set constitutional limits on property taxes. Also reflecting taxpayer resentment, New Jersey, Colorado, Tennessee, Arizona, and Michigan passed legislation restricting government spending. Maine, Minnesota, New Mexico, and New York lowered personal income tax rates. New York and Mississippi increased their standard de-

Taxpayers' Revolt

Proposition 13 is an eight-paragraph amendment to the California state constitution that sharply limits state and local authority to tax. When 1.3-million Californians signed petitions to put it on the ballot and 4.2 million voters passed it on June 6, 1978, it called dramatic attention to a nationwide revolt against rising taxes.

Proposition 13 was sponsored by Howard A. Jarvis, a prosperous 75-year-old industrialist who has been fighting for less government and lower taxes all his adult life. The co-author of the initiative was Paul Gann, a retired real estate broker.

The amendment cuts California's property taxes 57 per cent, to 1 per cent of the cash value of the property in 1976. It limits any tax on real property in California to 1 per cent of the full cash value of the property, and it limits increases in the assessed value of any property to 2 per cent a year unless the property changes hands. In addition, two-thirds of those voting in both houses of the state legislature must approve new state taxes, and two-thirds of all registered voters must approve new taxes levied by local governments.

Before the rollback, California property was taxed at 3.2 per cent of its assessed valuation. For some property owners, taxes had more than doubled in the last decade. The California property tax was particularly vulnerable to criticism because the state's real estate market is highly speculative. As the value of property rose – at 1 to 2 per cent per month for single homes in some parts of southern California – taxes jumped astronomically. By 1976, Californians were paying $63 for every $1,000 of personal income – a tax burden that was 142 per cent of the national average.

Statistics alone do not tell the full story. Middle-income taxpayers and property owners and especially senior citizens were increasingly hard-pressed to pay their taxes. Unlike most states, California used the property tax to finance welfare programs and its Medicare and Medicaid. Middle-income taxpayers saw their money going directly to finance these welfare programs for 2.2 million Californians, about 10 per cent of the

Support for 13

state's population. The taxpayers also knew that the state treasury had a surplus of about $5.3 billion in 1978.

Passage of Proposition 13 means about $7 billion in tax revenue will be lost in California in the fiscal year starting July 1, 1978, according to estimates. Private homeowners will save some $2.3 billion in taxes. Big property owners – various farmers and businessmen – will pocket about two-thirds of the tax saving.

Matching federal funds to California will decline, and the state may lose another $5.2 billion in federal funds. Taxpayers will pay somewhat higher federal and state income taxes because they will lose some of the deductions they previously claimed on federal income tax returns. California will thus collect an estimated $300-million more in state income taxes. And because of the tax cut, businesses may expand and bring more revenue into the state.

Proposition 13 cut the total revenue for local government and public schools in California about 22 per cent. Immediately after the vote, Governor Edmund G. (Jerry) Brown, Jr., announced a freeze on state hiring. Local services in many areas were also curtailed. Many school programs were cut back or eliminated because about half of all public school income in the state came from property taxes.

Some school districts, education groups, counties, and cities in California challenged the legality of the amendment after it was passed. California's Supreme Court, however, upheld its legality in a September ruling. It said Proposition 13 "survives each of the substantial challenges raised by the petitioners." Their main contention was that the legislation violated the equal-protection clause of the U.S. Constitution.

Four other states – Colorado, Michigan, New Jersey, and Tennessee – had already acted to limit state and local spending. Similar bills were under consideration in 17 other states, and 23 state legislatures have approved an amendment to the U.S. Constitution prohibiting federal deficit spending. Across party lines, across the nation, the taxpayers' revolt was gathering strength.   Carol L. Thompson

ductions, and Colorado included an inflation factor in computing the state income tax.

Antitax measures and spending ceilings were rejected when they appeared on the ballot only in Nebraska, Colorado, Maryland, and Oregon.

Fiscal 1978 state tax collections totaled $113.1-billion, an increase of 11.9 per cent over fiscal 1977. The largest source of state tax revenue continued to be sales and gross receipts taxes, which totaled $58.2-billion, 51.5 per cent of all state revenues. All 50 states collected some form of gross receipts and sales taxes. Individual income taxes were collected in 44 states, a total of $29.1 billion.

In fiscal 1978, eight states collected over half of all state revenue. Once again, California collected the most – $15.0 billion, followed by New York, $10.9 billion; Pennsylvania, $6.3 billion; Illinois, $5.8 billion; Texas, $5.4 billion; Michigan, $5.3-billion; Ohio, $4.1 billion; and Florida, $3.8 billion.

The U.S. Bureau of the Census reported in October that the states showed a budget surplus of $13.3-billion in fiscal 1977. State government expenditures in that period totaled $191.2 billion, including $64-billion for education, $32.8 billion for welfare, $17.5-billion for highway maintenance and construction, and $8.7 billion for hospital funding. Thirteen states collected almost $1.2 billion in state lotteries in fiscal 1977.   Carol L. Thompson

In WORLD BOOK, see TAXATION.

TELEVISION. The pre-eminent TV event of 1978 in the United States was "Holocaust," a harrowing dramatization of the Nazis' extermination of 6-million Jews. The National Broadcasting Company's (NBC) $6-million, 9½-hour mini-series was watched by an estimated 107 million viewers in the United States during its four-night run from April 16 to 19. In Israel, "Holocaust" was seen by 2-million of the country's 3.8 million people. The program was to be telecast in West Germany, where the networks had previously banned documentaries about Nazi atrocities. "Holocaust" won six Emmy awards on September 17, including best actor and best actress awards, which went to Michael Moriarty and Meryl Streep, and the best writer award, to Gerald Green.

Viewing Decline. In spite of the enormous success of "Holocaust," all three national networks – the American Broadcasting Companies (ABC), the Columbia Broadcasting System (CBS), and NBC – were generally disenchanted with their 1977 policy of *stunting*. Stunting is a trade term for pre-empting regular programs in favor of specials.

It became apparent that weekly series, not minis or specials, were the most consistently high-rated programs. For example, the first showing, on February 12, of the $5-million, six-hour mini-series "King," about civil rights leader Martin Luther King, Jr., rated last on a list of 64 programs.

Although TV viewing, which had declined slightly in 1977, was up again in 1978 and advertising sales were better than ever, the networks were "running scared." By June they had dropped 58 series, including several cited by the National Congress of Parents and Teachers (PTA) and other groups as "too violent" or "offensive sexually," or both.

Popular Favorites, such as the scantily clad "Charlie's Angels" and two risqué situation comedies – "Soap" and "Three's Company" – made the PTA's "10 worst" list. But all three of these top-rated shows were back on ABC's fall schedule along with such other high-rated, low-comedy series as "Happy Days" and "Laverne and Shirley."

Among the most popular of the 21 new fall shows were "Taxi," starring Judd Hirsch as a cynical New York cab driver, and two science-fiction entries – "Mork and Mindy" with engaging new comic Robin Williams as the alien Mork from the planet Ork, and "Battlestar Galactica," a lavish adventure series reminiscent of the film *Star Wars.* Another popular fantasy series was "The Incredible Hulk."

In June, Fred Silverman, the programming executive credited with making ABC the top-rated network, became president of NBC. Silverman said that NBC would schedule more weekly comedy and variety shows, and by October, the network had invested $50 million in pilots for potential new series.

Rosemary Harris as Berta Weiss and Fritz Weaver as her husband, Josef, portray the plight of Jews caught in the Nazi net in NBC's "Holocaust."

Pam Dawber as Mindy and Robin Williams as Mork from the planet Ork are surprised by each other's customs in the comedy series "Mork and Mindy."

In December, Silverman canceled all nine of NBC's new fall shows. See SILVERMAN, FRED.

Nostalgic Celebrations were rampant in 1978. All-star specials honored the 75th birthdays of Kraft Foods, the Ford Motor Company, and pianist Rudolf Serkin; and the 25th anniversaries of public television and the present ABC network.

The General Electric Company staged a centennial salute to the electric light bulb. Mickey Mouse's 50th year was celebrated on "The Wonderful World of Disney." NBC presented *The First 50 Years — A Closer Look, Part Two,* and CBS went all out with a star-studded weeklong, 9½-hour observation of its 50th anniversary.

Outstanding Specials included Emmy-winner Joanne Woodward as a 40-year-old Boston Marathon runner in *See How She Runs;* a moving performance by Lee Strasberg in *The Last Tenant;* an effective docu-drama, *The Defection of Simas Kudirka,* featuring Alan Arkin as the determined Lithuanian seaman; and a disturbing documentary on teen-age crime, *Youth Terror: The View Behind the Gun.* Multi-Emmy award winner Fred Astaire won his first Emmy for a dramatic role with his touching performance in *A Family Upside Down.*

American pioneer life was the theme of three impressive mini-series – "The Awakening Land," another "How the West Was Won" saga, and "Centennial," the longest (26 hours) and most

expensive ($30 million) mini-series to date, based on James Michener's novel.

In a class by itself was "The Muppet Show," the enchanting Emmy-winning puppet show. The syndicated series was the most popular first-run show in the world in 1978. It was telecast by 156 U.S. stations and 106 outlets in other countries.

Public Television aired the cream of the 1978 mini-series crop. As usual, most of it was imported from Great Britain. Among the superior British imports were a five-part biography of scientist Marie Curie, "The Mayor of Casterbridge," "Glittering Prizes," "Anna Karenina," "The Duchess of Duke Street," and "The Long Search."

The "Great Performances" series on public TV was highlighted by Sir Laurence Olivier and Alan Bates in Harold Pinter's *The Collection* and Sissy Spacek as *Verna: U.S.O. Girl.*

Public television also presented such fine "homegrown" productions as Frederick Wiseman's brilliant documentary, *Sinai Field Mission;* Jacques Cousteau's *Calypso's Search for "Atlantis";* and National Geographic's *The Living Sands of Namib.*

Sports Specials rated high in 1978. An estimated 102 million viewers saw the Dallas Cowboys beat the Denver Broncos in the first nighttime Super Bowl football game, on January 15. That audience, however, was dwarfed by the estimated worldwide total of 1 billion persons who saw Argentina defeat the

Netherlands in the World Cup championship soccer game, which was telecast from Buenos Aires, Argentina, in June.

On April 9, Gene F. Jankowski, president of the CBS/Broadcast Group, made an unprecedented on-the-air apology to the public for the network's "deceptive practices" in promoting four 1977 tennis matches as "winner take all" when, in fact, all the players were paid.

Cross Ownership. On June 12, the Supreme Court of the United States upheld a 1975 Federal Communications Commission rule on media cross-ownership requiring divestitures, which had been overturned by an appeals court in 1977. Under the 1975 rule, future cross ownerships of newspapers and stations were forbidden. Divestiture of current cross-ownership combinations would be required in only 16 markets where the only newspaper owned the only radio or TV station.

Cable Television continued to grow, and its 1978 annual gross income was expected to exceed $1-billion. As of May, close to 40 million Americans, including about 1.6 million pay-TV subscribers, were estimated to be seeing cable television in more than 12 million homes.

The U.S. House of Representatives voted in June to permit live television coverage of its debates beginning in 1979.   June Bundy Csida

In WORLD BOOK, see TELEVISION.

TENG HSIAO-P'ING (1904-   ), deputy premier, appeared to be the leading power in China in 1978. He was instrumental in negotiating a December agreement with the United States to normalize diplomatic relations. A highly flexible, pragmatic Communist official, Teng had twice been slated for a top government post and was ousted each time for "ideological errors." After Hua Kuo-feng was named premier in 1976, Teng became one of China's most powerful figures. See CHINA.

Teng was born in Chiating, Szechwan Province, in west China. After attending a special preparatory school in Chengtu, he was sent to France in 1920 to obtain a university education. He joined the French branch of the Chinese Communist Party while living in Paris. Teng returned to China in 1926 as a political instructor at a Communist military school in Shansi Province.

He was elected to the Central Committee of the Chinese Communist Party in 1945 and became general secretary of the party's Central Committee in 1956. But Teng was removed from all his offices during China's Cultural Revolution for allegedly failing to follow Chairman Mao Tse-tung's teachings. Teng returned to power in the early 1970s, but was again deposed in April 1976. By the end of that year he had regained power, and his critics were in disgrace.   Foster Stockwell

TENNESSEE. See STATE GOVERNMENT.

TENNIS. The best players in 1978 were familiar – Bjorn Borg of Sweden and Jimmy Connors among the men, Martina Navratilova and Chris Evert among the women. But there were major changes. The United States Open, which had been played at the staid West Side Tennis Club in Forest Hills, N.Y., for 54 years, was moved to the barely completed, $9.5-million National Tennis Center in Flushing, N.Y. The women's professional tour, sponsored by Virginia Slims cigarettes for its nine years, accepted a more lucrative offer, starting in 1979, from Avon Products, a cosmetics manufacturer.

Pro Tours. The Virginia Slims tour started in 1970 with one $7,500 tournament. The 1978 tour consisted of 12 tournaments from January to April worth $1,250,000. The 1979 Avon schedule listed 12 winter tournaments worth $2 million, with Avon continuing its satellite tour, the Futures Circuit.

The Colgate Grand Prix for men consisted of 99 tournaments throughout the world. Prize money exceeded $10 million, and more than $2 million was given in year-end bonuses to the leading players. The richest tournaments were the United States Open ($577,480 for men and women) and the Wimbledon championships in England ($512,240).

The Men. The 22-year-old Borg won his third straight Wimbledon title on grass and his second French and Italian opens on clay. As always, he was coldly efficient. "I'm playing probably my best tennis," he said. "I don't know if I can improve any the next couple of years, but I hope to stay at my peak for awhile." See BORG, BJORN.

The 26-year-old Connors, a left-hander from Belleville, Ill., lost to Borg on July 8 in the Wimbledon final, 6-2, 6-2, 6-3. But he beat Borg on September 10, 6-4, 6-2, 6-2, for his third United States Open title in five years. Borg, suffering his first defeat in 56 matches, played with an infected thumb on his racquet hand.

Vitas Gerulaitis of Kings Point, N.Y., won the Australian Open, the World Championship Tennis final, and the first prize of $100,000 in the new Forest Hills Invitational. He lost to Connors in the Wimbledon semifinals and to Borg in the U.S. Open.

The Women. In 1975, when Navratilova was 18, she defected from Czechoslovakia because she could not play when and where she wanted. In 1976, overweight, temperamental, and impatient, she lost in the first round of the United States Open.

In 1978, lighter, quicker, more in command of her emotions, and happy in her Dallas home, Navratilova won seven straight tournaments while Evert was taking a four-month winter vacation. She beat Evert on July 7 in the Wimbledon final, 2-6, 6-4, 7-5, but lost in the U.S. Open semifinals to 16-year-old Pam Shriver of Lutherville, Md., 7-6, 7-6. She won $500,757 in tournaments.

The 23-year-old Evert, from Fort Lauderdale, Fla., was more relaxed, saying, "It's not a life-or-death thing for me now whether I win a match." She won her fourth straight United States Open title to become the first woman to achieve that since Helen Jacobs in 1935. Evert beat Shriver, 7-5, 6-4, in the final on September 10.

Shriver, 6 feet (183 centimeters) tall, became the youngest semifinalist and finalist, male or female, in U.S. Open history. Ironically, she lost to Tracy Austin of Rolling Hills, Calif., in the finals of the United States championships for girls 18 years of age and younger and girls 16 and under. Austin turned pro late in the year, and her first tournament victory gave her $6,000 and a new automobile. She could not drive the car because she was only 15 years old.

Davis Cup. The United States, with such players as Gerulaitis, Arthur Ashe, Brian Gottfried, Harold Solomon, and John McEnroe, won the Davis Cup for the first time in six years. McEnroe starred in the defeat of Great Britain in December in the final round, played at Rancho Mirage, Calif.

World Team Tennis played its fifth season with 10 teams. The Los Angeles Strings, with Evert and Ilie Nastase, won the title. After the season, the New York, Boston, and Indiana teams suspended operations, but the league added teams in Dallas, Los Angeles, and San Diego.   Frank Litsky

In WORLD BOOK, see TENNIS.

TEXAS. See DALLAS-FORT WORTH; HOUSTON; STATE GOVERNMENT.

THAILAND followed a policy of active neutralism in 1978, reversing its previous staunch anti-Communist stand. Late in the year, Thailand welcomed senior government officials from Vietnam, Russia, the United States, and China.

Prime Minister Pham Van Dong of Vietnam visited Thai Prime Minister Kriangsak Chamanan in September. Dong said Vietnam would not interfere in Thai internal affairs and would "refrain from subversion either directly or indirectly." This was greeted with both relief and skepticism in Thailand because Vietnam was believed to have supported Communist insurgents there in the past.

China's Vice-Premier Teng Hsiao-p'ing warned while visiting Bangkok in November that Vietnam and Russia, which had just signed a friendship treaty, were a threat to regional peace. Teng avoided promising noninterference, trying to distinguish between state relations and peaceful support for the Thai Communist Party.

Border Clashes. Relations with its Communist neighbors Cambodia and Laos remained difficult. Clashes along the Cambodian border occurred sporadically. Kriangsak said on March 3 that some outbreaks were provoked by Thai Communist guerrillas operating near the border rather than by Cambodians.

Refugees from Laos, Cambodia, and Vietnam entered Thailand at an estimated 9,000 per month.

Despite United Nations efforts, homes outside Thailand could not be found for enough of them to avoid overcrowding refugee camps. The problem was aggravated by severe flooding along the Mekong River during unusually heavy summer rains.

Government Reorganization. Kriangsak reorganized the Cabinet on August 13. He gave up the interior ministry portfolio but took over as defense minister. The change enabled him to retain military influence after he retired on October 1 as supreme military commander. General Serm Na Nakorn replaced him as supreme commander, but the post's power was eroded by other appointments arranged by Kriangsak.

The appointed National Assembly worked during 1978 on a new constitution, which was scheduled to serve as the basis for elections for a new Assembly no later than April 1979. The revised draft, tabled on October 25, proposed a one-house legislature in which half the 269 members would be elected and half appointed by the head of the National Policy Council, with King Bhumibol Adulyadej's concurrence. The proposed constitution provided for council expansion from 23 to 40 members. A broad spectrum of civilian politicians opposed the constitution. They saw it as a way of continuing military control for at least four more years. Henry S. Bradsher

See also ASIA (Facts in Brief Table). In WORLD BOOK, see THAILAND.

THEATER. Necessity was the mother of theatrical invention in the United States in 1978. Soaring costs made producers more willing than ever before to give imagination a chance before the footlights. Small became beautiful, and the standard musical comedy that depends on a story, choruses, lavish costumes, and spectacular scenery gave way to "entertainments" relying on small casts and modest sets. In New York City, these included *Ain't Misbehavin'*, *Eubie!*, *The American Dance Machine,* and *Dancin'*. The best drama, *Da*, used six main actors and only one set, and the "hot" ticket for the fall was for a one-man show—Alec McCowen reading *St. Mark's Gospel*.

Ain't Misbehavin', a joyful song-and-dance evocation of the songs of jazz pianist Fats Waller, originated as a small cabaret revue in the Manhattan Theatre Club. Richard Maltby, Jr., and Murray Horwitz put the entertainment together, and Luther Henderson researched, supervised, and played the music, which was interpreted by five exceptional performing artists. Its success prompted the production of *Eubie!*, a revue of 23 songs from *Shuffle Along*, an all-black 1921 Broadway musical. The composer, 95-year-old Eubie Blake, was on stage as he had been 57 years earlier, to delight the opening-night audience.

Staged by choreographer Bob Fosse, *Dancin'*, with no plot, illustrated a wide variety of dances, including ballet, modern, soft-shoe, and disco. *Beatlemania* re-created songs by John Lennon and Paul McCartney against a background of projected photographs reflecting events of the 1960s. *The American Dance Machine* also revived the past, in dance numbers from earlier musical hits.

Lavish Musical Comedies were few. *Timbuktu!,* a remake of the 1950s musical *Kismet,* was directed, costumed, and choreographed by Geoffrey Holder. It was visually splendid but stifling in its opulence as it told a love story of king and commoner in 14th-century Timbuktu. Most successful of the traditional musicals was *On the Twentieth Century,* based upon the Ben Hecht-Charles MacArthur farce that was a hit on Broadway in the 1930s and again in the 1950s. The musical version adds music by Cy Coleman, lyrics by Betty Comden and Adolph Green, and stunning Art Deco sets by Robin Wagner, depicting the famous New York City-to-Chicago *Twentieth Century* train. John Cullum played the fading producer Oscar Jaffee, desperate to win the favor and contract of a movie queen, and Imogene Coca was a zany crusader for repentance.

Almost directly opposed to *On the Twentieth Century* in spirit and style, but equally entertaining, was *Runaways,* written, composed, and directed by 27-year-old Elizabeth Swados. In musical numbers on the serious themes of alienation and growing up,

young people tell why they have run away to the big city, to become its victims and victimizers.

Regional Theaters made an art of Broadway's financial necessity; from Los Angeles to Buffalo, N.Y., they tried out new plays that careful Broadway producers might view before embarking on costly New York City production ventures. Hugh Leonard's *Da* was first seen in the United States at the Olney (Md.) Theatre and at the Ivanhoe Theater in Chicago. The Broadway production was moved virtually intact from the stage of the Hudson Guild Theatre, which has been offering community and professional off-Broadway productions since 1922. Directed by Melvin Bernhardt and starring Barnard Hughes as Da and Brian Murray as the son, *Da* won Tony, Drama Critics' Circle, and Drama Desk awards. *Da* moves back and forth in time as a successful playwright returns to his Dublin home for his father's funeral and relives scenes from the past called up by mementos. The work is affectionate but never sentimental in its portraits of Da, a humble gardener of unshakable optimism and stubbornness, his well-meaning wife, and their impatient son.

Tribute by Bernard Slade, another Broadway hit, also mingles past and present imaginatively in treating the parent-son relationship. Jack Lemmon's interpretation of Scottie, the leading character, struck just the right note of charm, wit, and manipu-

Ain't Misbehavin' recalls the 1920s and 1930s, featuring 30 songs that jazz pianist Thomas (Fats) Waller either wrote or helped to make famous.

In the title role of *Da,* Barnard Hughes played a stubborn, optimistic Dublin gardener as he is recalled by his son, home for Da's funeral.

lation. Scottie, who has been unable to come to terms with his own son, is now dying of leukemia, and his friends have rented the theater – with the audience as participants – for a final "tribute."

From the American Place Theatre off-Broadway came *Cold Storage,* Ronald Ribman's perceptive drama about two cancer victims who clash verbally in the roof garden of a hospital. Martin Balsam was the outgoing Parmigian, who tries to help his defensive antagonist, played by Len Cariou, find peace.

Theatrical Chillers continued in 1978. Ira Levin's *Deathtrap* pitted John Wood as an aging writer of mystery plays against a young writer whose latest work promises to be a great success. The older man resolves to murder the younger and steal his play. Reversals, switches, and twists in the plot lead to a surprise ending. *The Crucifer of Blood* by Paul Giovanni is based on Sir Arthur Conan Doyle's novella "The Sign of the Four," dealing with the curse on a casket of jewels.

Most Distinguished Revival of the year was Eugene O'Neill's *A Touch of the Poet.* Jason Robards was effective in the leading role of Major Melody, an immigrant tavernkeeper who clings to his past glory as a military hero. Robards was unforgettable at the end when Melody, stripped of his illusions, shoots his horse and reverts to a "shanty Irishman."

Outstanding one-man shows included *Paul Robeson,* with James Earl Jones impressively conveying the humanity, dignity, and frustrations of the actor-singer; and Alec McCowen's *St. Mark's Gospel.* McCowen's performance in casual clothes on a bare stage was vividly theatrical. He created a character of Mark that made his telling of the ministry and death of Jesus contemporary, suspenseful, and moving.

Outside New York City, musical productions that gained national attention included *Zoot Suit* at the Mark Taper Forum in Los Angeles, concerning Chicanos in that city in the 1940s. An inventive production of *Joseph and the Amazing Technicolor Dreamcoat,* written by Tim Rice and Andrew Lloyd Webber and staged by the Hartke Theatre of Catholic University in Washington, D.C., proved so popular that it was moved to the Olney Theatre in Maryland. In Houston, Nina Vance's Alley Theater produced the U.S. première of *Echelon* by Mikhail Roschin, and brought Galina Volchyek, its Russian director, to Houston to stage the work. The play concerns the World War II evacuation of Russian women on trains called *echelons,* and makes a universal statement about female survival.   Alice Griffin

See also AWARDS AND PRIZES (Arts Awards). In WORLD BOOK, see DRAMA; THEATER.

TIMOR. See ASIA.

TOGO. See AFRICA.

TORNADO. See DISASTERS; WEATHER.

TOYS. See GAMES, MODELS, AND TOYS.

TRACK AND FIELD. Kenya has sent many outstanding runners to American colleges since the early 1970s. The most successful has been Henry Rono of Washington State University in Pullman.

In 1978, Rono shattered four world records in distance races. They came in the 5,000-meter run (13 minutes 8.4 seconds on April 8 in Berkeley, Calif.); 3,000-meter steeplechase (8 minutes 5.4 seconds on May 13 in Seattle); 10,000-meter run (27 minutes 22.5 seconds on June 11 in Vienna, Austria); and 3,000-meter run (7 minutes 32.1 seconds on June 27 in Oslo, Norway).

Rono, a 26-year-old sophomore, also won the steeplechase in the National Collegiate Athletic Association (NCAA) championships in June in Eugene, Ore. He won the steeplechase and 5,000-meter race in August in the Commonwealth Games in Edmonton, Canada.

European Championships. The European outdoor championships were held from August 29 to September 3 in Prague, Czechoslovakia, and attracted more than 1,000 men and women from 29 nations. Russia won 13 men's and women's events, and East Germany took 12. Between them, they won all women's events except the high jump.

The only man to win two titles was Pietro Mennea of Italy, who took the 100-meter and 200-meter dashes in 10.27 and 20.16 seconds. Steve Ovett of Great Britain won the 1,500-meter run in 3 minutes 35.6 seconds and finished second at 800 meters in 1 minute 44.1 seconds. Two weeks later, Ovett beat Rono and set an unofficial world record of 8 minutes 13.5 seconds for 2 miles.

The men broke no world records in the European championships. The women broke three and equaled one. The record breakers were Marita Koch of East Germany, who ran 400 meters in 48.94 seconds, and Vilhelmina Bardauskiene of Russia, who leaped 23 feet 3¼ inches (7.09 meters) in the long jump. Sara Simeoni of Italy high-jumped 6 feet 7 inches (2.01 meters), tying the world record she set four weeks earlier. Simeoni also set a world indoor record of 6 feet 4¾ inches (1.95 meters).

Koch broke or equaled world records at 200 and 400 meters five times during the year, and she was the first to better 49 seconds for 400 meters. Bardauskiene became the first woman to clear 23 feet (7.01 meters) in the long jump.

High-Jumpers. Vladimir Yashchenko of Russia, 19, set a world indoor high-jump record of 7 feet 8½ inches (2.35 meters) in March in Milan, Italy, and a world outdoor mark of 7 feet 8 inches (2.34 meters) in June in Tbilisi, Russia, using the old-fashioned straddle style. A confident, slender youth of 6 feet 2¾ inches (190 centimeters) and 165 pounds (75 kilograms), he felt his future was unlimited.

World Track and Field Records Established in 1978

Event	Holder	Country	Where made	Date	Record
Men					
3,000 meters	Henry Rono	Kenya	Oslo, Norway	June 27	7:32.1
3,000-meter steeplechase	Henry Rono	Kenya	Seattle, Wash.	May 13	8:05.4
5,000 meters	Henry Rono	Kenya	Berkeley, Calif.	April 8	13:08.4
10,000 meters	Henry Rono	Kenya	Vienna, Austria	June 11	27:22.5
800-meter relay	Univ. of Southern California (Andrews, Sanford, Mullins, Edwards)	U.S.A.	Tempe, Ariz.	May 27	1:20.3
3,200-meter	Podolyakov, Kirov, Malozemlin, Reshetnyak	Russia	Podolsk, Russia	August 12	7:08.1
High jump	Vladimir Yashchenko	Russia	Tbilisi, Russia	June 16	7 ft. 8 in. (2.34 meters)
Pole vault	Mike Tully	U.S.A.	Corvallis, Ore.	May 19	18 ft. 8¾ in. (5.71 meters)
Shot-put	Udo Beyer	E. Germany	Göteborg, Sweden	July 6	72 ft. 8 in. (22.15 meters)
Discus throw	Wolfgang Schmidt	E. Germany	East Berlin, E. Ger.	August 9	233 ft. 5 in. (71.16 meters)
Hammer throw	Karl-Hans Riehm	W. Germany	Heidenheim, W. Ger.	August 6	263 ft. 6 in. (80.32 meters)
Women					
200 meters	Marita Koch	E. Germany	Erfurt, E. Ger.	May 28	:22.06
	Marita Koch	E. Germany	East Berlin, E. Ger.	June 4	:22.06
400 meters	Marita Koch	E. Germany	Prague, Czechoslovakia	August 31	:48.94
*1,000 meters	Tatyana Providokhina	Russia	Podolsk, Russia	August 20	2:30.6
*3 miles	Kathy Mills	U.S.A.	Knoxville, Tenn.	May 26	15:03.9
*5,000 meters	Loa Olafsson	Denmark	Copenhagen, Denmark	May 31	15:08.8
*10,000 meters	Loa Olafsson	Denmark	Copenhagen, Denmark	April 6	31:45.4
*Marathon	Greta Waitz	Norway	New York	October 22	2:32.30
100-meter hurdles	Grazyna Rabsztyn	Poland	Furth, W. Ger.	June 10	:12.48
400-meter hurdles	Tatyana Zelencova	Russia	Prague, Czechoslovakia	September 2	:54.89
400-meter relay	Klier, Hamann, Bodendorf, Goehr	E. Germany	Potsdam, E. Ger.	August 19	:42.27
High jump	Sara Simeoni	Italy	Brescia, Italy	August 4	6 ft. 7 in. (2.01 meters)
	Sara Simeoni	Italy	Prague, Czechoslovakia	August 31	6 ft. 7 in. (2.01 meters)
Long jump	Vilhelmina Bardauskiene	Russia	Prague, Czechoslovakia	August 29	23 ft. 3¼ in. (7.09 meters)
Discus throw	Evelin Jahl	E. Germany	Dresden, E. Ger.	August 12	232 ft. (70.71 meters)

*No official world record at this distance.

In their only meeting, Yashchenko beat Franklin Jacobs in the United States-Russian outdoor meet on June 8 in Berkeley, though both cleared 7 feet 5½ inches (2.27 meters). Jacobs set a world indoor record of 7 feet 7¼ inches (2.32 meters) in New York City on January 27, only to have Yashchenko break it six weeks later in Milan.

The 20-year-old Jacobs, a Fairleigh Dickinson University sophomore from Paterson, N.J., flopped over the bar in a style he originated. Only 5 feet 8 inches (173 centimeters) tall, he jumped 23¼ inches (59 centimeters) over his head, itself a record.

Other Developments. Dwight Stones of Huntington Beach, Calif., the world's leading high-jumper before Yashchenko, was suspended by the Amateur Athletic Union (AAU), America's ruling body for the sport. The AAU also suspended javelin thrower Kathy Schmidt, miler Francie Larrieu, and pentathlon star Jane Frederick, all Californians who held world or U.S. records or both. The AAU said the four made themselves professionals by accepting money from the "Superstars" TV show. Larrieu was reinstated when she allowed the money to be distributed according to an AAU formula.

Mike Tully, a University of California, Los Angeles, senior, set world pole-vault records of 18 feet 5¼ inches (5.63 meters) indoors and 18 feet 8¾ inches (5.71 meters) outdoors.   Frank Litsky

In WORLD BOOK, see TRACK AND FIELD.

TRANSIT systems in United States cities enjoyed another ridership gain in 1978. The American Public Transit Association (APTA) said urban mass-transit operations carried 6.38 billion passengers in the first 10 months of the year, up 5.5 per cent from the first 10 months of 1977. New York City, which had suffered a continued patronage decline, showed a 3.2 per cent increase, as employment in the city improved. Ridership increased 4.4 per cent in Chicago; 5.4 per cent in Los Angeles; 9.8 per cent in Minneapolis, Minn.; and 18.5 per cent in Philadelphia, rebounding after a 1977 strike. But Detroit showed a 4.7 per cent decline, and Pittsburgh ridership was off 1.3 per cent.

Passenger totals rose as federal subsidies helped cities expand service. The Dallas Transit System, for example, added routes and boosted its bus-trip miles by 1.1 million (1.8 million bus-trip kilometers) through July. But deficits increased, too. The APTA said 1978 losses would exceed the 1977 deficit of $1.95 billion. About $700 million, or more than 33 per cent of the nationwide transit loss, was covered by federal subsidy, the rest by state and local funds. The U.S. Urban Mass Transportation Administration (UMTA) helped Denver finance a one-year fare-free experiment starting February 1, to decrease air pollution by encouraging motorists to ride buses in off-peak hours. The UMTA subsidized a similar trial in Trenton, N.J. On its own, the Transit Authority of River City in Louisville, Ky., provided free service during air-pollution alerts.

Systems tried fare increases to cover rising costs. Some California transit operators said fare boosts would be necessary to replace funds lost through cuts contained in the Proposition 13 property-tax proposal passed in June. See TAXATION (Close-Up).

Washington, D.C.'s Metro rapid-transit system opened a 5.7-mile (9.2-kilometer) extension of its Red Line on February 3 and a 7.4-mile (12-kilometer) start of its Orange Line on November 20 for a total of 30.7 miles (49.4 kilometers). Metro gained new federal support on August 17, when Secretary of Transportation Brock Adams pledged federal backing for the planned 100-mile (160-kilometer) system. He said money beyond the $5-billion committed would have to come from transfers of funds from canceled interstate highway projects in the Washington area. Atlanta, Ga., and Baltimore worked on federally financed rapid-transit systems; Miami, Fla., prepared to build a system; and Buffalo, N.Y., started a federally supported *light-rail* (trolley-type) line. The United States Department of Transportation (DOT), in an effort to dispel the belief that President Jimmy Carter's Administration disliked rail-transit systems, said on March 7 that some systems were valuable for urban development and energy savings.

New Legislation. President Carter signed the Surface Transportation Act of 1978 on November 6. The act provides highway and transit funding, including $16.4 billion in mass-transit aid, rising yearly through fiscal year 1982. The bill changed the capital-grant program to emphasize projects requiring major spending, and created a second operating-subsidy program emphasizing the biggest cities. Adams said in November that UMTA should merge with the Federal Highway Administration.

UMTA grants for rail projects included $135-million for New York City; $199 million for Washington, D.C.; $163 million for Boston; and $108-million for Philadelphia.

Accessibility Issue. Adams proposed rules on June 8 to make transit systems more accessible to the handicapped. Transit executives said the rules were unproductive and too costly. The rules, issued under the Rehabilitation Act of 1973, would require installation of elevators in existing subway stations, to accommodate wheelchairs, for example.

The Regulatory Analysis Review Group, a government committee that examines regulations before their adoption, said that the DOT program would cost $1.9 billion, of which $1.1 billion would be used mainly for elevators. It said that special buses on parallel routes would be cheaper than implementing the DOT program.   Albert R. Karr

See also TRANSPORTATION. In WORLD BOOK, see TRANSPORTATION.

TRANSKEI. See AFRICA.

TRANSPORTATION. The fortunes of United States transportation industries were mixed in 1978. Revenues increased amid rising calls for deregulation. Airlines prospered from increased traffic, spurred by decreased regulation; truck profits increased, but trucking companies feared deregulation; and railroads' lower earnings caused them to favor less regulation.

The Transportation Association of America estimated U.S. transportation revenues at $458 billion for 1978, up 11 per cent from 1977. Mainland intercity freight increased 5.8 per cent, with pipeline and railroad freight up 5 per cent; truck volume, 9 per cent; rivers and canals, 4 per cent; air cargo, 14 per cent; and Great Lakes traffic, 3 per cent.

Intercity passenger traffic increased 5.5 per cent, with air travel up 16 per cent and automobile travel up 4.3 per cent. Railroad passenger traffic held even, and bus travel decreased 7 per cent.

President Jimmy Carter signed a $54-billion Surface Transportation Act on November 6, raising the average authorizations for highway construction, repair, and safety from $7.1 billion for 1978 to $9.3-billion per year through 1982; and providing $16.4-billion for mass transit. The bill gave the states until 1983 to decide whether to use federal money to finish their interstate highway segments or use it for mass transit or other highway projects.

Government Action. Secretary of Transportation Brock Adams said in a policy statement on February 8 that the U.S. transportation system needed expensive improvements but "no major expansion within the next 10 to 15 years." Adams said the automobile would continue as the favored form of transportation, but emphasized the need for energy-saving alternatives.

The U.S. House of Representatives on July 19 rejected a bill giving coal-slurry pipelines *eminent domain* (the right to use private land for a purpose in the public interest). Coal slurry is powdered coal mixed with water. The Office of Technology Assessment had said on January 18 that slurry pipelines could transport coal more cheaply than railroads under certain conditions.

Congress imposed a tax of 10 cents per gallon (3.8 liters) on barge fuel by 1985. Barge lines opposed the bill, but railroads said it would correct an imbalance caused by government financing of inland-waterways improvements. A bill to help airlines pay for quieter new aircraft or reduce noise on existing aircraft failed, but Congress enacted an airline-deregulation measure that most airlines once opposed. The Carter Administration said it would push for similar truck and rail deregulation.

Rules and Standards. The Department of Transportation (DOT) on June 8 proposed rules to help

Transportation Secretary Brock Adams explains a proposed Amtrak cutback that would drop some 8,000 miles (13,000 kilometers) of passenger routes.

handicapped persons use mass transit, trains, and airports under guidelines set by the U.S. Department of Health, Education, and Welfare. The requirements would force refitting of subway stations, railcars, passenger terminals, and airports to provide easier access for disabled persons. Adams warned 14 states in February that they faced loss of highway funds unless they enforce truck-weight laws. He later dropped the threat. Adams also banned supertankers from Washington's Puget Sound on March 14, after the Supreme Court of the United States struck down a state ban imposed to prevent disastrous oil spills.

Federal safety, environmental, and trade regulators pushed motor vehicle manufacturers to recall more vehicles than the 1977 record of 12.6 million. Ford Motor Company decided on June 9 to recall almost 1.5 million Pinto and Mercury Bobcat cars. Some Pintos had been involved in fiery rear-end crashes. After a prolonged battle with the National Highway Traffic Safety Administration (NHTSA), Firestone Tire & Rubber Company agreed to recall about 13 million "500" steel-belted radial tires. NHTSA issued rules on July 14 requiring tire companies to grade tires according to tread wear, traction, and high-speed performance. Albert R. Karr

See also AUTOMOBILE; AVIATION; RAILROAD; SHIP AND SHIPPING; TRANSIT; TRUCK AND TRUCKING. In WORLD BOOK, see TRANSPORTATION.

TRAVEL. Changing factors made 1978 a record year for travel to the United States. The sagging U.S. dollar stimulated large numbers of travelers, particularly from Europe, South America, and Asia, to visit the United States. A record total of about 20-million persons from other countries visited the United States, up about 7 per cent. They spent $50-billion. Financially troubled New York City, for example, enjoyed the biggest tourism and hotel-building boom in its history. Nearly 17 million persons, many from other countries, visited the city, and 10 hotels were either underway, being renovated, or in various stages of development.

Lower promotional airfares and tour packages were another reason for the increase. Laker Airways' no-frills Skytrain carried more than 300,000 passengers round trip between New York and London for $246, and established scheduled carriers offered New York to London trips for as little as $269. The regular economy-class fare was $626.

United States embassies abroad were swamped with visa requests as travelers departed for America at the rate of 48,000 a day. They became a major factor in decreasing the trade deficit – the U.S. Travel Service estimated that tourists spent $17-million a day in America.

International Visits. There were about 245 million international arrivals throughout the world in 1978, an increase of 12 per cent. Some 22 million

Americans visited other countries, spending $12.2-billion. An estimated 12 million went to Canada, down 2.7 per cent; 2.7 million went to Mexico, down 2.7 per cent; and 7.2 million traveled overseas, a gain of 7 per cent. This included 406,132 air travelers to South America and 148,561 to the South Pacific. About 12.8 million Canadians visited the United States, up 8 per cent, and spent $2.5 billion. There were 2.2 million Mexican visitors to the United States, and they spent about $1.4 billion. The 900,-000 Japanese travelers spent $540 million. British visitors decreased 1 per cent to 533,000, while West Germans increased 22 per cent to 450,000. About 155,000 Australians visited the United States, down nearly 8 per cent.

Americans took about 750 million person-trips in 1978 in the United States, spending an estimated $100 billion. Highway traffic rose to 1.45 trillion vehicle-miles (2.33 trillion vehicle-kilometers).

In the Air. During the first eight months of the year, U.S. airlines carried 180 million passengers, up 16 per cent over 1977 and the largest gain in airline history. Earnings for the year were estimated at a record $1 billion. But neither airlines nor airports were prepared to cope with the flood. A two-hour wait for travelers to clear U.S. Customs was not uncommon.

Confusing Fares. The traveler's wait usually began at the telephone or airline ticket office, where it took up to 20 minutes to get through. For bargain hunters, the ticket agent's recital of some 20 alternative fares took another half an hour. Travel agents were not entirely pleased with the surge of cut-rate domestic fares. They claimed that though volume increased, the new fares decreased their overall commission profits. A study in May showed that U.S. retail travel agents received $420 million in commissions for domestic air travel, but costs of handling that portion of their business came to $443-million, a loss of $23 million. International air travel, on the other hand, showed a profit of $63 million, with commissions of $246 million and costs of $183-million.

Soaring Costs largely offset the low airfares to Europe. Deluxe hotel rooms in London, Paris, and many parts of Switzerland and West Germany ran as high as $100 per night. A cafeteria lunch for four of bratwurst and potato salad cost $20 in Berne, Switzerland. A stein of German beer sold for $2, and, on Sardinia's Costa Smeralda, a dinner tab of $175 per person was not uncommon.

On the other hand, millions of prosperous West Europeans flooded Mediterranean resorts and beaches. Transportation systems, campground facilities, and sanitation plants were strained beyond limits, adding to the problems of the already seriously polluted Mediterranean Sea. A slowdown by French air-traffic controllers in July and August stranded thousands at European airports.

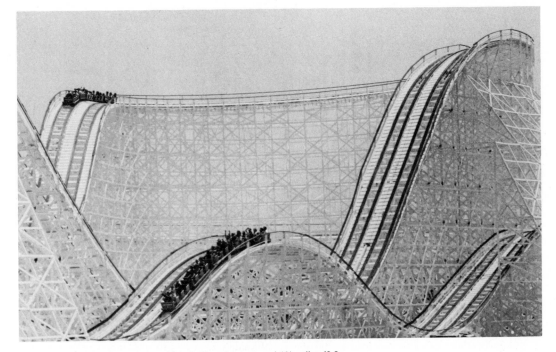

The new Colossus roller coaster whips thrill-seekers around 1³/₄ miles (2.8 kilometers) of track at Magic Mountain amusement park in Valencia, Calif.

On the Seas, Greece topped the list with 32 of a total of 140 cruise ships operating in 1978. Russia and Italy had 18 each; Great Britain, 13; Norway, 12; and Panama, 11. Only four ocean-going, passenger-carrying ships sailed under the U.S. flag. The 25 principal cruise lines carried about 1.7-million passengers out of U.S. ports.

Train and Bus. Amtrak, the U.S. National Railroad Passenger Corporation, carried some 19.2 million riders in fiscal 1978, a gain of 5.8 per cent. Amtrak served 524 stations on its 28,000-mile (45,000-kilometer) system. Unlimited-mileage passes were offered by both Greyhound Bus Lines and Continental Trailways Bus Lines.

Rising Bamboo Curtain. China lifted a long-standing ban on general tourism, but the bamboo curtain was raised somewhat gingerly because of limited tourist facilities. Only 10,000 visas were made available to Americans, and all of them were used. In November, Inter-Continental Hotels Corp. signed a memorandum of agreement with the China International Travel Service for the design, construction, financing, and operation of 5,000 hotel rooms in China, which will be owned by China.

A new U.S. customs code raised the duty-free allowance on overseas purchases to $300. Purchases up to $600 in Guam, American Samoa, or the U.S. Virgin Islands are duty-free.   Lynn Beaumont

In WORLD BOOK, see TRANSPORTATION.

TRAVOLTA, JOHN (1954-   ), became one of the most popular American actors in 1978 as the star of two hit motion pictures, *Saturday Night Fever* and *Grease.* An Oscar nominee as best actor for his portrayal of a young disco dancer in *Saturday Night Fever,* Travolta got good reviews for his footwork as well as for his sensitive interpretation of the character. He starred with Lily Tomlin in a third film, *Moment to Moment,* a May-September romance, which was released in December.

John Travolta was born on Feb. 18, 1954, in Englewood, N.J., the youngest of six children. His mother, a former actress and drama coach, encouraged all of her children to study music and acting. Travolta attended high school in Englewood but dropped out at 16 to try an acting career.

Travolta appeared in a number of Broadway productions, including the stage version of *Grease* and the Andrews Sisters' revival review, *Over There.* It was the role of "sweathog" Vinnie Barbarino in the popular television series "Welcome Back, Kotter," however, that first brought Travolta widespread recognition.

His acting has led to a second career as a singer. Travolta's duet with Olivia Newton-John, "You're the One That I Want," a song from *Grease,* became a hit in 1978. He has also recorded two solo albums.

Travolta lives in North Hollywood, Calif. He enjoys flying and has his own plane.   Beverly Merz

TRUCK AND TRUCKING. The United States trucking industry progressed financially in 1978, but the threat of government deregulation loomed larger. The American Trucking Associations, Incorporated (ATA), estimated that freight hauled increased 6 per cent to 970 million short tons (880-million metric tons), and motor-carrier revenues increased 16.5 per cent to $36 billion. Earnings increased 10 per cent from the 1977 profit of $850-million.

The Interstate Commerce Commission (ICC) approved freight-rate increases ranging up to 7.5 per cent in April, and added 2 to 3 per cent more in July and August. The ICC said in September that it would no longer automatically let truck or railroad companies recover higher costs by rate increases, but would require specific justification. The decision came as President Jimmy Carter's Administration pressed for holding down truck rates to fight inflation. The ICC on November 27 rejected a 6.2 per cent increase proposed by the Southern Motor Carriers Rate Conference and asked the conference to file for a 3.5 per cent increase.

The Deregulation Drive gathered momentum. Senator Edward M. Kennedy (D., Mass.) continued committee hearings on motor-carrier rate-making and market-entry limits. He advocated less regulation. The Administration, having rolled back airline regulations, began to plan truck deregulation. Its new inflation-fighting chief, Alfred E. Kahn, former Civil Aeronautics Board chairman, and the Department of Justice pushed to ease ICC control over trucking.

ICC Chairman A. Daniel O'Neal proposed on November 6 that ICC consider steps to ease its hold over trucking by eliminating most rate and entry regulation of specialized, full-truckload operations, and by rolling back controls on hauling less than full loads of general commodities. The ICC gave preliminary approval on November 30 to a proposal limiting the right of established trucking companies to protest the entry of new companies. Only companies providing the service the new companies proposed to provide would have the right to protest.

Truckers Opposed. The trucking industry argued that regulation is necessary for industry stability and planned legal and legislative action to block deregulation. ATA began drafting its own deregulation proposal.

Secretary of Transportation Brock Adams said on November 13 that the Administration would move quickly toward truck and railroad deregulation by proposing legislation to let trucking companies change rates with less ICC overview, to let new companies enter the trucking business more easily, and to prohibit companies from setting rates jointly, free of antitrust prosecution.   Albert R. Karr

See also TRANSPORTATION. In WORLD BOOK, see TRUCK AND TRUCKING.

TRUDEAU, PIERRE ELLIOTT (1919-   ), celebrated his 10th anniversary as prime minister of Canada on April 20, 1978. Victorious in three national elections, Trudeau had become one of the longest-serving leaders in the Western world. He was the best-known Canadian abroad, respected for his tough intellectual approach and forward-looking views, and admired for his flair and unconventional manner. His personal life, including the circumstances of his separation from his wife, Margaret, brought him celebrity status.

Yet most Canadians seemed to have a love-hate outlook toward the prime minister. The public adulation with which he had begun his administration in 1968 was followed by a disenchantment that almost drove him from office in 1972 and by a new surge of popularity after the 1976 election of a separatist government in Quebec. Many Canadians were deeply dissatisfied in 1978 with Trudeau's failure to cope with the problems of the economy.

Economic difficulties had plagued Trudeau for 10 years, a constant distraction from his deeply held objectives of reforming Canadian federalism and laying the foundations of a bicultural nation. Many of these problems were not of his making, but ultimately he would have to bear responsibility for the way he met them.   David M. L. Farr

See also CANADA; QUEBEC. In WORLD BOOK, see TRUDEAU, PIERRE ELLIOTT.

TUNISIA. A one-day general strike staged by the General Union of Tunisian Workers on Jan. 26, 1978, flared unexpectedly into riots. The strike was planned as a peaceful protest of government failure to implement the 1977 social contract with labor and of the ruling Destour Socialist Party's authoritarianism. But labor leader Habib Achour resigned on January 10, and other labor leaders left the striking workers essentially leaderless. Unemployed youths took over the streets and started looting.

The government called in troops and tanks and imposed martial law. It said 46 persons were killed during three days of violence. Other sources said about 200 were killed. About 1,000 persons were arrested, including Achour and other union leaders.

The embattled government tried to restore public confidence. A March 7 law set up a labor corps to reduce unemployment – running at 12 per cent overall and 50 per cent among young people. Unemployed persons between 18 and 30 were to be sent to areas that needed workers. Pay increases in May helped semiskilled and agricultural workers, but economic growth was slow and there were not enough jobs to absorb the growing population. The socioeconomic situation was as critical as the ongoing political struggle over succession to aging President Habib Bourguiba.   William Spencer

See also AFRICA (Facts in Brief Table). In WORLD BOOK, see TUNISIA.

TURBAY AYALA, JULIO CESAR (1916-   ), a diplomat and the candidate of the governing Liberal Party, narrowly won election as president of Colombia on June 4, 1978. The incumbent, Alfonso Lopez Michelsen, also a Liberal, was barred by the Constitution from seeking re-election. During the campaign, candidates exchanged personal attacks rather than dealing with pressing political and economic issues. See COLOMBIA.

Turbay Ayala was born in Bogotá, Colombia, on June 18, 1916, the son of Antonio and Rosaura Ayala Turbay. He studied law and worked for a time as a journalist. He was elected to a seat in Colombia's House of Representatives in 1943, and served there until 1953.

In 1957, Turbay Ayala was named minister of mines and energy. He served as minister of foreign affairs from 1958 until 1961, then resigned to run for a seat in the Senate. He served in the Senate from 1962 to 1970, and that body twice elected him vice-president.

In 1967, Turbay Ayala was named Colombia's permanent representative to the United Nations. He was appointed ambassador to Great Britain in 1970 and ambassador to the United States in 1974.

Turbay Ayala married Nydea Quintero in 1948. In 1957, he was awarded an honorary law and political science degree by the University of Cauza in Colombia.   Foster Stockwell

Turkish police arrest a young right wing demonstrator after protestors threw firecrackers at Ankara crowds in an antigovernment demonstration in January.

TURKEY. Troubled by sporadic violence, Prime Minister Bulent Ecevit struggled in 1978 to gain financial aid for the nation's ailing economy. However, increased violence forced the government to impose martial law in 13 cities on December 26.

In April, Marshall Nikolai Ogarkov, Russia's chief of general staff, became the first senior Soviet officer to visit Turkey since 1933. He offered military aid. Ecevit went to Moscow in June and signed nonagression, trade, and cultural agreements. The trade pacts would increase Turkish-Russian bilateral trade by 200 per cent over three years. Russia also agreed to supply Turkey with crude oil on a barter basis, payable in Turkish wheat and metal exports. The deal would enable Turkey to meet 25 per cent of its oil needs without spending scarce foreign hard-currency reserves.

Ecevit gathered additional financial aid on visits to Bulgaria, Romania, and Yugoslavia. Romania loaned $100 million for a new refinery and oil pipeline, and Bulgaria agreed to buy $150 million worth of Turkish farm products. With both the European Community (EC or Common Market) and the World Bank warning Turkey to put its economic house in order before more support for its five-year-plan would be granted, the Eastern bloc's unrestricted assistance was welcome.

Political Unrest. The growth of domestic violence was an important factor in the unwilling-ness of Western powers to bail out the Ecevit government. Between January and October, there were more than 500 politically motivated murders. Many of them, random attacks by unknown gunmen, were difficult to solve. The victims included university professors, bank officials, and civil servants. The violence included arson, numerous bombings, and gang battles.

The crimes were generally attributed to two rival extremist political organizations, a leftist group headed by Necmet Borbakan, a former engineering professor, and a rightist group led by Colonel Alpaslan Turkes. Borbakan sought a socialist revolution, and Turkes wanted a military-style Fascist republic. The street violence in Turkish cities was marked by battles between the two groups as well as by attacks on innocent bystanders.

Turkey's relations with the United States improved considerably from the low point reached in 1974 after Turkey invaded Cyprus. After a couple of false starts, the United States formally lifted the three-year embargo on arms sales to Turkey in September. In return, Turkey agreed in October to reopen four U.S. military bases that were closed in 1975. The dispute with Greece over Aegean Sea oil rights remained unsettled.   William Spencer

See also MIDDLE EAST (Facts in Brief Table). In WORLD BOOK, see TURKEY.

UGANDA. See AFRICA.

ULLSTEN, OLA (1931-   ), a leading member of the Liberal Party, became prime minister of Sweden on Oct. 13, 1978, following the resignation of Thorbjorn Falldin. See SWEDEN.

Ullsten was born on June 23, 1931, in Umeå. He was a social and temperance worker in Stockholm from 1952 to 1957. He received a degree as a social economist in 1956, at Stockholm's Social Institute. He then went into politics, being elected to the *Riksdag* (parliament) in 1956 and serving there until 1976. He became secretary of the Liberal Party in 1957. In 1962, he served on the Stockholm City Cultural Affairs Committee. From 1962 to 1964, he headed the Liberal Party Youth Federation.

Ullsten became federation chairman and chairman and executive chairman of the Stockholm County branch of the Liberal Party in 1972, posts he has held ever since. He was also vice-chairman of the parliamentary Liberal Party and a member of the party's executive, steering committee, and committee on foreign policy. Foreign affairs and international assistance have long been two of his principal interests.

In 1961, Ullsten married Evi Esko, a chemical engineer. They have two children.   Foster Stockwell

UNEMPLOYMENT. See ECONOMICS; LABOR.

UNION OF SOVIET SOCIALIST REPUBLICS (U.S.S.R.). See RUSSIA.

UNITED ARAB EMIRATES. See MIDDLE EAST.

UNITED NATIONS (UN) sent a peacekeeping force to Lebanon in 1978 after Israeli troops withdrew, and planned the most expensive operation in its history to supervise an election making Namibia (South West Africa) independent of South Africa.

Israeli troops entered southern Lebanon at midnight on March 14 to attack the Palestine Liberation Organization (PLO), which Israel accused of sending terrorists who had killed 37 civilians in Israel three days earlier. See ISRAEL; LEBANON; MIDDLE EAST.

After a three-day debate requested by Lebanon and Israel, the UN Security Council adopted a United States resolution on March 19 calling for an Israeli cease-fire and withdrawal and establishing the UN Interim Force in Lebanon (UNIFIL) to restore peace and help re-establish Lebanese government authority in the evacuated area. The Council then adopted a British resolution approving Secretary-General Kurt Waldheim's proposals that UNIFIL number 4,000 and stay in Lebanon for six months. The vote for both resolutions was 12 to 0, with China not participating and Czechoslovakia and Russia abstaining.

UNIFIL, commanded by Major General Emmanuel A. Erskine of Ghana, got troops from Canada, Fiji, France, Iran, Ireland, Nepal, Nigeria, Norway, and Senegal. By the same vote, the Security Council increased UNIFIL to 6,000 troops on May 3, as requested by Waldheim; extended UNIFIL's term by four months on September 18; and extended by six months the term of the UN Emergency Force (UNEF) in Sinai on October 23.

On May 31, the Council voted unanimously, except for China's nonparticipation, to give another six months to the UN Disengagement Observer Force (UNDOF) separating Israeli and Syrian troops on the Golan Heights. Waldheim had asked for another six months for UNIFIL and another year for UNEF. But France insisted on a shorter term for UNIFIL, to make it finish its job more quickly; and Russia insisted on a shorter term for UNEF, to prevent UNEF involvement in any agreement resulting from the Egyptian-Israeli peace talks. Waldheim said that when the Israeli soldiers left Lebanon on June 13, there were 6,100 troops in UNIFIL. UNEF had 4,198 troops, and UNDOF had 1,245.

UNIFIL could not restore government control in southern Lebanon. Dissident Lebanese Christian militiamen with Israeli supplies held a large part of the southern region and a narrow strip along the entire southern border. The UN General Assembly appropriated more than $168 million on November 2 to maintain UNIFIL until the Assembly's next regular session in September 1979, if necessary.

UN in Namibia. Namibia was the center of a 12-year-old UN dispute with South Africa. The General Assembly in 1966 had declared South Africa's mandate over the territory ended. Western members of the Security Council—Canada, France, Great Britain, the United States, and West Germany—proposed early in 1978 that the UN and South Africa plan and conduct a UN-supervised election as part of a seven-month process leading to Namibian independence by Dec. 31, 1978. South Africa accepted the proposal on April 25.

The South-West Africa People's Organization (SWAPO), a rebel group fighting to take over Namibia, delayed acceptance after a South African raid on a SWAPO camp in Angola on May 4. The Security Council condemned the attack unanimously in a May 6 resolution sponsored by Bolivia, India, Kuwait, Mauritius, Nigeria, and Venezuela. SWAPO finally agreed that the Western five should put their proposal to the Council. On July 27, the council voted 13 to 0, with Czechoslovakia and Russia abstaining, to take note of the proposal and ask Waldheim how he would carry it out. The Council also asked him to name a representative to manage supervision of the election.

Waldheim named Martti Ahtisaari of Finland and sent him to Namibia to investigate the situation and meet the South African administrator-general, Judge Marthinus Steyn. Ahtisaari kept his regular post as UN representative for Namibia. Waldheim on August 30 recommended establishing a UN Transition Assistance Group (UNTAG) of 7,500

International Year of The Child

Countries throughout the world, including many that promote programs to limit the number of children born to their citizens, will celebrate the International Year of the Child (IYC) in 1979. The United Nations (UN) General Assembly proclaimed the observance, expressing the hope that IYC and its programs would turn the world's attention to the needs of its children and spur action to meet those needs.

Noting that 1979 would be the 20th anniversary of its own Declaration of the Rights of the Child, the Assembly said IYC could serve to promote those rights. Every child, the declaration asserts, is entitled to a name and nationality, adequate nutrition, housing, recreation and medical services, parental care, education, and protection against neglect, cruelty, and exploitation. IYC planners added other needs to that general list — the need to avoid illiteracy, alcoholism, crime, unwanted pregnancy, and drug abuse, and the need to be helped when in trouble.

The UN Children's Fund, still known as UNICEF, is directing the IYC. Estefania Aldaba-Lim, a widowed mother of six children and a psychologist on leave from her position as secretary of the Department of Social Services in the Philippines, heads the program. A total of 151 nations planned to take part in IYC, and 121 of these had named national IYC commissions by the end of 1978.

The United States National Commission for IYC is headed by aptly named Jean Childs Young, former teacher, mother of four, and wife of UN Ambassador Andrew Young. Congress appropriated no funds for IYC, so all U.S. activities will be financed by local governments or private donors.

A variety of events, ranging from scholarly studies of child abuse to performances by children in the arts, will highlight the worldwide IYC observance. Young people in Poland will give the Order of the Smile, engraved with the motto, "All Children Are Ours," to an adult who has made a major contribution to the well-being of children. The award, an annual event in Poland, will keep to

IYC's theme by honoring an international figure for the first time.

Greece, Yugoslavia, and West Germany devised special programs for children of migrant workers. Spain put a provision in its constitution, promulgated on Dec. 27, 1978, saying, "Children will benefit from the protection stipulated in international agreements intended to protect their rights." Liberia began a Decade of the Liberian Child with IYC. Trinidad and Tobago concentrated on helping handicapped children. Sri Lanka plans to open 50 playgrounds and 50 children's libraries.

In the United States, hundreds of projects are underway. IYC activities are organized like the 1976 Bicentennial events — any group that wishes may participate, following the commission's broad guidelines.

The American Center of Films for Children in Los Angeles will sponsor a nationwide film tour. A National Youth Orchestra is being organized, and the Reading Is Fundamental program will distribute free books to libraries across the land.

Many corporations will participate in IYC. AMF, a sporting-goods manufacturer, will sponsor the U.S. Youth Games in Richmond, Va., in July, with tennis star Arthur Ashe as grand marshal, and Burger King will sponsor a fire-safety program, a physical-fitness program in cooperation with major-league baseball, and a reading-skills improvement program.

To make all programs associated with IYC immediately identifiable as such, Danish artist Erich Jerichau designed the official symbol, a stylized parent and child. The UN planned to put it on IYC commemorative postage stamps. In addition, a special gold coin will be minted. It will feature the likeness of entertainer Danny Kaye, who has volunteered his talents for the benefit of children in all countries for more than 25 years.

According to the latest UN estimate, about one-third of the people in the world will be under age 15 in 1980. The International Year of the Child aims to alert the world to their needs. William N. Oatis

International Year of the Child 1979

IYC symbol

troops, 1,200 civilians, and 360 police for one year extending through the election. The cost was estimated at $25 million per month, the highest in history for a UN operation. The pre-election period would involve a cease-fire, release of political prisoners, and return of political refugees.

The Council established UNTAG on September 29 in a resolution sponsored by all its Western and African members and adopted by a vote of 12 to 0, with Czechoslovakia and Russia abstaining and China not participating. The presumed election date had slipped to April 1979. South Africa withheld its approval and announced that it would hold its own election in Namibia from December 4 to 8, keeping its 1977 promise to the Democratic Turnhalle Alliance (DTA), the local interracial political coalition, to hold an election before 1979.

Top foreign-policy officials of the five Western countries, including U.S. Secretary of State Cyrus R. Vance, talked in Pretoria from October 16 to 18 with South Africa's Prime Minister Pieter Willem Botha. South Africa did not give up the December election but, in a statement issued by all six countries on October 19, downgraded it to "an internal process to elect leaders" and offered to start talks immediately with the UN on a later, UN-supervised election. The Africans were skeptical, however. On November 13, the Security Council called on South Africa to cancel the December election and warned that it would impose sanctions if South Africa did not cooperate in a UN-supervised election in Namibia. The vote was 10 to 0, with the five Western members abstaining. Waldheim reported on November 25 that South Africa would hold the December election but was willing to discuss a later, UN-supervised election. The December voting gave the DTA 41 of 50 assembly seats. South Africa consulted the Assembly and on December 22 asked Waldheim to send Ahtisaari back to settle all outstanding issues with Steyn in January so a UN-supervised election could be held by the end of September 1979. See NAMIBIA; SOUTH AFRICA.

In Rhodesia. The Council adopted a resolution on March 14 against the March 3 formation of a new biracial Rhodesian government. The vote was 10 to 0, with the Western five abstaining. The 49-nation African group had asked for the debate, afraid the new arrangement was a screen for continuing the white-minority rule that the Council's 12-year-old economic sanctions were aimed at eradicating.

Rhodesian troops entered Zambia on March 5 and 6 to attack bases they claimed were used for guerrilla raids on Rhodesia. On a Zambian complaint, the Council on March 17 unanimously condemned Rhodesia's attack.

After 27 United States senators invited Rhodesia's Prime Minister Ian D. Smith to the United States, the U.S. government admitted him. This violated UN sanctions against issuing visas to persons carry-

Some 200 French paratroopers march from Beirut airport after arriving in Lebanon on March 23 to serve in United Nations peacekeeping force.

ing Rhodesian passports, and the Council on October 10 adopted an Asian-African resolution saying the U.S. actions violated the sanctions against Rhodesia, but expressing hope that the United States would exert its influence to get "genuine majority rule" there. The vote was 11 to 0, with Canada, Great Britain, the United States, and West Germany abstaining but France voting "yes." While Smith and Ndabaningi Sithole, a black leader on the Rhodesian executive council, were in Washington, D.C., Rhodesian troops entered Zambia and Mozambique to attack bases of the Patriotic Front Rhodesian guerrilla alliance. United States and British officials met with Smith and Sithole in Washington on October 20 and said the two expressed readiness to attend a conference with the Patriotic Front. But the Patriotic Front, angry over the raids, withdrew its consent to an all-party conference. See RHODESIA.

Special Sessions. The UN General Assembly devoted 51 days to three special sessions, more than in any other year. The eighth special session in the Assembly's history, held on April 20 and 21, adopted a resolution to finance the new UN force in Lebanon; the ninth, April 24 through May 3, urged the Security Council to impose new sanctions to get South Africa out of Namibia; and the 10th, May 23 through June 30, agreed on a disarmament program, including a reorganization of the Geneva disarmament negotiating committee that ended France's 17-year boycott of that committee.

The Regular Session of the General Assembly began on September 19. Indalecio Lievano Aguirre of Colombia was elected president. The Assembly raised UN membership to 151 by admitting two former British territories – the Solomon Islands on September 19 and the Caribbean island of Dominica on December 18. It recessed on December 21 after agreeing to resume briefly on Jan. 15, 1979.

The Turkish Cypriots had given Waldheim proposals on April 13 for the constitution of a federal republic of Cyprus and the territories of separate Greek and Turkish Cypriot states. But the Greek Cypriots said the proposals were not worth discussing and refused to resume suspended intercommunal talks. The General Assembly on November 9 adopted a resolution by nonaligned countries calling for new intercommunal talks "on constructive proposals" and asked the Security Council to fix a schedule to carry out its Cyprus resolutions. The Council passed a unanimous resolution on November 27 setting a May 30, 1979, deadline for the withdrawal of Turkish troops from the island and resumption of intercommunal talks "on an agreed basis." The Turkish Cypriots rejected the resolution. The Greek Cypriots running Cyprus' government said their first object was to get the Turkish troops out.

The Assembly on November 10 unanimously approved a decision of the Committee on the Peaceful Uses of Outer Space to have an expert group study how to avoid accidents involving nuclear power sources on spacecraft. Canada made the proposal after a Russian satellite had fallen, scattering radioactive material over northern Canada, on January 24.

UN Conferences. Twelve Western countries walked out of a 13-day World Conference to Combat Racial Discrimination the night before the conference ended in Geneva, Switzerland, on August 26. They were protesting proposals to condemn relations between "the Zionist state of Israel and the racist regime of South Africa" and to applaud the Palestinians' "struggle for liberty and against racial discrimination." The 12 were Australia, Belgium, Canada, Denmark, France, Great Britain, Ireland, Italy, Luxembourg, the Netherlands, New Zealand, and West Germany. The United States and Israel boycotted the conference, which split 88 to 4 in adopting documents that included the protested passages. Austria, Finland, Sweden, and Switzerland voted against them.

The five-week 20th General Conference of the UN Educational, Scientific, and Cultural Organization (UNESCO) on November 22 unanimously adopted a compromise declaration on world news coverage. UNESCO Director-General Amadou-Mahtar M'Bow of Senegal presented the declaration as a softly worded substitute for an earlier draft calling for government control of the press. To meet Western concerns, the declaration advocated "freedom of opinion, expression, and information." To meet Third World wishes, it favored provision of "adequate conditions and resources" for expansion of mass media in developing countries and "more balanced dissemination of information."

The UN Law of the Sea Conference held its seventh session in Geneva from March 28 to May 19 and in New York City from August 21 to September 15 but failed to draft a treaty. It scheduled an eighth session for March 19 to April 27, 1979, in Geneva.

Russian Defector. Undersecretary-General for Political and Security Affairs Arkady N. Shevchenko, the highest-ranking Russian on the UN staff, resigned on April 25, saying he intended to stay in the United States. He cited serious political differences with the Soviet government as his reason for defecting. The UN and Shevchenko arranged a mutually satisfactory separation; he received more than $76,000 in severance pay and other benefits, including a pension.

He and his family had been scheduled to fly to Moscow on April 9. However, he disappeared from April 6 until April 10, when he renounced his Russian citizenship. Russia charged on April 11 that U.S. intelligence agents were holding him under duress.   William N. Oatis

In WORLD BOOK, see UNITED NATIONS.

UNITED STATES, GOVERNMENT OF THE. The danger of a national energy crisis was overshadowed in 1978 by inflation, a record trade deficit, a seriously unstable dollar, and a taxpayers' revolt. While struggling to slow inflation and stabilize the dollar, President Jimmy Carter chalked up two major achievements in foreign affairs with the signing of the Panama Canal treaties in June and the preliminary Middle East peace agreement in September. And on December 15, he announced that the United States and China would establish diplomatic relations on Jan. 1, 1979. See CHINA; MIDDLE EAST; PANAMA; PRESIDENT OF THE UNITED STATES.

Continuing prosperity and rising personal incomes did not appease Americans tired of higher taxes and irritated by the shrinking value of their paychecks. In a televised speech on October 24, President Carter outlined voluntary ceilings on wages and prices and pledged that his Administration would pare down administrative costs.

On November 1, the President announced a series of steps to steady the dollar. The Federal Reserve Board raised its discount rate to 9.5 per cent and increased reserve requirements for member banks by $3 billion to tighten credit; a $10-billion issue of U.S. securities was made available to buy up dollars in foreign markets if necessary; and, in December, the Department of the Treasury increased its monthly sale of gold from $300 million to $1.5 billion.

Foreign Policy. President Carter and Panamanian leader Omar Torrijos Herrera on June 16 signed two Panama Canal treaties that will turn over control of the canal to Panama on the last day of 1999 and ensure its neutrality. The Senate had ratified the treaties on March 16 and April 18.

After an intense, secluded meeting with Israel's Prime·Minister Menachem Begin and President Anwar al-Sadat of Egypt at Camp David in Maryland, President Carter announced on September 17 that the two leaders had agreed to establish a "framework" for peace in the Middle East.

Federal Agencies. Social Security System trustees announced on May 16 that the Social Security tax increase approved by Congress in 1977 has "restored fiscal soundness to the system until 2030."

On January 13, Joseph A. Califano, Jr., secretary of the Department of Health, Education, and Welfare (HEW), issued regulations barring discrimination against the handicapped in government agencies and all projects using federal funds (see HANDICAPPED). Califano announced on January 26 that federal funds may be used to pay for abortions only in cases of rape or incest and only if the crime is reported to law enforcement officers or a public health agency within 60 days.

Revelations of widespread corruption rocked the General Services Administration (GSA), the federal government's purchasing agency. Investigators estimated that fraud and mismanagement were costing taxpayers $66 million annually. Eighteen persons were indicted by a federal grand jury on September 29 on a charge of conspiracy to defraud the United States.

On July 10, Patricia R. Harris, secretary of the Department of Housing and Urban Development (HUD), declared that HUD and the Labor, Justice, and Interior departments plan to pool $209 million to rehabilitate recreation facilities and security and create jobs in public-housing projects.

The Postal Service raised the postage rate for first-class mail to 15 cents per ounce (28.3 grams) on May 29. Other postal rates were also raised.

Legislative Branch. President Carter vetoed a $37-billion defense bill on August 7 and a $10.2-billion public-works appropriation bill on October 5 on the grounds that both were inflationary. Congress approved an energy act and a tax-reform act, both diluted versions of programs sponsored by the Administration. The President abandoned efforts to persuade Congress to act on rising hospital costs, welfare reform, and election reform. See ENERGY; TAXATION.

In its second session, the 95th Congress passed an Age Discrimination in Employment Act raising the mandatory retirement age for most employees to 70 (see OLD AGE); extended the ratification period for the Equal Rights Amendment (ERA) to 1982; and passed and sent to the states a constitutional amend-

Major Agencies and Bureaus of the U.S. Government*

Executive Office of the President
President, Jimmy Carter

Vice-President, Walter F. Mondale
Presidential Press Secretary, Jody Powell
Central Intelligence Agency—Stansfield Turner, Director
Council of Economic Advisers—Charles L. Schultze, Chairman
Council on Environmental Quality—Charles H. Warren, Chairman
Council on Wage and Price Stability—Barry P. Bosworth, Director
Domestic Policy Staff—Stuart E. Eizenstat, Executive Director
Office of Management and Budget—James T. McIntyre, Jr., Director
Office of Science and Technology Policy—Frank Press, Director

State Department
Secretary of State, Cyrus R. Vance

Agency for International Development—John J. Gilligan, Administrator
U.S. Representative to the United Nations—Andrew Young

Department of the Treasury
Secretary of the Treasury, W. Michael Blumenthal

Bureau of Alcohol, Tobacco, and Firearms—(vacant)
Bureau of Engraving and Printing—Seymour Berry, Director
Bureau of the Mint—Stella B. Hackel, Director
Comptroller of the Currency—John G. Heimann
Internal Revenue Service—Jerome Kurtz, Commissioner
Treasurer of the United States—Azie T. Morton
U.S. Customs Service—Robert E. Chasen, Commissioner
U.S. Secret Service—H. Stuart Knight, Director

Department of Defense
Secretary of Defense, Harold Brown

Joint Chiefs of Staff—General David C. Jones, Chairman
Secretary of the Air Force—John Stetson
Secretary of the Army—Clifford L. Alexander, Jr.
Secretary of the Navy—W. Graham Claytor, Jr.

Department of Justice
Attorney General, Griffin B. Bell

Bureau of Prisons—Norman A. Carlson, Director
Drug Enforcement Administration—Peter Bensinger, Administrator
Federal Bureau of Investigation—William H. Webster, Director
Immigration and Naturalization Service—Leonel J. Castillo, Commissioner
Law Enforcement Assistance Administration—(vacant)
Solicitor General—Wade H. McCree, Jr.

Department of the Interior
Secretary of the Interior, Cecil D. Andrus

Bureau of Indian Affairs—Forrest J. Gerard, Commissioner
Bureau of Land Management—W. Frank Gregg, Director
Bureau of Mines—Roger A. Markle, Director
Bureau of Reclamation—R. Keith Higginson, Commissioner
Geological Survey—William Menard, Director
National Park Service—William J. Whalen, Director
Office of Territorial Affairs—Ruth Van Cleve, Director
U.S. Fish and Wildlife Service—Lynn A. Greenwalt, Director

Department of Agriculture
Secretary of Agriculture, Bob Bergland

Agricultural Economics—Howard W. Hjort, Director
Agricultural Marketing Service—Barbara Lindemann Schlei, Administrator
Agricultural Stabilization and Conservation Service—Ray V. Fitzgerald, Administrator
Farmers Home Administration—Gordon Cavanaugh, Administrator
Federal Crop Insurance Corporation—James D. Deal, Manager
Food and Consumer Services—Carol Tucker Foreman, Administrator
Forest Service—John R. McGuire, Chief

*As of Jan 1, 1979. † nominated but not yet confirmed

Rural Electrification Administration—Robert W. Feragen, Administrator

Soil Conservation Service—Ronello M. Davis, Administrator

Department of Commerce
Secretary of Commerce, Juanita M. Kreps

Bureau of the Census—Manuel D. Plotkin, Director

National Bureau of Standards—Ernest Ambler, Director

National Fire Prevention and Control Administration—Howard D. Tipton, Administrator

National Oceanic and Atmospheric Administration—Richard A. Frank, Administrator

Office of Minority Business Enterprise—Randolph T. Blackwell, Director

Patent and Trademark Office—Donald W. Banner, Commissioner

Department of Labor
Secretary of Labor, F. Ray Marshall

Bureau of Labor Statistics—(vacant)

Employment and Training Administration—Ernest G. Green, Administrator

Employment Standards Administration—Donald E. Elisburg, Administrator

Labor-Management Services Administration—(vacant)

Mine Safety and Health Administration—Robert B. Lagather, Administrator

Occupational Safety and Health Administration—Eula Bingham, Administrator

Women's Bureau—Alexis M. Herman, Director

Department of Health, Education, and Welfare
Secretary of Health, Education, and Welfare, Joseph A. Califano, Jr.

Administration on Aging—Robert C. Benedict, Commissioner

Alcohol, Drug Abuse, and Mental Health Administration—Gerald L. Klerman, Administrator

Center for Disease Control—William H. Foege, Director

Food and Drug Administration—Donald Kennedy, Commissioner

Health Care Financing Administration—(vacant)

Health Resources Administration—Henry A. Foley, Administrator

Health Services Administration—George Lythcott, Administrator

National Institute of Education—Patricia A. Graham, Director

National Institutes of Health—Donald S. Fredrickson, Director

Office of Consumer Affairs—Esther Peterson, Director

Office of Education—Ernest L. Boyer, Commissioner

Public Health Service—Julius B. Richmond, Administrator

Rehabilitation Services Administration—Robert R. Humphreys, Commissioner

Social Security Administration—Stanford G. Ross, Commissioner

Department of Housing and Urban Development
Secretary of Housing and Urban Development, Patricia Roberts Harris

Community Planning and Development—Robert C. Embry, Administrator

Federal Disaster Assistance Administration—William H. Wilcox, Administrator

Federal Housing Commissioner—Lawrence B. Simons

Federal Insurance Administration—Gloria M. Jimenez, Administrator

Government National Mortgage Association—John H. Dalton, President

Department of Transportation
Secretary of Transportation, Brock Adams

Federal Aviation Administration—Langhorne M. Bond, Administrator

Federal Highway Administration—Karl S. Bowers, Administrator

Federal Railroad Administration—John M. Sullivan, Administrator

National Highway Traffic Safety Administration—Joan B. Claybrook, Administrator

U.S. Coast Guard—Admiral John B. Hayes, Commandant

Urban Mass Transportation Administration—Richard S. Page, Administrator

Department of Energy
Secretary of Energy, James R. Schlesinger

Economic Regulatory Administration—David J. Bardin, Administrator

Energy Information Administration—Lincoln E. Moses, Administrator

Federal Energy Regulatory Commission—Charles B. Curtis, Chairman

Office of Energy Research—John M. Deutch, Director

Congressional Officials
President of the Senate pro tempore—Warren G. Magnuson

Speaker of the House—Thomas P. O'Neill, Jr.

Architect of the Capitol—George M. White

Comptroller General of the U.S.—Elmer B. Staats

Congressional Budget Office—Alice M. Rivlin, Director

Librarian of Congress—Daniel J. Boorstin

Office of Technology Assessment—Russell W. Peterson, Director

Public Printer of the U.S.—John J. Boyle

Independent Agencies
ACTION—Samuel W. Brown, Jr., Director

Civil Aeronautics Board—Marvin S. Cohen,† Chairman

Civil Service Commission—Alan K. Campbell, Chairman

Commodity Futures Trading Commission—(vacant)

Community Services Administration—Graciela Olivarez, Director

Consumer Product Safety Commission—Susan B. King, Chairman

Environmental Protection Agency—Douglas M. Costle, Administrator

Equal Employment Opportunity Commission—Eleanor Holmes Norton, Chair

Export-Import Bank—John L. Moore, President

Farm Credit Administration—Donald E. Wilkinson, Governor

Federal Communications Commission—Charles D. Ferris, Chairman

Federal Deposit Insurance Corporation—Irving Sprague,† Chairman

Federal Election Commission—Joan D. Aikens, Chairman

Federal Home Loan Bank Board—Robert H. McKinney, Chairman

Federal Maritime Commission—Richard J. Daschbach, Chairman

Federal Mediation and Conciliation Service—Wayne L. Horvitz, Director

Federal Reserve System—G. William Miller, Board of Governors Chairman

Federal Trade Commission—Michael Pertschuk, Chairman

General Services Administration—Jay Solomon, Administrator

International Communication Agency—John E. Reinhardt, Director

Interstate Commerce Commission—A. Daniel O'Neal, Chairman

National Aeronautics and Space Administration—Robert A. Frosch, Administrator

National Credit Union Administration—Lawrence Connell, Jr., Administrator

National Endowment for the Arts—Livingston L. Biddle, Chairman

National Endowment for the Humanities—Joseph D. Duffey, Chairman

National Labor Relations Board—John H. Fanning, Chairman

National Mediation Board—George S. Ives, Chairman

National Railroad Passenger Corporation (AMTRAK)—Alan S. Boyd, President

National Science Foundation—Richard C. Atkinson, Director

National Transportation Safety Board—James B. King, Chairman

Nuclear Regulatory Commission—Joseph M. Hendrie, Chairman

Occupational Safety and Health Review Commission—Timothy F. Cleary, Chairman

Overseas Private Investment Corporation—J. Bruce Llewellyn, President

Securities and Exchange Commission—Harold M. Williams, Chairman

Small Business Administration—A. Vernon Weaver, Jr., Administrator

Smithsonian Institution—S. Dillon Ripley, Secretary

Tennessee Valley Authority—S. David Freeman, Chairman

U.S. Arms Control and Disarmament Agency—George M. Seignious,† Director

U.S. Commission on Civil Rights—Arthur S. Flemming, Chairman

U.S. International Trade Commission—Daniel Minchew, Chairman

U.S. Metric Board—Louis F. Polk, Chairman

U.S. Postal Service—William F. Bolger, Postmaster General

Veterans Administration—Max Cleland, Administrator

Federal Spending and Revenue Receipts

Estimated U.S. Budget for Fiscal 1978*

	Billions of dollars
National defense	117.8
International affairs†	7.7
Science and space research	5.1
Natural resources, environment, energy	21.8
Agriculture	5.4
Commerce and transportation	20.4
Community and regional development	8.7
Education, employment, social services	30.4
Health	50.0
Income security	160.0
Veterans benefits and services	19.3
Law enforcement and justice	4.2
General government	4.3
Revenue sharing and federal aid	9.6
Interest	49.0
Allowances	2.8
Undistributed funds	−16.0
Total	500.2

*Oct. 1, 1978, to Sept. 30, 1979; all
previous years, except 1977 and 1978, July 1 to June 30

†Includes foreign aid.

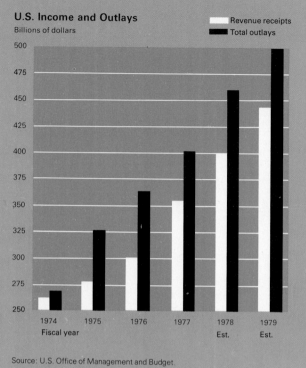

U.S. Income and Outlays
Billions of dollars

Revenue receipts
Total outlays

1974   1975   1976   1977   1978 Est.   1979 Est.
Fiscal year

Source: U.S. Office of Management and Budget.

ment giving residents of the District of Columbia voting representation in the House of Representatives and the Senate. See CONSTITUTION OF THE UNITED STATES.

Congress passed a modified version of the Humphrey-Hawkins "full employment" act, deregulated airline fares and routes, extended federal aid to education, authorized funds for highway construction and mass-transit facilities, and authorized $1.2 billion for parks and conservation programs. See CONGRESS OF THE UNITED STATES.

The Supreme Court of the United States issued a far-reaching decision on reverse discrimination on June 28. In *Regents of the University of California v. Bakke,* the high court ruled that the school's use of racial quotas to encourage nonwhite applicants violated Title VI of the Civil Rights Act of 1964, which forbids discrimination on racial grounds at any educational institution accepting federal funds. See SUPREME COURT OF THE UNITED STATES (Close-Up).

In a March 28 decision, the court ruled that the concept of judicial immunity protects a judge from a damage suit even in the event of a "grave procedural error." The case involved the sterilization of a 15-year-old girl in Indiana.

On April 25, the court ruled that an employer who charged women employees more than men to participate in a pension plan was guilty of illegal sex discrimination. On June 15, it upheld a lower court ruling that barred the completion of the Tellico Dam on the Little Tennessee River because the dam would endanger the survival of tiny snail darter fish, protected under the Endangered Species Act of 1973.

First Amendment rights were the subject of several 1978 rulings. On May 1, it ruled in *The Landmark Communication Company v. Virginia* that a state may not levy criminal sanctions against a newspaper carrying accurate reports of confidential disciplinary procedures against a judge. In a case involving media access to part of a California prison, the court ruled on June 26 that the press has no greater constitutional right than that granted to the general public to gain access to jails or other governmental institutions.

On November 27, the court said it would not review a sentence of the New Jersey Supreme Court against reporter Myron Farber of *The New York Times* who was jailed for contempt of court when he refused to surrender his confidential notes on a murder investigation. Farber was released after the defendant was acquitted. See COURTS AND LAWS; NEWSPAPER.   Carol L. Thompson

In WORLD BOOK, see UNITED STATES, GOVERNMENT OF THE.

UNITED STATES CONSTITUTION. See CONSTITUTION OF THE UNITED STATES.

UNSER, AL (1939-   ), youngest member of a famous auto-racing family, in 1978 became the first driver to win the United States Auto Club (USAC) Triple Crown. Unser won the Indianapolis 500-mile race for the third time on May 28. He also won the Schaefer 500-mile race at Mount Pocono, Pa., on June 25 and the California 500 at Ontario, Calif., on September 3, earning a record $591,599 during the year. See AUTOMOBILE RACING.

The 39-year-old Unser averaged 161.36 miles per hour (mph) or 259.68 kilometers per hour (kph) in finishing about 8 seconds ahead of Tom Sneva, the second-place finisher at Indianapolis. Unser's time was the second fastest in Indianapolis history. Mark Donohue averaged 162.962 mph (262.26 kph) in winning that race in 1972. Unser, whose earlier Indianapolis victories came in 1970 and 1971, earned $250,364 with his 1978 victory. He received $89,296 for his Schaefer victory, where he averaged 142.26 mph (228.95 kph). At Ontario, Unser's car was among only five to finish in a 31-car field. Unser averaged 145.16 mph (233.61 kph) there and won $73,400. He had also won the Schaefer 500 in 1976 and the California 500 in 1977.

Al Unser was born in Albuquerque, N. Mex., on May 29, 1939, and followed his brother Bobby into automobile racing. Bobby won the Indianapolis 500 in 1968 and 1975.   Joseph P. Spohn

UPPER VOLTA. See AFRICA.

URUGUAY. General Gregorio Alvarez became commander in chief of the army in February 1978, replacing General Julio Cesar Vadora, who had retired. The change, which was not announced until March 2, made Alvarez in effect the ruler of the country, since President Aparicio Mendez Manfredini is regarded as a figurehead who does the bidding of the armed forces.

General Alvarez came under attack by military hard-liners after he said in a speech on March 27 that civilian political leaders should be consulted about the nation's political reorganization. Military and police officers received an underground newsletter in April that accused Alvarez and officers associated with him of corruption and abuse of power. The attack was resumed in the next issue of the newsletter, mailed in June. General Amaury Prantl, chief of military intelligence, reportedly assumed full responsibility for the newsletter. He was said to be the leader of the military hard-liners who opposed Alvarez.

Prantl was fired on June 25 and placed under house arrest. Several of his junior officers reportedly were arrested or transferred.

In an apparent effort to counter speculation about a serious split within their ranks, the armed forces issued a communiqué on June 26 stressing their "full agreement on ideas, efforts, and feelings" and their determination to "reach the established goals, in order to achieve the moral and material recovery of the nation."

Outside Criticism. The government continued to come under attack from abroad for its alleged human rights abuses. On March 14, it was reported that the Inter-American Commission on Human Rights, an agency of the Organization of American States, had documented extensive human rights violations by the police and military. It claimed that 25 prisoners had been killed in Uruguay in recent years. Amnesty International appealed to President Mendez on May 3 to investigate charges that political prisoners were being tortured. The organization published details of 12 cases in which prisoners allegedly had died of torture in the past two years.

Soaring Inflation. For the second year in a row, consumer prices soared more than 50 per cent. Despite frequent general wage increases granted by the government during the year, real wages were said to have fallen more than 30 per cent below 1968 levels, and consumption was estimated to be 11.5 per cent less per person. The newspaper *El Día* claimed the drop in consumption was much more dramatic among low-income groups.   Everett G. Martin

See also LATIN AMERICA (Facts in Brief Table). In WORLD BOOK, see URUGUAY.

UTAH. See STATE GOVERNMENT.

UTILITIES. See COMMUNICATIONS; ENERGY; PETROLEUM AND GAS.

VANDEN BOEYNANTS, PAUL (1919-   ), began his second term as prime minister of Belgium on Oct. 20, 1978, succeeding Leo Tindemans, a fellow member of the Social Christian Party (PSC). Vanden Boeynants had been deputy prime minister since 1977 and minister of defense since 1972. He retained Tindemans' Cabinet. After indecisive general elections, he resigned on December 18, but was asked to stay in office until a new government was formed. See BELGIUM.

The prime minister was born in Vorst, a small town near Brussels, on May 5, 1919. He attended the College of St. Michel, a Jesuit secondary school, where he learned to speak French in addition to his native Flemish. After finishing school, he became a sausage maker and exporter.

He became interested in politics and was elected to parliament in 1949, and the Brussels Town Council made him one of its six aldermen in 1953. He served in the Cabinet as minister for the middle classes from 1958 to 1961, and he was elected president of the PSC in 1961.

Vanden Boeynants first became prime minister in 1966, succeeding Pierre Harmel. He resigned in 1968 after failing to resolve a language dispute between the Dutch-speaking Flemish and French-speaking Walloon members of the PSC.

Vanden Boeynants married Lucienne Deurinck in 1942, and they have three children.   Jay Myers

VENEZUELA. After a long and costly campaign, Luis Herrera Campins was elected president on Dec. 3, 1978, succeeding Carlos Andres Perez. Herrera received 88 per cent of the vote.

The presidential campaign opened officially on April 1, but Luis Pinerua Ordaz of the ruling Democratic Action Party (AD) and Herrera of the Social Christian Party (Copei) had been campaigning unofficially since January.

The Major Issues were waste and corruption in the Perez government's handling of Venezuela's sudden wealth that resulted from sharp increases in oil prices. Oil accounts for 95 per cent of the country's export income. Although Pinerua represented the AD party, he divorced himself from the Perez government. He could do this because Perez had alienated his followers by appointing Independents to his Cabinet and not consulting his party regularly during his term. In general there was little difference between the AD and other candidates on the issues.

Venezuela's oil riches had touched off a huge public and private spending binge that caused budgetary as well as trade deficits. This development worried many Venezuelans, who tend to be conservatives in fiscal matters. Despite Perez' announced intention of conserving the oil income for development purposes, imports soared 30 per cent, giving the country its first trade deficit in a decade. Many of the imports were capital goods for development, but vast quantities of luxury items were also imported. The country's harbors were clogged with incoming ships that took weeks to unload. Perez acted on April 6 to halt the inflow by banning the import of 500 consumer items.

Many Problems facing the government arose from trying to accelerate development beyond the ability of the country's small pool of technicians to handle it. A drop in oil production to about 2 million barrels per day (bpd) aggravated the situation because the fiscal budget had been based on the production of 2.2 million bpd. Competition in the United States market by Alaskan, Mexican, and Middle East oil was blamed for the drop.

In June, government security forces claimed that they had successfully contained a threat by left wing guerrillas in the eastern state of Anzoátegui. At least one soldier had been killed in clashes with the insurgents in late April. On June 8, security forces reported they had dismantled seven guerrilla bases and confiscated weapons.   Everett G. Martin

See also LATIN AMERICA (Facts in Brief Table). In WORLD BOOK, see VENEZUELA.

VERMONT. See STATE GOVERNMENT.

VETERANS. See COMMUNITY ORGANIZATIONS.

VICE-PRESIDENT OF THE UNITED STATES. See MONDALE, WALTER F.

VIETNAM followed a turbulent course in 1978. Conflict increased with neighboring Cambodia and China, while internal economic problems grew and the flow of refugees leaving the country increased. Clashes between the Vietnamese and Cambodian Communists that had started at least as early as 1970 became open warfare beginning in November 1977. Each side accused the other of responsibility for the fighting, and each refused the other's truce terms. Using captured United States arms and newly supplied Russian weapons, Vietnam seized most of Cambodia in early January 1979. See CAMBODIA.

Rift with China. The government announced on March 23 that private businesses in Saigon would be nationalized. This was a major blow to ethnic Chinese there. Many were in business, and some families had lived in Vietnam for more than 200 years. This announcement, combined with the government's decision to move middle-class residents out of the southern cities, caused many of Vietnam's 1 million Chinese to flee. Their flight across the border to China resulted in clashes there and soured relations with Peking. Relations had already been strained by disputes over South China Sea islands and by Hanoi's increasingly pro-Russian line.

China told Vietnam on May 12 that it was ending all economic aid and withdrawing its 800 technical advisers. Money allocated for future aid would be used to help Chinese refugees from Vietnam, Peking

President Jimmy Carter's March visit to Latin America includes a warm reunion with Venezuela's President Carlos Andres Perez.

said. China also reported that it had given Vietnam more than $18 billion in aid over an unspecified period. It accused Vietnam of deliberately expelling Chinese. Hanoi accused Peking of luring them out in order to cause trouble for Vietnam.

Ties to Moscow. Efforts to obtain foreign investments met with little success, and drought, typhoons, and devastating floods hurt the agriculture-based economy. So Vietnam joined the Moscow-led Council for Mutual Economic Assistance on June 29, tying its economy to the Russian bloc.

The turn to Moscow was culminated on November 3 with the signing of a treaty of friendship and cooperation. In addition, economic-aid agreements included Russian replacement for some Chinese aid.

Nationalization of private businesses was part of a tightening of controls because of bad crops and economic mismanagement. A number of Buddhist priests and lay leaders who had opposed the pre-Communist regime as dictatorial were imprisoned by the Communist government.

United States-Vietnamese relations deteriorated after the May 19 conviction of two men caught spying for Vietnam in Alexandria, Va., but showed some improvement until the Russian treaty raised new doubts in the United States.   Henry S. Bradsher

See also ASIA (Facts in Brief Table). In WORLD BOOK, see VIETNAM.

VIRGINIA. See STATE GOVERNMENT.

VISUAL ARTS. The opening of the East Building of the National Gallery of Art in Washington, D.C., on June 1, 1978, was symbolic of the growing government involvement in the arts and museums. A gift of the Andrew W. Mellon Foundation, the $94-million structure consists of exhibition areas and a Center for the Advanced Study of the Visual Arts. To celebrate the opening, the National Gallery of Art produced a cluster of exhibitions, capped by the 700-item loan show "The Splendor of Dresden: Five Centuries of Collecting."

Federal support to United States museums has risen from $5.7 million in 1973 to $30 million in fiscal 1979. However, the tax revolt that started in the United States with Proposition 13 in California troubled the art world with its implications of funding restrictions. The Detroit Institute of Arts furnished a possible reaction to economic instability. For the first time in its 93-year history, the institute purchased a work with funds from a $350,000 public subscription drive – a 1953 cut-paper collage, *The Wild Poppies,* by Henri Matisse.

Archaeological Shows. Public interest generated by the tour of the "Treasures of Tutankhamon" prompted several other important archaeological exhibitions. "Pompeii A.D. 79" was organized by the Boston Museum of Fine Arts. Asia House Gallery in New York City organized both "The Royal Hunt: Art of the Sassanian Empire," an exhibition of

Iranian art before Islam, and "The Ideal Image: Gupta Sculptural Tradition," Indian religious art.

Important Acquisitions. The Temple of Dendur, a first-century B.C. Egyptian temple, went on exhibition in September at New York City's Metropolitan Museum of Art in the largest enclosed museum space in the world. The building was given to the American people in 1967 by the Egyptian government in thanks for U.S. help in saving the Abu Simbel Temples from inundation by the Aswan High Dam. See MUSEUM.

The most dramatic museum acquisition was similarly ancient. The J. Paul Getty Museum in Malibu, Calif., bought a Greek bronze sculpture in almost perfect condition attributed to the great fourth-century B.C. sculptor, Lysippus. The $4-million sale was contingent upon approval by Italy, which may still declare the work an illegal export.

Other important acquisitions included 900 original paintings for *Time* magazine covers donated to the National Collection of Fine Arts in Washington, D.C.; the bequest by John D. Rockefeller III of his American art collection to the Fine Arts Museums of San Francisco; the gift of a large group of his works by the painter Ivan Albright to the Art Institute of Chicago; and the joint purchase by the Cleveland Museum of Art and a Swiss museum of the two Kingston Tureens, made in France in 1735 and called "the most important works in silver made in Europe since the Renaissance." In Mexico City, Mexico, the painter Rufino Tamayo donated a large collection of recent art to form the Museum of International Modern Art.

Great Auctions in 1978 included the most valuable private collection ever to go on the block, that of the late Swiss industrialist Robert von Hirsch. During the weeklong London auction, $38 million was paid for works that Von Hirsch did not wish to donate to museums. He said he wanted them to continue to give pleasure to private individuals as they had to him.

In the United States, *The Jolly Flatboatsman,* a mid-19th century painting by George Caleb Bingham, became the highest-priced American work ever auctioned. It brought $980,000. The McDonaugh collection of American art brought $1.8 million and 28 other record prices. The great auction houses of New York City reported sales-volume gains of about 50 per cent.

Three of the 48 Gutenberg Bibles still in existence were sold during 1978, each for about $2 million. The two-volume, mid-15th-century Bibles, named for their German printer, are considered to be among the most beautiful books ever made.

Photography Exhibitions throughout the United States emphasized the art's continuing climb in both public and museum esteem. The well-known fashion photographer Richard Avedon was honored by a show at the Metropolitan Museum of Art in New

York City. Lesser-known avant-gardist Robert Heinecken, who works with manipulated images, was seen in a traveling exhibition organized by the International Museum of Photography at the George Eastman House in Rochester, N.Y. Group exhibitions included both current surveys, such as "Mirrors and Windows: American Photography Since 1960," at the Museum of Modern Art in New York City, and the Art Institute of Chicago's "André Jammes Collection: The First 100 Years of Photography."

Exhibits of 19th-Century Art included two exhibits that focused on impressionism. "Frederick Bazille and Early Impressionism," at the Art Institute of Chicago, presented the artist along with his contemporaries, and the Metropolitan and St. Louis museums of art organized "Monet at Giverny 1883-1926," work done at Monet's estate outside Paris. Other 19th-century exhibitions included two large European displays. In London, the Tate Gallery held a comprehensive William Blake show, while the Royal Academy of Art continued the current interest in narrative academic art with "Great Victorian Pictures." The decorative arts of that era in France were seen at the Metropolitan Museum of Art in "The Arts Under Napoleon," and at the Philadelphia Museum of Art's "The Second Empire" exhibition.

Important survey displays of American art included "Munich and American Realism in the Nineteenth Century," illustrating German influence then, at the Crocker Art Gallery in Sacramento, Calif.; and New York City's Whitney Museum of American Art's two shows – "Abstract Expressionism: The Formative Years" and "Synchronism and American Color Abstraction 1910-1926."

Contemporary American artists were shown in large museum exhibitions, again pointing to the wide spectrum of style taken for granted in the visual arts. The super-realist sculpture of Duane Hanson attracted record crowds to the Whitney Museum. The Fort Worth Art Museum in Texas presented "Stella Since 1970," recent work of the premier U.S. abstract painter, Frank Stella. Similarly abstract and reductive was another exhibition, "Carl Andre: Sculpture 1959-1977," organized by the Laguna Gloria Art Museum, of Austin, Tex. In New York City, the Guggenheim Museum presented a retrospective display of Mark Rothko's poetic color; the Whitney Museum organized shows of both the well-known and witty Saul Steinberg and the lesser-known, but equally witty, H. C. Westermann. The Walker Art Center in Minneapolis, Minn., presented "Noguchi's Imaginary Landscapes," the environmental sculpture of the important Japanese-American artist Isamu Noguchi.

Branchini Madonna by the Italian painter Giovanni di Paolo, dated 1427, sells for almost $1 million at an auction in London in June.

European Modernist Art was seen in two Midwestern exhibitions. Both Chicago's Museum of Contemporary Art and the Indiana University Art Museum in Bloomington organized exhibitions of German and Austrian Expressionism. Similarly indicative of the fine and often overlooked exhibitions mounted at university museums was "El Quatre Gats: Art in Barcelona Around 1900" at the Princeton University Art Museum in New Jersey. In Buffalo, N.Y., the Albright-Knox Art Gallery staged exhibitions of English artists Bridget Riley, a major op-art practitioner, and Ben Nicholson, a pioneer cubist.

A vestige of avant-garde radicalism – somehow both discredited and yet now entrenched as a permanent aspect of the ongoing traditions of visual art – was seen at the Venice Biennale in Italy. The theme of the 75-year-old international art exhibition "Art and Nature/Nature and Art" brought out displays of real animals, primitive huts, and various types of multimedia and environmental art. For many observers, such "post-modernist" activities point to the current dilemma involved in producing significant art.   Joshua B. Kind

In WORLD BOOK, see ART AND THE ARTS; PAINTING; SCULPTURE.

VITAL STATISTICS. See CENSUS; POPULATION.

WALES. See GREAT BRITAIN.

WASHINGTON. See SEATTLE; STATE GOV'T.

Henry Moore waits as his sculpture is lowered into place outside the East Wing of the National Gallery of Art in Washington, D.C., in late spring.

WASHINGTON, D.C. A constitutional amendment that would give the District of Columbia voting representation in the Congress of the United States was approved by the Senate Aug. 22, 1978, and sent to the states for approval. The measure had been approved by the House of Representatives on March 2. It must be ratified by the legislatures of 38 states within seven years to become effective.

The amendment would give the district two U.S. senators and up to two members in the House of Representatives, depending upon the district's population. Currently, the capital is represented in the Congress by one nonvoting member of the House. The amendment would also give the district full voting representation in the electoral college.

A New Mayor. City Councilman Marion S. Barry, Jr., narrowly defeated Mayor Walter E. Washington in the Democratic Party primary on September 12. Washington's campaign was hurt by the indictment of one of his closest aides, Joseph P. Yeldell, former director of the city's Department of Human Resources, on bribery and conspiracy charges. Yeldell was convicted on October 24. Barry went on to defeat Republican candidate Arthur Fletcher in the November 7 general election.

The *Washington Post* reported in late August that the number of demonstrations in the city had increased by 1,500 per cent over the past 10 years, requiring a 400 per cent increase in U.S. Park Police budget for overtime pay. The year's largest demonstration was held on July 9 when an estimated 100,000 persons marched to the capital to urge Congress to extend the deadline for ratification of the Equal Rights Amendment (ERA). About 70,000 demonstrators gathered in the city on January 23 to protest the 1973 Supreme Court of the United States decision legalizing abortion. In other demonstrations, 10,000 persons gathered on April 15 urging the Supreme Court to rule against Allan Bakke's reverse discrimination suit, and 2,000 farmers demanded increased price supports on January 19.

A wildcat transit strike shut down the subway and bus systems in July. The strike started as a mechanics' walkout on July 19 and spread when 4,500 bus drivers and subway motormen refused to cross picket lines. It was settled by arbitration on July 25.

Quality of Life. Government reports released in November indicated that the population of the city had decreased by 7.6 per cent between 1970 and 1976, making Washington the nation's 12th largest city. It had ranked ninth in 1970.

Living costs rose 6.9 per cent in the area during the year ending in May 1978. Median family income in the city was $21,292, well above the $18,026 the Department of Labor estimated as a moderate budget for a family of four.   James M. Banovetz

See CITY. In WORLD BOOK, see WASHINGTON, D.C.

WATER. A battle between President Jimmy Carter and the Congress of the United States over water policy ended on Oct. 5, 1978, when Carter vetoed a $10.2-billion public-works and energy appropriations bill and the House sustained the veto. The bill included funds for six projects Congress agreed to cancel in 1977, when the President threatened to veto a similar bill. The House ignored veto threats and passed the measure produced by a House-Senate conference committee, 319 to 71, on September 14. The Senate followed on September 27 with a vote of 86 to 9.

Congress passed a revised bill on October 15, the last day of the session, eliminating the six projects and 11 others that Carter opposed. The cost of the projects was cut from $1.8 billion to $841 million.

New Water Policy. President Carter's water policy, announced on June 6, called for tougher standards for financing water projects to emphasize conservation and reduce pork-barrel spending. Western governors were pleased with what they called a "limited victory" in eliminating proposals from the policy that they thought would have adverse impacts in their states. They were split on Carter's proposal that the states assume 10 per cent of the costs of new irrigation and hydroelectrical projects and 5 per cent of new flood control projects.

Excess Lands. Secretary of the Interior Cecil D. Andrus urged Congress on April 13 to amend the 1902 Reclamation Act to allow an increase in the size of family farms receiving water from federal irrigation projects subsidized by the taxpayers. Andrus said, however, that those receiving water in excess of acreage limitations should be denied federally subsidized water after five years.

Under the 1902 act, one person can receive the cheap federal irrigation water for up to 160 acres (65 hectares) and a man and wife for 320 acres (130 hectares). Andrus proposed allowing two adults to receive water for 640 acres (260 hectares) of owned land and for up to 920 acres (370 hectares) of owned and leased land. Congress did not act on reforming the 1902 act, and the *de facto* absence of any size limits on farms using federal water is likely to continue for another year.

Drought Ends. United States water supplies increased rapidly early in 1978. The federal government declared on April 16 that the 1976-1977 drought had ended in most parts of the 17 Western states. America's five largest rivers recorded above-normal flows for the sixth straight month in August.

In California, which had suffered one of the most severe droughts in its history, state water experts reported on October 16 that water supplies were excellent. "If water is managed properly, we should not have any problem, regardless of what kind of weather we have this winter," the state Drought-Flood Center said. Federal experts warned, however, that it might take years to replenish supplies of ground water that were used up in the two dry years. See Section Two, COLDER WEATHER AHEAD – UNLESS IT'S WARMER.

The U.S. Department of Commerce warned on June 24 that flash floods have become America's number-one weather-related killer. The agency said that the average annual toll from flash floods in the last 10 years has been 200 lives lost and $1 billion in property damage.

Amazon Pact. The eight countries that share the Amazon River Basin agreed on July 3 to develop the area's resources and protect its environment. Bolivia, Brazil, Colombia, Ecuador, Guyana, Peru, Surinam, and Venezuela signed the Treaty of Amazonian Cooperation, agreeing to cooperate in building roads, to conduct multinational biological research, to exchange information, and to preserve the area's ethnic and archaeological wealth.

Court Decisions. The Supreme Court of the United States ruled on May 1 that a municipal utility may not cut off service for nonpayment of bills until it gives the customer a hearing. The court ruled on May 31 that water was not a valuable mineral resource and could not be used as the basis of a land claim under federal mining law, which states that citizens may file a claim on public land on which they have discovered valuable minerals such as gold and silver.   Andrew L. Newman

See also WEATHER. In WORLD BOOK, see WATER.

WEATHER. Storms and gales battered Europe during the first three months of 1978, and London narrowly escaped serious flooding as the River Thames came within 19 inches (48 centimeters) of overflowing its banks. Unprecedented monsoon rains in Southeast Asia caused widespread flooding that destroyed crops in this rice bowl for 100 million people in October. Severe drought withered southern Australia, and a record heat wave was reported at the South Pole in April.

The winter weather in the Eastern United States was much the same as in 1977 – cold. There was a heavier snowfall in the Midwest, where a series of snowstorms followed by extreme cold made it difficult to keep major thoroughfares open in some areas. The Western States had moderate winter temperatures with moderate to heavy mountain snows. Spring arrived with average to above-average precipitation across much of the Farm Belt. In some regions, such as the Northern Great Plains, the Midwest, the Southwestern Plains, and parts of the South, wet weather delayed spring planting. Even with this delay, yields were high because the summer was not especially severe and the ground was moist.

Colorado Drought. Nolan J. Doesken, Thomas B. McKee, and J. Owen Rhea of the Department of Atmospheric Science at Colorado State University published a detailed report in August that showed the winter of 1976-1977 was one of record-breaking drought in the mountains of Colorado, while the winter of 1977-1978 was one of record snows. Colorado and other Western mountain states depend more on mountain precipitation than on lowland precipitation for drinking and irrigation water because mountain snows and foothill reservoirs have great storage capacity, while moisture on the plains is quickly lost.

According to the Colorado state report, the mountains received less than 50 per cent of their average precipitation in the winter of 1976-1977. While the plains were also generally dry, they received relatively more precipitation during this period; some areas reported above normal amounts. In the summer of 1977, mountain water reserves were below normal, and a severe drought forced water restrictions.

In the winter of 1977-1978, the mountains received more than twice the normal amount of precipitation at most stations, while the plains were even drier than the year before. The summer of 1978 was exceptionally dry, but there was plenty of water, except for a few low reservoirs and dry wells. In fact, too much water became an occasional problem. Some rivers were filled to their banks in May, and Colorado's Big Thompson River carried so much silt and debris that intake pipes leading into the city of Loveland became clogged.

Roof on Hartford, Conn., Civic Center collapsed under heavy load of ice and snow on January 18, just hours after crowd viewed basketball game.

The storm track avoided the Rocky Mountain West almost entirely in the 1976-1977 season. Furthermore, air currents that normally carry moisture in from the Pacific Ocean were nearly nonexistent. In the 1977-1978 season the storm track came closer, but, more important, the area received copious amounts of moisture from the Pacific that produced heavy snows. It is unusual for a dry year to be followed by an unusually wet year, but that fact alone prevented the drought from being a disaster.

Automated Weather. Automation of Field Operations and Services (AFOS) became a reality on May 10 when two Pennsylvania National Weather Service offices approved a new data-handling system. AFOS will become nationwide in November 1980, automating more than 200 National Weather Service offices. The AFOS system transmits information faster by using video displays of data and maps rather than paper. Current weather maps take 10 minutes to relay, while AFOS will take only 15 seconds, and messages will travel at 3,000 words per minute, compared with the current speed of 100 words per minute.

The 52 Weather Service Forecast Offices will collect all weather information gathered from local automated offices. The offices will be able to call up just the information needed at a given time through a network of minicomputers. Weather-service personnel are being trained to operate the new system.

Tornado Detection. Doppler radar has been used at the National Severe Storms Laboratory (NSSL) in Norman, Okla., since 1971 to study how thunderstorms produce tornadoes. Doppler, or continuous wave radar, is used to determine the speed of moving objects. During the research, radar signals reflected by storms showed tornadic circulation embedded within them at heights of up to 30,000 feet (9,000 meters) above the earth. During the 1977 and 1978 tornado seasons, Donald W. Burgess at NSSL, Donald R. Devore of the Oklahoma City National Weather Service Office, and Air Force Captain Joel D. Bonewitz of Air Weather Service used Doppler radar for day-to-day weather forecasting. The results showed that tornadic circulation in severe thunderstorms can be detected by radar more than 20 minutes before it becomes visible as tornadoes to ground observers.

This early detection adds at least 10 minutes of lifesaving time for issuing tornado warnings. The Doppler radar may also be helpful in detecting the conditions that lead to flash floods. If the operational tests continue to be successful, then we can expect Doppler radar to be used more widely in weather forecasting in the 1980s.

Pollution. The Argonne National Laboratory near Chicago reported in July on a study that showed how weather plays a role in how much purification is needed to clean city water. A source of water pollution near Chicago at certain times is the

Indiana Harbor Canal, which links Lake Michigan to the port of Chicago. During the winter, the lake water cools to 39° F. (4°C), the temperature at which water is heaviest and sinks. Areas that are cooler or warmer remain close to the surface of the lake. Indiana Harbor Canal water is warmer and moves out near the surface of the lake, propelled by south or southeast winds. There it mixes with colder water until the mixture reaches 39° F. and sinks. The bottom water travels northwest along the western side of Lake Michigan. If south or southeast winds continue, lake currents carry the most polluted water along the bottom of the western edge of the lake to a major water-intake point for the city of Chicago.

The most severe pollution episodes occur following 24 hours of northwest winds combined with some rain in the canal watershed and followed by south or southeast winds for at least another 24 hours. The rain and southerly winds cause the canal to flush into Lake Michigan.

Typically, Lake Michigan is cold enough from December through April for severe pollution to occur. Although Chicago's water supply is not in danger of contamination, its water-purification costs rise at such times. The experiment to trace the water was performed in 1977.　　　　Edward W. Pearl

See also Section Two, COLDER WEATHER AHEAD – UNLESS IT'S WARMER. In WORLD BOOK, see METEOROLOGY; RADAR; WEATHER.

WEBSTER, WILLIAM HEDGCOCK (1924-　　), was appointed director of the United States Federal Bureau of Investigation (FBI) on Jan. 19, 1978. Webster was nominated for the post after district court Judge Frank M. Johnson, Jr., of Alabama, President Jimmy Carter's first nominee, withdrew for health reasons. Webster replaced Clarence M. Kelley, who retired on Feb. 15, 1978.

Webster has been interested in the criminal justice system throughout his career. After establishing a private law practice in St. Louis, he served as U.S. attorney there from 1959 to 1961. He was appointed to the federal district court bench in 1971, and in 1973 he was named to the U.S. court of appeals. He resigned on Feb. 23, 1978, to accept the FBI post. At his confirmation hearing, Webster pledged that, under his leadership, the FBI would no longer indulge in such activities as illegal wiretapping or mail opening.

Born in St. Louis in 1924, Webster received a Bachelor of Arts degree from Amherst College in Massachusetts in 1947 and a law degree in 1949 from Washington University Law School in St. Louis, where he now serves on the Board of Trustees. Webster served as a lieutenant in the U.S. Naval Reserve in both World War II and the Korean War.

Webster and his wife, Drusilla, have three children. He is an avid tennis player.　　Madelyn Krzak

WEIGHT LIFTING. See SPORTS.

WEST INDIES. The Caribbean Island of Dominica became independent on Nov. 3, 1978. The new nation, part of the Windward Islands chain, had been a British colony since the early 1800s and a British associated state since 1967. St. Lucia was promised independence on Feb. 22, 1979; no dates were set for St. Kitts/Nevis or St. Vincent.

Unemployment remained a major problem in the Bahamas. Island authorities ascribed part of the blame to an estimated 40,000 illegal Haitian immigrants. Subsequently, the government ordered all illegal aliens to leave by the end of June.

Elsewhere, a four-month strike by British West Indies Airlines International pilots seriously affected the tourist industry. When service in the area resumed in June, however, tourism made a major recovery.　　　　　　　Paul C. Tullier

See also LATIN AMERICA (Facts in Brief Table). In WORLD BOOK, see WEST INDIES; WEST INDIES ASSOCIATED STATES; WEST INDIES FEDERATION.

WEST VIRGINIA. See STATE GOVERNMENT.

WISCONSIN. See STATE GOVERNMENT.

WYOMING. See STATE GOVERNMENT.

YEMEN (ADEN). See MIDDLE EAST.

YEMEN (SANA). See MIDDLE EAST.

YOUNG MEN'S CHRISTIAN ASSOCIATION. See COMMUNITY ORGANIZATIONS.

YOUNG WOMEN'S CHRISTIAN ASSOCIATION. See COMMUNITY ORGANIZATIONS.

YOUTH ORGANIZATIONS carried out varied and vigorous athletic, educational, and social programs in the United States in 1978. As in 1977, they received encouraging support throughout the year from President Jimmy Carter.

Boy Scouts of America (BSA). Energy conservation was a dominant theme in Cub Scouts, Boy Scouts, and Explorers. Through community education programs, energy inventories of their own homes, and many other projects, members worked to reduce U.S. energy consumption in compliance with a request from Carter.

About 2,000 teen-age Explorers – both young men and women – competed in the fifth biennial National Explorer Olympics at Colorado State University in Fort Collins in August. There were 22 individual and team competitions, a general-knowledge test, and a public-speaking contest.

Nancy Winecoff, 19, of Albemarle, N.C., became the second woman president of the 400,000-member Explorers organization. She was elected at the National Explorer Presidents' Congress in Washington, D.C., in April.

The BSA ended age restrictions for handicapped members, permitting them to continue as Cub Scouts, Scouts, or Explorers beyond the usual age limits. See HANDICAPPED.

Boys' Clubs of America (BCA) was a founding member of the International Federation of Keystone

Youth Organizations in 1978. The new organization brings together Boys' Club organizations from such countries as Australia, Canada, Germany, Great Britain, Ireland, Jordan, New Zealand, Singapore, and the United States.

BCA's Alcohol Abuse Prevention project moved into its third and final year under a grant from the Department of Health, Education, and Welfare (HEW). More than 600 BCA staff members were trained to continue the program after the HEW funding stops.

President Carter declared March 12 to 18 as National Boys' Club Week and installed Ray Anthony Owens, a 17-year-old member of the Boys' Club in Austin, Tex., as National Boy of the Year during a White House ceremony on March 15.

BCA presented the Herbert Hoover Memorial Award for outstanding service to youth to two corporate leaders, DeWitt Wallace, founder and retired chairman of *Reader's Digest* magazine, and J. Paul Lyet, chairman and chief executive of the Sperry Rand Corporation.

Camp Fire held its first Congress in October 1978 under the organization's "New Day" program, which involves great changes in program, membership, and purpose. Camp Fire now includes both girls and boys. It serves nearly 750,000 youngsters up to 21 years of age in more than 35,000 communities.

The agency's New Day flexibility enabled local councils to respond to the needs of young people in their community. Local councils continued to offer traditional club programs, but they also provided such widely diverse activities as preschool programs, juvenile justice programs, career-education projects, family-life education classes, and day-care programs.

4-H Clubs. From the inner city of Newark, N.J., to the forests of Alaska, nearly 5.5 million young persons took part in the 4-H program in 1978 under the guidance of more than 575,000 adult and teen-age volunteer leaders. Members participated in programs in more than 3,000 counties of the United States, as well as in the District of Columbia, Puerto Rico, the U.S. Virgin Islands, and Guam.

President Carter congratulated 4-H'ers, their leaders, and the professional 4-H workers in October. "In learning-by-doing, through educational projects, and through community involvement efforts, 4-H is providing useful guidance and direction to young people and making them more responsible and sensitive adult citizens," the President said.

The most popular programs in 1978 dealt with consumer education, clothing and textiles, food and nutrition, home furnishings and equipment, and housing. Animal and poultry science continued to be of great interest to many 4-H'ers.

These boys are among more than 300 who chose to join the Klamath Falls, Ore., Camp Fire council when the national group became coeducational.

The Future Farmers of America (FFA) celebrated its 50th anniversary in 1978 with 8,200 FFA chapters participating in special activities during National FFA Week from February 18 to 25. The FFA had 507,248 students enrolled in high school vocational agriculture programs.

A record 21,668 FFA members and guests attended the golden anniversary national convention in Kansas City, Mo., in November. FFA's top awards, Star Farmer of America and Star Agribusinessman of America, went to Maynard Augst, 22, of Montgomery, Minn., and Mark Williams of Orlando, Fla., respectively. President Carter, a former FFA member, met for the second year with state presidents of FFA on July 20.

Girl Scouts of the United States of America (GSA) launched "From Dreams to Reality," a nationwide career education program for teen-age girls, in 1978. The program was designed to stimulate girls' interest in career possibilities and help them to explore as many as they desire.

Television viewers saw what Girl Scouts are doing to further conservation, preserve wildlife, and develop self-reliance in *Girl Scouting and the Wild Kingdom*, an episode of the "Wild Kingdom" TV series.

Membership in GSA reached 3 million in 1978. The number of girls, women, and men who have belonged to the organization since its founding in 1912 topped 40 million.

Girls Clubs of America (GCA) sponsored the seminar "Today's Girls: Tomorrow's Women" in June 1978, in cooperation with the Johnson Foundation of Racine, Wis. More than 50 experts on juvenile justice, human sexuality, employment, and education met with GCA participants to call national attention to the needs of today's girls and recommend action to meet those needs. More than 215,000 girls belong to 258 clubs in 36 states.

Junior Achievement (JA) helped more than 300,-000 young people in the United States and eight other countries in 1978 learn how the American business system operates. It provided the guidance of adult business volunteers who helped them to establish and operate small-scale businesses of their own.

North Star Enterprisers, a new company established in Westchester County, New York, was a typical JA project. Operated by 15 high school students, and sponsored by Consolidated Edison Company, the company manufactured shell jewelry, lucite penholders, and ice scrapers.

With the help of their advisers, the students formed the company and received a charter from National Junior Achievers. They sold stock at $1 a share to raise capital, then elected officers and set up a wage, salary, and commission scale. The students kept financial records, paid rent and taxes, and prepared an annual report.   Virginia E. Anderson

In WORLD BOOK, see entries on the individual organizations.

YUGOSLAVIA continued to prepare for the post-Tito era in 1978. President Josip Broz Tito visited the United States in March and obtained a public endorsement of Yugoslavia's nonaligned stance and territorial integrity from President Jimmy Carter. The United States authorized Yugoslav purchases of $1.4 billion in military equipment, and Defense Minister Nikola Ljubicic visited the United States in September to discuss more arms purchases.

Relations with Russia deteriorated after an August visit by China's Premier Hua Kuo-feng. Tito's planned meeting with Russia's Presidium Chairman Leonid I. Brezhnev was canceled. A dispute over Bulgarian Macedonians also damaged relations with Bulgaria.

Relations with Cuba deteriorated in July at the Belgrade conference of foreign ministers of nonaligned nations. Tito criticized what he saw as Cuba's domineering attitude toward nonaligned nations, especially in Africa.

Yugoslavia continued its close relations with the Communist parties in Western nations. Italian Communist Party leader Enrico Berlinguer visited Yugoslavia in October after a trip to Moscow.

New Leader. The Yugoslav League of Communists (Communist Party) reduced the size of its top body, the Presidium, from 48 seats to 24 at its 11th Congress in June. Stane Dolanc, chief secretary of the

President Tito gets a kiss from a Yugoslav girl and a smile from British Prime Minister James Callaghan during a visit to London in March.

Presidium's executive committee, was elected secretary-general of the league, putting him in charge of party administration. Edvard Kardelj, for years the party's second most important figure, went into virtual retirement because of ill health. The Presidium elected Branko Mikulic of Bosnia on October 19 as Tito's deputy for a year. The party congress elected 97 new members to the 165-member Central Committee. Many older members retired or were removed.

Opponents Jailed. Mileta Perovic was sentenced to 20 years in jail on April 13 for trying to bring Yugoslavia under foreign influence. The government said he was in the illegal New Communist Party of Yugoslavia, organized in 1974 to restore close ties with Russia. Perovic lived in Russia from 1958 to 1975.

A court in Sarajevo sentenced Wjenceslav Cizek, a Croatian nationalist who had disappeared from West Germany in 1977, to 15 years in prison on August 8.

West Germany rejected in September Yugoslavia's demand for extradition of three Croatians wanted in Yugoslavia on charges of terrorism. In retaliation, Yugoslavia refused to extradite four suspected West German terrorists. See EUROPE (Close-Up).   Chris Cviic

See also EUROPE (Facts in Brief Table). In WORLD BOOK, see TITO; YUGOSLAVIA.

YUKON TERRITORY. The $10-billion Alcan gas pipeline moved closer to construction in 1978 with Canada's decision to use thin-wall pipe 56 inches (142 centimeters) in diameter for the section running from Whitehorse in the Yukon to Caroline, Alta. The United States preferred a 48-inch (122-centimeter) pipe, but the National Energy Board of Canada decided that the larger size would provide greater safety and reliability.

It was decided that paving of parts of the Alaska and Haines highways would begin in August 1978.

Creation of a Yukon wildlife preserve of about 15,000 square miles (39,000 square kilometers), comprising the northern third of the territory, was announced on July 6. Mineral development will be prohibited, and the area will be a preserve for caribou, bear, and waterfowl. The region, one of the few areas in Canada not touched by glaciers in the past, contains remains of ancient human occupation.

Elections on November 20 gave 11 of the 16 legislative assembly seats to the Progressive Conservatives. Two Indians were elected for the first time. Yukon Commissioner Arthur Pearson's resignation was accepted on November 1 after the assembly council voted for his removal. He was accused of interfering in disciplinary action against a Whitehorse lawyer.   David M. L. Farr

See also CANADA. In WORLD BOOK, see YUKON TERRITORY.

ZAIRE. Rebels invaded Zaire's mineral-rich Shaba province from Angola for the second straight year in 1978, and once again French troops helped to drive the invaders out. Belgian troops also helped, and United States planes provided the airlift. The rebel force, estimated at 2,000 to 2,500, captured Kolwezi, Zaire's most important mining town, on May 13 and held it for eight days before French paratroopers drove them out. Mines and refineries in the Kolwezi area normally produce about 90 per cent of Zaire's cobalt and 75 per cent of its copper.

The attack on Kolwezi crippled both industries. Machinery was sabotaged, mines were flooded, and some immigrant engineers and technicians fled the area while others were killed. An estimated 855 persons, including 136 whites, died during the fight for Kolwezi, and about 2,200 whites, including virtually all the Europeans working in the mining sector, had been evacuated by May 22. They were slow to return, fearing a recurrence of violence.

Most of the rebels were members of the Lunda group living in Shaba province, once called Katanga and long known for its hostility to Zaire's central government. The Lunda-based rebel movement, the National Front for the Liberation of the Congo (FNLC), had mounted an 80-day invasion of Shaba from bases in neighboring Angola in 1977 before being turned back by government forces aided by troops from Morocco and France. The FNLC took responsibility for the 1978 attack, aimed at overthrowing President Mobutu Sese Seko.

Military Support. About 600 French Legionnaires landed in Kolwezi on May 19. The next day, 1,200 Belgian paratroopers were flown in to evacuate about 2,500 Europeans, most of whom were Belgians. See BELGIUM; FRANCE.

The FNLC rebels launched the attack from bases in Angola. Cuban President Fidel Castro Ruz denied U.S. charges that Cubans stationed in Angola had trained and equipped the FNLC guerrillas. He declared on May 17 that he had tried to prevent the invasion. See CUBA.

Angola supported the Shaba rebels in part because Mobutu had been helping three Angolan guerrilla groups that opposed President Agostinho Neto's government. However, Mobutu and Neto agreed in August to stop aiding each other's opposition. See ANGOLA.

Economic Aid. Mobutu asked Western countries for economic aid after the invasion. The United States and other donors agreed after Zaire promised to open diplomatic relations with Angola.

Mobutu's domestic political difficulties were not limited to the Shaba invasion. His government arrested 250 army officers in February for plotting his overthrow. Thirteen convicted in the alleged plot were executed on March 17.   John D. Esseks

See also AFRICA (Facts in Brief Table). In WORLD BOOK, see ANGOLA; ZAIRE.

ZAMBIA bowed to economic pressure on Oct. 6, 1978, and resumed exporting and importing goods through Rhodesia, its neighbor to the south. Zambia had closed its border in 1973 as part of black Africa's economic warfare against white rule in Rhodesia. General trade was not resumed with Rhodesia, but goods were once again shipped on its railroads, which provide the most direct route to the sea for landlocked Zambia.

An alternative rail route through Zaire and Angola was closed to Zambia in 1975 because of civil war in Angola, and severe bottlenecks had developed along the only other outlet, a 1,160-mile (1,860-kilometer) rail line through Tanzania. As a result, an estimated 140,000 short tons (127,000 metric tons) of Zambian copper exports had been tied up along this line by October.

Zambia depends heavily on copper, which provides about 90 per cent of the country's total export earnings. Low world copper prices added to the country's economic difficulties. Zambia was compelled to devalue its monetary unit, the kwacha, by 10 per cent on March 17 and to arrange two International Monetary Fund loans in April totaling $365 million to cover needed imports. Nevertheless, serious shortages of fertilizers, manufactured goods, and consumer essentials developed.　　John D. Esseks

See also AFRICA (Facts in Brief Table); RHODESIA. In WORLD BOOK, see ZAMBIA.

ZOOLOGY. Researchers reported new developments in 1978 in their efforts to teach languages to apes. Duane Rumbaugh of the Yerkes Regional Primate Center in Atlanta, Ga., has taught chimpanzees to communicate by using keyboards of geometric symbols that represent words. Rumbaugh and his coworkers, E. Sue Savage-Rumbaugh and Sally Boysen, reported in August what may be the first instance of symbolic communication between two chimpanzees.

Rumbaugh trained two chimps, Sherman and Austin, to recognize the symbols for certain foods as depicted on their keyboards. Then Sherman was taken away from his keyboard and shown some food that Austin, separated from Sherman by a glass wall, could not see. When Sherman returned to his keyboard, the researcher asked him to identify the food he had seen. Austin watched Sherman type out his reply and then requested the same food. Many other tests were equally successful.

Each chimp spontaneously used the keyboard to ask for a variety of foods that the researcher provided for the other chimp. The chimp who was given the food could pass it to the other chimp if he recognized the typed symbol and wished to do so. Austin always gave Sherman the food when he requested it, but Sherman, the more dominant of the two chimps, sometimes required some prodding before he handed over favorite foods to Austin.

Koko's Sign Language. Francine (Penny) Patterson of Stanford, Calif., has been teaching sign language to Koko, a 7-year-old female gorilla, for six years. Penny and Koko now communicate in ways that seem startlingly human. Koko jokes – she insists on calling a white towel "red" and then impishly points out a piece of red lint on the towel. She has a limited vocabulary of demeaning terms.

She even tries to lie to avoid troubles. When caught trying to poke a hole through a screen with a chopstick, she gives the sign for smoking and pretends to smoke. She also puts together signs denoting objects for which she has been taught no sign, such as "white tiger" for zebra and "eye hat" for mask. The most heartwarming response was her answer to the question, "Are you an animal or a person?" Koko replied, "Fine animal gorilla."

Chimp Warfare. Jane van Lawick-Goodall, who has studied a group of chimpanzees living in the Gombe Stream National Park in Tanzania since 1960, reported in April that a band of the apes had repeatedly attacked and eventually killed all of the apes in another band early in 1978. The two groups were originally part of the same band. Van Lawick-Goodall could not explain these attacks, but said, "I think they split up because there were too many males and too much tension."　　Barbara Benson

In WORLD BOOK, see CHIMPANZEE; GORILLA; ZOOLOGY.

ZOOS AND AQUARIUMS throughout the world continued to make rapid changes in exhibition, education, and conservation activities in 1978. The opening of the Minnesota Zoological Garden in Apple Valley in May was particularly notable. It has a large walk-through house for reptiles, birds, and mammals from tropical areas. It provides a contrast to other large outdoor exhibits of Northern Hemisphere mammals, such as beluga whales, snow monkeys, Siberian tigers, and musk oxen.

The Cincinnati (Ohio) Zoo opened a most unusual exhibit, its new Insect House, in August. Sixty-five insect exhibits are contained in a sunken building. The walk-through butterfly area is particularly interesting, as are the leaf-cutting ant colony and exhibits of goliath beetles and giant walking sticks. Some of the exhibits are developed around themes, such as insects' predators, insects' relatives, mimicry, metamorphosis, locomotion, and the economic effects of insect life on humans. In June, the Cincinnati Zoo dedicated a large open-air area for gorillas.

The St. Louis Zoological Park opened a completely renovated Reptile House in August. The National Zoological Park in Washington, D.C., completed its new quarters for bears in August, and the Shedd Aquarium in Chicago its refurbished 90,000-gallon (341,000-liter) reef tank in December.

Breeding Programs. A growing concern among zoo directors is the distribution of animals produced

Rare Look at China's Zoos

We saw some exotic animals rarely found outside China when our group of United States zoo and museum officials visited China's leading zoological parks in 1978. But the strangest sights we saw were caged household pets, including dogs, cats, and pigeons. Our group of 18 visited zoos in Peking, Nanking, Shanghai, and Canton (Kuang-chou) for three weeks in May 1978, the first official American zoological delegation to visit China in 30 years.

Theodore H. Reed, director of the National Zoological Park in Washington, D.C., asked the Chinese government in 1977 if we could make the trip to learn more about caring for giant pandas in captivity. The two pandas at the National Zoo were a gift to the American people by the Chinese in 1972. Reed was immediately invited to bring a group to China. I went as a representative of the Chicago Zoological Park – the Brookfield Zoo – near Chicago.

China's current public zoological parks were started when the People's Republic of China was established in 1949. Managed as units of municipal park districts, they closely resemble zoos in Europe and North America.

Typically, large moated enclosures with artificial or natural rocks house the bears, lions, tigers, and troops of monkeys. Lakes and canals are also prominent features, and many of them have large collections of cranes, ducks, pelicans, and other water birds. Their collections contain some African mammals and birds, a few Australian species, and occasional American animals, but they feature animals native to China.

Peking's golden langur

China's zoos have relatively large staffs. About 450 work at the Peking Zoo, including 170 keepers. Veterinarians are prominent among the professionals at the major zoos; animal care is generally adequate, and sanitation good. The animals get a wide variety of fresh foods. The zoos rarely use prepared or compounded foods, as ours do.

Zoo attendance figures are staggering. More than 8 million persons visit the Peking Zoo every year, and 5-million go to the Shanghai Zoo. Customarily, the zoos are open six days a week and charge a small admission fee to all persons over 3.3 feet (100 centimeters) tall. But on national holidays, the admission is free. Food stands and postcard and photograph kiosks are found in the zoos, but they do not offer the train or bus rides found in many U.S. zoos. There are no special children's sections.

Schools use the zoos extensively, however. Educational signs are prominent at the Peking Zoo. Some signs give the geographic distribution of the principal species of vertebrates around the world; others depict ecological, evolutionary, and economic aspects of animal life.

The giant panda is the most unusual species in Chinese zoos. About 25 of these animals are shown in 11 zoos. The rest of the world has only 11 in six zoos, including the pair at the National Zoo in Washington. Seven panda young have been bred and raised at the Peking Zoo, but no second-generation animals have yet been born. Scientists do not know much about how pandas live in the wild, partly because of the rugged nature of the animals' natural habitat in the bamboo stands of mountainous southwestern China. Several pandas in Peking are 25 or 26 years old. Other unusual species in the Peking Zoo include black-naped cranes, Chinese alligators, white-lipped deer, and golden leaf monkeys.

Because of a ban on pet animals in the cities, the Chinese exhibit familiar household pets alongside more exotic animals. We saw Mexican hairless dogs, Muscovy ducks, Persian cats, peacocks, and pigeons in regular exhibit cages. Goldfish are also displayed in a fascinating variety of mutant forms in zoo aquariums.

We observed major construction at three zoos. In Peking, a 15,000-square-foot (1,400-square-meter) reptile house, probably the largest in the world, was almost ready to open. A monkey house was under construction in Shanghai, and a new enclosure for hippopotamuses was being built in Canton.

We enjoyed the trip. We made new friends and gained an appreciation of China that only personal experience can supply.

George B. Rabb

Brown bear cub at Omaha's zoo feasts on whipped cream and wheat germ after keepers narrowly rescued it from the jaws of an adult male bear.

through breeding programs. Contraceptive devices have been used to prevent too many births of lions, tigers, and other large cats, but such techniques are not practical for most mammals. Population programs for many species will require national or international coordination among zoos. A conference at the National Zoo's Conservation and Research Center near Warrenton, Va., in May considered the population distribution of Père David's deer, and pedigree records of captive tigers were discussed at the International Union of Directors of Zoological Gardens meeting in Leipzig, East Germany, in October.

Gains in captive breeding were illustrated by three significant second-generation births in 1978 – a dolphin at Marineland in St. Augustine, Fla.; an orang-utan at the National Zoological Park in Washington; and a cheetah at the Cincinnati Zoo. Other births included the 19th Asian elephant at Washington Park Zoo in Portland, Ore.; two African elephants at the Knoxville (Tenn.) Zoo; bongos at the Cincinnati Zoo and the Gladys Porter Zoo in Brownsville, Tex.; and black and white ruffed lemurs at the Lincoln Park Zoo in Chicago. Twin orang-utans were born in Melbourne, Australia.

Rare birds included king vultures, hatched at zoos in Los Angeles; Birmingham, Ala.; and Jackson, Miss. Bald eagles were hatched at the Columbus (Ohio) Zoo and at the Central Texas Zoo in Waco.

Preservation Projects included the breeding of Arabian oryx at the Phoenix Zoo in Arizona, San Diego's Wild Animal Park, the Los Angeles Zoo, and the Gladys Porter Zoo. The species is probably extinct in the wild, and there are about 200 of these animals in zoos and conservation parks. Four Arabian oryx were sent from the United States to Israel, four to a desert reserve in Jordan, and several to European zoos. Plans were also underway to reintroduce this oryx into the wild in Oman.

Preservation of the seriously endangered golden lion marmoset has gone smoothly at the National Zoological Park in Washington, and offspring of that large colony are now being offered to other institutions. Unfortunately, a disease struck these marmosets at the Tijucas Biological Bank near São Paulo, Brazil, and the total captive population remained at 138 animals despite 34 births in 1977. Probably fewer than 400 of this species exist in the wild.

A breeding colony for another rare South American primate, Goeldi's monkey, was established at Brookfield Zoo (Chicago Zoological Park) near Chicago with five pairs received from the United States Fish and Wildlife Service, which had seized them in July 1977 as an illegal shipment. Eight successful Goeldi's monkey births have taken place in this colony.   George B. Rabb

In WORLD BOOK, see AQUARIUM; ZOO.

World Book Supplement

To help WORLD BOOK owners keep their encyclopedia up to date, the following new or revised articles are reprinted from the 1979 edition of the encyclopedia.

The North American Hognose Snake sometimes plays dead when threatened by an enemy. The illustration at the left above shows the hognose in a natural position. When playing dead, the snake rolls over on its back and hangs out its tongue, *right*.

One of the Largest Snakes is the anaconda of South America. It has a stout body and may grow about 30 feet (9 meters) long. Only the reticulate python of Asia rivals it in size.

SNAKE

SNAKE is a backboned animal with a long, legless body covered by dry scales. Snakes have many unusual body features and fascinating ways of life. To move about on land, a snake usually slides on its belly. Many snakes have such a flexible body that they can coil into a ball. The eyes of a snake are covered by clear scales instead of movable eyelids. As a result, its eyes are always open. Snakes have a narrow, forked tongue, which they repeatedly flick out. They use the tongue to bring odors to a special sense organ in the mouth. In this way, they can follow the scent trails of their prey.

Snakes belong to a group of animals called *reptiles*. Reptiles also include alligators, crocodiles, lizards, and

Donald W. Tinkle, the contributor of this article, is Professor of Zoology and Director of the Museum of Zoology at the University of Michigan.

turtles. Like other reptiles, snakes can maintain a fairly steady body temperature by external means. For example, they raise their body temperature by lying in the sun. In contrast, many other animals have internal mechanisms that regulate their body temperature.

Snakes developed gradually from lizards millions of years ago, and they resemble lizards more than they do other reptiles. But unlike most lizards, snakes lack legs, movable eyelids, and outer ears. Their scales and skulls also differ from those of lizards.

Snakes live almost everywhere on the earth. They live in deserts, forests, oceans, streams, and lakes. Many snakes are ground dwellers, and some live underground. Others dwell in trees, and still others spend most of their time in water. Only a few areas in the world have no snakes. Snakes cannot survive where the ground stays frozen the year around. Thus, no snakes live in the polar regions or at high elevations in mountains. In addition, no snakes live in Ireland or New Zealand.

There are about 2,700 kinds of snakes. The greatest variety dwell in the tropics. The largest snakes are the

San Diego Zoo

Fights Between Male Snakes occur often during the breeding season. In a typical fight, two males rear up and repeatedly lunge at each other. The combat continues until one of the snakes is forced down and retreats. The snakes shown above are red diamond rattlesnakes of North America.

Interesting Facts About Snakes

One of the Smallest Snakes is the Braminy blind snake, which lives in the tropics and grows only 6 inches (15 centimeters) long. It has tiny eyes that are covered by head scales.

An African Gaboon Viper in a zoo once fasted for 2½ years. Snakes in zoos sometimes do not eat for 6 months to 3 years.

Gaboon Viper

The Fastest Snake is probably the black mamba of Africa. It was timed moving at a speed of 7 miles (11 kilometers) per hour over a short distance.

Black Mamba

The African Ball Python protects itself from enemies by coiling into a ball with its head in the middle. Many other snakes also use this defense.

Ball Python

Green Tree Pythons may be yellow or brown when hatched. Snakes of both colors may hatch from the same batch of eggs. They turn green as they grow older. Green tree pythons live in New Guinea.

Green Tree Pythons

The Ringhals, or spitting cobra, of Africa can squirt venom 6 to 8 feet (1.8 to 2.4 meters). The snake aims for the eyes of its enemy. The venom causes a painful, burning sensation and can produce blindness.

Ringhals

WORLD BOOK illustrations by Alex Ebel

anaconda of South America and the reticulate python of Asia. Both may grow about 30 feet (9 meters) long. One of the smallest snakes is the Braminy blind snake, which lives in the tropics and grows only 6 inches (15 centimeters) long. Like other blind snakes, the Braminy blind snake has eyes, but they are covered by head scales. Blind snakes probably can distinguish only light and dark.

Some snakes are poisonous. They have two hollow or grooved fangs in the upper jaw. The snakes inject *venom* (poison) through their fangs when they bite. About 270 kinds of snakes have venom that is harmful or fatal to human beings. About 25 kinds cause most of the deaths from snakebites. These snakes include the Indian cobra of southern Asia, the black mamba and the saw-scaled viper of Africa, and the tiger snake of Australia.

Many people fear and dislike snakes, partly because some kinds are poisonous. But people probably regard snakes as frightening or "creepy" animals mostly because their appearance and ways of life seem strange. The fear of snakes also results from a lack of knowledge about the animals. Throughout history, snakes have been the subjects of many myths and superstitions.

Some people keep snakes as pets. But many people find that snakes do not make enjoyable pets. Snakes do not move around much and are hard to train. Many kinds stay hidden most of the time. In addition, some snakes have unusual feeding habits, which makes them difficult to care for.

The Bodies of Snakes

Body Shape. Snakes vary greatly in body shape. For example, some snakes have a stout body. Certain tree snakes, on the other hand, have an extremely thin, long body that resembles a vine. The bodies of sea snakes are flattened from side to side.

The males and females of most species of snakes do not differ greatly in body shape and appearance. However, among some species, the females are larger than the males. In some other species, the males are larger. One species in which the males and females differ greatly in appearance is the langaha of Madagascar.

537

How Body Shape Differs Among Snakes

The illustrations below show some of the variations in the body shape of snakes. The yellow-bellied sea snake is flattened sideways, and its tail forms an oarlike paddle. Vine snakes have an extremely long, thin body. The Malaysian short python is stubby. The Texas blind snake has a cylindrical body.

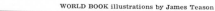

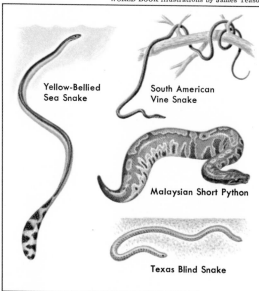

Yellow-Bellied Sea Snake

South American Vine Snake

Malaysian Short Python

Texas Blind Snake

Male langahas have a conelike stub on the snout. The females have a long snout shaped somewhat like a maple leaf.

Scales and Color. The body of a snake is covered with dry scales, which may be smooth or have ridges. The majority of snakes have overlapping scales that stretch apart. Among most species, the belly scales consist of one row of large scales extending from the neck to the tail. The side and back scales vary in size and shape among different species.

The scaly skin of a snake has two layers. The inner layer consists of cells that grow and divide. The cells die as they are pushed upward by new cells. The dead cells form the outer layer of skin. From time to time, a snake sheds the outer layer because it becomes worn.

The skin-shedding process is called *molting*. For a short time before molting, a snake is less active than usual. The animal's eyes become clouded and then clear again just before it molts. The snake loosens the skin around the mouth and head by rubbing its nose on a rough surface. The snake then crawls out of the old skin, turning it inside out in the process.

How often a snake molts depends chiefly on its age and how active it is. Young snakes shed more often than old ones. Snakes that live in warm climates are active for longer periods than those that live in cooler climates. As a result, they molt more frequently. Some pythons of the tropics shed six or more times a year. In contrast, some North American rattlesnakes average two or three molts a year. A new segment may be added to the rattle on the tail each time they molt.

A snake's color comes chiefly from special *pigment cells* in deep layers of the skin. But some color may be due to the way light is reflected from the surface of the

scales. Most snakes have a drab coloring that matches their surroundings. For example, the North American copperhead has brown bands that blend with the dead leaves on the forest floor where it lives.

Some snakes have bright colors. For example, the coral snakes of North America have bright bands of black, red, and yellow or white. In some cases, snakes of the same species have different color patterns. For example, some California king snakes are black with white bands across the width of the body. Others have white stripes that extend the length of the body. Great Plains ground snakes have a wide variety of markings. Some are tan or brown with many red bands, and some have a red band only around the neck. Others have a red stripe down the middle of the back. Still others are solid tan or brown, without any markings.

Skeleton. The main parts of a snake's skeleton are (1) the skull, (2) vertebrae, and (3) ribs. A few snakes, such as blind snakes, boas, and pythons, have *vestiges* of hind legs or hipbones. A vestige is a remaining trace of a body part that an animal has lost during its development through the ages. Snakes that have vestiges of hind legs or hipbones clearly show their close relationship to lizards.

Skull. The bones of a snake's skull are loosely connected. But the brain is completely enclosed by bone.

In most snakes, the lower jaw has two bones connected at the chin by an elastic tissue. These bones can be stretched widely apart. The lower jaw is loosely attached to the upper jaw. Several bones of the upper jaw and roof of the mouth also are loosely joined to one another and to the rest of the skull. The two sides of a snake's jaws can be moved separately. Some bones of the lower and upper jaws have pointed teeth that curve back toward the throat. These teeth are not suitable for chewing, and so snakes swallow their prey whole. Most snakes also eat their prey while it is alive.

The structure of their jaws enables most snakes to open the mouth widely and swallow animals that are larger than their own head. Some large pythons can swallow animals that weigh more than 100 pounds (45 kilograms). To swallow an animal, a snake moves first one side of its jaws forward and then the other side.

A Snake Sheds Its Skin by first rubbing its nose on a rough surface, which loosens the skin about the head. It then crawls out of the skin. This snake is a North American rainbow water snake.

The snake's curved teeth stick into the prey and prevent it from escaping. As the snake alternately draws each side of its jaws backward, it pulls the animal toward the throat. A large amount of saliva is produced in the snake's mouth and throat, which eases the passage of the animal.

In some cases, a snake may take more than half an hour to swallow an animal. A special feature prevents the windpipe from being blocked while the snake's mouth and throat are full. The windpipe can be pushed forward over the tongue and out the mouth.

Vertebrae. The backbone of snakes consists of an unusually large number of vertebrae. Snakes have about 150 to over 400 vertebrae, depending on the species. Strong, flexible joints connect the vertebrae and enable the body to make a wide range of movements.

Ribs. A pair of ribs is attached to each vertebra in front of the tail. The ribs are not joined together along the belly and so can be extended outward. After a snake has swallowed a bulky meal, the ribs thus spread out as the stomach expands.

Muscles. As many as 24 small muscles are attached to each vertebra and rib in a snake's body. These muscles connect one vertebra to another, the vertebrae to the ribs, one rib to another, and the ribs to the scales. Snakes use most of these muscles to move about. The section *Methods of Movement* describes the ways in which snakes move.

Internal Organs. The heart, lung, liver, and other major internal organs of snakes are long and slender. Most snakes have only one lung, though many have a vestige of another lung. Their paired organs—the kidneys and *ovaries* (female sex organs) or *testes* (male sex organs)—are arranged one on each side of the body. But each pair is staggered from front to back. Among many other animals, they are positioned one directly across from the other.

In most snakes, the digestive system, which includes the stomach and intestines, is specially suited for handling bulky food. The stomach can expand greatly. Substances called *enzymes* are produced in the stomach. The enzymes break down food into materials that can be absorbed in the intestines. Snakes can digest the entire body of their prey, except for hair or feathers. Bone may be completely digested within 72 hours. Waste products pass out of a snake's body through a cavity called the *cloaca* and out of an opening called the *vent.* In female snakes, the cloaca is also the cavity into which the *oviducts* (tubes from the ovaries) empty. In both males and females, the vent marks the end of the snake's trunk and the beginning of its tail.

Sense Organs. Snakes do not have especially keen senses of sight or hearing. They rely partly on special sense organs to provide them with information about their environment.

Snakes have an eye on each side of the head, which gives the animals a wide field of view. Clear scales cover the eyes. The scales are shed and replaced each time a snake molts. Snakes can easily see movements. But they cannot focus their eyes well, and they have sharp vision for only a short distance.

Snakes lack outer ears and eardrums. However, they have inner ears and can hear a limited range of sounds carried in the air. Certain bones in a snake's head re-

The Anatomy of a Snake
This drawing of a male water moccasin shows the skeleton and internal organs that most snakes have in common. A snake's skeleton consists of a skull and many vertebrae and ribs. Most of the animal's internal organs are long and thin. Only poisonous snakes have fangs and venom glands.

WORLD BOOK diagram by James Teason

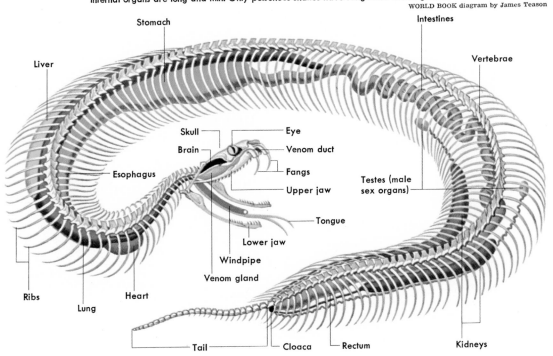

Stomach · Intestines · Vertebrae · Liver · Skull · Eye · Brain · Venom duct · Esophagus · Fangs · Upper jaw · Testes (male sex organs) · Tongue · Lower jaw · Windpipe · Venom gland · Ribs · Lung · Heart · Tail · Cloaca · Rectum · Kidneys

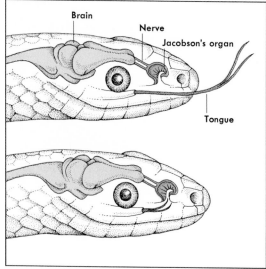

The Jacobson's Organ in snakes is used with the tongue to detect odors. The snake flicks out its tongue and picks up scent particles, *top.* When the snake pulls in its tongue, the particles are transferred to the odor-sensitive Jacobson's organ, *bottom.*

spond to sound waves and transmit them to the inner ear. Studies indicate that a snake's lung may also help transmit sounds.

A snake's tongue has few taste buds. The tongue is used with an organ of smell called the *Jacobson's organ.* The Jacobson's organ, along with the nostrils, provides snakes with a keen sense of smell. The Jacobson's organ consists of two hollow sacs in the roof of a snake's mouth. The sacs have many nerve endings that are extremely sensitive to odors. A snake sticks out its tongue to pick up scent particles in the air or on the ground or some other surface. When the snake pulls its tongue back into the mouth, these particles enter the Jacobson's organ. The organ enables a snake to follow the scent trail of its prey. In addition, a male snake can follow the trail of a female snake by using its tongue and Jacobson's organ.

Certain snakes have special heat-sensitive *pit organs.* Pit vipers have two pit organs, one on each side of the head between the eye and nostril. Some boas and pythons have many pits along the lip of the upper jaw. Pit organs enable a snake to detect the exact location of another animal by the body heat it gives off. Thus, the snake can accurately direct its strike at warm-blooded prey even in the dark. A snake with pit organs can sense a change in temperature near its head of less than 1° F. (0.5° C).

Researchers have found it difficult to test the intelligence of snakes. The animals are hard to train, partly because they have irregular feeding habits and so cannot be rewarded easily with food for performing correctly. In the few intelligence experiments that have been conducted, snakes showed little learning ability. However, most of the experiments did not test abilities that were important to the snakes' way of life. For example, the ability to learn mazes might be useful to

burrowing snakes. But burrowing snakes were not used in the experiments that tested this skill.

Fangs and Venom Glands. Only poisonous snakes have fangs and venom glands. They bite a victim with their fangs and inject venom into the wound. They use their fangs and venom chiefly to kill prey.

Among most poisonous snakes, the two teeth closest to the front of the mouth in the upper jaw form hollow fangs. The fangs are similar to hypodermic needles and may be shed and replaced several times a year. A narrow tube connects each fang to a venom gland on each side of the upper jaw. The fangs differ between the two main groups of poisonous snakes—*vipers* and *elapids.* Vipers, which include copperheads and rattlesnakes, have long, movable front fangs. When not in use, the fangs fold back into a sheath on the roof of the mouth. When the snake strikes, the fangs are erected. Elapids, which include cobras and coral snakes, have short front fangs that are fixed in place. Sea snakes have the same type of fangs that elapids have.

A few venomous snakes have one to three grooved fangs on the upper jaw in the rear of the mouth. However, most of these rear-fanged snakes are not dangerous to human beings.

A snake's venom glands produce a number of enzymes and other substances that can cause death. After a snake bites its prey, some of these enzymes begin the process of digestion even before the snake begins to swallow the animal. However, the snake usually waits for the venom to kill the animal before swallowing it.

In addition to enzymes, most snake venoms contain two kinds of poisons—*neurotoxins* and *hemotoxins.* Neurotoxins affect the nervous system. They cause difficulties in breathing and swallowing and disrupt the work of the heart. Hemotoxins damage blood vessels and body tissues. Sea snakes have an unusual type of venom that directly affects the muscles.

There is no easy way to distinguish all poisonous

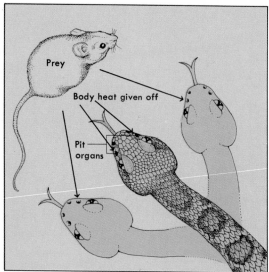

Pit Organs enable a snake to locate prey by the body heat the animal gives off. As the snake moves its head from side to side, the pit organs detect changes in the air temperature. The snake can accurately direct its strike even in the dark.

snakes from nonpoisonous ones. A person must either recognize the features of specific species or see whether the snake has fangs. For information on the treatment of snakebites, see the article SNAKEBITE.

Ways of Life Among Snakes

Snakes are difficult to observe in their natural surroundings because they stay hidden much of the time. Little is known about the ways of life among many species. Scientists who study snakes are called *herpetologists*. They have detailed information about the behavior of only a few species of snakes.

In general, the life of a snake consists mainly of moving about alone in search of food or a mate. Most snakes are active during the day. Others move about at night and rest during the day. Snakes are sometimes inactive for long periods because of cold or hot weather or a scarce supply of food.

Some snakes stay within a very limited area. For example, a study of prairie rattlesnakes showed that the males roamed an area about $\frac{3}{4}$ mile (1.2 kilometers) in diameter. The females roamed an area about $\frac{1}{6}$ mile (0.3 kilometer) in diameter.

Methods of Movement. Snakes often appear to slither swiftly across the ground. But they actually move slowly compared with many other animals. Garter snakes, pythons, and some other snakes have been timed at a speed of only 1 mile (1.6 kilometers) per hour. The fastest speed on record is that of an African black mamba. It was timed at a speed of 7 miles (11 kilometers) per hour over a short distance. In comparison, human beings can easily run short distances at 10 to 15 miles (16 to 24 kilometers) per hour.

Snakes have four main methods of moving about. They are (1) lateral undulation, (2) rectilinear movement, (3) concertina movement, and (4) sidewinding. Some snakes also move in other, unusual ways.

Lateral Undulation is the most common way in which snakes move about. The snake flexes its muscles and so produces a series of horizontal waves from head to tail. The loops of its body push against plants, rocks, twigs, or rough areas on a surface. In this manner, the snake's body is propelled forward.

All snakes can swim by producing the wavelike motions typical of lateral undulation. But sea snakes have a body shape that makes them especially good swimmers. The body is flattened from side to side, and the tail forms an oarlike paddle.

Rectilinear Movement is also known as creeping. Snakes often use this method to climb trees or move through narrow burrows. In addition, many thick-bodied snakes, such as puff adders and pythons, may use rectilinear movement when crawling along on the ground.

In rectilinear movement, the snake contracts certain muscles that pull its belly scales forward. The back edges of the scales catch on bark or rough areas in the soil. The snake then contracts other muscles, which pushes the scales against the bark or rough areas and so moves the body forward. Rectilinear movement is sometimes described as "walking on the ribs," but the snake does not actually move its ribs.

Rat snakes and many other climbing snakes have belly scales especially suited to rectilinear movement. The edges of the scales are squared, and they easily catch on bark as the snake creeps up a tree.

Some Ways Snakes Move About

Allan Power, Bruce Coleman Inc.

In Lateral Undulation, a snake moves its body in a series of horizontal waves. Snakes make these wavelike motions to move on the ground or, like the banded sea snake above, to swim.

Clem Haagner, Bruce Coleman Inc.

In Rectilinear Movement, the snake's body is kept straight. The snake crawls by pulling its belly scales forward and then pushing them backward. This snake is an African puff adder.

Karl H. Switak

In Sidewinding, a snake uses its head and tail as supports and lifts its trunk sideways. This North American sidewinder leaves distinctive tracks as it moves across the sand.

Concertina Movement is often used by snakes to climb through trees or move over smooth surfaces. The snake moves the front part of its body forward and coils it slightly, pressing against the surface to anchor itself. The snake then pulls its back end forward and coils it. The back end is pressed down, providing leverage for the front part to move forward again.

Sidewinding is used chiefly by certain snakes that live in areas with loose soil or sand. These snakes include the sidewinder of North America and the carpet viper and horned viper of Africa. In sidewinding, the snake's head and tail serve as supports. The snake lifts the trunk of its body off the ground and moves it sideways. The snake then moves its head and tail into position with the rest of its body. It then repeats the sequence.

Unusual Ways of Moving. Many small species of snakes seem to "jump" when trying to escape from danger. They hurl the body forward or to the side by rapidly straightening up from a coiled position. Two gliding snakes of southern Asia can "parachute" from a high limb to a lower one or from one tree to another. They spread their ribs, which flattens the body and so helps slow the fall.

Reproduction. All snakes reproduce sexually. In sexual reproduction, a *sperm* (male sex cell) unites with an *egg* (female sex cell), forming a *fertilized egg*. The fertilized egg develops into a new individual.

Male snakes have a pair of sex organs called *hemipenes*. They lie inside the tail and can be pushed out through the vent. During mating, the male curls his tail under the female's, inserts either hemipenis into her cloaca, and deposits sperm. Among some species, the sperm can live within the female's body from several months to more than a year. Thus, the eggs may become fertilized long after mating occurs. Male and female snakes do not stay together after mating.

In regions that have warm summers and cold winters, most snakes mate in the spring or fall. In the tropics, snakes may mate at any time of the year.

Most snakes lay eggs. The females generally lay them in shallow holes, rotten logs, tree stumps, or similar places. Sometimes, 100 or more females will lay their eggs at the same site. The number of eggs a female lays at one time varies greatly among different species. In many species, the female lays 6 to 30 eggs at a time. Large pythons usually lay about 50 eggs, but they occasionally produce more than 100.

Most female snakes leave their eggs after laying them. But among a few species, including Indian pythons and king cobras, the females may coil on top of their eggs and guard them.

The shells of snake eggs expand as the young grow inside. The young snakes hatch in about 8 to 10 weeks. The females of some species carry their eggs within the body several weeks before laying them. As a result, the eggs are well developed by the time they are laid and hatch within 2 to 4 weeks. When they are ready to hatch, young snakes slash their shells with a special tooth that grows on the upper jaw. The tooth is shed after the snakes crawl out of their shells.

About a fifth of all species of snakes bear live young. The pregnancy period among most of these species

© Zig Leszczynski, Animals Animals

Snakes Hatching from Eggs. Among most species of snakes, the young hatch from eggs outside the mother's body. The snakes shown above are northern pine snakes of North America.

© Zig Leszczynski, Animals Animals

A Female Snake Giving Birth to Live Young. About a fifth of all species of snakes bear live young. The mother and newborn above are northern copperheads of North America.

lasts about two or three months. Some species have more than 100 young at a time, but most bear far fewer.

Newly hatched or newly born snakes are entirely on their own. They grow rapidly. The young of some species reach maturity—that is, are able to reproduce—in one year. Among other species, the young mature in two to four years. Most snakes continue to grow after reaching maturity.

Regulation of Body Temperature. The body temperature of snakes varies with changes in the temperature of their surroundings. However, a snake's body temperature must be kept within a certain range for the animal to survive. Most snakes can be fully active only if their body temperature measures between 68° and 95° F. (20° and 35° C). They cannot move if it drops below about 39° F. (4° C). On the other hand, most snakes will die if they are exposed to temperatures above 104° F. (40° C).

Snakes maintain their body temperature within the necessary range by moving to warmer or cooler spots. Most of them raise their body temperature by lying in the sun. Snakes that live underground move to warmer areas in the soil. Snakes avoid high temperatures by seeking shelter under bushes, logs, or rocks. Some snakes that live in the tropics spend the hottest part of the year in a state of limited activity called *estivation*.

Snakes that live in regions with cold winters hibernate and so avoid freezing. They spend the winter in caves, holes in the ground, or other frost-free places. In most areas of the world, a snake sheltered 3 feet (91 centimeters) below the surface of the ground would be protected from freezing. During hibernation, a snake's body temperature may measure from about 39° to 41° F. (4° to 5° C).

Hundreds of snakes of different species may hibernate in the same place if suitable sites are scarce. In the fall and spring, they may be seen near their hibernating sites warming themselves in the sun.

Feeding Habits. Most snakes eat birds, fish, frogs, lizards, and such small mammals as rabbits and rats. Some snakes, including Asian king cobras and North American king snakes, eat other snakes.

Numerous snakes have highly specialized feeding habits. For example, some species eat chiefly snails. The teeth and lower jaw of some snail-eating snakes are specially adapted to pulling the snails from their shells. Thread snakes, which closely resemble blind snakes, have a tiny mouth and eat mainly termites. These snakes can suck the insides of the abdomen from a termite's body, leaving the less digestible parts. Certain snakes that eat eggs have long spines inside the throat on the neck vertebrae. After a snake swallows an egg, the shell is pierced by these spines and then crushed by the snake's muscle contractions. The contents of the egg pass through the throat, but the vertebral spines prevent the passage of the shell. The snake then spits out the shell.

Snakes have various ways of capturing prey. They may wait in ambush, stalk the animal, or pursue it. When a snake strikes, it lunges toward the animal with its mouth wide open. A snake's strike usually is effective only up to a distance equal to one-half to two-thirds of its body length.

Most snakes swallow their prey alive. However, poisonous snakes generally wait for their venom to kill an animal before they swallow it. Usually, *constrictors* also kill their prey before eating it. Constrictors include boas, bull snakes, king snakes, pythons, and rat snakes. A constrictor wraps two or more loops of its body around a victim and then contracts its muscles, squeezing the animal. Many people believe that constrictors kill by crushing the bones and internal organs of their victims. Actually, they kill animals by causing them to suffocate.

After feeding, a snake may lie in the sun. The warmth raises its body temperature, which speeds up the process of digestion. A meal may last a snake a long time. Snakes in zoos and laboratories sometimes do not eat for many months. Large snakes, such as boas and pythons, commonly go without food for more than a year. Even some small snakes may fast 6 to 12 months.

Snakes can survive a long time without food for several reasons. Unlike warm-blooded animals, snakes do not need much food energy to maintain a steady body temperature. Snakes also may remain inactive for extended periods and so use up little energy. In addition, snakes have extensive tissues that store fat. During long fasts, they live off this fat.

Protection Against Enemies. Many kinds of animals prey on snakes. The chief enemies of snakes include large birds, such as bustards and serpent eagles; certain mammals, such as mongooses and pigs; and certain

How a Snake Swallows Its Prey

The pictures below show a North American corn snake eating a mouse. The snake begins to swallow the mouse headfirst, *top picture*. Its scales stretch apart and its ribs spread out as it swallows the animal. The snake alternately moves each side of its jaws forward and backward, pulling the mouse through its throat, *center*. The mouse slides through the snake's esophagus, *bottom*.

© Zig Leszczynski, Animals Animals

other snakes, such as king cobras and king snakes.

Snakes have a wide variety of defenses against their enemies. Many species have color patterns that match their surroundings and so help conceal them. If threatened by an enemy, a snake may escape simply by fleeing into a burrow, pond, or some other place where the animal cannot follow. Some shield-tailed snakes of southern Asia can block the entrance to their burrow. They have a short, blunt tail, which they wedge against the opening.

Many snakes make threatening noises when an enemy approaches. Some can hiss loudly by expelling air from the lung. The rattlesnake makes a distinctive whirring sound by vibrating its tail rattle. The African saw-scaled viper produces a rasping sound by rubbing its side scales together.

Some snakes change their appearance and adopt a threatening posture that may frighten away enemies. For example, the cobra lifts its neck and spreads its

ribs, forming a broad hood. North American hognose snakes, indigo snakes, and some other species spread the neck ribs and inflate the lung, which makes them look larger and more fierce.

Many animals that prey on snakes have no interest in dead snakes. Thus, certain snakes defend themselves by playing dead. The North American hognose snake is especially well known for such behavior. The African ball python protects itself from enemies by coiling into a tight ball with its head in the middle. This defense is also used by North American ground snakes, rubber boas, and various other species.

Some harmless snakes resemble poisonous snakes and thus may gain protection from enemies that fear poisonous snakes. In addition, some kinds of harmless snakes imitate the behavior of poisonous snakes. For example, king snakes and rat snakes vibrate the tail among dry leaves and thereby produce a sound like that made by rattlesnakes. Some harmless snakes of Africa imitate the rasping sound of the saw-scaled viper by rubbing their side scales together. Certain harmless

Some Harmless Snakes of North America

WORLD BOOK illustrations by James Teason

Eastern Garter Snake
Thamnophis sirtalis sirtalis
18 to 26 inches (46 to 66 centimeters) long

Eastern Coachwhip
Masticophis flagellum flagellum
42 to 60 inches (107 to 152 centimeters) long

Prairie Ringneck Snake
Diadophis punctatus arnyi
10 to 14 inches (25 to 36 centimeters) long

Sonora Mountain Kingsnake
Lampropeltis pyromelana
18 to 41 inches (46 to 104 centimeters) long

Bull Snake
Pituophis melanoleucus sayi
50 to 72 inches (127 to 183 centimeters) long

Eastern Yellow-Bellied Racer
Coluber constrictor flaviventris
30 to 50 inches (76 to 127 centimeters) long

Rough Green Snake
Opheodrys aestivus
22 to 32 inches (56 to 81 centimeters) long

Corn Snake
Elaphe guttata guttata
30 to 48 inches (76 to 122 centimeters) long

Red Milk Snake
Lampropeltis triangulum syspila
21 to 28 inches (53 to 71 centimeters) long

Black Rat Snake
Elaphe obsoleta obsoleta
42 to 72 inches (107 to 183 centimeters) long

Northern Water Snake
Natrix sipedon sipedon
24 to 42 inches (61 to 107 centimeters) long

Asian snakes spread their ribs and form a hood like that of the Indian cobra.

If other defenses fail, a snake might attack and bite an enemy. The bite of a poisonous snake is an especially powerful weapon. But the snake could be seriously clawed or bitten before its venom takes effect. The African "spitting" cobra has added protection. It can squirt venom into the eyes of an enemy 6 to 8 feet (1.8 to 2.4 meters) away. The venom causes an immediate painful, burning sensation and can produce blindness. Large constrictors are also a powerful match for most of their enemies. They can quickly coil around an animal and suffocate it, just as they do prey.

Battles Among Male Snakes. Among some species of snakes, the adult males sometimes fight one another. In a typical battle, two snakes rear up, entwine their bodies, and try to push each other down. The combat continues until one snake gives up and retreats. Such battles are especially common among vipers. But they also occur among such small, harmless snakes as North American ground snakes and European smooth snakes.

Herpetologists do not know for certain why male snakes of some species fight one another. But most of the fights occur during the breeding season. They may be caused by rivalry over a mate or feeding area.

Life Span. Herpetologists do not know how long snakes live in the wild. Most snakes in zoos do not live longer than 15 years. But some have lived 20 years in captivity, and a few have lived over 30 years.

Classification of Snakes

There are about 2,700 species of snakes. They are classified into various families, based chiefly on common skeletal features. Herpetologists disagree on the number of families. Some list 11 families, and others list up to 15. The following discussion divides snakes into 11 families. The common names of these families are (1) colubrids, (2) blind snakes, (3) thread snakes, (4) boids, (5) elapids, (6) sea snakes, (7) vipers, (8) shield-tailed snakes, (9) pipe snakes, (10) sunbeam snakes, and

Some Poisonous Snakes of North America

Northern Copperhead
Agkistrodon contortrix mokason
24 to 36 inches (61 to 91 centimeters) long

Southern Copperhead
Agkistrodon contortrix contortrix
24 to 36 inches (61 to 91 centimeters) long

Broad-Banded Copperhead
Agkistrodon contortrix laticinctus
22 to 30 inches (56 to 76 centimeters) long

Western Pygmy Rattlesnake
Sistrurus miliarius streckeri
15 to 20 inches (38 to 51 centimeters) long

Black-Tailed Rattlesnake
Crotalus molossus molossus
30 to 42 inches (76 to 107 centimeters) long

Eastern Diamondback Rattlesnake
Crotalus adamanteus
33 to 72 inches (84 to 183 centimeters) long

Timber Rattlesnake
Crotalus horridus horridus
36 to 54 inches (91 to 137 centimeters) long

Eastern Cottonmouth
Agkistrodon piscivorus piscivorus
30 to 48 inches (76 to 122 centimeters) long

Eastern Massasauga
Sistrurus catenatus catenatus
20 to 30 inches (51 to 76 centimeters) long

Canebrake Rattlesnake
Crotalus horridus atricaudatus
42 to 60 inches (107 to 152 centimeters) long

Eastern Coral Snake
Micrurus fulvius fulvius
20 to 30 inches (51 to 76 centimeters) long

SNAKE

(11) elephant trunk snakes. The scientific name of each family of snakes is given in parentheses after the common name.

Colubrids (Colubridae) total about 2,000 species. They make up about two-thirds of all species of snakes. The family includes most of the common harmless snakes, such as the North American garter snakes and rat snakes. It also includes many species of venomous, rear-fanged snakes. However, only a few rear-fanged snakes, such as the African bird snakes and boomslangs, are dangerous to human beings.

Colubrids live throughout most of the world. The different species vary greatly in appearance and ways of life. They dwell on land, in trees, in water, or under the ground.

Blind Snakes (Typhlopidae) consist of about 200 species. They burrow underground and eat mainly ants and termites. Blind snakes look much like earthworms, though some species grow almost 3 feet (91 centimeters) long. Their eyes are covered by the head scales. Most blind snakes live in tropical and subtropical regions.

Thread Snakes (Leptotyphlopidae) make up about 50 species. They closely resemble blind snakes and have similar ways of life. A main difference between the two families is that blind snakes have teeth only on the upper jaw, and thread snakes have teeth only on the lower jaw. Thread snakes live in Africa, southern Asia, southwestern North America, and tropical areas of Central and South America.

Boids (Boidae) include the largest snakes—the anacondas, pythons, and boas. The family consists of about 100 species, most of which have a large, stout body. However, some species are less than 3 feet (91 centimeters) long. Most boids have external vestiges of hind legs. The majority of boids live in tropical and subtropical regions. Different species dwell on land, in trees, or in water.

Elapids (Elapidae) consist of nearly 200 species of venomous snakes. All have short, nonmovable front fangs. No elapids live in Europe, and coral snakes are the only members of the family found in North and South America. Elapids are most numerous in Australia, where they include the Australian black snake, death adder, taipan, and tiger snake. The cobras of

Some Snakes of Other Continents

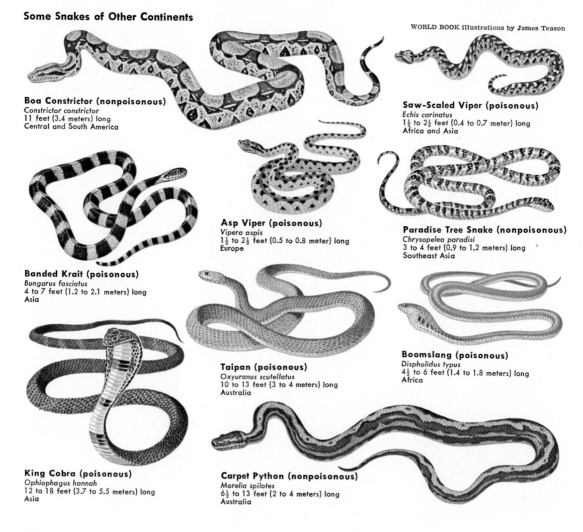

Boa Constrictor (nonpoisonous)
Constrictor constrictor
11 feet (3.4 meters) long
Central and South America

Saw-Scaled Viper (poisonous)
Echis carinatus
1⅓ to 2⅓ feet (0.4 to 0.7 meter) long
Africa and Asia

Asp Viper (poisonous)
Vipera aspis
1½ to 2½ feet (0.5 to 0.8 meter) long
Europe

Paradise Tree Snake (nonpoisonous)
Chrysopelea paradisi
3 to 4 feet (0.9 to 1.2 meters) long
Southeast Asia

Banded Krait (poisonous)
Bungarus fasciatus
4 to 7 feet (1.2 to 2.1 meters) long
Asia

Taipan (poisonous)
Oxyuranus scutellatus
10 to 13 feet (3 to 4 meters) long
Australia

Boomslang (poisonous)
Dispholidus typus
4½ to 6 feet (1.4 to 1.8 meters) long
Africa

King Cobra (poisonous)
Ophiophagus hannah
12 to 18 feet (3.7 to 5.5 meters) long
Asia

Carpet Python (nonpoisonous)
Morelia spilotes
6½ to 13 feet (2 to 4 meters) long
Australia

Africa and Asia, the kraits of southern Asia, and the mambas of Africa also are elapids. Most elapids dwell on land.

Sea Snakes (Hydrophiidae) consist of 50 to 60 species of venomous snakes. They are related to elapids. Most sea snakes are 3 to 4 feet (91 to 120 centimeters) long. In all species, the body is flattened sideways.

Most sea snakes live in the tropical areas of the Indian and Pacific oceans. They dwell in coastal waters and are rarely found at depths greater than 150 feet (46 meters). Occasionally, huge groups of sea snakes are spotted in the open sea. Scientists believe that the snakes may be massed together by tidal currents. No sea snakes dwell in the Atlantic Ocean, the Mediterranean Sea, or the Red Sea.

Most sea snakes give birth to live young in the water. However, a few species come ashore and lay eggs.

Vipers (Viperidae) have long fangs attached to the front of the upper jaw. The upper jaw rotates, enabling a viper to move its fangs forward and backward.

The fangs of vipers are much longer than those of elapids. The African Gaboon viper has perhaps the longest fangs of any venomous snake. They may grow up to 2 inches (5 centimeters) long.

Vipers are divided into two main groups—*pit vipers* and *true vipers*. The pit vipers have pit organs between their eyes and nostrils. Pit vipers consist of about 100 species, which are found on all the continents except Antarctica and Australia. They include North American copperheads, rattlesnakes, and water moccasins. True vipers do not have pit organs. They consist of about 50 species, which live in Africa, Asia, and Europe. True vipers include the African Gaboon viper and the European viper.

Shield-Tailed Snakes (Uropeltidae) consist of about 45 species of burrowing snakes, all of which live in Sri Lanka and southern India. They have a highly pointed or wedge-shaped snout; a short, blunt tail; and smooth scales. Most species dwell in humid mountain forests.

Pipe Snakes (Aniliidae) make up about 12 species of burrowing snakes. They have a stout body and short tail. They grow less than 3 feet (91 centimeters) long and live in southern Asia and South America.

Sunbeam Snakes (Xenopeltidae) consist of one species. The snakes live in southeastern Asia. They have highly polished scales, which sparkle in the sunlight. They usually stay under logs or stones or in burrows during the day and move about at night.

Elephant Trunk Snakes (Acrochordidae), also called wart snakes, consist of two species. They have a stout body and wrinkled skin. These snakes grow up to 8 feet (2.4 meters) long and are widely hunted for their leather-like skin. They live in the rivers and coastal waters of southern Asia, northern Australia, and the South Pacific islands.

The Importance of Snakes

The main value of snakes is that they form part of the environment and help preserve the balance of nature (see BALANCE OF NATURE). But people also gain economic benefits from snakes. The animals aid farmers by preying on such pests as mice and rats. In some countries, especially China and Japan, people eat the meat of snakes. The skin of boas, elephant trunk snakes, and pythons is used to make such items as belts and handbags. People also sell snakes as pets.

Snake venom has several uses in medicine and biological research. *Antivenin*, which is used to treat snakebite, is prepared from the blood serum of horses that have been injected with venom. Certain pain-killing drugs are prepared from neurotoxins in venom. Researchers use the powerful enzymes in venom to break down complex proteins for biochemical studies.

In general, snakes are abundant in most parts of the world. But human beings have caused a decline in the numbers of some species, partly through overhunting and by needlessly killing them. People also destroy the places where snakes live by clearing land for farms, houses, and industries. Human activities threaten the survival of a few species, including the Indian python, the Jamaica boa, and the San Francisco garter snake. In the United States, laws prohibit people from buying, selling, or killing endangered species.

Scientific Classification. Snakes belong to the order Squamata in the class Reptilia. They form the suborder Serpentes.   DONALD W. TINKLE

Related Articles in WORLD BOOK include:

KINDS OF SNAKES

Adder	Cobra	Mamba
Anaconda	Copperhead	Milk Snake
Asp	Coral Snake	Python
Blacksnake	Fer-de-Lance	Rattlesnake
Boa Constrictor	Garter Snake	Viper
Bushmaster	King Snake	Water Moccasin

OTHER RELATED ARTICLES

Herpetology	Pet (Unusual Pets)	Snake Charming
Molting	Reptile	Snakebite

Outline

I. The Bodies of Snakes
- A. Body Shape
- B. Scales and Color
- C. Skeleton
- D. Muscles
- E. Internal Organs
- F. Sense Organs
- G. Fangs and Venom Glands

II. Ways of Life Among Snakes
- A. Methods of Movement
- B. Reproduction
- C. Regulation of Body Temperature
- D. Feeding Habits
- E. Protection Against Enemies
- F. Battles Among Male Snakes
- G. Life Span

III. Classification of Snakes
- A. Colubrids
- B. Blind Snakes
- C. Thread Snakes
- D. Boids
- E. Elapids
- F. Sea Snakes
- G. Vipers
- H. Shield-Tailed Snakes
- I. Pipe Snakes
- J. Sunbeam Snakes
- K. Elephant Trunk Snakes

IV. The Importance of Snakes

Questions

What kind of fangs do vipers have?

Why can snakes survive a long time without food?

How do snakes swallow their prey?

What is the most common way that snakes move about?

How have human beings caused a decline in the numbers of some species of snakes?

How do most snakes raise their body temperature?

What is the Jacobson's organ? How is it used?

To what family do most species of snakes belong?

How do constrictors kill their prey?

How many kinds of snakes are there?

American Girls in a Track Meet

Frank Cezus, A. Devaney, Inc.

Kent Reno, Jeroboam, Inc.

Gerry Souter, Van Cleve, Inc.
English Schoolboys

Victor Englebert, De Wys, Inc.
Indonesian Girls Planting Rice

U.S. Teen-Agers Skateboarding

Adolescents of Different Cultures vary widely in their responsibilities. In agricultural societies, most young people must start work at an early age. They have little free time. In most industrial societies, boys and girls must attend school until they are 16 years of age or older. But they usually have ample opportunities for recreation.

ADOLESCENT

ADOLESCENT is a person who is no longer a child but not yet an adult. The word *adolescent* comes from the Latin term *adolescens*, which means *growing up* or *growing toward*. An adolescent is someone who is "growing toward" adulthood. Most Western societies consider a person to be an adolescent from about 13 to at least 18 years of age. In these societies, adolescence thus roughly corresponds to the teen-age years.

Nearly all societies consider boys and girls to have outgrown childhood when they start to mature sexually. Most young people begin this development in their late preteens or early teens. But the age when a person is expected or permitted to take on full adult responsibilities varies greatly among societies.

In agricultural societies, which need many workers, most boys and girls are expected to become economically productive when they reach sexual maturity or even before. Such societies are common in Africa, Asia, and Latin America. Adulthood begins early in these societies, and adolescence is brief or nonexistent.

On the other hand, industrial societies usually have a

James F. Adams, the contributor of this article, is Professor of Psychology at Temple University and the editor of Understanding Adolescence: Current Developments in Adolescent Psychology.

surplus of workers. They also have a higher standard of living than do agricultural societies. They can therefore delay the entry of young people into the labor force. In addition, the culture of industrial societies is far more complex than that of agricultural societies and takes far longer for a person to learn. For all these reasons, the laws of most industrial societies do not permit people to assume full adult responsibilities before the late teens. Nor are young people expected to be self-supporting. Legally, they are the responsibility of their parents.

In the past, nearly all industrial societies set the legal adult age at 21. Since the early 1960's, however, most of these societies have lowered the legal age to 18, 19, or 20. Today, a person legally becomes an adult at age 18 in most states of the United States, in most Canadian provinces, and in most European countries. The legal age is 19 or 21 in some states; 19 in some provinces; and 20 or 21 in Australia, Japan, New Zealand, and some European countries. Adolescence can thus be a fairly long period from a legal standpoint.

In addition to its legal aspects, adolescence may also be viewed as a stage of psychological development. To a psychologist, an adolescent is a person who is learning to be independent, like an adult, rather than remaining dependent, like a child. Some people reach this goal much faster than others. A teen-ager may thus become psychologically mature before reaching the legal adult age. However, most teen-agers mature psychologically at the rate set by their society. As a result, psychological adolescence normally lasts at least as long as the period of legal dependence.

In the United States, Canada, and other societies where adolescence is prolonged, teen-agers tend to form *subcultures*. A subculture is a group of people whose customs and values differ from those of society as a whole. However, teen-age subcultures often help shape the customs and values of the parent society.

There are about 29 million teen-agers in the United States. They make up about 13 per cent of the total population. But their influence on American life far exceeds their numbers. Teen-agers' preferences in such matters as music and clothing styles often affect the tastes of society as a whole. During the 1960's, the opposition of American teen-agers to established cultural values and institutions led to *countercultural movements*. The youth countercultures consisted mainly of older adolescents who wanted to set up a completely free and open society based on their ideals. They largely failed. However, their efforts contributed to the growing questioning of traditional institutions during the 1970's.

Growth and Development

Many studies of human development try to pinpoint the age at which most people develop a particular characteristic. These studies use data gathered in surveys to produce a statistical average called a *norm*. Development that approximates the norm is said to be normal. However, wide variations are not necessarily abnormal.

The norm is simply the average of many individual differences. For example, surveys have shown that, on the average, girls in the United States have their first menstrual period at the age of $12\frac{1}{2}$ years. Therefore, $12\frac{1}{2}$ years is said to be the "normal" age for an American girl to begin menstruation. However, few girls start menstruation at exactly this age, and many start it several years earlier or later. Parents and adolescents, therefore, should not be disturbed if the norm for a particular development is not met at a certain age.

Physical Growth and Development. Adolescence begins with a period of dramatic sexual development called *puberty*. Puberty is brought on by a sudden increase in the activity of certain glands, especially the hypothalamus, pineal, pituitary, and sex glands.

At the start of puberty, a girl's breasts become larger, her hips widen, and hair grows under her arms and around her *genitals* (external sex organs). A year or so after these changes begin, she has her first menstrual period. When a boy starts puberty, hair grows around his genitals, on his face, and on other parts of his body. His genitals become larger, his shoulders broaden, and his voice deepens. Most girls start puberty at about 11 years of age. Most boys start it at about age 13. Puberty ends when a girl or boy reaches sexual maturity—that is, becomes capable of reproduction. Most adolescents become sexually mature two or three years after they start puberty.

The increased glandular activity that brings on puberty also causes other physical changes in adolescents. These changes include rapid increases in height and weight. Most girls start to grow rapidly at about 9 to 12 years of age. Girls are normally taller and heavier than boys during these years. During the early teens, most boys start to grow rapidly, and the girls' rate of growth declines. After about age 14, males are heavier and taller, on the average, than females. Most males reach adult size during their late teens or early twenties. Most females reach it somewhat earlier.

Many younger adolescents become intensely concerned about their physical appearance. They may complain that they are too tall or too short, that their hands and feet are too big or too small, and that overall they are unattractive and awkward. A girl who matures early may feel self-conscious because her breasts are noticeably larger than those of other girls her age. A girl who matures late may feel self-conscious for the opposite reason. Late-maturing adolescents—especially boys—tend to have a poorer opinion of themselves than do adolescents who mature early or at an average rate. They may also have more difficulty making friends. In

Average Height and Weight for Adolescents

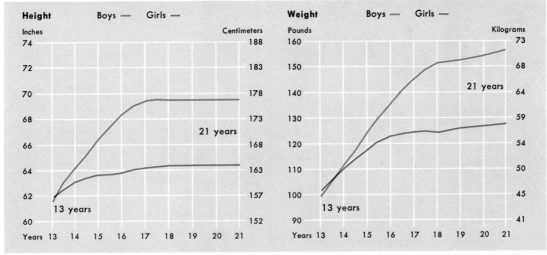

Source: National Center for Health Statistics, U.S. Public Health Service.

most cases, however, these difficulties disappear as the boy or girl matures physically. Many teen-agers are embarrassed by acne or pimples, though minor skin problems are common during adolescence.

The concern that younger teen-agers have about their appearance is understandable. Adolescents feel a strong need to compare favorably with others their age. Anything that makes them different will likely upset them. But differences in physical development are obvious during the early teen-age years, and so they naturally become a focus of attention. During middle and late adolescence, such differences fade in importance.

Social Development. Most young people mature sexually by the age of 14 or 15. They are thus physically able to have children. But a person this age lacks the experience and social maturity needed to function as an adult in most societies today. People are considered socially mature if they can act independently and accept full responsibility for their actions. Developing this ability is the chief task of an adolescent.

Most adolescents welcome the opportunity to take on more responsibility and become more independent. However, they may have difficulty at first in handling the challenge. To accept responsibility, a person needs self-confidence. But it is hard to develop self-confidence if the self seems to be constantly changing. Most younger adolescents have this difficulty because of the many physical changes they go through during puberty. These changes tend to interfere with an adolescent's sense of *personal identity*—that is, the awareness one has of oneself as a consistently whole person. As adolescents mature physically, they normally develop a stronger sense of personal identity and greater self-confidence. Their capacity for social development then increases.

Adolescents develop socially chiefly by expanding and testing their social relationships. A young child's social environment usually centers in the home. Children model themselves after their parents or other adults they admire. They may adopt bad traits as well as good ones, and so adults have a heavy responsibility in their behavior around children. In general, young children avoid types of behavior that their parents disapprove of. However, most adolescents become deeply involved with their *peer group*—that is, their circle of friends and acquaintances. These teen-agers look to their peer group, rather than to their parents, for approval, and they may change their behavior to win that approval. Within the peer group, adolescents also begin to define their relationships with the opposite sex.

Family Relationships are important to teen-agers, though in ways that are not always apparent. Most teen-agers prefer the company of their friends to that of their family. While at home, they often prefer being alone. These preferences are normal during adolescence, though they may not seem so to younger brothers and sisters and to parents. Conflicts between an adolescent and younger family members usually lessen as the family adjusts to the adolescent's need for independence and privacy. However, adolescents often have increasing conflicts with their parents over the amount of freedom they think they deserve.

Social development is easiest for adolescents who feel that their parents love and trust them. Parental love should include discipline, and so the teen-ager who is truly loved will receive guidance. Parents display trust by granting their children sufficient freedom. An over-protected adolescent may have great difficulty learning to act independently.

Peer Group Relationships help adolescents learn to deal with people on an equal basis. Developing this ability is an important part of becoming an adult. However, adolescents tend to measure social development chiefly in terms of their personal popularity. They assume they are developing normally if their peers accept and like them. Teen-agers thus become absorbed in matters they think affect their popularity, such as their style of dress, leadership ability, and success in dating. Parents may be annoyed by the amount of time and energy an adolescent devotes to such concerns. But these concerns are part of growing up, and teen-agers need freedom to pursue them.

Adolescents who have a strong need for peer group

Younger Adolescents become increasingly involved with their *peer group*—that is, their circle of friends and acquaintances, *left*. Peer group relationships play a major role in the social development of adolescents. Teen-agers need frequent contacts with their peers to help them learn to deal with people on an equal basis.

Dating normally begins during mid-adolescence. By the late teens, a boy and girl may have developed a special fondness for each other, *left*. But most young people do not restrict their dating to only one person until they are old enough and mature enough to consider marrying.

approval may feel forced to adopt all of the group's values. Problems arise if these values conflict with the ones taught at home. Parents should try to remember that the choice is not always easy for a teen-ager to make. Girls tend to have more difficulty resolving these conflicts than do boys, probably because girls are expected to be better behaved.

Boy-Girl Relationships. During early adolescence, boys and girls get together mainly in group activities, such as school or church dances, parties, and club meetings. By the mid-teens, most adolescents begin to date occasionally. Dating usually increases during late adolescence. In addition, many older teen-agers start to restrict their dating to one person.

The earliest age at which people may marry varies among societies. In most states of the United States, both partners must be at least 18 to marry without their parents' permission. Persons under 18 are generally not mature enough to take on the responsibilities of marriage and parenthood. But most adolescents mature sexually long before age 18, and many find it difficult to control their sexual desires. Studies of American teen-agers indicate that more than half the unmarried boys and nearly half the unmarried girls have sexual intercourse by the age of 19. However, sexual relationships involve moral and practical considerations. Many people regard intercourse outside marriage as morally wrong. In addition, such relationships may produce serious consequences, especially unwanted pregnancies.

In the United States, about 1 million teen-age girls become pregnant each year. Some are married at the time or marry soon after. A few have miscarriages, and a growing number have medical abortions. The rest have the child outside marriage. Teen-agers who have sexual relations also run a high risk of getting a venereal disease. The venereal disease rate among teen-agers is far greater than among adults.

Special Problems of Adolescence

All adolescents have problems from time to time. However, most young people pass through adolescence

without serious difficulty. They make new friends, join clubs, and take part in sports and social activities. For these young people, the teen-age years are generally happy and exciting.

Most of the problems that adolescents have are related to schoolwork, finances, or peer group and family relationships. The majority of such problems are minor, at least from an adult's point of view. However, a problem that appears unimportant to an adult may seem overwhelming to an adolescent. This difference in viewpoints may itself cause problems if it leads to a breakdown in communications between parents and their teen-age children. Parents accomplish little by lecturing. They help by being willing to listen and by avoiding the temptation to give instant advice.

Most personal problems of adolescents do not affect society as a whole. But certain other problems involving adolescents are so serious and widespread that they are considered social problems. These special problems include (1) attitudes toward schooling, (2) the use of drugs, and (3) delinquency.

Attitudes Toward Schooling. Education is increasingly important in today's complex industrial societies. More and more jobs in these societies require a high degree of specialized knowledge or technical skill. In addition, democratic societies, such as the United States, have traditionally relied on the schools to help produce well-informed, responsible citizens. Nearly every state of the United States requires young people to attend school until they are at least 16 years of age or until they graduate from high school.

Most adolescents finish high school, and many receive some type of advanced schooling. However, about 15 per cent of all U.S. high school students drop out of school when they meet the age requirement. Many others complete high school under protest and barely meet the requirements for graduation. Teen-agers who do not receive adequate schooling are likely to have great difficulty functioning as adults. About 15 per cent of all unemployed workers in the United States did not finish high school. Even everyday living can be difficult

Runk/Schoenberger from Grant Heilman

Cleaning Up a Polluted Waterway is a challenge gladly undertaken by these teen-age volunteers. Most young people are eager to devote time and energy to causes they believe in.

for adults who cannot read well, express themselves clearly, or do simple arithmetic.

Many teen-agers who drop out of school or neglect their studies come from homes where learning is not encouraged. But many students do not fully develop their abilities even though they receive ample encouragement at home. In some cases, parents may need to reevaluate the goals they have set for their children. Even able students may rebel if they feel that too much is demanded of them. Parents should try to encourage good performance in school without exerting unreasonable pressure.

The Use of Drugs. Surveys of U.S. teen-agers indicate that the great majority have at least experimented with such drugs as alcohol, barbiturates, cocaine, LSD, or marijuana. Some have experimented with heroin, morphine, or other narcotic drugs. Many of these drugs are physically harmful if taken regularly. A single overdose of some drugs, such as heroin or a barbiturate, can result in a coma or death.

Nearly all the drugs that teen-agers take cannot be obtained or used legally in the United States without a doctor's prescription. Alcohol is the major exception. It is the most widely used drug among both adults and teen-agers. Adults can obtain it legally. But alcoholic beverages cannot legally be sold to persons under 18 in any state, and in most states the legal drinking age is 19, 20, or 21. Marijuana is the second most widely used drug among American teen-agers. Unlike alcohol, it cannot legally be sold, possessed, or used by anyone in the United States.

Adolescents experiment with drugs for various reasons, including peer group pressure, the example of parents, and curiosity. Most teen-agers pass through the experimentation stage without developing a drug abuse problem. Others are not so fortunate. Alcohol is the most frequently abused drug among teen-agers, as it is among adults. Experts estimate that about 15 per cent of U.S. high school students may have a serious drinking problem.

The causes of teen-age drug abuse are not well understood. Some teen-agers may be led into it by boredom or by an unconscious desire to escape mental or emotional pressure. Teen-agers who feel genuinely useful are perhaps least likely to develop the problem.

Delinquency. About 25 per cent of all the persons arrested annually in the United States are under 18 years of age. In most states of the United States—and in most other societies—offenders under 18 are tried as juveniles rather than as adults. Many juvenile offenses are relatively minor. They include certain offenses, such as breaking curfew or running away from home, that apply only to juveniles. However, persons under 18 are charged with about 40 per cent of all the serious crimes in the United States. Most of these arrests are for automobile theft, burglary, larceny, or robbery. About 65 per cent of the teen-agers arrested for serious crimes are 15 through 17 years old. The rest are under 15. About 20 per cent of the serious offenders are girls. More than 60 per cent of the persons arrested for vandalism in the United States are juveniles.

In general, the juvenile delinquency rate is highest in urban areas that have many school dropouts and few employment and recreational opportunities for youth. Many juvenile delinquents, but by no means all of them, come from low-income families. Teen-agers are least likely to become delinquents if their parents have treated them with love and respect, have taught them discipline, and have themselves been models of responsible behavior. Extreme poverty does not favor these conditions. But they are also lacking in many well-to-do families. In numerous cases, juvenile delinquency results mainly from faulty parent-child relations and poor parental example, not from economic hardship. However, delinquency also has other causes. Pressure from the peer group may be a principal cause in many cases. Some juvenile offenders have strong antisocial feelings or other deep-seated psychological problems.

Preparation for the Future

During the final two years of high school, and often earlier, teen-agers must decide how they will support themselves after they are on their own. In planning a career, high school students should first decide what their goals are, what types of work they prefer, and what special skills they have. By comparing the answers to these questions with the descriptions of various careers, a student can narrow the range of possible choices. However, it is wise to keep the range as broad as possible at first. Either through choice or through necessity, many teen-agers change their goals as they grow older. They then need to be open to other career possibilities.

Teen-agers must also consider their financial resources when planning a career. Many jobs require a college education or other special training beyond high school. A college education may cost hundreds or thousands of dollars annually just for tuition. In some cases, parents can provide all or most of the money. Many students who need financial help apply for a scholarship. Scholarships provide money grants or free tuition on the basis of merit or financial need (see SCHOLARSHIP). Many students save enough money from part-time and summer jobs to enable them to continue their education. For detailed information on careers and career planning, see CAREERS.

Part-Time Employment gives high school students valuable experience and enables many of them to save enough money to attend college. These students work part-time in a library.

WORLD BOOK photo

Outline

I. Growth and Development
A. Physical Growth and Development
B. Social Development

II. Special Problems of Adolescence
A. Attitudes Toward Schooling
B. The Use of Drugs
C. Delinquency

III. Preparation for the Future

Questions

What is the chief task of an adolescent?

Why is adolescence usually shorter in agricultural societies than in industrial societies?

What is a *norm?* Why are norms not always a reliable measure of human development in individual cases?

How do adolescents tend to measure their social development?

What factors should high school students consider in planning a career?

Why is education especially important to adolescents in industrial societies?

How do boy-girl relationships vary from early to late adolescence?

How can parents help prevent their children from becoming juvenile delinquents?

Why do many teen-age marriages fail?

Why do many adolescents become intensely concerned about their physical appearance during the early teenage years?

Books to Read

ADAMS, JAMES F., ed. *Understanding Adolescence: Current Developments in Adolescent Psychology*, 3rd ed. Allyn & Bacon, 1976.

COLEMAN, JAMES S., and others. *The Adolescent Society: The Social Life of the Teenager and Its Impact on Education*. Macmillan, 1961.

CONGER, JOHN J. *Contemporary Issues in Adolescent Development*. Harper, 1975. *Adolescence and Youth: Psychological Development in a Changing World*. 2nd ed. 1977.

EAGAN, ANDREA B. *Why Am I So Miserable If These Are the Best Years of My Life? A Survival Guide for the Young Woman*. Lippincott, 1976.

FINE, LOUIS L. *"After All We've Done for Them": Understanding Adolescent Behavior*. Prentice-Hall, 1977.

FRIEDENBERG, EDGAR Z. *Vanishing Adolescent*. Beacon Press, 1959. *Coming of Age in America: Growth and Acquiescence*. Random House, 1965.

GINOTT, HAIM G. *Between Parent and Teenager*. Macmillan, 1969.

KAPPELMAN, MURRAY M. *Sex and the American Teenager: The Problems of Adolescent Sexuality—and How to Cope with Them—in Today's Changing World*. Crowell, 1977.

KETT, JOSEPH F. *Rites of Passage: Adolescence in America, 1790 to the Present*. Basic Books, 1977.

MINTON, LYNN. *Growing into Adolescence: A Sensible Guide for Parents of Children 11 to 14*. Parents' Magazine Press, 1972.

Some teen-agers plan to marry as soon as they are old enough. In the United States, about 15 per cent of all females and about 5 per cent of all males marry before the age of 20. The divorce rate among Americans who marry in their teens is six times as great as the overall U.S. divorce rate. For a marriage to work, both partners must have a high degree of emotional and intellectual maturity. Each also has to be willing to accept the other's faults. However, it usually takes time for two persons in love to see each other realistically. Many teen-age marriages fail because they were entered into too quickly. A marriage is more likely to succeed if the partners get to know each other well before they marry. JAMES F. ADAMS

Related Articles in WORLD BOOK include:

Djibouti, the capital of the country of Djibouti, is the home of more than half the nation's people. This photograph shows people walking in a public square next to the city's main *mosque* (Muslim house of worship).

Kay Honkanen

DJIBOUTI, *jih BOO tee,* is a small country in eastern Africa. It lies on the western shore of the Gulf of Aden. The gulf and the Red Sea and Suez Canal to the north link the Indian Ocean and the Mediterranean Sea. Djibouti's location has helped make the country's capital, also called Djibouti, a major port. The location also has potential strategic importance. Ships travel freely past Djibouti's coast. But it would be possible for a powerful nation that gained possession of the area to control the passage of vessels traveling between the Indian Ocean and the Mediterranean.

Djibouti is an extremely poor country with almost no natural resources. In 1977, it gained independence from France, which had ruled the area since the late 1800's. The French originally called Djibouti *French Somaliland,* but in 1967 they renamed it the *French Territory of the Afars and Issas.*

Government. Djibouti is a democratic republic. The people elect the nation's legislature, called the National Assembly, which has 65 members. The assembly elects Djibouti's president, who heads the government.

People. Djibouti has about 250,000 people. Two ethnic groups, the *Afars* and the *Issas,* make up most of the population. The Afars live in the north and west. The Issas, a Somali people, live in the south. Djibouti also has about 6,000 French and about 3,000 Arab residents.

The Afars and the Issas have traditionally been nomads. Today, many of them still wander over the desolate countryside with herds of goats, sheep, camels, and cattle. Scorching heat, a scarcity of water, and a shortage of grazing lands make life difficult for the nomads. As a result, about 100,000 Afars and Issas now live in the city of Djibouti. But poverty and an unemployment rate as high as 90 per cent plague the capital's people. Many people throughout the country chew *khat,* a leaf that produces a feeling of well-being. Large numbers of workers spend up to 40 per cent of their income for khat.

The official language of Djibouti is Arabic, but most of the people speak Afar or Somali. A large majority of the people are Muslims. Educational opportunities are limited in Djibouti, and only about 10 per cent of the population can read and write.

Land and Climate. The terrain of Djibouti is extremely desolate. A barren plain stretches along the coast. Farther inland is a mountain range that has a few peaks more than 5,000 feet (1,500 meters) above sea level. A rugged plateau lies beyond the mountains. Vegetation is scarce throughout the country.

Djibouti, which has been called "a valley of hell," has one of the hottest and driest climates in the world. The temperature averages 85° F. (29° C), and it some-

Djibouti

▭	International boundary
—	Road
▭	Railroad
✳	National capital
•	Other town
+	Elevation above sea level

WORLD BOOK map

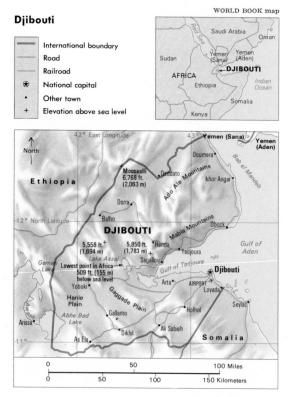

Capital: Djibouti (city).

Official Language: Arabic.

Form of Government: Republic.

Area: 8,494 sq. mi. (22,000 km²). *Greatest Distances—* east-west, 110 mi. (177 km); north-south, 125 mi. (201 km). *Coastline—*152 mi. (245 km).

Elevation: *Highest—*Mousaalli, 6,768 ft. (2,063 m) above sea level. *Lowest—*Lake Assal, 509 ft. (155 m) below sea level.

Population: *Estimated 1979 Population—*250,000; distribution, 50 per cent urban, 50 per cent rural; density, 28 persons per sq. mi. (11 persons per km²). *1960-1961 Census—*81,200.

Chief Products: Hides, skins.

Flag: The flag has a blue horizontal stripe at the top, a green horizontal stripe at the bottom, and a red star on a white triangle near the staff. Adopted in 1977. See FLAG (picture: Flags of Africa).

Money: *Basic Unit—*Djibouti franc.

times rises above 107° F. (42° C) from May to October. The country receives less than 5 inches (13 centimeters) of rain annually.

Economy. Djibouti is an extremely poor and underdeveloped country. It has no natural resources of any importance and no industry except for two soft-drink plants. Djibouti's only agricultural activity is livestock herding. The nation's economy is based almost entirely on the port of the capital and a railroad that links it with Addis Ababa, Ethiopia. Djibouti serves as a major port for Ethiopian trade. The country has an international airport and about 100 miles (160 kilometers) of paved roads.

History. People have lived in what is now Djibouti since prehistoric times. During the A.D. 800's, missionaries from Arabia converted the Afars who inhabited the area to Islam. The Afars then established several Islamic states, which fought a series of wars with Christian Ethiopia from the 1200's through the early 1600's. By the 1800's, the Issas had taken over a large part of the Afars' grazing lands, and hostility between the two groups was growing.

France purchased the Afar port of Obock in 1862 and established a coaling station for French ships there in 1881. The French signed agreements in 1884 with the Afar sultans of Obock and nearby Tadjoura. In 1888, the French occupied the uninhabited area that eventually became the city of Djibouti. They then united various small possessions in the area into a single territory and named it French Somaliland.

The French developed good relations with Emperor Menelik II of Ethiopia, who decided to have a railway built from his capital, Addis Ababa, to the city of Djibouti. In 1897, he made Djibouti the official port for Ethiopian trade. The city grew rapidly during the following years, but little development occurred elsewhere in the territory.

After World War II ended in 1945, the Issas and some other groups in French Somaliland began to demand independence from France. However, the French kept these groups under control. Against the opposition of the Issas, the territory voted in 1958 to join the French Community. This organization is an economic and cultural association linking France and its territories.

In 1967, French Somaliland voted to continue its association with France and was renamed the French Territory of the Afars and Issas. But opposition to French rule grew during the 1970's, when the Issa population increased rapidly. In May 1977, the people voted overwhelmingly for independence. As a result, the territory became the independent nation of Djibouti on June 27, 1977.   RICHARD PANKHURST

See also DJIBOUTI (city).

DJIBOUTI, *jih BOO tee* (pop. 100,000), is the capital of Djibouti, a country in eastern Africa. About 40 per cent of the nation's people live in the city of Djibouti. The city lies on the Gulf of Aden and has one of the best ports on the eastern coast of Africa. For location, see DJIBOUTI (map). A railroad connects Djibouti with Addis Ababa, the capital of Ethiopia, and many Ethiopian exports and imports pass through Djibouti's harbor.

In 1888, France took control of the Djibouti area, which was then uninhabited. The French founded the city that same year. In 1896, they made it the capital of French Somaliland (now the country of Djibouti). The French developed the city as a well-planned colonial capital with many fine public and commercial buildings. The population has grown rapidly since 1945, and large slums have developed.   RICHARD PANKHURST

INSULATION

INSULATION is the restriction of heat, sound, or electricity within a specific area. The term also refers to the materials used to block the flow of these elements.

This article discusses insulation for heat flow control and insulation against sound. For information about insulation against electricity, see INSULATOR, ELECTRIC.

Insulation for Heat Flow Control

Heat flows from a warm area to a cooler one by means of (1) conduction, (2) convection, and (3) radiation. Insulation stops this natural movement (see HEAT [How Heat Travels]). A Thermos bottle is a familiar example of such insulation. It keeps liquids hot or cold by preventing heat from passing in or out of the bottle. Thermos bottles have an inner container that consists of a bottle within a bottle. The bottles of the inner container are made of *borosilicate glass*, which is a poor conductor of heat. Thus, little heat can pass through. In addition, the glass has an aluminum coating that restricts the flow of heat by reflecting it back to its source. However, if heat does move through one of the glass bottles, further flow is limited by the vacuum between them. See VACUUM BOTTLE.

In homes and other buildings, insulation prevents heat from passing out of the structures during cold weather or into the structures during hot weather. In industry, insulation helps maintain certain temperatures necessary for processes used in manufacturing and other operations.

Materials used for insulation include fiberglass, metal foil, rock wool fibers, and certain plastics. These materials, like the borosilicate glass of a Thermos bottle, are poor conductors of heat. When placed against a heated surface, they provide a barrier to the flow of heat. In addition, most insulation materials consist of fibers with cell-like spaces that block the movement of hot or cold air.

In Buildings, insulation is installed in the areas where the greatest heat loss occurs. In most homes, these areas are the attic floor, the ceiling of an unheated basement, and the side walls. Insulation for the side walls is installed in the space between the interior and exterior walls. If a basement is heated, its side walls should be insulated.

There are five chief kinds of insulation for buildings: (1) batts and blankets, (2) loose-fill insulation, (3) cellular plastics, (4) rigid insulation boards, and (5) reflective insulation.

Batts and blankets are soft, flexible units made of fiberglass and rock wool fibers. Batts are cut to certain sizes by the manufacturer. Blankets are sold in long rolls that can be cut to any size during installation. Batts and blankets are used between the *joists*, the beams that support the floor and ceiling. They are also used between *wall studs*, which make up the vertical part of the building frame.

Loose-fill insulation consists of short fibers of cellulose, fiberglass, perlite, rock wool, or vermiculite. It is used chiefly in attics and side walls. Loose-fill insulation can be blown or poured into attics. It is installed between the interior and exterior walls by blowing it through small holes in one of the walls.

Cellular plastics are used to make plastic foam boards, which can be attached to a finished wall. These plastics are also used to make an insulating foam that can be injected into finished walls.

Rigid insulation boards are made from such materials as fiberglass, gypsum, and perlite. They can be attached to the ceiling, roof, or walls.

Reflective insulation consists of thin sheets of aluminum foil. The sheets are arranged in layers, and the layers are separated by spaces that trap warm air. Reflective insulation is used between the joists and between wall studs.

Almost all insulation needs a *vapor barrier* to prevent moisture from penetrating the insulation and decreasing its effectiveness. A vapor barrier can be a sheet of foil, plastic, or treated paper. It must be put on the side of the insulation that faces the heated area.

The effectiveness of an insulation material is designated by its *R-value*, a measurement of the material's resistance to the flow of heat. Materials with high R-values have the greatest heat flow resistance. Buildings in cold climates require greater resistance to heat flow than do structures in warm areas.

Insulation should be fireproof and able to resist any physical or chemical changes that could reduce its effectiveness. It should also be resistant to destructive small animals, such as insects, mice, and rats.

Insulation that is properly installed and has an adequate R-value can greatly reduce the amount of fuel needed to heat a building. During the 1970's, the cost of fuel used for heating rose drastically in the United States. As a result, many people installed insulation in their home or increased the insulation already there. Insulation can reduce the amount of fuel needed to heat or cool a home by as much as a third.

In Industry, insulation plays an important part in various operations. For example, some industrial furnaces are lined with blankets that resemble those used in home insulation. Industrial insulation blankets are made of ceramic fibers and can withstand temperatures as high as 2372° F. (1300° C). These blankets block the flow of heat from a furnace so that high tem-

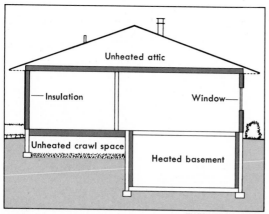

WORLD BOOK diagram

Insulation for Heat Control prevents heat from flowing through ceilings and walls to unheated parts of a house or to the outside. The insulation should be installed in the areas where such heat loss could occur, as shown in gray in this diagram of a well-insulated house. Adequate insulation can greatly reduce the amount of fuel needed to heat a home.

Some Kinds of Insulation for Heat Control

Owens-Corning Fiberglas Corporation

Batts and Blankets are soft, flexible units made of fiberglass or of mineral wool fibers. They are stapled between the joists that support the ceilings and floors, *above*.

CertainTeed Corporation

Loose-Fill Insulation consists of small pieces of fiberglass or other insulating material. It can be blown into unfinished floors, *above*, and walls, or through small holes into finished walls.

Scientific Applications, Inc.

The Upjohn Company

Cellular Plastics are used to make liquid insulating foam and rigid insulation boards. The plastic foam is injected into finished walls through small holes, *left*. The liquid foam hardens as it dries. Plastic boards are attached to finished roofs and walls, *right*.

peratures can be maintained during the heating process.

Furnaces used in steelmaking are insulated with ceramic bricks that can endure temperatures up to 3632° F. (2000° C). The bricks prevent the hot molten metal inside the furnace from damaging the furnace's metal parts. Ceramic insulation must also be able to withstand sudden changes in temperature and many types of chemical reactions.

Insulation is also used to maintain certain temperatures in pipelines that transport hot or cold substances. For example, fiberglass insulates the Trans-Alaska Pipeline, which carries hot crude oil a distance of about 800 miles (1,300 kilometers). This insulation helps maintain the high temperatures needed to pump crude oil through the pipeline. It also prevents the heat of the oil from penetrating the pipeline and damaging the surrounding frozen land.

Insulation Against Sound

Insulation against sound is used in buildings to reduce noise. Some kinds of such insulation block sound and thus prevent it from passing from one room to another. Other kinds, which absorb sound, reduce the noise level within a room. See ACOUSTICS.

Thick, heavy walls without cracks effectively block such sounds as loud music and noisy conversation. However, many modern buildings have thin, lightweight walls that sound can easily pass through. In such cases, sound-deadening boards made of wood fibers can be installed in the walls and ceilings. Such insulation must cover the entire surface because even a small gap allows much sound to pass through. Carpeting and other floor coverings help block the passage of sound to rooms below.

Noise in a room may be reduced by carpeting, draperies, and upholstered furniture, all of which absorb sound. For additional sound absorption, acoustical tiles may be installed on the ceilings and walls. These tiles have tiny holes that trap sound and prevent it from bouncing back into the room.

In industry, insulation against sound reduces noise in factories and in machines used at construction sites. Some factories have sound barriers between the workers and the machines. In others, sound-absorption materials are molded to the machines to lower their noise level. Insulation is also used to reduce noise in such construction machines as air compressors and pneumatic drills.   D. L. McELROY

Leonardi

Figure-Skaters Competing in a World Championship Meet

Royden Hobson

A Speed-Skater Racing over a Course

Robert Glaze, Artstreet

Professional Skaters Performing in an Ice Show

Ice Skating is a competitive sport, a dazzling entertainment in ice shows, and a form of recreation. Athletes compete in *speed-skating* or *figure-skating* events. Professional figure-skaters appear in ice shows. Recreational skaters enjoy skating outdoors or on indoor rinks.

ICE SKATING

ICE SKATING is the act of gliding over a smooth surface of ice on ice skates—boots with attached metal blades. For hundreds of years, people could ice-skate only during the winter months in cold climates. They skated on natural ice surfaces, such as frozen canals, lakes, ponds, and rivers. Today, machines produce ice mechanically in indoor rinks, making ice skating a year-round form of recreation in any climate.

People of almost any age can enjoy ice skating as healthful and relaxing exercise. Skaters use most of the muscles in the body, but especially the leg muscles. Skating also helps blood circulation by strengthening the heart.

Ice skating is an important competitive sport as well as a popular form of recreation. Athletes compete in two kinds of ice skating—*figure skating* and *speed skating*. Figure-skaters perform leaps, spins, and other graceful movements, usually to music. Speed-skaters compete in races of various distances. Many young people and adults also play hockey, a fast, rugged sport in which

Gregory R. Smith, the contributor of this article, is the Editor of Skating, *the official magazine of the United States Figure Skating Association.*

the players wear ice skates. Millions of people attend ice shows each year. An ice show is a colorful spectacle that emphasizes figure skating. Ice shows often feature champion figure-skaters.

Ice skating began many centuries ago in northern Europe. The earliest skaters tied polished animal bones to their boots with leather straps. Skates with iron blades attached to wooden soles probably appeared during the 1200's or 1300's in The Netherlands. A boot and blade were first made as a single unit in the 1870's by Jackson Haines, an American figure-skater.

For hundreds of years, ice skating was chiefly a means of travel in winter. About 1742, skaters in Edinburgh, Scotland, formed the first recreational-skating club. International figure-skating competition began in Austria in 1882. The first international speed-skating races took place in Germany in 1885.

This article describes basic safety rules for recreational skaters. It then discusses competitive figure skating and speed skating. For information on hockey, see the WORLD BOOK article HOCKEY.

Skating Safety

Use of the right equipment is essential to skating safety. The boots should fit properly—that is, they should be snug but not too tight. The blades should be attached securely to the boots and correctly positioned to distribute the weight of the body evenly

may also use the rope as a lifeline. Tie one end to a tree or to someone on shore and tie the other end around your waist before attempting a rescue.

You should also be careful when skating on a rink. Rinks generally attract more skaters than do natural ice sites, which increases the chance of collisions. For this reason, rinks forbid fast skating and require all skaters to move in the same direction.

Figure Skating

Figure-skating competitions are held on a rink about 200 feet (60 meters) long and 100 feet (30 meters) wide. The rink has gently rounded corners and is surrounded by a barrier about 4 feet (1.2 meters) high.

Figure skates have a special blade that enables competitors to perform the difficult moves required in figure skating. The blade is $\frac{1}{8}$ inch (3 millimeters) thick and about 12 inches (30 centimeters) long. The blade has

Anthony Tutrone, Focus on Sports Inc.

Recreational Skaters Having Fun on a Frozen River

Types of Ice Skates

WORLD BOOK diagram by Robert Keys

Figure Skates have boots with a high top. The front of the blade has several teeth.

Hooks

Eyelets

Boot

Blade

Speed Skates have boots with a low top. The blade is straight, flat, and thin.

Hockey Skates have strong, heavy boots with a low top. The blade curves at each end.

over the blades. Figure-skaters, speed-skaters, and hockey players use different types of skates. Many beginning skaters use figure skates. The boot has a high top for good ankle support. In addition, the design of the blade enables beginners to maneuver more easily than they could on speed or hockey blades.

Before going onto the ice, you should lace your boots properly, whether you are a beginning or experienced skater. Proper lacing provides needed support for the ankles. Lace each boot as tightly as possible in front of the ankle. Lace the boot more loosely near the top, leaving enough room to slip a finger through the top. Never skate, or even walk, in unlaced boots. Unlaced boots can result in a fall and a serious injury.

Skating on a natural ice surface is more dangerous than skating on an indoor rink or on an artificially created outdoor rink. The great danger is the risk of falling through thin ice. Therefore, never skate on a natural ice surface that is less than 4 inches (10 centimeters) thick. And never skate alone on natural ice. Every year, hundreds of skaters fall through thin ice. Many of them drown because nobody was nearby to rescue them. Always make sure a ladder and a rope are available for rescue purposes. To rescue a skater who has fallen through the ice, lie on the ladder as close as possible to the hole. The ladder spreads your weight evenly over the ice and prevents you from falling through. Use the rope to pull the skater to safety. You

Basic Figure-Skating Moves

A person must master certain basic moves to become a skilled figure-skater. The diagrams below illustrate the *figure 8* and the *axel*, two of the most important moves in singles competition.

WORLD BOOK diagrams by David Cunningham

The figure 8 is the basic design in figure skating. It consists of two circles. A skater begins and ends each circle at the same spot on the ice. One circle is skated on the right foot, and the other on the left foot. The diameter of the circles should be about three times the skater's height.

The axel is an acrobatic move. A skater begins the axel on the outside edge of one skate. After picking up speed, the skater spins one and a half turns in the air and lands on the outside edge of the other skate. Most skaters perform the axel in a counterclockwise direction.

an inside and an outside edge. Competitors skate on one edge at a time. The bottom of the blade is slightly curved. This curve permits only a small part of the edge to touch the ice at one time, and so enables a skater to maneuver more easily. The front of the blade has a number of teeth called *toe picks* or *toe rakes*. Skaters use the toe picks to bite into the ice when performing certain jumps and spins. The boots of figure skates have a high top.

Figure-skaters wear costumes that are comfortable and attractive and that permit freedom of movement. Women generally wear a simple dress with a short skirt and matching panties over tights. Men usually wear close-fitting, high-waisted pants with a matching shirt.

Figure-skaters may take part in three kinds of competitions: (1) singles skating, (2) pair skating, and (3) ice dancing. Men and women compete separately in singles skating, but they follow the same rules. In pair skating and ice dancing, teams consisting of a man and a woman compete against one another.

Judges score all figure-skating events on a scale of 0 to 6 *marks*, with 6 marks being the highest score. The judges carry the skaters' scores to one decimal place, as in a score of 3.7 marks.

Singles Skating is divided into three parts. They are, in the order in which they are performed: (1) compulsory figures, (2) the short program, and (3) free skating. Each part is judged separately and counts a certain percentage of a skater's total score. Skaters perform to music during the short program and free skating but not during the compulsory figures.

Compulsory Figures, also called *school figures*, count 30 per cent of a skater's score. The figures consist of designs based on the figure 8 that the skaters trace on the ice. There are 41 figures. The skaters perform 3 figures drawn by lot before the competition begins. They perform the figures in order of difficulty, from easiest to hardest. They skate each figure three times on each foot. A skater first traces the figure on clean ice and then retraces the figure twice over the original design. If the skater performs the figure properly, the three tracings will be almost identical.

Skaters receive three scores, one for each figure. The judges base the scores on such factors as the skater's

Elissa Baldwin

Compulsory Figures are designs based on the figure 8 that all competitors must skate at the start of a meet. Skaters trace each figure three times on each foot. Judges stand nearby.

Free Skating accounts for 50 per cent of the score in singles skating. In free-skating competition, skaters select and arrange their own jumps, spins, and other movements. They also choose their own music. Men may skate for five minutes, and women for four minutes. They lose marks if the program is too short or too long.

The judges award scores for technical merit and artistic impression. In scoring technical merit, they consider the difficulty and variety of the program as well as how accurately the skater performed the moves. In scoring artistic impression, the judges consider such factors as originality, creative use of music, and *choreography* (dance composition). The judges penalize a skater for falling only if the fall seriously interrupted the flow of the skater's program.

Pair Skating. In pair-skating events, the couples try to express a feeling of harmony and teamwork through their skating. Pair skating involves certain moves specifically designed for a man and woman skating together. The most spectacular moves are various *lifts*, in which the man picks up his partner and carries her above his head. Pair skaters perform most moves in unison. The partners may separate at times and perform individually, but the two must maintain the impression that they are performing as a true team. Competition in pair skating consists of two parts: (1) the short program and (2) free skating.

The Short Program counts about 30 per cent of each pair's score. The program calls for six moves that all the pairs must perform. However, each couple may arrange the moves and the steps that link them in any order and pattern. The pairs select their own music. The program must be completed within two minutes.

The judges score each couple on technical merit and artistic impression. They base the artistic impression score on such factors as how well the pair expressed a sense of unity and how smoothly their steps linked the various moves.

Free Skating makes up about 70 per cent of each pair's score. The couples select their own moves and their own music. Each pair's program may last up to five minutes.

technique and how closely the tracings of the figures resembled each other.

The Short Program makes up 20 per cent of a skater's score. The program consists of seven moves involving jumps, spins, step sequences, and jump-spin combinations. All competitors perform the same moves. However, the skaters arrange the moves in their own order and pattern. They also select their own music. Competitors must complete the short program within a two-minute period.

Each skater receives two scores. The first score reflects the *technical merit* of the skater's program—that is, how accurately the skater performed the moves. The second score reflects the program's *artistic impression*, which includes how skillfully the skater arranged the program and performed to the music.

Ice-Dancing Positions

Skaters use a number of basic positions in performing an ice dance. They include the hand-in-hand position, *left;* the Kilian position, *center;* and the closed, or waltz, position, *right.*

WORLD BOOK illustrations by David Cunningham

ICE SKATING

As in the short program, the judges give scores for technical merit and artistic impression. In scoring artistic impression, they rate each pair's program on composition and style. They also consider how well the couple express a feeling of "togetherness."

Ice Dancing combines skating with ballroom dancing. It differs from pair skating in several ways. In ice dancing, for example, the couple may separate only briefly to change direction or position. No high lifts are permitted. Each partner must have one skate on the ice at all times except during brief lifts and spins when the woman may have both skates off the ice. The couples perform many moves developed specifically for ice dancing. These moves closely resemble steps used in ballroom dancing.

Ice-dancing competition consists of three parts. They are, in the order performed: (1) compulsory dances, (2) the original set pattern dance, and (3) free dancing.

Compulsory Dances count 30 per cent of the score in ice dancing. All the couples perform three particular dances to the same music. A typical group of compulsory ice dances would be based on the waltz, the rumba, and the tango. Skaters must perform the dances according to official diagrams. Each couple must begin the first two dances, called *set pattern dances*, at the same place on the rink. For the third dance, called the *optional pattern dance*, a couple may begin anywhere on the rink they wish. The judges award a separate score for the performance of each of the three dances.

The Original Set Pattern Dance makes up 20 per cent of a couple's score. The partners select their own steps and music. However, all couples must choose music that follows a certain dance rhythm announced in advance. The dance may last up to three minutes.

Couples receive scores for technical merit and artistic impression. Artistic impression includes how well a couple expressed the music's tempo.

Free Dancing accounts for 50 per cent of the score. The couples select their own combinations of dance movements but may not repeat combinations. They also choose their own music, which must have variations in tempo and be suitable for dancing. Each couple must complete their program within four minutes.

The judges grade each couple's program on technical merit and artistic impression. In scoring artistic impression, they consider the composition of the dance and how well the partners interpreted the music.

Figure-Skating Organizations. The International Skating Union (I.S.U.) governs international figure skating. More than 30 countries belong to the I.S.U. Each member country has its own organization that supervises competition at the national level. In the United States, the sport is governed by the U.S. Figure Skating Association (USFSA). The Canadian Figure Skating Association (CFSA) supervises competition in the sport in Canada.

The USFSA holds figure-skating championships each winter. To reach the national championships, skaters first must qualify in regional and then sectional competition. The I.S.U. supervises three international meets each year. These meets are the world junior championships, the world championships, and the European championships. The I.S.U. also supervises figure-skating competition at the Winter Olympic Games, which are held every four years.

Speed Skating

Speed skating consists of races over various distances on oval, ice-covered tracks. Some skaters reach a speed of 30 miles (48 kilometers) per hour.

The blade and boot of speed skates are so designed that skaters can start quickly and maintain a high rate of speed throughout a race. The blade is flat, straight, and thin. It measures 12 to 18 inches (30 to 45 centimeters) long and only about $\frac{1}{32}$ inch (0.8 millimeter) wide. Steel tubing reinforces the blade for added strength. The boots are very lightweight and have a low-cut top.

Speed-skaters wear gloves or mittens and a one- or two-piece uniform with long sleeves. The uniform is made of lightweight synthetic fabric that gives a skater a streamlined appearance and offers little wind resistance. Skaters also wear a safety helmet.

Good speed-skating technique depends on three factors: (1) balance, (2) rhythm, and (3) drive. These factors enable a skater to produce smooth, powerful strokes.

A speed-skater's center of balance is in the hip over the forward skate. As the legs move back and forth, the center of balance shifts from hip to hip. Skaters keep the body relaxed and flexible. They lean forward from the waist with the back straight. They keep the head up and the eyes looking straight ahead.

A smooth, flowing motion produces the proper skating rhythm. The most obvious part of the rhythm is the arm swing. Skaters swing one arm forward across the chest and the other arm to the rear. The forward arm is always opposite the forward leg. The arm swing keeps the skater's balance steady and helps increase the power of the forward stroke.

The drive is the push from the legs during each stroke. Skaters use the entire surface of the blade to push forward. They try to bend their knees as much as possible to increase the length of the stroke. The longer the stroke, the more powerful will be the forward push.

In races up to 1,500 meters long, skaters swing their arms during each stroke. In races longer than 1,500 meters, many skaters save energy by swinging only one arm and keeping the other one behind them. Some skaters save energy by clasping both hands behind the back as they skate on the straight parts of the oval track. They use the arm swing only while skating around turns.

There are three types of speed skating: (1) Olympic-style speed skating, (2) pack skating, and (3) short-track skating. Men and women compete separately.

Olympic-Style Speed Skating is the most popular type of racing in international competitions. In Olympic-style speed skating, two skaters race against each other on a two-lane track. The track must be $333\frac{1}{3}$ to 400 meters (365 to 437 yards) around. Each lane should be about 5 meters (16 feet) wide. The lanes are divided by a band of snow or a painted line beneath the ice.

In most international championship meets, men's races are 500, 1,500, 5,000, and 10,000 meters long. A 1,000-meter race for men is added in the Olympics. Women's races cover 500, 1,000, 1,500, and 3,000 meters. Meets called *sprint championships* feature only 500- and 1,000-meter races. Races in all championship meets are held over a two-day period.

A speed-skater leans forward at the waist, keeping the knees bent, the head up, and the eyes looking straight ahead. For a more powerful stroke, the skater uses an arm swing. In races up to 1,500 meters, the skater swings both arms. In longer races, the skater saves energy by swinging only one arm.

WORLD BOOK illustrations by David Cunningham

Two-Arm Swing

One-Arm Swing

Before a race begins, the two skaters stand between the starting line and a line behind it called the *prestart line*. The lines are about 30 inches (75 centimeters) apart on a straight area of the track. Skaters may not cross the starting line before the starting gun is fired. A skater who begins ahead of the gun makes a *false start*. Three false starts disqualify a competitor.

During the race, the skaters must change lanes each time they reach the straightaway area opposite the starting line. This area is called the *crossing straight*. The only times skaters do not change lanes are on the first laps of 1,000- and 1,500-meter races run on a 400-meter track. Competitors change lanes so that each skater races the same distance. If they did not change lanes, the competitor on the inside lane would skate a shorter distance.

In most meets, skaters enter all the races. They skate once in each race. After all the competitors in a race have skated, the one with the fastest time wins the event. The skater who wins most of the events in a meet is the champion. If no skater wins a majority of the events, the championship is decided on a point system. Each skater receives points for the time taken to reach the finish line in each race. In the 500-meter race, a skater receives one point for each second. In the other races, the skater receives a fraction of a point for each second as follows: 1,000 meters, a half point; 1,500 meters, a third of a point; 3,000 meters, a sixth of a point; 5,000 meters, a tenth of a point; and 10,000 meters, a twentieth of a point. The points are totaled for each skater, and the competitor with the lowest score is declared the champion.

Pack Skating is the most popular type of speed skating in the United States. In pack skating, a number of competitors race at one time in a series of elimination races. Qualifiers then advance to final races that determine the winner.

Pack-skating meets are held on both indoor and outdoor tracks. Most outdoor tracks measure 400 meters around. Skaters use a hockey rink for indoor meets. They race on a track marked off on the rink. Most indoor tracks are $\frac{1}{16}$ mile (0.1 kilometer) around. Both indoor and outdoor tracks are 20 feet (6 meters) wide and have no lanes.

In organized meets, men and women and boys and girls compete separately in five age classes. These classes are senior (age 18 and older); intermediate (ages 16 and 17); junior (ages 14 and 15); juvenile (ages 12 and 13); and midget (ages 10 and 11). The midget class sometimes includes two additional groups. One is for skaters 8 or 9 years old, and the other for skaters 7 years of age or younger. Skaters may compete in older age classes but not in a younger one. For example, a 16-year-old may compete in the senior class but not the junior class.

The length of the races in a pack-skating meet depends on the age class. The youngest skaters take part in the shortest races. For example, boys and girls in the midget class compete in races up to 500 yards long. Senior men compete in races up to 5 miles long. Each contestant in an age group enters at least two events in a meet. Skaters in the senior class may compete in three or four races in a one-day meet and in as many as seven in a two-day meet.

ICE SKATING

W. Lee, St. Paul Winter Carnival Assn.

Pack Skating is a type of speed skating in which several skaters race at one time in elimination races called *heats*. Qualifiers from the heats compete in final races to decide the champion.

At a meet, the skaters in each class first compete in a series of qualifying races called *heats*. From 6 to 10 skaters race at one time in a heat. In most meets, the skaters who finish first and second in each heat qualify for the next heat. The number of heats depends on how many skaters entered the event. After the heats have been run, a number of skaters qualify for the final races. In most competitions, each final race has a maximum of six skaters.

The first four skaters to finish in each final race receive points. The winner of each race gets 5 points; the second-place skater, 3 points; the third-place skater, 2 points; and the fourth-place skater, 1 point. The skater with the most points is the class champion.

Short-Track Skating consists of two types of races: (1) individual races and (2) relay races. Men and women compete separately. This kind of racing is called *short track* because the races are held on a track shorter than those used in most Olympic-style and pack races. In international championship meets, the track is 110 meters (361 feet) around. The track must be at least 4.75 meters ($15\frac{1}{2}$ feet) wide on the straightaways and at least 4 meters (13 feet) wide on the turns. It has no lanes.

Individual Races. Speed-skaters take part in three kinds of individual races: (1) heat races, (2) elimination races, and (3) pursuit races. Heat and elimination races are each divided into five short events and one long one. The short events consist of 400-, 500-, 800-, 1,000-, and 1,500-meter races. The long event covers 3,000 meters.

In heat races, skaters must qualify in heats to compete in the final race. Up to four skaters compete in short events, and up to six skaters in the 3,000-meter race. First-place winners automatically qualify for the next heat. Skaters may also qualify if they are among a certain number of skaters with the fastest times or if they are among the fastest second-place winners. The skater who finishes first in the final wins the event.

In elimination races, a maximum of eight skaters compete. After the first two laps, the last-place skater is eliminated in each succeeding lap until three skaters remain. These skaters then race two laps to determine the first-, second-, and third-place winners in the event.

In pursuit races, two skaters compete. The skaters start opposite each other in the middle of the straightaway. The skater who passes the other wins. If neither skater is passed after a certain number of laps, the one with the faster time wins.

Relay Races involve two teams, each with four members. Men race in a 5,000-meter relay, and women in a 3,000-meter relay. One member from each team skates until replaced by a teammate. A teammate may replace a skater anytime except during the final two laps. Skaters may not begin to race until they touch, or are touched by, the teammate they replace. The team of the first skater to reach the finish line wins the race.

Speed-Skating Organizations. The International Skating Union governs international Olympic-style and short-track speed skating, as well as figure skating. It supervises many meets, including annual world championship meets and competition in the Winter Olympics. Many countries also hold national championships. The U.S. International Speed Skating Association governs Olympic-style and short-track speed skating in the United States. The Canadian Amateur Speed Skating Association governs the three types of speed-skating competitions in Canada.

The Amateur Skating Union supervises pack skating in the United States. It conducts national indoor and outdoor championship meets each year. It also supervises annual North American indoor and outdoor championship meets with the Canadian Amateur Speed Skating Association.   GREGORY R. SMITH

Questions

What is a pursuit race?

How do figure skates differ from speed skates?

What is the International Skating Union?

In figure-skating competition, what are compulsory figures? Compulsory dances?

How are champions determined in pack skating?

What is the short program in singles skating? In pair skating?

How should skaters lace their boots to get proper ankle support?

What are the three types of speed skating?

How does ice dancing differ from pair skating?

What safety procedures should a person follow in rescuing a skater who has fallen through the ice?

PESTICIDE is a chemical used to control or eliminate pests. Insects are probably the major pests. Many kinds of insects transmit serious diseases, such as malaria and typhus. Some insects destroy or cause heavy damage to valuable crops, such as corn and cotton. Other common pests include bacteria, fungi, rats, and such weeds as poison ivy and ragweed. Manufacturers use various chemicals in making pesticides.

Types of Pesticides. Pesticides are classified according to the pests they control. The four most widely used types of pesticides are (1) insecticides, (2) herbicides, (3) fungicides, and (4) rodenticides.

Insecticides. Farmers use insecticides to protect their crops. In urban areas, public health officials use these chemicals to fight mosquitoes and other insects. Insecticides are used in homes and other buildings to control various pests, including ants, flies, moths, roaches, and termites.

Herbicides control weeds or eliminate plants that grow where they are not wanted. Farmers use herbicides to reduce weeds among their crops. Herbicides are also used to control weeds in such public and recreational areas as parks, lakes, and ponds. People use herbicides in their yards to get rid of crab grass and dandelions.

Fungicides. Certain fungi are *pathogenic* (disease causing) and may infect both plants and animals, including human beings. Fungicides are used to control plant diseases that infect such food crops as apples and peanuts. Most disinfectants used in homes, hospitals, and restaurants contain fungicides.

Rodenticides are used chiefly in urban areas where rats and other rodents are a major health problem. Rats carry bacteria that cause such diseases as rabies, ratbite fever, tularemia, and typhus fever. Rats also destroy large amounts of food and grain, and rodenticides help protect areas where these products are stored.

Other Pesticides help control a variety of organisms. These pests include bacteria, mites and ticks, viruses, and roundworms called *nematodes.*

Pesticides and the Environment. Pesticides differ according to their effects on various organisms. *Se-* *lective pesticides* are toxic only to the target pests. They cause little or no harm to other organisms. However, *nonselective pesticides* can harm—or even kill—organisms that are not considered pests. Nonselective pesticides should be used only when no other method of control is available.

Most pesticides last only long enough to control the target pest. But some are *persistent* (long lasting) and remain in the environment long after that. The possible effects of persistent pesticides can be traced by means of a process called *biological concentration.* This process shows how living organisms retain a chemical deposit through a biological cycle known as a *food chain* (see ECOLOGY).

A pesticide is absorbed by organisms in a lower level of a food chain. Organisms in a higher level of the chain then eat many of the lower organisms and retain the chemical. This process continues until the highest organism in the chain retains the chemical. The amount of contamination in the highest organism is much greater than that in the lower organisms. The best-known case of biological concentration involved an insecticide called DDT. In 1972, the U.S. government banned the use of DDT almost completely (see DDT).

Some pests, such as cotton bollworms, mosquitoes, and rats, have developed increasing resistance to pesticides. New methods are being developed to control them. These methods, known as *integrated pest control systems,* combine the use of chemical pesticides with other effective but less harmful techniques. For example, a *sex attractant* is spread to control some insects, including gypsy moths and house flies. When the attractant is sprayed into the air, the insects become confused and cannot find members of their species with which to mate. Sex attractants may also be used to lure insects into traps.   HAROLD D. COBLE

See also FUNGICIDE; INSECTICIDE; WEED; CARSON, RACHEL.

How Pesticides Move Through a Food Chain

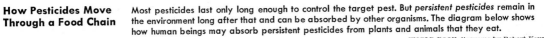
Most pesticides last only long enough to control the target pest. But *persistent pesticides* remain in the environment long after that and can be absorbed by other organisms. The diagram below shows how human beings may absorb persistent pesticides from plants and animals that they eat.

WORLD BOOK diagrams by Robert Keys

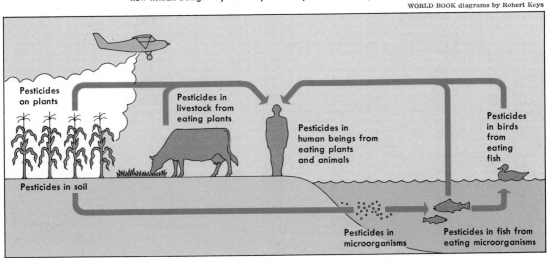

Pesticides on plants

Pesticides in livestock from eating plants

Pesticides in human beings from eating plants and animals

Pesticides in birds from eating fish

Pesticides in soil

Pesticides in microorganisms

Pesticides in fish from eating microorganisms

Fossil Ferns and a Lump of Coal, *left,* were both formed from the remains of plants that died many millions of years ago. While the plants lived, they stored up energy from the sun. The plants that became fossils gave up their store of energy in the process. Only the outline of their appearance remains. But the energy of the coal-forming plants is preserved in the coal. When the coal is burned, it releases this energy in the form of heat.

COAL

COAL is a black or brown rock that can be ignited and burned. As coal burns, it produces energy in the form of heat. The heat from coal can be used to heat buildings and to make or process various products. But the heat is used mainly to produce electricity. Coal-burning power plants supply about half the electricity used in the United States and nearly two-thirds of that used throughout the world. Coal is also used to make *coke,* an essential raw material in the manufacture of iron and steel. Other substances obtained in the coke-making process are used to manufacture such products as drugs, dyes, and fertilizers.

Coal was once the main source of energy in all industrial countries. Coal-burning steam engines provided most of the power in these countries from the early 1800's to the early 1900's. Since the early 1900's, petroleum and natural gas have become the leading sources of energy throughout much of the world. Unlike coal, petroleum can easily be made into gasoline and the other fuels needed to run modern transportation equipment. Natural gas is often used in place of coal to provide heat. But the world's supplies of petroleum and natural gas are being used up rapidly. If they continue to be used at the present rate, they may be nearly exhausted within 75 to 100 years. The world's

Joseph W. Leonard, the contributor of this article, is Professor of Mining Engineering and Director of the Coal Research Bureau at West Virginia University. The article was critically reviewed by the National Coal Association.

supply of coal can last 300 to 400 years at the present rate of use.

Increased use of coal, especially for producing electricity, could help relieve the growing shortage of gas and oil. However, the use of coal involves certain problems. The burning of coal has been a major cause of air pollution. Methods have been developed to reduce the pollution, but these methods are costly and not yet fully effective. They must be improved before the use of coal can be increased greatly. In addition, some coal lies deep underground and so is difficult to mine.

In the past, few jobs were harder or more dangerous than that of an underground coal miner. During the 1800's, many miners had to work underground 10 or more hours a day, six days a week. Picks were almost the only equipment they had to break the coal loose. The miners used shovels to load the coal into wagons. In many cases, children as young as 10 years of age hauled the coal from the mines. Women also worked in the mines as loaders and haulers. Over the years, thousands of men, women, and children were killed in mine accidents. Thousands more died of lung diseases from breathing coal dust.

Today, machines do most of the work in coal mines. Mine safety has been improved, work hours have been shortened, and child labor is prohibited. The death rate from mine accidents in the United States has dropped dramatically since 1900. However, coal mining remains a hazardous occupation.

This article discusses how coal was formed, where it is found, its uses, and how it is mined. The article also discusses the cleaning and shipping of coal, the coal industry, and the history of the use of coal.

Coal developed from the remains of plants that died 1 million to 440 million years ago. For this reason, it is often referred to as a *fossil fuel*. The coal-forming plants probably grew in swamps. As the plants died, they gradually formed a thick layer of matter on the swamp floor. Over the years, this matter hardened into a substance called *peat*. In time, the peat deposits became buried under sand or other mineral matter. As the mineral matter accumulated, some of it turned into such rocks as sandstone and shale. The increasing weight of the rock layers and of the other overlying materials began to change the peat into coal. Coal, sandstone, and other rocks formed from deposited materials are called *sedimentary rocks*.

The first stage in the formation of coal produces a dark brown type of coal called *lignite*. Lignite develops from buried peat deposits that have been under great pressure. The pressure results from the weight of the overlying materials and from movements within the earth's crust. As the pressure increases, lignite turns into a harder coal called *subbituminous coal*. Under greater pressure, subbituminous coal turns into a still harder coal called *bituminous coal*. Intense pressure changes bituminous coal into *anthracite*, the hardest of all coals.

Anthracites are the oldest coals in most cases, and lignites are the youngest. Some anthracites began to form as long as 440 million years ago. Some lignites developed within the last 1 million years. The greatest period of coal formation occurred about 300 million years ago, during a time in the earth's history called the *Carboniferous Period*. Swamps covered much of the earth during this period. Tall ferns and other treelike plants grew in the swamps and produced huge amounts of peat-forming matter after they died. Today's plentiful deposits of bituminous coal developed largely from the vast peat deposits formed during the Carboniferous Period. It took about 3 to 7 feet (0.9 to 2.1 meters) of compact plant matter to produce a bed of bituminous coal 1 foot (0.3 meter) thick.

Plant materials are still accumulating in such coal-forming environments as the Everglades, the huge swamplands of southern Florida. Under the proper conditions, these materials could eventually develop into peat and then, over hundreds of thousands of years, into the various kinds of coal.

Coal beds are also called *coal seams* or *coal veins*. Present-day seams range in thickness from less than 1 inch (2.5 centimeters) to 400 feet (120 meters) or more. The thickest seams are subbituminous coals and lignites. Many coal deposits consist of two or more seams separated by layers of rocks. These formations were produced by new coal-forming swamps developing over buried ones. Each new swamp became buried and developed into a separate seam of coal.

Some coal beds lie nearly parallel to the earth's surface. Other beds have been tilted by earth movements and lie at an angle to the surface. Most of the deepest beds consist of anthracites or bituminous coals. In many cases, earth movements have uplifted deep anthracite and bituminous beds to a position nearer the surface. Such movements also account for coal seams in hills and mountains.

The Development of Coal

The formation of coal involved three main steps. (1) The remains of dead plants turned into a substance called *peat*. (2) The peat became buried. (3) The buried peat was subjected to great pressure. After thousands or millions of years under pressure, the peat turned into coal. Each of these steps is illustrated below.

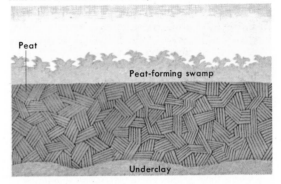

A Thick Layer of Peat developed as plant matter accumulated and hardened on the floor of a swamp. The matter built up as plants that grew in the swamp died and sank to the bottom. Peat-forming swamps once covered much of the earth.

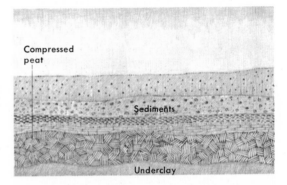

Deposits of Loose Mineral Matter, called *sediments*, completely covered the peat bed. As these sediments continued to pile up over the bed, they compressed the peat.

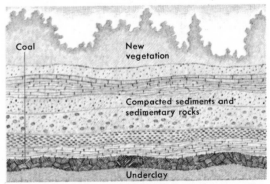

WORLD BOOK diagrams by Jean Helmer

Pressure on the Peat increased as the sediments became more compact and heavier. Some sediments hardened into rock. The ever-increasing weight and pressure turned the peat into coal.

Coal is found on every continent. Deposits occur as far north as the Arctic and as far south as Antarctica. Some coal deposits occur off ocean coastlines. However, deep underwater deposits have little value at this time because they are difficult to mine.

Coal deposits that can be mined profitably are called *coal reserves*. In most cases, a coal seam must be at least 24 inches (61 centimeters) thick for mining engineers to class it as a reserve. Some long-range estimates of coal reserves include beds 12 to 24 inches (30 to 61 centimeters) thick. But such thin beds would probably be mined only after more productive deposits were exhausted. Most estimates of coal reserves include only tested deposits. The reserves may actually be somewhat larger or smaller than the estimates.

To estimate coal reserves, mining engineers drill into the ground in suspected coal-bearing areas. A drill brings up samples of the rock formations in the order in which they occur. The depth and thickness of a coal seam can thus be estimated. By taking a number of such samples, engineers can estimate the extent of a particular deposit. A large area of tested reserves is called a *coal field*.

World Coal Reserves. Estimates of world coal reserves range from about 650 billion short tons (590 billion metric tons) to over 1,500 billion short tons (1,360 billion metric tons). The lower figure includes only the reserves that can be mined economically. The higher figure includes deposits that cannot now be mined profitably. The United States has 30 to 35 per cent of the world's coal reserves. Russia has about 25 per cent, and China has about 15 per cent. Most of the remaining reserves are in Australia, Canada, Great Britain, India, Poland, South Africa, and West Germany.

Location of U.S. and Canadian Reserves. About half of all U.S. coal reserves lie in the eastern half of the nation, from the Appalachian Highlands to the eastern edge of the Great Plains. The rest are in the western part of the country, especially the Rocky Mountain States, the northern Great Plains, and Alaska. The eastern reserves include nearly all the nation's anthracite deposits and more than three-fourths of its bituminous deposits. The western reserves include almost all the subbituminous coal and lignite in the United States.

Canada's coal reserves consist chiefly of bituminous coal. The nation also has large fields of subbituminous coal and lignite. But the deposits are much thinner than the bituminous deposits. More than 95 per cent of Canada's reserves are in its western provinces—British Columbia, Alberta, and Saskatchewan.

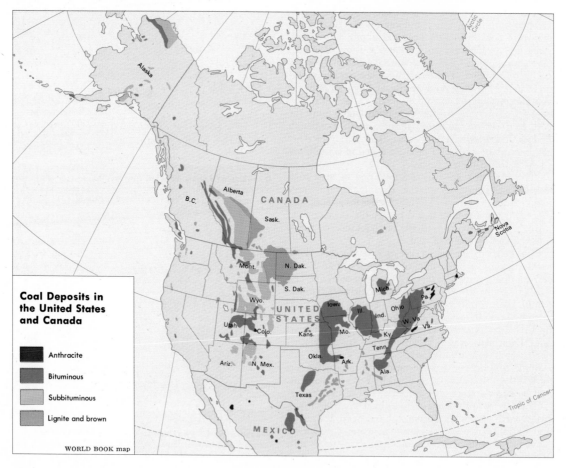

Coal Deposits in the United States and Canada

- Anthracite
- Bituminous
- Subbituminous
- Lignite and brown

WORLD BOOK map

The way in which coal is used depends on its chemical composition and moisture content. Coal is often referred to as a mineral. But unlike a true mineral, it has no fixed chemical formula. All coal consists of certain solids and moisture. The solids are composed chiefly of the elements carbon, hydrogen, nitrogen, oxygen, and sulfur. However, coal varies widely in the amount of each element it has as well as in its moisture content. In fact, no two deposits of coal are exactly alike in their makeup.

Coal is usually classified according to how much carbon it contains. Coal can thus be grouped into four main classes, or *ranks:* (1) anthracites; (2) bituminous coals; (3) subbituminous coals; and (4) lignites, or brown coals. The carbon content decreases down through the ranks. The highest-ranking anthracites contain about 98 per cent carbon. The lowest-ranking lignites have a carbon content of only about 30 per cent. The moisture content increases down through subbituminous coals and lignites. These coals have a lower *heating value* than do anthracites and bituminous coals. Heating value refers to the amount of heat a given amount of coal will produce when burned.

Bituminous coals are by far the most plentiful and widely used of the major ranks. They have a slightly higher heating value than do anthracites and are the only coals suited to making coke. Anthracites are hard to ignite. They also burn slowly and therefore are unsuited to today's standard method of producing electricity from coal. Anthracites are also the least plentiful of the four ranks. Less than 1 per cent of the coal found in the United States is anthracite.

Coal as a Fuel

Coal is a useful fuel because it is abundant and has a relatively high heating value. However, coal has certain impurities that limit its usefulness as a fuel. These impurities include sulfur and various minerals. As coal is burned, most of the sulfur combines with oxygen and forms a poisonous gas called *sulfur dioxide*. Most of the minerals turn into ash. The coal industry refers to ash-producing substances in coal as ash even before the coal is burned.

Some coals have a sulfur content of less than 1 per cent. These *low-sulfur coals* can be burned in fairly large quantities without adding harmful amounts of sulfur dioxide to the air. However, many coals have a sulfur content of more than 1 per cent. These *medium-* and *high-sulfur coals* can cause serious air pollution if they are burned in large quantities without proper safeguards. The difficulty and the high cost of developing safeguards have greatly restricted the use of coal as a fuel. Some of the ash produced by burning powdered coal may also escape into the air. Like sulfur dioxide, such *fly ash* can contribute to air pollution. However, devices have been developed to trap fly ash in smokestacks and so prevent it from polluting the air.

Coal is used as a fuel chiefly in the production of electricity. Electric power plants use more than two-thirds of the coal mined in the United States.

Electric Power Production. The great majority of electric power plants are *steam-turbine plants*. All nuclear

Uses of Coal in the United States

Total of all types of coal consumed or exported in 1976— 663,228,000 short tons (601,670,300 metric tons)

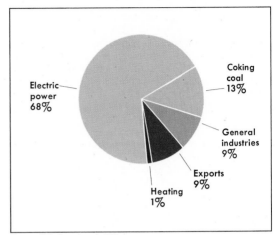

Electric power 68%

Coking coal 13%

General industries 9%

Exports 9%

Heating 1%

Source: U.S. Department of Energy.

power plants and almost all plants fueled by coal, gas, or oil are steam-turbine plants. They use high-pressure steam to generate electricity. The steam spins the wheels of turbines, which drive the generators that produce electricity. Steam-turbine plants differ mainly in how they create the heat to make steam. Nuclear plants create the heat by splitting uranium atoms. The other plants burn coal, gas, or fuel oil. Steam-turbine plants

National Coal Association

A Conveyor System at a Power Plant removes coal from a stockpile and carries it to the plant's boilers. Coal-burning power plants produce most of the electricity used in the world.

produce about 80 per cent of the electricity used in the United States. Coal-burning plants account for most of this output. See ELECTRIC GENERATOR; ELECTRIC POWER; TURBINE.

Bituminous coals have long been the preferred coals for electric power production because they are the most plentiful coals and have the highest heating value. Subbituminous coals and lignites have the lowest heating value. However, nearly all the subbituminous coal and about 90 per cent of the lignite in the United States have a sulfur content of less than 1 per cent. On the other hand, about 50 per cent of the nation's bituminous coal has a medium- or high-sulfur content. To meet federal and state pollution standards, more and more power plants have switched from bituminous coal to subbituminous coal or lignite.

Other Uses of Coal as a Fuel. In parts of Asia and Europe, coal is widely used for heating homes and other buildings. In the United States, natural gas and fuel oil have almost entirely replaced coal as a heating fuel. However, the rising cost of oil and natural gas has led some factories and other commercial buildings to switch back to coal. Anthracites are the cleanest-burning coals, and so they are the preferred coals for heating homes. However, anthracites are also the most expensive coals. For this reason, bituminous coals are often preferred to anthracites for heating factories and other commercial buildings. Subbituminous coals and lignites have such a low heating value that they must be burned in large amounts in order to heat effectively. As a result, they are seldom used for heating.

In the past, coal was also used to provide heat for the manufacture of a wide variety of products, from glass to canned foods. Since the early 1900's, manufacturers have come to prefer the use of natural gas in making most of these products. Coal is used mainly by the cement and paper industries. However, some industries have switched back to coal to avoid paying higher prices for natural gas.

Coal as a Raw Material

Many substances made from coal serve as raw materials in manufacturing. Coke is the most widely used of these substances. Coke is made by heating bituminous coal to about 2000° F. (1100° C) in an airtight oven. The lack of oxygen prevents the coal from burning. The heat changes some of the solids in the coal into gases. The remaining solid matter is coke—a hard, foamlike mass of nearly pure carbon. It takes about 1½ short tons (1.4 metric tons) of bituminous coal to produce 1 short ton (0.9 metric ton) of coke. For an illustration of the coke-making process, see COKE.

The coal used to make coke is called *coking coal*. To be suitable for coking, the coal must have various characteristics, such as a low-sulfur content and a specified amount of ash. Only certain types of bituminous coals have all the necessary characteristics.

About 90 per cent of the coke produced in the United States is used to make iron and steel. Most coking plants are a part of steel mills. The mills burn coke with iron ore and limestone to change the ore into the pure iron required to make steel. It takes about ⅝ short ton (0.5

National Coal Association

A Coking Plant heats coal in airtight ovens to make *coke,* an essential raw material in the manufacture of steel. This batch of red-hot coke is being released from an oven into a railcar. The car will carry it to another part of the plant to cool.

metric ton) of coke to produce 1 short ton (0.9 metric ton) of pure iron. For a description of the role of coke in ironmaking, see the article IRON AND STEEL (The "Recipe" for Making Iron; How Iron Is Made in a Blast Furnace).

The coke-making process is called *carbonization.* Some of the gases produced during carbonization turn into liquid ammonia and coal tar as they cool. Through further processing, some of the remaining gases change into light oil. Manufacturers use the ammonia, coal tar, and light oil to make such products as drugs, dyes, and fertilizers. Coal tar is also used for roofing and for road surfacing. Some of the gas produced during carbonization does not become liquid. This *coal gas,* or *coke oven gas,* burns like natural gas. But coal gas has a lower heating value and, unlike natural gas, gives off large amounts of soot as it burns. Coal gas is used chiefly at the plants where it is produced. It provides heat for the coke- and steel-making processes.

Gas can be produced from coal directly, without carbonization, by various methods. Such methods are known as *gasification.* The simplest gasification method involves burning coal in the presence of forced air or steam. The resulting gas, like coke oven gas, has a low heating value and produces soot. It is used chiefly in some manufacturing processes. Coal can be used to make high-energy gas and such high-energy liquid fuels as gasoline and fuel oil. But the present methods of producing these fuels from coal are costly and complex. Researchers are working to develop cheaper and simpler methods. The section *The Coal Industry* discusses this research.

Coal mines can be divided into two main groups: (1) surface mines and (2) underground mines. In most cases, surface mining involves stripping away the soil and rock that lie over a coal deposit. This material is known as *overburden*. After the overburden has been removed, the coal can easily be dug up and hauled away. Underground mining involves digging tunnels into a coal deposit. Miners must go into the tunnels to remove the coal.

Surface mining is usually limited to coal deposits within 100 to 200 feet (30 to 61 meters) of the earth's surface. The more overburden that must be removed, the more difficult and costly surface mining becomes. Most coal deposits deeper than 200 feet are mined underground. Surface mines produce about 60 per cent of the coal mined in the United States. Underground mines produce the rest.

Surface Mining

Nearly all surface mining is *strip mining*—that is, mining by first stripping away the overburden. Many coal seams are exposed on the sides of hills or mountains. In some cases, these seams are mined from the surface without removing any overburden. Miners use machines called *augers* to dig out the coal. This method of surface mining is known as *auger mining*.

Strip Mining depends on powerful machines that dig up the overburden and pile it out of the line of work. The dug-up overburden is called *spoils*. In time, a strip mine and its spoils may cover an enormous area. The digging up of vast areas of land has caused serious environmental problems in the past. As a result, the United States government now requires that all new strip-mined land must be *reclaimed*—that is, returned as closely as possible to its original condition. Strip mining thus involves methods of (1) mining the coal and (2) reclaiming the land.

Mining the Coal. Most strip mines follow the same basic steps to produce coal. First, bulldozers clear and level the mining area. Many small holes are then drilled through the overburden to the coal bed. Each hole is loaded with explosives. The explosives are set off, shattering the rock in the overburden. Giant power shovels or other earthmoving machines then start to clear away the soil and broken rock. Some of these earthmovers are as tall as a 20-story building and can remove more than 3,500 short tons (3,180 metric tons) of overburden per hour. After a fairly large area of coal is exposed, smaller power shovels or other coal-digging machines scoop up the coal and load it into trucks. The trucks carry the coal from the mine.

Although most strip mines follow the same basic steps, strip-mining methods vary according to whether the land is flat or hilly. Strip mining can thus be classed as either (1) area mining or (2) contour mining. Area mining is practiced where the land is relatively level. Contour mining is practiced in hilly or mountainous country. It involves mining on the *contour*—that is, around slopes.

In area mining, an earthmover digs up all the broken overburden from a long, narrow strip of land along the edge of the coal field. The resulting deep ditch is referred to as a *cut*. As the earthmover digs the cut, it piles the spoils along the side of the cut that is away from the mining area. The piled spoils form a ridge called a *spoil bank*. After the cut is completed, the coal is dug, loaded into trucks, and hauled away. The earthmover then digs an identical cut alongside the first one. It piles the spoils from this cut into the first cut. This process is repeated over and over across the width of the field until all the coal has been mined. The spoil banks form a series of long, parallel ridges that can later be leveled.

Area mining is impractical where coal seams are embedded in hills. If a seam lies near the top of a hill, an earthmover may simply remove the hilltop and so expose the coal. If a seam lies near the base of a hill, it must be mined on the contour.

In contour mining, an earthmover removes the shattered overburden immediately above the point where a seam *outcrops* (is exposed) all around a hill. The resulting cut forms a wide ledge on the hillside. The spoils may be stored temporarily on the hillside or used to fill in the cuts. After the exposed coal has been mined and hauled away, the earthmover may advance up the slope and dig another cut immediately above the first one. However, the depth of the overburden increases sharply with the rise of the slope. After the first or second cut,

Bucyrus-Erie Company

Strip Mining depends on giant earthmoving machines like the one at the top of this picture. The earthmover strips away the soil and rock that lie over a coal deposit. A coal-digging machine, center, then scoops up the coal and loads it into a truck.

the overburden may be too great for a coal company to remove profitably. But if the seam is thick enough, a company may dig an underground mine to remove the rest of the coal.

Reclaiming the Land. The chief environmental problems that strip mining can cause result from burying fertile soil under piles of rock. The rocks tend to give off acids when exposed to moisture. Rainwater runs down the bare slopes, carrying acids and mud with it. The runoff from the slopes may wash away fertile soil in surrounding areas and pollute streams and rivers with acids and mud.

The first step in reclaiming strip-mined land is to reduce the steep slopes formed by the spoils. The spoil banks created by area mining can be leveled by bulldozing. The spoils from contour mining can be used to fill in the cuts in the hillsides. As much topsoil as possible should then be returned to its original position so that the area can be replanted.

Mining companies have reclaimed much strip-mined land, which has been turned into farms and recreation areas in many cases. But much land has not been reclaimed. In 1977, the U.S. Congress passed a law requiring mine owners to reclaim all the land they use for strip mining after 1978. In every case, the mine owners must restore the land as nearly as possible to its original condition.

Auger Mining. A coal auger is a machine shaped like an enormous corkscrew. It bores into the side of a coal outcrop on a slope and twists out the coal in chunks. Contour mines often use augers when the overburden in a slope is too great to remove. An auger can penetrate the outcrop and recover coal that could not otherwise be mined. Some augers can bore 200 feet (61 meters) or more into a hillside.

A few companies specialize in auger mining, chiefly to mine outcrops of high-quality coal that cannot be mined economically by other methods. However, auger mining can recover only a small portion of the coal in a seam. The method is most efficient when used in combination with contour mining.

Underground Mining

Underground mining is more hazardous than surface mining. The miners may be injured or killed by cave-ins, falling rocks, accidental explosions, and poisonous gases. To prevent such disasters, every step in underground coal mining must be designed to safeguard the workers. Some of these safety measures are discussed in this subsection. For a detailed discussion, see the section *The Coal Industry.*

Underground mining requires more human labor than does surface mining. But even so, underground mines are highly mechanized. Machines do all the digging, loading, and hauling in nearly all the mines. Nonmechanized mines produce only about 1 per cent of the coal mined underground in the United States.

In most cases, miners begin an underground mine by digging two access passages from the surface to the coal bed. One passage will serve as an entrance and exit for the miners and their equipment. The other passage will be used to haul out the coal. Both passages will also serve to circulate air in and out of the mine. As the mining progresses, the workers dig tunnels from the access passages into the coal seam.

Underground mines can be divided into three main groups according to the angle at which the access passages are dug into the ground. The three groups are (1) shaft mines, (2) slope mines, and (3) drift mines. Some mines have two or all three types of passages.

In a shaft mine, the access passages run straight down from the surface to the coal seam. The entrance and exit shaft must have a hoist. Most extremely deep mines are shaft mines. In a slope mine, the access passages are dug on a slant. The passages may follow a slanting seam or slant down through a hillside to reach a seam under the hill. Drift mines are used to mine seams of coal that are embedded in hills or mountains. The access passages

Kinds of Underground Mines There are three main kinds of underground mines: (1) shaft mines, (2) slope mines, and (3) drift mines. In a shaft mine, the entrance and exit passages are vertical. In a slope mine, they are dug on a slant. In a drift mine, the passages are dug into the side of a coal bed exposed on a slope.

WORLD BOOK diagrams

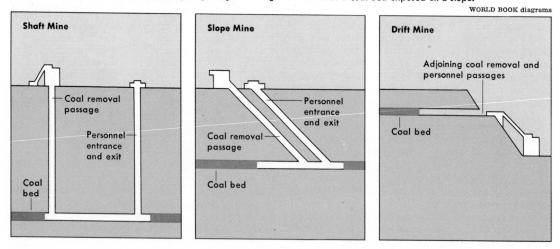

Shaft Mine — Coal removal passage — Personnel entrance and exit — Coal bed

Slope Mine — Personnel entrance and exit — Coal removal passage — Coal bed

Drift Mine — Adjoining coal removal and personnel passages — Coal bed

are dug directly into the side of a seam where it outcrops on a slope. They thus parallel the ground.

Two main systems of underground mining are used: (1) the room-and-pillar system and (2) the longwall system. Each system has its own set of mining techniques. Either system may be used in a shaft, slope, or drift mine. The room-and-pillar system is by far the more common system of underground mining in the United States. The longwall system is more widely used elsewhere, especially in European countries.

The Room-and-Pillar System involves leaving pillars of coal standing in a mine to support the overburden. Miners may begin a room-and-pillar mine by digging three or more long, parallel tunnels into the coal seam from the access passages. These tunnels are called *main entries*. In most cases, the walls of coal separating the main entries are 40 to 80 feet (12 to 24 meters) wide. Cuts are made through each wall every 40 to 80 feet. The cuts thus form square or rectangular pillars of coal that measure 40 to 80 feet on each side. The coal that the miners dig in building the entries is hauled to the surface.

The pillars help support the overburden in the main entries. But in addition, the tunnel roofs must be bolted to hold them in place. To bolt the roof, the miners first drill holes 3 to 6 feet (0.9 to 1.8 meters) or more into the roof. They then insert a long metal bolt into each hole and fasten the free end of each bolt to the roof. The bolts bind together the separate layers of rock just above the roof and so help prevent them from falling. The miners must also bolt the roof in all other parts of the mine as they are developed.

A railroad track or a conveyor belt is built in one of the main entries to carry the coal to the access passages. A mine railroad may also provide transportation for the miners along the main entries. At least two main entries serve chiefly to circulate air through the mine. An underground mine may also need such facilities as water drainage ditches, gas drainage pipes, compressed air pipes, and electric power cables. These facilities are built into the main entries and later extended to other parts of the mine.

After the main entries have been constructed, the miners dig sets of *subentries* at right angles from the main entries into the coal seam. Each set of subentries consists of three or more parallel tunnels, which serve the same purposes as the main entries. Cuts are made through the walls separating these tunnels, forming pillars like those between the main entries. At various points along each set of subentries, the miners dig *room entries* at right angles into the seam. They then begin to dig *rooms* into the seam from the room entries.

As the miners enlarge a room, they leave pillars of coal to support the overburden. A room is mined only a certain distance into the seam. When this distance is reached, the miners may remove the pillars. The room roof collapses as the pillars are removed, and so they must be removed in *retreat*—that is, from the back of the room toward the front. The miners' exit from the room thus remains open as the roof falls. Pillars are also sometimes removed from entries. Like room pillars, they must be removed in retreat to protect the miners.

All room-and-pillar mining involves leaving pillars in place. Room-and-pillar mines differ, however, in their mining methods. Mechanized room-and-pillar mines use two main methods: (1) the conventional mechanized method and (2) continuous mining.

The Conventional Mechanized Method produces about 30 per cent of the coal mined underground in the United States. This method was more widely practiced during the 1930's and 1940's than it is today. During the 1930's, it largely replaced the earlier method of digging coal by hand. Since about 1950, continuous mining has increasingly replaced the conventional method.

The Room-and-Pillar System

Most underground mines in the United States use the *room-and-pillar system* of mining. First, the miners dig tunnels called *main entries* into the coal bed from the entrance and exit passages. They then dig sets of *subentries* into the bed from the main entries and sets of *room entries* into the bed from the subentries. Pillars of coal are left standing in all the entries to support the mine roof. As the room entries are extended, they create large *panels* of coal. The miners eventually dig *rooms* into the panels to recover as much coal as possible from the bed. This floor plan of a room-and-pillar mine shows how the entries are developed.

WORLD BOOK diagram

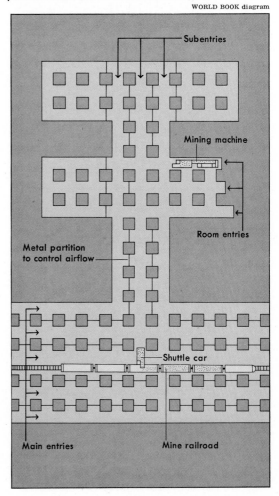

Subentries

Mining machine

Room entries

Metal partition to control airflow

Shuttle car

Main entries   Mine railroad

Types of Underground-Mining Equipment

The type of equipment that an underground mine requires depends on the method of mining it uses. Mechanized mines use three main methods: (1) the conventional method, (2) continuous mining, and (3) longwall mining. Each of the three methods calls for a different type of equipment.

WORLD BOOK illustrations by Robert Addison

Conventional-Mining Equipment. The conventional method of mining involves a series of steps, three of which require special machinery. First, a cutting machine, *left,* cuts a deep slit along the base of the coal *face* (coal exposed on the surface of a mine wall). Another machine, *center,* drills holes into the face. Miners load the holes with explosives and then set the explosives off. The undercutting along the bottom of the face causes the shattered coal to fall to the floor. A loading machine, *right,* gathers the coal onto a conveyor belt.

Continuous-Mining Equipment eliminates the need for separate steps in mining a face. A continuous-mining machine, *right,* gouges out the coal and loads it onto a shuttle car in one operation.

Longwall-Mining Equipment. Longwall mining differs from the other methods of underground mining in its system of roof support. The other methods are used only in room-and-pillar mines, where pillars of coal are left to support the mine roof. In the longwall method, movable steel props support the roof over one long coal face. The miners move a cutting machine back and forth across the face, shearing off coal. The coal falls onto a conveyor. As the miners advance the cutter into the bed, the roof supports are moved forward. The roof behind the miners is allowed to fall.

A Worker Operating a Continuous Miner can dig 12 short tons (11 metric tons) of coal a minute. These machines dig about 65 per cent of the coal mined underground in the United States.

The conventional method involves five main steps. (1) A machine that resembles a chain saw cuts a long, deep slit along the base of the coal face. (2) Another machine drills a number of holes into the face. (3) Each hole is loaded with explosives. The explosives are set off, shattering the coal. The undercutting along the bottom of the face causes the broken coal to fall to the floor. (4) A machine loads the coal onto shuttle cars or a conveyor. (5) Miners bolt the roof that has been exposed by the blast.

A separate crew of miners carries out each of the five steps. After a crew has completed its job on a particular face, the next crew moves in. The miners can thus work five faces of coal at a time. But there are frequent pauses in production as the crews change places.

Continuous Mining accounts for about 65 per cent of the output of U.S. underground coal mines. The method uses machines called *continuous miners*. A continuous miner gouges the coal from the *coal face*—that is, the coal exposed on the surface of a wall. One worker operating a continuous miner can dig as much as 12 short tons (11 metric tons) of coal per minute. The machine automatically loads the coal onto shuttle cars or a conveyor belt, which carries it to the railroad or conveyor in the main entries.

A continuous miner can usually dig and load coal much faster than the coal can be hauled out of a mine. The machine can work faster than the roof-bolting, ventilation, and drainage systems can be installed. As a result, a continuous miner must frequently be stopped to allow the other mine systems to catch up.

The Longwall System involves digging main tunnels or entries like those in a room-and-pillar mine. However, the coal is mined from one long face, called a *longwall*, rather than from many short faces in a number of rooms.

A longwall face is about 300 to 700 feet (91 to 210 meters) long. The miners move a cutting machine back and forth across the face, plowing or shearing off the coal. The coal falls onto a conveyor belt. Movable steel props support the roof over the immediate work area. As the miners work the machine farther into the seam, the roof supports are advanced. The roof behind the miners is allowed to fall. After a face has been dug out 4,000 to 6,000 feet (1,200 to 1,800 meters) into the seam, a new face is developed and mined. This process is repeated over and over until as much coal as possible has been removed from the seam.

The longwall system originated in Europe and is far more common there than in the United States. Underground mines in Europe are much deeper, on the average, than underground mines are in the United States. The pressure of the overburden becomes intense in an extremely deep mine. Longwall mining relieves the pressure by allowing the roof to cave in throughout most of a mine. In a European longwall mine, the roof remains in place only over the main entries, over the longwall face, and over two tunnels leading to the face. The mines can thus recover up to 90 per cent of the coal in a seam.

Mine safety laws in the United States require longwall mines to have fully developed subentries as well as main entries. Thus U.S. longwall mining includes some of the main features of the room-and-pillar system. But in many cases, the mines are more productive than room-and-pillar mines because less coal may be left in place.

Longwall mines produce about 5 per cent of the coal mined underground in the United States. However, more and more U.S. mines are adopting longwall techniques. Experts believe this trend will continue into the 1980's as mines are dug deeper and deeper to recover more coal. A few American mines have adopted a variation of the longwall method called *shortwall mining*. A shortwall face is only about 150 to 200 feet (46 to 61 meters) long, and it is mined with continuous-mining machines rather than with longwall equipment. This system, which was developed in Australia, is suited to coal seams whose structure prevents them from being divided into long faces.

Much coal is shipped to buyers exactly as it comes from the mine without any processing. In the coal industry, such coal is called *run-of-mine coal*. It ranges in size from fine particles to large chunks. About 40 per cent of the coal sold by U.S. mining companies is run-of-mine coal.

The two largest users of coal, the electric power industry and the coking industry, have definite quality requirements for the coal they buy. Much run-of-mine coal does not meet these requirements because it contains unacceptable amounts of impurities. Mining companies must *clean* this coal by removing the impurities before they can sell it. About 60 per cent of the coal mined in the United States is cleaned before it is shipped to buyers.

Cleaning Coal. Mining companies clean coal in specially designed *preparation plants*. Most large coal mines have a preparation plant on the mine property. The plants use a variety of machines and other equipment to remove the impurities from coal.

Ash and sulfur are the chief impurities in coal. The ash consists chiefly of mineral compounds of aluminum, calcium, iron, and silicon. Some of the sulfur in coal is also in the form of minerals, especially pyrite, or fool's gold. The rest is *organic sulfur*, which is closely combined with the carbon in coal. Run-of-mine coal may also contain pieces of rock or clay. These materials must be removed in addition to the other impurities.

Preparation plants rely on the principle of *specific gravity* to remove the impurities from run-of-mine coal. According to this principle, if two solid substances are placed in a solution, the heavier substance will settle to the bottom first. Most of the mineral impurities in coal are heavier than pure coal. As a result, these impurities can be separated from run-of-mine coal that is placed in a solution. The entire coal-cleaning process involves three main steps: (1) sorting, (2) washing, and (3) drying.

Sorting. Large pieces of pure coal may settle to the bottom of a solution faster than small pieces that have many impurities. Therefore, the pieces must first be sorted according to size. In many preparation plants, a screening device sorts the coal into three sizes—coarse, medium, and fine. Large chunks are crushed. The crushed pieces are then sorted into the three main batches according to size.

How Impurities Are Removed from Coal   Mining companies remove mineral impurities from coal by a process called *cleaning*. The process involves three main steps. (1) A screening device sorts the coal into batches of three sizes. (2) Each batch is piped into a separate washing device and mixed with water. The impurities in coal are heavier than pure coal. As a result, the first pieces of coal to settle to the bottom of each solution are those that contain the most impurities. Any loose pieces of rock or clay mixed in with the coal also sink to the bottom. All the waste pieces are discarded. (3) The clean pieces are dried with vibrators or hot-air blowers. The coal is then ready for shipment to buyers.

WORLD BOOK diagram

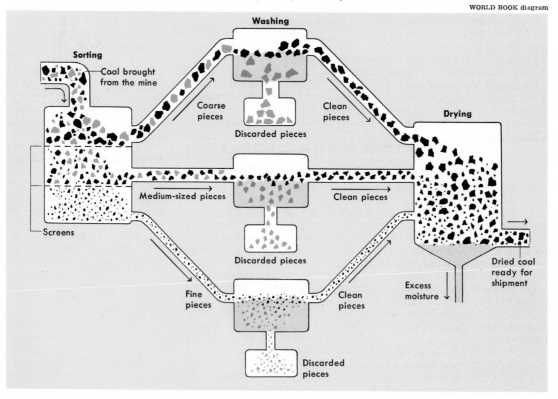

Sorting
Coal brought from the mine

Washing

Coarse pieces

Discarded pieces

Clean pieces

Drying

Screens

Medium-sized pieces

Clean pieces

Discarded pieces

Dried coal ready for shipment

Fine pieces

Clean pieces

Excess moisture

Discarded pieces

Unit Trains carry most large overland shipments of coal in the United States. A unit train normally carries only one kind of freight and travels nonstop from its loading point to its destination.

Dennis Brack, Black Star

Washing. The typical preparation plant uses water as the solution for separating the impurities from coal. Each batch of sorted coal is piped into a separate washing device, where it is mixed with water. The devices separate the impurities by means of specific gravity. The heaviest pieces—those containing the largest amounts of impurities—drop into a refuse bin. Washing removes much of the ash from coal. But the organic sulfur is so closely bound to the carbon that only small amounts can be removed.

Drying. The washing leaves the coal dripping wet. If this excess moisture is not removed, the heating value of the coal will be greatly reduced. Preparation plants use various devices, such as vibrators and hot-air blowers, to dry coal after it is washed.

In most cases, the separate batches of coal are mixed together again either before or after drying. The resulting mixture of various sizes of coal is shipped chiefly to electric power companies and coking plants. All coking plants and many power companies grind coal to a powder before they use it. They therefore accept shipments of mixed sizes. Some coal users require coal of a uniform size. Preparation plants that supply these users leave the cleaned coal in separate batches graded according to size.

Shipping Coal. Most coal shipments within a country are carried by rail, barge, or truck. In many cases, a particular shipment must travel by two or all three of these means to reach the buyer. Huge cargo ships transport coal across oceans, between coastal ports, and on large inland waterways, such as the Great Lakes.

Barges provide the cheapest way of shipping coal within a country. But they can operate only between river or coastal ports. Trucks are the least costly means of moving small shipments of coal short distances by land. Much coal, however, must be shipped long dis-

tances over land to reach buyers. Railroads offer the most economical means of making such shipments. About two-thirds of the coal shipped from mines in the United States goes by rail.

Many large shipments of coal in the United States are delivered to electric power companies and coking plants by *unit trains*. A unit train normally carries only one kind of freight and travels nonstop from its loading point to its destination. A 100-car unit train may carry 10,000 short tons (9,100 metric tons) or more of coal. To meet the need for low-sulfur coal, more and more power plants east of the Mississippi River are importing subbituminous coal from the West. Unit trains help speed such long-distance shipments.

A 273-mile (439-kilometer) underground pipeline carries coal from a mine in Arizona to a power plant in Nevada. The coal is crushed and mixed with water to form a *slurry* (soupy substance) that can be pumped through the pipeline. The coal and power industries are considering building other such pipelines in the United States. In some cases, however, pipelines are more costly and less efficient than the traditional methods of shipping coal.

In the past, nearly all coal shipments consisted of anthracite, bituminous coal, or subbituminous coal. It costs as much to ship a given amount of lignite as it costs to ship the same amount of a higher-ranking coal. But lignite has the lowest heating value of the four ranks. It therefore could not formerly compete with the higher-ranking coals in distant markets. Lignite was used chiefly by power plants built in the lignite fields. Conveyor belts or small railways carried the coal from the mines to the plants. However, the growing need for low-sulfur coal has increased the demand for lignite. Some lignite is now shipped by rail from mines in the Western United States to power plants in the Midwest.

In most countries, the central government owns all or nearly all the coal mines. The major exceptions are Australia, Canada, South Africa, the United States, and West Germany. In West Germany, the mines are jointly owned by the federal government, various state governments, and private investors. All or nearly all the coal mines in Australia, Canada, South Africa, and the United States are privately owned. In each of these countries, however, the central government regulates certain aspects of the coal industry.

The United States is the world's leading coal exporter. Nearly half of all coal exports come from U.S. mines. Other leading exporters include Australia, Poland, and Russia. Japan buys about a third of the world's coal exports—far more than any other country.

This section deals chiefly with the coal industry in the United States. However, much of the information also applies to other countries.

Coal Producers. The United States has about 6,000 coal mines and about 3,500 coal-mining companies. The great majority of the companies are small, independent firms that own and operate one or two small mines. All the small companies together supply less than a third of the coal mined in the United States. The 50 largest U.S. coal companies produce more than two-thirds of the nation's coal. Some of the companies are independently owned, but many are owned by corporations outside the coal industry. The chief outside owners include oil companies, railroads, and ore-mining firms.

Steel companies and electric utilities own many coal mines. These companies produce coal chiefly for their own use rather than to sell. Their mines are known as *captive mines*.

The National Coal Association (NCA) works to promote the interests of the major coal producers. The NCA is jointly sponsored by the producers and the firms that supply them with equipment, technical advice, and transportation. The association tries to increase efficiency within the industry, to encourage favorable legislation, and to inform the public about the industry. The National Independent Coal Operators Association represents the smaller coal producers.

Mineworkers. Most large coal-mining companies have a full-time staff of professional workers, including engineers, lawyers, and business experts. They also employ electricians, mechanics, and construction workers. Skilled miners, however, provide the labor on which the industry depends. Underground mining requires more miners than does surface mining. The United States has about 215,000 coal miners. About two-thirds of them work in underground mines.

Mechanization has helped miners become more productive. In 1950, each coal miner in the United States produced, on the average, about 7 short tons (6.4 metric tons) of coal daily. Today, the production rate averages about 15 short tons (14 metric tons) per miner per day. On the average, a strip miner produces about three times as much coal as does an underground miner.

Increased mechanization has also made miners' jobs more specialized. The job of most miners is to operate a certain type of machine, such as a continuous miner or a power shovel. A beginning miner must work as an apprentice for a specified period to qualify for a particular job. Mine supervisors must have a license from the department of mining in their state. The licenses are granted to miners who have two to five years' experience and who pass a written examination.

Most mining engineering jobs call for a college degree in engineering. If the job is directly related to mine safety, it may also require a state engineering license called a *P.E.* (professional engineer) *certificate*. Some mining engineering jobs require a P.E. certificate only. The states grant P.E. certificates to applicants who meet certain educational requirements, have a certain amount of on-the-job experience, and pass a written examination. The educational requirements vary from state to state. In some states, applicants must have an engineering degree. Other states require only a high school education.

Labor Unions. About 75 per cent of all coal miners in the United States belong to the United Mine Workers of America (UMW). The UMW was organized in 1890. At that time, the nation's coal miners lived and worked under miserable conditions. The mines were dangerously unsafe, and the miners earned barely enough to live on. Most miners and their families lived in *company towns*, which were owned and run by the mining companies. In many company towns, the housing and other facilities were far from adequate. Frequently, miners were not paid in cash. Instead, the mining companies gave them coupons that could be exchanged for goods at company-owned stores or used to pay rent on a company-owned house. The store prices and rents were unreasonably high in many cases, and some miners were always in debt to the mining companies.

During the first half of the 1900's, the UMW did much to improve the wages and working conditions of American coal miners. Through strikes and hard bar-

National Coal Association

Coal Miners provide the labor on which the coal industry depends. These miners have just finished their day's work in an underground mine. The train will carry them to the mine exit.

gaining, the union forced the mining companies to grant the miners increasingly favorable work contracts. The UMW owed much of its success to the vigorous leadership of John L. Lewis, who headed the union from 1919 to 1960. During Lewis' long term as UMW president, the union had the overwhelming support of its members.

Although the UMW is still strong, its influence has declined. This change partly reflects the rapid growth of strip mining. Strip mining requires fewer miners than does underground mining. It also requires a different type of miner. Strip miners are chiefly heavy-machine operators. Unlike underground miners, they have little need for traditional mining skills. Some strip miners are members of the UMW. But many belong to various building trades unions or to no union.

The UMW has also lost influence among its members. Many UMW members feel that their contracts with the mining companies are still far from satisfactory. The miners want better health and retirement benefits and stricter mine safety measures. During the 1970's, small groups of miners frequently took matters into their own hands and went out on *wildcat strikes*, which did not have the approval of union leaders.

Mine Safety. Since 1900, more than 100,000 workers have been killed in coal mine accidents in the United States. Many more have been injured or disabled. Because of this extremely high accident rate, more and more aspects of mine safety have been brought under government regulation. The federal government and the governments of the coal-mining states set minimum health and safety standards that the coal companies and miners have to follow. To make sure that all miners know their responsibilities, the companies must give every new miner a course in mine safety. The improvements in mine safety have greatly reduced the death rate from mine accidents. In the early 1900's, about 3.5 miners per 1,000 were killed in mine accidents annually. The annual death rate has dropped to about .5 today—an improvement of about 85 per cent.

Bolting the Roof is an essential safety practice in an underground mine. Roof bolts are long metal rods that are inserted into the mine roof. After a bolt is fastened to the roof, *above*, it helps prevent the rock layers immediately overhead from falling.

Leo Touchet, The Photo Circle

Mine safety involves four main types of problems. They are (1) accidents involving machinery, (2) roof and wall failures, (3) accumulations of gases, and (4) concentrations of coal dust.

Accidents Involving Machinery kill or injure more U.S. coal miners in a typical year than does any other kind of mining accident. Most strip mine accidents involve machinery. The machines in underground mines must often operate in cramped, dimly lit spaces. The miners must therefore be doubly alert to prevent accidents.

Roof and Wall Failures can be prevented in many cases if a mining company carries out a scientific roof support plan. The federal government requires all U.S. mining companies to draw up such a plan for any new mine. The government must then approve the plan before mining is begun. Mining engineers make a roof support plan after studying all the rock formations surrounding the coal bed. The plan deals with such matters as the number of pillars that must be left standing and the number of roof bolts that must be used.

Accumulations of Gases. Certain gases that occur in underground coal mines can become a serious hazard if they accumulate. *Methane* and *carbon monoxide* are especially dangerous. Methane is an explosive gas that occurs naturally in coal seams. It is harmless in small amounts. However, a mixture of 5 to 15 per cent methane in the air can cause a violent explosion. Carbon monoxide is a poisonous gas produced by the combustion of such fuels as coal and oil. Blasting in an underground mine may produce dangerous levels of carbon monoxide if the mine is improperly ventilated.

The air vents in a mine normally prevent harmful gases from accumulating. A powerful fan at the surface circulates fresh air through the mine. The circulating air forces polluted air to the surface. As an added precaution against methane, federal law requires all underground mines to have automatic methane detectors. A mine must shut down temporarily if a detector shows a methane accumulation of more than 2 per cent.

Concentrations of Coal Dust. Anyone who breathes large amounts of coal dust over a period of years may develop a disease called *pneumoconiosis* or *black lung*. The disease interferes with a person's breathing and may eventually cause death. Thousands of coal miners have been victims of the disease. In addition, high concentrations of coal dust are explosive. A mixture of coal dust and methane is especially dangerous.

Proper ventilation removes much of the coal dust from the air in a mine. However, mines must also use other dust control measures. In the United States, federal law requires that underground mines be *rock-dusted*. In this process, the miners spray powdered limestone on all exposed surfaces in the mine entries. The limestone dilutes the coal dust and so lessens the chance of an explosion. Mines use water sprays to hold down the dust along a face that is being mined.

Government Regulation. State departments of mining have traditionally set and enforced safety standards for American coal mines. In the past, the U.S. Bureau of Mines had this responsibility at the federal level. On occasion, Congress has made urgently needed standards a matter of law, as in the Federal Coal Mine

COAL

How Strip-Mined Land Is Reclaimed The law requires mine owners in the United States to reclaim all the land they use for strip mining. The first step is to level the piles of dug-up soil and rock, *left*. The area may then be reseeded, *center*. The project is finally completed when the new vegetation is fully grown, *right*.

Bucyrus-Erie Company

Health and Safety Act of 1969. This act strengthened the safety standards for mine ventilation, coal dust concentrations, roof supports, and mining equipment. The act also established a program to provide financial benefits to miners disabled by black lung. The responsibility for enforcing federal mine safety standards now belongs to the Mine Safety and Health Administration. The U.S. Department of the Interior, the U.S. Environmental Protection Agency (EPA), and similar state environmental protection agencies regulate the environmental aspects of coal mining in the United States.

Coal Research has become increasingly important. The U.S. Department of Energy and the EPA are the chief federal organizations that sponsor coal research. The leading industry sponsors include coal companies and oil companies.

The goal of most coal research is (1) to find ways to burn more coal without increasing air pollution and (2) to develop economical methods of converting coal into liquid fuels and synthetic natural gas.

Pollution Control. In 1977, Congress passed a law requiring all U.S. electric power plants built since 1971 to meet federal pollution standards by 1982. These standards prohibit the burning of medium- or high-sulfur coals without a means of controlling sulfur dioxide pollution. Medium- and high-sulfur coals

Leading Coal-Mining Countries

Tons of coal mined in 1976

Country	Tons
Russia	785,500,000 short tons (712,593,600 metric tons)
United States	684,913,000 short tons (621,342,600 metric tons)
China	532,000,000 short tons (482,622,300 metric tons)
East Germany	272,645,000 short tons (247,339,400 metric tons)
West Germany	246,701,000 short tons (223,803,400 metric tons)
Poland	240,977,000 short tons (218,610,600 metric tons)
Great Britain	136,504,000 short tons (123,834,300 metric tons)
Czechoslovakia	129,786,000 short tons (117,739,900 metric tons)
India	115,584,000 short tons (104,856,000 metric tons)
Australia	110,104,000 short tons (99,884,660 metric tons)

Source: U.S. Department of Energy.

Leading Coal-Mining States

Tons of coal mined in 1976

State	Tons
Kentucky	143,972,000 short tons (130,609,200 metric tons)
West Virginia	108,834,000 short tons (98,732,500 metric tons)
Pennsylvania	92,005,000 short tons (83,465,500 metric tons)
Illinois	58,239,000 short tons (52,833,500 metric tons)
Ohio	46,582,000 short tons (42,258,500 metric tons)
Virginia	39,996,000 short tons (36,283,800 metric tons)
Wyoming	30,836,000 short tons (27,973,900 metric tons)
Montana	26,231,000 short tons (23,796,400 metric tons)
Indiana	25,369,000 short tons (23,014,400 metric tons)
Alabama	21,537,000 short tons (19,538,000 metric tons)

Source: U.S. Department of Energy.

make up more than a third of all U.S. coal reserves. These resources can be used for electric power production only after ways have been found to control sulfur dioxide pollution.

Cleaning removes some of the sulfur from coal. But it does not remove enough from high-sulfur and some medium-sulfur coals to meet air quality standards. Sulfur dioxide can be controlled to some extent by devices called *scrubbers*. A scrubber absorbs sulfur dioxide fumes as they pass through a plant's smokestacks. Power plants are testing various types of scrubbers. But none of them is yet fully effective or economical.

Researchers are also working on an experimental sulfur control process called *fluidized-bed combustion*. In this process, crushed coal is burned in a bed of limestone. The limestone captures sulfur from the coal and so prevents sulfur dioxide from forming. The heat from the burning coal boils water that is circulated through the bed in metal coils. The boiling water produces steam, which may be used to produce electricity.

Coal Conversion. To turn coal into a high-energy fuel, the hydrogen content of the coal must be increased. Bituminous coals have the highest hydrogen content of the four ranks of coal. On the average, they consist of about 5 per cent hydrogen. The hydrogen must be increased to about 12 per cent to produce a high-energy liquid fuel and to about 25 per cent to produce synthetic natural gas.

The process of converting coal into a liquid fuel is called coal *hydrogenation* or *liquefaction*. Various methods of coal hydrogenation have been developed. In the typical method, a mixture of pulverized coal and oil is treated with hydrogen gas at high temperatures and under great pressure. The hydrogen gradually combines with the carbon molecules, forming a liquid fuel. This process can produce such high-energy fuels as gasoline and fuel oil if sufficient hydrogen is added.

Coal can easily be turned into low-energy gas by the carbonization and gasification methods described in the section *The Uses of Coal*. Low-energy gas can also be produced from unmined coal. This process, called *underground gasification*, involves digging two widely spaced wells from ground level to the base of a coal seam. The coal at the bottom of one well is ignited. Air is blown down the second well. The air seeps through pores in the seam, and the fire moves toward it. After a passage has been burned between the two wells, the air current forces the gases up the first well to the surface. Compared with natural gas, low-energy gas made from coal has limited uses. Low-energy gas must be enriched with hydrogen for its heating value to equal that of natural gas.

The present methods of obtaining high-energy fuels from coal cost too much for commercial use. Hydrogen is expensive to produce. In addition, most fuels made from coal contain unacceptable amounts of sulfur and ash. These fuels must be purified before they can be used in large quantities. The combined costs of hydrogen enrichment and purification make the synthetic fuels more expensive than natural gas or the fuels made from petroleum. Researchers are trying to develop cheaper methods of coal conversion.

No one knows where or when people discovered that coal can be burned to provide heat. The discovery may have been made independently in various parts of the world during prehistoric times. The Chinese were the first people to develop a coal industry. By the A.D. 300's, they were mining coal from surface deposits and using it to heat buildings and smelt metals. Coal had become the leading fuel in China by the 1000's.

Commercial coal mining developed more slowly in Europe. During the 1200's, a number of commercial mines were started in England and in what is now Belgium. The coal was dug from open pits and used mainly for smelting and forging metals. Most Europeans, however, regarded coal as a dirty fuel and objected to its use.

Wood, and charcoal made from wood, were the preferred fuels in Europe until the 1600's. During the 1600's, a severe shortage of wood occurred in western Europe. Many western European countries, but especially England, then sharply increased their coal output to relieve the fuel shortage.

Developments in England. During the 1500's, English factories burned huge quantities of charcoal in making such products as bricks, glass, salt, and soap. By the early 1600's, wood had become so scarce in England that most factories had to switch to coal. By the late 1600's, England produced about 80 per cent of the world's total coal output. The country remained the leading coal producer for the next 200 years.

Charcoal had also been widely used in England as a fuel for drying malt, the chief ingredient in beer. Brewers tried using coal for this process. But the gases it produced were absorbed by the malt and so spoiled the flavor of the beer. The brewers found, however, that the undesirable gases could be eliminated if they preheated the coal in an airtight oven. They thus developed the process for making coke. About 1710, an English ironmaker named Abraham Darby succeeded in using coke

A Pennsylvania Mine of the Late 1800's was like coal mines everywhere before mining became mechanized and child labor was abolished. Boys and mules provided much of the labor.

COAL

Coal Production in the United States Since 1800*

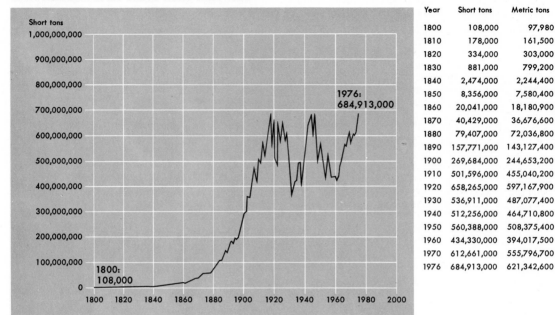

Year	Short tons	Metric tons
1800	108,000	97,980
1810	178,000	161,500
1820	334,000	303,000
1830	881,000	799,200
1840	2,474,000	2,244,400
1850	8,356,000	7,580,400
1860	20,041,000	18,180,900
1870	40,429,000	36,676,600
1880	79,407,000	72,036,800
1890	157,771,000	143,127,400
1900	269,684,000	244,653,200
1910	501,596,000	455,040,200
1920	658,265,000	597,167,900
1930	536,911,000	487,077,400
1940	512,256,000	464,710,800
1950	560,388,000	508,375,400
1960	434,330,000	394,017,500
1970	612,661,000	555,796,700
1976	684,913,000	621,342,600

*Includes all types of coal—anthracite, bituminous and subbituminous coals, and lignite.
Source: U.S. Department of Energy.

to smelt iron. Coke then gradually replaced charcoal as the preferred fuel for ironmaking.

The spread of the new ironmaking process became part of a much larger development in England—the Industrial Revolution. The revolution consisted chiefly of a huge increase in factory production. The increase was made possible by the development of the steam engine in England during the 1700's. Steam engines provided the power to run factory machinery. But they required a plentiful supply of energy. Coal was the only fuel available to meet this need. During the 1800's, the Industrial Revolution spread from England to other parts of the world. It succeeded chiefly in countries that had an abundance of coal. Coal thus played a key role in the growth of industrialization in Europe and North America.

Developments in North America. The North American Indians used coal long before the first white settlers arrived. For example, the Pueblo Indians in what is now the Southwestern United States dug coal from hillsides and used it for baking pottery. European explorers and settlers discovered coal in eastern North America during the last half of the 1600's. In the 1700's, a few small coal mines were opened in what are now Nova Scotia, Virginia, and Pennsylvania. The mines supplied coal chiefly to blacksmiths and ironmakers. Most settlers saw no advantage in using coal as long as wood was plentiful. Wood and charcoal remained the chief fuels in America throughout the 1700's.

The Industrial Revolution spread to the United States during the first half of the 1800's. By then, coal was essential not only to manufacturing but also to transportation. Steamships and steam-powered railroads

were becoming the chief means of transportation, and they required huge amounts of coal to fire their boilers. As industry and transportation grew in the United States, so did the production and use of coal. By the late 1800's, the United States had replaced England as the world's leading coal producer.

The United States led in coal production until the mid-1900's. The nation's demand for coal then declined as the use of petroleum and natural gas increased. Russia has surpassed the United States in coal production since the late 1950's.

Recent Developments. The growing scarcity of petroleum and natural gas has led to a sharp rise in the demand for coal. According to some U.S. government estimates, the production of coal will double in the United States by 1985. The increased output would be used mainly to produce electricity.

Today, electricity can be produced more cheaply from coal than from either natural gas or fuel oil. However, the cost of coal-generated electricity will almost certainly increase for several reasons. To meet environmental standards, power plants that burn medium- or high-sulfur coal must invest in costly sulfur dioxide scrubbers. To obtain low-sulfur coal, power plants must pay to have it shipped from the major producing areas. As coal deposits near the surface are used up, mines must be dug deeper and deeper. The high operating costs of extremely deep mines will add to the price of coal. Power companies, like other businesses, pass their added costs on to their customers. Thus, even though coal is plentiful, the energy it produces will become increasingly expensive.   JOSEPH W. LEONARD

Critically reviewed by the NATIONAL COAL ASSOCIATION

Section Six

Dictionary Supplement

This section lists important words from the 1979 edition of THE WORLD BOOK DICTIONARY. This dictionary, first published in 1963, keeps abreast of our living language with a program of continuous editorial revision. The following supplement has been prepared under the direction of the editors of THE WORLD BOOK ENCYCLOPEDIA and Clarence L. Barnhart, editor in chief of THE WORLD BOOK DICTIONARY. It is presented as a service to owners of the dictionary and as an informative feature to subscribers of THE WORLD BOOK YEAR BOOK.

A a

a|dri|a|my|cin (ā′drē ə mī′sən), *n.* a drug used as an antibiotic and experimentally in the treatment of cancer. It is derived from a kind of streptomyces. [< Italian *adriamicina* < *Adriàtico* Adriatic (Sea) + *-micina* -mycin, as in *streptomycin*]

ag|ro-in|dus|try (ag′rō in′də strē), *n., pl.* **-tries. 1** an agricultural industry. **2** an agro-industrial complex.

al|pha|fe|to|pro|tein (al′fə fē′tə prō′tēn, -tē in), *n.* a protein of undetermined function produced in the liver by the fetus and by persons suffering from some diseases, such as hepatitis. A high level of alphafetoprotein in the blood serum of a pregnant woman indicates possible defects of the brain and central nervous system in the fetus. *Abbr:* AFP (no periods).

alternative school, *Especially U.S.* a school that provides a different curriculum from the conventional elementary or high school program in an effort to educate students by changing the learning environment: *Alternative schools developed because of dissatisfaction with the quality and aims of public and private schools* (Beatrice and Ronald Gross). *New alternative schools are now coming on the scene—but they feature the basics* (Fred M. Hechinger).

angel dust, *U.S. Slang.* a powerful drug, phencyclidine or PCP, that acts as a depressant. It is used as a narcotic, especially by smoking it when sprinkled on marijuana, mint leaves, or parsley. *Angel dust has been linked to hundreds of murders, suicides and accidental deaths* (Time). *Angel dust ... can create paranoia, restlessness, manic agitation—and it can masquerade as other drugs because its effects sometimes resemble hallucinogens like LSD, or stimulants or depressants* (New York Daily News).

an|o|dyn|in (an′ə dī nin), *n.* a substance found in human blood and resembling a hormone. It has long-lasting pain-relieving properties. *Scientists at the National Institute of Mental Health who discovered it have named the blood substance anodynin from the word anodyne, meaning a medicine to relieve pain* (New York Times).

appropriate technology, the use of machinery and methods suited to available conditions, particularly to conditions of underdeveloped areas: *Although a lot of noise has been made in its favor, appropriate technology remains conspicuous only for its failure to have an impact on rural development in India* (New Scientist).

ar|chae|bac|te|ri|a (är′kē bak tir′ē ə), *n.pl.* microorganisms having a different chemical makeup and being genetically distinct from bacteria and higher living organisms; methanogens. *Archaebacteria exist in a warm, oxygen-free environment by ingesting carbon dioxide and hydrogen to produce methane. The identification of the archaebacteria's unique genetic structure suggests that there may be a third line of evolution. It also provides an important clue to the earth's early environment* (Time).

artificial gene, nucleic acids, sometimes in combination with other substances, that are joined under laboratory conditions to form nucleotides that will perform some genetic function in a living cell: *The researchers worked nine years to complete their artificial gene, and many*

biologists hailed the feat as proof that DNA molecules are indeed the basis of life (Earl A. Evans, Jr.).

B b

bargaining chip, an advantage held by any of the parties in a negotiation: *Bargaining from strength calls for arms programs that can serve as bargaining chips to trade for concessions that the other side might not otherwise make* (New York Times Magazine).

bi|o|mag|ni|fi|ca|tion (bī′ō mag′nə fə kā′shən), *n.* the increase in the concentration of toxic chemicals with each new link in the food chain: *Biomagnification is ... the process by which pesticides sprayed on vegetables and grains concentrate in the fat of animals and fish that eat them and then are further concentrated in the fat of meat and fish eaters further up in the food chain* (New York Times).

bi|o|mag|ni|fy (bī′ō mag′nə fī), *v.i.,* **-fied, -fy|ing.** to undergo biomagnification: *Probably the best news is that arsenic residues from soil and water do not biomagnify in the food chain* (Science News).

birr² (bir), *n., pl.* **birr** or **birrs.** the monetary unit of Ethiopia, divided into 100 cents. It replaced the Ethiopian dollar in 1976.

boat people, refugees from southeastern Asia, especially South Vietnam, who emigrate in small fishing boats for any country that will permit them entry: *The other nations in Asia did not want to take on the social and economic burden posed by the "boat people". ... The Carter administration said it would begin admitting 7,000 "boat people"* (John Sharkey).

C c

CAT scan, 1 an X-ray picture made by computerized axial tomography: *CAT scans depict cross sections or slices of any region of the body as seen looking down through the patient, head to foot* (Irwin J. Polk). **2** = CAT scanner. **3** = CAT scanning.

chro|mo|dy|nam|ics (krō′mō dī nam′iks), *n. Nuclear Physics.* the study of the action of forces by which the property of color binds quarks together: *An essential requirement of chromodynamics is that each species of quark possess three aspects called colors, which have to do with the way it combines with other quarks to form a larger particle* (New York Times Magazine).

comparative advertising, advertising that unfavorably compares a competitor's product by name: *The advertising community claimed that intense comparative advertising hurts the credibility of all advertising* (Edward Mark Mazze).

cluster headache, severe headache occurring repeatedly over a period of weeks followed by an interval of relief of several months: *Cluster headaches, unlike migraines, strike with little or no warning, affecting six times as many men as women* (New York Times).

computerized axial tomography, *Medicine.* X-ray photography in which images of an internal part of the body are made by a circling X-ray beam and syn-

thesized by computer into a single cross-sectional view; CAT scanning: *Computerized axial tomography ... is a technique that makes possible precise diagnosis in many cases where the abnormality is unclear or undetectable by conventional X-ray or radioactive scans* (Irwin J. Polk). *Abbr:* CAT (no periods).

Creutz|feldt-Ja|kob disease (kroits′felt yä′kop, -kob), a degenerative brain disease of middle and late life, caused by infection with a slow virus: *The scientists had noted that Creutzfeldt-Jakob disease causes changes in brain tissue similar to those caused by kuru* (Richard R. Johnson). [< Hans G. *Creutzfeldt* (born 1883) and Alfons M. *Jakob* (1884-1931), German neurologists who first described the disease]

D d

des|er|ti|fi|ca|tion (dez′ər tə fə kā′shən), *n.* the process of turning into arid or desert land: *An ugly word, desertification, has been coined to describe the relentless creep of the desert into the semiarid regions* (London Times). *Desertification is thought to result more from land mismanagement than from uncontrollable climatic changes* (New York Times).

dietary fiber, roughage in food, such as bran and fruit skins: *Some researchers feel that an adequate quantity of dietary fiber may protect against many noninfectious diseases of the large intestine* (G. Edward Damon).

dol|o|rol|o|gy (dol′ə rol′ə jē), *n.* the scientific study of pain: *Not until the specialty of dolorology began to emerge did the study of pain itself gain a new emphasis and respectability* (New York Times Magazine). [< Latin *dolor* pain + English *-logy*] — **dol′o|rol′o|gist,** *n.*

dou|ble-nick|el (dub′əl nik′əl), *n. U.S. Slang.* 55 miles per hour (the nationwide highway speed limit established in 1973): *If you are driving at 55, you are doing the double-nickel* (Michael Harwood).

drug|o|la (drə gō′lə), *n. U.S. Slang.* secret payment made to police or other authorities for permission to sell illegal narcotics without interference: *Federal investigators throughout the country are looking for friendly witnesses who will be granted immunity for telling what they know about payola and drugola* (Newsweek). [< *drug* + (pay)*ola*]

E e

exclusive economic zone, = economic zone: *Coastal countries would enjoy sovereign rights to prospect and exploit such natural resources as fisheries and offshore oil and gas fields in their exclusive economic zones* (Paul Hofmann).

ex|o|e|lec|tron (ek′sō i lek′tron), *n.* an electron emitted from surface atoms under conditions associated with such factors as heat, wear, cracks, and friction: *There were numerous studies ... to elucidate the properties of exoelectrons and to discover the mechanisms of their production* (Scientific American).

F f

fla|vor (flā′vər), *n., v.* — *n.* **5** *Nuclear Physics.* a hypothetical property, such as strangeness, that distinguishes one subatomic particle from another: *The different kinds of quarks or leptons are known technically as flavors* (Robert H. March).

fuzzy set, *Mathematics.* a set whose elements converge or overlap with those of other sets: *There are also situations in which the imprecision stems not from randomness but from the presence of a class or classes (that is, fuzzy sets) that do not possess sharply defined boundaries* (Science).

G g

gang of four, a faction within the Chinese Communist Party, that attempted to gain control of government after the death of Mao Tse-tung: *The "gang of four" was ... accused of ... sabotaging production with calls for more efforts to modernize revolution* (Mark Gayn). [in reference to Chiang Ching and three of her allies]

gene-splic|ing (jēn′splī′sing), *n. Informal.* the recombination of genetic material; production of recombinant DNA: *The basic process of ... gene-splicing is ... sufficiently developed to be a routine procedure in a properly equipped laboratory* (Edwin S. Weaver).

Gin|nie Mae (jin′ē mā′), *U.S.* **1** the Government National Mortgage Association (a mortgage-lending agency of the Department of Housing and Urban Development). **2** a stock certificate issued by this agency: *A cautious market in interest-rate futures ... found long-term Ginnie Mae's and Treasury contracts finished slightly lower in price* (New York Times). [< spelling for pronunciation of its abbreviation, *GNMA*]

give|back (giv′bak′), *n. U.S.* the cancellation of an employee benefit granted in a previous labor union contract, often in return for an increase in wages or other concession by management: *The long strike ... was tied to the company's demand for the giveback of plant seniority rights. New York City and its Transit Authority are both demanding givebacks to compensate for pay increases sought by their unions* (New York Times).

H h

HDL (no periods), high density lipoprotein: *High blood levels of HDL are ... associated with a reduced risk of atherosclerosis* (New Scientist).

HLA or **HL-A** (āch′el′ā′), *adj.* of or having to do with a system of tissue typing based on the presence in the body of certain antigens: *Studies of the many HLA types found in the population have also shown that some of them are associated with specific diseases: for example, a high proportion of all patients with some form of arthritis are found to have HLA B27 antigens* (London Times). [< *h*(uman) /(eucocyte) *a*(ntigen)]

hos|pice (hos′pis), *n.* **3** an institution devoted to the care of the terminally ill: *The hospice aims ... to make dying as pleasant as possible. The accent is on sun, fresh flowers, and open visiting hours even for young children and pets* (James Hassett). [< French, Old French *hospice*, learned borrowing from Latin *hospitium*

guest house; hospitality < *hospes, -itis* guest, host[1]. See etym. of doublet **hospitium**.]

hunter-killer satellite, an artificial earth satellite that destroys orbiting enemy satellites; killer satellite: *The Soviet Union and the United States have developed hunter-killer satellites armed with laser beams which can search out and destroy each other's reconnaissance satellites in the vast reaches of space* (New Yorker).

I i

IgA (no periods), immunoglobulin A: *The immunoglobulin known as IgA ... is found only in external secretions (saliva, tears, sweat ...)* (Lee Edson).

in|ter|nal|i|za|tion (in tėr′nə lə zā′shən), *n.* **1** *Psychology.* the act or process of internalizing. **2** *U.S. Finance.* a system of trading securities within brokerage offices rather than transmitting trading orders to the floor of an exchange: *For the public, moreover, internalization could lead to drastic changes in the way that securities are bought and sold* (Leonard Sloane).

J j

joint custody, a legal agreement between divorced or separated parents to share the custody of their offspring: *Where neither of two fit parents wants to be a weekend visitor, the alternative of joint custody cannot be dismissed as "disruptive" when compared with the damage suffered by children in an all-out custody war* (New York Times Magazine).

ju|ve|nile-on|set diabetes (jü′və nəl on′set′; -nīl; ôn′-), a mild form of diabetes usually occurring before the age of 20. It is caused by malfunction of the pancreas and is not a hereditary condition. *Juvenile-onset diabetes, which accounts for about 10 percent of all cases of the disease, ... is treated with injections of insulin* (Thomas H. Maugh II).

K k

ke|be|le (kə bā′lə), *n.* a unit of local government in Ethiopia, established after the deposition of Emperor Haile Selassie: *The radio announced that local neighborhood associations, or kebeles, would henceforth have the power to draft men and women and send them to military units* (New York Times). [< Amharic *kebele*]

killer satellite, = hunter-killer satellite: *A killer satellite carrying a laser weapon could ... move around the globe knocking out the Pentagon's communications satellites one by one* (Washington Post).

L l

LDL (no periods), low density lipoprotein: *LDLs carry cholesterol in their core and in man represent the major mode of transporting cholesterol from the liver to cells of various tissues* (New York Times).

li|lan|ge|ni (li läng′gə nē), *n., pl.* **emalangeni.** the unit of money of Swaziland, equal in value with the South African rand. [< siSwati *lilangeni*]

Lyme arthritis (līm), a form of arthritis accompanied by large reddened areas of the skin, believed to be caused by a virus carried by ticks: *Alerted by the Connecticut data, doctors in Massachusetts, Rhode Island and New York have since discovered instances of Lyme arthritis in their own areas* (Time). [< *Lyme*, Connecticut, where the illness was widespread]

M m

Mar|i|sat (mar′ə sat′), *n.* any one of a group of United States communications satellites positioned over the Atlantic, Pacific, and Indian oceans to transmit maritime weather conditions. [< *Mari*(time) + *sat*(ellite)]

Mars|quake (märz′kwāk′), *n.* a shaking or sliding on or beneath the surface of the planet Mars, similar to an earthquake: *The instrument can give information on the location of Marsquakes by comparing the data from both landers' seismometers* (J. Kelly Beatty).

ma|tur|i|ty-on|set diabetes (mə tùr′ə tē on′set′; -tyùr′-, -chùr′-; ôn′-), the widespread form of diabetes, occurring in adults usually after the age of 40. It is believed to be hereditary. *When one member of identical twins has documented maturity-onset diabetes, the other member is also found almost always to have diabetes* (George F. Cahill, Jr.).

media event, an event especially arranged to be publicized through the news media; pseudo-event: *His travels today ... were only the first leg of an elaborately extensive, two-day, 950-mile media event* (New York Times).

meth|an|o|gen (mə than′ə jen, -thā′nə-), *n.* one of the archaebacteria, microorganisms that are genetically distinct: *In this study the surprised scientists found that the methanogens' RNA sequences were unlike any other they had ever seen ... Microbiologist Wolfe detected chemicals inside the methanogens that are different from any in common bacteria* (Newsweek). [< *methane* + *-gen*]

N n

Now account (nou), *U.S.* a savings account from which a depositor may withdraw money by check for payment to a third party as in a commercial checking account: *Now accounts, which are actually a check-like method of withdrawing from a savings account* (New York Times). [< *N*(egotiated) *O*(rder) of *W*(ithdrawal)]

nu|me|ro u|no (nü′mə rō ü′nō), **1** *Informal.* the first or best of a group; number one: *Now along comes the 22-year-old Miss Evert, numero uno, a two-time defending champion* (New York Times).

Pronunciation Key: hat, āge, cāre, fär; let, ēqual, tėrm; it, īce; hot, ōpen, ôrder; oil, out; cup, pùt, rüle; child; long; thin; ᴛʜen; zh, measure; ə represents a in about, e in taken, i in pencil, o in lemon, u in circus.

Campaign jingoism can't cover up the fact that we're not Numero Uno (Time). **2** = oneself. [< Spanish or Italian *numero uno* number one]

O o

off-the-wall (ôf′тнə wôl′, of′-), *adj.*, or **off the wall**, *U.S. Informal.* not customary or usual; unconventional: *Brian knows how to startle the over-interviewed with off-the-wall questions that get surprising answers: Ever see a ghost? What makes you cry?* (National Review).

on|cor|na|vi|rus (ong kôr′nə vī′rəs), *n.* any one of a group of viruses that produce tumors and contain ribonucleic acid: *Professor W. F. H. Jarrett . . . spoke of the oncornaviruses particularly in fowls, mice and cats, in which they can lead to leukemia or sarcoma* (Nature). [< *onco*(genic) + *RNA* + *virus*]

OSHA (ō′shə), *n.* Occupational Safety and Health Administration (of the U.S. Department of Labor): *OSHA's permanent standards for worker exposure to vinyl chloride monomer—a cancer-causing material—went into effect in April* (Edward Abrams).

P p

passive restraint, a device in an automobile that automatically protects the occupants from dangerous injury in the event of an accident: *He suggested that at least two auto manufacturers agree to make and market . . . cars in various sizes equipped with passive restraints, either airbags or passive belt systems* (Charles C. Cain III).

plant|i|mal (plan′tə məl), *n.* a living cell or organism formed by the fusion of animal and plant cells: *Three separate research groups have now successfully fused animal cells with plant cells to form the first . . . "plantimals"* (Science News). [< *plant* + (an)*imal*]

Po|li|sa|rio (pō′li sär′yō), *n.* a guerrilla force fighting against the governments of Morocco and Mauritania for control of Western Sahara (the former Spanish Sahara): *Algeria . . . declared its firm support for Polisario* (Philippe Decraene). [< *Po*(pular Front for the *Li*(beration of) *Sa*(guia el Hamra and) *Rio* (de Oro), the two zones of Western Sahara]

post-mod|ern (pōst mod′ərn), *adj.* that develops after a period or movement called *modern.* In the arts the post-modern period is sometimes characterized by an appearance of spontaneous creation or by a markedly identifiable inclusion of elements from past developments of style and technique, *post-modern dance. By now, a large number of architects and critics have conceded that the glass, steel and concrete vocabulary of modern architecture has lost its potency and . . . a new, "post-modern" style is evolving* (Paul Goldberger).

Q q

quad|ro|min|i|um (kwod′rə min′ē əm), *n.* a building with four separately owned apartments: *In Chicago, Dayton and some West Coast areas, four-dwelling condominiums—or "quadrominiums"— have become the fastest selling form of*

housing (Time). [< *quadr-* four + (cond)*ominium*]

R r

RAM (no periods), random-access memory: *Appropriately programmed RAM's— up to 16 kbit [kilobit] per circuit—can store any program in the machine* (New Scientist).

read-on|ly memory (rēd′ōn′lē), a computer memory which stores permanent data: *Changing the program may require the physical replacement of a read-only memory* (Wallace B. Riley). *Abbr:* ROM (no periods).

re|jec|tion|ist (ri jek′shə nist), *n.* any one of the Arab leaders or states that refuse to negotiate or work out a settlement with Israel: *The "rejectionists" . . . have accused Syria of wanting to eliminate them so as to have a free hand to embark on what they call an Egyptian-type policy of accommodation with the United States and Israel* (Henry J. Tanner).

re|po (rē′pō), *n. U.S. Finance, Informal.* an agreement to buy back securities, especially government bonds, after a given period; repurchase agreement: *The Federal Reserve injected reserves into the banking system . . . , first by negotiating weekend repurchase agreements and then by arranging six-day fixed-term "repo's"* (John H. Allen). [short for *repurchase*]

S s

sam|bo² (sam′bō), *n.* a type of wrestling similar to judo, popular in international competitions. [< Russian *sambo*, acronym for *sam*(ooborona) *b*(ez) *o*(rushia) self-defense without weapons]

side-looking radar, radar used in an aircraft to transmit a microwave signal at an acute angle sufficient to reflect a profile image. Such an image recorded on film is used to substitute for aerial photography over obscured terrain. *The acute grazing angle of the microwave illumination of side-looking radar emphasizes the form of the land* (Scientific American).

South (south), *n., adj.* — *n.* **4** the developing countries of the world: *Today, any regional struggle over who is to become managing director of I.M.F. is far less likely to be one between the United States and Western Europe as between the "North" and "South"* (New York Times).

stra|ti|fied-charge engine (strat′ə fīd chärj′), an internal-combustion engine whose cylinders are divided into two chambers containing different mixtures of fuel and air: *In the stratified-charge engine . . . there are zones that are fuel-rich or fuel-poor* (H. Martin Malin, Jr.). *Fuel economy and reduced exhaust emissions can both be obtained in so-called stratified-charge engines* (London Times).

subsidized adoption, *U.S.* a government program that provides financial assistance to persons who adopt children: *Subsidized adoption is a way to increase the number of available adoptive homes* (Frances A. Mullen).

sunset law, *U.S.* **1** a law requiring a government regulatory agency to undergo

periodic review for its continued usefulness. **2** a law providing that state agencies created by a governor or a legislature be terminated after a specified period.

T t

thy|mo|sin (thī′mə sin), *n.* a hormone of the thymus gland, associated with the production of lymphocytes that cause cellular immunity: *Thymosin treatment has raised the T-cell count in more than 75 per cent of the cancer patients* (Allan L. Goldstein).

time warp, a distortion or suspension in the continuity of time: *Science-fiction writers, stymied by the laws of physics, turn to such literary devices as time warps to make interstellar travel possible* (Time). *Haiti is like a sustained hallucination imposed upon a time warp* (Harper's).

touch dancing, dancing in which the partners hold each other and usually move in a series of complementary steps: *Touch dancing is back, and with it a new demand for formal instruction in a genre less sensuously described as ballroom dancing* (Jane Davison).

tri|lat|er|al|ism (trī lat′ər ə liz′əm), *n.* a policy of fostering close cooperation between three nations or regions, especially such a policy applied to Western Europe, Japan, and North America: *Trilateralism . . . wants closer interaction, and, if possible, a united foreign front by the industrial nations of the non-Communist world* (Manchester Guardian). — **tri|lat′er|al|ist**, *n.*

U u

Ul|tra|suède (ul′trə swād′), *n. Trademark.* a synthetic, washable fabric that resembles suede: *Ultrasuède contained 60 per cent polyester and 40 per cent nonfibrous polyurethane* (Georgia Dulles).

U particle, an elementary particle belonging to the same class as the electron and mu-meson, but having a mass twice as great as that of proton; a heavy lepton: *Among the exotic new particles found in collisions of electrons and positrons are the U particles . . . , heavy members of the lepton family* (Science News).

V v

VLDL (no periods), very low density lipoprotein: *When the diet contains large amounts of saturated fats . . . , the liver makes more VLDLs and LDLs, which promote atherosclerosis* (New York Times).

W w

water hole, **2** *Astronomy.* a part of the electromagnetic spectrum, considered the most likely band for use in extraterrestrial contact with earth. It is almost free of radio noise and radiates interstellar hydrogen and oxygen (elements that combine to form water). *Radio telescopes in each hemisphere would sweep along the galactic plane every few minutes, transmitting in a noise-free band, such as the so-called water hole* (New Scientist).

Z z

ZBB (no periods), zero-based budgeting: *ZBB critics point to its cost in management time, and the mind-boggling paper work involved* (Maclean's).

Index

How to Use the Index

This index covers the contents of the 1977, 1978, and 1979 editions of THE WORLD BOOK YEAR BOOK.

Each index entry is followed by the edition year (in *italics*) and the page number, as:
ADVERTISING, *79-176, 78-174, 77-172*

This means, for example, that information about Advertising begins on page 176 in the 1979 edition of THE YEAR BOOK.

An index entry that is the title of an article appearing in THE YEAR BOOK is printed in capital letters, as: **AUTOMOBILE.** An entry that is not an article title, but a subject discussed in an article of some other title, is printed: **Pollution.**

The various "See" and "See also" cross references in the index list are to other entries within the index. Clue words or phrases are used when two or more references to the same subject appear in the same edition of THE YEAR BOOK. These make it easy to locate the material on the page, since they refer to an article title or article subsection in which the reference appears, as:
Mandatory retirement age: Congress, *79-265*; old age, *79-430, 78-425, 77-431*

The indication *"il."* means that the reference is to an illustration only. An index entry in capital letters followed by *"WBE"* refers to a new or revised WORLD BOOK ENCYCLOPEDIA article that is printed in the supplement section, as:
SNAKE, *WBE, 79-536*

Acknowledgments

The publishers acknowledge the following sources for illustrations. Credits read from left to right, top to bottom, on their respective pages. An asterisk (*) denotes illustrations created exclusively for THE YEAR BOOK. All maps, charts, and diagrams were prepared by THE YEAR BOOK staff unless otherwise noted.

3	Lois Wille*
8	Wide World
9	Wide World; Darquennes, Sygma; U.S. Air Force; Wide World
10	Keystone; United Press Int.; Wide World
11	Wide World
12	United Press Int.
13	Keystone; Keystone; Pictorial Parade
14-16	Wide World
18	Steve Hale*
20-22	Wide World
23	United Press Int.
24	Steve Hale*
26	United Press Int.
27	WORLD BOOK photo*
28	United Press Int.
30	Steve Hale*
33	United Press Int.
35	Wide World
36	Steve Hale*
38	Paul Conklin, Academy Forum
39-41	United Press Int.
42	Steve Hale*
44	United Press Int.
45	WORLD BOOK photo*
46	A. Devaney
47	WORLD BOOK photo*
48	Steve Hale*
50	Free Chin
51	WORLD BOOK photo*
52	Wide World
53	United Press Int.
54	Steve Hale*
56-58	United Press Int.
60-61	Computer Plot of Human Spine courtesy of University of Illinois, Circle Campus (photos by Steve Hale*)
63	The Syndics of Cambridge University Library, Cambridge, England
64-65	Barton Faist*
67	Low Back and Pain Clinic of the Rehabilitation Institute of Chicago (Steve Hale*)
68	Dan McCoy, Rainbow
69	Dan McCoy, Rainbow; Low Back and Pain Clinic of the Rehabilitation Institute of Chicago (Steve Hale*)
70-71	Steve Hale*
72	Barton Faist*
74-84	Steve Hale*
86	Tony Howarth, Woodfin Camp, Inc.; © David Hume Kennerly, De Wys, Inc.
87	© David Hume Kennerly, De Wys, Inc.
90-91	Arabian American Oil Company
92	Alain Nogues, Sygma; © Peter Carmichael, DPI
94	De Wys, Inc.
95	Arabian American Oil Company
96	Tony Howarth, Woodfin Camp, Inc.
97	Tony Howarth, Woodfin Camp, Inc.; © 1978 David Hume Kennerly, Contact; Fred Ward, Black Star
98	Arabian American Oil Company; Marc Riboud, Magnum
99	Alain Nogues, Sygma; © Peter Carmichael, DPI; Alain Nogues, Sygma; © Robert Azzi, Magnum
100	Arabian American Oil Company
102-103	George Suyeoka*
105	T. J. Dawson
106	Hans & Judy Beste, Tom Stack & Assoc.; John Wallis, Bruce Coleman Inc.; J. Brownlie, Bruce Coleman Inc.; Bay Picture Library
107	Hans & Judy Beste, Tom Stack & Assoc.; Hans & Judy Beste, Tom Stack & Assoc.; Bay Picture Library
108	Hans & Judy Beste, Tom Stack & Assoc.; Vincent Serventy
109	Hans & Judy Beste, Tom Stack & Assoc.; T.J. Dawson
110	George Suyeoka*
111	San Diego Zoo; G.R. Roberts; Vincent Serventy
112	George Suyeoka*; Fritz Prenzel
113	WORLD BOOK photo by Ivan Massar, Black Star*
114	George Suyeoka*
115	Bill N. Kleeman, Tom Stack & Assoc.; D.B. Croft
116	J. LaPuma, Bruce Coleman Inc.
118-122	Steve.Hale*
123	Bettmann Archive
125	Culver Pictures; Culver Pictures; Hope Enterprises, Inc.
126	Steve Hale*; Steve Hale*; Steve Hale*; Bettmann Archive; Bettmann Archive
127	Hope Enterprises, Inc.
128	Steve Hale*; Steve Hale*; Bettmann Archive; Hope Enterprises, Inc.
129	Bettmann Archive
130	U.S. Army
131	Wide World; CBS; © 1978 William H. Cosby, Filmation Studios; Bettmann Archive
132	Hope Enterprises, Inc.
133	Steve Hale*
134	Ellis Herwig, Stock, Boston; © Nik Wheeler, Black Star
137	Everett C. Johnson, De Wys, Inc.; Grant Kalivoda, Tom Stack & Assoc.
138	U.S. Naval Research Laboratory
139	Thomas P. Harlan, Laboratory of Tree-Ring Research, University of Arizona; Michael Hardy, Susan Griggs Picture Agency
140	Photri; Specimens courtesy of Dr. Peter Thompson of Lamont-Doherty Geological Observatory, and scanning electron micrograph by Dee Breger
142	NOAA; NASA
144	NOAA; Daniel Brody, Stock, Boston; NOAA; L.L.T. Rhodes, Taurus
148	Alfred B. Smith; © Philip Jon Bailey, Stock, Boston; Steve Hale*
151	© J.P. Laffont, Sygma; Brown Brothers
152	Steve Hale*
153	© Jim Anderson, Woodfin Camp, Inc.
154	© Eric Kroll, Taurus
155	Eric Kroll, Taurus; Stephen Kelley, Hour of Power; Oral Roberts University
156-157	© Chuck Fishman, Contact; © David Burnett, Contact
158	Lou Jones; © Olivier Rebbot, Stock, Boston
159	© David M. Campione, Taurus
162	Robert Keys*; The Newberry Library, Chicago; The Newberry Library, Chicago; The Newberry Library, Chicago; The Newberry Library, Chicago
165-173	The Newberry Library, Chicago
176	The Advertising Council, Inc.
177	Wide World
178	Campbell, Sygma
179	United Press Int.
182-184	Wide World
186	Alan Kamuda, *Detroit Free Press*
190	© 1978 National Geographic Society
192	Jadwiga Lopez
193	Wide World
195	McDonnell Douglas Corporation
196-197	© Sipa Press from Black Star
198	Wide World
201	U.S. Naval Observatory
202	Wide World
203	*The Bulletin,* Sydney
205	© Draper Hill from King Features Syndicate, Inc., 1978
207	Wide World
209	United Press Int.
213	Keith Meyers, NYT Pictures
214	Wide World
215	Wide World; William G. Fitzpatrick, The White House
216	Robert R. McElroy, *Newsweek*
218	Wide World
221	National Institutes of Health
222-223	Wide World
225	United Press Int.
226	Wide World
227	Tasi-Ying Cheng, Oregon Graduate Center
229-230	Wide World
231	Phillips Petroleum Company
232	Peter Steiner, *Saturday Review*
234-235	Wide World
236-237	J.P. Laffont, Sygma
238	Canadian Press
240	United Press Int.

These beautiful bookstands—
specially designed to hold your entire program, including YEAR BOOKS.

Height: 26⅜"
with 4" legs.
Width: 28¾"
Depth: 8³⁄₁₆"

Height: 9",
Width: 28½",
Depth: 8³⁄₁₆"

Most parents like having a convenient place to house their Year Books and their World Book library. A beautiful floor-model bookstand — constructed of solid hardwood — is available in either walnut or fruitwood finish.

You might prefer the attractive hardwood table racks, also available in either walnut or fruitwood finish. Let us know by writing us at the following address:

THE WORLD BOOK YEAR BOOK
Post Office Box 3564
Chicago, Illinois 60654

Cyclo-teacher®
The easy-to-use learning system
Features hundreds of cycles from seven valuable learning areas

Here's How Cyclo-Teacher® Works — in 3 easy steps!

STEP 1 — Asks a new question or poses a problem.

STEP 2 — Youngster writes in answer or response.

STEP 3 — Checks user's answer against correct response by flipping lever.

Cyclo-teacher® — the remarkable programmed learning system — comes right into your home to help stimulate and accelerate the learning of basic skills, concepts, and information. Housed in one specially designed file box, you'll find the Cyclo-teacher® machine, Study Wheels, Answer Wheels, a Manual, a Contents and Instruction Card, and Achievement Record sheets.

Your child will find this to be a new and fascinating game. Only, it's really so much more — for it teaches new things . . . reinforces learning . . . and challenges a youngster to go beyond!

Features hundreds of Study Cycles — to meet the individual needs of students — your entire family, just as Year Book is a valuable learning aid. And, best of all, lets you track your own progress — at your own pace! Cyclo-teacher® is available by writing us at the following address:

608

THE WORLD BOOK YEAR BOOK
Post Office Box 3564
Chicago, Illinois 60654